P9-DDX-474

Work Your Way around the World

Susan Griffith

Distributed in the USA by
The Globe Pequot Press, Guilford, Connecticut

 **VACATION WORK**
PUBLICATIONS

Published by Vacation Work, 9 Park End Street, Oxford
www.vacationwork.co.uk

WORK YOUR WAY AROUND THE WORLD

by Susan Griffith

First published 1983
Revised every other year
Twelfth edition 2005
Reprinted 2006

Copyright © 2005

ISBN 1-85458-329-8

No part of this publication may be reproduced or transmitted
in any form or by any means without the prior
written permission of the publisher

Cover design and chapter headings by mccdesign ltd

Maps by William Swan
The key to the symbols used on the maps
can be found on page 152

Typeset by Brendan Cole

Publicity: Charles Cutting

Printed and bound in Italy by Legoprint SpA, Trento

Contents

Work Your Way

Work Your Way in Europe

Work Your Way Worldwide

Preface

Because the world is always changing, a new edition of this book is necessary every two years. Since the last edition, ten new member states have been added to the European Union, and their citizens (especially from Poland) have wasted no time in dispersing to the far corners of Europe to take up casual work. Flows of travelling workers are always in flux. A recent phenomenon is the recruitment of westerners for work in India (mainly for training in call centres) and the number of working holiday visa schemes has increased for a range of destination countries.

There is nothing new in people leaving their homeland to find work abroad. In a single family to which I am distantly related, one brother went to Chile to work in the nitrate industry, his brother had some diplomatic role in China, a cousin took up farming in Canada and another emigrated to South Africa to recuperate from TB. Those 19th century reasons for travelling to distant lands may have changed but the same spirit of enterprise and adventure continues to entice the young and not-so-young to up sticks and seek paid or voluntary work in foreign parts.

My favourite film of the past year has been *Motorcycle Diaries* in which the young Che Guevara and a friend from medical school in Buenos Aires decide to take a 'gap year' and travel the length of South America. The way that they travel with very little money and close to the people, stopping to work, could be seen as a model for the readers of this book.

In the early 1980s when I wrote the first edition of *Work Your Way Around the World*, so few guidebooks about funding yourself on the road were available that travellers were grateful for any scrap of information and encouragement. Nowadays, working abroad has become such a mainstream idea that it has spawned scores of websites, been featured on primetime television and is serviced by a huge infrastructure for those who want to combine work and travel. This book has grown up with the travel industry and takes account of all those shortcuts to fixing up work abroad that now exist. The inclusion in its pages of hundreds if not thousands of potential employers, mediating agencies and useful internet sites sometimes makes me feel like a walking database.

Yet the swashbuckling kind of traveller who is prepared to carve out his or her own adventures is also alive and well and using this book to navigate. For this twelfth edition of *Work Your Way Around the World* my network of informants has encompassed an aspiring film maker who went to a Greek island to pursue this dream, a couple (now grandparents) who worked a season in a French ski chalet, an Irish airline worker who picked up hospitality jobs in Australia and New Zealand, a new graduate of philosophy who taught English in Bolivia, a man who made money by reading Tarot cards abroad, a journalist who recommends hostessing in Japan, a Canadian who overcame her nervousness of horses by working at a horse trekking farm in New Zealand, and an Englishwoman who participated in the paradigm of the working holiday by exchanging English conversation with Spanish language learners for a free fortnight in a resort near Madrid called "Englishtown". Almost with one voice, they urge people whatever their backgrounds to give it a go and expose themselves to the unexpected friendliness and generosity of foreign residents and fellow travellers.

Anybody who occasionally feels the call of the road, the spirit of adventure flicker will, I hope, enjoy reading this book and dreaming. My aim has been to make the information in these 576 pages as concrete and up-to-the-minute as possible, to cut all the vague generalities and waffle. But amongst all the specific contact addresses and realistic practical advice, the stories of working travellers are interwoven to inspire and encourage. This book is written to renew optimism and spark the imagination of all potential travellers.

Susan Griffith
Cambridge
February 2005

Acknowledgments

I never get tired of meeting and hearing from those intrepid travellers who are out there, sometimes living the life of Reilly, sometimes living on the edge. Their stories always enliven (and justify) my struggle to keep this book as up to date as possible. This new revised edition of *Work Your Way Around the World* would not have been possible without the help of hundreds of travellers who have generously shared their information over the years. Some have been writing to me over several editions, and their loyalty is greatly appreciated.

I would especially like to thank all those travellers who have crouched over keyboards in remote corners of the world and even (occasionally) bought a stamp to communicate with me since the last edition was prepared two years ago. All their pearls of travelling wisdom have been enthusiastically received and have been distilled into the pages that follow. My warmest thanks are owed to the following:

Hannah Adcock, Jonathan Alderman, Leona Baldwin, Susan Beney, Roger Blake, Till Bruckner, Catharine Carfoot, Bruce Clarke, Sara Coleman, Jon Cotterill, Paul Edmunds, Sarah Ellengorn, Sara Ellis-Owen, Martin Forbes, Debra Fuccio, Chris & Christine Giles, Alan Haden, Alan Hargreaves, Nigel Hollington, Keith Leishman, Sheona Mckay, Jason Motlagh, Colm Murphy, James Nibloe, Catherine Quinn, Barry Robinson, Sarah Smith and Sarah Zimmerman

While every effort has been made to ensure that the information contained in this book was accurate at the time of going to press, some details are bound to change within the lifetime of this edition. Wages, exchange rates and government policies are particularly susceptible to fluctuations, and the ones quoted here are intended merely as a guide.

If in the course of your travels you come across something which might be of interest to readers of the next edition, please write to Susan Griffith at Vacation-Work, 9 Park End Street, Oxford OX1 1HJ; susan@vacationwork.co.uk (who promises to reply). This book depends very much on up-to-date reports from travellers who have worked their way. The best contributions will be rewarded with a free copy of the next edition or any other Vacation-Work title (listed at the end of this book).

INTRODUCTION

The Decision to Go

For many, deciding to get up and go is the biggest stumbling-block. Often the hardest step is fixing a departure date. Once you have bought a ticket, explained to your friends and family that you are off to see the world (they will either be envious or disapproving) and packed away your possessions, the rest seems to look after itself. Inevitably first-time travellers suffer some separation anxieties and pre-departure blues as they contemplate leaving behind the comfortable routines of home. But these are usually much worse in anticipation than in retrospect. As long as you have enough motivation, together with some money and a copy of this book, you are all set to have a great time abroad.

Either you follow your first impulse and opt for an immediate change of scenery, or you plan a job and a route in advance. On the one hand people use working as a means to an end; they work in order to fund further travelling. Other people look upon a job abroad as an end in itself, a way to explore other cultures, a means of satisfying their curiosity about whether there is any truth in the clichés about other nationalities. Often it is the best way to shake off the boredom which comes with routine. Zoe Drew felt quite liberated when she decided to drop everything – her 'cushy secretarial job, Debenhams account card, stiletto heels' – and embark on a working holiday around Europe. Bruce Lawson finally kicked over the traces of the 'Office Job from Hell' and went off to Thailand to teach English.

When you are wondering whether you are the right sort to work abroad, do not imagine you are a special case. It is not only students, school-leavers and people on the dole who enjoy the chance to travel and work, but also a large number of people with a profession, craft or trade which they were happy to abandon temporarily. We have heard from a man who left the Met Office to pick grapes in Pauillac, a sixth former teaching in Nepal, a mechanical engineer crewing on yachts in the South Pacific, an Israeli busker in Switzerland, a career civil servant who enjoyed washing dishes in a Munich restaurant, a physiotherapist who has packed cod in Iceland, a nurse who busked in Norway and another who has worked on a sheep station in Australia, an Australian teacher who became a nanny in Istanbul, a Scottish lawyer who worked as a chalet girl in a French ski resort, a German tourism trainee who planted trees in Canada, a chartered surveyor who took more than two years off from his job to work his way around the world and a journalist and tour operator couple who picked up casual jobs to fund their 'Stuff Mammon World Tour' and ended up living quite comfortably in Hong Kong. They were motivated not by a desire to earn money but by a craving for new and different experiences, and a conviction that not all events which make up one's life need to be career-furthering or 'success'-oriented.

PREPARATION

It is not the Mr. Micawbers of this world who succeed at getting jobs. If you sit around 'waiting for something to turn up' you will soon find yourself penniless with no prospects for replenishing your travel funds. If you wait in idleness at home or if you sit in your *pension* all day worrying about your dwindling euros or pesos, hesitating and dithering because you are convinced the situation is hopeless or that you lack the necessary documents to work, you will get absolutely nowhere.

Every successful venture combines periodic flights of fancy with methodical planning. The majority of us lack the courage (or the recklessness) just to get up and go. And any homework you do ahead of time will benefit you later, if only because it will give you more confidence. But it is important to strike a good balance between slavishly following a predetermined itinerary which might prevent you from grasping opportunities as they arise and setting off with no idea of what you're looking for. Many travel converts regret their initial decision to buy an air ticket with a fixed return date.

For many people, a shortage of money is the main obstacle. It is the rare individual who, like Ian McArthur, specialises in 'reckless arrivals' (Istanbul with £5, Cairo with $20 between him and a friend, New York with $1). Other people wait until they have substantial savings before they dare leave home which gives them the enviable freedom to work only when they want to.

> **Sometimes pennilessness acts as a spur to action as it did in the case of Roger Blake:**
> *I left home with a substantial amount in savings. But they are long gone and for 18 months I have only been living off whatever I make locally. I have been down to just $50 more times than I'd care to remember. But somehow I always seem to come right. When I hear fellow travellers grumbling and sick with worry that they are down to $500, I cannot help but exclaim that they should enjoy it. In other words, when you've got it, flaunt it! Enjoy! There are those (usually with a few hundred dollars in the bank) who are 'looking for work' and those (including myself) who are looking for work. When your funds are REALLY low you WILL find a job, believe me.*

Anyone embarking on an extended trip will have to have a certain amount of capital to buy tickets, visas, insurance (see below), etc. But it is amazing how a little can go a long way if you are willing to take a wide variety of casual jobs en route and willing to weather the financial doldrums. Stephen Psallidas had £40 one December and four months later (most of which was spent working as a waiter in Paris) he had £1,600 for a planned year in Australia.

Money

It is of course always a good idea to have an emergency fund in reserve if possible, or at least access to money from home should you run into difficulties (see *In Extremis*). Yet a surprising number of our correspondents have written in with the advice not to bother saving money before leaving home. Adrian McCay is just one who advocates packing your bags and going even if you have only £10 (though he later confesses that he left for Australia with £300). How much you decide to set aside before leaving will depend on whether or not you have a gambling streak. But even gamblers should take only sensible risks. If you don't have much cash, it's probably advisable to have a return ticket. For example, if you decide to crew on a yacht from the Mediterranean and don't have much money, you could buy a very cheap last minute return flight to Rhodes or the Canaries. If you succeed and waste the return half of your charter, wonderful; if not, you will have had a few weeks in the sun – disappointing perhaps but not desperate.

Attitudes to saving vary too. A Malaysian student, T. P. Lye, thinks that there is no better feeling than planning travels while saving for them (assuming you realise your ambition). On the other hand, Ian McArthur finds saving over a long period depressing and starts to long for those pints of lager and late-night curries of which he has been deprived. But even Ian admits that 'living on the edge' is no fun when only a couple of hundreds of unattainable pounds stand between you and the air ticket you want to buy. When Xuela Edwards returned after two years of working her way around Europe, she tried to hang on to the travelling mentality which makes it much easier to save money: *'My advice is to consider your home country in the same way as others. It makes you more resourceful. Try to avoid the car loans and high living that usually make up home life. I'm sure that the reason bulb workers in Holland for example save so much money is because they live in tents (which I admit would be tricky at home).'*

Mike Tunnicliffe spent more on his world travels than he intended but didn't regret it:Originally, *'I intended to finance my year with casual work and return to England having spent only the price of my ticket. In the end, I delved far deeper into my life's savings than I had intended to do, but I was fortunate in having savings on which to draw, and I made the conscious decision to enjoy my year while I had the chance. In other words, fun now, pay later!'*

There's only one name you need to remember

SeasonWorkers.com

 The best ski resort jobs

 The best outdoor jobs

 The best summer jobs

 Best Recruitment 2004 Travel and Tourism web awards

 The best gap years

SeasonWorkers.com

Once you are resolved to travel, set a realistic target amount to save and then go for it wholeheartedly. Estimate how long it will take you to raise the desired amount and stick to the deadline as if your home country was going to sink into the ocean the day after. Don't get just any job, get one which is either highly paid (easier said than done of course) or one which offers as much overtime as you want. Dedicated working travellers consider a 70-hour week quite tolerable which will have the additional advantage of leaving you too tired to conduct an expensive social life. If you are already on the road and want to save, head for a place which allows this possibility, even if it won't be much fun. Adam Cook spent a miserable eight weeks picking peaches for an impossible French farmer but had saved £1,000 by the end of it. Murray Turner saved £4,000 in Hong Kong which soon made him forget the horrors of labouring on consecutive night shifts. If you have collected some assets before setting off, you are luckier than most. Property owners can arrange for the rental money to follow them at regular intervals.

The average budget of a travelling student is about £20 a day though many survive in some countries on half that. Whatever the size of your travelling fund, you should give some thought to how and in what form to carry your money. Travellers' cheques are much safer than cash, though they cost an extra 1% and banks for encashing them are not always near to hand. The most universally recognised brands are American Express, Thomas Cook and Visa. It is advisable also to keep a small amount of cash. Sterling is fine for most countries but US dollars or euros are preferred in much of the world such as Latin America, Eastern Europe and Israel. The easiest way to look up the exchange rate of any world currency is to check on the internet (e.g. www.xe.com/ucc) or to look at the Monday edition of the *Financial Times*. A Currency Conversion Chart is included in the Appendices.

Credit cards are useful for many purposes, provided you will not be tempted to abuse them. Few people think of crediting their Visa, Access, etc. account before leaving and then withdrawing cash on the credit card without incurring interest charges (since the money is not being borrowed). Visa has a TravelMoney service which works like a phone card; you credit it with cash and then access the money from cash machines worldwide with a PIN number. This is probably the most efficient way of transferring funds abroad, however find out whether your credit card charges a handling fee (typically 1.5%). Also find out in advance what charge there is for withdrawing from hole-in-the-wall machines abroad. For example the transaction fee for withdrawing foreign currency abroad or paying at point-of-sale with a standard Maestro card is 2.65% in addition to the ordinary exchange rate disadvantage plus cash machine withdrawals cost 2.25% of the sterling transaction up to a maximum £4 (no minimum) and POS fee is 75p.

Nevertheless a credit card is invaluable in an emergency and handy for showing at borders where the officials frown on penniless tourists, as Roger Blake discovered when he tried to leave Australia on a one-way ticket in 2004:

> On my world travels, I'm usually prepared to be challenged, by having printed bank statements (of borrowed money) at the ready. However, having never been asked before I didn't bother this time and, sods law, at Melbourne airport they weren't happy about allowing me to leave on a one-way ticket to New Zealand without proof of 'sufficient funds'. I pointed out that it states on my NZ work visa 'outward passage waived' but they were having none of it. I only had about A$400 in my pocket. But fortunately I have generous 'credit' available on my credit card. I was able to log onto my account via the internet and that was enough to persuade them to let me through...eventually, just one day short of a year to the day that I arrived.

If you have been slaving over a tepid sink full of washing up every day for the last few months, it would be disappointing to have your well-gotten gains stolen. From London to La Paz there are crooks lurking, ready to pounce upon the unsuspecting traveller. Theft takes many forms, from the highly trained gangs of gypsy children who artfully pick pockets all over Europe to violent attacks on the streets of American cities. Even more depressing is the theft which takes place by other travellers in youth hostels or on beaches. Risks can be reduced by carrying your wealth in several places including a comfortable money belt worn inside your clothing, steering clear of seedy or crowded areas and moderating your intake of alcohol. If you are mugged, and have an insurance policy which covers cash, you must obtain a police report (often for a fee) to stand any chance of recouping part of your loss.

While you are busy saving money to reach your desired target, you should be thinking of other ways in which to prepare yourself, including health, what to take and which contacts and skills you might cultivate.

Baggage

While aiming to travel as lightly as possible (leave the hair products behind) you should consider the advantage of taking certain extra pieces of equipment. For example many working travellers consider the extra weight of a tent and sleeping bag worthwhile in view of the independence and flexibility it gives them if they are offered work by a farmer who cannot provide accommodation. A comfortable pair of shoes is essential, since a job hunt abroad often involves a lot of pavement pounding. Stephen Hands had his shoes stolen while swimming at night and found that bleeding feet were a serious impediment to finding (never mind, doing) a job.

Mobile phones are now *de rigueur* for any job hunt on the road. Unless you are sure that you can use your phone from home on the cheapest network abroad, it is better to wait until you arrive to buy one. You might even pick up a bargain second hand one by scouring the notice boards at hostels and internet cafés. Make sure you keep it properly charged if you are waiting to be alerted of possible job openings.

Other items that can be packed that might be useful for a specific money-making project include a guitar for busking, a suit for getting work as an English teacher, a pair of fingerless gloves for cold-weather fruit-picking, and so on. Leave at home anything of value (monetary or sentimental). The general rule is stick to the bare essentials (including a Swiss army knife – but not in your hand luggage if you're flying or it will be confiscated at security). One travelling tip is to carry dental floss, useful not only for your teeth but as strong twine for mending backpacks, hanging up laundry, etc.

If you plan to work in one place for a long period of time, for instance on a kibbutz, you might allow yourself the odd (lightweight) luxury, such as an iPod (though theft will be a worry), short-wave radio or a jar of peanut butter. If you have prearranged a job, you can always post some belongings on ahead.

Good maps and guides always enhance one's enjoyment of a trip. If you are going to be based in a major city, buy a map ahead of time. If you are in London, visit the famous map and travel shop Stanfords in Covent Garden (12-14 Long Acre, London WC2E 9LP; 020-7836 1321; www.stanfords.co.uk), now with branches in Bristol and Manchester. Also recommended is Daunt Books for Travellers (83 Marylebone High Street, London W1; 020-7224 2295) which stocks fiction and travel writing alongside guide books and maps. The National Map Centre (22-24 Caxton St, London SW1H 0QU) is another place for Londoners to visit. The Map Shop (15 High St, Upton-on-Severn, Worcestershire WR8 0HJ; 01684 593146; themapshop@btinternet.com) does an extensive mail order business and will send you the relevant catalogue. Another online specialist is Maps Worldwide, Datum House, Lancaster Road, Melksham, Wilts. SN12 6TL (01225 707004; www.mapsworldwide.co.uk).

There are dozens of travel specialists throughout North America, including the Complete Traveller Bookstore (199 Madison Ave, New York, NY 10016; 212-685-9007) which also issues a free mail-order catalogue and, in Canada, the one-stop travel store Wanderlust (1929 West 4th Avenue, Kitsilano, Vancouver, BC, V6J 1M7; 604-739-2182; www.wanderlustore.com).

Health

No matter what country you are heading for, you should obtain the Department of Health leaflet T6 *Health Advice for Travellers*. This leaflet should be available from any post office or doctor's surgery. Alternatively you can request a free copy on the Health Literature Line 08701 555455 or read it online at www.dh.gov.uk, which also has country-by-country details.

In 2005 the United Kingdom will replace the form E111 with the new European Health Insurance Card (EHIC). The current phasing-in process involves an interim E111 form which became compulsory at the beginning of 2005 and will be valid until 31st December 2005. It is possible to apply in advance for the new EHIC by ticking the box on the new E111 application form (available from post offices). Your new card will then be automatically issued when the EHIC is introduced. In the first phase of introduction, the new card will cover health care for short stays and in the second phase, it will take the place of the current E128 and E119 which cover longer stays for job-seekers and students.

If you have a pre-existing medical condition it's important to anticipate what you might require in a crisis. Ask your GP or specialist support group for advice before you leave. If you're travelling with a tour operator let the company know about your condition in advance. Under extreme climatic conditions chronic or pre-existing conditions can be aggravated. Try to ascertain how easy it will be to access medicines on your trip, whether you'll be able to carry emergency supplies with you and how far you will be from specialist help. Always carry medications in their original containers and as a precaution you might carry a note from your doctor with an explanation of the drugs you're carrying and the relevant facts of your medical history. This could also include details of any allergies for example an intolerance of penicillin. This might be of use if you are involved in an accident or medical emergency.

If you plan to travel extensively in an area with poor medical standards and unreliable blood screening, you might want to consider equipping yourself with sterile syringes and needles. The Department of Travel Medicine at the Hospital for Tropical Diseases recommends that you should carry a specially prepared sterile needle kit in case local emergency treatment may require injections; MASTA (see below) sells these for £18.

Any visits beyond the developed world, particularly to tropical climates, require careful preparation. You will face the risk of contracting malaria or water-borne diseases like typhoid and cholera. You will need to provide your medical practitioner with precise details about where you intend to travel. Visit a travel medical centre at least a month before departure because some immunisations like those for yellow fever must be given well in advance. Expert medical advice is widely available on how to avoid tropical illness, so you should take advantage of modern medicine to protect yourself. And be prepared to pay for the necessary inoculations which are not normally covered by the NHS. It is always worth asking at your own surgery since if they are able to give good advice (and the Internet has made that possible for any doctor worth his or her salt), the injections may be considerably cheaper than at a private specialist clinic where you are likely to pay between £30 and £50 per vaccine.

Pre-eminent among specialist providers are Nomad Travel Clinics which specialise in longhaul travel; the Nomad Travel Stores can be found in Russell Square, Victoria and North London plus Bristol (www.nomadtravel.co.uk) all of which have travel clinics that can offer expert advice. The Hospital for Tropical Diseases (Mortimer Market, Capper St, Tottenham Court Road, London, WC1E 6AU; www.uclh.org) operates an automated information line on 09061 337733 (50p per minute and calls should last 7-8 minutes). To make an appointment ring 020-7388 9600. Consultations are offered at their clinic near Oxford Circus for £15 but if you have your jabs there, the fee is waived. The respected travel agent Trailfinders operates a Travel Clinic at 194 Kensington High St (020-7983 3999).

MASTA (Moorfield Road, Yeadon, Leeds LS19 7BN; enquiries@masta.org/ www.masta.org) is one of the most authoritative sources of travellers' health information in Britain and maintains a database of the latest information on the prevention of tropical and other diseases. Calls to the Travellers' Health Line (0906 822 4100) are charged at 60p per minute (average cost of call £2). MASTA can provide personalised advice depending on your destinations, which can be either e-mailed or posted to you. Here you can find explanations about protection against malaria, guidelines on what to eat and drink, and how to avoid motion sickness, jet lag and sunburn. MASTA's network of travel clinics administers inoculations and, like their online shop, sells medical kits and other specialist equipment like water purifiers and survival tools. MASTA also co-operates with the Blood Care Foundation, a charity that aims to deliver properly screened blood and sterile transfusion equipment to members in an emergency.

It is worth looking at a general guide to travel medicine such as *Bugs, Bites and Bowels* by Dr. Jane Wilson Howarth (Cadogan, £9.99) or *Traveller's Health: How to Stay Healthy Abroad* by Richard Dawood (OUP, £15.99). These books emphasise the necessity of avoiding tap water and recommend ways to purify your drinking water by filtering, boiling or chemical additives (iodine is more reliable than chlorine). MASTA and Nomad market various water purifiers; among the best are the 'Aquapure Traveller' (£40) and the 'Trekker Travel Well' (£65). Tap water throughout Western Europe is safe to drink.

Increasingly, people are seeking advice via the internet; check for example www.fitfortravel.scot.nhs.uk; www.tmb.ie and www.travelhealth.co.uk. The private internet-based medical service www.e-med.co.uk has a large travel section with a detailed immunisation schedule. A pre-travel consultation costs £40.

Americans seeking general travel health advice should ring the Center for Disease Control & Prevention Hotline in Atlanta on 404-332-4559; www.cdc.gov/travel.

Malaria is continuing to make a serious comeback in many parts of the world, due to the resistance of certain strains of mosquito to the pesticides and preventative medications which have been so extensively relied upon in the past. You must be particularly careful if travelling to a place where there is falciparum malaria which is potentially fatal. Out of up to 2,500 British travellers who return home to the UK with malaria each year, 10 to 20 will die. The two main drugs can be obtained over the counter: Chloroquine and Proguanil (brand name Paludrine). In regions resistant to these drugs, you will have to take both or a third line of defence such as Maloprim or Mefloquine available only on prescription. Because of possible side effects it is important that your doctor be able to vary the level of toxicity to match the risks prevalent in your destination. A newly licensed (and expensive) drug called Malarone is used as an alternative to mefloquine or doxycyline, and is recommended for short trips to highly chloroquine-resistant areas. New drugs are being developed all the time and sometimes there is a time lag before they are licensed in the UK or USA. For example in her gap year in Madagascar, Karen Hedges twice contracted malaria but was quickly treated with an effective drug called Coartem, expensive by local standards, and not yet licensed in the UK.

Unfortunately these prophylactic medications are not foolproof, and even those who have scrupulously swallowed their pills before and after their trip as well as during it have been known to contract the disease. It is therefore essential to take mechanical precautions against mosquitoes. Wearing fine silk clothes discourages bites. If possible, screen the windows and sleep under an permethrin-impregnated mosquito net since the offending mosquitoes feed between dusk and dawn. (Practise putting your mosquito net up before leaving home since some are tricky to assemble.) Some travellers have improvised with some netting intended for prams which takes up virtually no luggage space. If you don't have a net, cover your limbs at nightfall with light-coloured garments, apply insect repellent with the active ingredient DEET and sleep with a fan on to keep the air moving. Try to keep your room free of the insects too by using mosquito coils, vaporisers, etc.

Deet is strong enough to last many hours. Wrist and ankle bands impregnated with the chemical are available and easy to use. Cover your limbs as night falls (6pm on the equator). Wearing fine silk clothes discourages bites and keep the repellent topped up. Scientists have established that mosquitoes tend to be drawn to carbon dioxide vapours, heat and body odours. Avoid wherever possible using deodorants, soap and perfumes which can attract the insects.

A company which markets mosquito repellents and nets is Oasis Nets (High St, Stoke Ferry, Norfolk PE33 9SP; 01366 500466); they will send a free fact sheet about malaria in your destination country. Travelpharm (Unit 10 D, Mill Park Industrial Estate, White Cross Road, Woodbury Saiterton, Devon EX5 1EL; 01395 233771; www.travelpharm.com) sells an extensive range of mosquito nets, anti-malaria drugs, water purification equipment and travel accessories via its online store.

The International Association for Medical Assistance to Travellers (IAMAT) continues to collate news and information about health risks abroad. This organisation co-ordinates doctors and clinics around the world who maintain high medical standards at reasonable cost e.g. US$55 per consultation for IAMAT members. They will send you a directory listing IAMAT centres throughout the world as well as detailed leaflets about malaria and other tropical diseases and country-by-country climate and hygiene charts. There is no set fee for joining the association, but donations are welcome; at the very least you should cover their postage and printing costs. Further information is available on their website www.iamat.org including their world malaria chart and immunisation recommendations country-by-country.

Consider taking a first aid course before leaving. The St. John Ambulance (020-7324 4000; www.sja.org.uk) offers a range of Lifesaver and Lifesaver Plus courses. The standard half-day emergency first aid course costs from £20 (depending on region).

Insurance

Given the limitations of state-provided reciprocal health cover (i.e. that it covers only emergencies), you should certainly take out comprehensive private cover which will cover extras like loss of baggage and, more importantly, emergency repatriation. Every enterprise in the travel business is delighted to sell you insurance because of the commission earned. Shopping around can save you money. Ring several insurance companies with your specifications and compare prices. If you are going abroad to work, you are expected to inform your insurer ahead of time (which is often impossible). Many policies will be invalidated if you injure yourself at work, e.g. put out your back while picking plums or cut yourself in a restaurant kitchen, though it is not clear how they would know how or where the accident took place. If you snap your Achilles tendon, was it jumping off an orchard ladder or playing squash? There is no need to ask a broker to quote for a tailor-made policy since many of the backpacker policies specifically cover casual work.

Europ-Assistance Ltd (www.europ-assistance.co.uk) is the world's largest assistance organisation with a network of doctors, air ambulances, agents and vehicle rescue services in 208 countries worldwide offering emergency assistance abroad 24 hours a day. The Voyager Travel policy covering periods from 6 to 18 months costs £265 for 12 months in Europe and £545 worldwide. The policy is invalidated if you return home during the period insured. American readers can obtain details from Worldwide Assistance, 1825 K St NW, Suite 1000, Washington, DC 20006 (1-800-821-2828; www.worldwideassistance.com).

Many companies charge less, though you will have to decide whether you are satisfied with their level of cover. Most offer a standard rate that covers medical emergencies and a premium rate that covers personal baggage, cancellation, etc. Some travel policies list as one of their exclusions: 'any claims which arise while the Insured is engaged in any manual employment'. If you are not planning to visit North America, the premiums will be much less expensive. Some companies to consider are listed here with an estimate of their premiums for 12 months of worldwide cover (including the USA). Expect to pay roughly £20-£25 per month for basic cover and £35-£40 for more extensive cover.

Club Direct, Dominican House, St John's St, Chichester, W Sussex (0800 083 2455; www. clubdirect.com). Work abroad is included provided it does not involve using heavy machinery; £337 for year-long cover including baggage cover.

Columbus Direct, 17 Devonshire Square, London EC2M 4SQ (020-7375 0011; 08450 761030; www.columbusdirect.com). Globetrotter policy (basic medical cover only) costs about £200 for one year. More extensive cover is offered for £312 and £364.

Coverworks, 47a Barony Road, Nantwich, Cheshire CW5 7PB (08702 862828; www. coverworks.com). Policy specially designed for working holidays. In 2004 had a special offer of including a free working holiday visa for Australia with a 12-month worldwide policy costing £235 (€325).

Downunder Worldwide Travel Insurance. 3 Spring St, Paddington, London W2 3RA (0800 393908; www.dinsure.com). Backpacker policy covers working holidays (excluding ladders and heavy machinery) starts at £250. Adventurer policy covering adventure sports costs £340.

Endsleigh Insurance, Endsleigh House, Cheltenham, Glos GL50 3NR. Offices in most university towns. Twelve months of cover worldwide costs from £202, £305 for higher cover. Maximum age 35.

gosure.com – 0845 222 0020; www.gosure.com. Worldwide backpacker policy (which doesn't cover lost baggage) for just over £200 to cover 18 months including up to 3 months in North America.

MRL Insurance, Enterprise House, Station Parade, Chipstead, Surrey CR5 3TE; 0870 876 7677; www.mrlinsurance.co.uk. £210 for backpackers under 35.

Travel Insurance Agency, Suite 2, Percy News, 755B High Road, North Finchley, London N12 8JY (020-8446 5414/5; www.travelinsurers.com) £210/£290.

If you do have to make a claim, you may be unpleasantly surprised by the amount of the settlement eventually paid. Loss adjusters have ways of making calculations which prove that you are entitled to less than you think. For example when Caroline Langdon was mugged in Seville she suffered losses of about £100, for which her insurance company paid compensation of £22.30. The golden rule is to amass as much documentation as possible to support your application, most importantly a police report.

Recommended US insurers for extended stays abroad are International SOS Assistance Inc (8 Neshaminy Interplex, Suite 207, Trevose, PA 19053-6956; 1-800-523-8930; www.internationalsos.com) which is used by the Peace Corps and is designed for people working in remote areas. A firm which specialises in providing insurance for Americans living overseas is Wallach & Company (107 West Federal St, PO Box 480, Middleburg, VA 20118-0480; 1-800-237-6615; www.wallach.com).

Security

Travel inevitably involves balancing risks and navigating through hazards real or imagined. The Foreign & Commonwealth Office of the UK government provides updated travel information and cautions for every country in the world and additional risk assessment of current trouble spots and advice on how to find consular help and legal advice. You can contact the Travel Advice Unit by phone on 0870 606 0290 or check their website www.fco.gov.uk/travel. The FCO also runs a 'Know Before You Go' campaign to raise awareness among backpackers and independent travellers of potential risks and dangers and how to guard against them, principally by having a good insurance policy. According to FCO statistics, young travellers are twice as likely as the average to get into some kind of trouble abroad and yet many of them live to regret not having bothered with insurance.

A couple of specialist organisations put on courses to prepare clients for potential dangers and problems on a world trip or gap year. Needless to say, these are normally aimed at naïve 18 year olds whose parents are paying for the course though they are open to anyone willing to pay the fee of £150-£350. The newest provider is Safetrek (East Culme House, Cullompton, Devon EX15 1NX; 01884 839704; www.safetrek.co.uk). Two others are The Knowledge Gap Ltd (Pitt Farmhouse, Chevithorne, Nr Tiverton, Devon EX16 7PU; 0117-974 3217; www.kgap.co.uk) and Objective Team Ltd (Bragborough Lodge Farm, Braunston, Daventry, Northants NN11 7HA; 01788 899029; office@objectiveteam.com) run by a former member of the SAS.

Qualifications

These sensible precautions of purchasing maps, buying insurance, finding out about malaria, etc. are relatively straightforward and easy. Other specific ways of preparing yourself, such as studying a language, learning to sail or dive, cook, drive or type, or taking up a fitness programme, are a different kettle of fish. But the traveller who has a definite commitment may well consider embarking on a self-improvement scheme before setting off. Among the most useful qualifications you can acquire are a certificate in Teaching English as a Foreign Language (see chapter *Teaching*) and a knowledge of sailing or diving (see *Tourism* chapter for the address of a course which also offers job placement).

The person who has a definite job skill to offer increases his or her chances of success. After working his way from Paris to Cape Town via Queensland, Stephen Psallidas concluded '*There are several professions which are in demand anywhere in the world, and I would say that anyone who practises them would be laughing all the way to the 747. These are: secretary, cook/chef, accountant, nurse and hairdresser.*'

Nursing training is very useful and, after a year of working her way through Europe doing a variety of things, Mary Hall is glad she stuck the training since she has found that medical doors opened for her in Gibraltar, Uganda and South Africa. Childcare experience is also a highly portable skill.

It is a good idea to take documentary evidence of any qualifications you have earned. Also take along a sheaf of references, both character and work-related, if possible, all on headed notepaper. It is difficult to arrange for these to be sent once you're on the road. An even smarter move is to scan these documents before you depart and email them to yourself or carry a floppy disk. That way you can access them from any internet café around the world. It is a good idea to prepare your CV at the same time. When it comes time to apply for a job abroad, you'll have the template on the computer and can just tinker with it according to the vacancy you're going for.

Language

Having even a limited knowledge of a foreign language is especially valuable for the job-seeker. Stephen Hands thinks that this can't be over-emphasised; after an unsuccessful attempt to find work in France, he returned to Britain and, even before phoning home, signed up for a language course (and received the additional perk of a student card).

Evening language classes offered by local authorities usually follow the academic year and are aimed at hobby learners. Intensive courses offered privately are much more expensive. If you are really dedicated, consider using a self-study programme with books and tapes (which start at £30), correspondence course or broadcast language course. Even if you don't make much headway with the course at home, take it with you since you will have more incentive to learn once you are immersed in a language.

Although many people have been turning to the web to teach them a language, many conventional teach-yourself courses are still on the market for example from Berlitz (020-7518 8300), the BBC (08700 100222), Linguaphone (0800 282417; www.linguaphone.co.uk) and Audioforum (www.audioforum.com). All of them offer deluxe courses with refinements such as interactive videos and of course these cost much more (from £150). Linguaphone recommends half an hour of study a day for three months to master the basics of a language.

A more enjoyable way of learning a language (and normally a more successful one) is by speaking it with the natives. The cheapest way to do this is to link up with a native speaker living in your local area, possibly by putting an ad in a local paper or making contact through a local English language school. Numerous organisations offer 'in-country' language courses, though these tend to be expensive. CESA Languages Abroad (Pennance Road, Lanner, Cornwall TR16 5TQ; 01209 211800; www.cesalanguages.com) and Language Courses Abroad Ltd (67 Ashby Road, Loughborough, Leicestershire LE11 3AA; 01509 211612; www.languagesabroad.co.uk) offer the chance to learn languages on location. Caledonia Languages Abroad (The Clockhouse, Bonnington Mill, 72 Newhaven Rd, Edinburgh EH6 5QG; 0131-621 7721; www.caledonialanguages.co.uk) offers language courses worldwide and in Latin America combines language courses with voluntary placements. In the USA, language learners might like to contact the National Registration Center for Study Abroad (PO Box 1393, Milwaukee, WI 53201; info@nrcsa.com) for a listing of language schools in more than 25 countries. Many include options to participate in volunteer work or career-focused internships. Full-immersion courses are available at Eurocentres worldwide; ring 1-800-648-4809 for details. An effective search engine for locating courses is provided by the Institute of International Education on www.iiepassport.org. Alternatives are www.abroadlanguages.com and www.worldwide.edu.

Another possibility is to forgo structured lessons and simply live with a family, which has the further advantage of allowing you to become known in a community which might lead to job openings later. Several agencies arrange paying guest stays which are designed for people wishing to learn or improve language skills in the context of family life. EIL, a non-profit cultural and educational organisation, offers short-term homestay programmes in more than 30 countries; contact EIL for their fees (287 Worcester Road, Malvern, Worcestershire WR14 1AB; 01684 562577; www.eiluk.org).

Making Contacts

Based on her years of living on three continents, Till Bruckner thinks that learning the language is pivotal:
Learning the local language will not only help you find a job on the spot, it also makes life abroad so much more rewarding. As an extra bonus, you'll find work easier to come by when you return home too. The first thing I do when I arrive somewhere now is to get myself language lessons. The teacher will have met many other foreigners, have local connections and speak some English. In other words, he or she is the natural starting point on your job hunt. If you make clear that you can only continue paying for your lessons if you find a way of earning some money, you've found a highly motivated ally in your search for work.

The importance of knowing people, not necessarily in high places but on the spot, is stressed by many of our contributors. Some people are lucky enough to have family and friends scattered around the world in positions to offer advice or even employment. Others must create their own contacts by exploiting less obvious connections.

Dick Bird, who spent over a year travelling around South America, light-heartedly anticipates how this works:

In Bolivia we hope to start practising another survival technique known as 'having some addresses'. The procedure is quite simple. Before leaving one's country of origin, inform everyone you know from your immediate family to the most casual acquaintance, that you are about to leave for South America. With only a little cajoling they might volunteer the address of somebody they once met on the platform of Clapham Junction or some other tenuous connection who went out to South America to seek their fortunes. You then present your worthy self on the unsuspecting emigré's doorstep and announce that you have been in close and recent communication with their nearest and dearest. Although you won't necessarily be welcomed with open arms, the chances are they will be eager for your company and conversation. Furthermore these contacts are often useful for finding work: doing odd jobs, farming, tutoring people they know, etc.

Everyone has ways of developing links with people abroad. Think of distant cousins and family friends, foreign students met in your home town, pen friends, people in the town twinned with yours, etc. Maybe you dimly recall that someone you went to school with moved to Hong Kong or Tenerife and you could have a go at tracing them through the friendsreunited website. Human rights groups in your home country might have links with your destination or even know about opportunities for doing voluntary work in their offices abroad. Jacqueline Edwards placed a small notice in European vegetarian newsletters asking for a live-in position for herself and her young son. Tony Dalby of Swindon came up with an original way of forging links with Japan: '*I wrote off to the local Honda car plant and requested some contacts in order to gain some first-hand experience of Japanese culture and language before travelling. I now have links with a Japanese family.*'

School exchanges and membership in the Youth Hostels Association can also result in valuable contacts. To join in the UK, contact the YHA at Trevelyan House, Dimple Road, Matlock, Derbyshire DE4 3YH; (0870 770 8868; www.yha.org.uk). Annual membership costs £14 or £7 for the under-18s.

One way of developing contacts is to join a travel club such as the Globetrotters Club (BCM/Roving, London WC1N 3XX; info@globetrotters.co.uk) for £15/€27 a year. The Club has no office and so correspondence addressed to the above box office address is answered by volunteers. Members receive a bi-monthly travel newsletter and a list of members, many of whom are willing to extend hospitality to other globetrotters and possibly to advise them on local employment prospects.

Servas International is an organisation begun by an American Quaker, which runs a worldwide programme of free hospitality exchanges for travellers, to further world peace and understanding. Normally you don't stay with one host for more than a couple of days. To become a Servas traveller or host in the UK, contact Servas Britain, 68 Cadley Road, Collingbourne Ducis, Marlborough, Wilts. SN8 3EB; 020 8444 7778 (www.servasbritain. u-net.com) who can forward your enquiry to your Area Co-ordinator. Before a traveller can be given a list of hosts (which are drawn up every autumn), he or she must pay a fee of £25 (£35 for couples) and be interviewed by a co-ordinator. Servas US is at 11 John St, Suite 505, New York, NY 10038 (212-267-0252; www.usservas.org). There is a joining fee of US$85 and a refundable deposit of $25 for host lists in up to five countries.

Janet Renard from the US stayed with 21 Servas hosts during her six months in Europe
We call it 'Servas Magic'. Each visit was a great experience. The houses we visited ranged from a 16th century farmhouse in Wales to a cramped apartment in Naples. While we were on an archaeological dig in France, one family hosted us for three weekends, taking us to St. Malo and even sailing in a regatta. For some hosts, we gardened, chopped wood or cooked; others insisted on waiting on us completely.

Other hospitality clubs and exchanges are worth investigating. Women Welcome Women World Wide (88 Easton St, High Wycombe, Bucks. HP11 1LT; tel/fax 01494 465441; www.womenwelcomewomen.org.uk) enables women of different countries to visit one another. There is no set subscription, but the minimum donation requested is £25/$47, which covers the cost of the membership list and three newsletters in which members may publish announcements. There are currently 3,500 members (aged 16-80+) in 70 countries.

Hospitality exchange organisations crop up from time to time. Check out www.hospitalityclub.org (which has a special area for hitch-hikers) in which membership is free. A more commercial site is www.blue-home.com based in France; the membership fee of €16 entitles you to list yourself on the site for possible hospitality exchanges as well as house-sitting and home exchange. Other possibilities include the Hospitality Exchange, 822 W. Watson St, Lewistown, Montana 59457 (406-538-8770; www.hospex.net) which charges $20 for a year's membership.

The internet has of course revolutionised the way in which networks of contacts and friends can be developed. Catherine Carfoot spent a year after university in Australia and New Zealand:

> I thought you might be interested in the extent to which my adventures in cyber space have impacted on my real life exploits. For example the only genuine residents I met while travelling in the South Island (apart from people running hostels, which hardly counts) were either people I met on the net or their friends. It would make my mother's hair curl to say the least of it, but I stayed with a very nice chap (father of two) in Rotorua who took me out on his boat as well as making me dinner and letting me sleep in his spare room. Obviously one has to counsel caution in these matters but equally trust is a two-way street.

Online communications and electronic chat rooms may eventually replace corresponding with penpals but until then, pen friend organisations in Europe and North America charge varying fees for matching up correspondents. After years of corresponding with a girl in a small East German town, Kathy Merz from South Carolina paid what she thought would be a brief visit and instead turned into a six month stay while she worked in the family's butcher shop. The site www.pen-pals.net claims to be the largest penpal organisation in the world.

Travelling Alone

Many travellers emphasise the benefits of travelling alone, such as a chance to make friends with the locals more easily. Most are surprised that loneliness is hardly an issue, since there is always congenial company to be met in travellers' hostels, kibbutzim, etc. some of whom even team up with each other for short or long spells. Of course, if you are working in a remote rural area and don't speak the language fluently, you will inevitably miss having a companion and may steer away from this kind of situation if it bothers you. If you are anxious about the trials and traumas of being on your own, try a short trip and see how you like it.

Women can travel solo just as enjoyably as men, as Woden Teachout discovered:

> I'm 24, female, American and like to travel alone. I have travelled with friends on occasion which is definitely more 'fun' but it lacks the perilous sense of possibility and adventure that I love most about travelling. Whatever situations you get yourself into when you are on your own, you have to get out of. I have been terribly frightened: I spent the night of my 21st birthday huddled in a cellar hole in downtown Malmo Sweden, wet and shivering, knowing that a local rapist had claimed three victims within the fortnight. But by the same token, the glorious moments, the stick-out-your-thumb-and-be-glad-for-whatever-is-going-to-happen-next moments, the feelings of triumph and absolute freedom, are uniquely yours.

Try to seek out traditional female meeting places like produce markets, communal wash-houses, etc. The Women Welcome Women club mentioned above could be useful.

There will always be an element of risk in any adventurous endeavour. According to the most recent Foreign Office figures at least 50 women were raped in the previous year, over half of whom were in Spain, with incidents also reported in Thailand, Turkey, Cyprus and the US. It is unlikely that the numbers relative to the number of women abroad show any higher index of danger than women who stay in their home countries. As a point of comparison, more than 200 Britons were killed in traffic accidents abroad in the same year.

Travelling Companions

You have to be fairly lucky to have a friend who is both willing and available when you are to embark on a working trip. If you don't have a suitable companion and are convinced you need one, you can publish your request in the Connections column of *Wanderlust* magazine (www.wanderlust.co.uk), in the Globetrotters Club newsletter *Globe* (address on previous page) or the Youth Hostels Association's *Triangle* magazine.

Spending time in travel chatrooms like Lonely Planet's thorntree or (if appropriate) www.gapyear.com might turn up a like-minded companion. Start your search for a companion well in advance of your proposed departure date so there will be a chance to get to know the person a bit before the trip.

There are also a few agencies in the US which try to match up compatible travel companions for an annual or a one-off fee, for example TravelChums (www.travelchums.com) and the long-established Travel Companion Exchange, PO Box 833, Amityville, NY 11701 (516-454-0880; www.whytravelalone.com).

Sarah Clifford describes the easiest way of all to find companions: *'I think you should warn people that Work You Way Around the World is infectious. Even people who I would never have thought would want to go anywhere start flicking through the pages, then get more and more absorbed, become incredibly enthusiastic and demand to go with me on my travels!'*

Staying in Touch

The revolution in communication technology means that you are never far from home. Internet cafés can be found in almost every corner of the world, where you can check your e-mail and link up with other travellers. The easiest way to stay in touch is by e-mail, using free messaging services such as www.hotmail.com or www.yahoo.co.uk. If you prefer the human voice, don't rely on your mobile phone unless you have specifically bought a tri-band model; most European mobiles do not interface with the US roaming system. Instead, a plethora of companies in the UK and US sell pre-paid calling cards intended to simplify international phoning. You credit your card account with an amount of your choice (normally starting at £10 or £20), or buy a card for $10 or $20. You are given an access code which can be used from any phone. Lonely Planet, the travel publisher, has an easy-to-use communications card called eKno which offers low cost calls, voice mail and email (www.ekno.lonelyplanet.com). Rough Guides has just launched some reasonably priced travel planner software called intouch (www.roughguidesintouch.com) which might be worth investigating.

Clearly there are advantages to such easy communication, though there are also travellers out there who spend an inordinate amount of time tracking down and inhabiting cybercafés instead of looking around the country and meeting locals in the old-fashioned, strike-up-a-conversation way. Danny Jacobson from Madison is also ambivalent about its virtues (and committed his thoughts to paper): *'I've met loads of travellers using e-mail to meet people online, to keep in touch with people they've met travelling, to find out information about a place and to publish their own adventures. It all seems to be making the world an incredibly small place. Myself, I admit I've spent a fair share of money on e-mail and rely on it at times quite a bit. I worry that it is getting easier and easier to do everything from a sitting position.'*

It would be a shame if e-mail deprived long-term travellers of arriving at a poste restante address and having the pleasure (sweeter because it has been deferred) of reading their mail.

RED TAPE

Passports and Work Visas

A ten-year UK passport costs £42 for 32 pages and £54.50 for 48 pages, and should be processed by the Passport Agency within ten days, though it is safer to allow more time. The one-week fast track application procedures costs £70 and an existing passport can be renewed in person at a passport office but only if you have made a prior appointment by ringing the Passport Agency on 0870 521 0410 and are willing to pay £89 (£95.50 for 48 pages). Passport office addresses are listed on passport application forms available from main post office. All relevant information can be found on the website www.passports. gov.uk.

Most countries will want to see that your passport has at least 90 days to run beyond your proposed stay. If your passport is lost or stolen while travelling, contact first the police then your nearest Consulate. Obtaining replacement travel documents is easier if you have a record of the passport number and its date and place of issue, so keep these in a separate place, preferably a photocopy of the title page.

The free reciprocity of labour within the European Union means that the red tape has been simplified (though not done away with completely). See the chapter *EU Employment*. As will become clear as you read further in this book, work permits/work visas outside the EU are not readily available to ordinary mortals. In almost all cases, you must find an employer willing to apply to the immigration authorities on your behalf months in advance of the job's starting date, while you are in your home country. This is usually a next-to-impossible feat unless you are a high ranking nuclear physicist, a foreign correspondent or are participating in an organised exchange programme where the red tape is taken care of by your sponsoring organisation. Wherever possible, we have mentioned such possibilities throughout this book. The official visa information should be requested from the Embassy or Consulate (if only to be ignored); addresses and links are accessible via www.embassyworld.com. For general information about visas, see *Travel*.

Once you are installed in a country, be aware that any enemy you make who knows that your legal position is dodgy will be tempted to tip off the authorities. For example if you are trying to freelance as a guide and are resented by local operators, you may find yourself in trouble.

Student Cards

With an International Student Identity Card (ISIC; www.isiccard.com) it is often possible to obtain reduced fares on trains, planes and buses, £1 off each night's stay at a youth hostel in the UK, discounted admission to museums and theatres, and other perks. The ISIC is available to all students in full-time education. There is no age limit though some flight carriers do not apply discounts for students over 31. To obtain a card (which is valid for 15 months from September) you will need to complete the ISIC application form, provide a passport photo, proof of full-time student status (NUS card or official letter) and the fee of £7. Take these to any students' union, local student travel office or send a cheque for £7.50 to ISIC Mail Order, DPS Hull Ltd, Unit 132, Lois Perlman Centre, Goulden St, Hull HU3 4DL). When issued with an ISIC, students also receive a handbook containing travel tips, details of national and international discounts and how to get in touch with the ISIC helpline, a special service for travelling students who need advice in an emergency.

The fee for an ISIC card in the US is $22. An alternative card is the International Student Exchange Identity Card available from ISE Cards, 11043 North St Andrew's Way, Scottsdale, AZ 85254 (1-800-255-8000; www.isecard.com) at a cost of $25.

If you are not eligible, people have been known to walk into their local college, say that they are about to start a course and request a student card. There are a great many forgeries in circulation, most of which originate in Bangkok, Istanbul or Cairo.

Bureaucracy at Large

Having your papers in order is a recurring problem for the working traveller. Andrew Winwood thinks that this book underestimates the difficulties: *'I wish that you would be honest about immigration, obtaining the proper visas, etc. But having said that, I wouldn't have had the nerve to go in the first place if I'd known how hard it would be.'*

It is easy to understand why every country in the world has immigration policies which are principally job protection schemes for their own nationals. Nevertheless it can be frustrating to encounter bureaucratic hassles if you merely intend to teach English for a month or so, and there is really no local candidate available with your advantages (e.g. fluency). In all the countries with which we deal, we have tried to set out as clearly as possible the official position regarding visas and work and/or residence permits for both EU and non-EU readers.

If you are cautious by nature you may be very reluctant to transgress the regulations. People in this category will feel much happier if they can arrange things through official channels, such as approved exchange organisations or agencies which arrange permits for you, or by finding an employer willing to get them a work permit, which must normally be collected outside the country of employment. Arranging things this way will require extra reserves of patience.

It seems that a great many decisions are taken at the discretion (or whim) of the individual bureaucrat. Whether or not a document is issued seems to depend more on the mood of the official than on the rulebook. Leeson Clifton from Canada followed all the rules for getting official status as a temporary employee in Norway. When she took her passport to the police for their stamp she was told it would take two weeks and she could not work in the meantime. She returned to the same office the next day and got it done on the spot. She concludes: *'The left hand didn't know what the right hand was doing, but of course this is the same in any country. When dealing with government authorities always be patient and pleasant, but keep on asking for what you want and in most cases you'll get it (eventually). Losing your cool gets you nowhere; after all they have no obligations to you.'*

Other travellers are prepared to throw caution to the winds and echo Helen Welch's view that 'government bureaucracy is the same anywhere, i.e. notoriously slow; by the time the system discovers that you are an alien you can be long gone.' This is more serious in some countries and in certain circumstances than in others, and we have tried to give some idea in this book of the enthusiasm with which the immigration laws are enforced from country to country and the probable outcome for employer and employee if the rules are broken. The authorities will usually turn a blind eye in areas where there is a labour shortage and enforce the letter of the law when there is a glut of unemployed foreign workers. If you do land an unofficial job (helping a Greek islander build a taverna, picking kiwifruit in New Zealand, doing odd jobs at an orphanage in central Africa) try to be as discreet as possible. Noisy boasting has been the downfall of many a traveller who has attracted unwelcome attention. It is always important to be as sensitive as possible to local customs and expectations.

Julian Peachey is another veteran traveller who is suspicious of the value of using official channels: *'One of my conclusions is that going through the official channels and taking advice from officialdom is often a mistake. 'Officially' (i.e. the view of the British Council in Paris) it is very hard to get teaching work, as there are so many highly qualified English people living in Paris. The French agricultural information office warns that there is very little in the way of farm work for foreigners.'*

And yet Julian had a variety of teaching and agricultural jobs throughout France. He claims that if he had believed all that he had been told by officialdom and had taken all the suggested precautions, he would never have been able to go in the first place.

GETTING A JOB BEFORE YOU GO

The subsequent chapters contain a great deal of advice and a number of useful addresses for people wishing to fix up a job before they leave home. If you have ever worked for a firm with branches abroad (e.g. Virgin Records, Kelly Girl, even McDonalds) it may be worth writing in advance to ask about prospects. There is a lot to recommend prior planning especially to people who have never travelled abroad and who feel some trepidation at the prospect. There are lots of 'easy' ways to break into the world of working travellers, for instance working on an American summer camp, joining a two-week voluntary workcamp on the Continent or going on a kibbutz, all of which can be fixed up at home with few problems. Inevitably these will introduce you to an international circle of travellers whose experiences will entertain, instruct and inspire the novice traveller.

Professional or skilled people have a chance of prearranging a job. For example nurses, plumbers, architects, motor mechanics, piano tuners, teachers, divers, secretaries and computer programmers can sometimes find work abroad within their profession by answering adverts in British newspapers and specialist journals, by writing direct to hospitals, schools and businesses abroad, and by registering with the appropriate professional association.

But the majority of people who dream about working their way around the world do not have a professional or trade qualification. Many will be students who are on the way to becoming qualified, but are impatient to broaden their horizons before graduation. The main requirement seems to be perseverance. Dennis Bricault sent off 137 letters in order to fix up a summer job as a volunteer at an alpine youth hostel.

> **Rob Abblett recounts how doggedness worked in his favour:**
> *Armed with a couple of addresses of Corsican clementine farmers, I hounded them mercilessly over the years with my requests for work. The organic fruit farm wouldn't employ me on any terms and seemed a bit miffed when I phoned them. My present employer would throw my letters straight into the wastepaper basket. By pure chance one of them escaped his attention and got through to the sleeping partner who happened to have had an English nanny and spoke excellent English. He persuaded my boss to employ me on condition that he accepted full responsibility for kicking me off the orchard if I turned out to be like the last Brit that worked here many years ago. Apparently I have been an exemplary worker and have been wined and dined over the Christmas period with many a banquet.*

For many jobs, it is not at all easy to fix something up in advance. In an ideal world, you could stop in at your local branch of an international employment agency, impress them with your talent and keenness and be assigned your choice of job whether entertainments manager on a Caribbean cruise or ski tow operator in New Zealand. But it just isn't like that and people who expect jobs abroad to be handed to them on a platter by some agency or other are naïve in the extreme. Very very few employers anywhere in the world are willing to hire someone they haven't met. Some cynics would maintain that an employer who cannot fill vacancies locally, and who hires foreign people sight unseen, must be suspect. John Linnemeier worked at a Norwegian hotel, 'for a guy who had such a terrible reputation that none of the locals would work for him'.

Several editions ago, a reader and traveller (Stephen Hands) expressed his longing for a miraculous network of information for working travellers:

Wouldn't it be great if someone set up a scheme, whereby people could forward cor-

respondence to an exchange of some kind, for people to swap addresses of places they've worked abroad. For example someone planning to work in Nice could write to some agency to obtain the address of another traveller who could tell him what the manager's like or if the chef is an axe-wielding homicidal maniac or that the accommodation is a hole in the bottom of the local coal mine. This would enable working travellers to avoid the rip-off places; also it might save them turning up in places where the work potential is zero.

The scheme which Stephen thought was a pipedream just a few years ago now has a name, the Internet. Somewhere on the web, you can probably find out that the axe-wielding chef has been replaced by a Quaker and that the coal mine has been tastefully refurbished.

Employment Agencies

Adverts that offer glamorous jobs and high wages abroad should be treated with scepticism. They are often placed by one-man companies who are in fact selling printed bumph about jobs on cruise ships, in the United States or whatever, which will not get you much closer to any dream job whatever their ads promise (e.g. 'Earn up to £400 a week in Japan' or 'Would you like to work on a luxury cruise ship?'). A not infrequent con is to charge people for regular job listings and contacts in their chosen destination, which may consist of adverts lifted from newspapers or addresses from the *Yellow Pages* long out of date.

By law UK employment agencies are not permitted to charge job-seekers an upfront fee. They make their money from the company or organisation seeking staff. Every so often a bogus agency will place false recruitment advertisements in the tabloid press charging a 'registration fee', say of £15 for building workers in the Middle East, and possibly an extra sum for a magazine about living and working in the Middle East. They then disappear without trace. Some operate as clubs offering members certain services such as translating and circulating CVs. Before joining any such club, try to find out what their success rate is. You could even ask to be put in touch with someone whose membership resulted in their getting a job.

There are of course reputable international recruitment agencies in Britain, the USA and elsewhere. Specialist agencies for qualified personnel can be very useful, for example agencies for financial and IT vacancies with branches worldwide. Agencies with a range of specialities from disc jockeys for international hotels to English teachers for language schools abroad are mentioned in the relevant chapters which follow.

Do not neglect EURES, the state-run employment service within Europe (see chapter on *EU Employment*) which has been successfully helping even unskilled workers to find seasonal jobs in other member states.

International Placement Organisations

Established organisations that assist students and other young people to work abroad are invaluable for guiding people through the red tape problems and for providing a soft landing for first time travellers:

BUNAC, 16 Bowling Green Lane, London EC1R 0QH (020-7251-3472; www.bunac.org) is a student club (annual membership £5) which helps UK students to work abroad. It has a choice of programmes in the United States, Canada, Australia, New Zealand, South Africa, Ghana, Costa Rica and Peru plus Russia and China for English teachers willing to obtain a certificate. BUNAC USA (PO Box 430, Southbury, CT 06488; 203-264-0901; www.bunacusa.org) runs outgoing programmes for Americans to the UK, Ireland, etc.

Global Choices, Barkat House, 116-118 Finchley Road, London NW3 5HT (020-7433 2501; info@globalchoices.co.uk). Voluntary Work, internships, practical training and work experience worldwide from 2 weeks to 18 months. Placements are arranged for a fee in many fields in Australia, USA, New Zealand, Argentina, Ghana, France, South Africa, Brazil, Spain, Portugal, Austria, Tanzania, Costa Rica, Ukraine, Ecuador, Peru, Chile and India.

Be more than a tourist!™ **BUNAC**™

WORKING ADVENTURES WORLDWIDE

Make the most of your long summer holidays or 'time out' from work or studies with BUNAC's range of exciting work and travel programmes.

▶ Summer camp jobs in the US on *Summer Camp USA* or *KAMP*

▶ Work and travel for up to twelve months on *Work Canada, Work Australia, Work New Zealand* or *Work South Africa*

▶ Summer vacation work in the US on *Work America*

▶ Contribute to a volunteer project for eight weeks to twelve months on *Volunteer Ghana, Volunteer South Africa, Volunteer Costa Rica* or *Volunteer Peru*.

Valerie Williams, BUNAC, 16 Bowling Green Lane, London, EC1R 0QH. E-mail: enquiries@bunac.org.uk

020 7251 3472 www.bunac.org

IST Plus Ltd, Rosedale House, Rosedale Road, Richmond, Surrey TW9 2SZ (020-8939 9057; info@istplus.com; www.istplus.com). New partner agency of the Council for International Educational Exchange in the US. Working programmes for Britons in the USA, Australia, New Zealand, Thailand and China. Americans should contact CIEE, 7 Custom House Street, 3rd Floor, Portland, ME 04101; 207-553-7600; www.ciee.org/isp.

InterExchange Inc, 161 Sixth Avenue, New York, NY 10013 (212-924-0446; www.interexchange.org). Various work programmes including interning in Belgium, the UK and Costa Rica, au pairing in Germany, Netherlands and Spain, working in Australia and volunteering in Peru and South Africa.

Overseas Working Holidays, Level 1, 51 Fife Rd, Kingston, Surrey KT1 1SF (0845 344 0366; www.overseasworkingholidays.co.uk). Commercial agency that helps people to arrange volunteer programmes in Africa, working holidays in Australia and New Zealand, seasonal work in Canada, etc.

CCUSA, 1st Floor North, Devon House, 171/177 Great Portland St, London W1W 5PQ (020-7637 0779/ fax 020-7580 6209; www.ccusaweusa.co.uk). Work Experience programmes in the US (general and summer camps), in Australia/New Zealand and Brazil plus summer camp counselling in Russia. The US headquarters are at 2330 Marinship Way, Suite 250, Sausalito, CA 94965 (www.ccusa.com) which run outgoing programmes to Australia, New Zealand, Europe and Russia.

Youth exchange organisations and commercial agencies offer packages which help their nationals to take advantage of the work permit rules. For example Travel CUTS in Canada operate the SWAP programme (www.swap.ca) which sends Canadian students to work in the UK, Ireland, France, Germany, Australia, New Zealand, South Africa and Japan (45 Charles St E, Suite 100, Toronto, Ontario M4Y 1S2; 416-966-2887). Activity International does the same for Dutch and Belgian nationals (PO Box 7090, 9701 JB Groningen, Netherlands) and also Exis in Denmark, AIFS Germany and so forth.

Rita Hoek is one person who decided to participate in an organised programme, i.e. Travel Active's 'Work & Travel Australia' programme (PO Box 107, 5800 AC Venray, Netherlands):

> *Though I'm not suggesting these programmes are perfect for everybody's specific plans, it's been of great help to me. You join a discount-group airfare (cheaper and easier), they help with getting a visa and most programmes provide a first week of accommodation, assistance in getting a tax file number and opening a bank account, a service to forward your mail, general information about work and travelling and heaps more. If you don't want to feel completely lost at the airport while travelling for the first time (as I was), I can surely recommend it.*

IAESTE is the abbreviation for the International Association for the Exchange of Students for Technical Experience. It provides international course-related vacation training for thousands of university-level students in 80 member countries. Placements are available in engineering, science, agriculture, architecture and related fields. British undergraduates should apply directly to *IAESTE UK* at the British Council (www.iaeste.org.uk). The US affiliate is the Association for International Practical Training (AIPT, 10400 Little Patuxent Parkway, Suite 250, Columbia, Maryland 21044-3510; 410-997-3068; www.aipt.org or www. iaesteunitedstates.org,) which can make long and short-term placements of graduates and young professionals as well as college students in related fields.

In the US, several agencies offer a range of programmes for varying fees. The *Alliance Abroad Group* (1221 South Mopac Expressway, Suite 250, Austin, Texas 78746; 512-457-8062/ 1-888-6-ABROAD; www.allianceabroad.com) arranges volunteer placements in Latin America (Ecuador, Costa Rica, Peru, Brazil and Argentina) and paid work in Australia, China Costa Rica and the UK.

International Co-operative Education (15 Spiros Way, Menlo Park, CA 94025; 415-323-4944; www.icemenlo.com) arranges paid summer work for 2-3 months in Germany, Switzerland, Belgium, Singapore, Japan, China, Australia and South America. Jobs include retail sales, banking, computer technology, hotels and restaurants, offices, etc.; most require knowledge of relevant language. Placement fee is $700 plus application fee of $250.

Useful Sources of Information

Apart from contacting specific companies and organisations, you should consider consulting websites and reference books on the subject, directories of jobs and specialist journals. Publications covering specific countries or specific kinds of work (e.g. *Teaching English Abroad* or *Kibbutz Volunteer*) are mentioned in the relevant chapters. Of general interest are:

The Directory of Summer Jobs Abroad (Vacation Work, 9 Park End Street, Oxford OX1 1HJ; £10.99 plus £1.50 postage). Published each November.

Taking a Gap Year (Vacation-Work, 3ʳᵈ edition 2003; £11.95) by me. Covers all the specialist placement organisations as well as extensive county-by-country advice on how to wing it on your year off.

Prospects, Higher Education Careers Services Unit, Prospects House, Booth St E, Manchester M13 9EP (0161-277 5200; www.prospects.csu.man.ac.uk). Publishes huge amount of information for graduates and students in the UK. Links to 'Jobs Abroad'.

Transitions Abroad, (PO Box 745, Bennington, VT 05201; 802-442-4827; www. transitionsabroad.com). Annual subscription (six issues) costs $28 within the US. Valuable resource guide with range of work-abroad books as well. Their excellent website has a wealth of articles and links about working abroad.

The internet opens up lots of cheaper possibilities though there is a bewildering array of resources especially if you start with one of the giant search engines like the appropriately named monster.com.The University of Michigan maintains an excellent list of internships and work abroad programmes which are not exclusively of interest to Americans (see www.umich.edu/icenter/overseas/work/workabroad1.html).

A host of commercial websites promises to provide free online recruitment services for travellers. These include the admirable free Jobs Abroad Bulletin (www.jobsabroadbulletin.co.uk), www.seasonworkers.com, www.gapwork.com, www.anyworkanywhere.com, www.jobsmonkey.com (especially for North America), http://jobs.escapeartist.com, www.hotrecruit.co.uk, and so on. Everywhere you look on the internet potentially useful links can be found. Travel Tree (www.traveltree.co.uk) is a relatively new website directory aimed at people looking for educational travel, gap year ideas, internships, volunteering, etc.

A surprising number of company home pages feature an icon you can click to find out about jobs; often to be found under the heading 'About Us'. Elsewhere on the web, committed individuals around the world manage non-commercial sites on everything from kibbutzim to bar-tending.

Advertisements

If you are thinking of advertising your interest in working abroad, try to be as specific as possible. While surfing the net you will often come across postings along the lines of 'Looking for no-skills job anywhere. Please help me' which seems worse than hopeless. For a good example of a reader not targeting his self-advertisement carefully enough, see Fergus Cooney's story in the chapter on *Teaching English*. An increasing number of foreign newspapers can be read online making it much easier to reply to job advertisements as soon as they appear than in the old days when you had to track down a hard copy in a library or embassy reading room. Nevertheless any potential employer is likely to look askance at someone in Dudley or Kirkcaldy who answers an ad for someone to start immediately in a pub on Corfu or a fruit farm in Western Australia.

Unless you have very specialised skills, it is probably not worth advertising your services and availability for work in a foreign newspaper since anyone interested in hiring you would probably want to meet you first and advertising this way is expensive. For certain categories, it might be worth checking *LOOT* (24-32 Kilburn High Road, London NW6 5TF; 020-7328 1771) which bills itself as 'London's noticeboard,' although the *Loot* group publishes a total of 26 weekly publications throughout the UK. Among its many categories of classified ads (which are free to private advertisers) are 'International Jobs Offered/Wanted' (which doesn't usually contain anything very exciting) and 'Au Pair Jobs Offered/Wanted.' It is just one of many free newspapers worldwide in the Free Ads Paper International Association, usually printed on coloured newsprint. It is possible to advertise free of charge in any of these papers (from San Diego to Sofia, Rio to Ravenna) which are listed in each issue of *LOOT* with instructions for placing ads.

If you are in the process of negotiating a job with someone abroad, make sure you speak on the telephone and ascertain as many details as possible, to prevent what happened to Eric Mackness: *'I had an 'interesting' time in Hungary. I answered an ad in The Lady magazine for a house-sitter in a house mid-way between Budapest and Vienna. It was an absolute nightmare. A grubby little house, full of cats (there must have been 30) at the end of a mile-long mud track in the middle of a Hammer Horror forest, all dripping skeletal mist-enshrouded trees and howling dogs (wolves?). Quite an experience.'*

GETTING A JOB ON ARRIVAL

For those who leave home without something fixed up, a lot of initiative will be needed. Many travellers find it easier to locate casual work in country areas rather than cities, and outside the student holiday periods (although just before Christmas is a good time, when staff turnover is high). But it is possible in cities too, on building sites, in restaurants and in factories. If you go for the jobs which are least appealing (e.g. an orderly in a hospital for the criminally insane, a loo attendant, doing a street promotion dressed as a koala or a hamburger, a pylon painter, assistant in a battery chicken farm, salesman of encyclopaedia, dog meat factory worker, dog policemen (in Berlin, people are hired to follow dog-walkers) or just plain dogsbodies, the chances are you will be taken on sooner rather than later.

It always helps to have a neat appearance in order to dissociate yourself from the image of the hobo or hippy. You must show a keenness and persistence which may be out of character but are often essential. Even if a prospective employer turns you down at first, ask again since it is human nature to want to reward keenness and he or she may decide that an extra staff member could be useful after all. Polite pestering pays off. For example, if your requests for work down on the docks produce nothing one day, you must return the next day. After a week your face will be familiar and your eagerness and availability known to potential employers. If nothing seems to be materialising, volunteer to help mend nets (thereby adding a new skill to the ones you can offer) and if an opening does eventually arise, you will be the obvious choice. If you want a job teaching English in a school but there appear to be no openings, volunteer to assist with a class one day a week for no pay and if you prove yourself competent, you will have an excellent chance of filling any vacancy which does occur. So patience and persistence should become your watchwords, and before long you will belong to the fraternity of experienced, worldly-wise travellers who can maintain themselves on the road for extended periods.

Casual work by its very nature is changeable and unpredictable and can best be searched out on the spot. It pays to have your wits about you at all times. According to a collection of the oddest odd jobs spotted on the Lonely Planet website, a penniless traveller in Paris was nearly killed by a bag of tools falling from a construction site. He caught the bag, climbed the scaffolding with the tools, told the builders how they could easily arrange a pulley and was immediately hired as a mason's assistant for a month.

Despite her tender years when she first started travelling and fending for herself, Carisa Fey had learned the value of quiet observation: *'My motto was and still is watch the people that do the job you want and then copy them. So my first few days in London I spent walking through the city watching people. After I found out what the businesswomen wore, I went to the shops and bought as cheaply as possible a very neat suit and the right kinds of accessories.'*

You may follow the advice in this book to go to Avignon France in August, for example, to pick plums or to Magnetic Island Australia to get bar work. When you arrive you may be disappointed to learn that the harvest was unusually early or the resort has already hired enough staff. But your informant may go on to say that if you wait two weeks you can pick grapes or if you travel to the next reef island, there is a shortage of dining room staff. In other words, one thing leads to another once you are on the track.

A certain amount of bravado is a good, even a necessary, thing. If you must exaggerate the amount of experience you have had or the time you intend to stay in order to get a chance to do a job, then so be it. There is little room for shyness and self-effacement in the enterprise of working your way around the world. (On the other hand, bluffing is not recommended if it might result in danger, for example if you pretend to have more sailing experience than you really do for a transatlantic crossing.)

> **After circumnavigating the globe and working in a number of countries David Cooksley comments:**
> *All the information and contacts in the world are absolutely useless unless you make a personal approach to the particular situation. You must be resourceful and never retiring. If I were the manager of a large company which needed self-motivating sales people, I'd hire all the contributors to Work Your Way Around the World since they have the ability to communicate with anyone anywhere in any language.*

Meeting People

The most worthwhile source of information is without question your fellow travellers. After you have hurled yourself into the fray you will soon become connected up with kindred spirits more experienced at the game than you, whose advice you should heed. Other travellers are surprisingly generous with their information and assistance. David Hewitt claims that this cannot be overemphasised; he and his Brazilian wife have been consistently helped by their compatriots from Berlin to Miami. A Mexican correspondent who arrived in Toronto cold sought out the Latino community and, after taking their advice, was soon comfortably housed and employed.

Hitch-hiking is a good means for getting leads on work, providing you pump the local people who give you lifts for any useful information. If you arrive in a new place without a prearranged contact, there are many ways of meeting the locals and other travellers to find out about job possibilities. Backpackers hostels are universally recommended, especially out of season, and many hostel wardens will be well versed in the local opportunities for casual jobs. Check the websites www.hostels.com, www.hostels.net or www.hostelworld.com for a selection worldwide. The VIP Backpackers hostel group includes hundreds of hostels in Australia, New Zealand, South Africa and Europe; a membership card costs £16 (www.vipbackpackers.com).

Universities and polytechnics are good meeting places in term-time and also during the vacations when it is often possible to arrange cheap accommodation in student residences. Seek out the overseas student club to meet interesting people who are foreigners just like you. Investigate the student or bohemian parts of town where the itinerant community tends to congregate. Go to the pubs and cafés frequented by worldly-wise travellers (often the ones serving Guinness).

If you have a particular hobby or interest, ask if there is a local club, where you will meet like-minded people; join local ramblers, cyclists, cavers, environmental activists, train spotters, jazz buffs – the more obscure the more welcome you are likely to be. Join evening language courses, frequent the English language bookshop (which may well have a useful notice board) or visit the functions of the English language church, where you are likely to meet the expatriate community or be offered free advice by the vicar. Marta Eleniak introduced herself to the local Polish club, since she has a Polish surname and a fondness for the country, to ask if she could put up a notice asking for accommodation. The kindly soul to whom she was speaking told her not to worry about it; she'd find her something she could move into the next day. She has come to the conclusion that learning to be a 'fog-horn' is an invaluable characteristic.

Till Bruckner has (reluctantly) been persuaded that hobnobbing with the rich and powerful can be the key to job success:
The one lesson I have failed to learn over and over again is the value of socialising. In Bolivia, I shoved a pamphlet advertising myself as a trekking guide under the doors of dozens of agencies without ever getting a reply. It just doesn't work that way. Nobody will ever bother to ring you if they don't know you. A week before I left, I met an old Bolivian friend and when I told him that I'd been unable to find work, he said he couldn't believe it because his cousin had an agency and needed a German speaker. In the Sudan, I sent off my CV to all major NGOs offering myself as an unpaid volunteer. All I got was two negative replies. A week before I left (again) I went to a social event at a foreign embassy where I got talking with the head of a big charity. She told me about the problems they had with writing endless reports. I asked her why she hadn't replied to my application and it turned out she'd never seen it. The moral of the story is that in some countries the best place to start looking for a job is down the pub, especially the sort of pub where well-off locals and expats hang out. I absolutely loathe exactly that kind of establishment but you might well hit the jackpot in there. You're unlikely to get hired by someone poor after all.

Not that the people you will meet in this way will necessarily be able to give you a full-time job, but it sets the wheels in motion and before too long you will be earning your way by following their advice and leads. Provided your new friends speak the local language better than you, they can make telephone calls for you, translate newspaper advertisements, write out a message for you to show possible employers and even act as interpreters. One young Englishman was dragged along to the local radio station by his Italian hosts who persuaded the station to have him co-host an afternoon programme. The manager of another traveller's hostel in Cairo wrote out an Arabic notice for him, offering private English lessons.

If your contacts can't offer you a real job they might know of a 'pseudo job' or 'non-job' which can keep you afloat: guarding their yacht, doing odd jobs around their property, babysitting, typing, teaching the children English, or just staying for free. These neatly avoid the issue of work permits, too, since they are arranged on an entirely unofficial and personal basis. Human contacts are usually stronger than red tape.

Chance

When you first set off, the possibility of being a sheep-catcher in the Australian outback or an English tutor in Turkey may never have crossed your mind. Chance is a fine thing and is one of the traveller's greatest allies. Brigitte Albrech had saved up leave from her job in the German tourist industry to go on holiday in Mexico. While there, she became friendly with some Québecois who invited her to join them as tree planters in Western Canada, and she never made it back to her job.

There will be times when you will be amazed by the lucky chain of events which led you into a certain situation. 'Being in the right place at the right time' would have made a suitable subtitle to this book, though of course there are steps you can take to put yourself in the right place, and this book tries to point out what these might be. Here are some examples of how luck, often in combination with initiative, has resulted in travellers finding paid work:

- Mark Kilburn took up busking in a small Dutch town and was eventually asked to play a few nights a week in a nearby pub for a fee.
- Stuart Britton was befriended by a fisherman in a dusty little town in Mexico and was soon tutoring some of the fisherman's friends and acquaintances (and living in his house).
- While standing in a post office queue in the south of France, Brian Williams overheard the word boulot (which he knew to mean odd job) and cerises. He tapped the lady on the shoulder and offered his cherry picking expertise. After a protracted search for the address she had given him, he finally asked directions of someone who offered him a job in their orchard instead.
- On a flight to Reykjavik, Caroline Nicholls happened to sit next to the wife of the managing director of a large fish-packing cooperative in Iceland who told her they were short of staff.
- After finishing his summer stint as a camp counsellor in the US, Mark Kinder decided to try one parachute jump. He enjoyed it so much that he learned how to pack parachutes and was able to fund himself at the aerodrome for months afterwards.
- While looking for work on a boat in Antibes, Tom Morton found a job as a goatherd for six weeks in the mountains near Monte Carlo.
- Dominic Fitzgibbon mentioned to his landlady in Rome that he intended to leave soon for Greece since he had been unable to find a job locally in six weeks of looking. She decided he was far too nice to become a washer-up in a taverna and arranged for him to work as a hall porter at a friend's hotel.
- A. Gowing was a little startled to wake up one evening in Frankfurt station to find a middle-aged women staring down at him. She offered him the chance of working with her travelling fun-fair.
- While getting her jabs for Africa at a clinic in Gibraltar, Mary Hall (a nurse cycling across Europe) noticed a door marked 'District Nurses', barged in and the following week had moved in as a live-in private nurse for a failing

old lady.

o While shopping in a supermarket in Cyprus, Rhona Stannage noticed a local man with a trolley full of wine and beer, and assumed it could not be for his own consumption. She approached him, ascertained that he ran a restaurant and a day or two later was employed as a waitress.

o Connie Paraskeva shared a taxi in Bangkok with an American nurse who told her about a vacancy in a refugee camp.

o While sunbathing on an isolated Greek beach, Edward Peters was approached by a farmer and asked to pick his oranges.

The examples could be multiplied *ad infinitum* of how travellers, by keeping their ears open and by making their willingness to help obvious, have fallen into work. One of the keys to success is total flexibility. Within ten minutes of a chance conversation with a family sharing her breakfast table in an Amsterdam hotel, Caroline Langdon had paid her bill, packed her bags and was off to Portugal with them as their mother's help.

Of course there is always such a thing as bad luck too. You may have received all sorts of inside information about a job on a Greek island, a vineyard or in a ski resort. But if a war has decimated tourism (as the Gulf War did) or if there was a late frost which killed off the grapes or if the snowfalls have been poor, there will be far fewer jobs and your information may prove useless. Unpredictability is built into the kinds of jobs which travellers do.

Design

But you cannot rely on luck alone; you will have to create your own luck at times. You may have to apply to 20 hotels before one will accept you and you may have to inform 20 acquaintances of your general plans before one gives you the address of a useful contact. Public libraries can be helpful as proved by the traveller who found a directory of wildlife and environmental organisations in a South African library and went on to fix up a board-and-lodging job at a game reserve.

You must check notice boards and newspaper advertisements, register with agencies and most important of all use the unselective 'walk-in-and-ask' method, just like job-seekers anywhere. The most important tools for an on-the-spot job hunt are a copy of the Yellow Pages and a phone card. When Mary Hall was starting her job search in Switzerland, a friend gave her an odd piece of advice which she claims works, to smile while speaking on the phone. Some people say that all initial approaches are best made by telephone since refusals are less demoralising than in person and you need not worry about the scruffiness of your wardrobe.

One old hand Alan Corrie, describes his approach: 'The town of Annecy in the French Alps looked great so I found a fairly cheap hostel and got down to getting organised. This meant I was doing the rounds of the agencies, employment office, notice boards and cafés for a few days. After a matter of minutes in a town, I begin to sprout plastic bags full of maps, plans, lists, addresses and scraps of advice from people I have met on the road.' Alan sounds unusually cheerful and optimistic about job-hunting and the result is that he worked in Europe for the better part of a decade. He concludes '*Looking for work in Annecy was an enjoyable pastime in early autumn. Making contacts and job hunting in a new place is a whole lot more fun than actually working and worrying about the bills as I've often found before*'.

Our working wanderers have displayed remarkable initiative and found their jobs in a great variety of ways:

o Waiter in Northern Cyprus: I arranged my job by writing direct to the restaurant after seeing a two-minute clip on a BBC travel programme. Rita wrote back and here I am.

o Farmhand on a Danish farm: I placed an advert in Landsbladet, the farmers' weekly, and chose one from four replies.

o Au pair to a family in Helsinki: I found work as a nanny in Finland simply by placing advertisement cards in a few playgroups.

o Teacher at a language school in southern Italy: We used the Yellow Pages in a Sicilian Post Office and from our 30 speculative applications received four job offers without so much as an interview.

o Winery guide in Spain: I composed a modest and polite letter and sent it to an address copied from one of my father's wine labels. I was astonished at their favourable reply. Several years later the same contributor wrote to say, I sent a copy of the page in your book where I am mentioned to prospective employers in Australia, and I was offered a job on a vineyard near Melbourne.

o Factory assistant in Ghana: I asked the local Amnesty International representative for any leads.

Implicit in all these stories is that you must take positive action.

REWARDS AND RISKS

The Delights

The rewards of travelling are mostly self-evident: the interesting characters and lifestyles you are sure to meet, the wealth of anecdotes you will collect with which you can regale your grandchildren and photos with which you can bore your friends, a feeling of achievement, an increased self-reliance and maturity, learning to budget, a better perspective on your own country and your own habits, a good sun tan... the list could continue. Stephen Psallidas summed up his views on travelling: *'Meeting people from all over the world gives you a more tolerant attitude to other nationalities, races, etc. More importantly you learn to tolerate yourself, to learn more about your strengths and weaknesses. While we're on the clichés, you definitely 'find yourself, man'.'*

One traveller came back from a stint of working on the Continent feeling a part of Europe rather than just an Englishman. (Perhaps some Brussels bureaucrat should be subsidising this book.) Sometimes travels abroad change the direction of your life. After working his way around the world in many low-paid and exploitative jobs, Ken Smith decided to specialise in studying employment law. After deciding to cycle through Africa on an extended hospital, Mary Hall ended up working for aid organisations in Africa and the Middle East.

One of the best aspects of the travelling life is that you are a free and unfettered agent. Albert Schweizer might have been thinking of the working traveller instead of equatorial Africans when he wrote: *'He works well under certain circumstances so long as the circumstances require it. He is not idle, but he is a free man, hence he is always a casual worker.'*

The Dangers

Of course things can go desperately wrong, as they did for Louise Woodward. Several other young women and men who have been travelling and looking for work abroad have been murdered. Any women who are feeling especially anxious about the risks of travelling and working abroad might be cheered by the statistic that of all the letters addressed to the editor of this book (nearly half from women), not one hinted that she was sorry she had gone. In many ways a solo woman traveller gains extra respect from the people she meets and in many cases finds it easier to get work.

A much less remote possibility is that you might be robbed or lose your luggage. You may get sick or lonely or fed up. (Always arrange to keep in e-mail contact or to receive mail from time to time via poste restante or American Express to avoid becoming completely alienated from your roots.) You might have a demoralising run of bad luck and fail to find a job, and begin to run out of money (if this is the case, consult the chapter *In Extremis*).

Many unofficial jobs carry with them an element of insecurity. You may not be protected by employment legislation and may not be in a position to negotiate with the boss. Often the work may be available to travellers like you because the conditions are unacceptable to a stable local population (or because the place is too remote to have a local population). Phil New is probably right when he says that the travellers who worry that they won't get paid or won't get hired are the very ones who do encounter problems. If you have cultivated the right attitude, you will not hesitate to drift on to a new situation if the old one should become undesirable for any reason.

Exploitative working conditions will show you how much you are prepared to tolerate. Paul Bridgland was not sorry to have worked for a tyrannical and abusive boss in Crete, since he now thinks he has developed such a thick skin that no future employer could penetrate it.

Much is now said about 'socially responsible tourism' and perhaps working travellers who put up with dreadful employers are doing both their host community and other travellers a disservice. Stephen Psallidas's advice (based on his own experience of exploitative Greek bosses) is not to put up with it: *'My advice when you are mistreated or your employer acts unprofessionally is to shout back when they shout at you. If things don't improve threaten to walk out and then do so. You will be doing a favour to future working travellers, and you will almost certainly be able to find something else if you try hard enough.'*

Charlotte Jakobson's worst employer was a hotelier in the middle of nowhere in Norway. When she discovered how underpaid she was she contacted a union official who was shocked and wanted to take action. Today she regrets that she was so keen to get away that she didn't stay to present the case and thinks of other girls who were probably subjected to the same bad experiences as a result.

Some people set off with false expectations about the life of the working traveller. Armin Birrer (who has travelled long enough to have earned his right to make such pronouncements) says that some of the enthusiasm with which travel writers tend to glorify travel should be moderated a little. The travelling life is full of uncertainty and hardship. To quote the inveterate working traveller Stephen Psallidas once more, *'I would say that the bad times even outnumber the good times, but the good times are great and the bad times are good for you in the end.'*

Even when a planned working holiday does not work out successfully, the experience will be far more memorable than just staying at home. This view is held by Stephen Hands who didn't regret his decision to go abroad to look for work (although it didn't work out) but he did regret boasting to all his friends that he was off for an indefinite period to see the world. After writing pages about her dodgy and difficult jobs in Australia, Emma Dunnage concluded with a typical paradox: 'But we did have the best time of our lives'.

Though travelling itself is never dull, a job which you find to help out your finances along the way may well be. True 'working holidays' are rare: one example is to exchange your labour for a free trip with an outback Australian camping tour operator (see *Australia* chapter) or for a cruise to the midnight sun (see *Scandinavia*). But in many cases, the expression 'working holiday' is an oxymoron (like 'cruel kindness'). Jobs are jobs wherever you do them. David Anderson, who found himself working on an isolated Danish farm where he didn't feel at home in any way, recommends taking (a) your time to decide to accept a job, (b) a copy of *War and Peace* and (c) enough money to facilitate leaving if necessary. The best policy is to leave home only after you have the reserves to be able to work when you want to.

One of the unexpected drawbacks of becoming a global citizen was identified by Carisa Fey:
One of the blessings and the curses of travelling a lot is that your best friends live all over the world. Good, because you always have an excuse to go and visit a foreign country. But bad because you usually never have more than one close friend nearby.

Coming Home

Kristin Moen thinks that there should be a big warning at the beginning of *Work Your Way Around the World:* WHEN YOU FIRST START TO TRAVEL THERE IS NO WAY YOU CAN STOP! Correspondents have variously called travel an illness and an addiction. Once you set off you will probably come across a few restless souls for whom the idea of settling down is anathema and for whom the word 'vagabondage' was invented. One contributor met a 44 year old New Zealander in Sydney recently who had been travelling and working for 25 years. Undoubtedly some use it as a form of escapism, believing it to be a panacea for all their problems. But these are the exceptions.

In the majority of cases, homesickness eventually sets in, and the longing for a pint of bitter, a bacon sandwich, a baseball game, Radio 4's 'Today' programme, green fields, Marks & Spencer or Mum's home cooking will get the better of you. Or perhaps duty intervenes as in the case of Michael Tunison: *'I had planned to go on to South America this summer, but I had to return home under emergency circumstances. Not one, but two of my best friends were getting married. What is a poor globetrotter to do with people rather inconsiderately going on with their lives when he isn't even there? But after a year it was actually quite nice to have a chance to organise my things and repack for further adventures.'*

At some point your instinct will tell you that the time has come to hang up your ruck-sack (assuming you haven't sold it). After many years on the road Rob Abblett took stock last year: *'I decided to come back to England from Uruguay earlier than planned. I'd been robbed in Paraguay, got scared in Buenos Aires and decided that eight years of working around the world has been fantastic and worthwhile. But now I need to do something different.'*

Settling back will be difficult especially if you have not been able to set aside some money for 'The Return'. As soon as he left Asia en route back from Australia, Riwan Hafiz began to feel depressed and when he arrived at Heathrow wanted to put a blanket over his head. It can be a wretched feeling after some glorious adventures to find yourself with nothing to start over on. One travel writer has compared the post Travel Blues to SAD (Seasonal Affective Disorder). Life at home may seem dull and routine at first, while the outlook of your friends and family can strike you as narrow and limited. If you have been round the world between school and further study, you may find it difficult to bridge the gulf between you and your stay-at-home peers who may feel a little threatened or belittled by your experiences. If you have spent time in developing countries the reverse culture shock may be acute, as Chris Miksovsky from Colorado discovered:

> *Memories of the trip already come racing back at the oddest of times. A few days after returning to the US, I went to a large grocery store with my mother. It was overwhelming. Rows and rows of colours and logos all screaming to get your attention. I wandered over to the popcorn display and stood dumbfounded by the variety: buttered, lite, generic, Redenbacker, Paul Newman's au naturel, from single serving sachet through economy family popcorn-orgy size. I counted over 25 unique offerings... of popcorn.*

For a graphic and amusing description of reverse culture shock on returning to London after a long stay in West Africa, read *The Innocent Anthropologist* by Nigel Barley (Penguin).

But it passes. The reverse culture shock normally wears off soon enough and you will begin to feel reintegrated in your course or job. In some cases the changes which travel have brought about may be more than just psychological; for example David Hewitt set off on his travels a bachelor, married a fellow volunteer from Brazil met on his kibbutz and then had a child whom they were trying to make into a working traveller before she reached her first birthday by putting her forward for promotions in the US.

People often wonder whether a long spell of travelling or living abroad will damage their future job prospects. According to numerous surveys on graduate employment, most employers are sympathetic to people who defer entry to the labour market. Look what happened to J. K. Rowling who began writing Harry Potter while teaching English in Portugal.

In the majority of cases, travel seems to be considered an advantage, something that makes you stand out from the crowd. Marcus Scrace found that even in his profession of chartered surveying, employers looked favourably on someone who had had the get-up-and-go to work his way around the world. Jeremy Pack chose to join the computing industry upon his return and claimed that he did not meet one negative reaction to his two years off. Naturally it helps if you can present your experiences positively, if only to prevent the potential employer from imagining you out of your skull on a beach in Goa for 12 months. Your travels must be presented constructively and not as an extended doss. Stephen Psallidas, who returned after three years on the road, is convinced that he would never have got a good job (as Projects Manager in Computer Education) before he left. Not that he gained any relevant experience on his travels but he had learned how to be persistent and pester employers for an interview.

Some hostility is probably inevitable especially when the job market is shrinking making employers more conservative. Jane Thomas knew that it would be tough finding a job when she got back to England, but she didn't know how tough. Some interviewers did express their concern and suspicion that she would want to take off again (which at that time was exactly what she did want to do). But she also found that she could adapt the short-term jobs she had done in the US and Australia to fit whatever job she was trying to get. And after a certain period of time has elapsed, your absence from the conventional working world ceases to be an issue. At last report Jane had a job making videos with the possibility of some work with the BBC.

In some cases the jobs you have found abroad are a positive boost to your 'real life' prospects, as in the case of Michael Tunison from Michigan:

Newspaper work was exactly what I thought I was leaving behind by globetrotting. I'd temporarily sacrificed (I believed) my career as a journalist. The last place I thought I'd be working was at a daily in Mexico. But things never work out as planned and before I knew it I was the managing editor's assistant and a month or so later the managing editor of the paper's weekend editions. How ironic. By taking a step my newspaper friends believed to be an irresponsible career move, I was soon years ahead of where I'd have been following the old safe route back home.

Conclusion

While some identify the initial decision to go abroad as the hardest part, others find the inevitable troughs (such as finding yourself alone in a sleazy hotel room on your birthday, running out of money with no immediate prospect of work, etc.) more difficult to cope with. But if travelling requires a much greater investment of energy than staying at home, it will reward the effort many times over.

A host of travellers have mentioned how much they value their collection of memories. Since we have been guided by the experiences of ordinary travellers throughout the writing of this book, let one of their number, Steve Hendry, end the Introduction:
I left home with about £100 and no return ticket. I spent two years in Israel, three years in Thailand, one year in Japan. I have lived in the sun for years, with Arabs on the seashore and with wealthy Japanese. If I can do it, you can too. I've learned so very much. Travelling is 100% fun and educational. What are you waiting for?

WORKING A PASSAGE

Many people setting out on their world travels assume, not unreasonably, that a large chunk of their savings must inevitably be swallowed up by airlines, railways and shipping companies. This need not be so. With a little advance planning, a fair amount of bravado and a dose of good fortune you can follow the example of thousands of travellers who have successfully voyaged around the globe for next to nothing.

Hitch-hiking is one way of crossing landmasses (see *Travel*), but usually fails to solve the problem of sea crossings. Since it is a relatively slow means of travel, it also eats into your funds since you need to sustain yourself en route. Fortunately, if you are serious about travelling free or cheaply in ways other than hitch-hiking, there are several methods of working a passage by land, sea or air.

SEA

Commercial Shipping

Only registered seafarers are allowed to work on British-registered ships. The only realistic hope for casual employment and attendant transport lies with the more far-flung lines of Scandinavia and the Far East, or with the numerous ships sailing under flags of convenience e.g. Panama, Liberia and the great maritime nation of Liechtenstein. A high percentage of UK ships are flagged out (i.e. registered abroad) to avoid the high cost of unionised British labour. Very occasionally a medium-sized cargo ship takes on an individual with a skill such as catering or carpentry who has petitioned the captain for work, though in the vast majority of cases, merchant ships are fully staffed with low paid, non-unionised workers, many of whom are recruited from Third World countries.

We have heard of very few intrepid travellers who have succeeded with this method. After spending six months in India some years ago, one such traveller went down to the enormous bustling harbour of Bombay and asked the captain of a cargo boat from Ghana to take him on as an assistant; within an hour of asking he had set sail for Egypt. His duties were simply to run messages, keep watch and share the cooking duties. More recently Danny Jacobson and his girlfriend found themselves with an idle afternoon in Bangkok:

Marion and I caught a bus towards the port of Bangkok for a chance of a possible ocean journey to Japan aboard a cargo ship. After an open-windowed ride and a large wander on foot we found ourselves at the wide-open gates of the Royal Port Authority of Bangkok where the great tankers and cargo ships put in to drop and get loads. Cranes and tracks and trucks, the smell of a murky sea and the gray tint of a history of work. Several of those immensely large ships that crash and smash and traverse the mightiest of waves, and/or burn and sink to the Ocean floor, were parked along the concrete bank. A picture of a place one would imagine to be wholly off-limits to pedestrians and tourists yet we walked right past the guard office. Strolling along, admiring the ships, I mentioned how awesome it would be to go aboard and have a look around one, contemplating what it would be like to hitch a ride on a cargo ship. Marion called up to a couple of uniformed guys leaning on the railing of the deck of a nearby ship. 'Hey can we come up?' and they nodded back. We were greeted by a young man from the Philippines who introduced us to the Captain and crew members as though we were important guests. The whole crew was from the Philippines, as was the ship, and they were in Bangkok for a few days before sailing for Japan. Amid idle chat we dropped the idea of us going along to Japan with them. 'Yes, you should come with us,' he said, with an effort towards the end of the sen-

tence to disqualify the offer. We were not too motivated to push the idea either due to uncertainty as to whether we actually needed to be in Japan in the immediate future. Anyway, he shifted around the question a bit – have to ask the captain…no room… Soon after he escorted us back down to the deck and we thanked him for the tour.

The harbour authorities can be helpful, especially in countries off the beaten track. (Be careful not to confuse them with customs officers.) They will sometimes show enquirers a list of all the ships arriving and departing, since commercial shipping is almost as carefully regulated as air traffic. Sometimes you will have to ask their permission to go on to the docks, for example in Port Sudan you need to get a permit from the wharf police before you can ask captains for a lift to Mombasa or India. It is worth getting on the right side of the harbour-master since captains may tell him about their need of extra crew. At least, they can advise you about the tides. When it is coming up to high tide (spring tide) boats leave, and so this is a good time to ask around. Harbourside bars are not a good place to introduce yourself to captains since this is their off-duty time. They are more likely to consider your offer seriously when they are aboard their vessel. It is a good idea, however to chat up the barman in the local harbour bar, and ask him to keep his ears open.

Cruise Liners

The luxury cruise liner business is absolutely booming. More British holidaymakers go on cruises than take skiing holidays, despite the bad publicity in early 2005 when P&O's luxury cruise liner *The Aurora* had to abandon her round-the-world itinerary due to engine problems. Over a thousand liners sail the world's oceans at present, with more being built all the time. Every cruise ship requires a full range of staff, just as a fancy hotel does. Most recruitment takes place through agencies or 'concessionaires', all of whom say that they are looking only for qualified and experienced staff. But in many cases it is sufficient to be over 21 and have an extrovert personality and plenty of stamina for the very long hours of work on board.

Job-seekers with no experience or specialised skills should be wary of agencies that invite them to pay a fee to circulate their CV online; this may well work for the highly qualified but there are probably far more people looking for work than there are employers looking for staff this way. Websites to try are: Sea Cruise Enterprises (www.seacruiseent.com) and Ocean Crews Maritime Employment (www.maritimeemployment.com). The privately run site www.ucs.mun.ca/rklein/cruise.html calls itself a no frills page of cruise lines and cruise links, which includes contact details of cruise lines and concessionaires. Another useful list of links can be found in the Cruise Lines section of www.jobmonkey.com (which requires a subscription of $12.95 a month). Many cruise lines have special recruitment sites or pages which will set out how you should apply, e.g. Disney's site www.dcljobs.com advises phoning the dedicated Jobline 407-566-SHIP. For Radisson Seven Seas Cruises log on to www.rssc.com/employment and for Princess Cruises, check out http://employment.princess.com/employment/index.html).

According to Jane Roberts, who crossed the Atlantic from Venezuela to Estonia as a cruise line croupier, not all employees are experienced professionals:

I worked in the casino department of four different cruise ships and met many people doing jobs as waiters, bar tenders, stewards and stewardesses. These jobs are very easy to come by. In fact 80% of all crew members are people who have never done that particular job in their lives. The turn-over of staff is high, even when people sign year-long contracts, since few people complete them. It is difficult to live and work with the same people 24 hours a day. Crew don't get days off, perhaps just the odd breakfast or lunch off once a month. Patience levels have to be extremely high, since people who take holidays on cruise ships seem to think that they own the damn ship. Having to be sickeningly nice can take its toll very quickly.

Contract lengths (some as short as four months) and conditions vary from ship to ship.

Typically, crew are contracted for nine months and then get six weeks holiday. Wages are usually US$400-$550 a month but can be increased with tips or commission.

Some UK and European agencies that have advertised for cruise line staff in the past year include:

Crewships, V-Ships, Skypark, 8 Elliot Place, Glasgow G3 8EP (0141-243-2435; eileen. kelly@vships.com; www.vships.com). Also Vships Leisure, Hotel Dept, 24 Avenue de Fontvieille, PO Box 639, MC 98013 Monaco Cedex; +377-92-05-10-10; hotel. crew@vships.com.

Cruise Service Center Ltd, Palme & Associates, 9 Crown Lofts, Marsh St, Walsall WS2 9LB, U.K.; 01922 722356; www.cruiseservicecenter.com). Recruits middle and senior hotel management and service staff year round.

CTI Group Europe, Pinewood House, London Road, Send, Surrey GU23 7JX (0870 240 5208; CTI-Europe@cti-usa.com).Official recruiters of catering staff for Carnival, Celebrity, Crystal and Disney Cruise Lines. Head office is in Fort Lauderdale Florida: 3696 North Federal Highway, Suite 303, Fort Lauderdale, FL 33308-6262; CTI-USA@cti-usa.com).

Greatcruisejobs.co.uk – Berkeley Scott (01483 791291; www.greatcruisejobs.co.uk). Recruits for Cunard, Costa, Royal Caribbean, Carnival, P&O, Celebrity, Princess and Holland America.

International Cruise Management Ag A/S, PO Box 95, (Jernbanetorget 4B), Sentrum, 0101 Oslo, Norway (+47 23 35 79 00; office@icma.no; www.icma.no). Recruits staff with 2-3 years experience for four luxury vessels (Crystal Cruises). More than 1,700 people hired each year out of 12,000 applicants.

International Services, 11 rue du Commerce, St Pierre-du-Perray 91280, France (+33 1-60 75 95 95; fax 1-60 75 97 97; infos@internationalservices.fr; www.internationalservices. fr). Recruitment agency for Caribbean cruise ships including Disney.

Seefar Associates, 7 Berkeley Crescent, Gravesend, Kent DA12 2AH (01474 329990; seefarassociates@btclick.com; www.seefarassociates.co.uk). Hire casino and other staff for Disney Cruise Line, Festival Cruise Line, Royal Caribbean and Celebrity Cruise Lines.

There are also agencies worldwide, including in developing countries. For example Persohotel International (Pasaje La Victoria, Local E-15 Planta Alta, Plaza Bonita SM 28, Cancun, Quintana Roo 77509, Mexico; 998-892 4474; jmmendez@cancun.com.mx) recruits mainly but not exclusively Mexican nationals for cruise work.

Ads for professional hotel and catering staff for cruise lines appear in the specialist press like *The Caterer* and *Hotel Keeper.* Specialist catering agencies like VIP International (17 Charing Cross Road, London WC2H 0EP; 020-7930 0541; cruise@vipinternational. co.uk) supply experienced catering, management and other personnel for various cruise lines.

A plethora of books and websites provides a starting point for anyone interested in working on a cruise ship, e.g. *Working on Cruise Ships* by Sandra Bow (Vacation-Work, £10.99). Do not be misled by advertisements which read 'Cruise Ships are Hiring Now' or websites with names like shipjobs or cruiselinejobs. These are almost always placed by someone trying to sell a book about employment on cruise ships, and these are of varying quality. The *World Wide Cruise Ship and Yachting Career Guide* from Innovative Ideas Ltd (36 Midlothian Drive, Glasgow G41 3QU; 0141-649 8644/fax 0141-636 1016; info@cruiseservices.co.uk/ www.cruiseservices.co.uk) costs £32 which includes two years' access to Newsletters containing vacancy lists.

Anyone already in Florida might be able to arrange interviews with the cruise lines or their concessionaires. But do not get too excited if you see advertisements in newspapers or universities for people (including students) to work on cruise ships. Sander Meijsen from the Netherlands paid a fee of $150 to an agency he'd seen advertising, but in fact never got a job on a cruise line:

In my case I had to call the agent every day to find out if anything new came up which

*meant a huge phone bill (since they put you on hold all the time to retrieve your file).
So I quit calling which probably means that I will lose my fee. I chose this agency
because they told me you do not need a work permit. But when no cruise companies called me, I took the liberty of calling them and most told me that they hire only
people with work authorisations.*

The correct visa for working at sea is a C-1/D Crewman transit visa which is granted only
after you have a job contract, normally as a lifeguard, beautician or cruise ship entertainer.

Private Yachts

People who sail the seas for pleasure are not subject to the same restrictions as merchant
or cruise ship owners. They may hire and fire a crew member whenever they like, and
work permits are not a problem. If you display a reasonable level of common sense, vigour
and amiability, and take the trouble to observe yachting etiquette, you should find it possible to persuade a yachtsman that you will be an asset to his crew. It should be stressed
that inexperienced crew are almost never paid; in fact most skippers expect some contribution towards expenses; US$25 a day is a standard starting fee for food, drink, fuel,
harbour fees, etc. Safety is of paramount importance as was highlighted by the tragedy
in 2000 when several Cambridge University students crewing for an experienced skipper
were lost in the North Sea.

After crewing from Tonga to New Zealand and then on to Australia, Gerhard Flaig
summed up the pros and cons of ocean sailing:

*It definitely is adventurous to sail on the ocean. You usually meet dolphins, whales,
fish and birds. You get in close touch with nature to see and feel the waves and to
see wonderful sunsets. You learn about sailing, meteorology, navigation. But there
are also drawbacks. Maybe you get seasick, that's no fun. Then you have to deal
with pouring rain and heavy storms. You have to get up in the middle of the night
for the watch. The boat is wobbling all the time so that makes every little job more
difficult, even going to the toilet. Maybe there is no wind at all for days and then it's
frustrating not to move and to be far away from land. If you are willing to deal with all
that then a sailing trip can be most rewarding.*

Obviously, it is much easier to become a crew member if you have some experience. But
there are opportunities for people who lack experience at sea, and it is unwise to exaggerate your skills. Once you have worked on one yacht it will be much easier to get on
the next one. The yachting world is a small one. The more experience you have, the more
favourable arrangements you will be able to negotiate. Also, your chances are better of
having a financial contribution waived if you are prepared to crew on unpopular routes,
for example crossing the Atlantic west to east is much tougher than vice versa. If you are
embarking on a serious round-the-world-on-a-shoestring venture, read a yachting book
such as the *RYA Competent Crew Handbook* which contains invaluable information on
technical sea terms and the basics of navigation. If you demonstrate to a skipper that you
take safety seriously enough to have learned a little about the procedures and if you are
clean and sober, sensible and polite, you are probably well on your way to filling a crewing
vacancy.

Also consider doing a short sailing course (and take your certificate with you). The
first level, Competent Crew, can be reached in a five-day course at any Royal Yachting
Association recognised centre for £250-£400; details from the RYA, Ensign Way, Hamble,
Southampton, SO31 4YA (023 8060 4100; www.rya.org.uk), who can also send you a
leaflet 'Careers in Sailing' and a list of crew registers in Britain. Anyone who is a confident
cook, carpenter, electrician, mechanic or sewing machine operator (for sail-mending) may
be able to market those skills too. Since 2003 crew and skippers have needed an STCW
(Standards of Training, Certification and Watchkeeping for Seafarers; www.stcw.org).

If you can afford it, you might like to consider doing your sail training abroad, for instance in Croatia with Activity Yachting (01243 641304; www.activityyachting.com) where at the end of a week's hands-on sailing costing about £500, you should have earned the Mediterranean Cruising Association's Competent Crew Certificate.

Several firms specialise in preparing people for a career in sailing or watersports such as the UK Sailing Academy (West Cowes, Isle of Wight PO31 7PQ; 01983 294941;www.uksa.org) and Flying Fish (25 Union Road, Cowes, Isle of Wight PO31 7TW; 01983 280641; www.flyingfishonline.com) both of which also offer a follow-up careers service. If these courses are too expensive, go down to your nearest marina and offer to do some hard and tedious maintenance work, sanding, painting, varnishing or scraping barnacles from the hull, in exchange for sailing tuition. Later you can aim for an easier life looking after a boat for an absent skipper by living onboard and checking anchors and bilges. It is a good idea to buy a log book in which you can enter all relevant experience and voyages, and be sure to ask the captains of boats you have been on for a letter of reference.

As one skipper comments, 'A beginner ceases to be a passenger if he or she can tie half a dozen knots and hitches, knows how to read the lights of various kinds of ships and boats at night, and isn't permanently seasick.' Sometimes the arrangement is halfway between working and hitching a lift. There may not be much actual work to do but you could make cups of coffee, sand deck chairs, play Scrabble with the captain's wife or help look after the children of a cruising family. Some solo women sailors concentrate on job-hunting on cruisers sailed by retired couples partly for this reason and also because they are often the ones looking for a young deck hand.

Nearer destinations should be easier to reach than distant and exotic ones, both because of the larger numbers of yachts sailing short distances, and their greater willingness to take a chance on you. If you merely want to get from Tangiers to Gibraltar, from the Bahamas to the United States, from one Pacific Island to another or from Rhodes to Turkey, any small yacht harbour might provide the appropriate lift. On the other hand skippers are more likely to want extra crew on long journeys on the open seas (sometimes just to satisfy insurance requirements) rather than on the more enjoyable and leisurely coastal cruising.

If you are planning your trip a long way in advance, scour the classified columns of *Yachting Monthly, Yachting World* or *Practical Boat Owner*, though advertisers are likely to require a substantial payment or contribution towards expenses on your part. For example a 63ft yacht called the *Salamandra* was recently advertising its ongoing openings for paying crew on various legs of their voyage. At a cost of £600 a month this is closer to a holiday than a job; all details on www.geocities.com/apjbond or email sysalamandra@yahoo.co.uk.

You can also have a look at a book like *Working on Yachts and Superyachts* by Jennifer Errico (£10.99; www.vacationwork.co.uk). Lots of sites on the internet promise to match crew with captains, though as in the case of cruise ships, postings of jobs sought outnumber those offered. One worthwhile site is www.floatplan.com/crew.htm which carries details of actual vacancies, for example one taken at random in early 2005: 'Australia to Indonesia and Malaysia. Married couple (54/64) circumnavigating looking for a crew of one (M/F) to join us as we depart Brisbane, Australia in April/May up to the Great Barrier Reef, then to Townsville & Cairns and over the top to Darwin, then up to Indonesia and to Borneo. You will need to pay for your own transportation expenses to and from the boat'. A certain number of listings contain a lonely hearts element: 'Mexico and Beyond – Attractive fit slender female crew member wanted for Mexico, South Pacific and beyond. Seeking a smart, stable woman, who loves adventure, cruising, has a sense of humor and a good heart. Romance a possibility, but as we will be short-handed most of the time, the passion for sailing and a life of adventure is the crucial element.' Women should be warned that the yachting world is notoriously sexist. Even in a world where Ellen McArthur is a household name, it is often assumed that women aboard yachts are there to cook.

Crewing agencies in Britain, France, Denmark, the West Indies, the United States and elsewhere carry out the same function of matching yacht captains and crew (see regional sections below). These are mostly of use to professional experienced sailors.

The *Cruising Association* (CA House, 1 Northey St, Limehouse Basin, London E14 8BT; 020-7537 2828; www.cruising.org.uk/crewing.htm) runs a crewing service to put skippers in touch with unpaid crew. Meetings are held on the first Wednesday of the month at 6.30pm between March and July for this purpose. They claim to offer a variety of sailing (including two or three week cruises to the Mediterranean and transatlantic passages) to suit virtually every level of experience. The fee to non-members for this service is £25.

One of the best and largest crewing register in the UK is operated by *Crewseekers* (Crew Introduction Agency, Hawthorn House, Hawthorn Lane, Sarisbury Green, Southampton, Hants. SO31 7BD; tel/fax 01489 578319; sailing@crewseekers.co.uk). Their membership charges for UK members are £60 for six months, £85 for a year, £15 extra for joint members. Their web pages (www.crewseekers.co.uk) are updated daily showing the latest boats worldwide requiring crew. New members may also register online.

Alternatives include:

Crew Network Worldwide, www.crewnetwork.com. Interviews can be held at associate offices in Antibes, Palma de Mallorca, Fort Lauderdale and Auckland.

Global Crew Network, 23 Old Mill Gardens, Berkhamsted, Herts. HP4 2NZ (0870 9101 888; info@globalcrewnetwork.com). Specialises in crew recruitment for Tall Ships and traditional yachts. Membership is £35 for 6 months, £45 for 12.

JF Recruiting - www.jf-recruiting.com. Web-based recruitment. Website provides a useful list of crew accommodation worldwide.

Procrew Yachts and Crew Services, info@procrew.com; www.procrew.com. £25 for 6 months membership, £35 for 12 months.

Reliance Yacht Management, First Floor Suite, 127 Lynchford Road, Farnborough, Hampshire, GU14 6ET (01252 378239; info@reliance-yachts.com). Registration fee of £35. Specialises in yacht deliveries.

Once you're abroad, you'll have to track down your own sailing adventures. Frank Schiller split expenses with the New Zealand couple who took him (a complete sailing novice) aboard their yacht bound for Tonga and he ended up spending NZ$400 for four months of cruising. Always be sure to discuss the details of payment before setting sail. Many captains will ask you to pay a bond (say $500) for a long journey. Captains are responsible for making sure their crew can get back to their country of origin after the voyage is finished.

Whenever you end up finding a yacht to crew on, you may be letting yourself in for discomfort and danger, not to mention boredom, especially if you find yourself painting the boat in dock for the umpteenth time. Yachts require a surprising amount of maintenance. Offshore sailing is a risky business and you should be sure that the skipper to whom you have entrusted your life is a veteran sailor. A well-used but well-kept boat is a good sign.

Make sure before you leave the safety of dry land that your personality and politics do not clash with that of the captain. Quickly tiring of Gibraltar, Nicola Sarjeant and her Dutch boyfriend decided to join the hordes of people looking for a working passage on a yacht:

We asked around from boat to boat but most people weren't interested or wanted experienced people. We also put up a note in a shop in the harbour. This was answered by an Englishman who wanted a couple to help him crew to the Canaries and on to the West Indies. We had to contribute to food and expenses as well as do two four-hour watches per day. We also scrubbed and painted the bottom of the yacht. Because we were inexperienced we weren't paid which at the time seemed the best deal going in Gibraltar as there were many experienced people looking for crewing positions. I must caution anybody considering this kind of thing to think seriously about whether they can get along with the other people on the boat for a period of several weeks without throwing someone overboard. It turned out the captain had wanted a couple because he assumed a woman would cook dinner, wash dishes, etc. By the time we reached Gran Canaria (after three weeks because we made so many stops) the four of us were at each others' throats. My boyfriend and I hopped off (penniless). The trip had turned out to be quite expensive, though we saw islands I wouldn't otherwise have seen (Madeira in particular) and we got to learn a little about sailing. However the sailing is mostly quite boring (a yacht is very slow moving) and when you don't like the people, a lot of the fun goes out of the trip.

> **Bad weather can also get in the way of your romantic vision of sailing the oceans, as Dan Boothby found:**
> I ended up in Gib to look for a yacht to the Caribbean and instead ended up working in a supermarket, unloading freezer lorries and living on my wits. I got on a yacht eventually from Algeciras but we were late for the prevailing trade winds, hit a massive storm a few days out and turned tail back to Morocco. Adventurous days. I miss them.

Also try to ascertain in advance whether you will be subjected to any unfair pressures or unexpected fees. While travelling in Fiji, Melanie Grey met a man who had had a disastrous time crewing from Cairns:

> After having paid in full for the entire sail from Cairns to New Zealand, Derek was forced to leave the vessel in Vanuatu along with several other crew members. This was due to the Hitler-style regime of the Belgian skipper and his girlfriend. After parting with large amounts of money (A$25 a day), the crew were treated like slaves, every morsel of food consumed was closely monitored, and the female members of the crew were often reduced to tears. The skipper obviously took on crew purely for the financial gain and not for the company or the pleasure of sailing. The crew members who left the trip prematurely were not reimbursed.

It is also not unknown for crew to be thrown off a boat, perhaps on a remote island, if there is a personality clash. Never underestimate the stress of life afloat. Try to sign a contract entitling you to some compensation if you do not complete all the legs of the journey. And don't do anything which could get the captain into trouble. (Carrying drugs is the most extreme example; a boat that is found to be carrying drugs will be confiscated.)

Charming the Captain

In every marina and harbour there are people planning and preparing for long trips. There may be requests for crew posted on harbour notice boards, in yacht clubs or chandlery shops from Marina Bay in Gibraltar to Rushcutter's Bay in Sydney. Or you may have to approach skippers on spec. The most straightforward (and usually the most successful) method is to head for the nearest yacht marina and ask captains directly. To locate the yacht basin in an unfamiliar town, simply ask at your hotel or the tourist office. The harbour water supply or dinghy dock is usually a good place to meet yachties. One sailor looking for a berth in Thailand found that he had to swim out to the anchored yachts to knock on their hulls, which culminated in a free ride to Malaysia.

Since many of the yachts moored are used for local pleasure sailing only, concentrate on the yachts with foreign flags. Some travellers contend that boat-owners appreciate a straightforward approach: 'Good morning. I'd like to work for you.' Others think that this might catch captains off guard, and that it is better to approach the question in a more roundabout fashion. Many British, North American and Australian travellers are working their way around by cleaning boats and then participating as crew members as a means of alleviating travel expenses to their next destination. If you are not afraid to ask, your options can be greatly increased. Nothing can be lost by asking and much may be gained.

A yacht is a home, so an unwelcome intrusion on board is as bad as entering a house uninvited. The accepted phrase is 'permission to board?'. Once on board, behave as politely and as deferentially as you would in any stranger's home. Once you get to know both the boat and its owner, you can find ways to make yourself useful, whether washing up or scraping barnacles from the hull. You are then more likely to be offered a berth when the yacht finally sails.

Unless you are exceptionally lucky, you must expect to face a lot of competition for crewing positions and be prepared for repeated rejections and humiliations. Posting a notice on a marina notice board is usually not enough: you must visit the docks and sell yourself. This is one time when it is *not* a good idea to exaggerate your qualifications, since skippers who find out that they have been misled will be justifiably furious and, at worst, it could be life-endangering. Britons will probably do better with yachts sailing the British flag, and women often have an edge if only because of their relative novelty in a world dominated by men.

Women sailors encounter special problems and in fact are usually trying *not* to charm the captain to excess. Mirjam Koppelaars, who responded to a notice posted by a yachtsman in Gibraltar, spells out the problems:

> *I must put some words of warning, especially for the female sailors. Most captains who are actively looking for crew are not really interested in finding competent crew, but in finding female company for day – and nighttime. Be aware of this and think it over before boarding a boat. Elise from Norway and I sailed with this extremely peculiar captain and a third crew member (Simon from England) over to the Canary Islands. I shouldn't complain too much about it, since we were one of the only boats which actually made this trip without any damage that year, but anyway, we were all three very glad that we could jump over to another boat in Las Palmas.*

Crewing From Britain

There are many yacht basins along the south coast of Britain, from Burnham-on-Crouch in Essex to Falmouth, Cornwall, with Brighton, Chichester Harbour, Lymington, Hamble and other marinas in between. Cruising yachtsmen set sail from all these marinas to various destinations across the Channel or across the Atlantic. After finding out which bars the yachting fraternity frequents, you should make your face and your requirements known (assuming you do not use a crewing agency). The run-up to Cowes Week in early August is a good time to try since this is England's premier regatta.

Boat owners who leave in the spring are probably planning to cruise around the Mediterranean for the summer; those leaving in late October/early November may well be going to spend the winter in the Caribbean. Some are also heading to Scandinavia as Adam Cook reports: *'After a heart-stopping 11 days to windward from Gibraltar to Lymington, I stayed on as crew for the trip to Norway. Wow, the North Sea, it really is yellow sou'wester country out there. The sea is full of oil rigs, Danish fishing boats and the infamous 'stealth' tanker, the kind that only turns on its running lights when you're right up its blunt end.'*

Crewing in the Mediterranean

The standard pattern is for a traveller to get a job on a yacht for the summer charter season on the Mediterranean and then sail with the same yacht or power boat (the latter are generally more boring) to the Americas or (very occasionally) South Africa. Hundreds of boats descend on Gibraltar in the spring, many of which will be ready for a crew change. Hundreds more leave each autumn from the French Riviera, the Costa del Sol, the Canary Islands, etc. The annual ARC (Atlantic Rally for Cruisers) from the Canaries (departing the last Sunday in November in order to reach the West Indies for Christmas) is a convoy for the cautious more than a race, so this is an excellent time to be in Gran Canaria looking for a boat especially if you are willing to contribute $25 a day for the three week crossing. Gran Canaria is the last traditional victualling stop before the Atlantic crossing; the contemplation of thousands of miles of Atlantic Ocean often encourages owners and skippers to take on extra crew.

Asking from boat to boat is the only way of discovering who are the boat owners looking for someone to share the tiring night watches. In the Eastern Mediterranean the best place to pick up a yacht is Gouvia near Corfu town. The yacht basin here and facilities are large enough to service the so-called superyachts that need a lot of crew. From here, the favoured route to the Atlantic might include Malta, Palma, Alicante, Gibraltar, Las Palmas in the Canaries and the Azores before going on to the Caribbean, the Eastern Seaboard of the US or Brazil.

Yacht crew placement agencies are concentrated in Antibes. For example the Crew Network Worldwide with its HQ in Florida (see section below on the Americas) has an office in the south of France (12 Avenue Pasteur, 06600 Antibes; 04-97 21 13 13; antibes@crewnetwork.com) plus an affiliate in Mallorca (YachtHelp! C/ Joan de Saridakis, Edificio Goya, 1-A Marivent, 07015 Palma de Mallorca; 971-40 28 78; palma@crewnetwork. com). The main crewing agencies in Antibes are housed in the same building, viz. La Galerie du Port, 8 boulevard d'Aguillon, 06600 Antibes. One of the agencies there has stressed that they are attempting to fill professional vacancies and do not want to have their name publicised for fear of being inundated with applications from unsuitable candidates. Long established agencies in La Galerie du Port include Peter Insull's Crew Agency (04-93 34 64 64/fax 04-93 34 21 22; crew@insull.com) and the Blue Water Yacht Crew Agency (04-93 34 34 13/fax 04-93 34 28 89; crew@bluewateryachting.com). Competition for jobs on luxury yachts and super yachts is so acute that some candidates enrol in specialist training courses.

Tom Morton included a transatlantic sailing trip in his year between school and university: *'Anyone wishing to cross the Atlantic should seriously consider investigating the ARC. It's good to get down there at least two weeks before the start and get to know the people and boats. The atmosphere is extremely friendly and most hopefuls find a passage, even if it is only two days before departure. It must be borne in mind that nearly all the boats are run by families who will want a contribution towards food.'*

Crewing from the Caribbean

Yachts arrive in the Caribbean in the autumn (October to December) and leave again in April and May before the hurricane season begins (the official date is June 1st though plenty of boats stay around until July). A multitude of yachts gathers at the biggest end-of-season event, Antigua Race Week (end of April/beginning of May), which affords excellent opportunities to arrange a berth to Venezuela, Europe or the South Pacific. If you have accumulated experience during the season you should have little difficulty in finding a passage back to the Mediterranean or the UK.

According to Paul Crabb, Antigua is by far the most promising place to look for a crewing position. Now a professional sailor, he is an advocate of spending time in the yachties' bar and demonstrating what good company you are without drinking to excess. Paul was lucky enough to get day work on a yacht belonging to Richard Wright ex-keyboard player for Pink Floyd. When the skipper's wife had an accident and had to return to Britain for treatment, Paul was offered a free flight back to accompany her, though he was sorry to lose the chance of more musical evenings in the bar with his benefactor and Pink Floyd guitarist David Gilmour.

Other good places to look for a lift are Barbados between November and February and St Lucia at the beginning of December. Barbados is traditionally the place transatlantic vessels arrive, though vessels participating in the ARC often end up at Rodney Bay Marina on St Lucia in the first two weeks of December which makes this an ideal time and place to search for a crew position. After the long Atlantic crossing many skippers and crew are desperate to get away from each other.

Another excellent place to head is the Yacht Haven Marina in St Thomas, US Virgin Islands. Hanging around the Bridge pub and the yacht supply stores should result in contact with skippers. Pinning a note on the notice board outside the launderette should work. Also try Trinidad at Carnival time in February. This is the largest gathering of cruisers in the Caribbean and therefore offers some extraordinarily good crewing opportunities.

Kenneth Dichmann from Denmark spent a thoroughly enjoyable six months hitching lifts and working on six different sailboats in the Caribbean. His favourite crew-seeking method was the VHF radio. On several occasions he announced his intentions on the radio net (like a notice board on the airwaves) to which the majority of sailors tune in each morning. This worked for him in Trinidad and St. Martin. To gain access to the VHF Net, enquire at the marina office or bar.

His second method was the usual one of camping out at the dinghy dock and asking everyone who comes through. Take a notebook and pencil since you will be given leads to follow up later. On a few occasions Kenneth didn't wait for skippers to come to him but he went out to their yachts moored in the harbour either by swimming (as he did in Admiralty Bay on Bequia) which can be unpleasant if the harbour is polluted, or by hiring a pirogue (ocean kayak). Tireless in his searches, he made eye-catching notices for all the possible notice boards and checked them at least once a day. He talked to marina staff especially the dock master and travel lift master.

His general tips for inspiring confidence in skippers include dressing neatly, telling the skipper that you meet immigration requirements (and if you don't have an onward ticket offer to leave an equivalent deposit), showing your health insurance certificate, reassuring him that you are not carrying any illegal substances (inviting him to search your luggage if he would like), and finally if possible showing a reference from another skipper. Of the many yachts he joined, the daily fees for expenses varied from $18 to nil.

After crewing in the Caribbean for a year, Marcus Edwards-Jones summarised the experience: 'If you are keen on sun, sea and sand and do not have much money, crewing on yachts is a fantastic way of seeing the world, getting brown and enjoying yourself while being paid to do so.' See the chapter on the *Caribbean* for more information on crewing.

Crewing from the Americas

Apart from introducing yourself to boat-owners at the docks, the primary ways to find a crewing position in the US are by registering with a crewing agency, staying in a crew house where you are likely to hear of forthcoming vacancies, answering an advert in the yachting press or hanging around at a yachting supply store, some of which have notice boards. Great camaraderie and solidarity develops among yachties, many of whom get to know one another when staying in crew houses. Paul Crabb advises novices not to work for less than the going rate and never for nothing since this undervalues not only your labour but that of your colleagues who will resent you for it.

If intending to sign up with a crewing agency, it is virtually essential to do so in person. At that time you can enquire about visas, though you are likely to be told that it is permissible to join the crew of a foreign-registered yacht on a tourist visa provided you don't cruise in US waters for longer than 29 days (whereupon you should have a B-1 business visa). Many crewing agencies are located in Fort Lauderdale, the yachting capital of Florida. Here is a list of Fort Lauderdale crewing agencies, partly courtesy of Floyd's webpage (see reference to Floyd's Hostel below):

Crew Network Worldwide, 1800 SE 10th Ave, Suite 404, Fort Lauderdale, FL 33316 (954-467-9777/fax 954-527-4083; fortlauderdale@crewnetwork.com; www.crewnetwork.com).

Crew Unlimited, 2067 South Federal Highway, Fort Lauderdale, FL 32067 (954-462-4624/fax 954-523-6712; www.crewunlimited.com). One-time registration fee of $25. Summer office in Newport, Rhode Island.

Crewfinders International, 404-408 SE 17th St (954-522-2739; www.crewfinders.com). Also has summer office in Newport, Rhode Island (2 Dean Ave, Suite 5; 401-849-5227).

Luxury Yacht Group, 1362 SE 17th St, Fort Lauderdale 33316 (954-525-9959; www.luxyachts.com).

Palm Beach Yacht Crew, 4200 N Flagler Drive, West Palm Beach, FL 33407 (561-863-0082; www.yachtcrew.com).

Camper & Nicholson, The Quay, 1535 SE 17th St, Suite B No. 208 ,Fort Lauderdale, FL 33316 (954-760-5801; crew@ftl.cnyachts.com; www.cnconnect.com). Camper & Nicholson is one of the largest yacht brokerage companies in the world. Crew placement offices in Antibes, etc.

D & R Woods International, 500 SE 15th Street, Suite 102, Fort Lauderdale, FL 33316 (954-382-6125/524-0065; www.drwoodsintl.com).

The agencies normally charge job-seekers a fee of $25-$75. Experienced crew often bypass the agencies and simply ask captains directly. Chefs/cooks are especially in demand.

Boat supply stores are an excellent place to meet boat owners and pick up information. For example in South Florida, visit West Marine on Dixie Highway in Coconut Grove, Miami; Sailorman on State Road 87 in Fort Lauderdale or Smallwood's Yachting Supply at 1001 SE 17th St, Fort Lauderdale. A great place to stay in Fort Lauderdale is Floyd's Hostel and Crew House (954-462-0631; Floyd@floydshostel.com; www.floydshostel.com) which accepts only international travellers and yachties who should ring or email for the address; an overnight stay here costs about $17 plus tax. Floyd's Hostel also acts as a crewing agency. The two marinas in Fort Lauderdale are Bahia Mar Marina and Pier 66 a mile to the west. Just south of Pier 66 on SE 17th Street is an enormous collection of yacht brokers who sell a huge number of new yachts to sailors who might be nervous enough about their maiden voyage to take on a willing crew member.

Yachts sail from the west coast of North America to Hawaii, Tahiti and beyond in April/May or September/October. In October there are several organised gatherings of 'yachties' in California which provide an excellent chance to fix up a crewing position. As well as running relevant classified adverts, the monthly yachting magazine *Latitude 38* (15 Locust Ave, Mill Valley, CA 94941; 415-383-8200; www.latitude38.com) compiles a Mexico Only Crew List in October which costs just $5 for inclusion – the deadline is September 15th – and also hosts 'Crew List Parties' at the Golden Gate Yacht Club in San Francisco (see website for dates). Women job-seekers are advised by Latitute 38 to ask as many pertinent (but not impertinent) questions as possible about the duties (strictly sailing) which they will be expected to perform. Latitude 38's webpage provides contact details of skippers looking for crew. Many other crew registers and placement agencies can be discovered by researching the internet, for example try the Canada-based Yacht Crew Register (745 Tudor Ave, North Vancouver, BC V7R 1X1; 604-990-9901; www yachtcrewregister.com) or in Australia the Royal Queensland Yacht Squadron posts crew requests (www.rqys.com.au).

Ports along Baja California (the long Mexican peninsula) are surprisingly popular because skippers want to avoid the high mooring fees of California to the north. It has been estimated that there are as many as 400 foreign yachts moored in La Paz at any one time, a Baja town 22 hours by bus from Tijuana.

Further south, Panama is an excellent place to find a passage especially in March but any time between January and May. Apparently there are always a few sailboats stranded there for lack of crew. Helping yachts to negotiate the locks of the Panama Canal as a 'linehandler' enables you to make the acquaintance of prospective skippers. Try also the Cristobal Yacht Club or the Balboa Yacht Clubs in Panama City. Near the Balboa Club is a small white booth where you can find out which boats are departing the next day. A motor boat shuttles out to yachts from which you can make your requirements known to captains. The vast continent of South America may afford possibilities. Between May and August, hundreds of yachts congregate in Puerto la Cruz and Cumaná in Venezuela to avoid the hurricanes in the Caribbean. Elsewhere in South America try the yacht clubs in Buenos Aires and Rio.

Crewing in the South Pacific

After several exhausting but lucrative months of fruit-picking in Australia and New Zealand, Frank Schiller from Germany was all set to fulfil one of his dreams:

I was hellbent on scoring a ride on an ocean-going yacht for any Pacific destination – after all I'd read alluring stories of Joseph Conrad and Jack London. In June I stood in front of a 4-Square shop window in Russell in New Zealand's Bay of Islands when by pure chance a notice was put up by the shop keeper: 'Crew wanted for Tonga.' Less than an hour later I found myself sailing across the bay

> back to Opua. After a week of doing odd jobs on the boat I was en route to Nukua-
> lofa. Pure magic. All this despite never having set foot on a yacht before, once
> more stressing the theme of your book that nothing's impossible!
>
> Since the New Zealand owners had two kids, they needed someone to give
> them a hand. In no time I was doing night watches, taking sights with the sextant
> (the skipper taught me a few lessons on navigation which I was very keen on),
> cooking and washing up and most important of all – I became 'Uncle Frankie' to
> the kids. If you get along well with everyone on board, there are no worries going
> sailing in a matchbox. (But if there are hassles – no escape, even on a 100 footer.)
> Yachting, in fact, can be a very rewarding and adventurous thing to embark on.

The best season to ask around in Fiji, Samoa, Tonga, etc. is July to October when most boats leave to sail to Hawaii or New Zealand. Suva, the capital of Fiji, and Papeete in Tahiti are hubs of much yachting activity in the South Pacific. Try the Royal Suva Yacht Club or Tradewinds Marina (Suva). Frank Schiller provides more detailed advice on crewing between South Pacific Islands: 'As good as Neiafu harbour in Tonga is in July, Malolo-Lailai has got to be the best in September when the annual yacht race to Port Vilal/Vanuatu starts. There were quite a few 'crew wanted' signs in evidence, since everyone's getting the hell out of the Pacific at that time.' Other stops in the Pacific include Mauna Kea and Ala Wai (Hawaii) and Majuro in the Marshall Islands.

In New Zealand the best places by far to find crewing jobs are Opua in the Bay of Islands and Whangarei where the boats are close together and the people all know one another. Parties in the yacht club provide a good chance to meet sailors. Although the Westhaven Marina in Auckland Harbour is one of the biggest in the southern hemisphere, it can be more difficult to meet the right people because of the anonymity of a big city. You might try the Auckland office of the crewing agency Crew Network (37 South Ltd, 15 Halsey St, Westhaven, Auckland; 09-302 0178; newzealand@crewnetwork.com).

While in Auckland some years ago, Marcus Scrace saw many ads for crew (mostly on a share-expenses basis) bound for Australia, Tonga, Fiji, and the USA. As for the timing, March and April are the months to pick up a boat leaving Westhaven or the Bay of Islands. The early departures are usually heading further east (i.e. to Tahiti) while the later ones are likely to be destined for the Tonga/Samoa/Fiji triangle. Many end up in Australia at the end of the season, i.e. late October when all South Pacific sailors head for shelter from cyclones.

To leave eastern Australia, head for Airlie Beach and the Whitsunday Islands in Queensland (especially during the Fun Race held in September), Cairns or Townsville; check adverts in the Cairns Post most of which specify a payment of $15-$30 a day. Marcus Scrace, who was teaching at the Pacific Sailing School in Rushcutters Bay, Sydney, noticed an advert for crew on the notice board and was soon on his way to New Zealand. From Darwin boats leave for Indonesia from May; check the notice board at the Darwin Yacht Club in Fannie Bay. The Darwin-Ambon race between Australia and Indonesia in July is especially promising.

Crewing from Other Countries

Many yachts travelling around Africa lose their crew in Cape Town and need new crew for the onward journey, although January is not a good time to look judging from the number of notices from people looking for crewing positions which Stephen Psallidas noticed in the Cape Town Yacht Club. Durban Yacht Club is recommended though sailing from Cape Town to Durban against the ocean currents is a joyless endeavour. It's better to start in Durban or Maputo if you want to sail to Madagascar. Yachts leave the East African coast for the Seychelles in January or February and for Madagascar and South Africa in August/September. Visit the yacht clubs in Dar es Salaam and Mombasa. Similarly private yachts heading east or west from the Indian subcontinent which stop at tropical Sri Lanka are often short of hands. Ask around the visitors' yacht basins in Colombo or Galle. Both ports are part of the popular South-East Asia yachting circuit which also takes in Bali (Port

Benoa), Singapore (try the Changi Sailing Club or Sembawang Yacht Club), Penang and Phuket. The best time to try in South-East Asia is September/October. West of Sri Lanka there are crewing opportunities each spring to the Red Sea, Mauritius, the Seychelles and East Africa.

In fact the possibilities are infinite for people without a fixed timetable. For example the author of this book met by chance a charming sailor in a post office in Cochin, South India and could have crewed across the Indian Ocean to Dar es Salaam had it not been for the tyranny of publisher's deadlines (alas).

Yacht Delivery

Once you have some basic crewing experience you might go upmarket and try to get a job delivering yachts. Britain is still a major distributor and exporter of yachts and the easiest way to export a yacht is to sail it. This necessitates a crew, ideally one which considers the journey itself sufficient payment for the work, though licensed skippers often earn $1 a mile and the crew 50 cents. It is normally the purchaser's responsibility to arrange delivery and so he will want to get in touch with willing volunteers. Hence the yachting magazines and websites carry adverts requesting crew for such journeys; again *Yachting Monthly* offers the most scope and carries a number of advertisements for delivery agencies in Britain. A typical advert might read: 'Sailing Crew required for yacht deliveries to Tahiti departing October/November. All onboard expenses paid but not airfares. Crew must be experienced.'

LAND

If you possess a heavy goods vehicle (HGV) or passenger carrying vehicle (PCV) licence, you will have a distinct advantage wherever you go. These are costly in money and time to acquire, but open opportunities throughout the world. Anyone interested should compare costs, e.g. it is much cheaper and easier to obtain in New Zealand than in the UK. Most training centres will assess how much tuition you will need before trying the test, often 15-20 hours (at approximately £30-£35 an hour). You will also have to pay for a full medical examination from your doctor (from £50) and the test fees of about £100. People with enough mechanical knowledge to make running repairs to their vehicle are especially in demand.

Overland Tours

If you do have or are willing to train for one of the specialist licences and have some knowledge of mechanics, you may be eligible to work as an expedition driver. Competent expedition staff (including cooks) are greatly in demand by the many overland companies and youth travel specialists which advertise their tours and occasionally their vacancies in magazines like *TNT*. Look also in the glossy bi-monthly magazine *Wanderlust* (01753 620426; www.wanderlust.co.uk) for independent travellers (cover price £3.80 in selected newsagents; £22.80 annual subscription). It carries a few ads which might be relevant in its Jobshop column.

Leaders have to contend with vehicle breakdowns, border crossings, black market money exchanges and the trip whinger (usually the one with a calculator). It is always an advantage to have been on one of the tours of the company you want to work for.

Here is a selected list of overland operators some of whose websites include information on tour leader and/or driver recruitment. All UK employers are looking for staff who have the right to work in the UK/EU. For more companies, see the directory of tour operators maintained by Overland Expedition Resources (www.go-overland.com). Specialist companies which operate only in one region (e.g. Africa, Latin America) are mentioned in the relevant chapters.

Dragoman, Operations Department, Camp Green, Kenton Road, Debenham, Suffolk IP14 6LA (01728 861133; www.dragoman.co.uk). Incorporates Encounter (www.encounter.

co.uk). Have a good reputation and look for leader drivers over 25 willing to train for the PCV licence in their workshops (if they don't already have one). Minimum commitment of two years for expeditions to Africa, Asia, South and Central America.

Exodus, Grange Mills, 9 Weir Road, London SW12 0NE (nnikolsky@exodus.co.uk; www. exodus.co.uk). Suitable candidates (aged 25-32) for leader positions in Africa, Asia and the Americas can acquire the appropriate licence during the months of training. Knowledge of Italian, Spanish, French or Japanese highly valued.

Explore Worldwide Ltd, 1 Frederick St, Aldershot, Hants. GU11 1LQ (01252 760200; www.exploreworldwide.co.uk). Europe's largest adventure tour operator employing more than 100 tour leaders for Europe, Africa, Asia and the Americas. Must have first aid certificate and preferably a second language. Must be UK resident and over 25. Training given (refundable bond of £200).

First 48, Annapurna House, Victoria St, Featherstone, Pontefract, W. Yorks. WF7 5EZ (0845 130 48 49; www.first48.com/about/jobs). 18-month to 2 year contracts. Experience of driving in Egypt, Jordan, Syria, Turkey, Iran, Pakistan, India or Nepal would be useful.

Imaginative Traveller, 1 Betts Avenue, Martlesham Heath, Near Ipswich, Suffolk IP5 3RH (liddy@imtrav.net; www.imaginative-traveller.com/jobs). Tour leaders for at least 12 months for Middle East, China Thailand, Vietnam, etc. £250 good will deposit required.

Kumuka Expeditions, 40 Earl's Court Road, London W8 6EJ (020-7937 8855; www. kumuka.co.uk/employment.asp). Looking for qualified diesel mechanics with a PCV or HGV licence to be drivers. Tour leaders (minimum age 23) chosen according to experience and personality.

The Adventure Company, 15 Turk St, Alton, Hants. GU34 1AG (0870 794 1009; jobs@adventurecompany.co.uk). Tour leaders 25+ with first aid qualification and knowledge of languages (preferably) to lead tours worldwide.

After getting past the interview stage as an adventure tour leader, you may be invited to go on a training trip of at least six weeks at your expense (usually around £250). All or most of this bond is generally returned to you after you have been accepted and completed an agreed term of work. Procedures vary for choosing and training couriers. One old hand, writing in the *Traveller* magazine, claims that to be a good tour leader you have to be 'a cross between a Butlins redcoat and Scott of the Antarctic'.

The pay on your training trip will be low, say £70-£100 per week. Incidental expenses such as visas, passports, air tickets, etc. are paid for. Your company will also pay your food kitty contributions and will cover any compulsory money changes that may exist en route. Although it is hard work, it is undoubtedly an interesting and exciting job. Once you are a full expedition leader, you will be paid at a higher rate and have a chance of earning bonuses. Brett Archer from New Zealand enjoyed his stint of working for an African overland company though found it a little daunting to have 18 people dependent on him in such circumstances. After eight months, his contract was not renewed because of a drop in bookings.

Expeditions

One romantic idea for working your way around the world is to become part of an expedition venturing into the more remote and unspoiled parts of the world from Tierra del Fuego to Irian Jaya. It would be nice if you could be invited to join a party of latter-day explorers in exchange for some menial duty such as portering or cooking. However expedition organisers and leaders nowadays demand that participants have some special skills or expertise to contribute beyond mere eagerness. No one will accept you for the ride. For example an advert for people needed on an Arctic expedition included among its volunteer requirements a post-doctoral archaeologist, an electronics officer for proton magnetometer maintenance and an antenna theorist. One suspects that they weren't inundated with applications.

The Royal Geographical Society (1 Kensington Gore, London SW7 2AR) encourages and assists many British expeditions. Occasionally there are requests from expedition leaders for specialists with either scientific or medical skills, preferably with past expedition experience, and for this a register of personnel is maintained. Those who have a particular skill to offer and wish to be included on the register should send an s.a.e. to the Expedition Advisory Centre at the RGS for the appropriate form. The RGS distributes various titles of possible interest including the *Expedition Handbook* (2004, £16.95). A free guide to expedition planning can be read online at www.world-talks.co.uk/expeditionplanning.html. If you want personal advice on mounting an expedition, fundraising and budgeting for expeditions, you can make an appointment to visit the EAC (020-7591 3030; eac@rgs.org).

It is worth considering joining WEXAS The Traveller's Club (World Expeditionary Association, 45-49 Brompton Road, London SW3 1DE; 020-7589 3315) who not only make awards to worthwhile expeditions but, more to the point, carry advertisements and announcements in their quarterly publication *Traveller* where you can advertise your skills (free to members) and hope that a potential expedition leader sees it. WEXAS membership costs £53.50 though they often invite people to join at a reduced cost.

Raleigh International is a UK-based charity which aims to develop young people aged 17-25 (including Prince William a couple of years ago) by offering them the chance to undertake demanding environmental and community projects on expeditions overseas (see section on Gap Year Placement Organisations in the Volunteering chapter). They have an ongoing need for more experienced individuals (25+) to join expedition teams as self-funding staff, e.g. project manager, accountant, doctor, nurse, engineers, photographer, builder, trek leader and communications expert.

World Challenge Expeditions (The Leadership and Development Centre, Black Arrow House, 2 Chandos Road, London NW10 6NF; 020-8728 7200; www.world-challenge. co.uk) takes on about 300 expedition leaders to supervise school expeditions to developing countries. Trips take place in the summer and the minimum commitment is four weeks. Applicants must be at least 24, have a MLTB (Mountain Leader Training) and some experience of working with young people and preferably of travelling in the Third World. Remuneration is negotiable but at least all expenses will be covered.

When joining any expedition you are unlikely to escape a financial liability, for most expeditions levy a fee from each participant. Sponsorship, and the amount of it, from companies, trusts and other sources will depend upon the aims of the expedition and the benefits to the donor. And once the money and equipment are forthcoming the expedition then has obligations to its sponsors and forfeits much of its freedom. Raising sponsorship, a job with which all expedition members should help, is probably the biggest headache of all and involves endless letter-writing and the visiting, cap in hand, of dozens of commercial establishments and other possible sources of income.

AIR COURIERS

Changes in the international system of document delivery means that the role of the air courier has almost disappeared. In fact the man who runs the International Association of Air Travel Couriers (IAATC) in the UK predicts that the business will disappear completely in 2005 or 2006. In the old days international courier companies needed to lure casual couriers to accompany tons of 'time sensitive documents' between countries and continents which would then be cleared as excess passenger baggage. In many airports of the world it is no longer a requirement that someone physically accompany the documents. Furthermore, the universal use of e-mail has made it unnecessary for some of the documents to be shipped and alarm over airport security in the United States mean that the industry has seen a sharp decline. From the UK the only desinations that remain for air couriers are Sydney, Tokyo and Bangkok. In 2004 Air Cargo Partners stopped selling courier flights for Virgin Atlantic; and Bridges Worldwide, which at one time served 30 destinations, currently serves just Sydney. Transatlantic courier flights have all but disappeared.

The two companies in the UK left selling courier flights are:
Bridges Worldwide Wholesale Express, Jupiter House, 3 Horton Road, Colnbrook, Slough

SL3 0BB (tel/fax 01753 443747). Cheapest return fare to Sydney starts at £450 on Japan Airlines

British Airways Travel Shops, Room E328, E Block, BA Cranebrook S551, Off Jubilee Way, PO Box 10, Heathrow Airport, Hounslow, Middlesex TW6 2JA (0870 606 1133). Bangkok for £390, Tokyo from £340. No longer serve Miami or New York.

Once you have booked a courier flight the procedure is as follows: you turn up in plenty of time at the appointed meeting place with your passport, visa (if necessary), insurance and luggage (most companies nowadays allow their couriers the full 23kg allowance). There you will be met by the company's agent who is frequently very late, thereby causing severe anxiety to the hopeful courier. He shows the paperwork to airline staff, checks in up to a score of mail bags and sees you through customs. At the other end, another agent greets you (at least in theory), escorts you through customs and disappears with the packages.

The situation for outbound air couriers in the US has been hit hard by post-9/11 security concerns and the Federal Aviation Administration has withdrawn the licence for many destinations including those in South and Central America. However couriers are still being recruited for Far East destinations, but availability has been greatly reduced over the past two years. The courier broker Now Voyager (45 West 21st St, Suite 5A, New York 10019; 212-459-1616; www.nowvoyagertravel.com) no longer offers courier flights to Europe but sells return flights New York to Bangkok ($439-$599), Los Angeles to Singapore ($339-$579), Los Angeles to Hong Kong ($339-$519) and San Francisco to Manila (£389-$579). They concentrate on selling discounted or space-available flights (see Travel chapter). The survival of these few routes is reiterated on the Jupiter Air website www.jupiterair.com/courierflgt.htm. Their Los Angeles office can be contacted by telephone on 310-670-1197/8 and their New York office on 718-656-2883.

The situation changes so quickly that the following US contacts may be out of date:

International Courier Network, 212-741-8884.

Global Delivery Systems, 14725 176th St, Jamaica, NY 11434 (718-995-2708). Far East destinations only on Northwest Airlines. Saturday departures to Hong Kong, Tokyo, Bangkok, Singapore and Manila starting at $800 return for a stay of 3 months.

Micom America, Building 14, Suite 5, JFK International Airport, Jamaica, NY 11430 (718-656-6050; juajfk@cris.com).

World Courier, 1313 4th Ave, New Hyde Park, NY 11040 (516-354-2600).

ACP (Air Cargo Partners), 1983 Marcus Ave, Suite 108, Lake Success, NY 11042 (516-358-2025; www.acpww.com). Other offices in Chicago, Los Angeles and worldwide listed on website.

Air courier associations act as clearinghouses for courier flights though have understandably been diversifying into acting as regular travel agents. If considering joining one of these, make sure you understand exactly what you are paying for. All are heavily web-based since the fluctuating nature of this business means that printed books are soon obsolete. The three main associations are:

Air Courier Association, 1767A Denver West Blvd, Golden, Colorado 80401 (1-800-211-5119; www.aircourier.org). Annual membership costs $49 which allows access to travel bargains posted on the website.

International Association of Air Travel Couriers/IAATC, PO Box 847, Scottsbluff, Nebraska 69363-0847 (308-632-3273 Voicemail; fax 308-632-8267; www.courier.org). $45 annual membership.

Courier Travel, CT Web Technologies Inc, PO Box 3051, Nederland, CO 80466 (1-866-470-3061 or 303-642-7355; www.couriertravel.org). $50 annual membership. A recent example of a winter deal quoted on their website was $350 Los Angeles to Hong Kong.

Of course there are outfits not listed in the *Yellow Pages* which employ couriers to transport more exotic substances. Unless you want an extended holiday in one of H.M. prisons or a long vacation making licence plates in San Quentin, you should steer clear of this sort of operation.

TRAVEL

Not everyone has the time nor the stamina to work a passage. There follow some general guidelines for finding bargains in train, coach, ship and air travel. More detailed information on specific destinations can be found in travel guides from Lonely Planet and Rough Guides. The amount of travel information on the internet is staggering and this chapter cannot hope to tap its resources. There are websites on everything from sleeping in airports (www.sleepinginairports.net) to sharing lifts across North America (www.erideshare.com). Many sites have pages of intriguing links; to name just two, try www.bugeurope.com ('BUG' stands for Backpackers' Ultimate Guide) and www.budgettravel.com.

General advice on minimising the risks of independent travel is contained in the book *World Wise – Your Passport to Safer Travel* published by Thomas Cook in association with the Suzy Lamplugh Trust and the Foreign Office (www.suzylamplugh.org/worldwise; £7.99 plus £2 postage). Arguably its advice is over-cautious, advising travellers never to hitch-hike, ride a motorbike or accept an invitation to a private house. Travellers will have to decide for themselves when to follow this advice and when to ignore it.

Hitch-hiking

According to some die-hards, hitch-hiking is not only the best travel bargain around, it is the most rewarding. Yet over the past generation, hitch-hiking has fallen out of fashion, possibly because young travellers and students are generally more affluent and also because of a heightened sense of paranoia (though the dangers remain infinitesimal). However there are still enough people out there interested to support a number of websites.

In the experience of many travellers, hitching is cheap, safe and fascinating (and what else could anyone ask for?) The uncertainty of the destination is one of its great attractions to the footloose traveller. While hitching from France to Germany in pursuit of work, Kevin Boyd got a lift with a Russian truck bound for Leningrad. He was tempted to stay for the whole trip but, as the lorry averaged 35km an hour on the autoroute, he decided to stick with his original idea. Hitch-hiking has one positive virtue for job seekers: you can sound out the driver for advice on local job opportunities. Friendly drivers often go miles out of their way and may even ask in villages about work possibilities on your behalf, as happened to Andrew Winwood in Switzerland during the *vendange*. Lorry drivers often know of temporary jobs you could do.

Hitch-hiking is also good for the environment. As long ago as 1998, a UK government report was published to promote car-sharing. One of the suggested measures was to introduce hitch-hiker pick-up zones at motorway junctions which would be brightly lit and possibly equipped with closed circuit TVs. Some French roads already feature hitch-hiking zones. The popularity of hitch-hiking in the US has increased since single occupant cars were banned from the fast lanes in some American cities.

Some readers have expressed disapproval that we recommend hitch-hiking as a good way of getting around. Hitch-hiking, like any form of transport, has its dangers, but that is not a sufficient argument for a wholesale ban. The existence of road rage and air rage, of attacks on or derailment of trains, does not result in mass avoidance of these modes of travel. By following a few rules the risks of hitch-hiking can be minimised. Never accept a lift from a driver who seems drunk, drowsy or suspicious. Women should try not to hitch alone. A small dose of paranoia is not a bad thing, whether at midnight in Manchester or midday in Manila, especially in view of the murders of several hitch-hiking travellers in Australia and stories like the following from a reader of this book:

After my friend had decided to go back to Thailand and (by mistake) took most of my money, I continued on alone. I was offered a ride to Kuala Lumpur by what seemed like a very pleasant Malaysian guy. After about an hour he pulled over to the side of the road. I thought he was stopping to get a drink and something to eat. Before I knew it, he'd central-locked the doors (this truck was like Fort Knox) and pulled the curtains round, turned off the lights and undressed. For the next two hours he proceeded to tell me in graphic details how he was going to rape me and throw my dead body from the truck. Panic set in quickly, but I managed not to show it too much. I told the guy that he was frightening me and that I had people waiting for me in Singapore, and if I wasn't back by a certain time, they would not hesitate to call the police. I also started to tell him all about myself and my family. This makes the person see you as a human being and not just a lump of meat. Eventually he let me go.

Try to put the risks into perspective. It is worth mentioning that my friend Simon Calder, author of the now out-of-print *Hitch-hikers Manual: Britain* and *Europe: a Manual for Hitchhikers,* has found cycling in London a far more dangerous and damaging pursuit than thumbing lifts (and has lived to become the Travel Editor of the *Independent* newspaper). Usually the worst danger is of boredom and discouragement when you have a long wait. A few readers have written to say that they cannot understand how people manage to enjoy hitching especially across Europe. It is of course a game of patience. Eventually you will get a lift, but whether you have the stamina to wait for it is another matter.

But many hitchers have been amazed at their good fortune. Jakob Steixner reported that he had covered the 1,700km between Montpellier and Tangiers in three lifts. He had a different kind of luck when hitching out of Tallinn in Estonia: the woman who picked him up was going just a short distance but changed her mind and drove 50km out of her way to take him to his destination. Isak Maseide met nothing but nice people on the 3,200km between Oban in Scotland and Copenhagen via the Bavarian Alps. He was worried just once when he noticed a shoulder holster on a driver who had stopped for him; this man turned out to be an undercover policeman on his way home. On F. Dixon from Nottingham's first trip abroad, he hitched, and was pleasantly surprised by the ease with which great distances could be covered: *'I thought the odds were against me from the start. I am 6'6 tall, black and 18 stone. Who the hell is going to pick me up? Once in Denmark we got good lifts. One nice couple put me up at their home for the night and phoned her father who picked me up and took me to where I was going. I am now making my way to France getting good lifts. Can you tell other black people not to be afraid to travel?'*

In some Western countries organisations fix drivers up with cost-sharing passengers upon payment of a small fee (see the section on Europe below). An interesting variation is to prearrange a ride by talking to lorry drivers at local depots, lorry parks, truckers' cafés, pubs or wherever you see them. However in these nervous times when a stranger is considered a terrorist until proven innocent, this will take more patience and luck than it used to do.

Driving

In some countries you might decide to buy a cheap car and hope that it lasts long enough for you to see the country. This worked well for Frank Schiller, a German traveller in Australia:

How about becoming a car owner yourself if you just wanna roll along for a while? After two successful months of hitching in Tasmania (including a combined Landrover and yacht lift to Maria Island), the three of us decided to change our means of transport. We bought a Holden off a Canadian guy for $500 which included insurance, a few spare parts, a tool kit and some snorkelling equipment. (I'd suggest buying a standard model rather than an E-type Jaguar for ease of finding spares.) After ten weeks and 10,000 kilometres, we sold it to a wrecker in Alice Springs for $250. So each of us had paid $80 for the car plus about $120 for petrol – all in all a much better bargain than a bus pass.

A camper van is also an appealing idea, especially if you are interested in chasing fruit harvests around. It is possible to pick up a reliable vehicle for less than £1,000 if you're lucky.

> **Australians like Ben Hockley are devoted van users:**
> *My girlfriend and I were spending a lot of money looking for work in Spain so we decided we needed a campervan to help cut the accommodation costs. Vans are not very cheap in Spain and the casual relaxed attitude of the locals makes car hunting a nightmare. So we hopped a train to Amsterdam where I had learnt that vehicles were 40% cheaper. It was true and after three weeks we had an old Bedford camper for about £1,000. Life in the van was great, we could just park on any street and we had a home for the night.*

An informal van market takes place daily on York Way at Market Road, N7 near the Caledonian Road tube station. You might also check ads in *Auto Trader, Exchange & Mart* and *LOOT* or if starting in London on www.gumtree.com, London's online community.

Those who own their own vehicle might consider taking it with them. Certainly a car or motorcycle on the Continent will make life easier when it comes to visiting potential employers, especially in the countryside. On the negative side, it will be an expensive luxury (even if petrol is cheaper on the continent than in the UK) and a serious encumbrance if you decide to travel outside continental Europe. If you are considering taking your car, contact your local AA or RAC office for information about International Driving Permits, motor insurance, green cards, etc.

Train

The conventional wisdom is that trains are preferable to buses because they allow you to walk around or lie down on long journeys. Anyone who has experienced travelling unreserved on Indian trains or on long distance Italian trains in high summer (where theft is rife) will be aware of the limitations of this generalisation. Besides which, the traveller working his or her way around the world is more interested in financial considerations than in ones of comfort. So you will probably choose a slow, cheap bus in preference to a luxurious high-speed train. But in areas which have a dreadfully creaky and overcrowded rail service (running to a calendar rather than a timetable), it may well be the cheapest way of getting around. Even in developed nations, you may find rail fares rivalling coach ones especially if you are eligible for discounts. Rail passes are generally not much use to job-seeking travellers since they benefit people who want to do a great deal of travelling. The specialist UK agent Great Rail Journeys can book most rail journeys (01904 521900; www.greatrail.com) though nowadays most people do their research independently online.

The Inter Rail ticket is widely available. You must choose how many zones you intend to cover and bear in mind that seat reservations will cost extra; current prices for the under-26s are £159 for 16 days in one zone, £295 for a month's travel in all zones which includes 28 countries. Over 26s will pay £223/£415 for the same passes. Anyone intending to do some concentrated travelling by train should contact a specialist operator like Rail Europe (08705 848848; www.raileurope.co.uk) or Rail Choice (www.railchoice.co.uk) who sell a large range of European and international rail passes.

Other youth and student discounts can be very useful; for example the *Wochenendticket* (weekend ticket) in Germany is valid for the whole country on Saturdays and Sundays but only on regional trains. It costs €28 for up to five people which means that you can get from the Austrian to the Danish border for less than £4 each.

The Thomas Cook *World Timetable* is the bible for overland travellers outside Europe; within Europe, consult the *European Timetable* both for £13.99.

Coach

Coach travel has never enjoyed a favourable press. After buying a cheap coach ticket from London to Athens, Mark Hurley's conclusion was 'never again': even after the on-board loo packed up, there were only two rest stops every 24 hours. The last leg of the journey through Greece was done on another coach which was already full when Mark's lot turned up. On the other hand, coaches have some confirmed fans who positively relish long-distance journeys when life is reduced to its constituent pleasures of sleeping, eating, reading and socialising. The great advantage of course is the low cost.

In many areas of the world such as Nepal and Papua New Guinea, public road transport is the only way to get around the country short of flying. Fortunately this monopoly of the travel market is not generally reflected in high fares, usually because of competing companies. Such free enterprise is wonderfully apparent at the Topkapi Gate Bus Station in Istanbul where salesmen for a host of competing companies call out their destinations and prices. Bus prices are below a penny per mile in much of the Third World (possibly to compensate for the purgatory of non-stop Kung Fu videos in some parts of the world) and increase rapidly to nearly a pound for a half mile in Central London. Except where smooth air-conditioned buses provide an alternative to sub-third class rail travel, coaches are generally less expensive than trains. The Thomas Cook *Overseas Timetable* is valuable for coach as well as train travellers.

One of the most interesting revolutions in youth travel has been the explosion of backpackers' bus services which are hop-on hop-off coach services following prescribed routes. These can be found in New Zealand, Australia, Ireland, Scotland, England and the continent. Generally they are not really cheap enough to serve as a job-seeker's preferred mode of transport. For example a month long coach pass on Busabout Europe (258 Vauxhall Bridge Road, London SW1V 1BS; 020-7950 1661; www.busabout.com) costs £339 for those under 26. For 16 days of travel within the whole operating season between May and October on Busabout someone over 26 will pay £499.

Air

Scheduled airfares as laid down by IATA, the airlines' cartel, are best avoided. They are primarily designed for airline accountants and businessmen on expense accounts. You should be looking at no frills ticketless flying, cheap charters and last minute discounted tickets. Air travel within individual countries and continents is not always subject to this choice, though some special deals are available.

For longhaul flights, especially to Asia, Australasia and most recently Latin America, discounted tickets are available in plenty and there should never be any need to pay the official full fare. Previously the sale of these tickets was restricted to the original 'bucket shops', often seedy discount agencies. Now high street travel agents such as Thomas Cook and hundreds of travel websites are openly selling discounted tickets and because of their enormous turnover and sophisticated computer systems can often offer the best deals.

The very lowest fares are still found by doing some careful shopping around. Check adverts in the travel press like the Saturday *Independent* and in the London free magazine *TNT*. Phone a few outfits and pick the best price. A good start when browsing the internet is www.cheapflights.co.uk which is the brainchild of the well-respected travel journalist John Hatt and has links to other useful sources of travel information. Alternatives are www.travelocity.com, www.expedia.co.uk and www.lastminute.com which also owns www.flights4less.co.uk. When users log onto their destination, they must provide specific dates which makes the process of comparing fares, times and airlines time-consuming.

Unfilled seats are auctioned off to bidders by a US company called Priceline (www.priceline.com); you indicate where and when you want to go, how much you're prepared to pay (above a specified minimum), give them your credit card details and wait to see if any airline will bite. Of course very low fares are not available in busy seasons or on obscure routes. Priceline launched in the UK in 2001 but does not operate a name-your-own-price system for flights any more.

Another tip for finding the cheapest available fares is to tap into the expat community of the country to which you would like to fly. For example the cheapest flights from Toronto to Korea are probably found among the many travel agencies to be found in the city's 'Little

Korea' district on Bloor Street West.

The cheapest flights are available from airlines like Aeroflot and Garuda which do not enjoy good reputations when it comes to safety. East European and Asian carriers are worth investigating for low fares. Try to overcome your reluctance, since flying with the airlines perceived as dodgy is guaranteed to be more interesting than flying on KLM, Air Canada or British Airways. You may find that your flight leaves at 7am on a Sunday morning with a 12-hour stopover in Dhaka, but these inconveniences are a small price to pay for savings of a hundred pounds or more. The agency Eastways (6 Brick Lane, London E1 6RF: 020-7247 2424/3823) has the franchise for discounting tickets for Aeroflot, the Russian airline and deals with worldwide destinations.

Once you accept a price, check that the fare will not be increased between paying the deposit (typically £50 or £75) and handing over the balance in exchange for the ticket; if the agency is unable to make such a guarantee, ask for a written promise that you can reclaim the deposit in the event of a fare increase. Buying dodgy tickets is always worrying since it is impossible to grasp all the complexities of international air travel. Hand over the balance only when you are satisfied that the dates and times agree with what you anticipated. Roger Blake was pleased with the round-the-world ticket he bought from STA for £940 that took in Johannesburg, Australia and South America. But once he embarked he wanted to stay in Africa longer than he had anticipated and wanted to alter the onward flight dates:

> That is the biggest problem of having an air ticket. I had planned for six months in Africa but I've already spent five months in only three countries. I have been into the British Airways office here in Kampala to try my verbal skills but have been told the 12-month period of validity is non-negotiable. How stupid I was to presume I would get a refund when it states clearly on the back of the ticket that they may be able to offer refunds/credit. A lesson for me and a warning to future 'work your wayers' to check before they buy whether or not the ticket is refundable/extendable.

The price of round-the-world tickets has not risen too drastically over the past few years though taxes and fuel surcharges will add at least £100 and up to £180 to basic fares. Check www.roundtheworldflights.com for ideas (0870 442 4842) or the RTW section of www.thetravellerslounge.co.uk. The cheapest start at about £700 for under-26s in the low season and usually involve one or more gaps which you must cover overland e.g. Los Angeles to New York and/or Sydney to Melbourne. Most are valid for up to a year. An example of a good fare (available through STA) is £843 plus tax for a RTW fare from London to Sydney and Auckland with stopovers in Japan, Singapore and Fiji and on to the USA. The standard RTW stopovers are Singapore/Bangkok, Sydney, Los Angeles and London but there are endless combinations. If you don't want to include North America on your itinerary, you don't need a RTW ticket. An offbeat example of a route downunder used Emirates and SriLankan Airways to travel via Dubai to Mumbai (Bombay), overland to Trivandrum in Kerala, on to Colombo, Singapore, Sydney (or Melbourne or Perth) then back to London via Dubai for less than £1000.

Attempts are ongoing to launch a new airline specially catering for backpackers on routes from Europe to Australia via Southeast Asia. According to one website, BackpackersXpress.com is planning to start flying its 'funjet' service towards the end of 2005 but there have been so many delays that some have begun to suspect it will never materialise.

The principal agencies specialising in longhaul travel for student and budget travellers are:

STA Travel 0870 160 6070; www.statravel.co.uk. Leading agency for independent and youth travel with 450 branches worldwide including 65 in the UK. They can organise flexible deals, domestic flights, overland transport, accommodation and tours. Although they are aimed at the youth market, they can find cheap flights for the over-26s too. Note that many of their branches are so busy that it is possible to book an appointment free of charge (www.statravel.co.uk/c_aboutus/appointments.asp). Two

London branches at Victoria and Russell Square plus their Bristol branch offer a range of services including travel clinic and travel equipment shop.

Trailfinders Ltd, 194 Kensington High St, London W8 7RG (020-7938 3939 longhaul; 020-7937 5400 transatlantic; 020-7937 1234 Europe). Also travel centres in Birmingham, Manchester, Newcastle, Bristol, Cambridge, Glasgow, Dublin, Belfast, Sydney, Brisbane and Cairns Australia.

Marco Polo Travel Advisory Service, 24A Park St, Bristol BS1 5JA (0117-929 4123; www. marcopolotravel.co.uk). Discounted airfares worldwide.

Flight Centre, 0870 499 0040; www.flightcentre.co.uk. Many branches in London and around the UK (1200 shops worldwide). Cheap student flights and extra services (e.g. working holiday packages).

North South Travel, Moulsham Mill Centre, Parkway, Chelmsford, Essex CM2 7PX (01245 608291). Discount travel agency that donates all its profits to projects in the developing world.

Quest Travel – 0870 444 5552; www.questtravel.com.

Bridge the World – 0870 444 1716; www.bridgetheworld.com.

Travelbag, 15 Turk St, Alton, Hants. GU34 1AG (0870 814 4441; www.travelbag.co.uk). Australia & New Zealand specialist.

All of these offer a wide choice of fares including Round-the-World. Telephone bookings are possible, though these agencies are often so busy that it can be difficult to get through and sometimes the internet is preferable if you are a confident user.

In the US, check the discount flight listings in the back of the travel sections of the *New York Times* and *Los Angeles Times.* Contact any of STA's many offices throughout the country. Discount online tickets are available from Air Treks (301 Howard St, Fourth Floor, San Francisco, CA 94105; 1-800-350-0612/ 415-977-7100; www.AirTreks.com).

By far the cheapest airfares from the US are available to people who are flexible about departure dates and destinations, and are prepared to travel on a standby basis. The passenger chooses a block of possible dates (up to a five-day 'window') and preferred destinations. The company then tries to match these requirements with empty airline seats being released at knock-down prices. Air-Tech in New York (212-219-7000; www.airtech. com) advertises its fares by saying 'if you can beat these prices, start your own damn airline'. The transatlantic fares being advertised at the time of writing were $219 plus tax one way from the east coast and $229 from the west coast. Note that post September 11th regulations stipulate that US citizens must purchase a return ticket. Discounted fares of $250 return between the US and Mexico or to the Caribbean are also available. One satisfied customer is Lisa Russo who read about Air-Tech in an earlier edition of *Work Your Way Around the World,* used it to travel to Europe and went on to become Director of Marketing for a time.

Airhitch on the west coast also sells space-available vouchers online which can be turned into cheap paperless flights. Their fares to Europe are $165 from the east cost, $199 from the Midwest, and $233 from the west coast, plus taxes of $16 eastbound and $46 westbound plus a registration fee of $29 (www.airhitch.org). Compare a similar range of travel products advertised on www.air-hitch.org (note this website has a hyphen); more information is available by ringing 1-877-AIR-HITCH (1-877-247-4482).

Mig Urquhart was happy to take potluck with Airhitch and ended up in Dublin: *'I'd put down Paris, Amsterdam or Athens on the registration form and got offered Zurich or Dublin. In 30 seconds I had to decide that Switzerland was too expensive and I had never been to Ireland. I'm very happy with the decision and with life in Donnybrook, South Dublin.'*

While Britain, Benelux, Switzerland, the States, Australia and other bastions of the free world have highly developed discount ticket markets, most countries do not. While hundreds of agents in Britain will sell you a cheap flight to Rio, no Brazilian is able to reciprocate. So beware of being stranded if you fly out to an exotic destination on a one-way ticket. The rise and rise of no frills airline in Europe means that this is only a problem for longhaul flights.

You can get a friend in London to send you a discounted ticket for your homeward journey, but this is a tricky, risky and time-consuming business. On the other hand it is probably cheaper in the end and more flexible to piece together your own longhaul itinerary by buying cheap tickets en route, provided you have plenty of time to wait around for the best deals.

Reconfirmation is usually not necessary these days, though you will want to phone the airline or check their website a day or two before departure to check that the timings haven't changed. Also, find out whether airport tax is included in the fare or has to be paid upon departure. Air passenger duty in the UK is £5 for Europe and £20 for the rest of the world. In these days of sharply rising fuel costs, a last-minute fuel surcharge is not an impossibility.

An unusual way of locating cheap flights is available from Adventurair (PO Box 757, Maidenhead, SL6 7XD; 01293 405777; www.rideguide.com) who produce *The Ride Guide* as a CD which gives details of companies operating cargo planes, aircraft deliveries and private planes. Any of these may have seats available for bargain prices. The CD costs £11.99 in the UK ($16.99) plus £1.50 postage.

Bicycle

Cycling is not only healthy and free, it can simplify the business of finding work, as Adam Cook discovered in France:
Looking for work by bicycle is one of the very best methods as it allows you free unlimited travel far from the big towns and the competition. You can so easily visit the small villages and farms, some of which are off the beaten track.

In addition, employers may realise that people who have been cycling for a while are at least moderately fit and may choose them for the job, ahead of the flabbier vehicle-bound competition. In many parts of the world you will also become an object of fascination, which can only aid your job-finding chances. If you do decide to travel extensively by bicycle, you might consider joining the Cyclists' Touring Club (69 Meadrow, Godalming, Surrey GU7 3HS; 0870 873 0060; www.ctc.org.uk) which provides free technical, legal and touring information to members as well as third party insurance; membership costs £12 if you are a student under 26, £32 otherwise.

EUROPE

The European landmass is one of the most expensive areas of the world to traverse. Not all European countries are equally hitchable: Greece and Italy are fine – if you're blonde and female; Portugal is good, Spain is dreadful, Germany is far easier than France, while Ireland, Denmark and Switzerland are excellent, and so on. One of the best is Poland, as recently confirmed by Jakob Steixner, where many years ago the government encouraged lift-sharing by rewarding drivers and the tradition continues. Readers of this book (including Jakob whose record was mentioned earlier in this chapter) have turned in some impressive times: Jason Davies hitched from Barcelona to Frederikshavn in 3½ days, while in the opposite direction Tony Davies-Patrick got from Denmark to Avignon in a day. Meanwhile Kevin Vincent wonders if he might hold a world record: it took him nine days to hitch from Cadiz to Barcelona, a distance of less than 800 miles. The tollbooths on French and Italian motorways are recommended by seasoned hitchers as the best place to stand.

Often lifts can be arranged informally without having to stand out in the weather. Ride-sharing or 'Allostop' is not uncommon in Europe though normally you will have to make more than a token contribution to the driver's expenses, e.g.€50 for Amsterdam to Warsaw (as advertised February 2005). Check notice boards in hostels or youth travel bureaux or try websites such as http://europe.bugride.com which publicises long distance rides offered and sought on its site. There are dozens of lift-sharing outlets across Europe, especially in Germany, where there are Citynetz offices in Berlin, Düsseldorf, Freiburg, Hamburg, Munich, etc. Most require you to register which is free in some cases or costs

€10-20 in others.

Here are some details of European agencies:

France: Allostop, 30 rue Pierre Sémard, 75009 Paris (1-53 20 42 42 or 8-25 80 36 66; www. allostop.net or http://pcb.ecritel.fr/allostop/welcome.html). Prices are set according to distance of journey, e.g. €9 for less than 250km, €14 for up to 350km, up to €91 for a journey of 3000km plus a small registration fee on a sliding scale.

Belgium: Taxistop/Eurostop, 28 rue Fossé-aux-Loups, 1000 Brussels (+32 70-22 22 92; fax +32 2-223 22 32). Also has offices in Ghent and Ottignies (www.taxistop.be). The admin fee charged to passengers by Taxistop is 80 cents per 100km (minimum €6.20, maximum €20). In addition passengers pay drivers €2.50 per 100km.

Germany: Citynetz-Mitzfahrzentrale – www.citynetz-mitfahrzentrale.de. Website gives addresses, phone numbers and emails of offices around Germany. Prices are calculated at 6 Euro-cents per kilometre.

Matches can seldom be made straightaway, so this system is of interest to those who can plan ahead.

On the whole the railways of Europe are expensive and as noted above Inter Railing is not ideally suited to travellers who want to stop long enough to pick up work. Even with under-26 discounts available through specialist agents it is almost always cheaper to book a no-frills flight from Stansted or Luton. The explosion of competition on European routes has seen some amazingly low fares, though taxes and add-ons make it almost impossible to spend less than £30. As well as checking Ryanair and easyjet, don't forget foreign no-frills carriers like Air Berlin (www.airberlin.com).

No-frills airlines do not take bookings via travel agents so it is necessary to contact them directly, preferably booking over the internet since that invariably saves money, usually £5 per ticket. When comparing prices always factor the tax in which routinely adds £20-£30 to fares and often represents more than 100% of the fare cost:

Eurolines is the name given to all the separate national coach services of Europe working together and selling various coach passes. To find out about a straightforward journey from England to the Contiinent, just book through National Express offices or website (www.nationalexpress.com). Prices start at £49 return for London-Amsterdam. Passengers under the age of 26 are eligible for a 10% discount.

For smaller independent coach operators, check advertisements in London magazines like *TNT*. For example Kingscourt Express (125 Balham High Road, London SW12 9AJ; 020-8673 7500; www.kce.cz) runs daily between London and Prague or Brno; standby fares from £50.

NORTH AMERICA

Incredibly, the price of flying across the Atlantic has been steadily decreasing over the past decade. Off-peak student returns to New York start at £150 plus tax. Competition is fiercest and therefore prices lowest on the main routes between London and New York, Miami and Los Angeles. In many cases, summer fares will be twice as high as winter ones. One way fares are also available to eastern seaboard cities like Washington for £100-£150. When comparing fares, always take the taxes into consideration since they represent an extra £50-£90.

Outside summer and the Christmas period you should have no problems getting a seat; at peak times, a reliable alternative is to buy a discounted ticket on one of the less fashionable carriers which fly to New York, such as Air India or El Al. A one-year return London-New York on Kuwait Air might start at £250 plus taxes.

The USA and Canada share the longest common frontier in the world, which gives some idea of the potential problems and expense of getting around. You will want to consider Driveaway (see *United States* chapter) and also bus and air travel which are both cheaper than in Europe. In the US, consult any branch of STA (1-877-777-8717) and in Canada look for an office of Travel Cuts, the youth and student travel specialist (www. travelcuts.com). If you intend to travel widely in the States check out air passes. One working holidaymaker timed long journeys to coincide with night flights to save on accommodation and food. Hitch-hiking in the USA is often unnerving and sometimes fraught with danger, danger not only from crazy drivers but also from the law, especially where 'No Hitch-hiking' signs abound. It is a more reasonable proposition in Canada. Ride-sharing makes more sense on this continent. Try www.erideshare.com as mentioned above. The system of Allo-Stop is well developed in the province of Quebec but has been ruled illegal in Ontario after complaints were received from coach operators; check www.allostop.com for up-to-date information.

South of the Canadian border, bus passes (Ameripass) are a travel bargain for people who want to cover a lot of ground. Greyhound has no office in the UK but their US and Canada passes can be bought through STA and a few others such as Western Air Travel in Devon (0870 330 1100; www.westernair.co.uk). In 2005, Greyhound (www.greyhound.com) were offering 4, 7, 10, 15, 21, 30, 45 and 60 day passes in the low season to students and under 26s for £78, £98, £121, £140, £168, £186, £210 and £251; passes for over 26s about 12% more and high season passes add approximately another 20%. Once you are in the US timetable and fare information is available 24 hours a day on the toll-free number 1-800-231-2222. Greyhound also offer a Canada Pass which costs £130 for 7 days, £203 for 21 days up to £281 for 60 days (adult fares).

Other forms of transport in the USA are probably more expensive but may have their own attractions, such as the trips run by Green Tortoise (494 Broadway, San Francisco, California 94133; 800-867-8647; www.greentortoise.com) which use vehicles converted to sleep about 35 people and which make interesting detours and stopovers. There may even be an option to swap your labour for a free ride.

The deregulation of US domestic airlines has resulted in lunatic discounting. South-West Airlines based in Dallas (www.southwest.com) is one of the better known discount companies offering cheap fares and no-frills service. Normally the cheapest advance purchase coast-to-coast fares are about $200. The best advice within the USA is to ask locals and study local newspapers, as fare wars are usually fought using full page advertisements.

Attempts to revive long-distance train travel in the US have not been terribly successful and several grand old routes are threatened with closure. Amtrak (1-800-USA-RAIL/872-7245; www.amtrak.com) offers some good value rail passes such as 15 days around the western half of the country for £112 low season or 30 days for £143. The basic three-and-a-half day train trip from Toronto to Vancouver costs about C$550 in the summer, $416 off-season; these fares are slightly lower than they were two years ago. The Via Rail infoline in Canada is 1-888-842-7245 (www.viarail.ca).

In both Canada and the USA there is an alternative way to ride the rails, as Marcel Staats found (some years ago now):

An absolutely great way to see North America is by train. However, if you don't have that much money on you, do it the illegal way and 'hobo'. I left most of my luggage in a cloakroom and hoboed my way across the States. To hobo' (also known as freight-hopping' – Ed) means that you jump on goods trains (called freight trains) and stay there as long as possible. Hoboing is not what it was in the 40s and 50s. There's much tighter security, including frequent checks and padlocked doors. However there are possibilities.

For accommodation in North America (mainly Canada), get hold of the list of hostels from Backpackers Hostels Canada (Longhouse Village, RR 13, Thunder Bay, Ontario P7B 5E4; www.backpackers.ca). The list can be downloaded for free or sent by post in exchange for $5 or four IRCs.

LATIN AMERICA

In the low seasons of January to May and October-November, you can get from London to South America for under £200 one way, though this is rarely the best way to do it because international tickets bought out there are very expensive. Having a return ticket makes it much easier to cross borders. Open-dated returns are available as are open jaw tickets (where you fly into one point and back from another). It might be possible to extend these even if you decide to stay longer than a year; Nick Branch had an Alitalia ticket which he extended more than once for a $100 fee.

A fully-bonded agency that specialises in travel to and around this area of the world is Journey Latin America (12-13 Heathfield Terrace, Chiswick, London W4 4JE; 020-8747 3108; www.journeylatinamerica.co.uk) who consistently offer the lowest fares and the most expertise. Another advantage is that they deal exclusively with Latin America and hence are the best source of up-to-date travel information. One of the best deals at the time of writing was a six-month return to Rio on Air Portugal to Rio for £517. A plethora of airpasses is also available which can be cheaper if bought at the same time as your transatlantic ticket; request Journey Latin America's free newspaper *Papagaio* for an introduction to what's available. Another specialist in the field is South American Experience who offer an excellent service as well and whose prices should be compared: 47 Causton St, Pimlico, London SW1P 4AT (020-7976 5511; www.southamericanexperience.co.uk).

Taxes are levied on international flights within South America: the cheapest way to fly from one capital to another (assuming you have plenty of time) is to take a domestic flight (within, say, Brazil), cross the border by land and then buy another domestic ticket (within, say, Peru). The alternatives include the remnants of a British-built railway system and the ubiquitous bus, both of which are extremely cheap and interesting. A rough estimate of the price of bus travel in South America is US$1.50-$2 for every hour of travel.

Among the most reliable travel guides to the continent is the warhorse *South American Handbook* published annually by Footprint Handbooks (2005, £25). For information on travel in Latin America join South American Explorers (formerly the South American Explorers' Club). They maintain three clubhouses: Calle Piura 135, Miraflores (Postal Casilla 3714), Lima 100, Peru (1-445 3306); Choquechaca 188 No 4, Cusco; and Jorge Washington 311 y L. Plaza, Postal Apartado 21-431, Quito, Ecuador (2-225 5228). The US office is at 126 Indian Creek Rd, Ithaca, NY 14850 (607-277-0488; www.saexplorers.org) and membership costs $50, $80 per couple. In addition to travel information they are also developing extensive databases of voluntary and teaching jobs for members to access.

AFRICA

Flights to Cairo are advertised from £150 single, £200 return, while the special offers to Nairobi start as low as £280 single, £395 return. A specialist agency for Southern Africa is Melhart Travel in Manchester (0161-772 6900; info@melharttravel.com). A 12-month return to Johannesburg on Virgin in the low season (April-July) was costing about £590 including tax at the time of writing. Another agency to try is the Africa Travel Centre (21 Leigh St, London WC1H 9QX; 0845 450 1520; www.africatravel.co.uk). Note that there is no regular ferry service between Greece and Alexandria, Egypt.

The overland routes are fraught with difficulties, and careful research must be done before setting off via the Sahara (the route through the Sudan is of course impossible at present). Jennifer McKibben, who spent some time in East Africa, recommends trying to negotiate a cheap seat in one of the overland expedition vehicles which are so much in evidence in that part of the world, assuming 'half their number have stormed off the bus or truck, unable to bear each other any longer'.

ASIA

The famous hippy overland route to Nepal has been problematical for a very long time now, though not impossible. Although Afghanistan is still off-limits, it is possible to cross Iran into Pakistan (a very rigorous but very cheap trip, assuming you can get a transit visa for Iran). An alternative is to make the journey with an established overland company which charge between £100 and £150 a week not including the food kitty. Most travellers simply take advantage of the competitive discount flight market from London to Asian destinations. For example the cheapest quoted return price London to Delhi is £337 including tax on Etihad Airways (the airline of the UAE). The cheapest carrier to Bangkok is Tarom the Romanian airline which has a one-year return for £330 with a stopover in Bucharest. The price of flights to Japan has dropped significantly in the past few years, especially if you are willing to fly on Aeroflot. In London a wide range of travel agents advertises cheap fares to Asia. In the US, try Chisholm Travel (500 N. Clark Ave, Chicago, IL 60610; 1-800-631-2824; www.chisholmair.net).

Once you're installed in Asia, travel is highly affordable. The railways of the Indian sub-continent are a fascinating social phenomenon and also dirt cheap. Throughout Asia, air-fares are not expensive, particularly around the discount triangle of Bangkok, Hong Kong and Singapore. The notable exception to the generalisation about cheap public transport in Asia is Japan.

Travel within the People's Republic of China can initially be exasperating as you strug-gle with the inscrutable bureaucracy and the utterly incomprehensible nature of stations and airports (where no allowance is made for those who do not understand Chinese char-acters). But like most things in the East, once you come to terms with the people and their way of life, travelling once more becomes a pleasurable experience. With upheavals in Russia, the Trans-Siberian rail journey is not as cheap as it used to be.

AUSTRALASIA

Since 2001, the compulsory tourist visa for Australia has not been available free of charge. The paperless visa, the ETA (Electronic Travel Authority), must be obtained via a private agency like Visas Australia or the Australian Immigration Department's website (www.eta. immi.gov.au) which will incur a fee of A$20. The dispensing of visitor visas has in essence been privatised and specialist visa providers can charge a fee of their choice (none of which is passed on to the Australian government). Among the cheaper providers are www. fastozvisa.com (0800 096 4749) which charges US$12/£7.50 and www.australiavisas. com which charges US$15.

The Australian Tourist Commission's *Traveller's Guide* contains quite a bit of hard information and useful telephone numbers as well as all the advertising; request a copy by ringing 0906 863 3235 (60p a minute). An excellent guide for backpackers is the free *Australia & New Zealand Independent Travellers Guide* from TNT (14-15 Child's Place, London SW5 9RX; 020-7373 3377); although the booklet is called 'free', you must pay £2.95 for postage and packing via their website www.tntmagazine.com/uk or by post.

Per mile, the flight to the Antipodes is cheaper than most. Malaysia Airlines often turns out to be the cheapest; for example they were charging £616 including tax at the time of writing, which was £100 cheaper than Qantas or BA. The cheapest advertised fares become available when airlines offer promotional fares. Austravel (0870 166 2020) was offering return charter flights to Sydney for less than £500 before tax, though these fares allow a maximum stay of a month.

Your transport problems are by no means over when you land in Perth or Sydney. The distances in Australia may be much greater than you are accustomed to and so you will have to give some thought to how you intend to get around. Richard Branson's Virgin Blue (www.virginblue.com.au) has some good promotional deals whenever it launches a new route which seems to be about once a month. Sample fares in 2004 were A$200 Sydney to Alice Springs and $A170 Melbourne to Christchurch. Compare also the no frills domestic airline Jetstar (www.jetstar.com.au) which was recently conducting a price war with Virgin Blue. Substantial discounts are offered on Qantas domestic flights to overseas visitors who buy domestic flights in conjunction with their international flight.

If you plan a major tour of the country you might consider purchasing a Greyhound coach pass along a pre-set route (13 14 99/+61-7-4690 9950; www.greyhound.com.au). Sample prices are A$280 for the nearly 3,000km trip between Sydney and Cairns and the all-Australia pass costing $2,458 valid for 12 months; people with YHA or other cards should be entitled to a 10% discount. If you just want to get from one coast to another as quickly as possible and qualify for the very cheapest deals, you will pay around A$460 one way on the coach or train (excluding berth and meals). Students and backpackers are eligible for a very good deal on the railways: unlimited travel on the great transcontinental routes for six months costs $450 (www.railaustralia.com.au/rail_passes.htm). A multiplicity of private operators has sprung up to serve the backpacking market such as Oz Experience and Wayward Bus. Writing from New South Wales, Geertje Korf passed on the following warning: *'A guy I met from Canada arrived here on a bus whose driver had promised him guaranteed work for up to $100 a day. He paid $70 for transport from Sydney and had the impression that he would be taken to an orchard, shown where to pitch his tent, etc. But instead the driver simply dropped him off at the job centre. He could have saved money by just catching the ordinary bus and walking.'*

Having your own transport is a great advantage when job-hunting in Australia. Some places have second-hand cars and camper vans for sale which they will buy back at the end of your stay, for example Boomerang Cars in Adelaide (261 Currie St, 0414-882559; www.boomerangcars.com.au) or Travellers Auto Barn in Sydney, Melbourne, Brisbane and Cairns (www.travellers-autobarn.com). Expect to pay $2,000+ for an old car (like a gas-guzzling Ford Falcon) and more for a camper van; the more you spend the better your chance of its lasting the distance and being saleable at the end of your stay. Car hire is expensive, but occasionally 'relocations' are available, i.e. hire cars that need to be returned to their depots. Just pick up the *Yellow Pages* and phone through the rental companies and ask for relocation deals which is exactly what Roger Blake did in 2004 when he wanted to travel from Adelaide to Melbourne:

The Great Ocean Road is renowned as one of the most scenic drives in the world and I was determined not to see it from a tour bus window. I phoned a hundred and one rental companies looking for a relocation (taking a vehicle back to its state depot due to one-way rental demands). I got lucky because they desperately needed one to leave the next day. Only a $1 per day rental and so desperate that they even gave me a $100 for fuel. So I spent the following three days on my own in a flash 4/5 berth Mercedes-Benz motorhome on the spectacular Great Ocean Road along the coast of Victoria. The whole drive is dangerously scenic. And the cost to me? A whopping A$63!

A reader reported that Integra Car Hire in Brisbane was advertising relocation cars (07-3252 5752) and also says that Britz Campervans (03-8379 8890; www.britz.com) sometimes need people to reposition vehicles, sometimes charging drivers between $1 and $10 a day. Avis, Hertz and National Car Rental offer the same deal in New Zealand for drivers willing to take cars back north from Christchurch or Wellington.

If you can't afford the luxury of organised transport or buying your own vehicle, you might be drawn to the idea of hitch-hiking. A coast to coast journey won't take you much less than a week, so it's a major undertaking. Be careful about being dropped on isolated stretches of the road across the Nullarbor Plain where, without water, you might just expire before the next vehicle comes along. On the other hand, you might be lucky and get one of those not uncommon lifts which covers 3200km in 96 hours.

Many women travellers have expressed their reluctance to travel alone with a long-distance lorry driver in remote areas, especially after the well-publicised backpacker murders a few years ago. According to a policeman Lucy Slater spoke to, drivers are less inclined to pick up hitchers in view of the trouble. (Nevertheless, Lucy and her boyfriend hitched from Perth to Kalgoorlie and found that the people who gave them lifts were mines of information about job possibilities.) The Queensland coastal road is notoriously dangerous. Violence is rare, but if you are unlucky you might be evicted from the truck unless you comply with the driver's wishes. All backpackers' hostels are a good bet for finding drivers going your way, provided you are able to wait for a suitable ride. Try also the lift-sharing forum on www.backpackingaround.com.au.

You need not confine yourself to cars and lorries for hitching. Adrian McCay hitched a lift on a private plane from remote Kununurra to Mildura. While working at a remote property in Western Australia, David Irvine hitched a couple of lifts with the flying doctor service. Earlier in his travels he got stranded in Norseman after a truck ride across the Nullarbor. Here he met an aboriginal swagman who advised him to hop a freight which he did, which turned out to be a coal train. Suddenly there was a very rare rainstorm which turned the coal dust on which he was sitting in his open hopper to disgusting sludge.

Fortunately Virgin Blue has introduced Pacific Blue which has started flying across the Tasman making the cost of crossing between Australia and New Zealand much cheaper than it used to be. Canny shopping can bring the one-way fare down to not much more than $120; check out for example the agency www.travel.com.au or investigate the no-frills New Zealand airline Freedom Air (www.freedomair.co.nz) which flies into the smaller North Island cities of Palmerston North and Hamilton.

Once in New Zealand it is difficult to imagine a country more favourable to hitch-hikers and budget travellers. Travellers regularly cover the whole country, using youth hostels and hitching, and spend about £200 a month. Camping on beaches, fields and in woodlands is generally permitted. Hire cars can even be free. So many hirers leave their hire cars in Wellington before catching the ferry to the South Island, and in Christchurch after driving down from Picton that the major outlets need people to 'relocate' these cars north and often allow a few days for the journey.

FORMALITIES AT BORDERS

Whichever mode of transport you choose, there are a number of formalities that must be tackled before you set off, to ensure that your journey is not fraught with an unexpected range of disasters.

Visas

Outside the Schengen Area of Europe in which border controls have been largely abolished, you can't continue in one direction for very long before you are impeded by border guards demanding to see your papers. Post September 11th, immigration and security checks are tighter than ever before and many countries have imposed visa restrictions, particularly on North Americans in retaliation for all the new restrictions the US has implemented. Embassy websites are the best source of information or you can check online information posted by visa agencies. For example Thames Consular Services in London (www.thamesconsular.com) allows you to search visa requirements and costs for UK nationals visiting any country. An equivalent source of visa information in the US is Travisa (www.travisa.com) with offices in Washington, New York, Chicago, San Francisco and Miami. Travel Document Express in the US (www.traveldocument.com) provides visa, passport and travel information via fax or try Travel Document Systems in Washington and San Francisco (www.traveldocs.com).

Getting visas is a headache anywhere, and most travellers feel happier obtaining them in their home country. Set aside a chunk of your travel budget to cover the costs; to give just a few examples of charges for tourist visas for UK citizens applying in London: £30 for India, £30 for China, £11 for Jordan, £23 or £38 for Vietnam (depending on whether you have a letter of authorisation), £35 for Armenia, £45 for Pakistan, £50 for Rwanda, £42.40 for Nigeria, £30 for Haiti (visa recommended). Requirements for American travellers are completely different, for example no visa is required for Haiti (nor for the majority of Latin American countries), $115 for Brazil, $60 for India, $50 for China (or $80 for rush issuance), $16.50 for Jordan, $65 for Vietnam, $100 for Nigeria, $65.22 for Cameroon, $120 for Pakistan, etc. Last-minute applications often incur a much higher fee, for example a Russian visa costs £30/$100 if applied for at least two weeks in advance, but up to £150/$300 for same-day processing. If you do not want to pin yourself down to entry dates, you may decide to apply for visas as you travel for example from a neighbouring country, which in many cases is cheaper, though may cause delays.

If you are short of time or live a long way from the Embassies in London, private visa agencies like Thames Consular may be of interest. Others include the VisaService, 2 Northdown St, London N1 9BG (020-7833 2709/fax 020-7833 1857; www.visaservice. co.uk) and Global Visas (020-7009 3800; www.globalvisas.com). In addition to the fee charged by the country's embassy, there will be a service charge normally of £30-£35 per visa. Travel Document Systems in the US charges $40 per visa, $80 for express service.

If you intend to cross a great many borders, especially on an overland trip through Africa, ensure that you have all the relevant documentation and that your passport contains as many blank pages as frontiers which you intend to cross. Travellers have been turned back purely because the border guard refused to use a page with another stamp on it. Details of work permit regulations and so on can be found in the country chapters in this book. See also the introductory section *Red Tape*.

The Foreign and Commonwealth Office has reviewed its list of incompatible countries and the United Kingdom Passport Agency (Globe House, 89 Eccleston Square, Victoria, London SW1V 1PN 0870 521 0410; www.ukpa.gov.uk) has tightened up on issuing a second passport to people who intend to travel both to Israel and hostile Arab countries.

The Foreign Office has a Travel Advice Unit which can be contacted on 0870 606 0290; www.fco.gov.uk/travel. If you have access to BBC Ceefax look at pages 470 and following. North Americans may wish to obtain the relevant consular information sheet from the US State Department. Reports cover entry requirements, crime, terrorist activities, medical facilities, etc. Travel warnings are still issued for dangerous countries. Ring Overseas Citizen Services on 202-647-5225 for automated information.

Always reply simply and politely to any questions asked by immigration or customs officials. Roger Blake has a word of warning: *'Arriving in New Zealand was not really a problem other than a strange encounter with a customs officer: 'Are you bringing drugs into the country?' 'No!' 'Do you take drugs?' 'NO!' I reply. She asks 'Why not?' This is the kind of carefully planned (and corrupt) trap for would-be's that you occasionally come across. Anyway, no worries on my part. '*

Money

On arrival at a border, you may be asked to prove that a) you have enough to support yourself for the duration of your proposed stay, and b) that you have the means to leave the country without undermining the economy by engaging in unauthorised activities (e.g. working, changing money on the black market, smuggling, etc.). The authorities are more likely to take an interest in a scruffy impecunious looking backpacker. Sometimes border personnel wish to see proof of absurdly large sums such as $500 before you can board the boat between Greece and Israel or $1,000 for each month of your proposed stay in New Zealand. Remember that well-dressed travellers who carry suitcases rather than rucksacks will be challenged less often. Because Michel Falardeau was travelling on one-way tickets without all that much money, he wore a business suit whenever he was due to meet an immigration official, and this worked for him on his round-the-world trip. You can get away with having less money if you have an onward ticket, and the names and addresses of residents whom you intend to visit.

There are several ways round the problem. Some travellers have gone so far as to declare the loss of their travellers cheques, in order to use the duplicate set as 'flash money'. As soon as the duplicates have done their duty at the border, the supposedly lost originals can then be burned. A less dramatic technique is to show off your range of credit cards and make sure you know how to log on to the balance online so that if necessary you can prove instantly that you are in credit.

Find out beforehand whether there is a departure tax. For example to fly out of Kenya you must pay the equivalent of US$40, Peru $28, Ecuador $25, Hong Kong HK$120, Nepal 565 rupees ($8), Tanzania $20, India $20 and so on. This can be an unexpected nuisance or a total disaster. Information about transferring emergency funds from home is given in the chapter *In Extremis* at the end of this book.

ENTERPRISE

You don't have to spend eight hours a day washing dishes in order to earn money abroad. Many travellers have found or made opportunities to go into business for themselves, exchanging steady wage packets for less predictable sources of income. The people who have succeeded in this type of work tend to have a large degree of initiative, determination and often creativity; they have identified some local need and exploited it.

Often they find themselves on the borderline of the law. If you paint the sun setting over a harbour you are an artist; sell the painting to someone who stops to admire it and you may, in law, become a street trader requiring a permit. If you wash motorists' windscreens at traffic lights, you might be doing them a service, but the police might consider you an obstruction. At worst you will find yourself being moved on, though a few exceptions have been noted in the country chapters.

The chapter will first deal with importing and exporting: the ways in which you can make money by buying cheaply in one country and selling in another. The second part of the chapter will deal with the kinds of marketing opportunities which you should watch out for within the country you're visiting, many of which involve pandering to the desires of homesick tourists. The final two sections deal with odd-jobbing and gambling.

IMPORT/EXPORT

With experience, travellers come to know what items can be bought cheaply in one country and profitably sold in another. Wherever something is exorbitantly priced, it is possible to sell informally to local people or fellow tourists at a profit. But as the world shrinks and trade barriers dissolve, the possibilities are becoming fewer. After his extensive travels in Turkey and Asia, the American Tim Leffel concluded: *'The enterprise opportunities seem to be vanishing faster than you can say 'free trade'. There weren't many things in high demand that you could buy cheaper in the US or across a neighbouring border, at least where we were, unless you were dealing in big-ticket electronics. Bringing things back, of course, is a different story.'*

On the other hand niches can always be found. For example, a Derbyshire man realised that Germans in the town twinned with his loved British goods including the obvious like tea and marmalade. He went over with a supply of Union Jack beach towels and sold them at the local market in a very short time. Or a Scottish woman had T-shirts printed up with Gaelic motifs and sold them at the Canadian Highland Games. Another traveller found that condoms were in great demand in Malawi and traded them to advantage.

Past readers have recommended carrying around cigarette papers which are expensive in Scandinavia, for example, and hard to obtain in Greece, Brazil, etc. Ian McArthur planned to take about 500 packets to Goa where he'd heard that the selling price was five times higher than in Britain. Travellers in the Far East (Bangkok, Hong Kong and Japan) have been known to stock up on the newest play station games (which are often a third the price they are in the UK) with a view to selling them discreetly at home, possibly outside video shops. Only a buff would be able to make this work, since only certain UK computers are 'chipped up' (adapted) to cope with import games.

Some travellers think it's worthwhile to load up on bronze trinkets, alpaca sweaters, jade jewelry, rosewood boxes, sisal baskets from Kenya, Tibetan woollens, Turkish carpets or anything else which they know are more expensive or unobtainable elsewhere. Before engaging in this sort of activity you'll have to master the art of haggling, which involves patience and good humour. Usually it is difficult to make much of a profit on one-off trips abroad. Also, you should be thoroughly acquainted with customs regulations.

Do not believe every foreign trader who promises vast profits in your home country, for example selling Tahitian pearls or Sri Lankan gems, or who assures you that you will have no difficulty at customs. In fact do not believe any of them. Almost invariably they are inventing a story in order to make a bulk sale. No consumer protection is available to their gulls. Bangkok seems to be the capital of smooth-talking swindlers. A warning notice in a Bangkok hostel, which reads 'These people are vicious and evil and all they say is lies' was written by a German who parted with US$1,100 for '$3,000 plus' of sapphires, only to be told by his 'guaranteed buyer' (an unwitting jeweller in Sydney) that their true value was $250.

Yet there is a host of travellers successfully selling exotica as Kristen Moen reports: '*I was in Corfu selling jewelry I had bought in India, Nepal, Thailand and China. Quite a lot of my friends do similar things. When they come home from Asia and South America they sell jewelry and other things and they make almost enough money to finance their trip. Of course you have to be careful when you buy so you don't get cheated but you learn along the way.*'

You don't have to wait until you get home to sell. Many travellers successfully sell jewelry and knicknacks from Thailand and India in Taiwan and Hong Kong. Westerners can be seen selling leather goods and other items brought from India in European markets.

Duty-Free

Selling your duty-free tobacco, alcohol and consumer durables is an obvious and simple way of turning a profit. In some Asian and African countries, Scotch whisky and European cigarettes are hard to obtain and widely coveted. In other countries, these products are available in the shops but for a colossal price. In the past, people have made as much as four times their outlay, for example, after bringing back a box of high quality cigars from Cuba to Europe.

Be very cautious about taking alcohol into strict Islamic countries where it is forbidden. There is a good market in 'softer' Islamic countries; for example touts and guides in Tangiers and hostel owners in Egypt are willing buyers. Beware of highly organised local competition, for example along international trading routes where drivers and overland couriers will know all the tricks. Exploiting price differentials across international borders can be lucrative if you are well situated. For example people who live in Spain and work in Gibraltar can make a sizeable profit on cartons of Winston cigarettes bought in Gibraltar and sold in bars in La Linea. (Officially you are entitled to carry one carton a month across the border.)

Within Europe, duty-free differentials have been abolished, though this doesn't mean that cigarettes and wine aren't a lot cheaper in France than England. Tobacco and alcohol bought abroad must be for personal consumption, a law that is widely flouted. So many operators within Europe have been importing goods to sell at a profit that this illegal trade has seriously dented profits in the drinks trade of Southeast England and customs checks at British ports have become much tougher.

Currency Exchange

In countries where there is a soft currency, i.e. one that cannot officially be used to buy dollars or sterling, or where the government attaches an unjustifiably high value to its currency, a black market often develops. Tempting as the rewards might be, you should be aware of the pitfalls (in addition to the fact that it might be unethical to deprive banks of hard currency which helps poor economies to keep ticking over). The black market attracts all sorts of shady characters who very regularly cheat even the canniest travellers, making them regret their greed. Favourite ploys include handing the tourist an envelope full of shredded newspaper or one large denomination bill wrapped cleverly around a wad of lower bills, or pretending to spot a policeman and then vanishing after taking your dollars but before giving you your pesos, rupees, shillings, etc.

Even more worrying situations can arise if you realise that the black marketeer is an *agent provocateur* who is in cahoots with the police. The law will appear instantly either to arrest you (unlikely) or to demand some baksheesh. To guard against such an outcome, always avoid trading on the street. By asking around at budget hotels, you'll soon learn where to find legitimate traders, often in shops or travel agencies. Familiarise yourself with the appearance of all denominations of currency and take along a friend to assist you.

Second-hand Gear

Outside the consumer societies of the West, there is a fluctuating demand for gadgets and gewgaws, and various items we take for granted can be sold or traded. T-shirts with Western slogans have had spells of popularity in different places, though in most cases a local entrepreneur will have latched on to this market. Even if you don't get cash, you might trade for goods and services or an interesting souvenir. Writing in *Rough News*, the quarterly giveaway paper from Rough Guides, Justyn Evans from Milton Keynes described what he observed on an overland trip through Africa:

> We stopped in Nakuru in Kenya to do some shopping. One young vendor, trying to sell hand-painted cards, showed some unusual initiative. When I turned down his request to buy something, he asked if I had anything to trade. Jokingly I pulled my biro from a back pocket. Eagerly he tested it and offered me a card in return. While travelling around Kenya I had lots of requests to trade. On more than one occasional I could have walked away wearing only my underwear. Everyone wanted something I was wearing. When it comes to pens, however, most people are picky. Your standard biro just won't do any more, 'clicky' pens are the in thing. Watches are also popular. I had more offers for my watch than anything else and I wished I'd taken an old one with me.

If you are a frequent visitor to a country, you might try to learn what kinds of used items are in demand at markets. Foreigners in Britain could reserve a table at a car boot sale (for £5 or £10) to try to sell any items of interest from their country.

> **Elfed Guyatt from Wales thinks that Sweden is a particularly promising destination for any would-be entrepreneurs:**
> In the weekend market stalls people just set up their own table and sell off all sorts of odds and ends. The prices are incredibly high compared to Britain for certain things. You should make 500% profit on selling things like medals, caps, British and American books in subjects that interest the Swedes, in fact anything that looks different and not easily available in their country. They do like showing off possessions here. Souvenirs of London or Shakespeare go well. I saw a very cheap, small brass Big Ben table bell sell for £12.50 and an old battered cricket bat went for £25.

SPOTTING LOCAL OPPORTUNITIES

The opportunities for finding eager customers on whatever doorstep you find yourself are endless and we can only give some idea of the remarkable range of ways to earn money by using your initiative and your imagination. If you see a gap in the market, try to fill it. For example Stephen Psallidas toyed seriously with the idea of buying a bicycle in the tomato-growing capital of Queensland in order to hire it out to job-seeking tomato pickers since at the time Bowen was, if not a one-horse town, a one-bicycle town. After getting to know the Greek island of Levkas fairly well, Camilla Lambert hired a jeep at weekends for £35 a day and took three paying passengers out for a day's excursion. One Englishman acquired a chain saw in Spain and made a killing by hiring himself out to farmers to prune their olive trees. A Canadian who was having trouble being hired by a language school in a provincial city in Taiwan set up his own English immersion social club which easily covered his costs in the two months he ran it. You just need to exploit any manual or artistic or public relations skill you already have or which you have cultivated for the purpose.

Homemade Handicrafts

A number of people have successfully supported themselves abroad by selling homemade jewelry and other items on the street. Once you master a skill you can move around with it, perhaps following the festival circuit around Europe or wherever mobs of people gather (see section *Beaches and Mobs* below). Careful preparations can pay dividends; for example Jennifer Tong picked up shells from a beach near Eilat and invested £5 in a pair of pliers and some wire, clips and beads when she was in Israel. With these materials she made simple earrings which were bought for £2 a pair on the Greek Islands. Even more simply, Amy Ignatow collected smooth pebbles at her moshav, decorated them with a permanent pen and sold them on the street in Jerusalem for £3 each. Steve Pringle sold earrings in Madrid which he had made from a stock of cheap imitation diamonds he had brought over from London. Braided or knotted friendship bracelets are popular in travellers' resorts and can usually be sold for £2 or £3 and take 15 minutes to make. You have to find something that doesn't require too much time, which Emma Hoare failed to do while on her gap year:

> In the south of France I met up with a girl I had been previously travelling with, and decided to make money by selling bags that we'd sewn. We went on to Spain and quickly discovered that sitting in little pensione rooms stitching minuscule beads onto cheap, flimsy fabric was a recipe for mental deterioration and, at times, uncontrollable hysteria. Then I decided that I had put too much effort into my bags to sell them. They were my little works of art and I was damned if I was going to let some horrible young tourist have it for a fiver and then leave it on the floor in a club somewhere (see what I mean about mental deterioration?)

It is worth looking out for cheap and unusual raw materials such as beads from Morocco, shells from Papua New Guinea or bamboo from Crete. Grimly Corridor taught himself how to make pan pipes from the local bamboo and sold them for about £5 (which included a recitation of the Pan legend which American tourists found difficult to resist). One natural resource to avoid exploiting is coral. Corals are vulnerable living creatures and should not be removed from their habitat. An aspiring sculptress who makes copper wire sculptures found that business was slow at the beginning of the Edinburgh Festival but hotted up, allowing her to fund several months of post-Festival travels. You have to be good at what you do for this to be effective.

If you can draw, knit, sew, sculpt or work with wood or leather then you may be able to produce something that people want to buy in holiday resorts. The skill of braiding hair with beads or 'hair wraps' can make a lot of money. All you need is the expertise, some cheap multi-coloured beads and thread with which to tie off the ends. One contributor met a girl making the equivalent of £35 a day in a Cape Town market doing this. While on holiday on the island of Formentera near Ibiza, Georgina Bayliss-Duffield found that braiding people's hair was a lucrative pastime, especially with a companion on whom to demonstrate. Eventually she was able to complete a head whether male or female in about 20 minutes (depending on the hair) for which she charged the equivalent of £8. The weather will have an obvious effect on success or failure as Nicole Gluckstern from San Francisco found at the Edinburgh Fringe Festival: 'For cash I did hair wraps. But due to a number of circumstances (closure of the traditional place for setting up called the Mound, inconvenient show time right in the middle of the best selling part of the day and incessant rain), I did not even break even, although I made enough to cover most of my expenses and only spent about $200 of my own money in three weeks, not too bad for a fantastic time.'

Nicole is a seasoned follower of the festival circuit and manages to fund some exotic travels by doing this (in between working as a sound/light technician in San Francisco):

> As for the festival circuit, I do occasionally find work vending for other people when they would rather spend their time smoking dope with rock stars or whatever, when a specific festival/concert passes through where I am. Sometimes people will advertise for these positions at youth hostels, so if it's festival time, you might check the bulletin boards of your local hostel or whatever. 'Professional' vendors who go on

tour every year stand to make quite a lot of money (roughly $5,000-$10,000 in one or two months) but they have been doing it for years, have all the right contacts and work like absolute slaves for their wage. Established festivals like the world famous Oktoberfest in Munich are always looking for people to sell pretzels, wash glasses, take photos, etc. Leave your dignity at home if you want to work in the zoo-like atmosphere, but be prepared to make a tidy packet.

International sporting fixtures are a good bet too so creative craftsmen and women might think about heading for Germany for the World Cup in 2006. A Canadian whom Roger Blake met on his travels in Africa had made $500 painting flags on faces at the World Cup in Korea.

Beaches and Mobs

You should learn to look on any crowd of people as a potential market for what you have to sell. People emerging from a disco are often grateful for a hotdog or a sandwich or skiers queuing for a lift might appreciate some chocolate. If you loiter in a place where people regularly emerge from a remote place, as at the end of treks in Nepal or New Zealand, you could probably sell some interesting food and drink of which they have been deprived. Stephen Psallidas decided to become a portable off-licence with a view to selling wine to the devotees who flock to see Jim Morrison's grave in Paris. Unfortunately this was not a popular idea with the local cannabis sellers and he ended up drinking the wine himself.

Sunbathers on a wide unspoilt beach may be longing for a cold bottle of beer, sun tan lotion, a donut, or a few pre-stamped postcards and a ballpoint pen, and won't mind paying over the odds for them (especially if you have printed up your own postcards from your travel photos). Choose your beach carefully: if a beach is already swarming with cold drinks salesmen (as is the case along much of the French and Spanish Mediterranean), you're unlikely to be welcomed by potential customers. If a beach has none, selling may well be forbidden, as one reader discovered at Sydney's Bondi Beach, when the beach inspector chased them off after a few minutes.

If a crowd is scheduled to gather for a special occasion, think of the things they will want to buy. For example you could buy a few dozen roses in Niagara Falls, 'honeymoon capital of the world', and sell them individually to the happy couples at a high mark-up. The award for the most original salesman should go to the person who spotted an unruly crowd waiting for the arrival of the then Canadian Prime Minister in Sudbury, Ontario. He got hold of some eggs and sold them for use as missiles. Another situation which could be exploited is the refusal to allow scantily clad tourists into some European churches: renting out a pair of trousers would be a valuable service.

If you have the right product, you can sell to a wider market. One traveller earned his way in South America by selling peanut butter he'd made himself from local peanuts to American tourists outside the archaeological sites of Colombia. Ski bums regularly make pocket money by delivering croissants from the local bakery to self-catering holiday-makers. Meanwhile another traveller sold popcorn to fishermen in Crete. If you are a fisherman yourself, you can try to sell your catch door to door in residential areas. Tessa Shaw picked snails at night by the River Ardèche in southern France and then set up a stall in the market at Carpentras. She found that Fridays were particularly profitable, since restaurateurs and shopkeepers drove down from Paris to buy stock for the weekend.

Based on his recent travels Alan Haden wrote in 2005 with a suggestion for adding a string to your money-spinning bow:
Having been inspired by your book to work abroad, I felt that it might be of use for others to learn the skills of Palmistry or Tarot. These intuitive divination methods will allow a traveller to make plenty of money anywhere in the world. If you're a good palm reader and stuck for cash, just head down to the local tourist area or festival/market place and you'll find it easy to make a bundle of cash for your efforts. After arranging a job abroad, I used my skills to earn extra cash by charging

£5-£10 for a quick 5-minute reading. A good reader will quickly make more cash than you can shake a stick at. And you need not take any equipment with you, as all you need is a palm to read and the skill to do it.

Hostels

Julian Peachey landed a job as warden in a youth hostel in Marseille, and soon began supplementing his income by selling wine at the hostel. The local supermarket delivered supplies at 40p per bottle, which he sold to the hostellers for 80p. Even though they realised he was selling at a substantial profit, the hostellers were happy to patronise his store when their own supplies had run out late at night. Roger Blake in South Africa was taken on by a backpackers hostel to run the bar and help with the nightly ostrich barbecues. He also took the opportunity to serve breakfast which was like being self-employed. He was responsible for buying all the ingredients and was allowed to keep the profit, earning him after six weeks a 'small but worthwhile fortune'.

People staying in hostels often leave behind belongings (intentionally or otherwise) which could perhaps be sold, as Dustie Hickey did at an Avignon flea market earning herself £30 in an hour. At a backpackers in Byron Bay Australia last year, Roger Blake noticed that all the bikes for hire were in dire need of attention. Since he is a cyclist and familiar with bicycles, he decided to fix up one for his own use. When the manager saw this, he offered Roger the chance to fix all the bikes in exchange for free accommodation. Roger was able to fix all but two and earned himself A$110 worth of accommodation that week.

Writing and the Media

A few lucky people manage to subsidise their journeys abroad by selling articles or photographs based on their travels. There are two main markets for your creative work: local English language publications abroad, and newspapers and magazines in your home country. A trip to Northern Queensland might not seem newsworthy to you when you're there, but Frank Schiller sold an account of his trip to a German magazine for several hundred dollars. You can find out about local publications by studying news-stands when you are abroad.

For contacts in Britain, consult 2005 editions of *The Writers' and Artists' Yearbook* (A&C Black) and *The Writer's Handbook* by Barry Turner (Macmillan) both at £13.99 (less from Amazon). In the US consult the *Travel Writer's Handbook* by Louise Purwin Zobel (Surrey Books, $18.95) or *2005 Writer's Market* ($29.99) and *2005 Photographer's Market* ($24.99) both published by Writer's Digest Books. In-flight magazines of foreign airlines sometimes buy freelance pieces. Enterprising journalists have also set up sites on the worldwide web and have funded it or made a profit through sponsorship.

If you have already published, take along a cuttings book. Before you go abroad, it is a good idea to study the market, to get an idea of what editors are looking for. English language publications, whether print or online, might buy something from you. Here are some typical guidelines from *Egypt Today* (www.egypttoday.com) which could be applied to many similar expat (as opposed to tourist) publications that receive many speculative enquiries:

*The best way to get your foot in the door with us is to be in country and show us what you're made of by successfully completing some freelance work. We purchase both medium-length news pieces and profiles (775-1650 words) as well as feature-length work (2500 words and above, maximum 6000). From freelancers, our strong preference is for feature-length work with outstanding story telling. Pitches should give a strong sense of art, angle and sources, and indicate that you understand the sensibilities of our audience... Politics, social issues, culture, entertainment, celebrity interviews, anything goes, so long as it is current or a unique look back at a significant past incident. We are decidedly **not** interested in 'Exotic Egypt' pieces. All stories must be submitted electronically as Word attachments in Rich Text Format (Mac or PC). Photos may also be sent electronically as .EPS, .JPG or .TIF files.*

All magazines that accept freelance travel writing will be looking for a fresh view and new angle. Feel free to use the first person singular in a travel article. Describe interesting or curious incidents which, while not being of earth-shaking significance, help to brighten up the story. Quote the people you met on the trip: the innkeeper, the museum guard, as well as giving practical information on how to get there, what to see, where to stay and where to eat. Everything should be delivered in a light, readable manner. According to one experienced freelancer, sex really does sell abroad as at home, as do accounts of people coming through tragedies.

If at all possible, persuade an editor to give you a commission before you leave, as Tim Leffel did:

I had a few assignments set up before I left New Jersey as a travel writer and have started to sell a few other things from the trip now that I'm back. I've already made over $1,400 from various pieces, though none of the cheques were in hand until after my return. It's not something to do for quick money: 'quick' in an editor's mind means 'less than a year'. I've met lots of would-be writers and photographers who hit me up for advice on financing their travels, having not done the most basic research steps it takes to even get started. In my opinion, you must be someone who has something to say and be good at marketing it to even cover your costs, much less make a profit. I do make a profit now and then, but that's because of a trade publication I've written for for a few years (they pay me good money to review swank hotels).

Travelling adventures might provide just the right kind of material a writer needs to get started as it has for Mark Everleigh whose brief autobiography appeared on his personal website:

I have spent the last fifteen years travelling through remote regions of Latin America, South East Asia, Australia and Africa. At first I financed these trips as a pipe-layer, lorry driver, bouncer, security guard and perfume/oil-painting salesman. I had screen-printed T-shirts in Ecuador and sold time-share in the French West Indies before, at the age of 26, I decided that it was time to channel my 'travelling career' into the dog-eat-dog world of freelance photojournalism. My stories and photos have since appeared in magazines and newspapers in the UK, US, Canada, Spain and Africa and I have covered different, and often bizarre, aspects of many countries.

Illustrated travel articles are best of all. Black and white prints are good for this purpose, or colour transparencies. Remember that editors are less interested in arty effects than in photos which tell a story.

English language newspapers around the world are a real source of potential casual work from Japan to Eastern Europe, Mexico City to Bangkok. You can track down the ones with a web presence via the Kidon Media site (www.kidon.com/media-link/english.shtml) and the Internet Public Library (www.ipl.org/div/news), from the *Phnom Penh Post* to the *St Petersburg Times*. There is an entire sub-culture of bright young travellers working their way around these papers. Some are using it as a short-cut in a journalism career; others are merely adventurers. Many of the people working on these papers had never been inside a newsroom before. Business experience might well be appreciated in this context. Anyone who can get a job as a proofreader and show themselves competent will quickly advance to copy-editor or even reporter. Editors may not want to hire globetrotters, but staff turnover is often so high that they don't have much choice. Till Bruckner who wrote some freelance pieces for the *Bolivian Times* recommends making sure you will be paid for the work accepted.

International firms with branches abroad are less glamorous employers of writing skills, but they may need someone to edit their newsletter or brochures. An army of foreigners is employed in Beijing to polish the prose of journals and documents which have been translated into English. If you notice a badly written company report or piece of publicity it might be worth introducing yourself (especially in Japan), though make your point as tactfully as possible. Even such a long-established English language publication as the *Athens News* was so full of mistakes that a traveller from Los Angeles was taken on as a proof reader after circling and correcting all the errors in a randomly chosen issue and presenting it to the editor. You can always offer to correct the English of museum labels, menus or travel brochures. You might get a free meal in exchange for your grammatical expertise (though you may unwittingly be depriving future travellers of a source of amusement). When Carisa Fey translated into her native German the menu of an exclusive restaurant in the Mexican resort of Puerto Vallarta she was paid in margaritas. This piece of enterprise shaded into some structured busking so that she was invited to sing at the restaurant where she was fed superb food and given good tips by the customers. You do not have to know the local language perfectly in order to translate publicity brochures or the like, provided you have a dictionary.

One of the most remarkable literary coups was reported in the papers a few years ago. A student called Daniel Wilson sent his CV and an example of his verse to the president of Kiribati asking if he would like him to become the poet-in-residence. To his astonishment, he had a reply inviting him to occupy a beach hut and become their national poet for a time.

All you readers who imagine that the ideal job would be to write a travel guide should pay attention to the following description by Woden Teachout who spent one summer researching Ireland for the well-known *Let's Go* series:

> *I got lucky and was hired by Harvard Student Agency (which hires only students) to update their chapter on Ireland. They gave me $600 for air travel and $40 a day for expenses and profit. It was a mixed blessing. I spent most of each day visiting local historical societies and talking to all the Mrs. O'Learys who run B&Bs, checking their bathrooms for cleanliness and trying to figure out how to vary descriptions of fluffy white bedrooms. At night I would run around to three or four pubs, trying to encapsulate each atmosphere in a good one-liner and then back to the hostel to write up the day's work. When you're writing a guidebook you can never quite relax, since you are always evaluating in your head. And since you have a fixed itinerary, you are not as free to follow the whims of chance and circumstance. It was definitely nice to get paid to travel, and go to places I otherwise would have missed, but on the whole it felt like indentured servitude.*

For people who are very keen to get involved in journalism abroad and are willing to fund themselves to undertake some relevant work experience that might lead to better paid work, the mediating agencies i-to-i and Teaching & Projects Abroad (see *Volunteering: Gap Year Placements*) arrange journalism placements for fee-paying volunteers. Martin Forbes gave up his nine-to-five job as an accountant to take up a three-month voluntary placement in China with the English language *Shanghai Star*:

> *I wanted to try my hand at journalism. Shanghai seemed to be a happening city with all the economic reforms taking place - and so it proved! Having never done any journalism before it was pretty daunting to begin with (interviewing people, etc.) but I soon got the hang of it. Just over a month into the placement, I interviewed (albeit very briefly as it turned out!) Tessa Jowell, Secretary of State for Culture, Media and Sport_not something that a journalist starting out in the UK would have been in a position to do.*

Photography

A number of photo libraries in the UK accept high quality travel photographs. The photos are lent or leased to the agencies which in turn rent them to clients such as publishers and advertising agencies. Most photo libraries offer a 50-50 split of the earnings from the photographs. They also usually demand a minimum initial submission of at least 50 photos, a minimum period of time for keeping your photos with the agency and at least a year's notice of withdrawal. They also prefer a contributor to send photos regularly.

Stephen Psallidas decided to give it a go after he returned from spending time in Greece, Africa and Australia:

I'm not going to pretend that I'm a great photographer but out of 2,000 35mm slides, there were about 50 which I thought were quite good. I sent off a selection of my photos to a couple of well known photo libraries. However, both libraries returned my slides saying that they were too 'arty' and not commercially oriented enough. I would advise against having too high expectations, as the market is difficult in these days of cost-cutting and digital technology. At the same time, if you don't try you never get anywhere and readers of your book are unlikely to be daunted by poor odds!

Stephen concluded that it would have been better to contact some photo libraries before setting off to establish what kind of thing they are looking for. Many will offer useful technical advice. When sending in photos, make sure that they are presented well, e.g. in transparent sleeves with detailed captions, and it is a courtesy to include return postage. Many travel photo libraries accept only colour images which should be on slide film no faster than ISO 100 (Stephen recommends Fuji Velvia ISO 50). The larger the format, the better, though the standard 35mm is usually acceptable. Don't send in any poor shots just to make up the numbers since these will reflect badly on the overall submission. If a photo is used by a library it will generate between £50 and £150 every time it is used, so if you have 20 or 30 photos accepted, it could be quite lucrative. Stephen's story has a happy ending since he persevered and had some photos accepted by a third photo library, and made £160 in six months.

Even if you have no particular skill with a camera or pen you may be able to profit from being in the right place at the right time. Earl Young has strong opinions on the subject: *'Anyone who fails to carry a camera in foreign countries is a fool. What if an international incident happens to take place in the street in front of you one day and you don't happen to be carrying your camera?'*

If you do get a photo of a terrorist attack or any newsworthy event, don't waste a second contacting the news wire services; Reuters, Agence France Presse and Associated Press have offices or representatives in most capital cities. If your photograph is the one that's syndicated in newspapers worldwide, you need not work your way any further.

Although digital photography has brought about a revolution, there will always be tourists who will not have the necessary equipment with which to capture a key moment. With the right gadgetry it is possible to set yourself up as a portrait photographer on beaches, near monuments, where people try an adventure activity like parascending for the first time and so on. If potential customers like the image you show them on your digital camera, you can go ahead and print it out and sell it to them.

Another place to set yourself up as a freelance photographer is at a place that specialises in hosting weddings of holidaying couples. Certain places (and not just Las Vegas) become popular with couples looking for something different from the village church. Long-time working travellers Nicola and Peter Dickinson found just such a place on Rhodes where they tied the knot themselves and dream of returning as a freelance photographer and painter:

There is a little church on St Paul's Bay in Lindos where many people get married throughout the season. With 80 or 90 weddings a season somebody could set themselves up as a photographer. Obviously they would have to be good before offering their services to people getting married so you'd probably need to take a course on photography beforehand. With so many people getting married in Lindos and spending their honeymoons there, people would want photographs of the happy occasion.

You don't have to have a camera to make money from photographs. We have heard of two gap year students trying to raise money for a trip who travelled round car boot sales and junk shops buying old post cards and photos which they framed attractively and sold at a decent profit at antique markets.

Busking

If you can play an instrument, sing, tap dance, juggle, conjure, draw caricatures or act, you may be able to earn money on the streets. Most successful buskers say that musical talent is less important than the spot you choose and the way you collect. Two Americans busking in Morocco decided that the local man they employed to collect money for them was more entertaining than they were so gave him the money.

To busk, you need the tools of your trade, perhaps an accomplice to collect money and an audience. A favourable climate helps, though some of the most successful buskers we have heard from have played in Northern Europe in mid-winter. One of the keys to success (in addition to talent) is originality. We have had reports from opposite ends of the world (Sweden and Northern Queensland) that kilted bagpipe-playing buskers are always a hit. (We're assuming that it wasn't the same busking Scot.) Mary Hall is one busker who is convinced that talent is not essential, as she discovered in Bergen, Norway: *'I finally plucked up the courage to do a bit of busking on my pennywhistle. I'd only just bought it so was only able to play two songs 'Amazing Grace' and 'The Sounds of Silence'. Still I made £15 in 15 minutes. With a couple of extra songs I could well be on the way to my first million. It helped that my audience were pretty drunk.'*

Most international buskers say that people abroad (especially in Scandinavia, Germany, Switzerland and Spain) are more generous than in Britain, that there is less trouble with being moved on and it is not too difficult to keep yourself by busking around the cafés of Europe. Helen Chenery was very sorry that she had not taken her accordian with her to Greece, since she soon saw that she could have elevated her diet of bread and jam if she'd had her instrument with her. Some advise that if you have to choose between carting around an instrument or your luggage, leave your luggage at home. You need a great deal of confidence in your abilities, to go abroad specifically to busk; it may be better to regard performing as a possible way of subsidising a holiday.

Festivals and other large gatherings of merry-makers are potentially lucrative; bear in mind that the more potential a position has, the greater the competition is liable to be for it. Guitarist-cum-TEFL teacher Fergus Cooney found that competition can be acute, even at ordinary times: *'Please don't ever write a 'Guide to Busking'. We travelling folk would soon be out of business. It's bad enough as it is. For example this year 40 accordion players from Romania swamped Montpellier and killed busking for the rest of us.'*

Some years ago, Armin Birrer made a living by busking around Norway, Wales, Ireland and New Zealand (including a 15-hour stint in an Invercargill hair salon); in fact he even saved enough in Europe for his airfare to New Zealand. (One assumes he has more musical talent than most.) He generally found busking best in small towns where buskers were seldom seen. Your main enemies are the weather and the police. David Hughes who busked with a borrowed guitar in Taipei encountered a more mysterious obstacle in the form of red graffiti appearing near his spot in the subway and veiled threats from people he could only guess were local gangsters or traders. He didn't hang around to find out.

Regulations about street performing vary from country to country, but in general you will be tolerated if you are causing no obstruction or other harm. There are a few places where it is positively encouraged if you meet a high enough standard: buskers in the Covent Garden precinct in London and the Centre Georges Pompidou in Paris have to be judged worthy before they can perform. In contrast, you may be prosecuted if you perform in the London Underground (but are more likely to be moved on). You may even find that busking leads to better things: Mark Kilburn was offered a job playing guitar in a night club in Holland on the basis of his street performances, Armin Birrer was encouraged by a film writer who heard him to try for a job as a film extra in Melbourne, and Kev Vincent was invited to leave the streets of San Tropez behind to entertain on a millionaire's gin palace.

If you can perform, there is no harm in offering your talents, particularly to pubs in Ireland or in and bars and cafés in any resort frequented by what Ian McArthur calls the 'Marlboro, Levis and Coca Cola generation'.

Artists

An artist who paints local scenes or copies local post cards can do well in holiday resorts. Nicola Dickinson mentioned above would gladly have bought a painting of the church in Lindos where she and so many others got married, but none was for sale, so she has now taken an oil painting class in the hope of one day going back and making a profit.

If you can draw a reasonable likeness you could set yourself up as a street portraitist. Two friends Belinda and Pandora found it fairly easy to make money both in Britain and the Continent especially among holiday-makers. Belinda used unlined brown paper bought in an industrial roll and oil pastels or children's crayons. You can also use driftwood or smooth pebbles. It is awkward to carry around two chairs with you so she relied on borrowing them from an adjacent café or church hall. Artistically you shouldn't be ove-scrupulous; when a disappointed subject asked 'Do I really look that old?' Belinda didn't hesitate to erase a few wrinkles. Once you become known, you may get more lucrative portrait commissions in people's houses.

Apparently boat owners are a particularly vain bunch and will often jump at the chance to have their vessel immortalised on canvas, so loiter around yacht marinas with your sketchbook. Wealthy home owners might also be interested in commissioning a sketch of their homes and a professionally produced leaflet might unearth some customers. Stephen Psallidas noticed a trend in Mykonos for tavernas, banks and other public buildings to display paintings of themselves. John Kilmartin's decorations of buildings on his kibbutz were so highly valued they were praised in an Israeli newspaper which prompted people to pay him to draw their portraits.

Face painting is a portable skill and there is money to be made from organising children's parties wherever there is an expat community. Even if you can't make any money from your artistic endeavours, you may bring pleasure to the locals. While in Ching Kong in northern Thailand, Dustie Hickey sat outside a hut painting Winnie the Pooh and blowing up balloons for the children. When the local English teacher noticed how spellbound the children were, she asked Dustie if she would like to teach at the school on a voluntary basis. She did the same at a children's hospital in Calcutta which so impressed both the children and nuns that she was invited back as a longer term volunteer.

Film Extras

If you like the idea of mingling with the stars in Hollywood for a few days and being well paid for it – forget it. In most international film studios even extras belong to trade unions which exclude outsiders. When a film is being shot on location you may have the opportunity of helping to fill out a crowd scene – in fact the accepted term is 'crowd artist' – but it is a matter of luck coming across these, though your chances are better in some places than others. The picturesque streets of old Budapest together with the relatively lower shooting costs make it a favourite location (in fact the author once spotted Ben Kingsley in a restaurant in Budapest).

In the massive Asian film industry, film-makers actively seek out Caucasian faces, especially to be villains, dupes or dissolutes. Agents for film companies usually look for their supernumerary staff among the budget hotels of Bombay, Bangkok, Hong Kong, Cairo, etc. knowing that they will find plenty of travellers only too willing to spend one or two days hanging around a film set in exchange for a few rupees or dollars. In fact by local standards the wage is generous. (See the chapter on *Asia* for further details.) Japanese advertising companies are often on the lookout for European faces and pay extremely well, e.g. £130 for a half day's 'work'.

Although jobs are normally found by word of mouth there are agencies in some places that will register you as potential extras for example in Bangkok, one of which was successfully used by Vaughan Temby. Be wary of an agency that charges a fee. David Hughes found one in Vancouver which charged $50 and 'guaranteed' work. It turned out that if you didn't get hired by a film company, you didn't get a refund, your period of registration was simply extended.

Whether you work as an extra in the East or West you are unlikely to be given a part that will stretch your acting talents. But the work can still be demanding: hours can be erratic with long periods of idleness. Often you are expected to make do with ill-fitting costumes and shoes. Make sure you take along a good book to fill in the hours and possibly emergency rations of food.

If you hear rumours of a film being shot, try to find the crew and ask whom you should see about work. Dave Bamford asked at the police station in Geneva but their directions came to nothing. By chance the next day he found the film vans, talked to someone in charge and was paid £40 to appear in the background of *The Unbearable Lightness of Being*. He was also invited to a hotel meal where he made lots of contacts for future work.

Film-Making

Never mind just being a film extra... Aspiring film-makers might want to consider choosing a foreign location, as Outlook Productions did in the summer of 2004. Hannah Adcock and some friends (all twenty-somethings) had set up a semi-professional production company with a strong theatrical background, specialising in Greek tragedy and Shakespeare. Plans for making a film adaptation of Shakespeare's *Twelfth Night* had been discussed over a long period but it wasn't until the director and producer visited the Greek island of Patmos that they realised Patmos *was* the Illyria of their dreams (the magical island where all the action in *Twelfth Night* takes place). The island was so perfect that even one of *Twelfth Night's* more inconsequential lines took on a deeper meaning, "prithee foolish Greek, depart from me"!

Director of Photography and 'Wardrobe Mistress' Hannah Adcock describes the ins and out of organising one of the most enterprising and glamorous working holidays imaginable:

The company felt confident that they could sell the film, either to digital TV channels, educational institutions, even to a distributor, because Twelfth Night is a well known play, school children have to study it, and everyone will be so glad it is not Kenneth Branagh that they might just go out and buy it. The company failed to extract funding from organisations such as the Arts Council but it did attract private investors: people who had come to theatrical shows, liked what they saw and believed in the company. It is a really good idea if you are a theatre/production company to keep a mailing list of people who appreciate your work. However, private investment only goes so far when you are making a digital feature film. Paying wages was out of the question so cast and crew were invited to 'profit share'. This way all cast and crew rise or fall on the success or failure of the production, which is a huge risk but a good incentive to work hard!

The whole project took more than three years from idea to wrap. This included such necessary phases as location searching, formulating a shooting script, attracting finance, finding cast, crew and equipment, researching markets and organising post-production. The company let cast and crew make their own accommodation arrangements. This was fine but actors who are asked to work at 6am and have forgotten their breakfast will be difficult. The company also underestimated certain logistical difficulties, for example how to transport costumes and how much will this cost. The key seems to be a painful attention to detail.

The Director notified island officials about filming plans but they never replied. As long as the company didn't obstruct the public or tell them to move, red tape wasn't an issue. Once you have researched and then bought suitable equipment don't forget that it can (and will) break down. If possible have contingency plans since if you are miles from anywhere this is difficult. We had a dead mic for a week and will have to fall back on post production dubbing for some close-ups/medium close-ups.

It is important that you all have legally binding contracts and an agreed procedure for expenses, even if you are working with friends. The company learnt this the hard way and has unforeseen expenses claims. The company has tried to ensure that there will be enough money for a professional editing company to sharpen the rough cut. If you want to sell the film as 'professional' you need great sound and picture quality, together with slick editing.

In conclusion this is a great way to get into a tough sector (and not just by making the tea). You should get respect for initiative, but this is not a guaranteed money spinner.

Incidentally Hannah Adcock has far more than her fair share of 'enterprise' since she has also written and had published a very readable book called *20something: The Ultimate Survival Guide* (Discover Press, £9.99). Furthermore she is off to a Greek island in the summer of 2005 to man a bookshop.

ODD JOBS

If you can't or don't want to get a steady job you could consider offering your services as an odd job person. By all accounts there is a world shortage of emergency plumbers, car and bike mechanics and piano tuners, so someone with these special skills who put up notices locally should have no trouble finding paying customers. Brian Williams from North Wales, travelling with his partner Adrienne Robinson and their three year old son, found his skills as a mechanic in demand wherever he went, including Fiji, New Zealand and Australia, as Adrienne recounts:

Not only did we encounter fewer problems buying and selling cheap vehicles for us to tour around in but in some places Brian's skills as a mechanic could be used as leverage to get better prices or even in exchange for accommodation. In Fiji we negotiated a better price on the assumption that Brian would look at the 'new transport' which he did. Of course once he did this, the villagers wanted him to look at other things too. An orchard we stayed at in New Zealand only took us on when Bri said he was a mechanic – the tractor was broken.

If your sphere of expertise is domestic, you can often find a market for housework and ironing. Hand deliver a little printed notice in the neighbourhood where you're based and see what happens. When I was staying in Sydney one year, I was rather tempted by the leaflet that appeared in the mailbox 'Do you need a break?! Call Cathy's Home Help for housework and ironing now'.

Another skill which has proved popular is tattooing. One world traveller carried his tattooing gun with him to Australia and earned extra pocket money with it between fruit harvests. However there are plenty of jobs for the unskilled too: you don't have to study art to paint a garden fence. You may not earn a lot, but you should at least be promptly paid in cash, with no questions asked. There should be no problems about work permits unless you knock on the door of an immigration officer.

It is a good policy to suggest a specific job when you are on the doorstep, rather than just to ask vaguely if there is anything to be done. Householders are more likely to respond favourably if you tactfully suggest that their garden is not devoid of weeds, or that the hinges on the gate could be brought into the twenty-first century. You should never underestimate the laziness of other people: in summer lawns need mowing, garages need cleaning, cars need washing, and in winter snow needs clearing. If you propose to specialise in something like window cleaning you should invest in some basic equipment: people prefer to hire a window cleaner who has his own bucket, chamois and ladder. Some people have adopted a gimmick to attract custom, for example they offer their window-washing services while wearing roller skates.

> **Dean Fisher had none of these when he had a brainwave in the south of France:**
> *I was running out of money in Aix-en-Provence and got talking to an English guy who was working as a petrol attendant. I started washing windscreens for the people coming into the garage and ended up earning more money in tips than the petrol attendants' wages. Once a guy in a jeep gave me a £10 tip which was amazing. I was my own boss (and didn't tell the guys how much I was getting).*

The best areas to look for odd jobs and household maintenance jobs are in expatriate enclaves abroad (especially on the Mediterranean or in Mexico). Richard Adams did best in the semi-rural areas of Germany, where he found the population were less hasty to turn you away than fast-living city dwellers. You should consider your appearance carefully. An old age pensioner in Munich may not trust someone who looks as if has arrived on foot from Morocco. On the other hand, a housewife in Los Angeles has every right to be suspicious of someone wearing a three-piece suit who offers to clean her swimming pool.

It is also possible to fix up a low-level maintenance job before leaving home. Writing in the now defunct newspaper *Overseas Jobs Express,* Richard Ginger describes how he got hold of a brochure of holiday properties in France owned by expats (from a company called Chez Nous) and simply wrote to 20 of the most likely sounding ones. On the strength of a polite request for work, he was invited to stay in a chateau in the Pyrenees by a retired professor who turned out to be a first rate cook. Soon the professor's neighbours were asking Richard to do odd jobs for cash.

Susan and Eric Beney took a break from travelling with their daughters overland to Australia to spend a while on the small Greek island of Halki. They arrived in April, before the tourist rush, and there was no evidence of any work around. But they successfully created a job from scratch:

The beach was a terrible mess with rubbish washed up in the winter storms, so we set ourselves the task of cleaning it up and asked the Mayor for rubbish bags. After we had been here for five weeks and our funds were sadly depleted, Eric was asked if he would like the job of 'port cleaner'. This job entailed sweeping the harbour and cleaning the streets three days a week and cleaning the loos daily. The job hadn't been done for a month so was quite a task in the beginning but I helped Eric get the loos to a reasonable standard and after that the job was quite a nice little number with plenty of time off. The pay was more than £100 a month and of course it has endeared Eric to the locals, none of whom would do such a job. Apparently a council allowance is made for this job so it could be worthwhile searching out the local Mayor and offering your services. Even the police are happy about it or turn a blind eye. Because we have now been here a while Eric has also done lots of other odd jobs for people as there is very little spare labour on the Island (or the locals are too lazy!)

Apparently Halki's beaches are in good shape these days but, according to Tom Hawthorne, Gibraltar would benefit if some future traveller could talk the council into funding a clean-up operation.

Collecting bottles and cans for their deposits is mentioned in the chapter *In Extremis* but in some countries it is lucrative enough to count as an odd job, for instance in Scandinavia and Mexico. One unusual 'odd job' is to participate in medical trials, which is discussed in the chapters on the UK and USA. If you are accepted, it is possible to earn £100 a day.

GAMBLING

Many countries run state lotteries but the chance of winning a prize are mostly too remote for this to be a useful way of supplementing diminished funds. Casinos and gambling on horse racing may be slightly better bets but again the percentages are always against the punter.

If you must play roulette, bet with the wheel and never against it; it is always possible that there is a slight mechanical fault which favours certain players or numbers. If there are some really big players at the table, bet last and bet against them. Crooked wheels are not unknown and if the casino plans to wipe out the high rollers you stand to profit if you keep your chips well clear of theirs.

Well used by a practised operator, a pack of cards, a backgammon board or set of poker dice are a much more promising source of extra income. When Peter Stonemann was living in Copenhagen he noticed people gathered at the wall of Hallands Kirke where they offered to play fast games of chess for bets of 20 kroner. Poker, bridge and backgammon, but particularly poker, are widely played for money throughout the world; if you become proficient there is every reason to use your skills for profit. The great thing about poker and backgammon is that they are comparatively simple games in which at every stage there is a mathematically correct play. The vast majority of players in amateur schools never take the trouble to learn the percentages. If you do, and so long as you keep out of the professional games, you will win. If interested, get a copy of *The Education of a Poker Player* by Herbert O. Yardley, published by High Stakes Publishing for £9.99. Clearly if you learn to deal 'seconds' or off the bottom of the pack, you will increase your chance of winning though you may well diminish your prospects of longevity.

Another gambit is to become adept at less well known games that pack neatly into your luggage like cribbage, bezique or shut-the-box and then entice your unsuspecting pals to play with you. Lose the board when they look like catching up on your expertise.

The 'Three Card Trick' or 'Spot the Lady' requires a definite element of dexterity but with regular practice you will become competent in a few weeks and can confidently invite customers to place their money on the Lady which hopefully is never the card they choose. As if you were cutting the pack, you hold one card face down lengthwise between thumb and middle finger of the left hand and two cards in a similar manner with your right hand. When releasing the cards from the right hand the top card (i.e. nearer the palm) is released first thus reversing the apparent positions of the two right hand cards when placed on the table. Keep your elbows up and let your wrist hang loose. After a while your audience will start to get wise to the game which is the time to make your apologies and leave. If you are playing with only one person, give them the three cards and you double your previous winnings as they attempt what you have been practising for weeks.

Rolling two dice for someone and getting them to bet on what number will come up is also a possible ruse. The possible numbers are 2 to 12 so the odds about any one number appear to be 10/1. In fact they range from 35/1 for a 2 or 12 to 5/1 for a 7. Actually it is better to get the pigeon to roll the dice and let you bet on 6's 7's and 8's (6/1, 5/1, 6/1) and keep him paying out at 10/1 until he can stand it no longer.

Another ploy which can be used to advantage is to fleece a con-man. It never fails but has its dangerous side and it works like this. All over the world you will find pool halls, pubs or arcades where sharks try to induce mugs to play pool, darts or some other game for money. You put on your best clothes and go into one of these alone and quietly play by yourself – obviously you are not very good and the con-artist soon spots you as a possible touch.' He invites you to play. But con-men, like the rest of us, are greedy; they don't want just to take $1 off you; they want the lot and they aim to do this by letting you think you are a match for them and even raise your hopes that you may win some money. To do this they will always lose the first and probably the second game. You take the money and leave – and make sure you know where the exit is.

Amazingly the big operators in Las Vegas and Atlantic City in the US and the Gold Coast in Australia can also be taken for a few dollars on the same principle. Always looking to get new punters into their gaming palaces they subsidise day tours or return trips to their gleaming portals in the desert or by the sea. The fare (subsidised) may be $5 and when you get there they give you free food and possibly even some chips, say $20 worth, to play the tables or the machines. Cash these in and you are a day older with all expenses paid.

EU EMPLOYMENT AND TAX

Legislation has existed for many years guaranteeing the rights of all nationals of the European Union to compete for jobs in any member country. According to Article 8a of the Maastricht Treaty, every citizen of the European Union has the right to travel, reside and work in any member state. The only reason for refusing entry is on grounds of public security and public health. But this does not mean that all the red tape and attendant hassles have been done away with. Talk of the Single Europe should not lull Euro-jobseekers into thinking that they need not worry about the formalities.

The biggest change since the last edition is the accession of ten new member states to the Union in May 2004: Cyprus, Czech Republic, Estonia, Hungary, Latvia, Lithuania, Malta, Poland, Slovakia and Slovenia. Regulations affecting the free movement of labour in and out of these countries differ but in most cases reciprocal transitional controls have been implemented for two years in the first instance and up to a maximum of seven years before full mobility of labour will be allowed.

Even in the 'old Europe', practical barriers to the free movement of labour remain. The very idea of unimpeded movement of goods, services, capital and persons is utopian. The minute you have immigration laws of any kind, freedom is curtailed, especially when unemployment is a problem. But unemployment has been falling in many member states and in fact labour shortages are predicted in coming years (as currently in the UK), good news for the job-seeker in Europe. Interestingly, according to recent official figures, only 0.1% of Europe's population crossed a national border to look for work, though this figure is bound to increase steadily.

The EU now consists of 25 members; in addition to the ten new members listed above, the member states are Austria, Belgium, Denmark, Finland, France, Germany, Greece, Ireland, Italy, Luxembourg, the Netherlands, Portugal, Spain, Sweden and the United Kingdom. The free reciprocity extends to countries of the European Economic Area (EEA), which includes Iceland, Liechtenstein and Norway. Switzerland is a special case but has also been shedding restrictions (see chapter).

The standard situation among the original EU countries (and EEA countries, though the denotation EU is used throughout this book) is that nationals have the right to look for work in another member state for up to three months. At the end of that period they should apply to the police or the local authority for a residence permit, showing their passport and job contract. The residence permit will be valid for five years if the job is permanent or for the duration of the job if it is for less than one year.

Bureaucracies have a habit of getting in the way of progressive legislation though improvements are in evidence. For example EU nationals are no longer required to obtain the dreaded *carte de séjour* in France or *Tarjeta de Residencia* in Spain. Slowly the impediments are being dismantled.

Bureaucratic problems are still being encountered by travellers attempting to claim unemployment benefit (Job Seeker's Allowance in the UK); the procedures for claiming abroad are detailed below. I.A. Gowing attempted to claim unemployment benefit at the *arbeitsamt* in Frankfurt, having followed the correct procedure. He was told that this was not possible unless he could produce a residence permit, and to get this permit he would need letters proving that he had accommodation and a job, which resulted in a classic Catch-22 situation; he was not allowed to collect unemployment benefit to which he was entitled because he was unemployed. David Ramsdale compared his attempts to get benefit from the Danish *Komune* (municipality) to trying to get blood out of a stone. Unfortunately, it requires time and energy to appeal against such decisions, which may simply be the result of bureaucratic prejudice. The Department for Work and Pensions (0191-218 7777; www.dwp.gov.uk) has no control over its counterparts abroad when such problems arise and can only put forward a claimant's side of the argument, with no guarantee of success, though it is always worth a try.

Another Catch-22 affects self-employed workers, particularly self-employed building workers. Although there is a demand for bricklayers, plasterers, plumbers, etc. especially in Germany, the Netherlands and Belgium, employers are reluctant to hire anyone who does not have form E101, which proves that you are paying self-employed contributions in the UK and are therefore exempt from local tax and social security contributions for up to 24 months. The application form for an E101 is available from the Inland Revenue. However the form will only be granted to people who have been registered self-employed in the UK for six months making it difficult for people in paid employment at home to conduct a speculative job search abroad. A further problem is that some unscrupulous employers make sizeable deductions even though an E101 should mean that the worker is exempt.

Despite the fact that the system does not always work perfectly, a lot of labour does move freely over national borders. In fact approximately three-quarters of a million European Union nationals are employed outside their country of citizenship. This chapter is aimed exclusively at nationals of the original 15 European Union member states. (Schemes and exchanges relevant to other nationalities are mentioned throughout the rest of the book.) Nancy Mitford made the U and non-U distinction famous (upper class and not upper class) but for the purposes of this book EU and non-EU has replaced it as an individual's defining characteristic. Some Americans may have access to the EU if they are fortunate enough to be of Irish or Italian descent and can prove that they have a grandparent of either nationality, in which case they can obtain dual nationality. An increasing number of Americans are taking up this option for employment reasons and have been dubbed 'paper Europeans'. Americans of Greek extraction may be eligible for EU nationality, however they should first find out whether this will carry with it an obligation to do national service. (The United States allows its citizens to hold more than one passport, but does not recognise dual citizenship.)

From the European traveller's point of view there are many bureaucratic advantages to the EU. For many years the E111 was the certificate of entitlement to medical treatment within Europe which could be obtained free of charge from post offices. This is to be replaced by the European Health Insurance card which will be valid throughout the European Economic Area and Switzerland. The UK will start issuing these in 2005 in anticipation of the phasing out of the E111 by January 2006. In the first phase of introduction the new card will cover health care for short stays and in the second phase, it will take the place of the current E128 and E119 which cover longer stays for job-seekers and students.

Progress has been made on improving the mutual recognition of professional and vocational qualifications though the dream of Europe-wide recognition is a long way from realisation. The Department of Trade & Industry has a special Diplomas and Certificates Unit that can allocate Certificates of Experience to certain categories of worker. Further details are available in the DTI/DFES booklet *Europe Open for Professions* which can be obtained from Bay 212, Kingsgate House, Victoria St, London SW1E 6SW (020-7215 4648) or consulted online at www.dti.gov.uk/europe/open.pdf.

NATIONAL EMPLOYMENT SERVICES IN THE EU

Every EU country possesses a network of employment offices similar to British Jobcentre Plus, details of which are given in the individual country chapters. Although EU legislation requires national employment services to treat applicants from other member states in exactly the same way as their own citizens, it is impossible to prevent a certain amount of bias from entering the system. An employer is allowed to turn down an applicant who does not speak enough of the language to perform his job adequately for obvious reasons.

Average unemployment across Europe has been stable over the past couple of years and now stands at 8.9% in December 2004 (compared to 8.5% two years ago and 9.2% two years before that). But it is still high in some countries (e.g. 10.5% in Spain, 9.9% in Germany, 9.6% in France, 8.7% in Finland) and no amount of positive legislation will change the attitude of the official of the Amsterdam employment office who said 'How can we help the English to find work? We do not have enough jobs for our own people' or of the French ANPE (Jobcentre) employee who told Noel Kirkpatrick that he would prefer to give a job to any Moroccan or Algerian before someone from Britain. If there are two equally qualified job applicants of different nationalities, most employers will choose their fellow countryman/woman. In the words of experienced Euroworker Paul Winter: *'Please make it clear to your readers that all this talk of one Europe and a Europe without borders doesn't mean that jobs are easy and simple to get abroad. It's not easy. Plan ahead, try to learn a language and take as much money as you can. That being said, the chances of working around Europe are still there to be enjoyed, just use a little common sense.'*

Many developed nations welcome migrant workers who are prepared to take jobs that no local would consider. For example the bulb-packing factories of Holland and hotel kitchens in Germany have traditionally taken on large numbers of foreign workers during their busiest times of year. At one time many of those were Irish and British. Lately that trend has reversed, partly because the very low rates of unemployment in the UK and Ireland (just over 4%) mean that fewer people from those countries want to travel to find unskilled work. Also very large numbers of people from the accession countries are on the move to escape high unemployment (a staggering 18.4% in Poland and not much less in Slovakia) and low wages (e.g. a tenth of the Danish wage for an unskilled job).

The computerised, pan-European job information network EURES (EURopean Employment Service) is accessible through Jobcentre Plus offices around the UK and all national employment services in Europe. In the UK, expertise is centred in the International Job Search Advice department of Job Centre Plus (6th Floor, Whitehall II, Whitehall Quay, Leeds LS1 4HR; 0113 307 8090/91; fax 0113 307 8213; international-jobsearch-advice@jobcentreplus.gsi.gov.uk). Throughout Europe hundreds of specially trained EuroAdvisers can advise on vacancies within Europe. It is also possible to access the EURES database online via the EURES portal http://europa.eu.int/eures to see what kinds of vacancies are available in Iceland or Greece.

Vacancies are usually for six months or longer, and are often in the tourist industry or for skilled, semi-skilled and (increasingly) managerial jobs. Language skills are almost always a requirement. A random sample of job vacancies might include a nursery nurse for Finland, welders and chefs for Germany, a loom turner for Ireland and catering staff for a Spanish theme park. EURES can be used free by employers. On average, 500 new posts are registered with EURES each month though if you have a specific destination in mind, they are unlikely to be able to offer much choice of vacancy. If you are already abroad, make an appointment with the local EuroAdviser or you might ring them from home since they should have a lot of local knowledge and be able to communicate in English.

Euroguidance Centres covering European careers have been set up in all EU member states to provide information on training, education and employment in Europe, mostly to help careers services and their clients. Careers Europe (Onward House, Baptist Place, Bradford BD1 2PS; 01274 829600; www.careerseurope.co.uk) produce the Eurofacts series of International Careers Information, and Exodus, the Careers Europe database of international careers, all of which can be consulted at local Connexions careers offices and Jobcentre Plus in the UK.

Jobs with EU Organisations

The aim of the EU's *Leonardo da Vinci* programme is to improve the quality of vocational training systems and their capacity for innovation. It grants students and recent graduates mobility to undertake overseas work placements of between 3 and 12 months (for students) or between 2 and 12 months (recent graduates). It must be noted that applications for Leonardo funding must be submitted by organisations, not individuals. Details are available from university placement offices or International Relations Offices, or directly from the Education & Training Group (020-7389 4389; leonardo@britishcouncil.org/ www.leonardo.org.uk).

The office of the representation of the European Commission in the UK is at 8 Storey's

Gate, London SW1P 3AT (020-7973 1992/fax 020-7973 1900). Its website (www.cec.org. uk) has masses of links to potentially useful information on everything from Taxes in the Netherlands to Right of Residence in Portugal. The European Commission's literature can be requested on Europe Direct (freephone from all EU countries 00800 67891011) or check the web-site on http://europa.eu.int/citizensrights.

High flyers who would like to work for the European Commission as administrators, translators, secretaries, etc. must compete in recruitment procedures known as open competitions; the London office above can provide information (www.cec.org.uk/work/stage. htm). The Commission does not offer any work placements or summer jobs other than the 600+ five-month *stagiaire* positions for graduates in Brussels or Luxembourg. Applications must be submitted online not later than 31st August for positions starting in March (and 1st March for positions starting in October). Details and application forms can be obtained from the above website or from the Bureau de Stages, European Commission, 200 Rue de la Loi, 1049 Brussels, Belgium (02-299 23 39; eac-stages@cec.eu.int).

Short-term white-collar contracts may be available on the spot for people who are bilingual and/or have secretarial skills. Special rules govern the red tape of employees of international organisations.

CLAIMING JOB SEEKER'S ALLOWANCE IN EUROPE

It may come as a pleasant surprise to discover that it is possible to claim Job-Seeker's Allowance in other EU countries and also now Switzerland since it has signed up to the free movement of labour over its borders (www.europa.admin.ch). The two ways in which this benefit export can take place are covered in detail below: to understand them it is necessary to understand the principle behind what used to be known as unemployment benefit.

Payments are not paid automatically to people who are out of work. It is an entitlement that has to be 'bought' by paying a certain number of contributions into a country's unemployment insurance organisation. In Britain these contributions are represented by Class 1 National Insurance contributions. Class 1 contributions are paid only by people who are employees earning at least £91 per week. Other groups may pay either Class 2 and 4 contributions (for the self-employed) or Class 3 contributions (a voluntary payment for those who would otherwise not be covered by National Insurance) which entitle them to some social security benefits, but not Job-Seeker's Allowance.

Other EU countries have similar systems, and contributions paid in one country can be taken into account when building up an entitlement to unemployment benefit in another. Whichever of the two means of claiming benefit is relevant to you depends on where you last paid contributions, as you will be covered under that country's unemployment insurance scheme.

In Britain people who are not eligible to claim job-seeker's allowance may claim income support if they have no other means of support. The amount paid depends on the needs of the applicant – whether they have any relatives to support, how much is needed to pay for rent, etc. – and it is intended to cover only the essentials of life. Most EU countries have equivalents, but the right to claim these is not transferable between countries in the same way that unemployment benefit is. Normally it is handled by municipal authorities who stipulate that eligibility depends on a claimant having been resident in the district for several years. Applications for income support abroad are very unlikely to succeed.

Claiming UK Job-seeker's Allowance in Europe

Any EU national who has been registered unemployed for at least four weeks in the UK and is entitled to receive the UK allowance can arrange to receive it for up to three months, paid at the UK rate, while looking for work elsewhere in the EU. The applicant should inform Jobcentre Plus in Britain of his or her intention to look for work elsewhere well before departure, usually at least six weeks. It is helpful if you have a precise departure date and a definite destination, preferably with an address. Note that if you go abroad on holiday and decide to stay on to work, the benefit cannot be transferred. Your local Jobcentre should have a leaflet (ref. JSAL 22) for people going abroad or coming from abroad plus an application form for transferring benefit.

Austria: Local office of the national employment service *(arbeitsamt)*.
Belgium: Trade union members claim from the union's unemployment insurance division. Non-union members should go to CAPAC (the *Caisse auxiliaire de paiement des allocations de chômage*).
Denmark: Unemployment insurance is distributed by trade unions though non-union members may join an unemployment fund *(arbedjsløshedskammer)*.
Finland: Social Insurance Institution
France: Local office of the national employment service *(Agence Nationale pour l'Emploi)* or the local town hall if there is no *agence* nearby.
Germany: Local office of the national employment service *(arbeitsamt)*.
Greece: OAED (Labour Office).
Iceland: Unemployment Insurance Fund *(Atvinnuleysistryggingasjodur)* (Sudurlandsbraut 24, 150 Reykjavik; 588 2500).
Ireland: Local employment exchange or employment office.
Italy: Local employment office or the local office of the *Istituto della previdenza sociale* (national social welfare institution).
Luxembourg: National labour office *(Office National du Travail)* or the secretariat of the commune where you are living.
Netherlands: Previous employer's professional or trade association.
Norway: Local employment office *(Arbeidformidling)*
Portugal: Local office of the national employment service *(Centro de Emprego) and Centro Regional de Segurança* (CRSS).
Spain: Local office of the national employment service *(Oficina de Empleo)* or *Instituto Nacional de Seguridad Social* (INSS).
Sweden: Local employment office *(Arbetsfönmedlingen)*
United Kingdom: Local Jobcentre Plus.

When you have told your local Jobcentre Plus your plans, they will supply a letter in English and that of your destination country explaining that you are eligible to claim benefit. This introductory letter will be useful when you register with the appropriate authorities in your destination country, which must be done within seven days. Your local Jobcentre Plus will inform the Pension & Overseas Benefit Directorate of the Department for Work & Pensions who will then decide whether or not to issue a E303 which authorises the Employment Services in the other EU/EEA country to pay UK contribution-based JSA for up to three months. In the case of Denmark, Gibraltar, Ireland, Luxembourg and the Netherlands, the E303 is sent by the Department of Work & Pensions directly to a counterpart organisation. If you are heading for any other country, the E303 will be sent directly to you.

If someone tries to claim unemployment benefit abroad without making these preparations there may be delays of several months while the application is cleared. Be warned that even if the correct procedure is followed there may still be delays because of the time necessary to forward and translate correspondence.

Literature published by the Youth Information organisation Use It in Copenhagen sums it up
Transferring benefits can be a good way of tiding you over whilst you settle in, but it is essential that you are aware of the realities of the situation. Although it is your right and in theory a great way of encouraging young unemployed people to try their luck abroad, you should not expect to be handed a cheque on the day of arrival. The process can be long and painful so it is very important that you have plenty of money to get you started. It can take months before you see any of your benefits in hard cash.

In theory, people looking for work in more than one EU country can continue to receive unemployment benefit under this system in each country visited, as long as they register for work in each new country within seven days of arrival and have given adequate notice to the relevant office in the country from which they wish the benefit to be transferred. Overall however payment of unemployment benefit will not exceed the three month maximum. In fact complications and delays are bound to ensue if you country-hop.

Inside the United Kingdom employed persons who have paid the appropriate UK contributions can normally receive Job-Seeker's Allowance for up to six months. It is important to note that this maximum can be affected by the length of time you claim unemployment benefit abroad; if you claim benefit abroad for the maximum period of three months and then remain abroad for a further period of time, your right to claim JSA on your return to Britain lapses, according to EU regulations. But Jobcentre Plus staff have discretion to allow those who would still be allowed to claim if they had not left the country to do so on their return.

These arrangements are standard within the EU: thus, a German wishing to look for work in Britain must obtain a letter of authorisation and E303 from his or her local Arbeitsamt, and so on. The EU principle of equality of treatment means that an EU citizen claiming unemployment benefit under a foreign social security scheme who moves to another country including his own, can arrange to collect unemployment benefit at the rate set by the foreign unemployment insurance fund for up to three months. In the case of Britons who have worked abroad, the foreign rate might be higher or lower than the standard United Kingdom job-seeker's allowance. If after three months the applicant has still not found employment, he is no longer eligible for foreign unemployment benefit but may then apply for income support.

In countries where no Social Security agreement exists, the leaflet NI38 'Social Security Abroad' gives an outline of the arrangements and options open to you. If you fail to make National Insurance contributions while you are out of the UK, you will forfeit entitlement to benefits on your return. You can decide to pay voluntary contributions at regular intervals or in a lump sum in order to retain your rights to certain benefits. Unfortunately this entitles you only to a retirement/widow's pension, not to sickness benefit or unemployment benefit.

Anyone who is planning to quit work (to travel), go on the dole for the requisite four weeks and then head off to Europe to collect their benefit will be disappointed. Anyone who quits work voluntarily in the UK must wait 26 weeks before they are eligible to claim job-seeker's allowance.

If you are a national of a European Economic Area country working in another member state, you will be covered by European Social Security regulations. The information leaflet SA29 'Your Social Security Insurance, Benefits & Health Care Rights in the European Economic Area' was last updated October 2004 and can be read online at www.dwp. gov.uk/international/sa29 or obtained from the Centre for Non Residents, Room BP1301, Benton Park View, Newcastle-upon-Tyne NE98 1ZZ (0845 915 4811; www.inlandrevenue. gov.uk/nic). The leaflet explains that payments made in any EEA country count towards benefit entitlement when you return home.

Claiming Unemployment Benefit from Another EU Country

In order to claim unemployment benefit from another EU country you must have worked there and paid contributions into its unemployment insurance fund. The length of time for which you must have worked varies from country to country: the details are listed below. It cannot be emphasised too strongly that contributions paid in one country can be taken into account in another, and so for some people a very short period of work abroad may be sufficient to allow them to claim unemployment benefit there. Your history of paying contributions should be itemised on form E301 and sent to the corresponding office abroad. The UK authorities emphasise that possession of form E301 does not give the holder an automatic right to receive unemployment benefit in another European country. For the purposes of clarity the chart omits some of the complications, and mentions only the unemployment benefit that is normally paid to people who have just lost their jobs. In many cases, it will be necessary to join the relevant union which may be responsible for distributing benefit.

How Much?

Great Britain and Ireland differ from most other EU countries in paying a flat rate of job-seeker's allowance. In the UK this is currently £55.65 per week. Other member countries base their rates of unemployment benefit on a percentage of the wage most recently earned by the applicant, varying from 30.3% (plus a small daily allowance) in France to 90% in Denmark. In the Netherlands, claimants receive 70% of the minimum wage for up to six months. In Spain they receive 70% for the first 180 days and after that 60%. There are, of course, upper and lower limits on the amount paid to make sure that low earners do not suffer and the highly paid do not benefit excessively. Some Scandinavian countries pay a basic daily allowance to people who have not qualified for membership in an unemployment fund but who can prove that they are unemployed.

How to Claim Unemployment Benefit

The same principles apply when claiming unemployment benefit in all member states of the EU, although the names and procedures may vary from one country to another. In order to claim you must:

- Have become unemployed in that country through no fault of your own
- Be both fit and available to work
- Possess documentary proof of your last job and (normally) a residence permit
- Be registered as unemployed with the employment office
- Be aged under 65
- Have paid sufficient contributions into unemployment insurance organisations in the EU

Unemployment insurance funds are not always administered by a country's national employment service. A country by country guide is listed below:

Austria: Local office of the national employment service (arbeitsamt)
Belgium: Trade union members claim from the union's unemployment insurance division. Non-union members should go to CAPAC (the Caisse auxiliaire de paiement des allocations de chômage)
Denmark: Unemployment insurance is distributed by trade unions though non-union members may join an unemployment fund (arbedjsløshedskammer)
Finland: Social Insurance Institution
France: Local office of the national employment service (Agence Nationale pour l'Emploi) or the local town hall if there is no agence nearby
Germany: Local office of the national employment service (arbeitsamt).
Greece: OAED (Labour Office).
Iceland: Unemployment Insurance Fund (Atvinnuleysistryggingasjodur) (Sudurlandsbraut 24, 150 Reykjavik; 588 2500).
Ireland: Local employment exchange or employment office
Italy: Local employment office or the local office of the Istituto della previdenza sociale (national social welfare institution)
Luxembourg: National labour office (Office National du Travail) or the secretariat of the commune where you are living
Netherlands: Previous employer's professional or trade association.
Norway: Local employment office (Arbeidformidling)
Portugal: Local office of the national employment service (Centro de Emprego) and Centro Regional de Segurança (CRSS)
Spain: Local office of the national employment service (Oficina de Empleo) or Instituto Nacional de Seguridad Social (INSS)
Sweden: Local employment office (Arbetsfönmedlingen)
United Kingdom: Jobcentre Plus

ELIGIBILITY REQUIREMENTS FOR UNEMPLOYMENT BENEFIT IN EEA COUNTRIES

Country	Name of Unemployment Benefit	Qualifying Conditions
Austria	*Arbeitslosengeld*	At least 52 weeks (or 26 weeks if under the age of 25) in preceding 104 weeks
Belgium	*Allocations de chômage*	Between 75 days employment in last 10 months and 600 days employment in last 36 months, depending on age
Denmark	*Dagpenge*	Membership of an unemployment fund during the last 12 months and in employment for at least 6 of these months
Finland	*Työttömyysavustus*	At least 26 weeks in preceding 24 months
France	*Allocation d'assurance chômage* (also known as ASSEDIC)	Must be out of work or legitimately dismissed; must be capable of work and less than 60 years old, plus must have paid 3 months UB insurance in the last 12 months
Germany	*Arbeitslosengeld*	At least 480 days of insurable employment during the last 3 years
Gibraltar	Unemployment benefit	At least 30 paid contributions in the last 52 weeks
Greece	*Epidoma anergias*	At least 125 days of work during the 14 months preceding job loss
Iceland	*Tryggingastofnun*	425 hours in preceding 12 months
Ireland	Unemployment benefit	39 weeks paid insurance plus 48 contributions paid/credited in the year preceding the benefit year
Italy	*Indennita ordinaria*	One year during the previous 2 years; must also have been registered for at least 2 years with an unemployment insurance scheme
Luxembourg	*Allocations de chômage*	At least 26 weeks in the previous 12 months
Netherlands	*Werkloosheidswet* (also known as WW)	26 weeks in the previous 39 weeks
Norway	*Arbeidsledighetstrygd*	Must have earned approx. 22,000 Kroner in previous year
Spain	*Prestación por Desempleo*	At least 12 months employment within previous 6 years
Sweden	*Dagpenning*	At least 80 days spread over 5 months in preceding 12 months
United Kingdom	Job-seeker's allowance (flat rate)	Contributions must have been paid in one of the 2 tax years on which the claim is based amounting to at least 25 times the minimum contribution (i.e. 25 x £91)

In all countries it is essential to register as unemployed with the national employment service before claiming from the unemployment insurance fund. Unemployment benefit (see chart for appropriate name in different countries) is only paid from three days after the date when you first register as unemployed, so it is important to register as soon as you lose your job. You will also be required to continue to register as unemployed with the insurance fund at regular intervals.

If you need to have a period of work in another EU country taken into account to make you eligible for unemployment benefit you will need to provide proof of the contributions you paid there on form E301 which you should obtain from the unemployment insurance organisation of the country where you paid the contributions. If you do not have this form to hand when you apply for unemployment benefit the office at which you are claiming can obtain it for you, but this may lead to a delay in processing your application.

TAX

Calculating your liability to tax when working outside your home country is notoriously complicated so, if possible, check your position with an accountant, preferably one who specialises in expatriate matters.

There really isn't any such thing as legal tax-free income whatever an agency or employer promises. The only people who are not liable to pay any tax are those who earn less than the personal allowance (whatever that may be). However there are ways to minimise tax. Although the details of income tax systems vary from country to country, there are some common characteristics. In theory EU students working in the EU for less than six months are not liable for tax, so students should always show their employers documents to prove their status. The traveller who works for less than the full tax year will generally find himself paying too much in tax: this section outlines the circumstances when it may be possible to reclaim some of it. Individual cases should be discussed with the local tax authority.

If you are working on a longer term basis abroad, your UK tax liability depends on several factors, the principal one being whether you are classed as 'resident', 'ordinarily resident' or 'domiciled' in the UK. Working travellers are normally considered domiciled in the UK even if they are away for more than a year. Formerly it was possible to claim a 'foreign earnings deduction' (i.e. pay no tax) if you were out of the country for a full 365 days. However the legislation has changed so that you are eligible for this only if you have been out of the country for a complete tax year (6 April to 5 April) though you are allowed to spend up to 62 days (i.e. one-sixth) of the tax-year back in England without it affecting your tax postion. Anyone who is present in the UK for more than 182 days during a particular tax year will be treated as resident with no exceptions.

Inland Revenue leaflets which might be of assistance are IR20 'Residents and Non-Residents: Liability to Tax in the UK' and IR139 'Income from Abroad? A guide to UK tax on overseas income'. The Inland Revenue also has a good website if you have the patience to look for the information you need (www.inlandrevenue.gov.uk); it lists the relevant contact offices that deal with specific issues. If they can't help they will refer you to the appropriate section. General tax enquiries may be addressed to the Inland Revenue's Centre for Non Residents (as mentioned above): Benton Park View, Newcastle-upon-Tyne NE98 1ZZ (help-line 0845 915 4811).

If US citizens can establish that they are resident abroad, the first $80,000 of overseas earnings are tax-exempt in the US.

Why you can Reclaim Tax

Countries do not charge income tax on a person's income up to a certain figure, which is known as a personal allowance or a basic deduction. The exact size of this figure varies from country to country, but it is generally at least 20% of the national average wage. In theory, you won't have to pay any tax if your total earnings are below this figure.

In practice, however, most countries deduct tax under a withholding system or 'pay as you earn', which assumes that your weekly wage is typical of your annual earnings. Thus, if you were to work in Britain for two weeks earning the minimum wage of £4.85 for a weekly wage of £180, you would be taxed as if you were earning £9,360 a year. Sometimes you have the right to reclaim any tax you have paid on income up to the value of your personal allowance when you have finished work and are about to leave the country or at the end of that country's tax year. Unfortunately there are residential and other requirements in some countries which make this impossible.

This may seem to imply that you could escape from tax altogether by getting a series of short term jobs around the world and never exceeding your personal allowance in any one country. Unfortunately, there are a number of 'double taxation' agreements between most western countries which prevent this. Among other things, they ensure that the taxman can ultimately track you down in your 'country of permanent residence', where you will be liable to pay tax on all your earnings abroad at the local rate. Hence the popularity among tax exiles of countries with very low rates of tax.

How to Minimise Tax

Keep all pay slips, receipts and financial documents in case you need to plead your case at a later date. If your tax status abroad is not completely legitimate, you will be taxed in the UK as Jamie Masters found to his cost after nine months of English teaching in Crete:

> I didn't know that if you are working abroad for less than a year, you are liable to be taxed in Britain, and had cheerfully let the tax people know that I was working in Greece. The rules state that the tax you pay in Greece can be transferred to England to offset the tax you owe at home. But I didn't pay any tax in Greece (just bribes). Stupid, stupid. I should have just told the IR that I was travelling. Rule number one: if you're working illegally, deny everything.

In many countries where you can work legitimately (e.g. EU countries) your employer will expect you to clarify your tax position with the local tax office at the beginning of your work period. This can be to your advantage, for example in Denmark where, unless you obtain a tax card (skattekort), you will be put on the Danish equivalent of an emergency code and 60% of your earnings will be automatically deducted at source. Glyn Evans who picked apples in Denmark returned several times to the local Radhus to complain about the excessive tax, and finally obtained a skattekort entitling him to a taxation rate of 31%. Nowadays, the Danes offer significant tax concessions to foreign seasonal workers (see chapter). Germany is another country where it is customary for foreign workers to register at the tax office (Finanzamt). Be sure to get a tax code in Gibraltar since this, together with a tax return filled in before departure, will allow you to reclaim income tax once you're back in Britain.

France has an unusual tax system, and the general advice given in this section does not apply there. Instead of deducting tax on the 'pay as you earn' system, the French authorities charge tax retrospectively: in other words, with every pay packet French workers are paying off in instalments their tax bill from the previous year. So the working traveller in France will escape any deductions for tax unless he or she is unlucky enough to be working over the end of the tax year, which is from January 1st to December 31st. However he or she will have to pay social security contributions which are high in France, as much as a fifth of total earnings.

How to Reclaim Tax

When you have finished a job your employer should give you a form which will state the amount of tax he has taken from your wages. If he can't do this for any reason you should collect your pay slips. Even a scruffy piece of paper may be sufficient proof of your having paid tax if it states the dates you worked and the amount of tax deducted, and is signed by your employer. If your employer won't give you any written proof at all, the odds are that he has been pocketing the money he has deducted, in which case there is no point in trying to reclaim it from the tax office!

You then take this evidence to the local tax office and fill in a tax rebate form. On this form you will have to state that you will not be working in that country again during the tax year, and give the date of your departure. You may be asked to surrender your residence and/or work permit to prevent you from simply moving to another town and getting a new job or you may have to show your return ticket to prove that you are leaving. Bureaucratic delays often mean that your refund will have to be posted to you abroad. It can take weeks, and frequently months, for your claim to be processed. You therefore need to be sure that you will be at the address you give them for some length of time; if you are not sure of your future movements, give the address of a relative or friend.

Some countries, e.g. Germany, Denmark and the US, stipulate that you are not allowed to reclaim any tax until the end of the tax year. The rule in Germany as in Britain is that you must have resided in Germany for at least six months of the tax year in order to qualify for a rebate. In Denmark tax refunds can be issued only six months after the year in which the tax was paid.

It is not essential that you reclaim tax directly from the authorities of the country where you have been working, since double taxation agreements state that any tax you have paid on earnings abroad can be credited as if it had been paid in your own country. So, in principle, if you have paid too much tax you can reclaim it from your own national tax authority. In practice, however, this can turn into a long drawn out process as the bureaucracies of two countries attempt to communicate with each other: it took Tessa Shaw two years to obtain a refund of tax she had overpaid in Denmark through the British Inland Revenue. You are therefore strongly advised to deal directly with the tax offices of the countries in which you have worked whenever possible.

One way of making the whole process easier is to use a specialist agency. The Irish company ESS specialises in claiming rebates for clients who have worked abroad, specifically in the US, Canada, Netherlands, Germany, Ireland, the UK, Japan, Belgium and Australia. In the UK it trades as Taxback.com, 1st Floor, 277-281 Oxford St, London W1C 2DL (0800 018 4006; uk@taxback.com) and the Irish head office of ESS Tax Refunds is at 20 Eden Quay, Dublin 1 (www.ess.ie).

Work Your Way

Tourism   **Childcare**
Agriculture   **Volunteering**
Teaching English

TOURISM

The long-term prospects for the tourist industry are rosy. A staggering 19 million jobs in the European Union are travel and tourism-related which represents nearly 13% of the workforce. According to an estimate submitted to the European Commission, tourism could create between 2.2 and 3.3 million new jobs in the EU by 2010. The tourist industry, like agriculture, is a mainstay of the traveller-cum-worker. The seasonal nature of hotel and restaurant work discourages a stable working population, and so hotel proprietors often rely on foreign labour during the busy season. Also, many tourist destinations are in remote places where there is no local pool of labour. Travellers have ended up working in hotels in some of the most beautiful corners of the world from the South Island of New Zealand to Lapland.

Agencies and Websites

People with a background in hotels and catering may be able to fix up overseas contracts while still in the UK. The EURES European Employment Service registers quite a few foreign vacancies in the tourist industry (particularly in France and Italy) via JobcentrePlus. Specialist agencies will be of interest to qualified hotel staff including chefs, hotel receptionists and restaurant staff.

Specialist recruitment websites can be invaluable. One of the best is www.seasonworkers.com, a site that has been designed to help people find a summer job, outdoor sports job, gap year project or ski resort job quickly and easily. In 2004 it won in the 'Best Recruitment' category in the Travel and Tourism web awards. Dozens of sites may prove useful such as www.voovs.com and www.resortjobs.co.uk (part of natives.co.uk). Two US-based sites www.coolworks.com and www.jobmonkey.com are especially recommended for seasonal jobs in the tourist industry.

The agency Jobs in the Alps (17 High St, Gretton, Northants. NN17 3DE; 01536 771150; info@jobs-in-the-alps.co.uk) places young Britons in French, German and Swiss hotels for a minimum of three months during the summer season, for which the application deadline is April 15th. (See section below on Ski Resorts for further information.)

For people who are pursuing a career in travel and tourism, it would be worth looking at another Vacation-Work Publications title *Working in Tourism* (£11.95). Further information about training and recruitment for the industry is available from TTC Training (01483 727321; www.tttc.co.uk). Several specialist employment agencies such as T & T Recruitment & Resourcing (14 Bonhill St, London EC2A 4BX; www.ttrecruitment.demon.co.uk) specialise in placing candidates in travel agencies, administrative positions, ground-handling firms, etc. The website www.careerintravel.co.uk gives guidance on training to be a holiday rep, etc. and helps some of the major companies recruit staff.

If you have extensive experience of travelling on at least two continents (other than Europe and North America), you might be interested in working for one of the youth travel agencies like STA (Travel Recruitment, 6 Wrights Lane, London W8 6TA; 020-7361 6220; recruitment@statravel.co.uk).

The independent travellers' monthly magazine *Wanderlust* has a Jobshop column which advertises vacancies with adventure travel companies, e.g. as cycle or hill-walking tour leaders.

HOTELS AND RESTAURANTS

If you secure a hotel job without speaking the language of the country and lacking relevant experience, you will probably be placed at the bottom of the pecking order, e.g. in the laundry or washing dishes. Some hotels might confuse you by using fancy terms for menial jobs, for example 'valet runner' for collector-of-dirty-laundry or 'kitchen porter' for pot-washer. Reception and bar jobs are usually the most sought after and highly paid. However the lowly jobs have their saving graces. The usual hours of chamber staff (7am-2pm) allow plenty of free time. Some people prefer not to deal with guests (particularly if they are shaky in the language) and are happy to get on at their own speed with the job of room cleaning or laundering or vegetable chopping. The job of night porter can be excellently suited to an avid reader since there is often very little to do except let in the occasional late arrival.

Even the job of dish-washer, stereotyped as the most lowly of all jobs with visions of the down and out George Orwell as a *plongeur* washing dishes in a Paris café, should not be dismissed too easily. Nick Langley enjoyed life far more as a dish-washer in Munich than as a civil servant in Britain. Simon Canning saved enough money in five months of working as a dish-washer in an Amsterdam office block to fund a trip across Asia. Benjamin Fry spent a highly enjoyable two weeks washing dishes at the Land's End Hotel in Alaska and earned more per hour than he ever had in Britain. And Sean Macnamara was delighted with his job as dish-washer in a French hotel near Chamonix:

> *After a brief interview I was given the job of dish-washer. The conditions were excellent: £300 per month plus private accommodation and first class meals, including as much wine as I could drink. I earned my keep, though, working six days a week from 8am to 10pm with three hours off each afternoon. I was the only foreigner and was treated kindly by everyone. Indeed I can honestly say I enjoyed myself, but then I was permanently high on the thought of all that money.*

Many people thrive on the animated atmosphere and on kitchen conviviality. Nick Langley, who also worked in a German kitchen, loved the atmosphere. He maintains that once you're established you'll gain more respect by shouting back if unreasonable demands are made, but adds the proviso, 'but not at the powerful head cook, please!'. Heated tempers usually cool down after a couple of beers at the end of a shift.

Applications

The earlier you decide to apply for seasonal hotel work the better are your chances. Hotels in a country such as Switzerland recruit months before the summer season, and it is advisable to write to as many hotel addresses as possible by March, preferably in their own language. A knowledge of more than one language is an immense asset for work in Europe. If you have an interest in working in a particular country, get a list of hotels from their tourist office in London and write to the largest ones (e.g. the ones with over 100 rooms). If you know someone going to your chosen country, ask them to bring back local newspapers and check adverts. Enclose international reply coupons and try to write in the language of the country. Mass emailing of your CV will be much less effective than applying in writing or in person. Amanda Smallwood wrote to 20 hotels in a German resort and received seven job offers out of 15 replies.

On the other hand you might not be able to plan so far ahead, or you may have no luck with written applications, so it will be necessary to look for hotel work once you've arrived in a foreign country. All but the most desperate hoteliers are far more willing to consider a candidate who is standing there in the flesh than one who writes a letter out of the blue. One job-seeker recommends showing up bright and early (about 8am) to impress prospective employers. Perseverance is necessary when you're asking door to door at hotels. One of our contributors was repeatedly rejected by hotels in Amsterdam on the grounds that she was too late in the summer (i.e. August). Her last hope was the Hilton Hotel and she thought she might as well give it a try since it might be her only chance to see the inside of a Hilton. She was amazed when she was hired instantly as a chambermaid. It also might be necessary to return to the same hotel several times if you think there's a glimmer of hope.

> **Kathryn Halliwell described her job hunt in Les Gets in the Haute Savoie of France**
> *I had to ask from hotel to hotel for three days before finding the job, and experienced what I have come to know through experience and others' reports is the normal way to hire a casual worker. The boss told me blankly that he had no work. As I was leaving he said, what sort of work? I told him anything. He said I could come back the next day in case something came up. I did and was told he was out, come again tomorrow. I eventually did get the job and realised he had just been testing my attitude as he had every other employee when they first applied.*

When going door to door, you should start with the biggest hotels and restaurants. Try to get past the receptionist to ask the manager personally. If you are offered a position (either in person or in writing) try to get a signed contract setting out clearly the hours, salary and conditions of work. If this is not possible, you should at least discuss these issues with the boss.

Colm Murphy took a two-year leave of absence from his job in the airline industry of Ireland to work his way around Australia and New Zealand. He describes how it doesn't pay to be a wall flower in this business:

> *You have got to sell yourself. Nobody else is going to get you your first job, only your skills, experience and references and most importantly the first impression you make. The manager or human resources person who interviews you has to have a gut instinct that you will be honest and hardworking. When you get a trial or a job, it is very important to have a good attitude and create that vital first impression with work colleagues, management and, most importantly, the customers.*

One way to get a foothold in a resort is to cultivate the acquaintance of the reps from the big travel firms. Not only will they know of immediate openings, but they can establish your position with local hoteliers who normally know and respect the reps. This is a job-finding ploy which has to be used with care since reps are constantly being asked for favours. You might volunteer to help them, meeting a group or standing in for someone who is ill. Lisa Brophy met a local tour representative in an Austrian ski resort and was soon introduced to a restaurant manager with a staff vacancy.

Only in a handful of cases can agencies and leisure groups place people without any expertise in foreign hotels; however wages in these cases are normally negligible. For example First Choice (1st Floor, London Road, Crawley, W Sussex RH10 2GX; 0870 750 1204; overseas.recruitment@firstchoice.co.uk) send at least 250 summer staff and 750 winter staff to clubhotels and chalets in Austria and France; staff must have EU nationality but need not have relevant experience.

Advantages and Disadvantages

The same complaints crop up again and again among people who have worked in hotels: long and unsociable hours (often 8am-10pm with a few hours off in the afternoon plus lots of weekend work), exploitative wages, inadequate accommodation and food, and unbearably hot working conditions exacerbated by having to wear a nylon uniform. A great deal depends on whether or not you are the type to rough it. The working atmosphere can vary a lot from hotel to hotel. If you are lucky enough to get a job in a small friendly family hotel, you will probably enjoy the work more than if you are just one in a large anonymous group of workers in a sterile and impersonal institution where you have no job security.

It can be very aggravating to be asked to do extra duties beyond the ones specified in your contract. It seems to be a common occurrence, especially in French and German hotels, that the proprietor takes for granted that you will do unpaid overtime, without time off in lieu at a later date. If a contract is being breached in this way, you should try your best to sort it out with the employer. If this fails don't hesitate to go to the appropriate employment authorities to lodge an official complaint. This has far more chance of success if you have a written contract to show the authorities.

Not all hotels are like this and many people emphasise the benefits which they have found in the experience of working in a hotel: excellent camaraderie and team spirit, the opportunity to learn a foreign language, and the ease with which wages can be saved, including the possibility of an end-of-season bonus. Although Kathryn Halliwell was forced to share a windowless room which had an intermittently working light and water streaming down the roof beams into constantly overflowing buckets, she still enjoyed her time working at a hotel in Corsica, simply because of the conviviality of her 'fellow sufferers'. And Carisa Fey found somewhat to her surprise that a stint in a hotel was an asset to her CV: *'The human resources manager of a big company once told me that the greatest advantage in my CV was my job experience in a hotel because it showed that I am flexible and won't drop my pen at 4.30 sharp.'*

Other Catering

Hotels represent just one aspect of the tourist trade, and there are many more interesting venues for cooking and serving, including luxury yachts, prawn trawlers, holiday ranches, safari camps and ski chalets. (For information about working on cruise liners, see chapter *Working a Passage*.) People with some training in catering will find it much easier to work their way around the world than the rest of us. The serious traveller might even consider enrolling in a catering course before embarking on his or her journey. One of the most interesting opportunities spotted recently was with a small UK tour operator who was looking for a cook to work at a wilderness lodge in Northern Mongolia: no wage was to be paid but flights and expenses would be covered (www.4thworldadventure.com).

Of course, there are opportunities for the unskilled. You might find a job cooking hamburgers in a chain such as McDonalds or Burger King, which can be found from Tel Aviv to Toronto. (Bear in mind that the Oxford English Dictionary now includes the coinage 'Mcjob' to refer to any form of dead-end, low-paid employment.) Anyone who is not confident communicating in the language of the country can still hope for employment in a fast food kitchen. Pay is low, hours unreliable or inconvenient and the attitude to discipline more worthy of school children, however it is a good way of earning while you familiarise yourself with a new place. When you are applying for jobs like this, which are not seasonal, you should stress that you intend to work for an indefinite period, make a career of fast food catering, etc. In fact staff turnover is usually very high. This will also aid your case when you are obliged to badger them to give you extra hours.

A good way of gaining initial experience is to get a kitchen job with a large organisation in Britain such as Butlins (now owned by the Bourne Leisure Group; www.bournejobs.co.uk) with family holiday centres in Bognor Regis (01243 820202), Minehead (01643 703331) and Skegness (01754 714445) which offer a variety of jobs, including kitchen, restaurant, administration, entertainment, bar and shop work. Alternatively, consider PGL Adventure (Alton Court, Penyard Lane, Ross-on-Wye, Herefordshire HR9 5NR; 01989 767833; www.pgl.co.uk/people). Since they have so many vacancies (most of which pay only pocket money), the chances of being hired for a first season are reasonably good. PGL also have holiday centres abroad (mostly in France) which are staffed on the same principle.

You may also find catering jobs which have nothing to do with tourism, for example in canteens, on industrial sites, mining camps or army bases. These settings are not among the most congenial in the world, though they often have the advantage of offering more social hours than restaurants. Railway stations and airports have catering divisions which employ casual staff.

OTHER OPPORTUNITIES WITHIN TOURISM

Your average big-spending pampered tourist, so often ridiculed by budget travellers, indirectly provides a great number of employment opportunities. He wants to eat ice cream on the beach or croissants in his ski chalet, so you might be the one there to sell it to him.

He would be most distressed if he got dripped on in his hotel bed, so you may get hired to tar the roof before the season begins. He doesn't want to be pestered by his children, so you spend the day teaching them how to swim or draw at a holiday camp. He is not happy unless he goes home with a genuine sachet of Ardèche lavender or a Texan 10-gallon hat sold to him by a charming souvenir shop assistant, who will be you. He needs to be entertained so you get a job in an amusement arcade, the local disco or windsurfing school. His wife wants to keep up appearances so a freelance hairdresser's services are very welcome. And so it could continue. The point is that casual jobs proliferate in tourist centres.

Of course there are also many opportunities at the budget end of tourism, in travellers' hostels and so on.

Dustie Hickey describes the way she went about getting a job in the Avignon Youth Hostel

I checked out all the hostels in Avignon through the Minitel system. I had help to write a letter in French. Then I telephoned because I did not get a reply. The hostel could not promise me any work till they met me. Before I left the farm in Brittany where I was working, I telephoned again to remind them I was on my way. When I arrived the hostel was very busy. For free B & B, I just had to keep the dormitory clean, but I pitched in and helped with cleaning, laundry, breakfast, etc. The manager was pleased and gave me a little money. At the end of July the paid assistant left so I was given her job, and eventually I had a room to myself.

Many private travellers' hostels worldwide employ long-stay residents to act as PR reps at railway and bus stations, trying to persuade new arrivals to patronise their hostel. A free bed is always given and usually a small fee per successful 'catch'.

Several large Italian companies based on the continent recruit numbers of so-called 'animators', i.e. people to organise and lead the entertainment and sports programmes for adults or children in holiday resorts. For example Time Out Tourist Service places international staff in resorts in Greece, Spain, Tunisia and Egypt. Obviously there is a strong preference for good linguists as well as those with the right personalities. For further information contact the German office of Time Out at Prinzenalle 7, 40549 Dusseldorf (+49 211-523 91 149; www.timeoutourism.com). More are listed in the chapter on Italy.

Pubs and Clubs

Bars and nightclubs should not be omitted from your list of likely employers. Caroline Scott bought the club magazine *Mixmag* in the winter and contacted a number of Ibiza clubs, one of which hired her for the summer season. If you want to look for work after arrival, you might consider carrying a set of 'black and whites' (black trousers/skirt and white shirt) in case you pick up a job as a bartender or waiter. If you have no experience, it can be worthwhile volunteering to work at your local pub before you leave home for a week and then ask for a reference. Once you are abroad, ask at English-style pubs which are found from the Costa del Sol to the Zamalek district of Cairo, from Santa Monica California to Austrian ski resorts and try to exploit the British connection. Irish people are at an even greater advantage since there are Irish bars and pubs around the world from Molly Malone's in Paris to Fibber Magee's in Dubai. In ordinary bars on the Continent you may be expected to be proficient in the prevailing language, although exceptions are made, particularly in the case of glamorous-looking applicants. Women (especially blonde ones) can find jobs from Amsterdam to Hong Kong, but should be sure that they can distinguish between bars and brothels.

Places like the Canaries, Ibiza, Corfu and the Caribbean islands are bursting at the seams with 'nite spots' of one kind or another. Not only is there a high turn-over of staff but there is a rapid turn-over of clubs too, and you may not have much job security. As long as you investigate the establishments in the place you want to work before accepting a job, you should not encounter too many unpleasant surprises. Handing out promotional leaflets for bars and discos is a job which travellers frequently do, especially in Spain.

The idea that Britons know their way round the music scene better than other nationalities is fairly widespread, and anyone who knows how to use a turntable might get occasional work, not only in the obvious resorts but in farflung places like Bangkok (as Laurence Koe did). Experienced DJs who want to work abroad should request details from a specialist agency like Juliana's Leisure Services (15-17 Broadway, West Ealing, London W13 9DA; 020-8567 6765; www.julianas.com) which offers wages of £800-£1,000 per month for working in Europe, the Middle East or Far East (Juliana's has offices in Dubai and Hong Kong). They supply entertainment packages to 5-star hotels and other clients. The show business newspaper *The Stage* published every week sometimes carries adverts for dancers both respectable and otherwise for resorts abroad as well as in the UK.

Of course it is not necessary to go through an international agency to fix up a casual job as an entertainer in a club or restaurant. Carisa Fey was surviving in Mexico on a modest travel budget when she met the owner of an exclusive restaurant in Puerto Vallarta:

I could only afford the great margaritas not the food. I ended up first translating the menu into German and then singing in the restaurant. I got my food free (lobster and the like) and he always kept bringing me good wine and margaritas through the entire evening, plus tips from the guests up to €40 a night. And he invited me on a deep sea fishing expedition with his son and his teacher – a dream – I stayed there for a week, swimming in their pool, singing at night....

Special Events

Great bursts of tourist activity take place around major events. For example armies of volunteers will be needed for the World Cup in Germany in 2006. They will have to have a good command of German, basic knowledge of English, be 18 by the 1st of June 2006 and preferably have experience in sport or volunteering. Applications will be accepted via http://fifaworldcup.yahoo.com/06/en/o/volunteers/vbp.html over the summer of 2005 and again in January/February 2006. Sometimes recruitment for major events is contracted out to agencies, such as happened for the Sydney Olympics at which the Adecco Agency handled all hiring. No wage is paid and perks are few in many of these world events since the organisers know that there will be no shortage of eager participants.

On a smaller scale, annual arts festivals and sporting events, trade fairs and World Fairs are all useful providers of casual employment possibilities, both during and before or after when facilities are set up and then dismantled. It is not possible for an event such as Oktoberfest in Munich (held every year in late September) to host over 6 million visitors without a great deal of extra labour being enlisted to prepare the 560,000 barbecued chickens, 346,000 pairs of sausages and to dispense the 1,000,000 gallons of beer consumed. One source of information about when special events take place is the website www.whatsonwhen.com. Enterprising mechanics might consider taking their tools and some spare parts and setting up in the car park to fix and adjust the thousands of travel-weary vans and cars which assemble there. The main problem is finding affordable accommodation.

TOUR OPERATORS

Acting as a tour guide, rep or courier for a tour operator is one way of combining work with travel. Two-month jobs are rare in this field since in most cases employers want staff who will stay at least for the whole summer season April to October inclusive. The peak recruitment time is the preceding autumn, though strong candidates can be interviewed much later. Knowledge of a European language is always requested, though it is unusual for reps in Greece or Portugal to speak those languages. Debbie Harrison was taken aback at the ease with which she got a season's work as a rep in Greece without relevant experience or qualifications (see *Greece* chapter). Personality and maturity seem to be what count most and a commitment to the company, and possibly also to tourism as a career. By all accounts interviews can be fairly gruelling as they try to weed out the candidates who will crack under the pressure of holidaymakers' complaints and problems. It is estimated that only one in forty applicants gets a job, though sometimes your odds are much better than this.

Considering the rigours and pressures of the job of package tour company representative, wages are low, though of course accommodation is provided. Often wages (from £70 a week) are paid into a bank account at home. Employers usually expect their reps to supplement meagre wages by accepting commissions from restaurants, shops, car hire firms, etc. If this concept is unappealing, you can shop around to find companies that do not promote this idea (e.g. Open Holidays; personnel@openholidays.co.uk).

A qualification in childcare is highly marketable in this sphere since more and more tour operators are attempting to woo families. A specialist training and recruitment agency places qualified and/or experienced nannies with British tour operators on the Mediterranean or in the Alps; details from Nannies Abroad Ltd (Abbots Worthy House, Abbots Worthy, Winchester SO21 1DR; 01962 882299; enquiries@nanniesabroad.com).

In the first instance, search the internet or pick up a range of brochures from your local travel agent and see which tour operator's style suits you. Most big companies devote some of their web pages to recruitment, some with online application facilities. Alternatively you can send a large s.a.e. to the head office requesting their recruitment procedures. Here are some of the biggest UK tour operators:

Airtours, Holiday House, Sandbrook Park, Sandbrook Way, Rochdale, Lancs. OL11 5SA (24-hour Recruitment hotline 0870 241 2642; www.mytravelcareers.co.uk). Trading name of MyTravel Tour Operations, along with other tour operators Direct Holidays, Panorama and Manos Holidays. Hire customer services reps, children's reps 18-30s reps and many other kinds of staff between March and October in wide range of European resorts.

Club Med, International Recruitment, 11-12 place Jules Ferry, 69458 Lyon Cedex 06, France; recruit.uk@clubmed.com; 08453 676767 in the UK; www.clubmed-jobs. com). Range of staff (who must be able to speak French) to work as GO's *(Gentils Organisateurs)* for their upmarket holiday villages in Europe and North Africa. As well as general hotel and catering staff, they require sports instructors, children's reps, hostesses, shop staff and tour guides. North American applicants can apply online at www.clubmedjobs.com.

Cosmos, Wren Court, 17 London Road, Bromley, Kent BR1 1DE (020-8695 4724; www. cosmos-holidays.co.uk). 200 holiday consultants, 60 children's reps, admin staff, etc.

First Choice Summer Sun, 1st Floor, London Road, Crawley, W Sussex RH10 2GX (0870 750 1204; overseas.recruitment@firstchoice.co.uk; www.firstchoice4jobs.com). Hundreds of reps (resort, transfer, children's) needed for scores of hotels and chalets in alpine resorts winter and summer (mainly France and Austria).

Mark Warner Ltd, Resorts Recruitment Department, 61/65 Kensington Church St, London W8 4BA; 0870 033 0750; www.markwarner-recruitment.co.uk). Runs beachclub hotels in Corsica, Italy, Sardinia, Greece and Turkey for which it hires club managers, receptionists, chefs, bar and waiting staff, watersports and tennis instructors, pool attendants, laundry staff, handymen, drivers, gardeners and night watchmen (but not couriers or resort representatives). Childcare staff should contact separate department on 0870 033 0760. All staff must be over 19 and available from mid-April to mid-November, though there is a continuous need for replacements throughout the season. The wages run from £50-£250 per week; benefits include use of watersports facilities, travel, medical insurance and the potential for winter work at their ski chalet hotels in Europe.

Thomas Cook Tour Operations Ltd, Business Park, Units 13-14, Coningsby Road, Peterboroguh PE3 8SB (0870 607 0309; overseas.jobs@thomascook.com; www. thomascookjobs.com).Thomas Cook group includes Club 18-30 Holidays and Neilson. Hire large numbers of beach villa reps, creche reps, resort reps and transfer reps.

Thomson Holidays Ltd, Human Resources Overseas, Greater London House, Hampstead Road, London NW1 7SD (fax 020-7387 8733; overseas_careers@thomson.co.uk. Send s.a.e. for large-format leaflet about recruitment or check the requirements online; then email, fax or post your CV. Thomson is part of the World of TUI conglomerate which also hires staff via the Specialist Holidays Group (www.shgjobs.co.uk). As is the case with most of the major companies, Thomson employ reps, children's reps (minimum age 18) and entertainment reps for the summer season (June to mid-September). All the usual qualities required: flexibility, diplomacy, etc. A knowledge of French, Spanish, Italian, Greek, Portuguese or German would be an advantage.

A number of travellers who have done some casual hotel work abroad go on to take up jobs as reps with British tour companies. On her return from her extensive travels and numerous casual jobs en route, Xuela Edwards applied for various rep jobs in February:

> *They all told me that September is the best time to apply. But I managed to get a few interviews on the strength of my work abroad and ended up being sent to the Greek island of Paxos. I loved Paxos but I found I was too restless and used to independent travel to settle for seven months.*

Camping tour operators employ thousands of site representatives (see next section).

Different kinds of holiday company look for different kinds of staff. Drivers and cooks are needed to work for youth operator Top Deck Travel (2nd Floor, William House, 14 Worple Road, Wimbledon, SW19 4DD; fax 020-8944 9474; www.topdecktravel.co.uk). Prospective crew must be over 23 and willing to sign up for a six-week training trip in April at a cost of £350. Jayne Nash described her season with Top Deck as 'an amazing if exhausting experience': *'It enabled me to visit nearly every part of Europe, get involved in some really exciting events and meet some wonderful people, namely the South Africans (non-whites I might add) whom I later went to visit.'*

Bear in mind that the training bond of £200-400 charged by some companies is non-refundable and is no guarantee that you will be considered suitable. Driving positions normally require a European or international coach licence or at the very least a Passenger Carrying Vehicle (PCV) licence which takes about six weeks to obtain and costs at least £1,000. The Driving Standards Agency can offer advice on training (www.dsa.gov.uk). Note that unemployed people may be able to train and obtain a PCV licence through the New Deal Scheme; enquire at your local Jobcentre Plus.

Working in Africa, Asia and Latin America as an adventure tour leader is discussed in the chapter *Working a Passage: Overland Tours.* A list of special interest and activity tour operators (to whom people with specialist skills can apply) is available from AITO, the Association of Independent Tour Operators (33A St Margaret's Road, Twickenham TW1 1RG; www.aito.co.uk). In the US, consult the *Specialty Travel Index* (305 San Anselmo Ave, San Anselmo, CA 94960; www.specialtytravel.com); the directory is issued twice a year at a cost of $10 in the US, $22 abroad. Another useful directory of adventure holiday operators can be seen at www.wild-dog.com.

A number of companies specialise in tours for school children, both British and American. For example the London office of the American Council for International Studies (AIFS UK, 38 Queen's Gate, London SW7 5HR; 020-7590 7474; tmdepartment@acis.com) is looking for 100 clever linguists to become tour managers to lead groups of American high school students around Europe. Casterbridge Tours (Salcombe House, Long St, Sherborne, Dorset DT9 3BU; 01935 810810; tourops@casterbridge-tours.co.uk) employ guides to escort groups between March and June. Successful applicants must attend one of their weekend training courses for tour guides in the winter. Another major student group tour operator that takes on group leaders and couriers is Halsbury Travel Ltd. (35 Churchill Park, Colwick Business Estate, Nottingham NG4 2HF; 0115 940 4303; www.halsbury.com).

Contiki Holidays (Wells House, 15 Elmfield Road, Bromley, Kent BR1 1LS; 020-8290 6777 or 020-8225 4245; www.contiki.com) specialise in coach tours for clients aged 18-

35 and hire EU nationals as tour managers and coach drivers. Applications can be made online by candidates with independent travel experience who are able to join a 46-day European training programme. Two other youth-oriented European tour operators are Busabout (258 Vauxhall Bridge Rd, London SW1V 1BS; 020-7950 1661) which posts full recruitment information on its website (www.busabout.com) and Tracks Travel (The Flots, Brookland, Romney Marsh, Kent TN29 9TG; 01797 344164; www.tracks-travel. com) which advertise for road crew year round.

You need not confine your aspirations to Europe. While travelling in South-East Asia or South America several contributors have been invited to shepherd tourists around (e.g. the island resorts of Thailand and Venezuela) by a ground handling tour agency. You would have to be on hand to find out about this sort of opportunity. You can even set yourself up in business as a guide or courier, as Jennifer McKibben noticed long-stay travellers doing in East Africa.

Campsite Couriers

A different kind of courier is needed by the large camping holiday operators. British camping holiday firms (addresses below) hire large numbers of people to remain on one campsite on the Continent for several months. The Holidaybreak Group (Eurocamp, Keycamp) alone recruits up to 2,000 campsite couriers and children's couriers. The courier's job is to clean the tents and caravans between visitors, greet clients and deal with difficulties (particularly illness or car breakdowns) and introduce clients to the attractions of the area or even arrange and host social functions and amuse the children. All of this will be rewarded with on average £90-£114 a week in addition to free tent accommodation. Many companies offer half-season contracts April to mid-July and mid-July to the end of September. Setting up and dismantling the campsites in March/April and September (known as *montage* and *démontage*) is often done by a separate team (sometimes called 'squaddies'). The work is hard but the language requirements are nil.

Some camping holiday and tour operators based in Britain are as follows (with the European countries in which they are active):

Canvas Holidays, East Port House, 12 East Port, Dunfermline, Fife KY12 7JG (01383 629018; www.canvasholidays.com). Mainly France but also Germany, Austria, Switzerland, Italy, Luxembourg, Netherlands and Spain.

Club Cantabrica Holidays Ltd, 146/148 London Road, St. Albans, Herts. AL1 1PQ (01727 866177; www.cantabrica.co.uk). France, Austria, Greece (Corfu), Italy and Spain (including Majorca).

Eurocamp, Overseas Recruitment Department (Ref WW) - 01606 787525; www. holidaybreakjobs.com. Operate 200 campsites in most European countries. Applications accepted from October. Interviews held in Hartford, Cheshire over the winter. Also trade under Holidaybreak, Hartford Manor, Greenbank Lane, Northwich, Cheshire CW8 1HW (same telephone number).

Haven Europe, Overseas Recruitment Team, 1 Park Lane, Hemel Hempstead, Herts. HP2 4YL (01442 203970; www.haveneurope.com). Courier and children's courier staff for France, Spain and Italy.

Holidaybreak, see Eurocamp.

Keycamp Holidays, Overseas Recruitment Department, Hartford Manor, Greenbank Lane, Northwich, CV8 1HW (01606 787525; e-mail overseas-recruit@holidaybreak.co.uk). France, Italy, Spain, Germany.

Solaire Holidays, 1158 Stratford Road, Hall Green, Birmingham B28 8AF (0121-778 5061; jobs@solaire.co.uk; www.solaire.co.uk). France, Spain.

Be warned that an offer of a job may be more tentative than it seems, as Karen Martin describes: *'Before we left in May, we had both been interviewed for the job of campsite courier. We got the jobs and signed the contracts, and our rough start date was the 7th of July. They did not make the position clear that an offer 'subject to terms and conditions' means that it is possible that a week before the start date you can be told that there is no longer a job due to lack of customers, which is what happened to us. We really felt let*

THE KEY TO A SUMMER IN EUROPE... AND A CAREER IN LEISURE

If you are interested in working overseas but would like the security of being employed by an established UK-based Tour Operator, contact us today!

We are recruiting for vacancies in the following areas:

General Assistants	Mature Couples
Customer Service	Site Preparation*
Team Leaders	Site Closing*
Administration	Trainers
Children's Club*	Mature Singles

*Successful applicants will be asked to apply for a Standard or Enhanced Disclosure.

We will provide you with:

- RETURN TRAVEL
- UNIFORM
- FULL TRAINING
- ACCOMMODATION
- COMPETATIVE SALARY
- SUBSIDISED INSURANCE

To apply for one of these positions you will need to be:
- 18 or over, there's no upper age limit!
- Fit and healthy
- An EU passport holder
- Available to start work between March and May, contracts available until Mid July or September/October

If you think you have the qualities to provide our customers with the 'perfect family holiday' apply now!

Apply on-line at www.holidaybreakjobs.com or phone 01606 787525 for an application pack, quoting WW/05

*Further information about Disclosures can be found at www.disclosure.gov.uk or by phoning 0870 90 90 811 *down.'*

Successful couriers make the job look easy, but it does demand a lot of hard work and patience. Occasionally it is very hard to keep up the happy, smiling, never-ruffled courier look, but most seem to end up enjoying the job. Alison Cooper described her job with Eurocamp on a site in Corsica as immensely enjoyable, though it was not as easy as the clients thought:

> *Living on a campsite in high season had one or two drawbacks: the toilets and showers were dirty, with constant queues, the water was freezing cold, the campsite was very very noisy and if you're unfortunate enough to have your tent in sunlight, it turns into a tropical greenhouse. Of course we did get difficult customers who complained for a variety of reasons: they wanted to be nearer to the beach, off the main road, in a cooler tent with more grass around it, etc. etc. But mostly our customers were friendly and we soon discovered that the friendlier we were to them, the cleaner they left their tents.*
>
> *I found it difficult at first to get used to living, eating, working and socialising with the other two couriers 24 hours a day. But we all got on quite well and had a good time, unlike at a neighbouring campsite where the couriers hated each other. Our campsite had a swimming pool and direct beach access, though nightlife was limited. The one disco did get very repetitive.*

Despite all this, she sums up by highly recommending that others who have never travelled or worked abroad work for a company like Eurocamp which provides accommodation, a guaranteed weekly wage and the chance to work with like-minded people.

Caroline Nicholls' problems at a campsite in Brittany included frequent power failures, blocked loos and leaking tents: *'Every time there was a steady downpour, one of the tents developed an indoor lake, due to the unfortunate angle at which we had pitched it. I would appear, mop in hand, with cries of 'I don't understand. This has never happened before.' Working as a courier would be a good grounding for an acting career.'*

She goes on to say that despite enjoying the company of the client families, she was glad to have the use of a company bicycle to escape the insular life on the campsite every so often. Some companies guarantee one day off-site which is considered essential for maintaining sanity. The companies do vary in the conditions of work and some offer much better support than others. For example a company for which Hannah Start worked ignored her pleas for advice and assistance when one of her clients had appendicitis.

The big companies advertise in the travel supplements of the weekend papers and many are listed in the *Directory of Summer Jobs Abroad* which is published every November. They interview hundreds of candidates and have filled many posts by the end of January. But there is a very high dropout rate (over 50%) and vacancies are filled from a reserve list, so it is worth ringing around the companies as late as April for cancellations. Despite keen competition, anyone who has studied a European language and has an outgoing personality stands a good chance if he or she applies early and widely enough.

Activity Holidays

Many specialist tour companies employ leaders for their clients (children and/or adults) who want a walking, cycling, watersports holiday, etc. Companies that operate in only one country are included in the country chapters.

Acorn Adventure Ltd, 22 Worcester St, Stourbridge, W. Midlands DY8 1AN (01384 446057; www.acorn-jobs.co.uk; alternative contact 0121-504 2066; chris.lloyd@acornadventure.co.uk). Require 300 seasonal staff including catering, maintenance and admin as well as qualified canoeing, climbing, hillwalking, kayaking, sailing and windsurfing instructors to work in centres in the UK, France (Ardèche), Italy and Spain.

King's Camps, The Manor House, Ecclesall Road South, Sheffield S11 9PS (0870 345 0782; www.kingssportscamps.com/kscjobs). Recruit children's activity couriers on behalf of Eurocamps and Keycamp.

PGL Travel, Alton Court, Penyard Lane (874), Ross-on-Wye, Herefordshire HR9 5GL (01989 767833; pglpeople@pgl.co.uk; www.pgl.co.uk/people). Recruit for about 2,500 seasonal vacancies at their holiday centres throughout Britain plus France and Spain. They publish on their website and in a brochure their requirements for activity instructors, group leaders, catering and support staff. The norm is to pay pocket money of £50-£85 per week and to provide training opportunities and a fun lifestyle.

Ramblers' Holidays Ltd, PO Box 43, Welwyn Garden City, Herts. AL8 6PQ (01707 331133/ fax 01707 333276; mandy@ramblersholidays.co.uk). Tour leaders for programme of walking holidays worldwide. From £500 per month. Must hold walking qualifications (EML, ML or BHLC), First Aid Certificate and have language skills (Portuguese, Italian or Greek).

Sunsail International, The Port House, Port Solent, Portsmouth, Hants. PO6 4TH (02392 334600; hr@sunsail.com). Employs about 1,000 staff for their flotilla and bareboat sailing holidays and watersports hotels in the Mediterranean, especially Greece and Turkey. From March to October, positions are available as flotilla skippers, hostesses, diesel engineers, qualified dinghy, yacht and windsurfing instructors, receptionists, chefs, bar staff and qualified nannies. Wages vary from £200 to £800 a month plus food and accommodation and return flights on completion of contract. A knowledge of French or (especially) German is an advantage.

Tall Stories, Brassey House, New Zealand Ave, Walton-on-Thames, Surrey KT12 1QD (01932 252002; www.tallstories.co.uk/jobs.shtm). Adventure sports holidays in Austria, France, Spain, Corsica and Mallorca for adults and some families with teenagers. Resort hosts are employed from mid-May or mid-June to mid-September and are expected to join in the activities like paragliding, rafting and mountain biking.

Village Camps, Recruitment Office, Dept. 811, 14 rue de la Morache, 1260 Nyon, Switzerland (+41 22 990 9405; fax 22 990 9494; personnel@villagecamps.ch). Qualified and experienced staff needed to join international teams at spring, summer and autumn residential and day camps in Switzerland, Austria, Holland, France and England. Vacancies for activity specialists, facilities staff, language teachers and nurses. Room and board, accident/liability insurance and an expense allowance from €175 a week are provided. Staff must be at least 21 to apply. Visit www.villagecamps. com/personnel for application details.

Any competent sailor, canoeist, diver, climber, rider, etc. should have no difficulty marketing their skills abroad. If you would like to do a watersports course with a view to working abroad, you might be interested in one of the myriad instructors' courses offered by Flying Fish (25 Union Road, Cowes, Isle of Wight PO31 7TW; 0870 250 2500; www. flyingfishonline.com). They offer training as instructors in windsurfing, diving, dinghy sailing and yachting. A typical six-week sailing instructor course in Greece will cost about £5,500 all-inclusive though shorter courses, including some preliminary training in Poole England, are cheaper. The website allows access to water sport job vacancies around the world.

Diving resorts around the world from the Red Sea to the Great Barrier Reef are staffed by people who started out as recreational divers with the basic PADI (Professional Association of Diving Instructors) Open Water Diver qualification. The PADI website (www.padi. com) has an Employment Bulletin Board for paid-up PADI professionals, divided according to region of the world (USA, Asia/Pacific, Europe and so on). Dive centres in exotic locations around the world accept trainee divers willing to work in exchange for living expenses and dive training. To take two examples, Hurricane Divers in Playa Santa Cruz (Oaxaca, Mexico; www.hurricanedivers.com) operate a three-month work experience programme for anyone over 18 who is willing to spend long hours taking bookings, filling tanks and cleaning toilets. In Thailand PJ Scuba is allied to an internship programme called Learn in Asia Dive Internships Co. Ltd. (Mermaids Group, 75/124 Moo 12, Jomtien Beach Road Nongprue, Banglamung, Chonburi 20260; www.learn-in-asia.com).

WINTER RESORTS

Ski resort work is by no means confined to the Alps. Skiing centres can be found in Finnish Lapland and Argentine Patagonia, from the dormant volcanoes of North America to the active ones of New Zealand. If you are such an avid skier that it always depresses you to see the winter snows melt from the European Alps in April, you should consider going to seek work in the Australian and New Zealand Alps or the Chilean Andes, where the ski season lasts from late June until early October. And there are many ski resorts in North America, in addition to the most famous ones such as Banff in the Canadian Rockies, or Aspen in Colorado.

Winter tourism offers some variations on the usual theme of hotels and catering. Staff are needed to operate the ski tows and lifts, to be in charge of chalets, to patrol the slopes, to file, wax and mend hired skis, to groom and shovel snow, and of course to instruct would-be skiers. The season in the European Alps lasts from about Christmas until late April/early May. Between Christmas and the New Year is a terrifically busy time as is the middle two weeks of February during half-term. If you are lucky you might get a kitchen or dining room job in an establishment which does not serve lunch (since all the guests are out on the slopes). This means that you might have up to six hours free in the middle of the day for skiing, though three to four hours is more usual. However the hours in some large ski resort hotels are the same as in any hotel, i.e. eight to ten hours split up inconveniently throughout the day, and you should be prepared to have only one day off per week for skiing. Because jobs in ski resorts are so popular among the travelling community, wages can be low, though you should get the statutory minimum in Switzerland. Many employees are (or become) avid skiers and in their view it is recompense enough to have easy access to the slopes during their time off.

Either you can try to fix up a job with a British-based ski tour company before you leave (which has more security but lower wages and tends to isolate you in an English-speaking ghetto), or you can look for work on the spot.

Ski Holiday Companies

In the spring preceding the winter season in which you want to work, contact as many ski tour companies as possible including those listed below to request an application form. Increasingly recruitment takes place online and the websites of most major ski tour operators feature a 'Recruitment' icon. The range of positions and conditions of service are usually described in detail. These may vary slightly from company to company but most companies are looking for resort representatives (who will need language skills), chalet staff (described below), cleaners, qualified cooks, odd jobbers and ski guides/instructors. An increasing number of companies are offering nanny and creche facilities, so this is a further possibility for women and men with a childcare background. A certain number of staff have been hired by mid-June, though there are always vacancies until the beginning of the season and during it as well.

Specialist ski recruitment websites can be extremely helpful. The superb Natives.co.uk posts current vacancies on behalf of a selection of the major operators and also includes detailed resort descriptions and links to seasonal workers' email addresses. Try also Season Workers (www.seasonworkers.com), Free Radicals (www.freeradicals.co.uk) and findaskijob.com part of www.voovs.com which describe themselves as one-stop shops for recruitment of winter staff for Europe and North America. The smaller Ski Staff (www. skistaff.co.uk) specialises in placing staff with British ski tour operators in France.

Another way of fixing up a job in advance is to go through the agency Jobs in the Alps (17 High St, Gretton, Northants. NN17 3DE; info@jobs-in-the-alps.co.uk). They recruit about 250 staff for various positions in winter resorts especially in Switzerland, for which good German or French is usually required. You must arrange to be interviewed by the end of September and be prepared to sign a contract for the whole season, four months in the winter December-April. Wages are about £500 a month net for a five-day week. Under the name Alpotels, the agency carries out aptitude tests on behalf of German and French hotels for the winter season; candidates must have EU nationality.

The fifth edition of *Working in Ski Resorts* (Vacation Work, £11.95) contains many addresses of ski companies and details of the job hunt in individual European and North American resorts. In response to the thousands of enquiries about alpine jobs which the Ski Club of Great Britain receives, it distributes *The Alpine Employment Fact Sheet*; send £3 and an s.a.e. to the Ski Club GB, 57-63 Church Rd, Wimbledon SW19 5SB; 020-8410 2000; www.skiclub.co.uk). The Club also takes on intermediate skiers over the age of 22 with extensive experience of on- and off-piste skiing to work as ski reps in 43 European and North American resorts. Ski reps work for between one and three months after doing a two-week training course in Tignes in December (which costs £1,000 including airfares).

Here are some of the major UK companies. Some have a limited number of vacancies which they can fill from a list of people who have worked for them during the summer season or have been personally recommended by former employees, so you should not be too disappointed if you are initially unsuccessful.

Inghams Travel & Bladon Lines, 10-18 Putney Hill, London SW15 6AX (020-8780 4400 or 020-8780 8803; www.inghams.co.uk/general_pages/job.html). 450 winter staff including reps, chalet staff, hostess/cleaners, *plongeurs* and maintenance staff for chalets and club hotels in France, Italy, Austria, Switzerland and Finnish Lapland. Perks include free ski pass, ski and boot hire, meals, accommodation and return travel from the UK.

Crystal Holidays, King's Place, Wood St, Kingston-upon-Thames W4 5RT (020-7420 2081; www.shgjobs.co.uk). Part of Thomson Travel Group. 2,000 overseas staff in more than 100 ski resorts in Europe and North America (visa required). Resort reps, chalet staff and qualified nannies for France, Austria and Italy.

Esprit Holidays Ltd, 185 Fleet Road, Fleet, Hants. GU51 3BL (01252 618318; recruitment@esprit-holidays.co.uk). Vacancies for resort managers, hotel managers, chalet controllers, resort reps, chalet chefs and host/cooks, chalet and hotel assistants, nannies and snow rangers to work in resorts in France, Austria and Italy.

First Choice/Skibound, 1st Floor, London Road, Crawley, W Sussex RH10 2GX (0870 750 1204; overseas.recruitment@firstchoice.co.uk). 750 winter staff from EU employed in France, Italy, Austria, etc.

NBV Leisure Ltd., PO Box 371, Bromley BR1 2ZJ (0870 220 2148; www.nbvleisure.com/ recruitment.html). Catered chalet holidays in France and ski holidays in Austria.

Neilson Overseas, HR Department, Locksview, Brighton Marina, Brighton BN2 5HA (0870 241 2901; skijobs@neilson.com; www.neilson.co.uk/recruitment). Part of Thomas Cook Group. Resorts in Andorra, Austria, Bulgaria, Canada, France and Italy among others.

PGL Travel Ltd, Ski Department, Alton Court, Penyard Lane, Ross-on-Wye, Herefordshire HR9 5GL (01989 767311; skipersonnel@pgl.co.uk). School group operator with rep and snowboard instructor vacancies for 1-3 weeks during peak school holidays especially February half-term. Reps must be reasonable skiers with knowledge of French, Italian or German.

Powder Byrne, 250 Upper Richmond Road, London SW15 6TG (020-8246 5342; www. powderbyrne.com). Upmarket company operating in Switzerland, France, Austria. Compulsory 1-week training course in Switzerland for full-season staff. Also recruit staff for summer resorts programme in France, Cyprus, Italy, Portugal, Mallorca, Tunisia, Mauritius and Dubai.

Simply Ski, Kings House, 12-42 Wood St, Kingston upon Thames W4 5RT (0870 888 0028; www.shgjobs.co.uk). Part of TUI group. Chalet and other staff needed in Austria, France and Switzerland.

Skiworld, 3 Vencourt Place, London W6 9NU (0870 420 5914; recruitment@skiworld. ltd.uk; www.skiworld.ltd.uk). Catered chalet and hotel holidays in France, Austria, Switzerland, Canada and the USA.

Total Holidays, 185 Fleet Road, Fleet, Hampshire. GU51 3BL (01252 618 309;

recruitment@skitotal.com). Vacancies as above for Esprit Holidays in resorts in France, Austria, Italy, Switzerland and Canada.

You can find other ski company addresses by consulting ski guide books, magazines and travel agents. Another good idea is to attend the *Daily Mail* Ski Show held each October at Olympia in London where some ski companies hand out job descriptions and applications.

Rhona Stannage, a Scottish solicitor, and her husband Stuart applied to all the companies they could find addresses for and finally succeeded with Skibound (now part of First Choice):

Only one company gave us an interview. No one else would touch us because we were too old (i.e. 28), married and had no experience in the catering trade. The company gave us both jobs as chalet girls (yes, Stuart signed a 'chalet girl' contract) working in a four-person chalet with a manageress and a qualified chef. The wages were dire (as expected) but we got free ski passes, accommodation in our own apartment and food. Stuart was a bit worried about the uniform but it was only a purple T-shirt.

The wages paid by most tour operators are indeed dire, typically just £65-£75 a week plus bed, board and a ski pass. One of the excuses given for the low pay is that staff can supplement their wages with tips, something that made Susan Beney and her husband uncomfortable when they worked for Le Ski:

We did make good tips which became our spending money, so no tips, no treats. Being Aussies (with joint UK nationality), it goes against the grain to expect tips. And then you find yourself judging guests by how much they tip you – horrible way to be. We worked long hours six days a week, and were probably a bit too conscientious due to our age (we have just become grandparents). It's still a good way to experience a season in the Alps, but just be prepared to be overworked and underpaid. Listen to the young folk who have got the work down to a fine art and really know how to cut corners since they are there to ski and socialise.

Applying on the Spot

The best time to look is at the end of the preceding winter season though this has the disadvantage of committing you a long way in advance. The next best time is the first fortnight in September when the summer season is finishing and there are still plenty of foreign workers around who will have helpful advice. The final possibility is to turn up in the month before the season begins when you will be faced with many refusals. In November you will be told you're too early because everything's closed, in December you're too late because all the jobs are spoken for. Some disappointed job-seekers reckon there must be a 24-hour window between these two, and if you miss it, you're out of luck.

Assuming you can afford to finance yourself for several weeks, arrive as early as you can (say early November) so that you can get to know people and let them get to know your face. Weekends are better than weekdays since more shops and other tourist establishments will be open. Apply directly to hotels, equipment rental agencies, tourist offices, etc. It is also an idea to travel to the ski resorts out of season to look for work repairing or redecorating ski chalets, for instance, and then move on to a ski tow or bar job once the season begins. If you miss out on landing a job before the season, it could be worth trying again in early January, since workers tend to disappear after the holidays.

Every negative experience (see chapter on Switzerland for example) is counter-balanced by others like Mary Jelliffe's account of opportunities in the French resort of Méribel
At the beginning of the season there were many 'ski bums' looking for work in Méribel. Many found something. People earned money by clearing snow, clean-

ing, babysitting, etc. for which they were paid about £3 an hour. You do need some money to support yourself while looking for work but if you are determined enough, I'm sure you'll get something eventually. One group of ski bums organised a weekly slalom race from which they were able to make a living. Another set up a video service; another made and sold boxer shorts for £10 a pair.

Andy Winwood asked in over 200 places in Crans Montana, Verbier and Haute-Nendaz and came up with 10 or 12 possibilities. When he finally heard the magic words, 'You can start on December 15th', he rushed outside, let out a whoop of delight and headed for the nearest bar.

Chalet Staff

The number of chalets in the Alps has hugely increased over the past decade with the biggest areas of expansion being Méribel, Courchevel and Val d'Isère in France, Verbier in Switzerland and St Anton in Austria. Chalet clients in chalets are looked after by a chalet girl or (increasingly) chalet boy. The chalet host does everything (sometimes with an assistant) from cooking first-class meals for the ten or so guests to clearing the snow from the footpath (or delegating that job). She is responsible for keeping the chalet clean, preparing breakfast, packed lunches, tea and dinner, providing ice and advice, and generally keeping everybody happy. Fifteen-hour days are standard.

Although this sounds an impossible regimen, many chalet girls manage to fit in several hours of skiing in the middle of each day. The standards of cookery skills required vary from company to company depending on the degree of luxury (i.e. the price) of the holidays. Whereas some advertise good home cooking, others offer cordon bleu cookery every night of the week (except the one night which the chalet girl has off). In most cases, you will have to cook a trial meal for the tour company before being accepted for the job or at least submit detailed menu plans.

James Nibloe worked as a chalet host for Thomson Ski and Snowboard in Zell-am-See in Austria in 2003. As a trainee chef with a large hotel group, James was always going to be a strong contender and describes the whirlwind nature of his appointment. Using this book as a starting point he contacted several ski companies and favoured Thomson since they allow their cooks more flexibility with menus, etc.: *'We had to attend an assessment day for which we had to take with us a cake we had made. We were given basic literacy and numeracy tests and a kind of theoretical 'Ready Steady Cook' test. The best cake makers were summoned for interview and five days later I was told I had a job. Two days after that I was in Austria for the ten-day induction which took place in Ellmau.'*

Average pay starts at about £75 a week, plus perks. Obviously your accommodation and food are free. Also you should get a season's ticket to the slopes and lifts (called an *abonnement* and worth several hundred pounds), free ski hire and free travel from the UK. Recruitment of the 1,000+ chalet staff needed in Europe gets underway in May so early application is essential.

Ski Instructors

To become a fully-fledged ski instructor, qualified to work in foreign ski schools, costs a great deal of money (at least £2,000) and then competition is extremely stiff for jobs in recognised alpine ski schools. In France and to a lesser extent Italy there has been a great deal of resistance to foreign instructors, though banning them from the slopes has repeatedly been ruled illegal by the EU. Freelance or 'black' instructors – those who tout in bars offering a few hours of instruction in return for pocket money – are persecuted by the authorities in most alpine resorts. The main legitimate opportunities for British skiers without paper qualifications are as instructors for school parties or as ski guides/ski rangers.

If you are interested in qualifying as an instructor, contact the British Association of Snowsport Instructors or BASI (Glenmore, Aviemore, Inverness-shire PH22 1QU; 01479 861717; www.basi.org.uk). BASI runs training and grading courses throughout the year and also publishes a Newsletter in which job adverts appear. The most junior instructor's qualification is a Grade III which is awarded by BASI after a five-day foundation course following a two-week training course on the Continent or in Scotland. Courses take place throughout the season and also on the glacier in the summer. BASI also run courses in five disciplines: alpine skiing, snowboarding (which is gaining enormous popularity), Telemark, Nordic and Adaptive. Most instructors teach from two to six hours a day depending on demand. Pay can start from as little as £150 a week, though this often includes accommodation. Some participation in the evening entertainment programme is expected. It is of course much easier for Ski Teachers (Grade II) and National Ski Teachers (Grade I) to find lucrative work in Europe or beyond.

Several private firms have introduced snowsport instructors' courses abroad, particularly targeting the gap year market, though be warned that these are very expensive (for example £3,300-£6,000 for a 12-week course). Among the main players are the International Academy (St Hilary Court, Copthorne Way, Culverhouse Cross, Cardiff CF5 6ES; 02920 672500; www.theinternationalacademy.com) which offers instructor training in skiing and snowboarding in North American resorts plus one in Chile and another in New Zealand; Peak Leaders (Mansfield, Strathmiglo, Fife KY14 7QE; 01337 860755; www.peakleaders.com) which runs programmes in Canada, Argentina and New Zealand; and Base Camp Group (Howick, Balls Cross, Petworth, West Sussex GU28 9JY; 01403 820899; www.basecampgroup.com) whose instructor programmes are run in France, Switzerland and Canada.

Ski Resorts Worldwide

In conclusion, ski resorts create an enormous number of jobs from au pairing to cooking, guiding, selling, cleaning and so on. If you do end up in a resort looking for a job, try the ski equipment hire shops which may offer very short term work on change-over days when lots of skis need prompt attention, or the ski-lift offices preferably in the autumn. You might even find that the tourist office in the big resorts like Zermatt and Val d'Isère may be able to help. Outside the EU you will encounter work permit difficulties (details in individual country chapters), though when there is a labour shortage, there is usually a way round the difficulties. Unfortunately labour shortages these days are becoming rarer and the drifting population looking for jobs in ski resorts can be much greater in one area than the number of jobs available. You should therefore try as hard as you can to sign a contract ahead of time, or failing this, be prepared to move around to less popular areas to find work.

For a thorough list of 400+ ski resorts worldwide, consult the annually revised *Good Skiing & Snowboarding Guide* published by Which? Magazine (£15.99). Some major ski resorts are listed in the table that follows, though the list is by no means comprehensive.

SKI RESORTS AROUND THE WORLD

France
Chamonix
Les Contamines
Val d'Isère
Courchevel
Méribel
St Christoph
Flaine
Avoriaz
Les Arcs
La Plagne
Tignes
Montgenèvre

Switzerland
Davos
St.Moritz
Zermatt
Gstaad
Klosters
Villars
Wengen & Mürren
Crans-Montana
Kandersteg
Adelboden
Verbier
Grindelwald
Arosa
Saas Fee

Austria
Kitzbühel
Söll
Lech
Badgastein
St Anton
Mayrhofen
Kaprun
Alpbach
Brand
Kirchberg
St Johann
Solden
Obergurgl
Zell am See

Italy
Cortina d'Ampezzo
Courmayeur
Sestriere
Bormio
Campitello
Canazei
Livigno
Abetone
Corvara
Selva
Sauze d'Oulx
Asiago
S Stefano di Cadore
Alleghi

Spain
Sol y Nieve
Formigal
Cerler

Andorra
Arinsal
Soldeu
Pas de la Casa

Germany
Garmisch-
Partenkirchen
Oberstdorf
Berchtesgaden

Norway
Voss
Geilo
Telemark
Lillehammer
Gausdal
Synnfjell

Scotland
Aviemore
Glenshee (Glenisla)
Carrbridge
Glencoe

Finnish Lapland
Levi
Ylläs

New Zealand
Queenstown
Coronet Peak
Mount Hutt
Mount Ruapehu

Bulgaria
Borovets

Romania
Poiana Brasov

Australia
Falls Creek (VIC)
Mount Hotham
Mount Buffalo
Baw Baw
Mount Buller
Thredbo (NSW)
Perisher
Mount Field (Tas)
Ben Lomond

Canada
Banff
Lake Louise
Waterton
Ottawa
Huntsville
Collingwood
Barrie

USA
Aspen, Colorado
Copper Mountain
Steamboat Springs
Vail
Breckenridge
Alpine Meadows, CA
Lake Tahoe
Mt Batchelor, OR
Mount Hood
Aleyska, AK
Park City, UT
Sun Valley, ID
Jackson Hole, WY
Big Mountain, MO
Waterville Valley, NH
Stowe, VT
Killington, VT
Dore Mountain, NY

AGRICULTURE

HARVESTING

Historically, agricultural harvests have employed the greatest number of casual workers. Itinerant workers have traditionally travelled hundreds of miles to gather in the fruits of the land, from the tiny blueberry to the mighty watermelon. It might even be possible to pick your way around the world, by following the seasons and the ripening crops. The old-style gypsies, who roamed over Europe picking fruit as they went, have been joined both by nomadic young people and large numbers of East Europeans looking to earn western wages.

The well organised picker in Europe might find himself starting the year in Britain, picking mundane vegetables like cabbages and potatoes. He then moves on to strawberries and gooseberries in June, cherries, currants and raspberries in July, apples and plums in August and then on to choosing between the Kentish hop harvest in September or grape-picking in France. He could follow the *vendange* (grape harvest) north and then into Germany where grapes are picked into November, back to France for the chestnut harvest in late November and December. Tiring at last of the cold northern climate, our itinerant picker could flee south to pick oranges on the Greek Peloponnese.

Furthermore, living and working in rural areas is a more authentic way of experiencing an alien culture compared to working in tourism. It is easy to see why farms, vineyards and orchards play such a large part in the chapters that follow, since harvests provide so much scope for people working their way around the world. No serious self-funding traveller can afford to ignore the employment opportunities available at harvest time. When Gerhard Flaig was in New Zealand, he dedicated himself to the task of building up his travelling fund by accepting the hardest picking job of the three he was offered:

> I chose the squash packing job because it offered the highest wages, but it was bloody tough. Almost every day I had to move about 15,000 squash, which is about 25 tons of squash. After my season, which lasted about 14 weeks, I had moved more than one million single squash. I suffered from cuts and muscle strain. Very often I thought of giving up but the good wages kept me going. Now I am very proud that I could manage this tough job. And it was mainly this job that covered more than half of all the costs of my journey around the world.

Although the problem of work permits does dog the footsteps of fruit pickers abroad, there is always a good chance that the urgency of the farmers' needs will overrule the impulse to follow the regulations. But if you do end up picking fruit without a permit, it is best to keep a low profile in the village pub. Even locals who would not consider doing this kind of work might feel jealous of the imagined fortune you're earning while they are unemployed.

The availability of harvesting work for travellers in Europe has been greatly reduced by the large numbers of Romanians, Poles, Albanians, etc. now roaming every corner of Europe trying to earn the money their own struggling economies cannot provide. Often a certain amount of hostility exists between these economic migrants and working travellers, primarily because farmers have been dropping wages as a result of the new competition for jobs, and because impoverished Easterners will accept below-par wages. Now that Poland and a number of other Eastern European countries have joined the European Union, their nationals will all be legal workers in due course, though transitional barriers to the free movement of labour are in place in most of the EU-15 countries.

Where to look for work

The vast majority of this kind of work is found only after meeting the farmers face-to-face either well in advance of the busy season or once it's underway and the growers are desperate if they don't have enough labour. However, in a few isolated cases, specialist agencies try to match up farmers and travelling harvesters. While in Amsterdam Karen Martin made contact with a Dutch company called Appellation Controlée (www.apcon.nl) set up by two ex-travellers who wanted to help people find work on farms offering good pay and conditions in France, Britain and occasionally other countries. It was after paying the agency registration fee that she and her boyfriend Paul were assigned to maize castration jobs in the Loire Valley (see chapter on France). An agency in Australia called Grunt Labour Services specialises in harvesting work (see Australia chapter).

As usual the internet can play a key role. Check the website www.pickingjobs.com which brings together some of the harvests which are perennially short of workers as in the berry harvests of Scotland, cherry picking on the South Island of New Zealand and the massive fruit harvests of Victoria Australia. There are some country-specific sites as well such as www.seasonalwork.co.nz.

But mostly it will be a case of following leads in the countryside. Once you have arrived in the right area at the right time of year, the next step is to find out which farmers are short of help. Asking in the youth hostel or campsite and in the local pub is often successful, though not always; Jon Loop says this is great for people who are good at meeting prospective employers in pubs, unlike him who just gets drunk and falls over. The great advantage of job-hunting in rural areas rather then in cities is that people are more likely to know their neighbours' labour requirements and often are more sympathetic and helpful in their attitudes. Adam Cook interrupted a cycling tour of the South of France to look for fruit-picking work: *'Faced with having to decide between hurrying north to catch up with the cherries and going south to meet the first peaches, I decided to go south. It took ten good days of asking everywhere, cafés, bars, post offices, grocery shops – one of the best places I found to look as the owners very often know who is picking what and where.'*

If the word of mouth technique does not work at first, you will have to visit farmers personally. Since they will be generally working out of doors it is not difficult to approach them. Farm hands and people already picking in the fields will be able to offer advice as well. If farms are widely scattered, you may have to consider hiring or borrowing a bicycle, moped or car for a day of concentrated job-hunting.

Alternatively you might be able to get a list of farms and ring around. Farm co-operatives can be useful sources of this kind of information. Local newspapers may carry advertisements for pick-your-own farms or roadside fruit stands which may provide a job or at least a lead. If there is a weekly market or co-operative at which local farmers sell their produce, this is an ideal venue for job-hunting. Even if you don't find a farmer looking for pickers, they may need people to unload the lorries or man the market stall. They may also hold an auction and it may be possible to broadcast your request for work over the public address system, auctioning yourself off to the highest bidder as it were. If you are with several friends, you may find that it is difficult to find a farmer willing to offer work to all of you. You may then be able to work out a job-sharing arrangement, although this is more likely to be acceptable to the farmer if accommodation is not his responsibility.

One of the job-seeker's best allies is a very detailed map. Helpful locals can then point out their suggestions on a map rather than give verbal instructions (possibly in a language you barely know). An excellent reference book for prospective grape-pickers is Hugh Johnson's *World Atlas of Wine* (published by Mitchell Beazley) which includes splendidly detailed maps of wine-producing regions from Corsica to California. It is of course much too heavy and expensive to carry around, though you could perhaps take a few good photocopies of the regions you plan to try. Alternatively, get a list of vineyards from the regional tourist offices and write to (or visit) the proprietors, asking for work. Detailed maps can now be downloaded from the internet.

Mechanisation

Although harvesting techniques have become increasingly mechanised, human toil continues to play a large part. The recent mechanisation of the hop harvest for example has made a dramatic difference and yet a large number of helpers are still needed for various ancillary jobs. Although more and more vineyards are employing mechanical harvesters, often the rows of vines are too close together or on too steep a gradient for the machines to be of use. There are cherry-picking machines which work by shaking the fruit off the trees; these not only leave the fruit damaged but also loosen the roots and in the long run destroy the trees. Despite advances in agricultural technology, there is no immediate danger of humans being replaced altogether. That being said, it certainly can't hurt to go abroad with some tractor-driving experience.

One job which can't be done by machinery is selective picking. There are not many fruits and vegetables which ripen all at once. Pickers soon develop the ability to spot the lettuces, cauliflowers or strawberries that are ready and leave the rest for a later onslaught. Sometimes the process of selection becomes quite complicated if you are expected to sort the size and quality of the produce as you proceed; for example pickers must sometimes drop apples through a wire loop to determine the size.

Technique

Picking fruit may not be as easy as it sounds. For many people, their only experience of fruit picking may have been on family outings to a PYO orchard where most of the time was spent in tree-climbing or sibling-bombardment exploits. Picking fruit for your living will not be so idyllic. If you are part of a large team you may be expected to work at the same speed as the most experienced picker, which can be both exhausting and discouraging.

Having a little experience can make the whole business more enjoyable, not to mention more financially worthwhile if you are being paid piece work rates. The vast majority of picking jobs are paid piece work (with the notable exception of grape harvests in Europe), though a minimum level of productivity will be expected, particularly if you are being given room and board.

Try not to feel too discouraged at the end of the first day or even the first week of working in an orchard when you see that some old hands have picked three times as much as you. When Andrew Walford was tempted to feel envious of the people who could fill seven or eight bins of apples a day in Shepparton Australia, he consoled himself that, even if his record was only five, at least he wasn't as eccentric as they were. Rather than succumb to feelings of inferiority, watch their technique closely. Ask their advice about where to place the ladder, since moving a ladder can be time-consuming. (Note that this is not a job for anyone who suffers from vertigo.) After a week or two your confidence and your earnings will certainly have increased. Once you learn how to snap strawberries off with a quick twist of the wrist (leaving the floret intact) you will be surprised at how your speed improves. In the case of other fruits, shaking trees to dislodge fruit is almost always frowned upon by employers, though this does not prevent some pickers from resorting to it. There may even be scouts in large orchards patrolling in order to prevent this practice.

It is not merely technique which separates the professionals from the amateurs, but fitness as well. Richard Walford interrupted a cycling trip along the Rhine to pick grapes for a few weeks, and assumed that all his cycling would have prepared him for the work. He soon learned however that grape-picking uses different muscles entirely and he found the first few days gruelling.

There are often external limitations to the amount you can earn. Sometimes picking is called off in bad weather. Sometimes you are forced to take some days off while the next crop ripens fully or because the price on the market has dropped. Be prepared to amuse (and finance) yourself on idle days.

Some farmers prefer to hire men if the work is particularly taxing or if a lot of lifting is involved. But there are few actual picking jobs which women can't do equally well. Agility is often more important than strength and for some soft fruits, female pickers are preferred because they are assumed to have a gentler touch. If the fruit is very delicate, beginners are sometimes paid an hourly rate to discourage careless and damaging picking.

Informal competitions can enliven the tedium. Alan Corrie describes his fellow tomato-picker on a farm near Auch in the Gascony region of southern France, with undisguised admiration:

> In August I was taken on by a farmer to join his contracted Moroccan worker picking tomatoes. This is paid by the crate, and iron discipline and single-minded determination are needed to breach the fifty crates barrier per ten-hour day, and get in amongst the good earnings. When my first half century had been verified, I was punching the air in triumphant salute. The next day, toying with extremis, fifty-three was achieved, and I had the distinct feeling while unloading at the depot that the workers there nudging one another and confiding 'c'est lui, mon dieu, comme une tempête dans les tomates!'
>
> Ahmed, meanwhile, was touching seventy crates a day. Any day now, I reasoned, we'd be on a par, sending the boss off to buy a calculator and to order extra crates. This was not to be however. I had peaked. Desperation set in; the crates were becoming bigger, tomatoes always lying awkwardly, the heat blistering; I began to flounder, drained and dejected in the low forties. My colleague when I last asked him was turning in a cool eighty a day, which if you knew anything about tomato picking I would not ask you to believe. You would have to see it for yourself. I'm thinking of giving guided tours of the scene of his campaign for knowing seasonal workers and afficionados: 'Yup,' I'll nod my head – greyhaired as it now is after the experience – in the direction of a little altar-like structure, 'I was there, seen it wi' m'own eyes. I swear it, them little rascals wuz up'n jumpin' in that thaar bucket of his.' Anyway, good luck to him. It was with some relief that I was transferred to the shady plum groves across the road.

Equipment

During August in the South of France the only equipment you'll need is a sun hat. But if you are planning to pick apples in British Columbia or olives in the Greek winter, you will need warm clothing, waterproofs and possibly also rubber boots for muddy fields. When packing for your intercontinental fruit picking holiday, it might be an idea to pack a sturdy pair of gardening gloves for frosty mornings. Gloves can also be useful if you are picking fruit which has been sprayed with an insecticide that irritates cuts or stains your hands an unsightly colour. If it is too awkward to pick wearing gloves, you can tape up your hands with surgical tape to prevent blistering.

In each country chapter, we have dealt with the possibilities for willing and well-prepared pickers. Wherever possible we have included tables of crop locations and harvesting dates, so that you will know which specific areas to head for. This information can be more easily assimilated by examining the symbols on the sketch maps which should be used in conjunction with detailed country and regional maps.

FARMING

Not all casual work in rural areas revolves around fruit and vegetable harvests. There are a lot of miscellaneous seasonal jobs created by the agricultural industry, from castrating maize to crutching sheep, from scaring birds away from cherry orchards to herding goats (something which seems to reduce most novices to tears), from weeding olive groves to spraying banana plantations. There is always the chance of work if you knock on farmers' doors. Every working traveller ought to be able to turn his hand to the basic tasks of pruning, planting and harvesting.

Many farms, especially in Europe, are relatively small family-run businesses, and the farmer may not need to look any further than his own family for labour. But often farmers are looking for one able-bodied assistant over the summer months, and if you are fortunate to be that one, you will probably be treated as a member of the family, sharing their meals and their outings. It is more important to be able to communicate with the farmer than if you are hired as a fruit picker, since the instructions given to farm hands are more complicated. It also helps to have some tractor-driving or other farm experience or at least an aptitude for machinery.

Whereas picking a given crop can quickly become tedious, working as a general assistant provides much more variety as Ed Peters describes, based on his experience of working in mainland Greece: *'The work ranged from langorous to arduous – scattering chemical fertiliser, picking up wood, digging shallow ditches for water pipes, supervising irrigation (a sinecure if ever there was one) and spraying weed killer from ten litre containers on your back (murderous!).'*

But even if the work you are given is tedious, this might be exactly what you want, as was the case with Joseph Tame who spent a few weeks working on an organic farm in Switzerland in spring 2000 while waiting for his visa to come through for a summer job in a Swiss hotel: *'The type of work can at times be tremendously repetitive (such as the four hours a day every day spent scraping cow shit from the yard!). Yet in this repetitiveness you have a freedom, a freedom of the mind that enables you to mull over any thoughts or feelings that in England would be swept aside by the stress of everyday life. Here I have all the time in the world; and in this world, time is not money.'*

If you are spending an extended period on an isolated farm you should be prepared to enjoy your own company. Jakob Steixner has worked at a mountain farm in Austria for the past three summers and warns that it can be difficult in social terms when you have to spend three months in the company of the same two or three people, sometimes even sleeping in the same room.

> **As so much depends on the generosity of the hosts, Karen Martin and Paul Ansell were lucky at their maize and apple farm in France:**
> *It is, I imagine, like many farms out in the sticks, but the wife is happy to drive us to the supermarket or train station if you fancy going to big places like Angers or Saumur. They have given us loads of fresh fruit, washed our clothes, given us lots of their very good (very strong) drink, let us use their internet and even lent us money when we first arrived.*

Advertising and the Internet

Placing an advert in the national farmers' journal is especially worthwhile for people who have had some relevant experience. Gary Tennant placed the following advert in the Danish farmers' weekly *Landsbladet*: *'23 year old Englishman now in Denmark would like farm work. Have been working on a kibbutz (4 months) in the fields and tractor work. Just finished gardening work in England and want to try different farming. Telephone 06191679, ask for Gary.'*

Although he started his job hunt in the autumn (the worst time of year), he received four offers. An Englishwoman he met who had experience of dairy farming received 11 offers from such an advert.

Targeting small rural newspapers can also pay dividends partly because it will almost certainly be a novelty. Ken Smith noticed a small ad in the *Oamaru Mail* in New Zealand: 'Young German man seeks farm work. Has tractor experience and good work habits.' The scope of replies would be greater from New Zealand's national farming paper *Farm News* whose website allows free access to its classified ads (www.farmnews.co.nz).

You might prefer to advertise your availability for work abroad online. For example an agency in Bury St. Edmunds (www.4xtraHands.com) tries to ferret out farming vacancies for registered job-seekers in the UK, the Antipodes and elsewhere. It is mainly looking to place competent and experienced farm workers at busy periods downunder for harvests, silaging, lambing, etc.

Range of Opportunities

Many long-term itinerant workers meet up with people who are interested in alternative lifestyles which may include organic farming or goat cheese production as a way of earning a living. In rural areas, a polite request for room and board in exchange for half a day's work often succeeds. The 'small is beautiful' philosophy may mean that smallholders will not be able to pay wages, but this can be a congenial way to pass some time, as Rob Abblett has done all over the world from Mexico to Malawi, Sweden to Salt Spring Island, Canada. He simply gathers lists of contacts from organisations like the ones listed in this section and gets in touch with the ones that sound appealing:

I've visited, worked and had many varied experiences on over 30 communes around the world. I like them because they are so varied and full of interesting people, usually with alternative ideas, beliefs, but also because I almost always find someone that I can really connect with, for sometimes I need to be with like-minded folk.

Occasionally the specialist press (like *Farmers Weekly* published Fridays with an online edition at www.fwi.co.uk) contains advertisements for jobs abroad. Tree nurseries are often a good source of casual work and in some countries (especially Canada) tree planting is a job often done by nomadic types. If you find a job through an agency do not rely exclusively on the agency's information. It is better (if possible) to talk to your future employer direct to avoid the fate which befell Lee Morton when he was placed as a trainee groom in California: the employer was so demanding that he left the day after he arrived.

Equestrian Work

The International Exchange Program (IEP) is a scheme by which partner organisations in Britain, Ireland, Australia, New Zealand and the USA co-operate to offer work placements and rural exchanges to qualified candidates. They offer 300-400 agricultural, equine, horticultural and winemaking placements of varying lengths and also act as a recruitment agency making permanent and relief placements in the equestrian and agricultural industries. Equestrian staff require a suitable background. One year of practical experience is usually needed for all placements, though additional training is often available. Placements as nannies or general farm assistants may not require experience. The organisations to contact for information are:

IEP-UK, The Old Rectory, Belton-in-Rutland, Oakham, Rutland LE15 9LE, UK (01572 717383; fax 01572 717343; enquiries@iepuk.com; www.iepuk.com. Equine staff agency. Sample IEP fee for Australia is about £1,800 including airfares.

Stablemate Australia, PO Box 1206, Windsor, NSW 2756, Australia (02-4587 9770; www. stablemate.net.au).

Communicating for Agriculture Exchange Program, 112 East Lincoln Avenue, Fergus Falls, MN 56537; 218-739-3241; www.caepusa.com or http://ca.cainc.org). As well as arranging incoming programme, places US candidates aged 18-30 in agricultural, horticultural, equine or wine-making positions in many countries from Sweden to South Africa.

Experience International, PO Box 680, Everson, WA 98247 (360-966-3876; www.expint. org). Incoming placements in agriculture, forestry, fisheries mainly in Pacific North West of USA.

Experienced grooms, riding instructors and stable staff may consider registering with a specialist agency such as A World of Experience Equestrian Employment Agency (52 Kingston Deverill, Warminster, Wilts. BA12 7HF01985 844022; fax 01985 844102; www. equijobshop.com). For people with relevant experience, they have vacancies in 20 countries in Europe and worldwide which pay between £150 and £250 a week plus free accommodation for an 8-12 hour day, six days a week. All employers are English-speaking.

A more recently established equine agency online is Career Grooms (16E Randolph Crescent, London W9 1DR; 020-7289 6385; www.careergrooms.co.uk). In Ireland, one of the main agencies is Equipeople Ltd (Garryhinch, Portarlington, Co. Laois; fax 0502 43313; www.equipeoplestaff.com).

Other agencies advertise in the specialist press, for example *Horse & Hound*. Stable staff and lightweight riders are needed for work on studs and in racing establishments around the world. Check the situations vacant columns in *The Sporting Life* and *Racing Post*. For further leads, have a look at the book *Working with Animals: UK, Europe & Worldwide* by Victoria Pybus (Vacation-Work, £11.95).

For those who like horses but lack experience, becoming a volunteer at a riding stable might be the answer, which can be arranged in some countries through the WWOOF exchange.

Canadian Leona Baldwin and partner decided to go down this route to fix up a work-for-keep placement at a trekking centre in New Zealand:

From the Bay of Islands to Invercargill, WWOOF'ing opportunities were advertised everywhere, at Yoga retreats, ski resorts, cattle farms and horse trekking centres. Our preference was for the latter. Ever since my 'My Little Pony' days of youth, dazzled by storybook images of unicorns and Black Beauty, I had loved horses. As it transpired, it was destined to be a love affair from afar. My first riding experience at the age of ten had found me on the back of a temperamental horse named Chocolate Chip. Instead of following the path of its more obedient friends ahead, Chocolate 'Psycho' Chip decided to burn its own path at breakneck speed, leaving me clinging helplessly to the saddle and then face down in the snow. The best thing you can do in those circumstances is get right back on. But I hadn't, and now 15 years later, I decided to make amends.

Luckily, our first choice in horse trekking farms had a vacancy for two WWOOF-ers, and we were invited to come and stay in the scenic Ruapehu district. Soon after arrival I found myself in the paddock ready to confront the four-legged demons of my past. And there they stood, 14 Chocolate Chips, ears pricked up, eyes wild, muscles taut and ready for action. My knees went weak. Our task was each to walk a horse back to the main farmstead to be fed, groomed and saddled. Clutching the rope between my sweaty palms, they might as well have asked me to mount it bareback and gallop back for all the confidence I had. As I reached up over my head to attach the rope to its neck, heart in my throat, I took a step and to my great surprise, it moved obediently behind me. I was in control!

Gaining Experience

Without any formal training in agriculture, it is possible to get some preliminary experience. Many European countries have programmes whereby young people spend a month or two assisting on a farm, e.g. Norway and Switzerland. A farming background is not necessary for participating in these schemes, though of course it always helps. Israeli kibbutzim often give their volunteers exposure to a range of farming jobs. You might like to get an initial taste of farm life by having a 'farm holiday'. Rural tourism is gaining popularity and the tourist organisations of countries like Italy and New Zealand encourage tourists to take a holiday on a working farm and participate in the daily round of activities to whatever extent they like. You then have the chance not only of having a relatively inexpensive and interesting holiday, but also of learning a little about hay-baling, cheese-making and so on. One possibility for finding addresses of farms which might welcome working visitors is to obtain the *Green Guide* from ECEAT (European Centre for Eco-Agro Tourism, Postbox 10899, 1001 EW Amsterdam, Netherlands; www.eceat.nl). In order to promote eco-tourism and support small farmers, it publishes (in English) a directory for Britain and Ireland (€15), Poland (€10) and Spain & Portugal (€15). Its main publication is a 700-page guide to Europe which costs €25 but is only in Dutch.

It is not impossible to find work on farms and ranches which have diversified to accept paying visitors. This is particularly popular in the United States (where guest ranches are called 'dude ranches') and Australia. These establishments need both domestic and outdoor assistants to lead guests on trail rides, show them places or events of local interest, etc.

WWOOF

With growing fears of genetically modified foods, the organic farming movement is attracting more and more of a following around the world, from Toulouse to Turkey (to Prince Charles's Highgrove). It has been predicted that within five or ten years, one in six farms will have gone organic. Organic farms everywhere take on volunteers to help them minimise or abolish the use of chemicals and heavy machinery. There are various co-ordinating bodies, many of which go under the name of WWOOF.

WWOOF stands for World Wide Opportunities on Organic Farms, changed from Willing Workers on Organic Farms, with an eye to the sensitivities of immigration officers around the world who always bridle at the word 'work'. (If the topic arises at immigration, avoid the word 'working'; it is preferable to present yourself as a student of organic farming who is planning an educational farm visit or a cultural exchange.)

WWOOF has a global website www.wwoof.org with links to both the national organisations in the countries that have a WWOOF co-ordinator and to those which do not, known as WWOOF Independents. Each national group has its own aims, system, fees and rules but most expect applicants to have gained some experience on an organic farm in their own country first. WWOOF is an exchange: in return for your help on organic farms, gardens and homesteads, you receive meals, a place to sleep and a practical insight into organic growing. The work-for-keep exchange is a simple one that can be immensely satisfying. Visitors are expected to work around six hours per day in return for free accommodation and can stay from a few days to many months depending on whether or not they click with the owners and, of course, how much work needs to be done.

If you want to WWOOF in countries that have their own WWOOF organisation like Italy or Korea, it is necessary to join the national WWOOF organisation before you can obtain addresses of these properties. This usually costs €15 or €20 per year. At present the list of countries with their own WWOOF co-ordinators are: the UK, Denmark, Sweden, Germany, Switzerland, Austria, Italy, Slovenia, the Czech Republic, Australia, New Zealand, Canada, Ghana, Uganda, Japan, Korea, Nepal, Turkey and Mexico, many of which are mentioned in the following chapters of this book with the price of joining.

To obtain the addresses of properties in all the other countries, It is necessary to join WWOOF International. In the UK this can be done by sending £15 for Internet access, or £20 for a printed booklet, to WWOOF International c/o WWOOF UK, PO Box 2675, Lewes, East Sussex BN7 1RB (hello@wwoof.org.uk). WWOOF Australia also sells a similar list. This is a marvellous resource which can be obtained within Australia by sending A$22/£10/US$20 to WWOOF, Mt Murrindal Co-operative, Buchan, Vic 3885, Australia; +61-3-5155 0218/fax 3-5155 0342; www.wwoof.com.au. The price if posted overseas is A$27. (For their list of properties in Australia only, see that chapter.)

Mike Tunnicliffe joined the long-established WWOOF New Zealand to avoid work permit hassles and his experience is typical of WWOOFers' in other countries: *'My second choice of farm was a marvellous experience. For 15 days I earned no money but neither did I spend any, and I enjoyed life on the farm as part of the family. There is a wide variety of WWOOF farms and I thoroughly recommend the scheme to anyone who isn't desperate to earn money.'*

Before arranging a longish stay on an organic farm, consider whether or not you will find such an environment congenial. Many organic farmers are non-smoking vegetarians and living conditions may be primitive by some people's standards. Although positive experiences are typical, Craig Ashworth expressed reservations about WWOOF, based on his experiences in New Zealand, and claims that a proportion of WWOOF hosts are 'quite wacky'. (See Danish chapter for a first-hand account of total incompatibility in this context.) Bear in mind that the work you are given to do may not always be very salubrious: for example Armin Birrer, who has spent time on organic farms in many countries, claims that the weirdest job he ever did was to spend a day in New Zealand picking worms out of a pile of rabbit dung to be used to soften the soil around some melon plants. With such a loose network of individuals around the world, the system is bound to be hit and miss. Danny Jacobson was willing to take that gamble and on the whole was happy with his WWOOF experiences in South Australia:

> One was an organic fig/garlic farm and the other a vineyard. Both were great though the farmers can be really bizarre and sometimes anal about how things are done. On the fig farm, the lady even gave us grades according to how we'd done that day and it was pretty annoying. Still it was really beautiful and the work was good. On the vineyard, the guy was very nice and extremely enthusiastic about making the best wine in the world. But another experience was not so positive. We were heading to a village to meet a supposed orange farmer in northern South Australia. It was late and very dark so we had trouble finding the place. We stopped in a bar and asked for directions and were told that this guy didn't actually have his own orange grove. He would take WWOOFers and rent them out to other farmers, thus keeping the profit. It just goes to show that you have to be selective and careful in where you commit your time and be ready to run if the scene is leaking bad vibes.

Communities

Many communities (formerly called communes) welcome foreign visitors and willingly exchange hospitality for work. Although not all the work is agricultural, much of it is. Some are very radical or esoteric in their practices so find out as much as you can before planning to visit. The majority are vegetarian. The details and possible fees must be established on a case-by-case basis. The following resources are relevant:

Eurotopia, Okodorf Sieben Linden, 38486 Poppau, Germany (www.eurotopia.de). English version provides a comprehensive listing of 336 international communities in 23 countries (mainly Europe and the UK). The updated 2004 edition is only in German and Spanish. The English edition can be ordered from Edge of Time (BCM Edge, London WC1N 3XX; www.edgeoftime.co.uk) for £12.50.

Communities, 138 Twin Oaks Road, Louisa, VA 23093, USA (540-894-5798; http://directory.ic.org). Publish *Communities Directory: A Guide to Co-operative Living* (2000); price US$30 plus $4 US postage or $8 overseas by surface post. It lists about 600 communities in the US and about 100 abroad including 'ecovillages, rural land trusts, co-housing groups, kibbutzim, student co-ops, organic farms, monasteries, urban artist collectives, rural communes and Catholic Worker houses'. Annual updates are sold as supplements for $5 ($12.50 overseas). Some country-by-country listings are posted on their website (www.ic.org).

Global Ecovillage Network (GEN), based at ZEGG Community in Germany and at Findhorn in Scotland (info@gen-europe.org/ www.gen-europe.org). GEN functions as the umbrella organisation for a wide range of intentional communities and ecovillages all over the world, many of whom welcome guests and volunteers. (American contact: ecovillage@thefarm.org; Australiasia information: http://genoa.ecovillage.org).

Agricultural Exchanges

The international equestrian exchange IEP described above is also open to other categories of agricultural worker so it would be worth enquiring of IEP-Stablemate, etc. as listed above. In addition, opportunities exist worldwide for young people aged between 18 and 30 who have good practical farming experience. AgriVenture (run by the International Agricultural Exchange Association) arranges placements for British and European participants in the USA, Canada, Australia, New Zealand and Japan. Placements in the USA and Canada begin in February, March and April and last for seven or nine months. Placements for Australia and New Zealand begin in April, May, July, August and September and last for six to nine months. Placements in Japan begin in April and last four to twelve months. There are also several round-the-world itineraries which depart in the autumn to the southern hemisphere for six to seven months followed by another six to seven months in the northern hemisphere.

The cost of these programmes starts at around £2,000 but trainees are then paid a realistic wage. Included in the cost is a pre-departure information meeting, airline tickets, visas, insurance, stopover (if applicable), orientation seminar and board and lodging throughout with a host family. UK and Eire participants should contact Agriventure, IAEA, Avenue M, National Agricultural Centre, Stoneleigh Park, Kenilworth, Warwickshire CV8 2LR; 02476 696578; fax 02476 696684; uk@agriventure.com for a brochure; or check the website www.agriventure.com. Mainland European applicants should contact the Agriventure office in Denmark (+45 59 51 15 25; europe@agriventure.com).

MAST International (R395 VoTech Building, 1954 Buford Avenue, University of Minnesota, St. Paul, MN 55108; 800-346-6278; mast@umn.edu; http://mast.coafes.umn.edu) also runs a similar practical agriculture programme for Americans in Denmark, Sweden, Norway, Estonia, Finland, France, the UK, Germany, Switzerland, Netherlands, Spain, Greece, Hungary, Morocco, South Africa, Argentina, Australia and New Zealand. Participants must have had at least six months relevant experience and pay the modest programme fee of $400.

TEACHING ENGLISH

This chapter used to begin with a quotation from a traveller-turned-professional-EFL-teacher, Dick Bird:

> It is extremely difficult for anyone whose mother tongue is English to starve in an inhabited place, since there are always people who will pay good money to watch you display a talent as basic as talking. Throughout the world, native speakers of English are at a premium.

But this rosy view of the traveller's prospects must now be moderated somewhat. Although the English language is still the language which literally millions of people around the world want to learn, finding work as an English teacher is not as easy as many people assume. Furthermore there is a worrying trend even for people with a qualification to have difficulty. The number of both public and private institutes turning out certified TEFL teachers has greatly increased in the past ten years, creating a glut of teachers all chasing the same jobs, especially in the major cities of Europe.

Having sounded that warning note, it must be said that there are still areas of the world where the boom in English language learning seems to know no bounds, from Ecuador to China, the Ukraine to Vietnam. In cowboy schools and back-street agencies, being a native speaker and dressing neatly are sometimes sufficient qualifications to get a job. But for more stable teaching jobs in recognised language schools, you will have to sign a contract (minimum three months, usually nine) and have some kind of qualification which ranges from a university degree to a certificate in education with a specialisation in Teaching English as a Foreign Language (known as TEFL, pronounced 'teffle'). This chapter covers both possibilities.

One of the best sources of information about the whole topic of English teaching (if I may be permitted to say so) is the 2005 edition of *Teaching English Abroad* by Susan Griffith (Vacation-Work, £12.95). This chapter can only provide the most general introduction to such topics as TEFL training and commercial recruitment agencies; for specific information about individual countries, see the country chapters.

TEFL Training

The only way to outrival the competition and make the job hunt (not to mention the job itself) easier is to do a TEFL course. If interested, write to the English Information Centre of the British Council (Bridgewater House, 58 Whitworth St, Manchester M1 6BB; 0161-957 7755) for an information sheet 'How to Become a Teacher of EFL' and a list of approved Certificate centres.

There are two standard recognised qualifications that will improve your range of job options by an order of magnitude. The best known is the Cambridge Certificate in English Language Teaching to Adults (CELTA) administered and awarded by the University of Cambridge ESOL Examinations, 1 Hills Road, Cambridge CB1 2EU; 01223 553355; esol@ucles.org.uk; www.cambridgeESOL.org/teaching). The other is the Certificate in TESOL (Teaching English to Speakers of Other Languages) offered by Trinity College London, 89 Albert Embankment, London SE1 7TP (020-7820 6100; fax 020-7820 6161; tesol@trinitycollege.co.uk; www.trinitycollege.co.uk). Both are very intensive and expensive, averaging £850-£950. These courses involve at least 100 hours of rigorous training with a practical emphasis (full-time for four weeks or part-time over several months). Although there are no fixed pre-requisites apart from a suitable level of language awareness, not everyone who applies is accepted. And almost no one finds these intensive courses a breeze. Fergus Cooney says that on his CELTA course, they barely had time for a coffee during the day and that several trainees broke down in tears during breaks, himself (almost) included.

Other courses may be less challenging but the qualification not so widely recognised, though this didn't bother the self-confessedly unacademic Roger Blake who felt that he benefitted greatly from a short TEFL course:

Of the many things that I have achieved over the past two years, one of the most significant must be my certificate in TEFL. Partly inspired during a backpacker style holiday to New York in November 2000 where I saw a subway advertisement asking for English teachers, I followed it up and did a crash weekend course with i-to-i. To my surprise I enjoyed it so much that I then did their language awareness module by home study to improve my understanding and ability to teach. (It is worth noting that i-to-i's courses are aimed at casual would-be teachers not career professionals.) Not being the academic sort, I amazed myself in completing 40 hours but it was worth it. Since then I have been particularly keen to get off on my travels.

Roger's next communication came from Addis Ababa.

For people confused by the number of training courses jostling for attention in the marketplace, the language and teacher training consultancy Cactus (www.cactusteachers. com) can provide advice free of charge.

A list of the several hundred centres both in the UK and abroad offering the Cambridge Certificate course in Britain and abroad is available from UCLES in exchange for a large s.a.e. or can be browsed on the website as above. Here is a small selection of Cambridge CELTA training courses:

Basil Paterson Edinburgh Language Foundation, Dugdale-McAdam House, 22/23 Abercromby Place, Edinburgh EH3 6QE (0131-556 7695; www.basilpaterson.co.uk). 8-10 courses per year; £950.

Ealing, Hammersmith & West London College, Gliddon Road, London W14 9BL (020-8563 0063; www.wlc.ac.uk). £745.

International House, 106 Piccadilly, London W1V 9FL (020-7518 6999; www.ihlondon. com). IH centres also in Hastings, Newcastle and worldwide many of which offer CELTA courses.

Language Link Training, 181 Earl's Court Road, London SW5 9RB (020-7370 4755; www. languagelink.co.uk). £850. Can help place successful candidates in posts abroad especially in Central and Eastern Europe.

St Giles, 51 Shepherd's Hill, Highgate, London N6 5QP (020-8340 0828; www.tefl-stgiles. com). Sister schools in Brighton and San Francisco also offer CELTA.

Stanton Teacher Training, Stanton House, 167 Queensway, London W2 4SB (020-7221 7259; www.stanton-school.co.uk). £700.

Centres offering the Trinity College Certificate include:

Coventry TESOL Centre, City College Coventry, The Butts, Coventry CV1 3QD (02476 526700; c.fry@staff.covcollege.ac.uk). £695. Possibility of course being offered abroad as well.

Golders Green Teacher Training Centre, 11 Golders Green Road, London NW11 8DY (0800-074 0335; ggcol@easynet.co.uk). 5-week course £749.

The Language Project, 27 Oakfield Road, Clifton, Bristol BS8 2AT (0117-909 0911; www. languageproject.co.uk). £1,150. Also offer practical weekend introduction to TEFL/ TESL for £245.

A number of centres offer short introductory courses in TEFL, which vary enormously in quality and price. Although they are mainly intended to act as preparatory programmes for more serious courses, many people who hold just a short certificate go on to teach. Among the best known are:

EF English First Teaching Training, 36-38 St Aubyns, Hove, East Sussex BN3 2TD (01273 201433; www.englishfirst.com). 4-week EF Certificate course offered monthly in Brighton and occasionally other locations. Cost £400, subsidised for successful trainees who commit to working for EF afterwards, normally in China or Indonesia.

i-to-i, Woodside House, 261 Low Lane, Horsforth, Leeds LS18 5NY (0870 333 2332; www. teflcourses.com). Intensive TEFL weekend courses at venues in UK/Eire cities. Also an optional 20-hour home-study Grammar module. Online TEFL course also available from any location worldwide. Courses include online tutor back-up and CD-ROM. Price for both weekend and online course from £245.

Saxoncourt Teacher Training, 59 South Molton Street, London W1Y 1HH (020-7499 8533; www.saxoncourt.com). Introductory TEFL course throughout the year to prepare candidates for teaching contracts in China, Japan and Taiwan. Also offer CELTA courses monthly (£795).

Sussex Language Institute, University of Sussex, Falmer, Brighton, E. Sussex, BN1 9QN (01273 873234; www.sussex.ac.uk/languages/english). 1-week 'Introduction to ELT' course held in March. £175. Also offers the 4-week Trinity CertTESOL course (£895).

Cambridge CELTA courses are offered at nearly 100 overseas centres from the Middle East to Queensland, including several in the US:

Embassy CES, The Center for English Studies, 330 Seventh Ave, New York, NY 10001 (212-629-7300; www.embassyces.com). $2,545.

International House USA, 200 SW Market St, Suite 111, Portland, OR 97201 (503-224-1960; www.ih-usa.com). Also offers courses in San Francisco and LA. $2,250.

St Giles Language Teaching Center, One Hallidie Plaza, Suite 350, San Francisco, CA 94102 (415-788-3552; www.stgiles-usa.com). $2,790.

Other centres for American readers to consider are Transworld Schools, 701 Sutter St, 6th Floor, San Francisco, CA 94109 (1-888-588-8335/415-928-2835; www.transworld-schools.com) and the School of Teaching English as a Second Language (9620 Stone Ave N, Suite 101, Seattle, WA 98125 (206-781-8607; www.schooloftesl.com) which offer their own four-week Certificate courses. TEFL International (www.teflintl.com) is an expanding company offering its own 120-hour TESOL certificate in a number of locations (Ban Phe in Thailand, Zhuhai in China, Rome, Seville, etc.).

What English Teaching Involves

It is difficult to generalise about what work you will actually be required to do. At one extreme you have David Cooksley whose job it was to listen to Korean businessmen reading English novels aloud for him to correct their pronunciation. At the other extreme Gillian Forsyth, who taught for a private language school in the industrial north of Germany, had a gruelling schedule of 30 hours of teaching including evening classes, translation work and extensive preparation. Whatever the teaching you find, things probably won't go as smoothly as you would wish.

> **After a year of teaching English in Italy, Andrew Spence had this sensible advice**
> *Teaching is perhaps the best way there is of experiencing another country but you must be prepared for periods when not all is as it should be. The work is sometimes arduous and frustrating, or it can be very exhilarating. Be prepared to take the very rough with the fairly smooth.*

Native speaker teachers are nearly always employed to stimulate conversation rather than to teach grammar. Yet a basic knowledge of English grammar is a great asset when pupils come to ask awkward questions. The book *English Grammar in Use* by Raymond Murphy has been highly recommended for its clear explanations and accompanying student exercises.

Each level and age group brings its own rewards and difficulties. Beginners of all ages usually delight in their progress which will be much more rapid than it is later on. Not everyone, however, enjoys teaching young children (a booming area of TEFL from Portugal to Japan) which usually involves sing-songs, puzzles and games. Intermediate learners (especially if they are adolescents) can be difficult, since they will have reached a plateau and may be discouraged. Adults are usually well-motivated though may be inhibited about speaking. Teaching professionals and business people is almost always well paid. Discipline is seldom a problem at least outside Western Europe. In fact you may find your pupils disconcertingly docile and possibly also overly exam-oriented.

Only 18 himself, Sam James had to teach a variety of age groups in Barcelona during his gap year in 2002 and, despite the problems, ended up enjoying it:

> *The children I taught were fairly unruly and noisy. The teenagers were, as ever, pretty uninterested in learning, though if one struck on something they enjoyed they would work much better. Activities based on the lyrics of songs seemed to be good. They had a tendency to select answers at random in multiple choice exercises. On the other hand they were only ever loud rather than very rude or disobedient. The young children (8-12) were harder work. They tended to understand selectively, acting confused if they didn't like an instruction. Part of the problem was that the class was far too long (three hours) for children of that age and their concentration and behaviour tended to tail off as the time passed.*

Most schools practise the direct method (total immersion in English) so not knowing the language shouldn't prevent you from getting a job. Some employers may provide nothing more than a scratched blackboard and will expect you to dive in using the 'chalk and talk' method. If you are very alarmed at this prospect you could ask a sympathetic colleague if you could sit in on a few classes to give you some ideas. Brochures picked up from tourist offices or airlines can be a useful peg on which to hang a lesson.

The wages paid to English teachers are usually reasonable, and in developing countries are quite often well in excess of the average local wage, assuming you actually get them (for what to do if you don't, see Till Bruckner's account of teaching in Bolivia in the chapter on Latin America). In return you will be asked to teach some fairly unsociable hours since most private English classes take place after working hours, and so schedules split between early morning and evening are not at all uncommon. There may also be extracurricular duties and you should be prepared to do anything from making sausage rolls for an international food day to revising course materials. Even without these, hours will be very long, when you take into account class preparation time. Teaching of any kind is a demanding job and those who are doing it merely as a means of supporting their travelling habit may find it a disillusioning experience.

FINDING A JOB

Teaching jobs are either fixed up from home or sought out on location. Obviously it is less nerve-racking to have everything sorted out before you leave home, but this option is usually available only to the qualified. It also has the disadvantage that you don't know what you're letting yourself in for.

In Advance

Check the adverts in the Education section of the *Guardian* every Tuesday. The best time of year is between Easter and July. In some cases, a carefully crafted CV and enthusiastic personality are as important as EFL training and experience. The *Times Educational Supplement (TES)* published on Fridays carries very few ads for overseas EFL jobs.

Printed advertisements have been largely replaced by the internet with favourite recruitment sites like www.tefl.com, www.tefl.net and www.eslcafe.com. For schools, a website advert offers an easy and instantaneous means of publicising a vacancy to an international audience. Teachers looking for employment can use search engines to look for all pages with references to EFL, English language schools and recruitment. CVs can be e-mailed quickly and cheaply to advertising schools, who can then use e-mail themselves to chase up references. This presupposes a degree of IT awareness which the majority of job-seekers in this field now have. The internet has very quickly taken over as the primary means of recruitment.

Arguably it has become a little too easy to advertise and answer job adverts online. At the press of a button, your CV can be clogging up dozens, nay, hundreds of computers. But everywhere you look on the internet, potentially useful links can be found, many of them leading to Dave Sperling's ESL Café (www.eslcafe.com) which dominates the field. 'Dave' provides a mind-boggling but well organised amount of material for the future or current teacher including accounts of people's experiences of teaching abroad (but bear in mind that these are the opinions of individuals). It also provides links to specific institutes and chains in each country.

After sweating his way through a CELTA course one summer, Fergus Cooney turned to the internet to find a job:

After installing myself in the cheapest net café in Edinburgh I began reading and posting emails here, there and everywhere. I also posted a message on Dave's eslcafe.com, a message stating 'Qualified teacher seeking job'. Within two days I was inundated with many dozens of replies requesting my CV and, more surprising, with job offers everywhere from Andorra to Zonguldak, through Italy, Poland, Turkey, Russia and too many to count from Korea, Taiwan and China. Jackpot, I thought. (I have since realised that many schools/agents must have an automatic reply system that emails those who advertise in the way I did.) I quickly began sifting through the replies but not as quickly as they kept arriving in my inbox. Before a few days had passed, I had become utterly confused and had forgotten which school was which, which Mr. Lee-Soo was which, etc. So I deleted them all, got a new email address and posted a second more specific message on Dave's: 'Teacher with degree + CELTA seeks job in Italy/Spain.' This had the desired effect. A couple of days later my inbox began to fill though not overflow with replies. I still had to delete many from China etc. but could work with the rest and chose a school in Calabria...

A choice he later came to regret but that is another story (see Italy chapter).

The *Guardian* is especially strong on TEFL; see its dedicated pages http://education. guardian.co.uk/tefl where you can search for job vacancies. Other websites that are country specific e.g. www.ohayosensei.com (jobs in Japan) and www.ajarn.com (teaching in Thailand) are listed in the relevant country chapters. Recruitment agencies that at one time matched teachers CVs with international vacancies have been almost entirely supplanted by online recruitment. The major language school chains hire substantial numbers of teachers, many of whom will have graduated from in-house training courses. Among the major employers of EFL teachers are Bénédict Schools (www.benedict-schools.com), Berlitz (www.berlitz.com), EF English First (mentioned above), International House (www. ihworld.com), Language Link, 21 Harrington Road, London SW7 3EU (www.languagelink. co.uk), Linguarama (www.linguarama.com), Saxoncourt (www.saxoncourt.com) and Wall Street Institute International (www.wallstreetinstitute.com).

Scope for untrained but eager volunteers exists for those willing to pay an agency to place them in a language teaching situation abroad. In addition to those included here, see the chapter on *Eastern Europe*.

IST Plus Ltd, Rosedale House, Rosedale Road, Richmond, Surrey TW9 2SZ (020-8939 9057; info@istplus.com; www.istplus.com). Volunteers to teach English in China or Thailand. Must have a degree. Programme fee starts at £995 with the possibility of reimbursement for travel costs at the end of a 10-month contract.

i-to-i (address above). Placements for paying volunteers to teach English (and join other projects) in Latin America, Africa, Russia and Asia.

Teaching & Projects Abroad, Aldsworth Parade, Goring, Sussex BN12 4TX (01903 708300; fax 01903 501026; info@teaching-abroad.co.uk; www.teaching-abroad.co.uk. About 2,000 people are recruited annually, nearly half as volunteer English language teaching assistants in the Ukraine, Russia, India, Ghana, Mexico, China, Peru, Togo,

Nepal, Romania, Thailand, South Africa and others. No TEFL background required. Self-funded 3-month packages cost from £895 to £1,795 (excluding airfares).

Travellers, 7 Mulberry Close, Ferring, West Sussex BN12 5HY (tel/fax 01903 502595; www. travellersworldwide.com). Structured placements available for volunteers in Argentina, Brazil, Brunei, China, Cuba, Ghana, India, Malaysia, Russia, South Africa, Sri Lanka and Ukraine for teaching (as well as work experience and conservation). Sample charge of £1,345 for 3 months in Sri Lanka and £895 in Ukraine (excluding airfares).

The *Education & Training Group* at the British Council (10 Spring Gardens, London SW1A 2BN; 020-7389 4596; assistants@britishcouncil.org) administers language assistant placements to help local teachers of English in many countries from France to Venezuela. Applicants for assistant posts must be aged 20-30, native English speakers, with at least two years of university-level education, normally in the language of the destination country. In some countries (especially in Latin America) posts are of particular interest to graduates interested in a career in TEFL. Application forms are available from October; the deadline is December of the preceding academic year.

North American Organisations

A selection of key programmes and organisations in the US are:

ELTAP (English Language Teaching Assistant Program), University of Minnesota-Morris, Morris, Minnesota 56267 (320-589-6406; kissockc@mrs.umn.edu; www.eltap.org). Placement programme open to undergraduates, graduate students or as a non-credit certificate option for other adults. Participants sent to 32 countries on all continents for 4-11 weeks throughout the year. $300 placement fee, plus course fee and travel; total cost usually $3,500-$4,500. Accommodation and board provided by host schools.

Global Crossroad, 8738 Quarters Lake Road, Baton Rouge, LA 70809 (225-922 7854, fax 225-922 9114; info@globalcrossroad.com; www.globalcrossroad.com). Volunteer teaching and internships in various countries, including Tibet and Mongolia. Paid teaching in Thailand (3-12 months) and China (1-12 months). Placement fees from $699 for China to $2,599 for Mongolia.

TESOL (Teachers of English to Speakers of Other Languages, Inc.), 700 S Washington St, Suite 200, Alexandria, VA 22314 (703-836-0774; www.tesol.org). Basic membership is $75 ($51 for students). Members can receive a listing of job vacancies worldwide, or search jobs online.

WorldTeach Inc., Center for International Development, Harvard University, 79 John F Kennedy Street, Cambridge, MA 02138 (617-495-5527/800-4-TEACH-0; www. worldteach.org). Non-profit organisation that places several hundred paying volunteers as teachers of EFL or ESL in countries which request assistance. Currently, WorldTeach provides college graduates for 6 or 12 months to Costa Rica, Ecuador, China, Namibia, Honduras and the Marshall Islands.

On the Spot

Jobs in any field are difficult to get without an interview and English teaching is no different. In almost all cases it is more effective to go to your preferred destination, CV in hand, and call on language schools and companies. The director of the Mainz branch of a chain of language schools is just one language school director who has emphasised the importance of applying locally:

Schools like ours cannot under normal operating circumstances hire someone unseen merely on the basis of his/her resumé and photo. Moreover, when the need for a teacher arises, usually that vacancy must be filled within a matter of days which, for people applying from abroad, is a physical impossibility. I would suggest that an applicant should arrange for a face-to-face interview and make him/herself available at a moment's notice. Of course, I do appreciate the compromising situation to which anyone in need of employment would thus be exposed. Regrettably, I know of no other method.

When looking for work at private language schools, it is helpful if you can claim some qualifications, though you will seldom be asked to provide proof of same. If you happen to have a BA, take along the certificate. Steven Hendry, who taught English in Japan with no qualifications, stresses the importance of dressing smartly, having a respectable briefcase and a typed CV which exaggerates (if necessary) your experience. However these days it is rare for that to be enough.

There are many means by which you might fix up the odd spot of teaching during your travels. The names of specific language schools and methods of securing a job are mentioned in the various country chapters.

Accents can be important, especially in Latin America and the Far East where American English is favoured (though never to the exclusion of British). But many foreign language speakers cannot distinguish, and Geordies and Australians are as welcome as people who speak with a BBC accent. The important factor is whether or not you speak slowly and clearly. In a few cases, Americans may have an advantage, since some groups (e.g. Japanese and Middle Eastern businessmen) who hope to do business in the US, prefer to learn the language from an American speaker. In other countries (like Spain and Italy) an English accent is preferred.

Consult the British Council in your destination, and trawl the internet and the *Yellow Pages* (print or online) in order to draw up a list of addresses where you can ask for work. Business schools often need teachers of commercial English. Read the adverts in the English language papers. Visit centres where foreigners study the local language and check the notice board or befriend the secretary. Several factors will affect the length of time it will take before you find something: for example at what point of the term you begin your search (e.g. late August/September is usually best followed by Christmas-time; summers are usually hopeless), whether you know the vernacular language (especially an advantage in Spanish-speaking countries) and how convincing you look carrying a briefcase. If you have no luck in the major cities, consider trying resorts popular with English speaking tourists. Here you will find plenty of locals very eager to learn enough English to secure them a job in the local tourist industry.

An alternative to working for a language school is to set yourself up as a freelance private tutor. While undercutting the fees charged by the big schools, you can still earn more than as a contract teacher. Normally you will have to be fairly well established in a place before you can attempt to support yourself by private teaching, preferably with some decent premises in which to give lessons (either private or group) and with a telephone. Laurence Koe gave after-hours conversation classes in northern Italy and charged each child 50 pence. You should bear in mind the disadvantages of working for yourself, viz. frequent last-minute cancellations by clients, unpaid travelling time (if you teach in clients' homes or offices), no social security and an absence of professional support and teaching materials.

If you do decide to try this, you will have to promote yourself unashamedly. Try posting eye-catching bilingual notices all around town (especially the prosperous areas) or even leafletting door to door. You can be more selective, and concentrate on relevant notice boards. To find school-age pupils you could visit ordinary state schools, introduce yourself to the head teacher and ask him/her to announce your willingness to offer extra English tuition. If you are less interested in making money than integrating with a culture, exchanging conversation for board and lodging may be an appealing possibility, which usually relies on having a network of contacts. But not always. According to our contributors, invitations to participate in such an arrangement have come while chatting to a Parisian businesswoman, lying on a Turkish beach or sitting by the side of a road in Thailand.

CHILDCARE

The terms au pair, mother's help and nanny are often applied rather loosely, since all are primarily live-in jobs concerned with looking after children. Nannies may have some formal training and take full charge of the children. Mother's helps work full-time and undertake general housework and/or cooking as well as childcare. Au pairs are supposed to work for no more than 30 hours a week and are expected to learn a foreign language while living with a family.

One of the great advantages of these live-in positions generally is that demand is so great that they are relatively easy to get (at least for women). After proving to an agency or a family that you are reasonably sensible, you will in the majority of cases be able to find a placement, though it is much easier and quicker in some countries than others, e.g. easy in France, Austria, Italy and Israel, but more difficult in Scandinavia and Portugal. Furthermore au pairs can often benefit from legislation which exempts them from work permit requirements.

Usually the reasons for wanting to be an au pair are that you want to improve your knowledge of the country's language and culture, that you wish to take a break from the routine of studies, work or unemployment, or that you wish to get some experience of catering and children before pursuing a career along those lines. Occasionally, young men can find live-in jobs, and slowly the number of families and therefore agencies willing to entertain the possibility of having a male au pair is increasing.

The standard length of stay is for one academic year, typically September to June. Summer stays can also be arranged to coincide with the school holidays. The advantage of a summer placement is that the au pair will accompany the family to their holiday destination at the seaside or in the mountains; the disadvantage is that the children will be your responsibility for more hours than they would be if they were at school, and also most language classes will close for the summer. Make enquiries as early as possible, since there is a shortage of summer-only positions.

Anyone interested in finding out about all aspects of live-in childcare should consult the fifth edition of *The Au Pair & Nanny's Guide to Working Abroad* (Vacation-Work, £12.95).

PROS AND CONS

The relationship of au pair to family is not like the usual employer/employee relationship; in fact the term au pair means 'on equal terms' and often the terminology 'hostess' and 'hospitality' is used. Therefore the success of the arrangement depends more than usual on whether individuals hit it off, so there is always an element of risk when living in a family of strangers. The Council of Europe guidelines stipulate that au pairs should be aged 18-27 (though these limits are flexible), should be expected to work about five hours a day, five days per week plus a couple of evenings of babysitting, must be given a private room and full board, health insurance, opportunities to learn the language and pocket money.

Once you have arrived in the family, it is important to clarify immediately what your hours and duties will be, which day you will be paid, whether you can expect a rise and how much notice either party must give if they wish to terminate the arrangement. This gets everyone off to a business-like start. But no matter how well-defined your duties are, there are bound to be occasions when your extra services will be taken for granted. It may seem that your time is not your own. Kathryn Halliwell worked for a family in Vancouver, Canada for a year and describes this problem: *'A live-in job is a very committed one. It is extremely difficult to say no when the employers ring at 6pm to say they can't be home for another two hours. Children don't consider a nanny as an employee and tension develops if a child can't understand why you won't take him swimming on your day off.'*

So the standard working hours can soon turn into an unofficial string of 14 hour days.

Whether you can tolerate this depends entirely on your disposition and on the compensating benefits of the job, e.g. free use of car and telephone, nice kids, good food, lots of sunshine, etc.

No matter how carefully you try to determine your duties and privileges, there is still plenty of scope for different interpretations of how the arrangement should work. At one extreme you have the family (with one well-behaved child) who invites you along on skiing trips with them and asks you to do a mere 24 hours of child-minding and light housework a week. On the other hand you might be treated like a kitchen skivvy by the mother, and like a concubine by the father, while at the same time trying to look after their four spoiled brats. So it is advisable to find out as much as possible about the family before accepting the job. If you do not like the sound of the family at the beginning you should insist that the agency offer any available alternatives.

Even though an au pair does have her own room, there may be a definite lack of privacy. This can be the logical extension of being treated like a member of the family. For example Claire Robson, who spent a summer working as an au pair in Greece, described how the mother accused her of being unsociable because she wouldn't come and watch television (all in Greek!) when invited. Such unreasonable expectations are often the result of different national temperaments as well as simple personality clashes. In conservative countries (e.g. Turkey, Spain, southern Italy), it is unacceptable for young women to go out alone at night, so your social life may be very restricted.

> **On the other hand, Gillian Forsyth's experience when she au paired in Bavaria was a great success**
> *I had no official day off or free time but was treated as a member of the family. Wherever they went I went too. I found this much more interesting than being treated as an employee as I really got to know the country and the people. In the evenings I did not have to sit in my room, but chatted with the family. Three years later we still keep in close contact and I have been skiing with them twice since, on an au pair/friend basis.*

If you do not have such a friendly arrangement with your family, you may feel lonely and cut off in a foreign country. Many au pairs make friends at their language classes. Some agencies issue lists of other au pairs in the vicinity. For those wanting to meet other au pairs in a similar situation, Leeson Clifton, who came from Canada to be a mother's help in Britain, recommends placing an advertisement in the local paper for an au pair get-together. Despite all the possible problems, au pairing does provide an easy and often enjoyable introduction to living and travelling abroad. A family placement is a safe and stable environment for young, underconfident and impecunious people who want to work abroad.

Pay

You may enjoy being an au pair but you are unlikely to get rich quick. Mind you, things have improved since pre-war days when, according to one of our older contributors, you were liable not to be paid a penny until you had completed your six-month contract, and even then it would barely cover your train fare home from Switzerland. The standard pocket money paid to au pairs in Europe nowadays is £50-£60 per week, though it can be more, for example in Switzerland where it is £300-£350 a month.

Having some nursery training or childcare experience can open other doors and bring higher wages. Most large tour and campsite holiday operators like Mark Warner, Airtours and Thomson Holidays (addresses in *Tourism* chapter) employ nannies to look after the children of holidaymakers. Companies that specialise in arranging summer and winter holidays for families, such as Esprit Alpine Sun, employ a considerable number of childcare staff as well as other employees for their summer programme in the Alps (185 Fleet Road, Fleet, Hampshire GU51 3BL; 01252 618318; recruitment@esprit-holidays.co.uk).

Nannying can be an excellent passport to spending a season in a summer or winter resort for those with a qualification or experience. Nannies Abroad Ltd is a specialist agency with offices in Winchester and Les Gets in France that trains and recruits nannies for British tour operations in Europe (Nannies Abroad Ltd, Abbots Worthy House, Abbots Worthy, Winchester SO21 1DR; 01962 882299; enquiries@nanniesabroad.com).

Duties

Before accepting a position that involves cooking you should establish what standard your employer has in mind. Unless you do this you may end up like Sally Collins, who wrote about her experiences in the *New Zealand News*: *'I soon began to understand that simple cooking – which I had rashly said I could do, imagining boiled eggs and toast – in fact involved a certain amount of cordon bleu knowledge. I had no idea what to do with the pheasant which was presented to me.'* Perhaps it would be a good idea to ask for a *Delia Smith's Complete Cookery Course* or a Jamie Oliver book for your birthday.

Most au pairs' duties revolve around the children. For some, taking sole responsibility for a child can be even more alarming than cooking pheasant for the first time. You should be prepared to handle a few emergencies (for example sick or lost children) as well as the usual excursions to the park or collecting them from school. The agency questionnaire will ask you in detail what experience you have had with children and whether you are willing to look after newborn infants, etc., so your preferences should be made known early. You must also be prepared to hurt the children's feelings when you leave. Nicky Parker left a family in Majorca after just nine weeks and reported, 'I could only feel guilty and sad at the distress caused to the children by yet another in a long line of people whom they had learned to love, leaving them forever.'

APPLYING

Au pair and nanny agencies are never more than referral services. If you have a contract, it will be with the family not the agency, though the agency may facilitate drawing up a contract. Since 2003 agencies in the UK have not been allowed to charge the applicant a fee (till then the allowable maximum was £40 + VAT). Their only chance of making a profit is if their partner agencies abroad are willing to share the fees they collect from the client families employing au pairs. Agencies which at one time sent many British girls abroad are now concentrating almost exclusively on placing foreign girls with paying client families in the UK.

If you are already abroad, check in the local English language newspaper such as the *Athens News* or the *Anglo Portuguese News* in Lisbon, or visit an au pair agency office in the country where you are (addresses provided in country chapters). Other ways of hearing about openings are to check the notice boards at the local English-speaking churches, ask the headmistress of a junior school if she knows of any families wanting an au pair or visit a school at the end of the school day and chat with the mothers and au pairs who are there to collect their charges. One tip for finding babysitting jobs in resorts is to introduce yourself to the *portière* or receptionist on the desk of good hotels and ask them to refer guests looking for a babysitter to you, possibly offering 10-15% commission.

The Internet

Cyberspace buzzes with an exchange of information about live-in childcare. Finding agency details is very easy with several clicks of a mouse and some agencies now conduct most of their business on the web. Au pair placement was something that was always done by telephone and correspondence rather than requiring a face-to-face interview, so it is an activity that is very well suited to the web. Among the most popular sites are www.au-pair-box.com; www.aupairsearch.com, www.aupair-contact.com, www.aupairconnect.com/default.asp, www.aupair-world.net, www.findaupair.com and www.perfectaupair.com.

Internet agencies have enabled families and applicants to engage in DIY arrangements. They invite prospective au pairs to register their details, including age, nationality, relevant experience and in many cases a photo, to be uploaded onto a website which then becomes accessible to registered families. The families then make contact with suitable au pairs after paying an introduction fee to the web-based agency. Registration is usually free or reasonably priced for the job-seeker.

One problem identified by the traditional agencies is that this method makes it very difficult to carry out any effective screening of either party. On the other hand, the same could be said for sits vac advertising in the conventional way (see below). If relying on the internet it is essential to ascertain exactly the nature of the situation and the expectations of your new employer. Work out in your mind what you will do in the event the arrangement does not work out; if the agency is simply a database-provider, they will be able to offer no back-up.

Jayde Cahir turned to the internet, found an agency, was emailed several families' portfolios from which she was able to make direct contact, and eventually chose a family in Germany. In initial discussions with the host family, she was misled on several counts and found that she was expected to be more a paid companion for the neglected wife than an au pair. Even though she did develop a good relationship with the wife and boy, the husband took against her and unceremoniously dismissed her: *'I left the house within two hours of receiving his note asking me to leave or he would 'throw me out'. So I was left in a foreign country, unable to speak the language with nowhere to live. In most cases, the agencies are there to support you; however mine never returned my phone calls. This ended up being a very expensive experience as I am still owed unpaid wages.'*

Of course this lack of agency back-up is not confined to internet agencies; in-country partner agencies can also be derelict in a crisis.

Two internet-based agencies worth trying are www.au-pair.net which calls itself the 'No agency Au Pair Service' and the Almondbury Au Pair Agency (www.aupair-agency.com). Both act as international internet databases of au pair and other live-in vacancies. In 2005 Almondbury's site claimed that its database included 9,230 applicants and 689 registered families. Another possibility is the Kent-based Aupair-Select on www.aupair-select.com.

The old-fashioned way of looking for live-in vacancies was by answering or placing advertisements in *The Lady* magazine (39/40 Bedford St, London WC2E 9ER) published each Tuesday. Most of the major agencies continue to advertise in its pages.

Agencies

Arguably there is too little regulation in the world of au pair agencies, and things can go wrong in even the most tightly controlled programmes. Many leading au pair agencies and youth exchange organisations in Europe belong to IAPA, the International Au Pair Association (c/o FIYTO, Bredgade 25H, 1260 Copenhagen K, Denmark), an international body trying to regulate the industry. The IAPA website www.iapa.org has clear links to its member agencies around the world.

Agencies that specialise in one country are mentioned in the country chapters. The following UK au pair and/or nanny agencies all deal with a number of European countries:

Abacus Au Pair Agency, 2 Byron Terrace, Byron St, Hove, E. Sussex BN3 5AY (tel/fax 01273 203803; info@abacusaupairagency.co.uk).

Almondbury Agency, 4 Napier Road, Holland Park, London W14 8LQ (tel/fax 01288 359159; www.aupair-agency.com).

A-One Au Pairs & Nannies, Top Floor, Union House, Union St, Andover, Hampshire SP10 1PA (01264 332500; info@aupairsetc.co.uk). Some outgoing placements but mainly places incoming au pairs in the UK.

The Au Pair Agency, 231 Hale Lane, Edgware, Middlesex HA8 9QF (020-8958 1750; elaine@aupairagency.com). Mainly France, Spain (including Majorca) and Italy.

Au Pair Connections, 39 Tamarisk Road, Wildern Gate, Hedge End, Southampton SO30 4TN (01489 780438; www.aupair-connections.co.uk). France, Spain, Italy.

Bloomsbury Bureau, Rokeby House, 86-90 Lambs Conduit St, London WC1N 3LX; 020-7430 2280; fax 020-7430 2325; bloomsburo@aol.com; www.bloomsburyaupairs. co.uk). Specialises in Germany.

Childcare International Ltd., Trafalgar House, Grenville Place, London NW7 3SA (020-

8906 3116; www.childint.co.uk). Separate divisions for Europe, Canada, Australia and South Africa.

Childcare Solution & Worldnet UK, Emberton House, 26 Shakespeare Road, Bedford MK40 2ED or Avondale House, 63 Sydney Road, Haywards Heath, W Sussex RH16 1QD (0845 458 1550/1; www.worldnetuk.com or www.thechildcaresolution.com). Seasonal nannies placed in European resorts, among other placements.

Edgware & Solihull Au Pair & Nanny Agency, PO Box 147, Radlett, Herts. WD7 8WX (01923 289739; www.the-aupair-shop.com).

International Student Exchange Center, 89 Fleet Street London EC4; 020-7583 9116; fax 020-7583 9117; www.isecworld.co.uk/ap.htm. Au pair placements in Denmark, France, Germany, Netherlands, Norway and the USA.

Janet White Agency, 67 Jackson Avenue, Leeds LS8 1NS (0113-266 6507; www. janetwhite.com).

Jolaine Agency, 18 Escot Way, Barnet, Herts. EN5 3AN (020-8449 1334; aupair@jolaine. prestel.co.uk). Placements in France, Italy, Spain and Belgium.

Lucy Locketts & Vanessa Bancroft Nanny Agency, 400 Beacon Road, Wibsey, Bradford, BD6 3DJ (tel/fax 01274 402822; www.Lucylocketts.com).

Nannies Abroad, Abbots Worthy House, Abbots Worthy, Winchester SO21 1DR (01962 882299/fax 01962 881888; www.nanniesabroad.com).

Nanny & Au Pair Connection, 435 Chorley New Road, Horwich, Bolton BL6 6EJ (tel/fax 01204 694422; info@aupairs-nannies.co.uk; www.aupairs-nannies.co.uk). Placements in Belgium, France, Spain, Portugal, Switzerland, Austria, Germany, Greece, Turkey, and USA.

Quick Help Agency, 307A Finchley Road, London NW3 6EH (020-7794 8666; www. quickhelp.co.uk).

Worldnet UK, see Childcare Solution above.

UK & Overseas Agency Ltd, Vigilant House, 120 Wilton Road, London SW1V 1JZ (020-7808 7898; london@nannys.co.uk; www.nannys.co.uk). Au pairs placed in France, Italy, Spain, Switzerland, Germany, etc.

Agencies in North America

Americans and Canadians interested in an au pair placement in Europe should contact the following agencies:

InterExchange Inc., Au Pair USA Programme, 13th Floor, 161 Sixth Avenue, New York, NY 10013 (212-924-0446; fax 212-924-0575; info@interexchange.org; www. interexchange.org). Au pairs to France, Germany, Netherlands and Spain.

Au Pair Canada, 15 Goodacre Close, Red Deer, Alberta, Canada T4P 3A3 (tel/fax 403-343-1418; aupaircanada@shaw.ca). Au pairs to France, Netherlands, Switzerland and Germany.

Le Monde Au Pair/World Au Pair, 7 rue de la Commune Ouest, Bureau 204, Montréal, Québec H2Y 2C5, Canada (514-281-3045/fax 514-281-1525; aupair@generation. net; www.generation.net/aupair). Au pair placements in Denmark, France, Germany, Italy, Netherlands, Norway, Spain, Switzerland, Austria, UK, USA, Australia and New Zealand. $299 programme fee.

Scotia Personnel Ltd., Au Pair Section, 6045 Cherry St, Halifax, Nova Scotia B3H 2K4, Canada (902-422-1455/fax 902-423-6840; www.scotia-personnel-ltd.com). Au pairs to USA, England, France, Holland, Germany, Italy, Australia, Spain, Denmark, etc. Also placements in summer camps in Italy, teaching in Korea and work experience in Britain.

Au pairing is very popular among South Africans especially in the Netherlands for obvious linguistic reasons (since Akrikaans is based on the Dutch that the Boers took to southern Africa). One of the main sending agencies is Youth Discovery Programmes, Oxford Manor, Ground Floor, 196 Oxford Road, Illovo, Johannesburg; www.ydp.co.za) with offices in Cape Town, Jo'burg and Durban. Similarly, various agencies in Australia and New Zealand recruit live-in child-care staff for Britain and Europe such as Affordable Au-Pairs & Nannies (+61-7-5530 1123; www.nanny.net.au).

VOLUNTEERING

Volunteering can provide a unique stepping stone to further adventures abroad and is often an adventure in itself. Many schemes are open to all nationalities and avoid work permit hassles. By participating in a project such as digging wells in a Turkish village, looking after orphaned refugee children or just helping out at a youth hostel, you have the unique opportunity to live and work in a remote community, and the chance to meet up with young people from many countries who can point you towards new job prospects. You may be able to improve or acquire a language skill and to learn something of the customs of the society in which you are volunteering. You will also gain practical experience, for instance in the fields of construction, archaeology, or social welfare which will stand you in good stead when applying for paid jobs elsewhere.

It should be pointed out that the majority of unskilled voluntary jobs undertaken abroad leave the volunteer out-of-pocket. Many organisations charge volunteers large sums to cover the cost of recruiting, screening, interviewing, pre-departure orientation, insurance, etc. on top of travel, food and lodging. Many of these are profit-making companies though some do give a proportion of the fees paid by volunteers to support the projects with which they're linked. If you are thinking of signing up with an organisation with which you are not familiar, it is a wise precaution to check with former volunteers. Be sure that you are aware whether the agency is a charity/non-profit or a commercial enterprise and ask for a breakdown of the costs.

In any case it is worth giving careful thought to whether or not you need to go through a mediating organisation. After chunks of time spent working and travelling in Latin America and having fixed up a teaching placement in Africa that turned out not to be as it was described by the placement agency, Till Bruckner knows her mind on this question:

> It strikes me as weird to collect volunteers from Britain who have to pay a fee plus their airfares to teach the children of the better-off in universities. In a country with poverty on that scale, there's more useful things you can do with £500 to help people in need. If you want fun, go elsewhere. If you want to help, put the £500 in an Oxfam charity box. I can see that some people might appreciate organisational support if they want to volunteer, but except in very restrictive countries (like Sudan), it's not really necessary. I met two girls in Bolivia who had just walked into a home for street kids and volunteered there and then. They got free board and lodging and all they did was talk to the kids and play with them since nobody ever did that. Those girls really did something valuable there. But if they had found themselves not able to contribute anything they would have had the freedom to walk out on the spot.

After participating in several prearranged voluntary projects in the United States, Catherine Brewin did not resent the fee she had paid to Involvement Volunteers (whose activities are described below):

> The whole business of paying to do voluntary work is a bit hard to swallow. But having looked into the matter quite a bit, it does seem to be the norm. While it may be a bit unfair (who knows how much profit or loss these voluntary organisations make or how worthy their projects?), most people I've met did seem to feel good about the experience. The group I was with did raise the odd comment about it all, but did not seem unduly concerned. However I should mention that most were around 18 years old and their parents were paying some if not all the costs.

Sources of Information

If you are interested in short or long term voluntary projects you might like to start by browsing in the *International Directory of Voluntary Work* (Vacation-Work, £11.95) which describes the voluntary requirements of 700+ organisations. Another excellent compendium is *Worldwide Volunteering* published by How To Books (2004, £17.99) in co-operation with the organisation of the same name as the book (www.worldwidevolunteering. org.uk). As well as being a web-based resource of voluntary opportunities worldwide, the Brighton-based Workingabroad.com will prepare a personalised report after you complete a detailed request form; the fee is £29/$42 by email, £36/$53 by post. Their office address is 2nd Floor Office Suite, 59 Lansdowne Place, Hove, BN3 1FL (tel/fax 01273 711406).

The World Service Enquiry of the respected charity Christians Abroad, Bon Marche Centre, Suite 233, 241-251 Ferndale Road, London SW9 8BJ (020-7346 5950/ 0870-770 3274; wse@cabroad.org.uk; www.wse.org.uk) provides information and advice to people of any faith or none who are thinking of working overseas, whether short or long term, voluntary or paid. A frequently updated booklet *The Guide* contains a useful listing of organisations in the UK and overseas, and details how and where to begin a search for work abroad. It can be downloaded in its entirety from the WSE website or posted in exchange for a large s.a.e. with a 60p stamp and £3. For qualified and professional job-seekers, *Opportunities Abroad*, a monthly listing of vacancies through around 60 development agencies, is available on subscription from WSE (£15 for three months online subscription, £19.50 hard copy including UK postage).

The revolution in information technology has made it easier for the individual to become acquainted with the amazing range of possibilities. There are some superb websites with a multitude of links to organisations big and small that can make use of volunteers. For example www.idealist.org (from Action Without Borders) is an easily searchable site that will take you to the great monolithic charities like the Peace Corps as well as to small grassroots organisations in Armenia, Tenerife or anywhere else. It lists 43,000 organisations in 165 countries. Another impressive site is one from AVSO, the Association of Voluntary Services Organisations, in Belgium (www.avso.org) which is supported by the European Commission. Although TimeBank is primarily intended to match British volunteers with UK projects, it has developed an online overseas directory (www.timebank.org. uk/givetime/overseas.htm). A vast array of links to little known projects can be found on the website of Seek, a resource for anyone interested in backpacking, volunteering, working, learning and wandering around the world (www.bolt.icestorm.com/lyric). The Japan-based Go Make a Difference (www.go-mad.org) has links to unusual voluntary projects.

Christian Vocations (St James House, Trinity Road, Dudley, West Midlands DY1 1JB; 0870 745 4825; www.christianvocations.org) publishes a searchable online directory of short-term opportunities with Christian agencies.

The Tsunami Disaster of Boxing Day 2004 focused minds on helping in an emergency in an unprecedented way. The outpourings of financial help from around the world were reinforced by an upsurge in the number of people wanting to donate their time to help. As with all emergency relief work, skilled and experienced professionals are in demand while well-meaning amateurs potentially just get in the way. In the immediate aftermath, the United Nations Volunteers (www.unv.org) drew up an emergency roster of potential volunteers keen to help in the relief effort and reconstruction in Southeast Asia. To be included on that, you had to have had experience in disaster response, be available at short notice, have worked in South Asia, be at least 25 years of age with a completed technical/university degree and fluent in English with some knowledge of local languages. Quite a tall order.

Pros and Cons

Bear in mind that voluntary work, especially in the developing world, can be not only tough and character-building but also disillusioning (see Mary Hall's description of her year at a Uganda clinic in the *Africa* chapter). And just as the working traveller must be alert to exploitation in paid jobs, so he or she should be careful in voluntary situations as well. Misunderstandings can arise, and promises can be broken just as easily in the context of unpaid work. Occasionally eager young volunteers are forced to conclude that the people in charge of the organisation charge volunteers well in excess of essential running costs.

Fortunately the experiences of one volunteer in Africa are rare: he claims to have discovered that the community development projects described in the literature from an organisation in Sierra Leone did not exist and furthermore the director had previously jumped bail from Freetown CID. If you are in any doubt about an organisation you are considering working for, ask for the names of one or two past volunteers whom you can contact for an informal reference. Any worthy organisation should be happy to oblige.

Disillusionment can be a problem for even the most privileged volunteers working for the most respectable charities. When Danny Jacobson visited Bulgaria, he found the country stuffed full of Peace Corps volunteers:

I had always envisioned Peace Corps volunteers to be off in Third World countries living in huts, repairing trees and teaching English to tribal children. In fact, in Bulgaria they all had sly apartments, decent salaries and an average of about 20 hours a week to commit to the cause. Everything from toothpaste to toilet paper was provided and twice a year they were all carted out to some fancy hotel to practise the language and bond. Pretty much everyone we met had a similar story: they joined to try to make a difference and were now left disenchanted and feeling useless. Since the Peace Corps is pretty relaxed about assigning duties – basically you are dropped off in a town and left to your own resources with no supervision – Chris had to start teaching English and later worked with a couple of guys to help build mountain huts and maintain hiking trails. Everyone was pessimistic because it seemed to take forever to get anything done.

Morale might well be higher in other countries.

Gap Year Placements

Far more students have been taking a year out to volunteer, work and travel between school and university than used to be the case. Many organisations attempt to make it possible for school-leavers as well as older people taking a gap year to undertake useful voluntary work abroad. Normally anyone can join a project provided they can pay the programme fees. All volunteers are asked to fundraise substantial sums, normally £2500-£3500. This is a brief listing of the major specialist organisations; for more information see my book *Taking a Gap Year* (Vacation Work, £11.95) or the website www.gapyear.com. Note that the market in career breaks is growing faster.

A number of UK organisations make it possible for school-leavers in their gap year to work for 6-12 months abroad. Most of the organisations listed here are founder members of the Year Out Group (Queensfield, 28 Kings Road, Easterton, Wilts. SN10 4PX; 07980 395789; www.yearoutgroup.org) which was formed to promote well-structured gap year programmes and now has 34 members:

GAP Activity Projects, 44 Queen's Road, Reading, Berks. RG1 4BB (0118-959 4914; www.gap.org.uk). Posts are for between four and eleven months (six is average) and cost the volunteer from £1200 to £1600 plus airfares and insurance, while board, lodging and (sometimes) pocket money are provided.

Gap Challenge, Black Arrow House, 2 Chandos Road, London NW10 6NF (020-8537 7980; www.world-challenge.co.uk). Teaching and other placements in India, Malaysia, Madagascar, Tanzania, South Africa, Costa Rica, Ecuador, Mexico and Peru. Fees £1600-£2900 including airfares.

Africa & Asia Venture, 10 Market Place, Devizes, Wilts. SH10 1HT (01380 729009; www.aventure.co.uk). Voluntary teaching and other projects for year-out students in several African and Asian countries. From £2500 plus airfares.

Changing Worlds, Hodore Farm, Hartfield, East Sussex TN7 4AR (01892 770000; www.changingworlds.co.uk). Voluntary Placements in schools, orphanages, zoos, etc. and paid jobs in hotels. Destinations include Australia, New Zealand, Canada, Chile, India, Nepal, Tanzania and Romania.

Global Vision International (GVI), Amwell Farmhouse, Nomansland, Wheathampstead, St.

Broaden your horizons

Changing Worlds

AUSTRALIA CANADA CHILE INDIA LATVIA
MADAGASCAR NEPAL NEW ZEALAND ROMANIA TANZANIA

For details of our voluntary placements, visit www.changingworlds.co.uk
or telephone 01892 770000 Changing Worlds, Hodore Farm, Hartfield, East Sussex TN7 4AR

Albans, Herts. AL4 8EJ (0870 608 8898; www.gvi.co.uk). 30+ conservation expeditions, volunteer projects and internships throughout Africa, Latin America, Europe, Asia and the USA.

Global Volunteer Network, PO Box 2231, Wellington, New Zealand (+64-4-569 9080; www.volunteer.org.nz). Volunteer projects including English teaching, environmental work, animal welfare, health and sanitation and cultural homestays in China, Ecuador, El Salvador, Ghana, Nepal, New Zealand, Romania, Russia, Thailand, Uganda and Vietnam. Application fee of US$350 applies to all programmes plus varying fees from US$395 for one month in Ecuador to $3,600 for 6 months in Uganda.

i-to-i, Woodside House, 261 Low Lane, Horsforth, Leeds LS18 5NY (0870 333 2332; www.i-to-i.com). TEFL and conservation placements in Latin America, Africa, Russia and Asia. 300 projects in 24 countries.

Madventurer, Hawthorn House, Forth Banks, Newcastle-upon-Tyne NE1 3SG (0845 121 1996; www.madventurer.com). Rural projects in Africa including Uganda and Togo combined with overland adventure travel. Now also includes Tonga and Brazil on list of destinations.

MondoChallenge, Galliford Building, Gayton Rd, Milton Malsor, Northampton NN7 3AB (01604 858225; www.mondochallenge.org). Volunteer placements in Nepal, India, Sri Lanka, Tanzania, Kenya, the Gambia, Senegal and Chile. £900 for three months plus homestay expenses from £15 a week.

Outreach International, Bartletts Farm, Hayes Road, Compton Dundon, Somerset TA11 6PF (tel/fax 01458 274957; www.outreachinternational.co.uk). Tries to match the interests and skills of individual volunteers with selected projects in Mexico, Cambodia, Ecuador and the Galapagos Islands. Volunteers might teach English, computer or art skills, work with street children, help to conserve sea turtles, etc. Suitable for energetic volunteers who wish to immerse themselves in a foreign culture for 3-6 months. Fee of £3100 includes all flights, insurance, language training, food and accommodation

Outreach International

GAP Year and Voluntary Projects in
Cambodia, Mexico, Ecuador and
The Galapagos Islands

Volunteers are needed to work on the
following projects for three to six months:

- Orphanages and Street Children
- Art, craft and dance
- Disabled children centres
- Special needs school
- Teaching English and sport in Pacific coast villages
- Conservation work in the Amazon
- Work with whales, dolphins and giant sea turtles
- Rehabilitation centres for land mine and polio victims
- Humanitarian aid with NGOs

Do you have an interest in immersing yourself in a
fascinating foreign culture whilst working on an
important, locally initiated, grass roots project?

Gap@outreachinternational.co.uk www.outreachinternational.co.uk
Tel/Fax James Chapman on: 01458 274957

plus in-country support.

Project Trust, The Hebridean Centre, Ballyhough, Isle of Coll, Argyll PA78 6TE (01879 230444; info@projecttrust.org.uk). Educational charity that sends British school-leavers aged 17-19 overseas for a year to many countries. Fund-raising target for 2005 is £3950.

Quest Overseas, The North-West Stables, Borde Hill Estate, Balcombe Road, Haywards Heath, W. Sussex RH16 1XP; 01444 474744; www.questoverseas.com). Run gap year projects and expeditions in South America, Central America and South Africa.

Raleigh International, 27 Parsons Green Lane, London SW6 4HZ (020-7371 8585; www.raleigh.org.uk). Offers young people aged 17-25 the chance to undertake demanding environmental and community projects overseas. Destinations include Chile, Belize, Namibia, Ghana and Mongolia. The fundraising target is about £3500.

Students Partnership Worldwide (SPW), 17 Dean's Yard, London SW1P 3PB (020-7222 0138; www.spw.org). Educational and environmental programmes lasting 4-9 months in Africa and Asia for 18-28 year olds. Volunteers are paired with indigenous volunteers. Fee £2900-£3300 includes airfares.

Teaching & Projects Abroad, Aldsworth Parade, Goring, Sussex BN12 4TX (01903 708300; fax 01903 501026; info@teaching-abroad.co.uk; www.teaching-abroad.co.uk). About 2,000 people are recruited annually as English language teaching assistants, business interns, conservation volunteers and in other fields. Destination countries include Russia, India, Ghana, Mexico, China, Peru, Togo, Nepal, Thailand and South Africa.

Travellers, 7 Mulberry Close, Ferring, West Sussex BN12 5HY (tel/fax 01903 502595; www.travellersworldwide.com). Volunteers teach conversational English (and/or other subjects) among other projects in India, Sri Lanka, Russia, Cuba, South Africa, Ukraine, Malaysia, etc.

Venture Co Worldwide, The Ironyard, 64-66 The Market Place, Warwick CV34 4SD (01926 411122; www.ventureco-worldwide.com). 4-month gap year and career break programmes in Latin America and Africa that combine language learning, voluntary work and an expedition.

Workcamps and Other Placement Organisations

Voluntary work in developed countries often takes the form of workcamps that accept unskilled short-term labour. As part of an established international network of voluntary organisations they are not subject to the irregularities of some privately run projects. As well as providing volunteers with the means to live cheaply for two to four weeks in a foreign country, workcamps enable volunteers to become involved in what is usually useful work for the community, to meet people from many different backgrounds and to 'increase their awareness of other lifestyles, social problems and their responsibility to society' as one volunteer has described it. According to one of the leading organisers, workcamps are a 70-year-old programme of conflict resolution and community development and an inexpensive and personal way to travel, live and work in an international setting.

> **Andrew Boyle, who has done a variety of jobs abroad subsequently, got off to an excellent start by joining several European workcamps**
> *I participated in three voluntary workcamps: two in West Germany and one in the French Alps. The former, particularly, were excellent value, both in the nature of the work (Umweltschutz or environmental protection) and in that the group of about 20 became part of the local community – meeting the locals in the kneipen or socialising with the 'Ziwis' (conscientious objectors doing community service instead of military service). These camps are an excellent introduction to travelling for 16 to 20 year olds, say, sixth formers who have never been away from a family type social structure. I suspect that their value would be more limited to an experienced traveller.*

The European Voluntary Service is an initiative of the European Commission to encourage young Europeans (aged 18-25) to join short and long term projects in social care, youth work, outdoor recreation and rural development. This programme is remarkable because volunteers do not have to pay to participate; EVS provides free travel, food, accommodation and an allowance. The EVS programme offers 2,500 places for young volunteers in fully funded placements lasting six but preferably 12 months in EU countries plus central and Eastern Europe, the Mediterranean region and Latin America. The programme is delivered in the UK by several agencies, most importantly the British Council's Connect Youth International section, 10 Spring Gardens, London SW1A 2BN (020 7389-4030; www.britishcouncil.org/connectyouth-programmes-european-voluntary-service.htm) and EIL Cultural & Educational Travel, 287 Worcester Rd, Malvern, Worcs. WR14 1AB (0800 018 4015; www.eiluk.org).

Within Europe, and to a lesser extent further afield, there is a massive effort to co-ordinate workcamp programmes. This normally means that the prospective volunteer should apply in the first instance to the appropriate organisation in his or her own country, or to a centralised international headquarters. The vast majority of camps take place in the summer months, and camp details are normally published online in March/April with a flurry of placements made in the month or two following. It is necessary to pay a registration fee (usually £80-£130 for overseas camps) to join a workcamp, which includes board and lodging but not of course travel. In developing countries, there may be an extra charge to help finance future projects or to pay for specialised training.

The largest workcamp organisation is Service Civil International with branches in 25 countries. The UK branch is International Voluntary Service (IVS) (addresses below). Occasionally in the pages of this book, we have included foreign addresses of workcamp organisations for the benefit of long-term travellers who are already in the country in which they want to join a workcamp or for readers who do not know the address of their national partner organisation. Ideally you will be able to access details of the workcamps through the websites given below. When requesting information by post, always send a stamped self-addressed envelope or international reply coupon, since these organisations are charities that need to keep costs to a minimum.

International Voluntary Service (IVS Field Office), Old Hall, East Bergholt, Colchester, Essex CO7 6TQ (01206 298215/fax 01206 299043; www.ivs-gb.org.uk). IVS North: Castlehill House, 21 Otley Road, Headingley, Leeds LS6 3AA (0113-230 4600) and IVS Scotland: 7 Upper Bow, Edinburgh EH1 2JN (0131-226 6722). Programme of camps published in April for £4. The cost of registration on workcamps outside the UK is currently £135 which includes £30 membership in IVS.

Concordia Youth Service Volunteers Ltd, Heversham House, 20-22 Boundary Road, Hove, East Sussex BN3 4ET (tel/fax 01273 422218; info@concordia-iye.org.uk; www. concordia-iye.org.uk). Programme of workcamps in 30 countries.

UNA Exchange, Temple of Peace, Cathays Park, Cardiff CF10 3AP (029-20 223088; www. unaexchange.org). Majority of camps cost between £100 and £140 to join.

Youth Action for Peace/YAP, 8 Golden Ridge, Freshwater, Isle of Wight PO40 9LE; 01983 752577; fax 01983 756900; www.yap-uk.org). Formerly the Christian Movement for Peace. Workcamps held in many countries in Western and Eastern Europe, plus Mexico, the Middle East and Bangladesh.

American volunteers should apply to one of the major workcamp organisations in the US:

CIEE, Global Volunteer Projects, 7 Custom House Street, 3rd Floor, Portland, ME 04101; 1-800-40-STUDY/ 207-553-7600; fax 207-553-7699; www.ciee.org/isp). 500 International Volunteer Projects in 30 countries. Their directory of opportunities is posted on their website in early April. Programme fee is $350 if booked early, $395 otherwise.

SCI-IVS (Service Civil International-International Voluntary Service), 5474 Walnut Level Road, Crozet, VA 22932 (tel/fax 206-350-6585; info@sci-ivs.org; www.sci-ivs.org).

Volunteers for Peace, 1034 Tiffany Road, Belmont, Vermont 05730 (802-259-2759; vfp@vfp.org; www.vfp.org). Annual membership $20. VFP publishes an up-to-date *International Workcamp Directory* with over 2,000 programme listings in 80 countries, available from mid-April. Registration for most programmes is $200 ($250 if under 18).

The majority of workcamps projects are environmental or social. They may involve the conversion/reconstruction of historic buildings and building community facilities. Some of the more interesting projects recently include building adventure playgrounds for children, reno-vating an open-air museum in Latvia, organising youth concerts in Armenia, constructing boats for sea-cleaning in Japan, looking after a farm-school in Slovakia during the holidays, helping peasant farmers in central France to stay on their land, excavating a Roman villa in Germany, forest fire spotting in Italy, plus a whole range of schemes with the disabled and elderly, conservation work and the study of social and political issues. It is sometimes pos-sible to move from project to project throughout the summer, particularly in countries such as France or Morocco where the workcamp movement is highly developed.

Living conditions (and the quality of food in particular) vary greatly. The working week is 30 hours though it can stretch to a maximum of 40 hours, spread over five or six days. On the whole, camps are under the direction of one or two leaders but participants often help in the decision making. Social events and excursions are invariably included in the programme and some organisations arrange study sessions. Although English is the lan-guage of many international camps, some of them do require knowledge of a foreign language.

Some charities and companies organise short-term voluntary projects that resemble workcamps but operate independently. For example a small non-profit organisation Aid-Camps International (5 Simone Court, Dartmouth Road, London SE26 4RP; 020-8291 6181; www.aidcamps.org) sends teams of volunteers of all ages to various projects. Three weeks might be spent renovating a school for disabled children in India, Nepal, Sri Lanka or Cameroon. Participants pay £550, half of which goes directly to the aid project.

Archaeology

Taking part in archaeological excavations is another popular form of voluntary work, but volunteers are usually expected to make a contribution towards their board and lodging. Also, you may be asked to bring your own trowel, work clothes, tent, etc. Archaeology Abroad (31-34 Gordon Square, London WC1H 0PY; fax 020-7383 2527; www.britarch. ac.uk/archabroad) is an excellent source of information, as they publish bulletins in April and November with details of excavations needing volunteers; in the past year between 700 and 1,000 definite places on sites were offered to subscribers. They do stress however that applications from people with a definite interest in the subject are preferred. An annual subscription costs £18 (£20/£22 overseas).

Another valuable list of over 200 digs from Kentucky to Sri Lanka needing volunteers is the *Archaeological Fieldwork Opportunities Bulletin* which is now available online in a searchable format on the website of the Archaeological Institute of America in Boston (www.archaeological.org). The print copy becomes available each December and can be obtained from Oxbow/David Brown Books (www.oxbowbooks.com); 800-791-9354 in North America; 01865 241249 outside North America for £14.95.

An online source of dig information is the memorably named Shovelbums (www.shovelbums.org/archaeology-field-schools.html) run by an individual in Columbus Ohio whose aim is to maintain an up-to-date directory of field schools worldwide. Anyone who can navigate in German can also check www.archaeologie-online.de.

For those who are not students of archaeology, the chances of finding a place on an overseas dig will be greatly enhanced by having some digging experience nearer to home. Details of British excavations looking for volunteers are published in *British Archaeology* magazine from the Council for British Archaeology (see *UK: Voluntary Work*).

Anthony Blake joined a dig sponsored by the University of Reims and warns that 'archaeology is hard work, and applicants must be aware of what working for eight hours in the baking heat means!' Nevertheless Anthony found the company excellent and the opportunity to improve his French welcome.

Israel is a country particularly rich in archaeological opportunities, many of them organised through the universities. Digs provide an excellent means of seeing remote parts of the country though Israeli digs tend to be more expensive than most. Conditions vary, but can be fairly primitive. Jennifer McKibben found 'washing (apart from hands and face) was allowed only one day in four, when one enjoyed the luxury of a communal hose-pipe shower to remove all of the sand and grime that easily accumulates after four days of digging in the desert.'

Conservation

People interested in protecting the environment can often slot into conservation organisations abroad. One enterprising traveller in South Africa looked up the 'green directory' in a local library, contacted a few of the projects listed in the local area and was invited to work at a cheetah reserve near Johannesburg in exchange for accommodation and food.

For a directory of opportunities in this specialised area, consult the 2005 edition of *Green Volunteers: The World Guide to Voluntary Work in Nature Conservation* distributed by Vacation Work Publications in Europe (£10.99 plus £1.50 postage). Related titles from the same publisher are *Working with the Environment* and *Working with Animals*. Websites worth investigating include that of the Coral Reef Alliance (www.coral.org) whose members sometimes recruit volunteers for coral reef protection.

To fix up a short-term project ahead of time, contact BTCV (British Trust for Conservation Volunteers) which runs a programme of UK and International Conservation Holidays in 27 countries including America, Iceland, Lesotho, Australia and Hungary. Further details are available from BTCV Customer Service, Balby Road, Doncaster DN4 0RH (01302 572244; www.btcv.org/shop). Accommodation, meals and insurance are provided at a cost from £240 per week of international projects.

The international system of working-for-keep on organic farms is another good way of visiting unexplored corners of the world cheaply. A description of the organisation WWOOF (World Wide Opportunities on Organic Farms) may be found in the *Agriculture* chapter. Also, staying on communes, peace centres and the like may be of interest, as discussed in the same chapter.

Involvement Volunteers Association Inc (PO Box 218, Port Melbourne, Victoria 3207, Australia; +61-3-9646 9392; ivworldwide@volunteering.org.au; www.volunteering.org. au) arranges short-term individual, group and team voluntary placements worldwide. Opportunities are currently available in all the usual countries plus Argentina, Bangladesh, Botswana, Brazil, Cambodia, Estonia, Fiji, Fiji, Lebanon, Malaysia (Sabah), Mongolia, Namibia, and so on. Many projects are concerned with conservation, the environment, animal welfare, etc. though some are in social and community service, education and childcare. Programme fees start at €400 and cover any number of placements lasting 2-12 weeks within one year. The UK office is at 7 Bushmead Ave, Kingskerswell, Newton Abbot, Devon TQ12 5EN (01803 872594; ivengland@volunteering.org.au). The European office is at Volksdorfer Strasse 32, 22081 Hamburg (+49 41269450; ivgermany@volunteering. org.au).

Catherine Brewin from St. Albans joined two IV projects in the US. Her reaction is typi-cal of many people who undertake voluntary work of any kind in exotic locations:

After a fortnight of doing general maintenance at a Conference Centre in southern California, I flew to Hawaii to work at a centre for mentally handicapped people. This was a considerably more restrictive environment than LA and involved us living with the handicapped residents ('clients') in a fenced off complex some distance from the nearest town. Again we did some physical work such as tree planting and weeding, and also took the clients on day trips and organised a disco. It was not an easy place to be and could hardly have been more of an antithesis to what the mind conjures up when you think of Hawaii, but it's amazing how your sense of humour and the people around you can pull you through, and I think we all learned from the experience.

Both the projects demanded quite a bit of flexibility. Things were seldom appar-ent or well organised, and there were times when we were unsure as to what we were supposed to do, or felt that we were expected to work on tasks totally outside our brief. I think anyone considering joining a voluntary work project should be aware that this may be the case. I must admit that for me, two fortnight-long projects was enough and I was happy to move on, leave a group situation and start travelling and doing what I wanted to do.

Global Park Exchanges (www.globalparkexchanges.org) describes itself as an interna-tional sourcing agency which provides services to National Parks around the world includ-ing matching of volunteers. GPE is based in italy (Via P. Mascagni 15, 00199 Rome; +39 0686 01125) however its partner agency in the UK is Global Visions International mentioned above.

It is the function of several organisations to help and staff scientific expeditions by supplying fee-paying volunteers and it seems that there is a booming market for this sort of working holiday. Scientific expedition organisations that use self-financing volunteers include the following, some of whose expeditions are mentioned in the country chapters:

Biosphere Expeditions, Sprat's Water, Nr. Carlton Colville, The Broads National Park, Suffolk NR33 8BP (01502-583085; www.biosphere-expeditions.org). Volunteers of all backgrounds help scientists working on wildlife conservation projects lasting 2-8 weeks. Volunteers contribute £990-£1250. Projects in 2004/5 included wolf conservation in Ukraine, wildlife surveying on the Amazon and cheetah conservation in Namibia.

Coral Cay Conservation Ltd, 13th Floor, 125 High St, Colliers Wood, London SW19 2JG (0870 750 0668; www.coralcay.org). Non-profit organisation that sends teams of paying volunteers to survey endangered coral reefs and tropical forests in the Philippines, Fiji, Honduras, Cuba and Malaysia. Volunteers require no prior scientific or dive experience as full training is given. Sample six-week marine project costs £1800 (£2000 for dive trainee).

Earthwatch Institute (Europe), 267 Banbury Road Road, Oxford OX2 7HT (01865 318831; www.earthwatch.org/europe). International non-profit organisation that recruits volunteers to join more than 100 scientific research projects on which they assist professional, scientific field research expeditions around the world. Project contributions range from £155 for a short local project to £2195 for periods lasting 3-18 days. The contribution is a charitable donation that helps to fund the research and usually includes accommodation, food, equipment, local transport and training. Prices do not include air travel to location. Americans should request information from the Earthwatch Institute, 3 Clocktower Place, Suite 100, PO Box 75, Maynard, MA 01754, USA (1-800-776-0188; www.earthwatch.org).

Frontier, 50-52 Rivington St, London EC2A 3QP (020-7613 2422; www.frontierconservation. org). Places volunteers on 4, 8, 10 or 20-week phases on projects in Cambodia, Madagascar, Tanzania and Nicaragua. Fees for 20-week projects range from £3,600 to £3,950.

Greenforce, 11-15 Betterton Street, Covent Garden, London WC2H 9BP (020-7470 8888; www.greenforce.org). Recruits volunteer researchers to join biodiversity conservation aid projects in Malaysian Borneo, Fiji, Bahamas, Zambia, Ecuador and Nepal. 10-week stints as fieldwork assistants studying endangered species and habitats. No previous experience needed as training is provided. The cost is £2300-£2700 plus flights.

Trekforce Expeditions, 34 Buckingham Palace Road, London SW1W 0RE (020-7828 2275; www.trekforce.org.uk). Rainforest conservation charity that runs projects in Belize, Amazonian Guyana and East Malaysia (Sabah and Sarawak) concentrating on endangered rainforests. Fundraising targets begin at £2950 and go up to £3900 for 5-month programmes in Latin America.

Developing Countries

Commitment, no matter how fervent, is not enough to work in an aid project in the developing world. You must normally be able to offer some kind of useful training or skill unless you are prepared to fund yourself and don't mind that your effort to help will be more a token than of lasting benefit. Many organisations offer ordinary people the chance to experience life in the developing world by working alongside local people for a brief period and these are mentioned throughout the chapters on Africa, Asia and Latin America later in this book. Geoffroy Groleau from Quebec decided to spend some months in India and wanted to dedicate part of his time to volunteering in the development field. He stumbled across an Indian NGO on the internet and arranged to work for a month with Dakshinayan (see chapter on Asia).

> **Geoffroy ended up thinking that his enjoyment took precedence over his usefulness**
>
> *Volunteers should expect to learn more from the people than they will ever be able to teach. Remember that the villagers know much more about their needs than we do, and they have learned long ago to use effectively the resources around them. On the other hand, the contacts with the outside world that the volunteers provide is a valuable way for the villagers to begin to understand the world that surrounds them. In my experience, the hardest things were to adapt to the rather slow rhythm of life and to the fact that as a volunteer you will not manage to change significantly the life of the villagers other than by putting your brick in a collective work that has been going on for many years.*

Among the main voluntary and aid organisations in the UK and Europe are:

VSO, Enquiries Unit, 317 Putney Bridge Rd, London SW15 2PN (020-8780 7500; enquiry@vso.org.uk; www.vso.org.uk). Recruits professional volunteers in the fields of education, health, natural resources, technical trades and engineering, business and social work for two-year assignments. VSO pays a modest local wage, various grants, national insurance, provides accommodation, health insurance and return flights. Volunteers need to be aged 20-75, and qualified and experienced. A shortage of volunteers has prompted VSO to investigate shorter periods with companies keeping open the volunteer's job.

AFS Intercultural Programmes UK, Leeming House, Vicar Lane, Leeds LS2 7JF; 0113-242 6136; www.afsuk.org). Voluntary work opportunities for students and others aged 18-29 in Latin America, Africa and Asia. Placements last 6 months and involve living with a local family. Fee of £3300 including airfares.

Inter-Cultural Youth Exchange (ICYE), Latin American House, Kingsgate Place, London NW6 4TA (tel/fax 020-7681 0983; info@icye.co.uk). Students and others aged 18-30 spend 6 or 12 months abroad with a host family and undertake voluntary work placements, for example in drug rehabilitation, protection of street children and ecological projects in one of 30 countries in Latin America. Africa, Asia, and worldwide. No specific skills needed as this is a skills development programme. Fee is £2900 for 6-month placement, £3300 for full year.

World Exchange is a church-sponsored volunteer abroad programme based at St Colm's International House, 23 Inverleith Terrace, Edinburgh EH3 5NS (0131-315 4444; we@stcolms.org; www.worldexchange.org.uk) which sends skilled and unskilled volunteers to Malawi, Swaziland, India, Pakistan, Lebanon and others to work with schools and community organisations for 10-12 months. Programme provides all travel and living expenses; volunteers must fund-raise a minimum of £2500. Also organise study/workcamps for 4-6 weeks that cost £1000.

North American Opportunities

In the US, the website of the International Volunteer Programs Association has links to all the mainstream organisations (www.volunteerinternational.org). Note that volunteer-match.org is intended for Americans looking for local opportunities in the US. InterAction based in Washington DC posts vacancies in international relief and development agencies (www.interaction.org/jobs).

Companies that maintain databases of opportunities (mostly unpaid) and offer personalised consultations to fee-paying clients (often young people aged 16-25) attempt to match them with a suitable work, volunteer or study placement abroad. Many of the placement organisations to which candidates will be referred offer what are basically volunteer vacations, i.e. two or three week service programmes in developing countries for a substantial fee:

Taking Off - 617-424-1606; fax 617-344-0481; takingoff@takingoff.net; www.takingoff. net). Taking Off provides ongoing personal assistance to those looking for international experiences that include volunteer work, internships and custom-designed situations (not paying jobs). See website for up-to-date description of services and costs.

Center for Interim Programs LLC, PO Box 195 Nassau St, No 5, Princeton, NJ 08542 (609-683-4300; www.interimprograms.com). Consulting service based in Princeton NJ and Cambridge MA aimed primarily at pre-university and university students looking to arrange a worthwhile experience in the US or abroad that includes room and board, e.g. internships and volunteer work. Database with 5,000+ options. Consulting fee from $1,900.

LEAPNow, PO Box 1817, Sebastopol, CA 95473 (707-829-1142; www.leapnow.org). Structured programme for Americans aged 17-21 in Central America or India that can count as college credit.

Horizon Cosmopolite, 3011 Notre Dame Ouest, Montreal, Quebec, Canada H4C 1N9 (514-935-8436; www.horizoncosmopolite.com). Database of volunteer work, internships and Spanish immersion in 30 countries around the world. Tries to match clients with suitable placements. Registration fee (C$350-C$495) guarantees placement.

World Wide Volunteer Services (WWVS), PO Box 3242, West End, NJ 07740 (732-571-3210; http://welcome.to/volunteer_services). Individually arranged multi-cultural experiences and internships in a variety of settings around the world. Application fee

$50 plus placement fee $100.

The Quaker Information Center (1501 Cherry St, Philadelphia, PA 19102; 215-241-7024; www.quakerinfo.org) collates a great deal of information about volunteering which can be accessed online or by post for a $10 contribution ($12 if outside the US). The information, which is updated sporadically, covers what they aptly call a 'smorgasbord' of opportunities ranging from weekend workcamps through to two-year internships with aid agencies.

The first organisation that American volunteers think of is the *Peace Corps* (1111 20th St NW, Washington, DC 20526; 1-800-424 8580/202-692-1800; www.peacecorps.gov) which sends both skilled and unskilled volunteers on two-year assignments to 77 countries.

Kristie McComb was posted to Burkina Faso from 2001 to 2003 and gradually concluded that the Peace Corps programme places less emphasis on development than on cultural exchange, i.e. sharing American culture with the host country nationals and then sharing the culture of your host country with Americans on your return

The cool thing for Americans is that you don't have to be qualified in anything to be accepted by the Peace Corps. There are many generalist programmes where you can learn what you need to know once you get there through the three-month pre-service training. I would encourage interested parties to be honest about what they can and cannot tolerate since not all volunteers are sent to live in mud huts. In a world changed by terrorism it is comforting to know how much of an active interest the US government takes in the safety and well being of its citizens abroad. However some people might find this stifling and not adventurous enough. How well PC keeps tabs on volunteers in any given country depends on the local PC leadership but, regardless, you are still in a high profile group of well locatable people. Risk reduction is the buzz word in Washington these days.

Overall I am happy with my experience though I am often frustrated by the inertia, the corruption and bureaucracy that makes me question whether anything will ever change. But you do gain a lot by (if nothing else) witnessing poverty on a regular basis. You quickly learn to recognise the difference between a problem and an inconvenience and to see how lucky we are as Americans to have some of the 'problems' we have.

Not all volunteers can commit themselves for two years and are looking for shorter assignments. Sarah Smith from Newark, New Jersey describes herself as something of an expert volunteer vacationer, and no longer has any desire to go on a typical mass-tourist vacation. She assesses her varying expenses on five separate volunteering trips which highlights some of the issues to think about when choosing among the many companies offering trips and placements:

I spent about $1500 to go on an i-to-i trip for almost 3 months as an English teacher in a small village in Costa Rica. The people were just amazing, the rainforest was incredible, and I genuinely felt I was contributing. The only down side was that I also had to pay $300 a month for food, and I found out that not one dollar of my contribution went to the local community. I understand that the organisation must fund itself but was disappointed that NONE of the funds went to the community. The scheme did include some pretty decent Spanish lessons prior to the beginning of my volunteer work.

A two-week workcamp in Thailand through SCI was the least expensive trip I've been on by far and it showed. I hardly got any orientation materials, there seemed to be no communication whatsoever between SCI and the local community, and I was not able to get any answers to any of my pre-trip questions. Yet this is a great option for those who are willing to deal with a lot of unknowns. The work was good, though not particularly well organised, and I had to pay an additional 'meal fee' once I arrived.

Two years ago I went on a Global Volunteers trip to teach English in a charming little school in southern Italy - the cost was high - nearly $3000 before my airfare, however it was very well organised and our leader made the trip fun and meaningful. For those who have the money, these are well run trips.

This month I just returned from a volunteer vacation with Globe Aware to an orphanage in Cuzco, Peru. The one down side was that I really enjoy longer trips and this was only one week. Not only was it relatively cheap, but they help to per-suade your employer to foot part of the bill, which worked in my case. Our free time was well organised (and we got to see Machu Picchu), and the varied work with the children was deeply touching. I find myself so deeply grateful for the things in my life and I wish everyone could have the opportunity to do this.

Here is a selection of major organisations (most of whom favour the concept of being global, judging from their choice of names):

Cross-Cultural Solutions, 2 Clinton Place, New Rochelle, NY 10801 (1-800-380-4777; www.crossculturalsolutions.org). UK office: Tower Point, 44 North Road, Brighton BN1 1YR (0845 458 2781/2). Volunteers are placed in short-term volunteer projects in Ghana, India, China, Costa Rica, Guatemala, Peru, Brazil, Thailand, Tanzania and Russia.

Experiential Learning International, PO Box 9282, Denver, CO 80209 (303-321-8278; www.eliabroad.com). Volunteering programmes in Argentina, Ecuador, India, Ghana, Kenya, Mexico, Nepal, Philippines and Poland; plus intern placements in Ecuador, India, Ghana and Nepal. Sample price for 2 weeks of teaching English at Polish summer school is $995, or in the Philippines $495 placement fee plus $50 a week.

Explorations in Travel Inc, 2458 River Road, Guildford, VT 05301 (802-257 0152; www.volunteertravel.com). International volunteers for rainforest conservation, wildlife projects, etc. in Ecuador, Costa Rica, Belize, Guatemala and Puerto Rico. Other placements in animal shelters, on small farms and in schools. Placement fees start at around $800.

Global Volunteers, 375 E Little Canada Road, Little Canada, Minnesota 55117, USA (651-482-0915/toll-free 1-800-487-1074; www.globalvolunteers.org). Non-profit voluntary organisation that sends 1,500 paying volunteers a year to scores of projects lasting from one to three weeks in Africa, Asia, the Caribbean, the Americas and Europe. Service programmes cost between $500 (for projects in the US) and $2,395 excluding airfares.

Global Service Corps, 300 Broadway, Suite 28, San Francisco, CA 94133 (www.globalservicecorps.org). Co-operates with grass-roots organisations in Thailand and Tanzania and sends volunteers and interns for two or three weeks or longer.

Global Routes, 1 Short St, Northampton, MA 01060 (www.globalroutes.org). Offers 12-week voluntary internships to students over 17 who teach English and other subjects in village schools in Kenya, Costa Rica, Ecuador, Ghana and Thailand. Participation fee $3,550 for the summer and nearly $4,000 for the spring and autumn (excluding airfares.

Global Citizens Network, 130 N Howell St, St Paul, Minnesota 55104 (651-644-0960; www.globalcitizens.org). Sends volunteers to projects in Kenya, Nepal, Peru, Guatemala, Mexico and several US states.

Globe Aware, 7232 Fisher Road, Dallas, Texas 75214-1917 (214-823-0083; www.globeaware.org). Short volunteer vacations in Peru, Costa Rica, Brazil, Cuba, Nepal, Thailand and India.

International Cultural Adventures, Brunswick, Maine, USA; 888-339-0460; info@ICAdventures.com; www.ICAdventures.com. Cultural, educational and volunteer service experiences in Peru, India and Nepal. Fees for 6-week summer programmes from $2,200 and from $2,900 for 3+ months semester programmes beginning in

February, March, July and September.

Institute for Cultural Ecology, PO Box 991, Hilo, Hawaii 96721 (808-640-2333; www. cultural-ecology.com). Internships on several Hawaiian islands, Fiji and Thailand. Sample placements cost from $2,000 for four weeks, $4,000 for 12 weeks of reef-mapping on the Fiji coast.

Visions, PO Box 220, Newport, PA 17074-0220 (717-567-7313; www. visionsserviceadventures.pa.net). 3 or 4 week 'service adventures' in Dominican Republic, Guadeloupe, Ecuador, Montana, Alaska and Australia. Cost about $4,000.

Wildlands Studies, 3 Mosswood Circle, Cazadero, CA 95421 (707-632-5665; www. wildlandsstudies.com). Conservation projects lasting six weeks in the US (including Alaska and Hawaii), Belize, Thailand, Nepal, etc.

World Endeavors, 2518 29th Avenue South, Minneapolis, MN 55406 (612-729-3400; www. worldendeavours.com). Volunteer, internship and study programmes lasting 2 weeks to 2 months in Costa Rica, Ecuador, Philippines, Thailand, etc.

Going it Alone

In the course of your travels, you may come across wildlife projects, children's homes, special schools, etc. in which it will be possible to work voluntarily for a short or longer time. You may simply want to join your new Tongan, Bangladeshi or Guatemalan friends in the fields or wherever they are working. You may get the chance to trade your assistance for a straw mat and simple meals but more likely the only rewards will be the experience and the camaraderie.

Some travellers who find themselves in the vicinity of a major disaster think that their assistance will be welcomed. But with no practical skills, they often become a nuisance and a burden to professional aid workers. But if you are spending time in one place in the developing world you are bound to make the acquaintance of the aid community who will be plugged into the needs of local NGOs and international agencies. While Till Bruckner was staying in the Sudan she noticed that overseas branches of Oxfam, Save the Children, etc. had huge volumes of reports to write, something that the local staff sometimes struggled to do in polished English:

Till Bruckner reports:
Take your CV and walk into headquarters, suggesting you could help with report writing. Due to bureaucratic obstacles they can't give you a paid job. But if you've worked with them on a voluntary basis for a few months and there's a job coming up, chances are good that they'll take you on. If not, you've genuinely helped a good cause. My advice to anyone who wants to volunteer in Africa (or anywhere else) is to go first and volunteer second. That way you can travel until you've found a place you genuinely like and where you think you might be able to make a difference. You can also check out the work and accommodation for yourself before you settle down. If you're willing to work for free, you don't need a nanny to tell you where to go. Just go.

Work Your Way in Europe

United Kingdom	Greece & Cyprus
Ireland	Italy
Netherlands	Scandinavia
Belgium & Luxembourg	Spain & Portugal
France	Switzerland & Austria
Germany	Central Europe & Russia

Key to Symbols

working on grape harvest – picking, carrying, pressing

apple picking

cherry picking

berry picking

citrus fruit picking

picking mixed fruit (peaches, pears, bananas etc.)

working on olive harvests

work in agricultural nurseries

work on tobacco harvest – priming or planting

hop picking and tractor driving

vegetable picking and planting

stock and general farming

food canning and freezing

fishing; in combination with above, means fish processing

working in ski resorts

work in tourist centres – hotels, bars, resort complexes

work in yacht harbours, painting, crewing etc.

teaching English as a foreign language

building, factory or other industrial work

mining or (if in sea) oil drilling

United Kingdom

Many readers of this book will begin to plan their world travels in Britain, and it is in Britain that they will want to save up an initial travelling fund. The amount of savings will vary from a few pounds to more than a thousand, depending on the ambitiousness of the travel plans and on the individual's willingness to live rough and take risks once he or she sets out. Some people are lucky enough to have a reasonably well paid and stable job as a teacher, postman or software developer before they set out on their adventures and will be in a good position to save. Others will have to gather together as many funds as possible from doing casual work at home before pursuing the same activities abroad.

Readers in other countries will also be interested in the information contained in this chapter if they are planning a working holiday in Britain. Armies of young people, particularly Antipodeans, arrive year round and quickly plug into the network of like-minded travellers looking for work in London and beyond. Everyone knows that London is an expensive city and not a pleasant place for people with few funds. Joe Warnick from Washington arrived with $500 and within three weeks was down to a measly $30. But plenty of jobs are going begging with an unemployment rate among the lowest in Europe (4.7% in 2005).

RED TAPE

Nationals of the newly expanded European Union are not subject to immigration controls and are all entitled to enter Britain to look for work. The only restriction on nationals of the ten new countries applies to their right to claim benefit. For non-EU citizens, most of whom enter on six-month tourist visas (which can normally be renewed on re-entering the country after an absence), it is difficult to find legal work. In general the Department of Employment does not issue work permits to unskilled and semi-skilled workers. Until recently, employers seldom asked to see proof of status (though they would ask for your National Insurance number). However a law has been introduced to curb illegal employment by requiring employers to see documentary proof of status and not rely solely on verbal assurances. Still, the UK is not a very bureaucratic country so this practice is not universal.

The high levels of employment in southern England mean that seasonal employers are having a very hard time filling vacancies. In more skilled areas of employment (primarily information technology, especially in the London area), labour shortages are increasing to such an extent that the government introduced a new fast-track work permit for seasonal and temporary workers. Immigration rules are being relaxed on a number of fronts, for example in some cases it is no longer necessary to leave the country to apply for a work permit.

In 2003 Work Permits (UK) introduced a new low-skilled work permit scheme. The Sectors Based Scheme (SBS) operates in the food manufacturing sectors (fish, meat and mushroom processing) and the hotels and catering sector. As with all work permits, a limited number are granted to employers who can show that they have been unable to fill unskilled vacancies (i.e. below NVQ Level 3) with resident workers and have found suitable non-EU nationals aged 18-30. Last year, the total number of SBS work permits granted was 20,000. As usual it is the employer and not the employee who is responsible for obtaining the correct documentation while the prospective applicant is still in his or her home country. Further information is available at www.workingintheuk.gov.uk and any queries should be directed to their Customer Relations Team on 0114-259 4074. At the time of writing the scheme was under review.

Commonwealth nationals who can produce documentary evidence that a parent or grandparent was born in the UK can gain permission to stay and work. After completing four continuous years of work they can apply for permanent residency.

Working Holiday Visas

Working holiday-maker status may be obtained by members of Commonwealth countries between the ages of 18 and 30 inclusive with no dependants over the age of five. The working holiday permit entitles the holder to work in Britain with the primary intention of funding a holiday, for up to two years. It does not allow the holder to work for more than 25 hours a week, nor to work for more than a half of the total stay. For the period from June 2003 to February 2005, the rules were more liberal in allowing candidates to undertake career-type jobs over a continuous two year period, but that has now been revoked.

It is essential to apply in the country of origin rather than at the point of entry. Immigration officials will want to be reassured that the employment you will be seeking is incidental to your travels and that it is your firm intention to leave the UK after no more than a total of two years which must be continuous from the date of entry to Britain. You may be asked to prove that you have enough money to support yourself and fund a return airfare.

Other Visas

The Training & Work Experience Scheme (TWES) is a special arrangement within the Work Permit scheme which allows foreign nationals to do work-based training for a professional or specialist qualification, a graduate training programme or work experience. TWES permits are issued on the understanding that the individual will return overseas at the end of the agreed period and put the skills learned to use for at least two years. Normally, they will not be allowed to transfer to work permit employment. Applications for permits can only be made by employers based in the UK on behalf of the person they wish to employ.

Students in the UK who are not nationals of a European Economic Area (EEA) country and who have in their passports a stamp stating that they cannot work 'without the consent of the Secretary of State' are no longer required to obtain permission to take spare time and vacation work, or to undertake work or internship placements. Only students on courses lasting more than six months are eligible. They are allowed to work up to 20 hours a week during term-time and they should not fill a permanent full-time vacancy in pursuit of their career.

Anyone entering the country as a visitor or tourist who intends to stay longer than a few weeks should have a water-tight story, something Woden Teachout from Vermont had not prepared:

Coming into the UK I had a horribly distressing immigration experience. On the advice of my travel agent, I had bought a six-month return ticket rather than an open return and expected no problems. Everything went awry. I think it was when I wavered over how long I meant to be in the country that the immigration official

GREAT BRITAIN

Thurso

Ullapool

Inverness

Aviemore • Aberdeen

SCOTLAND

Ben Nevis Pitlochry Forfar

Blairgowrie

Firth of Tay

North Sea

GLASGOW EDINBURGH

Newcastle-upon-Tyne

Belfast

LAKE
DISTRICT

Isle
of Man

DUBLIN
Leixlip

IRELAND

Blackpool

York

Llandudno

Cheshire

BIRMINGHAM

THE
FENS King's Lynn

Wisbech

WALES

Stourport
Worcester

Pershore

Hereford

Evesham

Lowestoft

Cambridge

Saxmundham
Tiptree

Pembroke

Cardiff

BRISTOL Oxford

Abingdon

Henley

Chelmsford

LONDON

Westward Ho!

Bridgwater

Guildford

Tonbridge

Ramsgate
Maidstone Sandwich

WEST COUNTRY

Sidmouth

Southampton

Kent

Cornwall

Torquay

Plymouth

Bournemouth

Brighton

Isle
of Wight

Bognor

English Channel

WILLIAM SWAN

became suspicious. The lady-turned-ogre forced me to produce my passport, ticket, money, address book and wrote down my entire life's history in cramped cursive on the back of my entrance card. I portrayed myself as a spoilt and privileged child, funded by Mummy and Daddy in her aimless intercontinental wanderings. When she at last grudgingly stamped me into the country, she called after me in a voice thick with derision, 'Do you think you'll ever work for a living?'

A few weeks later Woden had five different jobs.

Special Schemes & Exchange Organisations

This chapter describes a number of special schemes for young people from the United States, Canada, Australia, New Zealand, Central and Eastern Europe, etc. which allow them to work legally in Britain. For example the Seasonal Agricultural Workers Scheme or SAWS (see section on Harvests) and BUNAC's reciprocal work exchanges are open to large numbers of young people from various countries.

The Home Office is the body which governs these schemes: Immigration & Nationality Directorate enquiry line 0870 606 7766 (www.ind.homeoffice.gov.uk). Students and others from EU and non-EU countries may be able to participate in work exchange programmes, many of which charge a substantial placement fee. Careers advisers in universities and colleges should be the best source of information.

Students from Central and Eastern Europe interested in temporary work in the UK should find out about the Harvesting Opportunity Permit Scheme (HOPS) which recruits a limited number of Central and East European full-time students aged 20 to 25 to pick fruit, vegetables or hops on HOPS (GB) registered farms for three months between May and November. The scheme has been very over-subscribed in the past, though the fact that nationals of Slovakia, Poland and the other new European countries are now entitled to work in Britain in any case may change that situation. (See the section below on the Seasonal Agricultural Workers Scheme.)

Interspeak, based in the north of England, undertakes to find traineeships *(stages)* for students mainly in the fields of marketing, retail, engineering, hotel work and computing. A fee of £340 is payable for placements which last from one to six months. Accommodation is arranged with host families which helps participants to improve their spoken English, though some knowledge of English is necessary before acceptance. Details will be sent on receipt of an s.a.e (A5) posted to Interspeak, Stretton Lower Hall, Stretton, Malpas, Cheshire SY14 7HS (01829 250641; www.interspeak.co.uk). They also organise *mini-stages* in the UK (as well as on the continent) whereby students aged 16-18 are found short work placements for one or two weeks.

Similarly Trident Transnational (The Smokehouse, Smokehouse Yard, 44-46 St John St, London EC1M 4DF; 020-7014 1420; www.trident-transnational.org) assists students and recent graduates to obtain internships and summer holiday jobs in the UK. Although they have in the past been able to assist non-EU nationals to obtain a TWES permit to do unpaid work experience in London and beyond, at the moment they have the staff only to help European candidates. In exchange for a fee of £235 (work experience) or £195 (working holidays), they will send CVs around relevant companies on behalf of people who want to work for up to 12 months.

The problem of work permits does not normally arise in the case of voluntary work, though participants will have to have a valid visa to be in Britain (where applicable). Conservation camps and other voluntary projects generally offer an enthusiastic welcome to foreign participants (see section on volunteering at the end of this chapter). For example CSV (5th Floor, Scala House, 36 Holloway Circus, Queensway, Birmingham B1 1EQ (0800 374991; www.csv.org.uk) run an overseas programme in the UK in which people from outside the UK aged 18+ are placed alongside British volunteers in projects with people who need help, such as children with special needs, adults with learning difficulties, teenagers at risk of offending and homeless people. Volunteers do not need any previous experience, special skills or minimum qualifications to join. During the projects which last from between four and 12 months, food, accommodation and £29 weekly allowance are paid together with travel expenses from the point of entry into the UK. All overseas CSV volunteers must pay a non-refundable placement fee of about £520 before receiving a placement.

Many recruitment agencies specialise in bringing EEA nationals to the UK (and to Jersey, the Isle of Man and the Republic of Ireland) to work in hotels (see *Tourism* section below). Lots of commercial agencies on the continent sell packaged working holidays to young people. Caution should be exercised when paying over large sums to a mediating agency since some offer a very poor service as Emiliano Giovannoni from Italy explains:

> *Every year there are hundreds of Italian, French, German and Spanish guys and girls who get to London, 'thanks' to the service of some unscrupulous agencies which operate in these countries and have the monopoly on 'advising' youngsters. These agencies charge enormous fees, promising jobs, accommodation and English lessons which they don't always deliver. I have met very many people in London who, after having paid a lot of money, had to live with rats and, after weeks, still haven't been given the chance of attending one interview for a job which they usually ended up finding themselves or thanks to the local Jobcentre. All this just because they did not have access to some genuine information.*

A number of English language schools in the UK run work placement schemes alongside language courses such as Twin School of English, 67/71 Lewisham High Street, London SE13 5JX (020-8297 1132; www.twinuk.com) which claims to have links with 700 companies and 1,000 hotels.

Working Holidays for Americans

The programme for American students wishing to work in Britain is called the Work in Britain Program, which allows about 3,750 full-time college students over the age of 18 to look for work before or after arriving in Britain. They must obtain a Blue Card (work permit) for a fee of about $275, which is authorised by the British Home Office. Participants may arrive at any time of the year and work for up to six months. Candidates must be US citizens enrolled at an accredited US or Canadian university or college or no more than one semester away from the most recent full-time semester. They must prove that they have access to at least £1,000. For further information contact BUNAC USA, PO Box 430, Southbury, CT 06488 (203-264-0901; info@bunacusa.org).

The *Work in Britain Participants' Handbook* contains the addresses of scores of potential employers. The BUNAC offices in London (16 Bowling Green Lane, EC1R 0QH) and Edinburgh have files of possible UK employers as well as current vacancy lists of cheap accommodation and job offers. The Work in Britain programme is the counterpart of BUNAC's Work America Programme for British students (see chapter *United States*).

According to statistics compiled on the Work in Britain programme, about a fifth of participants arrange their jobs before leaving the States. Some of these jobs are career-related, often fixed up through campus contacts. The remaining students wait until they arrive, and spend an average of four to five days job-hunting before finding work. The majority work in offices, hotels, restaurants, pubs and shops. It is not only American style establishments which hire them, but also bastions of English tradition like Harrods. The average wage for participants is £210 per week, though secretarial jobs pay up to £270. A single room in London will cost about £90 per week while a shared room will cost £70.

US citizens who have been offered a full-time position in the UK in their field of study or experience may apply for a work permit through the Association for International Practical Training (Career Development Exchanges, 10400 Little Patuxent Pkwy, Suite 250, Columbia, MD 21044-3510; www.aipt.org). The company Alliances Abroad can place American full-time students in live-in jobs in British pubs and hotels for between three and six months; details are available from the Alliance Abroad Group (1221 South Mopac Expressway, Suite 250, Austin, Texas 78746; 512-457-8062/ 1-888-6-ABROAD; www.allianceabroad.com) Similarly, an organisation called Cultural Embrace (1304 Hollow Creek Drive Suite B, Austin, TX 78704; 523-428-9089; www.culturalembrace.com) makes similar paid placements lasting three to six months of students and people within one semester of having been in full-time study. Jobs are mainly in pubs at a net wage of £145-£215 per week. A number of educational and commercial organisations in the US fix up internships for students in the UK, mainly London.

The Mountbatten Internship Programme (50 East 42nd Street, Suite 2000, New York, NY 10017-5405; www.mountbatten.org) offers a reciprocal programme to American students who want to acquire practical training in business in London for 12 months.

US citizens who wish to spend seven weeks from mid-June volunteering in a social service programme in Great Britain (e.g. working with inner city youth, the elderly, homeless and people with mental health problems) and then travel independently for two weeks should request an application from the Winant & Clayton Volunteers (109 E 50th St, New York, NY 10022; 212-378-0271; www.winantclaytonvolunteer.org); the application deadline is January 31st. Free room and board are provided, and the volunteer pays all travel expenses (approximately $3,500).

Working Holidays for Commonwealth Nationals

As mentioned, Canadian students can apply for a working holiday visa independently or, if they want the security of a package arrangement, they may participate in the Student Work Abroad Programme (SWAP) for C$320 which is comparable to the Work in Britain programme. It is administered by the Canadian Universities Travel Service (Travel CUTS) with many local offices across Canada.

Before prospective working holidaymakers leave home, a general starting place might be the tourist authority Visit Britain's website www.visitbritain.com which devotes some pages to working in Britain, covering lots of nitty-gritty topics like opening a bank account. Various backpacker agencies in Australia, South Africa, etc. have links with London agencies and sell packages that make arrival and the initial job hunt much easier. In Australia, a good source of preliminary information is Travellers Contact Point with offices in several Australian cities plus London (2-6 Inverness Terrace, London W2 3HX; www.travellers.com.au). New Zealanders should find out about the services offered by the agency Overseas Working Holidays (www.owh.co.nz). Like OWH NZ, the Australian branch of Overseas Working Holidays (www.owh.com.au) operates a scheme called Pubs UK which brings together many British pubs, mostly in London, looking to employ Australians and New Zealanders who either have a UK passport or a working holiday visa for the UK. OWH operates its own recruitment centre in London and promises to place new arrivals in a job within three days provided the applicant has experience in IT, finance/banking/accounting, legal, secretarial or call centres. South Africans might like to look into what the Overseas Visitors Club can offer (230 Long St, Cape Town 8001; +27 21-423 4477; www.ovc.co.za). Clients are encouraged to stay at the OVC hostel in Earls Court (30 Collingham Place, London SW5 0QA; 020-7244 8055) which has a job desk to help people find casual work in London.

Tax and Banking

One clear advantage of obtaining legal working holiday status is that you are entitled to apply for a National Insurance number which you should promptly do, from the local Contributions Agency (formerly the Department of Social Security or DSS) which can be found in any telephone directory. Most new employees are put onto the emergency tax code (denoted by 'X' at the end of your tax code) and immediately begin to forfeit a quarter of their wages. Since single people are entitled to a personal allowance of £4,745 per year (2004/5), it is likely that the maximum tax deducted under the PAYE system (Pay As You Earn) will be in excess of what you owe. The rate is 10% on the first £1,960 of taxable income and 22% after that. Some foreign workers have found it advantageous to set themselves up as a limited company (normally with the help of a tax advisory service as the rules have become stricter) and thereby avoid PAYE. PAYE is compulsorily deducted from the pay packets of all employees whose weekly earnings are in excess of £76 or £329 per month.

Foreign nationals can claim the personal allowances if they have been in the UK for at least 183 days in any tax year. If the total is less than 183 days, they may be able to claim as a foreign national and/or resident of a country with which the UK has a double taxation agreement. Inland Revenue operates a telephone information service for the public on 020-7667 4001 and an informative website (www.inlandrevenue.gov.uk). But in the world of taxation, rules are subject to discretionary interpretation, so even if you don't think you're eligible, it does no harm to put in a claim. Always keep tax documents such as the P60 (end-of-year tax certificate). When you finish work, send both parts of the P45 which your employer has to give you to your employer's tax office. When you are ready to leave Britain, complete and submit form P85, a leaving certificate which asks your intentions with respect to returning to the UK to work.

Always take the precaution of making photocopies of any forms you send to Inland Revenue for the purposes of chasing later, and be prepared to wait at least six weeks. If you leave Britain before the refund is processed, it may be better to nominate someone locally to forward the money to you. If you have worked briefly, then travelled for a while and started work again, your next employer may be able to arrange a tax rebate for you provided you can hand over the P45 from your previous job.

You can make things easier for yourself by using an accountancy firm that specialises in tax rebates. They normally keep a percentage (about 18%) of whatever they get back for you. Try for example one of the following London firms: 1st Contact (6th floor, Abford House, 15 Wilton Road, Victoria, London SW1V 1LT; 0800 039 3082/3; www.1stcontact.co.uk/live) and Taxback (167 Earls Court Road, London SW5 9RF; 020-7244 6666; www.taxback.co.uk).

Foreign students are treated the same as UK students and can be exempted from tax. They should ask their employer for a P38(S) form which exempts students from paying tax on vacation earnings.

In addition to income tax, you must also pay National Insurance Contributions of 11% on taxable earnings above £91 a week (up to a maximum of £595). Foreign students of English or agriculture (who can present a certificate in English from their institution proving that they are studying these subjects) can apply for an exemption.

British banks do not make it easy for people newly arrived in the country to open an account. If you can plan ahead, try to bring a letter of reference from your bank at home with some sample bank statements. Jakob Steixner from Austria came to England just for a holiday but decided to stay longer and work in rural Devon:

I registered with the only job agency around. Apparently they didn't quite know that EU citizens don't need a work permit and had to confirm with the authorities. The next time I saw them they offered me work to start one hour later at a dairy farm. Problems turned up when I tried to open a bank account to cash my pay cheques. Getting a letter from my bank back home might have taken weeks. I presented a letter from my host family but the local bank clerk would not accept it. So I ended up getting my wages paid into my host's bank account and they gave it to me in cash, a situation that seemed particularly absurd.

Claimants

It is estimated that the rate of unemployment among people under 25 is more than double the national average. If you are claiming Job-Seekers' Allowance and then find a temporary job, you will have to sign off, your rent-allowance will be stopped and your file closed. Similarly you are allowed to be away from home for no more than two weeks which means that you are not at liberty to travel to look for work even if it is voluntary. If you know in advance where your employment is going to be, you should ask for form A7 from your local benefit office which allows you to claim rent, etc. at your job destination. You may even be entitled to travel expenses to your new job (e.g. a Welsh hotel or fenland farm). Enquire at your local Jobcentre Plus.

Voluntary or part-time work may affect certain benefits. Further information on this subject is contained in the leaflet WK4 'Financial Help if you Work or are Doing Voluntary Work' from the Social Security Agency or accessible online at www.ssani.gov.uk. If you are doing voluntary work but are available for work at short notice, you may be required to fill in a special form. Check with your Jobcentre or with Volunteering England (www. volunteering.org.uk).

In an effort to crack down on so-called 'benefit tourism', the government introduced a test that must be passed before social security benefit will be paid. Anyone applying for benefit must prove that they are 'habitually resident' in the UK, though the definition seems to be discretionary. This has been catching out not only newly arrived foreign job-seekers but also British nationals returning from abroad.

EMPLOYMENT PROSPECTS

Although British manufacturing is in decline, many other sectors of the economy are booming. In some part of southern England there is close to full employment. But even in areas where unemployment is higher, seasonal and temporary work opportunities can usually be found. There are, for example, a multitude of harvests from the daffodils of Cornwall to periwinkles on the Isle of Mull for which the local work force is not sufficient and where acute labour shortages have been occurring. The tourist industry provides many opportunities for bar, catering and hotel staff in London, coastal resorts, the Lake District, Scotland and Wales. The increasing demand for childcare frequently outstrips the availability of willing candidates. In the South lots of office jobs can be seen advertised in the windows of employment agencies specialising in temporary work or in the 'Sits Vac' pages of local newspapers. Part-time and casual jobs are often advertised on cards posted in the windows of newsagents and sub-post offices (if you can find a sub-post office that hasn't closed).

The National Minimum Wage in 2005 is £4.85 per hour for workers over 22, £4.10 for workers aged 18-21. For details contact the NMW information line 0845 6000 678 or check the DTI website www.dti.gov.uk/er/nmw or www.tiger.gov.uk. Unless you are very lucky in finding cheap accommodation, it will still be very difficult to save on these wages especially in Southeast England where the cost of living is higher than elsewhere.

Temp Agencies

According to one estimate 6,000 employment agencies do business in the UK, though a large number of these are for specific professions. You should not be content to register with just one, since the degree of enthusiasm with which these numerous agencies try to find suitable work for their temps varies enormously, especially if the temps can't type 60 words a minute. Manpower and Select Recruitment are among the biggest general agencies with dozens of branches in London alone and many more nationwide. Blue Arrow has an industrial division that willingly signs up students and others to carry out casual cleaning, packing and warehouse work. Some agencies specially target backpackers such as www.linkindustrial.co.uk and Premiere People (www.premierepeople.com) with 21 branches around the UK.

A traveller from South Africa found industrial agency work a very satisfactory way to save for his future travels:

Though Colin Rothwell couldn't stomach all his assignments
In England I found the easiest way to find work was through temping agencies. However, it was also the most inconvenient way as they liked you to have an address and a phone number. They were also the biggest sharks around and you got paid half the going wage as they took a very healthy cut from your hard-earned blood, sweat and tears. It did have its advantages though; you worked when and

> *where it suited you, and some agencies sent you all over the place to do all kinds of weird jobs. For example, the worst job I did on my whole trip was at a dog meat factory. You arrived at the crack of dawn and were sent into a massive fridge where you were met with tons of semi-defrosting offal, with blood everywhere, and a stench like you wouldn't believe. So, as desperate for money as I was, I only lasted two days.*

If you are a trained nurse, nanny, chef, tractor driver, accountant, financial analyst, teacher, etc. there are specialist agencies eager to sign you up, especially in London and the Home Counties. Catering agencies abound and anyone with a background as a chef will probably be in demand. (See section below *Tourism & Catering*.) Temping allows a great deal of flexibility, though most agencies you approach will want to be reassured that you are not about to flit off somewhere. Most will ask foreign temps for evidence of permission to work.

Despite the agency fees, wages for labouring and warehouse jobs should be in excess of the minimum wage, usually more than £6 on a night shift. When you get a temp job through an agency, the agency generally becomes your employer and pays your wages. People who perform well on typing or shorthand tests will find that they are placed much more promptly than those who lack any office skills and will be paid accordingly. Skilled secretarial wages start at about £8 an hour, while unskilled clerical work pays not much more than the minimum wage.

One recommended agency for people with working holiday visas or EU nationality is Workabout, 43A East St, Wimborne, Dorset BH21 1DX (0871 222 4036/8/9; www.workabout.uk.com) which has separate departments for placing people in hospitality positions, as home helps or in farming or labouring jobs. The Australian-linked temp agency Bligh Appointments (70 North End Road, West Kensington, London W14 9EP; 020-7603 6123; info@bligh.co.uk) has vacancies for nannies, secretaries, etc. as well as an agricultural section to place people on farms throughout Britain.

Temping at any kind of job is a good way of exposing your skills to potential employers. It is a good idea to ask for an application form at those workplaces to which you are temporarily assigned which you enjoy, assuming you are looking for longer term work. The principal disadvantage of temping is the uncertainty of hours. Working for an agency can also be a good way to meet fellow travellers, since lots of people signed up with agencies are there to save money for an upcoming trip.

Ian Mitselburg from Sydney got so tired of the London scene that he repaired to Edinburgh where he found it was even easier to find work and that the lower wages were counterbalanced by the lower cost of living: *'I put my name down at almost every agency that would take it and had all sorts of temporary jobs including washing dishes, stuffing envelopes, transferring stocks and shares, labouring and unpacking delivery bags of foreign currency.'*

Another foreign visitor to Scotland, Cindy Roberts, was pleased that the agency she approached did not ask to see a work permit, nor did the dowager duchess for whom she worked on the west coast of Scotland, cooking, light housekeeping and errand-running.

Newspapers and Books

In addition to private agencies, you should make use of newspapers, where up to half of all job vacancies are advertised. There are several free weekly newspapers and magazines in London aimed at the ex-pat communities, mainly Australians, New Zealanders and South Africans. Yet these can prove to be excellent sources of casual jobs for anyone. You will find distribution boxes for *TNT* (14-15 Child's Place, Earls Court, SW5 9RX; 020-7373 3377; www.tntmagazine.com) and *New Zealand News UK* (South Bank House, Black Prince Road, London SE1 7SJ; www.nznewsuk.co.uk) in selected locations throughout London, e.g. outside travel agencies, tube stations, favoured pubs, etc. The majority of unskilled and semi-skilled jobs advertised are for mother's helps, sales people, call centres, in bars and on farms. Recruitment agencies advertise for nurses and professionals in accountancy, banking, IT, law, etc.

The *Yellow Pages* is much easier to use now that it is searchable online. For example a search for 'Fruit & Vegetable Growers' on www.yell.co.uk would turn up a long list of contact addresses. If you are looking for a summer job anywhere in Britain you should have a look at an annual publication which gives many addresses to which you can apply: *The Directory of Summer Jobs in Britain* (Vacation-Work, £10.99). The majority of jobs listed in *Summer Jobs in Britain* are in hotels or holiday camps, with a further emphasis on seasonal farm work. However there are also lots of unusual and interesting jobs like market researchers, travel reservation clerks, swimming pool life guards, English teachers and monitors, marquee erectors and conservation wardens.

Jobcentre Plus

Finally, in your job search, you should not omit the obvious step of visiting your local Jobcentre Plus (www.jobcentreplus.gov.uk). Jobcentres are notified of an estimated one-third of the job vacancies in Britain. Details of available jobs are posted on display boards so centres are primarily self-service. If things look grim one week, they might improve the next, especially in areas where there is a concentration of seasonal farm work.

HARVESTS

The principal fruit growing areas of Britain are: the Vale of Evesham over to the Wye and Usk Valleys; most of Kent; Lincolnshire and East Anglia, especially the Fens around Wisbech; and north of the Tay Estuary (Blairgowrie, Forfar). But there is intensive agricultural activity in most parts of Britain so always check with the Jobcentre or Farmers' Union in the area(s) where you are interested in finding farm work. Again *The Directory of Summer Jobs in Britain* lists many fruitgrowers, some of whom need more than 100 pickers. Harvest dates are not standard throughout the country, since the raspberries of Invernessshire ripen at least two or three weeks later than the raspberries on the Isle of Wight; nor are the starting dates the same from one year to the next.

Seasonal Agricultural Workers Scheme (SAWS)

SAWS is a scheme whereby full-time students from outside the EU are permitted to work in the UK. The programme is administered by nine approved agencies and overseen by the Home Office. The total number of foreign seasonal workers recruited is due to be capped now that the EU has expanded so dramatically.

New SAWS participants must be students in full-time education abroad however the upper age limit of 25 has been scrapped. Applicants are required to provide proof of status to the scheme operator. However participating operators may issue Home Office work cards to workers who have proved reliable in the past. The work card records the period for which the worker is required and at which farm and which operator issued the card. The scheme now operates year round instead of May to November so that daffodil growers in Cornwall, turkey producers and Christmas tree companies will be able to fill hard-to-fill seasonal vacancies. If no work is available at the original farm the worker may be transferred to another farm within the scheme. The Immigration Officer needs to be satisfied that the worker does not intend to take any other employment and that he or she intends to leave the country on completion of the period of work.

Among the approved operators of the SAWS scheme are:

Concordia (YSV) Ltd, Heversham House, 2nd Floor, 20-22 Boundary Road, Hove, East Sussex BN3 4ET (01273 422293/fax 01273 422443). Places foreign pickers on large number of farms.

HOPS (GB), YFC Centre, NAC Stoneleigh Park, Kenilworth, Warks. CV8 2LG (02476 857206; hopsgb@nfyfc.org.uk). Places foreign pickers on large number of farms.

Fridaybridge International Farm Camp, March Road, Fridaybridge, Wisbech, Cambridgeshire PE14 0LR (01945 860255).

G's Marketing Ltd, Hostel Office, Barway, Ely, Cambs. CB7 5TZ (01353 727314). Farm factory workers are paid at piecework rates (employer claims the average is £180 per week). People needed from October until after Easter to package salad and vegetable crops. Applications to Sharon Gudgeon, Hostel Recruitment Officer.

International Farm Camp, Hall Road, Tiptree, Colchester, Essex CO5 0QS (01621 815496; www.fruit-pickers.com).

R. & J. M. Place, International Farm Camp, Church Farm, Tunstead, Norwich, Norfolk NR12 8RQ (01692 536225).

Fruit Farms

Although the work is hard at the beginning (and also unreliable in bad weather), the international atmosphere can be enjoyable. Some farmers even organise a social and sporting programme. You are likely to meet some veteran travellers who can offer useful advice about job-hunting in their countries or whose names you can add to your address book.

Here is a selection of farms in addition to the ones listed above which hire at least 50 fruit pickers during the season, so it may be worthwhile for British and EU people to approach them directly:

Boxford (Suffolk) Farms Ltd., Hill Farm, Boxford, Sudbury, Suffolk CO10 5NY (01787 210348). Pickers and packers required.

Hill Farm Orchards, Droxford Road, Swanmore, Hants. SO32 2PY (01489 878616; hifol@eur-isp.com).

K.S. Coles, Chelston House Farm, Chelston, Wellington, Somerset TA21 9HP (01823 664244; lscoles@btinternet.com). 60+ pea pickers needed mid-June to mid-August.

Haygrove Fruit, Redbank, Ledbury, Herefordshire HR8 2JL (01531 633659; students@haygrove.co.uk). Large soft fruit farm.

Chandler & Dunn Ltd, Lower Goldstone, Ash, Canterbury, Kent CT3 2DY (01304 812262; fax 01304 812612; chandlerdunn@btopenworld.com; www.chandleranddunn.co.uk). Fruit pickers (numbers variable) for periods between the end of May and the end of September; most pickers needed for strawberries in June and apples in September.

F.W. Mansfield & Son, Nickle Farm, Chartham, Canterbury, Kent CT4 7PL (01227 731441; fax 01227 731795). Up to 100 workers to pick and pack apples, pears, strawberries, plums, cherries and pumpkins.

Newmafruit Farms Ltd, Howfield Farm, Howfield Lane, Chartham, Canterbury, Kent CT4 7HQ (01227 738221; fax 01227 738086; enquiries@newmafruit.co.uk). Pickers and packers required from June to September.

R.H. Nightingale & Partner, Gibbet Oak Farm, Appledore Road, Tenterden, Kent TN30 7DH (01580 763492; fax 01580 763938). Strawberry, apple and pear pickers required. Amenities, campsite and mobile homes with usual facilities provided.

Adrian Scripps Ltd., Moat Farm, Five Oak Green, Paddock Wood, Tonbridge, Kent TN12 6RR (01892 832406). Used to be a hop grower but now has apple and pear orchards and needs workers from the end of August to the end of October.

Stanley & Pickford, Rectory Farm, Stanton St John, Oxford OX33 1HF (01865 351214; fax 01865 351679; s.and.p@farmline.com; www.rectoryfarmpyo.co.uk). Fruit pickers to pick mainly strawberries and raspberries.

Scotland

Allanhill Farm, St. Andrews, Fife KY16 9XG (01334 473224; www.allanhill.co.uk. Employ more than 100 strawberry pickers on Scotland's east coast.

W.P Bruce Ltd., Balmyle, Meigle, Perthshire PH12 8QU (euan@wpbruceco.uk). Large strawbery farm offering reasonable harvest wages and facilities.

D & B Grant, Wester Essendy, Blairgowrie, Perthshire PH10 6RA (01250 884389; cmgrant99@yahoo.com). Berry picking and processing.

W. Henderson, Seggat, Auchterless, Turriff, Aberdeenshire AB5 8DL (01888 511223). Strawberry pickers and packers.

Peter Marshall & Co, Muirton, Alyth, Blairgowrie, Perthshire PH11 8JF (01828 632227;

megmarshall@aol.com). 200 raspberry pickers between June and August.

The raspberry harvest in Scotland usually begins in July, but can vary by as much as three weeks. About 3,000 pickers are at work throughout Perthshire (especially around Blairgowrie) and Angus at the peak of the harvest. On an exceptionally good day a picker might gather more than 150lb of fruit and earn £40. Even in the furthest corners of Scotland, there may be opportunities on farms. Heather McCulloch from Australia asked the owners of the hostel where she was staying on the Orkney island of South Ronaldsay if they had any work on their farm and, although she confessed to having no farm experience, was hired to join other travellers for various jobs including 'the sometimes farcical task of rounding up cattle and sheep' and cooking ('opening tins of beans and rice pudding'). For this she was paid a fair wage with food and accommodation thrown in.

One of the latest harvests is of apples which should be more lucrative than many others since the weather can be cold and wet between mid-September and mid-October. Unfortunately this is not always the case if you are inexperienced and being paid piece work. Advertised earnings are often only what a dedicated and experienced worker can achieve, as Lanka Dianova from Slovakia discovered when she abandoned the London rat race for life in rural Norfolk:

Together with an Aussie I met in a hostel, I found an advert in TNT magazine for strawberry pickers in Norfolk. It said you could make up to £55 a day, but when we got there, they sent us to a factory where we were folding boxes and packing tins for about £25 a day, working 12 hours. After one day, we said we wanted to leave, but they told us we gotta stay at least a week, otherwise we wouldn't get paid. So we stayed packing fresh salads (approximately £25 for an 8-hour day).

Canning and food processing plants go into high gear in fruit growing regions during the harvests and employ large numbers of seasonal workers. Lucrative overtime is often available. Among the largest in the country is Salvesen Food Services with freezing works in several Lincolnshire towns (Bourne, Easton and Spalding), plus Lowestoft, Peterborough, Grimsby, Hull, Edinburgh, Dundee and Inverness. Ask at local Jobcentres or check the papers in market towns like Wisbech and Kings Lynn.

Pay and Conditions

The two methods of payment used by farmers are piece rates (dependent on the quantity picked) or by the hour. In some cases farmers operate a combination of these two methods, paying an hourly rate plus a bonus for each bin of top quality fruit (which the supermarkets demand). If you are employed on a piece rate basis you must earn at least the minimum rates stipulated by the Agricultural Wages Board (which are in line with the minimum wage). The minimum rate for casual workers over 19 in England and Wales (different rates apply in Scotland and Northern Ireland) is £5.40 an hour (as of October 2004) and £8.10 overtime (for work above 39 hours a week or 8 a day or on Sundays and public holidays). Where an employer provides accommodation for workers (over the age of 19), no more than £3.75 per day worked can be deducted. Further details are available from the Agricultural Wages Team, Area 2 C, Ergon House, Horseferry Road, London SW1P 2AL or the Agricultural Wages helpline on 0845 0000134; www.defra.gov.uk/farm/agwork. htm#agwages).

Pickers being paid piecework sometimes overestimate their likely earnings. Legally they can't earn less than the minimum wage though in practice, pickers who are not picking enough (say 10 kilos of strawberries an hour) to reach that amount are summarily fired. Novices invariably find the work discouraging, especially if rain curtails picking and therefore earning potential. Piecework rates may not be standard in one fruit-picking area so it can be worth doing some comparison shopping before promising a farmer that you will work for him, preferably a month or so before the harvest is due to begin. Some crops pay more than others, usually because they're more difficult or painful to pick. Blackcurrants grow low on the ground and require hours of stooping at an uncomfortable height.

Gooseberries share this characteristic and in addition must be picked individually from among vicious thorns. Inexperienced pickers often leave after their first long gruelling day when they find they have not even earned enough to cover living expenses.

You cannot count on accommodation being provided on fruit farms. Even fruit growers who take on large numbers of pickers may provide nothing more than a field, which may or may not be properly levelled, well-drained or cleared of nettles. Sometimes you need to work a minimum number of hours per week, e.g. 15, to be allowed to use the campsite. Others provide completely equipped caravans or bunkhouses, but may make a deduction from your wages for this luxury.

If you do not independently enjoy camping, you are not likely to enjoy life on a Farm Camp. Mark Stephenson grew very fond of the 'wet sloping field' where he was directed to pitch his tent at a farm camp in Perthshire:

> After surveying the field which was to be my home for the next few weeks, I turned and noticed the terrific view; the sky may have been all grey clouds but this didn't diminish the magnificence. Social life thrived in and around this temporary community on the Scottish hillsides. Visits to the pub were usually musical events since traditional folk music was frequently played and often we visitors were invited to contribute a southern favourite like 'Maybe it's because I'm a Londoner.' Fruit-picking in Scotland may not leave you much richer in pocket but it gives you several weeks of camping surrounded by open fields and sky, combined with the chance to meet young people not only from Scotland but from all over the world.

While fruit harvests all take place between June and October, the daffodil harvest of Cornwall runs from late January to late March. Last year more than half the flowers rotted in the fields for lack of pickers, so it is very easy to find a job, as Till Bruckner discovered:

> Flower picking isn't bad at all. It's casual work so you just turn up in the morning if you want to pick (all week round). It's pure piecework and good pickers usually earn at least £50 a day; on good days, some earn up to £100. I'm very slow so it's no goldmine for me, but the flexibility makes up for the low pay. There are a few travellers (both New Age and international) working here and once you're on the circuit, you'll have no problems finding other work later on as many of the guys have been picking and harvesting around Britain and Europe for years. Anyone can turn up early and hop on a truck. I worked for Winchester Growers near Penzance. It's rough when the weather is bad but you can always stay in bed. I'd recommend it.

Agricultural Agencies

The soft fruit marketing company Advanced Marketing Services Ltd based in Evesham represents growers throughout the UK and assists its clients to find seasonal and other staff. AMS has set up a website to help match farmers and workers; check www.fruitfuljobs.com. Backpackers are encouraged to apply since most jobs both short and long term are live-in.

Jark Recruitment Ltd (22/28 Blackfriars St, Kings Lynn, Norfolk PE30 1NN; 01553 660888) recruits staff all year round for production work in and around the Norfolk and Suffolk area. Wages are from £4.20 to £6 per hour plus overtime and holiday pay. Self-catering accommodation is available for £57.50 per week. Catered accommodation is available for approximately £82.50 per week, including three meals, laundry, wake-ups and telephone/fax. Transport to and from work is charged at £2.50 a day. The minimum period of work is 12 weeks and applicants must be EEA nationals or working holiday visa holders between 18 and 35. A young man from Spain spent six months working for this company's precursor a few years ago and describes conditions: 'Outback hostels have a bar with subsidised beer and Sky TV. The lowest pay I earned was £2.97 at a broccoli factory in Ely while the highest was £5.25 for flower planting in Spalding. The hostels provided transport to the workplace, but £3 per day was deducted. At one of the hostels (in

Attleborough near Norwich), all the work was in chicken factories.'

> **Carisa Fey, an 18-year old German traveller, joined the ranks of the agri-
> cultural workers in the East of England after answering an advert in *TNT*
> magazine:**
> *Together with a South African girl I'd met in Scotland, I went to Wisbech, the most
> boring place on earth. So we didn't mind working 12 hours every day with 1½ hours
> to and from work. We managed to save around £100 each a week. And working
> in the factories wasn't that bad; one just has to entertain oneself. It is very easy to
> get a job in the factories through the agencies that advertise. The good thing is that
> they handle everything like accommodation, job, bank account, but you have to be
> lucky to find a fair one. If you have enough money for your own jobsearch, go to the
> Jobcentre in Peterborough or Wisbech or ask at the factories directly.*

Another agricultural agency which specialises in placing working holiday makers is called
Working Wonders or WoWo, Waspbourne Manor Farm, Sheffield Park, Uckfield, East
Sussex TN22 3QT (01825 723414; www.wowo.co.uk). Plenty of overtime is available and
caravan or other accommodation can be arranged. For other leads, check adverts in *TNT*
or *New Zealand News*. Caution is always required when accepting a picking job since conditions are notoriously rough and earnings can be disappointing if you are inexperienced.

The organisation WWOOF (World Wide Opportunities on Organic Farms) can put
members in touch with several hundred organic farmers throughout the UK who offer free
room and board in exchange for help. Membership costs £15; details from WWOOF UK,
PO Box 2675, Lewes, Sussex BN7 1RB (hello@wwoof.org).

Hop-Picking

Traditionally the hop fields of Kent and to a much smaller extent Herefordshire employed
large numbers of pickers in the month of September. However the industry is in serious
decline due to the inability of English producers to compete with cheap continental hops,
prompting quite a few farmers to switch to other crops, especially in Kent. Yet enough hop-
growers are optimistic that the demand will revive that there are still jobs left for pickers in
the hop industry. Take-home pay is often in excess of £150 per week. Tom Morton fixed
up a job well in advance: *'I wrote to hop farms in April and fixed up a job at Spelmonden
Estate. Work started at 7am and finished at 6pm. Accommodation (£8 per week) was in
'portakabins' with a large common room and kitchen for about 15 people. Take leather
gloves and bandages for your wrists or they will be lacerated by the hops in no time.
Although the work was hard there was a great atmosphere.'*

Here are some addresses of hop producers:

S.C. and J.H. Berry Ltd., Gushmere Court Farm, Selling, Faversham, Kent ME13 9RF
(01227 752205).

Redsell Group, Nash Court, Boughton, Faversham, Kent ME13 9SR (01227 751224 or
07889 308731; pat.goode@redsell.com; www.redsell.com). Hop pickers needed to
work on 200 acres of hops. Basic accommodation provided free of charge.

L. Wheeler & Sons (East Peckham) Ltd, Bullen Farm, East Peckham, Tonbridge, Kent
TN12 5LX (01622 871225).

TOURISM & CATERING

Despite its infamous weather and cuisine, Britain attracts millions of tourists from abroad. It
has been estimated that one in ten of the employed labour force of Britain is involved in the
tourist industry and that it is on the way to becoming the biggest employer in the country.
Furthermore more Britons have been holidaying at home, partly because of residual fears
about security abroad.

Somebody has to look after the needs of all those pleasure-seekers, whether selling
rock candy or playing the guitar to provide entertainment. (Many buskers have found holi-

day resorts during the season to be far more profitable than large urban areas.) Seaside hotels normally provide staff accommodation and food, though the standard will be considerably lower than that enjoyed by the paying guests at the hotel. There is also plenty of hotel work in London from the international hotels on Park Lane to the budget hotels of Earls Court, though it is the norm in London for staff to live out.

Wages in the hotel trade are notoriously low, and exploitation is common, though the introduction of the minimum wage has alleviated the situation for the lowest paid. Hotel staff with silver service or other specialist experience can expect to earn a decent wage as can restaurant staff in London who should earn at least £4.50 an hour plus free food. Waiting staff can supplement their wages with tips, however chamber and bar staff will generally have to be content with their hourly wage.

People who are available for the whole season, say April to October will find it much easier to land a job than those available only for the peak months of July and August. Most hotels prefer to receive a formal written application in the early part of the year, complete with photos and references; however it can never hurt to telephone (especially later in the spring) to find out what the situation is. You may work from the selective list of hotels in the *Directory of Summer Jobs in Britain* mentioned above or work systematically through a hotel guide such as those published by the Automobile Association, the Royal Automobile Club or the English Tourist Board. The more bedrooms listed in the hotel's entry, the better the chances of a vacancy.

It is worth contacting large hotel chains for up-to-date vacancy information, particularly if you have relevant experience. For example Hilton Group (Maple Court, Central Park, Reeds Crescent, Watford, Hertfordshire WD24 4QQ; 020-7856 8000) can give advice on which of their 41 UK hotels have current vacancies, although these should be applied to individually for employment. Similarly Choice Hotels Europe offer numerous opportunities in the UK and Ireland on a short-term (minimum four months) or long term basis to suitable applicants, qualified and/or experienced in the hotel business. A good working knowledge of English is essential. CVs and covering letter in English should be sent to the Human Resources Department, 112-114 Station Road, Edgware, Middlesex HA8 7BJ (hr@choicehotelseurope.com). Thistle Hotels Plc (2 The Calls, Leeds LS2 7JU; 0113-243 9111; careers@thistle.co.uk) have more than 50 hotels in the UK. Live-in accommodation is provided in some hotels but not all. The minimum period of work is three months and non-European nationals must possess a work permit before applying. Restaurant chains also have a huge turn-over of staff but of course do not provide accommodation. The TGI Friday chain, for example, pays its waiting staff well over the minimum wage.

Fast food restaurants around the world have many vacancies. If you are prepared to work overtime, you should be able to earn a living from McDonald's, Pizza Hut, etc. working as a 'crew member', though usually you have to be content with part-time work until you prove yourself reliable. A good bet over the next few years will be KFC who intend to create thousands of new jobs in the UK. A large percentage of workers is foreign. Having a reference from one of these chains can be useful if you want to move to another branch.

Anyone who can acquaint themselves with EU hygiene regulations before being interviewed would have the edge or, even better, the Basic Food Hygiene Certificate which can be obtained after a minimum of six hours training (£40-£60). Many employment agencies specialise in placing seasonal staff in the hospitality industry, for example:

Anglo-Continental Placements Agency, 9 Wish Road, Hove, E Sussex BN3 4LL (01273 776660; www.anglocontinentalplacements.com) place staff mainly from abroad in the hospitality industry (waiting, bar, housekeeping and kitchen staff, receptionists, porters, chefs and management). They will register anyone with an appropriate visa or Europeans with a reasonable knowledge of English.

*EuroCo*m, Suite 45, Surbiton Business Centre, 46 Victoria Road, Surbiton, Surrey KT6 4JL (020-8390 4512; post@europeancommunications.com). Provide staff to 4 and 5 star hotels; minimum contract 6 months year round.

Adria Recruitment, 24 Stourvale Gardens, Chandlers Ford, Hants. SO53 3NE (023 8025 4287; www.adriarecruitment.com). Live-in hotel and catering staff for minimum of six months can be arranged in conjunction with English classes. Also place nannies and au pairs.

Lucy Locketts & Vanessa Bancroft Agency, 400 Beacon Road, Wibsey, Bradford, West Yorks. BD6 3DJ; tel/fax 01274 402822. Placement of European waiters, porters, chambermaids, etc.

Many training and exchange organisations place foreign students in hotel jobs including the following:

European Work Experience Programme Ltd, Unit 1, Red Lion Court, Alexandra Road, Hounslow, Middlesex, TW3 1JS; 020-8 572 2993; www.ewep.com. Assist young EU nationals to find jobs in hotels, fast food restaurants, etc.

Exchange Training Communication International (ETCi), Otterburn House, 8-12 Bromley Road, Beckenham, Kent BR3 5JE (020-8663 0055; www.etci.co.uk).

Southern Work Experience, 12 Eversfield Road, Eastbourne, East Sussex BN21 2AS (swe@active-english.co.uk; www.yeseducation.co.uk). Hotel and industry work experience placements for 2-3 months.

Working holiday makers should be able to fix up work in bars, cafés, hotels, etc. with relative ease, without going through a mediating agency. Twenty-two year old Sarah Zimmerman from the US decided to support herself in the UK by picking up jobs in 2004, but encountered a few problems she hadn't anticipated when her first job was in a fancy hotel:

> You'd think it would be easier for me since I understand English, but no, the entire menu and bistro -- everything was in French, I couldn't even figure out what the word for green bean was! And, I know they said that the head chef was speaking English, but I begged to differ because I have yet to understand a word he shouted at me. The others whom I worked with from Austria, Poland, Sweden and Venezuela were very nice and seemed to grasp it all better.

Sarah set off to find a job in a non-French-speaking environment but wasn't convinced it was preferable: 'The English are self-proclaimed laid-back people, so maybe that is why it takes so long to secure something. I had a trial day at a funky/expensive bakery/restaurant that really was fun, minus the two-hour lunch rush where I was serving hot food and felt so much like a cafeteria lady from elementary school that I almost asked where my hair net was!'

Pubs

Live-in pub work is not hard to come by. You usually have to work throughout pub opening hours six days a week, and earn the minimum wage. Many people work some evenings in a pub in addition to their day job to boost their finances for future travelling. This is one job in which there is a good demand for working couples and (at least in London) for Australians and New Zealanders. The Original London Pub Company based in Brisbane (www.londonpubau.com) distributes information for Australians, New Zealanders and Canadians on working holidays: 'Live and Work in a London Pub'; their fixing fee is $595 (in Australian, Canadian or American dollars depending on country of origin). Women with bar experience normally find it easier to find a job than barmen, and can often negotiate a better package. As usual the greatest demand is for experienced chefs.

Waiting for an ad to appear is usually less productive than going pub to pub. An American traveller found himself nearly penniless in the popular tourist town of Pitlochry in Perthshire and made the rounds of the pubs asking for work. In each case the management were either fully staffed or were too concerned about his lack of a work permit. He claims that in the 34th and final pub, they asked him if he were free to start work that minute, and he gleefully stepped behind the bar and began work, without knowing shandy from Guinness. Americans may need to be reminded that you do not get tips in a British pub though you may be bought a drink now and then. Americans often have trouble with the different accents they will encounter as Woden Teachout found: 'I had a hard time deciphering the orders over the music; *'Bakes' does not sound remotely like 'Becks' to the American ear.'*

Pub jobs vary a great deal and it is better if you can find one which you find compatible. Ken Smith from New Zealand has extensive experience:

I worked in four pubs while in England, three of which were really good. I was regularly invited into the customers' homes for meals or tea and in one pub there was a retired gentleman who would drive me around historic country pubs. The six months I spent working in a pub near Russell Square were absolutely fantastic; the money was great (£130 a week cash-in-hand of which I could comfortably save £100), excellent food, great boss and brilliant customers. On the other hand I spent two months in a Surrey pub which was terrible in every conceivable way, but I was short on money and jobs were scarce. The final straw was when they started working on the roof in November and the freezing cold wind blew right into my bedroom. The job was only ever a roof over our heads and they even took that away.

Scotland

Although unemployment is higher in Scotland than England, plenty of tourist-related jobs are available.

Carisa Fey from Germany is just one traveller from the continent who was instantly smitten with Scotland:
Before all my money was gone I took the bus up to Scotland because I heard that it would be very easy to get a job in the highlands in a hotel. As the bus came through Aviemore on my way to Inverness it was love at first sight. One visit to the Jobcentre in Inverness and two days later I was back in Aviemore to work at the Freedom Inn Hotel plus extra nights at the Stakis Cairngorm Lodge (better paid but less fun). My planned stay of three months worked out to be ten and by the time I left I was speaking with a Scottish accent, could clean a room in record speed, carry four plates and still talk normally after consuming an amount of alcohol that would kill an average middle European man. I had a wonderful time.

Many foreign job-seekers in Britain tire of the London scene or are attracted to the peace and quiet of Scotland as Isak Maseide from Norway was:

We were originally going to Edinburgh to work at the Festival, but after Athens we preferred somewhere quieter, so went to the resort of Oban on the west coast of Scotland. Even though we arrived in the middle of the season (which lasts from mid-May to the end of September) we soon found work. Apparently McTavish's Kitchens is the place to go first since it is the biggest employer and has live-in facilities, pays well and employs quite a number of young people. My New Zealand girlfriend and I preferred to have a wee feeling of freedom so we rented a bedsit for £65 a week.

McTavish's has a restaurant in Oban (8 Argyll Square, PA4 4BA; oban@mctavishs.com) and another in Fort William (High Street, PH33 6AD; fortwilliam@mctavishs.com).

Agents sometimes advertise in London for live-in hotel work in Scotland. Keith Flynn answered such an ad and ended up working in an isolated place ten miles from the nearest town and with no public transport, which made it an ideal place to save money: *'I saw Dee Cooper's advert and decided to ring up. Basically you just call and say what job you do, e.g. kitchen porter, bar, waiter/waitress and she gives you a list of vacancies around Scotland at no cost to you.'*

Dee Cooper works for more than 1,000 hotels in Scotland, England and Wales supplying live-in staff; phone 01764 670071 or 01764 679765 or fax 01764 679728 (dee@livein-jobs.demon.co.uk/ www.livein-jobs.co.uk). Of course the online recruitment business is always expanding; try for example www.hotel-jobs-scotland.com or www.seasonalstaff.co.uk for live-in jobs in pubs and hotels (01543 672046).

Paul Binfield from Kent travelled further north in Scotland and was rewarded with a healthy choice of casual work in the Orkney Islands:

> *Unemployment here is about 5% and from March to September there is an absolute abundance of summer jobs. We worked in one of the several youth hostels on the islands, have done voluntary work for the Orkney Seal Rescue and I am currently earning a very nice wage working at the historical site Skara Brae on a three-month contract. There is loads of seasonal work available in hotels and bars, cutting grass for the Council and other garden contracts, etc.*

A surprising range of jobs can be found in Scotland from being a distillery guide (for example at the Glenfiddich Distillery, Dufftown, Banffshire AB55 4DH; 01340 820373) to pedalling tourists around in rickshaws in Edinburgh. For the distillery job it is necessary to attend an interview at your own expense before the end of April and to be available to work from at least the end of June till the end of August. For the rickshaw cycling, you have to hire the vehicle for £100 for a weekend and try to make a profit by working between 9pm and 4am. The job requires training, a street trading licence and has limits defined by the council.

Whelk and periwinkle collecting can apparently be done on the islands of Skye, Mull or elsewhere along the west coast. Conditions are best at low tide around the full and new moons. Agents provide bags, tide tables and a collection service (see *Yellow Pages*). Most people can earn up to £30 in one tide, double at Christmas when wellies and warm gloves must be worn.

The Channel Islands

In general, the Channel Islands are a favourite destination for seasonal workers in the hotel/hospitality industry. For a list of 100+ establishments, many offering accommodation in Guernsey, write to the States Tourist Board, PO Box 23, St. Peter Port, Guernsey GY1 3AN (enquiries@guernseytouristboard.com; www.guernseytouristboard.com). Several agencies specialise in recruiting catering and other staff for the Channel Islands, e.g. Towngate Personnel (3 Alum, Chine Road, Westbourne, Bournemouth BH4 8DT; 01202 752955; enquiries@towngate-personnel.co.uk). Towngate supply staff for permanent live-in vacancies in the Channel Islands and in the UK. Jersey Recruitment (La Rue le Masurier, St Helier, Jersey JE2 4YE; 01534 617373; www.jerseyholsjobs.com/main.html) cannot really process applications from students since their season finishes in October.

The tax status of the Channel Islands works to the advantage of seasonal workers (just as it does to offshore millionaires). The exemption limit for a single person is in the region of £11,000 per calendar year; further details are available from the CI Tax Department. The lovely island of Sark is also a magnet for itinerant workers.

Niamh Cordon is one of the many people who regularly returns to Jersey to work the season:

> *After returning home to Ireland from working on the Greek islands, I still had itchy feet. I had heard from friends that Jersey was a great place to go to pick up work easily. There is a job centre but more importantly a recruitment agency that deals with the catering trade and also has jobs for bar staff, waiting staff and receptionists. Accommodation is very expensive in Jersey but most hotels have live-in positions. You need to get over in early May before the hordes of students arrive. I spent two summer seasons as a receptionist and then signed up with the temping agencies and began clearing £300 working as a typist.*

Holiday Camps and Activity Centres

Anyone with a qualification in canoeing, yachting, climbing, etc. should be able to find summer work as an instructor. Since one or two high profile canoeing tragedies in the

1990s, directors have been looking for higher standards of training and experience. Centres that belong to the British Activity Holidays Association (tel/fax 01932 252994) submit to regular safety inspections. To find out whether a centre is licensed, contact the Adventure Activities Licensing Authority (17 Lambourne Crescent, Cardiff Business Park, Llanishen, Cardiff CF14 5GF; 029 20 755715; www.aala.org). Note that the British Activity Holidays Association website (www.baha.org.uk/workopps.asp) has a useful link to Job Vacancies.

Foreign equivalents of the British Canoe Union, Royal Yachting Association, etc. should suffice. There are also plenty of jobs as general assistants for sports-minded young people, especially at children's multi activity centres. Suzanne Phillips, who worked at an adventure centre in North Devon, claims that 'a person's character and personality are far more important than their qualifications.' The trouble is that the pay is not usually very much for this kind of work, though the minimum may be supplemented by an end-of-season bonus at some centres. Quite often foreign applicants will be asked to provide police clearance forms if the job involves working with children.

One of the largest employers is PGL Travel, with a staggering 2,500 vacancies during the season which extends from February to October. PGL's Seasonal Personnel Department can be contacted at: Alton Court, Penyard Lane, Ross-on-Wye, Herefordshire HR9 5GL (01989 767833; pglpeople@pgl.co.uk).

Here are some other activity centres which may require domestic as well as leadership staff:

Ardmore Language Schools, Hall Place, Berkshire College, Burchetts Green, Maidenhead, Berkshire SL6 6QR (01628 826699; info@theardmoregroup.com). Residential multi activity and English language camps for overseas children throughout the UK.

Barracudas Summer Activity Camps, Bridge House, Bridge Street, St Ives, Cambs. PE27 5EH (01480 497533; jops@barracudas.co.uk). Various residential and day camps in southern England.

EAC Activity Camps, First Floor, 59 George St, Edinburgh EH2 2LQ (0131-477 7574; www.activitycamps.com). 100 activity staff for July/August camps in Scotland and England. Accommodation is not provided.

EF Language Travel, EF House Castle Road, Torquay TQ1 3BG (01803 202940; ltrecruitment@ef.com). Residential courses for European students throughout Britain. Up to 1000 group leaders and EFL teachers are hired.

Kingswood Group, Group Operations, Kingswood Centres, West Runton, Cromer, Norfolk NR27 9NF (01263 835151; jobs@kingswood.co.uk). Employment at Camp Beaumont summer camps in Staffordshire, Isle of Wight and north Norfolk coast.

For catering, domestic and other work at family holiday centres contact the following:

Butlins Skyline, Roman Bank, Skegness, Lincolnshire PE25 1NJ (01754 761502) require receptionists, lifeguards, car park attendants, entertainers, shop assistants for Family Entertainment resorts. Application form and information pack available from regional offices: Bognor Regis 01243 820202; Minehead 01643 703331; Skegness (01754 614445).

HF Holidays, Redhills, Penrith, Cumbria CA11 0DT (01768 899988; hr@hfholidays.co.uk; www.hfholidays.co.uk/recruitment). Operate 19 country house hotels throughout the UK for people on walking and special interest holidays. Need children's activity leaders, walking leaders and domestic staff.

Pontin's Ltd, Sagar House, Eccleston, Nr. Chorley, Lancs. PR7 5PH (01768 454300; www. pontins.com). Hiring takes place for eight coastal family holiday centres.

Presthaven Sands Holiday Park, Shore Road, Gronant, Prestatyn, Flintshire, Wales LL19 9TT (01745 856471). 200 staff.

American-style theme parks have large seasonal staff requirements. As well as the usual skivvying jobs, they may also require ride operators, entertainers for both children and adults, lifeguards, DJs, shop assistants, etc. The main disadvantage is that accommodation is generally not provided. Among the largest are:

Alton Towers, Alton, North Staffordshire ST10 4DB (01538 704039). Approximately 1,000 vacancies between March and November.

American Adventure Theme Park, Pit Lane, Ilkeston, Derby DE7 5SX (01773 531521; www.americanadventure.co.uk). 150 ride operators, 70 retail staff, 120 catering assistants, etc.

Bourne Leisure Ltd, Park Lane, Hemel Hempstead, Herts. HP2 4YL. Staff needed at 40 holiday parks throughout Britain.

Chessington World of Adventures, Human Resources Department, Chessington, Surrey KT9 2NE (01372 731541; www.chessington.com). Employs between 500 and 1,000 people each year.

Frontierland Western Theme Park, The Promenade, Morecambe, Lancs. LA4 4DG (01524 410024). 40+ ride operators and general assistants in all departments.

Legoland Windsor, Winkfield Road, Windsor, Berks. SL4 4AY (01753 626150; jobs@legoland.co.uk). Over 300 seasonal workers needed in total.

Pleasureland Ltd, Marine Drive, Southport, Lancs. PR8 1RX (01704 532717; mail@pleasurelandltd.freeserve.co.uk).

Thorpe Park, Human Resources Department, PO Box 125, Staines Road, Chertsey, Surrey KT16 8PN (01932 577302; www.thorpepark.com). Limited accommodation provided for the 400+ ancillary staff.

Youth Hostels

Up to 200 seasonal assistant wardens are employed by the Youth Hostels Association (England and Wales) from March to October each year to help in the running of YHA's 230 youth hostels in the UK. The job can involve cooking for large numbers, general cleaning, cash handling and some clerical work. Accommodation and food are provided along with a basic salary from £370 per month. For an application form, apply in writing to the Person-nel & Training Department (Hostel Recruitment), YHA, PO Box 6030, Matlock, Derbyshire DE4 3XA (07626 939216; www.yha.org.uk), after which an interview may be scheduled, often at short notice.

There are also a number of independent hostels and budget accommodation around the country. Three hundred of these are listed in the pocket-sized *Independent Hostel Guide* from the Backpackers Press, Speedwell House, Upperwood, Matlock Bath, Der-byshire DE4 3PE (tel/fax 01629 580427; sam@backpackerspress.com), at a cost of £4.95 (plus £1 postage, £2 overseas). As of 2005 the hostel listings are accessible online at www.independenthostelguide.co.uk. Independent hostels are a good source of temporary work, often providing a few hours a day of work in return for bed and board. The Back-packers Press is able to circulate staff vacancy information to the hostels in its occasional newsletters.

Special Events

Events such as the Henley Regatta in June, Test Matches at Headingley in Leeds, the Edinburgh Festival in August/September and a host of golf tournaments and county shows need temporary staff to work as car park attendants, ticket sellers and in catering. Sporting events like the British Open and Wimbledon employ a myriad of casual workers. Ask the local tourist office for a list of upcoming events and contact the organisers. Outside cater-ing and other companies which hold the contracts for staffing special events include:

Events Staff Ltd, 25 York Road, Northampton NN1 5QA (01604 627775). 1000+ stewards, programme sellers, car park and security staff for racing fixtures, etc.

FMC (Facilities Management Catering Ltd), Church Road, Wimbledon, London SW19 5AE (020-8947 7430; www.fmccatering.co.uk). One of the largest outdoor caterers in Europe.

Leapfrog International, Riding Court Farm, Datchet, Berks. SL3 9JU (01753 589300; emt@leapfrog-int.co.uk). Up to 100 events crew for family fun days, etc.

If mass catering and cleaning seem a little tame, more interesting possibilities for entrepreneurs crop up at major events, especially at such a buzzy event as the Edinburgh

Fringe Festival:

As Nicole Gluckstern from the US discovered:
Work available breaks down into two basic categories: street vending and theatre work. Street vendors of jewelry, hairwraps, caricatures, etc. should bring their own supplies and a RAINCOAT. In theory you need a permit which has to be applied for one year in advance. In practice, as long as you don't set up on the high street, you can set up shop anywhere, until you get moved along by the (generally sympathetic) cops. Wait half an hour and set up again. 'The Mound' is the traditional place for setting up but it was closed this year (2002), to the dismay of dozens of unlicensed vendors who had to jockey for position along a single strip of stone benches nearby. But it should reopen possibly by next festival.

Theatre work itself is for technicians and flunkies who sell tix, make popcorn, mop floors (how much theatre experience do you need?) If you just breeze into town the week before the festival you can probably find work pasting up posters all over town; otherwise you probably have to do some advance planning. The Fringe Festival website has job listings and (I believe) the contact numbers for theatres. Alternatively, unless you live in Bohunk Montana, you might try to find a group in your hometown who's going and offer to be their stage manager. Every group is required to bring one but a lot of them find it hard to find one at the last minute. Unlike rock festivals or Christmas markets, working the Fringe is not going to make you any fortunes but the sheer value of the experience is well worth going out of your way for.

Adrian Little enjoyed the atmosphere of the British Open when it took place at the famous golf club in St. Andrews in Scotland. Jobs can be found as scoreboard operators, course scorers, radio operators, etc. In addition to earning about £100 for the one-week event, he got an excellent (free) view of the action. Look also for work during the Ryder Cup (when the tournament takes place in Britain).

Colin Rothwell from South Africa spent a few months in Nottingham trying to scrape together enough money to move on and recommends looking for work at fairs, horse races and rock concerts.

It's long hard work but the pay is usually not bad and there are sometimes good perks that go along with the job. I worked at a chicken and chips stand in Newcastle while Joe Cocker, Status Quo and Rod Stewart played away. During my short breaks I was allowed in to enjoy the concert. When it was all finished, there was a lot of roast chicken to take home (or sell). Then it was back to Nottingham in the early hours of the next morning with £40 in my back pocket.

Keith Larner recommends a variation on the classic summer job of erecting marquees for weddings and parties (see section Building and Other Seasonal Work below): *'Now I can tell you about another good avenue for casual work. I've just completed a job erecting temporary grandstands for sporting events such as golf, racing and tennis. It is very physical work, extremely heavy-going, but financially rewarding because you work 7 days per week (but only between April and October).'*

Less financially rewarding but probably a lot more fun would be to attend the Glastonbury Festival as a steward as part of a team of Oxfam volunteers. Last year Oxfam recruited 1,400 stewards who are guaranteed entry to the famous Gloucestershire festival that takes place in the third week of June. For details go to www.oxfam.org.uk and search for Glastonbury.

CHILDCARE & DOMESTIC

Au Pairs

One of the easiest ways for a European citizen between the ages of 17 and 27 to arrange to work in the United Kingdom is to become an au pair. The list of permitted nationalities includes all European Economic Area countries plus Turkey, the former Yugoslavia, Bulgaria and Romania. Anyone from outside the EEA seeking entry as an au pair has to show documents at entry proving that an arrangement has been made; changing status after entry as a visitor is not permitted. The maximum stay is two years, though it is possible to change families in this time.

The Home Office issues guidelines stipulating that the number of working days should be five and the weekly number of hours 25, not counting some evening babysitting. The work of an au pair consists of childcare and light housework duties. These guidelines cannot be enforced and many families ignore them, in which case the au pair should bring the Home Office directives to the attention of the host family.

The recommended pocket money for au pairs is currently £55 a week; this category of work has been declared exempt from minimum wage regulations. Details about working in Britain as an au pair are given in the *Au Pair & Nanny's Guide to Working Abroad* from Vacation Work (£12.95 or look in libraries). See the list in the introductory chapter Childcare for addresses of UK agencies, though normally foreign young people contact an agency in their own country in the first instance. In some areas it is easy to find live-in positions after arrival, but not in all areas, where there are more notices posted by foreign au pairs looking for jobs than families looking for au pairs.

Nannies

Young women (and very occasionally men) wishing to become mother's helps have a good chance of succeeding since the market in this field is also booming, especially in the Home Counties. An untrained, unqualified young woman can expect to be paid about £100 a week in addition to room and board. Mothers' helps with some experience often earn twice this amount and nannies even more.

Nannying in the UK is the option that many young women from Australia and New Zealand choose, partly because it takes care of accommodation and pays a good wage. Those with the working holiday visa can make use of agencies; others will have to answer private ads.

A less binding variation is to babysit, for which you should receive an hourly rate of £4-£5, more in London. Check notice boards, student broadsheets, etc. for such opportunities. A Malaysian student in London followed up a notice she spotted on a notice board next to Earls Court tube station and arranged free room and board in exchange for taking a child to and from school.

Many childcare agencies advertise in the weekly *Lady* magazine as well as in the free papers like *TNT* and *New Zealand News UK*. If you decide to register with one of the approved agencies, your references will be verified and a police check will be carried out on you. Two good websites to use with links to established nanny and au pair agencies are www.bestbear.co.uk and www.nannyjob.co.uk.

If you want a live-in position but not looking after children, many agencies specialise in providing carers for the elderly and disabled, for example Cura Domi-Care at Home (Guardian House, Borough Road, Godalming, Surrey GU7 2AE; 01483 420055; www.curadomi.co.uk) pays £350-£450 a week to residential care workers. Oxford Aunts is another venerable agency in this field (3 Cornmarket St, Oxford OX1 3EX; 01865 791017). Another national care provider is Complete Personal Assistance Ltd (www.completegroup.co.uk) which provide training. Obviously London is the best place for such an activity, though other provincial agencies offer this service such as Origin Care, 706 Cameron House, White Cross, Lancaster LA1 4XQ (www.origincare.com) who pay high wages to people aged 21-40 willing to assist people with spinal injuries on minimum 4-month contracts. Try also Active Assistance in Sevenoaks Kent (01732 746267; www.activeassistance.com) who promise wages of £400+ for a seven-day week.

TEACHING

Although there is a veritable epidemic of English language schools along the south coast and in places like Oxford and Cambridge, you may find it more difficult to get a job as a language tutor in Torquay than in Taipei, harder in Brighton than in Bogota. It takes more than a tidy appearance to get one of the well-paid summer jobs at one of the 600-800 summer language schools operating in Britain. And the situation has not been improved with the strong pound which has seen a falling off of numbers at many language schools. It is not uncommon for summer staff to be offered jobs which are contingent on student numbers, which makes it difficult to plan anything with certainty.

The majority of language schools in Britain insist that their teachers have a formal qualification in TEFL (Teaching English as a Foreign Language) or at the very least a university degree, teacher's certificate or fluency in a foreign language. If you satisfy any or all of these requirements you should apply to a number of language schools several months prior to the summer holiday period. The average starting salary for EFL teachers is £170-£200 per week, though Certificate-qualified teachers should earn £250-£300. Many employers provide staff accommodation for which there will be a deduction from wages.

If you lack the necessary qualifications to teach, you might still consider blitzing the language schools, since many of them also run a programme of outings and entertainments for their foreign students and they may need non-teaching supervisors and sports instructors. Working at one of these language summer schools is an excellent way of making contact with Italian, French and Spanish young people who might offer advice or even hospitality once you set off on your travels.

A list of 210 English language schools and colleges accredited by the British Council may be obtained from the Association of Recognised English Language Services (ARELS) at 56 Buckingham Gate, London SW1E 6AG (020-7802 9200; www.arels.org.uk). These schools employ only qualified or experienced teaching staff. Also check the Tuesday *Guardian* in the spring. Schools are located throughout the UK, but are concentrated in the South-East, London, Oxford and Cambridge. For further addresses, check in the following Yellow Pages under 'Language Schools' or 'Schools – Language': Bournemouth, Brighton, Cambridge, Canterbury, Exeter, Oxford and Tunbridge Wells. Two useful websites which list English language schools in Britain are www.EnglishinBritain.co.uk (accredited by the British Council) and www.tlcuk.com.

Here is a short list of major language course organisations which normally offer a large number of summer vacancies:

Alexanders International School, Bawdsey Manor, Bawdsey, Woodbridge, Suffolk IP12 3AZ (01394 411633; office@alexandersschool.com). Part of the Skola Group. International summer school for 11-18 year-olds mid-June to late August. Minimum 4 weeks. Activity staff also employed.

Anglo Continental Educational Group, 29-35 Wimborne Road, Bournemouth BH2 6NA 01202 557414/fax 01202 293944; English@anglo-continental.com). Up to 100 EFL teachers for adult summer courses and 20 for adolescents.

Anglo-European Study Tours, 8 Celbridge Mews, Porchester Road, London W2 6EU (020-7229 4435/fax 020-7792 8717; c.morris@aest.co.uk. Website: www.aest.co.uk). 200+ at centres throughout the UK for 2-6 weeks. £190-£220 per week. No accommodation.

Concorde International Summer Schools, Arnett House, Hawks Lane, Canterbury, Kent CT1 2NU (01227 451035/fax 01227 762760; www.concorde.ltd.uk). 150 teachers. £235-£280 a week depending on the course. Average 15 hours teaching and 20 supervising activities. Full board residential accommodation is available. Experience and TEFL qualification required.

EF Language Travel, EF House, Castle Road, Torquay TQ1 3BG (01803 202940). Large number of EFL teachers for residential courses.

Elizabeth Johnson Organisation, Passfield Business Centre, Lynchborough Rd, Passfield, Surrey GU30 7SB. With 35 centres around the UK. 85-90 teachers needed at peak time (July). Two weeks to a month minimum. £185-£270 per week. Three schools are residential.

Embassy CES, Lorna House, 103 Lorna Road, Hove, East Sussex BN3 3EL (01273-322353; vacjobsuk@embassyces.com). Summer schools from end of June to end of August at 21 centres around the UK. Employs several hundred teachers throughout UK and Ireland. Minimum requirement is a TEFL Cert. Accommodation can be provided.

English Language & Cultural Organisation, Lowlands, Chorleywood Road, Rickmansworth, Herts. WD3 4ES (01923 776731/fax 01923 774678; www.elco.co.uk). 20-30 EFL teachers to work at three locations in the south of England during the summer.

International Quest Centres, Havelock Chambers, 20/22 Queens Terrace, Southampton SO14 3BP (02380 338858; education@internationalquest.net). 400 vacancies in 30 centres for teachers and activity leaders. Period of work 2-6 weeks. Average wage from £10 per hour. Accommodation is not normally provided.

International Study Programmes, The Manor, Hazleton, Nr. Cheltenham, Glos. GL54 4EB (01451 860379; www.international-study-programmes.org.uk).

ISIS Educational Programmes, 259 Greenwich High Road, Greenwich, London SE10 8NB (020-8293 1188; recruitment@isisgroup.co.uk). 150 EFL teachers and 100 activity leaders.

OISE Youth Language Schools, Binsey Lane, Oxford OX2 0EY (01865 258300; younglearners@oise.com). Summer and Easter vacancies in dozens of locations. OISE offer their own training course to tutors.

Passport Language Schools, 37 Park Road, Bromley, Kent BR1 3HJ (020-8466 5925; dos@passport.uk.com). Employ about 150 teachers for schools in 30 towns in England and South Wales.

SUL Language Schools, 7 Woodland Avenue, Tywardreath, Par, Cornwall PL24 2PL (01726 814227; www.sul-schools.com). Employ 200-300 a year with degree and TEFL Cert. Minimum 2 weeks. Mornings only. From £23 per morning of 2½ hours. Residential.

TASIS England American School, Coldharbour Lane, Thorpe, Surrey TW20 8TE (01932 565252; www.tasis.com). Of special interest to American EFL teachers who want to teach in Britain from late June to late August; only suitably qualified Americans are eligible for work permits.

Thames Valley Cultural Centres, 13 Park St, Windsor, Berks. SL4 1LU (01753 852001/ fax 01753 831165; english@thamesvalleycultural.com). Up to 60 teachers around England.

Torbay Language Centre, Conway Road, Paignton, Devon T04 5LH (01803 558555; fax 01803 559606; laurie@tkc2.fsnet.co.uk). Employs about 40 teachers from the last week of June to the third week of August for a minimum of two weeks. Pay is £8.50 per hour; average 22½ hours per week.

The shortage of certified teachers for primary and secondary schools in deprived areas is still acute, both in London and elsewhere. Many local Education Authorities, mainly in inner and outer London, are constantly in need of supply or temporary short-term teachers who are paid a daily rate ranging from £80 to £126, though usually in the £90-£100 range.

APPLYING LOCALLY

British readers may decide that it is easiest to save money by working close to home. If you have had no luck through the Jobcentre, by answering newspaper adverts or by registering with private employment agencies, you may want to spread your net even wider. The *Yellow Pages* are an invaluable source of potential employers in anything from market gardening to market research. Personal visits are also a good idea, for example to the Personnel Managers of large department stores, supermarkets, national retailing chains, fast food restaurants or canneries in your area, especially as summer approaches. Staff turnover is high at DIY chain stores. Or you could approach the local council, most of which hire temporary staff during the summer or at Christmas. Look for small notices advertising for house cleaners.

Investigate every avenue for boosting your travel fund. Brendan Barker says the oddest odd job he had in England was in police identity parades. He got a few pounds for 15 minutes 'work' while Thames Valley Police pay £10 per appearance. You have more chance of being called back if you are male and look fairly scruffy, though the Cambridge Constabulary have been known to flag down dons cycling to the library to fill a last-minute vacancy in a parade. Ian Mitselburg several times replied to the police request received at his Edinburgh hostel but thought that the system was unfair to the suspect since the Australasians, North Americans and Germans invariably had a healthier appearance than the Scots.

After job-seekers from abroad have been based in one place for a time, they can normally find some work. Although Woden Teachout, a young travelling American woman, did not have the benefit of a work permit, she pieced together several jobs in Cambridge within a couple of weeks: 'In my terror at my shrinking funds, I accumulated five jobs: two cleaning, one nannying, one behind the bar at a red plush Turkish nightclub and one (which has stood me well) as a personal assistant to a professor.' The latter job, which was advertised on a notice board at the Graduate Student Centre, was by far the most interesting and also lucrative. Similar notices for research assistants are posted in universities around the world, mostly in department offices and teaching buildings rather than in student unions.

Medical Experiments

There are between 50 and 100 clinical research units in the UK according to the Association of Independent Clinical Research Contractors (AICRC), many of which rely on testing their drugs on human guinea pigs. The demand for willing volunteers is so great that some of the larger pharmaceutical companies like GlaxoSmithKline advertise in the mainstream media. Drug testing is overseen by ethical committees, but many people fear that the long-term consequences of taking unlicensed drugs cannot be safely predicted. The companies all give assurances that their tests are safe, but not everyone accepts this.

Nevertheless many people rely on drug testing as a regular source of income, earning as much as £200 a day. Most company literature states that expenses will be reimbursed, but payment is normally more generous than this. If interested, it is worth checking notice boards and making enquiries at any teaching hospital or asking any medical student you happen to meet. To obtain details from GlaxoSmithKline of their programme of experiments in Cambridge and elsewhere, ring the Volunteer Recruitment Line on 0800 328 4195. The website www.controlled-trials.com/mrct lists UK trial centres as well as international ones.

Some clinics to try include:

Charterhouse Clinical Research Unit, described below.

Chiltern Research Unit, Freepost SCE13234, Slough SL1 2BR (0800 783 0976/01753 642222).

Parexel Clinical Pharmacology Research Unit, Level 7, Northwick Park Hospital, Watford Road, Harrow HA1 3UT; 0800 085 1392; drugtrial@parexel.com; www.drugtrial. co.uk.

Hammersmith Medicines Research, Central Middlesex Hospital, Park Royal, Acton, London NW10 7NS (020 8961 4130; recruit@hmrlondon.com).

GDRU Ltd, – London, 020-7910 7777.

Kingshill Research Centre, Victoria Hospital, Okus Road, Swindon SN1 4HZ (01793 437518; info@kingshill-research.org).

LCG Bioscience, Bourn Hall Clinic, Bourn, Cambridge CB3 7TR (0800 833399).

Richmond Pharmacology Volunteer Recruitment - 0800 085 6464; www.trials4us.co.uk.
Royal Free Hospital, Clinical Trials Dept, Hampstead – 020-7830 2405.
Leicester Clinical Research – 0800 834435.
Covance Clinical Research Ltd. – Leeds, 0800 591570.
DDS Medicines Research Ltd. – Dundee, 0800 838249.
MDS Harris – Belfast, 01232 554000.
Indago Clinical Research – Stoke on Trent, 01782 555103.
Inveresk Clinical Research – Edinburgh, 0800 393855.
Medeval – Manchester, 0161-232 0391.
Simbec Research Ltd – Merthyr Tydfil, South Wales; 0800 691995.

In some cases, volunteer subjects must produce a medical certificate from their own doctor attesting to their good health, and in most cases foreign volunteers must prove that they are in the country legally. If you are not thoroughly screened, it may be that the research company does not comply with the rigorous standards set out by the Association of Independent Clinical Research Contractors and should be avoided.

Reluctantly Rob Abblett signed up for a study of hay fever tablets in his home town (Leicester) to revive his flagging fortunes between world trips: *'Lots of blood samples and lots of TV. Thankfully, my veins are too fine so I won't be making a career out of this. I'll get about £950 if I last the distance from 16th June to 11th July. This includes two nights residential and two return visits each week.'*

The majority of opportunities are in London. One of the well-regulated clinics which carries out tests on healthy volunteers is the Charterhouse Clinical Research Unit Ltd. located at the Ravenscourt Park Hospital, Ravenscourt Park, W6 0TN (020-8741 7170; www.charterhouse-clinical.com and www.volunteer4trials.com). If you qualify and they have places available on any experiment you will be asked to attend for screening by the Volunteer Recruitment Officer. After passing the screening (you must have taken no medications or drugs in the previous fortnight), you must undertake to abstain faithfully from nicotine, alcohol, tea, coffee, cola and chocolate for 48 hours on either side of the test. Between swallowing the experimental medications and having tests (e.g. blood tests, blood pressure, etc.), you will be given meals and entertained with videos (possibly *Zombie Flesheater, Coma* or *Love at First Bite*). If you don't want to subject yourself to all this, you can sell 600ml of your blood for £60, assuming you meet the specifications.

Guys Hospital also has a Drug Research Unit (6 Newcomen St, London SE1; 020-7910 7777) which is often looking for healthy volunteers and which pays on average £100 a day. On first arriving in London after a protracted round-the-world working trip, Jimmy Henderson signed up at Guys and did a 20-day experiment at £100 a day which set him and his girlfriend Bridgid up in London. The best time to ring is between 10am and noon during the week when you will be told when male volunteers and female volunteers should contact them.

If the thought of subjecting your body to unknown drugs upsets you, then psychological experiments provide an easier (if less lucrative) alternative. Psychology researchers constantly need large numbers of volunteers and often receive grants specifically to pay subjects. It is worth enquiring at any university's psychology department about this opportunity.

Men who at one time would have unthinkingly donated sperm in exchange for a small fee (normally £15 plus expenses) now have to register their details so that the children born subsequently can trace their genetic fathers. More than two-thirds of prospective donors are rejected. For the nearest clinic contact the Human Fertilisation and Embryology Authority on 020-7377 5077; their website www.hfea.gov.uk lists all clinics licensed to store sperm. The London Women's Clinic on Harley Street (www.lwclinic.co.uk/donor.htm) provides detailed information on how to become a sperm donor and what the process entails.

Job Creation
If you can't find anyone to hire you, you can set yourself up in a small odd-jobbing business.

Karen Weaving and Chris Blakeley, who claim to have no particular skills, set themselves up in Basingstoke as 'Spare Hands – Household & Domestic Services' and managed to save £4,000 in seven months, enough to fund a round-the-world trip. Within two months they were both working over 80 hours a week and earning an average of £2.50 an hour having found that gardening, decorating and catering were the most lucrative areas. After delivering and posting some publicity leaflets, they got a few customers, and word spread quickly that they were reliable and cheap. According to Karen and Chris, the question is not 'can I make a sandwich?' but 'can I sell a sandwich?'. Notice boards in newsagents' windows, colleges and unions sometimes give leads to potential dog-walkers, flat-cleaners, shirt-ironers, etc.

Anyone thinking of starting a new business should approach his or her local Business Link (formerly the Training & Enterprise Council) which can offer advice and in some cases financial support. Shell LiveWIRE, specialises in helping young people aged 16-30 to start their own business (Hawthorn House, Forth Banks, Newcastle-upon-Tyne NE1 3SG; 0845 757 3252/ www.shell-livewire.org).

Building and Other Seasonal Work

The building trade is flourishing. Ask around at new building sites to speak to the foreman (or gaffer) who may have powers of hiring or will at least be able to advise you on possibilities. There is more work for unskilled labourers as the foundations are being laid, though you might get hired at a later stage as a hodman carting the bricks and mortar up a ladder to the mason or bricklayer. Iain Kemble financed several trips abroad after a spell as a self-employed hod carrier. Wages, even for the unskilled, are above average. When you are asking for work, don't admit either to being a student or having no experience.

You may prefer to build temporary rather than permanent structures. The work of erecting marquees is strenuous and pays fairly well, especially since time spent travelling to the destination is also paid, and there is usually plenty of overtime. Try, for example, Field and Lawn (Marquees) Ltd who operate throughout the UK with offices near Leeds, Warrington, Edinburgh, Glasgow, London and Bristol (www.fieldandlawn.com). The company Danco has a history of hiring backpackers for marquee erecting (www.danco.co.uk/employment. htm). Check the local *Yellow Pages* for other firms to contact.

Certain agricultural jobs are very seasonal in nature, such as turkey plucking in December.

Eric Mackness braved the gruelling job of working on a Christmas tree plantation near Abingdon in Oxfordshire for one month from November 10th:
I was recruited at the end of the summer tourist season on Sark by an Irish company which has outlets in Ireland, Scotland and Kent as well as Abingdon near Oxford where I worked. The job consists of sorting, pricing and loading Christmas trees. It's not that well paid at £5 (now £5.50) an hour but because of the potential for working a hideous number of hours (80-90 a week with no days off) it is possible to earn a tidy sum. Accommodation is provided and the food is excellent. The work was the hardest I have ever done (and I have done some hard jobs). Working on top of a trailer loaded with frozen trees in a snowstorm is not for the faint-hearted.

Apparently many of the workers return from one year to the next in order to earn up to £1,500 in five weeks, but new vacancies do crop up with the Emerald Group; applications to Temple House, Templeshannon, Enniscorthy, Co. Wexford (+353 543 8333; davidbarrett@emeraldgroup.ie).

Tree-planting is a job normally associated with Canada however contractors have recently been recruiting tree planters to work in the Keilder Forest of Northumberland for five months. Piece work rates take time to build up, but some people earn £60-£70 a day.

Some of the best-paid jobs are the least desirable such as painting electricity pylons.

Mark Wilson was paid well for this job but he doesn't recommend it to anyone who can't handle heights:

> I've done unpleasant jobs before (including four years down a coal mine) but this job really was the pits. You are expected to catch six chickens in each hand at a rate of 600 an hour. You then carry them outside (the only time the chickens ever see daylight) and load them onto lorries. While they are pecking and clawing your arms, you can often feel their legs breaking. This together with the screams and cries of the chickens and the stench in the sheds meant that I didn't keep this job up very long and have since given up eating factory-farmed products.

Finally, don't overlook the obvious. The Post Office employs 100,000 temporary workers between the end of November and Christmas. The pay is well above the minimum wage.

LONDON

Most new arrivals in the capital report that there is no shortage of work. The problem is finding affordable accommodation which allows you to save from what is seldom a star-tlingly good wage. Ian Mitselburg from Sydney went through the usual processes: 'The first job I got was through a hostel notice board: labouring for a shifty hotel owner, who was restoring his hotel in the Paddington/Bayswater area (where else?) for a few weeks, paid cash-in-hand. After that I worked through the Everyman Agency in Earl's Court which was run by a couple of Kiwis who clearly favoured Australasians.'

With over 2,000 employment agencies, London is the best place to look for temporary work. The advertising pages of free magazines aimed at the ex-pat community (e.g. *TNT* and *New Zealand News*) all carry scores of ads for agencies specialising in everything from banquet catering to landscape gardening. It is normally pointless to write to agencies before arrival in the capital, especially foreign applicants who have no chance of obtaining a work permit and who do not speak fluent English.

You can expect to earn minimum wage as a kitchen porter (the most lowly job) and up to twice that as an assistant chef. Ask your agency about obtaining hygiene certificate training. Among the many agencies active in this field is Mayday. Mayday Exec Temporary Catering Staff has several offices including 2 Shoreditch High St, E1 6PG (020-7377 1352; www.maydaygroup.co.uk) and 21 Great Chapel St, W1F 8FW (020-7432 7000) for bar work.

Also check out cleaning and security work, for which there seems to be an insatiable demand in London. An active agency in the field of gardening and landscape labouring is Target Appointments (recruit@target-jobs.com; www.target-jobs.com).

Anyone who can speak a foreign language has an excellent chance of finding work at a tourist attraction. Young Europeans based in London should give this a go as Brigitte Albrech did:

> With basic English and a lot of courage, I applied for a job at Madame Tussauds Museum and was surprised they accepted me without a lot of questions. They are always in need of people speaking a foreign language to work as guides and are looking for people who appear clean and patient. There is an opportunity of being trained as a cashier or planetarium operator, which would mean more money. It can be hard work but getting a work reference from Madame Tussauds is not bad at all.

Apply to the Human Resources Officer, The Tussauds Group, Marylebone Road, NW1 5LR (020-7487 0289; www.madame-tussauds.com).

There is a very high turn-over of staff at pubs (see section on pub work above), shops, wine bars, station buffets, etc. Check the classified adverts in the *London Evening Standard* (which comes out at about 11am), the free weekly *TNT* and *LOOT*.

Modelling is a traditional way of earning cash; try the Chelsea School of Art, the St

Martin's School of Art or the London College of Printing for nude or clothed jobs. Aspiring film or television extras can register with a relevant agency that will ask for at least one recent professional quality photo (probably an 8 X 10 black and white) and a registration fee. Equity has a list of casting agencies (020-7379 6000). Beware of rogue agencies that take your money but fix up nothing.

Americans and others lacking working papers may find that agencies of any kind will not be prepared to help them. After watching his travel fund dwindle from $500 to $30 in just three weeks, American Joe Warnick was reduced to doing one of the sleaziest jobs around: he went to work for a prostitute posting her business cards in London phone booths. Just two days into the job, he managed to upset his plump, middle-aged, heavily made-up employer and told her to find someone else, using somewhat colourful language, whereupon she threatened to send round her pimp to teach him a lesson. Fortunately the thug never materialised and within a short while Joe had landed a job with a family-run window cleaning business which he thoroughly enjoyed for four months. *'I was treated extremely well by this wonderful family. Cleaning windows above the bustling streets of London was a real buzz. It afforded me countless opportunities to visit with Londoners in their flats and meet many of them at their places of work.'*

Pubs

Anyone who has been on a pub crawl in London will know that a huge percentage of the people working behind the bar are Australian. Although there are employment agencies specialising in bar work, they aren't usually very helpful to people looking for casual bar work.

> **Kristen Moen from Norway describes her job in a London pub**
> *I loved it: the atmosphere was great, I had so much fun and met so much nice people at work. The only thing I can complain about is that the money is not very good – or maybe the rents for flats in London are too high. If I had had a work permit, I would have gotten a job immediately, but it took me two weeks. First I went around asking in pubs and restaurants. Everybody was really helpful. They would always suggest another place I could go to or tell me to come back in a few weeks. At the same time I was also reading the job ads in the Evening Standard. 70% turned me down because of my missing work permit, but finally I got something and worked happily there for four months.*

Couriers

Driving is a standard stop-gap job, for example of vans and mini-cabs or as a courier. Motorcycle owners might be tempted by the money that can be earned by despatch riders. For those who don't own their own bikes, they can be leased from the firm. According to Ben Nakoneczny, despatch riders can earn up to £500 a week: *'Earnings are commission-only; they increase dramatically according to number of hours worked, knowledge of London streets and relationship with your controller. There is also a very high risk of serious injury, hence insurance premiums will be very high if you choose to declare your occupation for insurance and tax purposes, which many don't.'*

The firm City Sprint (www.citysprint.co.uk) is always looking for drivers, couriers and porters, and seems sympathetic to the erratic habits of people working for relatively short periods to fund their travels. Bicycle couriers are normally paid in the region of £2.70 per delivery. Top couriers earn in excess of £300 in a good week which means they have to cover up to 300 miles a day doing up to 40 jobs. The job carries on in all weathers (except snow which is considered too dangerous). Although cycle couriers don't earn as much as despatch riders, it appeals to some brave souls like T. P. Lye from Malaysia who claimed that you do it for love not money:

After the first few weeks of courier cycling (which is the best job I've ever had) it should be possible to earn a decent wage. Anyone who is reasonably fit, can endure from 20 to 30 miles of cycling in a day, knows London pretty well, can read a map and loves the thrill of dodging in and out of the London traffic should try it. It can be quite scary cycling in the rain when your brakes don't work and you have to cope with cretinous pedestrians who can't see beyond their brollies, but after a while that sort of experience is part of the whole fun of courier cycling. The company I worked for was always looking for new people since there is a high turnover especially during the winter months. The pay is always cash-in-hand and by the week. In my experience the most boring days have been fine, sunny ones when everyone wants to work and there aren't enough jobs to go round. One of the worst problems is punctured tyres.

Sales

People working in shops are often paid a commission in addition to the average weekly wage of £200+. Harrods is constantly looking for temporary staff to cover their busy sale periods (July and January) and the run-up to Christmas; contact the Recruitment Centre, 11 Brompton Place, SW3 1QE (020-7893 8793) for details.

Jobs in call centres and telesales are all too plentiful in London. Telesales involve telephoning complete strangers and persuading them to buy a product. Advertisements for this type of work frequently appear in the free local newspapers in the London area, although they may not always mention the nature of the job in the advert. The ones to look out for say things like: 'Do you want to earn up to £X/week in your spare time?'.

Accommodation in London

Most new arrivals in London go to one of the scores of (relatively) cheap hostels where overseas travellers congregate. Expect to pay £20 for a dorm bed. Your fellow hostellers will often prove invaluable sources of inside knowledge about the job market and hostels often serve as a launch pad for money-saving careers and shared houses. Carisa Fey arrived in London from Stuttgart at the tender age of 18 determined to make a go of long-term working and travelling, and soon moved out of a hostel and into rented accommodation:

> *Once in London I went – where else? – to Earls Court, and met my first fellow travellers in a hostel. I planned to be the very first one on Monday morning to grab the hostel copy of TNT and to start my hunt for a job. Well, unfortunately, we were in one of those, ehm, social hostels and until 3pm on Monday I couldn't even walk. I thought my chance was gone and that no one was going to give a job to me considering the state I was in. But just to practise I put on my suit and decided to look for a place to stay. The third letting agency I went into (I was still a spoiled brat then and believed in things like letting agencies) seemed nice, professional and not too expensive. While filling in the form, I left the space 'Occupation' empty and said that I was looking for a job. The agency's boss sat on the next desk, looked up and asked 'Do you want to work here?' So I found in one afternoon a job and a place to stay.*

A single room in a shared house will normally cost £250-£500 a month. Carisa's standard of accommodation changed considerably during her six months of doing various jobs in London:

> *I left my first nice room (too far outside the centre) and moved in first with a mentally ill Italian, then with 25 Swedish people in a tiny house where they played weird games at night, and then to the Indian quarter. I became ill and couldn't work and soon I had absolutely no money left. I did honestly starve. Great lesson for a girl that grew up safely in the comfortable middle class. To be hungry and not to have money to even buy a roll.*

Carisa may have turned her nose up at letting agencies but websites can be very useful (for London jobs as well as accommodation) especially www.gumtree.com and www. accommodationlondon.net.

Free food and accommodation in exchange for some duties is a great bonus in London. For example the charity SHAD recruits full-time volunteers to assist people with severe physical disabilities to live independently in the community. Volunteers are required to stay for a minimum of three or four months, and receive a place to live and an allowance of at least £60 a week plus expenses. A shift system is worked by volunteers allowing plenty of free time to explore London. SHAD's office is in Wandsworth at 5 Bedford Hill, Balham, SW12 9ET (020-8675 6095; www.shad.org.uk). Similarly Independent Living Alternatives (Trafalgar House, Grenville Place, NW7 3SA; 020-8906 9265; www.ILAnet.co.uk) pays its full-time volunteers £63.50 a week in addition to free accommodation.

Private agencies also employ live-in carers and pay £5-£9 an hour to people who have a qualification (e.g. NVQ level 2 or above).

Debbie Harrison arrived in London after a frenetic season as a holiday rep in Greece, eager to save some money:
After the constant dining out, excessive drinking and sunbathing, my current job as a live-in carer for an old lady in a quiet part of Surrey is quite a contrast. I went to the agency interview with no experience or qualifications but was introduced by a friend already employed by them and I was offered a job straightaway. The pay is good £336 for a week (with 12 hours off once a week) or £392 if I work seven days straight. These hours mean temporary death to the social life but it's a great way to save.

The kind of clientele served by certain agencies means that they will be selective, so you will need to look respectable and have a background to match with contactable references. A driving licence is often essential. Some agencies employ people on a casual basis to fill in for other carers; this pays from £50 a day.

VOLUNTARY OPPORTUNITIES

CSV mentioned at the beginning of this chapter guarantees a voluntary placement to anyone aged 16+ who commits him/herself to live away from home for 4-12 months supporting people who need help such as children with special needs and homeless people. Volunteers do not need any special skills, qualifications or experience. Volunteers receive £29 a week in addition to accommodation and meals; freephone the Volunteers' Hotline on 0800 374991 or consult the CSV homepage www.csv.org.uk. Another organisation which provides board, lodging and pocket money to volunteers willing to work at centres for the homeless is the Simon Community (PO Box 1187, London NW5 4HW; 020-7485 6639; www.simoncommunity.org.uk) whose preferred minimum stay is nine months. Volunteers receive an allowance of £33 a week in addition to room and board.

Many shorter term opportunities for volunteers can be found, especially during the summer months when disability charities recruit volunteers to assist at holiday centres to give disabled people and their carers a break. Vitalise (formerly the Winged Fellowship Trust) runs holiday centres in Southampton, Bodmin, Southport, Bridgford (Nottingham) and Chigwell that depend on willing volunteers (British or otherwise) from February to November. The charity pays all board, lodging and travel to the centres from within the UK; an application form can be downloaded from the site www.vitalise.org.uk or requested from the head office, 12 City Forum, 250 City Road, London EC1V 8AF (0845 345 1972). Break is another national charity that takes on volunteers for the holidays (Davison House, 1 Montague Road, Sheringham, Norfolk NR26 8WN; 01263 822161; www.break-charity. org). The organisation Young Disabled on Holiday also recruits summer volunteers (4 Parkgrove Neuk, Edinburgh EH4 7QT; 0131-332 1944).

If you are more interested in conservation work, several national bodies arrange one to three week working holidays where volunteers repair dry stone walls, clear overgrown ponds, undertake botanical surveys, archaeological digs or maintain traditional wood-land. You will be housed in comfortable volunteer basecamps with about a dozen other volunteers. For a free brochure listing the 450 projects organised by the National Trust, ring 0870 429 2428 for week-long and weekend residential projects or the Volunteering Department on 0870 609 5383 for long-term placements. Postal requests should be sent to the National Trust, Rowan, Kembrey Park, Swindon SN2 8YL (volunteers@nationaltr ust.org.uk; www.nationaltrust.org.uk/volunteering). Projects take place year round. Most summer projects cost £80 per week to join whereas out-of-season working holidays cost from £60.

BTCV (British Trust for Conservation Volunteers) organise over 350 conservation work-ing holidays throughout the UK from the Cornish coast to the Scottish Highlands. Accom-modation, meals and insurance are provided at a cost from £60 per week. All include relevant training, and many lead to qualifications and certificates. Visit the BTCV website www.btcv.org to view Volunteering Opportunities, or contact BTCV Customer Service (163 Balby Rd, Balby, Doncaster, S. Yorks. DN4 0RH; 01302 572244; information@btcv.org. uk).

For volunteers interested in the routine maintenance and conservation of old build-ings, contact Cathedral Camps at 16 Glebe Avenue, Flitwick, Beds. MK45 1HS (www. cathedralcamps.org.uk). These organisations charge a modest fee to cover expenses, e.g. £70 a week. Bird-lovers can become volunteer wardens for up to four weeks with the Royal Society for the Protection of Birds (RSPB, The Lodge, Sandy, Beds. SG19 2DL; 01767 680551; www.rspb.org.uk/volunteering). Accommodation is provided free but the volunteers must provide their own food. The Waterway Recovery Group Ltd (PO Box 114, Rickmansworth, Herts. WD3 1ZY; 01923 711114; enquiries@wrg.org.uk; www.wrg.org.uk) run week-long voluntary Canal Camps (from £42 a week for accommodation and meals).

A number of organisations in Britain which require volunteers for limited periods are listed in the *International Directory of Voluntary Work* (£11.95). Anyone who wants to par-ticipate on an archaeological dig should subscribe to *British Archaeology* for £27, avail-able from the Council for British Archaeology, St Mary's House, 66 Bootham, York YO30 7BZ(01904 671417; www.britarch.ac.uk). The magazine is produced six times a year and lists archaeological digs to which volunteers can apply.

Volunteering is an excellent solution for anyone who has work permit problems. Ameri-cans, and indeed anyone, can fix up voluntary jobs independently. Janet Renard and Luke Olivieri are two particularly enterprising American travellers who arranged several voluntary positions before they left home. One of the most unusual was working for the Festiniog Railway Company (Harbour Station, Porthmadog, Gwynedd LL49 9NF; www. festrail.co.uk) which operates a famous narrow gauge railway and provides hostel accom-modation to volunteers.

Many of the volunteers are railroad/steam engine fanatics, but accepted us even though we didn't know the first thing about it. We elected to work in the Parks & Gar-dens section and spent a week weeding, planting, clearing, etc. The work was hard and the evenings were busy too. We were taken to a pub one night, asked to dinner another, visited a Welsh male voice choir and went climbing in the area. Festiniog Railway depends completely on volunteers who come from all over, all ages, all pro-fessions. But they can always use more help, so we may just go back.

Other historic railways looking for volunteers, both in beautiful parts of the country, are the Strathspey Railway Co in Aviemore (01479 810725; information@strathspeyrailway. co.uk) and the Welshpool & Llanfair Railway (01938 810441; info@wllr.org.uk).

Communes (which are now properly called communities) may provide a good oppor-tunity for people sympathetic to a back-to-basics lifestyle. The Centre for Alternative Technology in Wales (Machynlleth, Powys SY20 9AZ; 01654 705950; www.cat.org.uk) takes on volunteers between March and September, many on a short-term basis, paying

£5.50 a day for food. Advance booking is essential. A directory called *Diggers & Dreamers* with details of communities both in Britain and abroad is available for £6.50 plus £1.50 UK postage from Edge of Time, BCM Edge, London WC1N 3XX (0800 083 0451; www.edgeoftime.co.uk).

Buddhist communities throughout Britain run retreats either for a modest fee or on a work-for-keep arrangement. For example the Losang Dragpa Buddhist Centre in the Pennines (Dobroyd Castle, Pexwood Road, Todmorden, W. Yorks. OL14 7JJ; 01706 812247 ext 201) requires volunteers to assist with various projects maintaining the Victorian castle in which it is housed. Also in Yorkshire is the Madhyamaka Centre (Kilnwick Percy Hall, Pocklington, Yorks. YO42 1UF; 01759 304832; www.madhyamaka.org) where Shona Williamson enjoyed a working holiday so much she decided to make it her home for an extended period. In exchange for 35 hours of work per week she got free dormitory accommodation, vegetarian meals and the chance to attend evening meditations and teachings. The Manjushri Mahayana Buddhist Centre in Ulverston, Cumbria advertises working holidays too (01229 584029; info@manjushri.org.uk).

Laura Hitchcock from New York state managed to fix up two three-month positions in the field of her career interest by agreeing to pay her own expenses if they would take her on and help her find accommodation in local homes. Her jobs were in the publicity departments of the Ironbridge Gorge Museum Trust (Coach Road, Coalbrookdale, Ironbridge, Telford, Shropshire TF8 7DQ) and then in a theatre-arts centre in East Anglia (The Quay Theatre at Quay Lane, Sudbury, Suffolk CO10 2AN): *'I learned when writing not to ask for 'internships' but rather for 'unpaid work experience'; otherwise the British will ask you what hospital you are with! The particularly good feature of my jobs was that the people were so friendly. If you were willing to help yourself they'd do all they could for you.'*

If you intend to become involved in the workcamps or organic farm movements abroad, it is advisable to get local experience first (see *Voluntary* chapter for addresses of internationally-active organisations and *Agriculture* for a description of the activities of WWOOF: World Wide Opportunities on Organic Farms).

Ireland

The rise in Ireland's fortunes over the past decade has been astonishing and the employment situation is far more promising than it has been for generations. (A dozen years ago Ireland's rate of unemployment was the worst in Europe.) No longer is the traffic of migrant labour one-way; nowadays lots of Europeans are flocking to Ireland for work since it has the second lowest rate of unemployment in the Eurozone (4.4%). The phenomenal amount of building work going on in Dublin is a reliable indicator of the vigour of the economy and justifies the description 'Celtic tiger'. Taxes and the cost of living are still high but wages are beginning to catch up. The hourly minimum wage at the beginning of 2005 was €7. Despite the go-ahead economy, the Irish have not changed out of recognition and most visitors come to prefer Irish habits at work and play to the uptight stressed-out life in many other countries.

The Irish government changed the rules governing work permits after the accession of ten new EU member states in 2004. Because Ireland implemented no barriers to the flow of labour from these countries Irish employers can expect to be able to fill the great majority of their vacancies with citizens of the enlarged EU, thus doing away with the need for work permits. Note that the government has a list of occupations that are not eligible for work permits which includes childcarers, hotel and bar staff, general labourers and sales staff. (Fish processors have just been removed from the list of ineligible job categories.)

Working Holiday Schemes

US nationals who can prove Irish ancestry may be eligible for unrestricted entry to Ireland

186 Work Your Way in Europe

and even Irish nationality (which would confer all EU rights). Enquiries should be directed to the relevant Irish Embassy.

Full-time North American students in tertiary education or recent graduates are eligible to apply for an 'Exchange Visitor Programme Work Permit'. For American students the permit is valid for up to four months at any time of the year and for Canadians the limit is 12 months. BUNAC USA (PO Box 430, Southbury, CT 06488; 203-264-0901; www.bunacusa.org) and CIEE (7 Custom House Street, 3rd Floor, Portland, ME 04101; 207-553-7600; www.ciee. org/isp) both administer the Work in Ireland programme while SWAP/Travelcuts (www. swap.ca) administer it in Canada. Whereas the number of visas for Canadians with student status is unlimited, the number available to non-students aged up to 35 is limited so early application to SWAP is advised.

Once in Ireland, the student and youth travel service Usit (19-21 Aston Quay, O'Connell Bridge, Dublin 2; 01-602 1777; www.usit.ie) will advise on job opportunities. Usit does not currently administer the working holiday scheme for Australians and New Zealanders who should apply for exchange visitor permits from the Irish embassy in their own country. The Usit website provides details of working holiday visa eligibility of other countries like Ghana and Argentina. If you visit the Usit office on the south side of the River Liffey, you can inspect a large notice board with many Jobs Available notices, including many for au pairs.

Obviously there will be many Americans and others who are not students and therefore not eligible for this programme. Again informal arrangements with private hostels can make it possible to extend your stay in Ireland. One enterprising Californian contacted hostels via www.hostels.com and, after a brief exchange of emails and references and a phone conversation, was hired by a start-up hostel which gave her accommodation plus $150 a week.

THE JOB HUNT

The Training & Employment Authority of Ireland is FAS (Foras Aiscanna Saothair) with about 70 offices throughout the country which EU nationals may consult. The best office for foreign enquiries is the EURES office in the FAS at 27-33 Upper Baggot Street, Dublin 4 (01-607 0903; www.fas.ie). There are a number of private employment agencies listed in the 'Irish Golden Pages' which is a better source of contacts than the Irish Department of Enterprise, Trade & Employment (www.entemp.ie) which oversees employment agencies in Ireland. Irishjob.ie is one of the country's biggest online recruitment services, which registers employers' vacancies and has many links to both general and specialised recruitment agencies.

Mig Urquhart from Glasgow ended up in Dublin by chance rather than choice since that was the cheapest flight she could get out of New York. She ended up staying for two years and says that the FAS is very useful for jobs if only because you can use their phones to follow up leads. The main newspapers are worth checking: the *Evening Herald* for more casual jobs and the *Irish Independent* (Thursdays and Sundays; www.loadza. com carries good though undated job listings, many with phone numbers and web links) and the *Irish Times* for more professional appointments; the online job classifieds can be found at http://jobs.nicemove.ie. The Dublin City Council Community & Youth Information Centre in Sackville Place off O'Connell St (01-878 6844; cyic@dublincity.ie) offers information on employment and careers as well as education and training, social welfare and travel information. They offer free internet access, free CV typing and provide the venue for a Free Legal Advice Centre every Saturday.

Note that some agencies arrange unpaid work experience placements for young people from the continent. One example in Cork is Interconnection (18 Mary St, Cork; 021-491 5298; www.interconnection-europe.com).

Tourism

The tourist industry is the main source of seasonal work in Ireland. Outside Dublin, the largest demand is in the southwestern counties of Cork and Kerry, especially the towns of Killarney (with well over 100 pubs) and Tralee. Vacancies are sometimes registered through EURES, for example hotel jobs paying about €250 a week plus accommodation were on offer at the time of writing to waiting staff with at least one year's experience. Write to the addresses in any guide to hotels in Ireland. One of the biggest employers is the Jurys Doyle Hotel Group (www.jurysdoyle.com).

When applying, you should mention any musical talent you have, since pubs and hotels may be glad to have a barman who can occasionally entertain at the piano. Directly approaching cafés, campsites and amusement arcades is usually more effective than writing. Two hundred thousand people a year visit the Aillwee Caves in County Clare; the company which manages the attraction recruits cave tour guides and support staff for a minimum of two months (Aillwee Cave Co. Ltd., Ballyvaughan, Co. Clare; 065-707 7036; www.aillweecave.ie).

Experienced assistants and instructors may be needed by riding stables and watersports centres throughout Ireland. The horse industry is still very strong in Ireland; experienced individuals looking for stable work should contact the National Stud Company (Tully, Co. Kildare; 045-521251). Anyone with experience of horses might have success by contacting stables, riding holiday centres or equestrian recruitment agencies. For example monitors, instructors and pony trek leaders are needed mainly for children at Errislannan Manor Connemara Pony Stud (Clifden, Co. Galway 095-21134; info@connemara-tourism.org; the minimum stay is three months and applications must be made before March. Children's adventure centres are a good bet for summer employment; try for example Delphi Adventure Holidays (Church Buildings, Church Lane, Main St, Rathfarnham, Dublin 14; www.delphiadventureholidays.ie) which has an adventure centre in Southwest Mayo employing seasonal staff.

Innumerable musical and cultural festivals take place throughout Ireland, mostly during the summer. Big-name bands often perform at concerts near Dublin. A small fortune can be made by amateur entrepreneurs (with or without a permit) who find a niche in the market. Heather McCulloch had two friends who sold filled rolls and sandwiches at a major concert and made a clear profit of over £1,000 in just a few hours.

'The Rose of Tralee', a large regional festival held in Tralee, Co. Kerry in the first week of September, provides various kinds of employment for enterprising workers, as Tracie Sheehan reports: *'As 50,000 people attend this festival each year, guest houses, hotels, restaurants and cafés all take on extra staff. Buskers make great money, as do mime artists, jugglers and artists. Pubs do a roaring business, so singing or performing in a pub can be very profitable.'*

Dublin

According to Mig Urquhart, 'crappy jobs are very easy to get in Dublin, whereas real jobs are scarce'. Mig has variously worked in a Dublin hostel, bed and breakfast, Irish-owned fast food company Supermacs, canteen of a government department and for the boat taxi on the River Liffey patronised by tourists, school groups and commuters. Check the notice boards in the main travellers' hostels like the Dublin International Youth Hostel at 61 Mountjoy Street.

Try the trendy spots in Temple Bar in the city centre. Writing from Dublin a couple of years ago, the American Dan Eldridge found the city to be a land of opportunity:

Restaurant and pub work is still exploding in Dublin especially in Temple Bar but also north of the river on and around Grafton Street, basically anywhere you see people. My experience has been that when your would-be employer asks if you have working papers (and they all do) your best bet is to say that you're in the process of getting them together, and they'll surely get the drift. For travellers who can't stand the idea of working in a pub, try the youth hostel in Temple Bar. The manager actually offered to sponsor me for a year.

But not everybody is as successful as Dan. Last year 19 year old Brazilian backpacker Manoel Netto headed for Dublin with €800 in savings and an optimistic outlook. His plan was to look for a job, save some money, make friends and go travelling afterwards. Writing his web diary (www.travelpunk.com/stories/manoel.htm) he recalls his hard landing:

I heard that Dublin was a good bet, as the job opportunities were massive and the Irish people were really friendly. The Irish never disappointed me! Temple Bar has tons of bars and the huge amounts of people, trying every tap. Walking around, look-ing for a job in every single place, I just could not find a job. In one week all I heard was 'no' and 'what's your insurance number?'. Nothing! After one week, the despair was in my face. Even though I made some friends with whom I used to go out, I knew that I wouldn't have enough money to keep this lifestyle for a long time. I felt humili-ated, tired and jaded. I needed to get out of Dublin in order not to get mad.

Heather McCulloch did a stint of door to door selling and reports that the Irish are more welcoming than most nations especially to someone with a foreign accent. Although she was enjoying this job, she soon quit, not only because it was on a commission-only basis but because she felt uncomfortable passing off mass-produced Taiwanese pictures as 'original oil paintings'.

Buskers and street entertainers can do well in and around Dublin's Grafton Street since the Irish are a generous nation and appreciate musical talent.

Au Pairing

Foreign women who want to learn English may wish to consider au pairing in Ireland via one of a number of agencies for example Au Pairs for Ireland, 27 Carysfort Downs, Blackrock, Co. Dublin (01-278 0199; www.aupairs4ireland.com) or the Job Options Bureau (Tourist House, 40-41 Grand Parade, Cork; 021-427 5369; www.joboptionsbureau.ie) which is a founder member of the International Au Pair Association. The Laurence Chérifat Au Pair Programme places a number of French au pairs with Irish families (95 Avenue Général Leclerc, Bat. B, 94700 Maison Alfort, France; +33-1-43 76 48 61). An au pair agency set up in 2000 soon after branched out into recruiting workers from outside the EU for jobs in hotels and restaurants, construction, etc. For details contact Cara International, Chancery, Turlough, Castlebar, Co. Mayo (014-903 1720; www.carainternational.net).

The recommended pocket money for au pairs is €70-€80 a week for 25 hours of duties, €80-€90 for 30 hours and up to €160 for a full-time six-day week. The agencies which are offshoots of language schools usually make it a requirement that au pairs sign up for Eng-lish courses with them.

Ireland is a popular destination for students of English from the Continent, so anyone with a background in TEFL might apply to one of the many language schools and camps for a summer job as an English teacher or monitor. Some language schools arrange work placements as well as courses; try for example the Centre of English Studies, 31 Dame St, Dublin 2 (01-671 4233; www.cesireland.ie), Pace Language Institute at 29/30 Dublin Road, Bray, Co. Wicklow (01-276 0922; www.paceinstitute.ie) who operate a work-study programme and Galway Cultural Institute (Salthill, Galway; 091-863100; info@gci.ie).

Agriculture

There is not much chance of finding paid work on farms because of high rural unemploy-ment. Even if the occasional vacancy does arise, the farms are small, widely dispersed and have no co-ordinating body to facilitate recruitment. However there is a good network of farms and smallholdings which allow people to work in exchange for keep. Unfortu-nately there is no longer a national WWOOF organisation in Ireland although you can join WWOOF Independents (see Introductory chapter on Agriculture) to gain access to the 80+ hosts in Ireland. Alternatively check out www.planorganic.com based in West Cork (although it is not updated regularly) and also the Irish Organic Farmers and Growers

Association in Co. Westmeath which posts details of about ten of their members looking for live-in helpers; www.irishorganic.ie/services/placelist.htm. People with agricultural experience looking for work on conventional farms could try placing a classified advert in the *Irish Farmer's Journal* (www.farmersjournal.ie).

Joe Warnick from the US was very grateful for the WWOOF arrangement after the tribulations of trying to find work in London
Your information on the WWOOF organisation was tremendously helpful. It was a superb way to experience rural Ireland, and make friends with so many good people. I stayed on a traditional farm one hour from Galway where I picked potatoes and herded dairy cows down an old lane surrounded by stone fences. My carpentry skills were handy when repairing the attic floor as well. At night the old farmer Tom would play his accordion and sing Irish songs. We'd take shots of moonshine and exchange tales. Tom's wife Maureen was a wonderful cook. Her homemade bread was out of this world. It was great to eat such healthy food and fresh vegetables after the excesses of London's nightlife.

Another American, David Stamboulis, writing in the magazine *Transitions Abroad,* also found the opportunities in rural Ireland to offer plenty of non-financial rewards:

I discovered farmers, three nursery owners and small communities with plenty of work to be done. Just politely asking was usually all it took to get four hours of work per day in exchange for room and board. Always, the work was fun, challenging and unpressured, because I was not doing it for money. The food was usually self-produced and self-prepared; and the accommodations were always interesting, ranging from small crofts to large farms.

Ken Smith from New Zealand worked as a farmhand for several stretches of a couple of months:

For me it has proved invaluable as a way to plan my next move while in a family environment. I enjoy the work which involves cleaning out the cattle houses, cutting silage, fencing and a thousand and one other odd jobs which need doing on a farm. The work is for board and lodging only and I'm very happy with the arrangement. It's great to be outside in the fresh air and at the ground level of Irish rural life. I am now a familiar face in the local community. When the work's done the Irish like to enjoy themselves, and the atmosphere in country pubs is great, with story-telling and music.

Outdoor work can be found in the Christmas tree industry. Having failed to secure work on the apple harvest in England due to early frosts, Robert Abblett contacted Emerald Trees (Temple House, Templeshannon, Enniscorthy, Co. Wexford; www.emeraldgroup.ie); their website has employment information. By arriving in September, Rob was assured a place on the harvest in December. Working conditions were just as tough as those described in the UK chapter (see section on Seasonal Work) but he managed to save £750 including a tax rebate. Those who prove themselves on the harvest might then be taken on for pruning and planting which is fairly lucrative and much more civilised.

More recently Rob returned to the Beara Peninsula to take up a job collecting rhododendron stems but soon regretted it:

I usually make it a rule never to work outside in Northern Europe during winter and, after one week of scrabbling up the slippery hills of Ireland in the cold, I stopped on the hillside and looked around me at the awesome scenery. I thought, yes, it's good to be here. But the hard work and icebox of a house shared with two Latvians on a work exchange programme who couldn't speak English and saving next to nothing from my labours seemed a mistake at my age.

Ireland has its share of big fruit farms that hire people for the harvest season. For instance The Berry Farm south of Dublin takes on strawberry harvesters in June/July (contact John Brennan on nobilis@indigo.ie). The website www.pickingjobs.com has links to the recruitment needs of Ballybin Fruit Farm in County Meath and Prices Fruit Farm in Northern Ireland.

Fishing

Robert Abblett gave a lift to an Irish fisherman who passed on some tips on finding work in the fishing industry:

> He mentioned three places to try. I visited Rossaveal fish factory west of Galway and could have got a job easily extracting the roe from herrings. The work was paid piece work and the boss told me that the average experienced worker earns £50 a day, and the fastest worker double that, for a maximum of five days a week (weather permitting). Most people only last a few days as the work is dirty, smelly and boring. The season here lasts from mid-October till February only. I then visited Dingle and enquired at the fish factory, where the wages were £3 plus bonus. I didn't bother checking Castletownbere on the Beara peninsula which is a large whitefish port. Work on the fishing boats and factories is apparently available most of the year.

Robert showed admirable enterprise in tracking down these opportunities. He picked out likely looking village names from the Michelin map, and dialled Directory Enquiries (1190) to phone the local post office. They were usually able to give the telephone numbers of the local fish factories. To make things easier for readers, the Rossaveal factory can be contacted at Iasc Mara Teoranta, Rossaveal, Co. Galway (091-572136/fax 572271; iascmara@iol.ie). Their vacancies as general operatives can sometimes be found posted on the EURES website. Work on the fishing boats can be very well paid but it is normally necessary to have experience.

Voluntary Opportunities

Volunteering Ireland aims to match individuals who wish to volunteer with organisations that offer suitable volunteering opportunities. They are located in Coleraine House, Coleraine St, Dublin 7 (01-872 2622; www.volunteeringireland.com).

A range of 2-3 week voluntary workcamps are held all over Ireland from June to October. Projects include for example playschemes for inner city, refugee and traveller children, environmental work and holiday schemes for wheelchair users. Projects in Ireland are organised by Voluntary Service International (30 Mountjoy Square, Dublin 1; 01-855 1011; www.vsiireland.org). Applicants in Britain should contact IVS in Colchester, Leeds or Edinburgh. Volunteers can expect to pay from €100 to cover board, insurance and administration.

The Simon Community of Ireland (St. Andrew's House, 28-30 Exchequer St, Dublin 2; 01-671 1606; info@simoncommunity.com) takes on committed volunteers with an excellent standard of spoken English for a minimum of six months to live and work with long-term homeless people at their shelters and residential houses in four Irish cities. Volunteers work and live on-site for three days and then get two days off where they stay in a separate flat. Pocket allowance of €50+ per week is paid.

The Corrymeela Community (Drumroan Rd, Ballycastle, Co. Antrim BT54 6QU; enquiries@corrymeela.org; www.corrymeela.org) is an ecumenical Christian organisation committed to reconciliation in Ireland that has been accepting volunteers for more than a generation. Approximately 25 volunteers per week are needed in the summer to work in arts and crafts, recreation, housekeeping, etc. as well as some longer term volunteers from March or September. All volunteers receive free board and lodging plus a stipend of about €35 a week if they stay for six months or more. The deadline for summer applications is April 1st.

An Oige, the Irish Youth Hostel Association (61 Mountjoy St, Dublin 7; 01-830 4555; www.anoige.ie) has 23 hostels throughout the country and relies to a large extent on voluntary help. Assistant wardens are needed June to September and general assistants to help with maintenance, office work, conservation, etc. year round. As throughout the world, you can always approach busy hostels to see if they need an assistant. The hostel just outside Killarney often employs foreign travellers.

Conservation Volunteers Ireland (The Steward's House, Rathfarnham Castle, Dublin 14; 01-495 2878; www.cvi.ie) aims to protect and enhance Ireland's natural and cultural heritage through practical conservation projects. These are operated year-round throughout the country and include nature trail construction, pond restoration and tree planting. Membership costs €25 (€18 unwaged) and volunteers must pay a nominal charge for food, accommodation and transport (from €25 for a weekend).

The Irish Wildlife Trust for Volunteers, Groundwork, organises summer workcamps for volunteers to tackle the problem of the invasive rhododendron in two national parks (Killarney and Glenveagh); details from Groundwork, 21 Northumberland Rd, Dublin 4; www.groundwork.ie). Volunteers pay only €30 a week for food and accommodation (or €45 for two friends).

Netherlands

British and Irish young people continue to pour off ferries, check into hostels and begin looking for the highly paid jobs and liberal attitudes (e.g. to drugs and prostitution) they've heard about. Some draw benefit while they look and in some cases Dutch tolerance has been tested. Yet the market for unskilled non-Dutch-speaking workers is far from saturated since unemployment is 4.6%, among the lowest in Europe.

The job search should not be confined to Amsterdam. Scores of temporary employment agencies can be found in Rotterdam, The Hague, Haarlem, Leiden and Utrecht. Unemployment is highest in the south and north-west, so these areas should probably be avoided. Competition for work is much less outside the summer.

REGULATIONS

The Dutch have been tightening up the regulations in an attempt to clamp down on squatters, drug abusers and other undesirables. All new employees can be asked by their employers to show suitable proof of identification such as a passport. They should carry ID around at work in case of spot checks by tax, social security or immigration inspectors.

EU Nationals

All job-seeking EU nationals must follow the bureaucratic procedures which the majority of agencies and employers follow. Nationals of the new EU countries will have to obtain a work permit for the first two years after accession, however lobbying from certain sectors, mainly agricultural, has forced the government to backtrack slightly and promise to be flexible in the case of seasonal agricultural work. This has resulted in a substantial influx of workers from the newly-enlarged EU.

For EU nationals who intend to stay for more than three months, the first step is to acquire a sticker in your passport from the local aliens police (*Vreemdelingenpolitie*) or Town Hall, normally over-the-counter. They will expect you to provide a local address

– hostel addresses will normally suffice – and it is best to use this same address throughout your stay. For a job lasting longer than three months but less than one year, the sticker will be issued for the duration of the contract, and for a job lasting longer than one year, a residence card can be obtained for five years. Employers often request this document before signing any contract.

The passport should then be taken to the local tax office to apply for a *sofinummer* or *'sofi'* (social/fiscal number). In Amsterdam go to the big black building outside the train station in Sloterdijk. For the address of the nearest tax office, ring 0800 0534. It is also possible to apply for a *sofi* from outside the Netherlands, though this will take at least six weeks; send a copy of your passport details to Belastingdienst Particulieren/Ondernemingen Buitenland, Postbus 2865, 6401 DH Heerlen; +31 800 0543 (www.belastingdienst.nl).

Normally you will have to complete both these steps before being allowed to register with employment bureaux or take up a job, though in some cases the *sofi* will suffice. To turn the initial sticker into a residence permit *(Verblijfsvergunning* or *verblijfskaart)* after three months (which can be extended for a further three months if you can prove you are still searching for work), you will have to show a genuine work contract or letter of employment from an employer (not an agency). The cost to Community nationals of a permit or an extension is €28. The contract will have to show that the legal minimum wage and holiday pay are being paid and the proper tax and deductions are being made. The registration office for foreigners in Amsterdam *(Dienst Vreemdelingenpolitie)* is at Johan Huizingalaan 757, 1066 VH Amsterdam (020-559 63 00), while the tax office *(Belastingdienst)* is at Kingsfordweg 1, 1043 GN Amsterdam (020-687 77 77). In rural parts of Holland, satisfying the bureaucrats may take several days and use up lots of petrol.

A further complicating factor is that job agencies may not be willing to sign you up unless you have a bank account and banks in areas frequented by short-stay workers have become reluctant to open accounts. Look for the Fortis PostBank which allows you to open a giro account.

Non-EU Nationals

The situation for non-EU nationals is predictably more difficult. North Americans, Antipodeans and others who require no visa to travel to the Netherlands are allowed to work for less than three months, provided they report to the Aliens Police within three days of arrival and their employer has obtained a *tewerkstellingsvergunning* (work permit) for them. Non-EU nationals wishing to stay for longer than three months must obtain a provisional residence permit *(machtiging tot voorlopig verblijf* or MVV) before their arrival in the Netherlands and before their employer can apply for an employment permit from the CBA (Centraal Bestuur Arbeidsvoorziening). The MVV must be applied for through the Dutch Embassy in your country and then can be turned into a Residence Permit after arrival. The current price of a time-limited permit for non-EU nationals is a steep €430 and €285 for an extension. In practice, the *tewerkstellingsvergunning* is unlikely to be issued for casual work.

Chris Miksovsky is one of those rare Americans who has found a European employer willing to back an application for a work permit:

I've been here in Holland the past two months doing marketing work for a company that makes radio-controlled model racing cars, a long-time hobby of mine. It was pure luck that they were looking for someone just like me when I faxed them out of the blue (from Auckland). It's been two months already and the company is still paying me in cash while all the red tape is processed. The company has really had to back me up with lots of explaining as to why the position can only be filled by me and not a native citizen. It can be done, but you need to be damn lucky, damn qualified or (preferably) both.

Information on working and living in the Netherlands is available on the Dutch Embassy website (www.netherlands-embassy.org.uk/econfaq_eng.htm) which has lots of potentially useful links. The expatriate support organisation Access publishes a booklet called

Working in the Netherlands (€9.50 via www.access-nl.org) which is recommended by the British Embassy in the Hague. For detailed information, contact the Dutch Immigration Service, Immigratie- and NaturalisatieDienst (IND), Postbus 5800, 2280 HV Rijsvijk (0900-1234561); its website www.ind.nl or www.immigratiedienst.nl can be accessed in English.

Canadians, Australians and New Zealanders up to the age of 30 can obtain a working holiday visa valid for up to a year.

Red Tape

The Dutch have some of the most progressive laws in the world to minimise exploitation of workers, though the minimum wage no longer seems much higher than the rest of Europe as it did a few years ago. Because the minimum wage is lower for younger workers, employers often prefer to hire younger people whenever possible, often Dutch school children.

Compulsory holiday pay of at least 8% of your gross salary should also be paid on all but the most temporary casual jobs. Do not count on receiving the holiday pay immediately after finishing a job. Although one of Ian Govan's friends received his holiday pay two weeks after the vegetable harvest in Westland, Ian and another friend were told that it would be sent to their UK bank account several months later. Sure enough £250 arrived in time for Christmas. Similarly tax rebates may be owing at the end of the tax year, and so employees should save all pay slips showing income and deductions.

Health insurance *(Ziekenfonds)* is compulsory. The cost is shared between you and your employer/agency but deductions are not usually large, e.g. €15 a month. You will have to register with a local insurance provider.

If you feel that you are not being treated fairly by an employer or landlord, you can get free legal advice from any Jongeren Informatie Punt or JIP (Youth Information Points) or you can make enquiries at any employment office.

A potentially useful web forum can be found at www.nlplanet.com which bills itself as the English language resource for the Netherlands and all things Dutch. As well as maintaining a forum on Work & Travel, the site provides up-to-date information on the bureaucracy of working in the Netherlands.

Private Employment Agencies

The majority of employers turn to private employment agencies (*uitzendbureaux* – pronounced and meaning 'out-send') for temporary workers, partly to avoid the complicated paperwork of hiring a foreigner directly. Therefore they can be a very useful source of temporary work in Holland. They proliferate in large towns, for example there are nearly 250 in Amsterdam alone.

Look up *Uitzendbureau* in the telephone directory or the *Gouden Gids* (Yellow Pages; www.goudengids.nl) and register with as many as you can in your area. Not all will accept non-Dutch-speaking applicants. You should visit or at least phone the office daily at opening time and perhaps twice a day since often the allocation of jobs is not systematic and once the phone is put down the agency forgets about you. Do not expect to be offered a job instantly, for the competition is stiff, especially in Amsterdam and especially during school holidays in August.

While looking for dock work north of Haarlem, Murray Turner concluded that the *uitzendbureaux* were in the habit of promising more than they could deliver. He had just five days of work out of three weeks, and those were found by asking around at the docks, while the agencies produced nothing.

By contrast, Martyn Rutter was pleased with the service he received:
It's still quite easy to find work with the agencies. It took me two days of trying at the Manpower agency before they gave me a job in a warehouse. Most people get a job within three or four days. In fact I must have met 25 English and Irish people in the two months I was in Amsterdam, all of whom had found work through agencies. The only must is to be clean and tidy when applying.

BENELUX

Friesland

North Sea

NETHERLANDS

Groningen

De Koog

Emmeloord

Andijk
Zwolle
Alkmaar

Haarlem
Heemstede AMSTERDAM
Hillegom
Lisse
Apeldoorn
Enschede

Sassenheim
Nieuwveen
Katuijk a/Zee
Leiden
Ter Aar
The Hague
Utrecht
Arnhem
Delft
Wageningen
Naaldwijk
Nijmegen
Hook of Holland
Rotterdam
Gorinchem
Tiel

Breda

Vlissingen
Baarland
Knokke-Heist
Antwerp

GERMANY

Bruges
Hasselt
Ostend
Ghent
Vilvoorde
BRUSSELS
Rixensart
Liege

BELGIUM

Namur
Charleroi

FRANCE

Wiltz
Diekirch

LUXEMBOURG

Bouillon
LUXEMBOURG
Esch
Remich

The symbol for flowers
refers to packing and processing bulbs
as well as picking flowers.

WILLIAM SWAN

Uitzendbureaux deal only with jobs lasting less than six months. Most of the work on their books will be unskilled work such as stocking warehouse shelves, production line work in factories, washing dishes in canteens, cleaning, hotel work or fixing roofs in the snow. Most agencies are accustomed to foreign job-seekers and even in the so-called 'boon-docks' will have an English-speaking member of staff.

Like all employment agencies *uitzendbureaux* gain their income by charging the employer a percentage of the wage, which in some cases is 100% or more. Allan Kirkpat-rick, who worked in the pre-Euro days for a company in Arnhem as an 'order picker,' is just one of the many clients who is puzzled by the economics of the system:

> *I tried to understand the whole uitzendbureau thing. I was paid 10 guilders an hour while the agency got 26 guilders. So why doesn't the company (and it was a very good company) pay me 18 guilders and save themselves some money, and cut out the crazy uitzendbureau altogether? Insurance purposes I think was the problem. I made this point to the very nice but hard-working boss and he said 'That's a good idea' and no more was said about the matter until I reminded him again, and again, and again. I gave up in the end and got a cheap coach to London.*

Allan was less critical of the system a few months later when his *uitzendbureau* (Olympia in Arnhem; www.olympia-uitzendburo.nl) sent on a cheque for £200, his entitlement to holiday pay.

Among the largest *uitzendbureaux* are Randstad with about 300 branches (www.rand-stad.nl), Unique (www.uniquemls.com) for multilingual jobseekers, Manpower (www.man-power.nl), Vedior (www.vedior.nl), Creyfs Interim (www.creyfs.nl) and Tempo Team (www.tempoteam.nl).

Another potentially useful kind of agency is a private relocation agency such as Dutch-Down (075-640 1495) whose website www.dutchdown.nl contains reasonably sound infor-mation about applying for a residence permit, etc.

State Employment Service

Dutch job centres are called Centra voor Werk en Inkomen (CWI) and offer job placement services, advice on employment in the Netherlands and help to prospective entrepre-neurs. A full list of CWIs is available on their website www.cwinet.nl/nl. Dutch Euroadvisers can also be helpful since they have an overview of the range of temporary and permanent possibilities for EEA nationals.

BULB INDUSTRY

Traditionally, the horticultural sector has had difficulty in finding enough seasonal labour for the processing of flower bulbs for export and related activities. Hordes of young travel-lers descend on the area between Leiden and Haarlem in the summer and there aren't enough jobs to go around. Still, large numbers of unskilled workers are employed in fields and factories to dig, peel, sort, count and pack bulbs, especially in the early spring and through the autumn. Other important export companies *(Bloembollen Groothandel)* can be found in the north around Andijk and Breezand. The Dutch Yellow Pages, online at www.goudengids.nl, can be a useful ally in the search for work. For example a search for bulb companies links to a map of Hillegom.

Finding the Work

Increasingly, farmers use agents or middlemen to recruit casual labour. Links are espe-cially strong between Holland and Ireland as Garrett Mohan from County Monaghan discovered. Garrett's first agricultural job in the Netherlands resulted from answering an advert in the Irish *Sunday Independent* placed by an agency in Breda (see next section) whereas his job in the bulb industry was connected with an Irish agency affiliated to ICDS

Recruitment (www.icdsuk.com):

> *After receiving a phone call from a friend who was working in the bulbs around Ven-huizen (40km northwest of Amsterdam), I phoned the farmer directly but he put me onto the agent that he uses and I was offered the job as long as I could get there the next day. Because we are working through an agent, we're being paid the minimum and 20% of our wages are held back as a deposit against the house which is pro-vided free of charge. I think that most of the farmers around here are using agents so it may be hard to find a well-paid job. Our farmer pays the agent in Dublin more than twice what we were paid per hour.*

Darren Slevin worked at a bulb factory in Voorhout 3km from Leiden. He did not appreci-ate the way the Irish workers were treated as thieves and drug-users (which they weren't) nor did he enjoy the mind-numbing work which caused pain in back, legs and feet. His boss's favourite word was 'snell, snell' (faster, faster). But he did enjoy the international camaraderie. Darren has come across similar agencies offering work in bulb factories and glasshouses such as Atlanco Ltd (221/223 Lower Rathmines Road, Rathmines, Dublin 6; 01-491 0555; www.atlanco.ie) whose partner in Holland is Rimec b.v. (Raadhuisstraat 15, 1016 DB Amsterdam; info@rimec.nl).

A couple of years ago Rob Abblett travelled to Holland after the *vendange* in Switzer-land, just because he'd never been before. He headed for Andijk near Enkhuizen north of Amsterdam: *'By great luck and effort I managed to find a job on foot, but later discovered that I had to go through a job agency anyway, unless I had worked there the year before. The job agencies helped me and, now that I have their telephone numbers, I can even phone them from England, say, to check on work availability.'*

Work in the Andijk factories is available mid-July to September and mid-October till February/March. He returned to Hillegom in September armed with an address bestowed on him by a fellow traveller, and this connection made it much easier to land a job. Eighty caravans were parked behind the factory, full of Polish workers with German passports. His job was to sprinkle glitter on waxed pinecones for the Christmas market, at a rate about equivalent to the UK minimum wage (though no one received any wage slips). After a month, he couldn't face it any more and returned home.

The busy times differ among bulb employers according to their markets. For exam-ple mail-order companies (like P. Bakker mentioned below) need employees to pick and pack customers' orders from February until the end of April and again from September to December. The busy time for bulb peeling is the second half of June. Ask at the local *CWI* or look for signs *(Bollenpellers Gevraagd)* in Hillegom, Lisse, Noordwijk, etc. Because you are paid only according to how much you do, many workers take time off to visit the bulb factories in the neighbourhood to put their names on various waiting lists, in an attempt to secure a more lucrative job as a bulb packer. This doesn't start until the end of July or even early August and lasts to October, when many factories and associated campsites close down.

The best towns to head for are Hillegom, Lisse, Noordwijkerhout, Sassenheim and Bennebroek. New arrivals will have no trouble locating the properties of the bulb barons once they arrive. In Hillegom head for Pastoorslaan or Leidsestraat where many of the factories are concentrated and in Lisse, look along Heereweg. Note that the greenhouses and flower auction houses in and around Aalsmeer also provide employment but not so seasonal.

The majority of bulb exporters consider only candidates who are around when there are vacancies and with changes in immigration patterns more of them are able to find enough workers already resident in the Netherlands. It is always worth trying the famous bulb exporter P. Bakker B.V., Meer en Duin 1-5, 2163 HA Lisse (0252-438438/fax 438300; www.bakker-hillegom.nl) which employs up to 2,000 people at busy times doing shift work (3.30pm-11.30pm and 6.30am-2.30pm). Unauthorised days off are grounds for instant dismissal.

The Dutch Bulb Exporters Association in Hillegom may be able to offer useful contacts as can the Royal Dutch Wholesalers Association (www.kbgbb.nl). The long established firm Frijlink b.v. (s'Gravendamseweg 71, 2211 WH Noordwijkerhout; 0252 343143) receives plenty of applications via word of mouth as do Baartman & Koning b.v. (Teylingerlaan 7, 2215 RT Voorhout; 0252-211141) and Van de Groot b.v. (Leidsevaart 151, 2211 WD Noordwijkerhout; 0252-373891). Try also Van Zanten B.V. in Den Helder and Hillegom.

It should be noted that like all employers the bulb companies can accept applications only from European Union nationals; people from outside the EU who write are wasting their time and money. Even if you do receive a job offer in advance, you cannot be sure that the company will honour its promise. It costs them nothing to promise jobs to enquirers, to cover themselves in case of a worker shortage, as happened to Gordon Robertson from Glasgow a couple of years ago:

> The bulb exporter sent some details of the work during the flower bulb season which appeared to be quite interesting. I then confirmed my interest in the position and within a couple of weeks received my start date and was invited to go over and work for them. I also telephoned them a couple of times to enquire about a few minor details and they were quite helpful. I then saved up some money to pay for the flight and a week's spending money and travelled on the start date. I settled down and prepared for the next day's work but was told I would start work a day later. Then on that day, I was told in no uncertain terms that there was no employment for me. I was then instructed to find work elsewhere and later informed to leave their premises. These events totally ruined my working holiday and I don't understand how they could let me go all that way and let me pay all that money to go to Holland just to be told to go away.
>
> Traditionally seasonal workers congregate on big campsites, and will normally be willing to advise newcomers. The job hunt will be easier if you're carrying a tent. At times the need for workers is so urgent that employers have to find some way round the problem of accommodation. Martin and Shirine from Crawley worked for a farmer who risked trouble from the police by letting them camp in a disused field. Renting a flat is even more problematical since foreign workers have such a bad reputation for rowdiness and irresponsibility that few landlords will risk it.

In Robert Abblett's experience, this reputation is not undeserved: *'Lots of the workers smoke dope from waking up, at work (if they can) and the rest of the day. Coming back to my house and finding my three co-habitants totally stoned is quite normal. But I can't blame them, for the work requires a positive mental attitude to withstand the boredom and if you haven't got it, then you must choose insanity, oblivion or just leave.'* Obviously if the competition is like this, it is not too surprising that his boss at De Jongs Lily Factory made him supervisor of the night shift line (Kerkepad 28, 1619 AE Andijk; 0228-591400; info@dejonglelies.nl).

Yet competition for jobs remains acute, though less so at the more far-flung factories. Mark Wilson recommends having some transport: *'Along with a tent, a necessity when looking for bulb work is a bicycle. While out exploring on my bike I came across an area full of factories just outside Noordwijkerhout, a village west of Lisse.'* Second-hand bicycles can be picked up fairly easily and affordably.

Pay and Conditions

The bulb industry is better regulated than it once was which means that there is much less black work around. The hiring of non-EU nationals has virtually ceased and exploitation is less common than it was, though membership in the bulb workers' union (Voedingsbond FNV) is not generally available to foreigners.

Excellent earnings are possible: Iona and Steve Dwyer return every year because in their opinion they can earn twice or three times more than they could in an equivalent time anywhere else. Overtime paid at a premium rate is what makes the big savings possible. Like most agricultural work, earnings fluctuate according to the weather; on a rainy day when the flowers don't open people are lucky to get four hours work.

The most commonly heard complaint about packing is how boring it is, 'worse for your head than boxing' according to one veteran. But most workers receive enough breaks throughout the long day to make it bearable. Naturally there are good employers and bad employers and Garrett Mohan felt himself lucky to be working for one of the former: *'Our boss is quite easy-going but, like the rest of the Dutch, very big on punctuality. He has provided us with a TV and VCR and regularly records English films for us. We have heard of another local farmer who separates the Irish so they can't talk to each other, won't allow music to be played in the factory and actually stands on the conveyor belts as they move to ensure everyone is working.'*

Bulb-peeling is a much more unpleasant job as Martin and Shirine recall: *'The work was hard on our hands and we soon resorted to wearing rubber gloves or plasters. The hours of work were 8am-5pm with an hour's lunch break and the choice to work until 10pm. That was a long time to spend crouched over a table, sitting on an old wobbly stool that was the wrong height for you.'*

Mark Wilson had an even more miserable experience as a bulb peeler: *'The first job I had was peeling the skin off the bulbs which was the most mind-numbingly boring job I have ever done. Later I was condemned to two weeks in the hyacinth shed which is kept away from the main factory. While working on a sorting machine in a loose T-shirt I found to my horror and my Dutch workmates' amusement that bulb dust is a very powerful irritant, so after a couple of hours of itching like a madman, I resigned on the spot, ran back to the campsite and dived into the shower to relieve my tormented skin.'*

AGRICULTURE

According to information from the European Employment Service EURES, there are plenty of opportunities for seasonal agricultural workers:

> *From mid-April to October jobs might be available picking asparagus, strawberries, gherkins, apples and pears. During the same period of time there are also jobs in greenhouses and mushrooms, though these jobs are popular with locals and usually can be filled with local job-seekers.*

Many harvests take place in fertile pockets of southern Holland for example in the Baarland in the extreme south-west and in Limburg to the east along the Belgian border (see section below). Garrett Mohan travelled to the tiny village of Kwadendamme near Goes in the Baarland (Zeeland) in early September (after local school children had returned to school) to join the apple and pear harvest which ends in early November. An agency which may be able to assist is Creyf's Interim (Voorstad 3, 4461 KK Goes; 113-211223/fax 113-216911; goes@creyfsinterim.nl).

Although Garrett Mohan's boss was a 'Jekyll and Hyde' type (laughing and joking one minute and shouting 'pick, pick, quickly and with two hands' the next), he grew to like Dutch people and rural life in Holland enough to want to move from the hard fruit harvest to bulb work in the north. In seven weeks of hard work, he had saved more than £400 after buying a rucksack and a camera out of his earnings.

Another area where hard fruits are harvested in the autumn is the area south of Utrecht called Betuwe (which means 'Good Land') around the towns of Culemborg and Buren.

Limburg and Brabant

The 'deep south' of Holland is known among working travellers as more than the place where the Maastricht Treaty was signed. The area around Roermond (about 50km southeast of Eindhoven and north of Maastricht in the province of Limburg) is populated by asparagus growers and other farmers who need people to harvest their crops of strawberries (June to mid-July), potatoes and other vegetables, especially in the spring. You can travel south from Roermond (on the N271) to villages such as Linne, St. Odilienberg, Montfort, Posterholt and as far as Susteren to find work. Going north, head for Venlo, Helden and nearby Panningen. If possible find someone to translate ads in the local paper *De Limburger*. The agencies around here are less accustomed to dealing with non-Dutch applicants but can be all the more helpful for that. Independently Joanne Patrick and Steve Conneely found work picking potatoes and earned a tidy sum between them in two weeks in late February and early March. They were so taken aback to earn so much money that they spent it all on good times across the German border.

Asparagus picking starts just after the middle of April and lasts through to mid-June. A tent is a great advantage here to be able to stay at campsites like the one Murray Turner stayed at in Helden north of Roermond. Despite initial hopes that earnings would be high in the peak season, he ended up earning a modest wage based on piece work rates. He moved on to the strawberry harvest where earnings from piecework were very unreliable because of the weather. The asparagus harvest is similarly affected by weather; if it's hot you can work as long as you are able.

Westland

The area between Rotterdam, the Hook of Holland and Den Haag is known as the Westland. K. ('Moondog') McCausland recommends tomato picking here as another good alternative to bulb packing. The principal villages in the area are Naaldwijk, Westerlee, De Lier and Maasdijk, but the whole region is a honeycomb of greenhouses.

The tomato harvest begins in early to mid-April and this is the best time to arrive, although work is generally available all year round if you are prepared to work for at least one month. Although the work was boring and dirty with long hours – it was normal to start work at 5am and finish at 7pm or 8pm – conditions were usually good and accommodation was provided in a barn.

Once again a lot of the work in the area is registered with *uitzendbureaux*. Ian Govan recommends trying the ones in Naaldwijk, 's-Gravenzande and Poeldijk for work picking cucumbers, peppers, flowers, etc. Also try the flower and vegetable auctions *(bloemenveiling/groenteveiling)* in Westerlee/de Lier and Honselersdijk which need people to load the stock for auction buyers, etc. Ian Govan's overtime pay (in cash) increased his basic earnings for a 38-hour week by about two-thirds.

Work in tree and other nurseries abounds in and around Boskoop, 11km from Gouda north of Rotterdam. Anyone with any relevant experience should aim to arrive in the area between February and April. Nurseries are concentrated along Reijerskoop and Laag Boskoop. Job agencies will help, such as Creyf's Interim at Bootstraat 7, 2771 DL Boskoop (0172 212424/fax 0172-216401; boskoop@creyfsinterim.nl), one of 88 branches of Creyf's Interim throughout the Netherlands in addition to its affiliate ASA Student. It could also be worth advertising in the free local paper, as Dermot Campbell recommends: 'I think it would be worthwhile putting an advert in the Boomkwekerij section of the 'Gouwe Kourier' even if one hasn't any experience. Nobody ever really asked if I had any experience whatsoever. Only if you appear to be enthusiastic.'

Food Processing

Onion pickling in Baarland, near Vlissingen in Southern Holland, sounds fairly grim, so you might follow James Pollock's advice and work in apple, cherry and green bean factories instead:

> *There were many advantages. We did not reek of onions; we were paid fairly and directly by the factory owners rather than being ripped off by an agency; plus there were perks like the 'dead animal reward', a sum of £5 for any animal (from slugs to rabbits) found dead or alive amongst the green beans. As you can imagine many of the unfortunate creatures (often picked off roads on the way to work) completed many rounds on the conveyor belt. Some of us managed to double our wages so it*

was no mean perk.

There are several food canning factories in Zuid Holland (between Amsterdam and Rotterdam); make enquiries at uitzendbureaux in Nieuwveen, Ter Aar and Roelofarendsveen.

TOURISM

Dutch hotels and other tourist establishments often employ foreigners, especially those with a knowledge of more than one European language. A few tour operators like Holidaybreak and Village Camps (see *Tourism* chapter) employ British young people as staff at their day camps for the summer season.

In Adam Skuse's year off before university, he almost succeeded in finding hotel work but not quite:

> *One very useful resource I found was the web-site www.visitholland.com, where I got a list of hotels and then systematically emailed them all asking for a job. Most had no vacancies, a couple told me to call them when I was in Amsterdam, and one actually arranged an interview with me. But even the knockbacks were pleasant. Quite a few offered to buy me a drink anyway. Alas, I never managed to find the hotel in time, ran out of funds and am now back in Blighty. I had plans for my gap year, but just ended up sitting around on the dole.*

According to Simon Whitehead, foreigners are the last to be hired and the first to be fired, so do not expect job security in a hotel job. Although you may be lucky enough to obtain a hotel job through an *uitzendbureau,* your chances will normally be better if you visit hotels and ask if any work is available, or keep your ears open in pubs frequented by working travellers.

While visiting a friend in the seaside resort of Zaandvoort south of Haarlem, Martin and Shirine tried to find work washing dishes for one of the many bars which line the beach. They knew that without speaking Dutch this was the only job they could reasonably expect to get.

A little known opportunity for people who can communicate in German or Dutch is to work on one of the 250 *Platbodems,* traditional sailing boats that cruise the waters of Ijsselmeer and Waddensea off the north coast of the Netherlands in spring, summer and autumn. They cater mainly to school groups and are staffed by a skipper and one mate *(maat)* one of whose jobs is to offer simple instruction to the guests, though he or she must also help the skipper on watch, carry out repairs and so on. Even without any background in sailing, Felix Fernandez was offered ten jobs after adding his CV to the databank *(vacature bank)* of job-seekers and ended up working on the two-masted ship *Citore.* The company that owns *Citore* is Hanzestad Compagnie, Bataviahaven 1, Postbus 300, 8200 AH Lelystad, Netherlands (0320-292100; www.hanzestad.com in Dutch only).

OTHER WORK

Labouring work may be available in some of the massive docks of Rotterdam and Ijmuiden north of Haarlem. According to Shelly Harris's partner Terry, who got work straightaway unloading fishing boats, it's just a case of turning up at the offices on the docks early (about 5.30am) and asking for work. The money is good but the work is hard, cold and irregular. It used to take Terry two hours to thaw out in front of a fire after knocking off work about 3.30pm.

> **Skilled tradesmen may find lucrative contracts as Steven Dodd, a welder/fabricator from County Durham did:**
> *I have been working for the same company in the Netherlands for ten months, getting an excellent wage plus paid accommodation, the use of a Mercedes Benz and VW camper van plus free flights home every eight weeks. Our agent reimburses us for fuel and food (but not beer) if we show the receipts. We are expected to work*

for our money but I have found that if you do a good job they do not hound you to work faster. I have found the country to be a nice place with friendly people though they cannot understand the British custom of getting very drunk and noisy. But we have had very few complaints – they love our money and our humour.

Teaching

Urban Dutch people have such a high degree of competence in English after they finish their schooling that there is not much of a market for EFL teaching. What language schools there are tend to provide business English, and people with extensive commercial or government experience as well as a teaching qualification might find an opening, for example at Feedback (Lassusstraat 9a, 1075 GV Amsterdam; 020-671 67 09; www.feedbacktalen.nl) and PCI (Pimental Communications International, Bachlaan 43, 1817 GH Alkmaar; 072-512 11 90; www.pcitalen.nl) where experience in technical writing would be useful.

The agency Franglais Language Services, Molenstraat 15, 2513 BH The Hague (070-361 1703; jobs@franglais.nl) claims that it is often looking for native English speakers to edit texts by e-mail written in English by non-native speakers. The pay is 4 eurocents per word.

Opportunities in Amsterdam

As throughout the world, hostels employ people to clean, cook, do maintenance and night porter duties. Carolyn Edwards was not dissatisfied with the wage which was paid in addition to room and board since it was equivalent to what she had been earning as a temp in London (minus the food and accommodation). More usually, people work a few hours a day for a free bed and breakfast but no wage. Saffery Ruddock enjoyed this arrangement as a *whapper* (worker) at the Flying Pig hostel near the Vondelpark; she exchanged 3½ hours of work a day cleaning, serving breakfast and doing odd jobs for a dorm bed and a 'brilliant atmosphere, busy, friendly and relaxed'. There are two other Flying Pig hostels, one downtown and one at the beach (www.flyingpig.nl) which were advertising jobs at the time of going to print: *'We are offering jobs at our Beach Hostels. You can work with us for food and accommodation. We need drivers to drive the shuttle, EU passport holders to do reception or bar work and handy people who like to do construction jobs. Interested people should give us a call on 0031713622533 or just pop by at the Beach Hostel.'*

As in Athens some Amsterdam hotels and hostelries hire 'runners' to meet the morning and afternoon international trains to persuade travellers to patronise the hostel. Enquire at budget hotels and hostels near the station. Without a job, it is easy to squander a lot of your travelling funds in Amsterdam, as Karen Martin from Grimsby and Paul Ansell from Derry found out:

We started out in Amsterdam and in all honesty we went a bit mad with the lifestyle. Word of warning: Amsterdam is a great place to be if you have the means to fund yourself but is not nice for those who are penniless and jobless. If it wasn't for the goodness of friends we had made there and of my uncle who lives there, we would have been on our way back home from our planned trip to work our way around Europe before we'd even started.

But after three weeks of self-indulgence Karen and Paul signed up with a few agencies including one called Undutchables (see below) which finds work for non-Dutch people. Soon Karen found a job at the London Bridge pub which she tolerated for a time, while Paul began work as a kitchen porter at the Boom Chicago Comedy Club in the Leidseplein which he found congenial and reasonably well paid. Another place they recommend is the St. James Gate Irish pub in Rembrandtplein.

You might want to contact office cleaning services directly (see 'Schoonmaakbedrijf' in the *Gouden Gids* which are kept in public libraries but not in phone boxes), or ask cafés, of which there is no shortage in Amsterdam, if they would like you to clean their windows on a weekly or regular basis. (The Dutch are very particular about the cleanliness of their windows.)

Interview-NSS is an international market research agency that advertises for native-speaking personnel from throughout Western and Eastern Europe (www.interview-nss.com in English). From the call centre in Amsterdam they conduct surveys in around 17 European countries. They are looking for people with computer experience and a polite voice who are willing to work for a minimum of 8-12 hours a week for at least three months. The working hours are divided into three shifts: morning, afternoon and evening, Monday to Saturday. Interview-NSS is located close to the centre of Amsterdam (Overtoom 519-521, 1054 LH Amsterdam; 020-60 70 707; info@interview-nss.com). It is reputed to be a fun and relaxed place to work and a good place to meet people from many countries. For other possibilities look up 'Telemarketing' in the *Gouden Gids*.

Busking is an ever-popular way to earn some money and the tolerance for which the Dutch are famous extends to street entertainers. The best venues are in the Vondelpark (where many Amsterdammers stroll on a Sunday) and in the city squares like Stadsplein and Leidseplein. Some pitches (like the one outside the 'smoking' coffee shop the Bulldog) are in such demand that you may have to wait your turn.

Schiphol Airport is a major employer. Try the employment agency Adecco at the airport (020-316 3040) or indeed anywhere in Amsterdam; recent travellers have found the Adecco branch on Rokin helpful for call centre jobs. You can check out the Undutchables Recruitment Agency, whose Amsterdam office is at Singel 80, 1015 AC Amsterdam (020-62 31 300; amsterdam@undutchables.nl; www.undutchables.nl) with five or six branches around the country.

Au Pairs

Since Dutch is not a language which attracts a large number of students, au pairing in the Netherlands is not well known and in fact one of the two longest establised agencies (Activity International) cancelled its incoming programme last year. However a number of private agencies can place au pairs with Dutch or international families. Working conditions are favourable (e.g. pocket money of €250-€340 per month and insurance costs are met by the host family) but you must stay at least six months with the family. The main agencies are reputed to offer solid back-up, guidance on contacting fellow au pairs and advice on local courses.

The international exchange organisation Travel Active (PO Box 107, 5800 Venray; 0478-551900; aupair@travelactive.nl) has the largest incoming programme for foreign au pairs aged 18 to 30 as well as sending Dutch young people abroad on various work exchanges. The programme costs €600 for 12 months.

Jill Weseman from the States was very pleased with her au pair placement in a village of just 500 people 30km from Groningen:

After graduation I accepted an au pairing position in Holland, mainly because there is no prior language requirement here. I really lucked out and ended up with a family who has been great to me. Though the situation sounds difficult at best – four children aged 1½, 3, 5 and 7, one day off a week and a rather remote location in the very north of Holland – I have benefitted a great deal. The social life is surprisingly good for such a rural area.

Two other agencies are located in the Hague: Au Pair Agency Mondial, PO Box 17123, 2500 CC The Hague (www.aupair-agency.nl/doc) and the House o Orange Au Pairs, Oostduinlaan 115, 2596 JJ The Hague (06-45 98 80 62; house-o-orange@planet.nl; www.house-o-orange.nl). For others see the website for the Dutch Au Pair Association NAPO (Nederlandse Au Pair Organisatie; www.napoweb.nl).

Voluntary Opportunities

Although the Netherlands is in so many ways a progressive country, there are still undeveloped corners as Joan Regan found when she joined a farm-based project not far from Rotterdam which was affiliated to International Voluntary Service. In fact all the major workcamp organisations arrange camps in Holland over the summer. If you are in the Netherlands you might also make enquiries of SIW Internationale Vrijwilligersprojekten whose office is a five-minute walk from the Utrecht station but keeps limited opening hours (Willemstraat 7, 3511 RJ Utrecht; 030-231 7721; www.siw.nl); otherwise apply through affiliated workcamp organisations at home, e.g. IVS, Concordia and UNA Exchange in Britain. The registration fee for most Dutch workcamps is about €100.The other work-camps organisation in the Netherlands is SCI's partner VIJ (Vrijwillige Internationale Aktie, M. v. Bouwdijk Bastiaansestraat 56, 1054 SP Amsterdam; www.werkkamp.nl).

Archaeological and building restoration camps are arranged by NJBG (Nederlandse Jeugdbond voor Geschiedenis, Prins Willem Alexanderhof 5, 2595 BE Den Haag; fax 070-335 2536; www.njbg.nl). The worldwide charity International Building Companions is particularly active in the Netherlands and has its headquarters in Nijmegen: Postbus 1194, 6501 BD Nijmegen (024-322 6074; www.bouworde.nl).

The youth portal www.markt.nl describes in English voluntary openings *(Vrijwilliger-swerk)* in the Netherlands ranging from hospital filming to a multicultural home for the elderly. Volunteers are needed to collect bottles and glasses after weekend concerts in Eindhoven (info@effenaar.nl).

Belgium

Belgium is a country that is often ignored. Sandwiched between France and the Netherlands, its population of just over 10 million can be broadly divided between the French-speaking people of Wallonia in the south (about 42% of the total population) and those who speak Flemish (which is almost identical to Dutch) in the north. The wages in Belgium fall somewhere between the high wages of Holland and those of France.

Belgium has no large agricultural industry comparable to those of its neighbours: it needs neither the extra fruit pickers that France does, nor the unskilled processors of Dutch bulbs. Furthermore the unemployment rate in Belgium is considerably higher than in the UK, standing at 8% in 2005.

As in neighbouring Holland, employment legislation is strictly enforced in Belgium with favourable minimum wages, compulsory bonuses, sickness and holiday pay for all legal workers. The demand for temporary workers is especially strong in Belgium because of the generous redundancy regulations which discourage employers from hiring permanent staff. Of course the many multinational companies, attracted by the headquarters of the European Union in Brussels, have a constant and fluctuating demand for bilingual office and other workers.

Regulations

The usual rules apply to EU nationals coming to work or live in Belgium: EU nationals arriving in Belgium to look for work and who intend to stay for a period of three months or more should register within eight days at the local Town Hall where the *administration communale* will issue either a temporary *certificat d'immatriculation* valid for three months or the one year certificate of registration (*certificat d'inscription au registre des étrangers* – CIRE).

Non-EU citizens will have to find an employer willing to apply for a work permit on their behalf from the Office National de l'Emploi. They must be in possession of a residence entry visa and a work permit before arrival, when they can then apply for an authorisation of provisional sojourn. Americans can apply through Interexchange (161 Sixth Avenue,

New York, NY 10013; info@interexchange.org) to be placed in an internship in Belgium. Applicants over 18 with a working knowledge of French or Dutch can be placed in companies or organisations for between one and three months. The programme fee is $750 and the application deadline is three months before the desired start date, so late April for summer positions; full details on the website (www.interexchange.org).

Seasonal Work

Although Belgium's seaside resorts like Knokke-Heist, Blankenberge and De Panne, and other holiday centres like Bouillon in the Ardennes are hardly household names, there is a sizeable tourist industry in Belgium where seasonal work is available. The more mainstream tourist centre of Bruges is very busy in the summer. Travellers have a chance of being given free accommodation in exchange for some duties at one of the city's four or five private hostels. According to Brett Archer, who worked several seasons at the Bauhaus International Youth Hostel at Langestraat 35, there are never enough people around to work in restaurants and bars during the summer. Venture Abroad (Rayburn House, Parcel Terrace, Derby DE1 1LY; 01332 224951; www.ventureabroad.co.uk) employs reps, including students with a background in scouting or guiding, for its programme in Belgium. Ski-Ten International takes on French-speaking tennis instructors and monitors to work at summer camps (081-21 30 51; martine@ski-ten.be).

One harvest which has need of seasonal labour is the hop harvest centred on the town of Poperinge in Flanders close to the French border. Every September Belgian students, Polish migrant labourers and a handful of other nationalities gather for three weeks to bring in the harvest which services Belgium's renowned brewing industry. Most farmers are well set up to welcome foreign pickers and offer comfortable accommodation and a good atmosphere.

The best way of finding short-term general work, apart from contacting possible employers directly, is to visit a branch of the Belgian employment service *Agences Locales pour l'Emploi* or ALEs. A special division called T-Interim (www.tserviceinterim.be) specialises in placing people in temporary jobs. Most jobs obtained through the T-Interim service will be unskilled manual ones such as stocking supermarket shelves. They may also be able to help skilled secretaries who can function in French to find temporary office positions.

The employment services in Belgium are divided into three regional branches: Greater Brussels (ORBEM for French speakers, BGDA for Flemish), French-speaking Belgium (Office Wallon de la Formation Professionnelle et de l'Emploi) and Flemish-speaking Belgium (VDAB), with addresses as follows:

ORBEM (Office Régional Bruxellois de l'Emploi) and BGDA (Brusselse Gewestelijke Dienst voor Arbeidsbemiddeling), Boulevard Anspach 65, 1000 Brussels (02-505 14 11; www.orbem.be or www.bgda.be) which has several EURES Advisers on hand. The T-Interim office is next door at number 69 (02-511 23 85).

Office Wallon de la Formation Professionnelle et de l'Emploi, Boulevard Zoe Drion 25, 6000 Charleroi (071-20 50 40). There are more than 30 T-Interim offices in Wallonia.

VDAB, Keizerslaan 11, 1000 Brussels (02-506 15 11/ www.vdab.be). The 40+ Flemish-speaking T-Interim offices are listed at www.t-interim.be/over/kantoren/index.shtm.

People who live in the south-east of England can make use of EURES Crossborder HNFK based at South Kent College (Maison Dieu Road, Dover CT16 1DH; 01304 244356) which assists people looking for jobs in Belgium, especially in West-Vlaanderen and Hainaut (western Belgium). Two bilingual Euro-Advisers can put job-seekers in touch with network partners on the continent and can also give advice and information about living and working conditions.

Au Pairs

Anyone who wishes to be an au pair in Belgium will find it much harder than it once was. The government has brought in stringent requirements that families pay a very high wage for only 20 hours of work: €400 a month for au pairs from the EU, €450 for non-EU au pairs. A further disincentive to employ a non-EU au pair is that the authorities have been taking up to five months to process work permit applications. Non-EU au pairs must join their families only between July and September and stay no more than 12 months altogether. They are also required to study a language for at least two hours a day, and 15 hours a week. These changes forced several Belgian agencies to cancel their incoming programme, though Stufam VZW (Vierwindenlaan 7, 1780 Wemmel; 02-460 33 95; aupair. stufam@pi.be; www.aupair-stufam.be) and the Catholic organisation Services de la Jeunesse Feminine (29 rue Faider, 1050 Brussels; 02-539 35 14; or rue de Dave, 174, 5100 Jambes-Namur; fax 081-30 91 35) still make placements inside Belgium.

The free weekly newspaper *Vlan* with *'petites annonces'* (www.vlan.be) is an effective advertising medium for prospective au pairs under the heading *Gens de Maison*.

Teaching

The casual EFL teacher will probably have trouble finding work in Belgium where there is a great deal of competition from highly qualified expatriates. A number of language schools advertise in *The Bulletin* (see next section); the magazine publishes an annual 'Schools Guide' in April containing a section on language schools, though there is not much point in applying to the kind of school which teaches senior EU bureaucrats unless you have professional qualifications. Almost all foreign teachers who begin to work for an institute do so on a freelance basis and will have to deal with their own tax and social security. The starting pay at most schools falls between €10 and €20 an hour.

Berlitz have several schools in Belgium which employ up to 100 native English speakers with a university degree after they have done the compulsory 8-day pre-service training course in the Berlitz Method; contact Berlitz at Avenue Louise 306, 1050 Brussels (02-649 61 75; info@berlitz.be). They pay €8.92 for a 40-minute lesson. Other schools to try if you have a TEFL background include Kiddy & Junior Classes asbl (rue du Marteau 8, 1210 Brussels; www.kiddyclasses.net), May International Training Consultants (55 rue de Bordeaux, 1060 Brussels; www.mayintl.com), Ceran Lingua International (Av. du Chateau 16, 4900 Spa; www.ceran.com), Euro Business Languages (Leuvensesteenweg 325, 1932 Zaventem), Call International (Boulevard de la Cense 41, 1410 Waterloo & Avenue des Drapiers 25, 1050 Brussels) and Phone Languages (rue des Echevins 65, 1050 Brussels; www.phonelanguages.com). The latter employs people with American or British accents to teach over the phone and pays about £10 an hour.

Contacts

The Federation Infor Jeunes Wallonie-Bruxelles is a non-profit making organisation which co-ordinates 12 youth information offices in French-speaking Belgium (070-233 444). These can give advice on work as well as leisure, youth rights, accommodation, etc. Their headquarters are in Namur (081-71 15 90; federation@inforjeunes.be) though much of their information is published on their website www.inforjeunes.be. A related organisation with a more useful site for job seekers is www.bruxelles-j.be. Advising on temporary and holiday jobs is among Infor Jeunes' services.

Belgium's English language weekly publication *The Bulletin* carries job adverts such as live-in positions and language tuition. Its address is 1038 Chaussée de Waterloo, 1180 Brussels (02-373 99 09; www.ackroyd.be); the magazine is published on Thursdays and can be bought from newsstands. *Newcomer* is a bi-annual publication (available from the above address for €3) which is aimed at new arrivals in Belgium and carries useful sections called 'Getting to Grips with the Red Tape' and 'Job-Seekers' Guide'.

Voluntary Opportunities

The Flemish association of young environmentalists called Natuur 2000 (Bervoetstraat 33, 2000 Antwerp; 03-231 26 04; natuur2000@telenet.be; www.natuur2000.be) is a Flemish conservation organization that hosts summer workcamps and study projects throughout Belgium open to all nationalities. Volunteers must pay a sizeable fee to cover accommodation, food, insurance and local transport. Other possibilities exist in their bat reserve-cum-nature education centre situated in an old WWI fortress near Antwerp (May till September).

Those interested in participating in residential archaeological digs in Namur province for three weeks in July should contact Archeolo-j (Avenue Paul Terlinden 23, 1330 Rixensart; 02-653 8268/fax 02-673 40 85; archeolo-J@skynet.be; www.skene.be). Residential archaeological digs accept paying volunteers in July; the fee is €220 Euros for 8 days, €372 Euros for 15 days.

The system of volunteering to work on organic farms is still in its infancy in Belgium. The Flemish organisation Velt (Uitbreidingstraat 392c, 2600 Berchem; 03-281 74 75; http://old.velt.be) publishes a bi-monthly newsletter *Seizoenen* which contains a sprinkling of adverts for organic farms with which individuals could make contact asking for work.

Luxembourg

If Belgium is sometimes neglected, Luxembourg is completely by-passed. Yet it is an independent country with an unemployment rate of just over 4% (almost the lowest in the EU) and a number of useful facilities for foreigners. The national employment service (Administration de l'Emploi or ADEM) at 10 rue Bender, L-1229 Luxembourg (352-478 53 00; www.etat.lu/ADEM/adem.htm) operates a *Service Vacances* (8002 4646; info.jeu@adem. public.lu) for students and young people looking for summer jobs in warehouses, restaurants, etc. To find out about possibilities, you must visit this office in person, although EU nationals looking for long-term jobs may receive some assistance from EURES counsellors. Other branches of the employment service are located in Esch-sur-Alzette (54 10 54), Diekirch (80 29 29) and Wiltz (95 83 84), but the headquarters is the only one to have a *Service Vacances* section. Paul Newcombe found the service very helpful and was delighted to be given details of a job vacancy at an American bar in the capital.

While cycling through the country, Mary Hall was struck by the number of travellers working on campsites and in restaurants in Luxembourg City. More recently Danny Jacobson was hitch-hiking through Luxembourg and stayed at the main hostel, a big affair full of groups of kids during the summer. He noticed a sign at the desk for dishwashers so he enquired and worked three hours on several mornings. In return he received a free bed and meals. He hinted that he might be prepared to stay on if there was any chance of a small wage being paid, but his hint was not taken up, so the arrangement is strictly work-for-keep.

Anyone who wants to reside in Luxembourg must register with the authorities and prove that they have sufficient means to support themselves. Non-EU nationals must obtain a work permit *(Déclaration Patronale)* from an employer which has been approved by the Administration de l'Emploi and by the Ministère de la Justice, Police des Etrangers, 16 Bd. Royal, L-1333 Luxembourg.

The Range of Jobs

With a total population of 463,000, job opportunities are understandably limited, but they do exist especially in the tourist industry. Even the Embassy in London at 27 Wilton Crescent, London SW1X 8SD (020-7235 6961) maintains that seasonal jobs are often to be found in the hotels of the Grand Duchy of Luxembourg and will send a list of the 250+ hotels in exchange for an A4 envelope and a 50p stamp. Alternatively check an online directory of hotels such as www.hotels.lu. Wages are fairly good in this sector, often about £500 per month after room and board.

The main language is Luxembourgish (variously called Luxembourgeois and Letzeburgesch) but both German and French are spoken and understood by virtually everyone. Casual workers will normally need a reasonable knowledge of at least one of these. Temporary office work abounds since many multinational companies are based in Luxembourg, some of which may regard a knowledge of fluent English in addition to a local language an advantage. Addresses of potential employers can be obtained from the Luxembourg Embassy who on receipt of an s.a.e. will send a list of British firms, as well as of the largest local companies. Several agencies specialise in temporary work. Manpower-Aide Temporaire, 42 rue Glesener, L-1630 Luxembourg (48 23 23/fax 40 35 52; manpower. lux@manpower.lu) handles all types of temporary work.

Prolinguis runs summer language courses for teenagers near Arlon though its offices are in Belgium (228 Place de l'Eglise, 6717 Thiaumont; 063-22 04 62; www.prolinguis.be). Philip Dray, an EFL teacher from Ireland, worked for them one summer:

> *I was employed in a freelance capacity to work 90 days between April 5th and September 15th. The salary was the equivalent of £60 a day and I had a sort of hotel room in a building that housed the students' dorms. For my keep I had to check the dorms twice a week, which was not too bad since most of the kids were co-operative. The work was grammar-based but with some emphasis on games and role play.*

EFL-trained teachers are hired by Prolinguis on 12-month or 2-month contracts and are paid €40-€50 a day plus full board and lodging on campus.

Helpful Organisations

The Centre Information Jeunes (CIJ), 26 Place de la Gare, Geleria Kons, 1616 Luxembourg (+352-26 29 32 00; www.cij.lu) runs a holiday job service between January and August for students from the EU. They can also inform you what the national minimum wage is for someone of your age. As of 2005 students 18 or over earn €6.65 an hour or €1150 a month.

Luxembourg Accueil Information (10 Bisserwee, L-1238 Luxembourg-Grund; 24 17 17) is a centre for new arrivals and residents. They put on courses and workshops and may have resources available that will help newcomers to conduct their own job search. Requests for leads on au pair placements might meet with a favourable response. There seems to be no dedicated au pair agency in Luxembourg though plenty of demand so the best way is to browse through all the online au pair matching services such as www.aupair-world. net. Since 2003 Luxembourg has not recognised the special legal status of au pairs so that they are treated like all foreign workers which means they must have a written contract of employment and pay social security contributions. Non-EU citizens who would like to come as au pairs must satisfy all the requirements of foreign workers which is likely to prove next to impossible.

If you want to check newspaper adverts which will mainly be for professionals, buy the *Luxemburger Wort* (especially on Saturdays), or the English language weekly named after the country's telephone code *352* (info@352.lu). *Le Jeudi* (www.le-jeudi.lu), a French language paper aimed at foreigners living in Luxembourg, appears every Thursday and contains a section of job ads.

Grape-Picking

Luxembourgeois wine producers need help in the vineyards along the Moselle in the southeast of the country around the town of Remich. The harvest normally begins around the middle of September and continues for two or more weeks. The Institut Viti-Vinicole, B.P. 50, 5501 Remich (23 69 92 88; info@vins-cremants.lu) does not arrange jobs, though it may be able to estimate the starting date of the harvest and give more precise dates closer to the time. Starting dates fluctuate from about the 13th to the 25th of September though the average is usually the 16th. Its website www.vins-cremants.lu has an alphabetical list of all the growers and their addresses plus map of the vineyards.

The only way of finding out about harvest jobs, as Ian Black discovered, is to go straight to the region and ask the farmers directly. Kristof Szymczak picked grapes in Luxembourg for a number of seasons in a row: *'It was very easy to find work just walking along the Moselle valley from the villages of Schengen and Wasserbillig. People are really wonderful. I always received board, lodging and about £25 per day.'*

France

Although you may occasionally encounter the legendary hostility of the French towards the English, more often you will be treated with warmth and helpfulness especially in the countryside. So many English-speaking people reside in France that expatriate grapevines are an invaluable source of job information. Unemployment is among the highest in Europe, just a shade under 10% at the beginning of 2005, and the rate among young people is much higher. It would be a mistake to expect to walk into a job just because you have a GCSE in French and enjoy eating *pains au chocolat*.

Although the French tourist industry offers many seasonal jobs, there are even more in agriculture: approximately 100,000 foreign workers are employed on the grape harvest alone. Workers come from all over, but mainly from Eastern Europe, North Africa and Southern Europe. You may find yourself working in the fields next to a mature student from Québec (on the exchange scheme mentioned below), an Armenian migrant worker, an office worker from Basingstoke or a young Dane or Scot who is touring Europe as a nomadic worker. It is possible to support yourself throughout the year in France by combining work in the various fruit harvests with either conventional jobs such as tutoring in English, or more unusual occupations from busking to gathering snails.

One important feature of working in France is that you should be paid at least the *SMIC (salaire minimum interprofessionel de croissance)* or national minimum wage. There are slightly different rates for seasonal agricultural work and full-time employees; at present the basic SMIC is €7.61 per hour gross or €1,154.18 per month based on a working week of 35 hours. These are adjusted annually to take account of inflation.

REGULATIONS

Tax inspectors and immigration officers carry out spot checks in tourist resorts, and employers in even the most out-of-the-way places have refused to hire anyone who lacks the right documents. Wine-makers in Bordeaux have been told that if they are caught employing people without papers, they will not be allowed to bring in their harvest the following year.

French workers enjoy some of the most generous employment legislation in Europe The cut in the working week from 39 to 35 (for anyone working in a firm with more than 20 employees) continues to be controversial. This legislation alarms the large number of UK tour operators with staff in France since they do not offer their campsite couriers, chalet girls, etc. SMIC-level wages nor statutory perks. It has now been decided that because of the short-term nature of the contracts and because their employees are paid in sterling into British bank accounts, they are exempt.

For European Union Nationals

In November 2003, the government abolished the obligation for EU citizens to acquire a *carte de séjour* (residence permit). No longer will it be the case that people without the permit (which was always strangely elusive) will be disadvantaged in the job hunt. The official word is that Europeans can still apply for one, since it can be a useful piece of ID for long-term stayers, but they will have to provide the battery of translated documents as before, and so the majority won't bother.

Once you take up paid employment in France, your employer must complete all the necessary formalities for registering you with social security *(sécu)* and you will be issued with a registration card and then pay a percentage of your wages as contributions. After working a summer season at Disneyland Paris in 2003 (described later), Keith Leishman offered what he considers a crucial piece of advice, which is to take a certified copy of your birth certificate translated into French. It must include your father's full name and your mother's maiden name. Keith arrived without this abstruse document and as a result had trouble registering for social security and furthermore in getting paid.

Self-employed workers *(travailleurs indépendants),* however little they earn, are obliged to register at the social security office (URSSAF). Some employers may claim that they cannot hire you without a *sécu,* and employment agencies may not be willing to register you without one, however you should insist on your rights.

Legal employers will deduct as much as 18% for social security payments, even before you have a number. These can be counted towards National Insurance in Britain, if you subsequently need to claim benefit. You may also lose a further 5% in tax. It is worth pointing out that legal residents of France may be able to reduce their rent bill significantly, provided their earnings two years prior to applying were low. The benefit is administered by the Caisse d'Allocations Familiales (CAF) to whom you must furnish a signed/stamped declaration from your landlord, a declaration of income for the calendar year preceding the year of benefit, a *Fiche Individual d'Etat Civile* and various other bits and pieces.

A problem for some legal workers crops up when they try to cash pay cheques. After the plum harvest finished, Brendan Barker was told that he would have to wait eight days to be paid and that the cheque could be cashed only at the local village Credit Agricole. Stephen Psallidas reports that it is so difficult for foreigners to open a bank account, that you'll have to eat your pay cheques before you can cash them. His solution was to open an account at the Post Office for which it was necessary to show an *attestation de domicile* (letter from your landlord saying that you really do live there) plus a photocopy of a recent gas or electricity bill. More recently Keith Leishman wishes that he had not followed the advice set out for employees by Disneyland Paris in opening a French bank account which was a hassle and as it turned out a waste of time. He found that cheques could easily be cashed at a local bank.

A useful source of information is the leaflet published by the CIDJ (address and description below) called *Travailler en France: ressortissants de l'Union Européenne* (fiche no. 5.5702) which can be searched on their website (www.cidj.com) or paid for if picked up in person.

Non-EU Formalities

Australians and New Zealanders under 30 are eligible for one-year working holiday visas for France. Non-EU nationals must obtain work documents before they leave their home country in order to work legally and this is fiendishly difficult since it depends on finding an employer who can argue that no French or EU national could do the job. A more manageable approach is to turn yourself into a student. After an initial year of study, people on a student visa are permitted to work 10-20 hours a week in term-time and up to 39 hours in vacations. In order to obtain a student visa, you will have to have good French language skills, two years of higher education (which may be waived if attending art college) and proof of financial support in the form of a notarised statement from a bank or benefactor that you can access enough per month to live on. With a student visa and stable accommodation, you can apply for a *carte de séjour* and after that for jobs, preferably jobs that French people can't do like teaching English, guiding groups of foreign students, etc.

Special Schemes for North Americans

The Council on International Educational Exchange no longer administers the Work in France scheme for students. A Paris organisation, Centre d'Echanges Internationaux (CEI), has take over the programme. Its Work in France department can assist higher education students over 18 (or occasionally new graduates) from outside Europe to obtain temporary work permits *(autorisation provisoire de travail)* to work in France for up to three months starting any time. Those participating in training programmes may stay for up to one year. All candidates must be conversant in French. The basic placement fee for independent job-seekers is €330. CEI can also arrange jobs for a fee of €700 and internships for €450 or €600. Details are available from CEI Paris, 1 rue Gozlin, 75006 Paris (01-40 51 11 81, fax 01-43 29 06 21; wif@cei4vents.com; www.cei4vents.com).

The Cultural Service of the French Embassy (4101 Reservoir Road NW, Washington, DC 20007; 202-944-6011; www.frenchculture.org) collates information of use to Americans who wish to study or intern in France. It oversees an internship programme (www.frenchculture.org/education/support/internship/index.html) and also a teaching programme (assistant.washington-amba@diplomatie.fr). The English Teaching Assistantship programme runs from Oct 1st to Apr 30th and is for those who have a good working knowledge of French. The monthly stipend is €890 (gross) a month.

Americans who are interested in arranging an internship in France may also contact AIPT (see Introduction) or the French American Chamber of Commerce which oversees an International Career Development Program (6th Floor, 1350 Avenue of the Americas, New York, NY 10019; 212-765-4460; icdp@faccnyc.org; www.faccnyc.org). The programme is for graduates aged 18-35 with relevant professional experience. The Chamber can assist suitable candidates arrange a six-month visa that can be renewed twice.

The French American Center in Montpellier (4 rue St. Louis, Montpellier 34000; 04-67 92 30 66; www.frenchamericancenter.com) arranges au pair placements for Americans aged 18-25 with families in the Languedoc region plus internships in local businesses. Details are available from the French-American Center of Provence, Inc., 198 Avenue of the Americas, New York, NY 10013; 212-343-2675; jhr2001@aol.com.

The Alliance Abroad Group has started to offer new internship positions to qualified French-speaking candidates in small hotels and campgrounds. Work experience candidates receive free room and board and a stipend of €180 per month. Details of the programme and fees are available by emailing CPrieto@allianceabroad.com. Another source of internships for eligible Americans is Experiment Paris, 89 rue de Turbigo, 75003 Paris (01-44 54 58 03; incoming@experiment-france.org; www.experiment-france.org). Their placements are also in hotels/restaurants or businesses, e.g. advertising, computing, import/export, etc. for a maximum of three months; the placement fee is €425-€625.

A one-year visa is at present available to Canadians aged 18-35; however, according to the SWAP 2005 literature, this may be dropped in favour of a three-month maximum (www.swap.ca). In addition to paying the registration fee of $265, SWAP participants must have access to support funds of C$2,000-$3,000. Special exchange visas are available for students who are residents of Québec through the Association Québec-France (9 Place Royale, Québec G1K 4G2; prog@quebecfrance.qc.ca). They can issue special work permits to cover the grape harvest or a summer job in holiday camps.

The symbol for flowers refers to the castration of maize flowers

THE JOB HUNT

Internet browsers might start with several useful websites: www.paris-anglo.com in English has articles and links on working in France; www.angloinfo.com has reams of practical information specific to three regions (Normandy, Brittany and the Riviera), while the French-language youth information site www.phosphore.com incorporates a job search function with quite a lot of hard information and contact details. Offers of internships and student jobs may be found at www.directetudiant.com and www.optioncarriere.com.

French speakers should be aware of the widely used French Telecom subscriber service *Minitel*. Minitel is a computerised information system which operates via a small screen plugged into an ordinary telephone. Minitel screens may be available at information centres and main post offices. With it, ordinary people can access a variety of databases including one for job vacancies or even to advertise their own availability for work. CIDJ's query number is 3615 CIDJ and you can also try 3615 TOPJOBS. Note that the Yellow Pages can be accessed by dialling 3611 on the Minitel which is free for the first three minutes but €.06 per minute thereafter. As usual the *Pages Jaunes* are available online (www.pagesjaunes.fr and in English) which can prove a great help when drawing up a list of relevant places to ask for work.

Not all hitch-hikers rank France very highly but once you get into the countryside, the French can be remarkably generous not only in offering lifts but in helping their passengers to find work. If you are offered seasonal work ahead of the job starting date and plan to leave the area in the meantime, stay in constant touch with the employer; not only can starting dates vary but farmers and hotel managers don't always keep their promises.

ANPE

The *Agence National pour l'Emploi* or ANPE is the national employment service of France, with dozens of offices in Paris and 600 others throughout the country. The headquarters are at 4 rue Galilée, 93198 Noisy-le-Grand (01-49 31 74 00/49 31 77 11) and their website lists all the branches by region or postcode (www.anpe.fr/contacts), providing addresses, telephone and fax numbers. For example the ANPE in Narbonne (ANPE, BP 802, 29 rue Mazzini, 11108 Narbonne Cedex) has seasonal hotel vacancies from May to September, and others can provide details of when agricultural work is available. Although EU nationals are supposed to have equal access to the employment facilities in other member states, this is not always the case in France unless the job-seeker speaks good French and has a stable local address. If possible foreign job-seekers should work with a EURES Adviser.

EURES advisers throughout Europe have knowledge of vacancies; in France, most of these are in the tourist industry. It has a regional branch in south-eastern England (EURES Crossborder HNFK, South Kent College, Maison Dieu Road, Dover CT16 1DH; 01304 244356/7; www.eureschannel.org) which assists people looking for jobs in the northern French region of Nord-Pas-de-Calais (as well as West Flanders in Belgium). Two bilingual Euro-Advisers can put job-seekers in touch with network partners on the continent and can also give advice and information about living and working conditions.

Seasonal offices are set up in key regions to deal with seasonal demands like the *Service Vendanges* for the grape harvest and the *Antennes Saisonnières* set up in ski resorts. These may be more likely to assist working travellers than the permanent offices which deal primarily in full-time jobs for French citizens. The addresses of ANPE offices recommended as offering seasonal work are listed in the relevant sections later in this chapter.

CIJ

There are 32 regional *Centres d'Information Jeunesse* (CIJ) and 1,500 smaller youth information points in France which may be of use to the working traveller. Helping people to find jobs is only one of their activities: they can also advise on cheap accommodation, the legal rights of temporary workers, etc. The main Paris branch is CIDJ *(Centre d'Information et de Documentation Jeunesse)* whose foyer notice board is a useful starting place for the job-seeker in Paris. It can also provide booklets and leaflets for varying fees on such sub-jects as seasonal agricultural work, possibilities for work in the summer or winter, and the regulations that affect foreign students in France. Check the site www.cidj-librairie.com for a complete list which includes a recent publication *Etrangers en France: Vos Droits* for €22. CIDJ may be visited at 101 Quai Branly, 75740 Paris Cedex 15 (01-44 49 12 00; www.cidj.com). In order to find out about actual vacancies you must visit the CIDJ offices in person, preferably first thing in the morning. Employers notify centres of their temporary vacancies; some offices just display the details on notice boards, while others operate a more formal system in co-operation with the local ANPE (e.g., CIDJ in Paris registers about 10,000 summer jobs).

Some CIJs publish free lists of potential employers. For example Stuart Bellworthy made good use of a list given out by the CIJ in Angers (now closed) which gave all the *producteurs* in the area with estimated harvest dates. About a third of the vacancies with which the CIJs deal are for mothers' helps, for which good French is not a prerequisite.

A similar range of jobs is notified to the Centres Régional des Oeuvres Universitaires et Scolaires (CROUS) in all university towns. Although they primarily assist registered stu-dents to find part-time and holiday jobs, they have been known to help foreign travellers who approach them in the right way.

Private Employment Agencies

Private employment agencies in France are prohibited from dealing with permanant jobs and so all are *agences de travail temporaire* (temporary work bureaux) or *agences d'intérim*. Among the largest are Manpower (www.manpower.fr) and Adecco (www.adecco. fr); others can be found in the Yellow Pages under the heading *Travail Intérimaire* or from the Franco-British Chamber of Commerce (31, rue Boissy d'Anglas, 75008 Paris; 01-53 30 81 30; www.francobritishchamber.com). Many specialise in a field such as industrial, medical or office work, and vacancies for unskilled jobs are few and far between. To find a job through an agency you first need to register, which is not as easy as it sounds, especially if you haven't worked in France before and don't have a French social security number. Yet some travellers have made good use of agencies.

> **On his year abroad during his degree course, Matthew Binns went to a job agency in Paris without high hopes of success:**
> *I foolishly said I was prepared to do anything. The bloke in the agency looked astonished and gave me, I think, the most unpopular job on his books – plongeur in a factory canteen in the suburbs. George Orwell's account in Down and Out in Paris and London about his time as a plongeur should be required reading for all would-be dishwashers in Paris. I did three weeks in this job until the regular plon-geur came back, poor sod. The worst bit is arriving at work with a hangover and putting on yesterday's wet clothes. But the pay was excellent.*

TOURISM

The best areas to look for work in the tourist industry of France are the Alps for the winter season, December-April, and the Côte d'Azur for the summer season, June-September, though jobs exist throughout the country. The least stressful course is to fix up work ahead of time with a UK campsite or barge holiday company in summer or ski company in winter. For example the giant First Choice Holidays (see *Tourism* chapter) hires people, not nec-essarily with qualifications, to work in hotels in the Alps and Normandy. Esprit Alpine Sun hires resort managers, chalet hosts and childcare staff for their summer programme in the Alps; contact them at 185 Fleet Road, Fleet, Hants. GU51 3BL (01252 618318; www. esprit-holidays.co.uk/Recruiting).

Horizon HPL (Signet House, 49/51 Farringdon Road, London EC1M 3JP; 020-7404 9192; horizonhpl.london@btinternet.com; http://horizon1.club.fr/index.htm) is an Anglo-French training organisation which offers packages lasting between three and 12 months combining language tuition and live-in hotel work placements and company placements all over France. The wages are on a trainee scale, from £50 per week plus accommodation, while the package fee starts at £240. Candidates can choose to prepare for Sorbonne University exams. Horizon's office in France is at 22-26 rue du Sergent Bauchat, 75012 Paris (01-40 01 07 07; horizon1@club-internet.fr) while the Dublin office is at 3 Lower Abbey St, Dublin 1 (01-8745 002).

Eurolingua offers hotel work experience in the south of France lasting two months in summer, three or six months at other times. The work is paid and comes with free accommodation and meals in the hotel. The programme involves French language tuition (individually or in a group) at the Eurolingua Institute in Montpellier (5 rue Henri Guinier, 34000 Montpellier; tel/fax 04-67 58 20 17). Other locations include Nice (Côte d'Azur) and Toulon (Provence). These programmes are suitable for both EU and non-EU students meeting French immigration requirements; details at www.eurolingua.com/Work_Experience(France).htm. The programme fee is €750 for 2-3 months €950 for 6 months.

An online recruitment agency that specialises in France is irecruit at www.irecruitltd.com: 0870 990 8890 in the UK and tel/fax 05-61 73 34 13 in France.

If you set off without anything pre-arranged, one of the easiest places to find work is at fast food establishments like Pizza Hut France or Quick Restaurants (www.quick-restaurants.com); the latter employ a staggering 12,000 people in France (recrute@quick.fr). Americana is still quite trendy in France and English-speaking staff fit well with the image. The hardest place to find work, except at the lowest level (e.g. dishwasher) is with reputable French-owned hotels and restaurants, where high standards are maintained. Your best chances will be in small family-run hotels where the hours and conditions vary according to the temperament of the *patron*. One reader met an English couple hitch-hiking through the rain to take up jobs as silver service waiting staff at a hotel in the Médoc, despite not speaking French or having had any relevant experience. The jobs had been pre-arranged through the ANPE in Pauillac.

Hotels and Restaurants

People with enough time to make long term plans can write directly to the hotels in the region which interests them, listed in any tourist hotel guide. Remember that the vast majority of restaurants are staffed by waiters rather than waitresses. Newspapers in holiday towns may carry adverts, e.g. *Nice Matin*.

But most people succeed by turning up at a resort and asking door to door, and in the opinion of veteran British traveller Jason Davies, 'door-to-door' should be just that:

> Before I was down to my last few francs I had been choosy about which establishments to ask at. 'That doesn't look very nice' or 'that's too posh' or 'that's probably closed' were all thoughts which ensured that I walked past at least three in five. But in Nice I discovered that the only way to do it is to pick a main street (like the pedestrianised area in Nice with its high density of restaurants) and ask at EVERY SINGLE place. I visited 30-40 one morning and I would say that at least 20 of those needed more employees. But only one was satisfied with my standard of French, and I got the job of commis waiter.

Speaking French to a reasonable standard greatly improves chances of finding a job, though fluency is by no means a requirement. Kimberly Ladone from the American east coast spent a summer working as a receptionist/chambermaid, also in Nice, though her job hunt did not require the same dogged determination as Jason Davies did:

> I found the job in April, at the first hotel I approached, and promised to return at the start of the season in June. While there, I met many English-speaking working travellers employed in various hotels. No one seemed bothered by work permit regulations as most jobs paid cash in hand. My advice to anyone seeking a job on the French Riviera would be to go as early in the season as possible and ask at

hotels featured in English guidebooks such as Let's Go: France, since these tend to need English-speaking staff. My boss hired me primarily because I could handle the summer influx of clueless tourists who need help with everything from making a phone call to reading a train schedule.

Beach restaurants are another hopeful possibility. Julian Peachey put on his one white shirt and pair of smart trousers and began visiting the restaurants along the beach by Avenue Montredon in the eastern part of Marseille. After the third request for work he was handed a tea towel, and proceeded to work 14-16 hours a day, seven days a week. Only the thought of the money kept him sane. The wage was severely cut on days when it rained or the mistral blew and no one came to the beach.

It must be said that not everyone finds work so easily, as Alison Cooper found: *'Last summer I tried to find work along the French Riviera, but was unsuccessful. I met many people at campsites who were in the same position as myself. From my experience most employers wanted people who could speak fluent French, and German as well. Otherwise you have to be very very lucky.'*

Many people think the Riviera has lost its glamour and is hardly worth job-hunting. In the opinion of Andrew Giles the best time to look for work on the Côte d'Azur is the end of February when campsites well known to working travellers, such as Prairies de la Mer and La Plage at Port Grimaud near St Tropez host representatives from camping holiday companies trying to get organised in time for Easter. If you are on the spot you can often wangle free accommodation in exchange for three or four hours of work a day. If you can't be there then, try the middle of May at the beginning of the peak season. Bars recommended by Andrew where you can meet local workers and residents include Marilyns (Prairies de la Mer), Mulligans (Holiday Marina), Finnigans (Port Grimaud) and L'Utopée (Marines Cogolin). Emiliano Giovannoni found the McMahon's Pub in central Nice was a meeting place for Brits, Americans and Aussies. Also, try to listen to the English station Radio Riviera based in Nice, which at 9.30am and 4.30pm broadcasts job vacancies along the coast and will also announce your request for a job free of charge. (Its website includes some job postings: www.rivieraradio.mc/jobs.html). When Peter Goldman couldn't find work on boats as he had hoped (because of rainy September weather) he tuned in to Radio Riviera and got a job stripping wallpaper from luxury apartments in Monte Carlo.

Campsite Holidays

An estimated 7,000 campsites in France employ an army of seasonal staff even though some of them are small family-run operations which need one or two assistants. You can write directly to the individual campsite addresses listed in any guide to French campsites (e.g. the Michelin *Camping and Caravanning Guide*), or you can simply show up. Robert Mallakee and a friend found campsite jobs as they hitched along the Mediterranean coast in August which is the month when almost everyone in France takes their annual holiday. There is a point in the summer at which workers who have been there since the beginning of the season are getting bored and restless, which creates a demand for emergency substitution to cover the last two months of the season. Jobs included cleaning the loos, manning the bar or snack bar, doing some maintenance, etc. Some will be especially interested in people with musical ability. Even if there are no actual jobs, you may be given the use of a tent in exchange for minimal duties.

A number of British-based travel companies offer holidaymakers a complete package providing pre-assembled tents and a campsite courier to look after any problems that arise. Since this kind of holiday appeals to families, people with a childcare background or who can organise children's activities are especially in demand. In addition to the Europewide companies like Eurocamp (addresses in *Tourism* chapter), the following all take on campsite reps/couriers and other seasonal staff:

Carisma Holidays, Bethel House, Heronsgate, Chorleywood, Herts. WD3 5BB (01923 284235; personnel@carisma.co.uk).

Fleur Holidays, 4 All Hallows Road, Bispham, Blackpool FY2 0AS (01253 593333;

employment@fleur-holidays.com).

French Life/Camping Life, Unit 2, Rawdon Park Industrial Estate, Green Lane, Rawdon, Leeds LS19 6RW (0870 197 6541; overseasemployment@frenchlife.co.uk).

Ian Mearns Holidays, Tannery Yard, Witney St, Burford, Oxon. OX18 4DP (01993 822655; enquiries@ianmearnsholidays.co.uk). People able to start work by Easter especially in demand.

Select France, Fiveacres, Murcott, Kidlington, Oxford OX5 2RE (01865 331350; jobs@selectfrance.co.uk).

Venue Holidays, 1 Norwood St, Ashford, Kent TN23 1QU (01233 629950; www.venueholidays.co.uk). Website carries job information.

The best time to start looking for summer season jobs from England is between November and February. In most cases candidates are expected to have at least A-level standard French, though some companies claim that a knowledge of French is merely 'preferred'. It is amazing how far a good dictionary and a knack for making polite noises in French can get you. Many impose a minimum age of 21.

The massive camping holiday industry generates winter work as well. Brad Agencies Ltd. has a depot in Beaucaire near Avignon that cleans and repairs tents and bedding on behalf of many of the major companies. Staff (who need not speak French though it is an advantage) are needed for the laundry and distribution between September and May. Gite accommodation is provided and a wage negotiated. A driving licence is essential and your own transport helpful. Brad International's UK office is at Abbey Lakes Hall, Orrell Road, Wigan WN5 8QZ (01695 632797; ian.b@bradint.co.uk).

Another behind-the-scenes agency which maintains holiday caravans in and outside the season is called European Services (54 Oaklands Road Trading Estate, Rodley, Leeds LS13 1LQ; 0113 236 1577; europserve@aol.com).

Short bursts of work are available in the spring (about three weeks in May) and autumn (three weeks in September) to teams of people who put up and take down the tents at campsites, known as *montage* and *démontage*. Sometimes the camping tour operators contract out this work to specialist firms like Mark Hammerton Travel (Spelmonden Old Oast, Spelmonden Road, Goudhurst, Kent TN1 1HE; 01580 214000; enquiries@markhammerton.co.uk) who pay their crews nearly £95 a week in addition to board, lodging and travel expenses.

Holiday Centres

Outdoor activity centres are another major employer of summer staff, both general domestic staff and sports instructors. Try the companies mentioned in the chapter *Tourism* such as PGL and Acorn Adventure (01384 446057; www.acorn-jobs.co.uk). The NST Travel Group (Chiltern House, Bristol Ave, Blackpool FY2 0FA; 01253 503011; www.nstjobs.co.uk) hires catering and instructing staff for its activity holiday centres in the Pas de Calais and the Ardèche.

Keen cyclists could try to get a job with a cycling holiday company active in France such as Belle France (same address as Mark Hammerton Travel above; 0870 405 4056), Bent's Bicycle & Walking Tours (The Blue Cross, Orleton, Ludlow, Shropshire SY8 4HN; info@bentstours.com) and Susi Madron's Cycling for Softies (2-4 Birch Polygon, Rush-olme, Manchester M14 5HX; 0161-248 8282; www.cycling-for-softies.co.uk) whose staff are over 25. Headwater Holidays (The Old School House, Chester Rd, Castle Northwich, Cheshire CW8 1LE (01606 720033; www.headwater.com) looks to hire French-speaking reps (minimum age 21) and British Canoe Union qualified canoe instructors.

For work in a more unusual activity holiday, contact Bombard Balloon Adventures, Chateau de LaBorde, 21200 Beaune (03-80 26 63 30; www.bombardsociety.com/jobs) who hire hot-air balloon ground crew for their summer season May to October. The job requires excellent physical fitness and strength, a cheerful personality, clean-cut appearance and year-old clean driving licence. Another balloon holiday company to try is France Montgolfieres (24 rue Nationale, 41400 Montrichard; 02-54 32 20 48; jane@franceballoons.com); they promise wages of £500-£600 per month.

The Youth Hostels Association of France (FUAJ) employs hostellers for short periods at various hostels to work in the kitchen, reception and as sports leaders. The headquarters of the Fédération Unie des Auberges de Jeunesse (27 rue Pajol, 75018 Paris; www.fuaj.org) distributes a guide to the 185 French hostels to which interested workers must apply directly. FUAJ also organises workcamps for volunteers to renovate hostels.

Those with fluent French who want to work in a theme park or resort centre can find links to the major holiday parks that belong to SNELAC (Syndicat Espaces de Loisirs, d'Attractions et Culturels) on www.snelac.com.

Ski Resorts

France is the best of all countries in Europe for British and Irish people to find jobs in ski resorts, mainly because it is the number one country for British skiers, 200,000 of whom go there every year. Most of the resorts are high enough to create reliable snow conditions throughout the season. The main problem is the shortage of worker accommodation; unless you find a live-in job you will have to pay nearly holiday prices or find a friend willing to rent out his or her sofa. Since many top French resorts are purpose-built, a high proportion of the holiday accommodation is in self-catering flats or designed for chalet parties. This means that not only is there a shortage of rental accommodation, but there are fewer jobs as waiters, bar and chamber staff for those who arrive in the resorts to look for work. There is an increasing number of English and Irish style pubs which are good places to find out about work.

If you are employed by a British tour operator, be aware that you will not be paid according to French employment law. The French authorities have estimated that 10,000 staff are employed to work for ski chalet companies and all of them are being paid much less than the SMIC, typically between £50 and £65 plus living expenses and lift pass. If trying to fix up a job from Britain, there are one or two agencies that arrange for young people with a very good knowledge of French to work in ski resorts. Alpotels (17 High St, Gretton, Northants. NN17 3DE; www.jobs-in-the-alps.co.uk) carry out aptitude tests on behalf of various resort employers and liaise between suitable candidates and prospective employers who pay a net salary of approximately £500. Enquirers (EU nationality only) must send an s.a.e.

A London-based recruitment company to contact for work in French resorts is UK Overseas Handling (UKOH, PO Box 2791, London W1A 5JU; 020-7629 3064; vacancies@ukoh.co.uk) which provides seasonal and annual staff to the French tour operator Eurogroup which owns hotels, restaurant and chalets in ski and beach resorts in France (and the rest of Europe). Applicants must be EU-passport holders. Three excellent recruitment websites are www.natives.co.uk, www.seasonworkers.com and www.freeradicals.co.uk which match job-seekers with alpine and other vacancies. Qualified/experienced nannies are especially sought after. Specialist nanny agencies supply nannies to holidaying British families such as Jack Frosts in the Portes du Soleil (06-13 79 07 17).

Up to 30 British tour companies are present in Méribel alone, so this is one of the best resorts in which to conduct a job hunt. It may even be worth calling into the tourist office to ask about seasonal employment, though it is more promising to ask for work in person at hotels, bars, etc. Looking for work out-of-season in October and November has the added advantage that well-placed youth hostels (like the one in Séez les Arcs where Matthew Binns stayed) are empty and relatively cheap. Matthew also recommends the free Red Cross hostel in Bourg-St Maurice.

Resorts like Méribel are flooded with British workers just before the season and eventually by British guests, many of them school groups. The functioning language of many establishments is English. Since the infrastructure work was done for the Olympics, British chalet operators have established a strong presence in Courchevel; at least one UK tour operators has its French office in the picturesque village of Le Praz, one of the five villages that comprise the resort of Courchevel. If you are not already familiar with the resorts, try to do some research beforehand, something Susan Beney regretted failing to do: 'We took pot luck with the resort and on reflection would have done a bit more homework on *resorts we might have preferred. La Tania was very limited; La Plagne would have been one hundred percent better.'*

Most jobs with British companies pay low wages but allow workers to ski or snowboard between 10am and 4pm. UK operators that recruit staff for Méribel and France generally include the following:

Esprit Holidays, 185 Fleet Road, Fleet, Hants. GU51 3BL (01252 618309; recruitment@esprit-holidays.co.uk).

Eurogroup Vacances, 1091 Avenue de la Boisse, 73000 Chambéry (04-79 62 36 63; www. eurogroup-jobs.com). Staff needed for hotel and tourist properties in French Alps in winter and summer.

Family Ski Company, Bank Chambers, Walwyn Road, Colwall, Malvern WR13 6QG (01684 541444; www.familyski.co.uk/Jobs.htm). Offer many jobs in the French Alps.

Inghams, 020-8780 8803; www.inghams.co.uk.

Le Ski, 25 Holly Terrace, Huddersfield, HD1 6JW (0870 754 4444; www.leski.com). Jobs in Courchevel, La Tania and Val d'Isère.

Lotus Supertravel, Sandpiper House, 39 Queen Elizabeth St, London SE1 2BT (020-7962 1369; alice@lotusgroup.co.uk; www.supertravel.co.uk/jobs.htm). Takes on winter staff for France, primarily chalet hosts with excellent cooking skills, reps fluent in French, qualified masseurs, nannies and handymen. All applicants must hold an EU passport and be over 21.

Meriski, 01285 648518; www.meriski.co.uk. Chalet cooks and nannies in greatest demand.

Scott Dunn, Fovant Mews, 12 Noyna Road, London SW17 7PH (020-8682 5005; recruitment@scottdunn.com).

Simon Butler Skiing, 01483 212726; info@simonbutlerskiing.co.uk. Jobs for nannies, chalet people, cooks and ski instructors in Megève.

Ski Armadillo, 07781 411820; www.skiarmadillo.com. For chalets in Verbier.

Ski Beat, Metro House, Northgate, Chichester, Sussex PO19 1BE (01243 780405; www. skibeat.co.uk). Jobs in La Plagne, Tignes, Val d'Isère and La Tania.

Ski Olympic, PO Box 396, Doncaster DN5 7YS (01302 328820; www.skiolympic.co.uk).

Nannying is a very promising area of employment in ski resorts. Matt Tomlinson, who spent a year near Paris as an au pair, spent the winter season in Courchevel:

> *I'm not sure if I just luck out getting work or whether it is a question of having done most jobs, being presentable and enthusiastic. There certainly doesn't seem to be any shortage of employment opportunities in Courchevel and Le Praz during the busy periods. My first job was as a private nanny: easy work, £100 for the week plus another £70 for extra babysitting. I moved on to doing Children's Club with Simply Ski and then Snow Club with Ski Esprit. Not everyone was NNEB qualified though all had substantial childcare experience and most were hired in England. I would recommend anyone thinking of doing a nanny job in the Alps to think seriously before taking it on. The days were very long and tiring, especially when you have to keep track of 18 sets of ski gear.*

In Tignes, Harri's Bar (Evolution 2, Le Lavachet, 73320 Tignes, 04-79 06 48 11; info@skibarjobs.com; www.skibarjobs.com) encourages applications from ski bums to work in a hotel/bar complex. Another promising resort is Chamonix, where Sean Macnamara obtained a series of manual jobs as a dishwasher and handyman through the local ANPE office. In fact the ANPE mount a concerted campaign every winter called the A3 Network (ANPE Alpes Action) to attract qualified resort staff. Contact details for the relevant offices are:

- ◦ Plagne – 04-79 09 01 14; A3.la-plagne@wanadoo.fr
- ◦ Bourg St Maurice – 04-79 07 25 34; A3.bourg-st-maurice@wanadoo.fr
- ◦ Meribel – 04-79 00 51 75; A3.meribel@wanadoo.fr

- Tignes – 04-79 06 42 08; A3.tignes@wanadoo.fr
- Courchevel – 04-79 08 00 48; A3-courchevel@wanadoo.fr
- Menuires – 04-79 00 71 32; A3.les-menuires@wanadoo.fr
- Valle d'Isère – 04-79 06 16 00; A3.val-d-isere@wanadoo.fr

Also try the permanent ANPE offices in Albertville, Annecy, Cluses and so on. For example the Albertville ANPE in the Savoie (45 ave Jean Jaurès, BP96, 73203 Albertville Cedex; 04-79 32 20 03) has a centralised placement service for vacancies in a range of resorts including Tignes, Val d'Isère and Méribel.

Some other relevant offices that open year-round include:

Annecy ANPE, Immeuble Genève Bellevue, 105 Av de Genève, 74000 Annecy (04-50 51 00 42)

Cluses ANPE, 1115 Av George Clemenceau, 74300 Cluses (04-50 98 92 88)

St Jean-de-Maurienne ANPE, rue Louis Sibue, 73300 St Jean de Maurienne (04-79 64 17 88)

Chambery ANPE, 32 rue Paulette Besson, 73000 Chambery (04-79 60 24 70)

Thonon les Bains ANPE, 5 place de la Gare, 74207 Thonon les Bains Cedex (04-50 71 31 73)

Success is far from guaranteed in any ski resort job hunt and competition for work is increasing. Val d'Isère attracts as many as 500 ski bums every November/December, many of whom hang around bars or the ANPE for days in the vain hope that work will come their way. With such an inexhaustible supply of ski bums, some employers are ready to hire people for Christmas, work them non-stop over the high season, pay them less than the *SMIC* if they think they can get away with it and fire them if they complain. If looking for work in Val, try Radio Val which broadcasts from next door to the tourist office. Job vacancies are announced in the morning (mostly babysitting and kitchen portering) and then posted in French outside the studio or check online www.radiovaldisere.com/jobs.php. A related job site of possible interest is www.jobvaldisere.com.

A problem that recurs every winter is the dispute between British tour operators and French ski schools. The rules state that only qualified instructors and guides can accompany holidaymakers which means that English-speaking ski guides or ski-hosts (part rep, part guide) hired by UK tour companies face arrest on the slopes. But for the past few years, the French have at least accepted (under pressure from the European Commission) that BASI-qualified British ski instructors have an equal right to work in the Alps.

Selling to Tourists

A well known job in the south of France consists of selling refreshments on beaches. You may find foreigners doing this on beaches in and around Port Grimaud, San Tropez, Fréjus, Pampelonne and indeed all along the Mediterranean coast. Buy one of them a drink and he or she will direct you to their boss. Many bosses allow sellers to camp on their land. Sellers are paid on commission and earnings differ enormously. It helps if you are a raging extrovert with the gift of the gab.

Entrepreneurial activities often meet with opposition from those who have already staked a claim, as Stephen Psallidas found in Père Lachaise cemetery in Paris:
I really was penniless so I thought up a scheme to make (I thought) vast profits. I would sell wine to all the hippies and camera-wielding tourists around Jim Morrison's grave. Macabre huh? So I bought a few bottles of el cheapo vin rouge and set up shop, complete with a sign in six languages. Unfortunately I was very quickly moved on by the established operators, who were mostly selling more exotic substances. So I drank the wine myself and had a very jolly time for the rest of the day.

Selling treats to tourists in ski resorts, e.g. chocoate to the ski queues, has also proved a lucrative sideline for some travellers-cum-ski bums. Enterprising individuals have made money by delivering croissants to chalets and inns either as an independent business or as an employee of the local bakery.

As usual you might be able to sell your talent to tourists as a busker. Leda Meredith made about £30 an hour as a dancer/mime in Avignon before and during the festival in August. Dustie Hickey also found work during the festival doing promotions (i.e. selling tickets and T-shirts) for an American theatre group. After the festival is over, however, street performers need a permit, and will be moved on by the police otherwise.

Yachts

Kevin Gorringe headed for the south of France in June several years ago with the intention of finding work on a private yacht. His destination was Antibes, where so many British congregate, and began frequenting likely meeting places like the Gaffe Bar and the Irish bar as well as the agencies like Adrian Fisher and Blue Water. A number of crewing agencies are housed in the same building, La Galerie du Port, 8 Blvd d'Aguillon, 06600 Antibes (see *Working a Passage*).

Kevin recommends staying at one of the cheap campsites at Biot on the other side of Antibes, which is easily reached by public transport, though Stella's (04- 93 13 64 30) and the usual crew houses are also possibilities. He and his girlfriend went round the quays asking for work but soon tired of begging for scrubbing jobs and decided to move on. They concluded that to find work in Antibes you have to be 'persistent, focused and able to get into the click'. Bill Garfield is one traveller who stuck at it. After a week of failure, Bill began asking at every single boat including the ones already swarming with workers and also all the boats big and small in the 'graveyard' (refitting area). Two weeks after leaving Solihull this tactic paid off and he was hired for a nine-week period to help refit a yacht in preparation for the summer charter season.

Look tidy and neat, be polite and when you get a job work hard. The first job is the hardest to get, but once you get in with this integrated community, captains will help you find other jobs after the refitting is finished. Of course many continue through the summer as deckhands on charter yachts and are paid £100 a week plus tips (which sometimes match the wage). The charter season ends in late September when many yachts begin organising their crew for the trip to the West Indies.

A British tour company which hires instructors and reps for its sailing holidays in Southwest France is Sail France, Rockley Watersports, Poole, Dorset BH15 4RW (0870 777 0541; personnel@rockleywatersports.com). They operate out of two of the largest RYA recognised watersports centres in Europe.

Barges

The holiday barges that ply the rivers and canals of France hire cooks, hostesses, deckhands and captains. The best time to apply to the companies is in the new year; addresses may be found in the travel advertisement sections of English Sunday papers. All prefer to employ only people who feel comfortable functioning in French even if the majority of their clientele is American.

European Waterways employs staff for its hotel barges in Europe. Steward/stewardess salaries can be substantially increased with tips. The UK address is European Waterways Ltd, 35 Wharf Road, Wraysbury, Staines, Middlesex TW19 5JQ; fax 01784 483072; www.GoBarging.com). Vacancies also exist throughout the year for chefs, housekeepers, deck hands, tour guides and barge pilots for the luxury barge fleet. All applicants must have an EU passport (or have the right to work in the UK), be at least 21 and possess a current driving licence. A knowledge of French is useful.

Continental Waterways was bought by the American company Grand Circle Travel in 2004 but still wants to recruit English-speaking staff from the EU. For recruitment information see Continental's website www.continentalwaterways.co.uk or contact them on 03-80 53 05 34 or jstark@GCT.com. They need seasonal crew including chefs, driver/guides, stewardesses and deckhands in five regions of France to work with a mainly American clientele. Long hours are rewarded with from £600 a month.

Other possibilities include Croisieres Touristiques Francaises (2 Route de Semur, 21150 Venarey-les-Laumes; 03-80 96 17 10; boat@club-internet.fr) which operates five luxury barges employing chefs, guides, stewardesses, deckhands and pilots. Canals of France operates luxury barges between Toulouse and Sete (www.canalsoffrance.com) and Afloat in France (06-86 27 35 26; www.argeaif.com) also hire qualified staff.

GRAPE-PICKING

Every year the lure of the *vendange* attracts countless hopefuls whether for financial gain or the romance of participating in an ancient ritual. Past participants agree about the negative aspects of the job: the eight or nine hours a day of back-breaking work, often for seven days a week, and the weather, which is too cold and damp in the early autumn mornings and too hot at mid-day. Waterproofs are essential because you will be expected to continue picking in the pouring rain. The accommodation may consist of a space in a barn for a sleeping bag, and the sanitation arrangements of a cold water tap. But despite all this, every year the grape-growing regions of France are flooded with job-seekers.

Part of the attraction is the wage. Although it is not usually much higher than *le SMIC* of €7.61 (porters sometimes earn more especially when the vineyards are located on steep hills), there is little opportunity to spend your earnings on an isolated farm and most people save several hundred pounds during a typical fortnight-long harvest. Martin and Shirine from Crawley earned £1,550 between them during the ten-day harvest of white grapes followed a week later by the red harvest in the first half of October. More typically, Rob Abblett walked away from the *vendange* in Chateauneuf de Pape a couple of years ago with cut fingers, an aching back and £250. If you work for the same *patron* for seven consecutive days, you should be paid an overtime rate. Be prepared for at least 15% to be deducted for social security.

The major threat to jobs at present comes from mechanisation. A great many farmers are clubbing together to invest in the great noisy juggernauts harvesting day and night, which have almost completely replaced human beings in some areas like Cognac and south of Bordeaux. However predictions that hand-picking will completely disappear are unlikely to come to pass. Prestige chateaux which produce Grand Cru wines and Champagne are sticking with hand-picking.

> **Jon Loop describes the relationship with machines at the chateau where he picked grapes:**
> *They had started using machines at Pontet Canet in the 1980s, but returned to using grape-pickers in the 1990s. The reasons they gave were purely economic: the machines lie idle over much of the year; they pick up stones, small animals, dirt and destroy the vines. They must be very certain of this because they have completely refurbished the dormitories and cooking facilities for 150 pickers.*

Contact details for Chateau Pontet Canet in Bordeaux are 05-56 59 04 04; fax 05-56-59-26-63; pontet-canet@wanadoo.fr.

Work and Conditions

The working and living conditions can vary greatly from farm to farm. Often the size of the farm has a bearing on this: obviously it is easier for the owner of a small vineyard with a handful of workers to provide decent accommodation than for the owner of a chateau who may have over 100 workers to consider. Farmers almost always provide some sort of accommodation, but this can vary from a rough and ready dormitory to a comfortable room in his own house. Food is normally provided, but again this can vary from the barely adequate to the sublime: one picker can write that 'the food was better than that in a 5-star hotel, so we bought flowers for the cook at the end of the harvest', while another may complain of instant mashed potatoes or of having to depend on whatever he or she can manage to buy and prepare. When both food and accommodation are provided there is normally a deduction of one or two hours' pay from each day's wage.

Free wine is a frequent feature of the job, though Martin and Shirine looked in vain for it at their chateau. In addition to her wage, Dustie Hickey was allowed a seemingly endless supply of wine which 'lifted up the workers' spirits but often left me falling into the bushes'. (When she was offered the same perk during the olive harvest later in the autumn, she wisely sold her daily two litres of wine.)

Hours also vary. Whereas one traveller found the structuring of the working day ridiculous, with a 1½ hour lunch break and no other breaks between 7.45am and 6pm, others have found themselves finishing the day's picking at lunchtime, especially in the far south near the Spanish border, where the sun is unbearably hot in the afternoon.

The work itself will consist either of picking or portering. Picking involves bending to get the grapes from a vine that may be only three and a half feet tall, and filling a pannier that you drag along behind you. New regulations have resulted in the use of new secateurs which make it much less hard to cut yourself than with the old *vendangettes* but also make it harder to pick the grapes. Plastic gloves are useful if you don't want your hands stained by grape juice (white grapes are the worst). The panniers full of grapes are emptied into an *hotte* a large basket weighing up to 100lb which the porters carry to a trailer.

The first few days as a *cueilleur/cueilleuse* or *coupeur* (picker) are the worst, as you adjust to the stooping posture and begin to use muscles you never knew you had. The job of porter is sought after, since it does not require the constant bending and is less boring because you move around the vineyard.

The further south you go the more likely you are to find yourself competing with migrant workers from Spain, Portugal, Morocco and Algeria. Large and famous chateaux (like Lafite) often use a contracted team of pickers who return every season and who can stand the fast and furious pace. These immigrant workers tend to return to the same large vineyards year after year, where they work in highly efficient teams which are normally preferred to individual travellers. Meanwhile migrant workers from Eastern Europe especially Poland have been coming in large numbers (an estimated 110,000 each year), often via agents in their countries, and accepting lower wages than the SMIC.

How to Find Work

ANPEs are not always the best informed source of temporary job information. Jason Davies describes his experiences with them:

> At the end of August I phoned the ANPE at Bordeaux and was informed that the vendange was going to start early, about September 4th or 5th. So I worked a week's notice at my restaurant in Nice and set off for Bordeaux. When I arrived I went to the ANPE for addresses to contact. 'Oh no, not yet,' said the pretty girl behind the desk (whom I would have liked to put through the window). 'The vendange won't be starting until the 25th at the earliest. It's a bit late this year,' she added. In Avignon the ANPE was just as unhelpful. 'We are no longer concerned with the vendange here'. Altogether I was amazed at the incompetence and uselessness of the ANPEs. If I ever use them again, I will be very cautious with the advice they offer.

Provided you are prepared to disregard their negative advice, there is no harm in visiting the local ANPE in a wine-growing region on the off-chance that they will be able (and willing) to tell you which farmers need workers. Rizla Plus was told by the ANPE in Saumur, as well as the tourist office, a *maison de vin* and a private employment agency 'C'est complet.' Undaunted he headed east along the Loire and, after a ten-mile walk though the vineyards, found a job.

When Michael Jordan (not the basketball legend) was looking for grape-picking work in Alsace, he noticed that every *mairie* had a poster up advising job-seekers to present themselves to the ANPE in Colmar. That office had set up a special *Service Vendanges* in a courtyard where addresses were given out at the discretion of ANPE staff. They wouldn't give Michael any addresses, not because he was American but because he confessed that he didn't have a car and there were no more vacancies at farms with accommodation. David Loveless was told by the ANPE in Sélestat (16A pl. Marche aux Choux) also in the Alsace region that 50 people searching for *vendange* jobs were being turned away daily. David happened to meet some travellers in Riquewihr (near the main Alsatian town of Colmar) who advised him to try the local wine-grower. He was promptly hired for three weeks and was even offered a bonus as an incentive to come back the next season. Because of its more northerly location, Alsace can be very cold during the harvest, which puts some potential competition off.

Below are listed the addresses of major ANPEs in the wine-producing regions, with rough guidelines as to the starting dates of the harvest. It should be stressed that these dates can vary by days or even weeks from year to year. In the very hot summer of 2003, the harvest in Beaujolais started a full month early. Even vineyards a few miles apart may start picking up to a week apart.

Alsace – October 15th
ANPE, 20 rue Georges Wodli, 67081 Strasbourg Cedex (03-88 21 42 70).
ANPE, 54 ave de la République, 68021 Colmar Cedex (tel/fax 03-89 20 80 70)
Beaujolais – September 10th
ANPE, 1 Place Faubert, 69665 Villefranche-sur-Saone Cedex (04-74 60 30 03).
Bordeaux – September 25th
ANPE, 1 Terrasse du Front du Médoc, 33076 Bordeaux (05-56 90 85 20).
ANPE, 19 rue A. Chauvet, 33250 Pauillac (05-56 73 20 50/fax 05-56 59 62 49; ale. pauillac@anpe.fr).
Burgundy – October 6th
ANPE, Maison de l'Emploi, 1000 Av Mallattre de Tassigny, 71000 Macon Cedex (03-85 21 93 20).
ANPE, 7 rue des Corroyeurs, 21000 Dijon (03-80 72 67 90).
Champagne – October 1st
ANPE, 33 bis rue Hincmar, 51057 Reims Cedex (03-26 89 52 70).
ANPE, 11 rue Jean Moet, 51331 Epernay Cedex (03-26 51 01 33).
Languedoc-Roussillon – September 15th
ANPE, 10 rue Léon Paul Fargue, 66042 Perpignan Cedex (04-68 63 69 00).
ANPE, 90 avenue Pierre Sémard, 11009 Carcassonne Cedex (04-68 10 30 00).
ANPE, 79 rue Christian Martinez, 30910 Nimes Cedex 2 (04-66 04 90 90).
ANPE, rue du 19 Mars 1962, 30205 Bagnols sur Cèze Cedex (04-66 90 59 80).
ANPE, 31 quai du Port Neuf, CS 641, 34536 Beziers Cedex (04-67 11 80 60).
Loire – October 6th
ANPE, 9 rue du Docteur Herpin, 37027 Tours Cedex (02-47 60 58 58).
ANPE, 6 Square Lafayette, 49000 Angers (02-41 24 17 20).

These are the most famous wine-making regions but there are many others. K. McCausland recommends the Savoie as being off the beaten track of job-seekers. The villages of Apremont, Montmélian and Les Marches near Chambery are recommended. The harvest here begins approximately October 1st. He also recommends trying to get a job picking table grapes in the département of Lot. It is harder work (because you have to be careful not to damage the fruit) but the wages are higher and the work lasts longer than for the *vendange*.

For those who do not want to beard the ANPE lion, there is an easier way. A Dutch agency called Appellation Controllée (+31 50-549 2434; project2@bart.nl; www.apcon.nl) mediates between grape-growers (in Beaujolais, Maconnais, Burgundy and Chablis) and Europeans looking for jobs in the *vendange*. Work lasts between one and three weeks in September. In exchange for working eight hours a day, seven days a week you will earn €50 a day plus get full board and lodging. The ApCon agency fee is £85 (€99).

The demand for pickers in all regions is highly unpredictable. Whereas there is usually a glut of pickers looking for work at the beginning of the harvest (early to mid-September), there is sometimes a shortage later on in the month. Harvests differ dramatically from year to year; a late spring frost can wreak havoc. The element of uncertainty makes it very difficult to fix a starting date from afar.

Experienced grape-pickers recommend visiting or phoning farms well before the harvest starts and asking the farmer to keep a job open. According to Jon Loop the key to success is serial phoning: *'The best time to phone is July. Then phone in August to ask when to phone for starting dates. Then phone in September to say you are coming, to ask when it starts. You may also have to phone a week before the start to confirm.'*

If you are hunting in person, it is advisable to visit farmers in small villages far from the big towns where there is a superfluity of job seekers once the harvest starts. Also check the CIJ and university notice boards, for example the one in the cafeteria at the University of Dijon. As usual, a village bar is often the hub of activity during the *vendange* as Keith Flynn found to be the case in Chateauneuf de Pape (which incidentally is where the famous system of *appellation controlée* was invented): *'One of the easiest ways of finding work is to go to the one and only bar in town across from the tourist office. All the workers go there in the evening and a lot of the bosses so just ask everybody. There were at least 30 or 40 pickers in town in the middle of September and more arriving; yet everybody seemed to have plenty of work.'*

While some job-seekers do succeed by trudging from vineyard to vineyard on foot to ask for work, there are alternatives. After badly blistering his feet on the country roads near Montpellier, Stephen Hands recommends borrowing or hiring a bicycle. More recently Rob Abblett spent a very discouraging few days hunting in several regions, including near Nimes: 'On foot without a tent I had no luck at all as no one had accommodation'. He did eventually find work in Chateauneuf du Pape but had to live in a big shed with no facilities. He later learned from some regular *vendangeurs* that he might have found it easier to find work in Beaujolais.

Phoning is a more leisurely option for French speakers though it too can be discouraging, as one working traveller found: *'I had nothing fixed up in advance and the ANPE in Bordeaux was no help. So I got a Yellow Pages from the main post office, picked the famous appellation controlée of Margaux and started phoning. I got about 25 chateaux down the list, which was pretty disheartening, when Chateau Prieure-Lachine told me I could start on Monday.'* Look up *viticulteurs* or *producteurs négociants*.

Jon Loop found the Syndicat d'Initiative (tourist office) in Cursac Fort Médoc very helpful in obtaining vineyard addresses. Always enquire at the *départementale* office rather than the city one. Many rural towns have a *chambre d'agriculture, maison d'agriculture,* a *syndicat général des vignerons* or a *conseil inter-professionel du vin,* all of which may have leads.

Alison Cooper was not immediately successful when she doggedly tried to find a job through the Co-op in Limoux (between Perpignan and Toulouse). Success came in the end not through the Co-op but by a stroke of good fortune: *'Fate intervened when a Portuguese and a Frenchman turned up at the Co-op in a car, with an address of a vineyard which might need five workers. I got into that car immediately with two Spaniards and we all ended up with jobs. First class French cuisine and a bed were provided (for a deduction of £10 a day) and I earned £250 tax free in ten days.'*

OTHER HARVESTS

Although the *vendange* may produce the highest concentration of seasonal work, there are tremendous opportunities for participating in other harvests and with potentially less competition for the available work. While increasing mechanisation threatens the future of grape-picking by hand, there are not yet any machines which can cope with apples, plums, peaches and olives.

One longstanding source of seasonal work is maize castration or maize topping *(l'écimage)* which consists of picking off the flowers of the male maize plants. Demand for temporary workers has fallen sharply over the years partly because of the introduction of a sterile maize plant. According to the ANPE in Riom in the Auvergne (4 allée des Tilleuls, 63201 Riom Cedex; 04-73 64 45 10), the working period lasts only three to seven days, no accommodation is provided and the starting date is not known until the very last minute, which make it impractical for people from outside the region to look for work with maize farmers. Nevertheless travellers do still find maize work (see section on the Loire Valley below).

France is an overwhelmingly rural country. The *départements* of Hérault, Drôme and Gers are among the most prolific fruit and vegetable producers, especially of plums, cherries, strawberries and apples. Crops ripen first in the south of the country, and first at lower altitudes, so it is difficult to generalise about starting dates. For example the strawberry harvest on the coastal plain around Beziers normally takes place between mid-May and late June, whereas 60km inland in the Haut Languedoc near Sauclieres, it starts in mid-July. Cherries and strawberries are the first harvests, normally taking place between May and July. Blueberries are picked throughout July and August. Peaches are picked from June after the trees have been pruned, while pears are picked throughout the summer but especially (like apples) from mid-September to mid-October. Apples are grown throughout France including in Normandy.

> **The Belgian traveller Vincent Crombez wrote from the village of Monetier-Allemont (between Gap and Sisteron) to recommend this area of the Hautes-Alpes south of Grenoble:**
> *Apple picking starts about the 1st of September and lasts until the end of October. I was paid the SMIC and worked 9 or 10 hours a day every day except Sunday. It's no problem to save £400+ a month if you don't go to the only pub in this wonderful village every day. Now I'm back here for the apple thinning. I'm working 9 hours a day, but it's easy, always sunny and I will save £800 for the two months.*

Sarit Moas from Israel found it very worthwhile asking a fruit weigher at one of the open markets in Paris about harvesting work: *'The owner of the market stand answered, 'Why do you want to do tedious backbreaking picking?' In the end he offered me a job working with him selling from 6am to 2pm. I'd assemble the fruit stands with him five days a week and receive £25 daily.'*

Harvest work is paid either hourly (normally the SMIC) or by piece rates. If you are floundering with piece work, you may be transferred to a different job where you can earn an hourly wage as happened to Brendan Barker a few years ago when he was picking plums in the Bordeaux area:

> *For the first two days we were on picking duty as part of a team, though we were marked down individually for each crate we filled. The rate was roughly £1 a crate and some of the people were doing 30-35 even 40 crates a day. My girlfriend and I were hitting a measly 15 crates – inexperienced and unfit. So on the third day we were put on the factory line where the incoming wounded plums were sorted out and put onto wooden trays for the three giant furnaces that would shrivel them into prunes. For this work we were put on the SMIC which was better for us financially though we had the patron (an ex-military man) barking down our necks 'Allez vite, quick, rapido' for the benefit of the French, the Portuguese and us.*

It is normally up to workers to provide their own food and accommodation, and so a tent and camping equipment are essential. If a farmer does provide board and lodging he will normally deduct the equivalent of two hours' wages from your daily pay packet. If you are planning to leave as soon as the harvest is over, bear in mind that agricultural wages are often not paid until seven to ten days after the harvest finishes (to ensure workers do not leave prematurely). Furthermore the wages may have to be cashed at a local bank, so be prepared to hang around.

In addition to fruit picking there are many other kinds of work which travellers end up doing, from cheese making to haymaking. There may be late autumn work pruning vines and orchards. Poultry farms (especially in the Anjou area) are often looking for chicken-catchers-cum-lorry-loaders who are (not surprisingly) paid fairly well.

The Avignon Region

All manner of fruit is grown in the Rhône Valley in the vicinity of Avignon. Working travellers have achieved long spells of continuous employment in the *départements* of Vaucluse and Ardèche by following the different harvests. In late July go to the Ile de Barthelasse, which is a 16km-long island in the River Rhône near Avignon which is entirely given over to fruit and vegetable growing. The village of Aubignan has several sheds where melons, courgettes, peppers and apricots are packed in September. Grape-picking could follow in nearby Vacqueyras and carries on till mid-November on the high slopes of Mont Ventoux. Those with stamina could head north to Privas in the Ardèche where chestnuts are picked in the frost.

Stuart Bellworthy looked for work in this area. Having started in Lyon, it wasn't until he got to Avignon with its massive fruit distribution centres and the Ile de Barthelasse with its promising sounding street names (Chemin des Vignes, Chemins des Raisins) that he became optimistic:

> I spent a whole (very hot!) day wandering around the Ile de Barthelasse, without any luck (though I have never eaten so much fruit in my life free of charge). Just up the road from Camping Etoile (a very cheap campsite near Avignon just on the island) there is a map of the island and a list of all the producteurs. It is worth starting at the north of the island since the farmers nearest Avignon probably get asked for jobs about every ten minutes. After I was convinced there were no jobs, I travelled 10km south to Chateaurenard and found a pear-picking job. All the roads to the north of Chateaurenard are lined with farms. The villages of St Remy, Barbentane and Rognons are also good. The pear season lasts from mid-July to early August.

Stuart goes on to recommend visiting the nearby Marché d'International (preferably at about 5am) and asking the farmers for work either on their farms or helping with their market stalls.

Through meeting people at the Koala Bar in Avignon Dustie Hickey fixed up a job picking olives between early November and late December in St Remy. She says that she would happily do this work again since it was so peaceful, and furthermore she earned some decent money:

> We worked at Mas de la Dame, a place where Van Gogh painted. The job involved climbing ladders but as I'm light I would climb right into the trees (best view!) and comb, comb, comb the branches so the olives would fall into the net below. When the tree is cleared, you have to pick out all the twigs and leaves and roll the olives into the crates. It's very satisfying to fill a few crates from one tree (but not at all satisfying when the net turns out to be too small. It is easy to rent cheap accommodation in St Remy at this time of year. The only problem was transport: although there is a bus to Avignon there is no off-season service south to Les Baux de Provence.

The Loire Valley

Strawberries, apples, pears and many other crops can be found along the River Loire: the towns of Segré, Angers and Saumur are especially recommended. For example the strawberry harvest around Varennes-sur-Loire lasts six to eight weeks from early/mid April.

Two unusual crops are grown round Saumur, both of which are picked from the beginning of July, mushrooms and blueberries. While working on a farm in Kent, Andrew Pattinson-Hughes found out that the farm secretary owned a blueberry farm in Brain-sur-Allonnes, a few kilometres north of Saumur:

> After hounding her to write us a letter of recommendation, she gave in. I borrowed

*money from my dad for the coach fare to Tours, then caught a train to Saumur and
an over-priced taxi to the farm, Anjou Myrtilles (myrtille is French for blueberry). The
farmer spoke fluent English and agreed to hire us. It's easy to earn £40 a day. We
stayed on a campsite in Brain-sur Allonnes about a 40 minute walk away, as the farm
is in the middle of the sticks.*

They continued picking until the end of August and then moved on to the apple harvest in the
nearby village of Parcay les Pins where earnings were around £500 per month for up to two
months. In these circumstances it is very easy to save most of your earnings.

Karen Martin and Paul Ansell found work castrating maize in the Loire Valley which
was paid at SMIC rates:

*While we were in Amsterdam we looked on the internet and found the Dutch agency
Appellation Controllé who mediate between workers and farmers in England, Denmark, Holland and France. They charged a fee and got us work doing maize castration on a farm where two people had dropped out (God bless 'em). We made our
way by hitching from Angers and were greeted by the farmer Bernard and his wife
Merielle with lovely cherry wine. They speak little English but it was not an obstacle.
You camp on the farm for a pound a day and have good facilities.*

The proprietors cooked barbecues for them, washed clothes and were generally very
hospitable and Karen and Paul were delighted to be invited back soon afterwards for a
month's apple picking which allowed them to save £1,000 between them. Karen thinks
that they were among the first non-French workers here but the farmer expressed interest
in hosting more foreign young people at this farm which is about 20 miles east of Angers;
contact Earl le Chêne du Mensonge, Hye, Bernard, Porteau, 49350 Les Rosiers sur Loire;
02-41 51 90 27.

Apple picking takes place around Tour throughout September and October. In the village of Breches try M. Sohier (02-47 24 03 05; msohier@terre-net.fr).

Organic Farms

The national organisation Sésame fixes up *stages* or work experience placements for agricultural trainees of all nationalities on French organic farms (9 Square Gabriel Fauré, Paris
75017; 01-40 54 07 08; sesame@agriplanete.com; www.agriplanete.com). Their brochure
and website are in English as well as French.

Although the organic movement is powerful in France, there is no independent
WWOOF organisation that maintains an up-to-date list of organic farmers looking for
volunteers. However the International List from WWOOF Australia (see *Agriculture*) lists
more than 260 addresses in France, many of them farms run by expatriates or by exiles
from the big city; descriptions without addresses can be seen on the web page wwoof.
org/frdepart.html. The atmosphere on this kind of farm is often different from that on purely
commercial farms, though you will still be expected to work hard. Most temporary workers
hear of farms like this by word of mouth *(de bouche à l'oreille)*, but it is always polite to ring
or write ahead rather than show up unannounced. The kind of information they are interested in includes your background, age, experience, whether or not you are vegetarian,
mode of travel (preferably a bicycle) and of course dates of intended visit.

TEACHING

So many expatriates live in Paris and throughout France that being a native speaker of
English does not cut much ice with prospective employers of English teachers. Without a
TEFL qualification, BA or commercial flair (preferably all three) it is very difficult to get a
teaching contract. Of course if you can make yourself look ultra-presentable and have an
impressive CV, you should ring to make appointments and then tramp round all the possible schools to leave your CV. (As is usual in Europe, there is virtually no hope of success

in July and August.)

The technique of making a personal approach to schools in the months preceding the one in which you would like to teach is often successful. On the strength of her Cambridge Certificate from International House, Fiona Paton had been hoping to find teaching work in the south of France in the summer but quickly discovered that there are very few opportunities outside the academic year. On her way back to England, she disembarked from the train in the picturesque town of Vichy in the Auvergne just long enough to distribute a few self-promotional leaflets to three language schools. She was very surprised to receive a favourable reply from one of them once she was home, and so returned a few weeks later for a happy year of teaching.

In Paris many schools advertise in the *métro*, or you can look up addresses in the Yellow Pages under *Enseignements Privé de Langues* or *Ecoles de Langues*. A great many of these cater for the business market, so anything relevant in your background should be emphasised. Most schools pay between €15 and €25 (gross) per lesson. As is increasingly common, schools are reluctant to take on contract teachers for whom they would be obliged to pay taxes and social security, and so there is a bustling market in freelance teachers who work for themselves and are prepared to teach just a few hours a week for one employer.

Partly because of France's proximity to a seemingly inexhaustible supply of willing English teachers, working conditions in France are seldom brilliant. Although Andrew Boyle enjoyed his year teaching English in Lyon and the chance to become integrated into an otherwise impenetrable community, he concluded that even respectable schools treated teachers as their most expendable commodity, a view corroborated by the veteran traveller Jayne Nash who lasted only three months in Le Havre: *'Thirty plus hour weeks (not including preparation time), irregular hours at any time between 8am and 8pm with last-minute classes to cover for absent colleagues, and classes of mixed ability, soon took their toll. The money wasn't that good either. I felt my employer cared little for his employees. After three months I found myself under so much stress that I was obliged to leave, although I am normally not someone to shun a challenge or responsibility.'*

A more realistic possibility is to offset the high cost of living in Paris by doing some tutoring which sometimes shades into au pairing. Language exchanges for room and board are commonplace in Paris and are usually arranged through advertisements (in the places described below in the section on Paris) or by word of mouth.

This is a good way for Americans and others to circumvent red tape difficulties as Beth Mayer from New York found in Paris:

> I tried to get a job at a school teaching, but they asked for working papers which I didn't have. I checked with several schools who told me that working papers and a university degree were more important than TEFL qualifications. So I placed an ad to teach English and offer editing services (I was an editor in New York City before moving here) and received many responses. I charged a decent fee but after I had spent time going and coming, I earned only half that. It would be better to have the lessons at your apartment if centrally located. I not only 'taught' English but offered English conversation to French people who wanted practice. I met a lot of nice people this way and earned money to boot.

This is most commonly done in Paris though it can work just as easily in other French cities. The usual methods of advertising in local newspapers, sticking up photocopied ads in libraries and stores such as Prisunic supermarkets could work. A telephone and answering machine are great assets in the initial stages. Conversation classes with adults are easier than teaching children but tend to pay less well.

University language students who would like to spend a year as an English language *assistant* in a French school should contact the Language Assistants Team of the Education & Training Group of the British Council, 10 Spring Gardens, London SW1A 2BN; 020-7389 4596; assistants@britishcouncil.org). They send hundreds of undergraduates studying French at British universities and recent graduates aged 20-30 to spend an academic year in primary or secondary schools throughout France. Assistants only work 12 hours a week and are paid about €900 (gross) a month. Similar posts are also available in other francophone countries, i.e. Belgium, Québec (Canada), Switzerland, Tunisia and Senegal. As mentioned earlier, Americans can also become *assistants* for seven months from October to April through the French Embassy.

CHILDCARE

Au pairing has always been a favoured way for young women to learn French and, increasingly, for young men too. The pocket money for au pairs in France is linked to the *SMIC* and is currently €65-€75 per 30-hour week plus a city transport pass. Au pairs plus should earn €95 for a 35-hour week and nannies far more. Dozens of agencies both in Britain (see list in *Childcare* chapter) and in France arrange placements. Most agencies make enrolling in a French course a necessary condition.

CIJ offices and even ANPEs may have a list of families looking for live-in help, and this is the one category of work for which fluent French is unlikely to be a necessity. In Paris, the notice boards described below are always crammed with announcements of live-in positions and so there is little chance of being left jobless if you wait until arrival to look.

Quite a few foreigners are too hasty in arranging what seems at the outset a cushy number and only gradually realise how little they enjoy the company of children and how isolated they are if their family lives in the suburbs (as most do). Unless you actively like small children, it might be better to look for a free room in exchange for minimal babysitting (e.g. 12 hours a week). Matt Tomlinson went into his au pair job with his eyes open:

I'd heard too many horror stories from overworked and underpaid au pair friends to be careless, so chose quite carefully from the people who replied to my notice on the upstairs notice board of the British Church (just off the rue de Faubourg St Honoré). My employers were really laid back, in their mid-20s so more like living with an older brother and sister. The little boy was just over two whilst the little girl was three months old, and they were both completely adorable. On the whole it was great fun. Baking chocolate brownies, playing football and finger-painting may not be everybody's idea of a good time but there are certainly worse ways to earn a living (and learn French at the same time).

Although it is still more difficult for men than women to find au pair placements, France seems to be streets ahead of Britain in this respect, as Iain Croker reports:
I have had a thoroughly rewarding and enjoyable year as an au pair in France – so much so that I'm going back again in September for another year. Certainly in France there are quite a few male au pairs – four in my village near Fontainebleau alone. In my experience the boys tend to get placed in families with a lot of energetic children or families that have traditionally had a large turn-over of au pairs. After a year in the sticks with four kids I feel I have proved myself and my agency have offered me one of their best placements in Paris, one child and my own apartment. By the way, my agency (Soames International) is great.

Applying directly through a French agency is commonplace. The most established agencies are members of UFAAP, the Union Francaise des Associations Au Pair, an umbrella group set up in 1999, currently with its headquarters in the Oliver Twist Association agency below (www.ufaap.org). Member agencies are linked from their website. While some agencies charge nothing, others charge a registration fee which can be steep (€160+). The online matching service www.frenchaupairs.com is free to au pairs.

Here are some agencies to contact:

Alliance Francaise, 310 rue Paradie, 13008 Marseille (04-96 10 24 60;

info@alliancefrmarseille.org).

L'Arche, 53 rue de Gergovie, 75014 Paris (tel/fax 01-45 45 46 39).

Association Familles & Jeunesse, 4 rue Masséna, 06000 Nice (04-93 82 28 22; info@afj-aupair.org; www.afj-aupair.org). Places more than 300 au pair girls and boys, mainly in the South of France plus the French Riviera and Corsica.

Association Mary Poppins, 4 place de la Fontaine, 38120 la Fontanil, St Egrève (04-76 75 57 33; Mary.Poppins@wanadoo.fr; http://assoc.wanadoo.fr/marypoppins.aupair).

Butterfly et Papillon, 5 avenue de Genève, 74000 Annecy (04-50 67 01 33; aupair.france@wanadoo.fr).

Euro Pair Services, 13 rue Vavin, 75006 Paris (01-43 29 80 01; europairservices@wanadoo.fr).

France Au Pair - Eurojobs, 6 Allée des Saules, BP 29, 17420 Saint Palais sur Mer (05-46 23 99 88; contact@eurojob.fr; www.eurojob.fr).

Institut Euro'Provence, 69 rue de Rome, 13001 Marseille (04-91 33 90 60; euro.provence@wanadoo.fr; http://perso.wanadoo.fr/euro.provence). Largest au pair agency in southern France.

Inter-Séjours, 179 rue de Courcelles, 75017 Paris (01-47 63 06 81; http://asso.intersejours.free.fr).

Nurse Au Pair Placement, 16 rue Le Sueur, 75116 Paris (1-45 00 33 88; nappsarl@aol.com/ www.napp.fr). Australian-run agency for nannies, maternity nurses, mother's helps and au pairs.

Oliver Twist Association, 7 rue Léon Morin, 33600 Pessac (05-57 26 93 26; fax 05-56 36 21 85; oliver.twist@wanadoo.fr).

Soames Paris Nannies, 64 rue Anatole France, 92300 Levallois Perrec (01-47 30 44 04; contact@soamesparisnannies.com).

By law, families are supposed to make social security payments to the local URSSAF office on the au pair's behalf, though not all do and you might want to enquire about this when applying. Au pairs in or near Paris should receive the *carte orange* (monthly travel pass) which is worth about €50.

North Americans can fix up au pair placements directly with a French agency, bearing in mind that the placement fees must be paid in advance and that in some cases little information about the family is available in advance.

BUSINESS & INDUSTRY

You will normally need impeccable French in order to work in a French office which eliminates the sort of temping jobs you may have had back home. If you are lucky enough to get a job in a French office – as Ben Nakoneczny did through a family connection – you may find yourself benefitting from such perks as a subsidised canteen serving French food and wine. With no contacts, Michael Jordan from St Louis Missouri had no luck when he mounted a job search in his field in Strasbourg which involved cycling round all the bakeries at 2am.

Fee-paying training programmes can provide an opening to employment and boost the quality of a participant's CV. Andy Green participated in a scheme run by Interspeak and spent two months in an office in Limoges. As is usual with placements in France, Andy's *stage* was on an unpaid basis, yet he still considered the £1,000 investment worthwhile for the experience. Interspeak also offer *mini-stages* which last just one or two weeks. These appeal mostly to 16-18 year olds whose parents are willing to spend £340 on the placement fee.

A cheaper way to find a base in France from which to improve your knowledge of the language is to participate in the work exchange programme offered by the Centre International d'Antibes, a French language school on the Côte d'Azur. Volunteers with the right to work in Europe do administrative or domestic work in exchange for board and lodging and/or French tuition. Details of the scheme are available from CIA, 38 Boulevard d'Aguillon,

06600 Antibes (04-92 90 71 70; info@cia-france.com).

Anyone with secretarial skills and a knowledge of French has a chance of finding office work, particularly in Paris. The Syndicat des Entreprises de Travail Temporaire (SETT, 54-56 rue Lafitte, 75009 Paris) should be able to provide a list of temporary agencies specialising in bilingual secretarial staff. The Sheila Burgess Agency in Paris specialises in placing bilingual secretaries (62 rue St Lazare, 75009 Paris; 01-44 63 02 57).

A number of British-run building firms (not all of them licensed) are active in areas like the Dordogne where many English people build homes. You are more likely to come across building work informally as the American Peter Goldman did:

I was hitching south from Paris when a kind woman stopped near Tours. She was heading to her farm house near Bordeaux where a Dutchman was putting a new roof on the house. I explained that I had some experience in construction and I was hired on the spot. I worked for ten days, received good wages plus tons of food, beer and wine and a bed. The Dutchman was happy with my work and took me to Biddary near Bayonne to help him renovate another house. There I earned a small wage on top of all living expenses, learned a lot about European building methods, rural France and met some great people.

It can be profitable to let your fingers do the walking when you are in France: the telephone directory (www.pagesjaunes.fr) can be an invaluable ally when you are looking for new addresses to contact. Here are a few headings to look under: *Publicité direct* and *Distributeurs en publicité* for jobs handing out leaflets (a job which www.phosphore.com describes accurately as 'un job harassant mais facile à trouver'), *Démenagement* for house removals, *Entreprises de nettoyage* for domestic work cleaning houses and *Surveillance* for security work. Leaflet distribution pays either according to the number you offload or by the day, typically €60 for seven hours plus overtime. Another job readily available to French speakers is *animateur de supermarché*, i.e. product promotion in supermarkets.

VOLUNTARY OPPORTUNITIES

France has as wide a range of opportunities for voluntary work as any European country, and anyone who is prepared to exchange work for subsidised board and lodging should consider joining a voluntary project. Projects normally last two or three weeks during the summer and cost between €8 and €18 a day. Many foreign young people join one of these to learn basic French and make French contacts as well as to have fun.

Archaeology

A great many archaeological digs and building restoration projects are carried out each year. Every May the Ministry of Culture (Direction de l'Architecture et du Patrimoine, Sous-Direction de l'Archéologie, 4 rue d'Aboukir, 75002 Paris; 01-40 15 77 81) publishes a national list of summer excavations throughout France requiring up to 5,000 volunteers which can be consulted on its website (www.culture.gouv.fr/fouilles). Most *départements* have *Services Archéologiques* which organise digs. Without relevant experience you will probably be given only menial jobs but many like to share in the satisfaction of seeing progress made.

Anthony Blake describes the dig he joined which the History Department of the University of Le Mans runs every summer: *'Archaeology is hard work. Applicants must be aware of what working 8.30am-noon and 2-6.30pm in baking heat means! That said, I thoroughly enjoyed the working holiday: excellent company (75% French so fine opportunity to practise French), weekends free after noon on Saturday, good lunches in SNCF canteen, evening meals more haphazard as prepared by fellow diggers. Accommodation simple but adequate.'*

Unskilled volunteers are charged a small contribution for their board and lodging. For example every July M. Louis Roussel (28 rue du Bourg, 21000 Dijon; malain_gam@hotmail.com) takes 20 volunteers to work on a Gallo-Roman site outside Dijon; volunteers contribute €15 per week. Further north the Service Archéologique of the Musée de la Chartreuse (191 rue St-Albin, 59500 Douai; 03-27 71 38 90; p.demolou@douaisis-agglo.com) carries out summer digs on a Mérovingian abbey and mediaeval town. The registration fee here is €22.87.

Conservation

France takes the preservation of its heritage *(patrimoine)* very seriously and there are numerous groups both local and national engaged in restoring churches, windmills, forts and other historic monuments. Many are set up to accept foreign volunteers, though they tend to charge more than archaeological digs:

APARE/GEC, Association pour la Participation et l'Action Régionale, 25 Boulevard Paul Pors, 84800 L'Isle sur la Sorgue (04-90 85 51 15; www.apare-gec.org). An umbrella organisation that runs volunteer workcamps at historic sites in Provence (plus a few in Morocco and Lebanon). Cost of €91 for 2 weeks, €124 for 3 weeks.

Chantier Histoire et Architecture Médiévale (CHAM), 5-7 rue Guilleminot, Paris 75014 (01-43 35 15 51; www.cham.asso.fr). Paris-based organisation that runs volunteer projects to protect historic buildings, not just in mainland France but in farflung places including Reunion Island (a *département* of France in the Indian Ocean near Mauritius) and in Africa. The address of the delegation in La Réunion is 25 rue Mahé, La Mare, 97438 Sainte Marie, Ile de la Réunion (02-62 53 27 98; CHAM-REUNION@wanadoo.fr). See the CHAM website (which is in English) for details.

Club du Vieux Manoir, Ancienne Abbaye du Moncel, 60700 Pontpoint (03-44 72 33 98; www.clubduvieuxmanoir.free.fr). 15-day summer workcamp to restore ancient monuments. Board and lodging cost €14 per day.

REMPART, 1 rue des Guillemites, 75004 Paris (01-42 71 96 55; www.rempart.com). Similar to the National Trust in Britain, in charge of endangered monuments throughout France. Most projects charge €7 per day plus €40 for membership and insurance. Registration must be done by post.

La Sabranenque, Centre International, rue de la Tour de l'Oume, 30290 Saint Victor la Coste (04-66 50 05 05; www.sabranenque.com). $630-$710 per fortnight. US applicants should contact Jacqueline Simon, 124 Bondcroft Drive, Buffalo, NY 14226 (716-836-8698).

UNAREC (Etudes et Chantiers), Délégué International, 3 rue des Petits Gras, 63000 Clermont-Ferrand (04-73 31 98 04; www.unarec.org). Hundreds of international volunteers for short-term conservation projects and longer-term professional training. €115 fee includes accommodation and insurance for 2-3 week workcamps.

Try to be patient if the project you choose turns out to have its drawbacks, since these organisations depend on voluntary leaders as well as participants. Judy Greene volunteered to work with a conservation organisation and felt herself to be 'personally victimised by the lack of organisation and leadership' or more specifically by one unpleasantly racist individual on her project. Tolerance may be called for, especially if your fellow volunteers lack it.

PARIS

Like all major cities in the developed world, Paris presents thousands of ways to earn your keep, while being difficult to afford from day to day. Unless you are very lucky, you will have to arrive with some money with which to support yourself while you look around. When house-hunting, check notice boards (see below) and local papers or (if you can afford it) use an agency which will cost you at least a month's rent but will help to ensure that you get your deposit of two months' rent back.

The Grapevine

Expatriate grapevines flourish all over Paris and are very helpful for finding work and accommodation. Most people find their jobs as well as accommodation through one of the city's many notice boards *(panneaux)*. The one in the foyer of the CIDJ at 101 Quai Branly (*métro* Bir-Hakeim) is good for occasional studenty-type jobs such as extras in movies, but sometimes there are adverts for full-time jobs or *soutien scolaire en Anglais* (English tutor). It is worth arriving early to check for new notices (the hours for most CIDJ services are Monday-Friday 9.30am-6pm and Saturday 9.30am-1pm). They also have a telephone information service now on 0825 09 06 30.

The other mecca for job and flat-hunters is the American Church at 65 Quai d'Orsay (01-40 62 05 00; *métro* Invalides). Official notices are posted on various notice boards inside and out; the cork board in the basement is a free board where anybody can stick up a notice. You will bump into lots of other people studying the board here, and so it is a good place to make contacts. Obviously it is necessary to consult the notices in person; they are not available by phoning the church or on the internet. Also pick up the free monthly magazine *Paris Voice*.

The American Cathedral in Paris at 23 avenue George V (www.us.net/amcathedral-paris; *métro* Alma Marceau or George V) has a notice board featuring employment opportunities and housing listings. The Cathedral also offers volunteering opportunities as well as career forums for job-seekers. Also check the two British churches though there are few employment or language exchange notices: St Georges Anglican at 7 rue Auguste-Vacquerie in the 16th *arrondissement* and its sister church St Michael's at 5 rue d'Aguesseau in the 8th (*Métro* Madeleine). These churches are happy to provide notice boards as a way of helping people get settled in Paris but they are churches not employment agencies.

The British Institute at 11 rue de Constantine has a notice board with some live-in tutoring and au pair jobs. Although the notice board at the Alliance Francaise (101 Boulevard Raspail near the *métro* Notre Dame des Champs; www.alliancefr.org) is for the use of registered students of French, you may be able to persuade a student to look at the adverts for you, many of which are exchanges of room for some babysitting and/or teaching. The notice board is in the annex around the corner at 34 rue de Fleurus.

Arguably the most eccentric bookshop in Europe is Shakespeare and Company at 37 rue de la Bûcherie in the fifth *arrondissement* (on the south side of the Seine). It has a large notice board and is also useful as a place to chat to other expats about work and accommodation. The shop operates as a writer's guest house. If you are prepared to write a short account of yourself and pitch in with a few chores you can stay free for a limited period, assuming there is space. The elderly American expat owner George Whitman still hosts weekly Sunday open house for aspiring *literati* and also hires English-speaking staff to clean, run errands and work behind the till.

Hannah Adcock describes herself as a 'rather solemn' eighteen year old when she read an earlier edition of this book and set off for Paris:
Soon after, I found myself living at this hippy Parisien bookstore with a view of Notre Dame, a treat of inedible pancakes to look forward to and orders to clean the floor using newspaper and cold water. Kids staying at Shakespeare's do most of the jobs for free. You'll only get a paid job if (a) the owner really likes you, (b) you went to a university like Cambridge or Harvard and (c) you're really cute. The room overlooking Notre Dame is lovely but when I was there it smelt foul and a highly evolved species of bed bug lurked, as big as rats (ok – exaggeration). Shakespeare's is brilliant, but working there has its 'interesting' aspects!

Most expat places like WH Smith Bookshop near the Place de la Concorde and the Virgin Megastore on the Champs Elysées distribute the free bilingual English newsletter *France-USA Contacts* or *FUSAC* (www.fusac.org) which comes out every other Wednesday. *FUSAC* comprises mainly classified adverts including some for English teachers which are best followed up on the day the paper appears. It is possible to place an ad before your arrival in France. An advert under the heading 'Work Wanted in France' costs US$24 for 20 words, and can be e-mailed to franceusa@aol.com or sent in the US to France Contacts at PO Box 115, Coopers Station, New York, NY 10276; 212-777-5553/fax 212-

777-5554). Another possible source of job and accommodation leads is the weekly free ads paper *J'Annonce*.

The online community noticeboard Gumtree that has been so successful in London has just started up in Paris at www.gumtree.fr. As usual, pubs are a good place to pick up job tips. Try any of Paris's growing number of Irish pubs including Tigh Johnny's (55 rue Montmartre), Molly Malone's (21 rue de Godot de Maure in the 9th arrondissement) or Kitty O'Shea's at 10 rue des Capucines on the right bank.

Disneyland Paris

The enormous complex of Disneyland Paris, 30km east of Paris at Marne-la-Vallée, employs about 12,000 people in high season, both on long-term and seasonal contracts. Seasonal positions from March or May to September are open to EU nationals or others with permission to work in the EU. The minimum period covers the high season from the end of June to the end of August.

'Cast members' (Disneyspeak for employees) must all have a conversational level of French and preferably a third European language. The only positions for which you might get away with weak French is in the parades (where the emphasis is on dancing ability) or in the more menial positions as sweepers, etc. Working conditions are reasonably good, with two consecutive days off a week, reimbursed travel (most recently €76 each way from the UK) and accommodation provided in shared flats a bus-ride away from the park.

The majority of jobs are in food and beverage, housekeeping, merchandising and cus-todial departments, though one of the best jobs is as a character like Micky Mouse. The French standard working week is 35 hours long for which staff are paid a salary starting at €1,103.39 a month (gross) depending on job; social security deductions will be at least €160 and staff accommodation costs €230.20 per month. Further details are available from Service du Recrutement-Casting, Disneyland Paris, BP 110, 77777 Marne-la-Vallée Cedex 4 (www.disneylandparis.com/uk/employment).

Specific vacancies at Disneyland Paris are often registered with EURES, the Euro-pean Employment Service which can be accessed through any Jobcentre. For all jobs the well-scrubbed look is required (though the no-facial-hair rule has been dropped), and of course they are looking for the usual friendly, cheerful and outgoing personalities. Whether you will be impressed by the fringe benefits is a matter of individual taste; they consist of discounts on merchandise and in the hotels and some free entrances to the theme park itself.

Keith Leishman from Dundee was a cast member during the summer of 2003:

Getting the job was initially quite frustrating. I first sent a letter to the company around November. After another couple of letters and e-mails without reply I was just about giving up hope. Finally around March I received notification of an inter-view in Edinburgh and was offered the job. After that you are pretty much left to your own devices and simply expected to turn up at Disney the day before your contract begins. (This was rather a shock to me after working for Eurocamp the year before who provided transport to France and some preparatory material beforehand.)

I was employed on the ticketing side of operations. I had to wear a Prince Charming costume and supervise the entrance of guests to the Park, stamping their hands for readmission. This meant standing for the whole shift in what were often scorching conditions. This was very beneficial for my French as people would ask a whole range of weird and wonderful questions.

The staff apartments were comfortable enough and equipped with kitchens, though I did not cook much due to the cheapness and accessibility of Disney can-teens. I could eat well for 3 or 4 euros a day. Another of the main advantages of working at Disneyland is the mixture of nationalities. The sheer number of young people from all over the world means there are always lots of parties and bar-

becues in the residences. On days off I usually went into Paris which is only 40 minutes away on the train. I stayed for two months of the peak summer season and found it quite hard to keep up the Disney smile when I was hot and tired. The job is demanding because you are creating an illusion. All the same I would urge anybody with an interest in people and a desire to improve their French to try the experience. I intend to return at Christmas or Easter.

Specific Jobs

The job hunt in Paris doesn't get any easier, as Mark Davies described:

Although it has taken me five and a half weeks to find paid employment (plongeur in a creperie) I console myself with the fact that there is high unemployment here at the moment. To give you an example, I turned up as stated on the job notice at 5pm for a dishwashing job, and there were eight other people doing the same, and they were by no means all poor-looking immigrants. The pay for the job I'm doing now is lousy but it pays the rent while I look for something better. But as long as I'm in the Jardin du Luxembourg and the sun is shining I can't complain.

Sarit Moas from Israel doggedly enquired at all the restaurants and street food stalls until she got a job selling crepes and taffy in the Tuilleries amusement parks. Since that time Haagen-Dasz ice cream outlets have sprung up in various locations and are often hiring staff.

Pay is usually *SMIC* plus tips and one or two meals a day, although an experienced waiter with excellent French could make over €75 per night. There are many American-style fast food restaurants which employ a majority of non-French staff. Among the best known employers are the Quick chain mentioned earlier with outlets in high profile places like the Boulevard St. Michel, Boulevard Poissonniere and Place de la République, and the Chicago Pizza Pie Factory (5 rue de Berri, 75008 Paris; métro George V; 01-45 62 50 23). The related Chicago Meatpackers at 8 rue Coquillière (01-40 28 02 33; métro Les Halles) also has a high staff turnover. If you write in advance, the most that will happen is that they will write to assure you that you will be offered an interview after arrival in Paris. If you show up, you will be asked to fill out an application form before seeing the manager on duty. If you can function in French and there is a vacancy (as there often is) you could be offered a full or part-time job at SMIC rates plus tips and one meal a day.

Another chain that likes to hire English speakers is Frog Pubs (www.frogpubs.com) with five pubs in Paris (plus one in Toulouse and another in Bordeaux). They normally offer only part-time work to people who are already resident and who will work for at least six months.

Survival

Talented musicians should consider joining the army of buskers on the Left Bank on a Friday or Saturday night and graduating to the highly competitive métro. Transit authorities issue licences (free of charge) which allow you to perform in prescribed locations. Playing on the trains themselves is not allowed, though many ignore the regulations. Some of the most lucrative destinations for buskers have been proving disappointing, as talented guitarist Fergus Cooney discovered a couple of years ago:

This year, 40 accordion players from Romania swamped Montpellier and killed busking for the rest of us. Even old blokes who have played there for 20 years couldn't. The problem is that the Romanians are happy to play for pennies, which are worth a lot in Romania when they go home after the summer. And they do play – all day long. They have incredible toleration of the afternoon heat. Romanians have really swamped France, in fact. I couldn't believe it when I heard the Parisian prostitutes had gone on strike and went on a demo/march through the streets protesting about the Romanian women stealing their customers.

It has been mentioned elsewhere in this book that English churches are often helpful sources of contacts. Jonathan Poulton found himself very short of money in Menton (near Monte Carlo) after discovering that the starting date of his job in a patisserie had been postponed. He wandered into the English church which happened to be next door, explained his situation to the vicar and within five minutes had secured a job as a gardener for one of the congregation. Religious foundations also run many emergency shelters and free hostels throughout France, mostly for men only.

Julian Peachey made use of the Night Shelter in Marseille when he arrived to look for work: *'I looked around for likely helpful characters and asked a young man, obviously penniless, where to stay. He told me to go to the Accueil de Nuit in rue Plumier near Vieil-leport. This was run by a Catholic order and the routine was very strict: entry between 7.00 and 7.10pm, in bed by 9pm, up at 5am, and out by 6.30am. This did however allow me to recover from my long hitch-hiking journey, without having to spend my emergency fund.'*
Look up Foyers/Asiles de Nuit in the telephone directory or ask a gendarme on the beat. According to the BBC 1 documentary 'Brits Abroad', begging is legal in France and people are generous. One British beggar who was interviewed on the Cote d'Azur claimed to be raking in £300 a week while his accommodation and meals were paid for by the council.

If you would like to survive in rural France, communal living is a possibility. Roberta Wedge enjoyed several months at the 'bleakly beautiful' Le Cun de Larzac Peace Centre (Route de Saint-Martin, 12100 Millau; 05-65 60 62 33) and says that they need work-for-keep volunteers in the summer to look after visitors, tend the gardens, preserve the fruit, etc.

Several Gandhian Communities of the Ark accept volunteers, including La Borie Noble (34650 Roqueredonde; 04-67 44 09 89) and La Flayssière (34650 Joncels; 04-67 44 40 90). Robert Abblett moved from one community to another with mixed results:

From the Australian WWOOF list, I found the address of Les Courmettes. This was my favourite WWOOF for it was situated on an 800 metre plateau above the Côte d'Azur. I spent a wonderful 3½ weeks here one August in a most peaceful place camping and swinging in my hammock, contemplating life and exploring the top of the mountain nearby naked. On my days off I would go swimming in some of the most beautiful rivers and swimming holes with the other volunteers. I would work four days washing up followed by three days off. My French really helped me enjoy the experience.

Then I hitched down to an anarchist commune called Longo Mai near Forcalquier with its own radio station and met some of the most unfriendly people, who openly criticised my lifestyle and goals. This was hard, but I stuck it out and did find a few gentle souls amongst them.

If you are more into private enterprise, you may wish to follow Tessa Shaw's example. She learned that there were many edible snails to be found along the canal and river banks in the *département* of Vaucluse which she could sell in the market. The snails move about only on still, dank nights: so Tessa would be found between the hours of 2am and 7am scouring the waterside with the help of a torch. She would then keep them in a sack or bin for four or five days until they exuded all the poison in their systems, and then sell them in the market of Carpentras. There is a closed season for snail collecting between April 1st and June 30th.

While you're waiting for something to turn up, it is possible to sleep in parks, railway stations or on beaches, though this is unlikely to be trouble-free. Do not consider spending the night at the Gare de Lyons unless you can produce a current ticket since the patrolling police will not be over-gentle when evicting you. T. J. Coles recommends the pebble beach at Nice, though the police regularly arrived at 2.30am shouting *'Debout Debout'*.

Lee Merrick found the UCRIF Etapes Jeunes (27 rue de Turbigo, BP 6407, 75064 Paris Cedex 02; 01-40 26 57 64; www.ucrif.asso.fr) very helpful for accommodation both in Paris and beyond. They have 50 residential centres throughout France, including a dozen in and around Paris, which are about the cheapest hostel accommodation available and largely frequented by young people from overseas. Try also C.H.E.A.P. Hostels (fax 01-42 64 22 04; www.cheaphostel.com) for affordable Paris accommodation and the possibility of work for a minimum of six months.

CORSICA

Although the island of Corsica is officially a French *département,* the inhabitants have more in common with Sardinians than with the mainland French. There will always be competition for casual work from the large North African contingent. Corsica is a relatively poor and undeveloped region, but its warm climate does create a few opportunities in farming and tourism for the working traveller.

K. McCausland found the ANPE in Porto Vecchio (Route d'Arca, 20538 Porto Vecchio; 04-95 70 21 65) to be surprisingly helpful, given that there is quite a measure of local animosity to incomers. In the end, he was so put off by the frequent spectacle of road signs riddled with bullet holes that he didn't pursue the idea of working in Corsica. The Corsican separatist movement is active, so caution is advised.

Tourism

The tourist industry is concentrated in a small number of towns: Ajaccio the capital, Bastia, Bonifacio, Calvi, Ile Rousse and Propriano. Unfortunately these have been the occasional targets of separatists' bombs though things have been fairly quiet recently. Anyone with a knowledge of German would be at an advantage since the level of German tourism in Corsica is very high. Kathryn Halliwell found her job in the hotel Sofitel Thalassa in Porticcio (04-95 29 40 40), a resort about 12km down the coast from Ajaccio, by the time-honoured method of asking from door to door. She worked as a chambermaid on a hotel staff of 150, and mentioned that the worst problem faced by the female members of staff was the level of unwelcome attention from local Arab men.

Alison Cooper found the heat to be a more serious impediment to her enjoyment of her summer as a Eurocamp courier in Corsica, but managed to have a great season: *'I enjoyed this job immensely even if it did get unbearably hot when it's 40°C and you're trying to clean a tent in direct sunlight with a hangover. We had one and a half days off a week on average with a fantastic beach to go and chill out on, or a quick dip in the campsite pool after cleaning. On the whole it was a good summer.'*

The British tour company Simply Corsica (King's House, Wood St, Kingston-upon-Thames, Surrey KT1 1SG; www.shgjobs.co.uk) employs resort reps who are over 24 and fluent in French plus more junior staff in resorts throughout the island. The latter receive only pocket money in addition to living expenses. Contact the Overseas Recruitment line 0870-888 0028. Another British tour operator with beachclub hotels on Corsica is Mark Warner (08700 330750; www.markwarner-recruitment.co.uk) which hires many seasonal receptionists, watersports and tennis instructors, chefs, kitchen porters, waiting and bar staff, nannies, handymen and nightwatchmen. A long-established French specialist operator is VFB Holidays, Normandy House, High St, Cheltenham, Glos. GL50 3FB (personnel@vfbholidays.co.uk) which employs French-speaking reps for the whole season from late April to early October.

Farm Work

Although Corsica is not as far south as Greece, many sub-tropical fruits such as kiwifruit, clementines and avocados thrive. Most of this fruit ripens in mid-November and is picked through January. There is also an important grape harvest that takes place in September/early October.

The best region to try for fruit-picking work is the fertile area on the east coast especially around Bastia and half-way down around Aleria. Vineyards are concentrated along the coast to the north of Calvi, around Ajaccio and Sartene. Grapes are picked around Pianottoli Caldarello, a town between Sartene and Bonifacio. Ask at the local farming co-operative, though be prepared for stiff competition. If you can't speak French, it will be very difficult to get someone to accommodate and employ you when there are dozens of North African migrant workers to do the job.

Perseverance paid off for Rob Abblett who had the address of a farmer in northern Corsica to whom he had written three times over the years, enclosing French references and s.a.e.

Finally, one autumn, the phone call came and Rob took a no-frills flight to Sardinia on Ryanair and ferry on to Corsica:
I arrived at the orchard and am now living in a little simple one-bed building with kitchen, loo and shower on the property. It's really quiet and peaceful (no TV, radio or people), only the third time in my life that I have experienced this solitude. A time to shore up my 'battered timbers' from years of travel. My days are spent quietly snipping away at the clementines with the pungent aroma of oranges in the air and the cool sunshine on my head. I work hard and long and my boss seems to have taken a shine to me and lets me have the accommodation rent-free. I started in mid-November and have signed a contract to stay until the end of the harvest about 10th January although I have been offered the chance of staying until May doing the pruning. It's a hell of a long time to live so quietly with only the sound of a fire to occupy me. But I hope at some point to get some time off to go exploring this beautiful (though expensive) island with its history of violence and rebellion.

Germany

Ever since the reunification of Germany 15 years ago, foreign workers have been flocking to Germany especially from Poland, the former Yugoslavia and now from the new accession countries which were admitted to the EU in May 2004. Many casual jobs are no long available to the British students (and other nationalities) who at one time might have done them.

Since about 2003, German hotels have turned in great numbers to eastern and central Europe for their staff, leaving few vacancies for British and other students. Marianne Dix, whose agency the Bloomsbury Bureau in London has been sending au pairs and hotel staff to Germany since 1971, described in 2005 the recent changes she has noticed:

> The hotels I have worked with for many years have told me that staff are now delivered to their doors by the busload from the countries bordering Germany, with the help of the local official job centres. Unfortunately we no longer receive notice of vacancies from German hoteliers, as they are now inundated with workers from the new EU countries. It is a shame for the western European students that this opportunity no longer exists.

The very high rate of unemployment – 10.3%, the highest since 1990 – compounds the problem, painting a gloomy picture for working travellers thinking of job-hunting in Germany. Work experience placements for students of German are on the increase but in most cases positions are unpaid (and furthermore participants have to pay agency fees).

And yet perseverance by anyone who has a reasonable command of German may still be rewarded with a decently paid job at some level in Germany.

The Regulations

If you are an EU national you are free to travel to Germany to look for work. However if you want to stay more than three months, you will be subject to the labyrinthine bureaucracy, as David Hughes from the UK discovered when he went to Frankfurt to take up a job as a nurse: *'I believe (hope) we've finished our dealings with those German bureaucrats. Cumbersome is the exact adjective. I'm not sure about why or what we were doing some of the time. After establishing myself here as a legal worker, I fully understand the writings of Franz Kafka! On the opening times of offices: absurd, ridiculous, inconvenient and too bloody early are thoughts that spring to mind.'*

The first step is to obtain the *Anmeldebestätigung* (the registration document required by Germans as well as foreigners) from the local authority *(Einwohnermeldeamt)* or *Meldenstelle*. Go to your local town hall *(Ortsamt* or *Rathaus)* to pick up the right form *(Anmeldung)* which will have to be signed by your landlord as proof that you have a German address and are therefore entitled to an ID card. People who are not in rented or owned accommodation will have problems. One young job-seeker staying at a youth hostel in Berlin described it, 'I was trapped for a week in a vicious circle of no job – no papers – no accommodation; without one of these it is very difficult to get the others.'

If you do have a job and accommodation, the application for a residence permit should be straightforward. Go to the aliens' authority *(Ausländerbehorde* or *Ausländeramt)* to apply for an *Aufenthaltserlaubnis* (residence permit) or *Aufenthaltsgenehmigung* (valid up to three years). Take all your processed documents, your passport and three photos.

The accession of the new member states to the EU in 2004 has not yet had an impact on the labour pool because transitional measures still require citizens of Slovakia, Hungary and the rest to obtain work permits. There is still a high level of people working black *(Schwarzarbeiter)* and employers who hire large numbers of workers under-the-table are subject to raids and huge fines if caught. For many jobs (e.g. childcare, food service, etc.) you must also acquire a *Gesundheitszeugnis* (health certificate) from the local *Gesundheitsamt* (health department). Again, restaurants will be heavily fined if they are caught employing anyone without it. When you go for the medical examination, you will have to produce the proper form *(Anmeldung)* which you have purchased earlier as well as a hefty fee. You return a week later, and then your *Gesundheitszeugnis* will be posted.

Australians and New Zealanders under 30 are eligible for one-year working holiday visas for Germany. Other citizens of Australia and New Zealand plus Canada and the US are permitted to apply for a work permit after arrival in Germany provided they have found an employer willing to support their application. Other nationalities will have to apply to a German consulate in their home country.

Non-Europeans wishing to stay in Germany for an extended period require an *Aufenthaltserlaubnis* or residence permit. For this, applicants will require a notarised certificate of good conduct, evidence of health insurance as well as a *Gesundheitszeugnis* (as above), proof of accommodation and means of support. The permit must specify that employment is permitted before the bearer has any chance of going on to obtain an *Arbeitslaubnis* (work permit) from the *Arbeitsamt* (Employment Office, described below).

Special Schemes

Internships for American students and graduates up to the age of 30 who can function in German are available in business, finance, engineering or technical fields through CDS International Inc. (871 United Nations Plaza, 15th Floor, New York, NY 10017-1814; 212-497-3502; www.cdsintl.org). If appropriate, the first month can be spent at an intensive language course in Cologne, after which participants undertake a paid or unpaid internship which they have secured previously with the help of CDS's partner agency InWEnt (Internationale Weiterbildung und Entwicklung gGmbH) with offices in Bonn and Cologne (www.inwent.org). The summer programme is open only to enrolled students (whose placement must be less than six months) whereas graduates are permitted to stay up to 12 months, extendable to 18. The average monthly compensation is €500, which will cover living expenses. The CDS programme fee is $700 and the deadline for the summer programme is mid-December.

CIEE in the US no longer administer a work abroad programme for American students. InterExchange in New York runs Au Pair in Germany whereby young Americans aged

North Sea

Fehmarn ☀

Heiligenhafen • • Burg

Timmendorf • Baltic Sea

Travemunde ☀

Stade • Rostock

HAMBURG

Altland

NETHERLANDS

Verden •

Munster • Minden • Hannover •

BERLIN

Rhine

Paderborn •

GERMANY

Iserlohn •

Dusseldorf • Göttingen •

Cologne •
Bonn • Eschwege •

B

Giessen •

Koblenz •

Mosel Piesport • Rheingau

Bernkastel • Ruwer Rheingau

L Trier • Nahe

Saarburg • Rudesheim • Mainz • FRANKFURT

Nierstein • Darmstadt

Rheinhessen

Saar Alzey • Franconia

Bergstrasse • Wurzburg • Bamberg •

Neustadt • Deidesheim •

Heidelberg • Nürnberg •

Zirndorf •

Böhmer Wald

FRANCE

Baden-Baden •

• Stuttgart

Baden Wurttemburg

Black Forest Neckar Valley

Neu-Ulm •

Freiburg • Augsburg •

Passau •

Bavaria

Ravensburg • MUNICH

Friedrichshafen •

Fussen • Chiemsee

Lake Constance Oberstdorf • Bavarian Alps Garmisch Partenkirchen

SWITZERLAND Mittenwald

AUSTRIA

WILLIAM SWAN

18-25 spend 6 or 12 months living in a Germany family (see below). SWAP in Canada dispenses three-month work permits to eligible students and recent graduates. Work must be taken up between mid-May and mid-October. A German language evaluation is required.

A list of opportunities to live and work in Germany can be found in the Jobs section of the British Council-hosted British German Youth portal The Voyage (www.the-voyage. com). Among the listings are work experience placements, au pairing and voluntary work. They suggest links (among others) to Eurostage (www.eurostage.org/de/accueiluk.htm).

The IJAB (International Youth Exchange) in Bonn has a EuroDesk which administers European student exchanges (Heussallee 30, 53170 Bonn; 0228-95 06 208; www. eurodesk.de). The website www.prabo.de, available in English, describes itself as the leading free internship database for companies, students and anyone else who is looking for an internship in Germany. If you can read German fluently try the job search sites arbeitsplaza.de and jobware.de.

The Happy Hands working holiday scheme places language and gap year students from the UK and the old EU countries in the field of rural tourism. Participants are given weekly pocket money of €51 and full board and lodging with families on farms or in country hotels. In return they look after children and/or horses and farm animals or take up serving and kitchen duties. The preferred stay is three to six months though a two-month commitment is also allowed; details available from Working Holidays in Germany, c/o Anne von Gleichen, Römerberg 8, 60311 Frankfurt; 069-293733; Anne.Gleichen@t-online.de; www. workingholidays.de. A fee of €180 must be paid after the placement is agreed and two weeks before it starts.

Work Experience

Work placements can be organised in a wide range of sectors including tourism, trade, telecommunications, marketing and banking depending on timing and availability. Most internships are organised in conjunction with an intensive language course. Normally an upper intermediate level of language ability is required for work experience to be successful. Most are unpaid or are rewarded only with a subsistence wage. Board and lodging will generally be provided only in the tourism sector.

DID-Deutsch Institute (Hauptstrasse 26, 63811 Stockstadt am Main; 6027 41770; www.did.de) is a major language course provider which can also arrange two to six month internships following their language courses in Berlin, Frankfurt, Munich and Wiesbaden; the processing fee for an unskilled work placement is €300 while a qualified internship placement will cost €415 in addition to the preceding language course (e.g. €1,609 for 8 weeks). Similarly *GLS (Global Language Services)* combines a minimum 4-week language course with an internship in a Berlin-based company of 4, 8 or 12 weeks. Host companies want their trainees to speak German to at least an intermediate level.

Astur GmbH (Sturmiusstrasse 2, 36037 Fulda; 661-92802-0; www.astur-gmbh.de/ work_1.html) organises linguistic stays in about 50 cities and towns around Germany with work experience placements lasting four or eight weeks for EU nationals. An excellent standard of German is required to work in a German company, normally in industry, sales, marketing, administration, accountancy, tourism, law, translation or computers. Astur also arrange hotel experience placements for which candidates need an intermediate standard of German after a compulsory pre-placement language course.

The internship department of Euroacademy has recently been christened *Gwendalyne* (c/o Twin Training & Travel, 67-71 Lewisham High St, London SE13 5JX; 020-8297 3251; www.gwendalyne.com); it matches students' area of interest with work placements in companies in Berlin. Participants do a 4-week German course first. A sample internship placement lasting ten weeks (including the language course) would cost £1,500.

Interspeak is a UK-based work placement agency that can arrange placements for young people who have studied German in hotels, offices and in any specific type of placement required. Placements last 1-24 weeks year round and include full board accommodation, though the positions are mainly unpaid. The agency's registration fee is £80 and the placement fee is £340, plus the client pays for accommodation with a host family.

Details will be sent on receipt of an s.a.e (A5) posted to Interspeak, Stretton Lower Hall, Stretton, Malpas, Cheshire SY14 7HS (01829 250641; www.interspeak.co.uk).

Tax

You can use the *Anmeldebestätigung* (residence permit) to obtain a *Lohnsteuerkarte* (tax card) or a *Steuernummer* (tax number). Legal workers can expect to lose between 33% and 40% of their gross wages in tax and social security contributions unless they earn less than the personal allowance (about €640 per month). One of the taxes included in the tax bill is a church tax *(Kirchensteuer)* which accounts for 8-9% of income tax, unless you claim an exemption due to atheism (and thereby forego the possibility of ever being married or buried in a German church).

Emma Forster visited the tax office *(Finanzamt)* in Hamburg after working for two months and was told that she was entitled to all her tax back. When you finish work in Germany, take your *Lohnsteuerkarte* to the tax office and complete a declaration of earnings *(Steuerklärung)* and hope that you are eligible to receive a rebate, which will be transferred to your home bank account.

Students taking up a short-term job in the Federal Republic of Germany during their university vacations for not longer than 183 days should be exempt from German income tax, provided they can prove to their German employer that they are enrolled in higher education. Students who are eligible should go the local German tax office before completing their summer contracts and file a claim. They should also make their student status known to prospective employers, for whom student employees are cheaper than non-students. Other categories which are exempted from tax (but not social security contributions of about 13%) are teachers and professors (from the EU) who work in Germany for less than two years.

You will need your processed *Anmeldung* to open a bank account. Anyone who can show a student card will be exempt from bank charges.

German National Employment Service

The whole of Germany is covered by the network of employment offices run by the state *Bundesanstalt für Arbeit* (www.arbeitsamt.de). There are nearly 200 principal *Arbeitsamter* (job centres) and a further 650+ branch offices. These are all connected by a number of co-ordinating offices that handle both applications and vacancies that cannot be filled locally.

Arbeitsamter are entitled to refuse to help you if you do not have residence papers though the self-service system (SIS) means that anyone can inspect job vacancy information updated daily on SIS computer terminals and in many cases make use of free telephones. Even before this computerised system was introduced, many praised the efficiency of the *Arbeitsamt*:

> **Amongst them was Nick Langley who used the one in Munich near the U-bahn station Goetheplatz**
> *Germany has one of the most efficient National Employment Services in the world. In Munich there is a massive modern complex which is organised on the basis of different departments handling job vacancies for different work categories such as building and construction, engineering, restaurant work, hotel work, etc. It may be necessary to visit several departments to maximise your chances of a job. Each department has counsellors to handle enquiries, tell you what's on offer and arrange interviews. There is also a microfiche reader listing hundreds of vacancies in the area. I was immediately offered a job at a new Burger King restaurant about to open in the main station.*

If you speak German and aren't in a hurry, it's probably worth registering. Look for their weekly publication *Markt + Chance* which lists job vacancies.

It is possible to use the Federal Employment Service from outside Germany. The

Zentralstelle für Arbeitsvermittlung (Central Placement Office) has an international department *(Auslandsabteilung)* for dealing with applications from German-speaking students
abroad. Details and application forms are available from ZAV, Villemombler Str. 76, 53123
Bonn (0228-713-1330; fax 0228-713 1111; Bonn-ZAV@arbeitsamt.de); the deadline is the
end of February.

All applications from abroad are handled by this office. Although people of any nationality can apply through the Zentralstelle, only citizens of EU countries who have German
language skills are entitled to expect the same treatment as a German. People of other
nationalities are accepted only within the framework of special exchange programmes and
government-approved schemes.

There is one exception to this rule. The Zentralstelle has a special department which
finds summer jobs for students of any nationality *(Studentenvermittlung),* because this
is felt to be mutually beneficial to employers and employees alike. Students who wish to
participate in this scheme should contact ZAV before March. Students must be at least
18 years old, have a good command of German and be available to work for at least two
months. ZAV places students in all kinds of jobs, but mainly in hotels and restaurants, in
industry and agriculture. The Zentralstelle assigns jobs centrally, according to employers'
demands and the level of the candidate's spoken German. For example those with fluent
German may be found service jobs while those without will be given jobs such as chambermaiding and dishwashing. If you decline the first job offered by the Zentralstelle, you
may not be offered another.

The Bundesanstalt also operates mobile temporary employment offices, called *Ser-
vice-Vermittlung* in addition to permanent *Arbeitsamter.* These are set up as an emergency measure where employers need extra workers immediately for short periods of
time. It is, however, worth looking for them at any of the trade exhibitions and wine or beer
festivals in which the Germans take such delight.

Other Sources of Work

Anyone with office experience and a knowledge of German should look for branches of
private employment agencies such as Adecco, Manpower and Interim in the big cities;
these will be listed in the *Gelbe Seiten* (Yellow Pages) under *Personalberatung* or *Stellen-
vermittlungsburo.* A German reader Carisa Fey recommends the temp agency she used
on her return to Stuttgart: Dr. Stern GmbH, Rotebühlplatz 11, 70178 Stuttgart, which fills
office vacancies with fluent German speakers and factory workers with a basic understanding of the language. Carisa thinks that world travellers are uncommon in the conventional workplace and attract a lot of curiosity and in a few cases jealousy.

To avoid bureaucracy completely, EU nationals with a student card should try the *stu-
dentische arbeitsvermittlung* in all German universities. Casual jobs like babysitting and
cleaning are registered with the student job service attached to the ASTA students' council.
One traveller from Glasgow visited the Student *Arbeitsamt* in Munich (with a forged student card) and within an hour was working on a building site.

Most of the main dailies like *Frankfurter Allgemeine Zeitung* carry their job supplements on Saturdays which go on sale on Friday evening. *BZ* in Berlin has a good selection
of vacancies for unskilled people.

The Irish agency ICDS mentioned in the chapter on the Netherlands recruits workers
for Germany too, as described by Darren Slevin from County Westmeath who worked at
various trees nurseries in the region of Specken:

*I am working in a baumschule (tree nursery) in the village of Rostrop near Oldenburg
in northern Germany. I got the job through an agency at 24 Upper Fitzwilliam St in
Dublin 2. Accommodation, transport to and from work and insurance are provided.
We receive half of what our boss pays the agency, which seems very unfair, but the
working conditions are quite good. Before I came to Germany, I assumed the people
would be cold and aloof but I've found them to be very friendly and generous people.
On cold mornings, my supervisor gives us brandy or rum to warm us up. Even those*

with only a few words of English make the effort to talk and on St. Patrick's Day, our boss came with us to an Irish pub in Oldenburg.

Darren describes the various jobs at Bruns – the largest tree nursery company in Europe – including tree-planting, removing the trees with a mechanised digger, wrapping the trees in netting (very hard on the back) and the cushiest job working on the trailer, guiding the netted trees into position. Conditions were much tougher at his next assignment in the same area where he and his Polish colleagues were obliged to do a huge amount of overtime (one day they worked for 20 hours) and were told that if they stopped work at 10pm they would be fired. The worst job was weeding which had to be done bending or kneeling, both painful after 9½ hours. Tree nurseries in the area include Container Baumschule near Bad Zwischenahn, Marken and Jeddeloh. It is almost obligatory to be hired via an agent rather than directly.

If you are looking for labouring or other casual work after arriving in Germany, seek out the local Irish bar or British pub. There are dozens of these from the Oscar Wilde in Berlin to Mulligans in Oldenburg (as mentioned above). Many tend to be staffed by British and Irish people and are often meeting places for expat workers.

Accommodation

Flats and apartments are not as scarce as they were but accommodation is still expensive. Many find it necessary to go through an agency. *Mitwohnzentralen* are helpful and charge less than many other agencies (some charge two months' rent); in Emma Forster's case the fee charged by the *Mitwohnzentral* in Hamburg was a quarter of a month's rent. There is even a facility for people who are looking for flat-mates. Some agencies will not take you onto their books without a *Burgschaft*, the name and address of a local referee. If you are chasing a flat through the classifieds of a local paper, be warned that the competition will probably buy the first edition in the wee small hours and not wait until morning to ring potential landlords. Free listings newspapers are useful for those seeking accommodation, for instance the *Zypresse* in Freiburg.

TOURISM AND CATERING

The German tourist industry depends heavily on immigrants and students during the busy summer months. Despite the huge number of (illegal) immigrants from the former Yugoslavia who are often willing to work for exploitative wages, many other nationalities do find jobs in hotels and restaurants.

If you are conducting a door-to-door search of hotels and restaurants in the cities, you will be at an enormous advantage if you speak decent German. For example every time Danny Jacobson turned around in Freiburg (after a fruitless search for harvesting work in the countryside), he met young people from around the world working at campsites and in bars. You may be lucky and find a manager who speaks English and who needs someone behind the scenes to wash dishes, etc. When Robert Lofts worked in a hotel kitchen, he had to phone up his German-speaking brother who was living nearby every time he received a new instruction ('He wants you to peel the cucumbers'). Robin Gray was not so lucky as to have a linguistically talented sibling and he accepted a job in a kitchen without really understanding what he was meant to do:

The manageress told me she was looking for a salad chef and I said I was a chef. The waitresses were coming in with the orders, but I didn't know there were about seven different salads. I was just putting a couple of slices of lettuce, tomatoes, bit of cucumber, etc. on all the plates and they were going off their heads because there wasn't enough watercress or no tomatoes with that certain salad. I started at 10am and got the sack at 2pm, but I got paid for it so I wasn't too bothered.

As well as trying the Zentralstelle beforehand, you can try to fix up a summer job ahead of time by sending off speculative applications. This worked for Dean Fisher, an unemployed engineering apprentice, who went to wash dishes in Berchtesgaden on the Austrian border: *'I spent 2½ months working in a very orderly and efficient kitchen on the top of a mountain in the Kehlsteinhaus (Eagle's Nest) with the most amazing view I've ever seen. I actually enjoyed the work even though it was hard going. I met loads of good people and learned a lot of German.'*

Get hotel addresses from websites or, if you know anyone going to Germany on holiday in the spring, ask them to bring back local newspapers. The wage range for general catering work should start at €8 an hour though some employers have been known to pay €6.

Munich is estimated to have more than 2,000 pubs and restaurants (especially in the fashionable suburb of Schwabing) and Berlin is similarly well endowed with eateries (try the American style places on Kurfürstendamm). The Munich beer gardens, especially the massive open-air Chinese Tower Biergarten, pay glass collectors and washers-up (most of whom have lined their jobs up at the beginning of the season) €70-€80 a day tax free at the height of the season, when people work 14-hour days. Look for adverts in the local press, especially *Abendzeitung* in Munich or on the website www.az-gastro. de. Key words to look for on notices and in adverts are *Notkoch und Küchelhilfe gesucht* (relief and kitchen assistant required), *Spüler* (dishwasher), *Kellner, Bedienigung* (waiters/waitresses), *Schenkekellner* (pub type barman); *Büffetier* (barman in a restaurant), *Büffetkräfte* (fast food server), or simply *Services*.

Be prepared for hard work. In hotels, it is not unusual to work 10 or 12 hours a day and to have only a day or two off a month. Those whose only experience of hotels and catering has been in Britain are usually taken aback by German discipline. Waitresses are normally expected to keep all customers' payments until the end of a shift, when the total is calculated and handed over as a lump sum. Those who lose track while being shouted at in German will not last long.

The punitive hygiene laws do not help matters. Once you realise that restaurants and hotels are frequently visited by the health department you will appreciate why it is that the head cook orders you to scrub the floors, clean the fat filters regularly, etc. But the high wages make it worthwhile.

Paul Winter has worked several seasons on the lakes near Munich:

I found that it is best to apply around April/May in person if possible. What they usually do is to tell you to come back at the beginning of June and work for a couple of days to see how you get on. As long as you are not a complete idiot they always keep you on until September. Even as late as July I knew of places looking for extra staff but as a rule most places are full by the end of May. I worked for the summer as a barman/waiter earning a good net wage. With the tips I got I generally managed to double this.

Both Amersee and Starnbergersee can be reached by S-Bahn from Munich. These two lakes are ringed by towns and villages which all have hotels and restaurants, popular mainly with German tourists. Be warned that competition for work from German students (especially from the old East Germany) will make it difficult.

Other recommended areas to try for a summer job are the Bavarian Alps (along the border with Austria), the shores of Lake Constance, the Bohmer Wald (along the Czech border), the Black Forest (in south-west Germany), and the seaside resorts along the Baltic and North Seas. One employer on the Baltic coast hires a number of general assistants, food and beverage staff, child carers and sports instructors at a coastal campsite/golf and holiday park. The hours are long and you must be able to speak German but the wages are good. Students only should apply in the spring to Riechey Freizeitanlagan GmbH, 23769 Wulfen/Fehmarn (04371 86280; www.wulfenerhals.de/ENGLISCH/jobs.shtml).

The UK agency Alpotels (affiliated to Jobs-in-the-Alps) carries out aptitude tests on behalf of German hoteliers looking for about 50 English-speaking staff (with EU nationality) for the summer and winter seasons. If interested in this scheme, you must have an A level in German, an EU passport and be interviewed in London. Send an s.a.e. to Alpotels, 17 High St, Gretton, Northants. NN17 3DE (www.jobs-in-the-alps.co.uk).

Movie World (part of the American-owned Six Flags Theme Parks group) employs between 400 and 500 staff for food concessions (restaurants, bakeries, ice cream stalls, fast food, etc.). Applicants should be able to converse in German and preferably Dutch as well as English. Accommodation is not provided. Applications can be submitted online or sent to Warner Allee 1, 46244 Bottrop-Kirchellen (02045-899540; www.movieworld.de); note that the 'Jobs' page is available in English as well as German and Dutch.

Anyone with some experience working in hotels or restaurants might check the website www.eurotoques.de (click on *Chefkoche* and then on *Jobborse)* where top chefs offer unpaid work experience placements.

Winter Resorts

Germany is a good place to pick up jobs in ski resorts although few British tour companies operate there compared to France and Austria. Jobs-in-the-Alps mentioned above helps in the recruitment of chambermaids and kitchen staff for the winter season in Germany; fluent German is not always required. The two main skiing areas are Garmisch-Partenkirchen (which also has hotels and services for the American Army) on the Austrian border 50 miles southeast of Munich, and the spa resort of Oberstdorf in the mountains south of Kempten. Seasonal vacancies are mostly in the kitchen or housekeeping departments.

As always, timing is crucial. One highly qualified job-seeker (with experience in hotels and restaurants, a knowledge of German, French and English, and a good skier) went on the old 'hotel-trot' in Garmisch Partenkirchen and was repeatedly told that they wouldn't be hiring until the beginning of the season (circa December 15th).

Work on Military Bases

Cutbacks in military spending have necessitated the withdrawal of both American and British troops and resources from military bases in Germany. Many large US bases such as the ones in Munich and Berlin have closed. Yet there are still jobs around for Americans and Britons on the relevant bases. Heidelberg is the HQ for the U.S. Army in Europe, home to about 16,000 serving soldiers and their families, which creates many ancillary jobs.

Military bases throughout Germany have Civilian Personnel Offices (CPOs) that are responsible for recruiting auxiliary staff to work in bars, shops, etc., on base and as ski instructors. The best bet for shorter term openings is at the Army's recreational centres at Garmisch-Partenkirchen and Chiemsee. The Armed Forces Recreation Center Europe is know known as Edelweiss Lodge and Resort (www.edelweisslodgeandresort.com/employment) which offers entry-level jobs only in the hotel and recreation departments for a period of 18 months. They recruit exclusively in the United States, and candidates must go through rigorous interviews and background checks before being selected. Edelweiss never hires Americans who are already in Europe. Americans do not require work permits to work on US bases. For a searchable list of civilian vacancies throughout the US military see http://acpol.army.mil/employment. The site www.armygermany.com also has links to job opportunities in bases around Europe.

Every base in Europe and Asia has a food court in the commissary area where you will find a Burger King, KFC, Baskin-Robbins, Pizza Hut and other fast food outlets. In addition to the large base at Heidelberg, large commissaries can be found in Mannheim, Kaiserslautern (the largest American community outside the US) and Hanau. Each base also has an officers' club and hotel facilities for Armed Forces personnel where they need waiters and chamber staff.

The *Stars and Stripes* is the US Army newspaper and is worth checking for jobs, especially as nannies or au pairs (www.estripes.com). Ana Güemes from Mexico answered an advert and was hired over the phone by a service family in Beibesheim near Darmstadt. The low pay and loss of freedom meant that Ana did not stay long, but it would be easy to move to a better family once you were on a base.

Jobs on British Forces Germany bases along the Rhine such as Münster/Osnabruck and Paderborn are now very scarce though British nationals are occasionally still hired at the Berlin base for waitressing, bar work, cleaning and administration. The Rhine Area Labour Support Unit (RALSU; www.army.mod.uk/ralsu) is responsible for the recruitment and administration of civilian labour.

Special Events

Anyone who wants to volunteer to work at the World Cup in 2006 needs to have a good command of German, basic knowledge of English, be 18 by the 1st of June 2006 and preferably have experience in sport or volunteering. Applications will be accepted via http://fifaworldcup.yahoo.com/06/en/o/volunteers/vbp.html over the summer of 2005 and again in January/February 2006.

Oktoberfest starts each year on the last Saturday in September and lasts a fortnight. They begin to erect the giant tents for the festival about three months ahead so you can begin your enquiries any time in the summer. Some of the hiring is done directly by the breweries, so it is worth contacting the Hofbräuhaus and Löwenbräu for work, as well as pubs, restaurants and hotels. Nicole Gluckstern from California wrote (from Togo!) two years ago to confirm that Oktoberfest is always looking for people to sell pretzels, wash glasses, take photos, etc. but she advises job-seekers to set their dignity temporarily aside since the atmosphere will be zoo-like. There is also work after the festival finishes as Brad Allemand from Australia discovered: *'On the Monday after Oktoberfest finished I went around to all of the Beer Halls which were being taken down asking for some work. The first one I went to was Spatenbräu and the boss obliged. Even though my German was almost non-existent, I managed to understand what was needed of me. Many other foreigners were also on the site – English, Australian, Yugoslav, etc.'*
Brad enjoyed the work, which lasted about six weeks. He worked 7am-5pm five days a week.

Many other international trade fairs and special events may need large numbers of people to set up stands and deal with maintenance, catering, etc. Some of the major ones are listed below, for example the Frankfurt Trade Fair in March, the Hannover Trade Fair in April, etc. Armin Birrer reported from Hamburg that they hold a fair ('Dom') three times a year, for a month after Christmas, Easter and late summer. He helped to dismantle the place at the end of the Easter fair after seeing a 'Worker Wanted' sign on some of the stalls. Opportunities for casual work also exist before the fairs open.

Many high-profile trade fairs are held at the huge Frankfurt Exhibition Hall *(Messe)*, such as the Frankfurt Book Fair in mid-October. Applications for work at one of the numerous fairs held in Frankfurt can be addressed to Messe Frankfurt GmbH, Ludwig-Erhard-Anlage 1, 60327 Frankfurt; 069-75750). Only people with a stable base in Frankfurt and a good command of languages (for example for running messages) can be considered.

BUSINESS AND INDUSTRY

Germany is once again becoming a mecca for foreigners looking for work in the manufacturing industries though, as in Britain, some of the traditional heavy industry of the Ruhr Valley has been struggling to compete lately. Very high wages are no longer universal, and most production line work pays €8-€12 an hour.

You generally need to be on the spot to find this sort of job or have contacts. The best advice is simply to head for large industrial towns such as Stuttgart, Cologne, Düsseldorf, Munich and Hannover, and start asking for work in *Arbeitsamter* and at factory gates. You should also check the sits vac columns, for example in the *Rheinische Post* in Düsseldorf and *Süddeutsche Zeitung* and *Munchner Merkur* in Munich (particularly the Wednesday and Saturday editions which can be bought the previous evening in stations).

In Munich Robin Gray found a better job quite by chance: *'I went in to a factory next to the building site (where I'd worked for a couple of days) for a drink of water since there was none on site. The owner of this factory which made mirrors warned me that the guy I was working for was disreputable and offered me a job which I did for a month. There is a lot of work in Munich. I met people from all over the world doing everything from labouring to welding, tree surgeons to bar work.'*

TEACHING

If you enquire at an *Arbeitsamt* about teaching, translation or secretarial work in the major cities, you will probably be told (truthfully) that there is a surplus of people offering those services. However you may find that they are more helpful in smaller cities like Ravensburg in southern Germany where Nick Barton (writing in the now-defunct *Overseas Jobs Express*) found teaching work within days. He was surprised that the staff were so helpful considering how much trouble he was having with the local dialect, Schwabisch. After working for a local language institute, he began to acquire a number of private clients and ended up staying for nearly two years.

Graduates with a background in economics or business who can speak German have a better chance of finding teaching work in a German city than arts graduates, since most of the demand comes from companies. Private language schools have multiplied in the eastern *Lander*, many with an American bias, though it seems that demand peaked in the late 1990s. Try for example Sprache und Wirtschaft (Sternwartenstr. 4-6, 04103 Leipzig; 0341-257 7127; www.spracheundwirtschaft.de) which employs about 40 teachers; and Lingua Franca (Mauer Strasse 77, 10117 Berlin; 030-863 98 080; www.lingua-franca.de).

A TEFL Certificate has less clout than relevant experience, as Kevin Boyd found when he arrived in Munich in September, clutching his brand new Cambridge Certificate: *'I was persuaded by a teaching friend to go to Munich with him to try to get highly paid jobs together. As he spoke some German and had about a year's teaching experience, he got a job straightaway. Every school I went to in Munich just didn't want to know as I couldn't speak German and only had four weeks teaching experience.'*

If you do intend to look for a teaching job take evidence of any qualifications and some good references *(zeugnisse)* which are essential in Germany. You can always try to arrange private English lessons to augment your income, though you are unlikely to be able to make a living this way. During the four winter months Ann Barkett spent in Munich, she put up flyers for private and group lessons but received no response.

Many secondary schools in Germany (including the former East) employ native English-speaking *assistenten*. Posts are normally reserved for students of German who apply to the Language Assistants Team of the Education & Training Group of the British Council (10 Spring Gardens, London SW1A 2BN; 020-7389 4596; assistants@britishcouncil.org; www.languageassistant.co.uk.). They send undergraduates studying German at British universities and recent graduates aged 20-30 to spend an academic year in primary or secondary schools throughout Germany. Altogether they place about 300-400 assistants who work 12 hours a week and are paid about €700 a month. American students and graduates can participate in the assistants scheme in Germany by applying through the Fulbright Program (administered by the Institute of International Education, 809 UN Plaza, New York, NY 10017-3580; www.iie.org). Candidates planning to go on to become teachers of German are strongly preferred for this programme, which pays the monthly stipend as above in addition to free flights and insurance.

Language teaching organisations whose addresses are included in the introductory chapter *Teaching English* have a sizeable presence in Germany: Berlitz Deutschland (http://careers.berlitz.com) with 48 institutes in 41 cities, Bénédict with 37 branches, Language Link, inlingua with 50 branches and Linguarama which specialises in language training for business. Linguarama Spracheninstitut Deutschland (Rindermarkt 16, 80331 Munich; 089-260 70 40; munich@linguarama.com) employs between 25 and 70 teachers at each of its eight centres in Germany.

Many commercial institutes employ teachers on a freelance basis, often resident expatriates willing to work just a few hours a week. The best source of language school addresses is once again the *Yellow Pages* which can be consulted online (www.gelbe-seiten.de). Another way of accessing potential employers is via the local English Language Teachers Association, a branch of which can be found in most major cities. The Munich Association (MELTA) is especially vigorous and devotes one page of its website to potential jobseekers (www.melta.de/jobs.htm). Look for English-language magazines aimed at expats and you should come across some relevant adverts. For example the English-language magazine *Munich Found* (www.munichfound.com) carries occasional TEFL vacancies.

Childcare

Most UK au pair agencies have partner organisations in Germany which make family placements. Some, like the Bloomsbury Bureau (Rokeby House, 86-90 Lambs Conduit St, London WC1N 3LX; 020-7430 2280; fax 020-7430 2325; bloomsburo@aol.com; www.bloomsburyaupairs.co.uk), specialise in Germany. Au pairs must have some knowledge of German and experience of childcare and those from outside the European Union must be aged 18-24.

Among the longest established agencies is the non-profit Roman Catholic agency IN VIA with 42 branches throughout Germany (Karlstrasse 40, Postfach 420, 79004 Freiburg (0761-200206; au-pair-invia@caritas.de; www.aupair-invia.de). Its Protestant counterpart is affiliated to the YWCA: Verein für Internationale Jugendarbeit (Goetheallee 10, 53225 Bonn; 0228-698952; www.vij-Deutschland.de). VIJ has 23 offices in Germany and places both male and female au pairs for a preferred minimum stay of one year though six months can be considered.

With the deregulation of employment and recruitment agencies that took place in Germany several years ago, dozens of private agents have popped up all over Germany, many of them members of the Aupair Society (www.au-pair-society.org) which carries contact details for its nearly 50 members (some of which specialise in sending German au pairs abroad). Commercial au pair agencies do not charge a placement fee to incoming au pairs.

Au-Pair Vermittlung, AMS Anna-Maria Schlegel, Postfach 5166, 79018 Freiburg (0761-70 76 917; info@aupair-ams.de; www.aupair-ams.de). Information in English on website.

Au Pair Interconnection, Staufenstr. 17, 86899 Landsberg am Lech (08191-941378; www.aupair-interconnection.de).

MultiKultur AuPair Service, Von-Werth-Str.48-50, 50670 Köln (0221-921 30 40; www.aupair.com). Places international au pairs throughout Germany.

Perfect Partners Au Pair Agency, Am Sonnenhügel 2, 97450 Arnstein (09363-994291; www.perfect-partners.de).

The minimum monthly pocket money for an au pair in Germany has been pegged at €210 a month for a long time, though a proposal to raise it to €280 is awaiting ratification by German states. Some families offer to pay for a monthly travel pass or even cover your fare home if you have stayed for the promised period of nine months, typically up to €150. In return they will expect hard work which usually involves more housework than au pairs normally do, as Maree Lakey found during her year as an au pair in Frankfurt:

> *I found that Germans do indeed seem to be obsessed with cleanliness, something which made my duties as an au pair often very hard. I also found that from first impressions Germans seem to be unfriendly and arrogant, however once you get to know them and are a guest in their home, they can be the most wonderful and generous people. The Germans I met were sincerely impressed by my willingness to learn their language and at the same time genuinely curious about life in Australia, my home country.*

It is possible for non-EU citizens to become au pairs through one of the above organisations provided they are not older than 24. Interexchange in New York simplifies placement for eligible young Americans willing to pay the $400 programme fee. Upon arrival, Americans will need to apply for a temporary residence permit that allows them to live and work in Germany as an au pair for up to 12 months

FARM WORK

Farms in Germany tend to be small and highly mechanised: most farm work is done by the owner and his family, with perhaps the help of some locals at busy times. Only on rare occasions are harvesting vacancies registered with the local *Arbeitsamt*.

Grape production is the only branch of agriculture that employs casual workers in any great number. The harvest, which takes place mostly in the west of the country, is usually later than the one in France, taking place throughout the month of October. The vast majority of harvesting jobs is taken by East Europeans. While hitching through the Rhine Valley a couple of years ago, Danny Jacobson asked repeatedly about grape-picking and every response included a reference to Polish migrant workers who appear to have a monopoly on the harvest work. Philip O'Hara was not prepared for the competition when he set off by bicycle to look for grapes to pick along the River Mosel:

> I had to travel 20km from Trier before I found a Weingut that hadn't already finished its harvest. When I finally caught the harvest up, I found the place littered with Polish cars and vans. There were hundreds of little Polski Fiat 126s with muscle-bound Poles crammed inside. Believe me when I say that finding work is hard. I was told by many vineyard owners that they had plenty of workers and there was no advantage in employing an Englishman in preference to a Pole. Poles were viewed as being honest, tolerant of poor pay and conditions, strong, friendly, hard-working – it is hard work – and hard-drinking. Strangely enough it seems that Irishmen are viewed the same way here. Since I had an Irish passport, I began to boast of my Irishness. That and the bicycle were enough. I worked only with Polish people on the grape harvest at Leiwen/Mosel.

Wages on the steep slopes of the Rhine and Mosel have not risen for a number of years and in some cases have even declined because of the availability of East European workers.

As usual your chances are better if you can visit the vineyards a month or two before the harvest to fix up work. Ask any German tourist office for a free leaflet about wine festivals which is bound to include sketch maps of all the grape-growing regions of Germany. The main concentration of vineyards is along the Rivers Saar, Ruwer, Mosel and Nahe, centred on places familiar from wine labels like Bernkastel, Bingen, Piesport and Kasel. There are ten other areas, principally the Rheingau (around Rüdesheim and Eltville), Rheinpfalz (around Deidesheim, Wachenheim and Bad Dürkheim) and Rheinhessen (around Oppenheim and Nierstein).

Apart from grapes, the most important area for fruit picking is the Altland, which lies between Stade and Hamburg to the south of the River Elbe and includes the towns of Steinkirchen, Jork and Horneburg. The main crops are cherries, which are picked in July and August, and apples in September and October. Apples and other fruit are grown in an area between Heidelberg and Darmstadt called the Bergstrasse, and also in the very south of the country, around Friederichshafen and Ravensburg near Lake Constance. Peter Radomski recommends the Bodensee area for apple picking: small villages such as Oberdorf, Eriskirch and Leimau sometimes employ migrant workers.

An account of the strawberry harvest near Wilhelmshaven in northern Germany from another Polish contributor Kristof Szymczak goes some way to explaining why so few travellers work on German fruit harvests: '*I was strawberry-picking in June/July, and I don't recommend this kind of work to anybody who isn't desperately short of money. Strawberry picking for me is really hard work, almost all day under the sun or rain. Of course it's piece work. The pickers are only from Vietnam and Turkey (already resident in Germany) and of course Poles like me. After travel and living costs, there wasn't much left.*'

Those who wish to volunteer to work on organic farms should contact the German branch of WWOOF (Willing Workers on Organic Farms), Postfach 210 259, 01263 Dresden (info@wwoof.de). Membership costs €18 plus two international reply coupons whereupon the farm list containing about 150 addresses in Germany will be sent to you within about three weeks.

VOLUNTARY OPPORTUNITIES

Most of the international organisations mentioned in the introductory chapter *Volunteering* operate schemes of one sort or another in Germany. Justin Robinson joined a workcamp to restore an old fortress used by the Nazis as a concentration camp. The green movement in Germany is very strong and many organisations concentrate their efforts on arranging projects to protect the environment or preserve old buildings. For example Internationale Jugendgemeinschaftsdienste (IJGD) organise summer 'eco-camps' and assist with city fringe recreational activities. This organisation was highly praised by a former volunteer Andrew Boyle who wrote: *'The camp was excellent value both in the nature of the work and in that the group became part of the local community. These camps are an excellent introduction to travelling for 16 to 26 year olds.'*

As usual workcamps organisations in Germany normally recruit through national partners:

IJGD, Kasernenstrasse 48, 53113 Bonn (0228-22 80 00; www.ijgd.de). Scores of camps in Germany (fee about €100). British applications accepted by Concordia and UNA Exchange.

Internationale Begegnung in Gemeinschaftsdiensten (IBG), Schlosserstrasse 28, 70180 Stuttgart (0711-649 11 28/ www.workcamps.com). Publish a booklet in English of their projects in both eastern and western Germany. Applications via CIEE or VFP (vfp@vfp.org).

Mountain Forest Project (Bergwald Projekt e.V.), Hauptstr. 24, 7014 Trin, Switzerland (081-630 4145; www.bergwaldprojekt.ch). One-week forest conservation projects in the alpine regions of southern Germany. Basic knowledge of German is useful since the foresters conduct the camps in German. Hut accommodation, food and insurance are provided free though participants must pay an annual membership fee of SFr60/€40.

Norddeutsche Jugend im Internationalen Gemeinschaftsdient (NIG), Am Gerberbruch 13A, 18055 Rostock (0381-492 2914; www.campline.de). Range of environmental and social projects in northeastern Germany.

Pro International, Bahnhofstr. 26A, 35037 Marburg/Lahn (06421-65277; www.pro-international.de). Social projects published in English (booklet and website). Application fee €65.

Vereinigung Junger Freiwilliger (VJF), Hans-Otto-Str. 7, 10407 Berlin (030-428 506 03; office@vjf.de). Camps take place in the former East Germany. Registration fee for applicants who apply directly is €220-€250.

There are some longer term possibilities as well. Internationaler Bund (IB, Burgstrasse 106, 60389 Frankfurt am Main; www.Internationaler-Bund.de) takes on young people for a period of six or twelve months in various social institutions such as hospitals, kindergartens, homes for the elderly or disabled people. In some German states, young people may also work on ecological projects. Volunteers are paid pocket money plus full board and accommodation. Their literature is published in English but their website is only in German.

An international conference centre in the Harz Mountains employs young Europeans both short term (for the duration of a conference) or longer (up to one year) as domestic staff, looking after children and as conference assistants. Contact Internationales Haus Sonnenberg, Clausthalerstr. 11, 37444 St Andreasberg (www.sonnenberg-international.de)

Survival

Living close to the edge is even less fun in Germany than it is elsewhere. Joe Warnick was reduced to sleeping in a doorway for a few nights in the ski resort of Garmisch-Parten-kirchen since there was no cheap accommodation at all. Fortunately he found a job in a hotel before he froze to death.

Medical clinics in Germany such as the AAI Human Pharmacology Centres in Munich and Neu-Ulm are reputed to pay well for medical trials, but it is increasingly difficult for foreigners to be accepted on to these lucrative pharmacological experiments. Clinics insist that you speak and read fluent German, so they can be sure you understand and legally agree to any risks involved. But the American Rod Fricker reported that he had spent several weeks in various medical testing centres in Germany, thanks to this book. Some blood donor clinics pay about €25 and you are allowed to donate every six weeks.

If you do happen to speak German watch out for media market researchers who are sometimes on the lookout for guinea pigs, as Isak Maseide discovered some years ago:

> The different agencies working for TV and movie companies were picking people at random off the streets of Munich when we were there to show them a cut of an episode of a TV series or new film before release. They then interview you to find out what the public thinks. We were accosted by an interviewer just near the Toy Museum and were paid £3 each for a nice hour in a warm room with plenty of coffee and tea and a rotten German TV series. According to the interviewer, you can make quite a lot of money going from agency to agency. Some pay as much as £8.

Not as many travellers work for hostels as in some other countries. In Berlin try either of the Circus hostels in the Mitte district (www.circus-berlin.de) which are staffed by international travellers or the Helter Skelter Hostel (www.helterskelterhostel.com).

Finding affordable accommodation in Germany is a challenge and travellers solve this problem in various ways. Dave Hewitt managed to find a room in a *Studentenheim* (university residence) in Berlin. The international youth camp under canvas Kapuzinerhölzl (in den Kirschen 30, 80992 Munich; 089-1414 300; www.the-tent.de) costs €8.50 to stay on a mat on the floor or €11 per night in the bed tent, both including breakfast. It is open only from early June till early September.

If you are really in straitened circumstances, you might like to investigate the Bahnhof mission (Travellers' Aid) which can be found at most mainline stations. But even these cannot be relied upon, as Nicola Hall discovered one cold and hungry night in Munich when she found the Bahnhofmission closed. Station waiting rooms are not recommended either, at least not by Philip O'Hara: '*I personally don't recommend Berlin Hauptbahnhof as a jolly sleeping experience unless you get your kicks from watching baton-wielding policemen removing the drunks every hour or so through the night, interspersed with said drunks returning to wake you to offer you a drink or try to cadge a fag.*'

Greece

Greece has countless attractions: beautiful scenery and climate, friendly and carefree people, memorable wine and food, a much lower cost of living than in the UK. It is no wonder that at least 11,000 Britons have settled in Greece and that so many travellers join the general drift to Greece from Northern Europe in the autumn, and the second migration from Israel and elsewhere after Easter. Many would like to extend their stay in Greece by picking up casual work, such as orange picking, dishwashing or building. Once you become a confirmed Graecophile, working will seem infinitely preferable to spending your remaining travel fund on a ticket home. Greece seems to be the country where travellers are most willing to gamble their last few euros on getting a job.

The complicating factor over the past decade has been the influx of Albanians, Serbs, Romanians, Bulgarians and Georgians. At first most of these people were working in Greece illegally and would regularly be rounded up and sent back over the border. However in 1998 and again in 2001, the Greek government implemented measures by which migrant workers who had been in the country for more than a year could obtain a white card (temporary residence permit) and eventually reside and work legally. The slow processing of applications caused chaos resulting in mass demonstrations. Large numbers of Eastern and Central Europeans have monopolised the vast bulk of casual work on farms, building sites, etc. (jobs that Greeks are unwilling to do) since they are willing to work for half of the standard daily wage and are very hard workers. With the evaporation of all the jobs created by the 2004 Olympics, many of these migrant workers are now looking for work in a country where the rate of unemployment is about 11.2%.

The work that remains for Western Europeans is mainly for women in bars and tavernas, in English language schools, as holiday reps and in private households looking after children. Outside Athens the hiring of itinerant workers to pick fruit, build houses, unload lorries, etc., often on a day-to-day basis, generally takes place in the main café or square of the town or village, where all the locals congregate to find out what's going on and possibly offer a day's work to willing new arrivals.

REGULATIONS

When EU nationals stay in any member country longer than three months, they are supposed to apply for a residence permit at least three weeks before that period expires. To get a residence permit in Greece, take your passport and a letter from your employer to the local police station or, in Athens, to the Aliens Department (Sofokleous 70 & Pireos Street, 210-523 5671). EU citizens will soon be able to file applications at their nearest Citizens' Service Centre (KEP). The English language newspaper The Athens News makes a brave attempt to summarise the regulations governing foreigner residents (www. athensnews.gr/Directory2004/1dir43.htm).

EU nationals in employment should make sure that their employer registers them with the Greek social security scheme (IKA). Contributions will be between 11% and 16% of earnings. After 60 days of paying contributions, you must go with your employer to apply for an IKA book; thereafter you are entitled to free medical treatment and reduced cost prescriptions. The IKA office in Athens at 125-127, Kifissias Avenue (210-691 4131; www. ika.gr) will give you a list of participating doctors who treat IKA patients free of charge.

Because of the expense, employers are sometimes in no hurry to regularise the status of their foreign workers. For example Julian Richards, a British graduate who went to teach English in the town of Veria, went to the trouble and expense of getting certified and translated copies of his degree certificate in order to obtain a teacher's licence and hence a residence permit; however by the end of his nine-month contract his school had still not got the documents nor had any of his IKA contributions been paid, which all employers are obliged to do.

The official literature states that even EU nationals who intend to work for periods of less than three months are supposed to report to the police within eight days of arrival in the country. But work in Greece is normally undertaken so sporadically that many decide that it is not worthwhile changing their status from that of tourist. Many working travellers who want an extended stay find it easier to pop over a border and re-enter on another three-month tourist visa. Be careful not to stay longer than the three months or you risk a hefty fine when leaving; Debbie Harrison from Australia was fined €150 when she left Greece after her season as a rep extended beyond three months. Although most casual jobs are illegal because employers aren't paying contributions, the police mostly turn a blind eye, at least to EU citizens. On the other hand, officials do sometimes visit places known to pay their staff under-the-counter and it is common for a taverna to close for the evening when they hear the 'control' is coming to visit or they ask their illegal staff to pretend to be customers or run out the back door when the police arrive.

Detailed information sheets on the procedures for EU nationals intending to work in Greece and on the social security system can be requested from the Economic & Commercial Section of the Greek Embassy, 1a Holland Park, London W11 3TP (020-7727 8860; commercial@greekembassy.org.uk).

The Greek government employment office is OAED whose headquarters are at Ethnikis Antistasis 8 str., 174 56 Alimos; 210-998 9131/2) through which EURES counsellors can be contacted.

Non-EU Nationals

Based on the new immigration law of 2001, seasonal work is categorised as any lasting less than six months in one year. Non-EU nationals can apply for permission to take a seasonal job only from outside the country, after the employer has applied to the local authorities and has posted a bond to cover the worker's return to their home country if they break the terms of the permit. Needless to say not every barmaid and English tutor goes through this process. Of course the local police will not hesitate to invoke the law if they want to get rid of someone, as happened to some aggressive Antipodeans in Santorini who were hassling tourists. They were jailed overnight and deported the next day.

The immigration police seem to target some places and not others. For more high profile and longer-term jobs like English teaching, it seems that most employers will hire outside the EU only if they are desperate, at least according to the American Richard Spacer, who taught English in Corfu until he was fired after the police talked to his employer.

Non-EU citizens working in Athens should regularise their status at the Aliens Bureau at Antigonis Street 99, Kolonos, Athens (210-510 2706).

TOURISM

Millions of tourists choose Greece for their annual hols. Anyone who looks for work at the beginning of the season (from early May) should be able to find an opening somewhere. A good time to look is just before the Orthodox Easter when the locals are beginning to gear up for the season. If you do fix up a job that early, you will have to be prepared to support yourself until the job starts. In a few cases there is work outside the May to September period especially if you are willing to work on a commission-only basis.

You are more likely to find work in places that are isolated from the local culture, in American/European style bars in the cities and resorts, where disco music is played and package tourists willingly pay over the odds for imported Scotch and gin. The monthly electronic jobs listing *Jobs Abroad Bulletin* (www.jobsabroadbulletin.co.uk) carries a sprinkling of vacancies in Greece most recently by Naxos Camping (zorosia@otenet.gr), Hotel Coral in Roda, Corfu (coralhot@otenet.gr), No Limits watersports centre on the north coast of Crete (thoma3@otenet.gr) and the British-style Flying Pig pub in Piraeus (flying_pig_pub@yahoo.com).

Jobs in cafés patronised by local Greeks are not an impossibility as Rhiannon Bryant from Dorset discovered in Crete some years ago:

> *I was the only bar girl in Palaiokhora who enjoyed working at the Jam Bar; all the others had left within a month. The only customers were Greek men, no English-speaking types, just local 'cowboys'. Late each night the cowboy saloon doors would swing open and in they'd step, always in a group with synchronised movements. The right foot, a twiddle of their moustaches, then the left foot, followed by a flick of their worry beads, their pockets bulging with pistols and bullets. I was fascinated. The Cretan music would drive them to a frenzy, smashing bottles, glasses and on one occasion, a guy was so excited he shot the toilet. The atmosphere was explosive. If I wasn't dodging bullets and glass, I'd stare mesmerised. Actually one of them is now my boyfriend. Beneath their macho exteriors they are very kind-hearted, gentle guys.*

Women travellers will find it much easier than men to land a casual job in a bar or restaurant. As one disgruntled male traveller wrote to us: *'In general I would say that if you're a girl you have a 50% better chance of finding work in the tourist industry abroad. In Greece I would say women have a 500% better chance. Every pub I went into on Corfu seemed to have an English barmaid.'*

Alison Cooper describes the transience she experienced working in the tourist industry:'I spent the summer on the island of Ios doing the typical touristy work: waitressing, touting, dishwashing, etc. It was very common to have worked at four different places in a week due to being sacked for not flirting with your boss, but I had a great time partying all night and sunbathing all day long.' Think of Shirley Valentine. Undoubtedly the motives of some employers in hiring women are less than honourable. If you get bad vibes, move on.

A typical starting wage would be €15-€20 (cash-in-hand) plus tips and two meals for an eight-hour shift (5pm-1am). This is enough to fund quite a good time if you are camping or sharing a cheap room. Bar work is more difficult to find because it is better paid and usually involves cocktail-mixing experience. Hotel work (chambermaiding and cleaning) is not so well paid.

Some women find the legendary attention paid by prowling male Greeks intolerable; others have said this unwanted admiration is not unduly difficult to handle. Once you

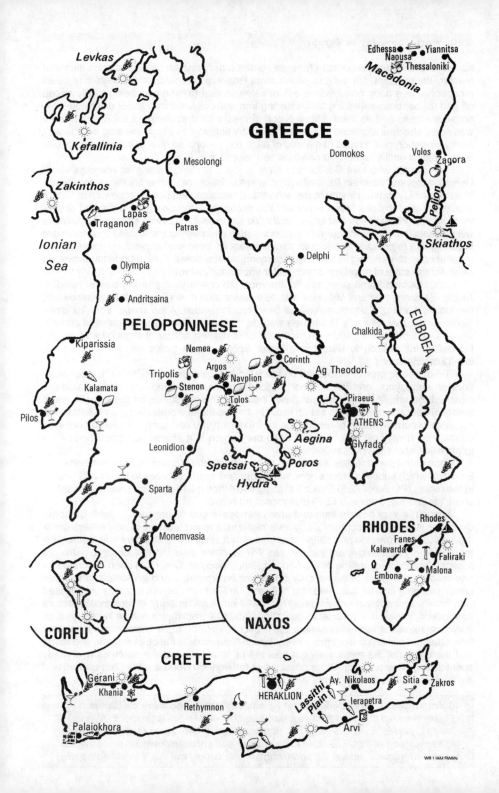

have established your reputation (one way or the other) you will be treated accordingly, at least by the regulars. On her gap year, Emma Hoare lasted precisely 20 days in a job as receptionist in a hotel on Mykonos before realising that (a) she was being totally ripped off and (b) her boss was a big fat disgusting immoral bully, whom another disgruntled ex-employee described as 'feral'. When Nicola Sarjeant's bar at Perissa Beach on Santorini was quiet, she was expected to liven things up by dancing, to which she said 'No thanks'. Always insist on getting paid at the end of each day's work, so no misunderstandings can arise, at least until you feel you can trust your employer.

Even people who love Greece and have enjoyed working there offer warnings about Greek employers. Stephen Psallidas (who speaks Greek) describes his life as a waiter on Mykonos as idyllic but goes on to describe the 'down side' and how to cope with it: *'Greek employers are the worst I've ever known! You should be very careful since they will always try to rip you off when you first arrive. You must stand up for yourself, since any weakness will be exploited. Greek restaurant bosses are also often very unprofessional, for example requiring you to present 'fiddled' bills to customers or, even worse, pinching your tips.'* He recommends threatening to leave and carrying out the threat if things don't improve, as much for the sake of travellers coming after you as for your own.

Corfu, Ios and Paros seem to offer the most job openings in tourism, though Rhodes, Naxos, Santorini, Kos and Mykonos and, to a lesser extent, Aegina, Spetsai, Skiathos and the Ionian island of Zakynthos have all been recommended. A job-seeker from Yorkshire reported on Lonely Planet's Thorn Tree website that when she was in Kardamena on Kos, she passed a number of bars/restaurants with 'Staff Wanted' notices. It might be worth applying before the season to Kardamena Water Sports Centre (voicemail/fax 22420-91341; info@koswatersports.gr).

The meteoric growth of tourism on the island of Zakynthos (or Zante) has put pressure on employers, and the number of good workers (including entertainers) has not matched the employment opportunities. Check out the classifieds on the website www. zanteconnect.com which was set up recently by two expat women living on the island. It carries a decent selection of resort-type jobs to which you can apply, workers' accommodation (which will cost roughly €150-€170 per person in a shared apartment) and local information about the bureaucracy.

Flamboyant personalities might want to investigate the Remarc Agency in Athens and Belgrade which supplies entertainers, animators and sports services to hotels and resorts in the region (PO Box 77260, Paleo Faliro, 17510 Athens; 210-985 8553; www.sunseafun. com); the promised wage is €550 plus room and board.

Working in very heavily touristed areas can leave you feeling jaded. Scott Corcoran describes Kavos in the south of Corfu as a 'nightmare resort town full of northerners drinking Newcastle brown ale and eating chip butties' but since it has 200 bars and restaurants there is plenty of employment including as 'PR' workers, persuading tourists to patronise a certain establishment. The 1,000-bedded Pink Palace on Corfu has been described by one reader as a cross between a Club Med for backpackers and an American summer camp, though it is to be assumed that neither Club Med nor children's camps are plagued with brawls and noisy drunkenness. The hostel employs an army of foreign workers as bartenders, cooks, receptionists, etc. (26610-53103; root@pink-palace.ker.forthnet.gr; www.thepinkpalace.com/employment.asp). Michel Falardeau, a more mature traveller from Quebec, picked up work there even though November is the quiet season, and found that the wage (all the employees got less than €10 a day) was not much as everybody spent their money partying. Other possibilities for work on Corfu are the Club Barbati and the yachting centre Gouvia near Corfu town.

Safra Wightman was delighted at how easily she found work on Naxos:
Finally I cashed my last travellers cheque and headed for the largest of the Cycladic islands, Naxos, to find a job. The numerous bars, cafés and tavernas seemed quite daunting at first. I decided to be choosy and approach only the places which appealed to me. I strolled the paralia and a café caught my eye. I marched up to a

> *Greek guy standing in the doorway and asked him if he had a job for me. He simply said yes and I started work that evening. The Greeks appreciate a direct approach. They are kind, welcoming, generous people.*

Safra went on to recommend going to the favourite haunts of working travellers on Naxos to find out about openings, such as the Ocean Club Disco on the road to Agios Georgios and the Musique Café in the main square.

On Paros, there are jobs in the main town of Parikia and also in the quieter town of Naoussa where the season is shorter, accommodation less expensive and wages higher. The Sani Beach Holiday Resort on the Halkidiki peninsula east of Thessaloniki (www. saniresort.gr) employs a large number of hospitality trainees aged 18-20 for a minimum of five or six months on a 'training wage' of €16-€18 per eight-hour shift (63077 Kassandra, Halkidiki; 23740-99447; groutsou@saniresort.gr).

Foreigners (especially women) may also be hired in tourist resorts to deliver cars for car rental firms or to act as transfer couriers. Xuela Edwards and her companion Nicky Brown went to the package resort of Lindos on Rhodes in April and were offered several jobs on the first day. They worked as 'escorts' on day-trips from the village and also did airport transfers for British tour companies which paid a flat fee whether or not an arriving flight was delayed. They found this work by asking around at those local travel agencies which acted as the headquarters for overseas reps. According to Xuela this work requires that you be 'presentable, reliable, able to work all night and get up very early in the morning'. When Debbie Harrison was repping on Kos, they were so desperate for more transfer reps that they attempted to recruit their customers.

Another long-time contributor Camilla Lambert was based on the Ionian island of Levkas for five months working for Sunsail (see section *Boating* below) and acted as an occasional freelance guide on the side: *'I also earned money driving tourists round the island in a hired jeep, as many had forgotten their driving licences and I knew which roads were passable and where the cheapest tavernas were. It cost me about £30 a day to rent a 4-wheel drive vehicle so if you take three passengers and they pay £15 each you make a profit while getting away from base.'*

Seasonal jobs can be arranged from the UK. Mark Warner (08700 330750/760) run several beachclub hotels in Greece which require British staff who are paid from £50 per week depending on the position, in addition to full board and accommodation and use of watersport facilities. Good possibilities exist with Olympic Holidays (1 Torrington Park, Finchley, London N12 9SU; 0870 499 6742; www.olympicholidays.co.uk) who are always on the lookout for outgoing EU nationals over 21 to work a season as resort reps (candidates must be over 21) or transfer reps (for those over 20). Pavilion Tours (Lynnem House, 1 Victoria Way, Burgess Hill, West Sussex RH15 9NF; 0870 241 0425; www.paviliontours.com) which need windsurfing, kayaking and sailing instructors for children. They must be qualified to RYA/BCU Level 2 and have teaching experience.

Tour operators seem to be more interested in finding the right attitude rather than experience when recruiting reps, as Debbie Harrison discovered:
Despite the fact that I had no qualifications or relevant experience, had never been to Greece and had never even been on a package holiday, I was offered a job on the island of Kos immediately at the end of my interview. Perhaps this had something to do with the fact that it was mid-March, less than a month before training began and they obviously still had positions to fill. However tour operators do hire reps as late as May or June to help out with the extra workload of high season. Six or seven months is a long time to stay in one place. One of the reasons I stuck it out to the end was so I'd get my £100 deposit refunded. As a rep my wages were about £300 per month on top of accommodation. The youngest full-time rep was an 18 year old who had just finished a college course in Tourism, and at the other end of the scale, one of my colleagues was 28 and had resigned from her position at an advertising agency to work in the sun for a bit.

Note that the tour operator for which Debbie worked was Golden Sun Holidays which went bust in September 2004.

Hostels

The competition for business among hostels and cheap pensions is so intense that many hostel owners employ travellers to entice/bully new arrivals into staying at their hostel. In exchange for meeting the relevant boat, train or bus, 'runners' (otherwise known as couriers, touts or hawkers) receive a bed, a small amount of cash-in-hand and a small commission for every 'catch.' The system of hustling or touting is well established in Athens (especially among the hostels around Omonia Square) and to some extent on the islands, but is not necessarily to be recommended. Kathy Hood from New Zealand describes her experience on Naxos:

> My boyfriend and I unfortunately became enlightened as to the illegality of 'hawking' people for hotels. It is illegal to hawk on boats or on the port past a certain line which is usually made clear by hordes of screaming hotel owners. Having spent a night in the port police offices and an afternoon in court, I would strongly recommend that travellers don't take up such an opportunity should it arise. We were, however, let off on the grounds of traveller's naïveté.

The situation in Athens can be cut-throat. There will be as many as 30 hostels vying for custom at Athens station, not to mention further competition and much animosity from taxi drivers (who want to earn a commission from hotels). Working conditions vary among the hostels and you soon learn which are the bad ones. If you are looking for this work, it is easier making enquiries at the station where the runners congregate rather than going from hostel to hostel.

Many enjoy the hostel atmosphere and the camaraderie among hostel workers (at least the ones who do not take the job too seriously), and they regard the job as a useful stop-gap while travel plans are formulated, often based on the advice of fellow travellers. Anyone who sticks at it for any length of time may find themselves 'promoted' to reception; in this business a fortnight might qualify you for the honour of being a long-term employee.

A great many hostels offer the same wage and perks to people who will spend a few hours a day cleaning. This work is easy-come, easy-go, and is seldom secure even when you want it to be. Consolas Travel near Omonia Square (100 Eolou St, 105 64 Athens; 210-324 1751; consolas@hol.gr; www.consolas.gr) is a travel agency that may be able to offer work in hostels, etc. in Athens and the islands including Paros and Gavdos.

Selling & Enterprise

When taking advantage of the opportunities afforded by tourism, you need not confine yourself to hotels, restaurants and cafés. Mandy Blumenthal funded her island-hopping by selling 500 pairs of sunglasses brought from England. If you have any handicraft skills like making jewelry, the tourist areas of Greece could provide a lucrative market for your wares. Safra Wightman was very glad she had remembered to take her scissors to Naxos where she was able to market her training as a hairdresser. Hannah Adcock and her partner were heading to Santorini for the summer of 2005 to run a bookshop set up by friends of theirs. If you are arriving from Asia, you can stock up on cheap Eastern jewelry as Kristen Moen did. She found Corfu a very successful market for Indian, Nepali, Thai and Chinese jewelry.

You may try to sell your product to souvenir shops, set up an independent market stall or sell on the streets. If you choose the latter, make sure that it is allowed, since the police in busy resorts have been cracking down on this as Nicola Hall (now Dickinson) reported from Crete several years ago:

We came across a young lad who had been making friendship bangles and hair pieces and street trading in Hersonisos (on the coast east of Heraklion). It is now illegal to sell on the street here, as it is in Malia, the next town along. The police give you three warnings and then fine you dr60,000 and if you can't pay they put you in jail for 22 days where all you are given is bread and water. He was paid to look out for the cops and, if they came, to clear up the stuff and run with it.

Anyone who can paint portraits may be in for a bonanza. Street artists in the main resorts charge £10 for a 15-minute portrait and can expect to do four in an evening. You can also try to sell paintings of restaurants, banks, etc. to the establishment concerned. There is often work to be had painting signs and notice boards (primarily at the beginning of the season) or decorating the walls and doors of tourist places themselves. This can be quite well paid if you are good at it and get a good reputation. Nicola saw so many misspelled signs on Zakynthos (her favourite advertised 'daft Cider') she was sure someone with both artistic and orthographic talents could persuade Greek bar owners to pay for a sign.

On her most recent trip to Greece, Nicola Hall became Nicola Dickinson in a picturesque little church on St. Paul's Bay, Rhodes: *'Many people get married here throughout the season including us. We noticed that of all the oil paintings there was none of St. Paul's Bay and the church, which was a shame because it is so lovely and we would gladly have bought a picture of it. So I've taken up oil painting classes in the hope of one day going back there and providing a service for newly weds.'*

Boating

Yachting holiday companies are a possible source of jobs, which can be fixed up either ahead of time or on the spot. Camilla Lambert greatly enjoyed her season with the sailing holiday operator Sunsail (The Port House, Port Solent, Portsmouth, Hants. PO6 4TH; 02392 222308; www.sunsail.com) which started in April with a two-week refit of the clubhouse and scrubbing and painting the boats. Sunsail hire sailors, hostesses, clubhouse staff, cooks and nannies.

Sailing Holidays Ltd (105 Mount Pleasant Road, London NW10 3EH; 020-8459 8787; www.sailingholidays.com) look to hire flotilla skippers and hostesses, boat builders and marine engineers for their upmarket holiday programme in the Greek and Dalmatian islands. The specialist tour operator Setsail Holidays (PO Box 5524, Sudbury, Suffolk CO10 2ED; 01787 310445; boats@setsail.co.uk) recruits a similar range of staff for the six-month season in the eastern Med.

In the past people have found work by visiting skippering brokers and yacht agencies around Piraeus. Some may require boat cleaners and general help which could lead to better things. English companies such as Camper & Nicholson prefer to hire English speakers, as do many local firms. Two yacht charterers identified on the website of the Jobs Abroad Bulletin (www.payaway.co.uk/greece.shtml) may need occasional staff: Polco Yachts Ltd, 124 Papadiamanti St, Koridallis, 181 21 Piraeus (www polco.net) and Seahorse Yacht Brokers, 83 Kon. Karamanlis Avenue, Voula Marina 166 73, Athens (210-895 2212; www.seahorse.gr).

On islands where there is a lot of yachting traffic, you might find a job living on a boat. Mary Falls frequented a popular bar in Rhodes Town and soon found a half day's work polishing the brass of a boat. Someone who happened to notice how industriously she worked invited her to stay on his boat, working in exchange for her keep. After that she was taken on as the cook while the boat cruised the Turkish coast. Gouvia on Corfu is another place full of yachties coming and going, with harbour facilities sophisticated enough to handle the super luxury yachts that often take on hostesses and crew.

The numerous cruise ships which ply the Aegean Sea are occasionally looking for personnel to replace people who have left their jobs in the ship's restaurants, bars or in the entertainment programme. Phone numbers of the relevant companies can be obtained from travel agents or found in the Yellow Pages under *Krouazieres*.

AGRICULTURE

Working in the English-speaking environment of tourism is not for everyone and certainly does not conform to Ben Nakoneczny's philosophy of travel:

> *If you are to work abroad it is preferable to be employed in a capacity which allows an insight into the people of the country you are visiting. To serve English tourists bottled beer in a western-style bar is merely to experience the company of those travellers who cling to what they know, unprepared to risk the unfamiliarity of an alien culture. I believe that the best way of breaking cultural boundaries is to work outside the tourist areas, probably in agriculture.*
>
> *Unfortunately these days you might end up deserting an English-speaking environment only to find yourself in an Albanian or Romanian one. Most of the feedback received over the past couple of editions of this book has read more like an epitaph than a how-to guide.*

For example Siôn from Wales revisited the Peloponnese on a sentimental journey, recalling his experiences as a fruitpicker and casual worker when he was a contributor to this book in its infancy: *'The citrus pickers I watched in the Sparta region seemed to be Romanians and Greeks. I didn't notice any of the sort of seasonal workers in Kalamata, Mystras and Sparta that I knew in the early eighties in Greece. I remembered my time on the mainland when I and others had been offered seasonal work by drivers merely by walking along roads.'*

Inevitably, travellers will continue to meet farmers in cafés and be asked to lend a hand here and there in the harvesting of oranges, olives, grapes and other crops. But the employment of young international travellers does not take place on the massive scale it once did and so the lengthy sections in previous editions on fruit harvesting in Greece have been cut.

Jane McNally suggests mastering the following few words: *kopse* (cut), *sheera* (drill/row), *ilea* (olives), *thermo keepio* (greenhouse), *kafasi* (crate), none of which will be found in a conventional phrase book (which is more likely to translate for you 'Excuse me, does Yorkshire pudding come with my roast beef?' or 'I'm going to be sick' rather than 'Do you need help in your fields?') Make very sure of your instructions before tackling the task. Rhiannon Bryant's Greek was not very advanced but she did decipher the word *kopse* when she went to the Cretan village of Kondouras to help in one of the many tomato greenhouses. She proceeded to hack her way through the plants, but was never paid for her stint since in five hours she had managed to destroy an entire crop.

The orange harvest between Corinth and Argos and south to Tolo runs from late November or early December to late February, with the crop at its peak between mid-December and mid-January.

The Mani peninsula on mainland Greece is famed for its olives. Visitors may be welcomed to help with the December harvest more for local colour than for money. A journalist writing in *The Times* a couple of years ago described how she fulfilled her romantic ambition to 'commune with the olive groves' by staying in Areopoli and helping an expatriate Austrian olive farmer in Pyrgos Dirou to harvest his organic olive crop on a hospitality basis, i.e. free room and board but no wage.

Crete and the Islands

Crete, the largest of the Greek islands, was once able to provide a huge amount of work to travellers, from the bananas in Arvi on the south coast (the most northerly commercial banana plantations in the world) to the potato harvest around Ayios Georgios in the Lassithi Plain in August, but mainly involving the grape and olive crops. The olive harvest normally begins in late November but can be delayed if the rains are late. In the old days, the villagers waited for the ripe olives to fall by themselves into nets beneath but nowadays the trees are beaten with sticks and branches are shaken to dislodge the olives. A pair of pickers can strip about five trees in a day.

Men may be able to find jobs in olive processing plants as Scott Corcoran did one December: *'I eventually got a job at an olive oil processing shed in the village of Kallithea (5km southwest of Heraklion). This involved working 16 hours a day (8am till midnight) carrying sacks of olives and processing them in the factory. I was given free room and board in addition to a decent wage. By Christmas I had had enough and moved on.'*

The two areas that absorb the most pickers are around the two largest cities: a few kilometres south of Heraklion you will hit valley after valley of grapes which are picked from mid-August and just west of Khania, crops are grown around Platanias and Gerani. The village of Voukolies south-west of Khania has been recommended both for olives (from late November to mid-February) and oranges (January to April). Tomatoes are grown in hothouses around Palaiokhora and in the village of Stomio on the south coast; the picking mainly takes place from April to June.

Northern Greece

Although much of northern Greece is rugged and forbidding, some of it is very fertile. It is also closer to the Yugoslav, Albanian and Bulgarian borders. The area west of Thessaloniki, encompassing the market towns of Veria and Yiannitsa, is a major peach growing area, centred on the villages of Makrohoria, Diavato, Kavasila, Kasmena and Stavros all near Veria. The harvest gets started in mid-July but peaks after August 1st. Tomatoes are picked in the village of Kavasila. A good worker who can stand the sun can make a lot as piece work rates are paid.

Yiannitsa 50km northwest of Thessaloniki is the centre of a rich agricultural area, especially known for its tobacco crop. Further west there is apple and pear picking in September/October around the towns of Skedra and Edhessa. Another region to try is the Pelion peninsula south of Volos. This area is very fertile and green with apple trees, pears, walnuts and blackberries fruiting in September. Most of the apple picking is centred on Zagora, though work can be found in the much smaller town of Makrirakhi.

OTHER WORK

It is sometimes worth checking the Situations Vacant column of the English daily *Athens News* (9 Christou Lada, 102 37 Athens; an-classified@dolnet.gr). You can check the classified ads on the internet (www.athensnews.gr). Adverts range from the distinctly dodgy ('Smart-looking girls required for co-operation in luxury bar') to the legitimate ('English girl wanted for babysitting'). Most are for au pair, nanny or English-tutoring jobs in private households. Obviously these jobs may not be the most desirable in the world as Vaughan Temby discovered: he left his 'hideous valet/houseboy job' after just two days. You could also try placing your own advertisement in the Situations Wanted. The minimum rate for advertising is €10 for 15 words.

Also check out the American-biased www.ads-in-greece.com which lists a few job vacancies, though these are outnumbered by 'Services Offered' (Employment Wanted) postings. One interesting opportunity was listed at the beginning of 2005: an agency called InGlobe O.E. was promoting a Work & Travel in Greece programme. Jobs were promised in hotels, restaurants, bars, clubs and families all over Greece for English speaking people aged 18-45 years old. The contact name was Maria Tsilempi (Karaoli & Dimitriou 193, Evosmos, Thessaloniki (2310-588200; fax 2310-588202; inglobe@axiom.gr).

The Athens Chamber of Commerce and Industry (7 Academias Str, 106 71 Athens (210-360 4815-9/ fax: 210-361 6408; info@acci.gr/ www.acci.gr) may be able to advise skilled candidates on jobs with Greek companies.

Childcare

The Nine Muses Agency accepts postal applications from young Europeans and American women for au pair positions and can also place candidates after arrival in Athens. Hotel positions are also sometimes available. Contact the agency at PO Box 76080, 171 10 Nea Smyrni, (El. Venizelou 4b, 171 21 Nea Smyrni), Athens; 210-931 6588; www.ninemuses. gr). The owner Kalliope Raekou prides herself on her after-placement service, meeting regularly with au pairs at coffee afternoons. There is no fee to au pairs. Among her satisfied au pairs is Riitta Koivula from Finland who, from an unsatisfactory situation on Kos, moved with Popy Raekou's help to a much better one in Athens:

> *I started my work as an au pair on Kos when I was 19. At first I was so excited about my new family and the new place since I had never been to Greece before and I loved the sun and the beach. I lived in a small village called Pili where almost no one spoke English. But soon I got tired of the village because winter came, tourists left and it wasn't so warm to spend time on the beach any more. I also got tired of the family. The three little girls didn't speak English and they were very lively. The working hours were also terrible: 8 to 12 in the morning and then 4 to 10 in the evening every day except Sundays. I was very homesick on Kos and decided I wanted things to change. So I went to Athens in November and was soon given a new family. I fell in love with Athens and its people right away. My new family was the best and we are still very close. I met other au pairs and one Finnish au pair became my best friend. I learned so many things, even to read and write and speak Greek because we took Greek lessons during the spring with Popy. I have many happy memories of Athens and friends who are still dear to me.*

At the time of writing the Athenian Domestic Agency was advertising that it could place qualified and/or experienced nannies, au pairs and maternity nurses in Greece for a minimum period of a year (ezelda@otenet.gr). The last available address for the ADA is K. Kotta 28, Neo Psyhico, Athens 11525 (tel/fax 210-672 3974). Positions are primarily for childcare professionals willing to provide good references.

Au pair and mother's help positions may of course be booked through agencies in Britain. Lucy Locketts & Vanessa Bancroft Nanny Agency (400 Beacon Road, Wibsey, Bradford, BD6 3DJ; tel/fax 01274 402822) has a few summer vacancies for mothers' helps in the Greek islands and mainland.

The main advantage of waiting until you get to Greece to look for a live-in job is that you can meet your prospective family first. It is far better for both parties if you can chat over a cup of coffee and bargain in a leisurely fashion for wages, time off, duties, etc. Most families looking for nannies live in the well-off suburbs of Athens like Kifissia, Politia, Pangrati and Kolonaki as well as in Thessaloniki, Patras and the islands. The Greek attitude to privacy differs from the British one, but in most cases the au pair is given a private room except on summer holidays where she might be expected to share with the children.

Teaching English

Thousands of private language schools called *frontisteria* are scattered throughout Greece, creating a huge demand for native English speaker teachers. This is one job for which there will be no competition from Albanians, though it should be noted that Australians, South Africans and North Americans of Greek ancestry are often given teaching jobs in preference to people with non-Greek surnames.

Standards at *frontisteria* vary from indifferent to excellent, but the run-of-the-mill variety is usually a reasonable place to work for nine months. By no means all of the foreign teachers hired by *frontisteria* hold a TEFL qualification, though all but the most dodgy schools will expect to see a university degree (which is a government requirement for a teacher's licence) and EU nationality.

The majority of jobs are in towns and cities in mainland Greece. Athens has such a large expatriate community that most of the large central schools are able to hire well-qualified staff locally. But this is not the case in Edessa, Larisa, Preveza or any of numerous towns of which the tourist to Greece is unlikely to have heard. The minimum hourly wage is currently about €6 gross. Anyone with some training or experience should be able to ask for a slightly higher rate. Earnings can be increased substantially by compulsory bonuses at Christmas and Easter and holiday pay at the end of the contract. Be prepared for long hours by normal English teaching standards, often 30 or 32 hours per week.

Chains of schools are always worth approaching with your CV. Try for example ISON Foreign Language Centres part of the Strategakis Group (24 Proxenou Koromila St, 546 22 Thessaloniki; 2310-264276; www.ison.edu.gr) which employs 25 British and Irish teachers for 100 schools all over northern Greece. Application can be made online and are especially welcomed in May/June and August/September.

Several teacher recruitment agencies actively seek teachers to work for one academic year. Interviews are carried out in Greece or the UK during the summer for contracts starting in September. These agencies are looking for people with at least a BA and normally a TEFL certificate (depending on the client *frontisterion's* requirements). The following undertake to match EU teachers with *frontisteria* and do not charge teachers a fee:

Anglo-Hellenic Teacher Recruitment, PO Box 263, 201 00 Corinth (27410-53511; jobs@anglo-hellenic.com; www.anglo-hellenic.com). Dozens of posts in wide choice of locations for university graduates from the UK, preferably with a CELTA or Trinity TESOL. Interviews conducted in London, Corinth or Athens during the summer.

Cambridge Teachers Recruitment, 17 Metron St, New Philadelphia, 143 42 Athens (tel/fax 210-258 5155; macleod_smith_andrew@hotmail.com). One of the largest agencies, placing 75 teachers per year in vetted schools. Applicants must have a degree and in most cases a TEFL Certificate, a friendly personality and conscientious attitude.

After travelling and working in Greece for a couple of years, Jane McNally wrote from a school in Macedonia with some advice:

> Most English speakers find work in private English schools. It can be difficult to find work by just knocking on school doors. Most school owners recruit their staff through agents two or three months in advance of the new term. If you want to bring a partner check first with your employer in case you are expected to share a flat or even a room with another teacher. All my colleagues and myself have had discipline problems in the classroom. Be prepared for employers that range from nutty to demented!

By the time Jamie Masters decided to go to Crete to teach English, it was too late to register with the agencies. He arrived in Heraklion in October:

> I advertised (in Greek) in the Cretan newspapers, no joy. I lowered my sights and started knocking on doors of frontisteria. I was put onto some guy who ran an English-language bookshop and went to see him. Turned out he was some kind of lynchpin in the frontisterion business and in fact I got my first job through him. Simultaneously I went to something which roughly translates as the 'Council for owners of frontisteria' and was given a list of schools which were looking for people. The list, it turned out, was pretty much out of date. But I had insisted on leaving my name with the Council (they certainly didn't offer) and that's how I found my second job.

Private lessons, at least in the provinces, are possible to find. The going rate is about €15 an hour for First Certificate teaching, more for Cambridge Proficiency. Rates are higher in Athens. Most employed teachers do at least three or four hours a week of private undeclared teaching – more than enough to cover their Retsina bill.

Volunteering

Conservation Volunteers Greece (Veranzerou 15, 106 77 Athens; 210-382 5506; marina@cvgpeep.gr; www.cvgpeep.gr) is a non-profit organisation promoting intercultural exchanges and nature and heritage conservation. Projects include work in protected landscapes, conservation of traditional buildings and work on archaeological sites. Applications should be sent to a partner workcamp organisation in your country (e.g. UNA Exchange in the UK). The participation fee for people applying directly is €120 for two or three weeks (possible extra fee for special cultural camps).

Organisations involved in the protection of sea turtles actively use volunteer helpers. Archelon is the Sea Turtle Protection Society of Greece (Solomou 57, 104 32 Athens; tel/fax 210-523 1342; stps@archelon.gr; www.archelon.gr) which carries out research and conservation on the loggerhead turtle on Zakynthos, Crete and the Peloponnese. A free campsite is provided for those who stay at least a month; volunteers will need at least €15 a day for food plus pay a registration fee of €100.

Voluntary Action for Youth (Athinas 13, Agia Varvara, Athens 123 51 (210-561 0728; www.youthcamp.gr) organises summer workcamps lasting 2-3 weeks in both Greece and Cyprus. Camp details are released mid-March. The participation fee is €130 which covers free accommodation and meals for the camp.

MEDASSET (Mediterranean Association to Save the Sea Turtles), 1c Licavitou Str, 106 72 Athens (210-361 3572; medasset@medasset.org; www.euroturtle.org/medasset) offers volunteers free accommodation in central Athens in exchange for working for a minimum of three weeks in the Medasset office providing administrative back-up for a sea turtle rescue project in Zakintos and elsewhere in the eastern Mediterranean.

Bears are even more threatened than marine turtles. *Arcturos* accepts short-term volunteers at its bear protection centre. The office is at Victor Hugo 3, 546 25 Thessaloniki (2310-55 59 20; arcturos@arcturos.gr) whereas the Arcturos Environmental Centre is in the northwest corner of Greece (530 75 Aetos, Prefecture of Florina; 23860-41500, aec@arcturos.gr).

Another interesting possibility for people with specific skills willing to work for pocket money for at least three months (May to July or August to October) is at the holistic holiday centre on the island of *Skyros* in the northern Aegean. A number of 'work scholars' help with cleaning, bar work and domestic and maintenance duties in exchange for full board and accommodation and £50 a week for three months. (Bilingual nurses and chefs are preferred.) The main perk is that they are welcome to join one or more of the 250 courses on offer from yoga to windsurfing. Details are available from Skyros, 92 Prince of Wales Road, London NW5 3NE (020-7267 4424; connect@skyros.com).

Cyprus

The Cypriot economy like its Greek counterpart relies heavily on tourism (nearly three million tourists visited the island last year) and agriculture which can normally be counted on to provide work for travellers. In the early 1990s it is registering a remarkably low rate of unemployment of 4% - less than 1% long-term unemployed - which bodes well for job-seekers. The accession of Cyprus to the European Union in 2004 has dispensed with the bureaucracy of work permits since it elected not to implement a transitional period before labour could move freely in and out of the country. With Turkey energetically pursuing its hopes of joining the EU (which is unlikely to be within a decade) there is also hope that the problem of Turkish Cyprus may be resolved. (Northern Cyprus is dealt with separately at the end of this chapter.)

A visitor to Greek Cyprus will be struck by the similarities with Greece (language, cuisine, architecture, landscapes and culture) but then surprised by the relative prominence of English and the widespread British influence. Because Britain was the island's colonial master until 1960, almost everybody speaks English as a second language, which means that there is less demand for native speaker English teachers in private institutes. However the tourist industry requires a huge influx of seasonal labour. Note that the cost of living is higher than in Greece.

Regulations

According to a letter from the Cypriot Department of Labour written after accession in 2004 (as posted on the internet) the formalities are as follows:

Nationals from member states of the European Economic Area have the right to enter Cyprus by simply showing a valid EU passport or ID Card without having to register upon arrival. No work permit is required. However, the applicant must get the ARC (Alien Residence Certificate) by showing up at the nearest police station. If they intend to stay longer than three months and take up employment they will need a residence permit. They must apply for the residence permit before the initial three months expires by going in person to the Civil Registration & Migration Department at the local police station. One of the document required is a document of engagement of employment from the employer, stamped by the Labour Dept. The residence permit is issued within six months of the date of application and will be valid for a five-year period; the applicant is permitted to work while waiting for the residence permit to be processed.

Australians are lucky that there is a reciprocal working holiday scheme whereby people aged 18-25 can apply in Australia for a one-year working holiday visa for Cyprus.

The Tourist Industry

Most big tour operators consider placement in Cyprus as a perk to be offered to staff who have worked well for the company elsewhere, especially if they have worked in Greece and picked up some of the language. Cyprus has the advantage of offering work during the winter as well as the summer, though it has special short seasonal attractions when it is especially busy, such as for the spring flowers.

For a list of tour operators to Cyprus in addition to Olympic Holidays mentioned earlier, see the listing on www.tourist-offices.org.uk/Cyprus/uktourops.html. Specialists include Cyplon Holidays (561-563 Green Lanes, London N8 0RL; www.cyplon.com) and Amathus Holidays (2 Leather Lane, London EC1N 7RA; www.amathusholidays.co.uk). Cyprus features in most Winter Sun brochures such as that of the Christian tour operator Mastersun (63-67 Kingston Road, New Malden, Surrey KT3 3PB; 020-8942 9442) whose website describes its job vacancies (www.mastersun.co.uk/jobs.asp)

Also check specialist recruitment websites such as www.jobs.com.cy and www.cyprus-jobs.com. The chain of Louis Hotels (www.louishotels.com) is often hiring either for their hotels or for their cruise division based in Limassol (www.louiscruises.com). Luxury hotels like the Coral Beach Hotel in Paphos (www.coral.com.cy) and the Amathus Beach Hotel in Limassol have frequent vacancies (check websites for an employment icon).

As in Greece, women are at a great advantage when looking for work in cafés, bars and restaurants, but they should exercise caution according to Karen Holman:

In my two years there I heard stories about Cypriot employers expecting more of their barmaids than just bar work. I worked in two pubs and I would say that both bosses employed me with an ulterior motive. I was lucky – both of them were shy. By the time they realised I wasn't going to be their girlfriend, they had found me to be a good worker and were used to me being around. Many employers will sack the girls, or threaten to report them for stealing.

Just such a serious case of exploitation and harassment was reported in the British press a few years ago. A 23 year old trainee lawyer who had met her employer on a previous holiday found herself working 15 hours a day without a day off in temperatures of over 100°. The final straw came when the manager hit her after she rebuffed his advances. She instantly quit and was paid C£40 for 15 days work.

Rhona Stannage was much luckier: her boss (whom she met in a novel way) was gay. In the supermarket in Protaras she and her husband Stuart introduced themselves to a man whose trolley was so full of bottles, they reckoned he must run a restaurant. He practically offered Rhona a job on the spot as waitress and cleaner, and offered Stuart a cooking job two days later.

Tom Parker had little success with a job search along the seafront in Limassol in April:

> We headed for the tourist area and were soon told that we would stand a better chance if we bought a drink for the manager before asking about jobs. The only concrete result was that we got very drunk. No job opportunities (they told us we were too early). The next day we concentrated on the small cafés in the back streets of the old town. Here my two companions (both girls) were offered jobs in separate cafés. The kitchen job paid £13 a shift and the waiting job £16, both plus tips. They both also worked in a bar in the evening, sitting round talking to the mainly local customers and being bought drinks for which the customer was charged £6.50 whether it was water or vodka and they earned a commission of £1 per drink, in addition to the evening shift fee of £13.

Outdoor Work

Because he was male, Tom Parker did not find a restaurant job. But on the advice of his guest house landlady he found two weeks of (backbreaking) weeding work with a landscape gardener, which paid £20 a day. Work on the boats in Limassol or Larnaca harbours might also materialise.

Moving away from the tourist resorts, grape-picking takes place between August and October. Olives are also picked in the autumn. There are two strawberry harvests a year, one in May/June and another in November/December. Oranges are picked for up to three months around Limassol. Women's wages are lower than men's. Men interested in labouring work should look for new tourist developments in resorts along the south-east coast. Arrange to be paid daily or weekly rather than monthly, since it can be difficult to extract earned money.

TURKISH REPUBLIC OF NORTHERN CYPRUS

As is well known, Cyprus is a divided island. The southern part is the Republic of Cyprus, a member of the British Commonwealth and European Union. The north, occupied by Turkey since the intervention of 1974, is called the Turkish Republic of Northern Cyprus (Kibris). It is not recognised by any country except Turkey. Surprisingly, there is a sizeable expat community here and an expanding tourist industry, hampered by the lack of direct flights (incoming tourists must travel via Turkey). Because it is off the beaten track, the pool of potential seasonal or casual labour is much smaller than it is elsewhere on the Mediterranean.

The red tape for foreign workers is relatively straightforward, though the morality of the situation may give you pause. Before working in the TRNC, you will first have to overcome your qualms about working in a place whose regime was responsible for the forcible eviction of so many Greek Cypriots and destruction of property and artefacts following the invasion of 1974. On the other hand, the easing of border restrictions began in 2003 and looks set to continue.

Eric Mackness, a correspondent of long standing, reiterates his enthusiasm for Northern Cyprus as a destination for job-seekers:
I think that Turkish Cyprus is quite a unique location work-wise. I don't want to make light of my undoubted charm and my ability to chop a tomato into four pieces, but I think anyone with a little common sense can always find a job here. I hear of job vacancies literally every day. Of course it is early in the year and as the season progresses the vacancies won't be quite so numerous. But if you work hard, prove yourself to be honest and reliable, there are always vacancies here in the North. Quite a few new restaurants have opened since I was last here, all looking for chefs and bar and waiting staff.

Turkish Cyprus is a very small place (population 210,000) and job vacancies become known as soon as they exist. For every one advertised in the English language paper *Cyprus Today* there are six heard of on the grapevine. The notice board outside the Post Office in the main town of Kyrenia is a good source of information on jobs, accommodation, etc. Most opportunities lie in the catering trade and are open to men and women. Many are in restaurants, etc. owned or managed by expats. The wages are poor by British standards, i.e. less than £200 per month. But this is on top of food and accommodation (which is offered in 99% of cases) and tips.

Eric fixed up his first job in an amazing way: he simply wrote directly to a restaurant in the village of Lapta 10km from the capital Kyrenia (Girne in Turkish) which he had heard mentioned briefly on a BBC travel programme. Even without any catering experience apart from some part-time dish-washing when he was a mature student, he was offered a job. The highest concentration of restaurants and bars is along the picturesque harbour of Kyrenia, with a further concentration in Lapta, Karaman and Alsancak to the west.

The pre-season spruce-up normally takes place in February to prepare for an opening date in early March. So this is a good time to make enquiries. The season doesn't get very busy until June but by then most of the vacancies will be filled. Independent accommodation is available; two-bedroomed houses can be rented for £200 a month out-of-season, while Eric Mackness was offered a number of chances to house-sit.

Tour Companies

Pat Kennard is another reader who found work in Northern Cyprus. While her husband found a technical job at the Acapulco Casino (5 miles west of Kyrenia), she landed a job with Kibris Travel Service, the ground handling agent for ten UK tour operators. She enjoyed a fantastic season as a holiday rep even though, as she admits, it is a very demanding job having to do early morning and late night airport runs, sort out clients' problems with their accommodation and conduct tours of the island. The Anglo-Cypriot Association has a noticeboard in front of the Girne post office where it might be worth posting your interest in finding work.

Northern Cyprus is not a cheap package holiday destination and tends to attract a more discerning clientele, who are interested in visiting the sites as well as enjoying the marvellous scenery and climate. It is a popular destination for Germans, so some knowledge of German would be an advantage. After making friends with several residents, Theresa Thomas (a trained teacher) accepted a job with a local tour operator. Typically, the interview took place in a café:

> My job was to take out daily coach tours (the clients were mostly professionals from the UK) six days a week, explain the history of the island and liaise with bus drivers, restaurateurs, etc. The good features were that I was able to see so much of this beautiful island and mix with interesting people. The bad features were poor pay for long working hours (sometimes in extreme heat), having no workers' rights and always having to deal with sexual harassment.

Other jobs can be found on boats as well as on land, leading tours, hiring sports equipment, etc.

Red Tape

As in Turkey it will be necessary to leave Cyprus every three months to renew your tourist visa; this entails a two-hour catamaran trip to mainland Turkey at a cost of at least £20.

Italy

Italy is a remarkably welcoming country. Once Italians accept you, they will go out of their way to find you a place in their communities, without any emphasis on the barriers of nationality. Once you get a toehold, you will find that a friendly network of contacts and possible employers will quickly develop. Without contacts, if only a sympathetic landlady at your pension, it is virtually impossible to find work.

Some travellers mistakenly expect Italy to be backward in some respects. They are surprised, especially in the north, to discover that the cost of living is considerably higher than in other Mediterranean countries. They find the best-dressed and most sophisticated people in the world. Image counts for a great deal in Italy, and it has to be said that good-looking smartly dressed people have far more chance of success than their dowdy counterparts. With an unemployment rate of about 8.5%, it is going to take time to find a job no matter what your dress sense. The situation for casual job-seekers has been made more difficult by the arrival of Albanians and refugees from the old Yugoslavia. Because of its anxiety about high immigration, Italy has imposed a quota on the total number of immigrants (to include citizens of the new accession countries) of 20,000 a year.

The Regulations

The bureaucratic procedures for EU nationals have become easier in recent years. Once you are hired you should take your passport and letter of employment to the local *Questura* (police department) to obtain a *permesso di soggiorno* (residence permit). Procedures vary from place to place, and even from official to official. Legislation intended to prevent an influx of refugees from outside the European Union has created problems for all job-seekers who have encountered reluctance on the part of potential employers to face the bureaucracy. Persistence and patience will be needed in all cases.

Even farmers eager to hire people for a very temporary period will ask to see your papers for fear of being caught and fined, as Xuela Edwards found when she looked for grape-picking work in the Chianti region:

Several vineyard owners were keen to take us on but insisted we get the correct papers. As EU citizens we were entitled to work and so set out to get our papers. We were told to apply for a Libretto di Lavoro from the Town Hall on the Piazza del Campo in Siena. When we found the right office they said we needed a Permesso di Soggiorno first and directed us to another part of Siena. On application we were told that it would take 60 days to come through, by which time of course the grape harvest would be over. We did hear that it was possible to get a Permesso by queuing all day in Rome; arrive very early, take a couple of passport photos and a packed lunch.

Ideally, you will also be able to obtain a *libretto di lavoro* (work registration card) from the local *Ispettorato del Lavoro* and/or *Ufficio Collocamento* which generally involves much queuing and a wait of several months. Depending on the circumstances, they may want to see your university diploma, qualifications if relevant and birth certificate – originals rather than copies, and preferably authenticated by the Italian Consulate in your home country.

Once the paperwork has been dealt with, your employer will have to pay contributions on your behalf which can be very substantial in Italy. As usual, all of this should be more straightforward for EU nationals than in fact it is. When Ian McArthur tried to get a *libretto di lavoro* he was treated little better than an illegal immigrant (but nevertheless has embarked on a 'lifelong love affair with Italy'). Roberta Wedge who taught English for a year in Bari recalls the red tape: *'I had to visit three different government offices about eight times in total. Not exactly the free movement of labour! My health card arrived six months after the wheels were set in motion.'*

Australian and New Zealand citizens aged 18-30 have recently become eligible for a 12-month working holiday visa in Italy. The best chances for other non-EU citizens *(extra-comunitari)* of getting their papers in order are to be a dual national, to obtain a student visa which permits 20 hours or work a week (living in or out) or to arrange a firm offer of a job while they are still in their home country. According to the Italian Embassy in Washington, some jobs may be eligible for a *lavoro subordinato* visa. To qualify they must first obtain from their employer in Italy an authorisation to work issued by the Ministry of Labour or a Provincial Office of Labour *(Servizio politiche del lavoro)* plus an authorisation from the local *Questura*. The originals of these plus a passport and one photo must be sent to the applicant's nearest Embassy or Consulate. The book *Living, Studying and Working in Italy* by Travis Neighbor Ward and Monica Larner ($17 from Owl Books, 2003) is aimed specifically at Americans and contains much practical advice about coping with the bureaucracy.

Note that American citizens may be able to avoid work permit hassles by working for the US military. The large base in Vicenza sometimes hires catering and other staff; contact the Vicenza Civilian Personnel Advisory Center's Job Information Centre on 0444-6351 7266.

Do not be too discouraged by the regulations and the red tape since there is a great deal of unofficial, cash-in-hand work or *lavoro al nero* available in Italy. One young working holidaymaker from Berkshire who spent part of the winter season working in a ski resort bar kept a drink strategically placed at the end of the bar so she could vault over and pose as a punter should the *carabinieri* come in. She decided that this was preferable to making four separate train journeys down from the mountains to get the appropriate *bolli* (stamps).

If you want to open a bank account, you need to register at the registry office *(Ufficio Anagrafe)*; in Rome the address is Via Luigi Petroselli 50 (behind Piazza Venezia). Tax is a further headache for long-stay workers. As soon as you sort out the work documents, you should obtain a tax number *(codice fiscale)*. The rate of income tax *(Ritenuta d'Acconto)* is usually about 20% in addition to social security deductions of up to 10%.

Remember that medical expenses can be very high if you're not covered by the Italian Medical Health Scheme (USL or *Unita Sanitaria Locale*). If your employer is not paying contributions, you might want to take out private insurance.

In some areas, anyone who gets a job in the food and beverage sector must obtain a *Tessera Sanitaria* (hygiene certificate) even if they are not handling food themselves. Even the most laid-back employers insist on it since they can be in serious trouble if found employing people without it.

FINDING WORK

If you can't speak a word of Italian, you will be at a distinct disadvantage. Provided you can afford it and are sufficiently interested, you should consider studying a little Italian before you set off on your travels or enrolling in one of the many short Italian language courses offered in most Italian cities. Italian is one of the easiest languages to learn, especially if you already have some knowledge of a Latin-based language.

However your inability to speak Italian need not be an absolute barrier, as Ian Moody found when he got a job as a door-to-door salesman of English books and language courses, without himself knowing any Italian. His technique was more amusing in retrospect than it was successful:

> I was given the spiel in phonetic Italian and told to learn it off by heart before knocking on the doors of middle class, professional Italians in various northern Italian towns. Reeling off the sales pitch parrot-fashion was okay until they asked a question which I couldn't make head nor tail of. I found it was often easier to run away. So it was extremely difficult to make many sales. For those who persevered at the door, sales were often promised just to get rid of the rep. Still the working conditions were good, mainly because it was permanently sunny. And you were able to meet people (even if you couldn't actually understand a word they were saying).

Although you should not neglect scouring the newspapers and online recruitment sites for job adverts, you may be disappointed. Sometimes requests by *stranieri* (foreigners) for work outnumber the situations vacant. The following publications might be of use to Italian-speaking job-seekers:

Il Sole 24 Ore, Via Lomazzo 52, 20154 Milan (fax 02-310 3426/341062). Newspaper with a careers supplement in October.

Corriere della Sera – the Friday edition of this major Italian daily has the employment adverts.

Campus, *Tuttolavoro*, *Trovalavoro* and *Bollettino del lavoro* are all monthly employment magazines.

The first free-ads papers in Europe were published in Italy in 1977. *Secondamano* (meaning Second Hand) is published in ten regional editions covering the industrialised north of the country.

Some foreigners have topped up their travel funds by doing life modelling for which there is a great demand in Florence and other cities. Simply visit art schools and ask to sit in on a life drawing class to make sure that the situation is one you can cope with.

In Vacanza Lavorando (IVL) maintains a database of information on working holidays, voluntary work, traineeships and language courses in Italy and all around the world. It is possible to consult the IVL databank at Youth Information Centres in Italy. Every region has a *Centro Informazione Giovani* which may be in a position to advise on local holiday work. The addresses of these youth centres are provided on the website www.in-vacanza-lavorando.it which also carries other useful information for those who wish to travel or work in Italy. Their literature includes the addresses of the Centro per l'impiego in several northern cities including Trento and Riva del Garda. Contact details for these regional offices for seasonal work in agriculture and hotels in the Alps can also be found online at www.agenzialavoro.tn.it/agenzia/indirizzi and current vacancies (mainly in hotels) are listed at www2.agenzialavoro.tn.it/intranet/public/lavoro.

The national youth agency Informagiovani (www.informagiovani.it) is aimed at Ital-

ians but could prove useful to anyone who speaks Italian. It posts job offers with email addresses at www.informagiovani.it/lavoro/lavoro.htm and has links to voluntary work.

The job that is most prolifically advertised among students and young people, often in English, is *for animatori turistici*, i.e. holiday animators and entertainers (see section on Tourism below).

The Employment Service

Unless you are fluent in Italian, the state employment service *(Ufficio di Collocamento)* is unlikely to be much use to you. It is normally necessary to visit them regularly (preferably every day) to make your presence felt. The employment offices in the smaller towns might be more helpful than the ones in the main cities being less accustomed to foreign job-seekers. For example before the summer season, the ones in seaside resorts often have lists of hotel and restaurant jobs.

People with a professional profile and knowledge of Italian might wish to register their CV at the British Chamber of Commerce in Milan (www.britchamitaly.com). For example for a fee of €62, the BCC will make your details available online to relevant companies. Anyone can search vacancies on their website which has employment-related links.

Contacts

Contacts are even more important in Italy than in other countries. Many of the people we have heard from who have worked in Italy (apart from TEFL teachers, au pairs, etc.) have got their work through friends. They may not necessarily have had the friends or contacts when they arrived, but they formed friendships while they were there as visitors. Louise Rollett, for example, first went out as a paying guest to a town near Bologna (an arrangement made through EIL UK, mentioned in the *Introduction*) and then extended her stay on a work-for-keep basis as an English tutor. Dustie Hickey went for treatment to a doctor in Milan who immediately offered to pay her a good hourly wage to tutor his children in English.

You can't expect preferment over the locals' own friends and relatives however as Allan Kirkpatrick found a couple of years ago: *'I took a flight to Rome to visit an old Italian friend who lives in Anzio near Rome. I stayed in her house and found some bar work for only ten days out of my total stay of two months, due to the fact that my Italian wasn't too good. The school holidays must have been a big factor too in my lack of success; friends, relatives and next door neighbours come first before a young backpacking, English-speaking Scot.'*

Staff at the local CTS branch may be helpful. CTS (Centro Turistico Studentesco e Giovanile) is the main student travel agency which does far more than arrange flights and travel, e.g. its website www.cts.it has links to language courses *(corsi di lingua)* and conservation volunteering as well as to its offices *(sedi)* throughout Italy.

In Rome try the notice boards in the following locations: the English language Lion Bookshop at Via dei Greci 33/36, the Church of England on nearby Via del Babuino and CTS at Via Genova 16, 00184 Rome (06-462 0431). Language school notice boards are always worth checking; at the *Centro di Lingua & Cultura Italiana per Stranieri* where Dustie Hickie took cheap Italian lessons in Milan, there was a good notice board with adverts for au pairs, dog-walkers, etc. Dustie got a cleaning job this way.

Laurence Koe had collected the addresses of many of his pupils at a summer school where he had worked on the south coast of England. The first one he looked up was in Como and the family promptly invited him to stay until he found work (an invitation which made him marvel at the contrast with English habits of hospitality). One of the daughters had the idea of asking the local radio station to employ Laurence, mainly for novelty value. She accompanied Laurence to the station and stood in for him at the interview, inventing freely about his past history as a DJ. They put him on a jointly presented afternoon music programme and his task seemed to be to adjudicate the correct English pronunciation of song titles. No wage was paid, but it was good experience and good fun. Also he became very well known in the town, a kind of celebrity, and felt that he was giving something to the community instead of just taking. He would let it slip on the radio that he was there to teach English and opportunities began to present themselves.

Even with contacts you are not guaranteed of finding work, as Edward Peters found one summer: *'After travelling through Eastern Europe and Austria, we had hoped to find something in Italy; but three sets of contacts were unable to find us anything – perhaps because it was August (national holidays) or perhaps because we were too busy enjoying ourselves in Milan, Rome and Ischia.'*

TOURISM

Italy's tourist industry employs between 6% and 7% of the Italian workforce and has limited openings for unskilled non-Italians. Anyone who has had the pleasure of dining out in Italy or even buying 200 grams of cheese or salami at a delicatessen will know that Italian standards of service are very professional and indeed people (usually men) consider waiting on tables as a career. Any openings for casual bar staff that come along are likely to be in (for example) Irish themed pubs or American-style bistros. It is also difficult to find work with a UK tour company, since there are severe legal restrictions on the hiring of non-Italian staff.

Of course some readers have succeeded. The Australian Dominic Gibbon found a job in a hotel in Rome (in the days before Australians could get a working holiday visa):

After six weeks of no luck I told my landlady that perhaps I would head off to Greece. She said I was far too nice to look for dishwashing work and told me about a friend who needed help running his seasonal hotel off Piazza Barberini. Within 20 minutes I was behind the counter having the telephone system explained to me and was told the wage for six nights a week as a night porter. After praying the telephone wouldn't ring for the first few weeks, everything settled down. It's quiet, a little boring, but allows me to read and study Italian, more than the few key words related to the hotel trade I knew before. My boss is even going to lend me a TV to help me improve my Italian. I now know how lucky I was to find my place and this job.

Although less well known than the seaside resorts of other Mediterranean countries, there may be seaside possibilities for foreign job-seekers, especially in the resorts near Venice, as an Italian reader Lara Giavi confirms. She is familiar with two holiday regions: the Lake Garda resorts like Desenzano, Malcesine, Sirmione and Riva del Garda; and the seaside resorts near Venice like Lido di Jesolo (which she says is a great resort for young people), Bibione, Lignano, Caorle and Chioggiaa, all of which are more popular with German and Austrian tourists than Britons so a knowledge of German would be a good selling point. Lara disagrees that there are few opportunities for foreigners in catering, bars and hotels in Italy, though she admits that a knowledge of Italian is necessary in most cases, apart from the job of *donna ai piani* (chambermaid).

The seaside resorts are full of people (including Italians) working black and not being paid the going wage, overtime or holiday pay, but earning plenty of tips. It is difficult enough for an Italian, never mind a foreigner, to find an employer who pays by the book. In Lara's opinion, travellers looking for a 'working holiday experience' who don't mind about the money should certainly pursue this possibility. Try to track down local hotel associations or hotel chains, for example the following along the Adriatic:

Alberghi Consorziatai, 61032 Fano (0721-827376)
Associazione Albergatori di Rimini, Viale Baldini 14, 47037 Rimini (fax 0541-56519)
Associazione Pesarese Albergatori, 61100 Pesaro (0721-67959)
Associazione Balneare Azienda Turismo – 0733-811600
Associazione Bagnini di Numana e Sirolo, 60026 Numana Ancona (0721-827376).

The relatively low rate of unemployment in the Veneto region makes it a better bet than some of the other tourist regions of Italy such as the Adriatic coastal resorts of Rimini and Pescara and the Italian Riviera between Nice and Genoa (Portofino, San Remo, etc.), though it may be worth trying resorts in Italy's lake region, like Stresa and Cannero on Lake Maggiore. The Blu Hotels chain has hotels and holiday villages in Lake Garda, Sardinia, Umbria, Abruzzo, Tuscany, Rome, Palinuro and Calabria (as well as Austria); its website www.bluhotels.it has a Jobs icon. Michael Cullen worked in three hotels around Como and Bellagio and found 'a nice friendly and warm atmosphere, despite the heat and long hours'. Even in flourishing resorts like Rimini, there seems to be nearly enough locals and Italian students to fill the jobs in hotels, bars and on the beach, although one company has been advertising heavily in the English-speaking media. The Life Disco Club (Via Regina Margherita 11, 47900 Rimini; www.lifedisco.com/job.php) hires lots of young people to work in the club scene over the summer.

Assistance in Rimini may be available from the employment agency Sinterim (www.sinterim.it) which deals with seasonal and temporary work and also has branches in other offices in northern Italian cities. High unemployment in the south of Italy together with a huge population of migrant workers from poor countries means that it is probably not worth trying the resorts south of Naples, viz. Capri, Sorrento and Amalfi.

If you don't get a job in a hotel, you might get work servicing holiday flats or gardening. If you plan far enough in advance (and speak some Italian) you might get a job as a campsite courier with one of the major British camping holiday organisers such as Canvas Holidays (see the chapter on *Tourism*). The smaller Venue Holidays (01233 629950; www.venueholidays.co.uk) employs summer season reps at campsites on the Venetian Riviera, Lake Garda and in Tuscany. Catherine Dawes enjoyed her campsite job near Albenga on the Italian Riviera – 'a fairly uninspiring part of Italy' – even more than she did her previous summer's work on a French campsite. She reports that the Italians seemed to be more relaxed than the French, especially under high season pressure, and would always go out of their way to help her when she was trying to translate tourists' problems to the mechanic or the doctor.

Many mountain resorts with busy ski seasons (see section below) also need workers from outside the area for the summer. One UK tour operator that takes on domestic staff and summer reps is Collett's Mountain Holidays (01763 289660; www.colletts.co.uk).

You can also try Italian-run campsites which have a large staff to man the on-site restaurants, bars and shops. Stephen Venner noticed that the two main campsites in Rome including the Flaminio take on English help before the season begins (i.e. March). With the help of some Argentinian friends, Andrea Militello rounded up a job at a campsite Santa Teresa di Gallura in northern Sardinia for the summer season. Boat mechanics and other staff can approach holiday barge companies; for example the British company Connoisseur Holidays Afloat (0870 160 5648; www.connoisseurafloat.com) keep six boats at Casier and Porto Levante south of Venice in the Po delta.

Holiday Animators & Entertainers

Various agencies recruit musicians, singers, DJs and entertainers for summer jobs around Italy. Italian companies would be unlikely to hire anyone unless they spoke more than just English. Here are a handful of companies that hire on quite a major scale:

R.I.S.I.C.O. srl, Via del Portonaccio 1, 47100 Forlì (FC) (0543 26199; www.risicoweb. it). Offers services for the tourist industry, mainly entertainers. The most important qualifications in candidates (who must be between 18 and 35) are availability, professionality, kindness and creativity.

Planet srl, Animazione e Spettacolo, Via Circonvallazione Occidentale n° 102, 47900 Rimini (RN) (0541 787597; fax 0541 786159; www.planetvillager.com). This company recruits hundreds of staff not only in Italy but on recruiting trips to Belgium, Switzerland and the Czech Republic.

Anderson Animatore, Via Tevere 44, 00198 Rome (fax 06-884 4664; animazione@andersonclub.it). Employs more than 100 staff for tour operators and holiday villages.

Darwin srl, Turismo e Spettacolo, Piazza del Pesce 1, 50122, Florence (055 292114; darwinstaff@yahoo.it; www.darwinstaff.com). Large numbers of staff needed, e.g. 150

mini club animators to arrange children's holiday programme plus hostesses, DJs, musicians, etc.

Equipe Smile srl, Via Fioravanti 5/F, 40129 Bologna (051-370774; www.equipesmile.com). 150 animateurs/entertainers for Italian resorts such as Lake Garda and Sardinia.

Associazione Nazionale Animatori, Via Sicilia, 166/B, 00187 ROMA (06-678 16 47; www. ilportaledegliartisti.it/ana.htm).

Hostels

As throughout the world, backpackers' haunts often employ travellers for short periods. Jill Weseman recommends trying the Fawlty Towers hostel at Via Magenta 39, 00184 Rome; 06-445 0374) near the Termini Station in Rome where she noticed several Antipodeans working in reception, maintenance and cleaning. While planning her escape route from a less-than-satisfactory summer au pairing job in Naples, Jacqueline Edwards asked in the Sorrento youth hostel about job possibilities and a few weeks later moved in to take over breakfast duties in exchange for free bed and breakfast.

Raised in New York and largely cut off from her family's Italian roots, one traveller decided at age 30 to spend some time in Italy.

> **By making use of www.hostels.com Debra Fuccio had little difficulty pre-arranging a hostel job:**
> *Never in a million years did I think that watching MTV would be part of my daily life in Rome, Italy. But it was. I was working at a really cute, small hostel in Rome during April 2002. The hostel was Hostel Casanavova (Via Ottorino Lazzarini, 12, 00136 Rome; 06-397 45228; hostelcasanova@yahoo.com). I was working 7 days a week (since I was a bit scared about running out of money since this was the first leg of the trip). The shifts would alternate from evening to morning everyday: one day doing the morning shift when the hostel was cleaned and the next day the evening shift. As well as getting to stay there for free, they paid me and my co-worker 20 euros per day in cash which was really nice. Rome was so cheap (from a San Francisco point of view) and with great weather, it was easy to save. I came to Italy with $700 cash and a plane ticket, I left with about $600 and a plane ticket to England and Ireland. I was there about 5 weeks total.*

So smitten was Debra with the life of an itinerant hostel worker that she moved on to other hostels in Ireland and San Francisco and set up an e-magazine about travelling.

Oikos hostel in Rome is even cheaper (€10.50 per night) and is also the head-quarters of an environmental protection agency which organises summer workcamps (volontariato@oikos.org; www.oikos.org). Oikos is located in the quiet suburb of Rome, Spinaceto, at Paolo Renzi 55 (06-508 0280). Free board and lodging are given in exchange for 20 hours of work per week mainly in horticulture and general maintenance.

Winter Resorts

On-the-spot opportunities are possible if not plentiful in the winter resorts of the Alps, Dolomites and Apennines. Many of the jobs are part-time and not very well paid, but provide time for skiing and in many cases a free pass to the ski-lifts for the season. Sauze d'Oulx and Courmayeur are the best resorts for job hunting, particularly the former according to Jaime Burnell who, while in her gap year, left an exploitative job with a British ski tour operator near Trento to job-hunt in Sauze d'Oulx: *'I cannot recommend enough winter work in Sauze d'Oulx. I arrived on the 14th of January. Everyone tells you that the turnover is high but that is an understatement. Going out every night you couldn't be sure who would be behind the bar that day.'* Jaime goes on to offer one more nugget of information which proves once and for all that blondes really do have more fun: *'The best investment you can make in Italy is a bottle of blonde hair dye. My tips tripled'.*

Cathy Salt describes her success in Sauze d'Oulx:

Upon arrival at Sauze d'Oulx on 14th November, we found we were much too early for on-the-spot jobs. The place was practically dead. Only a few bars were open. Fortunately an English guy working in a bar informed us that the carpenter was looking for help. My partner Jon was able to get four weeks work with him, sanding down and varnishing, also enabling him to be on the spot for other work that would come up. The same day I found a babysitting job for a shop owner's son, but I wouldn't start until 5th December. We were both fortunate in finding this since we came up on a Thursday and have since found out that the weekend is a much better time to look because the ski shops and restaurants are open.

Such stories are counterbalanced by the inevitable failures: Susanna Macmillan gave up her job hunt in the Italian Alps after two weeks when she had to admit that her non-existent Italian and just passable French were not getting her anywhere. Perhaps she was looking in the wrong resorts like Cortina which is sophisticated and expensive and has a high percentage of year-round workers.

Crystal Holidays, part of the Thomson Travel Group (King's Place, Wood St, Kingston-upon-Thames W4 5RT; 020-7420 2081; www.shgjobs.co.uk) hire resort reps and chalet staff for work in the Italian Alps as well as staff for summer holidays. The Ski Department of PGL Travel Ltd (Alton Court, Penyard Lane, Ross-on-Wye, Herefordshire HR9 5GL) offer some jobs as ski reps, leaders and ski/snowboard instructors (to BASI-qualified skiers), especially for short periods during half-term and Easter holidays.

Not nearly as many chalet jobs can be found in Italy as in France, due to the very strict regulations that govern chalets in Italy. You are more likely to find a job in a small family-run bar or hotel than in one of the big concerns. The large hotels usually recruit their staff in southern Italy and then move them en masse from the sea to the mountains in the autumn.

AU PAIRS

The majority of European au pair agencies deal with Italy, so you should have no trouble arranging a family placement. Au pairs coming from outside Europe should consider enrolling in a language course and obtaining a student visa which will allow them to work for up to 20 hours a week. Australians and New Zealanders under 30 are free to work as nannies or au pairs under the provisions of the working holiday scheme.

Angie Copley was delighted with the situation to which her British agency sent her:
After finding the address of agencies in your book, I wrote to one and before I knew it they had found me a family in Sardinia. I couldn't believe it was so easy. All I had to do was pay for a flight out there and that was that. When I arrived, the family met me and took me to their house. Some house. It wasn't just a house but a castle where the Italian royal family used to spend their holidays. What was even better was that the family had turned it into a hotel, the best possible place for meeting people. I ended up having the best summer of my life in Sardinia. Once I picked up the language I went out, met lots of people, had beach parties. My work involved not much more than playing with their two-year old boy all day and speaking English to him. Basically it was one big holiday.

Summer-only positions are readily available. Most Italian families in the class that can afford live-in childcare go to holiday homes by the sea or in the mountains during the summer and at other holiday times which did not prove as idyllic as it sounds for Jacqueline Edwards:

My first job as an au pair in Italy was with a family who were staying in the middle of nowhere with their extended family. It was a total nightmare for me. I could just about say hello in Italian and couldn't understand a word of what was going on. After three weeks I was fed up, homesick and ready to jump on the next plane to England. But a few days later we moved back to town (Modena) and from then on things improved dramatically. I was able to go out and meet other au pairs and nannies at the park, etc. and we all socialised together. I ended up learning Italian quite well, making lots of friends (partly through my language school, which was free by the way) and visiting most of the Italian cities. The only part that I didn't like in that job was going away with the family to their holiday houses for skiing, etc. You end up working twice your usual hours for the same pay, have no social life as you don't have any friends there, can't go skiing as you are minding the baby and then they tell you to cheer up because you're on holiday.

The average wage for au pairs is in the range €60-€70 per week, au pairs plus earn around €420 per month, mothers' helps €500-€800 and trained nannies €1000+. Wages are slightly higher in the north of Italy than central and southern parts of the country because the cost of living is higher. The demand for nannies and mothers' helps able to work 40+ hours is especially strong since a high percentage of families in Italy have two working parents.

Most of the Italian agencies speak English and welcome applications from British au pairs. Although it is illegal in Italy to charge candidates a registration fee, some agencies charge for ancillary services so always enquire. Try any of the following:

ARCE (Attivita Relazioni Culturali con l'Estero), Via XX Settembre 20/124 16121 Genoa (010-583020; fax 010-583092; www.arceaupair.it). Long established agency makes placements throughout the country.

Au Pair International, Via S. Stefano 32, 40125 Bologna (051-267575/238320; www.au-pair-international.com). Member of IAPA.

Au Pairs Recruitment, Via Gaeta 22, 10133 Turin (329-211 6277; annaparavia@tin.it).

Euroma, Viale B Buozzi 19 AA, int 3, 00197 Roma (06-806 92 130; www.euroma.info). According to their website, they charge a fee of €130.

Euro-Placements Italy srl, Via Felica Cavallotti 15, 20122 Milan (02-760 18 357; euro placements@studioventimiglia.it; www.euro-placements.com). Jobs available for trained/experienced nannies in Rome, Milan, Tuscany, Trento and Lugano as well as Switzerland. Summer positions for au pairs always available.

Intermediate SNC, Via Bramante 13, 00153 Rome (06-57 47 444; www.intermediateonline. com). Intermediate has its own language school in the Aventino district of Rome.

Mix Culture Roma, Via Nazionale 204, 00184 Rome (06-4788 2289; mixculture@tiscalinet.it).

TEACHING

Hundreds of language schools around Italy employ native English speakers. Unfortunately for the ordinary traveller, the vast majority of the jobs require a degree, TEFL qualifications and knowledge of Italian. Xuela Edwards arrived with a friend who was a qualified English teacher at the right time (September) and reported that the language schools were flooded with teachers and just being able to speak English was not enough. This view has to be set against P.G. Penn's experience. After he left a selling job, he went to Turin to find TEFL work and after putting in some effort he succeeded without any experience whatsoever and recommends Turin over the more glamorous and popular cities of Milan and Rome.

Doing an introductory TEFL course at home simplifies the job search, especially since many of the training organisations feed their 'graduates' to Italian schools. After 'stessing and sweating' his way through a CELTA course in Edinburgh one summer, Fergus Cooney posted a message on Dave's ESL Café (see intro chapter *Teaching English*) 'Teacher with degree + CELTA seeks job in Italy/Spain' and soon his inbox began to fill (and not only with job offers from Korea). He chose a school in Calabria (and it is unlikely that the Calabria Tourist Promotion Board will be giving him a job in the near future):

To cut it short (forgive the pun), I was sacked after two months for what might well be the most unreasonable reason ever in the field of TEFL, for falling ill with appendicitis. My appendix burst and I nearly died. The small private school in the village far from anywhere wanted me back at work two days after the operation. I could barely walk and couldn't talk for a week. I certainly couldn't shout loudly which was necessary in the south of Italy in a class full of screaming 12 year olds. After a week, the bosses told me that I was no longer needed and that I had to be out of their flat by Monday. I found a job in a nice school run by two English guys in the city 50km away although I had problems there too trying to obtain a contract. I now know that getting a contract is of the utmost importance and next time I will not plunge into a job before researching the school, town, amenities, etc. To inexperienced teachers: don't go to Reggio Calabria. It has to be Europe's most boring and ugly city. There is nowhere to eat during the day except Mc-bloody-Donald's; there is nowhere in the city centre to sit down, no cinema, no pubs, no live music and a general lack of culture. OK the local food and, especially the oranges in winter, are fantastic. But I would definitely NOT go back to Calabria.

Without any TEFL training whatsoever, the job hunt will be an uphill struggle as Laurence Koe discovered in both Como and Lecco. He visited all the language schools, some of them three times, and was always told he needed a TEFL qualification or that he was there at the wrong time (October). After three weeks of making the rounds he was asked to stand in for an absent teacher on one occasion, and this was enough to secure him further part-time work. After a few more weeks he found work teaching an evening class of adults. He began to attend the weekly English club (a good source of contacts and leads) and was offered a few thousand lire to answer questions on the plot after English film shows.

Similarly Natalia de Cuba could not persuade any of the language schools in the northern town of Rovereto where she was based to hire her without qualifications. So she decided to enrol in the Cambridge Certificate course run by International House in Rome (Viale Manzoni 22, 00185 Rome). She found the month-long course strenuous but not terribly difficult, and worth the fee (which now stands at €1,500). Job offers come into IH from all over Italy and no one seems to have a problem getting a job immediately after the course. Natalia went back to a teaching job in Rovereto where she was well paid for 18 hours of fairly enjoyable teaching a week. A starting salary for a full-time timetable should be €850-€900 (net) per month.

Fortunately the online version of the Italian Yellow Pages is reasonably user-friendly. Go to www.paginegialle.it and search under *Scuole di Lingue* in the cities and towns in which you're hoping to work. Make sure you use the Italian version of the name, e.g. Napoli, Torino, Venezia, etc. (although you can also search in English). The ones listed first have email and web addresses. International language school groups like Benedict Schools, Linguarama, Berlitz and inlingua are major providers of English language teaching in Italy. Wall Street Institutes now have about 50 centres in Italy and actively recruit native speakers; the headquarters are in Udine at Via Maniago 2 (0432-481464; www.wsi.it).

Several Italian-based chains of language schools account for a large number of teaching jobs. But because many of them operate as independent franchises, it is difficult to get a master list of addresses. Chains include the British Schools Group (www.britishschool.com) with more than 70 member schools who carry out a lot of their recruitment through the British recruitment agency Saxoncourt. Other chains include British Institutes with 200 associated schools (www.britishinstitutes.it) and Oxford Schools (Via S. Pertini 14, Mirano 30035 Mirano, Venice; 041-570 23 55; www.oxforditalia.it) with 15 schools in northeastern Italy.

Another possibility is to set up as a freelance tutor, though a knowledge of Italian is even more of an asset here than it is for jobs in schools. You can post notices in supermarkets, tobacconists, primary and secondary schools and advertise in a free paper. As long as you have access to some premises, you can try to arrange both individual and group lessons, and undercut the language institutes significantly. The ever-enterprising Laurence Koe presented himself to a classroom teacher who asked her class of 12 and 13 years olds if they would like to learn English from a native. They all said Yes and paid a small sum to attend his after-school class.

As in other European countries, summer camps for unaccompanied young people usually offer English as well as a range of sports. The organisation called A.C.L.E. Summer & City Camps (Via Roma 54, 18038 San Remo, Liguria; tel/fax 0184-506070; www.acle. org) advertises heavily in the UK for more than 150 young people with a genuine interest in children who must be 'fun-loving, energetic and have high moral standards' to teach English and organise activities including drama for two, four or more weeks. The promised wage is €170-€190 per week plus board, lodging, insurance and travel between camps within Italy. However summer staff must enrol in a compulsory three or four-day introductory TEFL course for which a deduction of €170 for city camps or €190 for summer camps is made from earned wages.

A less well known organisation also based in San Remo might be worth comparing: Lingue Senza Frontiere, Corso Inglesi 172, 18038 Sanremo (info@linguesenzafrontiere. org). They promise to pay their tutors €1750 plus board and lodging for eight weeks work in their English immersion summer camps. Another company that hires native English speakers to work at summer language camps is Smile (Via Vignolese 454, 41100 Modena; tel/fax 059-363868). The period of work is just three weeks from late August.

AGRICULTURE

In most Italian harvests, there is no tradition of hiring large numbers of foreign young people. With the arrival of so many migrant workers from the Balkans and elsewhere joining the traditional Moroccan workers, the situation has become even less promising. Seasonal jobs in the grape and olive harvests are reserved and carefully regulated among locals and other Italian unemployed. However if you have local friends and contacts or if you speak some Italian it is worth trying to participate in one of the autumn harvests which by most accounts are thoroughly enjoyable. Wages are also good.

Val di Non Apple Harvest

The main exception to the shortage of harvest jobs for foreign travellers is the apple harvest in the Val di Non around the town of Cles in the valley of the River Adige north of Trento. It is one of those famous destinations for migrant workers which a number of readers have praised, most recently Marisa Wharton from Argentina who met the Englishman there who became her husband a year or two later.

> **Andrea Militello (from another part of Italy) has participated in harvests from Spain to Tasmania, but his favourite is the apple harvest in Revo near Cles where he has picked fruit for many years:**
> *This year I had a great time with the other pickers. The harvest starts about the 20th-25th September and last until 25th October, but it's better to arrive at least ten days early. In the beginning it's best to go to Cles and talk with Padre Tiziano, one of the best people I have ever met. He helps everybody. This harvest unites people from everywhere, South America, Spanish, black people... so there's a meeting of many cultures.*

Without waxing quite so lyrical, Amanda Bridle from Hampshire also enjoyed the 'short sharp shock of physical labour with a large pay packet at the end of it' in the Val di Non. Women normally sort the apples which the men have picked (for a slightly higher wage). To get the crop picked as quickly as possible, the farmers expect workers to pick ten hours a day with no days off (nine hours after the clocks go back). The standard arrangement is for a proportion of the hourly wage to be deducted for lunch and accommodation. According to Amanda, it is becoming increasingly difficult to find work without a *libretto di lavoro* though in her experience some farmers afraid of a clampdown by the *Guardia di Finance* are willing to traipse around with people they have hired to the various offices chasing the necessary documents (see introductory section on *Regulations*).

Of course not everyone is successful at finding a job. Kristof Szymczak from Poland described the area as a tower of babel and couldn't find an orchard owner willing to hire him. But if you do manage to break in, it sounds one of the most enjoyable harvests in this book, at least as described by the American Natalia de Cuba:

> *Apple picking is great on the ground. The ladders require much more concentration (beware of drinking too much wine!) and are considered a man's job. Lunch with the family was included – pasta, salad, wine and a shot of grappa. It was delicious and friendly, as all the pickers – many of them family members – ate together and gossiped and joked. There is always plenty of opportunity to chat while working, especially if you are assigned the job of sorting the fruit. The Italian pickers really do sing opera in the orchards.*

Grape-Picking

Several people have succeeded in finding a place on the grape harvest *(vendemmia)*. Italy was called *Oenotria* by the ancient Greeks meaning 'the land of wine' and it remains the biggest producer of wine in the world. Today there are no regions of Italy which are without vineyards. Xuela Edwards and Nicky Brown made enquiries at vineyards in the Chianti region and met several growers who were keen to pay them the equivalent of £30 a day for the three weeks of the harvest. Although there seemed to be no prejudice against women pickers, the employers did insist that they obtain the proper papers which, as reported earlier in this chapter, turned out to be impracticable.

Once you are in a fruit-growing area, a good place to look for work is the warehouse run by the local cooperative where all the local farmers sell their produce to the public. There may even be a list of farmers who are looking for pickers. Natalia de Cuba found her job picking grapes (and also apples) this way, by going to the *Societá Agricultura Val-lagarina* in Rovereto in the region of Trentino, a major agricultural area.

The style of grape-picking is reputed to be easier than in France since the plants are trained upwards onto wire frames, rather than allowed to droop to the ground, so that pickers reach up with a clipper and catch the bunch of grapes in a funnel-type object, which is less strenuous than having to bend double for hours at a stretch. The worst problems that Natalia de Cuba encountered were stained hands (which could be avoided by wearing rubber gloves) and bee stings (which apparently can be soothed with grated potato, bound in place and left as long as possible). Accommodation can also be a problem since it is not normally provided by farmers.

Tomatoes are supposed to be a well-paid picking crop in Italy. Also there may be seasonal agricultural work in the strawberry harvests of Emilia Romagna. Cherries are grown around Vignola (just west of Bologna) and are also picked in June. The Valtellina area, near the Swiss border, is another area with a multitude of orchards. Olives are almost never picked by foreigners. Andrea Militello investigated possibilities for olive pickers in Tuscany (around San Miniato) but the wages were so low he didn't pursue the idea.

The contact for World Wide Opportunities on Organic Farms (WWOOF) in Italy is Bridget Matthews, 109 Via Casavecchia, 57022 Castegneto Carducci (LI); 0565-765001 (info@wwoof.it; www.wwoof.it). WWOOF volunteers in Italy must join the national association at a cost of €25 for insurance purposes and in return will be sent the list of more than 50 organic farmers in Italy looking for volunteers.

VOLUNTARY OPPORTUNITIES

Many Italian organisations arrange summer work projects which are as disparate as selling recyclable materials to finance development projects in the developing world to restoring old convents or preventing forest fires. Here is a selection of voluntary organisations that run working holidays. In some cases, it will be necessary to apply through a partner organisation in your home country:

Abruzzo, Lazio and Molise National Park, c/o National Parks Office, Viale Santa Lucia, 67032 Pescasseroli (AQ) (0863-91131; info@parcoabruzzo.it). Volunteers carry out research and protection of flora and fauna in remote locations. Further details are available by contacting the local park offices in Pescasseroli (0863-911 3242) or Villetta Barrea (0864-89102; fax 0864-89132).

AGAPE, Centro Ecumenico, 10060 Prali (Torino) (0121-807514; www. agapecentroecumenico.org). Volunteers help run this ecumenical conference centre in the Alps, about 80 miles from Turin. Stays usually last 3-5 weeks.

CTS, Dipartimento per la Conservazione della Natura, Via A. Vesalio 6, 00161 Rome (06-4411 1476; www.cts.it).

Emmaus Italia, Campi di lavoro, Via Mellana 55, 12012 Boves (CN) (tel/fax 0171-387834; www.cuneo.net/emmaus/giovanni/index.htm). Workcamps to collect, sort and sell second hand equipment to raise funds for social and community projects worldwide.

International Building Companions (Soci Costruttori), Via Montebello 46A, 44100 Ferrara (0532-243279; www.iboitalia.org). Renovation projects in deprived communities.

LIPU, Lega Italiana Protezione Uccelli, 0521-273043; www.lipu.it). Long-established environmental and bird conservation association which publishes a catalogue of summer projects at its bird reserves *(oasi)* throughout Italy. Volunteer camps cost approximately €150 per week.

Mani Tese, P. le Gambara 7/9, 20146 Milan (02-407 5165; www.manitese.it). International campaigning organisation raises funds for projects in developing countries and hosts study camps for which a basic knowledge of Italian is needed.

La Sabranenque, Centre International, rue de la Tour de l'Oume, 30290 Saint Victor la Coste, France (04-66 50 05 05; www.sabranenque.com). French-based organisation uses voluntary labour to restore village and monuments in Altamura (inland from Bari in Southern Italy). The cost of participation is $630 for two weeks in July.

WWF Italia, Servizio Campi, Via Po 25/C, 00198 Rome (06-844971; www.wwf.it/ENG/holiday/listcamps.asp). A few environmental conservation camps, though the emphasis is on holidays. Sample 9-day fire-watching camps in Sicily cost €233.

Volunteers can also join archaeological camps. The national organisation Gruppi Archeologici d'Italia is the umbrella group for regional archaeological units that co-ordinate 2-week digs (Via Baldo degli Ubaldi 168, 00165 Rome; tel/fax 06-3937 6711; segreteriagai@infinito.it; www.gruppiarcheologici.org) Paying volunteers may join these digs (e.g. €350).

Malta

Since Malta joined the European Union in May 2004, EU nationals have been entitled to work in Malta. However because of its small size and population and fear of having its labour market swamped, Malta has retained the right to control inward migration. Therefore non-Maltese citizens must still apply for an employment permit and will be obliged to do so for the next seven years. Australians (but not New Zealanders) under the age of 30 may apply for a working holiday visa to Malta valid for one year.

Although small in area (30km by 15km), Malta has much of interest for the traveller. Its economy is in good shape with a relatively healthy rate of unemployment of 7% (down from 8% in 2003). The procedure for obtaining an employment licence is to obtain a signed form (Employment Engagement Form) from your prospective employer and submit it to the Department of Citizenship and Expatriates (3 Castille Place, Valletta CMR 02; 356-212 24259; citizenship@gov.mt). The Department is at its busiest after Easter and through the summer when many permit applications for seasonal employment and then English teaching are being processed. A range of questions on the red tape requirements is addressed on the website of the Maltese Employment & Training Corporation: www.etc.gov.mt.

Tourist Industry

Tourism plays such a large part in the island's economy that it may be possible to get a job on the spot. Try cafés, bars, hotels and shops in Sliema, Bugibba and beach resorts in the south. Although Robin Gray was in Malta to enjoy a holiday rather than to work, he met a number of people who were working in tourist establishments, some of whom had set up their jobs ahead of time by writing to prospective employers. Wages are far from high.

The Employment & Training Corporation (ETC) maintains an up-to-date online vacancy database. Many vacancies were posted at the time of writing (February 2005), the majority for skilled tradesmen and labourers, though with a fair number for hotel and restaurant staff.

The Malta Youth Hostels Association (17 Triq Tal-Borg, Pawla PLA 06; +356 2169 3957; myha@keyworld.net) can put unpaid volunteers aged between 16 and 30 to work for three hours a day over a short period. A longer-term commitment of full-time work over 6, 9 or 12 months is open to EU nationals only aged 18-25 who will receive free room and board. Jobs to be done include administration, decorating, building, etc. MYHA obtains work permits for participants, a process that takes many months for long-term volunteers who should submit an application six months before they intend to go to Malta.

Teaching

Malta has undergone an EFL boom over the past decade and a number of private language schools cater to groups of language learners from around the Mediterranean. Their interests are represented by FELTOM, the Federation of English Language Teaching Organisations Malta (Foundation for International Studies, Old University Building, St. Paul St, Valletta VLT 07) whose website www.feltom.org has good links to its 16 members schools including Inlingua (9 Triq Guzi, off Bisazza St, Sliema SLM 15; www.inlinguamalta.com) and the Global Village (St. George's St, St. Paul's Bay SPB 02; 2157 3417; info@gvmalta.com).

The student and youth travel organisation NSTS (220 St Paul St, Valletta VLT 07; 2124 4983/fax 2123 0330; www.nsts.org) markets English courses in conjunction with sports holidays for young tourists to Malta. NSTS runs weekly vacation courses from June to August, and it might be worth approaching them for a job, particularly if you are a water sports enthusiast. NSTS was keen to hire Robert Mizzi from Canada, especially when they learned he was half-Maltese:

> I was offered a job quite casually when NSTS found out I was volunteering conversational English in the main youth hostel in Valletta. Perhaps one reason they wanted to hire me was they knew the visa would not be a problem. However I was surprised by how relaxed the offer was. It was just mentioned in passing rather than at an actual interview. I guess it is the Maltese way; once you are one of them, then everything is gravy.

Since that time, language teachers have become obliged to obtain a permit from the Ministry of Education after having been vetted.

Scandinavia

Denmark, Sweden and Finland are full members of the European Union, whereas Norway and Iceland have decided to stay outside the Union but are part of the European Economic Area (EEA) which permits the free movement of goods, services and people within the EU. European citizens are entitled to enter any Scandinavian country for up to three months to look for work. When they find a job and get a 'Confirmation of Employment' from their employer, they can then apply to the police for a residence permit which, in the case of open-ended (i.e. permanent) jobs, will be for five years; otherwise it will be for the duration of the job. At least in principle, the only prohibition in the two non-EU countries is that foreign workers are not entitled to claim social security.

The accession of the ten new member countries into the European Union in 2004 has had a major impact on the job markets of Scandinavia. A large number of students from Poland and the other countries have been attracted to the high wages and low unemployment that contrast so strongly with their home countries. For example the hourly rate in Norway for an unskilled job like cleaning, house renovations or in hotels would be 100 Norwegian kroner, ten times more than would be paid in Poland.

This has made the employment prospects of non-EEA nationals even gloomier than they were, with one major exception. Australian and New Zealand citizens aged 18-30 may obtain a working holiday visa valid for one year for Denmark, Sweden and Finland; and Australians only can enter Norway as working holidaymakers. In all the programmes, participants must undertake not to work for the whole 12-month validity of the visa and be able to show sufficient back-up funds, e.g. 18,000 Danish kroner (A$4,000) for Denmark.

No such reciprocal schemes exist for Americans or Canadians. In order to work legally, North Americans and others will have to obtain work permits before leaving home, which is well-nigh impossible. The American-Scandinavian Foundation (Exchange Division, 58 Park Avenue, New York, NY 10016; 212-879-9779/fax 212-249-3444; trainscan@amscan.org; www.amscan.org) places about 30 American trainees aged 21-30 each summer in the fields of engineering, chemistry, computer science and business in Scandinavia, primarily Finland and Sweden. (It also has an English teaching programme in Finland – see below.) Work experience assignments usually last 8 to 12 weeks in the summer, though longer place-ments are also possible. A non-refundable application fee of $50 must accompany applica-tions which are normally due by the beginning of January. Trainees are paid the going wage but accommodation is not paid for. The ASF can also help 'self-placed trainees', i.e. those who have fixed up their own job or traineeship in a Scandinavian country, to obtain a work permit.

A knowledge of a Scandinavian language is not essential since English is so widely used throughout Scandinavia. One contributor humorously points to the few areas where English will not cut any ice (literally): 'among migratory Lapp shepherds, among polar Eskimo hunters in North Greenland and among Russian coal miners in Spitzbergen'.

One of the features that unifies these countries is that the cost of living and of travel is very high. But some people manage to keep costs down by sleeping in a tent and cooking over a campfire, like Jakob Steixner's sister who lived on £70 during her four-week holiday in Sweden. Yet another possibility is to join WWOOF and work four hours a day in return for bed and board at organic farms (national contact details below). Susan and Eric Beney, a couple from Australia with two grown-up daughters, did this when they found themselves 'pretty broke' driving their camper van from Norway to France where they had been hired as chalet hosts for the winter season. As for travel, Woden Teachout concluded that hitch-hiking is the only way to keep down the expense: *'As far as transport goes, I hitched all over Norway and Sweden without incident, except for one ominous truck driver who told me leeringly that he himself was virtuous, but he had friends who were not so reliable. My other experiences with truck drivers have been universally positive. I got rides very quickly since I was something of a curiosity. In five months I didn't see another soul hitching.'* Watch out for the mosquitoes in summer and the short daylight hours in winter.

Voluntary workcamps are not very numerous in Scandinavia but a few voluntary organisations are mentioned in the country sections. If you see adverts for an international organisation that goes under the names Humana People to People, Tvind or One World, check the website www.tvindalert.org.uk.

Busking, begging and street-selling are illegal in many places, however prosecutions are rare. As long as you are not causing a nuisance or blocking traffic you should be left alone by the authorities but will attract the attention of many passers-by for whom busking is a novelty. Scandinavians have the reputation of being both rich and generous.

Au Pairing

The demand for English-speaking au pairs is not vast but remains steady, especially in Denmark, where a certain number of young women over 18 are placed with families for 10-12 months. The au pair placement activities of the Danish exchange agency Exis were taken over in 2004 by Au Pairs International, Sixtusvej 15, 2300 Copenhagen S (+45 32-841002; info@aupairsinternational.dk). It makes placements in Denmark, Norway, Iceland and Sweden as well as worldwide.

Another possible source of au pair vacancies is the searchable online database www.aupairforum.com, which has a selection of current family listings in Scandinavia whom interested candidates can contact directly. Searches take into account religious affilia-tion, and in Scandinavia there is a much higher proportion of requests for Protestant than Catholic au pairs (and almost none for atheists). Weekly wages vary a lot but many are around €100.

Another possibility is the Scandinavian Au-Pair Service Center (scandinavian@aupair.se; www.aupair.se) whose website provides contact names, phone numbers and email addresses for its representatives in Helsingborg (Sweden), Oslo and Hamar (Norway) and Aalborg (Denmark) among others.

SCANDINAVIA

ICELAND

Höfn
Isafjordur
Vopnafjordur
Akureyri
Seydisfjordur
Djupivogur
Pingeyri
Skaftafell
Tromso
REYKJAVIK
Hafnarfjordur
Vestmannaeyjar

NORWAY

Hammerfest
Finnmark
Vardo
Karasjok
Lapland

SWEDEN

FINLAND

Savonlinna
Hameenlinna
Lahti
Saimaa Lakes
Turku
HELSINKI

Are
Trondheim
Ostersund
Geiranger
Romsdal Fjord
Nordfjord
Vaga
Hovringen
Loen
Lillehammer
Bergen
Geilo
Gol
Hardanger
OSLO
STOCKHOLM
Orebro
Ski
Tonsberg
Stavanger
Kristiansand
Gotland
Skagen
Goteborg
Hirtshals
Oland
Mors
Frederikshavn
Jutland
Logstrup
DENMARK
COPENHAGEN
Skane
Roskilde
Malmo
North Sea
Esbjerg
Ørbaek
Dragør
Fejo

WILLIAM SWAN

Denmark

Denmark has the highest average wage of any EU country with a minimum hourly wage of about 90 Danish kroner (£8.35/€12). It also has a reasonable rate of unemployment (6.1% in 2005) though the rate is higher among people aged 16-24 in Copenhagen. Denmark is an undeniably rich country and there are many opportunities for casual work. Employers are obliged to pay legal workers an extra 12.5% holiday pay *(feriepenge)*.

Work exists on farms and in factories, offices and hotels: the main problem is persuading an employer to take you on in preference to a Danish speaker. May Grant from Glasgow corroborated that the attitude in the job centres seemed to be 'Denmark for the Danes' and to find work it was necessary to explore other avenues.

Any job-seeker in Copenhagen should take advantage of the youth information centre Use It, Rädhusstraede 13, 1466 Copenhagen K (33 73 06 20; fax 33 73 06 49; www.useit. dk). Their primary function is to help newcomers find affordable accommodation but they also distribute a booklet *Working in Denmark* with information about red tape procedures and some realistic tips for those trying to find a job or study Danish. It covers everything from the hours and locations where busking is permitted to how to register for a social security number. If requesting the booklet before arrival, send two IRCs and an s.a.e. Newly arrived job-seekers can visit Use It to consult their files, newspapers and *fagboden* (Yellow Pages) and to check their notice board for lift-shares (there is no jobs board). The helpful staff will even translate ads on request, though Use It is a tourist information centre for budget travellers, not an employment agency, and cannot offer or arrange employment.

Peter Anthony Stonemann is one foreigner who made good use of Use It's facilities during his long stay in Copenhagen. Although initial impressions are that non-Danish speakers have little chance of finding work, Mr. Stonemann claims that the reality is not so bad, provided you speak English. Partly because benefits are so generous in Denmark, many unemployed people are reluctant to move to find work, to take on unpleasant jobs or work at unsocial hours, which leaves plenty of opportunities for the energetic foreigner.

It is possible to place a free advertisement in English or Danish in the twice-weekly Copenhagen paper *Den Bla Avis* (meaning The Blue Paper), a member of the Free Ads Paper International Association; it comes out on Monday and Thursday. The free Copenhagen paper *Sondagsavisen* carries a good number of ads for casual work and is distributed on Sundays. If you know a Danish speaker, check adverts in the job *(erhvervs)* section of the Sunday and Wednesday editions of *Berlingske Tidende* and *Politiken* newspapers, though these are mostly for qualified people. Advertisements in English are accepted by these papers.

The Regulations

EU nationals who intend to stay longer than three months should apply for a residence permit *(Opholdsbevis)* from the Copenhagen Overpraesidium (Hammerensgade 1, 1267 Copenhagen K; 33 12 23 80). Although the office stays open until 3pm most days, it is better to go as close to opening time at 10am as possible. Take the approved form, two photos, passport and, if possible, a contract of employment or, alternatively, proof of means of support. The contract should show that you are employed for a minimum of 20 hours a week and that your wages are at least kr7,200 per month before taxes. If your application is straightforward, you should be sent the permit within a week.

Non-EU nationals will find it much more difficult, though certain categories may be eligible (such as au pairs). As usual, work and residence permits must be applied for at a Danish consular representative in the applicant's home country. The cost of applying in the US is currently $45. Details of the procedures are posted in English on the Danish Immigration Service website (www.udlst.dk). The office of the Immigration Service or *Udlaendingestyrelsen* is at Ryesgade 53, 2100 Copenhagen Ø; 35 30 84 50.

Another essential document you will need if you will be staying in Denmark for more than three months is a Civil Registration Number (CPR or *personnummer*) which is simply a personal registration number which you are supposed to apply for within five days of finding a place to live (other than a hostel or hotel). In Copenhagen this can be obtained from the Folkeregistret, Dahlerupsgade 6, 1640 Copenhagen V (70 80 70 10). This will entitle you to open a bank account (essential for some jobs and for accepting the return of rent deposits), to register for tax purposes and eventually to use the Danish health service.

The minute you find employment, even if it is going to be very temporary, apply for a tax card in the municipality where you are working (or where your employer has his head office). In Copenhagen, the *Skatteforvaltning* (tax office) is at Gyldenløvesgade 15, 1639 Copenhagen V; 33 66 33 66). You will need a *personnummer* in order to apply. Give your tax card to your employer the day you get it. Without one, you will be taxed at a punitive 60% on all earnings. The tax card entitles you to a monthly personal allowance of kr36,800 per year (and then a tax rate of 30%-35%). If you do end up overpaying, you won't have a chance of getting a rebate until six months after the calendar year in which you worked. The office is open 9.30am-2.30pm Monday to Wednesday, 9.30am-5.30pm Thursday and 9.30am-1pm Friday.

Because of the acute shortage of workers especially in seasonal harvests, the authorities have taken the unprecedented step of bestowing significant tax breaks on foreign workers. They are entitled to a tax deduction of kr583 per day (assuming accommodation is not provided by your employer) to cover expenses in their home country. In other words the exemption is calculated according to how much it would cost you in your home country per month so you may need to show documents to prove your home situation. In some locales, the worker will be given a *frikort* (tax card) which shows the exemption; in others the tax will be deducted at source and will have to be reclaimed after leaving Denmark. Tax can also be set against travel expenses as well; the 2005 rate is kr0.84 per kilometre travelled from home including the ferry.

If successful, seasonal workers should end up paying only the 8% plus 5% of earnings which is compulsory for all workers in this sector. The EURES website (www.seasonalwork.dk) explains the new scheme in detail.

Copenhagen

Copenhagen, the commercial and industrial centre of the country, is by far the best place to look for work. It is also the centre of the tourist industry, so in summer it is worth looking for jobs door to door in hotels, restaurants and the Tivoli Amusement Park. The highest concentration of restaurants is located from Vesterbros Torv to Amalienborg Slot and from Sø Torvet to Christiansborg Slot. Many of the large hotels have personnel offices at the rear of the hotel which should be visited frequently until a vacancy comes up. The Mercur Hotel is reputed to have a high turnover of staff. Also try the English Pub, the Scottish Pub and Rosie McGee's near Tivoli Gardens.

Some job-seekers may have no trouble finding hotel work, as in the case of the Dutch traveller Mirjam Koppelaars:

> *My Norwegian friend Elise and I rather liked Copenhagen but realised that money was going quick again and decided to try to find some work. After filling in an application form and having a very brief interview at the Sheraton, we both got offered jobs as chambermaids starting the next day. To get a permit, we only needed an address. The next five weeks I cleaned 16 rooms and 16 bathrooms a day in a very funny uniform. Although I had to pay over half in tax, I was able to save for more travels.*

Fast food restaurants, such as Burger King and McDonalds are also recommended, though they will expect you to fill in an application form in Danish and not all consider people who don't speak the language.

The Jobcenter in Copenhagen at Kultorvet 17 (33 55 17 14/33 55 10 20) should be able to assist EU nationals with a sought-after skill and a knowledge of Danish. They can do nothing for people who send their CVs. The casual work centre *(Løsarbejderformidling)* is at Tøndergade 14, Vesterbro (33 55 10 09), next door to the *Studenterformidlingen* (Student Job Centre). People gather inside the main entrance on Vesterbro early in the morning (between 6am and 8.30am) Monday to Friday to be assigned casual work such as cleaning and furniture removal; however a knowledge of Danish is a pre-requisite.

Private employment agencies *(vikarbureauer)* will also expect clients to speak Danish. It may still be worth registering with a few of those listed in the Yellow Pages such as the multinational Adecco.

Among the largest employers of casual staff in Denmark are newspaper distribution companies. More than 100,000 Danes subscribe to a daily or weekly newspaper and an army of 3,000 workers is needed to deliver them. This job is not done by school children as in Britain and North America because most of the deliveries are done at night. Typically, papers must be collected from a local depot at midnight and delivered by 7am. The job is much easier if you have invested in a second-hand bicycle or a wagon.

Bear in mind that the reason for the chronic shortage of workers is that the work is no doddle. Mr. Stonemann describes what is involved:

Few buildings in Denmark have private mail boxes at the entrance, so deliverers must go up to the fourth or fifth floor to put the paper through the right slots. Hence this is physically demanding work, especially in winter. Payment is according to quantity of work done. New workers take only one or two routes, whereas some veteran workers can do six or seven by themselves. After the first week of practice, a new worker can usually earn kr500 per night (before losing half in taxes). So in less than two nights he has financed his bicycle, especially if he chooses to work on Sundays and holidays. In winter the payment is 10% more. Payment is made every 14 days by bank transfer, so the worker needs to open a bank account before beginning a contract.

To get a job as an *omdeler* or 'paper boy/girl', contact A/S Bladkompagniet (Islevdalvej 205, 2610 Rødovre; 70 20 72 25; bladkompagniet@bladkompagniet.dk) or check the *Yellow Pages* under the heading 'Aviser Distriktsblade' for other companies. Another big hiring company is the morning paper *Morgenavisen Jyllands-Posten.* They employ 4,000 people on weekdays and 5,000 on Sundays to deliver all their papers before 6.30am (8am on weekends). Ring 80 81 80 82 or email avisbud@jp.dk for details; their website www2. jp.dk/avisbud/eng/index.htm is in English.

Agriculture

Farming plays an important part in the Danish economy and farm work is arguably the easiest door by which to enter the working life of Denmark. The main crops are straw-berries (picked in June and July), cherries (picked in July and August), apples (picked in September and October), maize (month of August) and tomatoes (picked throughout the summer). The Danish fruit industry is flourishing and worker shortages are a problem, something that is being energetically addressed by EURES whose website (www.eures. dk) provides a wealth of information about harvest work. EURES estimates that 1,500 foreigners are offered jobs in seasonal harvests and invites applications to be submitted to Arbejdsformidlingen EURES, Smedelundsgade 16, 4300 Holbaek (70 33 07 07; fax 59 48 13 10; euresjue@post6.tele.dk).

The hours of strawberry picking are normally early in the morning until noon or 1pm leaving the afternoons free for cycling, swimming and socialising. Most employers expect you to bring your own tent and cooking equipment but do not charge for camping. The island of Fyn has often been recommended for fruit-picking work, especially the area around Faaborg. But Samsø is where most pickers head in June. The website www.sam-sobaer.dk is a central resource for six Samsø farms which are included in the list that follow. All the farmers stress that they can accept only EU nationals with an E-111 form.

Birkholm Frugt & Baer ApS, Hornelandeveg 2D, 5600 Faaborg (62 60 22 62; fax 62 60 22 63; birkholm@strawberrypicking.dk; www.strawberrypicking.dk). Season lasts from early June to nearly the end of July and applications are processed between 1ˢᵗ April and 15ᵗʰ May. Piecework rates are calculated over the whole season, varying from kr5.40 per kilo if you pick less than 500kg during the season up to 7.25kr if you pick a superhuman 2,500kg or more, with an average falling between these two. Minimum period of work is two weeks. Picking starts at 5am. Free campsite available. Minimum age 18.

Danfrugt, Skaelskør, Lodshusvej 13, 4230 Skælskør (58 16 86 96; fax 58 16 88 80; post@danfrugt.dk). Largest orchard in Denmark with 300 hectares of fruit and more being planted, stretching from the island of Lolland to the town of Jyllinge.

Else Lysgaard & Ingvar Jørgensen, Alstrup 2, 8305 Samsø (86 59 03 45; fax 86 59 03 46; else-ingvar@samso.com; www.else-ingvar.dk).

Guldborgland Frugtplantage, Vigsnæsvej 36, Guldborg L., 4862 Guldborg (54 77 01 01; guldborgland-frugt@post.tele.dk).

Holmgaard, Sildeballe 35, 8305 Samsø (86 59 14 30; holmgaard@brdr-madsen.dk). 70-100 pickers needed.

Maries Minde, Permelille 26, 8305 Samsø (86 59 08 72; mahlers@tdcspace.dk; www.mahlers.dk). 100 pickers needed. Daily charge of kr10 for use of campsite facilities.

Morten Alexandersen, Storgade 34, Pillemark, 8305 Samsø (86 59 22 64; morten@samsobaer.com). 80-100 pickers employed from early June for six weeks.

Gordon Robertson from Glasgow wrote to a couple of addresses but received an enthusiastic reply from a different farmer on Samsø. The farmers know one another and can direct you to one of their colleagues with vacancies.

Starting dates and picking hours are unpredictable so do not count on making a quick fortune. Whereas you will get 40 or 50 hours of work one week (and can expect to pick between 5kg and 20kg of strawberries an hour), you might only get 10 hours the next. Be sure to take wet weather gear since picking carries on through the rain. And even in July the 5am starts can be chilly. Other crops like apples, pears and cherries are paid either by the hour (which because of the high minimum wage is usually very worthwhile) or by piece work.

Anyone with a farming background and time to plan ahead could place an advertisement in the main farming journal *Lands Bladet* or one of its four sister publications, all published by De Danske Landbo Foreninger at Vester Farimagsgade 6, 1606 Copenhagen V. Gary Tennant's advert was instantly successful (see introductory chapter *Farming*). He was paid about £400 a month after tax, living expenses and Danish lessons since the latter were provided free by the commune.

Another possibility is to contact WWOOF Denmark (VHH) to obtain a list of their approximately 30 members, most of whom speak English. Most members are organic farmers but people involved in other environmentally friendly activities are also included. In return for three or four hours of work per day, you get free food and lodging. Always phone, email or write before arriving. The list can be obtained only after sending €10/£5/US$10/kr50 to Inga Nielsen, Asenvej 35, 9881 Bindslev (98 93 86 07; info@wwoof.dk; www.wwoof.dk). May Grant and her boyfriend Ian visited two VHH places, one very relaxed where they only had to weed the garden, the other more strenuous. Rob Abblett had a very positive experience working briefly for a friendly farmer who took him to Copenhagen to visit the Botanical Gardens and other sites.

If communal living appeals, you may want to visit the Svanholm Community which consists of about 120 people including lots of children. Numbers are swelled in the summer when more volunteers arrive to help with the harvest of the organic produce. This possibility is open only to EU nationals. Guests work 30-40 hours a week for food, lodging and (if no other income is available) pocket money. If interested, write to the Visitors Group, Svanholm Gods, 4050 Skibby (47 56 66 19; www.svanholm.dk).

As usual it is best to find out as much as you can about what you're letting yourself in for.

> **David Anderson made private arrangements to work on an organic farm on Mors in the north of Jutland. He regretted his haste in deciding to take the job**
>
> *I arrived at the doorstep with the equivalent of £10. The owner was a strict vegetarian (all home-grown) and expected me to be the same. And there was no hot water. I was the only staff to pick the fruit and vegetables plus I had to help him build a greenhouse in the shape of a pyramid since he was convinced pyramids have some special power. When I received my pay for the first three weeks, I left and headed straight for the McDonald's in Esbjerg.*

Unlike most organic farms, this one paid a wage of about £50 a week, but this was not nearly enough to make up for the culture shock David was experiencing in the 'back of beyond,' as he no doubt described it to his fellow diners at McDonald's.

Voluntary Opportunities

You can arrange to spend a few weeks during the summer on a voluntary workcamp in Denmark by applying through the organisations mentioned in the chapter on *Volunteering* (IVS and UNA) or, only if you are already in Denmark, Mellemfolkeligt Samvirke, Borgergade 14, 1300 Copenhagen K (ms@ms.dk). MS organise summer workcamps in Denmark which last two or three weeks. The main objective of these camps, which carry out projects such as building playgrounds, conservation work, etc., is to bring participants into contact with the social problems found in every society. Four 4-week summer workcamps in Greenland are planned for 2005 (minimum age 20). The participation fee for Greenland is approximately €1,500 (www.mstravels.dk/greenland). Among recent tasks in Greenland was the renovation of a Viking village.

Survival

Contributors have suggested various ways to survive including bottle-collecting from bins early in the morning or from annual festivals like the Roskilde Festival. The pickings are rich along certain Copenhagen streets especially on Sunday morning when only a few supermarkets are open to accept returns; try for example the one at Rantzausgade.

After he had had an HIV blood test and been in the country for three months, May Grant's boyfriend Ian earned £20 (tax-free) by donating sperm at Cryos. You are allowed to donate three times a week but are asked to stop after conceiving 30 children. (Unfortunately Ian's sperm did not freeze well so he never got this far.) If women are excluded from this money-making wheeze, men are not in demand to hand out promotional leaflets outside the Museum Erotica. Doing a similar job for the Little Mermaid English Theatre would be more wholesome.

Buskers head for the pedestrian streets of Central Copenhagen like Købmagergade and Strøget where, on a busy summer's day, it is not unusual for a talented musician, juggler or acrobat to earn 200kr in an hour. Buskers must not use amplifiers and must not perform in groups of more than three. Hours are restricted in some places, though Radhuspladsen and Kogens Nytorv by Krinsen are open to buskers between 7am and 10pm. For more detailed information, contact Copenhagen Police (33 14 14 48) and Copenhagen City Council, Vej og Park (33 66 35 13). Whereas most musicians need not apply for a licence, street performers like magicians and jugglers do.

Finland

Finland offers about 1,800 short-term paid training opportunities to foreign students every year. The International Trainee Exchange programme in Finland is administered by CIMO, the Centre for International Mobility, PO Box 343, 00531 Helsinki, Finland; +358-1080

6767; http://finland.cimo.fi (which is in English). British students and graduates who want on-the-job training in their field (agriculture, tourism, teaching, IT, etc.) lasting between one and 18 months should apply directly to CIMO. Short-term training takes place between May and September, while long-term training is available year round. Applications for summer positions must be in to CIMO by the middle of February. To qualify for the trainee exchange, you must have studied for at least one year, preferably with a year's experience as well, in a related subject. Despite the designation 'trainee', wages are on a par with local Finnish wages for the same work. Among CIMO's programmes is a language teaching programme for a month, a term or preferably an academic year, open to native speakers who are university students or recent graduates in arts or education.

Applicants in the US should contact the American-Scandinavian Foundation mentioned above. If an individual does succeed in fixing up a traineeship, work and residence permits are granted for the specific training period offered by a named Finnish employer. Immigration queries can probably be answered by looking at the English language website of the Directorate of Immigration (UVI), PO Box 18, 00581 Helsinki or in person at Lautatarhankatu 10 in Helsinki (09-476 5500; www.uvi.fi).

Teaching

One of the programmes offered by the American-Scandinavian Foundation (58 Park Avenue, New York, NY 10016; 212-879-9779/fax 212-249-3444; trainscan@amscan.org; www.amscan.org/tefl.html) is an English teaching programme in Finland. American students and recent graduates over 21 teach in a variety of companies and educational establishments from kindergartens to colleges, for a minimum of three months but normally from the end of August or beginning of September until the end of May. The Foundation's role is merely to circulate vacancy details, mainly online, between April and June. Monthly salaries in 2004 varied from $400 to $1,000 (paid in Euros) with monthly rent bills falling between $250 and $310 for accommodation arranged by the employer. Flights, insurance and internal travel are also at the teacher's expense. The application deadline is March 1st for placement the following autumn.

Anyone with experience of the business world might persuade Richard Lewis Communications (Länsituulentie 10, 02100 Espoo, Helsinki; 09-4157 4700; www.crossculture.com) to hire them to teach English to corporate clients. RLC has offices in five other Finnish cities and one in the UK at Riversdown House, Warnford, Southampton, Hants. SO32 3LH (01962 771111).

Casual Work

Finland's rate of employment is over 8% which is nearly double the rates in Norway and Sweden, so job opportunities are never going to be abundant. However certain areas of employment do experience occasional labour shortages, such as the flower nurseries around Helsinki, language tutoring and the 500 hotels included in the Tourist Board's list of hotels, especially in resorts like Hämeenlinna and Lahti. Jobs with UK tour operators are rare but possible: Esprit Santa's Lapland have positions for tour reps, chalet hosts and child care staff for their Finnish Lapland programme which operates for the month of December (Esprit Holidays; 01252 618318; recruitment@esprit-holidays.co.uk).

Some time ago, Natasha Fox fixed up her own work with private families:

I found work as a nanny in Finland simply by placing advertisement cards in a few playgroups. The best area to place them if you are in Helsinki, is Westend Espoo, the most affluent area of the capital. My job paid £110 a week for working Monday to Friday 8am-4pm.

If you have Finnish friends, ask them to translate newspaper advertisements for you. Helsingin Sanomat, Finland's daily newspaper, has several vacancies for domestic positions each day. It's certainly worth ringing up and asking if they would like an English speaker for the children's benefit. (Since so many Finnish parents want their children to learn English, this often works.) If you advertise yourself, try to

write in Finnish; it shows you aren't an arrogant foreigner. You probably won't have
to speak a word of it in the job.
Here is the advert I put up:
Haluaisitko vaihtaa vapaale', lasten hoidon lomassa? Iloinen, vastuullinen England-
tilais-tytto antaa sinulle mahdollisuuden! Olen vapaa useimpina päivinä/iltoina.
This translates as, 'How would you like a break from the kids? Responsible cheerful
English girl will give you the chance! I am free most days and evenings.'

There is no reason why male readers could not advertise themselves likewise. In fact anyone could try this technique for any kind of job, especially teaching English.

On a more frivolous note, busking might be one way of stretching your travel fund, especially outside Helsinki. According to a correspondent in Finland, buskers are an unfamiliar sight, which means that they attract great crowds and a lot of money can be made. As in Denmark, collecting empty bottles, both alcoholic and non-alcoholic, can be profitable.

Voluntary Opportunities

The co-ordinating workcamp organisation in Helsinki is called KVT, the Finnish branch of Service Civil International (Rauhanasema, Veturitori, 00520 Helsinki; www.kaapeli.fi). They organise about 15 summer camps each year. Allianssi (Olymdiastadion, Eteläkaarre, 00250 Helsinki; 9-34824 305; info@alli.fi) co-operates with the members of the Alliance of European Voluntary Service Organisations placing volunteers sent by their counterparts in other countries in workcamps in Finland (though the vast majority of their work involves sending Finnish young people abroad).

Iceland

Iceland has a tiny population of about 293,000 and a low rate of unemployment 2.6% (December 2004). Demand is greatest within the fish, farming, tourism and construction industries and often during the summer season only. There is also a demand for skilled labour in certain service industries, health care and IT. But the greatest number of vacancies open for those who do not speak Icelandic is in the fish industry, agriculture and unskilled hotel jobs. Generally employers wish to hire people for at least three months but preferably 6-12.

There are eight regional Employment Offices in Iceland and the EURES Advisers can be consulted at the main office EES-Vinnumiðlun, Engjateigi 11, 105 Reykjavík (+354 554 7600; eures@svm.is). The Icelandic Directorate of Labour's website includes a job application form in English: www.vinnumalastofnun.is. Efforts are also concentrated on recruiting workers from other Scandinavian countries primarily through the Nordjobb scheme which arranges summer jobs for Nordic citizens aged 18-28 in other Nordic countries for at least four weeks (www.nordjobb.net).

The private employment agency Ninukot (Skeggjastadir 861, Hvolsvöllur; 487 8576; ninukot@islandia.is; www.ninukot.is) originally specialised in agricultural and horticultural jobs throughout Iceland but has branched out to offer jobs in babysitting, fisheries, gardening, horse training and tourism as well. Their welcoming website is in English and holds out the prospect of an easy-to-arrange working holiday in Iceland.

If staying more than three months, you must register at the Immigration Office (Utlendigaeftirlitid), Skógarhlíð 6, 105 Reykjavik (510 5400; www.utl.is). If you are planning to take advantage of the freedom of all EEA nationals to go to Iceland to look for work, take plenty of money to cover the notoriously high cost of living. If touring, accommodation costs can be very high unless you are hardy enough to camp (and it is often cold). An alternative is *svefnpokaplass* which means 'sleeping bag accommodation' whereby you pay £10-£15 for a mattress in a school, farm, etc. Another way of solving the problem is to arrange to live with a family in exchange for minimal duties (housekeeping, English conversation, etc.). Check the adverts in the main national daily *Morgunbladid*.

Au Pairing

Exit-IS (Bankastraeti 10, 101 Reykjavik, Iceland; 562 2362/fax 562 9662; info@exit.is; www.exit.is) is a leading exchange agency in Iceland, the only agency certified to bring foreign au pairs to Iceland for six to twelve months. The Au Pair in Iceland programme accepts au pairs aged 18-25 for periods of 9-12 months starting in August/September or for 6, 8 or 12 months from January. Families undertake to reimburse half the cost of your flights if you stay 6-9 months and all your travel expenses if you stay 9-12 months. The rate of weekly pocket money in Iceland can be as high as kr9,500 (£80) for a 30-hour week. The partner agency in Iceland promises close supervision, opportunities to meet other au pairs and hiking and riding trips offered at a discount.

The Ninukot Employment Agency is always filling vacancies for live-in childcarers who are promised a minimum of €1,150 a month gross, with a deduction of €18 a day for room and board. After completing six months, the family pays for one way airfare to Iceland and after 12 months return.

THE FISHING INDUSTRY

The fishing industry is fairly labour intensive, employing 14% of the working population directly and many more indirectly. Fish products account for three-quarters of the country's exports. It is a seasonal industry and the busiest season coincides with the long dark winter. The demarcation of jobs seems to be strictly adhered to according to sex: men go to sea or do the heavy lifting and loading in the factories and women do the processing.

Work on fishing trawlers was available a generation ago, but not any more as Tim Wetherall described after a fruitless search for work:

> I was in Reykjavik for three weeks in October/November and failed to find work of any kind. Maybe I was unlucky but I don't think so. I'm normally pretty good at finding work when I need it but couldn't manage to pull it off in Iceland. I was ideally looking for work aboard a trawler but then realised that experienced Icelandic trawlermen were unemployed. Years ago casual labour was available to many foreigners aboard trawlers but now Icelandic people are very keen to get taken on because of the excellent money to be earned (around £3,000 per month). A resident Englishman told me that in order to get work on a trawler these days you need to marry the skipper's daughter. I couldn't get a job in a fish factory either. One consolation is that the people of Iceland are very friendly.

Fish Processing

Fish processing in Iceland was once upon a time one of those classic travellers' jobs where you could earn a lot in a relatively short time in an interesting part of the world. The labour shortage still exists but the work is much less popular and not as well paid was it once was. Yet there is enough demand from employers in the fish processing industry and from foreign job-seekers to justify the involvement of the Ninukot Agency mentioned above. Provided you are prepared to stay at least six months in an Icelandic town or village, the agency will try to find a job in a fish factory. The minimum pay promised is a handsome €1,400 a month gross with the possibility of earning overtime wages. The employer always provided accommodation.

The factories are always located by the seaport. Work is pressurised because the fish must be processed quickly to maintain freshness. Shifts of 12 or 14 hours with few breaks are the rule. The peak season is February and April/May and again in September/October.

Tasks to be done in a fish-processing plant include sorting, cleaning, filleting, weighing, deworming and packaging. The worst job is in the *Klevi* or freezer where the temperature is around -43°C (-45°F). The work of packing and shifting boxes of fish would not be too bad were it not for the intense cold. Without proper gear including fur-lined boots and gloves, a balaclava and layers of sheepskin, this work is unendurable. In the rest of the factory the temperature is 10°C-16°C (50°F-62°F).

It takes weeks of practice before you can fillet and pack fish expertly. Standards are usually very high and if the supervisor finds more than two bones or worms, the whole case will be returned to you to be checked again. Since pay is normally according to performance, your earnings will increase as your technique improves, but the wages will not be wonderful in view of the high cost of living. Debbie Mathieson described her work at a small factory in Hnfisdal as 'not really difficult, but mind-blowingly boring'. One of the compensating features of the job for Debbie was that she was eligible for a tax rebate at the end of her contract which amounted to several hundred pounds.

Conventional social life is almost non-existent in the fishing villages of northern Iceland, though many are so prosperous that they offer facilities that would be unheard of in a village of similar size elsewhere. The five dark months of winter, when villages are cut off from their neighbours, can be depressing. Vicki Matchett signed a six-month contract with a factory in the village of Vopnafjörd in north-east Iceland and describes the life: *'Fishing villages usually have about 800 inhabitants with almost no social life, no pubs, not even any wildlife, and the weather between December and May made sightseeing risky. For the sake of saving £1,000 I'm not sure it's worth vegetating for six months. I must admit I spent most of my spare time reading travel journals to remind myself that civilisation still existed.'*

OTHER

Agriculture is a major enterprise in Iceland. Hay-making is an important summer job; much of the grass is cut by scythe as tractors cannot work the steep slopes, particularly in the narrow valleys where many of the farms are located. However this work is mainly done by school children.

Ninukot specialises in finding agricultural and horticultural jobs throughout Iceland. These are normally in picking and packing plants in the south and west of the country, but can also be with riding stables or on holiday farms between May and September. The pay and terms for flight reimbursement are the same as for au pairs mentioned earlier.

It is also possible to fix up this kind of summer job independently or through EURES, especially if you know more than one European language. Janet Bridgeport was staying as a tourist at a guesthouse in Hvolsvöllur which happened to be next door to a horse trekking centre: *'Because I'd worked with horses and wasn't in any rush to get home, I knocked on the door of the trekking centre and asked if they needed any casual help for the summer. I was really amazed when they said they'd take me on (for board and lodging only). A lot of the riding guests spoke English so I suppose that weighed in my favour.'*

The Icelandic Environment Agency in partnership with BTCV (British Trust for Conservation Volunteers) runs a summer programme of projects (not for the faint-hearted!) at eight locations throughout Iceland lasting from between one and 16 days, which are open to everyone. Transport from Reykjavik is usually provided, as is the food and accommodation in huts or (weather permitting) tents. Recent projects have been mainly involved with building paths and steps in national parks such as Jökulsárgljúfur National Park. You can fix this up ahead of time through www.btcv.org or call BTCV Customer Services 01302 572244. The cost is from £570 including flights or £320 if you arrange your own travel.

A splendid new voluntary organisation called Worldwide Friends (WF) offers an interesting range of two-week projects which international volunteers can join. Many are concerned with the environment but others revolve around the national festival on the first weekend of August when Icelanders celebrate the granting of sovereignty to their country in 1874. Volunteers help prepare for and work during the festival in several towns including Heimaey on one of the remote Vestmannaeyjar Islands. WF can be contacted at Hafnarstræti 15, 101 Reykjavík; (551 8222; fax 561 4617; wf@wf.is; www.wf.is). The participation fee is €50, €120 or €170 depending on the project and the duration.

Norway

Norway has been more resistant than most countries to embracing Europe and sometimes this attitude is apparent when foreigners look for jobs in Norway. Robert Abblett is not convinced that equality of opportunities is being taken seriously enough in employment offices in Norway:

> Before I flew out to Norway, I thought I would test the water a bit by phoning the Oslo Jobcentre and a private employment agency. I think I was a bit naïve, really, wasted loads of money on phone calls and got a bit wound up about it. I even wrote to the Norwegian Embassy in London pointing out that their booklet 'Looking for Work in Norway' is misleading. When I phoned Oslo I was passed on to three different people each of whom flatly refused to give me any information because I could not speak Norwegian. The same happened when I phoned Manpower in Bergen. In perfect English we argued over the point that this was a racist barrier against foreign workers from Europe from claiming their legal right to work in Norway.

The EURES department of the Norwegian Employment Service (called Aetat; www.aetat. no) may be more willing to assist job-seekers in person; contact the Euroadviser, Postboks 360 Sentrum, 0101 Oslo; 22 86 22 63/65/67). The Aetat Servicecenter operates a telephone information line (toll free within Norway) providing information on vacancies throughout the country; ring +47 800 33 166.

No matter how long the duration of your employment, you will need to apply for a tax card from the local tax office (*Likningskontor*) before starting work; otherwise 50% of your wages will be withheld for tax. In Oslo, you can get a tax card at Hagegata 23 near Tøyen Underground station or request one by phoning 815 444 55 (www.skatteetaten.no). EU nationals intending to stay longer than three months must apply for a resident permit; see www.udi.no for general immigration information.

To make contact with private temp agencies, look up *Vikartjenester* in the Yellow Pages (www.gulesider.no) or look for the usual suspects like Manpower, Adecco and Kelly Services. Also check ads in the main daily paper *Aftenposten* or try placing one yourself. (As in Denmark, the delivery departments of the main newspapers employ lots of people; ring 22 93 36 40 for *Aftenposten's* delivery or 'Avisbud' department.)

As throughout Scandinavia, wages are high, though the high cost of living makes it difficult to save. Travellers have commented on how friendly and generous Norwegian people are. Because buskers are a relative novelty, earnings can be remarkably high. Mary Hall plucked up the courage to do some busking in Bergen on her newly acquired penny whistle. Although she knew only two songs, she made £15 in 15 minutes, mostly due to the fact that her audience was drunk.

Oslo also has a Use It office (Ungdomsinformasjonen) one of whose aims is to find work and accommodation for young visitors while offering a range of services, all free of charge, as in Copenhagen. Use It is located at Møllergata 3, 0179 Oslo (224 14 98 20; use-it@ung.info) and is open year round from 11am to 5pm with longer opening hours during the summer. Their online guide to Norway called 'Streetwise' (www.unginfo.oslo. no/useit/index.php) in English has lots of concrete tips for living and working in Oslo. Among its listings is a cleaning agency with offices in Oslo, Sandnes (Stavanger), Nyborg (Bergen) and Tiller (Trondheim) called City Maid part of whose website is in English (81 50 03 70; www.citymaid.no).

Tourism

A reasonable number of English-speaking tourists visit Norway each summer, so there are some openings for English-speaking staff. You can also try winter resorts like Geilo, Hemsedal, Lillehammer, Nordseter, Susjoen, Gausdal and Voss. For either season, you can try to get something fixed up ahead of time by emailing or writing to hotels listed on websites such as www.hotelsinnorway.com or in the accommodation brochure available from the Norwegian Tourist Office. There is a greater density of hotels in the south of Norway including beach resorts along the south coast around Kristiansand, and inland from the fjords north of Bergen (Geilo, Gol, Vaga, Lillehammer, and in the Hardanger region generally). Remember that even in the height of summer, the mountainous areas can be very chilly.

Wages and deductions for board and lodging for the hotel industry are revised annually. The starting net monthly wage of an unskilled hotel worker is about NOK9,000 (£750) after a deduction for board and lodging. Wages are lower outside the big cities, but the work may be more pleasant.

The Norwegian Hiking Association take on some people to be caretakers at their network of mountain huts, though the only foreigner we have heard of who did this job was studying at the University of Oslo and therefore was on the spot.

The ski holiday market is much smaller in Norway than in the Alps and few British tour operators hire staff for holidays in Norway. Neil Tallantyre, who spent several winter seasons in Lillehammer, found that there is quite a demand for British workers. He was amazed at the resourcefulness of travellers who have extended their time in ski resorts (primarily to ski), by doing odd jobs like snow clearing and car-cleaning, waitressing, DJing (especially common since the British are thought to know their way around the music scene), au pairing and English teaching. One traveller who happened upon a short-term opportunity for teaching is David Moor: *'I saw an advert in a supermarket in Lillehammer for a native English speaker to teach for a month and jumped at the chance, although I had gone there for a skiing holiday. I'd intended to stay in the hostel or a cheap hotel but was finding Norway expensive, and was lucky that another teacher was able to put me up and feed me. I was just working for keep, but only teaching three days a week, so I had lots of spare time.*

Woden Teachout describes one intriguing avenue you might pursue:

The other opportunity I know of is something I nearly did. There is a very posh cruise during the summer months that sails up the coast past the Arctic Circle, touring the fjords under the midnight sun. Because it is such a luxury liner they need a lot of staff to pander to the passengers. I called the offices and asked if they needed help; they said to meet the boat in Bergen at the docks and ask the captain. I did this on three successive days and none of the captains wanted help. But they didn't laugh at me (as I'd expected) and in fact were quite encouraging, saying that chances were I'd get something within the week. I imagine the trick is to catch them quite early in the season. I don't know what the wages were but the trip is supposed to be so spectacular that it would be worth doing one 14-day run for nothing. Ask as early in the season as possible.

You can find out more about the Norwegian Coastal Voyage on the internet at www.norwegiancoastalvoyage.com.

Norwegian Working Guest Programme

Atlantis Youth Exchange at Kirkegata 32, 0153 Oslo (tel/fax 22 47 71 79; atlantis@atlantis.no; www.atlantis.no) runs an excellent 'Working Guest Programme' which allows people aged between 18 and 30 of any nationality to spend two to six months in rural Norway (Americans and other non-Europeans may stay for no more than three months). The only requirement is that they speak English. In addition to the farming programme open to all volunteers, placements in family-run tourist accommodation are available to European nationals.

Farm guests receive full board and lodging plus pocket money of at least NOK825 a week (£70) for a maximum of 35 hours of work. The idea is that you participate in the daily life, both work and leisure, of the family: haymaking, weeding, milking, animal-tending, berry-picking, painting, house-cleaning, babysitting, etc. A wardrobe of old rugged clothes and wellington boots is recommended.

After receiving the official application form you must send off a reference, two smiling photos, a medical certificate confirming that you are in good health and a substantial registration fee which varies according to country of origin and mediating agency (and which therefore does not appear on the Atlantis website). British applicants are asked to apply through Gwendalyne, c/o Twin Training & Travel, 67-71 Lewisham High St, London SE13 5JX (020-8297 3251; www.gwendalyne.com) and Americans through InterExchange (161 6th Avenue, New York, NY 10013; 212-924 0446; www.interexchange.org).

Atlantis will try to take into account individual preferences and preferred part of the country. There are about 400 places (for all nationalities), so try to apply at least four months before your desired date of arrival. If they are unable to place you, all but NOK250 will be refunded.

> **Robert Olsen enjoyed his stay so much that he went back to the same family another summer:**
> *The work consisted of picking fruit and weeds (the fruit tasted better). The working day started at 8am and continued till 4pm, when we stopped for the main meal of the day. After that we were free to swim in the sea, borrow a bike to go into town or whatever. I was made to feel very much at home in somebody else's home. The farmer and his daughter were members of a folk dance music band, which was great to listen to. Now and then they entrusted me to look after the house while they went off to play at festivals. Such holidays as these are perhaps the most economical and most memorable possible.*

Outdoor Work

One of the best areas to head for is the strawberry growing area around Lier, accessible by bus from Drammen. Wages are notoriously bad in this area, and as a result the majority of harvesters are foreign. Kristin Moen and her Italian friend Maurizio were given jobs at the first farm phoned, but earned only NOK120 between them after 2½ hours, and then quit. The strawberry season here reaches its peak in early July.

Further north the harvest is a little later. For example in Steinkjer (north of Trondheim), it goes from mid-July to August. Wages are a little higher here since the fruit is smaller, and accommodation may be available, unlike in the south where you normally have to provide a tent. Nordfjord, south of Romsdal, is also a possibility. The raspberry harvest starts at the beginning of August at Andebu near Tansberg. Potatoes and other vegetables are harvested in early September; try the village of Loen, in the Romsdal area and inland around Hamar.

The steep hillsides on either side of the many fjords support abundant wild blueberries. It is possible to freelance as a berry picker and then sell the fruit to the local produce and jam co-operatives. In Lapland it is not permitted to pick certain berries in certain seasons, since only native Lapps have the right, so make local enquiries first. Autumn brings wild mushrooms – Norway has about 2,500 varieties. In some of the larger towns, there are weekend mushroom controls where you can have what you have picked checked.

The Norwegian organic farm organisations Oikos and the Biodynamic Association distribute a list of about 40 organic/biodynamic farms using trainees for shorter or longer periods during the year. The list (which is in Norwegian, though most of the farmers will be able to communicate in English) can be sent by email or post or found on the relevant homepages: www.oikos.no or www.biodynamisk.no. The contact address for APØG is

Elias Hofgaardsgate 43, 2318 Hamar (62 53 36 16; biodynfo@frisurf.no).

The harvest season is not the only time when extra help is needed. Jill Weseman and seven others found themselves having to help round up some sheep for slaughter: *'Sheep-herding was one of the most difficult things I have every attempted. Armed with walkie-talkies, binoculars and backpacks stuffed with energy-giving chocolate and coffee, we banded together and hit the hills. We strategically chased the stupid animals down from the mountain and into the valley where they marched back to the farm and towards their deaths.'*

The major industry in the far north of Norway is fishing. Not enough locals are prepared to work in the fish processing plants, as Rob Abblett had confirmed when he rang a fish factory (PO Box 51, 9951 Vardø):

> *I spoke to a manager called Leis who had picked up an American accent somewhere and he told me almost everyone at the factory was Finnish because the local people don't want to do the work. Speaking Norwegian was not a pre-requisite here (hurray) but he did say that he would only consider long-term applicants, minimum one year, as it takes up to six months to train someone the finer arts of fish processing, which sounded a little incredible to me. He was probably gently trying to put me off wasting my money on the effort of making the huge journey only to be disappointed with the work and leave. But I was sorely tempted to send my CV which he said he'd consider. I like the idea of experiencing the aurora borealis and weeks of nighttime/daytime, wild coastline and very very nippy weather for most of the year.*

Accommodation is provided cheaply and the wage is NOK90 an hour. The website www.fishroute.net/norg lists fish processing companies with email addresses according to region (e.g. Bergen, Trondheim).

Au Pairs

The situation is promising for au pairs of all nationalities (provided they speak some English), though the red tape is still considerable for non-Europeans and the majority of au pairs are from the EU. Atlantis runs a programme for 200 incoming au pairs who must be aged 18-30 and willing to stay at least six months but preferably 8-12 months. The programme has become so popular that applications are accepted only through partner agencies, and at the moment there is none in the UK. Interested Britons should seek advice from Atlantis since it may be possible to apply through an agency in another country such as Activity International in the Netherlands.

Information about the programme is readily available on their website www.atlantis.no. Atlantis charges a sizeable registration fee, a quarter of which is non-refundable if the placement doesn't go ahead. Au pairs from an EEA country can obtain the residence permit after arrival. When a family has been found for someone from outside Western Europe, the co-operating agency in Norway obtains an agreement of which four copies are forwarded to the au pair, together with an invitation letter. These must be presented to the Norwegian Embassy in the applicant's home country, together with an original birth certificate. At least three months should be allowed for these procedures. Upon arrival in Norway you must register with the local police within a week.

The pocket money in Norway is at least NOK3,000 per month which sounds generous until you realise that it could be taxed at 25%-30% (depending on the region), leaving a net amount of NOK1,800-2,200. Atlantis can advise on possibilities for minimising tax by obtaining a *frikort* which entitles you to a personal allowance of NOK30,100.

The majority of families are in and around Oslo, Bergen or the other cities in southern Norway, although applicants are invited to indicate a preference of north, south, east or west on their initial application. Virtually all employers will be able to communicate in English. Au pairs are given a travel card worth NOK400 a month.

The Oslo *Yellow Pages* contain several au pair agency addresses, though these are primarily for Norwegians wanting to go abroad as au pairs.

Voluntary Opportunities

The workcamp organisation in Norway is called Internasjonal Dugnad at Nordahl Brunsgate 22, 0165 Oslo. If you're in Norway and want to spend two or three weeks volunteering, for example at a peace centre or an experimental farm, contact them; otherwise you must apply through the Service Civil International/IVS branch in your own country.

Norway has seven Camphill Villages for people with special needs that rely on international volunteers. For example Kristoffertunet (Hans Collins vei 5 N-7053 Ranheim; 73 82 68 60; www.kristoffertunet.no) welcomes applications from anyone who wants to live in their community for short or long periods.

Sweden

EU/EEA nationals may enter Sweden to look for work as in any other member state. Non-Europeans who have the offer of a seasonal job lasting no more than three months may apply for a temporary work permit. All the requirements are set out in the admirably clear English-language website of the Swedish Migration Board: Migrationsverket (www.migrationsverket.se/english.jsp). According to this information, every year Swedish employers apply to hire a number of seasonal workers who wish to take up short-term employment such as picking fruit, vegetables or berries. There are area quotas so early application is advised, especially since the application fee of SEK1,000 (£75) is not refunded if the application is denied. Immigration queries should be addressed to Migrationsverket, 601 70 Norrköping (0771 19 44 00; upplysningen@migrationsverket.se; www.migrationsverket.se). Since September 2004 it has been possible to apply for work and au permit permits electronically.

The addresses of employment offices *(Länsarbetsnämnden)* around Sweden can be found on the website of the Swedish Employment Service (www.ams.se). The job centre in Stockholm might be worth visiting at 45 Kungstensgatan. Once you find work, you must register at the local taxation office *(Skattemyndigheten)* within three days and get a *personnummer;* full information is in English on the taxation website http://skatteverket.se/english/index.html.

Casual Work

State handouts are so generous in Sweden that many natives are unwilling to undertake jobs like dishwashing and fruit picking for a few kroner an hour. Even without the benefit of having the right stamp in your passport, there are possibilities, as the American Woden Teachout discovered:

> *In southern Sweden I did the cleaning lady's tour of Swedish mansions. I found the first job through a couple who picked me up hitch-hiking and who contacted a friend of theirs. There are a great number of large country houses in Skane, and the Swedes who live in them find it no luxury to pay for household help. All the families I worked for were the acme of respectability, and a neat appearance in probably very important. So I had several weeks of sweeping out from behind stoves, washing windows, and generally helping with the spring clean. Housework has never been my great speciality, but the living was easy since the relics of Swedish gentry are both rich and hospitable. I had my own room, four-course meals under the evening sun and they took me merrily along to celebrate midsummer, or on outings to the beach or theatre.*

A rather more elevated casual job has been found by well-educated foreigners as proofreaders and polishers. So many documents in Sweden are translated into English that it is worthwhile phoning publishing companies for freelance work which should pay about £20 an hour.

Some years ago Elfed Guyatt from Wales chanced his luck by looking for work after arrival in Sweden and soon found work as a barman in both Malmö and Lund. In Malmö he worked as a barman in a sports club where the pay was negligible but he was given all the beer and food he wanted plus accommodation shared with one of the club members. Lund was also a good place to look for work and shared accommodation through the student grapevine.

It may be worth trying to find work in hotels, usually in the kitchen. Your best bets are hotels in remote areas where if you are touring before the season begins you may find lots of jobs going. Jakob Steixner met a fellow Austrian who had strolled into her job in the Fjälls area. She had had three job offers within a week of asking around, even before she had decided whether or not to work. Elsewhere you might try areas where tourism is well established. Try the Sunshine Coast of western Sweden including the seaside resorts between Malmö and Göteborg, especially Hölsingborg, Varberg and Falkenberg. Other popular holiday centres with a large number of hotels include Orebro, Västeras, Are, Ostersund, Jönköping and Linköping. The chances of fixing up a hotel job in advance are remote. After writing to dozens of Scandinavian hotels, Dennis Bricault's conclusion was 'Forget Sweden!'.

If you are interested in outdoor work, try the southern counties, especially Skane, where a wide variety of crop is grown. Woden Teachout found morning work at a strawberry farm near Skane: *'Strawberry picking jobs are incredibly easy to come by. Our motley crew consisted of six spindly Swedish teenagers, most of whom quit over the course of the harvest, myself and a carload of Polish students. We worked from 7am till lunch and could make up to $3.50 an hour if we worked fast.'*
With wages like that, it is obvious why few Swedes would want to accept such jobs.

Vacancies also exist in the market gardening sector. Peas, cucumbers, spinach and many other vegetables are grown under contract to canneries and if you can't find work in the fields, you might find it in the processing plants. In the eastern part of Skane there is specialised fruit growing: apples, pears, plums, cherries, strawberries and raspberries. The islands of Oland and Gotland are also very fertile and you might find a farming family short of a helper.

If you can't find an employer willing to take you on, you could consider freelancing as a berry picker. Wild strawberries, blueberries and raspberries can be found in the forests of Sweden from June till September and might be successfully sold at weekend street markets, in youth hostels, etc. In the late summer there are mushrooms and loganberries to pick, though you should be knowledgeable about which mushrooms are edible before trying to market them and also be sensitive about local laws which protect the livelihood of Laplanders. Be warned that forested areas in Sweden are commonly mosquito-ridden, so be prepared. Either remain fully clothed at all times (despite the summer heat) or apply liberal lashings of a powerful repellent.

Au Pairs

Au pairs are subject to the same regulations as all other foreign employees so non-EU nationals must obtain a work permit before leaving their home country. As mentioned it is possible to apply online or by post, provided you have the necessary documents including a job offer from a family (showing hours and pay) and a certificate of intended studies in Swedish. You can also pay the fee of SEK1000 (£75) by credit card. The Swedish Migration Board stipulates that au pairs must work no more than 25 hours a week, must be serious about studying Swedish and must earn at least SEK3,500 a month before tax (currently £265).

Two domestic agencies that send many Swedish au pairs abroad will try to place British and other girls as au pairs in Sweden: Au-Pair World Agency Sweden (Box 299, 461 26 Trollhättan; 520 309 53; www.interteam.se/au-pair.html) and Swede Au Pair (Nämndemansvägen 32, 64332 Vingaker; swedeaupair@swipnet.se). The Scandinavian Institute for International Work and Study (SIIS, formerly EXIS) in Malmö (Box 3085, 20022 Malmö; 40-93 94 40/fax 40-93 93 07; info@scandinavianinst.com) makes a few au pair placements in Swedish families and throughout Scandinavia, though its website describes only its outgoing programmes for Scandinavians.

Once you arrive, it is worth checking university notice boards for baby-sitting openings. The same social class that employed Woden Teachout as a cleaner is often willing to hire live-in childcare. In fact the last family for whom Woden cleaned gave her free room and board in exchange for acting as a companion to their ten year old daughter.

Teaching

Casual work teaching English is rarely available. The Folk University of Sweden runs an adult English language programme in many towns throughout the country in which native speaker teachers are placed for one academic year (nine months). There are five trusts closely linked to the universities of Stockholm, Gothenburg, Lund, Uppsala and Umeå, with branches in many smaller towns. Anyone interested in teaching in Sweden on this scheme should contact the programme co-ordinator, Peter Baston, Folkuniversitetet, Box 2116, S-22002 Lund; 46-19 77 00/fax 46-19 77 80; peter.baston@folkuniversitetet. se; www.folkuniversitetet.se. Interviews can sometimes be held in the UK at the Salisbury School of English (36 Fowler's Road, Salisbury, Wilts. SP1 2QU; 01722 331011). They look for candidates with a first degree or recognised teaching qualification or initial TEFL certificate and two years experience. Classroom experience is essential and experience in other fields is an advantage.

Voluntary Opportunities

The main workcamps organiser in Sweden is Internationella Arbetslag (IAL), Tegelviksgatan 40, 11641 Stockholm, which is the Swedish branch of SCI (ial@algonet.se). It is essential to apply for one of their camps (which are mostly on an ecological theme) through your local branch of Service Civil International (IVS in Britain).

WWOOF is now represented in Sweden: Teleskopsg. 2 Lgh 6,5, 41518 Götebord (Jesper_Lagerman@spray.se). In order to obtain the list of 28 WWOOF farms you must send SEK50/€5/$7. Susan and Eric Beney enjoyed rural Sweden a few summers ago:

> When we were looking for work in Sweden the number we rang no longer took Wwoofers but they put us on to someone who did. Lotte and Matthias had a small-holding with a lovely old farmhouse not far from Orebro. Their greenhouse had collapsed after a huge snowfall so our jobs was to dismantle it so they could erect a new one. They were very friendly, fed as very well and sent us on our way with fresh meat and vegetables. During our time off we would explore the local area - beautiful forest walks were close by.

Stiftelsen Stjärnsund (Bruksallén 16, 77071 Stjärnsund; 225-80001/fax 80301; fridhempost@hotmail.com; www.frid.nu) is located amongst the forests, lakes and hills of central Sweden. Founded in 1984, the community aims to encourage personal, social and spiritual development in an ecologically sustainable environment. It operates an international working guest programme throughout the year, but is at its busiest between May and September when most of the community's courses are offered. Carpenters, builders, trained gardeners and cooks are especially welcome. First-time working guests pay SEK500 for their first week of work and if the arrangement suits both sides it can be continued with a negotiable contribution according to hours worked and length of stay. Enquiries should be made well in advance of a proposed summer visit.

The Taiga Rescue Network relies to a large extent on volunteers and interns to help in the office, co-ordinating the work of this environmental NGO in Jokkmokk, arctic Sweden. Attachments are for at least three months and come with accommodation; details from TRN International Co-ordination Centre, Box 116, 96223 Jokkmokk (971 17039;

info@taigarescue.org).

Another possibility for lovers of the outdoors is the Falsterbo Bird Observatory on the southwestern tip of Sweden, where they need people who can recognise birds to help with the ringing during the autumn migration. Volunteers who stay for several weeks are given an allowance of SEK150 a day, free accommodation and travel expenses within Sweden; details from the FOB, Fryen, 23940 Falsterbo (040-470688; www.skof.se/fbo/index_e.html).

Survival

Collecting discarded bottles and cans can be a fairly profitable way to earn some money anywhere in the country. The carnivals that take place in July and August are recommended as prime targets for bottle-collecting; Elfed Guyatt earned around £50 a day during three days in Norrköping. British and American souvenirs are trendy, so you can make up to 500% profit by selling such things at local weekend markets. Medals, caps, books, etc. are worth stocking up on at home for possible sale in Sweden.

Spain & Portugal

Although unemployment remains one of the highest in the EU (10.5%), the rate has been coming down and the demand for foreign labour, particularly in English language teaching, persists. Spain's tourist industry continues to absorb thousands of foreign young people in a temporary and part-time capacity. Otherwise there is not much job mobility, due to a legal requirement that anyone (employer or employee) who signs a contract must pay compensation if he or she breaks the contract.

The Regulations

EU nationals no longer need to apply for a residence card *(Tarjeta de Residencia)* though it may be useful to take up the option of applying for one from the local police headquarters *(Comisaría de Policia)* or to a Foreigners' Registration Office *(Oficina de Extranjería)* which in Madrid is at Calle General Pardiñas; ring the toll-free number 900 150 000 for information about the documents needed which include a contract of employment, three photos, a passport and in some cases a medical certificate.

As soon as you start a job you should also apply to the police for an NIF (national insurance number). Further details are available from the Ministry of the Interior website (www.mir.es/sites/mir/extranje/index.html) in Spanish only or can be checked with the Labour & Social Affairs Counsellor's Office of the Spanish Embassy (20 Peel St, London W8 7PD; 020-7221 0098; conspalon@mail.mae/ constrab.uk@mtas.es; www.conspalon. org/indexeng.html); and with the British Consulate-General in Spain (Paseo de Recoletos 7-9, 4º, 28004 Madrid; 91-524 9700; www.ukinspain.com). The procedures involved in applying for permanent residence in Spain can be daunting if you do not have a working knowledge of the language which is why so many people pay for the services of a *Gestoria Administrava,* an expert in Spanish documentation.

The immigration situation for non-EU citizens has become increasingly difficult. Employers who want to hire an American teacher or New Zealand tour manager will have to go through an expensive, complex and very lengthy rigamarole. Non-EU nationals must first obtain a *visado especial* from the Spanish Embassy in their country of residence after submitting a copy of their contract, medical certificate in duplicate and authenticated copies of qualifications. In some cases a further document is needed, an *antecedente penale* (certificate proving that they have no criminal record). Invariably the Spanish authorities take months to process this and then quite often reject the application if they think that a Spanish or EU national could do the job. If a visa is issued (normally Type A which is for one specific job), it must be collected from a Spanish consulate in the applicant's home country.

One way for North Americans to get round the draconian immigration laws is to join an organised cultural exchange. For example InterExchange (161 Sixth Avenue, New York, NY 10013; www.interexchange.org) and Alliances Abroad (1221 South Mopac Expressway, Suite 250, Austin, Texas 78746; 512-457-8062; www.allianceabroad.com) arrange Teach in Spain programmes whereby young American women live with a family in exchange for speaking English and providing 15 hours of tutoring a week. The Californian company Adelante LLC (601 Taper Drive, Seal Beach, CA 90740; 562-799-9133; www. adelantespain.com) places interns who are learning Spanish in Barcelona, Madrid, Seville and Marbella. Other live-in programmes are discussed in the section on Teaching below.

Americans, Canadians, Australians, etc. do sometimes find paid work as monitors in children's camps, tutors at language schools and in private households, touts for bars and discos, etc. When their tourist visas are about to expire, they usually follow the example of those who simply cross into France or Portugal to extend their tourist visa for a further three months on their return to Spain.

The strict rules make it almost impossible for people from outside Western Europe to pick up casual work legally as Ana Güemes from Mexico found: *'Although we Latin Americans speak Spanish, I insist on saying that Spain is one of the hardest countries to find a job in. Everywhere you go they ask to see your identity card because of the problems they have with Moroccans.'* That being said, Ana did make friends with the daughters of a vineyard owner and picked grapes in exchange for free food, wine and tours of the area.

Online recruitment agencies might be of some use to those looking for permanent jobs, such as the Malaga-based www.jobfinderspain.com which deals with vacancies along the south coast and Gibraltar.

TEEMING TOURISM

Spain hosts a staggering 40 million visitors a year, including 12 million Britons, making Spain the most popular destination for British tourists by far. Of the top ten package holiday destinations for Britons, five are Spanish: Majorca, Tenerife, Ibiza, Menorca and the Costa Blanca. Spain's coastal resorts continue to draw hordes of tourists, especially Lloret de Mar, Calella (Costa Brava), Benidorm (Costa Blanca), Torremolinos, Benalmadena, Fuengirola (Costa del Sol), Mojacar (Costa de Almeria) and Ibiza and Palma (Majorca). The proverbial British tourist in Spain is not looking for undiscovered villages but wants to have the familiar comforts of home along with the Mediterranean sunshine. The Spanish tourist industry has recognised this preference for a long time and has employed large numbers of English-speaking young people to make the tourists feel at home.

It is always worth checking the English language press for the sits vac columns which sometimes carry adverts for cleaners, live-in babysitters, chefs, bar staff, etc. Look for the giveaway weekly *Ibizasun* (www.theibizasun.net), the *Lanzarote Gazette* (www.gazettelive.com/classified/class-employment.htm) and *SUR in English* (www. surinenglish.com) which has an employment section and is used by foreign and local residents throughout southern Spain including Gibraltar. It is published free on Fridays and distributed through supermarkets, bars, travel agencies, etc. If you want to place your own ad, contact the paper at Avenida Doctor Marañón 48, 29009 Malaga (952-

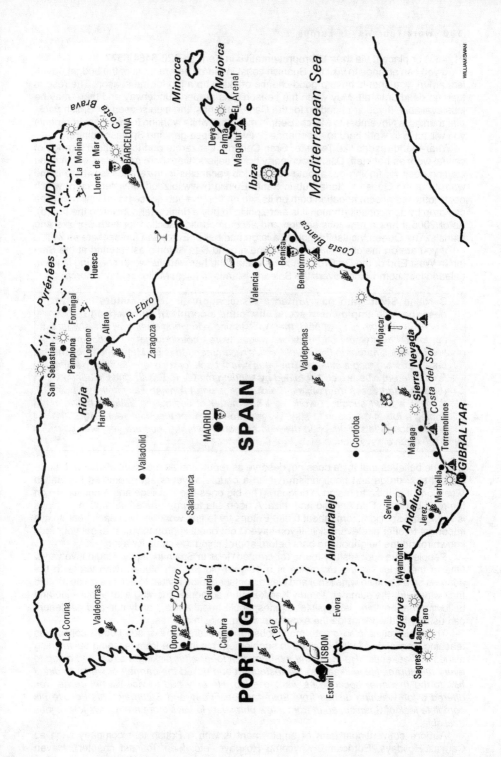

WILLIAM SWAN

212463) or place it via their UK representative in Kent on 020-8464 5577.

If you can arrange to visit the Spanish coast in March before most of the budget travellers arrive, you should have a good chance of fixing up a job for the season. The resorts then go dead until late May when the season gets properly underway and there may be jobs available. If you are heading for the Canary Islands, the high season for British package tourists is November to March. Bear in mind that while working in these environments you will have to work hard to experience or even glimpse genuine Spanish culture.

Year-round resorts like Tenerife, Gran Canaria, Lanzarote and Ibiza afford a range of casual work as bar staff, DJs, beach party ticket sellers, timeshare salesmen, etc. A good starting point for finding out about seasonal job vacancies in Ibiza and elsewhere is the website of the Queen Victoria Pub in Santa Eulalia (www.ibizaqueenvictoria.com) which posts jobs and accommodation both on its site and on the pub notice board which anyone can drop by and consult (though it is more polite to buy a drink after consulting the board). As of 2005 it has a new jobs section and accommodation section for both workers and tourists. The Queen Vic itself employs a large number of European fun-seekers as well.

If you are on the other side of the island around San Antonio ask around at the Ship Inn in West End or the Do Drop Inn in Es Cana. Another website worth checking is www.balearic-jobs.com which covers the Balearic Islands of Ibiza, Mallorca and Minorca.

> **Caroline Scott, who has written a dissertation on youth culture in Ibiza, describes the employment scene she found a couple of summers ago:**
> *Bar work was the highest paid, then waitressing and worst touting which is what I did for the club Godskitchen, where wages were enough to get by. Accommodation becomes harder to find in July, so it's recommended to go May/June when the better jobs are also available. This year I went back for a second season working for a different club, which I obtained by sending my CV to British clubs in January. (I got the addresses from Mixmag, a club magazine.) Arriving early in the season, there is a short supply of work, so it's a matter of finding the balance between finding a job and a place to stay. Wages are low, lower than last year, £40-£50 a week, though this picks up in the high season. Postering jobs are very well paid, £120 for five days work.*

Caroline believes that Ibiza does not deserve its reputation as a cesspit of vice with nothing but sex, drugs and hooliganism (which a couple of years ago prompted the British Vice Consul in Ibiza to resign in disgust). The big ones like Privilege and Amnesia are on the road between San Antonio and Ibiza. A good site for up-to-date information on clubs is www.ibiza-spotlight.com. About 6,000 Britons try to find work on Ibiza each year so it is important to offer a relevant skill. If you haven't got one it is probably best to get your face known round the neighbouring bars before approaching the clubs for a job.

People have successfully found (or created) jobs in Spain in highly imaginative ways. One of the most striking examples is a 19-year-old Finnish student who wrote to the address on a Spanish wine label and was astonished to be invited to act as a guide around their winery for the summer. Tommy Karske returned home 'knowing a lot about wine and believing that anything is possible'. Tradespeople, mechanics, handymen and gardeners can usually find work inside the expatriate community in any resort.

The major cities also create many jobs for travellers. One of Jon Loop's colleagues teaching English in Madrid decided to supplement his income from teaching by washing dishes at weekends: *'He found the job in mid-October after picking a street and going to every restaurant. He walked into the restaurant and asked the barman or waiter to direct him to the manager because he wanted a job. He only had to visit six before he was offered a job washing dishes from 9pm-4am on Friday and Saturday. This despite his complete lack of Spanish, apart from a few phrases. He says there are always lots of jobs available.'*

A more conventional form of employment is with a British tour company such as Canvas Holidays, Eurocamp, Keycamp Holidays, etc. (see *Tourism* chapter). Haven

Europe (www.haveneurope.com) and Solaire Holidays (1158 Stratford Road, Hall Green, Birmingham B28 8AF; 0121-778 5061; jobs@solaire.co.uk) need Spanish-speaking couriers and children's staff to work at mobile home and tent parks from early May to the end of September. Open Holidays (29 Guildbourne Centre, Chapel Rd, Worthing, W. Sussex BN11 1LZ; 01903 201864; personnel@openholidays.co.uk) specialise in Balearic resorts in Menorca and Majorca. And don't ignore the possibility of winter work with a British tour company in a Pyreneen ski resort either in the Spanish province of Huesca or in the principality of Andorra. Andorra Holidays (www.andorra-holidays.com) is a leading company with a range of self-catering holiday apartments and a handful of catered chalets requiring cooks.

Agencies in the major Spanish cities may be able to assist, for example the Easy Way Association (www.easywayspain.com) in Madrid (see Au Pairing section for details) charges a fee of €300 for placing Spanish-speaking or hospitality-trained people in restaurant jobs for a minimum of two months.

A different kind of agency called Animatur supplies teams of entertainers to Spanish resorts; contact international.recruitment@animatur.com or check out actual vacancies with start dates on www.animacion.net/en.

Odd Jobs and Touting

There is a job which is peculiar to the Spanish resorts and which allows a great many working travellers to earn their keep for the season. The job is known variously as 'PRing', 'propping,' 'blagging' or touting, that is to entice/bully tourists to patronise a certain bar or disco.

Many readers have found propping a good way to spend the season, among them Ian Govan from Glasgow in Lloret de Mar
There are literally hundreds of British props and a fair number of Commonwealth and other European nationals. I worked as a prop for over a dozen bars in three months and by the end I was earning up to £280 a month with free beer to boot. Be warned that saving is virtually impossible, but you will have one hell of a social life, and will soon enjoy the job and the challenges which arise as you try to match the experienced props and develop your own routine. The highest compliment is when the old hands start using your lines. It's pure unadulterated showbiz.

The job can involve dressing up to promote a themed event, putting up posters or sticking leaflets under windscreen wipers, as well as simply leafleting and chatting up passers-by. The nightly wage varies of course but tends to be in the range €20-€25 per night. Other places pay a commission, e.g. €1 or €2 for every capture plus a bonus after every 20. Sometimes new people are taken on on a drinks-only basis for one or two sessions and, after they have proved their effectiveness in drawing in customers, begin to earn a wage. When you first arrive, try to get a toe-hold by working at one of the less sought-after places. The authorities normally turn a blind eye to this activity provided props carry out their work discreetly. The hours of work are usually midnight onwards, as late as 7am.

After leaving Lloret de Mar (which Alison Cooper describes as a 'nightmare resort') she moved to the much smaller resort of Estartit where she managed to get a job as a dishwasher in a restaurant. She worked from 6pm to 2am every day for £75 a week: *'Although it was backbreaking work, it certainly was a laugh. I worked with three Moroccans and one Spaniard, and we all had to communicate by sign language and by drawing pictures. In September my Spanish boss gave me a lift to Perpignan and invited me back to work anytime. I was pleased to feel appreciated.'*

Also in the vicinity of Barcelona is Salou, site of Spain's largest theme park Port Aventura at which it might be worth enquiring for seasonal jobs. Universal Studios (Universal Mediterránea) at Port Aventura employs 3,000 people (fax 977-77 90 97; recursos. humans@portaventura.es). In 2005 they were recruiting English speakers via Jobscentre Plus/EURES.

Timeshare touting is another of those jobs that some find objectionable but others recommend. The industry is much better regulated than it was a decade ago, and there are fewer shady practices. Respectable companies like Thomas Cook are involved and do not employ the hard-sell which gave timeshare such a bad name. Many companies provide a one-week sales training course beforehand.

Outside Personal Contacts or OPCs have the job of persuading holidaymakers to visit the holiday development, where they are handed over to a sales rep. Those who succeed have to be aggressive and prepared to face a lot of rejection. Instead of buttonholing people on beaches (which in some cases is against the law), a more common practice for timeshare reps is to visit package holidaymakers in their rooms and invite them to a welcome meeting. The commission paid is 8%-10% which, on an investment of thousands of pounds, means that high earnings for the reps are possible. Writing in a quality Sunday paper, one former timeshare rep in Tenerife claims to have made £20,000 tax-free in ten months.

Most companies will pay for your accommodation for the first two to four weeks or even reimburse your flight after they've seen whether you're any good. No one should expect to make a lot of money at the beginning, nor should they be too cavalier about the police (*guardia civil*) who can come down very hard on anyone openly working the beaches or streets. A company that markets properties in Fuerteventura was advertising its employment packages for OPCs and sales staff at the end of 2004: details are available from Sunshine Horizons (01489 569442; www.sunshinehorizons-ltd.co.uk/Recruitment.htm).

Selling oil paintings may seem easier than selling property but travellers who have done this job on commission in other countries seldom last long. A company called Spainjoy in Madrid (spainjoy@hotmail.com; www.spainjoy.com) sends out teams of young sales staff who start at any time of the year and travel to various towns to sell the company's wares door to door. A vehicle is provided and accommodation costs €40-€70 a week.

Exploiting the Tourist Market

As in all areas of heavy tourism, selling your handicrafts and busking should prove to be profitable. Martin and Shirine's money-making schemes in Benalmadena are typical: while she made money on the promenade making hairwraps each evening, he plied the English bars with a bag of rune stones and some well-placed rhetoric.

If your skills are literary, rather than manual or musical, you should try to sell an article to one of the many English language magazines and newspapers which thrive on tourism and resident expatriates. Get hold of, for example, the *Costa Blanca Post & Mail* in Alicante, the *Costa Blanca News* in Benidorm (www.costablanca-news.com includes employment classifieds), *Lookout Monthly Magazine* in Fuengirola, the *Iberian Daily Sun* in Madrid, the *Majorca Daily Bulletin* or the *Island Gazette* in Tenerife, and see what type of article would suit.

Barcelona is especially popular among buskers, partly because it is not a prohibitively expensive city in which to make ends meet. Although there will be plenty of foreign buskers already installed, the majority of tourists and locals will pay to be serenaded as they sip their drinks in one of the hidden squares in the Old Town, provided the quality is sufficiently high.

Boats

Many yachts are moored along the Costa del Sol and all along the south coast. It might be possible to get work cleaning, painting or even guarding these luxury craft. There are also crewing possibilities as Peter Goldman discovered:

> In Alicante I was taking a day off from hitching and was engrossed in the sunset when I noticed some folks coming off a sailboat. I asked them if they needed crew and they said they did. I hinted that I had little experience (really none) but they said that was no problem and I was on. We sailed around Spain including Ibiza and settled in Palma de Majorca. There were five of us and we decided we would look for

work in Palma and live on the boat, but we soon discovered that Palma is a terrible place to look for work in January/February.

Acorn Adventure (22 Worcester St, Stourbridge, West Midlands DY8 1AN; 01384 446057; www.acorn-jobs.co.uk) need seasonal staff for their two watersports and multi activity centres on the Costa Brava. RYA qualified windsurfing and sailing instructors, BCU qualified kayak instructors and SPSA qualified climbing instructors are especially in demand, for the season April/May to September. Minorca Sailing Holidays (58 Kew Road, Richmond TW9 2PQ; recruitment@minorcasailing.co.uk) hire qualified sailing and windsurfing instructors as well as nannies and other staff for their sailing centre in the Bay of Fornells on the north coast of Minorca.

Pavilion Tours (Lynnem House, 1 Victoria Way, Burgess Hill, West Sussex RH15 9NF; 0870 241 0425; www.paviliontours.com) need windsurfing, kayaking and sailing instructors for children. They must be qualified to RYA/BCU Level 2 and have teaching experience.

TEACHING ENGLISH

The boom in English language teaching has subsided somewhat, apart from in the area of teaching children as young as pre-school (for which a knowledge of Spanish is virtually essential, not to mention songs and games). However there are of course thousands of foreigners still teaching English in language institutes from the Basque north (where there is a surprisingly high concentration) to the Balearic and Canary Islands. The entries for language schools occupy 18 pages of the Madrid Yellow Pages. But the days are gone when any native speaker of English without a TEFL background could reasonably expect to be hired by a language academy.

Job Hunting on-the-Spot

Most teaching jobs in Spain are found on the spot and, with increasing competition, it is necessary to exert yourself to land a decent job. Most people simply use the usual method of consulting the Yellow Pages *(Las Paginas Amarillas)* available online at www.paginasamarillas.es and pounding the pavements of the place where they are staying. The best time to look is at the beginning of September, after the summer holidays are ended and before most terms begin on October 1st. Spanish students sign up for English classes during September and into early October. Consequently the academies do not know how many classes they will offer nor how many teachers they will need until quite late. It can become a war of nerves; anyone who is willing and can afford to stay on has an increasingly good chance of becoming established.

After finishing A levels in Yorkshire, Sam James and Sophie Ellison decided to spend their gap year in Barcelona if possible. After acquiring their Trinity Certificates from Oxford House in their destination city, they did the rounds of the language schools:

Though tedious, this did work and we doubt we would have found work any other way. Job availability didn't seem that high in Barcelona when we were looking in October and we both accepted our only job offers. (Our age may have put off some employers.) Most schools seem to have recruited in September, so October was a bit of a lean month. I got my job by covering a class at two hours notice for a teacher who had called in sick. When this teacher decided to leave Barcelona, I was interviewed and offered her classes on a permanent basis. I got the job permanently about a fortnight after handing out CVs. Sophie was asked to her first interview after about three weeks of job-hunting. She was selected but then had to wait for several more weeks while her contract was finalised.

The great cities of Madrid and Barcelona act as magnets to thousands of hopeful teachers. Sam James blamed his lack of job security and bitty hours on Barcelona's popularity, 'the result of the great supply of willing teachers here keeping working conditions down and making it hard to exert any leverage on an employer when one is so easily replaced.' For this reason other towns may answer your requirements better. There are language academies all along the north coast and a door-to-door job hunt in September might pay off. This is the time when tourists are departing so accommodation may be available at a reasonable rent on a nine-month lease.

Ben Hockley from Australia recommends trying Wall Street Institutes, whose head office in Spain is at Rambla de Catalunya 2-4, 08007 Barcelona (902-399399; www.wsi.es). With 100+ academies in Spain, this chain is reputed to have a high staff turnover, partly because the pay is at the lower end of the spectrum. Ben had no trouble fixing up a job with them on his second visit to Madrid; the first time he had no luck job-hunting because he had no TEFL qualification and no Spanish. Try also Berlitz, whose five Madrid branches including the main one at Gran Via 80 4°, 28013 Madrid (91-541 6103) recruit EFL teachers with a degree but not necessarily any teaching experience or qualifications.

Other sources of job vacancy information include the Madrid daily *El Pais* which usually has a few relevant classifieds under the heading *Trabajo – Idiomas.* Also try *Segundamano,* Madrid's free ads paper which comes out Monday, Wednesday and Friday. The English and Irish pubs that advertise in the English language press are usually good places in which to make contact with like-minded job-seekers, for example Kitty O'Shea's, the Shamrock and the Haddock pub in Barcelona and Finbar's, Finnegans and the Irish Rover near the Santiago Bernebeu metro station in Madrid. Another way to make contact with the local community is to attend (or organise) an *intercambio* in which Spanish speakers and English speakers exchange conversation in both languages. Some are listed on the English-language site www.catalunya-classified.com which is linked to the online magazine *Barcelona Metropolitan* (www.barcelona-metropolitan.com).

In Advance

Anyone with an EFL component on his or her CV might try to fix up work ahead of time. School addresses can be found in the online Yellow Pages and in the seventh edition of *Teaching English Abroad* (Vacation-Work Publications, 2005) which has about 120 addresses of language schools that hire native speaker teachers. One option which makes the job hunt easier is to do a TEFL training course in Spain, of which there is a considerable choice.

Summer-only positions are available at language camps for children. The Educational Consortium of Spain (TECS), Apdo Correos 85, 11500 El Puerto de Santa María, Cádiz (956-853000; tecscamp@tecs.es; www.tecs.es) hires native English speakers for summer work or for longer-term work in the academy.

For voluntary work as an English assistant on summer language/sports camps, try Relaciones Culturales, the youth exchange organisation at Calle Ferraz 82, 28008 Madrid (91-541 71 03; spain@clubrci.es), which also places native speakers with Spanish families who want to practise their English in exchange for providing room and board. Another language agency involved in making this sort of live-in placement is Castrum, Ctra. Ruedas 33, 47008 Valladolid (983-222213; info@castrum.org). The latter makes placements of people aged 18-30 in Castille and Leon whereby participants undertake to spend three or four hours a day teaching English to members of the family and to enrol in a Spanish course (minimum five hours a week). The cost of this student-teacher exchange is €244 for 15-45 days.

Michelle Manion from Australia was happy with the language exchange arranged for her by Elena Garcia Perez of Castrum:

I would recommend the programme to anyone in my situation, i.e. anyone who wants to live in Spain but not as an au pair and is not entitled to a work permit. I was placed with a family with two boys aged 11 and 14. In the morning I went off for my Spanish lesson and then gave a lesson to the boys in turn. Spanish boys are notorious for being spoilt and impossible to control, but also for possessing wonderful personalities and great senses of humour. Carlos and César were typically Spanish and always managed to be both delightful and infuriating. Anyone interested in undertaking this venture should try to ascertain the children's level of English before arriving in Spain and to bring textbooks, magazines and children's books to work with, since English books are difficult to find in Spain. Also, when you arrive in Spain try to make as many friends and take up every opportunity you're given as this is the best way to learn Spanish.

It is also possible to arrange an informal exchange of English conversation for a free week in Spain. Englishtown is a unique programme whereby a holiday village in Spain (between Madrid and Barcelona) is 'stocked' with native English speakers and Spanish clients who want to improve their English. The English native-speaking volunteers participate alongside the Spanish adults in an intensive week of activities, sports, games and group dynamics and, in exchange for making English conversation, receive free room and board. All they have to do is cover the travel expenses to Madrid and then agree to chat and exchange stories. Participants come from all over the world and the average age is 40. More information is available from Vaughan Systems (Eduardo Dato 3, 1ª planta, 28010 Madrid, Spain; +34 91-591 4840; www.vaughanvillage.com).

> **Catharine Carfoot went on what amounts to a classic working holiday at the Vaughan Village in the summer of 2004:**
> *Back in June I took part in an English Language immersion programme in Spain. They want native English speakers (any flavour, although in practice North Americans predominate) to go and talk a lot of English to Spaniards. The Spaniards are generally professional manager-types paid to be there by their companies to improve their English. Last year there were problems finding people to fill the programme due to the Madrid bombings, but since both locations are out in the mountains in formerly abandoned villages I think they are fairly safe! All people have to do is get themselves to Madrid in time for the pick-up (by the way the cheapest option for getting to Madrid is to fly with Ryanair to Valladolid and then take a bus from there). At the end of the week, you will be delivered back to Madrid, unless you have extraordinary stamina and can manage two (or more) continuous weeks in the programme. It isn't a way to make money, but of course people can and do make friends and contacts both with the other 'Anglos' and with the Spaniards. It's also a week off worrying about food, drink and where to sleep.*

Catharine was rather amused when she was told by a number of the Spanish participants (and one or two of her fellow English speakers) that understanding her received pronunciation accent would be their 'challenge'. It seems that many of the Spanish participants had been learning via the Vaughan system, which seems to be staffed largely by Texans. A Swedish friend of Catharine's was accepted as an 'Anglo' which would suggest that being a native English speaker isn't strictly necessary.

Qualified TEFL applicants from the EU might want to make use of a recruitment agency, whether a general one or one that specialises in Spain, such as English Educational Services (Alcalá 20-2°, 28014 Madrid; +34 91-532 9734/ 91-531 4783; fax 91-531 5298; movingparts@wanadoo.es). The owner Richard Harrison recommends that candidates with just a degree and Cambridge Certificate come to Spain in early September and contact his agency on arrival. He also runs a small English-speaking theatre company. Anyone with a theatrical bent who wants to teach English through drama might contact the Moving Parts Theatre Company (same address as EES; www.movingonsl.com) which takes on young British and Irish actors and musicians full-time to perform plays and storytelling sessions to schools all over Spain entirely in English.

Conditions of Work

Salaries for English teachers are not high in Spain. The minimum gross salary is about

€850 per month with many schools offering €950 for a full-time load (i.e. 21 hours a week). Compulsory social security *(seguridad social)* payments of 4%-7% will be deducted; 6% is typical. Tax deductions are paid in arrears and do not normally affect teachers on nine-month contracts. A full-time contract normally consists of 25 contact hours or in some cases 30, which can feel gruelling, especially if the teacher teaches in off-site locations and has to travel around a big city like Madrid.

One of the worst problems in the classroom is the difficulty in motivating students. Many are children or teenagers whose parents enrol them in classes in order to improve their performance in school exams. David Bourne echoes this complaint after completing a nine-month contract in Gijón: *'I have found it very hard work trying to inject life into a class of bored ten year olds, particularly when the course books provided are equally uninteresting. The children themselves would much rather be outside playing football. So you spend most of the lesson trying (unsuccessfully in my case) to keep them quiet.'*
Despite this he still sums up his job in Spain as exhilarating.

A reluctance to learn is not confined to the youth of Spain as Jon Loop found when he spent a year teaching at a Madrid language academy: *'A lot of my groups were civil servants. They were excruciating because they didn't want to be there. The government has to spend its language training budget and picks people at random. I taught other classes including some university students who were very enthusiastic and great to work with, and also a group of technicians from the meteorological office who were keen because it was linked to their work.'*

Jon recommends taking advantage of the friendliness and helpfulness of students who may be in a position to lend you an unoccupied holiday house or put you in touch with their friends who want private tuition in English. In Jon's case, one of his students arranged for him to spend the harvest at a family vineyard and another helped him fix up work editing technical papers.

Private Tutoring

As usual, private tutoring pays much better than contract teaching because there is no middle man. The going rate for teaching individuals is about €30 per hour. Freelance rates in Madrid are higher to take account of travelling time.

It is difficult to start up without contacts and a good knowledge of Spanish; and when you do get started it is difficult to earn a stable income due to the frequency with which pupils cancel. Getting private lessons is a marketing exercise and you will have to explore all the avenues that seem appropriate to your circumstances. Obviously you can advertise on relevant websites as well as on notice boards e.g. at universities, corner shops and wherever else you think there is a market. Send neat notices to local state schools asking them to pin it up broadcasting your willingness to ensure the children's linguistic future.

AU PAIRS

Gone are the days when all the live-in positions in Spain were taken by Irish girls because of their Catholicism (so that it is said that the aristocracy of Spain regularly used such expressions as 'Begorra', according to Maura Laverty's amusing book about being a governess in Spain in the 1920s and 30s called *No More Than Human*).

The pocket money for au pairs in the big cities at present is €55-€65 a week. Au pair links between Spanish agencies and those in the rest of Europe have been increasing partly because Spanish is gaining popularity as a modern foreign language. As mentioned in the section above on teaching, people can also arrange to stay with Spanish families without having to do much domestic or childcare duties. If you deal directly with a Spanish agency, you may have to pay a placement fee though mostly the agencies charge large fees for outgoing placements:
ABB Au Pair Family Service, Via Alemania 2, 5°A, 07003 Palma de Mallorca (971-752027; abbaupair@telefonica.net).
B.E.S.T., Calle Solano 11, 3°C, Pozuelo de Alarcón, 28223 Madrid (www.bestprograms.

org). Au pair placements for Americans and Europeans; fee $970 for three months. B.E.S.T. also organises internship and work-study programmes for varying fees, e.g. €1,370 for a 2-month internship in Seville or €1,615 for a 3-month internship in Barcelona including a one-month language course.

Centros Europeos Galve, Calle Principe 12-6°A, 28012 Madrid (91-532 7230; centros-principe@telefonica.net). Mainly places au pairs in the Madrid, Valencia, Alicante and Pamplona areas.

Easy Way Association, C/ Gran Via 80, Planta 10, oficina 1017, 28013 Madrid (91-548 8679; www.easywayspain.com). Also makes hotel and restaurant placements.

GIC Educational Consultants, Centro Comercial Arenal, Avda. del Pla 126, 2.22, 03730 Javea (Alicante); 096-646 20 15 (ecsl@telefonica.net). Au pair placements and live-in language tutors (registration fee €180).

Globus Idiomas, C/ Gómez Cortina 5, 2°1B, 30005 Murcia (968-295661; globus@ono.com; globusidiomas.com). Member of IAPA.

Instituto Hemingway de Español, Bailén 5, 2°dcha, Bilbao 48003 (94-416 7901; www.institutohemingway.com). Accepts most nationalities. Also places interns in local companies, volunteers and English teachers.

Interclass, C/ Bori y Fontestá 14, 6° 4°, 08021 Barcelona (93-414 2921; www.interclass.es).

Relaciones Culturales, Calle Ferraz 82, 28008 Madrid (91-541 71 03; spain@clubrci.es).

Anyone with a childcare qualification or reasonable experience should approach tour operators that offer creche facilities or a dedicated babysitting and childcare agency like the British-run company Cosytoes in Majorca; fax 01252 370451 in England, telephone 630 457486 in Spain or email employment@cosytoes-mallorca.com.

Non-EU nationals who wish to work as au pairs should apply for a student visa before leaving their country of residence. Officially the Embassy requires both an offer of employment from the family and a letter from the school where the au pair is enrolled to study Spanish but in fact only the former is required, since the authorities recognise that it is usually impracticable for au pairs to enrol in classes before arrival in Spain.

AGRICULTURE

Reports of people finding harvesting work in Spain are far less common than in France and Greece, but they do filter through every so often. Traditionally there is an excess of exploited immigrant labour from North Africa and landless Spanish workers especially from Andalucia to pick the massive amounts of oranges, olives, grapes, and latterly avocados and winter strawberries. In places where migrant pickers congregate like Almeria, the Caritas charity often sets up a temporary food stall or even arranges basic accommodation. Andrea Militello from Italy went to the Valencia area at the beginning of November and did succeed in arranging work on an orange farm. But because of the many problems created by competition from Moroccans and low market prices for oranges, he left after a few days.

Brendan Barker hitched to an organic farm near Granada (whose address he had noticed on a card displayed in a health food shop in Brixton!) and worked happily there on a work-for-keep arrangement for six months, while picking olives at a neighbouring farm in his free time. He describes the job as 'not particularly hard work but a little boring' and was told of a local superstition which claimed that having olive trees on your land means that you have been cursed by God.

The strawberry harvest lasts from Easter to June around Huelva on the southwest coast of Spain. Dozens of strawberry farms are located around the village of Moguer (from which half of Columbus's sailors came), plus Cartaya and Lepe. The usual struggle to find work pertains; newcomers must go to the hiring café at 6am each morning until a farmer picks them up. Then there is the usual struggle to earn decent money. It is possible to earn £50 a day in the latter part of the season, though £30 would be the average for a practised picker and a measly £10 for a beginner who is not yet used to bending double in the broiling sun.

When the strawberry harvest finishes in June, the apricots in the area are ready for harvesting. Elsewhere try the Lorca area for pepper picking in early November followed by artichoke picking (bearing in mind that an estimated 5,000-6,000 migrant workers from Africa and Latin America will be competing with you). You might also try the famous wine-making region of Spain, the Rioja Alta which is centred on Logrono, Haro, Cenicero and Fuenmayor. The local councils in some of these towns along the River Ebro have been known to allow migrant grape-pickers to camp free of charge in a public space.

Tomatoes and many other crops are grown on Tenerife. The Canaries are normally valued by working travellers only for their potential in the tourist industry, but there is a thriving agricultural life outside the resorts. Just a bus ride away from Los Cristianos, the farms around Granadilla, Buzanada, San Isidro and San Lorenzo may take on extra help between September and June. Most pickers camp and work on three-month contracts. Although a few foreigners have discovered these harvests, most of the locals will consider it a novelty to employ a traveller and will help you to improve your Spanish.

Spanish lessons are on offer on a working holiday noticed in the Jobs Abroad Bulletin (November 2004). Workers for an olive and almond farm (Lo Vela; info@yourbackonline.com) were being sought to clear land and pick the crops. Food and lodging are provided in addition to some free time to learn Spanish or hike in the area.

The Spanish organic farm movement is AEAM (Amics de l'Escola Agrària de Manresa, Ramon d'Iglésies 5-7, (Edifici FUB), 08242 Manresa; 93-878 70 35; fax 93-877 16 34; aeam@agrariamanresa.org; www.agrariamanresa.org). It is primarily concerned with campaigning though anyone who can communicate in Spanish could ask to be put in touch with member farmers looking for trainees in organic farming. The WWOOF Independents list contains 171 addresses in Spain.

Jon Loop is one contributor who succeeded in linking up with an organic farmer in southern Spain where he soon got down to some serious work weeding, building a pig enclosure, searching for water when the mountain stream dried up, etc. with no days off. But the surroundings were stunning, and the desolate beauty and harshness of the semi-desert made his stay very enjoyable. He even managed to enjoy goat-herding, that most challenging of rural activities:

This could be quite difficult since their range was 10km by 5km, and they could get through dense undergrowth while I had to follow dried-up rivers and footpaths. Also they had a habit of disappearing, even though they wore bells. The family were quite friendly, the food was exquisite, the accommodation adequate but the temperatures were unbearable. Walking out of the house at 5pm for the evening stint was like walking into a Swedish sauna without the steam. After three weeks I decided to call it a day, and headed up north in search of rain.

Sunseed Trust, an arid land recovery trust, has a remote research centre in southeast Spain where new ways are explored of reclaiming deserts. The centre is run by both full-time volunteers (minimum five weeks) and working visitors who stay two to five weeks and spend half the day working. Weekly charges for part-time volunteers are £65-£118 according to season and for full-time volunteers £49-£70; students and those on unemployment benefit get a discount. Typical work for volunteers might involve germination procedures, forestry trials, hydroponic growing, organic gardening, designing and building solar ovens and stills, and building and maintenance. Living conditions are basic and the cooking is vegetarian. Occasionally workers with a relevant qualification in appropriate technology, etc. are needed who are paid a small stipend. The address of the centre is Apdo. 9, 04270 Sorbas, Almeria (tel/fax 950-525770; www.sunseed.org.uk).

VOLUNTEERING

International workcamp organisations recruit for environmental and other projects in Spain for programmes as various as carrying out an archaeological dig of a Roman settlement in Tarragona to traditional stone quarrying in Menorca. The co-ordinating workcamp organisation in Spain is the Instituto de la Juventud or INJUVE (José Ortega y Gasset 71, 28006 Madrid; 91-363 76 23; fax 91-309 30 66; svi@mtas.es) which oversees scores of camps every year. You can approach them independently as well as through a partner organisation in your own country. Note that many camps are restricted to volunteers aged 18-26 with a few accepting volunteers up to the age of 30.

The Atlantic Whale Foundation is working to protect whales and dolphins in the Canary Islands. Volunteers join the project for 1-8 weeks and contribute $160-$250 per fortnight towards expenses. Contact 59 St Martins Lane, Covent Garden, London WC2H 4JS (edb@whalenation.org; edb@whalefoundation.org.uk).

A small fruit farm in southern Spain, EcoForest (Apdo Correos 29, 29100 Coin, Malaga, Spain; 661-079 950; info@ecoforest.org, www.ecoforest.org) offers a place to live for people striving to embrace a healthy, sustainable way of life at low cost. Non-working visitors pay €10 per day to camp while working visitors exchange four hours a day of their labour for accommodation. The centre runs two-week permaculture courses and the diet is vegan (raw food only).

Jacqueline Edwards wanted a live-in position but her status as the single mother of a two-year old boy made her quest more complicated. She used her initiative and contacted vegetarian/vegan societies around Europe, asking them to put her details in their newsletter. Several of the replies she received were from Spain including from a natural therapies retreat centre in Zamora.

Gibraltar

Gibraltar is an anomaly, an accident of history. It is a tiny British dependent territory on the Spanish coast, less than three miles square and with a population of just 28,000. Until the 1980s, Gibraltar was inaccessible from Spain and is still separated by a wire fence and border guards. It has the same currency, the same institutions, the same language (though with a unique accent) as the UK. Although Gibraltarians do not necessarily want to be a British colony, they have little choice. Under the 1713 Treaty of Utrecht Gibraltar must revert to Spain if Britain ever gives up sovereignty, a claim Spain would be unlikely to give up.

No feedback from travellers working in Gibraltar has been received for this edition, however a posting on the website virtualtourist.com dated December 2004 from someone who has been working there for two years reiterated the position that the 'jobs available to foreign citizens are in the bars and clubs of Gibraltar - and there are a lot'. In a place with a rate of unemployment less than 2%, opportunities must exist particularly in the busy summer tourist season. A few years ago, Allan Griffith and Paula Kershaw found work easily between the new year and July:

We both got work in Gib. Paula was working as a chef and getting in 12 hours a day, six days a week. Hard work but she saved £3,000 in five months. I got a job on one of the tug boats working alongside the world's biggest cargo ships. Funny hours but a great job. Both jobs paid cash in hand.

But not everyone has found it easy. Pat and Martin Kennard went to Gib with the intention of finding crewing positions on a transatlantic yacht (see *Working a Passage*). But when they arrived in September, the boat owners they talked to already had their crew. So they changed their tactics and tried to find land jobs. Not only was it the end of the season so bar work and related employment was scarce, they felt themselves to be discriminated against for being British. They found job-seekers from Morocco being given a warmer welcome than they were. Furthermore the wage of did not inspire enthusiasm for persisting in the struggle (though they liked Gibraltar and wanted to stay over the winter). In the end they were forced to purchase expensive one-way tickets home to England, declaring Gibraltar a disaster.

EU nationals of the original member states plus Cyprus and Malta are free to take up any offer of employment made to them in Gibraltar. Until 2009, citizens of the other new accession countries along with all other non-EU nationals must apply for a work permit from the Ministry of Education, Employment & Training, Unit 76-77 New Harbours (40408/ fax 73981) after first obtaining a Terms of Engagement form. To have an application for a work permit approved, the prospective employer must prove that no Gibraltarian or EU national is available to fill the vacancy, undertake to repatriate the worker if necessary and show that suitable accommodation has been found.

Tourism continues to flourish, partly because Gibraltar is a shopping destination because of its tax-free status. There are hundreds of bars and restaurants in Gib, many with job vacancies during the busy summer season that can't be filled by locals. If you were to start at one end of Gibraltar and work through, asking at all the bars and restaurants, it should take about two or three days. You will have a chance of work if you look tidy and sell yourself.

Out of the scores of drinking holes, Andrew Giles recommends Charlie's Tavern on Admiral's Walk as a good source of job information. Charlie's is favoured by the owners and crews of boats moored in Marina Bay.

Even Adam Cook, who complained of the shortage of work in 'that litter-strewn blob of all that's undesirably British', managed to find a little yacht-varnishing work, and then was taken on to help redecorate a restaurant, before his big break came and he was taken on as paid crew back to England.

Accommodation

There are neither campsites nor youth hostels on the Rock and free camping is completely prohibited on the beaches. Camper vans are not even permitted in after midnight. A property boom in the wake of the expanding gambling businesses means that rental property is almost non-existent. The cheapest accommodation we have heard of is at a very basic hostel run by the charity TOC H (Line Wall Road; 73431). Most non-resident workers are therefore forced to commute from La Linea, the port town in Spain just across the border, which has been described by many as a cesspool of seediness and crime.

Sheppards Marina is where most of the yacht work is carried out, whereas Marina Bay is where the long distance yachts are moored. A good source of information on jobs and lodgings in the marinas is the newsagents next door to Bianca's Bistro in Marina Bay and to a lesser extent the Star Bar on Parliament Lane or Aragon Bar on Bell Lane in central Gibraltar. A notice board worth using is located in Sheppards Marina equipment shop at the Old Marina.

Opportunities for fixing up a crewing position on a yacht exist, though normally on a shared-expenses basis; see the chapter *Working a Passage.*

Portugal

Although Portugal's economy is reasonably healthy and the rate of unemployment (at 6.7%) is well below the EU average, wages are low. The minimum wage in Portugal is €498 per month, the lowest among the original EU member states (compared to around €1,180 in Britain and France). Chances of finding work are best with tour operators or in hotels, restaurants and clubs along the Algarve coast. Euro 2004 created many short-term jobs in Portugal, though the long-term effects have not been noticeable. The new anxiety is that EU money that might once have come to Portugal will now be diverted to the poorer accession countries.

There is a long and vigorous tradition of British people settling in Portugal, and the links between the two countries are strong. Large numbers of expatriates live around Lisbon and on the Algarve, many of whom are retired. English-speaking travellers might expect to find odd jobs in this community, but the friendly relations between foreigners and locals mean that the former are quite happy to employ the latter for many such jobs.

Ask expatriates for help and advice. Probably the best idea is to scan the advertisements in the English language press or place an ad yourself. The long-established English-language weekly *Anglo-Portuguese News* (Apartado 113, 2766-902 Estoril; tel 214-66 15 51; fax 214-66 03 58; apn@mail.telepac.pt) carries job adverts. The classified sections of the weekly *Resident* (published weekly in an Algarve and a Greater Lisbon edition; www.portugalresident.com) does not usually include many useful listings.

The Regulations

Portugal has always had comparatively liberal immigration policies, possibly because it has never been rich enough to attract a lot of foreign job-seekers. EU citizens are supposed to apply for a residence permit if they intend to stay for more than three months. The usual documents will be needed: proof of accommodation and means of support plus adequate health insurance or proof of paying social security contributions. Wage earners must prove that they are being paid at least the Portuguese minimum monthly wage. The permit should be obtained from the nearest immigration office (*Serviço de Estrangeiros e Fronteiras*). The address of the headquarters of the *Serviço de Estrangeiros* is Rua Conselheiro José Silvestre Ribeiro 4, 1649-007 Lisbon (217-11 50 00).

The Consular Section of the British Embassy in Portugal (Rua de S. Bernardo 33, 1249-082 Lisbon; 213-92 41 88) distributes information on taking up residence in Portugal which goes into more detail than the information from the Portuguese Consulate-General in London.

Non-EU nationals must provide the usual battery of documents before they can be granted a residence visa, including a residence visa obtained from the Portuguese Consulate in their home country, a document showing that the Ministry of Labour *(Ministerio do Trabalho)* has approved the job and a medical certificate in Portuguese. The final stage is to take a letter of good conduct provided by the applicant's own embassy to the police for the work and residence permit. There are stories of non-Europeans arranging a residence permit after finding a job on arrival, but this is difficult.

Tourism

Thousands of Britons and other Europeans take their holidays on the Algarve creating many job opportunities in bars and restaurants.

> **According to many travellers like Emma-Louise Parkes, the Albufeira area is the place to head:**
> *I arrived at Faro Airport in June last year, and went straight to the Montechoro area of Albufeira. A job hunter here will be like a kid in a sweet shop. By 12.15pm I was in the resort, by 12.30pm I had found somewhere to stay and had been offered at least four jobs by the evening, one of which I started at 6pm. All the English workers were really friendly individuals and were a goldmine of information. Jobs-wise, I was offered bar work, touting, waitressing, cleaning, packing ice cubes into bags, karaoke singing, nannying for an English bar owner, timeshare tout, nightclub dancer…I'm sure there were more. Touts can earn £16 a night with all the drink they can stomach while waitresses can expect a little less for working 10am-1pm and 6pm-10pm. Attractive females (like myself!) will be head-hunted by lively bars, whereas British men are seen by the locals as trouble and are usually kept behind bars (serving bars that is) and in cellars.*

Emma-Louise recommends visiting the many bars and diners along Av. De Carneiro, known as the Strip.

Kevin Gorringe agrees that Albufeira holds limitless possibilities for a working holiday. He met with nothing but a friendly warm response and there was no sign of red tape anywhere: *'I left home in June as an engineer and now I am cooking English food in a place called Fat Frank's Fryer, just one of the many places to find work and friends. Other places are Casa da Fonte, Simply Delicious, Ludo's, Fernandos, the Rock Bar, Vegas Bar, Twist bar, etc. etc.'*

Finding somewhere to stay can be more difficult than finding employment. Not surprisingly, accommodation is quite expensive during the high season. Ask around so you can avoid the dodgy landlords. It would be cheaper to do what Kevin Gorringe and his girlfriend did which was to stay at Campismo Albufeira. Discounts may be available to long-stay campers.

The bullring does not offer much scope to working travellers, but it is has been known for an English person to work in it. Some years ago, Virginia Montesol (her ring name) went to Spain, made contacts, moved on to Portugal and for two years fought as a *Rejoneador* in the Portuguese bullrings. In Portugal the bullfighter is usually on a horse and the bull is not killed. Virginia was an amateur and therefore unpaid but stayed free with a country family; the qualifications are to be an excellent rider with nerves of steel.

Teaching

The market for English tuition is fairly buoyant, especially in the teaching of young children and especially in northern Portugal. Apart from in the main cities of Lisbon and Oporto, both of which have British Council offices, jobs crop up in historic provincial centres such as Coimbra (where there is also a British Council) and Braga and in small seaside towns like Aveiro and Póvoa do Varzim. The Cambridge Certificate (CELTA) is widely requested by schools, but a number (especially those advertising vacancies in June, July and August) seem willing to consider candidates with a BA plus a promising CV and photo.

One of the most well-established groups of schools is the Cambridge School group (Avenida da Liberdade 173, 1250-141 Lisbon; 21-312 46 00; www.cambridge.pt) which every year imports about 100 British teachers for its eight schools. Other chains of language schools to try are the Bristol School Group (Instituto de Linguas da Maia, Trav. Dr. Carlos Pires Felgueiras 12-3°, 4470-158 Maia; 229-48 88 03; www.bristolschool.pt); Royal School of Languages (Rue José Rabumba 2, 3810-125 Aveiro; 234-42 91 56; www.royalschooloflanguages.pt) and Novo Instituto de Linguas in Lisbon (Rua Cordeiro Ferreira, 19C 1°Dto, 1750-071 Lisbon; tel/fax 21-759 07 70; www.nil.edu.pt).

The consensus seems to be that wages are low, but have been improving at a favourable rate in view of the cost of living. On the positive side, working conditions are generally relaxed. The normal salary range is €750-€1,000 net per month. Some schools pay lower salaries but subsidise or pay for flights and accommodation. Teachers being paid on an hourly basis should expect to earn between €10 and €15 an hour.

Business

If you know some Portuguese, you might find an opening in an office; without knowing the language, chances are remote. For agencies specialising in temporary work, look up the Yellow Pages or *Paginas Amarelas* (www.paginasamarelas.pt) under the heading *Trabalho Temporário*. For temporary office or manual vacancies, try Manpower in Lisbon at Praça José Fontana 9c (21-313 40 00; lisboa.sede@manpower.pt) and also in Oporto (222-00 24 26), Braga (253-21 43 74) and in the Azores (296-63 63 41). See also www.manpower.pt. Two of the other main agencies are SELGEC, Rua Alexandre Herculano 39-1°, 1205-009 Lisbon (213-51 14 90; www.selgec.net) and Adecco (www.adecco.pt).

The British-Portuguese Chamber of Commerce (*Camara de Comércio Luso-Britanica*) is in Lisbon (Rua da Estrela 8, 1200-669 Lisbon; 21-394 20 20; www.bilateral.biz). CVs may be sent by e-mail to info@bpcc.pt though the Chamber cannot respond unless they have already been notified of a relevant opportunity. They attempt to match qualified job-seekers with their members who might be looking for staff.

Agriculture

Although it is the fifth largest wine producer in the world, we have never heard of any traveller picking grapes. The farms are generally so small that hiring help from beyond the local community is simply not done. On the other hand, a large strawberry farm (www. wellpict-portugal.com) on the west coast of Portugal was advertising recently on the website www.fruitfuljobs.com. It needs people between the beginning of February and May or (preferably) June. Jobs include picking and general farm work as well as supervisors.

Your best chance of success is to follow up leads passed on by the army of Portuguese migrant workers you might come across elsewhere in Europe, though even this is no guarantee as described by Jon Loop, who had become friendly with Portuguese workers during the French *vendange*:

> Two friends and I decided to try our luck with the chestnut harvest in northern Portugal. We had been assured that there was lots of work picking chestnuts near Bragança near a place called (I think) Carrazedo. We got a lift in one of the Portuguese workers' coaches and eventually made it to the chestnut area. Sure enough there were lots of chestnuts just waiting to jump into our baskets.
>
> However we never managed to get a job. First we had trouble with the local policeman who took an immediate dislike to us. All the people we'd got to know at the grape harvest would meet us, then disappear, promising to return but they never did. Our last hope for work was a guy who had been very friendly when we'd bought him drinks during the grape harvest. He turned out to be the local thug and petty criminal who had just come out of jail after five years for (we think) drug smuggling. Not a good reference! ('Hey, we're looking for work. We're good friends with Pedro,' at which the prospective employer's eyes would narrow and he'd be thinking about calling the police.)

The WWOOF Independents list (www.wwoof.org) includes 40 properties in Portugal including romantic sounding olive plantations and cork tree woodlands.

Voluntary and Au Pair

The voluntary movement in Portugal is not particularly strong nor is it easy to find out about. The state-supported Instituto Portugues da Juventude (IPJ), Av. da Liberdade No. 194, 1269-051 Lisbon (213-17 92 00; geral@juventude.gov.pt; http://juventude.gov.pt) oversees a programme of heritage protection and other short-term voluntary projects. Applications should normally be sent through a partner organisation in the applicant's own country, for example Concordia and UNA Exchange in the UK which may also have links with other Portuguese voluntary agencies.

Au pairing is not at all common in Portugal, and very few placements are made by UK agencies to Portugal. A few positions with expat families may be advertised on the internet. Summer openings are most likely to occur in the school holidays between the end of July and end of September.

Switzerland

Switzerland is not a member of the European Union. However a bilateral agreement with the European Union has been concluded and the main obstacles to free movement of persons were removed in 2004. This means that the Swiss have had to undergo a huge shift in their attitudes to immigration and employment. The abolition of the category of seasonal worker (a lynchpin of the old system and of great interest to the readers of this book) has been abolished. Now the system is more in line with the rest of Europe so that EU job-seekers can enter Switzerland for up to three months (extendable) to look for work. If they succeed they must show a contract of employment to the authorities and are then eligible for a short-term residence permit (valid for up to one year and renewable) or a long-term permit (up to five years) depending on the contract.

With a low rate of unemployment of 3.7% in 2004 (though that is double what it has been in the past) and a high proportion of foreign workers (estimated at nearly a fifth of the workforce), it is easy to understand why the Swiss want to tread carefully when it comes to integrating with Europe. The continuing quota system together with the very high cost of living while you are job-hunting and the (deserved) Swiss reputation for hard work discourage many travellers from going to Switzerland to look for work. But many people who have spent time working in Switzerland and have come to know the Swiss have nothing but compliments. According to Tony Mason who picked grapes four seasons running and worked as a builder: *'The Swiss are a genuinely friendly and hospitable people and we are often invited to local homes for meals and on outings to the mountains. Hitching here is excellent and also a valuable source of potential employers. I can't say enough good things about the Swiss.'*

The Regulations

No permit is needed for EU nationals who stay for less than three months. If they want to stay for a further three months, e.g. to continue job-hunting or to do a seasonal job, they must apply for an L permit (short-term residence permit). The L-EC/EFTA permit *(Kurza-ufenhalter/Autorisation de Courte Durée)* is issued for four, six or up to twelve months, depending on the job. EU nationals simply need to take their passport and contract of employment to the local cantonal office. L-permits are no longer tied to a particular job or canton.

If the contract of employment is going to extend beyond a year, it is possible to apply for a B-permit, valid for between one and five years. Note that until 2007, Switzerland will continue to impose quotas on the number of permits granted, i.e. 115,000 L-permits and only 15,000 B-permits per year. After 2007 Switzerland plans to do away with quotas and prepare for the unfettered movement of workers.

Since 2004, employers have been under an obligation to treat Swiss and EU applicants equally – an admirable principle though it will undoubtedly take many years before it becomes a reality. Detailed information about the new regulations can be found online at www.europa.admin.ch and www.auslaender.ch. The document entitled *European Nationals in Switzerland* – accessible at www.europa.admin.ch – is not as dry-as-dust as might be expected. Not only is it clearly presented but its contents are enlivened by the inclusion of true life stories of foreigners currently resident in Switzerland.

All of these changes are of course bad news for non-EU citizens who will now find it harder to gain access to Switzerland's labour market unless they apply in special categories like au pair or the trainee permit (which is unchanged under the new dispensation). Even before the signing of the agreement with Europe, non-EU workers were finding things difficult as Danny Jacobson from the US reported: *'I lost my pizza chef job in Bulle back in November due to the boss freaking out that she was going to get raided. All the permit-less workers were booted, some without notice, and replaced with other foreigners who had the luck of European passports or asylum.'*
If a non-European does find an employer willing to sponsor their application, the applicant will have to collect the documents from the Swiss Embassy in his or her home country.

With the new L and B permits, workers become eligible for the minimum wage (approximatelySFr3,000/€2,000 a month) and the excellent legal tribunal for foreign workers which arbitrates in disputes over working conditions, pay and dismissals. Accident insurance is compulsory for all foreign workers and often the employer pays this. However health insurance, also compulsory, is the responsibility of the individual. Certain perks of having a permit differ from region to region, for example the entitlement to public transport or seasonal ski passes at a subsidised local rate.

Trainee exchanges between Switzerland and a number of non-EU countries including the US continue. Permits for temporary trainee placements *(stagiaires)* can be obtained from the Swiss Federal Office for Migration, Emigration and Trainees, Quellenweg 15, 3003 Bern (031-322 42 02; swiss.emigration@bfm.admin.ch; www.swissemigration.ch/elias.en (in English). The website provides a list of co-operating partner organisations, e g. CDS in the USA (www.cdsintl.org). Guidance may be given to applicants on how to find an employer, though the programme is for individuals who can find a suitable position independently. The trainee position arranged must be in the vocational field of the applicant, who must be aged 18-30.

Students from outside Western Europe who wish to apply for short-term voluntary work may have a chance if they can obtain a letter of confirmation from their university stating that the work is important for their course of study. The chances for other non-Europeans are diminishing fast as Switzerland forms closer ties with Europe.

Casual Work

Particularly in the building trade and for agricultural work, the local supply of labour is so clearly inadequate that people without a residence permit do find jobs.

> **Danny Jacobson from Wisconsin has spent several successful seasons piecing together odd jobs in the town of Bulle:**
> *I still feel Switzerland is a working traveller's best friend in Europe. If you're willing to get dirty, there's tons of work around. If you can speak French or German, head into the more rural parts or the less touristy towns. I've based myself in Bulle, an over-sized village in the Préalpes. The word on the street is that in the off-the-beaten-track parts of Switzerland, the authorities look the other way because the hotels and restaurants are usually desperate for workers. The hotel owner has offered me a full-time position cleaning the staircases and washing dishes five days a week for a generous wage paid cash in hand plus food. If I choose to stay here for a bit, I shouldn't need to work again for a long long time when I hit the road again.*

He clearly preferred this boss to a previous one, a 'drunken mad man with 800 ways to mop a floor, of which a new one would be demonstrated each day because I was too inept to realise I was using yesterday's'.

Although Switzerland doesn't go so far as to demand that buskers get a work permit, Leda Meredith was surprised to find that the city of Bern (a 'goldmine for buskers') publishes a leaflet about when and where busking is permitted. Merchants keep a supply and will not hesitate to give you one if you transgress. Assaf de Hazan from Israel also found Switzerland a Shangri-La for buskers: *'If you have a guitar (and can play it) here in Geneva, you are a king. If you have a bit of impudence and are willing to go around cafés and bars (not too fancy) and ask to play three songs, you are more than a king. I was getting more than £50 for a day's playing around the train station part of the lake. You just go and ask and they always say yes. After playing just three songs, you go around with an ash-tray and get money, and lots of it.'*

TOURISM

It has been said that the Swiss invented tourism. Certainly their hotels and tourism courses are still the training ground and model for hoteliers worldwide. For the hotels and catering industry, a rapid short-term injection of labour is an economic necessity both for the summer and winter season – June/July to September and December to April.

Swiss hotels are very efficient and tend to be impersonal, since you will be one in an endless stream of seasonal workers from many countries. The very intense attitude to work among the Swiss means that hours are long (often longer than stipulated in the contract): a typical working week would consist of at least five nine-hour days working split shifts.

Whether humble or palatial, the Swiss hotel or restaurant in which you find a job will probably insist on very high standards of cleanliness and productivity. After working at an independent hostel and then a 3-star restaurant in Interlaken, Kathy Russell from Australia concluded that 'the Swiss are very picky to work for, so a good temperament is needed'.

On the other hand, the majority are *korrekt*, i.e. scrupulous about keeping track of your overtime and pay you handsomely at the end of your contract. Alison May summarised her summer at the Novotel-Zürich-Airporthotel: 'On balance, the wages were good but we really had to earn them'. Remember that from the gross *(brutto)* monthly wage of just less than SFr2,800, up to half will be lost in deductions for board and lodging, tax and insurance (with slight cantonal variations).

The Job Hunt

Provided you have a reasonable CV and a knowledge of languages (preferably German), a speculative job hunt in advance is worthwhile. One hotel group worth trying (provided you are a European national) is Mövenpick on www.moevenpick-hotels.com (with a link to current vacancies) while the Park Hotel Waldhaus, 7018 Flims-Waldhaus (081-928 48

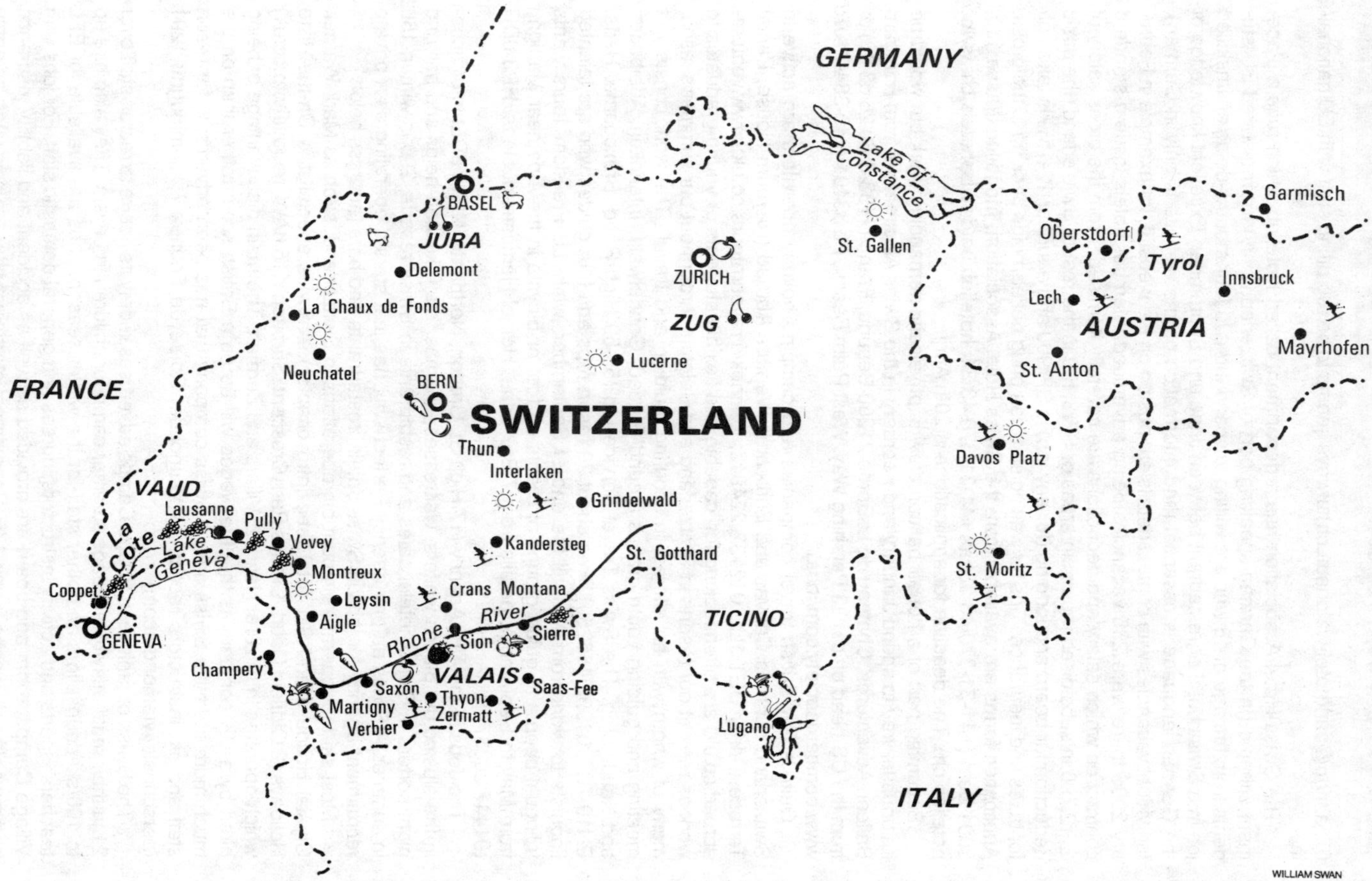

WILLIAM SWAN

GERMANY

AUSTRIA

ITALY

FRANCE

SWITZERLAND

Garmisch
Mayrhofen
Innsbruck
Tyrol
Oberstdorf
Lech
St. Anton
Davos Platz
St. Moritz

Lake of Constance
St. Gallen

ZURICH
ZUG
Lucerne
Grindelwald
St. Gotthard
TICINO
Lugano

Thun
Interlaken
Kandersteg
Crans Montana
Sierre
Saas-Fee
Rhone River
VALAIS
Sion
Zermatt
Thyon

BASEL
JURA
Delemont
BERN
La Chaux de Fonds
Neuchatel

Saxon
Martigny
Verbier
Leysin
Aigle
Vevey
Pully
Montreux
Lausanne
VAUD
Champery

Cote
Lake Geneva
GENEVA
Coppet

07; a.frigo@parkhotel-waldhaus.ch) always seems to be recruiting staff with EU nationality.

The Swiss Hotel Association has a department called Hoteljob which runs a placement scheme (in the German-speaking part of Switzerland only) for registered EU students from the age of 18 who are willing to spend three to four months doing an unskilled job in a Swiss hotel or restaurant between June and September. Excellent knowledge of the German language is essential (and information on the website is only in German). Individual vacancies with contact details are posted on the website; for example in February 2005 there were 235 vacancies being advertised. Member hotels issue a standard contract on which salary and deductions are carefully itemised. From the gross salary of SFr2,790 in subsidised mountain areas or SFr3,100 in the rest of Switzerland, the basic deduction for board and lodging (for any job) is SFr900 and a further 12-15% is taken off for taxes and insurance. Tips for waiting staff can bring net earnings back up to the gross. Application forms are available from the Swiss Hotel Association, Monbijoustrasse 130, 3001 Bern (+41-31-370 43 33/fax +41-31-370 43 34; hoteljob.be@swisshotels.ch; www. hoteljob.ch). The deadline for applications is 20th April.

Becoming part of a hot-air balloon crew is physically demanding work but would be an unusual way to spend January and February in the Swiss Alps; details from Bombard Balloon Adventures, Chateau de LaBorde 21200 Beaune, France (+33-3-80 26 63 30) or from the US head office, 33 Pershing Way, West Palm Beach, FL 33401 (240-384-7107; www.bombardsociety.com/jobs).

Quite a few British travel companies and camping holiday operators are active in Switzerland such as Canvas and Eurocamp. Venture Abroad (Rayburn House, Parcel Terrace, Derby DE1 1LY; 012132 224942; joannek@rayburntours.co.uk; www.venture-abroad.co.uk) are often looking for 'capable and flexible students or young graduates to work as reps at our resorts in Switzerland and Belgium throughout our summer season, many of whom with an interest in scouting, guiding and travel'. The work consists of meeting and guiding youth groups around Gstaad, Grindelwald, Interlaken, Adelboden and Kandersteg. The Swiss Travel Service Ltd (55-59 High Road, Broxbourne, Herts. EN10 7DT; 01992 456250) hires about 20 resort reps and tour guides who are talented linguists to work from April till the end of September, while LB Freedom Tours wants trilingual people to guide groups of clients on foot or bicycle in the Alps near Martigny from May to September; details from 7 Box Lane, Hemel Hempstead, Herts. HP3 0DH (01442 263377).

The Jobs in the Alps Agency (17 High St, Gretton, Northants. NN17 3DE; info@jobs-in-the-alps.co.uk) places waiters, waitresses, chamber staff, kitchen helps and hall and night porters in Swiss hotels, cafés and restaurants in Swiss resorts, 200 in winter, 150 in summer. A Swiss au pair agency Perfect Way has just started operating as a private recruitment agency for jobs in Swiss hotels, restaurants and bars (address below).

Most ski tour operators mount big operations in Switzerland, such as Mark Warner, Crystal Holidays and Ski Total (see intro chapter). A Swiss specialist is On-the-Piste Holidays (2 Oldfield Court, Cranes Park Crescent, Surbiton KT5 8AW; recruit@otp.co.uk) which operates in Anzère, Nendaz, Villars and Zermatt. The main disadvantage of being hired by a UK company is that the wages will be on a British scale rather than on the much more lucrative Swiss one. A Swiss company that has been advertising for resort staff and ski instructors recently is Viamonde, Route de Founex 7, Commugny 1291 (personnel@viamonde.com).

The Swiss organisation Village Camps advertises widely its desire to recruit staff over 21 in their multi-activity language summer camp for children in Leysin. They also hire up to 100 ski counsellors and other staff for the winter season. Jobs are available for EFL teachers, sports and activity instructors, nurses and general domestic staff. For jobs with Village Camps, room and board are provided as well as accident and liability insurance and a weekly allowance from €175. Recruitment starts just after the new year; an application pack is available from Village Camps, Recruitment Office, Dept 811, 14 rue de la Morache, 1260 Nyon (+41 22 990 9405; fax 22 990 9494; personnel@villagecamps.ch).

Applications from North Americans and Antipodeans are welcome.

Another camp operator looking for seasonal summer or winter staff is Les Elfes (CP 174, 1936 Verbier (027-775 35 90; leselfes@axiom.ch; www.leselfes.com). Winter contracts for ski/snowboard instructors and activity staff are from 1st December to 30th April. They also hire kitchen and domestic staff for their various camps.

On-the-Spot

Most people go out and fix up their jobs in person, as recommended in the introductory section on *Winter Resorts*. Steve Rout, a resort expert, has always found this to be the most satisfactory way to find work. He recommends looking in Les Portes de Soleil at Champery, Les Crosets as well as the major resorts of Leysin, Verbier, Thyon and Crans Montana. This valley is a major road and rail route and is ideal for concentrated job hunting. Another area which has been recommended is the Jura between La Chaux-de-Fonds and Delémont.

Surprisingly, tourist offices may be of use. Naturally their lists of local accommodation are a useful starting point, but tourist information staff may be of more specific assistance. Joseph Tame found that it was possible to register your name and details with the tourist office in Grindelwald for a small fee. These would then be circulated to all the hotels in town on a weekly basis (this was in September). It is useful to have a reference or two to show. Also check notice boards and adverts in local papers like *Le Nouvelliste* in the Rhone Valley.

Like most people, Andrew Winwood found the job hunt tough going:

All in all I asked in over 200 places for ski-season work, but eventually could have counted 10-12 possibilities. Going on that rate, it would be possible to get work after asking at 50 or 60 places, but of course the 'Grand Law of Sod' would prevail. As far as I can see, it's a simple case of ask, ask, ask and ask again until you get work. It was costing me about £80 a week to live in Switzerland, so I couldn't let up until I definitely had a way of getting the money back.

The most promising time to introduce yourself to potential employers is about a week before the end of the previous season, so late April/early May for the summer season and September for the winter. November is a bad time to arrive since most of the hotels are closed, the owners away on holiday and most have already promised winter season jobs to people they know from previous seasons or ones who approached them at the end of the summer season.

Rob Jefferson had no luck whatsoever and describes his discouraging experiences job-hunting in Swiss resorts:

We arrived in Grindelwald in mid-December, and stayed in the youth hostel (along with 11 others all looking for work). After ten days, only one of the hostellers had found work, and so we left for Saas Fee with half-promises of work from seven hotels of the many we'd phoned. We were flatly refused by six but the seventh promised Sonja my girlfriend a job as a waitress if the pre-contracted waiter did not show up the next day. Sonja is very attractive, speaks near perfect English and good German. We had been around about 70 hotels in all and it took a late arrival for her to get a job. If this was the case for her, what about me? No chance.

Danny Jacobson's tip is to bypass the large ski stations in favour of the less tourist-filled smaller stations and the surrounding villages. Joseph Tame's surprising tip is to go up as high as possible in the mountains. After being told by virtually every hotel in Grindelwald in mid-September that they had already hired their winter season staff, he despaired and decided to waste his last SFr40 on a trip up the rack railway. At the top he approached the only hotel and couldn't believe it when they asked him when he could start. Although he had never worked in a hotel before, they were willing to take him on as a trainee waiter, give him full bed and board plus the standard Swiss wage. At first he found the job a little boring since there were few guests apart from Japanese groups on whirlwind European tours. But things changed at Christmas:

> *Christmas and New Year was an absolute nightmare. Three shifts a day for everyone with very little sleep and no time off. When a promised pay rise didn't materialise, I decided I had had enough and handed in my notice. But by January 5th, business had slumped and we had at least two hours off daily to ski. When my overdue pay rise came through I withdrew my notice. If you can stick the Christmas rush, things do get better. Switzerland was definitely the best thing that ever happened to me.*

So good that Joseph returned for three subsequent seasons and says that he is very glad that he stumbled across this 160-year old hotel in a blizzard. The proprietors sometimes have trouble filling vacancies and so he recommends sending a CV with photo to Hotel Bellevue des Alpes, Scheidegg Hotels AG, 3801 Kleine Scheidegg (info@scheidegg-hotels. ch; fax +41 33 855 12 94).

The intriguingly named Hiking Sheep Aubergerie (Villa La Joux, 1854 Leysin; 024-494 35 35; fax 024-494 35 36; info@hikingsheep.com) hires general staff who speak French and English (and preferably German) to work on reception for at least a month.

Another recommended meeting place is Balmer's Herberge in Interlaken (Hauptstrasse 23-25, 3800 Interlaken; 033-822 19 61; mail@balmers.ch). They take on English-speaking staff for a minimum of six months and only after interviewing them in person. The owner is pleased to pass on information about other job openings in the area, as the hostel is often contacted by local hotels asking for workers.

Casual work opportunities crop up in some alternative establishments in Bern and the other big cities. According to Danny Jacobson there are a number of socialist, hippy/punk type restaurant/cafés around town that the police don't bother much due to their tricky politics. Danny found weekend bar work at the Reithalle in Bern, a socialist collective art centre housed in the former city stables, where he had some fairly wild and woolly times. For serving drinks over the pounding electro-beats and cleaning up as dawn broke, he was paid SFr15 an hour cash-in-hand.

AGRICULTURE

Official Schemes

Young people who are more interested in rural experiences than in money may wish to do a stint on a Swiss farm. The Landdienst located at Mühlegasse 13 (Postfach 728), 8025 Zürich (01-261 44 88/fax 01-261 44 32; admin@landdienst.ch) fixes up farm placements for a minimum of three weeks for young people from Western Europe who know some German or French. Last year about 600 foreign young people and 3,000 Swiss were placed through the Landdienst. The scheme is open to European nationals only. Workers are called 'volunteers' and can work for up to two months without a work permit. They must pay a registration fee of SFr50.

In addition to the good farm food and comfortable bed, you will be paid at least SFr20 per day worked. Necessary qualifications for participating in this scheme are that you be between 18 and 25 and that you have a basic grounding in French or German. On these small Swiss farms, English is rarely spoken and many farmers speak a dialect which some find incomprehensible.

Most places in German-speaking Switzerland are available from the beginning of March to the end of October and in the French part from March to June and mid-August to the end of October, though there are a few places in the winter too. Each canton has a farm placement representative who liaises with the Zürich headquarters.

Despite Switzerland's reputation as an advanced nation, thousands of small family farms practise traditional farming methods, especially in the German-speaking cantons. Part of the reason for this is that not many mechanical threshers or harvesters can function on near vertical slopes (neither can every human harvester for that matter).

The hours are long, the work is hard and much depends on the volunteer's relationship with the family. Most people who have worked on a Swiss farm report that they are treated like one of the family, which means both that they are up by 6am or 7am and working till 9pm alongside the farmer and that they are invited to accompany the family on any excursions, such as the weekly visit to the market to sell the farm-produced cheeses. The arrangement is similar in many way to the au pair arrangement; in fact young women who get placed on a Swiss farm may be asked to do more chores inside the house than out. Life on an isolated farm can be lonely with few chances to improve speak German or French if you are alone in the house with a baby or in the fields with the goats.

Ruth McCarthy gives an idea of the range of tasks to do on the farm, and a taste of village life, which sounds like something out of *Heidi*:

The work on my farm in the Jura included cleaning out cow stalls, hay making, grass cutting, poultry feeding, manure spreading, vegetable and fruit-picking, wood cutting, earth moving, corn threshing and also housework, cooking and looking after the children. The food was very wholesome and all produced on the farm: cheeses, fresh milk, home-made jam, fresh fruit, etc. The church bells struck throughout the day and peeled at 6am and 9pm to open and close each day. As well as church bells the sound of cow bells was also present so that it was quite noisy at times. There was little night life unless you went to a gasthof bar in the village. Anyway it's probably better to get a good night's sleep.

Paul Barton arranged to work for the same farmer he'd worked for through the Landdienst the previous year. He was given a work permit and paid nearly three times his previous summer's wage. He was also expected to do twice as much work, which was impossible when he'd already been working 16 hours a day. For his own amusement he kept track of the number of hours worked and counted up to a staggering 1,250 in ten weeks before returning home for some essential rest and relaxation.

The Swiss Farmers' Union runs a programme for trainees in agriculture from Europe, North America, Brazil, the Antipodes, South Africa and Japan. Participants who want to work for 3 to 12 months must have professional training in agriculture or horticulture, or at least three years' practical experience or relevant training and be able to speak some English, French or German. Further details are available from Agroimpuls, c/o Farmers' Union, Laustrasse 10, 5201 Brugg, Switzerland (056-462 51 44; www.agroimpuls.ch).

WWOOF Switzerland (Postfach 59, 8124 Maur) keeps a constantly updated list of farmers around the country, currently 45. To obtain the list you must join WWOOF at a cost of SFr20/€15/$20/£10 in cash. Details are available on WWOOF's web-site www.wwoof.org/switzerland. Volunteers must apply with a photocopy of their passport and an accompanying letter stating why they want to become unpaid volunteers.

Joseph Tame made use of the WWOOF website to fix up a place on a farm in the spring:
I can honestly say that it has been an absolutely fantastic experience. The hours could be thought fairly long by some (perhaps 35 per week) considering there is no money involved, but I absolutely love the chance to work outside in this land that reminds me so much of the final setting in 'The Hobbit.' From our farm your eyes take you down the hillside, over the meadows covered in flowers, down to the vast Lake Luzern below and over to the huge snow-capped mountain Pilatus. It really is paradise here. The family have been so kind, and as I put my heart into learning all that I can about the farm they are only too happy to treat me with generosity. I really feel a part of the family.

The charity Caritas Schweiz (Freiwilligeneinsatz, Löwenstrasse 3, Postfach, 6002 Lucerne; caritas@caritas.ch) accepts volunteers who want to help mountain farmers with renovating their farms or to support them in agriculture.

Grape-Picking

Like every country in Europe south of Scotland, Switzerland produces wine. The main area is in the Vaud north of Lake Geneva, but also in Valais around Sion and Sierre, where the harvest begins in late September though sometimes a few days in October. Every year scores of hopeful *vendangeurs* begin pouring into the region. Robert Abblett calculated that if he had arrived in time to catch the beginning of the harvest, he could have saved £350 from 11 days of work:

> From Chateauneuf du Pape we headed north to find later grape work, but it took us three days of searching before we ended up at a place called Aigle in Switzerland. By sheer luck we found three days work at the end of the harvest and lived (free) with 100 other workers in some army barracks. They were an international collection of seasonal travellers who liked to party till 2am every night, so I ended up sleeping in the front of the van to get some sleep. The grapes were so much easier to pick here than in France and I had to stop myself from racing along the lines and leaving the others behind. It was a really pretty place to work, and the owners of the smaller vineyards were very generous with tea, coffee, wine and food. On one family vine-yard we would all be swigging wine while we worked to keep the boss happy.

Almost everyone who over the years has written about the Swiss harvest writes in similarly glowing terms. In Salgesh, the third farm which Robin Gray tried told him to come back at 8am the next morning:

> I worked there for two weeks and had a fantastic time. When I told the boss I was camping, he offered me his garage which was like a comfortable house. I ended up being given free food and accommodation and the equivalent of £5 an hour. What a job. The family were unbelievably nice. Every night we had a different traditional Swiss meal. The boss's mother did my washing for me and it would come back not only ironed but with the rips sewed up. Of all the places I've been, Switzerland has been the friendliest of them all. I earned about £400 in two weeks.

Vineyards are found along the north shores of Lake Geneva on either side of Lausanne. One district is known as La Cote, between Coppet and Morges west of Lausanne, and the other is the Lavaux, a remarkably beautiful region of vineyards, rising up the hillside along the 25km between Pully on the outskirts of Lausanne and the tourist city of Montreux. The vineyards, enclosed within low stone walls, slope so steeply that all the work must be done by hand, and the job of portering is recommended only for the very fit. The harvest here is later than in France (early to mid-October) when the weather is beginning to get cold and rainy (the latter curtails work). Also the harvest is shorter (a week to ten days), because of the lower density of grapes per hectare.

One suggestion is to visit the tourist office outside the railway station in Biel on the Lake of Biel (Bielersee) and obtain the leaflet about wine in the region, which gives the names, addresses and phone numbers of nearly 50 vineyard owners *(weinbauern)*. September can be a good time to ask, since you might be taken on early to help with netting the grapes, to minimise bird damage. Try also the northern shores of the two adjoining lakes Murtensee and Lac de Neuchâtel.

Although the harvest is the time of year when there are the most vacancies, grape farmers also need people to help prune, something which Andrea Militello found very lucrative in June around Aigle. He claims that the technique is easy enough for anyone to master, though it is hard physical labour and even harder to land the job in the face of a lot of competition. He earned SFr2,880 on top of bed and board for working six days a week for four weeks.

BUILDING

Far fewer Swiss nationals than foreigners work as building labourers. In addition to building improvement in residential areas, resorts have a continual demand for painters and builders out of season. Ask the migrant workers you come across doing this work for advice or visit timber yards or estate agents *(agences immobilieres)*.

In winter you may be able to find occasional work chopping firewood or mending roofs. Danny Jacobson found out just how much wood is needed to keep a farming family warm through the Swiss winter when he spent a few weeks chopping and carting enough wood to give him a lifetime's phobia of trees. (But he was paid a handsome SFr100 per day for his trouble as well as free room and board.) A special opportunity for odd jobbers is afforded by the Swiss law that prohibits snow on roofs from reaching more than two metres depth. Apparently casual labourers are needed at the giant vegetable market in Zürich (near the football stadium). The wage for shifting heavy sacks of produce is £8 an hour. It will probably be necessary to sleep at the market since farmers start arriving long before dawn breaks.

TUTORS AND AU PAIRS

Private tutoring is a possibility for those who lack a permit, as an American world traveller discovered when he was living with his Swiss girlfriend (now wife) in Bern:

> **Danny Jacobson found that**
> *A Swiss friend advised me to apply at one of the English schools but I didn't think it would work without a permit. So I just made my own flyer and put it up around town and the next thing I knew I had a bunch of people calling me up to help with proof-reading seminar papers/assignments and to give private lessons. I figured I'd go for quantity and low-ball the market, charging only SFr20 per hour. But I found a few adverts for people looking for teachers and with those, I went with their offered price which was sometimes twice as much.*

For those interested in a domestic position with a Swiss family there are rules laid down by each Swiss canton, so there are variations. Now that European citizens no longer require a work permit, the au pair system has become more relaxed. However the agencies still work to the old requirements and place females between the ages of 17 and 29 (minimum 18 in Geneva) for at least 12 and up to 18 months. All nationalities will have to obtain the L-EC/EFTA permit whereas only non-EFTA au pairs are obliged to attend at least three hours a week of language classes in Zürich, four in Geneva. Families in most places are required to pay half the language school fees for six months and half the compulsory health insurance. The agencies are at pains to remind potential au pairs that Swiss German is very different from the German learned in school which often causes disappointment and difficulties.

Au pairs in Switzerland work for a maximum of 30 hours per week, plus babysitting once or twice a week. The monthly salary varies among cantons but the normal minimum is SFr700-800. Rates may be slightly higher for older girls and are generally higher in Geneva than Zürich. In addition, the au pair gets a four or five week paid holiday plus SFr18-20 for days off (to cover food). Au pairs are liable to pay tax and contributions which can mean a deduction of up to a fifth of their wages.

Pro Filia is a long-established Catholic au pair agency with about 15 branches including 32 Av de Rumine, 1005 Lausanne (021-323 77 66) for French-speaking Switzerland, and Beckenhofstr. 16, 8035 Zürich (01-363 55 00; www.profilia.ch) for the German part. The agency registration fee is SFr30–35 plus a further SFr100-150 to be paid within a month of taking up the placement.

Independent au pair placement agencies include Sunshine Au Pair Agency, 15, Vy des Crêts, 1295 Mies (tel/fax 022-755 20 81; www.au-pair-sunshine.ch); Swissaupair Agence de Placement Au Pair, Quai Maria Belgia 8, 1800 Vevey (tel/fax 021 921 28 47; www.swissaupair.ch) and Perfect Way, Hafnerweg 10, 5200 Brugg (+41 56 281 39 12; info@perfectway.ch) which vets all families and distributes a list of other au pairs and their contact details. The agency Wind Connections in Erlenbach near Zurich (01-915 4104; fax 01-915 4105; info@windconnections.ch; www.canadalink.ch) accepts au pairs only from Australia and Canada.

The Haut-Lac International Centre (1669 Les Sciernes; 026-928 4200; info@haut-lac.com; www.haut-lac.com) employs teachers and monitors of any nationality for both their summer and winter camps for teenagers. The American School in Switzerland (TASIS) also employs TEFL tutors and children's counselors for their Summer Language Programs, 6926 Montagnola-Lugano (091-960 5151; summer@tasis.ch; www.tasis.ch).

VOLUNTEERING

Several of the international workcamp organisations operate in Switzerland mainly to carry out conservation work. For example Gruppo Volontari dalla Svizzera Italiana (C.P. 12, 6517 Arbedo; 077-354 01 61; fmari@vtx.ch; www.gvsi.org/en) organises camps on which groups of volunteers who can speak one of Switzerland's official languages help mountain communities in Maggia, Fusio and Borgogne. Volunteers pay about SFr100 per week for living expenses.

The Mountain Forest Project (Bergwald Projekt e.V.) publishes its literature and website in English and is welcoming to foreign volunteers who know some German. It provides hut accommodation, food and insurance for the one-week projects:

> People from overseas travelling in Europe will surely enjoy a week's workcamp with MFP in Switzerland, Germany or Austria. You will learn a lot about alpine forests and nature in general. We do not, however, consider it reasonable to fly to Europe just for one week to work with us. We all know that airplanes pollute the air and endanger our atmosphere, climate and forests. For these reasons we offer our workcamps only to people who are in Europe anyway.

For details send two IRCs to MFP, Hauptstr.24, 7014 Trin (081-630 41 45) or register online (www.bergwaldprojekt.ch). An annual membership of the organisation costs SFr60/€40.

Austria

For many years Austria has offered seasonal employment in its summer and winter tourist industries. Its rate of unemployment is among the lowest in Europe at 4.5% (December 2004) and an estimated 25% of people employed in tourism are not Austrian citizens. A good knowledge of German will be necessary for most jobs, apart from those with UK tour operators. The government website www.help.gv.at/Content.Node/144/Seite.1440000.html gives information about immigration and social security procedures for those working in Austria.

Once you are in Austria, you should visit the state-run regional employment office AMS (Arbeitsmarktservice) though it would be virtually essential to speak German before they could assist. The AMS web pages might be of assistance to German speakers (www.ams.or.at) and the links to EURES Advisers could be followed up. Offices that specialise in seasonal work are called BerufsInfoZentren or BIZ. There are 60 in the country including three in Vienna, eight in the Tyrol and so on. For example many hotel and catering vacancies in the South Tyrol are registered with the Euro BIZ Jobcentre at Schöpfstrasse 5, 6020 Innsbruck (eurobiz.innsbruck@702.ams.or.at). Most Saisonstellen im Hotel und

Gastewerbe (seasonal hotel jobs) for the winter season are notified in November for the start of the season at the end of November. The Ufficio di Lavoro is responsible for job information in the Italian-speaking region of South Tyrol.

Private employment agencies exist in Austria, mostly registering professional vacancies for chefs, restaurant managers, etc. Nationals of non-European countries must obtain a work permit before departing from their home country which, as usual, is virtually impossible for casual and seasonal work. Special rules apply to au pairs (see section below). At present each region of Austria has a quota of foreign workers from outside Europe, and when the annual quota is filled, no more permits are granted that year.

If working legally, you can expect to have 15% of your gross wage deducted for contributions to the compulsory Health and Social Security Scheme provided you earn more than €550 a month.

THE JOB HUNT

Because of its shared borders and proximity to several of the new accession countries, Austria has been particularly concerned to implement the transition phase of the free movement of labour within an enlarged Europe. For many years Austria has been the destination of choice for thousands of East Europeans, many of whom are still there working in unskilled jobs. There is also a large community of guest-workers from Turkey and Bosnia-Herzogovina. Immigrants from the Balkans are often hired in preference to ski bums, and hotels and bars draw their staff from the pool of employees willing to work extremely hard to maintain their relatives at home.

Tourism

There is no shortage of hotels to which you can apply either for the summer or the winter season. Get a list from the local tourist office or on the net. The largest concentration is in the Tyrol though there are also many in the Vorarlberg region in western Austria. Wages in hotels and restaurants are lower than they are in Switzerland but reasonable.

If you want to improve your chances of finding work in a ski resort, you could consider joining the two-week 'Learn German and Get a Seasonal Job in the Snow' course at Club Habitat in Kirchberg/Kitzbühel in the Austrian Tyrol. Details are available from Club Habitat Ski Chalet, Kohlgrub 9, 6365 Kirchberg; 05357 2254; info@clubhabitat.at; www.clubhabitat.at). The course takes place from the last week of November and costs from £250 which includes bed and breakfast accommodation and two hours of tuition a day. In fact Kirchberg is such a popular tourist destination that it might be worth job-hunting there in winter or summer. In the summer season Club Habitat works with local suppliers of adventure activities who often require guides for white-water rafting, mountain biking or hiking. For example Fankhauser Rafting has been seen in recent years advertising for rafting, cycling, and hiking guides as well as support staff (Dorfstrasse 17, 6832 Kirchdorf; info@tirolrafting.com).

The main winter resorts to try are St Anton, Kitzbühel, Mayrhofen, St. Johann-im-Pongau which is a popular destination for British holidaymakers creating a demand for English-speaking staff, St. Johann in Tyrol, Lech and Söll. Once you are in a resort like St Anton or Brand which, during the season, has to accommodate and service thousands of holidaymakers, it should be easy to find an opening. Try putting an ad in the *Tiroler Tageszeitung* newspaper.

As usual, it will be necessary to enquire everywhere for jobs in hotels, shops, as an au pair, in specialist areas like the 'skiverleih' (ski hire) as a technician or just working on the drag-lifts. It is probably best to target one or two villages where there are a lot of guesthouses and hotels. The Tourist Information office and the bus drivers who convey skiers from hotels to slopes are both good sources of information. Needless to say, there are more jobs when the resorts are busy, which in turn depends on snow conditions. The ski season in the Innsbruck region is fairly reliable since the Stubai Glacier normally ensures snow from early December until the end of April.

Pubs, clubs and discos should not be overlooked since many of them regularly hire foreigners. Karin Huber, a native of Zell am See, reckons there are plenty of openings for foreigners, especially in the winter, since she found herself the only Austrian working in a club. The best time to arrive is late November.

You could try to fix up a job with a British tour operator beforehand, ideally in September. Because Austria is a very popular destination for British skiers, there is a large choice, for example Esprit Alpine Sun, Equity Travel, Inghams and Travelbound (see introductory chapter *Tourism* for addresses). For example Equity Travel (01273 886911; www.equity.co.uk/employment) recruit chefs, housekeeping and waiting staff, handymen, night porters, plongeurs and bar staff (EU nationality essential) for its sizeable operation in the Austrian Alps. Lotus Supertravel (Sandpiper House, 39 Queen Elizabeth St, London SE1 2BT; 020-7962 1369; www.supertravel.co.uk/jobs.htm) takes on winter staff for Austria, primarily chalet hosts with excellent cooking skills, reps fluent in German, qualified masseurs, nannies and handymen. All applicants must hold an EU passport and be over 21.

Tall Stories (Brassey House, New Zealand Avenue, Walton on Thames, Surrey KT12 1QD; 01932 252970; www.tallstories.co.uk/jobs.shtm) require resort staff in Austria among other countries. Another possibility for both seasons is First Choice Holidays (London Road, Crawley, West Sussex RH10 9GX; 01293 588585; skijobs@firstchoice. co.uk; www.firstchoice4jobs.co.uk) which hires hundreds of people to work in hotels and resorts in Austria; no qualifications are required because staff are given in-house training, but you must be available to stay for the whole season from May to September.

> **One of the more unusual casual jobs in Austria was described on a post card from Fionna Rutledge**
>
> *I thought you might be interested in my summer job in Vienna. I spent two months working for a classical music concert company (Strauss). There are loads of these in Vienna and most of them employ students. I was paid on commission and spent the day dressed up in Mozart costume in the main Vienna tourist spots. Hard work, but a great opportunity to meet people. You have to sell the concert to complete strangers. And I earned about £1,300 in six weeks. All you need to do is approach the 'Mozarts' on the street and ask them to introduce you to their boss.*

English Teaching

As in Germany, the market for EFL in Austrian cities is primarily for business English, particularly in-company. Most private language institutes such as SPIDI (Mariahilferstr. 32, 1070 Vienna; 01-524 17 17/40; www.spidi.at) depend on freelance part-time teachers drawn from the sizeable resident international community. The hourly rate at reputable institutes starts at €22, which is none-too-generous when the high cost of living in Vienna is taken into account.

Berlitz is well represented with four separate premises in Vienna alone, including the one at Graben 13, 1010 Vienna (01-512 82 86; www.berlitz.at). In fact the Instructional Supervision department at the regional head office (Mariahilferstrasse 27, 1060 Vienna) recruits new English teachers for Berlitz centres in Austria, Slovakia and Slovenia. They are looking for people with British, Irish, American or Australian nationality who are at least 23 and with a good degree.

Inlingua also has operations in the major cities (www.inlingua.at). According to an American teacher-traveller, Richard Spacer, who taught privately in Vienna for two months, the manager of inlingua in Vienna was very welcoming and informed him that the two-week methods course was offered to promising teachers free of charge. Richard earned his hourly wage cash-in-hand.

Summer language and sport camps provide more scope for EFL teachers and others. Village Camps (14 rue de la Morache, 1260 Nyon, Switzerland; www.villagecamps.ch) run a summer activity camp at Piesendorf near Zell-am-See. Activity counsellors over 21 receive €240 per week in addition to room and board and insurance. The season lasts from the end of June to mid-August. Some experience of teaching children and a knowledge of a second European language are the basic requirements.

Two other organisations active in this field are the similarly named English for Children (Weichselweb 4, 1220 Vienna; 01-958 1972; www.englishforchildren.com) and English for Kids (Postgasse 11/19, 1010 Vienna; 01-667 45 79; www.e4kids.co.at) both of which are looking for young monitors and English teachers with experience of working with children and preferably some TEFL background.

The organisation Young Austria, Ferienhöfe GmbH, Alpenstrasse 108a, A-5020 Salzburg; 0662-62 58 59-0) run summer camps *(Osterreichisches Ferienwerk)* that employ about 30 teachers and monitors to work at summer language and sports camps near Salzburg. For about three or four hours of each day of the two-week camp, 10 to 17 year old children receive English tuition from teachers (who must have teaching experience). Monitors organise the outdoor programme and help the teachers with the social programme as well as with the lessons. Teachers receive about €240 per fortnight and monitors receive €160 in their first year. Applications forms are available from December and should be submitted to gudrun.doringer@youngaustria.at by mid-March.

The American camp counsellor company CCUSA (2330 Marinship Way, Suite 250, Sausalito, CA 94965; 415-339-2740; www.ccusa.com) places English teachers on day camps in Austria and Germany as well for a minimum of six weeks.

Au Pairs

Austria, together with Switzerland, was one of the first countries to host au pairs so there is a well-developed tradition and several well-established and respectable agencies place hundreds of au pairs in Austria each year. Most of the families live in Vienna and Salzburg.

Au pairs from EU countries will have no trouble sorting out the paperwork in Austria. Officially au pairs from outside the EU must obtain both a work and residence permit *(Beschäftigungsbewilligung)*. Alien au pairs are allowed to stay in Austria for no more then a year and must renew their permit a month before the first six months is up. In order for a host family to obtain a *Beschäftigungsbewilligung* for their non-EU au pair, they should apply to the local employment office *(Arbeitsmarktservice)* at least two weeks before the au pair is due to arrive. Before the permit can be approved and an *Anzeigebestätigung* issued, the authorities must see an agreement or contract (signed by the employer and the au pair) and proof that health and accident insurance cover has been obtained by the au pair. A template of the contract is available on the Austrian Employment Service website (www.ams.or.at/download/aupair-vertrag.pdf). The agency should help with this process and tell the au pair where to take the documents to be stamped. The current fee is about €70.

The main agency is the Catholic-affiliated Auslands-Sozialdienst, Au-Pair Vermittlung, Johannesgasse 16/1, 1010 Vienna; 01-512 7941; www.volunteer.at/aupair/f-contact.htm) which is accustomed to dealing with direct applications from abroad for au pair placements lasting an academic year. Most agencies charge an upfront registration fee of €100-€150. The minimum weekly pocket money is about €60 a week. The Austrian employment service posts a useful list of agencies at www.ams.or.at/neu/tirol/1889.htm including:

Au Pair Austria, Vermittlungs-agentur, Mariahilfer Strasse 99/2/37, 1060 Vienna (tel/fax 01-920 38 42; www.aupairaustria.com). Registration fee of €30 plus completion fee of €70.

AuPair4You, Hasnerstrasse 31/22, 1160 Vienna (01/990 15 74; www.au-pair4you.at).

Au-pair Corner, Josef Buchinger Strasse 3, 3100 St. Pölten (02742/25 85 36; www.au-pair-corner.at).

It should be possible to find babysitting work if you are based in a resort. Ask for permission in the big hotels to put up a notice. The going rate is about €6.50 an hour.

Voluntary Opportunities

Service Civil International is an international peace organisation which, as a part of its work, organises two to three week workcamps mostly in summer. Work can take place indoors or out, for example working with children, elderly or disabled people, helping at peace or other festivals, farm work, renovation work, etc. SCI also offers the possibility of longer periods of voluntary work, e.g. three to six months in which case pocket money is paid. Contact IVS/SCI in your own country or if in Austria, SCI at Schottengasse 3a/1/4/59, 1010 Vienna (01-535 9108; www.sci.or.at).

For information about WWOOF Austria, contact Hildegard Gottlieb, Einödhofweg 48, 8042 Graz (tel/fax 0316-464951; wwoof.welcome@telering.at; www.wwoof.welcome.at.tf). Membership costs €20/$25 per year plus two IRCs which entitles you to the list of around 160 Austrian organic farmers looking for work-for-keep volunteer helpers.

Outdoor Work

A native of Doren in the Vorarlberg region of Austria thinks that it should be possible to find work on a mountain farm:

> **For three separate seasons Jakob Steixner has worked in the mountains:**
> *There is one sort of job available to everybody who doesn't mind working long hours in agriculture in Austria and Switzerland (and probably everywhere along the Alps). It's working temporarily on livestock farms in the mountains. It can be quite interesting not only because it involves so many different activities but also you're outside a lot of the time, often in extraordinarily beautiful surroundings. Pay is by the day and might seem very little by European standards (around £20-£30 in my area, but more if you get deeper into the mountains). But you can save a lot as there is nowhere to spend the money and you get free food and accommodation. Depending on your bosses you might have to work quite long hours though, sometimes searching for lost cattle for hours in the pouring rain or hail, 5000ft above sea level, or repairing fences when it's snowing in the middle of July. But that can be quite hilarious when you think about it later.*

The best time to ask around for work is March, well ahead of the season which lasts from June till early September. But as the farmers are often short of helpers it might be possible to pick up a job on the spot. Increasingly these jobs are done by foreigners (e.g. Brazilians and Poles) though the farmers prefer workers who know some German since few of them speak any English. Normally you will be expected to stay for the whole season though people who are free to work for the first four weeks are in great demand before the school holidays begin, since many students do this as a summer job. Try the large co-operatively run farms rather than the small ones that usually rely on family members. One idea is to place an advert in the agricultural journals. Jakob Steixner heard of someone who, after she did this, was so bothered by phone calls all day long in response to her ad that she had to unplug her phone, even though she didn't have any agricultural experience.

Central Europe & Russia

Political change in Eastern and Central Europe provoked revolutions in many spheres. One of the most important was the enthusiasm with which the governments and citizens of those countries embraced the English language giving rise to an enormous demand for native speakers to teach English. The vast majority of working opportunities in the region is in the field of English language teaching.

Despite having moved past making 'Western' synonymous with 'desirable,' East Europeans are still remarkably welcoming to British and American English language teachers. On most street corners, private language schools employ native speaker teachers. Working in Central and Eastern Europe may not seem as sexy as it did just after the 'revolution', but thousands of foreigners continue to fall under the spell of Prague, Budapest and Kraków. Even those who find themselves in the less prepossessing industrial cities normally come away beguiled by Central European charm.

The English language teaching industry in those countries has grown up, and is now much more likely to hire teachers with proven experience or an appropriate qualification. As schools and language training organisations have become more choosy, so too the governments have made visas more difficult to obtain. Even in countries where English native speakers are sought after, the red tape can be offputting. For example in Russia, visas and residence permits are specific to a given employer. When a pre-arranged job turns out to be less satisfactory than expected, foreign teachers who find a much better job encounter difficulties in switching employers.

In Russia, the Baltic states of Latvia, Lithuania and Estonia and the other (not-so-newly) independent states of the old Soviet Union, the English teaching situation is more fluid. Almost any native speaker can arrange some kind of teaching, often on a private basis, but with no guarantee of earning a living wage from it.

While opportunities vary from place to place, it is true to say that there will be a demand for native EFL teachers for many years ahead. And though these may not be the best paid EFL jobs in the world, Eastern Europe can offer historic and beautiful cities, genuinely friendly people and a unique chance to experience life in the 'other Europe' before it turns into just another group of free-market democracies.

TEACHING ENGLISH

While some foreigners teach in state schools where there is a guaranteed salary, access to state health insurance, a long-term contract and a light teaching load after exams are over in late May, most teach in the private sector which offers less financial and job security but better pay.

Fewer vacancies in Central and Eastern Europe are being advertised in the educational press and on the internet, even in Poland, but it is still worth checking the Tuesday *Guardian*. A certain number of commercial recruitment agencies are involved with filling vacancies in Eastern Europe with certificate-holding EFL teachers, and educational charities or gap year placement organisations send untrained volunteer teachers who normally pay a placement fee. Here are the main organisations based in the UK which continue to recruit teachers for more than one country in the region:

Language Link, 21 Harrington Road, London SW7 3EU (020-7225 1065; fax 020-7584 3518; recruitment@languagelink.co.uk; www.languagelink.co.uk). Mainly active in Russia and Slovakia but also have occasional positions elsewhere for newly qualified teachers as well as experienced ones.

Services for Open Learning (SOL), 2 Bridge Chambers, The Strand, Barnstaple, Devon EX31 1HB (01271 327319/fax 01271 376650; info@sol.org.uk; www.sol.org.uk). Non-profit-making organisation which annually recruits about 30 graduates with a recognised TEFL Certificate to teach in schools in the state sector in most Eastern and Central European countries, especially Hungary and Romania. Contracts with individual schools are mostly for a complete academic year September to June.

Teaching & Projects Abroad, Aldsworth Parade, Goring, Sussex BN12 4TX (01903 708300; fax 01903 501026; info@teaching-abroad.co.uk; www.teaching-abroad.co.uk). Recruits volunteers to work as English language teaching assistants for the summer or during the academic year in Russia (Moscow) and Romania. No TEFL background required. Flexible start dates for stays lasting up to three months; extensions can be arranged for a further fee.

Travellers Worldwide, 7 Mulberry Close, Ferring, West Sussex BN12 5HY (tel/fax 01903 502595; www.travellersworldwide.com). Paying volunteers teach conversational English in Russia (Moscow, St. Petersburg and Siberia) and the Ukraine (Kiev and Crimea). Sample prices for 3 months: Ukraine £995 and St Petersburg, Russia £1,495 including food and accommodation.

US Organisations

Several US organisations are actively involved in teacher recruitment for the region:

Bridges for Education, 94 Lamarck Drive, Buffalo, NY 14226, USA (716-839-0180; www.bridges4edu.org). Organise international summer peace camps which involve 180 volunteers teaching English for three weeks in July followed by one week of travel in Belarus, Hungary, Poland and Romania. Volunteers are given basic ESL training before departure. Participants pay their airfare and programme administration fee from $875.

Central European Teaching Program, 3800 NE 72nd Avenue, Portland, OR 97213, USA (503-287-4977) or Holgy u.34 fsz. 1, Budapest 1102, Hungary; +36-30-922-8867; vhajnalka@matavnet.hu; www.ticon.net/cetp. Supplies about 40 English teachers to state schools in Hungary and Romania. Placement fee of $2,000 for 10-month placement or $1,500 for one semester.

International TEFL Certificate, ITC, Kaprova 14, 110 00 Prague (02-2481 4791; info@itc-training.com). Graduates of the 4-week ITC certificate in TEFL are guaranteed a job in the Czech Republic or elsewhere in the region.

Once you have a work base, the supply of private teaching is usually plentiful. The pay for private lessons can be excellent compared to wages offered by schools. A small notice placed on a prominent university notice board or in a daily newspaper would have a good chance of producing results. Sometimes notices are posted in less likely places: Hannah Start reported that when she was teaching in the Russian city of Yaroslavl, locals pinned notices to trees.

CZECH & SLOVAK REPUBLICS

There seems to be an equal demand for English in both the Czech and Slovak Republics, though the majority of TEFL teachers gravitate to the former, particularly Prague.

Teaching in the Czech Republic

The centralised contact for recruitment of teachers for state primary and secondary schools is the *Academic Information Agency (AIA)* in Prague (Dum zahranicních sluzeb, Senovázné nám. 26, 111 21 Prague 1 or PO Box 8, 110 06 Prague; 02-24 22 96 98; aia@dzs.cz; www. dzs.cz/scripts/detail.asp?id=599). AIA is part of the Ministry of Education and acts as a go-between, circulating CVs and applications (due by the end of April) among state primary and secondary schools that have requested a teacher. Schools (mostly in small Czech towns) then contact applicants directly to discuss contractual details. They place university graduates, preferably with TEFL training or experience, in schools from September 1st to June 30th. The net salary per month is 8,000-11,000 crowns plus free or subsidised accommodation.

Brian Farrelly was satisfied with the arrangement made for him by Services for Open Learning (address above):

> I taught in two state schools in the Czech Republic. I had a really great time in both those schools and I felt really privileged to teach the students there. SOL placed me in a 'gymnazium' secondary school in the small town of Sedicany 60km south of Prague where I taught English conversation and regular English classes. Both the staff and the students made me tremendously welcome. I also greatly enjoyed the freedom I had to teach as I saw fit, although initially I felt very daunted by the lack of guidance regarding what I should be doing.

Most people wait until they arrive in Prague before trying to find teaching work, which is what Linda Harrison did: *'The best time to apply is before June (I arrived in September which was too late) but if you persevere there are jobs around. A lot of teaching work here seems to be in companies. Schools employ you to go into offices, etc. to teach English (though not usually business English). After a short job hunt, I have been hired by Languages at Work.'* Languages at Work is at Pobrezni 4, 186 21 Prague 8 (tel/fax 02-248 11 379; www.languagesatwork.cz).

Most private language schools can count on receiving plenty of CVs on spec from which to fill any vacancies that arise. Anyone who is well qualified or experienced should have few difficulties in finding a job on the spot and obtaining a work permit. The Yellow Pages *(Zlaty Stranky)* are an excellent source of addresses under the heading *Jazykove skoly*. Among the schools with the largest demand for teachers are:

Akcent International House, Bitovská 3, 140 00 Prague 4 (02-6126 16 38; www.akcent.cz).
CELTA or equivalent is minimum requirement.

Akademie J.A. Komenskeho, Trziste 20, Mala Strana, 118 43 Prague 1 (02-5753 1232; www.akademie.cz). Many posts in 50 adult education centres and schools throughout the Czech Republic where British native speakers (including gap year students) are employed. Monthly net wage is 8,000 crowns.

Anglictina Expres, Korunni 2, 120 00 Prague 2 (tel/fax 02-2251 3040; www.anexpres.cz).

15-20 graduates employed for morning and evening freelance work.

Caledonian School, Vltavská 24, 15000 Prague 5 (tel 02-57313650; jobs@caledonianschool. com). Employ 170+ teachers who must have a BA plus Cambridge Certificate or equivalent. Approximate salary of 20,000 crowns per month for qualified teachers; accommodation provided for 4,500 crowns per month.

Compared to the starting monthly wage in state schools of 8,000 crowns, private sector wages are normally over 10,000 crowns (also net). But this does not include accommodation which will account for between a quarter and a third of a teaching salary. Hourly fees are normally in the region of 220-250 crowns less 20%-30% for tax and deductions. A full-time salary should be adequate to live on by local standards but will not allow you to save anything, unless you take on lots of private tutoring.

Since accession and the passing of the Amendment of the Employment Act, EU nationals no longer have to apply for a work permit. Other foreigners who want to stay more than 90 days must apply for a long-stay Czech visa before arrival in the country. This requires gathering a raft of documents including a work permit issued by the employer, proof of accommodation, etc. all presented in the original or a notarised copy.

Teaching in Slovakia

As the poor cousin in the former Czechoslovakia, the republic of the Slovaks has been somewhat neglected not only by tourists but by teachers as well. As one language school director put it: *'Many teachers are heading for Prague, which is why Slovakia stands aside of the main flow of the teachers. That's a pity as Prague is crowded with British and Americans while there's a lack of the teachers here in Slovakia.'*

The density of private language schools in the capital Bratislava and in the other main cities like Banska Bystrika makes an on-the-ground job hunt promising.

A UK agency that actively recruits up to 100 teachers for Slovakia is Language Link (21 Harrington Road, London SW7 3EU; 020-7225 1065) which is affiliated with the largest semi-private language school in Slovakia, the Akadémia Vzdelávania, Gorkého 10, 815 17 Bratislava (02-5441 0040; centrum@aveducation.sk; www.aveducation.sk). It offers approximately 50 posts in adult education centres and schools throughout Slovakia, with a wage of about 10,000 koruna per month in the first year in Bratislava, 12,500 crowns in the second.

Although Slovakia is now inside the European Union, the obligation to apply for a Long-term Stay Permit will not disappear for two years or more. Already teachers from the EU have been allowed to apply for a work permit after arrival in Slovakia by producing evidence of health insurance, a work contract and proof of accommodation. For non-EU candidates, the by-now-familiar story of bureaucratic complexity awaits, i.e. the employer must put a strong case for the necessity to hire a non-European and then all documents must be officially translated including medical report, criminal clearance, bank statements and so on.

HUNGARY

English is compulsory for all Hungarian students who wish to apply for college or university entrance, and university students in both the Arts and Sciences must take courses in English, creating a huge market for English teachers. But because of the high calibre of Hungary's home-grown teachers, native speakers do not have the cachet they have in other central European countries.

Yet native speakers continue to find teaching opportunities in Hungary, especially in the business market. The invasion of foreigners in Budapest was never as overwhelming as it was (and is) in Prague, but still Budapest has a glut of teachers. The opportunities that do exist now are mostly in the provinces.

Teachers are poorly paid in Hungary, aside from in the top-notch private schools and the British Council. A typical hourly wage for a qualified TEFL teacher would be 1200 forints (less than £3.50). Wages and the exchange rate have remained stable over the past few years, though Budapest rents have continued to climb and take a major proportion of a teacher's salary; some schools help by subsidising accommodation, or it may be possible to arrange accommodation in return for English lessons.

Money is not the point for everybody. Trudie Darch spent her gap year teaching in Hungary through GAP Activity Projects (see *Volunteering: Gap Year Placements*):

> *I had been there three weeks and with very little notice I was told that I'd be teaching on my own for one whole week. This was the scariest thing that had happened so far. Virtually unprepared, I walked into a classroom full of 18 year olds (I was 19) and had to teach. The first lesson was not very good and I had some difficulties getting them to listen to me. It was hard to get over the fact that these were my students not people who were supposed to be my friends. However I overcame this and learnt that to be a more professional teacher, I had to distance myself from trying to be their friend. The school was basic, the food was interesting (pasta and icing sugar was one I hated) and my accommodation left a lot to be desired. But even the bad things I wouldn't swap because they taught me a lot.*

In the US, the Central European Teaching Program (description in introduction to this chapter) has its strongest base in Hungary. CETP liaises with the relevant government department in Hungary to place teachers in state schools throughout the country.

The Regulations

Since Hungary's accession in 2004, EU nationals no longer require a work permit, only a residence permit, as throughout member states. The requirements for obtaining a residence permit are relatively undemanding, so the immigration procedures overall have been much simplified. However for the first time EU nationals working full-time in Hungary are subject to the same social security and pension obligations as Hungarians. Payments must now be made into the National Health Insurance Fund and into a pension fund. Together these contributions amount to 12.5% of the employee's monthly salary and a massive 29% from employers. This is likely to result in fewer teaching contracts being given and most people hired as part-timers and freelancers

Non-EU citizens must arrange work permits before leaving their country of residence. A foreign employee cannot be legally paid until she or he has a labour permit. General information in English is available on the website of the Hungarian Ministry of Foreign Affairs (www.mfa.gov.hu). A good source of information is the Expat Relocation Center in Budapest (www.ercglobal.com).

POLAND

Prospects for English teachers in Poland, western Poland in particular, remain the most promising in Europe. Even the major cities of Warsaw, Wroclaw, Kraków, Poznan and Gdansk are worthwhile destinations, though the job hunt is of course easier in the many lesser known towns and cities of Poland. As in the Czech and Slovak Republics numerous possibilities exist in both state and private schools. School directors are often willing to interview native English speakers who present themselves in a professional manner. The reverence for 'native speakerhood' still runs high in Poland.

APASS UK North is the acronym for the Anglo-Polish Universities Teaching Project, which supplies native-speaker tutors to summer language camps and schools. The programme invites both mature students and teachers from British universities and young volunteers over 16 (with parental permission) to spend July, August or both in Poland. Furnished accommodation and food are provided for three weeks teaching (2½ hours of English conversation and instruction per day) and there is one week allocated for a tour of Poland. All expenses and pocket money are paid by the Polish host. An information pack about the programme including placement fee can be requested by sending an s.a.e. (45p stamp) and £3 postal order to APASS, UK North, 93 Victoria Road, Leeds LS6 1DR; fax 020-7498 7608 (they have no website). Reports have been received that details of these summer placements are finalised not long before departure, so be prepared to endure some suspense.

Wayne Stimson feels that this excellent scheme is not widely enough known:

I had always wanted to teach English and, as a politics student, I also had an interest in the history and politics of the former Eastern Bloc states. I got the opportunity last summer to combine these two when APASS arranged for me to spend seven weeks in a village near the Czech border called Dusniki Zdroj. Here I worked on two camps that gave children an activity-based holiday alongside English teaching. The children were mainly from middle class, professional backgrounds and their English skills were often quite developed so teaching and general communication was not difficult. I tried to teach a little about the customs, culture and politics of the UK. I was treated very graciously by my hosts and found Polish people to be very warm and friendly.

Private language teaching organisations run short-term holiday courses which require native speakers, including the English School of Communication Skills (Personnel Department, ul. Walowa 2, 33-100 Tarnów; 607-616-605; personnel@escs.pl; www.escs.pl) which hires 100 EFL teachers for five language schools in southern Poland and summer language camps at the Polish seaside. Pay at ESCS is 2200 zloties a month. Candidates with no TEFL training are obliged to take a pre-term methodology course plus it offers its own three-week TEFL training course in September. Will Gardner was full of praise for this organisation when he worked for them one summer, having fixed up the position from England in the spring:

I spent one month working for ESCS at their summer camp on Poland's Baltic Coast. The camps were well organised and great fun. As an experienced teacher who has worked in several different countries for a range of schools, I would just like to say what a pleasure it was to work with such a well organised group of people and for a school that completely lived up to its promises. The school supplied a wide range of resources to assist teachers, although a lot of emphasis was placed on originality. The focus was always on communication and fun. The camp facilities were perfect for the situation. Food and accommodation were supplied and the weather was beautiful. Although the students were attending lessons daily, a holiday atmosphere prevailed over all activities.

International House (www.ih.com.pl) maintains a large contingent of language schools in Poland employing many certificate-qualified EFL teachers, including IH Katowice (ul. Sokolska 78/80, 40-128 Katowice), IH Kraków (ul. Pilsudskiego 6, 31-109 Kraków), IH Opole (ul. Reymonta 29, 45-072 Opole), IH Wroclaw (ul. Leszczynskiego 3, 50-078 Wroclaw), IH Bielsko-Biala (ul. Zielona 32, 43-300 Bielsko Biala) and IH Bydgoszcz (ul. Dworcowa 81, 85-009 Bydgoszcz).

On the Spot

Semesters begin on October 1st and February 15th, and the best time to arrive is a month or two beforehand. After arrival, try to establish some contacts, possibly by visiting the English department at the university. Although some school directors state a preference for British or American accents, many are neutral. After obtaining some addresses, would-be teachers should dutifully 'do the rounds' of the *Dyrektors*. Some of the bigger schools include:

Angloschool, ul. Ks. J. Popieluszki 7, 01-786 Warsaw (tel/fax 022-664 77 00; www. angloschool.com.pl).

Multischool, Ul. Olawska 5, 01-494 Warsaw (022-638 23 39; fax 022-638 2340; biuro@multischool.pl; www.atut.edu.pl). 20-25 native speakers with degree and TEFL training.

Cambridge School of English, Millennium Plaza, al. Jerozolimskie 123, 00-0176 Warsaw (022-635 24 66; www.cambridge.com.pl).

EF English First, ul. Marszaldowska 1p, 00-624 Warsaw (022-825 0070). Teachers for 4 schools in Warsaw and 11 elsewhere in Poland.

Greenwich School of English, ul. Gdanska 2, 01-633 Warsaw (022-833 2431; www. greenwich.edu.pl).

Lektor Szkola Jezykow Obcych, ul. Olawska 25, 50-123 Wroclaw (071-343 2599; rmyszkowski@lektor.com.pl). 50 British, American, Canadian or Australian teachers with certificate in TEFL.

YES School of Language, ul. Reformacka 4, 35-026 Rzeszów (017-852 0720; www. yes.pl). Recruitment details can be downloaded from website for summer jobs in the mountains or for the academic year.

If you base yourself in Warsaw and wish to advertise your availability for private English tuition, try placing a notice just to the right of the main gate of Warsaw University or in one of the main dailies, *Gazeta Wyborcza* or *Zycie Warszawy.*

The Regulations

On the basis of reciprocity, Poland has implemented barriers to the free movement of labour apart from British, Irish and Swedish citizens who do not require a work permit to work in Poland. Everyone else must still apply in their country of origin. You will need to present original or a notarised copy of your degree diploma and TEFL Certificate (if applicable) and a promissory work permit from your future employer to the Polish Consulate in your country of residence.

Generally speaking, private language schools in Poland offer reasonable working conditions, with fewer reports of profit-mongers and sharks than in other countries experiencing a TEFL boom. Wages are reasonably high and the terms of service are seldom exploitative. It is not uncommon for overtime to be paid to teachers for hours worked in excess of the contracted number (typically 24).

RUSSIA & the Independent States

The language school market shrank drastically due to an economic crisis several years ago and as a result the number of full-time job opportunities for native English-speaking teachers decreased. The situation (like the rouble) has since stabilised and there are still ample English teaching opportunities for those wishing to experience the real Russia.

Apart from the qualified teachers working for the major foreign-owned language chains like Benedict, Language Link and EF English First (see below) and other established schools like Polyglot and the American Academy of Foreign Languages (www.aafl.ru), the majority of English teachers in Russia and the former Soviet Republics, including the Baltics and the Ukraine, have come through voluntary placement organisations or are students of Russian with an interest in the language and culture. The situation in the Central Asian Republics is somewhat different because demand for English there is largely funded by international oil investment and so highly qualified teacher trainers are needed.

Many foreign teachers prefer the security of working for a western-owned company where the support and fringe benefits are favourable. Barry Robinson has spent the past seven years in Moscow working the EFL circuit:

When living in Moscow patience is priceless. Expect to queue, wait longer, and endure a certain amount of discomfort when travelling around the city from lesson to lesson. Yet Moscow is an expansive, vibrant, culturally rewarding city in which to live. The people at first appear a tad abrupt, but this is usually just to cope with the breakneck pace of life in Russia's capital. When you make friends - and you will as

Russians are quite sociable and always interested in native English speakers - you'll find them warm and generous people, who will let you into their hearts and homes if they genuinely like you.

Be warned: Moscow is a very expensive city. Increasing prosperity and the influx of foreigners have driven up rents so, if you don't want to rent a roach-infested shed, you'll have to spend $300-$400 on some living space. Often teaching contracts will include a flat, but these tend to be rather manky and often shared with another teacher. A reasonable salary for Moscow should be in the range of $800-$900 without a flat or at least $550-$600 including one. Freelance opportunities are abundant, and extremely lucrative. However you'll have to wade through the quagmire that is Russia's ever-muddled, ever-changing visa and entry requirements.

Finding a Job

Anyone with contacts anywhere in the region or who is prepared to go in order to make contacts should be able to arrange a teaching niche on an individual basis. Most educational institutes are suffering such serious financial hardships that they can't attract local teachers let alone Western ones. Alternatively teaching jobs are sometimes registered on the main recruitment websites.

A thriving English language press has established itself in Moscow and St. Petersburg. Check adverts in the *Moscow Times, Moscow Tribune* and the weekly *St. Petersburg Press*.

Among the major language teaching organisations, the following employ substantial numbers of native speaking teachers with a TEFL qualification:

Benedict Schools, 23 ul. Pskovskaya, St. Petersburg 190008 (812-113 85 68/114 10 90/fax 812-114 44 45; www.benedictinternational.co.uk). Employ 40-60 teachers including about 20 for St. Petersburg (main franchise holder) and others in Novosibirsk, Tomsk, Murmansk and Kemerovo. Run a Work-Study Programme for which no TEFL background is required; details from Benedict International Ltd (74 Baxter Court, Norwich NR3 2ST; 01603 301522; info@benedictinternational.co.uk).

EF English First, 5th Fl, Building 15, 125 Brestskaya 1st Street, 125047 Moscow (095-937 3883/fax 095-937 3889; www.englishfirst.com/teacherinfo/recruitment/russia.asp). 25 teachers for 19 schools in Moscow, St. Petersburg, Vladivostok, etc.

Language Link Russia, Novoslobodskaya ul. 5, bld. 2, 127030 Moscow (tel 095-232 0225; jobs@language.ru). 200 teachers throughout Russia (Moscow, St. Petersburg, Volgograd, Siberia, Urals, etc.) BUNAC have a Russian programme in partnership with Language Link Russia whereby freshly certified EFL teachers are placed in Russia; details from BUNAC on 020-7251 3472 (www.bunac.org.uk).

Robert Jensky, Director of Language Link Russia, is convinced that high standards are essential:
I have personally seen many unqualified teachers fail because they did not fully realise the difference between speaking English and teaching English. Although Russians can vary in temperament and personality, they share a respect for education. Russians who under Communism did not have to pay for education have come to accept the fact that it is now necessary to do so. Their only concern is that they get their full money's worth from each and every lesson. Russian students are demanding and place high expectations on their teachers, and so do the companies which employ them (including those that hire EFL teachers illegally). Given these circumstances, it is strongly recommended that any teacher coming to Russia has with him or her a good grammar book, a dictionary and a concise guide to TEFL methodology.

Russians have taken to the internet with unbounded enthusiasm and opportunities may be discovered by doing some concerted surfing. For example the website of the Svezhy Veter Travel Agency (www.sv-agency.udm.ru) describes in detail a scheme by which native speakers can go to the city of Izhevsk, several time zones east of Moscow, simply to live with a family on an au pair basis or to teach mornings plus an evening course at Secondary School No. 27 in exchange for homestay with meals and visa support. They now charge a registration fee for the scheme of €148. Jim Clost from Canada does not have a TEFL certificate but had studied Russian at university and really enjoyed his stint of giving conversation and teaching practice to his students while staying with a local family free of charge.

Koober Grob from Chicago was also impressed with the arrangement and found lots of scope for initiative

> I corresponded with Vladimir Bykov (the teacher I would eventually work with) for seven months before I went to Izhevsk. The students and I would discuss various topics such as domestic violence, cooking, nature, war or even manure and choco-late-covered ants. There was never any pretence in any of the classes. Eventually I started a theatre club for teenagers at a local school and then accompanied a six-week school trip around Siberia helping students individually with their English. The students were all so motivated, respectful and friendly. I only spent $600 for the three-month period that I was in Russia since Russia is very inexpensive and my students and friends paid for most of my expenses.

Further information about this scheme in Izhevsk can be obtained from SV, PO Box 2040, 426000 Izhevsk, Russia (tel/fax 3412-450037; sv@sv-agency.udm.ru).

Other organisations offer volunteers the chance to teach English at any level from university to businesses to summer camps. For example the youth exchange company CCUSA runs a Summer Camp Russia Programme whereby teacher/counsellors are placed on youth camps in Russia lasting four or eight weeks between mid-June and mid-August. Participants must be between the ages of 18 and 35, have experience working with children and/or abroad, and have an interest in learning about the Russian language and culture. The programme fee of £699 includes round-trip travel from London to Moscow, visa, travel insurance, orientations on arrival and room and board. In the UK contact CCUSA at 1st Floor North, Devon House, 171/177 Great Portland St, London W1W 5PQ (020-7637 0779; www.ccusaweusa.co.uk/ccrussia/programme.html) or in the US: 2330 Marinship Way, Suite 250, Sausalito, CA 94965 (1-800-449-3872; www.ccusa.com).

The International Exchange Center in Latvia (20 Kalku St, LV-1050 Riga; 722 8228; fax 783 0257; info@iec.lv) recruits young people with a TEFL qualification for summer language camps in Russia as well as Ukraine, Belarus and a few in Latvia. It offers between 20 and 40 hours of teaching in return for a salary equivalent to local rates or free board and lodging. The application fee is $150. Further information is available through the partner agency in the UK: International Student Exchange Center, 89 Fleet St, London EC4Y 1DH; 020-7583 9116; fax 020-7583 9117; www.isecworld.co.uk).

For Americans the Petro-Teach Program (www.petroteach.com) places interns in state secondary schools and private institutes in St. Petersburg for ten months. An intensive pre-teaching Russian language course is part of the programme. The deadline for autumn departure is mid-March and the programme fee for the academic year is $6,000 or $825 per month.

Regulations

For people participating in established international exchanges, the red tape is usually straightforward. Russia at the moment is a place where the regulations change as often as the government ministries responsible. In the commercial sector, work permits are problematic, because few Russian companies are willing to embark on the time-consuming process.

If you are an ex-pat and want to teach English in Russia, you must have permission to work and only the company that has invited you to Russia (the visa sponsor) has the right to obtain this for you. Language schools which are unable to provide teachers with legal working status usually elect to use the services of any one of a number of firms which specialise in inviting 'foreigners' to Russia (as distinct from *employing* foreigners in Russia). These visas will be registered with the local police but this is not the same as obtaining permission to work. The process takes about a month from the time the visa-sponsoring firm applies to the Ministry of Internal Affairs for an invitation.

Companies with the right to invite and employ foreign teachers in Russia are no longer obliged to obtain work permits for their teachers. Legislation enacted in 2004 stipulates that foreign specialists (including teachers) are not required to have work permits, provided they are employed by a company that has the right to do so. Companies without the right to invite and employ teachers opt for the one-year multiple entry visa. The disadvantage of working for these schools is that despite holding a year-long visa, teachers are required to leave the country after six months and then return, a real hassle when the nearest border can be hundreds, if not thousands of miles away.

Numerous foreigners do work without proper authorisation, but run a constant risk of being fined or even deported. Rhys Sage became suspicious of an employer who sent him the wrong visa:

> *After a fiasco in Latvia, it has become apparent to me that if a company is not willing to obtain the proper visa then they must be up to something dodgy. When I negotiated my contract with a school in Novosibirsk, they accepted some pretty excessive demands on my part which made me suspicious that the contract was worthless. This, combined with the fact that they sent me a visa form for a transit visa claiming it was a work visa, resulted in my complete loss of interest in them. A transit visa means nothing. It just means that you have permission to cross Russia, and therefore you have no redress if the employer decides to withhold your wages.*

Baltic States

As traditionally the most westernised part of the old Russian Empire, the Baltic countries of Lithuania, Latvia and Estonia were all admitted to the European Union in May 2004. Their rates of unemployment have dropped sharply over the past two years (e.g. from 16.5% to 9.7% in Latvia) and the economies are strengthening. The English language teaching industry may well experience growth over the next few years.

Rhys Sage worked at a summer camp through the International Exchange Center mentioned earlier and, despite finding the food and working conditions barely tolerable, returned to the same camp several summers later after receiving a faxed invitation from the camp director: *'I spent two months as an English teacher. Well, that's what they called it. I was merely a token English speaker and was not allowed to do any actual teaching or any real assisting. It was a typically Soviet experience where people were not expected to do anything but were paid and criticised for anything they actually did.'*

The most promising time to make contact with schools is just before the summer holidays in June. There are more opportunities for teachers in Kaunas, the second city of Lithuania, and the surrounding areas than in the capital.

Ukraine

With the (eventual) election of the new pro-Western government at Christmas 2004, the market for English may increase over the next few years. At the moment the voracious demand for teachers in the Ukraine is similar to the way it was in Central Europe just after the quiet revolutions of 1991. Teaching in the Ukraine can be a very rewarding experience, especially as one of the biggest problems encountered by Ukrainians studying English is the lack of contact with native speakers, as Sara Coleman discovered when she went to teach in Kiev though Teaching and Projects Abroad:

> *The main concern of Ukrainian English teachers and pupils alike was pronunciation. There are very few exchange programmes for students or teachers and it is almost impossible to receive a visa to visit England even if they could afford it. As I was one*

of the few English people to have visited the school I was in great demand. I never took over one class for a long time, as they wanted me to go around as many classes as possible, to give everybody the chance to hear a real native speaker!

I was fairly shocked by the country's poverty and had to endure difficult living conditions. I was staying in a small apartment in a tower block in Kiev's suburbs. Whilst my host family were very hospitable and tried to make me as comfortable as possible, the flat would regularly run out of water and conditions were very cramped. The lift regularly broke down and the fact that most of the lights on the stairwell were broken made the long climb to the eighth floor fairly daunting.

Many of the younger pupils express an adoration for native teachers which can be overwhelming, and prospective teachers should be prepared for an abundance of invitations to students' homes in order to meet their families. Although this can initially be a little unnerving, most teachers find that the generous hospitality of people so poor is one of the things that makes teaching in the Ukraine such a worthwhile experience.

Several emigré organisations in the US recruit volunteers including the Ukrainian National Association (2200 Route 10, PO Box 280, Parsippany, NJ 07054; 973-292-9800; www.unamember.com) which sponsors an English-teaching programme for qualified teachers who stay for at least four weeks between May and August.

CENTRAL EUROPE

Romania

English was barely taught before the downfall of Ceaucescu in 1989 and the collapse of communism. Demand for English has been intense ever since as the country seeks to attract foreign investment and to modernise antiquated industries in order to be ready to join the European Union in the next wave of accessions. Anyone seriously intent on teaching in Romania regardless of remuneration should be able to find an opening. Paul Converse from Oregon travelled in the country one summer a few years ago: *'I doubt that anyone could make any money teaching English but they would certainly get a free place to live and food and appreciation. When I was in Felenc, the entire village wanted me to stay and teach English.'*

There are very few private language schools in Romania at present. The association of quality language services (QUEST Romania; www.quest.ro) based at the Prosper-ASE Language Centre in Bucharest has seven founder members.

Wages on a volunteer placement scheme will be equivalent to those earned by Romanian teachers, from US$100 a month. Pupils are lively and curious about life in the West, and children are often up-to-date with the latest Western fashions and music from MTV. Photocopiers are scarce and paper is in short supply, if available at all. Teachers would be advised to take as many teaching materials as possible, e.g. magazine articles, postcards, language games, photos, pictures. Information about the teacher's hometown always goes down well.

Bulgaria

Opportunities in the private sector are still very scarce. A Bulgarian agency of long standing appoints 60-80 native speakers to teach in specialist English language secondary schools for one academic year. Details are available from Teachers for Central and Eastern Europe (21 V 5 Rakovski Blvd, Dimitrovgrad 6400; tel/fax 391-27174; tfcee@usa.net; www.tfcee.8m.com). University students, preferably with a TEFL background, are accepted from the US, UK, Canada and Australia. A summer programme is also available at Black Sea resorts for which the application deadline is June 15th.

Slovenia

Slovenia joined the European Union in 2004. As in Croatia, there are a good many private schools and many opportunities can be created by energetic native speakers both as freelance teachers for institutes or as private tutors.

The English Studies Resource Centre at the British Council in Ljubljana (www.brit-ishcouncil.si) has a list of private language schools throughout the country. The Council remains closely in touch with language schools and may be prepared to refer qualified candidates to possible employers. The average hourly wage is 2,000-2,500 tolars (about €9-€10) net.

After answering an advert in the *Guardian*, Adam Cook spent a year working at a *Gimnazija* in the town of Ajdovscina. He was hired with a BA plus an introductory one-week TEFL course:

> *The work is great and Slovenia is a fabulous country: good standard of living, good wages. My contract stipulates 20 hours a week but I work more, to save myself from boredom if nothing else. I'm paid by the Slovene Ministry of Education but am answerable to the British Council who recruited me in the first place. Slovene students are great and I have no discipline problems.*

Two private language schools which hire native speaker teachers are Berlitz Language Center (Gosposvetska 2, 1000 Ljubljana; 061-133 13 25; beatrice.slamberger@berlitz.si) and Nista Language School (6 Smarska C.5D, 6000 Koper; 0562 50400; nista@siol.net).

Albania

Information about teaching in this neglected and troubled European country wedged between Greece and the former Yugoslavia has been in short supply in recent years. A few years ago it was a rather desperate and lawless place, but its economy is now growing and the country is more stable. Private schools have begun to open, though are staffed almost exclusively by Albanian teachers. Wages are low while the cost of living is rising. A couple of years ago, Wade McReynolds from Michigan decided to take a bus from Athens to Tirana and see if he could uncover any teaching possibilities:

> *Shortly after my arrival in Tirana a Baptist missionary told me that there was, quite simply, almost no chance of my finding work in Albania. Apart from the volunteers working in his organisation, there were no native speakers teaching anywhere in the capital. Rather than take this as a sign that I should be moving on, I pounded the pavement for several days up and down the city (injuring my knee in the process), armed only with a short list of schools I'd requested in the well-appointed British Council office. Several days and many phone calls later I got an interview (my first and only) with one of the directors of the Wisdom Centre, who was quite eager to take me on as the school's speaking instructor. Equally keen to accept the offer, I made my decision before seriously considering what the position would require of me, or whether I could live on US$5 an hour in what turned out to be a surprisingly expensive city (my rent was upwards of $170). I will say that I have never met anyone so excited to talk to a native speaker as the students I taught during my short time in Albania who were some of the most gregarious people I have met in my travels. Very few of them had ever spoken English to a foreigner, and their enthusiasm lent a holiday air to the proceedings. Yet despite their chattiness I still found it hard to keep them occupied; there were virtually no teacher resource books or workspace for preparing my lessons and, as the director continued adding classes to my schedule, little time in which to plan them.*

Unable to cope with these various problems, Wade left just after signing a contract which he admits was a 'shameful course of action' after the people had gone to such lengths to find him a flat, get him working papers and change the sign over the door advertising a native speaker.

Butrint National Park in the far south of Albania has impressive archaeological remains and extensive wetlands. It accepts international volunteers to help preserve the ancient monuments, teach English and take on other roles; details from Butrint National Park, Office for Administration and Coordination to the Ministry of Culture, Youth and Sports, Blvd. 'Deshmoret e Kombit,' Tirana (visitbutrint@albmail.com).

VOLUNTARY OPPORTUNITIES

Workcamps

The main workcamp organisations in Britain (IVS, Concordia, Youth Action for Peace, and UNA Exchange) and in the US (SCI-USA, VFP and CIEE) can provide up-to-date details of projects and camps in all the countries of the region including some of the former Soviet states. In many cases the projects are a pretext for bringing together young people from East and West in an effort to dismantle prejudice on both sides. Often discussion sessions and excursions are a major part of the three or four week workcamps and some volunteers have been surprised to find that their experiences are more like a holiday, with very little work expected. The people of Eastern Europe are repeatedly praised for their generosity and hospitality.

Some preparation is recommended by all the recruiting organisations and participants are encouraged to get some workcamp experience closer to home first and to attend orientations. The registration fee is normally higher than for Western Europe, say £140, though Concordia's fee is £85. The national workcamp partners normally handle the travel and insurance arrangements once you arrive in their country. The language in which camps are conducted is usually English. Projects vary from excavating the ancient capital of Bulgaria to organising sport for gypsy children in Slovenia. Many projects, especially in the former satellite states of Russia, concern themselves with the reconstruction of ancient churches and other buildings which fell into ruin under Communism. There is also a high proportion of much-needed environmental workcamps.

Applications for workcamps should be sent through the partner organisation in the applicant's own country (see introductory chapter on Volunteering). A search of the internet will produce national representatives (e.g. www.avso.org or Eastlinks on www.volunt. net/east/usr). A number of organisations have sprung up especially in the ex-Russian Federation; to take just one example SVIT in the Ukraine (www.svit.org.ua) arranges tented camps to clean up environmental contamination among other projects (applications accepted through partner agencies only). If you are particularly interested in one country it is worth checking the websites of their main voluntary organisations at regular intervals. The Zavod Voluntariat in Slovenia, now part of Service Civil International (Resljeva 20, 1000 Ljubljana; placement@zavod-voluntariat.si) runs ecological workcamps but also works with Croatian and Bosnian refugees.

While Russia continues to experience socio-economic and organisational problems, anyone interested in volunteering there would be advised to keep abreast of developments through a local workcamp organisation. For example the annual *Workcamp Directory* from VFP in the US (online at www.vfp.org) provides detailed advice on obtaining a visa for Russia, explaining that workcamp volunteers should obtain a business visa through an invitation from the Russian camp organisers, a process which takes several months. The alternative is to buy a tourist visa (for $170+) through a visa agency. The visa must then be stamped after arrival at your accommodation. The Russian Youth Hostels Association might be able to arrange the appropriate visa for people who want to have an extended stay (www.ryh.ru) though they can assist only with tourist visas.

Environmental Volunteering

A number of voluntary organisations are involved in protecting the ecology of Lake Baikal in Siberia. For example the Baikal Federation for Ecotourism and Mountaineering co-operates with the Earth Island Institute (300 Broadway, Suite 28, San Francisco, CA 94133; 415-788-3666 ext 109; www.earthisland.org) in the creation of the Great Baikal Trail joining several national parks in Siberia by means of summer workcamps for paying volunteers; (see also www.baikal.eastsib.ru/gbt/volunt/volunt_en.html). REAP stands for the Rural Enterprise Adaptation Program which runs a 3-4 week village volunteer programme and internships for Americans in the Lake Baikal region. Placement and visa fee of $450 plus $150-$200 per month homestay; contact REAP at 1109 31st St NE, Cedar Rapids, Iowa 52402 (319-366-4230; www.reapintl.com).

Volunteers/interns are needed to stay for at least two months to work with at-risk youths on an outdoor education programme in the mountains of Kyrgyzstan; details from the Alpine Fund, 2 Erkindik 262, Bishkek 720001, Kyrgyzstan (+966-312-66-55-67; info@alpinefund.org; www.alpinefund.org).

Organisations in the countries of the region organise workcamps independently, such as the Association for Educational, Cultural and Work International Exchange Programs, 42 Yeznik Coghbatsi St, Room 22, Yerevan 375002, Armenia (+374 1-584733; aiep@arminco.com; www.aiep.am) sponsors camps to restore and maintain mediaeval buildings in Armenia and runs an internship programme. The British agency Cultural Cube (16 Acland Road, Ivybridge, Devon PL21 9UR; www.culturalcube.co.uk) mediates these placements for a sliding scale of charges; sample programme fee is £230/$370 for 20-day summer project.

The organic movement is gaining ground (so to speak) in Central Europe. One possibility for finding addresses of farms which might welcome working visitors is to obtain one of the *Green Holidays Guides* from ECEAT (European Centre for Eco-Agro Tourism, Postbox 10899, 1001 EW Amsterdam, Netherlands; www.eceat.nl) who publish their Poland guide in English for €10/£5; the Czech one is in Dutch only.

A relatively new WWOOF branch has been set up in Slovenia (c/o Polona Gostan, Pajerjeva 10, 4208 Sencur, Slovenia; polona.gostan@s5.net; www.svetduhovnosti.org/wwoofing/all.htm). The joining fee is €10 in cash.

Rob Abblett had a short but very enjoyable stay in Hungary after looking up addresses of organic farms and communities:

I had a great ten days living and working in a small self-sufficient village in Felsonyék (Béke u. 15, 7099 Felsonyék; 74-478 345). The only problem I found with Hungary was that hardly anyone speaks English. The organic farm experience was great. I had a house all to myself and I enjoyed the work, going to the market and being treated so well by the family and my workmates. The whole village was virtually self-sufficient, vegetable patches, ducks, geese, chickens, rabbits, vines. How I wish my mother had taught me Hungarian. I moved on to an eco-village at Gyürüfü where I spent five hard days helping to construct a rammed earth house; shovelling earth into a wooden framework in 35°C was a somewhat sweaty affair. It is mainly professional-type folk wanting to live here, and many spoke English. Great if you want to get hands-on experience of alternative building, though I preferred the traditional village lifestyle.

The Ormánság Foundation (Arany János u. 4, H-7967 Drávafok; tel/fax 073-352333), cannot offer paid employment at its farm dedicated to sustainable development located 60km southwest of Pécs. But it does offer accommodation and some voluntary work gardening, tending an orchard, etc. to suitable candidates for a minimum of a week and preferably two. It can also put volunteers in touch with neighbouring sustainable farms looking for helpers.

The working holiday programme of the British Trust for Conservation Volunteers includes Hungary, Poland, Slovakia, Bulgaria, Albania, Romania and all three Baltic countries; tasks include protecting rare bird reserves in Bulgaria and building hiking trails in Lithuania.

Volunteers who are willing to pay €600-€700 for 11-12 days spent assisting researchers to monitor dolphin behaviour and habitats along the coast of Croatia should contact the Adriatic Dolphin Project (adp@blue-world.org; http://adp.hpm.hr). The Eco-Centre Caput on the Croatian island of Cres (Insulae-Beli: Beli 4, 51559 Beli, Cres; +385-51 840 525; caput.insulae@ri.htnet.hr; www.caput-insulae.com) welcomes conservation volunteers to assist in the conservation of the Eurasian griffon vulture, repairing dry stone walls, saving small ponds, picking olives and helping local shepherds. Volunteers pay €149 for one week in summer or €271 for 2 weeks; winter fees are much less, €98/€122.

The region of South Eastern Europe includes Croatia, Macedonia, Serbia and Bosnia Herzogovina. For volunteering opportunities in these countries, look at www.seeyouth. info/eng/engine.php.

The Institute of Archaeology of Almaty recruits international volunteers for archaeological fieldwork. Details are available from the Department of International Scientific Projects, Tole Bi 21, Room 31, 480100 Almaty, Kazakhstan (07-3272 914386; ispkz@nursat.kz). The programme lasts 15-30 days between May and October and costs $300 per week.

The Center for the Study of Eurasian Nomads in California carries out fieldwork in Southern Russia and Mongolia which paying volunteers may join. A contribution of $1,100 is requested to join the three-week Chastiy Kurgany Excavation; details from CSEN, 2158 Palomar Ave, Ventura, CA 93001 (www.csen.org).

Social Projects

Kitezh Children's Community for orphans in Kaluga 300km south of Moscow has close links with the Ecologia Trust in Scotland (The Park, Forres, Moray IV36 3TZ; 01309 690995; www.ecologia.org.uk). The Trust specifically recruits students in their gap year to spend between one and three months at Kitezh and provides extensive preparatory information, including profiles of the individual residents. The joining fee is £540 for one month, £710 for two months, including visa support but not airfares to Moscow. Knowledge of Russian or TEFL is preferred.

> **Many recent volunteers have found Kitezh a friendly, welcoming and relaxing place to spend some time, among them Sarah Moy:**
> *Kitezh life is so different from the rest of the world that it took a while to know where you could go, how to get involved in work/play with the children, etc. I felt very much a part of the community and enjoyed sharing my talents (but would have liked to have taught more English). Apart from the obvious benefits of improving Russian and learning more about Russian culture and people, I gained much from the slower pace of life. I was very impressed by the idea of people who have made a career out of genuinely caring and giving. I learnt more about a rural way of life and appreciated being reminded how many luxuries we have here. Altogether it was a fantastic experience.*

Of the many charities that were formed to help the children of Romania, the Nightingales Children's Project operates a full-time volunteer programme. Volunteers spend from one to three months working at an orphanage in Cernavoda, 80km from the Black Sea resort of Constanta. Volunteers work with the children, some of whom are disabled and have special needs, some with the HIV virus. Accommodation is shared with eight volunteers in a flat; volunteers contribute £2.50 a day to cover their rent and food. For further information contact the director on info@nightingaleschildrensproject.co.uk (www.nightingaleschildrensproject.co.uk).

British-Romanian Connections, PO Box 86, Birkenhead, Merseyside CH41 8FU (tel/fax 0151-512 3355; brc@pascu-tulbure.freeserve.co.uk) operates summer language camps in Romania as well as English clubs year round in Piatra-Neamt. Native speakers are welcome at camps but language clubs are looking for teachers with a TEFL qualification (minimum stay three months).

Voluntary organisations working with displaced persons inside the former Yugoslavia sometimes take on foreign volunteers. One of the most important is Balkan Sunflowers which works for social reconstruction in the Balkans and is always looking for volunteers; BSF, Mother Teresa Society Building, Agim Ramadani Street, Prishtina, Kosovo (+381-38

245 785; www.balkansunflowers.org). The Global Children's Organization in the US (PO Box 67583, Los Angeles, CA 90067; 310-581-2234; www.globalchild.org) sends volunteer camp counsellors to work with Croatian children for two weeks in July on the Adriatic island of Badija. The application fee is $35 plus participation fee is $1,500.

OTHER OPPORTUNITIES

Many people based in the cities of Eastern Europe over the past decade have taken advantage of the new entrepreneurial spirit by engaging in conventional employment. Companies and recruitment agencies advertise in the English language papers and on the internet for computer programmers, administrators, etc.

The westernising democracies of Eastern Europe are all targeting tourism as a means of aiding their economies and are encouraging foreign tour operators to develop resorts, etc. that in time may have large staff requirements. Ski tour operators like Balkan Holidays (Sofia House, 19 Conduit St, London W1S 2BH; www.balkanholidays.co.uk) recruit some children's reps outside the countries, but mostly try to hire locals.

Young people in east European capitals are so eager to embrace western culture that American-style restaurants and Irish pubs have sprung up everywhere, some of which hire English speakers, as attested by Bruce Collier whose British wife Sharon was hired by a restaurant near Red Square some years ago. Such jobs will be heard about by word-of-mouth or possibly advertised in the English-language press. Turn-over of foreign students is high so if you are staying for a while your chances are reasonable. The trendy area of Moscow is on New Arbat.

If you are looking for some casual work, ask discreetly in hostels, around the universities or among expatriates teaching English. Your services as anything from a disc jockey to a freelance business consultant may be in demand. English-language papers may carry relevant adverts. For example the classified section of the *The Prague Post* (Stepanska 20, 110 00 Prague 1; 02-9633 4411/4400) can be read online at www.praguepost.com/classifieds. An advert of 25 words or less can be placed quite cheaply.

Marta Eleniak started as a volunteer in Warsaw teaching English in a primary school and within a year listed her various paid activities as assistant to the Vice-President of a consulting firm, translator and teacher at a real estate agency, UK representative of a Polish musician and exporter of paragliders. She concludes that 'England seems so sleepy in comparison'. Obviously there are many niches which keen foreigners willing to stay for a while can fill.

Work Your Way Worldwide

Australia
New Zealand
The USA
Canada
Latin America

Caribbean
Africa
Israel
Asia
Middle East

Australia

In some ways this chapter is superfluous. Australia has developed a magnificent industry to cater specifically for backpackers and working holidaymakers. Most hostels both in the cities and the countryside are well informed about local jobs available to travellers; some act as informal employment agencies. Bus companies have routes that shuttle between fruit-picking regions for the benefit of working travellers. Outback properties offer training in the skills necessary to work on a station and then double as a placement agency. Recruitment agencies and employers with seasonal requirements target the backpacking community by advertising in the places they frequent. Free newspapers, magazines and websites specifically address an audience of backpackers, carrying employment advertisements. Employers even co-operate with regional tourist offices to find seasonal staff, as in the South Australian fruit-growing region of the Riverina. So there is no shortage of information and assistance available for the newly arrived working holidaymaker.

A report published in Canberra recently claimed that working holidaymakers annually add £450 million to the Australian economy and create 8,000 jobs. The number of working holiday visas granted has been rising steadily from 33,000 in 1995 and 65,000 in 1999 to 88,750 in 2004, demonstrating the strength of the Australian economy. On the negative side, there is a lobby in Australia that argues that the working holiday scheme deprives Australian nationals of jobs. However with a rate of unemployment (currently 5.3%) continuing to fall, this lobby is not very powerful. The vast majority of unemployed Australians do not want to pick fruit, collect for charity, work on a sheep station, or do any of the other kinds of work visitors to Australia do. This is the conclusion to which a longstanding contributor to *Work Your Way Around the World*, Armin Birrer, came when he worked as recruiting officer at a vineyard in northern Victoria:

> *Local unemployment was high at that time, and yet I had severe problems getting pickers. Most of the unemployed didn't want to pick grapes because it is too hard for them. Plus lots of them don't think it's worthwhile to go off the dole for three to four weeks and then wait to go back on again. I came to the conclusion in Mildura that I can always find some work even if unemployment rises to 20%, if I go to where the work is. People who can work hard and don't make trouble are always in demand.*

Those same people are probably the ones who arrive with just a few pounds after having travelled across Asia or the States and earn enough in a few months to fund further months of travel. This is not too difficult in a country where unskilled workers are generally paid $10-$13 an hour, sometimes cash-in-hand, and people with keyboard skills (for example) can earn $20 an hour in the big cities. Provided you arrive with the right visa, some references (most Australian employers are sticklers for references and will check them) and some decent clothes, you should find a way to earn a crust.

But do not expect the job hunt to be a doddle. Partly because of the overwhelming numbers of young foreigners on working holiday visas, it is an employer's rather than a job-seeker's market and the job hunt can be a struggle. Working holidaymakers often find themselves at the bottom of the heap in the job market, principally because they are limited to jobs of less than three months so that no serious jobs are available to them. Because there is such a glut of job-seeking backpackers, employers can get away with treating them badly. So the note of optimism struck in this chapter needs to be tempered with some realism. An article appeared in *Rough News* in the autumn of 2004 entitled 'Working Holiday Hell' written by a disgruntled traveller, though the following issue carried some spirited rebuttals (www.roughguides.com; click on Spotlight Archive).

Roger Blake who has spent two separate spells as a working holidaymaker in Australia is someone who is willing to turn his hand to anything and has successfully 'blagged' (talked) his way into all manner of jobs around the world. Yet he finds Australia an uphill struggle, certainly compared to New Zealand. Although he managed to survive on his occasional earnings (having arrived with next to nothing), he warns to expect a 'rough ride' in the Australia of 2004/5: *'I have met SO many travellers who are leaving Australia after just 3 months or less of their WHV, thoroughly disgusted with the attitude of employers towards backpackers and the associated struggles of finding an (often lousy) job in the first place. .... But it is not all doom and gloom and I've had fun between troublesome times.'*

First-time visitors to Australia are often surprised by the degree to which that far-off continent is an imitation of Britain. Despite their reputation as 'pommy-bashers', most Australians take for granted a strong link with Britain, and this may be one reason why British travellers are so often welcomed as prospective employees. Being Scottish is even better, according to Melanie Grey from Edinburgh, especially in tele-sales since 'you always end up speaking to someone who has a granny in Dundee'.

The kinds of job you are likely to get in the rural areas are of a very different nature from city jobs. To discover Australia's more exotic features, you will have to penetrate into the countryside. While some experienced travellers declare that the big cities are the only places you can work on a steady basis at reasonably good wages, others advise heading out of Sydney as soon as you've seen the harbour. Chris Miksovsky from Connecticut found computer work in both Sydney and Melbourne offices with ease. However after a few months he realised that the reason he had left home was to get away from spending his days in an office, so he headed north to look for station work. Work in the country or the outback often comes with accommodation whereas city rents can eat into your wages, as can the social life.

Working Holiday Visas

Australia has reciprocal working holiday arrangements with Britain, Ireland, Canada, Netherlands, Germany, Japan, Korea, SAR of Hong Kong, Taiwan, Sweden, Denmark, Finland, Norway, Cyprus, Malta, France, Belgium, Italy and most recently Estonia. Americans aged 18-30 are eligible for a four-month working stay in Australia (see below).

The visa is for people intending to use any money they earn in Australia to supplement their holiday funds. Working full-time for more than three months for the same employer is not permitted, though you are now allowed to engage in up to three months of studies/ training. You are eligible for a working holiday visa only once. Applicants must be between the ages of 18 and 30 and without children.

The Working Holiday visa is valid for 12 months after entry, which must be within 12 months of issue. The visa is not extendable or renewable either in Australia or at home. You can leave and re-enter Australia during that 12 months but this does not alter the maximum duration of the visa.

It is now possible to apply for an electronic working holiday visa as described below. The High Commission in London is located in Australia House, Strand, London WC2B 4LA (020-7379 4334; www.australia.org.uk) and in the north the Australian Consulate is located at Chatsworth House, Lever St, Manchester M1 2DL. It is not possible to apply in person, so you must get organised well in advance if you are going to apply in the conventional way, preferably at least eight to ten weeks before you plan to travel. British people (and Irish, Dutch and Canadians) can also apply at Australian Consulates outside the UK.

Assuming you are using the traditional paper method, the first step is to get the working holiday information sheet and form 1150 Application for a Working Holiday Makers (WHM) visa from a specialist travel agent or from a visa agent like Visa Australia in Cheshire (01270 626626) or Consyl Publishing (3 Buckhurst Road, Bexhill-on-Sea, East Sussex TN40 1QF; 01424 223111/premium line 0906 863 3464) enclosing an A4 stamped addressed envelope (66p stamp). The non-refundable processing fee in the UK is currently £70; this can be checked online with the Australian Immigration website (www.immi. gov.au) or by ringing the Australian Immigration and Citizenship Information line 09065 508 900 (charged at £1 per minute).

A top tip when filling out the application form is to answer the question: What type of employment do you intend to seek in Australia? with the reply 'fruit harvest/seasonal work'. This is primarily what the government wants WHM's to do while in Australia and therefore they are more likely to approve a visa application on this basis. Once you have the visa you are free to seek any job and do any kind of work (within the terms of the visa).

The second step is to get as much money in the bank as possible. Each application is assessed on its own merits, but the most important requirement is a healthy bank balance. You must have enough money for your return fare, although it is not essential to have a return ticket at the time of entry. You must show evidence of having saved a minimum of A$5,000/£2,000. If your bank statements do not show steady saving, you may have to submit documents showing where the money came from (e.g. sale of a car, gift from a relative).

Now that ticketless flights are well established, paperless visas are now a possibility and are being heavily marketed by the visa agencies who don't like to handle passports. For an e-WHM visa there is no need to provide proof of funds nor do you send in your passport. Your passport isn't physically inspected until you arrive in Australia when you must take it along to an office of the Department of Immigration. Applying online via www. immi.gov.au is normally straightforward and hassle-free and should result in an emailed confirmation well inside the promised 48 hours which is sufficient to get you into the country. To obtain the visa label in your passport, you must visit a DIMIA office, preferably not the busy downtown Sydney or Melbourne offices. Elsewhere it should be easier as Roger Blake found in Brisbane where he was 'in and out of the office within half an hour' with no request to show sufficient funds and no fee charged. In either case the fee for the WH visa is A$170 (£70). Specialist agents like Visas Australia (www.visas-australia.com) or Travellers Contact Point will add a premium of about £15. Either way you will have the authorisation within a couple of days.

Anyone intending to work in catering and hospitality, health care, education or the pharmaceutical industry must provide a recent medical report assuring the authorities that they are fit enough to travel to Australia and back again at the end of the proposed stay. (Some GPs charge for this service.)

Some people worry that if their application for a working holiday visa is turned down for some reason, they won't be granted a tourist visa. But the High Commission maintains that this is an unfounded anxiety. If you overstay your visa and they notice on the way out, you will be automatically barred from returning to Australia for a minimum of three years. People found working without the necessary visa will be placed on the Movement Alert List (whose acronym means 'bad' in French) which may count against them in future visa applications.

The Department of Immigration & Multicultural & Indigenous Affairs is a valuable

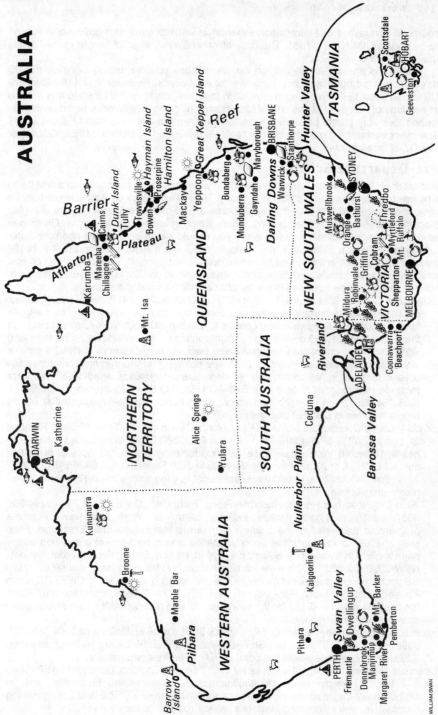

AUSTRALIA

TASMANIA
Scottsdale
HOBART
Geeveston

Barrier
Reef

Hayman Island
Dunk Island
Great Keppel Island
Hamilton Island

QUEENSLAND

Atherton
Plateau

Karumba
Mareeba
Chillagoe
Cairns
Tully
Townsville
Bowen
Proserpine
Mackay
Yeppoon
Bundaberg
Maryborough
Gayndah
Munduberra

Mt. Isa

BRISBANE
Warwick
Stanthorpe
Darling Downs

Hunter Valley

NEW SOUTH WALES

Muswellbrook
SYDNEY
Orange
Bathurst
Thredbo
Cobram
Griffith
Myrtleford
Robinvale
Mt. Buffalo
Mildura
Shepparton
MELBOURNE

VICTORIA

Coonawarra
Beachport

ADELAIDE

Riverland

SOUTH AUSTRALIA

Ceduna

Barossa Valley

NORTHERN TERRITORY

Alice Springs

Yulara

DARWIN
Katherine

Kununurra

WESTERN AUSTRALIA

Nullarbor Plain

Broome

Marble Bar

Pilbara

Barrow
Island

Kalgoorlie

Pithara

PERTH
Fremantle
Swan Valley
Dwellingup
Donnybrook
Manjimup
Mt. Barker
Pemberton
Margaret River

WILLIAM SWAN

source of all relevant visa information either on its website www.immi.gov.au or in Australia by ringing DIMIA on 131881. The busy office in Sydney is at 26 Lee St in the Central Business District.

Americans are not yet part of the working holiday scheme, mainly because the US has implemented no reciprocal programme for Australians. However Visa 416 allows any US citizen aged 18-30 (residing in the US) to take any jobs they find for up to four months at any time of the year. At the end of four months of doing casual work participants may extend their stay purely as tourists for a further three months (at a cost of about $200). The major exchange organisations can facilitate this including BUNAC, CIEE, CCUSA or VisitOZ all listed below.

Pre-Departure Schemes

A number of UK and North American travel and youth exchange agencies can assist those who want some back-up on a working holiday. They offer various packages which may be of special interest to first-time travellers. Some are all-inclusive (especially the gap year placement organisations listed below); others simply give back-up on arrival. Given how easy it is to orient yourself and find work, you should weigh up the pros and cons carefully before paying a substantial fee. Typically, the fee will include airport pick-up, hostel accommodation for the first few nights and a post-arrival orientation which advises on how to obtain a tax-file card, suggestions of employers and so on. Some even guarantee a job. Various perks may be thrown in like a telephone calling card and free maps.

BUNAC, 16 Bowling Green Lane, London EC1R 0BD (020-7251 3472; downunder@bunac. org.uk) features Australia as one of its destination countries. Anyone who is eligible for the working holiday visa may choose to join the BUNAC Work Australia package that costs from £1,750 depending on flight routings. This includes a round-the-world flight, WH visa, orientation on arrival and back-up services from BUNAC's partner International Exchange Programs (IEP, see below). The programme sometimes fills up and reopens in March for summer departures. Americans aged 18-30 can work for up to four months; details from BUNAC USA, PO Box 430 Southbury, CT 06488 (203-264-0901; enquiries@bunacusa.org; www.bunac.org/usa/workaustralia) whose programme fee is US$550 plus insurance.

CCUSA, Camp Counsellors USA, 1st Floor North, Devon House, 171/177 Great Portland St, London W1W 5PQ (020-7637 0779/ fax 020-7580 6209; www.ccusaweusa.co.uk) has a 12-month Work Experience Downunder programme. US applicants should contact CCUSA at 2330 Marinship Way, Suite 250, Sausalito, CA 94965 (1-800-449-3872; downunder@ccusa.com; www.ccusa.com). Programme fee is $365 for the four-month programme.

IST Plus Ltd, Rosedale House, Rosedale Road, Richmond, Surrey TW9 2SZ (020-8939 9057; info@istplus.com; www.istplus.com) offers the Work and Travel Australia programme on behalf of the Council on International Educational Exchange. Fees start at £320 to include initial accommodation and a post-arrival orientation at the partner office in Sydney: AIFS Australia Pty Ltd, 91 York Street, Ground Floor, Sydney, NSW 2000 (02-8235 7000; www.workinaustralia.net) but not visa or insurance costs. US young people may apply for the four-month working visa (416) to CIEE, 7 Custom House Street, 3rd Floor, Portland, ME 04101 (1-800-407-8839; www.ciee.org). For a fee of US$425 (plus A$170 for the visa), participants receive work documentation and access to job-finding assistance.

International Exchange Programs (IEP), Level 3, 362 Latrobe St, Melbourne 3000 (03-9329 3866) or Level 3, 333 George St, Sydney 2000 (02-9299 0400). National enquiries 1300 300912; www.iep-australia.com. BUNAC's partner organisation.

Overseas Working Holidays (OWH), Level 1, 51 Fife Rd, Kingston, Surrey KT1 1SF (0845 344 0366; www.overseasworkingholidays.co.uk). Guaranteed hospitality work in Melbourne at major sporting events such as Australian Grand Prix and Spring Racing Carnival, as well as ongoing corporate work. Programme fees from £189.

VisitOZ Scheme, Springbrook Farm, MS188, Goomeri, 4601 Queensland (fax 07-4168

6106; www.visitoz.org) sends participants with the working holiday visa to a station on the Queensland/NSW border for a 4-day crash course in outback working techniques (or in hospitality industry skills if preferred) and then guarantees paid employment on outback properties as tractor drivers, stock and horse workers, hospitality assistants on cattle and sheep stations and mothers' helps. The cost is A$1,680. The UK contact can be reached on 07966 528664; jules@visitoz.org. A handful of places are available to people who seek to book after arrival in Australia.

Stablemate Staff Agency UK – see description below in section on Rural Australia.

Changing Worlds, Hodore Farm, Hartfield, East Sussex TN7 4AR (01892 770000; www. changingworlds.co.uk). Paid placements in Queensland hotels. Placements last 3 or 6 months starting September, March and July. Fee £1,895 for hotel and farm work, £2,395 for zoos. Farm and zoo work provides accommodation but no wage. The hotel jobs are paid.

Gap Activity Projects (GAP) Ltd, 44 Queen's Road, Reading, Berks. RG1 4BB (0118-959 4914/fax 0118-957 6634; Volunteer@gap.org.uk/ www.gap.org.uk). 5-12 month placements in schools throughout Australia and 5-month conservation placements through the Conservation Volunteers Australia (described later). Placement fee £1,650 or £1,500 plus travel and insurance.

Gap Challenge, Black Arrow House, 2 Chandos Road, London NW10 6NF (020-8728 7205; welcome@world-challenge.co.uk; www.world-challenge.co.uk). Arranges three-month jobs in youth recreation programmes, on cattle stations, horse ranches or trail ride farms in New South Wales and Victoria departing September and January.

i-to-i International Projects, Woodside House, 261 Low Lane, Horsforth, Leeds LS18 5NY (www.i-to-i.com) can fix up conservation packages with Conservation Volunteers Australia lasting 4-24 weeks for a fee starting at £795 excluding travel.

Involvement Volunteers Association Inc, PO Box 218, Port Melbourne, VIC 3207 (03-9646 9392; ivworldwide@volunteering.org.au) runs a programme by which volunteers are placed within a network of voluntary projects around Australia (and worldwide) for up to a year. Past placements have included assisting zoology research in Queensland, working at a zoo and reptile park in South Australia, and social service work with children, elderly and disabled people. To register with IVI, a fee of A$275 must be paid.

SWAP (Student Work Abroad Program), 45 Charles St. E., Suite 100, Toronto, Ontario M4Y 1S2, Canada (416-996-2887, www.swap.ca). Working holiday programme administered by the Canadian Federation of Students. Participants must be Canadians aged 18-30 but need not be students.

Increasingly, Australian recruitment agencies are actively looking for people in the UK with at least a year's relevant experience and office skills to fill their clients' temporary vacancies in Australia and are geared up to advise people with working holiday visas. For example, Options Consulting in Sydney (02-9221 7733) co-operates with Victoria Wall Associates in London (www.vwa.com/workinaus.htm). The Robert Walters agency (55 Strand, London WC2N 5WR; 020-7379 3333; www.robertwalters.com) has a dedicated international team located in its offices in London, Dublin and Johannesburg who can arrange interviews for candidates at their city of arrival. Similarly Joslin Rowe in London (overseas@joslinrowe.com; www.working-worldwide.com) co-operates with several specialist agencies in Australia in the financial sector, as does Geoffrey Nathan International (3rd Floor, Hill House, Highgate Hill, London N19 5NA) which co-operates with AA Appointments in Brisbane (www.aaappointments.com).

Backpacker Agencies

Any travel agency that specialises in the backpacker market will almost certainly promote their ability to assist clients on working holidays, since such a high proportion of that market wants to work. There are a maze of alliances between travel and recruitment agencies, hostel groups and working holiday providers though most of them seem to be offering similar services. Try to shop around if you have the stamina.

Travellers Contact Point (2-6 Inverness Terrace, Bayswater, London W2 3HX; 020-7243 7887; www.travellers.com.au) operates a free job search centre in connection with recruitment agencies in eight offices around Australia and New Zealand. Other services include flat-share, bank accounts and mobile phones. Membership for £25 includes 12 months mail forwarding, e-mail and word processing access. They also sell an arrival package for £75 which includes your first two nights in Sydney, airport pick-up, membership, plus a working holiday information kit among other things. In Sydney the TCP office is at Level 7, Dymocks Building, 428 George St, Sydney 2000 (02-9221 8744/fax 9221 3746).

The Backpacker's Resource Centre will help people with the working holiday visa to set up work as well as providing a range of other back-up services for a fee of A$330. Send for an information pack from Hotel Bakpak Group (167 Franklin St, Melbourne 3000; 03-9329 7525; info@bakpakgroup.com).

Worldwide Workers (www.worldwideworkers.com) is a dedicated recruitment service for travellers and backpackers coming to Australia and New Zealand, located at 234 Sussex Street in Sydney's Central Business District (02-8268 6001). They specialise in placing working holiday visa holders in jobs lasting anything from one shift up to three months. Jobs are mainly in hospitality, labour/factory/warehouse, call centre and white collar. In 2004, they set up a 'JobText' service whereby registered members are sent text messages of suitable jobs as soon as they come in.

A Perth-based company Workstay WA (www.workstay.com.au) has marketed itself aggressively as a source of work for backpackers. Its office is on the 9th Floor of the Carillon City Arcade Tower opposite Myers Department Store in the Murray Street Mall in downtown Perth (workstayperth@westnet.com.au). As well as fruitpicking jobs in Western Australia via their affiliated Workstay hostels, this company also places barmaids in country pubs.

The international hostel group Nomads (www.nomadsworld.com) sells a Travel Guide & Adventure Card for £16 (A$39) through specialist travel agents abroad and in Australia. Nomads operate a number of working hostels (for example in Bundaberg) and sell a Job Package to new arrivals for A$199 (Sydney and Adelaide) or A$159 (Melbourne). They also maintain a database of job vacancies updated weekly, accessible by members via telephone.

Many working holidaymakers entertain the possibility of staying on. The regulations have been loosened so that people with a skill in short supply (often in the field of information technology) and an employer who wants to employ them for longer than the three months allowed under the working holiday visa can apply for a four year business visa while still in the country. Immigration law firms like Parish Patience in Sydney (02-9286 8700) specialise in assisting clients with visa applications; its up-to-date website on www.parishpatience.com.au is worth checking for recent changes to the legislation.

Obtaining a resident's visa (for permanent migration) is, predictably, much more difficult, though not impossible if you have a skill in short supply (like nursing or teaching and are prepared to work in a rural area) and/or a close relative in Australia. Note that working on a more 'serious' visa would have definite tax advantages too (described below). Form 1126 is the initial migration form, available online at www.immi.gov.au or from Consyl Publishing mentioned above which includes notes on how to obtain one or more migration application packs (for which fees will be charged). Rhona Stannage was very surprised to learn that three states in Australia recognise a Scottish law degree and she considered the seven-month wait and the fee of several hundred pounds for a resident's visa worthwhile, although she and her husband were really interested only in a working holiday.

Unofficial Work

Those who don't qualify for a working visa should not despair, though escalating concern at all levels of Australian society and government about illegal immigration means that new measures to prevent visa-less workers are making it harder. Rarely now does a 'no worries' attitude prevail especially since tax file numbers are compulsory (see below). Many areas, from the most remote farms to George Street in downtown Sydney, have been subject to immigration raids. The Department of Immigration takes the restrictions very seriously. There is now a helpline for employers to ring to check workers' visa status and anyone who is suspicious is urged to inform on ('dob in' in Australian parlance) suspected illegal workers via a special telephone number or internet feedback site. Discretion is therefore essential. Employers who at one time did not ask to see the stamp in your passport are more likely to do so these days to avoid paying huge fines if caught - up to $66,000 and two years in prison for persistent offenders. One suggestion made in 2004 by the leader of the opposition was to introduce compulsory photo ID for all legal foreign workers to root out the illegals.

New schemes are afoot to supply severe labour shortages especially in agricultural harvests with Asian workers on short-term visas. For example mango growers in the Northern Territory were lobbying in late 2004 for teams of East Timorese workers to be brought in as guest workers. At the beginning of 2005, the Australian press was reporting that Chinese labour could soon be picking fruit under a new labour treaty. Naturally these proposed solutions were being resisted by the powerful Australian Workers' Union but, if implemented, could in the long run reduce the number of jobs available to backpackers and solve the crisis described by one of the hostel staff in the great fruit growing area of Mildura: *'It's great for someone to sit in their office and make these decisions, but we have such a shortage of workers quite often during the year, that I do not believe they could police it. There is no way our harvest (January to April) could operate without taking people who do not have work visas.'*

The same situation pertains in Queensland where labour shortages cost the fruit and vegetable industry tens of millions of dollars every year i.e. up to a tenth of the total value of production, according to a spokesman for Growcom (formerly the Queensland Fruit & Vegetable Growers Association; www.growcom.com.au) as reported in October 2004.

High-profile summer raids in Victoria and Queensland can uncover scores of workers in breach of their visa conditions. The usual procedure is to extract a bond of $2,000 to $5,000 from people with expired visas, and give a week to leave the country.

Jane Harris thinks it should be stressed that anyone working without a visa alongside others in a similar position should be very careful, and suspicious of anyone nosing around. She describes what happened at the campsite she was staying on in Stanthorpe Queensland:

I got back to our campsite to discover that Immigration had raided farms throughout the area. Apparently, a local man had been running an illegal bus service to all the local farms from the three campsites in town. Someone from Immigration started checking the visas of everyone on the bus, and found seven people with tourist visas. They were told to leave the country within two weeks. That evening, four car loads of Immigration officials turned up at the campsite. They had lists of local farm employees and were matching these with people's passports, so it seems best to work under a false name (especially as the local pubs will cash salary cheques without seeing any ID). Meanwhile we stayed inside our campervan and hid all signs we'd been working (e.g. gloves, boots, pay slips). It seems that they do not have to see you physically working but can act on circumstantial evidence.

Another colourful tale of a raid on a strawberry farm in Caboolture north of Brisbane emerged in 2004:

On my second day there the farm was raided by officials from both DIMIA and the ATO (tax office). It was like a scene from a movie as they came out of nowhere in big Holden Commodores with tinted windows and blocked in all of the workers' vehicles so there was no way out. They flashed their silver warrant cards in leather cases and one by one were checking all of our identities/passports via two way radio to ensure that we had the work rights. Fortunately for the farmer (as he had never asked anyone) we all had work visas. Meanwhile the ATO were going through all of the tax declarations meticulously and gave an informal warning to a few that they had made a false claim on their form (resident for tax purposes). Once they had gone we all gave a sigh of relief. A German guy I worked with says the farm he worked on in Mackay was raided 5 times in 3 months and people were deported. DIMIA take it all very seriously (unlike their NZ counterparts).

Without a working holiday visa you might decide to steer clear of farms where you are relatively exposed, and find work inside the relatively safe and anonymous walls of the urban jungle or on smaller family farms where the immigration people are unlikely to bother you.

One old hand American who has worked his way around Australia recommends changing one letter in your last name every place you go which is guaranteed to confuse the bureaucracy. Real ID can be used to cash cheques (if that is necessary) and a clerical error blamed if the bank clerk notices the discrepancy.

Tax

All people in employment in Australia must either provide their employer with a 9-digit tax file number or be taxed at a punitive 49% for non-residents. Therefore it is greatly to your advantage to obtain one. We have heard of several cases of people being deported for inventing tax file numbers (but giving their real names). You may come across people selling on the tax file numbers of people who have left the country.

Foreigners must apply at a tax office, for example at 100 Market St in Sydney, where queues are long (national telephone number 132861; www.ato.gov.au). Processing normally takes between four and six weeks. You must submit a passport with appropriate visa plus one of a number of documents such as an original or certified copy of your birth certificate, Australian driving licence, bank statement at an Australian address, etc.

The ultimate tax liability for non-residents of Australia is 29% of all earnings (assuming you earn less than $21,600 in the tax year) whereas residents are taxed at 17% of earnings. Non-residents are not eligible for the tax-free threshold of $6,000 nor for concessional rebates (for example residents who work in a 'remote zone' and those who work in seasonal harvests pay only 13% tax). For many years, people with Working Holiday visas were able to claim to be 'resident' – and therefore eligible for the much lower rate of tax – on the grounds that temporary visits can turn into longer-term ones. However it now seems clear that this will no longer wash with the Australian Tax Office and all working holidaymakers are now categorised Non-Resident. The tax implications are huge: the Seasonal Work Guide on the Wayward Bus Company website (www.waywardbus.com. au/seaswork.html) calculates that out of $10,000 of earnings, tax of $2,900 will be lost as opposed to $700 under the old dispensation, so that travellers have an estimated 40%-45% of disposable savings at the end of four or five months of working.

If you are lucky enough to have obtained a Resident's Visa on the basis of your education and skills, you can legitimately claim the tax status of a resident. In this case, you should obtain a Group Certificate (statement of earnings and tax deducted, equivalent to a P45) after you leave each job, arranging to have it posted on to you if necessary. If you have earned less than your tax-free threshold of $6,000 during the tax year (starting July 1st), you could be eligible for a refund. All earners are supposed to submit a tax return by October 31st.

A small consolation is that 70% of the compulsory deduction made for superannuation (retirement) can be reclaimed.

Anyone who can show that they will be resident in a certain place for more than three months is eligible for a Medicare card which allows you refunds on doctors' fees and prescriptions.

THE JOB HUNT

Although everybody finds some kind of job in the end, it isn't always easy. You are likely to encounter a surprising degree of competition from others on working holidays, many of whom are chasing the same kinds of job. For example a company which operates tours of Sydney Harbour received 50 replies to an advertisement for waiting staff and a receptionist, 42 of which were from Poms. The glut of travelling workers is especially bad in Sydney, Perth and in Queensland resorts before Christmas. In addition to asking potential employers directly (which is the method used by at least a third of successful job-seekers in Australia), the main ways of finding work are via the internet, newspaper advertisements, notice boards (especially at travellers' hostels) and private employment agencies. Note that the government's Employment National jobcentres closed last year to everyone except the long-term unemployed (www.workplace.gov.au).

Anyone intending to work in Australia should have an up-to-date and properly thought out CV. With few exceptions (like fruit picking) prospective employers will ask to see your résumé before they'll so much as entertain your application and often they'll also ask for references from an Australian too. A further frustration is the rampant bureaucracy and government insistence on paper qualifications which means that employees must have specific certificates to work in certain industries, for example the RSA (Responsible Service of Alcohol) and/or RCG (Responsible Conduct of Gambling) for jobs in hospitality and the Occupational Health & Safety (OHS) green or blue card for the building and construction industry. Most training courses last one day and cost $75-$125. A certificate issued in one state is often not recognised in another; one never knows whether an employer will strictly enforce the regulations or be willing to flout them (and risk a fine).

The door-to-door job hunt will require huge reserves of stamina and patience, as Roger Blake discovered:

Another frustrating aspect of the job hunt downunder is the oh-so-frequent scenario where I have walked into a bar, restaurant or where ever (CV/resumé in hand) to express an interest in the job seen advertised in their window. The response has varied from: 'Sorry, the job has been taken, we just haven't taken the sign down' (yet two weeks later the sign is still up in their window) to 'Sorry, we're looking for a female' to 'We want a local, sorry, mate'. Obviously they're not allowed to put that on their advertisements.

Private Employment Agencies

As in Britain, private employment agencies are very widespread and are a good potential source of jobs for travellers, especially those with hospitality experience or office skills, computer, data processing or financial experience. In addition to the specialist backpacker agencies mentioned earlier, a surprising number of mainstream temp agencies positively encourage UK people on working holidays, often by circulating their details to hostel managers. This is more common in Sydney and Melbourne than in Perth where most recruitment agencies are just not interested in working holidaymakers. Competition will be most acute at those agencies that court the backpacking market so some people purposely avoid those. The offered wages are good too: from $12 an hour for clerical work, $14 for secretarial and $15 for computer work.

An ability to type 50 words per minute is a great advantage and, at least in Stephen Psallidas's experience, virtually essential: *'I went round the temping offices, but alas. Despite my extensive experience with computers, well-prepared CV, shirt and tie, etc. I had no luck. All of them required at least 60 words a minute typing for any office work. I would recommend anyone to take a short typing course before coming over since there is plenty of work.'*

Major agencies include Drake, Bligh and Adecco. Most agencies do not occupy the equivalent of high street premises, and you will often find yourself in some obscure office block. You should make an appointment to register and allow up to an hour for each one to have your skills assessed. Your chances of being accepted will be increased if you can produce some good references from previous employment at home or elsewhere in Australia. Even when you do get an assignment, there is no guarantee that work will be continuous and you should be prepared for a certain amount of hanging around between jobs.

George Street in Sydney has dozens of agencies including the long established Bligh Appointments (Level 7, Dymocks Building, 428 George St, Sydney 2000; 02-9235 3699; http://jobs.careerone.com.au/bligh) who welcome working holidaymakers, and Goldstein & Martens Recruitment Consultants (Level 4, 285 George St; 02-9262 3088; www.goldsteinmartens.com.au) which pays $2-$3 above the average hourly wage.

Periodic shortages of temporary secretaries crop up, so if you've got decent skills, you're practically guaranteed work. Drake International/Drake Overload (www.drakeintl.com) has been recommended by several readers; the company has offices in all the major cities including Sydney (02-9273 0500), Melbourne (03-9245 0215) and Brisbane (07-3291 6099). Because they have offices all over the world, it can be useful having one of their Career Passports which will serve as a letter of introduction to other branches. Debbie Harrison, with a lot of secretarial experience, reported from Parramatta, a suburb of Sydney, that the hourly rates she had been offered by her agency for short-term assignments varied from $15 to $18 with an average of $17.

In Sydney good secretaries can expect to get around $20 per hour and occasionally up to $30. In Sydney and Melbourne, the agencies almost always ask about your visa status. Carolyn Edwards side-stepped the issue with one agency by saying she had just moved into a flat and couldn't locate her passport and another time claiming that she had left it in a safety deposit box in Queensland and was arranging for it to be sent. After she had proved herself a reliable worker and was getting called back by companies, the agency seemed conveniently to forget about it. The two temp agencies in Kalgoorlie for whom Lucy Slater worked didn't even ask to see her passport. They were more interested in whether or not she could drive since most secretarial work there is with the mines and involves driving a company car between sites.

Some agencies specialise in certain kinds of work for example work on stations and farms, in tourist resorts or as nannies and au pairs (see relevant sections). Troys Hospitality Staff (Suite 1, Level 11, 89 York St, NSW 2000; 02-9290 2955; www.troys.com.au) and Alseasons (Level 6, 225 Clarence St; 02-9324 4666) have been recommended for placing casual catering staff in Sydney. Pinnacle Hospitality and Travel People recruitment agency have offices in Melbourne, Sydney, Perth and Brisbane for Queensland resorts (www.pinnaclepeople.com.au).

Advertisements

Either before you leave Britain or once you are in one of the major cities, get hold of the free booklet *Australia & New Zealand Independent Travellers Guide* published by the London-based travel magazine TNT (14-15 Child's Place, London SW5 9RX; £2.95 charge for postage and packing) or consult their online classified section on www.tntclassifieds.com.au. The same company (www.tntmagazine.com.au) publishes a specific weekly magazine for Sydney and monthly magazines for NSW/ACT, Queensland/Northern Territory, Victoria/Tasmania/SA/WA and the Outback, available free at airports, bus and train stations as well as from the TNT office, Level 4, 46-48 York St, Sydney (02-9299 4811). They carry a certain number of classified ads for job-seekers and a section called 'Finding Work'.

The main daily newspapers have job supplements once or twice a week, for example on Wednesday and Saturday in the *Sydney Morning Herald* (www.smh.com.au), the *West Australian* (Perth), *Adelaide Advertiser* or the *Courier-Mail* (Brisbane). The Monday Job Market in the Melbourne *Age* is particularly worthwhile while the *Herald Sun* carries a number of telemarketing/sales/customer service jobs, many commission-only. The agency website www.mycareer.com.au permits access to up-to-date job ads in the *SMH*, the *Age*, etc. Remember that these wide-circulation papers generate a lot of competition for jobs and, increasingly, ads say 'No travellers'. Try to buy the paper the preceding evening so you can start your job at the crack of dawn. For example the *Herald* in Sydney goes on sale about 2am from outlets in Taylor Square (Darlinghurst) and near King's Cross Station. Colm Murphy from County Cork spent eight days after arrival in Melbourne replying to all the ads before he got occasional Sunday work catering at weddings and parties and after a further blitz of answering ads got a probationary contract as a casual drinks waiter at a suburban restaurant.

Ken Smith was so dismayed by the level of competition that he decided to check out the more local papers:

> Any jobs that are advertised in the 'Sydney Morning Herald' are normally so flooded with replies that your chances are minimal. I replied to a bar vacancy along with 119 other people and was very honoured to make it to the final selection stages. I then started looking through the smaller papers and replied to an advertisement for labourer/factory cleaner. In this case, four people applied for two jobs and I soon was working from 7am to 3.30pm with the prospect of daily overtime and Saturday work if I proved myself a good worker. Soon I was taking home just under $500 a week. The work (which was often very physical) was for an engineering firm in Botany Bay which designed and manufactured abattoirs.

The range of jobs advertised in the newspaper can be discouraging. Sarah Snell describes the choice in the Darwin paper:

> Jobs that were advertised included cooking on prawn trawlers (and I gathered through various accounts that this may have included rather more demanding activities than merely preparing meals for the hardy crew), jillarooing (the female counterpart of the jackaroo, who is a kind of cowboy on sheep and cattle stations in the outback), training as a croupier for a new casino, and nude modelling for aspiring life artists at the local college.

Meanwhile the 'Casual Work Available' columns in other cities can carry an equally unpromising range of opportunities including 'promoting art' (i.e. selling prints door-to-door), delivering junk mail for a pittance, telephone sales and working as a film extra (where you will be asked to pay a registration fee with little immediate prospect of work). Furthermore all these jobs are gone by 6am.

However it is worth persevering since there will also be adverts for bar and restaurant jobs (especially under the specific heading 'Positions Vacant – Hospitality Industry'), for work on guest ranches, for factory jobs and so on. Posts for live-in child-carers are sometimes advertised in daily papers; check under the 'Situations Vacant – Domestic and Rural' column (though almost all the jobs are urban not rural).

If you think you might be a successful door-to-door salesman, the newspaper is the place to look. Unless you're prepared to exaggerate the virtues of your product you might last no longer than Simon Whalley from Hull did after answering an advert in the *West Australian,* for salesmen of paintings, i.e. two hours. Adam Jones found this work more congenial and managed to make about $400 a week by selling an average of seven paintings an evening. The ex-girlfriend of an American reader told him she was earning a cool $1,000 a week as a rep for a cleaning company in Brisbane. More recently Colm Murphy worked for various sales companies in Melbourne selling everything from raffle tickets on behalf of the Victorian Football Club to mobile telephones. It took a long time but eventually he saw that it was possible to earn £300 a week. One company that hires backpacking sales people is ABC (A Better Chance) which distributes Time Life books in Australia. They send sales teams (called 'Interview Teams') all around Australia (expenses paid) to sell on commission for a minimum of 12 weeks; in Sydney ring 02-9299 9933 and in Brisbane 07-3228 2233 (www.abetterchance.com.au).

Some charities are perennial advertisers for paid fund-raisers. For example in Sydney Spinal Cord Injuries Australia (PO Box 397, Matraville, NSW 2036; 02 9281 8214; fundraising@spinalcordinjuries.com.au) pays collectors a quarter of donations collected, which should work out to be $50-$100 a day. Another charity worth investigating is the not-for-profit environmental organisation the Wilderness Society which gets its collectors to dress up in koala suits. The Sydney branch is on Level 2, 64-76 Kippax St, Surry Hills, NSW 2010 (02-9282 9553 or 1300 138 174; wd.recruitment@wilderness.org.au); hourly earnings average $15-$20. A good reference from the Wilderness Society might someday come in handy in impressing a personnel officer at Disneyland. One of the Wilderness Society's campaigns is a door-to-door canvas which is suitable for English-speaking backpackers with some knowledge of environmental issues. The job pays a base salary of $60 per four-hour shift plus canvassers can keep a quarter of takings above a set target.

Chris Miksovsky is amusing on the subject of dressing up as a koala in Brisbane:

My year in Australia ended with a rather fitting and hilarious job, collecting for the Wilderness Society, a sort of Australian Greenpeace, wearing a koala costume. After a brief interview with the Koala Co-ordinator ('So, Chris, do you have any experience walking around as a big furry animal?'), I found myself in a busy square wearing a full-body fluffy grey koala suit complete with fake felt claws and droopy oversize ears. Actually it works. Takings per hour were about $25 on average. For me, probably the best thing was that you learned to not take yourself so seriously. I have an Ivy League degree in Political Science but there I was dancing around a city centre dressed as a koala.

Danny Jacobson also from the States was not so enthusiastic about his stint as a charity collector: *'For a few weeks I shook the bucket on street corners and quietly snuck up on people in city parks asking for donations. It was a very enlightening experience and it very nearly made me go nuts. Collecting money for a charity is a real mind-game. I chatted with the AIDS charity collectors and they seemed to have it made. They were paid $15 an hour plus commissions. They get uniforms and huge buckets and everyone gives.'*

Hostels and Notice Boards

Youth hostels and backpackers' lodges everywhere are a goldmine of information for people working their way around the world. And nowhere are they better than in Australia. A growing number of hostel managers, especially in the major fruit and vegetable growing areas of Queensland, run their own informal job-finding service and try to put backpackers in touch with local employers. The disadvantage of being hard to contact when based in a big city hostel has largely been overcome by the mobile phone.

You may find employment in the hostels themselves of course. Stephen Psallidas describes the proliferation of work, especially on the 'Route' between Sydney and Cairns:

I've met loads of people working in backpackers' hostels. Typically you work two hours a day in exchange for your bed and a meal. Work may be cleaning, driving the minibus, reception, etc. and is always on an informal basis so there are no worries about visas, etc. I will be jumping on the bandwagon myself soon. I'll be completely shattered from picking tomatoes so I'm going to 'work' in a hostel in Mission Beach, where the owners invited me to work when I stayed there earlier. I'm going to rest up in a beautiful place before continuing my travels, and not spend any of my hard-earned dollars.

There might be night work, especially at the big city hostels, for those who are up to the job of keeping non-residents out and rounding up residents swilling beer in the garden at 4am.

Australia has 131 YHA hostels, many of which distribute details about employment available within their region. A free booklet listing all hostels and state offices is widely available (www.yha.com.au). One of the most successful groups of non-YHA backpackers' hostels is VIP Backpackers Resorts of Australia which is especially strong in New South Wales and Queensland. A booklet listing their 146 Australian hostels is distributed far and wide or can be obtained from overseas by purchasing their VIP kit for A$41 (£16 in the UK) which gives $1 off each hostel stay among other discounts; contact VIP Backpackers in the UK: Riverbank House, 1 Putney Bridge Approach, London SW6 3JD; 020-7736 4200; www.vipbackpackers.com). Almost all VIP hostels have notice boards advertising jobs, flats, car shares, etc. and most charge about $20 a night for a dorm bed.

The Nomad's Backpacker chain has already been mentioned, with about 50 hostels, many of them renovated pubs. Their membership card ('Adventure Card') costs £16 per year and entitles users to access job advice. It is possible to join both these hostel groups in advance through backpacker agents outside Australia such as Travellers Contact Point in London (address above).

The disadvantage of using hostels as your main source of jobs is that they are full of your main competition for available work. Andrew Owen was discouraged to find that every backpackers' hostel seemed to be populated almost entirely with Brits on working holidays. Also be a little suspicious of claims such as 'Plenty of farm work available for guests' since this may just be a marketing ploy on the part of the hostel (see section on Queensland Harvests).

Most Sydney hostels are well clued up on the local job scene, especially in the three main backpackers' areas, King's Cross (which is beginning to lose its sleazy image), trendy Glebe and Coogee Beach. Some even sell working holiday packages such as the often-recommended Footprints Westend (412 Pitt St, Sydney NSW 2000; freecall 1800 013 186/02-9211 4588); see their website www.footprintswestend.com.au for what the package costing $243 includes.

One recommended Sydney backpackers is Kangaroo Bakpak at 665 South Dowling Street in Surry Hills (02-9319 5915; www.kangaroobakpak.com.au/employment.htm). The 556-bed YHA hostel opposite the Central Railway Station (corner of Pitt and Rawson Sts) features an employment bureau among a range of state-of-the-art facilities. In King's Cross, the Pink House at 6-8 Barncleuth Square (02-9358 1689) has good work contacts.

Roger Blake could not afford to be tempted by the social life of Sydney and got straight down to finding a job:

Having enjoyed the East Coast to the full, I arrived in Sydney at make or break point with $70 to my name, leaving me with no choice but to sort myself out and quickly. I found a reasonable and certainly affordable place to stay on day one. First Resort (191 Darlinghurst Rd, in King's Cross; 02-9332 3213; www.firstresort.com.au) is more a large shared home than a backpackers hostel. At $75 per week (more in the summer) it's a steal. I found a job on day two, once again through scouring the backpacker noticeboards and making a hundred and one phone calls. A desperate backpacker is willing to turn his or her hand to anything for a dollar (no choice but). I spent six hours a day, seven days a week parading the city streets in a sandwich board handing out flyers promoting of all things, tapestry, knitting and needlecraft. This went on for about three weeks and I was one of the few who stuck it out from start to finish. I only made it through this mind-numbing, leg-cramping job because of the comedy moments and observations of life on Sydney's streets. We attracted a lot of attention and I enjoyed watching passers-by including irate taxi drivers, ladies tripping over their high heels and businessmen running like the clappers to a meeting. A couple of times I saw buskers being casually thrown a $50 note and on several occasions beggars being given $10-$20 as if they were 20 cent coins. The owners took us out for a nice meal and all drinks paid for at the end of the sale. I did quite well out of it actually and didn't mind being paid to parade the city streets looking like a fool...all too easy and good fun. I do have to find work for this venture to continue. I did two brilliant tours of the outback paid for by my antics in Sydney.

The Cronulla Beach YHA (02-9527 7772; www.cronullabeachyha.com) actively assists backpackers to find local jobs as waiting staff, labourers, nannies, etc. and invites them to submit an online employment request form. In the beach suburb of Coogee (pronounced Coodjee) try the Wizard of Oz at 172 Coogee Bay Road (02-9315 7876) and Sydney Beachside next door. Both are regularly contacted for casual workers. People looking for day labour regularly come in early (7.30am). Apparently it helps if you are built like a barn, especially if they are looking for someone to move grand pianos. It is also worth sticking close to reception in the evenings when employers ring with their requirements for the next day. When working like this, insist on being paid daily.

Rizwan Hafiz was amazed by the speed with which work came his way through his hostel:

> You can't help but meet people in Oz. I arranged for a Coogee hostel to pick me up from Sydney Airport and they said 'if you go to your left you'll meet another bloke from Britain who's just phoned us'. I found work in two days. The warden asked 'what are you doing in 10 minutes?' There's a job in a café down the road washing dishes'. I did nine hours of backbreaking work but received $14 in tips and a huge burger for lunch. Great way to offset the jetlag.

In Melbourne, Enfield House Backpackers in St Kilda (03-9534 8159) was once a good place to find out about work but now is more a party hostel. The Hotel Bakpak in downtown Melbourne is attached to the Backpacker's Resource Centre which can assist people with a working holiday visa as well as provide a range of other back-up services for a fee. In Adelaide, try Rucksackers Riders International at 257 Gilles Street (08-8232 0823) or any of the others along the same road, which try to direct travellers to relevant agencies and seasonal fruit picking as well as to jobs at show time. Another recommended Adelaide hostel is Sunny's at 139 Franklin St (1800-225725). In Perth, try Club Red Backpackers, 496 Newcastle St, West Perth (08-9227 9969; www.redbackpackers.com.au) which has strong links with local employers and keeps a job register.

In fruit-picking areas, certain hostels and campsites are populated almost exclusively by workers; see the relevant sections below.

The Internet

Searching the web for employment leads is especially productive in Australia. Dozens of routes exist for finding out about job vacancies. Before leaving home, you might like to register (free) with www.gapwork.com which is updated regularly and lists employers who hire working holidaymakers. Gapwork also sell an Australia/New Zealand Gap Pack for £12.99 (or £9.99 with promotional discount).

The government's www.jobsearch.gov.au is a superb resource listing up-to-date vacancies throughout the country in an easily searchable format with contact details, normally to a local employment agency. Another good site is a free service by the Wayward Bus Company (www.waywardbus.com.au/seaswork.htm) which has an index of actual employers, hostels and pubs recommended for job-seekers and agents.

Free Spirit (www.freespirit.com.au) specially targets travelling workers as well as professionals and is recommended by backpacking agencies such as the Traveller's Club in Perth. Free Spirit has offices in Sydney and Perth plus London (london@freespirit.com. au). Another site to try is www.workaboutaustralia.com.au run by a man in Dubbo NSW; the latter is run as a club whose membership costs A$55 although some information is available free on the website. Also have a look at www.recruitoz.com specially for working holiday visa holders and www.jobmap.com.au affiliated to Worldwide Workers mentioned above. Plenty of other sites cater for more corporate job-seekers, such as www.seek.com. au or www.mycareer.com.au.

RURAL AUSTRALIA and the OUTBACK

Most of Australia's area is sparsely populated, scorched land which is known loosely as the outback. Beyond the rich farming and grazing land surrounding the largest cities, there are immense properties supporting thousands of animals and acres of crops. Many of these stations (farms) are so remote that flying is the only practical means of access, though having a vehicle can be a great help in an outback job search. Sandra Gray describes the drawbacks of spending time on a station:

> Be warned! Station life can be severely boring after a while. I managed to land myself on one in the Northern Territory with very little else to do but watch the grass grow. If you have to save a lot of money quickly station work is the way to do it since there's nothing to spend it on. But make sure the place is within reasonable distance of a town or at least a roadhouse, so you have somewhere to go to let off steam occasionally.

Your chances of getting a job as a station assistant (a jackaroo or jillaroo) will be improved if you have had experience with sheep, riding or any farming or mechanical experience. Several farmers are in the business of giving you that experience before helping you to find outback work, like the one mentioned above in the Visitoz Scheme. Shaun Armstrong thoroughly enjoyed a similar four-day Jackaroo/Jillaroo course in Queensland:

> Should any traveller wish to discover an introduction to authentic rural Australia, no better window of opportunity exists than Pat and Pete Worsley's Rocky Creek Experience. I braved the jackaroo course with three other travellers (all Dutch). Horse riding, cattle mustering, ute driving, trail biking (the 'ings' were numerous) and other tasks occupied our days: wonderful hospitality ended each evening. Memorable days. Station placement was arranged afterwards as was transport if needed. I was sorry to leave really. I'd say the course did prepare me for most experiences encountered in the job. For example I was able to muster cattle on horseback with four experienced riders having spent only 15 hours in the saddle. It wasn't easy, but I did it.

The course fee is $484 including job placement afterwards with one of more than 300 employers, plus ongoing back-up. Rocky Creek is located inland from Bundaberg (Isis Highway MS 698, Biggenden, Qld 4621; 07-4127 1377; www.isisol.com.au/rockycrkfarm-stay).

Another outback training courses is offered by the Leconfield Jackaroo and Jillaroo School in Kootingal NSW 2352 not far from Tamworth/Armidale (tel/fax 02-6769 1230; www.leconfieldjackaroo.com/info.html). On completion of the group course lasting 11 days and costing $850, successful participants will be guided in the direction of paying jobs.

Shearing is out of the question for the uninitiated. Although the post of roustabout is open to the inexperienced, jobs are generally scarce on sheep stations at present because of the decline in the wool industry due to changes in fashion and the collapse of the Asian market. Roustabouts fetch, carry, sweep and trim stained bits from the fleeces. Check adverts under the heading 'Stock and Land' for shearing team recruitment in agricultural journals like Land or Queensland Country Life (searchable on http://qcl.farmonline.com. au). Many of the jobs on a sheep station verge on the stomach-churning, as the Dutch woman Geertje Korf vividly describes, after spending a short time on a 10,000 acre sheep farm owned by the friend of her former employer:

> My main tasks were bringing the rubbish to the tip (including dead sheep and the waste from the killing shed, sheep guts, skins, heads, etc.) and branding the sheep after shearing which included a lot of running up and down the race trying to get

those frustratingly stupid sheep where I wanted them to be. At the end of the day I was covered with sweat, dust, branding paint, sheep grease, sweat and blood. You shouldn't be too faint-hearted since often you see the bone glistening between the blood where the shearers had accidentally cut the skin off the legs. I didn't often get the chance to help with mustering (rounding up the sheep on motorbikes, which is quite fun) and I did not learn to ride a horse as I had hoped. Nevertheless, I enjoyed doing something completely different. I wouldn't have minded the hard work if I had been paid decently for it (I was working 11 hours a day for $100 a week.)

Chris Miksovsky was not impressed with the assistance he received from two outback placement services in Alice Springs so resorted to cold-calling stations after looking them up in the phone book for northern Western Australia. After making more than 40 calls (and spending as many dollars on phone cards) he found a cattle station willing (or desperate enough) to take him on. He advises against exaggerating your experience: if you say you can ride a horse, the station manager will probably put you on 'Satan the Psycho-mare' your first day.

Chris describes station life as he experienced it:
The days were long (breakfast sometimes at 3am), never-ending (I worked 32 days straight once), often painful and sometimes gruesome. But then again, where else can you gallop across the outback chasing (or being chased by) a Brahman bull and sleep out under the stars listening to other jackaroos spinning yarns around a campfire, all while getting paid? Three months on the station earned me $2,700 net. It was the best thing I've done since I started travelling.

Australia's first specialist harvesting recruitment agency is flourishing: Grunt Labour Services has offices in Darwin, Katherine, Kununurra, Broome, Childers, Cairns, Bundaberg and Brisbane (www.gruntlabour.com).

Some city-based employment agencies deal with jobs in country and outback areas, primarily farming, station, hotel/motel and roadhouse work. In Western Australia try PGA Personnel, a division of the Pastoralists & Graziers Association of WA Inc (08-9479 4544; www.pgapersonnel.org.au) or Pollitt's (251 Adelaide Terrace, 13th Floor, Perth 6000; 08-9325 2544) who say that experienced farmworkers and tractor drivers are paid $13-$15 an hour for 10-12 hour days, seven days a week at seeding time (April to June) and harvest time (October to December). Housekeeping, nannying and cooking positions are available for two or three months at a time throughout the year. The standard wage is $300-$350 a week after board, most of which can be saved. For work in outback roadhouses and hotels, previous experience is essential to earn $400+ a week after lodging. The three-month commitment enables travellers to experience the regional country towns, and save $4,000-$5,000 during their stay.

While travelling back from Ayers Rock Sara Runnalls popped into an employment office in the Northern Territory town of Katherine to ask about local jobs. That day she was driven 80km to a property at Scott Creek:

Here I found 15 hungry workers and a disgustingly dirty, dusty, insect haven for a kitchen. I had few fresh ingredients, ample beef, plenty of salt and tomato ketchup. My mission was to feed them five times a day with a variety of beef dishes and homemade cakes. I came up with some typically English cuisine and no complaints. I saw plenty of wildlife and enjoyed my two weeks on the cattle station. They asked me to stay the whole season but I'm here to travel.

Outback International (PO Box 8042, Allenstown, Queensland 4700; 07-4927 4300; www.outbackinternational.com) is an Australia-wide rural employment agency which places tractor drivers, cotton workers, cooks and seasonal staff. The minimum period of work is only two weeks.

Anyone with experience of the horse industry should contact the Stablemate Staff Agency in the UK (The Old Rectory, Belton-in-Rutland, Oakham, Rutland LE15 9LE; enquiries@iepuk.com), whose Australian partner is Stablemate, PO Box 1206, Windsor, NSW 2756 (02-4576 4444; info@stablemate.net.au). They deal exclusively with placing equestrian and thoroughbred staff but are sometimes able to assist people with limited experience with horses if they want to work as a nanny, general farm assistant or even in unskilled harvest work sometimes. People over 18 with a year's practical experience should enquire of the UK office about the International Exchange Programme in Australia for which the fee is about £1,800 including airfares.

Although you may not be forced to eat witchetty grubs for tea, there are some obvious disadvantages to life in the outback, viz. the isolation, the heat and to some extent the dangers. Even if you have had experience of living in the rural areas of Europe, it may be hard to adjust to life in the outback. Lots of towns have nothing more than a post office and small shop combined, a hotel (pub) and petrol pump. The sun's heat must not be under-estimated. It is important to cover your head with a cowboy hat or a towel and to carry a large water bottle with you. Droughts are not uncommon in the outback. On Tricia Clancy's guest ranch near Sofala NSW, where it hadn't rained for a year and a half, both guests and staff were permitted to have one shower a week (in spite of the terrible heat and dust) and this water had to be recycled for laundry.

Finally there is the ever-present hazard of spiders and snakes which Tricia describes: 'The hay barn attracted mice and the mice attracted snakes, so whenever we entered the barn we had to make a loud rumpus to frighten them away. Huntsmen spiders proliferated. These great tarantula-like creatures were not poisonous, however it was still frightening when they emerged from behind the picture frames in the evenings.' Once you get into the habit of checking inside your boots and behind logs for snakes, and under the loo seat for redback spiders, the dangers are minimised. The outback is often a rough male-domi-nated world, and not suited to fragile personalities.

Conservation Volunteers

Several organisations give visitors a chance to experience the Australian countryside or bush. The main not-for-profit conservation organisation in Australia is called, predictably enough, Conservation Volunteers Australia (CVA) and it places volunteers from overseas in its 'Conservation Experience' projects, though the charges are quite steep. Sample projects include tree planting, erosion and salinity control, seed collection from indigenous plants, building and maintaining bushwalking tracks, etc. Overseas volunteers are wel-come to become involved by booking a four-week or six-week package which includes food and accommodation and some transport at a cost of A$815 and $1,200 respectively (which works out at less than $30 a day for accommodation, food and transport). Further details are available from the National Head Office, Box 423, Ballarat, Vic 3353 (03-5330 2600; www.conservationvolunteers.com.au). There are volunteer offices in all the states.

> **Daniele Arena from Italy stumbled across an independent project on the coast of Queensland that appealed to him:**
> *One of the most amazing experiences I had in Oz was the time I was volunteering at the Turtle Rookery in Mon Repos Beach. We could pitch our tent for free, and gave a small contribution of $5 a day for food. The work was to patrol the beach waiting for nesting turtles and, when they come in, to tag and measure them and the nest. This goes on between November and March. I was fortunate enough to get this by chance but normally there's quite a few people who want to do it, so you should probably contact the Queensland Parks & Wildlife Service for info.*

The World Wide Opportunities on Organic Farms organisation is very active in Austra-lia. WWOOF headquarters are at Mt Murrindal Co-operative, Buchan, Vic 3885 (03-5155 0218; www.wwoof.com.au) though their publicity is distributed at many hostels. The Aus-tralian WWOOF Book that they publish contains more than 1,500 addresses throughout

Australia of organic farmers and hosts looking for short or long term voluntary help or to promote cultural exchange. The list is sold with accident insurance at a cost of A$50 within Australia, A$60 for a couple ($55 and $65 if members join from outside Australia).

A free internet-based exchange of work-for-keep volunteers can be found at www.helpx.net where nearly 200 Australian hosts are listed.

Before becoming a Long Term volunteer with CVA, Susan Gray joined WWOOF Australia and worked on several farms on a work-for-keep basis. *'They are all growing food organically and usually in beautiful countryside. Most are very keen to show you around and show off their home region to you. The work was as hard as you wanted it to be, but about four hours of work were expected. I usually did more as I enjoyed it, and I learned a lot from those experiences.'*

Interesting research projects take place throughout Australia and some may be willing to include unpaid staff looking for work experience. For example a research station in northern Queensland operated by the Australian Tropical Research Foundation (PMB 5, Cape Tribulation, Qld 4873; 07-4098 0063; www.austrop.org.au) welcomes 50 volunteers a year to carry out all sorts of tasks to conserve the rainforest. Volunteers are asked to pay US$15 a day to cover food and accommodation. It might be worth trying the Heron Island Research Station (Great Barrier Reef, via Gladstone, Qld 4680; www.marine.uq.edu.au/hirs) which has been known to offer free accommodation in exchange for about four hours of work a day.

The Australian Institute of Marine Science (AIMS) at Cape Ferguson near Townsville (07-4753 4240; visitor_coord@aims.gov.au/ www.aims.gov.au) runs a Prospective Visitors Scheme which encompasses volunteers; applicants with their own research projects or a scuba diving certificate are especially welcome. Application must be done online.

Often the state conservation organisation organises a voluntary programme, as is the case in Western Australia with the Conservation & Land Management Department of CALM (www.calm.wa.gov.au). The programme is open to anyone though it can't provide accommodation in remote places; write to the Volunteer Co-ordinator at CALM for details (Locked Bag 104, Bentley Delivery Centre, WA 6983; 08-9334 0333). For people with a conservation background or relevant skills, CALM also runs an Educational Work Experience Programme, though none of the positions involves working with wildlife.

FRUIT PICKING

In the rich agricultural land between the coastal ribbon of urban development and the outback, a multitude of crops is grown: grapes around Adelaide and in the Hunter Valley of New South Wales, tropical fruit on the Queensland coast and north of Perth, apples in the southwest part of Western Australia and in Tasmania, etc. Although fruit farms may be more fertile than the outback, the same considerations as to isolation, heat and dangers from the fauna hold true. The standard hours for a fruit picker working in the heat are approximately 6am-6pm with two or three hours off in the middle of the day.

During certain harvests, the farmers are desperate for labour and put out appeals over the radio, on the notice boards of backpackers' hostels and via harvest employment agencies. On one Queensland farm where Mary Anne Mackle from Northern Ireland worked, the farmer had to bring in a team of prisoners to finish off the cucumber harvest since there was such a shortage of pickers. Just as in Europe and North America, there are professional pickers who follow the harvests around the continent, though it may be possible to spend seven or eight months in one region such as the valley of the Murray River. So if you find yourself falling behind your fellow-workers during the first few days of the harvest, you should console yourself that you are competing with years of experience.

OzJobs is a division of the Australian recruitment agency Forstaff Group which publicises harvest vacancies online and via the telephone; contact the Go Harvest hotline on 1300 720126 or check www.goharvest.com or www.oz-jobs.com.au/harvest/destinationsDB.cfm. Also contact the National Harvest Labour Information Service based in Victoria (PO Box 5055, Mildura, Vic 3502; 1800 062 332; nhlis@madec.edu.au/ www.jobsearch.

gov.au/harvesttrail).

Harvest seasons are often diverse: crops ripen first in Queensland and finish in Tasmania as you move further away from the equator. Even the two major grape harvests take place consecutively rather than simultaneously. For easy reference, we have included tables showing crops, regions and times of harvest (omitting grapes which appear on a separate chart) for the most important fruit-growing states of New South Wales, Victoria, South Australia, Western Australia and Queensland.

Quite often farmers will offer a shack or caravan for little or no money. Not all fruit farmers can supply accommodation, however, so serious job-seekers carry a tent. You should be able to buy a decent two-man tent for $100. On the other hand backpackers' hostels are never far away and in the main picking districts organise minibus transport between hostels and farms. Campervans are of course very versatile and comfortable but expensive to run and expensive to buy.

Women on their own tend to encounter resistance among farmers (known as 'blockies'). Many of the growers are of Italian or Greek descent and the old Mediterranean sexism creeps in. Certain jobs such as cutting apricots and work in the shed generally are considered 'women's work' and with these jobs it is usually impossible to earn the big money. Louisa Fitzgerald was disgusted by the blatant discrimination:

> I was all ready to go and pick fruit down in Victoria, but when I phoned the farm to check if work was still available and they discovered I was a girl intending to go alone, they said unless I was accompanied by a male, I couldn't pick fruit! It seems that under union rules, females are not allowed to lift over a certain weight which means that for fruit picking a man has to be with you to lift weights – typically chauvinist I'd say!

Mary Anne Mackle participated in a number of harvests during her working holiday and offers these tips to unsuspecting fruit pickers:

1. Although a car is not essential, it is often necessary in looking for work, and then getting to town to shop.
2. Be prepared for extremes of temperature. Although it may be in the 80s during the day, the nights are often very cold.
3. Don't expect any nightlife. A typical evening for us involved showering, washing dishes, making dinner, reading, writing and chatting with fellow fruit pickers.
4. Forget about vanity. You will stink at all times even after a shower. Your socks will never be the same again and your skin won't like the sunblock and build-up of dirt either.
5. Forget about modesty. Don't expect to have the use of toilet facilities out in the fields.
6. On an optimistic note, you will be a fitter person and, if things go well, a wealthier one too. You can then go off and take a dive course on the Great Barrier Reef, snorkel in Coral Bay, canoe down Katherine Gorge, get drunk in Darwin, hike in national parks, swim in waterfalls, until your money runs out and you start all over again.

Mary Anne's conclusion is that harvesting is certainly preferable to packing videos in a warehouse in Sydney or selling hotdogs for $11 or $12 an hour.

The Grape Harvest

Australian wines have made a startling impact on the rest of the world as the volume, quality and consumption increase each year. Regardless of their quality, the important fact for itinerant workers is that there is a large quantity of grapes to be picked. The main centres for grape-picking are the Mildura region of Victoria, the Riverland of South Australia (between Renmark and Waikerie) and the Hunter Valley of New South Wales (around

Pokolbin and Muswellbrook), though they are grown in every state including Tasmania. Detailed tables are set out below. The harvests usually get under way some time in February and last through March or into April. Earnings can be impressive: Raymond Oliver from Co. Durham made $2,200 during the five or six week harvest near Mildura.

Many grape varieties are grown in Australia and all demand different styles of picking which (like any fruit-picking) take some time to master before you can earn the big money. The amount you can earn depends on the condition of the vines, the type of grape, whether you have tough enough hands to pull the grapes off (which is much faster than cutting with a knife or snips), whether you have a hard-working partner (which is faster and less demoralising than picking on your own), how fit you are and of course how competitive (or desperate for money) you are.

Normally they start with sultanas and currants moving through different grape types as the wineries demand. Picking for a winery is easiest; it doesn't matter too much if the grapes are squashed or there are a few leaves left in (a blockie would have a fit if he read that). Picking for drying means the grapes shouldn't be squashed and picking for market (i.e. table grapes) demands extreme care and is usually paid as wages or at a higher rate per box.

You will be paid by tin, by bucket (25% more) or by weight. To take an example, an average picker of sultanas around Mildura can pick 200 buckets in eight hours thereby earning $100. The fairest way to pick is by weight. The idea that you can pick as long as you want or take a break in the afternoon is a misconception. The only time you are likely to get a break in the afternoon is when it is too hot to leave the grapes out in the sun. Around Perth this cut-off might come at a roasting 36°C (97°F) which can be a determining factor when you are deciding whether or not to persevere with the work. Pickers often resort to hosing each other down before they can face the afternoon. In many places Saturday is the day off.

Certainly the demand for pickers is intense in many regions. After deciding that the Sydney employment scene was unremittingly grim, Henry Pearce phoned some employment agencies in mid-February and decided that Griffith in New South Wales was the best bet. When he arrived, he was delighted to see that the job board was full of grape-picking jobs. He was hustled into the harvest office, allocated to a farmer and driven to a farm in the region, where he began work the next morning. The International Hostel at 112 Binya Street in Griffith (02-6964 4236; info@griffithinternational.com.au) helps with finding work.

Across the River Murray the situation is the same around Mildura in Victoria, the grape capital of the area. Armin Birrer reported from the town of Cardross that, despite high local unemployment, 300 picking jobs were advertised in the local papers and on roadside signs. This is the area to which agencies in Melbourne are most likely to send you if you arrive in January/February. Although Caroline Perry had to wait for a month, she was eventually sent to work for an Italian grape-grower:

The owner met us at the bus station as promised and took us to our accommodation on the farm. We were dumbfounded when we saw where we had to live: it was worse than a shed with rats and cockroaches. The dunny was a tin shed with no lights and so we worried about redback spiders.

It was very tough work, which killed your back and arms before you got used to it. We could work whatever hours we liked, but because we needed the money we worked from 7am-7pm, seven days a week. We usually managed 150-200 buckets a day which isn't bad since the crop was poor that year and we were inexperienced. We were paid a very low rate per bucket.

After describing all these privations Caroline goes on to say that they had a good time working for an employer in Nichols Point, Victoria.

The Tasmanian wine industry has really taken off and the sparseness of population in rural areas means that travellers are in demand during the harvest. For example a vineyard in Lebrina north of Launceston posted 40 vacancies on the internet for its harvest which lasts eight to ten weeks from late March.

Grape-picking isn't for everyone but usually a degree of camaraderie develops between pickers and blockies and hassles about weights, buckets, etc. are more in the nature of a game. If you are lucky enough to find a friendly employer, there may even be an end-of-harvest party or barbecue.

Related employment includes grape trimming and grape packing, both of which were done by Alison Cooper in Robinvale southeast of Mildura:

> The exciting job of grape trimming involves standing at a conveyor belt all day, trimming the bad grapes off bunches. I soon got 'promoted' to grape packing whereby I had to stand at the end of the conveyor belt being bombarded by thousands of grapes which I then had to pack nicely into boxes. At first I thought there was no way I could do this job as I'd die from boredom first, but I managed to stick it out for the season and saved $2,500.

If you aren't around at the right time for the harvest there may be out-of-season jobs, as Daniele Arena found:
My stroke of luck was in Jugiong NSW in November where I worked at a vineyard, not to harvest grapes but to work on the vines. The work of disbudding and training the vines was paid more than $14 an hour and I took home $500 a week. Just great. I stayed at the Blueheeler Guesthouse in Gundagai where the owners helped me find work.

GRAPE HARVESTS

South Australia

	Dates of Harvest
Clare-Watervale	February-April
Barossa Valley	February-April
Adelaide and Southern Vales	February-March
Coonawarra	February-April
Langhorne Creek	February-April
Riverland (Waikerie, Berri, Loxton, Renmark)	February-April

New South Wales

Orchard Hills	late Jan-mid March
Camden	early February-mid March
Wedderburn	mid February-mid March
Nolong	late February-April
Orange	March-April
Mudgee	late February-April
Hunter Valley (Pokolbin, Bulga, Denman, Broke, Muswellbrook)	early February-March
Murrumbidgee Irrigation area (Griffith, Leeton)	mid February-March
Dareton	Jan-April
Curlwaa	Mar-April
Buronga	February-June
Mid-Murray (Koraleigh, Goodnight)	late February-April
Corowa	February-March

Victoria

Goulburn Valley	February-March
Swan Hill	February-March
Lilydale	February-March

Mildura/Robinvale	February-March
Great Western-Avoca	February-March
Drumborg	February-March
Glenrowan-Milawa	February-March
Rutherglen	February-March
Western Australia	
Swan Valley (near Perth)	February-April
Margaret River	February-April
Mount Barker	February-April

The Apple Harvest

Although apple-picking is notoriously slow going for the beginner, you can usually pick up enough speed within a few days to make it rewarding. Seasonal pickers are needed in Western Australia throughout the year but especially between November and May, with the peak of the apple harvest falling in the summer. In harvests where the conditions seem at the outset to be unattractive, it is not hard to get work especially when it is the time of year (normally February to May) when students return to college and the weather is getting colder.

Many travellers flock to the Western Australian harvest that takes place around Donnybrook, Manjimup and Pemberton. Hourly wages are generally reasonable. Brook Lodge Backpacker Accommodation (3 Bridge St, PO Box 175, Donnybrook, WA 6239; 08-9731 1520; www.brooklodge.com.au) maintains a register of job vacancies in the area. It can take between a couple of hours and seven to ten days to find work locally, depending on the time of year. The season starts in November with thinning out the immature apples and plums and progresses to stone fruit picking December to March, though apple picking carries on until July. Other crops are grown in the vicinity such as tomatoes (picked January to March) and pears (February to April). During the picking season, a contract rate is the norm, ranging from $550 to $700 for a six-day week. Otherwise a straight hourly wage is paid of $14-$15. Transport to work is arranged by Brook Lodge.

A number of other hostels in the area help guests to find seasonal fruit-picking work at most times of the year. The hostel-cum-caravan park is another popular place for apple pickers to stay between March and June. Immigration raids take place at least once a year in this area, but a few farmers continue to employ foreign holidaymakers who have a tax file number.

Climatic conditions will determine what else you take in addition to a long novel to keep you amused until work materialises. High summer temperatures mean that you will need to take water, sunblock and a brimmed hat into the orchards. Later on warm clothes will come in handy as Armin Birrer discovered one chilly autumn: *'The only problem with the south of WA is that the wet season starts in May which lasts till August. And as the season progresses it gets colder and colder and more and more miserable. It's very hard work when you get wet and cold every day, and the trees give you a nice shower when they're wet. I had to buy a heater for my van mostly for drying wet clothes.'*

Mary Anne Mackle spent six weeks picking in Manjimup and found that being paid by the bin was a great motivator to work long hard hours. She and her companion started on a meagre three bins a day but by the end they were filling 16 a day, which shows what a difference some practice can make. By the time she finished, her clothes were in shreds and her body not far behind but she had saved $2,000.

Tasmania is not known as the 'Apple Island' for its shape alone. The apple harvest takes place between March and early May, though other fruit harvests start at the beginning of November with strawberries and apple thinning, followed by cherries and blueberries in late December. Grape picking is available in March/ April. The work is available in the Huon region around Cygnet and Geeveston not far south of Hobart. Like many before him, Robert Abblett recommends the Nomads hostel 'Balfes Hill,' Huon Valley Backpackers, Main Road & Sandhill Road, Cradoc 7109 (03-6295 1551; huonvalley@tassie.net.au): *'As the main accommodation in the area, the hostel finds work for guests and provides transport too. I spent two months working hard for several different orchards, as the crop was intermittent. With previous experience, I saved £1,000. I was put with 20 other strange people for the whole season. The owners (bless 'em) thought I would have a calming influence on them because of my age. No chance.*

Working travellers are charged $140 per week and transport/shopping costs $20 per week.

With years of experience of picking fruit throughout Europe and in other states of Australia, Andrea Militello was as enthusiastic about Tasmania as any place. He spent the month of March picking apples in Cygnet: 'wonderful place, great boss, small trees and big apples so you can get good good money.' The area also offers work picking berry fruit and cherries from November to April.

By February/March Rob Abblett was the only foreigner picking apples at his orchard on the Mornington Peninsula in Victoria. He was delighted to be earning a good hourly wage and not piecework rates plus having free accommodation and the use of a ute for shopping.

Apple orchards also need to be thinned and pruned from mid-December before the picking starts in March. One of the most famous places for this work is Batlow NSW, near the Snowy Mountains where there are a number of orchards, though two of the biggest including the Fruits of Batlow are teetering on the brink of collapse (2004/5) due to mounting debts. Ken Smith is just one traveller to have travelled to nearby Tumut to secure a job before travelling to the area. Pay and conditions in Batlow have in the past been better than in Griffith and Young (see section below on New South Wales Harvests).

OTHER HARVESTS

From asparagus to zucchini there is an abundance of crops to be picked from one end of Australia to the other, and the energetic itinerant picker can do very nicely. Australia has such an enormous agricultural economy that there will always be jobs. Gordon Mitchell from Aberdeen is just one Briton who has worked out a profitable route:

> *I've been picking fruit in Australia for a few years. I make the best money between November and April/May, starting at Young NSW picking cherries. When they finish I do the smaller cherry harvest in Orange NSW, then on to Shepparton Victoria in early January for the pear picking. When the sultanas start in Mildura in early February I do them, though most people stay in Shepparton to finish the pears and apples. This takes me to early or mid-March when the apples start in Orange and finish in late April or early May. Sometimes it's very hectic but that's when the picking is good.*

Queensland

As you travel north the produce, like the weather, gets more tropical so that citrus, pineapples, bananas and mangoes grow in profusion in the north, while stone fruits, apples and potatoes grow in the Darling Downs, 220km inland from Brisbane. In the tropics there are not always definite harvest seasons since crops grow year round. A good clue to the available work can be deduced from the excessively large artificial fruits by the roadside, for example the big pineapple near Nambour.

The prying eyes of immigration are everywhere along the Queensland coast and anyone whose papers are not in order should feel discouraged. From time to time the Immigration Department co-ordinates early morning raids on farms from Bundaberg in the south to Tully in the north, which catch and deport illegal fruit pickers.

Work in the Queensland harvests is strongly monopolised by the hostels. Farmers for the most part rely on hostel wardens to supply them with a workforce, making it hard to fix up a job directly with a farmer and accommodation on farms is rare. Shuttle transport between hostel and farms is often laid on. Make sure you get paid a decent wage and pay a fair price for your transport and accommodation.

About 400km north of Brisbane, the agricultural and rum-producing centre of Bundaberg absorbs a great many travelling workers. All the hostels in town advertise help with employment including Federal Backpackers (07-4153 3711) and City Centre Backpackers (07-4151 3501) both on Bourbong St. The Nomads hostel at 64 Barolin St (07-4151 6097) calls itself a Workers & Diving Hostel. Bundaberg is such a magnet for working travellers that it is often bursting at the seams. Bridgid Seymour-East was not impressed with the scene: *'There are too many hostels and too few jobs to go around. Hostels take about 100 people each so lots of desperate people all together. Most people get only one or two days of work a week, just enough to pay for their hostel bed and food. You cannot choose your jobs and if you quit or get fired they might not give you a job for another week.'*

Roger Blake was no more positive when he arrived as a refugee from the depressing job scene in Brisbane. Sure enough, he started work picking zucchinis at 5am the day after he arrived and hated every minute of it. He managed just over a week of back breaking work before he could no longer tolerate the 'boot camp' attitude of the farmers towards their workers.

The town of Childers is the centre of a harvesting area, though since the tragic fire in June 2000 that killed 15 backpackers at the Childer's Palace Backpackers (a hostel that was used almost exclusively by workers), it has lost much of its appeal. The best paying job in the area is sugarcane planting; Bridgid Seymour-East and her boyfriend managed to save $3,500 in six weeks.

The town of Bowen, centre of a fruit and vegetable-growing region (especially tomatoes) 600km south of Cairns, is another very well known destination for aspiring pickers. Julian Graham spent part of his working holiday in Australia as manager of Barnacles Backpackers in Bowen, which sounds an excellent place to find out about work:

Part of my duties consisted of finding work for travellers at the many local farms. All sorts of picking and packing are available and Bowen is a superb place to recover considerable funds. My girlfriend and I arrived broke and left with enough money to fly to Tasmania for the Sydney-Hobart race and finance a month's travelling in Tas. Anyone arriving in Bowen should do themselves a favour and go straight to Barnacles where they will find you work (May-December) and make you more welcome than anywhere else in the town by a large margin.

Another working hostel in Bowen is Reefers at the Beach on the corner of Soldiers Rd and Horseshore Bay Rd (07) 4786 4199; www.reefers.com.au/work.htm). In fact all the hostels in Bowen cater for working travellers. As always, count on paying $120 a week for a dorm bed, or $150 a week in a double.

Picking and packing work is normally paid hourly – sometimes a dollar or two more for men in sexist Queensland. It is possible to make more with contract picking especially if you are experienced. At a rate of $1 a bucket, a professional tomato picker can earn up to $350 a day, but even inexperienced pickers can hit $100. A good time to arrive is the end of August. If the backpackers' hostels in Bowen are full, accommodation is limited so having a tent is an advantage.

The farmers usually provide a minibus once the picking really gets going, which costs a couple of dollars from Bowen. Otherwise a bicycle would be handy. If you're job-hunting farm-to-farm, go out on the Bootooloo or Collinsville Roads or to the Delta or Euri Creek areas. Apparently the tail end of the harvest in November can be a good time to show up, when lots of seasonal workers are beginning to drift south. If the farmers are desperate enough, they pay premium rates, sometimes even double.

Caroline Perry got off the harvest-workers' minibus at the last stop called Climate Capital Packers (Collinsville Road, Bowen, Qld 4805; or PO Box 908, Bowen 4805; 07-4785 2622). This is a packing and freezing shed for four of the largest farms in the area, mainly capsicum and rock melons. While they do not guarantee work to backpackers, they do regularly employ them (with working holiday visas). Caroline's job earned her $3,274 net in two and a half months. In the busy season (between May and November packers can earn $500 a week. At other times, hours are shorter and therefore earnings are less. Weekly pay cheques are paid directly into a bank account (Caroline recommends the ANZ Bank.)

Heading north, vegetables are picked around Ayr south of Townsville between June and September. Mary Anne Mackle recommends staying at the Silverlink Caravan Park in Ayr, whose owners gave her a list of farmers and where all new arrivals looking for work found it within a couple of days, picking squash, zucchini, cucumbers, peppers, pumpkins and rock melons. Apparently locals prefer to work on the better paid sugar cane harvest which takes place over the same period. Frank Schiller saved a cool $1,400 after four weeks of capsicum-picking near Ayr. Among their recreations, the pickers went dancing in Ayr 'where they've got both kinds of music – Country and Western.'

Further north, Cardwell, Innisfail and Tully offer work in banana and sometimes sugar plantations. Farmers around Tully (the wettest place in Australia) organise transport between town and the properties. Try asking at the purpose-built working hostel Banana Barracks at 21 Richardson St (07-4068 0455; info@bananabarracks.com). Henry Pearce describes his gruelling job as a banana cutter in October:

The bananas all grew together on a single stem which could weigh up to 60kg. The farmer cut into the trunk to weaken it and, once I had pulled the fruit down onto my shoulder, he cut the stem and I staggered off to place them on a 'nearby' trailer. The work was physically shattering and the presence of large frogs and rats inside the bunch (thankfully no snakes) jumping out at the last minute didn't do anything to increase my enjoyment. We were paid by the hour and worked an eight hour day, five days a week which was standard for the area.

Working with Queensland fruits seems to be an activity fraught with danger. If you decide to pick pineapples, you have to wear long-sleeved shirts and jeans (despite the sizzling heat between January and April) as protection from the prickles and spines. Caroline Perry advises anyone who packs rock melons to wear gloves; otherwise the abrasive skin rips your hands to shreds. Worst of all apparently is that lovely fruit, the mango, as Julian Graham explains:

One in three pickers is allergic to the sap contained in mangoes, and in some cases contact with the fruit produces an extreme reaction. Having sent pickers out to the fields and seen at first hand the state they come back in I feel duty-bound to warn people that they may be that unfortunate one in three. One girl's face and limbs became so swollen she had to fly home where it took several injections of steroids to cure her. Remarkably, the hospital at Bowen proved completely incompetent in dealing with this problem and offered no remedy at all. Having spoken to many farmers, it became evident that if the sap squirts into your eyes, serious damage can occur.

Still, if you don't react badly, mango picking can be less strenuous than other harvests since the mangoes are picked off the ground after the trees have been shaken. Whereas the four-week mango harvest around Bowen starts in November, the harvest in the Atherton Tablelands (around Mareeba) starts in early to mid-December.

Southern Queensland is also a good destination. Head for Stanthorpe almost on the NSW border in November for peach and pear picking and January/February for tomato picking. Summit Backpackers (07-4683 2044) and Stanthorpe Backpackers (07-4681 8888) are good sources of job information and transport. Just after the new year Jane Harris and her friend Pete drove to Stanthorpe. During their first day of driving farm to farm and asking for work, they were hired as tomato pickers:

We spent the hardest day of our lives picking egg tomatoes. By the end of the day

382 Work Your Way Worldwide

neither of us could stand up straight without feeling pain. So, we decided picking wasn't for us and left. Short of money, we later decided to give the place another go, knowing that the employment office was about to open for harvest work. This time was a lot more successful, sorting tomatoes for me and 'bucketing' for Pete. Bucketing means carrying empty buckets to the pickers and taking the full ones away to be sorted. When Pete told the farmer he wasn't sure he could keep it up, as the farmer employed the fastest tomato picker in Australia who was picking well over 350 buckets a day, surprise surprise, the farmer said he'd give him some easier work.

Potatoes and onions are harvested in the Lockyer Valley in the Darling Downs. The harvest around Gatton lasts from August to November, although problems caused by the increasing saltiness of the soil have been cutting yields. Head for the Tenthill Caravan Park (M.S. 149, Mount Sylvia Road, Tenthill, Qld 4343; 07-5462 7200) near Gatton where the owner knows about local opportunities. In most cases you will have to have your own transport. Potato and onion picking is paid piece work, and many travellers find that they have to work intolerably hard to make a decent wage. Contract jobs with local growers of lettuce, etc. are also available but will probably pay no more than $12 an hour.

New South Wales

The southern part of the state around Wagga Wagga is known is the Riverina. Seasonal work opportunities can be found in Batlow, Jugiong, Leeton and Young as well as Darlington Point, Gundagai, Hay and so on. The OzJobs offices in Griffith at 108 Yambil Street (02-6961 8405) or Young 145 Boorowa Street (02-6382 1547) should be able to assist.

The asparagus harvest at Jugiong on the Hume Highway northwest of Canberra attracts many seasonal pickers, as does the cherry harvest around Young half an hour north of Jugiong which starts as the asparagus finishes. The packing season is a long one from about late September to at least mid-November. The work is notoriously back-breaking but can be lucrative, as much as $500 a week net. Note that Powers Asparagus mentioned in previous editions closed in 2003.

Conflicting accounts of the cherry harvest near Young between mid-November and Christmas have been received. Whereas some recommend its money-making potential and good camp atmosphere, others advise steering clear and say that the magic figure of $100 a day in earnings is exaggerated. The unpredictable weather and piece work pay rates make it difficult to make good money. Mary Anne Mackle thought it the worst job she did in Australia (while admitting that it was her first harvesting job). She had her hands cut to ribbons trying to avoid picking the buds along with the fruit and was terrorised by bull ants which swarmed in the branches; for all this she earned $300 a week. No wonder work is so easy to obtain here. When Geertje Korf turned up at an employment agency in Young, not only did a helpful member of staff find her a friendly orchard with cooking facilities, but drove her to the farm personally. One of the main ones is Cherry Haven Orchards on Cowra Road (02-6382 4023).

The cotton harvest in the extreme north of New South Wales needs workers from the first week of November and occasionally advertises in Sydney to attract them. The Tandara Caravan Park in Trangie (02-6888 7330) advertises job vacancies in the area November to May. Richard Edwards discovered that the possibilities for cotton workers around Wee Waa were extensive year-round but especially in October/November which is the cotton-chipping season. Richard earned $600 a week.

Of all the many picking jobs that Henry Pearce found, the best money was earned working on onions around Griffith, where he and his girlfriend saved an impressive $5,000 in ten weeks between early January and March. For a short time Henry was paid $11 a bin and could manage 17 bins a day, alongside a clan of Turks who return every year. However, mostly he was paid the agreed daily rate (however many hours he worked) but the reliability of work made up for the low pay. You have to be lucky to find work in this harvest particularly if you don't have your own transport. Ask at all the onion-packing sheds in Griffith.

Leeton near Griffith is the centre of a citrus-growing area where Vince Crombez from Belgium headed as soon as he arrived in Australia in December. He earned $14 per bin of oranges but could pick only one every two hours because the harvest was a poor one. Ask at the campsite (where an on-site van will cost a pair of people about $130 a week).

Victoria

The summer fruit harvests in northern Victoria annually attract many participants on working holidays. The best time to arrive is mid to late January and work should continue until the end of March. As well as contacting the National Harvest Labour Information Service mentioned above, contact can also be made with the Northern Victoria Fruitgrowers' Association Ltd, PO Box 612, Mooroopna, (2 Rumbalara Rd, Mooroopna) Victoria 3629 (03-5825 3700; www.nvfa.com.au), with the Victorian Peach and Apricot Growers' Association, (vpaga@cnl.com.au) or OzJobs (361 Wyndham St, Shepparton; 03-5833 4800). Victorian farmers are noted for providing accommodation more often than elsewhere, though anyone with camping gear will be placed more easily. Once again, some people make a killing while others complain of pathetic earnings. Whereas Vince Crombez earned $80 in six hours picking pears, Alison Cooper made $25 in nine hours. The current casual hourly rate is $15.07 and the piece work rate (for example of pears and peaches) is $29.62 per half-ton bin.

Mooroopna is just outside Shepparton and is a good place to look for work. Ask in the pub about tomato-picking possibilities in February and March. You might want to buy a second-hand bicycle from the shop on the main street of Shepparton to get around the area. McCamish Bros. in Mooroopna are big growers of apricots, peaches and pears which are picked between January and April. R J Cornish & Co in Cobram are massive employers too (03-5872 2055; jobs@rjcornish.com) as are Plunkett Orchards in Ardmona in the Goulburn Valley (03-5829 0015; www.plunkettorchards.com.au) and McNab & Son also in Ardmona (03-5829 0016; www.fruitpicking.com.au). Pickers coming to the area can stay at the Cobram Willows Caravan Park on the Murray Valley Highway (03-5872 1074) where they will meet lots of people earning $60-$100 a day between December and March. The hourly rate for fruit grading (for instance at Plunkett Orchards) is over $15.

In the northwestern corner of the state, Mildura (mentioned above as a centre for grape-growing) is a major agricultural district and Cardross across the river is also a promising destination. Work is available virtually year-round (May is the slowest month) due to the sunny climate and epic irrigation schemes. Contact the MADEC Harvest Jobs Australia office in Mildura (03-5022 1797; www.MADEC.edu.au). A high proportion of the travellers staying in Mildura's hostels take advantage of the job-finding and transport-providing services of places like the Riverboat Bungalow (27 Chaffey Avenue; 03-5021 5315; bungalow@vic.ozland.net.au) where the majority of guests are working or looking for work. Jane Inckle took advantage of her hostel's job-finding and transport-providing services:

The managers arrange work for everyone; consequently you're less likely to get dodgy deals, which is especially good for female travellers who, incidentally, are preferred for packing, sorting and grafting work. At the moment (spring) we've been planting vines, picking citrus fruit, packing asparagus. Rock melons start soon for good money, so I'm told. The place is a magnet for international working holidaymakers, with Poms a little thin on the ground, which makes a pleasant change.

Work is also available nearer Melbourne for example at the nurseries in the Dandenong Ranges (all year round) and fruit picking in November/December. Emerald Backpackers Hostel (2 Lakeview Crescent, Emerald, Vic 3782; 03-5968 4086) one hour east of Melbourne is renowned for finding work year-round in local nurseries. Robert Abblett stayed here while working for a cut flower grower in the winter (July/August). He spent each day bent double collecting bunches of hyacinths and tulips but was well rewarded, saving £800 in six weeks. Most of the other people in the hostel (including, for obvious reasons, many Dutch people) were also working in nurseries and factories, and using the transport provided to the farms.

Although harvesting work is often not hard to get, some find it hard to make any money. The pear crates may look quite small at the outset but will soon seem unfillable with mysterious false bottoms. Many eager first-timers do not realise how hard the work will be physically, and give up before their bodies acclimatise. But you should have faith that your speed will increase fairly rapidly.

South Australia

The Riverland region of South Australia (not to be confused with the Riverina in NSW) consists of Renmark, Loxton and Waikerie but is centred on Berri where most of the backpacker accommodation and job agencies like Select and Rivskills are located. In recent years work has been available all year round due to the expansion of the wine and citrus industries. Berri Backpackers (Box 203, Berri, SA 5343; 08-8582 3144) continues to get rave reviews from long-stay residents. Daniele Arena called this hostel 'the most wonderful probably in the whole world' since he greatly enjoyed their regular barbecues for $6-$7.

According to an earlier report from Bridgid Seymour-East who also loved this hostel, landing some work is a bit of a free-for-all:

> Whoever answers the phone first gets a job first, which can seem a bit daunting at first (survival of the fittest). We started on citrus picking for a big company Yandilla Park. Whilst the contract rate is high, you don't get that many hours in the long run because you can't pick citrus until the fruit is dry on the tree. Often you can't start picking until 11am or 12 noon, which can be very frustrating. But it gives you enough money to survive until the vine work begins. At the end of June I got a job cutting canes which involves taking a cutting from the grape vines, trimming it to size and bundling it in bunches of 100. Whilst extremely boring, I never made less than $120 a day after tax and on good days $200, so I was getting pay cheques of $800-$900 a week.

The biggest employers in the Berri area are:

Angas Park – 08-8561 0800; www.angaspark.com.au. Apricots and peaches are picked December to April. Men only. 7 days a week, 10 hours a day. Extra money paid at weekends. No days off (or you're fired).

Simarloo – 08-8583 8269. Apricots and plums picked in Lyrup December to March. Contract work (i.e. per bin).

Solora – 08-8584 1322; www.solora.com.au. Citrus work from mid-May till March. Untrained pickers take at least a week to get the hang of it.

Yandilla Park – 08-8586 1200; www.yandillapark.com.au. Peak period April-November.

In addition to these big companies, there are at least 1,000 small family blocks which need helpers. Other accommodation for pickers is available on campsites.

Nearer Adelaide, a major employer of travellers and casual fruit pickers is Torrens Valley Orchards (Forreston Rd, Gumeracha; 08-8389 1405; www.tvo.com.au), located just south of the Barossa Valley wine region and only a $5 bus ride from the state capital. Cherry picking and packing takes place in December/January, pear picking and packing from February to September, tree planting and training, pruning, maintenance and office work year round. Most recruitment is conducted over the internet.

Western Australia

The area around Donnybrook is not just good for apple-picking as described earlier. Sara Runnalls picked grapes one January for $2.50 a bin before moving on to work in a nursery for five weeks planting gum seedlings. Vegetables are extensively grown in this area creating jobs in the fields and packing sheds. Armin Birrer packed onions around Manjimup just long enough to remind himself how much he dislikes indoor work, especially in dusty and smelly conditions. Cauliflower picking work is available in winter to those who can stand the freezing conditions. More appealing because warmer is the orange harvest around Harvey (north of Bunbury) which starts in June.

There are over 100 vegetable and banana plantations around the cities of Geraldton and Carnarvon north of Perth, many of which are very short of pickers in the winter when they are busy supplying the markets of Perth. The tomato harvest lasts from early August until mid-November, with the month of September being the easiest time to find work. The banana harvest starts in October, but there is casual work available anytime between April and November, most of which pays roughly $10 an hour. This is such a well known area for casual workers that immigration raids are not unknown. One way of meeting farmers is to go to the warehouses or packing depots where growers come to drop off their produce.

Agricultural development around Kununurra in the extreme north of the state is extensive, and every traveller passing through seems to stop to consider the possibility of working in the banana, melon, citrus or vegetable harvests. Travellers are regularly hired during the first part of 'The Dry' (the dry season lasts from May to July) and beyond. If you can't fix up work through the Youth Hostel or the Backpackers Resort hostel, contact Ord River Bananas, Bonza Bananas and Oasis Bananas. For the melon harvest between May and October contact Bluey's Outback Farm (08-9168 2177; www.blueysoutbackfarm.com.au). Other melon farm contacts are listed on www.kimberleyagriculture.com/ordrivermelons/farm-contacts.html.

There is a lot more work for men in Kununurra than for women, especially picking melons and bananas. Packing jobs are usually in shorter supply and are therefore quickly snapped up. You can also try to find work 'topping' or detassling corn, which may take place in temperatures of 35°C. To exacerbate the suffering of an 11-hour day, the corn gives pickers a rash on their arms and legs.

AUSTRALIAN HARVESTS		
Crop	**New South Wales**	**Dates of Harvest**
Strawberries	Glenorie & Campbelltown	Sep-Dec
Cherries	Orange	Nov-Jan
	Young	Oct-Dec
Peaches &	Glenorie	Oct-Jan
Nectarines	Campbelltown	Nov-Jan
	Orange	Feb-Mar
	Bathurst	Jan-Mar
	Leeton & Griffith, Forbes	Feb-Apr
	Young	Feb-Mar
Plums	Glenorie	Nov-Jan
	Orange	Jan-Mar
	Young	Jan-Mar
Apricots	Leeton & Griffith	Dec-Jan
	Kurrajong	Nov
Apples & Pears	Oakland, Glenorie & Bilpin	Jan-Apr
	Armidale	Feb-May
	Orange	Feb-May
	Bathurst	Mar-May
	Forbes	Feb-Apr
	Batlow	Feb-May
	Griffith & Leeton	Jan-Apr
	Young	Mar-Apr
Crop	**New South Wales (cont.)**	**Dates of Harvest**
Oranges (Valencia)	Outer Sydney	Sep-Feb

	Riverina, Mid-Murray	Sep-Mar
	Narromine	Sep-Feb
	Leeton	Dec-Jan
Lemons	Outer Sydney, Riverina, Mid-Murray, Coomealla	Jul-Oct
Grapefruits	Mid-Murray	Nov-Apr
	Curlwaa	Jun-Feb
Asparagus	Dubbo, Bathurst, Cowra, Jugiong	Sep-Dec
Wheat	Narrabri, Walgett	Nov-Dec
Cotton	Warren & Nevertire, Wee Waa	Nov-Mar
Onions	Griffith	Nov-Mar

Crop	**South Australia**	**Dates of Harvest**
Apricots	Riverland (Waikerie, Barmera, Berri, Loxton, Renmark)	Dec-Jan
Peaches	Riverland	Jan-Feb
Pumpkins &	Riverland	May-Jul
Oranges	Riverland	Jun-Apr

Crop	**Victoria**	**Dates of Harvest**
Pears & Peaches	Shepparton, Ardmona, Mooroopna Kyabram Invergordon, Cobram	Jan-Mar
Tomatoes	Shepparton/Mooroopna, Tatura Kyabram Echuca, Tongala Rochester Swan Hill Elmore	Jan-Apr
Tobacco	Ovens & Kiewa Valley	Feb-Apr
Potatoes	Warragul, Neerim	Feb-May
Cherries	Silvan, Lilydale, Warburton, Lilydale	Nov-Dec
Berries	Silvan, Wandin, Monbulk, Macclesfield, Hoddles Creek, Daylesford	Nov-Feb
Apples & Pears	Myrtleford	Mar-May
	Goulburn Valley	Jan-Apr
	Mornington Peninsula	Mar-May
Flowers & Bulbs	Emerald	Jan-Dec

Crop	**Western Australia**	**Dates of Harvest**
Apples & Pears	Donnybrook, Manjimup, Balingup, Pemberton	Mar-Jun
Oranges	Bindoon, Lower Chittering	Aug-Sept
	Harvey	Jun-Jul
Lemons &	Bindoon, Lower Chittering	Nov-Feb
Grapefruit	Harvey	
Apricots, Peaches & Plums	Kalamunda, Walliston, Pickering Brook	Dec-Mar
Tomatoes, vegetables	Carnarvon, Geraldton	Aug-Nov
Bananas	Carnarvon	Oct
Melons, Bananas, etc.	Kununurra/Lake Argyle	May-Oct

Crop	Queensland	Dates of Harvest
Bananas	Tully	October
Tomatoes	Bowen	Aug-Nov
Peaches & Plums	Stanthorpe	Dec-Mar
Watermelons	Bundaberg	Nov-Dec
Potatoes	Lockyer Valley	Oct-Dec
Onions	Lockyer Valley	Sep-Oct
Pineapples	Nambour, Maryborough, Bundaberg, Yeppoon	Jan-Apr
Apples	Stanthorpe	Feb-Mar
Citrus	Gayndah, Mundubbera	May-Sep
Strawberries	Redlands	Jul-Nov
Mangoes	Bowen	Nov-Dec
	Mareeba	Dec-Jan
Cucumbers, etc.	Ayr	May-Nov
Courgettes	Mackay	Aug-Sep

INDUSTRY

Factory and cannery jobs are occasionally advertised in newspapers or you may hear about openings from other working travellers. City employment agencies like Drake Industrial are a good bet.

Ken Smith took the unusual step of visiting factories in Sydney door-to-door:
There are huge industrial estates all over Sydney and really some of them have staff turnovers that are almost daily. My advice would be to get a 336 bus from Circular Quay, get off at Matraville or Botany Bay and just walk around the factories asking if they have any vacancies. Overall Sydney is a wonderfully cosmopolitan place. Of the 23 people who worked for the engineering firm I worked for, only three were Anglo-Australians. The rest were Indians, Fijians, Indians and Chinese.

Mining

The mining industry of Australia does offer some opportunities to travellers, particularly to those with a background in catering. Whereas some people take a chance on fronting up in the mining towns of Western Australia (e.g. Dampier, Karratha, Port Hedland, Kalgoorlie) to look for work, others approach the head offices in Perth. Melanie Grey reported that she earned $600 a week working as a breakfast chef for a catering company on a nickel mine. She recommends tracking down the head office of catering companies in Perth, 'armed with references from home and a big cheesy smile'. The wages paid on mines are generally high to compensate workers for working in a remote place. Most of the offices of sub-contracting companies are located in or near Mt Newman House at 200 St George's Terrace in downtown Perth.

Gold mining continues in Western Australia, and union membership is seldom a prerequisite of employment. The gold mining town of Kalgoorlie is a place which past contributors have recommended for year-round employment, among them Lucy Slater:

I know everyone tells you not to hitch but we found that people who gave us lifts between Perth and Kalgoorlie were mines of information with ideas of companies to try, people to ask for, etc. Through a hitching contact my boyfriend got a job in the gold mines. The work was hard going but the hours were long and so there was a lot of money to be made. There seemed to be quite a lot of work going, which did not surprise me since the place is a hellhole. The red dust gets everywhere, it's hot, loads of flies and is quite dead.

Employment in survey and drilling is available, provided you make certain preparations. You must undergo a drugs test, a criminal record check with the police and take a half-day safety induction course which costs $130-$150 from the Mining and Resource Contractors Safety Training Association (www.marcsta.com). Once you have completed these steps, the accepted way of finding work in Kalgoorlie is to go around or phone all the relevant companies listed in the *Yellow Pages* or on the Access list of mines, drilling, surveying and lab companies. Exploration companies occasionally hire unskilled assistants (known as 'fieldies', 'TAs' or 'offsiders') who are sometimes sent into remote areas (like Norseman and Leonora at the end of the sealed road heading north) where pay starts at $500 per week in the hand plus free caravan or motel accommodation. Most people work nearer town and earn $11-$13 an hour, with weekend work being particularly lucrative. Some offsider work requires a truck driving licence, which is very easy to get, assuming you can afford the $200 fee for about three lessons and the test (see Driving below). Jeremy Pack describes his job: *'As an offsider, I have been going off into the bush with a walkie talkie, axe, tape measure and stakes, while the boss stays behind his instrument making sure my pegs are in straight. Sometimes we camp out in the really nowhere bush.'*

It is possible to find opals by 'noodling', i.e. sifting through the slag heaps around Coober Pedy. Anne Wakeford had a go and found seven opals in two days of careful searching, one of which was worth $100. Other recommended places are Mintabie and Andamooka, which are on Aboriginal land in remote South Australia, but can be visited after purchasing a permit for $5 from the police in Marla.

You might also find a job in areas related to mining. For example there is a firm called SGS Australia (formerly Analabs) whose headquarters are at 1/3 de Laeter Way, Technology Park, Bentley WA 6102 (08-9472 5555) which occasionally takes on temporary staff. The work involves the preparation of rock samples for chemical analysis, a job which is reported to be dirty and monotonous. Some laboratory work is occasionally available too. The pay for casual workers is about $15 an hour. The company also maintains a lab in Townsville.

Construction and Labouring

Darwin has always been a mecca for drifters, deportees and drop-outs looking for labouring work, though there are fewer job adverts in the Territory's papers than there once were. As the rains recede in May, the human deluge begins and competition for jobs is intense. It is better to be around at the end of the Wet (April) to fix something up beforehand.

If you do happen to get a building job in Australia, you may benefit from some of the interesting perks which the strong unions have negotiated. Workers on buildings over eight storeys high earn a height allowance, even if their work keeps them firmly on the ground.

Tradesmen of all descriptions usually find it easy to get work in Australia, especially if they bring their papers and tools. Plumbers, electricians and carpenters have been having a field day, particularly of course in Sydney. A pair of steel-capped boots would also be a useful accessory.

Mechanics are in great demand as Brian Williams from Wales found when he toured the country. Potential employers in Sydney were not too bothered that he lacked a working holiday visa but they did want to have his British qualifications verified (which would have necessitated showing a work visa). So he and his partner and their three year old son headed up to Darwin where, through meeting someone in a pub, he was soon working in a bodyshop.

Driving and Vehicles

Several travellers have found it possible to get driving jobs after they have gone to the trouble of acquiring an Australian licence especially the 'B' class licence which permits you to drive trucks. The possibility of failing the test didn't worry Dan Ould: *'The test mainly involves driving a truck around the block while the examiner gazes out of the window. If you don't crash you've passed. But the process of taking a few lessons and the test will cost several hundred dollars, worth it in my view since it opens up lots of job opportunities.'* In the South Australian town of Ceduna on the Nullarbor highway, Dan heard of lots of driving jobs, mainly because so many locals had lost their licences for drunk driving.

An ability to drive can be a handy asset in the cities too, since papers like the Melbourne *Age* are full of adverts for furniture removers, drivers and cab mates (called 'jockeys' in Victoria). Stephen Psallidas observed that there seemed to be more bicycle and motorcycle couriers in Sydney than cars, so you might investigate possibilities.

Buying and selling vehicles can also be profitable for anyone who understands engines. Mechanic Brian Williams and Adrienne Robinson bought three vehicles for touring the country and sold two at a profit: *'We bought one van for $950 to sell but decided to keep it and moved on. It saw us good for 12,000km and we sold it for $1,500 to a dealer.'*

Private enterprise does not always pay off like this, as Chris Miksovsky found in Brisbane. He tried his hand at being an intersection windscreen washer but was bluntly made to stop by the police after his second windscreen.

Another vehicle-related job is 'detailing cars' i.e. washing, polishing and hoovering. Rhona Stannage met two English women in Darwin who had both found this job by asking at car garages and sales offices.

TOURISM AND CATERING

This category of employment might include anything from cooking on prawn trawlers out of Darwin (read the fine print), to acting as a temporary warden in a Tasmanian youth hostel. You might find yourself serving beer at a roadhouse along the nearly uninhabited road through the Australian north-west or serving at a Sizzler diner in the big cities. Casual employees make up 60% of the 140,000 workforce employed in the hospitality industry. Whatever the job, expect to present yourself as a serious candidate. According to Ken Smith who noticed plenty of 'Help Wanted' signs up in restaurant and shop windows in Melbourne, 'even a job washing dishes usually requires several months relevant experience.'

Casual catering wages both in the cities and in remote areas are higher than the equivalent British wage. The award rate for waiting staff in New South Wales is about $12.50 an hour, with weekend loadings of time and a half on Saturdays and time and three-quarters on Sundays and holidays. People being paid cash-in-hand may be offered less. Although tipping was not traditionally practised in Australia, it is gradually becoming more common and waiting staff in trendy city establishments can expect to augment their basic wage to some extent.

Standards tend to be fairly high especially in popular tourist haunts. A common practice among restaurant bosses in popular places from Bondi Beach to the Sunshine Coast is to give a job-seeker an hour's trial or a trial shift and decide at the end whether or not to employ them. Stephen Psallidas was taken aback when he approached a hospitality employment agency in Cairns: *'I was in Cairns in April and thought I'd have little trouble getting work. But though I had a visa and experience I had no references, having worked as a waiter in Greece, where they wouldn't know a reference if one walked up and said 'Hi, I'm a reference', so I was doomed from the start. The agency told me that if I'd had references they could have given me work immediately. Curses.'*

Sara Runnalls, a qualified chef, was more successful with her agency in Cairns who sent her to four and five star hotels in Cairns and Port Douglas. She enjoyed this, but not half as much as working as a chef at the Olympics where she served afternoon tea to Princess Anne.

Those with experience as cooks or chefs will probably find themselves in demand all over Australia. One tourist area which is not normally inundated with backpacking job-seekers is the stretch of Victorian coast between Dromana and Portsea on the Mornington

Peninsula near Melbourne. Although most jobs don't start until after Christmas, the best time to look is late November/early December.

If exploring Australia is your target rather than earning high wages, it is worth trying to exchange your labour for the chance to join an otherwise unaffordable tour. For example camping tour operators in Kakadu and Litchfield Park have been known to do this; try Billy Can Tours (www.billycan.com.au).

Australia has a number of external island territories including Christmas Island, the Coral Sea Islands and Cocos Islands all of which have a tourist industry. According to a newspaper article a couple of years ago, employment possibilities exist on tiny Christmas Island (population 2,564) south of Java. Bars, restaurants and discos cater to the well-heeled tourists who come, mainly for the gambling. Trained croupiers and chefs are always in demand especially if they convince the resort company that they will stay for a reasonable length of time.

Queensland

Because of Queensland's attractions for all visitors to Australia, the competition for jobs comes mostly from travellers, who are more interested in having a good time than in earning a high wage. The pay is generally so low in seasonal jobs in the Queensland tourist industry that the work does not appeal to many Australians, since they can earn nearly as much as on the dole. When employers need to fill a vacancy, they tend to hire whomever is handy that day, rather than sift through applications. For example if you phone from Sydney to enquire about possibilities, the advice will normally be to come and see.

If you want a live-in position, you should try the coastal resorts such as Surfers Paradise and Noosa Heads and islands all along the Queensland coast where the season lasts from March, after the cyclones, until Christmas. If Cairns is choc-a-bloc with job-seekers try the huge resort of Palm Cove just north of the city. Many of the small islands along the Barrier Reef are completely given over to tourist complexes. You might make initial enquiries at employment offices on the mainland for example in Proserpine, Cannonvale, Mackay or Townsville, though normally you will have to visit an island in person (and therefore pay for the ferry). Among the many possibilities are the Kingfisher Bay Resort on Fraser Island (human_resources@kingfisherbay.com) and the Heron Island Tourist Resort. Even if you don't land a proper full-time job you might be able to negotiate a few hours of work a day in exchange for free accommodation as sometimes happens at the Great Keppel Island Holiday Village (www.gkiholidayvillage.com.au).

Voyages Hotels & Resorts bought out P&O Australian Resorts in 2004 but the resorts on Heron Island, Lizard Island, Bedarra, Brampton and Dunk Islands plus Silky Oaks Lodge in the Daintree Rainforest of North Queensland and Wrotham Park Station in the Far North Gulf region are still run in the same way. They employ large numbers of seasonal staff, mainly with relevant experience in hospitality. Their employment website (www.poresorts.com/careers) includes detailed fact sheets on living and working in each of their resorts including number of employees, perks and accommodation (most resorts charge $32-$50 a week for staff accommodation plus $78 for meals) and contact details for job-seekers in each resort, e.g. careers@heron.poresorts.com. You could also try in advance Rydges Capricorn International Resort (Farnborough Road, PO Box 350, Yeppoon, Qld 4703; www.rydges.com/about/jobs.asp).

Be warned that Queensland employers are notorious for laying off their staff at a moment's notice without compensation, holiday pay, etc. Emma Dunnage was disillusioned with one of the six backpackers hostels on Magnetic Island where she worked for ten weeks as a catamaran instructor-cum-general dogsbody. She was paid $100 a week, half of what most of the other staff were getting. In fact there is an 'Offshore Islands Award' for workers in isolated places which is a minimum of $350 a week in addition to board and lodging, though it seems that it is often ignored.

Tourist development along the Queensland coast is progressing at an alarming rate, especially with an eye to the Japanese market. Anyone who has travelled in Japan or who has a smattering of Japanese might have the edge over the competition (unless the competition happens to be a Japanese working holidaymaker of whom there are many in Cairns and elsewhere). James Blackman, who hadn't studied any Oriental languages, describes how he got his job at a resort in the Whitsunday Islands:

Giving up on Airlie Beach I went to Hamilton Island to search for work. I went to practically every establishment and was turned away. However I persevered and the second last place gave me a job as a kitchen hand in a restaurant which was on the beach front. Lots of different people staffed the resort and most were quite friendly, always asking, 'How're ya going?' I spent ten weeks there earning about $150-200 per five-day week.

James also noticed that working holiday visas were expected on these resort islands.

Roger Blake was luckier in Airlie Beach and the initial two weeks of work as a handyman, gardener, labourer and jack-of-all-trades at some swanky apartments was extended to six:

I saved a tidy sum and figured I had enough to do the East Coast. I loved Airlie Beach and not without good reasons. Besides the obvious - the climate, crystal clear and turquoise Whitsunday waters and stunning ocean views - being a familiar face in this one-street town also had perks. I made good friends with many locals and was treated as one. For example I qualified for $2 beers at a popular bar which otherwise charges absurd resort prices.

Caroline Perry was fairly confident that a commercial resort like Surfers Paradise would offer opportunities to work but didn't have much luck filling in forms and waiting for the phone to ring. Eventually she and a friend got work in Movie World, 21km from Surfers Paradise on the Pacific Highway.

The Gold Coast has a number of theme parks with good opportunities for casual work during holiday periods, mainly in food and beverage and retail service. It will be difficult to save any money since wages are not high and you will have to pay for transport between a hostel in town. Check for adverts in the *Gold Coast Bulletin* on Saturdays or in the Brisbane *Courier Mail*. Alternatively contact the Warner Bros. Theme Parks Employment Hotline on 07-5573 8350 which services Movieworld, Sea World and Wet 'n' Wild (the latter is being massively expanded in 2005). The contact address for the Human Resources Department is Warner Village Theme Parks, Pacific Motorway, Oxenford, Queensland 4217 (hr@wvtp.com.au); they will keep your application on file for up to three months. Another big employer is Dreamworld in Coomera which welcomes applications by post or in person only.

Yet another possibility for work on the Gold Coast is Conrad Jupiters casino resort; the Recruitment Centre is at PO Box 1515, Broadbeach Island, Broadbeach, Qld 4218 (cjhrd@conrad.com.au).

Diving and Watersports

One of the larger employers is the dive industry. Although not many visitors would have the qualifications which got Ian Mudge a job as Dive Master on *Nimrod III* operating out of Cookstown (i.e. qualified mechanical engineer, diver and student of Japanese), his assessment of opportunities for mere mortals is heartening:

Anyone wishing to try their luck as a hostess could do no worse than to approach all the dive operators with live-aboard boats such as Mike Ball Water Sports in Townsville, Down Under Dive, etc. 'Hosties' make beds, clean cabins and generally tidy up. Culinary skills and an ability to speak Japanese would be definite pluses. A non-diver would almost certainly be able to fix up some free dive lessons and thus obtain their basic Open Water Diver qualification while being paid to do so. Normally females only are considered for hostie jobs.

Travellers with a sailing qualification might find temporary work instructing. The sailing season in Sydney lasts from October to April with the peak in December. There is no point in looking for work in the Antipodean winter. To take one example Northside Sailing School at Spit Bridge in the Sydney suburb of Mosman (02-9969 3972; www.northsidesailing.com.au) offers casual instructing work during school holidays to travellers who have experience in teaching dinghy sailing especially to kids. There is often a shortage of staff in early September though opportunities would not be full-time. Flying Fish (see Tourism chapter) run a structured Work Experience programme in Australia. After yacht and dive training, graduates can be helped to find work in the industry. Many trainees who have completed Professional Dive Training with the Pro Dive Academy in Sydney (www.academy.prodive.com) go on to work at Pro Dive's network of resorts in Australia and the South Pacific.

Ski Resorts

Another holiday area to consider is the Australian Alps where ski resorts are expanding and gaining in popularity. Jindabyne (NSW) on the edge of Kosciuszko National Park and Thredbo are the ski job capitals, though Mount Buller, Falls Creek, Baw Baw and Hotham in the state of Victoria are relatively developed ski centres too. The best time to look is a couple of weeks before the season opens which in Jindabyne is usually around the 11th of June. The employment offices in Wangaratta and Cooma can advise, though most successful job-seekers use the walk-in-and-ask method. In 'Jindy' try the Brumby Bar, Aspen Chalet Hotel, Kookaburra Lodge or any of the dozens of other hotels and pubs.

Denise Crofts went straight from a waitressing job in King's Cross Sydney to the large Hotel Arlberg in Mount Buller, where she had a terrific season, since that year the resort had the best snow it had had in a decade. The hotel accepts applications for vacancies posted online (www.arlberg.com.au/jobs.html). In Mount Hotham try the tourist establishments like the Jack Frost Bar & Restaurant, the General Bar or Herbies. There is considerable staff turn-over mid-season, though obviously May/June is a better time to look.

Henry Pearce's experiences looking for work were not so positive, despite heavy radio advertising:

> When we hitched to Cooma on June 2nd, we enquired about the progress of the applications we had sent in April. We were told that there had been 4,000 applications and two vacancies for bar staff to date. We carried on up to Thredbo and half-heartedly asked around a few chalets and hotels and it seemed most of them had already fixed up their basic requirements. We were told of several definite posts available once the snow fell. In Jindabyne we were hired to work at the 'highest restaurant in Australia' (at the top of the ski lift). But accommodation was uniformly expensive in Jindabyne ($100+ a week) as was the cost of lift passes and ski hire.

Anyone qualified as a ski instructor should attend the hiring clinics held in the big resorts before the season gets underway. Kosciuszko Thredbo Pty Ltd. at the Alpine Ski Village Thredbo (PO Box 92, Thredbo 2625; 02-6459 4100; recruitment@thredbo.com.au) hire the full range of ski resort staff in three categories: on-the-mountain, hotel and instruction. Their website www.thredbo.com.au provides detailed information about recruitment procedures; applications must be in by 21st April (2005). The names of short-listed candidates will be listed on the website shortly afterwards; interviews take place in Sydney, Brisbane and Thredbo in early May.

Nannies can also find openings as Matt Tomlinson recounts:

> I arrived in Mount Buller hopelessly late and found it very difficult to get work. In the end my resourcefulness called upon my experience a few years back as a nanny and I got some work with the resort's nanny agency looking after the under fours. I was about the only person to stick with the job for the whole season. Despite the lack of a lift pass or accommodation, I stayed because it suited me to go out snowboard-

*ing when I had no work. I also enjoyed the irony of being paid to build snow people,
read stories and go tobogganing.*

Cities

Melbourne is arguably better for work than Sydney, partly because it is much less packed
with working travellers and also the cost of living is lower. Apart from restaurants and
cafés, pubs and clubs, catering jobs crop up in cricket grounds, theatres, yacht clubs and
(in Sydney) on harbour cruises. Function work is usually easy to come by via specialist
agencies provided you can claim to have silver service experience. It is worth applying to
catering companies as Fiona Cox did in Sydney, though she was not impressed with the
weekly take-home pay of $200.

Easy success at job hunting in Perth is far from automatic, particularly without a working visa. Several correspondents have recently given up on the city and moved on. Nothing much turned up even for Sara Runnalls, a qualified chef, who was job-hunting in
January. Jenni and Eric Holland spent six weeks in Perth before they gave up, moved
north and immediately found work on a melon farm. Jenni, a qualified welder, met with a
discouragingly sexist response when applying for welding work, 'If you want to visit your
husband here, just f***ing call first',

Looking for work in a Sydney suburb apart from the ones inundated by backpackers
might prove more successful. For example Danny Jacobson, a pizza chef from Chicago,
had better luck in Newtown than he did in Bondi. He also was hired as a walking advertisement for a designer clothing sale:

> *I just approached a guy on Oxford Street holding a huge sign on a wooden stick. This
> backpacker told me his boss doesn't fuss about work permits and he pays $10 an
> hour cash. The work consists of just standing for up to ten hours a day on a specific
> street corner or sometimes walking a beat. It's not bad because you get to people-
> watch and meet all the street freaks. They also hire the more attractive people to
> work in store selling clothes or checking bags. Check around the Town Hall in the
> city or in Paddington. The best way to tap into these jobs is to talk to the people with
> the signs who will send you straight up to the boss.*

The best opportunities for bar and waiting staff in Perth are in the city centre, Fremantle
and Northbridge, the area around William and James Streets. Rhona Stannage and her
husband Stuart Blackwell arrived in Perth in November, and having had chalet experience
in the French Alps and restaurant experience in Cyprus en route, were in a strong position
to find hospitality work:

> *Since there were lots of adverts in the newspapers for bar/restaurant staff we didn't
> go door-knocking, but we did meet a Canadian guy who had been in Perth one week
> and who had immediately found work in Northbridge just by asking around in the res-
> taurants, bars and nightclubs. We both got jobs fairly quickly – me within a week and
> Stuart a couple of weeks later. (I put my relative success down to the usual sexism
> in the hospitality trade since we have virtually the same experience.) I'm working in
> an Irish pub called Rosie O'Gradys (they prefer Irish accents but stretched a point
> when it came to my Scottish one). I would also recommend the 'traditional British
> pub' the Moon and Sixpence on Murray St in the City, since they seem to have only
> Poms and no Aussies working there.*

Rhona was also offered a job at the Burswood Resort Casino (www.burswood.com.au
which has an Employment page) which often needs staff willing to work shifts (it is open
24 hours). To attract 'permanent' staff, they pay twice the going wage and offer their staff
lots of perks such as free meals and a staff gym. One contributor describes how he took
advantage of these same perks at the Crown Casino in Melbourne without going to the

trouble of being hired. He claims that penniless starving backpackers should tell security at the staff entrance that they are from 'Pinnacle' or 'Hoban', the two main catering agencies that supply staff to the casino, proceed to the uniform issuer up the escalator, claiming to be a new waiter/chef/kitchen staff working in the King's Bistro/Georges, and make the trek to the staff canteen. The more honest among this book's readers might prefer to try actually being hired by the catering agencies mentioned (www.pinnaclepeople.com.au and www.hoban.com.au). Alternatively they might like to have a slap-up meal at a bargain price; for example many RSL (Returned Services League) clubs offer cheap eats, perhaps a Sunday roast for well under $10 or an affordable mid-week all-you-can-eat Chinese buffet.

The preference for females is strong in places like Kalgoorlie where waitresses are sometimes known by the offensive name 'skimpies' (after their uniforms). Partly because Darwin has such a small population (107,000), tourist bars and restaurants rely heavily on transients for their staff. As well as being easier to find work than in Sydney or Melbourne, the cost of accommodation is substantially less.

Call centres are constantly recruiting, often through agencies. In Sydney try Telus (Level 12, 2 Park St; www.telus.com.au). Bridgid Seymour-East thinks that new arrivals should be warned of the dangers which Sydney poses to the traveller: *'You may plan to stay a week or two and set off to travel or find work. However one or two months later, after a lot of fun, you find yourself still there and your funds severely depleted. Sydney traps you because you do have so much fun. Jimmy and I met in a youth hostel in Glebe and love blossomed.'*

Holiday Language Courses

Travellers with a TEFL certificate can take advantage of the seasonal demand for English tuition created by 'study tours,' popular among Japanese, Indonesian and other Asian students during their autumn and winter holidays. Demand for these holiday English courses has been increasing ever since the Australian immigration authorities relaxed the restrictions on visas, allowing foreign students to undertake short courses on a tourist visa. With a working holiday visa and a dash of luck, Simon Brooks fixed up several short contracts for February/March and July/August with no difficulty at all:

> It's just a question of timing really and getting an interview two or three weeks before a new course starts. It took me two weeks to get work in Sydney but only five days in Perth where I had five offers on the same day. Even if you don't get a three-month contract straightaway, get yourself on the relief list and get a mobile phone (or at least stay in a backpackers' hostel with a reliable receptionist) and persist. Talking to one Director of Studies in Sydney whom I met by chance socially, there's no doubt that effort counts a lot with them and tells them something about you.

In Sydney Simon worked for Universal English College (Level 12, 222 Pitt St, Sydney 2000; 2-9283 1088; www.uec.edu.au) and Sydney English Language Centre (Level 2, 19-23 Hollywood Avenue, Bondi Junction, NSW 2022; 2-8305 5600; www.selc.com.au) while in Perth he happily worked for Milner International College (379 Hay Street, Perth, WA 6000; 08-9325 5444; www.milner.wa.edu.au). Hourly rates of pay start at $25. Access Language Centre in Sydney (english@access.nsw.edu.au) employs certified TEFL teachers for periods as short as four weeks.

Special Events

Special events like test matches and race meetings can be seen as possible sources of employment. If you happen to be in Melbourne in late October or early November for the Melbourne Cup (held on the first Tuesday of November which is a public holiday in Victoria) or for the Grand Prix, your chances of finding casual work escalate remarkably. An army of sweepers and cleaners is recruited to go through the whole course clearing the huge piles of debris left by 15,000 race-goers. Hotels, restaurants and bars become frantically busy in the period leading up to the Cup, and private catering firms are also often desperate for staff.

At a swanky new backpackers in the hip suburb of St Kilda, an opportunity came up for Roger Blake to do some work. A company setting up exhibition stands at the MEC (Melbourne Exhibition Centre) were short-staffed so came looking for casual workers to earn $10 per hour. He worked for them on and off throughout his stay in Melbourne which meant that he could move on to New Zealand with a few hundred dollars saved up.

A couple of years ago Daniele Arena had the chance to work at the Phillip Island Racing Circuit just south of Melbourne. They are especially keen to employ casuals before the Australian Motorcycle Grand Prix in October and the Superbikes in March. Odd jobs like scrubbing floors, hosing the pit lanes and even painting tyre walls pay well (Daniele earned $14 gross) and you get long hours. Telephone enquiries can be made on 03-5952 2710.

Special events agencies should be a first port of call. For instance Skilled Hospitality & Events (18 Humphries Terrace, Kilkenny, SA 5009; fax 08-8345 0461) accepts written applications for ancillary jobs over the four days of the Clipsal 500 Motorsport Festival in Adelaide in March (clipsal500@skilled.com.au).

All the major cities have important horse races. Rowena Caverly was hired for the Darwin Cup Races 'mainly to check that none of the Lady Members had passed out in the loos'.

Travelling fairs are very popular and have frequent vacancies. Richard Davies joined the Melbourne Show in September and was paid $100 a day tax-free (to work 12-14 hours). It travels from Adelaide to Melbourne, Sydney and on up the Gold Coast staying a week or ten days. Ask at the local tourist office. Geertje Korf was at first thrilled to land a job with a travelling fair but it wasn't all as exciting as she had hoped:

> The work itself was good enough, helping to build up the stalls and working on the Laughing Clowns game. But the family I got to work for were not extremely sociable company. As a result, when we left a place and headed for the next I would spend time (about a week) until the next show day wandering lonely around incredibly hot and dusty little country towns where there was absolutely nothing to do while the showmen sat in a little circle drinking beer and not even talking to me. Also, the public toilets on the showgrounds were not usually open until showday, never cleaned since the last showday and usually provided some company (at last!) such as frogs, flies and redback spiders. I got paid $200 a week plus the use of a little caravan and evening meals which was not bad. Apparently a Dutch guy had spent six months with them the year before and had a great time, so I suppose it all depends on your personality.

Loneliness was not a problem for Sam Martell from the Orkneys and he earned nearly four times as much on a fair:
A girl I met on a tour at Byron Bay got me a job in Brisbane at the Queensland State Fair in the second week of August. I was paid $10 cash-in-hand working on a bouncy castle rescuing scared kids from the slide and chatting to the mums – it was great. In seven days I clocked up 73½ hours and took home $735 which meant I could afford the Whitsundays sailing trip.

The Interior

Uluru or Ayers Rock is a place of pilgrimage for more than a third of a million visitors a year. The nearest facilities are in the Ayers Rock Resort village about 20km north of the Rock. Ayers Rock Resort (formerly known as Yulara) is the fourth largest settlement in the Northern Territory and a good place to look for a job. Although the resort has a waiting list of job-seekers, many people have moved on before they reach the top of the list. The resort employs about 1,000 people in catering and cleaning and many other departments.

Staff accommodation is available. It would be worth sending your CV if you have a catering qualification or two years experience in a four-star hotel (Human Resources Department, Ayers Rock Resort, PO Box 46, Ayers Rock Resort, NT 0872; fax 08- 8957 7381; www. voyages.com.au/corporate/employment.asp).

Alice Springs is a very popular tourist destination because of Ayers Rock. One traveller who stayed at one of the many backpackers' lodges reported that 8 out of the 12 women staying there were working as waitresses or bar staff. Occasional vacancies occur for hostesses to work on upmarket special interest tours. Personality and presentation are more important than qualifications and experience for jobs as hostesses and cooks.

Coober Pedy (opal capital of Australia in the South Australian outback), Alice Springs, Kununurra and Broome are other places worth trying for tourist work in the Dry (May to October). Broome hosts a big festival in early September just prior to the monsoon (when travel becomes hazardous and uncomfortable) which is a good time to try.

As a general rule the lower the wage the higher the staff turnover. However low wages are not the only reason for people staying a short time at any one job. Working at a road station can be a very lonely business. A typical station consists of a shop, a petrol pump and a bar, and they occur every couple of hundred miles along the seemingly endless straight highways through the Australian desert. The more remote the place (and these are often the ones that are unbearably hot) the more likely there will be a vacancy. If you see a job going in Marble Bar, for example, remind yourself that it is arguably the world's hottest inhabited town with summer temperatures reaching 50°C (122°F).

The Australian Pub

Until the early 1970s, pubs were licensed only from 5pm to 6pm, which resulted in some fairly barbaric drinking habits known as the 'six o'clock swill.' Now that the licensing hours are more civilised (from about 10am-10pm on weekdays and until midnight on Friday and Saturday) many Australian pubs or 'hotels' are now quite genteel establishments where the staff are treated courteously. An increasing number are becoming trendy and yuppi-fied. But there still is a strong preference for hiring women rather than men. The tradition in male-dominated pubs of heavy drinking and barmaid-taunting continues, so you should be prepared for this sometimes irritating (though almost always good-natured) treatment. You may get especially tired of hearing sporting comparisons between Australia and Britain (though at least in 2005, British cricket does not look as hopeless as it has of late).

Standards of service are high and many hotel managers will be looking for some experience or training. Only those desperate for staff will be willing to train. Even if you have had experience of working in a British pub, it may take you some time to master the technique of pouring Australian lager properly. There is a bewildering array of beer glasses ranging from the 115ml small beer of Tasmania to the 575ml pint of New South Wales with middies, schooners, pots and butchers falling in between. Names and measures vary from state to state.

The local pub is always a good place to find out about local opportunities, from the 'Animal Bar' where trawlermen and jackaroos foregather in Karumba Queensland to the hotel in Waikerie SA where fruit pickers congregate on a Friday night.

CHILDCARE

The demand for live-in and live-out childcare is enormous in Australia and a few agencies in Britain cater to the demand, such as Childcare International (Trafalgar House, Grenville Place, London NW7 3SA; www.childint.co.uk). But it is easy to conduct the job hunt on arrival. Applicants are often interviewed a day or two after registering with an agency and start work immediately. Nanny and au pair agencies are very interested in hearing from young women and men with working holiday visas. Geertje Korf's experience in Tasmania illustrates the ease with which childcare work can be found: *'I decided to go to Tasmania for a cycling holiday. At the second place I stopped I got offered a job as a nanny to four children, just by mentioning I had been nannying in Sydney. The place had beautiful sur-*

roundings, restaurants, etc. so I decided to accept. It was a good job and I left quite a bit richer.'

A number of au pair agencies place European and Asian women with working holiday visas in live-in positions, normally for a minimum of three months. Not all placements require childcare experience. Try any of the following:

AAA Nannies, PO Box 157, Sanctuary Cove, Queensland 4212 (07-5530 1123; www. nanny.net.au). Charges registration fee of $396 for international applicants.

Australian Nanny & Au Pair Connection, 404 Glenferrie Road, Kooyong, Melbourne, Vic 3144 (tel/fax 03-9824 8857; www.australiannannies.info).

Dial-an-Angel, PO Box 543, Edgecliff, NSW 2027 (1300 721111/ 02-9362 4225; adminis tration@dialanangel.com; www.dial-an-angel.com.au). Long established agency with franchised branches throughout Australia. Wages offered $250-$500 per week.

Family Match Au Pairs & Nannies, PO Box 6406, Kincumber, NSW 2251 (02-4363 2500; www.familymatch.com.au). Online service for live-in positions including for working holidaymakers. 20-30 hours per week for pocket money of $150-$180 plus all live-in expenses.

People for People, PO Box W271, Warringah Mall, Brookvale, NSW 2100 (02-9972 0488; www.peopleforpeople.com.au). Welcome working holidaymakers for three month summer positions.

Most agencies will expect to interview applicants and check their references before placement. As in America, a driving licence is a valuable asset. As well as long term posts, holiday positions for the summer (December-February) and for the ski season (July-September) are available. As mentioned earlier Matt Tomlinson worked as a nanny in a ski resort, on the strength of the year he'd spent as an au pair in Paris: *'Being a male nanny in Australia was an interesting experience. I got used to being asked if I was a child molester. On the upside, I was also offered a number of live-in jobs in Melbourne. And in case you're wondering, yes, I did get a lot of ribbing from the guys when I told them what job I was doing.*

Anyone considering a childcare position may be interested in Rowena Caverly's experiences: *'I looked after a 15-month old boy at a permaculture farm set in a rainforest. The job taught me new skills daily, such as how to persuade a baby that the Huntsman Spider on the wall really does not want to play. My task in summer was to teach him to toddle heavily to scare off snakes. Otherwise a nasty situation might have developed (and my money would not necessarily be on the baby as the victim).'*

Casual work in nurseries, daycare centres and pre-schools might be available as it was to Catharine Carfoot in Sydney
One surprisingly successful route to employment was through Select Education (Level 1, 109 Pitt St). Whether you decide to go for this work would depend on how you feel about being left in sole charge of e.g. 16 3-4 year olds or six babies while your colleague goes on lunch-break. I should emphasise that I was never left as the only member of staff at a centre but I have been alone in a room with only an intercom to connect me to back-up. There was an interview and they did ask for references but I was asked during my interview whether I wanted to work that afternoon.

FISHING & BOATING

It is sometimes possible to get work on prawn fishing vessels out of Broome, Darwin, Cairns, Townsville, Bowen or even Karumba on the Gulf of Carpentaria. Stephen Psallidas noticed lots of trawler and yachting jobs in the *Cairns Post* (especially on Wednesday and Saturday) and on noticeboards in town. You can either try to get work with one of the big companies like Raptis (www.raptis.com.au) in Queensland, South Australia, etc. or on smaller privately-owned boats. Fishing trips from Queensland tend to be day trips.

The main jobs assigned to male deckhands are net-mending and prawn-sorting. Work is especially demanding during the banana prawn season of April/May, since banana prawns travel in huge schools which are caught in one fell swoop, requiring immediate attention. Women are taken on as cooks. They should make it quite clear before leaving harbour whether or not they wish to be counted among the recreational facilities of the boat, since numerous stories are told of the unfair pressures placed on women crew members at sea, though Anne Wakeford encountered no problems of this kind when she went out on a small fishing boat from Darwin. The most that some women have had to complain about is that they were expected not only to cook but to help sort out sea snakes and jelly fish from the catch. Men are not immune to problems, of course: if the skipper takes a dislike to any of his crew, he can simply leave them stranded on an island or beach.

Ian Mudge, who worked on a diving boat in northern Queensland, heard terrible things about prawn trawler work and thinks that it would be safer for a woman to work in a King's Cross brothel than to sign up on one. He also thinks that the general working conditions are very unsafe, though he does admit that the money can be excellent. The backpacker press has in the past carried a rather alarming ad placed by the Queensland Transport and Whitsunday Charter Boat Industry Association, headed 'At sea, no one can hear you scream.' The ad goes on to warn backpackers to be wary of predatory boat owners who chat them up at pubs and clubs and entice them on to unseaworthy boats. The relevant government website (www.msq.qld.gov.au/qt/msq.nsf/index/lookb4ugetonboard) quotes the recent experience of one unhappily duped customer from the UK, Andy Duckworth:

> I got ripped-off by pirates. I replied to an ad in Cairns for crew for a one-off boat trip to Airlie Beach. $500 each. A private cruise along the coast and the Whitsundays sounded unforgettable. It was. The boat was unsafe and unregistered. Our hosts were obnoxious. We had to supply our own food and drinks. We were given a long list of chores, couldn't use the shower and were left stranded on islands for hours. When I overheard the skipper planning another trip from Cairns, it was obvious the whole thing was a scam. Pass the word around about dodgy, unregistered operators - I like to call them the pirates of the coast. You'll have a much better time with an authorised operator.

The prawn fishing season in Darwin starts on April 15th and continues through till Christmas. Any traveller who goes down to the docks at the beginning of the season has a good chance of being taken on for a one or two week trip, even without experience, though wages will be a fraction of those earned by the old hands, as Sam Martell learned:

> After chatting to some Aussies in Darwin, the allure of $15,000 over six weeks was too tempting. So I trooped down to the harbour with a few beers to bribe my way and chatted to some fishermen and got shown around a couple of boats. Unfortunately I found that because I was 'green' I would not be paid what everyone else was. Rather than $2,500 a week it would be $300 – definitely not worth it as it works out at about $4 an hour. Only those who are gluttons for punishment or with experience should try the prawn trawlers. There are other fishing boats around though.

If you don't manage to join a crew, try for work in the fish-processing plants. For example the Bundaberg fishing fleet keeps three processing plants supplied, especially with scallops while Carnarvon also has a prawn and scallop industry. The season lasts from March to October and accommodation is available in caravan parks. The rock lobster season around Geraldton WA also starts in March but lasts only three months. Sometimes you see advertisements for oyster openers, a skill worth cultivating if only for your own consumption. Scallop-splitting was at one time a favourite among casual workers, e.g. around Bicheno on the east coast of Tasmania, though the quantities have been drastically curtailed recently by overfishing.

Conclusion

Ian Fleming sums up what many working travellers have observed about Australians:

> *The opinion that we formed regarding Australian employers is that they are hard but fair. They demand a good day's work for a fair day's pay, and if you do not measure up to their expectations they will have no hesitation in telling you so. But generally we found that the British worker is held in quite high esteem in Australia. I also found the Aussies to be much more friendly and helpful than anticipated and very easy to socialise with (in spite of the fact that I was nicknamed 'P.B.' for Pommy Bastard).*

Most people are struck by what a good standard of living can be enjoyed for not very much money. As Gawain Paling put it so graphically, 'If you're poor in Britain it's the pits; if you're poor in Australia you can have a nice comfortable life'. There is a marvellous range of jobs even if you are unlikely to repeat Sandra Grey's coup of being paid $50 for three hours 'work' testing a sunscreen on her lily-white back, or Jane Thomas's bizarre jobs, one in a sex change clinic, the other in a morgue typing up the labels for dismembered parts of bodies.

Even after several setbacks with bosses and jobs, Louise Fitzgerald concludes: *'To anybody not sure about going, I'd say, go, you'd be stupid not to. Australia is a wonderful country and the Australians are great people, even if the males do have a tendency to be chauvinists. If you prove to them you're as good as they are, they tend to like you for it!*

New Zealand

New Zealand is a charmingly rural country where just short of four million human beings are substantially outnumbered by sheep. While the main cities become more sophisticated by the year, they remain friendly and manageable in scale. Travellers have found hitch-hiking easy, the backpackers hostels congenial, camping idyllic (when it's dry) and the natives very hospitable. The minimum wage is NZ$9.50 (from March 2005), equivalent at the time of writing to £3.62, which represents a substantial increase over the past five years. Furthermore the NZ cost of living is low and therefore you should aim to spend your earnings before leaving the shores of New Zealand.

The New Zealand economy is booming, unemployment is at a 15 year low and labour shortages are widespread. According to a survey of companies published in the *New Zealand Herald* in 2005, 40% of companies reported that they had difficulties recruiting unskilled workers with the figure rising to 61% for skilled workers. It is a job-seeker's market at present. Supplementing your travel fund with temporary jobs, cash-in-hand work, odd jobs or work-for-keep arrangements is usually good fun. Camping on beaches, fields and in woodlands is generally permitted. In addition to official youth hostels, there is a wealth of budget accommodation, where you can often learn of local opportunities for casual work, particularly the ubiquitous fruit-picking.

The Regulations

New Zealand deserves its national reputation for friendliness to visitors. Tourists from the UK need no visa to stay for up to six months, while Americans, Canadians and Europeans can stay for three visa-free months. Tourists entering the country may be asked to show an onward ticket and about NZ$1,000 per month of their proposed stay (unless they have pre-paid accommodation or a New Zealand backer who has pledged support in a crisis). In practice, respectable-looking travellers are most unlikely to be quizzed at entry.

The UK Citizens' Working Holiday Scheme has been deemed such a success in addressing severe labour shortages in seasonal work that from July 2005 the maximum duration will be extended from one year to two years, and the quota of 9,000 removed. The scheme allows any eligible Briton aged 18-30 to obtain a working holiday visa, allowing him or her to do temporary or full-time jobs in New Zealand. Participants are permitted to work for up to 12 months of the two-year visa validity, either consecutively or cumulatively. The elimination of a cap on the number of WH visas issued means that the old first come, first served system has disappeared and applications are welcomed throughout the year. Information can be obtained from the New Zealand Immigration Service, Mezzanine Floor, New Zealand House, 80 Haymarket, London SW1Y 4TE (fax 020-7973 0370) in person, by phone on 09069 100100 (charged at £1 per minute) or via the internet at www.immigration.govt.nz. This is an admirably clear and thoroughly up-to-date website.

From 2005, applications for all working holiday schemes will have to be done online so that there will no longer be a requirement to apply from your home country. The fee (currently NZ$120/£50) will be payable by credit card at the time of application. The New Zealand Immigration Service intends to stay in touch with WH-makers via email, sending information about jobs and requesting feedback on the scheme. Other working holiday schemes (maximum duration one year) are open to Irish, Canadian, Dutch, Japanese and many other nationalities, mostly on a reciprocal basis. The number of working holiday visas granted to US citizens by the NZ Embassy in Washington or Consulate in Los Angeles is fixed at 500 (no fee is charged). A new requirement will be that working holiday applicants from the UK must undergo a medical check and X-ray. Britons and other nationalities on working holidays are allowed to apply to extend their stay or even for residence without leaving New Zealand

A possible alternative to the working holiday visa for those who have contacts in New Zealand or special skills and can obtain a firm offer of employment before leaving the UK is to apply for a temporary work visa (for a non-refundable fee of £80/NZ$200). Your sponsoring employer in New Zealand must be prepared to prove to the NZIS (NZ Immigration Service) that it is necessary to hire a foreigner rather than an unemployed New Zealander. The work visa does not in itself entitle you to work, but does make it easier to obtain a work permit after arrival. If you are granted a work visa before departure it will allow you to stay for up to three years.

Applicants with skills in demand may apply for a work permit only at one of the seven Immigration Service offices in New Zealand for a fee of NZ$90. To be considered for a work permit in these circumstances you must have a written job offer from a prospective employer confirming that the position offered is temporary, a full description of the position, salary, evidence that you are suitably qualified (originals or certified copies of work references, qualification certificates, etc.) and evidence that the employer has made every effort to recruit local people (proof of advertising, vacancy lodged with Employment Service, etc.) As usual there are no hard and fast rules and no guarantee of success, as Ken Smith (a native New Zealander) found when he worked alongside foreigners at Franz Josef resort:

> There was a Northern Irish girl working there who had been granted a work permit to work as a waitress. She was assured of the job over the phone having told them that her application for a work permit was being processed (which it wasn't) and when assured of the job she promptly set about applying for a work permit before arriving at the hotel. The work permit was granted three months later, a week or so before she was due to move on, so she was quite annoyed because it cost a lot of money. On a previous occasion working at the same resort I remember an English fellow who was working as a barman. His application for a work permit was flatly refused, so I guess it depends on 'Do you feel lucky?'

The problem of long queues at the three busy Department of Labour offices in and around Auckland (Central, Henderson and Manukau), has been solved since 2004 by the replacement of a counter service with an online or drop-box facility. The other five offices around the country (Wellington, Palmerston North, Hamilton, Christchurch and Dunedin) continue to operate a face-to-face service.

Sometimes you have to show real grit and determination, as Emiliano Giovannoni from Italy found:

> When I was offered a job I decided to apply for a work permit on that basis rather than on my de facto relationship with a kiwi (girl not fruit) which had been rejected because I didn't submit my full birth certificate. I go to the NZIS in Wellington (about the eighth time) with a letter from the prospective employer and the contract, and they explain that I have to come back with my CV and qualifications and they will send it to another department to establish that no NZ citizen is available for that post. So I leave and come back the next day (ninth time) with all the necessary papers and the officer that sees me this time says she can't understand why my de facto application for residency had been rejected and that I didn't need the extra documentation for my work permit application. She just stamped my passport there and then with a full work permit, contradicting everything her colleagues had told me before. The trick is to go back to the NZIS office as often as you can (every day) and hope to see a different officer and hope for some luck. There is absolutely no logic in the way the NZIS operate and whether an application is accepted or rejected does not depend on the documentation but rather a complete luck of the draw.

If you think that permanent migration is a possibility, you must first submit an Expression of Interest to the New Zealand Immigration Service (the fee for an online application is NZ$315 or hard copy $465). The application fee for residence in the Skilled Migrant category is £560 (NZ$1,360). Consyl Publishing (www.consylpublishing.co.uk) specialises in publishing information for potential migrants; their information line 09068 633464 is charged at 60p a minute.

Because so many employers are desperate for workers, especially in the fruit-growing sector (in which it is estimated that up to 30% of horticultural workers have invalid permits), working without a visa (and with impunity) is widespread. However the Minister of Immigration and Labour stated that he planned to crack down in orchards and vineyards from the summer of 2005/6,

Special Schemes

BUNAC (downunder@bunac.org.uk) has a Work New Zealand programme that provides the usual range of services – flights, stopovers, initial hostel accommodation and ongoing support for up to 12 months from their partner International Exchange Programs in New Zealand (www.iep.co.nz); the inclusive fee is from £1,900. The Work Experience Downunder programme from CCUSA (1st Floor North, Devon House, 171/177 Great Portland St, London W1W 5PQ; 020-7637 0779/ fax 020 7580 6209; www.ccusaweusa.co.uk) operates to New Zealand as well as Australia. The application and programme fees come to £230 plus insurance, travel and visas. IST Plus (Rosedale House, Rosedale Road, Richmond, Surrey TW9 2SZ; 020-8939 9057; info@istplus.com) offers UK residents the Work and Travel New Zealand programme. Fees start at £320 to include initial accommodation and a post-arrival orientation at the partner office in Auckland (Backpackers World).

One of the gap year placement companies to operate in New Zealand is Changing Worlds (Hodore Farm, Hartfield, E Sussex TN7 4AR; 01892 770000; www.changingworlds.co.uk) which offers 3 or 6-month job placements in hotels in Paihia or Queenstown and on farms in the North Island, or the chance to volunteer on a tall ship based in the Bay of Islands. The programme fee including flights is £2,495.

Americans aged 18-30 are eligible to apply for a 12-month work exchange visa through approved organisations like BUNAC USA (www.bunac.org), CIEE (www.ciee.org/isp) and CCUSA (www.ccusa.com). Canadians aged 18-35 may obtain a 12-month working holiday

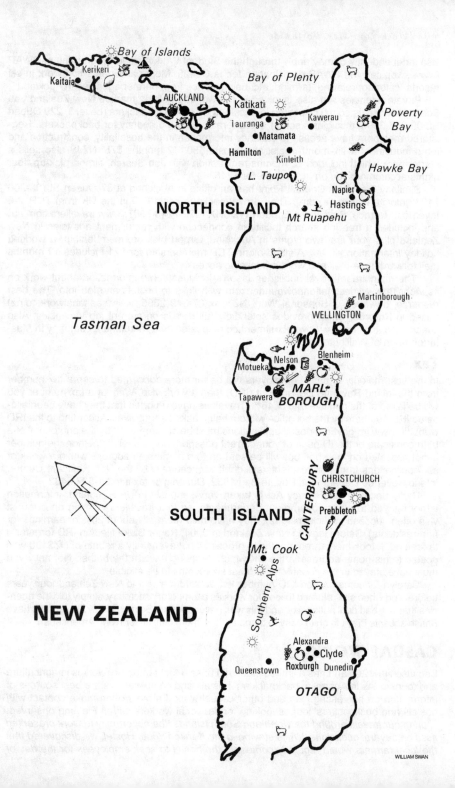

☀️ Bay of Islands

Kerikeri

Kaitaia

Bay of Plenty

AUCKLAND

Katikati ☀️

Poverty
Bay

Tauranga

Kawerau

Matamata

Hamilton

Kinleith

Hawke Bay

L. Taupo ☀️

Napier

Hastings

NORTH ISLAND

Mt Ruapehu

Martinborough

Tasman Sea

WELLINGTON

Nelson ☀️

Blenheim

Motueka

*MARL-
BOROUGH*

Tapawera

CHRISTCHURCH

SOUTH ISLAND

Prebbleton

Mt. Cook ☀️

Southern Alps

Alexandra

Clyde

NEW ZEALAND

Queenstown

Roxburgh

Dunedin

OTAGO

WILLIAM SWAN

visa independently or may apply through the Student Work Abroad Programme or SWAP (www.swap.ca); the SWAP participation fee is C$425. Most participants find work in ski resorts, catering, retailing, farming, etc. using advice from partner agencies in Auckland.

Private agencies are also involved in the working holiday market. New Zealand Job Search (www.nzjs.co.nz) is located in Auckland Central Backpackers (Level 3, 229 Queen St; 09-357 3996; jobs@nzjs.co.nz) and operates as a job agency for backpackers. Registered members have access to vacancy information in the hospitality, construction and temp industries; a six-month registration costs $50, 12 months $75. NZJS also sells a starter pack which includes 12 months registration with Job Search, airport pick-up, four nights accommodation on arrival, etc. for $245.

Similarly Travellers Contact Point has an office in Auckland at 87 Queen St (09-300 7197; info@travellersnz.com). Their arrival package costs £60 in the UK from TCP, 2-6 Inverness Terrace, Bayswater, London W2 3HX (020-7243 7887; www.travellers.com.au) and includes a free job search facility in connection with recruitment agencies in New Zealand plus your first two nights in Auckland, airport pick-up, membership, a working holiday information kit, etc. A stand-alone TCP membership for £21 includes 12 months mail forwarding, e-mail and word processing access.

The mainstream travel publisher Jason's includes some information about work on its website www.destinationdownunder.com with links to hostels and job info. The best resource, however, is Seasonal Work NZ (fax 07-349 2865; www.seasonalwork.co.nz) based in Rotorua, which provides splendidly full details on current job vacancies. Also check vacancies on www.kiwirecruitment.co.nz posted by a recruitment company in Masterton north of Wellington.

Tax

In the vast majority of cases employers will be far more concerned to see a tax number from the Inland Revenue Department (IRD) than a work visa. Without a tax number you will be taxed at the punitive rate of 46%. Travellers have reported that they have been allocated IRD numbers by the tax office without being asked about visas. According to the IRD website (www.ird.govt.nz) postal applications must be accompanied by the photocopy of a birth certificate or the ID page of your current passport. If you apply in person the number is not allocated on the spot, but will be sent on to a nominated address within a week or so. Applications from non-residents are dealt with centrally by the Non-Resident Centre, Inland Revenue Department, Private Bag 1932, Dunedin or fax it to 04-527 6432.

Partly because the Privacy Act is taken very seriously in New Zealand, information is not relayed to other government departments, so that travellers working on a tourist visa often succeed in reclaiming tax they have paid (normally about 20% of earnings for non-residents). Before leaving New Zealand in 2004, Roger Blake filed an IRD form for a tax refund. It took them three months to process it but eventually a rebate of NZ$130 was posted to his home address in the UK which he thought worth the bother. Normally you must have stayed in the country for at least six months to be eligible.

Carolyn Edwards had an IRD number left over from a visit to New Zealand four years before, and when she returned to look for work as a temporary secretary, simply told the agencies that she had dual nationality, and this was never queried. So many New Zealanders have British accents that it is quite easy to blend in. (It is more difficult for North Americans.)

CASUAL WORK

Because New Zealand has a limited industrial base, most temporary work is in agriculture and tourism. As in Australia, backpackers' hostels and campsites are the best sources of information on harvesting jobs and other casual work. Farmers often make contact with hostels and backpackers' lodges looking for seasonal workers as Ian Fleming observed: *'During our travels around the North and South Islands, the opportunity to work presented itself on several occasions. While staying in the Kerikeri Youth Hostel, we discovered that the local farmers would regularly come into the hostel to seek employees for the day or longer. (This was in July, which is out-of-season.) My advice to any person looking for farm work would be to get up early as the farmers are often in the hostel by 8.30am.'*

Alternatively local farmers co-operate with hostel wardens who collate information about job vacancies or they may circulate notices around youth hostels, for example, 'Orchard Work Available January to March; apply Tauranga Hostel' so always check the hostel board. At the same time, be on your guard as Roger Blake warns:

> *After a couple of weeks in Auckland with a little work here and there I was barely breaking even as the cost of living is quite high. Acting on an ad I had seen on the YHA notice board, I phoned a hostel in Hastings which had placed an ad for 30 apple pickers 'Needed Immediately' which they confirmed. So the following day I jumped on a bus to Hastings. Although a few of the travellers there were working, the others were hanging on for another day as work was assured, 'maybe tomorrow'. After a week I had learned for myself that the season was late. A warning that hostels can and do use these tactics to fill their beds.*

A website maintained by the Budget Backpackers Hostels group includes job information (www.bbhnet.co.nz/billboard_home.asp). At the time of writing (2005) there were 19 vacancies for hostel jobs listed plus 14 other vacancies. Hostels often employ travellers for short periods, either part-time in exchange for free accommodation or full-time for a wage as well. After the engine of Roger Blake's campervan blew up, he scoured the hostel notice boards of Wellington and fixed himself up with a cleaning job on a work-for-accommodation basis at Wildlife House Backpackers on Tory Street. Many travellers are dotted around New Zealand cleaning in hostels for three hours each morning six days a week in return for a free dorm bed. The job is usually not difficult. The main BBH site (www.backpack.co.nz) links to its 350 member hostels.

Matt Tomlinson recommends buying a vehicle to travel and job hunt in New Zealand. He bought one for a few hundred pounds at a Sunday morning car market in the Auckland suburb of Manukau City. Backpackers' car markets take place in Auckland at 20 East Street in the city centre and in Christchurch (near the corner of Colombo and Battersea Streets); details on http://backpackerscarmarket.co.nz. Look for a vehicle with a couple of months of WOF remaining (equivalent to MOT).

Hitching has already been extolled. Cycling is another attractive alternative. The Belgian world traveller Vince Crombez, who had no trouble finding work around New Zealand, is sure that the fact that he presented himself to possible employers on his loaded bicycle convinced them that he would not be a lazy worker.

If planning to be in or near Dunedin for a period of time, you could see if Zenith Technology is conducting any clinical trials in which you might be able to pick up $200 for a weekend's volunteering: Zenith Technology, 156 Frederick St, Dunedin (03-477 9669; www.zenithtechnology.co.nz).

Rural & Conservation Volunteering

World Wide Opportunities on Organic Farms (WWOOF) NZ is active and popular, with 780 farms and smallholdings on its fix-it-yourself list which welcome volunteers in exchange for food and accommodation. The list can be obtained from Jane and Andrew Strange, PO Box 1172, Nelson (tel/fax 03-544 9890; wwoof@wwoof.co.nz/ www.wwoof.co.nz) for a fee of £16/US$30/NZ$40. WWOOF hosts often have leads for paid work in market gardens, nurseries and other farms.

Farm Helpers in New Zealand lists about 190 farmers around New Zealand where working travellers can arrange a farmstay lasting from three days to several months. FHiNZ (16 Aspen Way, Palmerston North; tel/fax 06-355 0448; www.fhinz.co.nz) charges NZ$25 for their membership booklet and list of farms which is updated monthly. No experience is necessary and between four and six hours of work a day are requested. The coordinator advises that hosts in the Auckland area tend to be oversubscribed, so that it is best to head into the countryside. Another possibility is the free internet-based exchange of work-for-keep volunteers which can be found at www.helpx.net where nearly 250 hosts in New Zealand are listed. Originally set up by a British backpacker in New Zealand, the scheme is flourishing and expanding.

Adrienne Robinson and her partner and young son joined FHiNZ and arranged two enjoyable farmstays. Because they were looking for farms at the height of the summer and at Christmas, they found that many of the listed farms were already booked up for that period. They found that the general picking, weeding and mulching work they were asked to do was fairly easy to manage alongside three year old Jordan.

Leona Baldwin thought she would try something completely alien to her, a WWOOF stay on a New Zealand farm:
Growing up in Toronto, the closest I'd ever come to experiencing life on a farm was driving past deserted cornfields on my way into the city with billboards boasting 'Prime Site for Housing Development'. The appeal of one day 'getting back to nature' lingered. Taking leave of the neurotic 9 to 5 existence and all its anxieties, and exchanging my designer jeans and stiletto shoes for a pair of overalls and some 'gum boots' was an idea that I had often entertained, though usually in the context of planning for a retirement that is still over three decades away.

After touring New Zealand we began to long for a taste of real life in Kiwiland. Becoming a WWOOF volunteer presented the ideal scenario, satisfying our need to take a break from the ordinary, and our bank balance's need to take a break from all the spending. Luckily, our first choice in horse trekking farms had a vacancy for two Wwoofers, and after a brief informal telephone interview, we were invited to come and stay at a farm just outside the ski resort of Ohakune.

My apprehensions about being asked to fit a horse with shoes, or kill a chicken for dinner, were apparently unfounded. Our first task was to walk the horses back to the main farmstead to be fed, groomed and saddled. Conscious of not appearing totally inept on my first day, I plucked up whatever reserves of bravery I had, took a deep breath, and slowly walked towards the only horse that hadn't already been snagged.

The self-sufficiency of life on this farm was quite amazing. Seeing firsthand how easy and economical it is to live without the aid of supermarkets and pre-packaging builds an inarguable case for sustainable living. But admittedly, after weeks without even a glimpse of the golden arches and its chemically enhanced flavor additives, I was craving a Mc Anything. I guess old habits die hard. For someone who was not entirely sure what the term 'organic' even meant prior to my stay, being a part of the daily regime on an organic farm truly was a breath of fresh air. I learned more about gardening than I ever thought possible, I developed muscles in places no amount of circuit training or yoga has ever come close to and I formed friendships with people from around the world.

The New Zealand Department of Conservation (DOC) carries out habitat and wildlife management projects throughout New Zealand and publishes a detailed Calendar of Volunteer Opportunities; see their website www.doc.govt.nz/community/006volunteers/index.asp which lists all sorts of interesting sounding projects from counting bats to cleaning up remote beaches to helping to maintain historic buildings. Most require a good level of fitness and a contribution to expenses, though not always. The DOC also needs volunteer hut wardens at a variety of locations. Details are available from any office of the Department of Conservation (all addresses are listed on website).

The New Zealand Trust for Conservation Volunteers was set up in 1999 to match both local and international volunteers with conservation projects of all kinds to counteract the loss of native bush and wildlife. Whereas DOC projects take place only on DOC lands, NZTCV registers projects run by many local and national organisations as well as DOC projects. Details are available on their website www.conservationvolunteers.org.nz (tel/fax 09-415 9336; conservol@clear.net.nz). NZTCV has created a central database on which individuals can register in order to be put in touch with organisations running conservation projects.

> **Paul Bagshaw from Kent and his girlfriend spent a thoroughly enjoyable week on an uninhabited island in Marlborough Sound monitoring kiwis, the flightless bird whose numbers have been seriously depleted. An ongoing programme removes them from the mainland to small islands where there are no predators**
> *The object of the exercise was to estimate the number of kiwis on Long Island north of Picton. As the kiwi is nocturnal, we had to work in the small hours. As it's dark, it's impossible to count them so we had to spread out and walk up a long slope listening for their high-pitched whistling call. During the day they hide in burrows and foliage so it is very rare to see one. One night, when we heard one rustling around our camp, my girlfriend went outside with a torch and actually managed to see it. She was so excited that she couldn't speak and resorted to wild gesticulations to describe its big feet and long beak. The island has no water source except rainwater which collects in tanks, all very basic. We lived in tents and prepared our own meals from supplies brought over from the mainland. Our one luxury was a portaloo.*

Involvement Volunteers New Zealand (PO Box 153, Helensville; ivns@xtra.co.nz) places volunteers in conservation and farming as well as social projects for a placement fee.

FRUIT PICKING

The climate of New Zealand lends itself to fruit and vegetable growing of many kinds including not only the apples and kiwifruit well known from every British supermarket but carrots, citrus fruit and other produce. Just turning up in towns and asking around is usually a safe bet for work while the season is on. Expect to earn between $300 and $400 a week. Below are some general guidelines as to what areas to head for in the appropriate seasons. Motueka/Nelson, Tauranga/Katikati, Hawke's Bay and Kerikeri are the favourites among travellers.

Most farmers are able to provide some kind of shack or cottage accommodation (known as a 'bach' in the North Island, a 'crib' in the South), though the spring and summer weather is suitable for camping provided you have a good waterproof tent. Many others stay in backpackers hostels. Farmers often provide fresh fruit and vegetables, milk and sometimes lamb, or organise end-of-harvest barbecues with free drinks. As Roger Blake concluded after picking pears in Motueka, 'Very nice people Kiwis!'.

FRUIT AND VEGETABLE HARVESTS

Place	Crop	Season
Nelson/Blenheim/Motueka	apples (also pears & peaches)	Feb/Mar/Apr
Motueka	apple thinning	mid-Nov/Dec
Blenheim	cherries	late Dec/Jan
Motueka	apple thinning	Feb/Mar/Apr
Wairau Valley (Marlborough area)	cherries, grapes	Dec
Nelson/Tapawera	raspberries	Dec
Kerikeri (Bay of Islands)	peaches, apricots	Dec/Jan
	citrus packing	Oct/Nov
	kiwifruit	late Apr
Northland (peninsula north of Auckland)	kiwifruit	May
	strawberries	mid-Oct
Paiumhhue (just south of	kiwifruit	May

Auckland)		
Poverty Bay (Gisborne)	*kiwifruit*	May
Poverty Bay Flats	*grapes*	from Feb
Tauranga/Te Puke (Bay of Plenty)	*citrus*	Oct/Nov
	kiwifruit	May-Jul
Clive/Napier (Hawke's Bay)	*apples, pears &* *grapes*	late Feb/Apr
	pruning work	Jun
Hastings	*tomatoes*	
	apples	late Feb/Apr
Ohakune	*carrots*	June
Martinborough (north of Wellington in the Wairarapa area)	*grapes*	Mar
Central Otago (Alexandra & Roxburgh)	*plums, apricots*	Jan/Feb
	apples & pears	Mar/Apr
Christchurch area	*peaches*	Mar
	apples, berries & *mixed fruit*	Jan-May
	potatoes	Jan-Mar
Invercargill	*tulips*	early Dec

Bay of Plenty

The Bay of Plenty is where the majority of New Zealand's kiwifruit is grown. The tiny community of Te Puke swells in number from 6,000 to 10,000 for the harvest which traditionally starts on May 1st (though it is best to arrive a week or two early to line up a job). Picking lasts four or five weeks and the packing season extends to August. Workaholics can work an evening shift packing after a day in the orchards. An hourly wage is paid for this boring work (5pm-11pm).

Just as quickly as Vince Crombez got a job in the Te Puke harvest, he quit, after deciding that the rate he was paid was a rip off. So he cycled on to Katikati (65km to the north) and visited the very helpful tourist information office who phoned two or three farmers for him and found him a job the same day. He stayed until the season ended (6th June) and cleared an average of $350 a week working in a gang which was not particularly dedicated. Unlike most picking jobs, this one allows leisurely morning starts, since the fruit must be dry before it can be picked, starting about 10am. Rates of pay are either by the bucket ('contract') or by the hour (called 'award rate,' as in Australia).

Hawke's Bay

Local students are not available for autumn harvests such as apples and pears in the Hawke's Bay area, so you may be able to pick up casual work in the apple orchards around Napier. This is one area in which it is wise to keep an eye out for immigration officials. Craig Ashworth arrived in late February and found that there was lots of no-questions-asked apple picking work around. He found it tough at first but was eventually earning about $500 for five days of work. There is also pruning work in the area in June. Hawke's Bay fruit growers launched a website in the summer of 2005 in their ceaseless attempts to find staff to work on their pip fruit, stone fruit, berry and grape harvests. Pick NZ, which will post all seasonal and permanent jobs in Hawke's Bay Bay horticulture, can be found at www.picknz.co.nz. In the future, vacancies elsewhere in New Zealand will also be included. Also you can check with the Hawke's Bay Fruit Growers' Association which keeps track of their members with job vacancies (www.hbfruitgrowers.co.nz/work_info.html).

Vince Crombez did well in Hastings in April:

Except for Granny Smiths, it is always picking according to colour which pays more. I got between $22 and $25 a bin for picking Braeburns, Fujis and other varieties. A ganger checked every hour to see if the apples were coloured enough, though usually it's 'no worries, mate', especially if you are the only traveller amongst Polynesians and Maoris. I could fill five bins between 8am and 2pm working non-stop (I was on muesli bars and energy drinks).

Apollo Fruit Ltd (www.fruitpack.co.nz/fruit_pack) operates a large apple packhouse in Whakatu in Hawke's Bay (06-873 0404) employing about 260 staff in the season between mid-February and July.

A harvest of boysenberries takes place in Hastings on Hawke's Bay between early December and mid-January. The fruit cannot be picked in the heat of the day so working holidaymakers are invited to swim and fish in the Ngaruroro River during the day.

Travelling east, the largest carrot-producing region in the southern hemisphere is around Ohakune. Work is available for up to nine months of the year here. While waiting for the ski season to begin, Matt Tomlinson rang some farmers out of the *Yellow Pages* and was soon hired to pack carrots. High staff turnover means that hiring goes on continuously. The work is boring and hard and pays not much more than minimum wage.

Northland

The tropical far north of the country, which specialises in citrus growing, is another favourite destination. In addition to growers in the region, several major packing sheds employ a large number of casual workers in November/December. Contract pruning can be more lucrative than picking. Kiwifruit pickers normally work in gangs of ten and are paid piece work, while kiwifruit packers and citrus pickers are paid by the hour. The six weeks between early April and mid-May is a busy kiwifruit season. Any of the hostels in Kaitaia and Kerikeri will be able to advise. Especially recommended is the Aranga Holiday Park in Kerikeri (opposite the BP Service Station; 09-407-9326; www.aranga.co.nz). It provides transport to the kiwifruit and mandarin orchards for a small fee and has tent sites which are available at discounted weekly rates in the off season; the weekly charge for a dorm bed is $86. Similarly Pukenui Holiday Park in Kaitaia (09-409 8803) recruits and runs the mandarin gangs on behalf of Kerifresh, the company that manages the four largest mandarin orchards in the area.

Armin Birrer picked fruit from October to January and reports: *'There is work in Kerikeri almost year round. The best way is to hire a bicycle and ask from orchard to orchard. Usually you have to work for various orchards at the same time since farmers can't afford to put too much fruit on the market at once.'*

Nelson/Motueka/Blenheim

The Nelson/Motueka area is a great area for travellers for its jobs as well as its beaches. Many foreign travellers are hired for the apple harvest, and also at the apple packing and processing works in Stoke, just outside Nelson. The union has succeeded in making it obligatory for farmers to provide accommodation other than just a campsite; some charge will be made though often the deduction is negligible. Orchard workers must join the union. The negotiated rate is $25-$30 per bin; the average picker fills three to four bins a day, though star pickers manage 6-8½ bins a day.

In Blenheim, make enquiries at the Grapevine hostel (29 Park Terrace; rob.diana@xtra. co.nz) about local picking, packing and pruning work in local vineyards. Rob Abblett spent several months earning money in the South Island. Apple thinning between mid-November and Christmas was fairly lucrative though more recently he fared less well with contract cherry picking around Blenheim for six weeks from late November or early December:

The season starts with select picking (on November 20th) on which nobody made any wages worth bothering about. Things picked up after the first two or three weeks *but unfortunately many backpackers were paid by the kilo throughout the season, even on select picking. I was aghast to earn about £40 in the first week, £60 in the second. Way too fickle a fruit. Yeah, in an excellent year with good pollination, ideal weather and a good orchard, it might be possible to earn $800 a week (the figure used by the orchard owners to motivate the thoroughly disillusioned backpackers). But in a bad or average year, I would stick with apple thinning.*

Many employers can be found by trawling the internet as well as asking locally. For example Birdhurst Ltd employs 250 pickers and shed staff near Motueka from February to June (61 High St North; 03-528 8492).Meanwhile the wine giant Allied Domecq Wines NZ (www.adwnz.com/Pages/profile/career_vacancies.html) needs about 700 people to prune vines in their Marlborough and North Canterbury vineyards from mid-May to August.

Our most recent correspondent from 'Mot,' as Motueka is known locally, is Roger Blake who stayed on until the season ended in June:

It has been three months since I arrived in this small town which is a haven for working travellers(plenty of hippies in these parts). Surrounded by the marvellous Mount Arthur, Motueka is the gateway to the world famous Abel Tasman National Park which has fantastic walking trails. I came to Mot to work with a friend and have been flat out ever since. The first job was a three-week stint picking pears which was good as it goes (fruit picking is really fun, not!) then went to an orchard to pick apples. But I hated every minute of it and quit on my first day and was ready to up and leave the town, thoroughly disillusioned with this fruit picking lark. As if by fate I got a job in a packing shed (apples and pears) and have been packing ever since. The job is work as work is meant to be - monotonous and semi-hard labour. But for some reason I have enjoyed spending 8-14 hours a day for six days per week running back and forth between conveyer belts, sorting, standing tirelessly at a grader throwing out bad apples and (my preference) stacking the boxes after they are packed. And that for a pittance of a wage. Worked with a great crowd of people though which made work more of a social thing.

Although Roger calls his wage a pittance, he was earning $10 an hour and $15 for any overtime over 44 hours which gave him a weekly after-tax pay packet of $425. He saved $2,000 in three months of hard work in Motueka and by living in a tent pitched at Fearon's Bush Holiday Park (tel/fax 03-528 7189) which charges seasonal workers a very affordable $55 a week.

Southland

Cherries are picked in Otago over the winter with the peak period from December 10 to January 20th. Bennie & Son Orchards in Alexandra (025-293 6893) accepts up to 200 pickers who camp on the farm, some of whom stay on for the apple harvest from mid-March to late April. It is also worth travelling to the far south of the South Island in late December for the tulip bulb harvest during the month of January at Van Eeden Tulips, 370 West Plains Road, R.D.4, Invercargill; vaneedentulips@xtra.co.nz).

Another Otago farm which extends a welcome to overseas working holidaymakers is Schist Mountain Orchards Ltd (PO Box 302, Alexandra; tel/fax 03-449 2083) where the cherry harvest begins in mid-December followed by soft fruit harvests through the autumn. Massive investment in cherry production around Cromwell (not far from Alexandra) has created many additional seasonal jobs for the area. For instance Molyneux Fruit Growers in Cromwell in Otago (03-445 1402) employ 100-200 picking and packing staff between mid-October and May; for details move to the Employment page from www.orchardfresh. co.nz.

Other Farm Work

Without wishing to state the obvious, there is a great deal of sheep and dairy farming in New Zealand. Wages on sheep stations are not likely to be high, perhaps $300 a week in addition to room and board. The International Agricultural Exchange Association (uk@agriventure.com) offers seven or eight month placements in New Zealand to trained agriculturalists from the UK or Ireland, which will cost at least £2,500.

> **Gerhard Flaig from Germany followed up a lead from another traveller and was invited to stay on the farm, which is a very typical New Zealand scenario:**
> *Very soon we all liked each other and I ended up staying five weeks on the sheep farm. I helped muster the sheep, sort the wool, repair fences, make firewood, do some construction work and gardening, mow the lawn, do some washing and cleaning. I didn't get money but got free board and lodging and in addition I had a wonderful time in rural countryside. We went for day trips to visit sights, we rode horses, we hunted wild pigs... There are many farmers in New Zealand willing to have travellers for some time to help them in their daily work.*

The Saturday edition of the *New Zealand Herald* and the *Waikato Times* in Hamilton are recommended for people looking for work on the land. Philippa Andrews noticed that there were almost daily adverts for milkers in the latter paper between July and Christmas. Usually experience is required. Small town New Zealanders would be intrigued by an advert placed by a young traveller in their local paper. Ken Smith was impressed with the initiative of the traveller who placed an ad in the *Oamaru Mail:* 'Young German man seeks farm work. Has tractor experience and good work habits;' Ken is sure that the novelty value of this approach would almost certainly bring success.

Gina Farmer (possibly a pseudonym?) describes her reasonably well paid job as a 'rousie':

> *Some of the jobs I have done in New Zealand have not been at all easy. For example, as a rousie, you get up at 4am, are working by 5am and don't stop until 5pm, with no guarantee of a day off until it rains so much that the sheep get wet. If you work with a slow gang where the average number of sheep shorn is about 250 a day per shearer then life can be quite fun. However if you land with a gang where the average is 350 and you have to look after two shearers, then life get decidedly tough. So anybody considering this sort of job would be wise to make some enquiries first. Whatever the case this is not a job for the faint-hearted.*

TOURISM

Openings in New Zealand's flourishing tourist industry generally continue to proliferate. Waiters and waitresses are usually paid $10-$13 an hour. On the plus side, restaurant kitchens tend to be more relaxed places than they are in Europe. In preparation for the America's Cup of 2000, Auckland's waterfront was transformed by a range of upmarket tourist facilities. International sporting events like these not only create employment opportunities before and during the event but for years afterwards. Colm Murphy from Ireland was looking for catering work there in 2003 and recommends cold calling at all the bars and restaurants in the Viaduct Harbour, Princes Wharf, Parnell, Ponsonby and Jervois Road areas. Remember that there is only a very recent tradition of tipping in New Zealand, though it is possible to make a little extra. Colm Murphy made $80-$100 a week in tips, especially when foreign tourists came to dine: *'Admittedly waiting on Kiwis is soul destroying. On numerous occasions I had big tables of 10-12 Kiwis and they never tipped me. They will thank you profusely for the service but they will not tip. To a certain type of Kiwi (especially those from south of the Bombay Hills, i.e. south of Auckland) tipping is an alien concept.'*

Well south of the Bombay Hills, the capital Wellington is not the first city you think of in the context of New Zealand tourism. But the base used by Peter Jackson in the making of the *Lord of the Rings* trilogy has brought fame and fortune to the city. It has a remarkably high ratio of cafés to citizen and a booming job market. Catharine Carfoot showed up there one November with a working holiday visa (though she wasn't always asked to show it) and easily found work first and accommodation second:

> I worked weekends driving for Wellington Cable Cars which has its ups and downs (cable car joke). And I was doing various things during the week, mostly temping through Select Appointments, and life modelling at the Inverlochy Art School and Vincents Art workshop ($80 cash for five hours). Bizarrely, I ended up practising my French conversation skills more than I had done for years, both at the Cable Car and with people met on the street asking for directions. It seems very odd that even the bigger hotels here don't always have a francophone on duty.

Note that the cable car and many tourist operations become very busy in February which marks the cruise ship season. The tourist industry in New Zealand adopts many adventurous and sporting guises. You might get taken on by a camping tour operator as a cook; perhaps you could find a job on a yacht or in a ski resort (see below).

Queenstown & the South Island

The lakeside resort of Queenstown is particularly brimming with opportunities. It is a town whose economy is booming due to tourism and whose population is largely young and transient. It is now almost as common to hear foreign accents among seasonal workers as New Zealand ones, though bear in mind that for this reason Queenstown has become a target for immigration investigations. It is one of the few places in which restaurants and bars (especially those that have been burned in the past) may ask to see your passport.

The central town notice board in the pedestrian mall and the notice board in supermarkets often carry adverts for waitresses, kitchen help, etc., as do the boards in the Queenstown Youth Hostel and backpacker haunts. Writing from Queenstown in January 2005, 28 year old Roger Blake describes how he had set about the job hunt a few months earlier:

> I arrived in Queenstown late one night with only NZ$90 in my pocket (and to my name). I immediately set about studying the internet café/backpackers notice boards and phoned for every job going, no matter what. Early the following morning I got a call asking me if I could start work right now. (A mobile phone really is the most valuable asset to gaining work.) Since then I have been a builder's mate, a landscape gardener, deliveries off-sider, done house & furniture removals, dug holes for scientists, dug trenches, planted trees, been a refuse collector and much more besides. Generally only working Mon to Fri, my average week was around 45 hours (optional weekend work is available but I chose to enjoy them otherwise). Quite an achievement to save money in Queenstown with so much temptation and so many establishments willing to take your money. After 4 months here (and having had a damn good time in the process) I have saved a little over $3000. On Monday I will attempt to leave (if I can get away from the lure Queenstown has over so many of us) to start my trip cycling around NZ this summer.

Roger claims not to have met anyone who had a problem obtaining work in Queenstown whatever their nationality or visa status. As always in travellers' meccas, finding affordable accommodation is the main challenge. Roger shared a house with seven like-minded working travellers.

One of the perks of being a worker in Queenstown and therefore an honorary resident (instead of a 'loopy', the local term for tourist), is that often workers can get discounts on local activities like rafting or 'zorbing' (rolling down a hill in a plastic ball). On the other hand, the town's popularity means that there are often more people (including New Zealanders) looking for work than there are jobs, so it might be advisable to try more remote tourist areas, like sparsely populated but heavily visited Milford Sound. It is accepted practice to phone the resort hotels and ask if they have any immediate vacancies. Good resorts to phone in addition to Milford Sound are Fox Glacier, Franz Josef and Mount Cook.

Ski Resorts

The ski season lasts roughly from July to October. Of the dozen commercial ski fields in the country, the main ones on the South Island are Coronet Peak and the Remarkables (serviced by Queenstown), Mount Hutt and Treble Cone (with access from Wanaka). On the North Island, Mount Ruapehu is the main ski area, at least when its volcanic activity is dormant. The ski field at Turoa is serviced by the resort of Ohakune and the ski area of Whakapapa by the settlement called National Park.

Catering and related jobs are widely available in these resort towns. Altogether NZ ski resorts employ about a thousand seasonal staff. In addition to the hourly wage of $10-$15 you may be given a lift pass and subsidised food and drink. Matt Tomlinson enjoyed his two jobs in Ohakune as a barman in the ski resort bar and a waiter in a restaurant, though he came to the conclusion that New Zealand bosses like to get their money's worth. When there weren't many customers, he was put to work building shelves, chopping wood and cleaning drains. He found the jobs by checking notice boards (by the library in Ohakune and in the supermarket), reading the local newspapers and asking around. Altogether the Ruapehu/Ohakune area absorbs about 700 seasonal workers so there is plenty of scope. One of the main employers in the area is Ruapehu Alpine Lifts Ltd (Private Bag, Mount Ruapehu; 07-892 3738; employment@mtruapehu.com) which accepts applications until mid-April and interviews candidates in the first week of May. You will also have to keep your ears open if you are to find affordable accommodation.

If you have a specific skill, e.g. ski instructor, ski patroller, ski hire technician, snow-cat/plough driver, then it is worth applying to the resort in advance. Resort addresses are listed in the *Travel Survival Kit New Zealand* from Lonely Planet and most are linked from http://skicentral.com/newzealand.html. The site www3.nzski.com/nzskicom/employ_intro. asp has an online application for ski resort work. Opportunities also exist for carpenters and painters in the months before the season begins; ask around in the pubs.

To get a job as a ski instructor, request a place on one of the hiring clinics held at the beginning of July in most resorts, for which you will have to pay (but not much). A BASI certificate or equivalent (see introductory chapter *Tourism: Winter Resorts*) is essential to get full-time instructing work. Part-timers or rookie instructors usually get a lift pass plus instructor training sessions and loggable hours of practice. Snowboard instructors are in heavy demand and may not need advanced qualifications to be hired.

Fishing

Fishing is a profitable business for New Zealand and fishermen can be found in most coastal towns. Nelson is one of the important centres for fishing and fish processing, and one of the largest processing operations is called Sealords where you might get a job (though it's a long shot) filleting, freezing and packing fish in the block freezer. If you can, try to get taken on instead as a 'wharfie,' transferring the fish from the boats to the chiller, since the pay will be better. Go down to the docks before 6am to see if any casual work is available.

The oyster season runs from April to December and oyster shelling work is available especially in Whangarei on the North Island, Orongo Bay near Russell and in Kerikeri. Fiona Cox enjoyed this work far more than fruit picking:

We found work the day after we arrived in Whangarei in December and worked for the three weeks of the Christmas rush. We phoned about four fisheries, none of which asked about visas. We even got a gumboot allowance! Loads of overtime and in terms of perks and fairness to the workers, it was one of the best places I've worked in, even if we did work in a bloody cold disco. Managed to save enough money to do some touring in the North Island.

Of course recreational fishing creates work, as the American Chris Miksovsky describes:

> Queenstown was such a nice place that I decided to stay for a while. I happened upon a job with a chartered fishing boat business. We'd take small groups of angler-wanna-be's out in a motorboat and try to help them catch some rainbow trout or lake salmon. I got to go on several outings but mostly I sat at a small desk by our dock in the town harbour giving information to people about the trips and getting a commission on the trips I booked. The money was excellent some days ($150 was my record) and nil others, all paid cash-in-hand. It was probably the most relaxing and scenic job I've ever had, right on the water, surrounded by mountains, watching the tourists of the world go by. The only downside was that I often had to listen to die-hard fishermen go on and on about all the fish they'd caught around the world. The Americans were the worst: 'Now y'all see that there Barracuuuuda?' (pointing to photo) 'I caught that big ol' boy in Faayjaay. Tuk me fowr hours to brang that there sucker in.'

BUSINESS & INDUSTRY

Experienced secretaries are in constant demand in Auckland and Wellington, though temp agencies like Adecco (www.adecco.co.nz) will want to be reassured that you have a legal right to work in the country. A mobile phone makes it much easier to stay in touch with employment agencies. Temping secretaries in the main cities earn $16-$18 an hour, data entry pays $13-$15 while clerks start at $10 and telemarketers earn $13. Holiday pay of 6% is also accrued.

> **Emiliano Giovannoni spent several successful months in telesales in Wellington**
> There are lots of opportunities for travellers in Wellington to get a little job. The big thing seems to be telesales and telemarketing. There are loads of agencies recruiting people for that sort of job and no particular skills are required but to be able to 'blag' it. The money is reasonably good for New Zealand ($13-$15 per hour) and it is easy clean work.

One specialist agency in Wellington is Select Teleresources, Level 6, Clayton Ford House, 132 The Terrace. Agencies in Auckland to try for a range of jobs include Kelly Services (Level 9, Gen-i Tower, 66 Wyndham St; 09-303 3122; www.kellyservices.co.nz) and Robert Walters (Level 9, 22 Fanshawe St; 09-302 2280).

Without secretarial skills, try market research and labouring agencies, which sometimes require only an IRD number. Building work abounds in Auckland and in other areas of the North Island. Labouring agencies can be a good bet such as Allied Workforce which is the largest casual labour supplier in New Zealand. Check the Saturday, Monday and Wednesday editions of the *New Zealand Herald* and the *Dominion Post* from Wellington on Saturdays, the Saturday *Nelson Times* and the Wednesday *Christchurch Press,* which carry adverts for labourers, clerks, waiters, drivers, receptionists, etc.

Scouring the ads paid off for Jane Harris who hadn't been having much luck doing the rounds of the cafés and sandwich shops in Auckland. She answered an ad placed by a direct marketing company in the *Herald* and was soon selling charity pens and key rings door-to-door:

> The pay for my job was commission only, but it was easy to earn $90-$100 per day. People were much more welcoming than I expected. And I enjoyed working out of doors. I did that job for two months before getting fed up with it. So I went after a job as manager of another backpackers hostel which I got and was given free accommodation with my boyfriend Pete. I also managed to get a second part-time job (which paid $11.33 an hour) as a telephone interviewer for a market research

company. Easy work. In all cases, I told them I had a work permit (though I'm 34 and therefore ineligible); all they wanted was my IRD number and bank account details.

The shortage of primary teachers in New Zealand has been somewhat reduced over the past few years but there is still great demand for secondary teachers of certain targeted subjects (maths, sciences, English, ICT, PE). The NZ government has been providing incentives such as a $3,000 relocation grant in order to attract teachers from overseas, many from Britain, on two-year visas; details on www.teachnz.govt.nz/overseas_index. html. Most of the schools experiencing a shortage are rural schools off the beaten track that would afford an excellent opportunity to experience country life.

Useful websites which list actual job vacancies (most of them permanent) and dates of posting are www.seek.co.nz, www.netcheck.co.nz and www.workingin-newzealand.com. The latter company produces a glossy recruitment magazine (Working In Ltd, PO Box 3394, Shortland St, Auckland; 09-302 0977).

Greenpeace frequently recruits fund-raisers. The job involves standing around in a busy shopping area and trying to persuade people to sign up for a monthly direct debit donation to Greenpeace. After Catharine Carfoot was selected and given a three-hour training session by Greenpeace in Wellington, she was paid an hourly rate plus a commission for 30 hours a week and was happy to be earning money while not turning into a 'corporate nazi'.

ANTARCTICA

There are probably very few corporate nazis 25° latitude to the south either. As well as the highly trained scientists and others needed to run an Antarctic research station such as McMurdo Station, a certain number of dogsbodies are needed. The Raytheon Polar Services Company is subcontracted by the US government's National Science Foundation to hire between 800 and 1,000 Americans to run the station, a third of whom are women. Of these, a certain number are general assistants (GAs) who, among many tasks, do quite a lot of snow shovelling. Openings also exist for chefs, electricians, computer programmers, typists, construction workers and so on. Contracts are for four, six or twelve months.

Raytheon (www.rpsc.raytheon.com) begin considering applications in April though may not choose their summer season personnel (to work October to mid-February) until the last moment. Even though the work schedule is nine hours a day, six days a week, these jobs are massively oversubscribed, so perseverance will be needed, plus excellent health (physical, mental and dental) and a willingness to travel at short notice. It is now necessary to submit an application online through www.rayjobs.com since applications will not be accepted by email or post.

Britain's five research stations and two research vessels in Antarctica are overseen by the British Antarctic Survey (High Cross, Madingley Road, Cambridge CB3 0ET; 01223 221508; employment@bas.ac.uk/ www.antarctica.ac.uk/Employment/index.html). Most vacancies are for tradespeople like plumbers and electricians plus IT engineers at the BAS stations of Rothera and Halley. All support staff hired by BAS must be suitably qualified or experienced and willing to sign a fixed term or open-ended contrac, usually for up to 18 months. They also offer short-term vacation and casual labour contracts, which range for a period of weeks up to a maximum of one year, usually to committed students.

United States

The great American Dream has beckoned countless people who have left their homelands in eager pursuit of the economic miracle. Whether Latin Americans fleeing poverty at home or East Europeans seeking a brave new world, generations of foreigners have become part of the American population which is often described as a 'melting pot'. But post 9/11 regulations have made it even more difficult to obtain permission to live and work in the US. The authorities continue to make a concerted effort to protect their borders, partly in the interests of 'homeland security' but also because the economy is still uncertain. The dollar has been weakening over the past couple of years and the rate of unemployment has not dropped significantly (5.5% at the end of 2004).

Despite the wide open spaces and warm hospitality so often associated with America, their official policies are discouraging for the traveller who plans to pick up some casual work along the way. The choice of the word 'alien' in official use to describe foreigners may not be intentionally symbolic, however it does convey the suspicion with which non-Americans are treated by the authorities. It is very difficult to get permission to work. But as we have found in so many other countries, there are some special provisions and exceptions to the rule.

The most important exception to the gloomy generalisation is the special work visa available through work and travel programmes like the ones run by BUNAC, the British Universities North America Club (16 Bowling Green Lane, London EC1R 0QH; 020-7251 3472; www.bunac.org.uk) and Usit, the Irish student travel service (19-21 Aston Quay, Dublin 2; www.usit.ie). All of these programmes, including the summer camp agencies, are described in detail since they arrange for large numbers of people to work legitimately in the USA. This is because they are authorised by the US State Department to give out J-1 exchange visas. Other possibilities include joining the one-year Au Pair in America Programme (see section on Childcare below) or joining one of the work exchange or internship programmes, which require you to find your own position in your field of study. The brief list of approved Work Exchange Programmes in the US published by the Fulbright Commission on its website was out-of-date at the time of writing (Educational Advisory Service, Fulbright Commission, 62 Doughty St, London WC1N 2JZ; 020-7404 6994; www. fulbright.co.uk/eas/workexchange).

The other side of the coin is the possibility of working without permission, which carries a number of risks and penalties to be carefully considered beforehand. As described below, the laws are always changing in order to tighten up on security in general and black work in particular. The missing link between you and a whole world of employment prospects is a social security number to which you will not be legally entitled unless you have a recognised work visa.

VISAS

Most British citizens and those of 27 other countries do not need to apply for a tourist visa in advance. Tourists can wait until arrival to obtain a visa-waiver which is valid for one entry to the US for a maximum of 90 days. Individuals entering visa-free or with a visitor visa for business or tourism are prohibited from engaging in paid or unpaid employment in the US. Those planning trips of more than 90 days, including those who wish to work or study, must obtain a visa in advance from the Embassy. This has become much more complicated than it once was and requires a face-to-face interview and a £60 fee (even if the visa is denied) as well as completing a long and detailed form.

British travellers and tourists arriving in the US on the visa waiver programme face increasingly rigorous restrictions. Upon arrival you will have a digital photograph and an inkless fingerprint taken, before being given permission to enter for three months. Since October 2004, the US authorities have insisted that all incoming visa-less visitors have a machine-readable passport (which most European passports are). In the future everyone will need a 'smart' passport, i.e. one that has a chip containing your biometric data including an iris scan. The US authorities say that they will accept travel documents issued after 26 October 2005 only if they are 'smart' or contain a visa.

Check the Embassy website (www.usembassy.org.uk) or dial the premium line 09055 444546 for full visa information and application forms or request an outline of non-immigrant visas from the Visa Branch of the US Embassy (5 Upper Grosvenor St, London W1A 2JB).

The non-immigrant visa of most interest to the readers of this book is the J-1 which is available to participants of government-authorised programmes, known as Exchange Visitor Programmes (EVP). The J-1 visa is a valuable and coveted addition to any passport since it entitles the holder to take legal paid employment. You cannot apply for the J-1 without the right form and you cannot get form DS2019 (formerly IAP-66) without going through a recognised Exchange Visitor Programme (like BUNAC and Camp America) which have approved sponsors in the US.

The programmes are allowed to exist because of their educational value. These exchanges and their quotas are reviewed regularly by the government, though with constant lobbying and proof from employers of staff shortages, the quotas have been increasing. Still it is important that the arrangement not be abused (e.g. participants breaking the terms of the programme, or even worse, breaking the law) since this will damage the reputation of the entire programme.

Other Visas

Apart from the J-1 visa available to people on approved EVPs, there are three possible visa categories to consider, all of which must be applied for by the employer on the applicant's behalf and will take at least three months. The H category covers non-immigrant work visas in special circumstances. The H2-B is for temporary or seasonal vacancies that employers have trouble filling with US citizens. For example, the chronic shortage of workers on the ski fields of Colorado means that many employers can obtain the necessary Labor Certification confirming that there are no qualified American workers available to do the jobs. A petition must be submitted by the employer to the Immigration and Naturaliza-tion Service. The maximum duration of the H2-B visa is ten months though most come in for about six months to work at amusement parks, as lifeguards, in retail and fast food, construction, landscaping and fish processing. They must work only for the employer that has petitioned for their visa. The seasonal work visa for agriculture is the H-2A valid for between three and ten months.

The H-1B 'Specialty Occupation' visa for professionals with a university degree is available for 'prearranged professional or highly skilled jobs' for which there are no suit-ably qualified Americans. H-1B visas allow skilled foreigners to live and work in the US for up to six years. The number of allocations of H1-B visas has been rising, mainly to IT spe-cialists and more recently to nurses. Last year's allocation was 65,000, all of which were snapped up soon after the quota was released on October 1st. All the paperwork must be carried out by the American employer who must pay a new application fee of $1,500 as of December 2004.

The H-3 'Trainee' visa is another possibility. Applying employers must indicate in detail the breakdown between classroom and on-the-job time, and why equivalent training is not available in the foreign trainee's own country. The validity of this visa is 18 or 24 months.

The Q visa is the 'International Cultural Exchange Visa', affectionately dubbed the 'Disney' visa, since it was introduced partly in response to their lobbying. After working at Disney World on a Q visa, Paul Binfield concluded that the main difference between the J-1 and the Q-1 was that the latter obliges you to pay more tax. If you find a job in which it can be argued that you will be providing practical training or sharing the history, culture and traditions of your country with interested members of the American public, you might be eligible to work legally for up to 15 months. This is potentially possible in amusement parks, restaurants, museums, summer schools, etc. As usual this visa must be applied for by the prospective employer in the US and approved in advance by an office of the Immi-gration and Naturalization Service (INS).

Another possibility is the B-1 'Voluntary Service' visa. Applications must be sponsored by a charitable or religious organisation which undertakes not to pay you but may reim-burse you for incidental expenses. Applicants must do work of a traditional charitable nature. Foreign students on an F-1 visa are allowed to work up to 20 hours a week.

It is exceedingly difficult (not to mention expensive) to get an immigrant visa or 'green card' (actually it's off-white) which allows foreigners to live and work in the US as 'resident aliens'. Nearly all the permanent resident visas which are issued each year are given to close relations of American citizens or world experts in their field. Money and love are not the only reasons to marry, though this course of action is too drastic for most. More than a few foreigners have in the past been tempted to counterfeit ID. However the US govern-ment post 9-11 has invested heavily in tightening up on potential fraud.

Every autumn, the US government holds a Green Card Lottery or 'Diversity Immigrant Visa Program' whereby applications are drawn from a hat. Strict quotas operate for differ-ent nationalities and, in recent years, Britons have been barred from entering (apart from people from Northern Ireland).

Arrival

If you have a visa, a return ticket and look tidy and confident, chances are you will whizz through immigration. But American immigration is so notoriously tough and unpleasant that it is worth describing some of the techniques used by readers to avoid possible catas-trophe. If you are sure that you will not want to stay longer than 90 days, you can sign the visa waiver form at entry. One reader wrote to say that she had trouble crossing back from Mexico with a visa waiver; however the official word is that you can cross borders as long as the crossing takes place within 90 days of your return ticket from North America to Europe.

Whichever method you choose, be prepared for a gruelling inquisition when you first arrive. It is probably better to ask for a relatively short stay since the authorities are bound to be suspicious of someone who says he or she plans to be a tourist for five months.

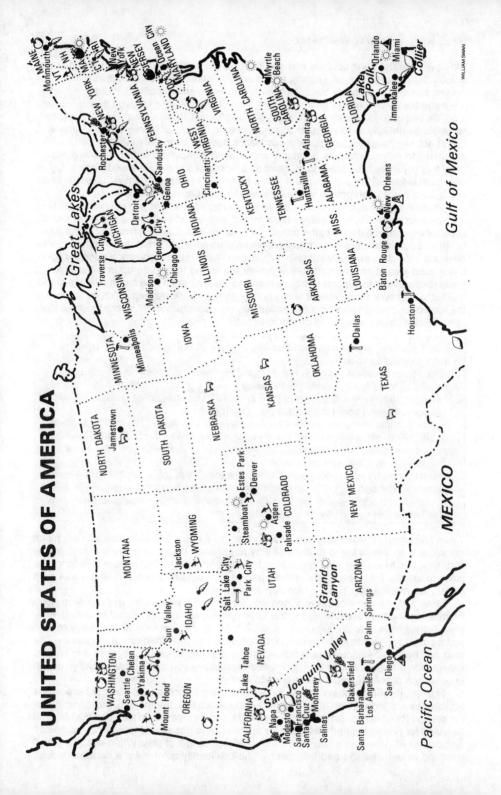

Whatever you do, don't confess that you hope to find work. Dress neatly but remember to look like a tourist, not an aspiring professional. Sander Meijsen was pulled out of the immigration queue probably because he was carrying a smart laptop computer.

If you are taken away to be interviewed, expect to have your luggage minutely examined. Be prepared to explain anything in your luggage which an average sightseeing tourist would be unlikely to have, such as smart clothes (for possible interviews). Better still, don't pack anything which could be incriminating such as letters of reference, letters from an American referring to jobs or interviews, or even a copy of this book. Having written proof that you have a full-time job to return to, property ties or a guaranteed place in higher education in the UK are also an asset. It can be helpful to provide them with a travel itinerary, a list of places and people you want to see in your capacity of tourist.

Although having a return or onward ticket is no guarantee that you will not be hassled, it helps your case. Many travellers recommend entering the US on a short-term return ticket which can be extended after arrival, for instance with Kuwait Airways or Virgin Atlantic. (If you do choose this option, make sure before you buy a ticket that the date can be changed without an excessive penalty.) If you don't have much money or an onward ticket, it is a good idea to have the names of Americans willing to put you up or a letter from a friend, undertaking to support you for a month or so. Laurence Koe had asked his grandmother to type up a list of all their family connections on the continent which he showed to the suspicious immigration officer at Hawaii Airport, accompanying it with a touching story of how it had been his boyhood dream to encircle the globe.

> **Rilda Maxwell wants to stress the importance of being adequately prepared for a possible ordeal**
> *People (especially if they are black, travelling alone or staying more than three months) should have at hand the following:*
> 1) *at least $500 for every month of their proposed stay plus credit cards. Don't lie, since you have to count the money out in front of them.*
> 2) *names, addresses and telephone numbers (work and home) of your contacts or hosts. If they are suspicious, they won't hesitate to ring the numbers. Have several numbers in case the first people are away or out. Otherwise you'll be stuck at Immigration until they get an answer.*
> 3) *be prepared for your luggage and handbag to be thoroughly searched. They read letters, go through your diary and address book with a fine tooth comb. A CV and reference are a give-away, so be sure to send these on ahead if you think that you'll need them. Don't leave anything to chance.*

When Mig Urquhart was flying into New York from Athens via Casablanca with not much money, she phoned a friend to say that if by any chance immigration were to ring, to say that, yes, her friend Mig was coming on holiday and no she didn't know how long she planned to stay. Fortunately this priming proved unnecessary since all she got was a 'Hi there'... Stamp, stamp...'Have a nice day' and she was in.

Steve King has an innovative suggestion for proving how wealthy you are. Many British building societies are affiliated to the 'Link' system, which entitles card holders to withdraw money from over 20,000 cash dispensers in the US. Get friends and family to lend you money for a few days, bring the passbook up to date and then return the money. The card and healthy balance in the account can be paraded before the eyes of any curious immigration officers. Despite taking all these precautions you may still be unlucky enough to get only a couple of weeks permission to stay.

The length of time given seems to be completely discretionary. Marcus Scrace has entered the US three times: the first time he asked for two months and was given three; the second time his request was for three weeks and they gave him two; and the last time he asked for two weeks and was given six months! Jane Roberts adopted a coy approach. She did not fill in the part of the form about proposed length of stay. When she was pulled over and asked why she had left it blank, she confidently gave them a detailed (though fictitious) itinerary and list of contacts (also fictitious) and asked them what period of time they would recommend. With the tables so flatteringly turned, she was given 90 days although she had with her only $280.

Visa Extensions

It is possible though time-consuming to extend your tourist visa. Before your permitted time is up, ask the local office of the Immigration and Naturalization Service for the form entitled 'Application for Issuance or Extension of Permit to Re-enter the United States.' To get a renewal you will have to show adequate means of support and have a reason for wishing to prolong your stay. Merely saying you wish to travel longer may work, or you might claim that your parents are arriving soon and you wish to show them around. (Note that it is almost always a waste of time to ring INS offices since you will spend hours listening to irrelevant recorded messages.)

One tactic that has been brought to our attention is for those with a J-1 visa about to expire to apply to have it extended. This application will be denied, but it normally takes the INS three months to return your passport during which time you are not working illegally.

Alternatively you can slip over the Canadian or Mexican border and recross the border and hope that the immigration officer on your return will automatically extend your stay. If you overstay, you can 'lose' the immigration card showing your date of entry from your passport and exit by land to Mexico or Canada where there is no US immigration control.

WORK AND TRAVEL PROGRAMMES

Obviously it is preferable to avoid all this anxiety about visas by participating in an approved exchange programme. *BUNAC* (16 Bowling Green Lane, London EC1R 0QH; 020-7251 3472; www.bunac.org.uk) administers three basic programmes in the US: one is the 'Work America Programme' which allows full-time university students to do any summer job they are able to find; the second is 'Summer Camp USA' which is open to anyone over 18 interested in working on a summer camp as a counsellor; the third is 'KAMP' (Kitchen & Maintenance Programme) which is open to students who want to work at a summer camp in a catering and maintenance capacity. (The camp programmes are described below under the heading 'Summer Camps'.) All participants must join the BUNAC Club (£5), travel on BUNAC flights between June and the beginning of October and purchase compulsory insurance (about £130). BUNAC runs its own loan scheme.

If you are considering a summer job in America, it is worth contacting BUNAC headquarters or your local club branch (in most universities) as early as possible for their detailed brochure setting out the various and potentially confusing procedures. There is no easy way of circumventing the red tape and accompanying uncertainty though BUNAC are very experienced at guiding applicants as gently as possible through the processes. With tightening US security it is essential that you keep abreast of changes, for example the SEVIS tracking programme means that if you intend to leave the country temporarily (e.g. to visit Canada), you have to register your intention at least two weeks in advance by sending your DS2019 form to your sponsoring organisation.

BUNAC's *Work America* programme (www.bunac.org/uk/workamerica) offers about 4,000 places to students who may take virtually any job anywhere in the US over the summer. To assist applicants in finding work, BUNAC publishes an annual Job Directory with thousands of job listings in the US from hundreds of employers, many of whom have taken on BUNAC participants in the past. The Directory is available to all potential applicants and is free of charge. Accommodation may be provided by the employer, particularly if a British student takes a job in the hospitality industry. Jobs can be pre-arranged through the directory or other resources, or they can be found on-the-spot, though it should be noted that this latter route is now heavily discouraged after the US government considered prohibiting it.

In addition to the registration fee of £114 for first-time applicants (£89 for early applicants) and the flight package from £450, you must submit a letter from your principal, registrar or tutor on college headed paper showing that you are a full-time student in the year of travel. You are also required to take at least $400 in travellers cheques. If you are going over with a commission sales job or plan to job hunt on arrival, you must take at least $800. The J-1 visa application fee is $100 and the SEVIS fee is a further $35 (as of September 2004).

In addition to BUNAC, the principal work and travel programmes (as distinct from career-oriented internship programmes described in the next section) are broadly comparable. These programmes provide full-time or deferred place students aged 19 to 30 with the opportunity to live and work in the US for a maximum of four months.

IST Plus Ltd, Rosedale House, Rosedale Road, Richmond, Surrey TW9 2SZ (020-8939 9057; info@istplus.com; www.istplus.com) is the agency appointed in 2004 to operate programmes on behalf of CIEE (Council on International Educational Exchange) based in Boston, USA, including Work and Travel in the USA and Internship USA (described later). Participants, who must be students returning to full-time education, are free to find their own summer jobs before departure and are required to show minimum back-up funds. The fee starts at £365 excluding travel.

Work & Travel Company, 45 High St, Tunbridge Wells, Kent TN1 1XL (01892 516164; www.worktravelcompany.co.uk). Choice of programme: self-arranged job costs £349-£399 depending on date of registration or the full-service option in which a job is arranged for you through Interexchange in New York costs an extra £100 (approximately) and is available only up until the end of February.

CCUSA, 1st Floor North, Devon House, 171/177 Great Portland St, London W1W 5PQ (020-7637 0779/ fax 020-7580 6209; www.ccusaweusa.co.uk). In addition to its summer camp programme (described below), CCUSA has a sizeable Work Experience programme whereby participants can work on a J-1 visa in any job for up to four months between June 1st and October 19th or for the winter season (see section on Ski Resorts below). Candidates choose whether to find their own job before or after arrival or to have CCUSA find a job for them. CCUSA works with a number of employers in resort and vacation centres throughout the United States to find placements for participants so that a job offer is guaranteed to those who are accepted onto the Placement programme (fee £540). It is also possible to arrange your own job for a lower fee (£360). The package cost includes a Directory of Employers, four months insurance, meeting on arrival and two-day orientation in New York with accommodation. Interested individuals in Scotland and the north of England should contact the CCUSA office at 27 Woodside Gardens, Musselburgh, Scotland EH21 7LJ (0131-665 5843). Most recruitment takes place before April 1st. The company has a network of 45 interviewers around the UK and organises various open houses and recruitment fairs. The US headquarters of CCUSA are at 2330 Marinship Way, Suite 250, Sausalito, CA 94965 who run several outgoing programmes for American students.

Global Choices, Barkat House, 116-118 Finchley Road, London NW3 5HT (020-7433 2501; info@globalchoices.co.uk) arranges basic, entry level summer jobs mainly in housekeeping, as restaurant support staff, and in amusement parks for UK students. A job is guaranteed though it is pot-luck as to where you'll be and what you'll be doing. The fee is £400-£480 for assisted placements (the earlier the application, the cheaper the fee) while the fees are £100 cheaper if you arrange your own job.

Camp America (contact details given in section on Summer Camps below) offers the Resort America programme whereby people are placed in hotels or holiday resorts for a minimum of 12 weeks and are paid $1,400 for the whole period in addition to a free transatlantic flight.

CIEE Australia, 91 York St, Sydney, NSW 2000 (02-8235 7000; www.councilex-changes.org.au) organises Work and Travel USA for Australian students, while New Zealanders should contact Backpackers World Travel, Level 2, Base Travel, 16-20 Fort St, Auckland; 09-379 4126; WATUSA@backpackersworld.com/ www.backpackersworld.com). Antipodeans are permitted to work in the US between November 15th and April 15th only but participants can stay on for an extra month on a tourist visa.

Note that a number of other student travel organisations place students from around the world in similar work and travel programmes. For example Sayit is an Irish student travel agency with offices in Dublin and Cork which operates a J-1 programme (01-671 5900; www.sayit.ie). APEX USA Ltd (PO Box 8, Clinton, Oklahoma 73601; www.apexusa. org) has partners in Sofia, Tallinn, Gdansk, Kingston (Jamaica), Denpassar (Bali) and many others that conduct interviews on its behalf. Spirit Cultural Exchange (2011 West Concord, Suite B, Chicago, IL 60047; 723-862-9449; www.spiritexchange.com) pre-arranges summer jobs in hotels and restaurants for university students while American Work Experience (335 Greenwich Avenue, Greenwich, CT 06830; info@aweusa.com) recruits actively in Eastern Europe and has its European office in Bratislava. Typically participants are placed in summer jobs in big leisure attractions like Six Flags Parks (see section on Tourism below).

Internships

Internship is the American term for traineeship, providing a chance to get some experience in your career interest as part of your academic course. These are typically available to undergraduates, recent graduates and young professionals, and are almost always unpaid. The 750+ page book *Internships* published by Peterson's Guides (address below) lists intern positions which are paid or unpaid, can last for the summer, for a semester or for a year. The book offers general advice (including a section called 'Foreign Applicants for US Internships') and specific listings organised according to field of interest, e.g. Advertising, Museums, Radio, Social Services, Law, etc. This annually revised book is available in the UK from Vacation Work for £18.99 plus £3 postage (www.vacationwork.co.uk).

Several organisations in the UK are authorised to help candidates find work placements in the USA and obtain a J-1 visa valid for up to 18 months. IST Plus in the UK (address above) helps full-time students and recent graduates to arrange course-related placements in the US lasting from 3 to 18 months. The placement can take place at any time during your studies, during the summer, as a sandwich year or up to 12 months after graduating. Although you are responsible for finding your own course-related position, CIEE through its partner agencies like IST Plus supplies practical advice on applying for work and a searchable database of internships/work placements. Those who qualify get a J-1 visa. The programme fees start at £350.

The UK/US Career Development Programme is administered by the Association for International Practical Training (AIPT) in Maryland (www.aipt.org). This programme is for people aged 18-35 with relevant qualifications and/or at least one year of work experience in their career field. A separate section of the programme is for full-time students in Hospitality & Tourism or Equine Studies.

International Employment Training, a division of the Work & Travel Company, assists anyone with a degree from a recognised UK university and some work experience in a chosen field to find a placement with a US company for 3-18 months; details from IET, 45 High St, Tunbridge Wells, Kent TN1 1XL (www.jobsamerica.co.uk). Fees vary from free (for arborists) to £1,178 for 18 months of a self-arranged placement, for example in the hotels industry. Wages are paid on a par with US co-workers.

CDS International (871 United Nations Plaza, 15th floor, New York, NY 10017-1814; 212-497-3500; www.cdsintl.org) offers practical training placements in the US lasting 3-18 months in a variety of fields including business, engineering and technology. The opportunities for internships are open to young professionals, aged 21-35.

Cultural Cube (16 Acland Rd, Ivybridge, Devon PO21 9UR; www.culturalcube.co.uk) runs two internship programmes, one for the hospitality industry, the other for business. Hospitality internships are available for 12 months in and around Atlanta (programme fee £1,490; monthly stipend $400 on top of accommodation). The business placement in Washington DC (minimum age 21) consists of an optional 1-month business training workshop plus 6 or 12 month placements (fee of £1,500 or £1,900).

Intrax has a Work/Travel Program (but no representation in the UK) though they have recently been designated by the US Department of State as an official sponsor for the

International Career Training Program (also J-1) for which British candidates would be eligible to apply. Intrax can be contacted at 2226 Bush St, San Francisco, CA 94115 (415-674-5260; www.intraxcareertraining.com) and have links with large summer employers such as national park concessionaires.

Other internship sponsors include InterExchange (161 Sixth Avenue, New York, NY 10013; www.interexchange.org) and the Alliance Abroad Group (1221 South Mopac Expressway, Suite 250, Austin, Texas 78746; 512-457-8062/ 1-888-6-ABROAD; www.allianceabroad.com) both of which are accredited to grant J-1 visas to European candidates. Alliances Abroad arrange internships in Denver, San Francisco and Washington DC. The International Trainee Network (www.internationaltrainee.com) has its headquarters in LA and branch office in Miami and co-operates with partner agencies in France and Ireland.

A programme of the British-American Chamber of Commerce (8 Staple Inn, Holborn, London WC1V 7QH; 020-7404 6400) provides training opportunities in the US for qualified foreign trainees in business-related fields to promote the general interest of international educational and cultural change. The programme fee is $1,200.

The Mountbatten Internship Programme (Abbey House, 74-76 St John St, 5th Floor, London EC1M 4DZ; www.mountbatten.org) provides work experience in New York City for people aged 21-28 with business training and in the majority of cases a university degree. Placements last one year and provide free accommodation as well as a monthly allowance of about $900. Interns pay a participation fee of £1,955 (from September 2005).

SUMMER CAMPS

Summer camps are uniquely American in atmosphere, even if the idea has spread to Europe. An estimated 8 million American children are sent to 10,000 summer camps each year for a week or more to participate in outdoor activities and sports, arts and crafts and generally have a wholesome experience. The type of camp varies from plush sports camps for the very rich to more or less charitable camps for the handicapped or under-privileged.

It is estimated that summer camps employ nearly a third of a million people. Thousands of 'counsellors' are needed each summer to be in charge of a cabinful of youngsters and to instruct or supervise some activity, from the ordinary (swimming and boating) to the esoteric (puppet-making and ham radio). Several summer camp organisations are authorised to issue J-1 visas, primarily Camp America and BUNAC, but some smaller ones are also mentioned below.

After camp finishes, counsellors have up to six weeks' free time and normally return on organised flights between late August and the end of September. Camp counselling regularly wins enthusiastic fans and is worth considering if you enjoy children (even the rambunctious American variety who might sue you if you shout at them) and don't mind hard work. As Hannah Start concluded after a summer at an expensive camp in upstate New York, primarily for Jewish kids, 'If you can survive the bugs and the kids, camp counselling is a healthy, rewarding way to spend the summer.' Some camps are staffed almost entirely by young people from overseas, which can be useful if you are looking for a post-camp travelling companion. Others have a reasonable proportion of American employees, in which case there is a good chance that you will be invited to visit their homes when camp finishes. In Hannah's view, whatever happens at camp is compensated by the amazing travel opportunities afterwards.

If the idea of working at a remote lakeside or mountain location appeals to you but the 24-hour-a-day responsibility for keeping children entertained and well-behaved does not, you might be interested in a behind-the-scenes job in the kitchen or maintenance. Camp directors often find it difficult to attract Americans to do these jobs, partly because the wages are low, and both BUNAC and Camp America can arrange this for British and European students.

Bear in mind that your enjoyment of a summer camp job will be largely determined by the style of the camp, the standard of facilities and its proximity to interesting places to visit on your days off. (Note that a day off is often 24 hours, so can be from 5pm one day to 5pm the next.) Signing up with one of the big organisations like BUNACAMP or Camp America is a lottery. If you happen to have had a camp recommended, you are free to contact them independently, fix up a job and then ask one of the exchange visitor programmes to expedite the paperwork. Another way of making an informed choice is to attend one of the recruitment fairs held in the new year by Camp America where you can meet camp directors. This might have helped Amy Jones, a student at Nottingham University, to avert her disastrous experience:

> On arrival we were launched into a 75 hour week, looking after the children and the 37 horses. This increased to 85 when the only American counsellor quit after just two weeks. Apart from the exhaustion, this might have been tolerable. But the couple who ran the camp were intimidating. They seemed worried we might run away (which we did often think about). One of the new rules they imposed was that we were not allowed to speak to each other unless it concerned camp organisation. There was no privacy and no freedom. The atmosphere was filled with tension.

Amy's conclusion was that, seen from one point of view, the recruitment agencies supply cheap labour who are not at liberty to leave because they then forfeit their free flight.

Camps have to impose rules and in many cases these are quite strict, such as no alcohol (apparently Irish and Australian counsellors, true to their reputations, are the most likely to be fined for drinking at camp.)

BUNAC

With its *Summer Camp USA* programme, BUNAC is one of the two biggest counsellor placement organisations in the field, sending between 3,000 and 4,000 people aged between 19 (occasionally 18 year olds are accepted) and 35 as counsellors at children's camps. The registration fee of £67 includes camp placement, return flight and land transport to camp and pocket money of $820-$880 (depending on age) for the whole nine-week period. The fact that you do not have to raise the money for the flight is a great attraction for many; the camp which decides to hire you advances the amount from your wages to BUNAC who in turn put it towards your flight. Interviews, which are compulsory, are held in university towns throughout Britain between November and May.

Summer camps provide more scope for employment than looking after the kids. BUNAC's Kitchen and Maintenance Programme, otherwise known as *KAMP*, is open only to students who are given ancillary jobs in the kitchen, laundry or maintenance department, for which they will be advanced their airfare and in some cases paid more than the counsellors, i.e. a guaranteed minimum of $1,225 for the eight or nine-week period of work. Again initial registration costs £67.

Camp America

Camp America (37a Queen's Gate, Dept. WW, London SW7 5HR; 020-7581 7333; brochure@campamerica.co.uk/ www.campamerica.co.uk) is another major recruitment organisation in Britain, which arranges for a massive 9,000 people aged 18 or over, from around the world, to work on children's summer camps in the USA. The work is for nine weeks between June and August where you could be teaching activities such as tennis, swimming and arts and crafts. Camp America provides a free return flight from London to New York and guidance on applying for a J-1 visa. The camp provides free board and lodging plus pocket money.

At the end of your contract, you will be given a lump sum of pocket money which will range from $600 to $1,100 depending on your age (as of 1st June), experience, qualifications and whether you've been a camp counsellor in the US before. Upfront charges include the registration fee of £299 which rises in increments if you are interviewed after December 6th to £365, and the J-1 visa fee of £60.

> **After the first year of her software engineering course at Birmingham University, Victoria Jossel spent a wonderful summer in the US with Camp America which she felt really enhanced her CV:**
> *On June 9th, I apprehensively boarded my flight to Blue Star camp in North Carolina. Not only did I have the privilege of bonding with the children in my cabin from whom you receive constant love, caring and attention, but I also met new people from all over the world and received amazing references for my future career. I learned how to organise, motivate and lead people as well as negotiate positive outcomes to conflicts. From a normal 19 year old girl, I became a responsible, motivated, adaptable and independent person with 14 children who were my responsibility. I had never been camping and had never wanted to go camping. Yet it was the most amazing experience: I learned to start a fire on my own, cook food for all 14 girls and organise it so the kids all got EXACTLY the same amount of Hershey's chocolate.*

One way to secure a placement early and avoid last-minute uncertainty is to attend one of Camp America's recruitment fairs in London, Birmingham, Manchester, Edinburgh or Belfast in February and March, which is what Colin Rothwell did: *'At the recruitment fair at Manchester Poly, you could actually meet the camp directors from all over the States and find out more about particular camps. If you are lucky, like me and a thousand others, you can sign a contract on the spot. Then you leave all the 'dirty work' to Camp America and wait until they call you to the airport in June sometime.'*

Camp America also offers two other summer programmes: Campower for students who would like to work in the kitchen/maintenance areas at camp and the Resort America programme mentioned earlier.

Other Summer Camp Organisations

Camp Counselors USA (CCUSA) works with 850 camps in 48 states and since 1986 has placed 100,000 young people aged 18-30 from over 60 countries. CCUSA's programme includes return flight to the US, one night's accommodation in New York City, visas and insurance, full board and lodging during placement as well as the chance to earn up to $600 as a first year counsellor. CCUSA tries to place counsellors at camps which suit their skills and personality. Enquiries should be made as early as possible to Camp Counselors (CCUSA), 1st Floor North, Devon House, 171/177 Great Portland St, London W1W 5PQ (020-7637 0779). Early applicants pay a lower registration fee than later ones. The deadline for applications is April 1st.

The pocket money for first year participants aged 18 is $675 for the nine-week programme rising to $875 for those over 21 in addition to flights and living expenses. CCUSA is reputed to offer a good service, as reported by Joseph Tame: *'CCUSA were very good to me. They visited us during the summer and were very efficient when it came to my flight home. All I did was call their freefone number with the date I wanted to return; there and then they said yes. The overall impression I got was that CCUSA offered a good service, being relatively small and friendly.'*

Several au pair agencies co-operate with Interexchange in New York by placing candidates over the age of 19 on the Camp USA programme: contact Worldnet UK (Emberton House, 26 Shakespeare Road, Bedford MK40 2ED; 0845 458 1551; www.worldnetuk. com). Other possibilities include the International Camp Counsellor Program run by YMCA International (5 West 63 St, New York, NY 10023-9197; www.ymcaiccp.org) which does not have a UK partner; Camp Leaders in America (CLIA) about which details can be requested from 59 Seel St, Liverpool L1 4AZ (0845 430 1219; www.campleaders.com); and International Counselor Exchange Program, 38 West 88th St, New York, NY 10024 (212-787-7706; www.international-counselors.org) with no British representative. Note that some of the less publicised programmes may charge lower fees than the big companies.

Many organisations in the rest of Europe send young people to the USA as camp counsellors; for example Travel Active Programmes in the Netherlands (PO Box 107, 5800

AC Venray; www.travelactive.nl) have up to 1,000 places for counsellors. Readers on the Continent should follow links from the websites given here or enquire of their national youth exchange organisation for details.

CASUAL WORK

A law stipulates that all employers must physically examine documents of prospective employees within three working days, proving that they are either a US citizen or an authorised alien (see *Documents* below). All US employers are obliged to complete an I-9 form which verifies the employee's right to work. Employers who are discovered by the Immigration and Naturalization Service to be hiring illegal aliens are subject to huge fines. Yet it is estimated that there are up to 200,000 British workers living and working illegally in California alone.

The law is unenforceable in seasonal industries such as fruit growing and resort tourism where it is still not uncommon for more than half of all employees to be illegal. Farmers and restaurateurs have claimed that they can barely stay in business without hiring casual workers without permits. Yet those who are caught working illegally run the risk of being deported, prohibited from travelling to the US for five years and in some cases for good. If your place of work is raided and you are caught, you will be detained while your case is being 'processed', which can take up to three weeks. If you are 'in-status' (which means your tourist visa has not expired) you are given the option of departing voluntarily. If not, you will be automatically deported.

The law seems to be more strictly enforced in areas like California, Texas and Florida which are traditional strongholds for 'wetbacks', illegal workers from Mexico and the rest of Latin America. Several years ago, Iain Kemble spent 11 lucrative weeks packing oranges in southern Florida. When he returned at the end of the year hoping to be hired again by the boss who had promised him a job, he was turned away, because the INS had visited the farms in the area putting a stop to cash-in-hand work.

On the other hand, when the authorities are targeting illegal hispanic workers, they may not notice others, as Jan Christensen from Denmark found when he worked in southern Florida on and off for two years, in which time he had no run-ins with the INS:

> *I arrived in southern Florida very low on cash. So I was very pleased to be offered a job on the second farm I went to and started the same day. No one seemed to care about my status. After about two weeks I was asked by the manager to fill out an employment form which had me worried for a while. I managed to avoid the question about the form for three more weeks until the manager finally cornered me. So I laid down the cards. Apparently he couldn't care less about permits. He was only bothered that I had tried to take him for a ride, and not told him the truth right away. I ended up working there for about six months, without paying tax and earning an average of $500 a week cash-in-hand.*

Documents

Every American can reel off his social security number by heart. J-1 visa holders are entitled to apply for one though recently a new regulation has come into force requiring social security offices to check the J-1 visa with the INS database and this has inevitably caused some delays which in turn can mean delays in being paid by your employer. Other routes to obtaining a social security number apart from having an approved visa include getting one for the purposes of banking but this will be stamped 'Not Valid for Employment'.

Some travellers have managed to get away with inventing a nine digit number (3-2-4) with the first three digits taken from the holder's home town zip code. Others have 'borrowed' an American friend's number, especially if they're out of the country, or out of work, since if social security payments are deducted, they will benefit someone. If the false number is traced, the friend can claim that he lost his card and never suspected that some miscreant would find and use it. But this is risky: any foreigner caught by the authorities will be deported.

According to Maria Perez from Peru, show your passport, take a driving test and obtain a US driving licence as ID. (A driving licence is an advantage for many jobs anyway.) False social security cards still circulate, though security is much tighter than it was a decade ago.

One of the easiest ways for the authorities to realise you are working illegally is when the Internal Revenue Service (IRS) processes your W-4 form which all employees must fill in when they start work. Some wily travellers recommend using a false name on the W-4 in case the INS and Internal Revenue compare notes. The danger of being caught out is greatest at the end of the tax year (December 31st). Although students should be exempt from some state and city income taxes (but not normally federal tax which is 15%), these are normally withheld at source. If you think you might have overpaid, ask your employer to send a W-2 form (statement of earnings, equivalent to a P45) to your home address. This will not arrive until after the end of the tax year, before the middle of February. The non-resident tax form (104ONR) can be requested from the IRS or downloaded from their website (www.irs.gov) and file your claim accordingly. Those who enlist the help of a tax firm like www.taxback.com can expect to pay 10% of any tax refunds.

Hostels

The first step that many travellers take in the job hunt in America is to find a hostel that will trade food and a bed for some work to spare them having to spend $16-$22 a night. This provides an excellent base from which to look for paid work elsewhere. Occasionally notices of casual jobs appear on the bulletin boards of youth hostels and backpackers' haunts, such as the Hostelling International hostel in New Orleans, Marquette House, 2253 Carondelet St, New Orleans (504-523-3014; HINewOrlns@aol.com). Many international travellers make it their base while they look for a job or an apartment and Marquette House has furnished apartments as well as dormitory accommodation for longer stay visitors. The Green Tortoise Hostel at 494 Broadway in San Francisco sometimes has strange odd jobs for pleasant and persistent travellers.

Other popular hostels worth considering are the Washington DC YHA Hostel on the corner of 11th and K Streets, and Boston International YHA Hostel, 12 Hemenway St, 02115 Boston (www.bostonhostel.org). In New York, Hostelling International have a hostel at 891 Amsterdam Ave at 103rd St (212-932-2300) which is a good place to make contacts. These big city hostels do hire foreigners but only those with legal working papers.

Carolyn Edwards had a discouraging time looking for work in Hawaii, but came across plenty of travellers spending four hours a day cleaning in hostels in exchange for bed and board. Richard Davies was given free accommodation and paid $10 an hour to clean toilets at his Los Angeles hostel which allowed him time to look for other work. Employment in your hostel is always worth asking about since many operate an informal work-for-keep system. After giving up a depressing job hunt in California, Jane Roberts phoned some hostels on her proposed route and was not only offered a job by one in Flagstaff, Arizona, she was even advanced her flight. Ask at privately owned travellers' lodges in the Grand Canyon area; according to Iona and Steve Dwyer they pay $4-6 per hour in addition to allowing you to stay free in beautiful surroundings.

Mark Horobin patronised a different sort of hostel when he found himself skint in California:

Males who line up in the early afternoon outside the San Diego Rescue Mission on 12th and Market Streets have a good chance of being given a bed and meals for three days. If you need a longer stay you may consider signing up as a helper as I did, but to do this you'll have to explain your reason (claiming to be an ex-alcoholic goes over well) and attend a compulsory daily Bible study session. If you are accepted you work about four hours a day. Later I stayed at the Prince of Peace Monastery in Oceanside.

San Diego seems well supplied with such places. Steve Bastick wrote more recently describing how to arrange to stay at the St Vincent de Paul homeless shelter at 1501 Imperial Ave:

> Single men and women receive an initial four-month stay at the Center. It sometimes takes up to ten days for a person to get in. Every day at 10am a person should call the Info-line (619-230-0997) to ask for a referral to the PMC and must be ready to be there by noon if the referral comes through. The requirements for acceptance are an on-site TB test, a one-hour orientation and five hours of chores (usually an hour a day for five days each week). A 9.30pm curfew exists and residents who miss this will lose their bed. Residents do not have to leave the facility at any time except for the monthly field day. Laundry service, 24 hour showers, telephone message service, health care assistance and three meals a day are all available free. All in all a good deal for a layover or to recuperate.

Drive-Aways

The term 'drive-away' applies to the widespread practice of delivering private cars within North America. Prosperous Americans and Canadians and also companies are prepared to pay several hundred dollars to delivery firms who agree to arrange delivery of private vehicles to a different city, usually because the car-owner wants his or her car available at their holiday destination but doesn't want to drive it personally. The companies find drivers (an estimated three-quarters of whom are not American), arrange insurance and arbitrate in the event of mishaps. You get free use of a car (subject to mileage and time restrictions) and pay for all gas after the first tankful and tolls on the interstates. Usually a deadline and mileage limit are fixed (e.g. 400 miles or 650km a day), though these are often flexible and checks lax. When there is a shortage of drivers you may even get a fee; Michael McDonnell was paid $150 on his first of many deliveries which was from Orlando to Ottawa. A good time to be travelling east to west or north to south (e.g. Chicago to Phoenix) is September/October when a lot of older people head to a warmer climate. On the other hand, when there is a shortage of vehicles (e.g. leaving New York in the summer), you will be lucky to get a car on any terms.

The only requirements are that you be over 21 (25 in some cases), have a driving licence, preferably an International Driving Permit, and able to pay a deposit in cash or travellers cheques (generally $300-$350) which will be refunded on successful delivery. First of all look up 'Automobile Transporters and Driveaway Companies' in the Yellow Pages of any big city or check the Internet Directory of Automobile Transporters at www. movecars.com. Companies to try are:

Auto Driveaway Company – www.autodriveaway.com; 1-800-621-4155. More than 50 offices around North America. Available cars are listed on the website in real time and it is possible to sign up online. In some cases fuel costs are covered. Website gives numbers of branch offices from Salt Lake City to Syracuse, Tucson to Toronto (Canada).

Blue Angels Auto Transport Inc. – 888-735-6996 (toll-free); www.autotransporter.com. Website does not include information for prospective drivers.

Across America Driveaway – www.transportautos.com/driveaway.htm; 1-800-677-6686.

An alternative to the internet and the Yellow Pages is to ask at a travel information centre for car rental agencies which arrange delivery of rental cars to the places where there is a seasonal demand, for example to Florida or to ski resorts in the winter.

If no company has what you want, then try to leave a number where they can reach you, or arrange to phone the most promising ones daily. If you actually call in to register with the company, they are more likely to take you seriously. When establishing your criteria, try not to be too fussy. The greater your flexibility of destination, the quicker you'll be out of town. Bridgid Seymour-East and Jimmy Henderson enjoyed a wonderful 'potluck' trip around the USA, picking up a car in Los Angeles and driving to a town in Minnesota. If you want to go coast to coast, it's probably worth waiting for a through vehicle; but if you have plenty of time and people and places to visit en route, you can piece together shorter runs which will eventually bring you to your destination.

If you are travelling with one or more people, you can save money by splitting the cost of the gas. The company allows you to take co-drivers and/or passengers provided they register for insurance purposes. The type of vehicle you are assigned to drive can make a significant difference to the overall cost. Since you are normally paying for gas, the more fuel-efficient the car, the cheaper your trip will be. Fuel-efficient cars are much less prevalent than gas guzzlers, especially among the kind of people who pay to have their cars moved for them.

Eventually a company will have something going in the right direction and summon you to their office where you are told the details of pick-up, drop-off, time and distance restrictions. You will probably have to present your passport showing that you are entitled to be in the US plus possibly two passport size photos, a returnable cash deposit (about $350) and your thumb prints. You will be given two copies of the way-bill, an insurance claim form and a notice informing you of the FBI's penalties for delay, diversion and other atrocities. Make sure the company is ICC bonded. You will be expected to nominate a final destination where your deposit can be returned to you. But if you change your mind, you may have to make alternative arrangements; in Carl Griffiths' case, his $350 deposit was sent to his home address in Bristol.

Few agencies store cars themselves so you will need to get a bus to the car's home. When you are introduced to the vehicle, check through a list of existing damage with the owner (or agent) and fill in a 'Condition Report'. Be very thorough, since otherwise you may be held liable for existing damage or faults. If you do have mechanical problems on the road, you pay for any repairs costing less than a specified sum (perhaps $75), which you reclaim from the recipient of the vehicle. For more expensive work you should call the owner (collect) and discuss how he will arrange payment for the repairs. Ten minutes spent checking and going for a short test ride can save an awful lot later. Even if you know nothing about cars, you should be able to check the lights, oil, battery, brakes, and seat belts and also look for rust. If you do know some elementary mechanics, look for a worn fan belt and a leaky radiator which can cause serious problems during your trip. You should point out to the owner/agent anything you are unhappy about. Also check that there is a full tank of petrol, pointing out this requirement on the way-bill if necessary.

Many travellers have concluded it is an excellent wheeze, among them Mig Urquhart:

> One day somebody in Fort Lauderdale was talking about fishing in Alaska and about a week later three of us had a driveaway to Seattle. It was the most outstanding car to do the journey in – a Mitsubishi Montero, one of those big jeep-type 4X4s. Only two of us could drive. We did 4,700 miles in nine days which included a birthday party for me in Tampa, lunch in New Orleans, the Grand Canyon, Las Vegas, a weekend with a friend in San Francisco and finally the glorious drive from SF to Seattle. The trip cost each of us $200 including food, gas, the motel in Vegas and a really nice meal in SF. It can be tough going driving all the time and there can be personality clashes if you go with people you've just met up with. I know that my very slow, cautious driving annoyed the other driver and we didn't become best buddies, but overall I thoroughly enjoyed the expedition.

THE JOB HUNT

Working holidaymakers from Britain and countries worldwide can capitalise on current employee shortages during the summer season by participating in one of the approved Work & Travel programmes mentioned earlier. A headline in the *Sunday Telegraph* revealed the extent of the problem for employers: 'US Students Say No to Summer Jobs,' with the article claiming that nearly a third of America's 16 million teenagers are choosing not to take up a summer job. This has resulted in BUNAC and similar organisations being besieged with calls from employers eager to hire foreign students and offering perks like subsidised accommodation, transport and free food. The majority of seasonal jobs will pay the minimum wage of $5.15, though some states have legislated a higher wage, e.g. California and Massachusetts ($6.75), Connecticut ($7.10), Washington DC ($6.15) Maine and Vermont ($6.25), Washington state ($7.01), etc. However trainee workers aged under 20 may be paid the youth minimum of $4.25 for the first 90 days of their employment. These can be checked on the Department of Labor's website (www.dol.gov/esa/minwage/america.htm).

Prospects for job-hunters in the cities are not so rosy. Dan Jacobson returned to his home town of Chicago after several years of roaming the globe but was not welcomed back with open arms by local employers:

With all the experiences I've had getting work all over the place, when I'm finally legal I can't find a job. It's a laugh really... I've applied around town like crazy and nothing's come up so far. Temp agencies don't call back and won't let you come in to interview any more. I've hit I don't know how many cafés and restos, all to no avail, plus plenty of shops and various other stuff (like a dog daycare centre) but nobody's hiring me. I guess all the anecdotes about a bad economy are for real. I'm heading back to the mountains of Switzerland.

But if you're prepared to travel and to work for a whole summer season, you will have better luck. Time can productively be spent searching the internet. Dozens of sites may prove useful, though www.coolworks.com and www.jobmonkey.com are especially recommended for seasonal jobs in the tourist industry. You might also look at the bi-annually revised book *Summer Jobs in the USA* published by Peterson's Guides (PO Box 67005, Lawrenceville, NJ 08648-4764; www.petersons.com) and distributed in Britain by Vacation Work at £12.99. Each employer's entry indicates whether applications from foreign students are encouraged. The categories for each state cover specific job listings in business and industry, summer camps and summer theatres, resorts, ranches, restaurants and lodgings, commercial attractions, as well as in government for which only American citizens are eligible.

If you wait until you arrive in the States to look for a job, bear in mind that it is more difficult to lead a hand-to-mouth existence in North America than elsewhere. If you are intending to pick up a little work here and there and get by on a pittance, you may find that such a lifestyle puts you at risk of going on the streets where you are vulnerable to what one reader describes as 'the geeks and weirdos of this cutthroat society'. Finding suitable accommodation should be a priority especially in a place where you can't stay long-term at the youth hostel. It may be worth investigating university residences, although in central city locations these will not be cheap; e.g. it costs $2,400 for a single room at Columbia University in Manhattan for the period May 30 to August 7. Adda Macchich was driven out of Boston because she found it was difficult to rent a room without undergoing a credit check and proving that she had a job (and concluded that this explains why there are large numbers of homeless people begging everywhere). Peter Stonemann recommends sticking to rural areas where you can camp, while admitting that a lack of public transport outside cities makes this difficult.

You should try to avoid arriving in the States without enough money to support yourself for several months. Depending on how long you plan to stay you might think about investing in an old car (normally available for less than $1,300). Even in cities, a car is a great asset from the start when you may be house-hunting and job-hunting. A mobile phone is also essential.

As in any place, job-seekers will rely on newspaper adverts for leads. However this tends to be less productive than walking in and asking. Similarly, placing your own advert in order to prearrange a job is not recommended since the chances of attracting undesirables are high. Kev Vincent flew all the way to Hawaii supposedly to work on the farm of the woman who had answered his advert, only to find that she had two fruit trees and was proposing to charge him $150 a month for a cupboard off the garage. Pre-arranging a job

432 Work Your Way Worldwide

from so far away is always a danger as Lee Morton found when he arranged a position as a trainee groom in California through an agency in England. Although the house and setting were beautiful, he lasted only a couple of days because the woman for whom he was working was so unreasonably demanding.

Word of mouth and personal contact are particularly important in the States. Again and again we have heard from travellers who have been offered some casual work while hitching or chatting to local residents. Many of these jobs have been in building, landscape gardening, furniture removal, etc.

Other jobs are less conventional. Paul Donut didn't have to look too hard for work in the capital of Louisiana, but the opportunities that presented themselves were distinctly unappealing:

> When I arrived in Baton Rouge I looked up a friend of a friend who, I was told, might be able to help me find work. She did. She found me a job escorting customers from a bar called the Chimes at the gates of Louisiana State University to their cars, as many of them had been mugged on this short but perilous journey. After considering this job for about 30 seconds, I declined it, since the murder rate in Baton Rouge is among the highest in the country. The only other job opportunity to arise was helping out on an alligator farm which I wasn't sure would be any safer than protecting people from mugging.

TOURISM AND CATERING

Labour demands in summer resorts and national parks sometimes reach crisis proportions especially along the eastern seaboard. Because tipping is so generous, employers in many states are allowed to pay a mere $2.13 per hour, provided tips bring the take-home pay up to at least $5.15. This means that you can earn the derisory wage of $10 for an evening shift. An average weekly take in tips for a full-time waiter/waitress might be $120 with possibilities of earning twice that. Bar staff can earn as much as $200 a night (but note that bar staff have to be the legal drinking age of 21). Apparently a British accent helps, except in the case of Jane Thomas who was accused of putting it on to attract a higher tip! Even if you don't get a job as a barman or 'waitperson', busboys (table clearers) are usually given a proportion of tips by the waiter whom they are helping, typically 10%. Jobs which do not earn tips (like dishwashing) often earn above the minimum wage, especially when restaurants are desperate.

The recruitment needs of national and state parks can often be found on the internet, for example Glacier National Park in Montana near the Canadian border on www.gpihr. com and Denali Park in Alaska (www.nps.gov/dena/home/employment/index.htm); the latter hires nearly 1,000 people each summer (early May to mid-September). Facilities in the famous national parks of Utah (Bryce Canyon, Zion Canyon and the Grand Canyon North Rim) are run by Xanterra Recreational Services (www.xanterra-corporate.com or www.coolworks.com/utahparks). Xanterra also recruit for the even more famous Yellowstone National Park in Wyoming which offers 2,500 seasonal jobs (www.yellowstonejobs. com). The DNC Parks & Resorts concessionaire at Yosemite National Park in California can be contacted by ringing 209-372-1236 or checking the Employment section on www. yosemitepark.com) about its 800 open summer vacancies.

The majority of food-related jobs in the US are in fast food establishments where labour is not unionised. It is always worth enquiring at the local KFC, McDonalds or Pizza Hut for jobs, since there is a very high turnover of staff. (It was recently estimated that a staggering one in eight of all Americans will work for McDonalds at some point in their lives.) These major chains will invariably ask to see your social security card. Try to carry out your search before local college students finish their term, usually in May. The two main disadvantages of working in this kind of job are the lack of accommodation (some are even stingy about the food) and the unreliability of working hours, making it difficult to save. If you want more hours, keep pestering the manager to give you some. One British traveller says: *'Fast food restaurants offer a great chance to settle into a place. You won't make great money but they're always looking for people, and you'll get to find out what's happening in a place.'*

At the other end of the tourism spectrum, the hotel trade is not easy to get into because of the number of people intending to make 'hospitality vending' their career. Liam Lynch tried six or seven plush hotels in downtown Seattle and got the definite impression that the management were not looking for bearded round-the-world latter-day hippies. Europeans aged 19 to 35 beginning a career in the hotel and food service industry or students studying a hotel/catering course with relevant work experience who want to train for up to 18 months in the US should write to AIPT (10400 Little Patuxent Parkway, Suite 250, Columbia, Maryland 21044-3510; info@aipt.org; www.aipt.org) for information about the Hospitality and Tourism Exchange. AIPT will advertise your specifications in a newsletter distributed to relevant organisations in the US.

Plenty of Brits and other foreigners find work in Los Angeles, in the restaurants, bistros and cafés of North Beach, San Francisco and also in the cafés of Greenwich Village New York, though you'll have to serve a great many generous tippers before you'll be able to afford accommodation in Manhattan. As an aside, Jane Thomas solved this problem by getting on a house-sitting circuit via contacts. Through a friend, she met various people who were only too glad to have a nice reliable English girl live in their houses while they were away on holiday, to discourage burglars, water the plants, etc. One of the places she stayed in was a luxury apartment overlooking Central Park. The incongruity of passing the commissionaire every morning arrayed in the tacky orange uniform of Burger Heaven (where she had finally got a job after much searching and exaggeration of her experience) struck her as highly amusing. The more people she got to know, the more offers of accommodation came her way, including some of pure hospitality.

Live-in jobs are probably preferable, and are often available to British students whose term-times allow them to stay beyond Labor Day, the first Monday in September, when most American students resume their studies. After working a season at a large resort in Wisconsin, Timothy Payne concluded: *'Without doubt the best jobs in the USA are to be found in the resorts, simply because they pay a reasonable wage as well as providing free food and accommodation. Since many resorts are located in remote spots, it is possible to save most of your wages and tips, and also enjoy free use of the resort's facilities. Whatever job you end up with you should have a good time due to the large number of students working there.'*

New Orleans is repeatedly described as a casual workers' paradise. Any of the cheap travellers' hotels (for example along Charles St or Prytania St) should be able to recommend places to try or offer work themselves. After fleeing from a boring job in Arizona, Jane Roberts headed for New Orleans in time for the Jazz Festival in late April: *'After 15 minutes of desperate job-hunting I landed a job in a restaurant in the French Quarter. The following day I moved my pack into the apartment above and began work over the Festival. When it ended, business dropped. I was told I could carry on working, but only for tips. No customers meant no tips, so I left.'*

In most cases the minimum wage is paid in addition to free accommodation.

Seaside Resorts

Popular resorts are often a sure bet, especially if you arrive in mid-August (when American students begin to leave jobs), or in April/May (before they arrive).

Katherine Smith, who got her J-1 visa through BUNAC, describes the range of jobs she found in Ocean City, a popular seaside resort in Maryland which absorbs a large number of Britons

I decided to spend my summer in Ocean Beach because I knew the job scene would be favourable. I found a job as a waitress in a steak restaurant and another full-time job as a reservations clerk in a hotel by approaching employers on an informal basis and enquiring about possible job vacancies. In my case this was

> *very fruitful and I found two relatively well-paid jobs which I enjoyed very much. Other jobs available included fairground attendant, fast food sales assistant, lifeguard, kitchen assistant, chambermaid and every other possible type of work associated with a busy oceanside town. Ocean City was packed with foreign workers. As far as I know, none had any trouble finding work; anyone could have obtained half a dozen jobs. Obviously the employers are used to a high turnover of workers, especially if the job is boring. So it's not difficult to walk out of a job on a day's notice and into another one. It really was a great place to spend the summer. I would recommend a holiday resort to anyone wishing to work hard but to have a really wild time.*

According to Andrew Boyle, there seemed to be more BUNACers in Ocean City than natives and in fact he noticed considerable tension and a 'clash of ideologies' between the party-loving young workers and the older year-round residents, outnumbered fifty to one. In fact a lot of young foreigners go to resorts like this simply to party and anyone who is willing to work really hard stands out and is usually treated better.

In Atlantic City, the only gambling town in the US outside Nevada, a number of travellers (who must be fit) earn up to $400 a week by pushing punters in rolling chairs along the Boardwalk. Nearby, Wildwood New Jersey (four hours south of New York City) is another mecca for holiday job-seekers. A very high percentage of the people working in the fast-food outlets, ice cream parlours, slot machine arcades and fun piers are UK and Irish students especially from Scotland and Northern Ireland. As long as you arrive by the Memorial Day weekend (the last one in May) there is every chance of finding work. The New Zealander Ken Smith heard about Wildwood when he was working on a farm in Northern Ireland and found it just as easy to find a job as he had been told: *'I was just strolling along the boardwalk when I stopped for an ice cream at a store and was offered a job by its owner. The pay is just the minimum wage but by working 80+ hours a week, it soon adds up. The most hours I worked in a day was 19, and then was told to be back the next day at 8.30am. The other workers told me the boss ripped them off but I must say he always paid me in full.'*

Shared accommodation is cheap and easy to find in Wildwood. On days when the boardwalk is rained out, you can eat cheap buffet meals at the casinos in Atlantic City. While admitting that he was exploited and maltreated to some extent, Ken made enough that season to pay for nearly two months of 'quality travelling' throughout New England as well as paying for his airfares and insurance. (He has subsequently studied law, specialising in employment law.)

The tourism and catering business is not known for its generous treatment of its employees and America is no exception. Adda Maccich described working conditions at a 4-star hotel on Cape Cod as terrible:

> *I found a waitressing job despite my non-existent work visa and made-up social security number. Off-duty staff were not allowed anywhere within the hotel grounds (including the beach). The accommodation turned out to be some three miles away without any public transport. I had to hitch a ride with my fellow workers every morning for the 6am start. A lot of the staff were Jamaicans brought over for the season. Staff were expected to walk long distances with a huge tray piled up with dishes held in one hand. Afraid of injury, I reduced the load as much as possible, but soon my colleagues complained and I was fired without notice and asked to move out of the housing unit the following morning.*

Other resorts to try are Virginia Beach (Virginia), Myrtle Beach (South Carolina) and Atlantic Beach (North Carolina). David Hewitt found work at a specialised kind of restaurant largely on the strength of his knowledge of kosher food gained while working on a kibbutz. He worked in Jewish hotels in Miami Beach and later in the Catskill Mountains north of New York. Earnings over Passover were spectacular.

Boats

For a yachting job, Florida is the best place to look. Innumerable pleasure craft and also fishing boats depart from the Florida Keys (at the southern tip of the state) bound for the Caribbean, especially between Christmas and Easter. You might also try for work on a cruise ship (see section on the Caribbean). There is usually plenty of bar and kitchen work in the Keys, the second largest gay centre in North America and, according to Kev Vincent, many of the jobs had certain conditions attached. The area is swamped by tens of thousands of students during their spring breaks, so accommodation is almost impossible to find in March and early April.

Fort Lauderdale creates plenty of casual work on yachts year round which regularly pays $10 an hour. A good place to hear about day work on yachts, as well as opportunities in landscaping and restaurants, is Floyd's Hostel and Crew House in the southeast section of town, which accepts only international travellers. Floyd Creamer, the owner/manager (who contributed to an earlier edition of this book), invites people to ring 954-462-0631 to find out about bed availability and arrange a free pick-up from bus or train station.

Tim Pask describes his experiences in Huntingdon Beach, California:

My first job was in a boat broker's yard. I found this job after days of walking around the area asking in every shop, garage, restaurant and marina. My work involved cleaning all the boats which were on display as well as any minor maintenance jobs. The job suited me perfectly as I was able to stay in the local hostel cheaply. The boat yard was situated next to the beach, so I was able to earn whilst developing an enviable tan. From then on I accepted work which came my way even though I was not actually looking for it. I would pick up odd day jobs which included roofing, cleaning, and kitchen work, often heard about at my hostel.

Ski Resorts

There is plenty of winter work in ski resorts, especially in Colorado, between December and the 'Mud Season' in May. Aspen, Vail and Steamboat Springs Colorado have all been recommended. Much of it can be investigated online, e.g. through www.jobmonkey.com/ski or www.skiingthenet.com/jobs.htm.

If you are prepared to travel in person, the best time to arrive is October/November when the big resorts hold job fairs. Jobs are available as lift operators, restaurant workers, ticket clerks, basket check (like left luggage for skiers) assistants, etc. The main problem in big resorts (especially Vail) is a lack of employee accommodation. Unless you arrive in August/September, you will have to be very lucky to find a room of any kind. Check adverts in the local papers for example in *Steamboat Pilot & Today* whose employment classifieds are posted online (www.steamboatpilot.com). Hundreds of help wanted ads appear in the winter months and even more in the summer. Also check the resorts' websites which have links from the employment website www.coolworks.com/ski-resort-jobs. You should also be aware that immigration raids are frequent, which make employers reluctant to hire people without papers even when desperate for staff. This danger is less likely at small out-of-the-way resorts like Purgatory or Crested Butte in Colorado (where of course there will be fewer jobs).

The Steamboat Springs Chamber Resort Association (PO Box 77408, 1255 Lincoln Ave, Steamboat Springs, CO 80477; 970-879-0880; www.steamboatchamber.com) is helpful to job-seekers. It publishes a free leaflet 'Live, Work & Play in Ski Town USA' which includes an Employment Resource List and includes on its website information about visas for international applicants. Job Fairs are held around the first weekend of November where employers can meet job-seekers. The Colorado Workforce Center at 425 Anglers Drive (PO Box 881419, Steamboat Springs, CO 80488; 970-879-3075; www.yourworkforcecenter.com) assists documented job-seekers to find full-time, part-time and seasonal employment. Neil Hibberd worked a season as a ski lift operator for the Steamboat Corporation on a J-1 visa fixed up through CIEE's Internship Programme (now IST

Plus described at the beginning of the chapter). According to Neil the Corporation offers subsidised rental accommodation to its employees.

Condominiums or 'condos' are sometimes a good bet for casual employment. Hotels aren't a big feature of American resorts (though two of the principal ones at Steamboat, the Sheraton and the Ptarmigan Inn, hire large numbers of non-local workers). Resort companies like Mountain Resorts and the Steamboat Ski and Resort Corporation hire chambermaids, maintenance men, drivers, etc. It is common for one company to own all the facilities and control all employment in one resort, and in some cases provide accommodation to all staff. In Vail try Vail Resorts Inc. PO Box 7, Vail, CO 81658 which also has a dedicated freephone jobs line 1-888-Ski-Job-1 and an employment website http://skijob1.snow.com. If you're just looking for occasional work, chopping wood in late autumn is a simple way of making a quick profit and contracts for clearing snow from roofs are sometimes available.

Aspen is one of the wealthiest resorts and supports a large transient working population. The Aspen Skiing Company is heavily involved with the hiring of foreign workers through CCUSA. Due to popularity of the programme they encourage interested candidates to start the application procedures as early as May for the following ski season. The company is permitted to submit visa applications in July; the website www.aspensnowmass.com/companyinfo/employment/visa.cfm contains a wealth of detailed information about the recruitment procedures for non-US citizens. One of the major employers in Aspen for the summer as well as the winter season is the Gant Condominium Resort (610 West End St, Aspen, CO 81611; 970-925-5000; www.gantaspen.com/employ/positions.cfm).

If you decide to show up in Aspen, visit the Cooper Street Pier bar and listen for foreign accents. Unfortunately wages tend to be low in this setting; one worker reported that he saved less than $100 a month after room and board, ski pass and equipment rental. This figure would have more than doubled if he had been able to stay until the end of the season and had been able to collect his share of the season's tips. Another major Colorado resort is Winter Park Resort, PO Box 36, Winter Park, CO 80482 (1-800-979-0332/970-726-1536; www.skiwinterpark.com/employment). Californian ski resorts that also hire in large numbers include Sugar Bowl (PO Box 5, Norden, CA 95724; Job Hotline 530-426-6731) and Mammoth Mountain Resort (PO Box 24, Mammoth Lakes, CA 93546; 760-934-0654; http://jobs.mammothmountain.com). For a list of major American ski resorts see the end of the section on Winter Resorts in the introductory chapter *Tourism*.

Theme Parks

Although British people are acquainted with fun fairs and theme parks, they will be amazed at the grand scale on which many American amusement parks and carnivals operate, sometimes employing up to 3,000 summer assistants to work on the rides and games, food service, parking lot and maintenance, warehouse, wardrobe and security. One chain of parks is Six Flags Theme Parks which have huge operations in a few states, including New Jersey and Illinois near Chicago. Some of the biggest employers of this kind co-operate with the work and travel programme organisers described earlier. Representatives from Six Flags sometimes liaise with the major summer work agencies and recruit summer staff abroad. One of the biggest amusement parks is Cedar Point (One Cedar Point Drive, Sandusky, Ohio 44870-5259; www.cedarpoint.com) which hires international students via CIEE and CCUSA. The opportunities afforded to young people looking for summer work by just one of these enormous commercial complexes are enormous and dwarf Butlins and Alton Towers entirely. The present shortage of student labour has forced some Florida theme parks to offer generous bonuses of up to $1,000.

On a smaller scale, travelling carnivals and fun fairs may need a few assistants to set up, operate and dismantle game stands and rides. Since the keynote of American business is to encourage competition and provide incentives, many of these carnival operators let you take home a cut of the profits on your particular stall, and these can be high. The trouble is that a lot depends on the type of concession you are allotted in the first place, as well as on your personality. Whether you get rich or not, you will certainly experience a uniquely American way of life and meet some authentic American characters. Chris Daniels got a job through the BUNAC job directory with a small travelling fair in the mid-West:

> The convoy of trucks made an impressive sight, taking 'all the fun of the fair' from one sleepy town to another linked by miles of straight, often deserted roads. The romance of this nomadic lifestyle could not unfortunately offset the harsh realities of working 18 solid hours whenever we moved on to the next town, permanently dirty truck accommodation and a low fixed wage. The other employees were a strange mixture: the fellow who ran a ride called the 'Tilt & Whirl' was called 'Rosebud' and was something out of the days of the Wild West (or at least out of a Saturday night TV Western); he chewed tobacco incessantly and spoke with an almost unintelligible drawl. The fair was owned by one man, an elderly gentleman, patriot and entrepreneur with the frontier spirit which had built it up from scratch.

The International Casting Department of Walt Disney's EPCOT Center (PO Box 10090, Lake Buena Vista, Florida 32830-0090; fax 407-828-3330; http://disney.go.com/disneycareers/wdwcareers/international/index.html) prefers to rely on the word-of-mouth network rather than to publicise their six-month or one-year vacancies for young people to work as 'cultural representatives'. People aged 18-28 from the UK and about a dozen other countries are hired to represent the culture and customs of their countries; in the case of the UK this means olde worlde pubs, Scotch eggs and Royal Doulton china. Anyone applying will have to wait until a Disney recruiter comes to your country. Contact details are provided on the above website. In the UK, the annual recruiting presentations normally take place in March and October; for details contact Yummy Jobs (The Georgian Village, Unit 5, 100 Wood Street, London, E17 3HX; 020-7691-7820; enquiries@ymmmyjobs.com). Any job which involves tips is usually more lucrative than others; wages can be swelled by more than $100 in a five-hour shift. The staff facilities are attractive with pools, jacuzzis, tennis courts and subsidised rent.

Paul Binfield from Kent describes the process of being hired by Disney as 'a long and patient' one
I initially wrote to Disney in October and started my contract in January, 15 months later. It was the most enjoyable year of my life, experiencing so many excellent things and making the best friends from all over the world. The pros far outweigh the cons, though some people did hate the work. Disney are a strict company with many rules which are vigorously enforced. The work in merchandising or the pub/restaurant is taken extremely seriously and sometimes it can be hard to manufacture a big cheesy Disney smile. There are dress codes, and verbal and written warnings for matters which would be considered very trivial in Britain, and indeed terminations (which is a very nasty word for being fired). If you go with the right attitude it can be great fun.

Any major theme park is worth trying well before the season. For example Universal Studios have an ongoing need to hire staff for their operations in California and Florida (http://corp.universalstudios.com).

FISHING AND HUNTING

Alaskan Fishing

Fishing off the coast of Alaska and fish-processing are classic money-spinning summer jobs in the US, still widely advertised in west coast newspapers, though the possible earnings are often exaggerated since the Alaskan salmon industry has been in decline for some time. During the boom years of the mid-eighties, pink salmon were fetching 55 cents a pound. In a typical summer on a decent boat at that time, a deckhand making an 8% share of the boat's catch could expect to walk away with at least $20,000 for three months work. Due to the rise of farmed fishing and changing market demands abroad, the days of making money hand over fist are long gone. In 2004, pink salmon yielded a criminal 5 cents a pound at the dock. It is not unknown for deckhands to weather full three-month seasons on mediocre boats and go home with less than $3,000 for their effort.

Therefore think carefully before buying a one-way ticket to Alaska where the cost of living is very high and the competition for work intense, particularly from American students. Be sure your expectations are realistic. There is no guarantee of finding a job on a productive boat and, even if you do get work, it's unlikely that you'll make any more than minimum wage considering the long hours. What is certain is that you will work harder, longer and faster than you ever have or ever will; you will be cold, beyond exhausted, made to feel stupid, and at times, miserable. Yet the determined can still succeed.

Do not rely on the promises of websites that offer to arrange jobs in the fishing industry for a fee. With profits and the safety of all onboard at stake, boat captains cannot afford to rely on email or long distance phone calls to size up potential crew. The only reliable way to land a deckhand job in Alaska is to show up before the season begins and beat the docks. Novices can be found frequenting the docks at Kodiak, Ketchikan, Homer and Petersburg in Alaska as well as Astoria and Newport in Oregon. Due to the proximity to the mainland US, work is generally harder to find in the ports of the Southeast. Venturing further north to Kodiak Island or the Bristol Bay fisheries, which boast large fleets and are less accessible, holds more promise. In Kodiak, check the ever-popular job board at Harborside Coffee, perpetually plastered with post-it notes like 'Deckhand needed immediately, no experience necessary'.

The first halibut are caught over a 24-hour period in early May and this opens the fishing season. It is easier to pin down job openings between then and early June when salmon crews are doing pre-season gear work. Often a skipper will take inexperienced newcomers on a trial basis. If you are willing to do prep work without pay, e.g. mending nets, scrubbing hulls, chances are you will have the job when the season opens in early June. By putting in some hard time for free, a skipper can better discern if you have the necessary tenacity as Jason Motlagh puts it 'to grind through sleepless two-day benders, jellyfish facials, raw hands and screaming muscles'.

This is a way of life for the boat owners, not a summer job. Try to convey that you will take your work seriously, but are easygoing enough to live with under cramped conditions for months at a time. Do not forget that taking orders and insults on the chin is a rite of passage; take it personally and you'll soon find yourself back on the dock.

Rejection is an inevitable part of the deckhand job search; never take no for an answer. Many skippers will turn you down several times before taking you on. If you can pass this initial test of your resolve, the prevailing logic is that it may reflect your work ethic, which will be tested like never before.

If you start your job search late, be wary of boats with crew vacancies deep into the season. Some skippers are notorious for being abusive, reckless, withholding pay, or simply bad at catching fish. Ask around the docks to get the straight story on which boats are reputable and which ones to avoid. Deckhands like to talk and you'll generally get a consensus. Boats talk too. If a vessel looks like it hasn't seen a fresh coat of paint since the Cold War, move on. Safety should be a top priority. Between 1991 and 1998, 239 boats sank and 97 people died fishing Alaskan waters. Each year a lot of fingers and a few lives are lost usually because of irresponsible captains cutting corners.

Most of the newcomers that flock to Alaskan ports each summer looking for deckhand jobs have no idea what they are letting themselves in for. Fishing is dangerous work in which adrenaline and fatigue are in constant conflict. A salmon boat crew typically numbers four or five men; each must pull his weight under monotonous, often brutal conditions that push the limits of physical and mental endurance. Amazingly, it is not impossible for women to find work as deckhands, though they will be spared none of the harshness of life at sea. Needless to say, privacy is in short supply, while crude language and pornography are not.

To remain in business fishermen must offset lower prices with higher volume, which translates to even longer hours. Unable to cope, many naïve hopefuls quit their jobs within the first few days which is how Jason Motlagh managed to get a job on board a 'high-liner'.

After finishing a degree in foreign affairs, American Jason Motlagh caught the fishing bug. On returning from Kodiak in the autumn of 2004, he wrote about the 'gruelling, tedious work aboard a commercial fishing vessel with rewards few other jobs could hope to offer':

Like countless others before me, I decided to head north to be a 'greenhorn' for a crack at fortune and adventure as an Alaskan fisherman. Three months later, I returned to the lower 48 a lean-mean-fishing machine with a respectable pay cheque, a wealth of stories, and the self-knowledge that while I could brave 20+ hour work days on the water, 9 to 5 at a desk would never again be as easy.

Less than ten hours after landing in Kodiak on a puddle jumper from Anchorage, with nothing more than a backpack and blind faith, I walked onto one of the top five boats in the entire fleet. A skipper who had come into port to refuel that morning got word on the dock that I was looking for deckhand work and told me he 'might be short a man, check back in two hours'. Apparently, after three rough weeks on the fish, one of his deckhands wanted off the boat. When I returned I was instructed to get some new rain gear and a fisherman's license, as we'd be leaving in less than an hour. This was all the more remarkable as it was already weeks into the summer salmon season. The first guy I'd spoken with told me he had beaten the docks for eight days without success. But I didn't take his word for it, and neither should you. Make it happen.

If you can cook well, this is also the time to show your expertise in the galley. After a long day in foul weather, a tasty meal might be all a crew has to look forward to. Cooking duties invariably fall on greenhorns. Bad cooks are hated, skilled ones will be cut some slack. During my first weeks, when I could do no right on deck, some extra effort preparing meals kept me in my skipper's good graces.

If you are fortunate enough to find a job on the right boat, fishing can still be safe and lucrative. Thanks to a little bit of initiative and a lot of dumb luck, I walked away with just under $10,000 for ten weeks' work on a boat that netted well over one million pounds of salmon for the season. But you must not forget that the good jobs are likely to be filled by return crew, who know just how rare they are.

But if you go in search of an experience that will sharpen life's edge, you will not be disappointed. Think of your pay cheque in terms of learning a real trade, earning the respect of hardened men, of gazing out over calm seas as humpback whales breach under a midnight sun. A moment's rest, a fresh cut of fish, the feel of solid land under your feet after two weeks on the water, will never be as sweet. And when the season finally comes to a close, you'll walk away with the unmistakable swagger of an Alaskan fisherman.

Fish Canneries

Finding work in an Alaskan fish processing plant is easier but it offers low wages relative to the unpleasant working conditions. Major seafood companies have their headquarters in Seattle where much of the seasonal hiring takes place. Most companies pay the Alaska minimum wage of $7.15 per hour and usually $9-$10.75 for overtime. Perks can include free housing, food, gear, laundry and transport costs from the point of hire to the job site, which means you get a free cruise up the Inside Passage. But first-timers may get few of these benefits and end up camping. The companies hire a range of ancillary staff, as well, for the laundry, mail room, kitchens, etc. and there is some movement between departments. They all warn that fish processing ('working the slime line') is repetitive and gruelling and the hours can be cruelly long (up to 18 hours a day) in cold, wet and smelly conditions. To find out the current employment situation concerning the operations of Kodiak Salmon Packers, such as the one at remote Larsen Bay on the west side of Kodiak island, contact them at PO Box 38, Larsen Bay, AK 99624 (907-847-2250/ fax 907-847-2244; www.kspi.net).

A specialist website AlaskaJobFinder.com (affiliated with www.jobmonkey.com/alaska) has a database of thousands of employers. However this is available only on subscription: a five-day trial membership costs $3.95. Other useful sources of information are www.fishermansexpress.com/alaska-fishing-jobs.html and the state employment service www.labor.state.ak.us (follow the link to Seafood/Fishing Jobs). The Pacific Seafood Processors Association (www.pspafish.net/employment.htm) has links to several major employers including the following:

Alaska General Seafoods, Cannery Recruiting, 6425 NE 175th St, Kenmore, Seattle, WA 98028 (425-485-7755; www.akgen.com/employment.htm). 700 jobs, especially June 16-July 22 in Bristol Bay and July 1-September 5 in Ketchikan. Accepts postal applications only (January 1-June 1).

Peter Pan Seafoods, 10th Floor, 2200 Sixth Ave, Seattle, WA 98121-1820 (206-728-6000; humanresources@ppsf.com). Fifth largest employer in Alaska.

UniSea Inc., PO Box 97109, 15400 NW 90th St, Redmond, WA 98073-9719 (UniSea Jobline 425-861-5330; jobs@unisea.com/ www.unisea.com/jobs.htm). Large canning operations in Dutch Harbor (Alaska) and Redmond (Washington).

Westward Seafoods Inc, Jobline 888-562-7974; jobs@westwardseafoods.com/ www.westwardseafoods.com. Website has extensive recruitment information.

Processing takes place on shore or on special processing ships. Work shifts can vary from 16 hours on with 8 hours off to 6 hours on with 6 hours off. This schedule continues day after day until the end of the season leading to fatigue and (occasionally) accidents. Some processing vessels travel to link up with trawlers, possibly as far as Russia or Japan. Stephen Bastick from San Diego did not go so far afield but was not discontented:

I have worked in some pristine locations in Alaska. My processor vessel pulled into some small remote Alaska towns where I was able to hike around. I go to enjoy wilderness, and the paycheck is a necessary benefit. Often processors can volunteer to stay on between seasons and get paid work assisting the engineers or carpenters. I averaged $1,000 for every nine-day period of 16-hour shifts. Many processors belong to and are despatched out of the Inland Boatmans Union (IBU) in Seattle. Once a member, a person can anticipate continuous seasonal employment.

Information about the IBU can be found at www.ibu.org/employment.htm.

If you go to Alaska on spec, you should go to each cannery and put in an application (before the salmon run begins in the beginning of July for the Kenai area). After that, it is a question of waiting, preferably outside the canneries every day, to see if they are hiring. Kenai south of Anchorage has a large number of processing factories which hire hundreds of workers during the latter half of June. A fever of hiring takes place on the days when a catch is landed. The right number of people will be picked from the waiting crowd, more or less at random, which can be very frustrating. A lot of people give up and leave, so the longer you wait the better your chances. The salmon run at different times during the summer, depending on the area of Alaska. The farther west you go in Alaska, the earlier the run is; for instance it takes place in August on the Panhandle.

Aaron Rabinovitz spent several hundred dollars on the ferry from Bellingham in northern Washington state to Petersburg Alaska at the beginning of June to look for a job to pay for his university education. Although it didn't quite work out that way, he concluded that everybody passing through the States should try to get to Alaska:

The ferry is an interesting place to meet fellow travellers. There is no youth hostel *in town but rather a place known as tent city (reminiscent of the squalor found in moshav housing). Tent city is a series of wooden platforms covered with tarpaulins, inhabited by a mass of strange people: travellers, hippies, vagrants, migrant workers. But it is unusually cheap at $100 a month [$125, 2004, Ed]*

Unfortunately I arrived in town a month too early. The fishing season starts on July 5th this year. In the meantime I've been supporting myself with odd jobs around town. Several places worth checking are Harbor Lights Pizza, the Homestead Cafe and the Hammer & Wikan grocery store. By asking around and becoming friendly with the natives, I've gotten day jobs washing cars and mowing lawns: at least it's money for beer. Alaska is truly a beautiful place. Everywhere in this quaint town you can see mountains, eagles and an occasional bear. The rivers are relatively clean and if you are low on funds you can catch your dinner out of the water. Visas will be a problem for undocumented foreigners. Every application form without exception asks for ID.

Hunting

A number of years ago David Irvine caught a standby flight to Anchorage in mid-July hoping to get a fishing job. After looking into the situation, he decided against fishing and tried hunting lodges instead. He got a list of recognised guides from the Alaska Department of Fish & Game and began phoning. Partly because of the difficulty of talking to the hunters (who are often out in the bush) this method did not work. Although the tourist season was already underway, a job was advertised in the *Anchorage Times* for a lodge assistant which David had the good fortune to get. He worked at a fly-in fly-out lodge in the Alaskan interior for two months, landscaping and doing maintenance work for the benefit of the JR clones and German millionaires who patronised the lodge. He had the impression that women cooks were in considerable demand at other lodges.

David also gained experience of 'moose-packing' which means lugging the shot game (often weighing over 100lbs) out of the bush. Because the carcasses attract bears, it is dangerous to do this job unarmed. By the end of September it had started to snow so David collected his meagre wages and left.

A related field in which assistants and dog handlers are needed is to work in kennels preparing for dog sled races such as the Iditarod Race in Alaska or the Yukon Quest. (Incredibly) the website www.sleddogcentral.com has a Classified section that lists vacancies for dog handlers and racers. One potential employer is Ozone Sled Dogs based in Michigan in 2004/5 who were advertising for people to care for, feed, and train 40 sled dogs between October and April (ozonesleddogs@yahoo.com).

OTHER POPULAR JOBS

Selling

By reputation, anyway, American salesmen are a hardbitten lot. Some travellers have found that their foreign charm makes selling surprisingly effortless. ('Are you really English? I just love that accent.') Americans are not as suspicious of salesmen as other nationalities and you may be pleasantly surprised by the tolerance with which you are received on the doorstep and, even more, by the high earnings which are possible. The BUNAC Job Directory contains details of a number of selling jobs but you must have at least $800 on arrival to tide you over the low periods.

Advertisements for sales positions proliferate. You may find telesales less off-putting than door-to-door salesmanship, but it will also be less lucrative. On the other hand, some working holiday makers and gap year students do not shy away from the hard edge of selling and tackle commission-only jobs. The Southwestern Company with its headquarters in Nashville markets educational books and software door-to-door throughout the US and has a recruitment office in the UK (Unit 4, Bakers Park, Cater Rd, Bishopworth, Bristol BS13

7TT; 0117-978 2121) which targets gap year students. Its website (www.southwestern.com) contains glowing reports from past students whose earnings have been impressive. They claim that the average seller earns more than $100 a day. Their statistics possibly exclude all the students who give up in disgust after a few weeks of failure.

Advertisements for salesmen, especially of magazine subscriptions and cleaning products, proliferate in local papers. Many employers will not be too concerned if your visa is not in order as long as you inspire them with faith in your selling ability. Another travellers' standby is selling ice cream though nowadays the work is available only to men because of the danger of urban crime. An International Driving Permit is an asset when looking for this work.

For general comments on the pros and cons (sic) of selling, see the chapter *Business and Industry*. It can be tough if you have to rely solely on commission. If training is promised, be prepared to be subjected to a quasi-religious indoctrination.

Soccer Coaching

Soccer is fast gaining popularity in North America, and demand is strong for young British coaches to work on summer coaching schemes. A number of companies recruit players to work all over the States including Hawaii:

ProExcel, 10281 Frosty Court, Suite 100, Manassas, VA 20109, USA (703-330-2532; www.proexcel.com). Network of various soccer coaching companies like Britannia (www.britanniasoccerusa.com) and Noga Soccer that recruit seasonal coaches via BUNAC.

Goal-Line Soccer Inc, PO Box 1642, Corvallis, OR 97339 (541-753-5833; info@goal-line.com; www.goal-line.com). Minimum age 21. Mostly in Oregon and Washington. Recruits through BUNAC for July and early August only.

Major League Soccer Camps, 47 Water St, Mystic, CT 06355, USA. UK corporate office: MLS Camps, Malmarc House, 116 Dewsbury Rd, Leeds LS11 6XD (0113 272 0616/ 0113 270 4200; employment@mlscamps.com. The largest and best known. Registration fee of £310 includes flights from UK, rental car and gas expenses plus at least $150 per week. MLSC assists with processing of H-2B visas.

Soccer Academy Inc, PO Box 3046, Manassas, VA 20108, USA (703-385-0150; socceracademype@aol.com/ www.soccer-academy.com).

Others advertise in the specialist press. BUNAC knows about these companies, since they normally process the necessary J-1 visa. It is more important to be good at working with kids than to be a great football player, though of course it is easier to command the respect of the kids if you can show them good skills and a few tricks.

Theo West spent part of his gap year before going to Liverpool University, as a soccer coach and describes the application process and the job itself:

The procedure involved in getting a place is time-consuming and difficult but well worth the effort. It includes an interview to see if you have the right personality and experience in coaching followed by a couple of coaching days where you are evaluated at close quarters by senior coaches (which proved a slight problem for me since my home is in Inverness and the nearest coaching day was in Newcastle). Finally you accept a contract, list preferred working locations, pay a membership (which covers flights to the US), apply for a J-1 visa through BUNAC and attend an induction. On arrival in America we were briefed on where our first week-long assignment was to be and given our coaching equipment. The next day we headed off in hire cars for Monroe Woodbury, a rich area in upstate New York where we were introduced to the families that were to put us up for a week. The pay as a first year coach is around $140 a week for a three hour session each day and occasional adult coaching clinics. In terms of pay it was not great but the benefits generally come from the families that house you, feed you and entertain you. The benefits of an English accent in America are still many. I spent five weeks coaching in New

York, Connecticut and finally worked with under-privileged kids in New Jersey. It was an amazing and draining experience as I got to meet many great people, saw some wonderful sights and negotiated myself with some difficulty into a number of bars (the strictness of the adherence to the 21 age limit for drinking proved annoying).

Manual Work

Cash-in-hand work can be found, especially as a loader with removal firms (wages of up to $15 an hour), as security guards and in construction (especially for those with skills). The best time (for men) to look for removal work is just before the end of the month when many leases expire and more people tend to move house. Dan Eldridge worked at a hostel in San Francisco for a year and so knows the working scene well: 'An interesting option is to open up the phone book to 'Movers' and personally visit them, especially any with Irish names. They all employ foreigners paying at least $10 an hour cash-in-hand. It's tough work but $10 an hour is incredible if you're just starting out. I sent many people to the moving companies and most quit after a couple of weeks, but were happy to have the cash.'

Since houses throughout the States are wood-framed, carpenters can do well, even those without much experience. It is common practice to pay employees as contract labour, which leaves them with the responsibility of paying taxes, social security, etc.; this is a definite advantage if your papers are not in order. Even if you can't find work building new houses, you can offer your painting or maintenance skills to any householder, preferably one whose house is looking the worse for wear.

The USA has more than its fair share of natural disasters which always create a lot of urgent work. Paul Donut found work in Florida clearing up after a hurricane; the authorities were so desperate for workers that no questions were asked about permits.

A more definite but offbeat suggestion has been proffered by Mark Kinder who wrote from rural Maryland:

After spending the summer on the Camp America programme, a friend and I decided to do a parachute jump. Once you have made about ten jumps, the instructors expect you to learn how to pack parachutes, which takes about five hours to learn. Once you have learnt how to pack you get paid $5 per chute cash and with a bit of practice can pack three or four chutes an hour which is good money. I would say that 90% of parachute centres in the US pay people cash for packing the chutes but you generally have to be a skydiver to do the job. It is definitely a fun way of earning money. Skydivers are very friendly people and are thrilled to meet foreigners, so they will often offer a place to stay. If not, you can always camp at the parachute centre.

A list of the 275 parachute centres in the US can be obtained from the national association USPA, 1440 Duke St, Alexandria, VA 22314 or via the Drop Zone Directory section of their website www.uspa.org/dz.

Medical

Nurse shortages are chronic in the US and qualified nurses might like to investigate possibilities through a specialist UK agency. For people with a more casual interest in medicine, there is the possibility of testing new drugs as well as donating blood.

While filling in the time until her flight out of Seattle, Mig Urquhart sold plasma at the Plasma Center. She was turned down on her first visit since there was too much protein in her urine (she reckoned it was because she had been living on peanut butter sandwiches). But it was fine the next time and she earned $10, $15 or $20 depending on how often she went in a week.

When Lindsay Watt arrived in the US, he intended to sustain himself with conventional kinds of employment. But almost immediately he discovered that the longish-stay male travellers staying at his hostel in New York were all earning money solely through medical studies. Invariably, a social security number is needed though it can bear the stamp 'Not

Valid for Work'. Most studies pay at least $100 a day and provide all food, accommodation and entertainment. On the three studies in which Lindsay participated, he earned $300 in five days in New York, $475 for four days in Philadelphia and $3,000 for a month in West Palm Beach (Florida). Together these funded a tour of South America. The best he ever heard of was a three-day study in Baltimore which paid $800. (It must have involved some fairly unpleasant tests, such as a spinal tap.) There are Drug Research Centers in many American cities especially Massachusetts, New York, New Jersey, Pennsylvania, Maryland and Florida. Women are seldom accepted unless they are sterile.

Two excellent sources of information on drug testing centres are the websites www.centerwatch.com, a listing service for clinical trials, and www.gpgp.net, a free online directory of clinics and research centres. Try also www.clinicaltrials.gov which lists thousands of clinical studies sponsored by the National Institutes of Health, other Federal agencies and the pharmaceutical industry; they indicate which ones are recruiting but mainly they are looking for people who are actually suffering from the relevant disorder or disease. Healthy volunteers are needed only for Phase 1 trials.

For example at the end of 2004 the University of Pennsylvania (215-662-4652) was paying smokers and non-smokers $150 to submit to a health check-up and blood work (and referral to a stop-smoking clinic if desired). For certain studies you are paid hourly, for example the Berkley Olfactory Research Project (http://socrates.berkeley.edu/borp/volunteerinfo1.htm) pays an hourly fee of $10-$30 to volunteers who undergo MRI scans.

Here is a brief list of possible contacts, going from east to west:

Boston University Medical Center, Massachusetts – 617-414-1325

Clinical Trials Office, SUNY Upstate Medical University, Syracuse NY – 315-464-5476

Cornell Clinical Trials Unit, New York – 212-746-4166

Warren Magnuson Clinical Center, Bethesda, Maryland – 1-800-411 1222

Johns Hopkins University School of Medicine, Baltimore, Maryland – www.hopkinsclinicaltrials.com.

Advanced Research Institute, Florida – 727-845-0589; www.urologyhealthcenter.com.

Ohio State University, General Clinic Research Center, Columbus, Ohio – 614-293-8750; http://gcrc.osu.edu.

Vanderbilt Clinical Trials Center – Nashville, Tennessee – 615-343-8010; www.clinicaltrials.vanderbilt.edu.

University of Kansas Medical Center Research Institute, Kansas City, KS 66160-7702 (913-588-1242).

University of Texas Medical Branch, Galveston, TX 77555-0671 (409-747-0749).

CEDRA Research, Austin, Texas – 512-345-0032; www.cedraresearch.com.

University of Utah Medical Center, Salt Lake City – 801-581-5036

Advanced Clinical Research Institute (ACRI), Anaheim, California (also in Orange, CA) – 714-778-1309; http://advancedtrials.com/home.

Northwest Kinetics, Tacoma, Washington – 253-779-8815 or toll free 1-877-697-8839; recruiters@nwkinetics.com. Was offering $1,100 to healthy volunteers for an 8-day study (December 2004).

University of Washington, Seattle, Washington – 206-543-2317; www.washington.edu/healthresearch.

Radiant Research – Headquarters in Bellevue Washington; 1-866-429-3707; www.radiantresearch.com. Trials conducted at clinical research centres throughout the US.

CHILDCARE & DOMESTIC WORK

The US State Department administers the au pair placement programme which allows thousands of young Europeans with childcare experience to work for American families for exactly one year on a J-1 visa. They apply through a small number of sponsoring organisations (currently there are six) who must follow the guidelines which govern the programme, so there is not much difference between them.

The basic requirements are that you be between 18 and 26, speak English, show at least 200 hours of recent childcare experience, have a full clean driving licence and provide a criminal record check. The childcare experience can consist of regular babysitting, helping at a local creche or school, etc. Anyone wanting to care for a child under two must have 200 hours of experience looking after children under two and must expect the programme interviewers to test their claims carefully. The majority of candidates are young women though men with relevant experience (e.g. sole care of children under five) may be placed. (It is still not unusual to have just a handful of blokes out of hundreds of au pairs.)

The job entails working a maximum of 45 hours a week (including babysitting) with at least one and a half days off per week plus one complete weekend off a month. Successful applicants receive free return flights from one of many cities, four-day orientation in New York and support from a community counsellor. The time lag between applying and flying is usually at least two months. The counsellor's role is to advise on any problems and organise meetings with other au pairs in your area. Applicants are required to pay a good faith deposit of $400 which is returned to them at the end of 12 months but which is forfeit if the terms of the programme are broken.

The fixed amount of pocket money for au pairs is $139.05 a week which, although it hasn't changed for six years, is a reasonable wage on top of room, board and perks. On arrival participants must receive a four-day orientation which covers child safety and development. Legislation has made first aid a compulsory component. An additional $500 is paid by the host family to cover the cost of educational courses (three hours a week during term-time) which must be attended as a condition of the visa. Au pairs are at liberty to travel for a month after their contract is over but no visa extension is available beyond that.

A separate programme exists for qualified child carers/nannies, called by Au Pair in America the 'Au Pair Extraordinaire' programme or 'Premiere Au Pairs', 'Au Pair Elite', etc. by other companies. Candidates with the appropriate NNEB, BTEC, Diploma in Nursing or NVQ3 qualification are eligible to earn $200 a week plus a $1,000 completion bonus (including the return of the $400 deposit). A new Nanny in America programme was introduced in 2004 in which professional nannies earn $350 per week. Another 12-month programme is called Educare for students who want to have shorter working hours and more time for formal studies. In this programme the pocket money is $105, the family's contribution to non-degree studies is $1,000 and the upfront fee $825 plus airfare.

At any one time 12,000 American families are hosting a foreign au pair and the vast majority of placements are reasonably successful. This is not to say that problems do not occur, because it is not at all unusual for au pairs to chafe against rules, curfews and unreasonable expectations in housework, etc. When speaking to your family on the telephone during the application period, ask as many day-to-day questions as possible, and try to establish exactly what will be expected of you, how many nights babysitting at weekends, restrictions on social life, use of the car, how private are the living arrangements, etc. The counsellors and advisers provided by the sending organisations should be able to sort out problems and in some cases can find alternative families.

Consider carefully the pros and cons of the city you will be going to. Emma Purcell was not altogether happy to be sent to Memphis Tennessee which she describes as the 'most backward and redneck city in the USA':

I was a very naïve 18 year old applying to be an au pair for a deferred year before university. I have been very lucky with my host family who have made me feel one of the family. I have travelled the USA and Mexico frequently staying in suites and being treated as royalty since my host dad is president of Holiday Inn. On the bad side, I have lost numerous friends who have not had such good luck. One was working 60 hours a week (for no extra pay) with the brattiest children, so she left. Another girl from Australia lasted six months with her neurotic family who yelled at her for not cleaning the toaster daily and for folding the socks wrong. Finally she plucked up the courage to talk to her host parents and their immediate response was to throw her out. A very strong personality is required to be an au pair for a year in the States.

Several agencies accept au pairs into the US, and it is worth comparing their literature. Au Pair in America is the largest organisation making in excess of 4,500 au pair and nanny placements throughout the country. Brochures and application forms can be ordered online (www.aupairamerica.co.uk) or by phone in the UK on 020-7581 7322/7300. The programme operates under the auspices of the American Institute for Foreign Study or AIFS (37 Queens Gate, London SW7 5HR) though some of the selection has been devolved to independent au pair agencies such as Childcare International Ltd, Trafalgar House, Grenville Place, London NW7 3SA (0870 774 7475; 020-8906 3116; www.childint.co.uk). Au Pair in America also has representatives in 45 countries and agent/interviewers throughout the UK.

Other active au pair Exchange Visitor Programmes are listed on the US Embassy website (www.usembassy.org.uk). All are smaller than Au Pair in America but may be able to offer a more personal service and more choice in the destination and family you work for:

Au Pair Care, 2226 Bush St, San Francisco, CA 94115; 415-434-8788/1-800-428-7246; www.aupaircare.com.

EurAupair, 238 North Coast Highway, Laguna Beach, CA 92651; 949-494-7355. Plus three other regional offices in US; www.euraupair.com. UK partner is EurAupair UK, 17 Wheatfield Drive, Shifnal, Shropshire TF11 8HL; 01952 460733/ maureen@asseuk.freeserve.co.uk.

goAUPAIR, 111 East 12300 South, Draper, UT 84020; 1-888-287-2471; 2baupair@goaupair.com; www.goaupair.com.

InterExchange, 13th Floor, 161 Sixth Avenue, New York, NY 10013; 212-926-0446; www.interexchange.org.

Increasingly, au pairs and families are bypassing conventional agencies by using the internet to engage in DIY arrangements. Prospective au pairs are invited to register their details, including age, nationality, relevant experience and in many cases a photo, to be uploaded onto a website which then becomes accessible to registered families. The families then make contact with suitable au pairs after paying an introduction fee to the web-based agency. Registration is usually free or reasonably priced for the job-seeker. Two internet-based agencies to try are www.aupair-agency.com operated by the Almondbury Au Pair Agency in the UK and www.aupair-world.net based in Germany.

It should be possible to fix up a job working with a family after arrival in the States, though the penalties for working illegally described earlier in this chapter apply equally. There are many job notices for au pairs and nannies on hostel notice boards (especially in San Francisco) and in big city dailies. After finding it impossible to get a job without a social security card in Houston, Ana Maria Güemes from Mexico started reading the ads and soon had a live-in job as a babysitter.

After having been in California for a while, Paul Young decided to try to market himself as an informal butler, willing to drive and cook in a household. After advertising in the rich county of San Anselmo, he received a disappointing response, mostly from disabled people offering $100 a week. He chose the most lucrative position paying $320 a week cash-in-hand, but was far from thrilled with his choice. His employer sounds the worst kind of snobbish spoiled American; even the dog was horrible and, in Paul's view, needed (and probably got!) a psychiatrist. He concludes that a sane wealthy American is a contradiction in terms, and recommends checking out the situation carefully before committing yourself.

Gerhard Flaig found a much more congenial employer by the simple expedient of pestering a contact he had (organist in the church next to his hostel in Los Angeles who had kindly let him play the organ) until he finally introduced him to the church secretary who did have an idea:

The secretary arranged a meeting with an old man who wanted someone to organise his files and house, to do some transcriptions and other odd jobs. He gave me *my own room and free food plus paid me $5 an hour. I was overjoyed and left the hostel at once. After I'd done the transcribing, he wanted me to paint his rooms. His landlady was so satisfied with the job I did that she asked me to paint her house and then a friend of his asked me as well. I got one job after the other and was very busy working as a painter. I had a wonderful time in Hollywood and earned quite a lot of money to travel on. And I still keep in touch with the man.*

AGRICULTURE

Students of agriculture may find various schemes which allow them to receive further training in the US (see information for instance on the International Agricultural Exchange Association in the introductory chapter on *Agriculture*). Also described in the introduction is the International Exchange Programme which allows equine and horticultural trainees to be placed in the US by the international agency, Stablemate (www.iepuk.com).

Like everything else in America, many farms (often agribusinesses rather than farms) tend to be on the grand scale, especially in California and the Midwest. This means that the phenomenon of cycling along a country road, finding the farmer in his field and being asked to start work in an adjoining field is virtually unknown in the US. Furthermore it could be dangerous, since anyone wandering up a farmer's driveway would be suspected of being a trespasser and liable to be threatened with a vicious dog or a gun.

In many important agricultural areas, much of the fruit and vegetable harvesting has been traditionally done by gangs of illegal Mexicans or legal Chicanos (naturalised Americans of Spanish descent) for notoriously low wages. It is very common for an agent to contract a whole gang, so that there may be no room for individuals and pairs of travellers.

A gentler form of agriculture is practised on organic farms that flourish in many corners of the USA. One centralised place to make contact with them is via the WWOOF website www.organicvolunteers.com where members can contact organic farmers throughout the country who are looking for volunteers. Alternatively WWOOF USA has recently established a national organisation (PO Box 510, Felton, CA 95018; 831-425-3276 *voicemail*; info@wwoofusa.org; www.wwoofusa.org); individual membership costs $20 and dual membership $30. After joining you will be sent the list of 250 member farms by post. WWOOF Hawaii is a separate organisation run by the Canadian branch of WWOOF; membership of $15 plus postage entitles you to receive the booklet listing 70 host farms, 43 of which are on the Big Island (see www.wwoofhawaii.org).

Unfortunately working for keep on a farm counts as employment for the purposes of Immigration so as usual it is important not to mention the word 'work' or 'employment' in any immigration context but rather cultural exchange.

People who visit a rural coastal hostel in California, Bill's Home Hostel (1040 Cielo Lane, Nipomo, CA 93444-9039; 805-929-3647; bdenneen@slonet.org) can work for two or three hours a day in lieu of payment for accommodation and food.

In the world of conventional agriculture, there is scope for finding work. While working at parachute centres in rural Delaware and Maryland, Mark Kinder from Blackpool found that farm work was easy to come by on an intermittent basis with free caravan accommodation. In every state in the Union (except perhaps Nevada, Montana and Alaska) there is some fruit or vegetable being picked throughout the summer months.

Both in large-scale harvests and on small family farms there is a chance that no one will be concerned about your legal status. This is what Jan Christensen from Denmark found when he looked for summer farm work in Minnesota a few years ago:

The farmers seemed to have a very relaxed attitude towards permits. The best places to look are along route 210 just off Interstate 94 at Fergus Falls which is a rich farm area with good employment prospects from April/May till mid-October. But it's best to have some experience in tractor driving and combine harvester work. If you try to bluff, you will find yourself on the road PDQ. I found that my farmer expected me to know just about everything about farming and had no time to train me.

Fruit pickers congregate in the counties of Yakima, Chelan, Douglas and Okanogan in Washington State. Another example of a large-scale harvest is the peach harvest in Western Colorado around Palisade. A few thousand pickers are suddenly needed between 20th July and 4th September and especially during the second fortnight in August. One large hiring peach farm is Rancho Durazno, 3940 G 2/10 Road, Palisade, CO 81526; rdurazno@aol.com; www.ranchodurazno.com/rd/FarmLabor.htm. Cherries are also grown here and must be picked in June. Similarly the three-week cherry harvest around Traverse City Michigan in late June/early July employs large numbers of non-locals. The employment site www.michaglabor.org has links to growers throughout Michigan. Deep in the cornfields of the Midwest, crews are recruited to detassel corn by a company called Sunshine Enterprises based in Iowa; email sunshine@corn-jobs.com for details of these itinerant positions that last three weeks in July and require no experience.

California and Florida are the leading states for agricultural production, especially citrus, plums, avocados, apricots and grapes. Most of these are grown along the Central Valley particularly the San Joaquin Valley around Fresno. The work is notoriously poorly paid. Some have fared better in the Salinas Valley on the California coast, which is a huge vegetable growing area, again predominantly Spanish-speaking.

Florida Harvests

Most citrus fruit in Florida is still picked by hand though mechanical harvesting is slowly gaining momentum. For the time being, massive numbers of itinerant pickers or local casuals must be enlisted over the winter and spring, when the Florida climate is at its most pleasant. Citrus production is greatest in the central counties of Lake and Polk, inland from Tampa and north past Orlando, where more than 25 million boxes of fruit are picked annually. The surrounding counties of Marion, Volusia, Orange, Hillsborough, Hardee, De Soto, Highlands, Indian River and St. Lucie are also major producers. Another good area is around Arcadia and Nocatee in Desoto County where there are about 5,000 citrus pickers in the peak season.

The harvest season for all citrus crops broadly lasts from mid-October until early July, exactly opposite from the usual summer harvesting season. As far as individual crops are concerned, oranges normally start up in November and peak in January, February and March with another peak in May with the late Valencia orange crop.

Buses drive into large local towns at around 6am and anybody who wants to pick fruit that day can get on and be driven to that contractor's grove. Ask around in bars what the form is as regards buses, rates of pay and good groves. To them you are nothing more than a box number in a given row and so, with luck, visas won't be a problem, unless there are rumours of an impending immigration raid.

Wages are based on piece rates, the basic unit being a bin or box. You determine your own work level and nobody rushes you. Pay is given out by the day or by the week if you want, and it is cash in hand. Steve and Iona Dwyer were distinctly unimpressed with the earning potential of picking oranges in Florida: *'We got ourselves a car in Florida which became very necessary during our jaunt. I would say that unless you are almost broke, don't bother with the orange harvest. The Hispanics have kept the wages very low. When we were there the rate was $7 per half-ton bin. For one and half days we toiled in sweltering heat to earn $60 between us.'*

The speed at which you can fill boxes is heavily dependent upon your ability to place your ladder cleverly. A lot of time is wasted moving ladders around from branch to branch and this means fewer boxes filled and hence less money earned. A good picker can clear half a tree from one position – as a novice you will not be able to do so. An alternative method operates in the groves which supply juice factories. In this case you knock the fruit from five or six trees onto the ground, pick them up and fill a big sack which is dumped into a giant bin. Picking is organised by the foreman assigning each picker or pair of pickers a row of trees to clear. Once he realises a particular picker is keen, he or she should be given the better rows.

The picking season is divided into early, middle and late. Early picking means selecting

	May	June	July	August	September	October
Alabama	potatoes, tomatoes					
Arizona	carrots, lettuce		cotton			
Arkansas		peaches				
California		cherries	peaches, broccoli, peppers	grapes, apples		
Colorado			cherries	apricots, peaches	peas, apples	
Florida	(winter: citrus and most vegetables)				cucumbers	
Georgia		peaches		peanuts		
Idaho			cherries	onions	apples, potatoes, sugar beets	
Illinois	asparagus (April) corn detassling					
Indiana		corn detassling		tomatoes, corn		
Iowa	asparagus	corn detassling	beans			
Kentucky		strawberries		tobacco		
Louisiana		strawberries			sugar cane	
Maine		asparagus (April)		blueberry-raking		apples
Maryland		strawberries, cabbages				
Michigan		strawberries	cherries	haying	peaches	apples
Minnesota					beetroot, potatoes	
Missouri				peaches	apples	
Montana			cherries		sugar beets, potatoes	
New Hampshire					apples	
New Jersey		strawberries		cranberries	blueberries	apples
New York		strawberries, peas, cherries		apples		
North Carolin			tobacco			
North Dakota		sugar beets				
Pennsylvania					peaches, apples, grapes	
Ohio			field vegetables			
Oklahoma	wheat cutting			corn detassling		
Oregon		strawberries, cherries	peaches		apples, nuts, hops	
South Carolina		peaches				
South Dakota			wheat	hay, potatoes		
Utah		cherries		apricots	apples, sugar beets,	
Vermont					apples	potatoes
Virginia			tobacco	apples, peaches		
Washington		cherries	berries, hops		apples	
Wisconsin		lettuce, onions, peppers				
Wyoming					sugar beets	

the ripe fruit which is slow and hence badly paid. Much the same applies to late picking when one takes what is left on the trees. Middle picking starts up when the fruit demand is high and involves virtual stripping of the fruit. This is the best paid part of the season. The price being paid per box varies per week, per grove and per fruit type. The only way to make the most of the grove variation in price is to have your own car and drive around a few groves and offer yourself for work at the best paid grove or the one that looks fullest in fruit. Sometimes you may have to drive 30 miles to work. Many people do this, though the majority rely on the labour buses.

Although citrus is the most important crop in Florida, the state also produces a whole range of vegetables. Southern Florida is the only place in the nation where vegetables can be grown between December and March (e.g. tomatoes, peppers, cucumbers). The best areas are Collier County centred around Naples on the Gulf of Mexico and the area around Homestead south of Miami. The September cucumber harvest is reputed to be the best paid work in the area ($100 a day) but the work is incredibly hard and most travellers barely survive their first day. Apparently cabbages and watermelons are none too easy either.

A lot of the produce is designed for markets outside Florida and there are dozens of packing houses in these two areas which employ thousands of seasonal workers. Contact the Southwest Florida Growers Association in Immokalee Florida for more details of times and locations of harvests and job availability in the packing factories. Try growers along Route 31 around Arcadia.

Farms and packing houses are easy to locate near Homestead along US 1 from Miami. The bean season runs from November 1st till April and the potatoes from New Years to the middle of May, so the best time to arrive is October. Tomato harvesters in Florida fluctuate between receiving just $48 for picking two tons in one day to earning $7 to $12 per hour for a few days in the peak season.

The Apple Harvest of Maine

In the early autumn, the local newspaper in south central Maine (around the town of Monmouth) is full of apple picker ads in the 'Help Wanted' columns. The season lasts two months, starting in early September and continuing until the first deep frost near the end of October. Pickers start out at the minimum wage, but graduate to piece work per bushel as soon as their speed reaches a certain level. Rates of pay are standard among orchards, as is the custom of paying a bonus to people who complete the harvest for one grower. Hours are flexible, though people who put in 70 hours a week are preferred. Crews are formed by the orchard foremen according to speed of picking; the French Canadian professional crews are a sight to behold and they earn well over $100 a day right from the beginning. The website of the *Apple Journal* (www.applejournal.com) gives contact details for apple orchards worldwide including about 50 in Maine.

Once you get a little fitter and master the techniques, apple picking can be enjoyable, as Roger Brown comments:

> *Standing on top of an apple tree in the bright sunshine and chatting away to a colleague became a very pleasant way of passing the time. It was good too that the apple-picking season falls during the 'season of mists and mellow fruitfulness'. You get to the top of an apple tree on the top of a hill in Maine and the whole world seems to unroll at your feet. Beyond the white wooden church and steeple of Monmouth, ranges of hills can be seen in the distance creating a rainbow of colours with the bright leaves of the autumnal maples.*

VOLUNTEERING

The main workcamp organisations in the US such as VFP (www.vfp.org) listed in the chapter *Volunteering* have incoming programmes. Prospective volunteers must register through a workcamp organisation in their own country. For example Volunteers for Peace place most than 500 volunteers on 50-60 workcamps in the US. In the past, volunteers have been placed on environmental projects in San Francisco's Golden Gate National Park and the Hawaii Volcanoes National Park, assisted with urban renovation and preservation of historic landmarks in New York and New Jersey, and worked with disabled children and adults on their summer holidays.

Voluntary opportunities in the US range from the intensely urban to the decidedly rural. In the former category, you can build houses in deprived areas throughout the US with Habitat for Humanity (Global Village, 121 Habitat St, Americus, GA 31709; www.habitat. org). Each summer Winant-Clayton Volunteers place 20 participants in community projects in the USA, mainly in New York, working with inner city youth, the elderly, homeless people and people with mental health problems. Volunteers with a British passport are taken on to work for eight weeks from mid or late June followed by two or three weeks of travel. For an application pack send an s.a.e. to WCVA, St. Margaret's House, 21 Old Ford Road, Bethnal Green, London E2 9PI (020-8983 3834; wcva@dircon.co.uk) in advance of the application deadline of mid-January. If you want a less structured spell of volunteering in New York City, go along to the University Soup Kitchen at the Church of the Nativity at 44 Second Avenue, on Saturdays from 11.45am-3.30pm (www.streetproject.org). Volunteers receive a free lunch.

Hostelling International (8401 Colesville Road, Suite 600, Silver Spring, MD 20910; 301-495-1240) relies on volunteers and interns from around the world who stay for at least ten weeks and often many months. Interns receive free accommodation at the hostel plus possibly a small weekly payment. The website www.hiayh.org has links to hostels around America. Hostels sometimes link up with local national parks in volunteer programmes. For example in 2004, the Everglades Hostel in Florida City paired up with Biscayne National Park to bring volunteers to this marine park to work on a coral protection project and another one to clean up a sea turtle nesting area; contact the hostel for details (305-248-1122; gladeshostel@hotmail.com).

Working outside the big cities is an attractive prospect. For example the US Forest Service organises workcamps to maintain trails, campsites and wildlife throughout the country; volunteers should apply to the individual parks; state-by-state opportunities are posted on the internet at www.volunteer.gov/gov or also try www.usafreedomcorps.gov. The Heritage Resource Management department of the US Forest Service operates a volunteer programme called 'Passport in Time' to conduct archaeological surveys, record oral histories, etc.; details from 800-281-9176; pit@sricrm.com/ www.passportintime.com. Alternatively contact the Volunteer Co-ordinator's office in Modoc National Forest (800 West 12th St, Alturas, CA 96101; 530-233-5811; ggates@fs.fed.us). This office sends out application forms, tries to match volunteers with appropriate vacancies and assists with obtaining a J-1 visa. Volunteers/trainees are paid a stipend of about $120 a week in addition to free accommodation. Archaeological digs that need volunteers are listed in the *Archaeological Fieldwork Opportunities Bulletin* (see *Voluntary* chapter for details).

The General Convention of Sioux YMCAs in South Dakota offers summer camp and longer positions (February-October). Volunteers live in rural Native American communities in order to help run the local YMCA Youth Center, working with Lakota children, families and schools. The Y provides housing, a small living stipend and cultural training. Contact the YMCA for details: PO Box 218, Dupree, South Dakota 57623 (605-365-5232; www. siouxymca.org/volunteers.htm). International applications are accepted via the YMCA International Camp Counselor Program (ICCP) mentioned earlier (www.ymcaiccp.org).

The American Hiking Society collates volunteer opportunities from around the United States to build, maintain and restore foot trails in America's backcountry. No prior trail work experience is necessary, but volunteers should be able to hike at least five miles a day, supply their own backpacking equipment (including tent), pay a $120 registration fee ($95 for AHS members) and arrange transport to and from the work site. Food is provided on some projects. For a schedule of projects, go to www.AmericanHiking.org or send an s.a.e. to AHS, Volunteer Vacations, 1422 Fenwick Lane, Silver Spring, MD 20910

(301-565-6704). AHS also publish *Get Outside,* a directory published in 2002 of volunteer opportunities in America's great outdoors which costs $10.95 (US dollars only) excluding international postage.

The Student Conservation Association Inc. (SCA, 689 River Road, PO Box 550, Charlestown, NH 03603-0550; 603-543-1700; www.thesca.org) places anyone 18 or older in conservation and environmental internships in national parks and forests nationwide. Position lengths vary from 12 weeks to 12 months and travel expenses, housing, training and a weekly stipend are provided. The SCA website includes a searchable database of open positions as well as an application form.

It might also be worth trying the Appalachian Trail Conservancy (PO Box 807, 799 Washington St, Harpers Ferry, WV 25425-0807; 304-535-6331; crews@appalachiantrail. org; www.appalachiantrail.org) which organises work parties to maintain the Appalachian Trail lasting one to six weeks. Volunteers receive food, accommodation and insurance.

In her year out between school and university, Elisabeth Weiskittel from New York State fixed up a short internship at the Ocean Mammal Institute (www.oceanmammalinst. com) on the island of Maui in Hawaii. Every January, the woman in charge of the Institute takes some of her students and a few interns (often people taking a year off) to Hawaii for three weeks for a fee of about $2,000:

> *The purpose of the Institute was to study humpbacked whales and the effects of nearby boats on their behaviour. Our data was intended to support a pending law restricting the use of speedboats and other craft in these small bays where the whales and calves were swimming. One group watched and recorded the whales' behaviour in the morning and had the afternoon off, and the other group watched in the afternoon and had the morning off. I had no problem adjusting to life in Hawaii. Most people were there to get a tan and go to bars, but even if that's not your scene it's still lots of fun in Hawaii. During our last week there was a large conference on environmental issues, which all the interns were invited to attend. Some of the speakers were well-known, and one or two spoke to our group, such as the founder of Greenpeace.*

CONCLUSION

This chapter has only scratched the surface, but has been written in the hope that it will spark a few new ideas for your trans-American trip. As one of our less intrepid correspondents recalls: *'When we first arrived in the States we went immediately to visit the parents of a friend. I'd never met them before but they made us welcome. A good thing too, because America seemed so strange to me and expensive, that I just wanted to get on the first plane back. I think it was because everything seemed so big and in advance of us. I was used to being in more 'backward' places (i.e. Ghana and Scotland) and America was much more complicated.'*

There is no denying that it is preferable to qualify for an Exchange Visitor Programme like BUNAC, Au Pair in America or the Work & Travel Co. One of the advantages is that they choose a comprehensive insurance policy for you. If you go on your own, make sure you have purchased enough insurance cover since medical care is astronomically expensive in the US.

You must balance caution with a spirit of adventure, accepting and even revelling in the bizarre. When you learn that it is possible to get a night's lodging in a police cell, at a rescue mission or Salvation Army hostel, you need not necessarily shy away. You might have an experience similar to Benjamin Fry's in Alaska: *'I stayed in another rescue mission in Anchorage and there witnessed an amazing spectacle: a tearful Indian or perhaps Eskimo confessing his sins in his native language. We were also fed – revolting food but free.'*

You may end up in some unlikely situations, but some of them may also lead to a few days of work helping a trucker with his deliveries, joining an impromptu pop group to perform at private parties, gardening on a Californian commune, building solar houses, and so on. If you aren't lucky enough to have the appropriate visa, you should grasp every opportunity to take advantage of offers of genuine hospitality.

If you do conduct a proper on-the-spot job hunt, the two most useful tools you can have are a car and a tidy appearance. Writing from small-town North Carolina after a stint of working in a pizzeria in Ohio, Peter Stonemann summarises the situation: *'North America still offers good possibilities of life, but it is not at all the 'dream' that the chauvinistic Yankee propaganda tries to present to the world. Perhaps it was in the past, but certainly it is now extremely difficult to progress here if you do not even have your own motor vehicle. You can only survive, with many poorly paid jobs.'*

Even so, you should be able to get some kind of job which will introduce you to the striking cultural differences between Europe and America and which will provide you with some capital with which to explore this amazing country.

Canada

Countries like Canada which are favoured with a high standard of living and a reputation for unlimited job opportunities have traditionally attracted many travellers and emigrants. But, alas, it is not easy to work in Canada, both because of strictly enforced 'Canada-only' immigration policies and high unemployment of 7.3% where it has remained for more than two years. However Canadians are hospitable and eager for visitors to like their country. Even the immigration officer who deported one of our contributors expressed regret that the offender had not had a chance to see more of the country.

RED TAPE

British citizens require only a valid passport to enter Canada. Normally on arrival they will be given permission to stay as tourists for six months; incoming tourists may be requested to show that they have sufficient funds, adequate medical insurance and a return ticket or, failing that, some Canadian contacts. Although Canadian Immigration is reputed to be less savage than its American counterpart, many young travellers without much money have been given a rough ride.

The working holiday programme for Britons who want to work in Canada has recently become more flexible. The upper age limit has been raised from 30 to 35 and, more significantly, it is no longer compulsory to be a full-time student. The General Working Holiday Programme allows any UK national under 35 to apply for a 12-month Employment Authorization via BUNAC (the British Universities North America Club). A second BUNAC programme is open to full-time students, and another one to gap year students. Participants of programmes via BUNAC do not require a definite job offer but must show sufficient funds. It is also possible for students and those who have graduated within the past 12 months to apply for a temporary authorisation directly to the Canadian High Commission but in this case they must show proof of a job offer from a Canadian employer and be prepared to work only for that named employer for the duration of their visa.

The Canadian government offers in the neighbourhood of 15,000 temporary authorisations each year to students and non-students from eligible countries The Canadian High Commission in London administers the programme for students of British, Irish, Swedish and Finnish nationality. Other nationalities (like Australian and New Zealand) should consult the Canadian Consulate locally or check www.whpcanada.org.au. The quotas are allocated on the basis of reciprocal agreements between Canada and the partner countries and can fluctuate from year to year. To take one example, the quota for Australians in 2005 was 7,500.

Interested students should check the website www.canada.org.uk/visa-info or obtain the general leaflet 'Student Temporary Employment in Canada' by sending a large s.a.e. with a 50p stamp and marked 'SGWHP' in the top left-hand corner to the Canadian High Commission (Immigration Section, 38 Grosvenor St, London W1K 4AA); the visa Info number is 020-7258 6699. You can have full programme details and an application form faxed back to you by ringing 020-7258 6350 and giving your fax number. Processing of work authorisations normally takes ten working days and is free of charge. Note that anyone with a job fixed up in Quebec must comply with separate and additional Quebec immigration procedures.

Certain special categories of work may be eligible for authorisation, such as nannies who are in great demand but must be qualified (see *Childcare* section below). There is also a category of work permits for voluntary work which takes about a month to process if you have found a placement through a recognised charitable or religious organisation.

Americans do not require a passport to visit Canada (only proof of US citizenship if requested) but they are not allowed to enter in order to look for work. Like all foreign nationals, they must fix up a job (before arrival) which has been approved by the employer's local Human Resource Development Centre or HRDC (the name for employment offices). The one difference is that they can apply for an Employment Authorization at the port of entry rather than having to apply through a Canadian consulate in the US.

Australians should write to the Canadian Consulate General, Immigration Office, Level 5, 111 Harrington St, Sydney, NSW 2000 (02-9364 3082; whpcanada.sydney@international. gc.ca; www.whpcanada.org.au) to request an application form for a working holiday visa which is an open Employment Authorization valid for a year, available to young people (not necessarily students) aged 18-30 with no criminal record. Application forms will be accepted only after January 2nd of each year when the programme opens, and will close as soon as the quota is filled, which is often within the first six months of the year. Processing normally takes 4-6 weeks. Applicants must submit their application before their 31st birthday. Anyone with a criminal record (including alcohol-related driving offences) or with dependants is not eligible to apply. The Consulate issues a Letter of Introduction that allows the holder to obtain an open Employment Authorization at the Canadian port of entry within 12 months (non-extendable) of the date of issue. Only one of these letters is issued to a given individual. The Employment Authorization issued at the port of entry usually has a one-year validity and is a multiple entry visa. At entry Australian working holiday makers will also have to prove that they have access to A$4,000 (recent bank statements, cash, credit card, etc.).

People with an employment authorization are entitled to apply for the essential Social Insurance Number. This should be done at an HRDC office in one of the big cities, listed in the government pages of telephone directories. Health insurance regulations differ from province to province for foreign workers. For example new arrivals in Ontario cannot join the Ontario Health Insurance Plan (OHIP) for the first three months, during which they will need to buy private cover. Approved workers in Alberta are eligible to join the Alberta Health Care plan as long as they apply within 90 days of arrival in the province; ring 403-427-1432 for details.

Special Schemes

As mentioned, BUNAC (16 Bowling Green Lane, London EC1R 0QH; 020-7251 3472) offers three programmes: for students, gap year students and non-students. Work Canada is for both full-time tertiary level students aged 18-30 (departures mostly in summer) and for non-students aged 18-35, and Gap Canada is for candidates with a confirmed place at university who depart between October and December. Altogether about 1,500 students obtain Employment Authorizations through BUNAC, including finalists with proof that they will return to the UK. Early application is advised because of the quotas set by the Canadian government. The great majority of participants go to Canada without a pre-arranged job and spend their first week or two job-hunting.

Anyone intending to work in childcare, teaching or healthcare must undergo a medical examination with a designated doctor which will cost an estimated £130 and add up to five weeks to the application process. The BUNAC programme fee is £156, and insurance from £152 for four months. Participants can choose to travel on a BUNAC group flight (costing approximately £470 return to Toronto, £570 to the west coast) or independently which would be cheaper. Places are allocated on a first come, first served basis so early application is advantageous (from December). Departure for Canada can be anytime between the beginning of February and the end of the calendar year. Note that Gap Canada application forms are not available until May and the visa cannot be issued until after A level results are known and university offers accepted in August.

BUNAC distributes to Work Canada participants a free guide called *The Vital Info Handbook* which includes contact details for companies that have employed foreign students in the past. The majority of jobs are in hotels and tourist attractions in the Rockies, a beautiful part of the world in which to spend a summer. British university students have an edge over their North American counterparts in this sphere of employment since they don't have to return to their studies until mid to late September rather than the beginning of September.

Changing Worlds arranges paid hotel jobs for students in the two main Canadian ski resorts of Banff and Whistler. The six-month jobs start in November or March and cost £1,975 or £2,075 including airfares. Hotel staff are paid on average $9 an hour and will have $12 a day deducted for room and board. Details of the programme are available from Changing Worlds (Hodore Farm, Hartfield, East Sussex TN7 4AR; 01892 770000; www. changingworlds.co.uk).

Another gap year placement organisation offers a similar scheme. Gap Challenge (Black Arrow House, 2 Chandos Road, London NW10 6NF; 020-8728 7272; www.world-challenge.co.uk) places a number of British students between school and university in resort jobs in the Rockies both summer and winter. As with BUNAC, school leavers must have unconditional acceptance from a college or university. Note that when time is short, it is sometimes possible to obtain an Employment Authorization in person by queuing all day at the Canadian High Commission.

Overseas Working Holidays (OWH) which is part of the Flight Centre Travel Agency (Level 1, 51 Fife Rd, Kingston, Surrey KT1 1SF; 0845 344 0366; www.overseasworkingholidays. co.uk) offers a working holiday package for the summer. The programme fee of £349 includes access to scheduled job interviews in London in March for summer jobs lasting from May/June to October. Their partner tourist industry employers are located mainly in the Muskoka holiday region of Ontario, i.e. Deerhurst Resort, Clevelands House and Delawana Inn plus Fairmont Hotels (see section on Tourist Jobs below).

CIEE in the US (www.ciee.org) operates a student work exchange to Canada for American students and recent graduates for a maximum of six months starting year round. The application fee is US$350. You can also apply via a SWAP partner office in Fort Lauderdale (800-592-2887).

International Exchange Programmes in Australia liaise with the Canadian Consulate in Sydney to administer the Canada Working Holiday scheme for Australian nationals (www.iep.org.au/workcanada). Applications for the working holiday authorisation can be

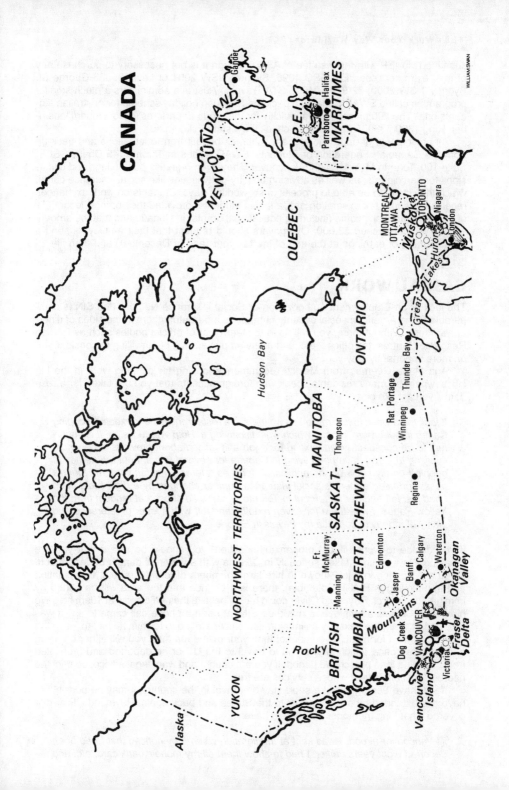

CANADA

NEWFOUNDLAND

Gander

P.E.I.
Halifax
Parrsboro
MARITIMES

QUEBEC

Hudson Bay

MONTREAL
OTTAWA
Muskoka
TORONTO
Niagara
L. Huron
London
Great Lakes

ONTARIO

MANITOBA

Rat Portage
Thunder Bay
Thompson
Winnipeg

SASKAT-
CHEWAN

NORTHWEST TERRITORIES

Regina

ALBERTA

Ft.
McMurray
Manning
Edmonton
Jasper
Banff
Calgary
Waterton

Rocky
Mountains

BRITISH
COLUMBIA

YUKON

Dog Creek
VANCOUVER
Victoria
Vancouver
Island
Fraser
Delta
Okanagan
Valley

Alaska

WILLIAM SWAN

submitted via IEP with the visa fee of A$170 though it is not necessary to purchase any of their extra services (IEP, GPO 4096, Sydney, NSW 2001 or Level 3, 333 George St, Sydney, NSW 2000; 02-9299 0400). STA Travel in Australia administers a much smaller programme called SWAP Canada, a packaged working holiday scheme for Australian students only. The 200 places sell out quickly for the group departures in November/December. Ring 1300 733035 for details or check www.statravel.com.au.

All participants of approved student schemes benefit from orientations and back-up from the Canadian Federation of Students' SWAP offices in Toronto (45 Charles St E, Suite 100, Toronto M4Y 1S2) and Vancouver. They even organise pub outings and excursions for participants, as well as advising on nitty-gritty issues like social insurance cards, which they claim to be able to process in six working days. Students on work exchanges receive the same tax exemption as Canadian students, provided they earn at least 90% of their total annual income (including educational grants) in Canada and that the amount earned will not exceed $3,000. Overpayers should request that their employers send a T4 statement of earnings at the end of the tax year (end of December) and then file an income tax return.

CASUAL WORK

The lack of an Employment Authorization or Social Insurance Number (the SIN is comparable to the American social security number) is a perpetual thorn in the sides of itinerant workers. Without them, you will have to steer clear of official bodies such as Human Resource Centres, tax offices, etc. and many employers will be unwilling to consider you or, more importantly, pay you.

Ana Maria Güemes from Mexico recommends looking for catering work in the big cities, where so many residents speak with foreign accents that you are taken for a resident if you act like one:

> It took me a week to find my job as waitress at a restaurant in the Yorkdale Shopping Centre in suburban Toronto, which was displaying a 'Help Wanted' sign. It is important to be confident when looking for a job and talking about previous experience, implying that you have been living in Canada for several years. I put the names of people I hardly knew on the application form as referees (my landlord, my friend's boss) and used a friend's social insurance number changed by a digit. I told them I had just left another restaurant in Toronto, a name I'd chosen at random from the Yellow Pages. I was there for seven months and left with a letter of reference and plenty of money to continue my travels in Europe.

If you decide to work without proper authorisation, you should be aware that you are breaking a law which is taken seriously in Canada with a very real danger of deportation. If you are working in a job known to hire large numbers of foreigners (e.g. tree-planting and fruit-picking in British Columbia), there is a chance that the area will be raided by immigration control. Raymond Oliver could hardly believe their efficiency: at 10am he gave his British Columbia employer a made-up SIN, at noon a phone call came to say it was fake and at 11am the next day an immigration officer arrived to tell him he had to leave the country within a fortnight. If you cannot fund your own departure, you will either be given a 'departure notice' which allows you to travel to the US or be deported and prohibited from returning for a prescribed period. If you are caught and want legal advice, contact the nearest legal aid lawyer whose services are free.

If you have been granted a short stay on arrival in the country, it may be possible to have this extended by crossing over to the States and back again. Raymond Oliver discovered what long memories computers have:

> At Vancouver airport, I was kept at Immigration when they noticed that I had been deported eight years earlier. I had to show them all my money, bank card, etc. and

the immigration officer even telephoned the friend I was planning to stay with (even though her sons were at the airport to meet me). I was only given a 17-day visa to cover the length of my holiday. Having said that, I went to Vancouver Island and by ship to Anacortes Island in Washington state. When I came back into Canada at Osoyoos, the immigration officer asked how long I wanted to stay. I could have stayed a year if I could prove I had the funds.

Prospective employers seldom ask to check the actual SIN card but will certainly ask for the number. Numbers issued to foreign workers begin with a 9, though this might prompt an employer to ask to see proof that your status is legitimate. The efficiency of Canadian bureaucracy means that few employers will conveniently forget about your lack of ID. For example a skilled baker from Manchester, who kept telling employers his number was in the post, was dismissed every couple of months when they became suspicious. Obliging employers might be prepared to pay your wages to a workmate who will hand over the cash, so that your name stays out of the books. A variation is to work under a Canadian friend's name and number and ask him or her to cash your pay cheques for you.

Anyone on shaky legal ground should keep a very low profile. It is rumoured that it is not difficult for people without permits to find winter work in ski resorts in the Rockies but not on the slopes. Brigitte Albrech worked as a tree planter in Prince George B.C. using a SIN number given to her by her employer. But because she was German, it was hard to blend in and the authorities somehow heard of her (after she had been working for three months) and sent her a request in writing to leave within six weeks or face a court hearing.

Wages are fairly good in Canada with statutory minimum wages, e.g. $7.45 per hour in Ontario (from February 2005) and $5-$7 in most of the other provinces except British Columbia where it is $8. Most working holiday makers (like most Canadian students) earn the minimum wage, with an average weekly wage of $300 and average accommodation costs of $115-$170 per week.

Iain Kemble earned well in excess of the average when he got a few days work ferrying buckets of cement to a crew of fence-builders in Alberta. Because this was a government contract (to prevent animals from being killed on the Icefield Parkway between Banff and Jasper), the wage was excellent. Iain concluded that after earning $450 in five days, he must have been the best paid illegal worker in the Banff Youth Hostel.

THE JOB HUNT

The job hunt is tougher in Canada than almost anywhere else; it takes BUNACers a discouraging average of nine days to find a job in Canada. Even Canadian students find it hard to get summer jobs and there will be stiff competition for most kinds of seasonal work. As well as having to cope with the inevitable rejections, remember the weather in summer is often very hot and humid. It will be necessary to look presentable, eager to please, positive and cheerful, even if the responses are negative or the employers rude. Adda Macchich recounts the job hunt that nearly saw her giving up:

I decided to settle in Ottawa one February and spent five weeks looking for work, with no luck. I filled out about 50 applications; the answer was invariably 'leave it with me; we'll get back to you' and they never did. You never even get to see the manager. I returned to Canada in June, hoping things had improved as the summer approached. I went to Niagara Falls expecting as many summer jobs as in Cape Cod but was disappointed at the total absence of Help Wanted signs or ads in the local paper, so I returned to Toronto. Spent a whole month on an unsuccessful job hunt, constantly being asked to submit resumés for menial jobs in restaurants and cafés and tramping from one end of town to the other merely to fill in more forms. The only available jobs were those paid on commission, which were advertised everywhere.

Not too surprisingly Niagara Falls was a dead loss since it has among the highest unemployment rates in the country. Just as Adda had decided it was time to fly back to London she stumbled across a commission-only ice cream vending job which was open to virtually anyone willing to man a stationary or bicycle-powered ice cream unit. At first the money wasn't very good but as the season picked up so did the sales. The most lucrative areas are around the base of the CN Tower, the Skydome and Harbourfront in downtown Toronto. On average, Adda earned between $20 and $60 daily and on good days $100+. The best times are during Caribana, the annual Caribbean festival at the end of July (when she made $200 in a single afternoon) and over the Labour Day weekend at the beginning of September. If interested, ask the vendors for the name and number of their boss. Toronto also has a fleet of rickshaws which employ runners. Matthew Shiel from the University of Swansea did it for the summer and at one point was saving an astonishing C$1,000 a week. One company with rickshaws in Toronto, Kingston and Ottawa is Orient Express which operates between Easter and September (416-410 7433; hoibak@newdirectionmedia.ca; www.rickshaws.net). Runners must rent the rickshaw from the company and work as independent contractors.

Downtown Toronto is the favourite stomping group for job-seekers since it is bursting with restaurants, cafés and shops with high staff turnover. According to one gap year traveller's personal website:

With only two nights accommodation provided by BUNAC in a local youth hostel and no job, the whole initial experience proved to be somewhat daunting. As luck would have it, our small party of five soon all secured jobs in a restaurant in downtown Toronto, at the Marche Mövenpick at the corner of Bay and Wellington. Each of us took on different roles, mine being that of 'Marche Guide' (which simply meant I seated customers) in this 750-person capacity self-service market-style restaurant. Within the restaurant I made many friends, which was fairly easy to do, since I was one amongst a staff of 250.

Employment enquiries can be addressed to Mövenpick on 416-366-8122/ hr@movenpickcanada.com.

As ever, youth hostel notice boards are recommended for information on jobs. According to Preeti Sharma, staff at the Edmonton Youth Hostel can advise on local work opportunities (10647, 81 Ave Edmonton, Alberta T6E 1Y1). Only students with working holiday permits will be allowed to work in hostels. Note also that the Double You Internet Café & Job Shop in Banff was promising to help job-seekers in November 2004; it is located in the Wolf and Bear Mall next to the Lux Cinema (403-760-7650).

To illustrate the stringency of immigration regulations, even work-for-keep arrangements are difficult to find, as described by the Jericho Beach Youth Hostel in Vancouver (1515 Discovery St, Vancouver, B.C. V6R 4K5; 604-224-3208): *'Unfortunately, due to Canadian employment regulations, we are unable to have foreign nationals participate in our work exchange programme at the hostel (two hours work in exchange for a free overnight). We do have an employment board at the hostel where we post notices from local companies and individuals offering employment. In addition, the front desk staff are a valuable resource for finding employment in the city.'*

In addition to Vancouver, the best cities to look for work are Toronto, Calgary and Edmonton. Jobs for sales staff are advertised wherever you go in Canada. One of the easiest ways to get a job is to apply to branches of European companies like the Body Shop and Gap. Tanufa Kotecha joined BUNAC's Work Canada programme and quickly learned that Canadian selling techniques are just as aggressive as American ones: *'I landed a job within a week in Toronto working in a French Canadian clothing store. In my store as soon as a customer walked in, they had to be greeted by a 'sales associate' within 15 seconds! The North American way of selling is pushy and upfront, but it does get results. One must have confidence to sell.'* Almost all shop jobs of this kind pay the minimum wage.

Selling in a shop is too high profile for people without permits, but door-to-door and telephone selling are possible and once again your British accent should work in your favour as it did for Helen Welch in Barrie Ontario when she was hired to persuade people to buy photographic portraits of themselves. This was working well until the last day of May when a freak tornado hit Barrie and the people whom she had been telephoning suddenly didn't have any walls left on which to hang their pictures. So she was forced to move to Toronto in her quest for a roof over her head.

TOURISM

Newspapers are always worth scouring such as the *Toronto Sun*, *Vancouver Sun*, *Province*, *Westender* and *Calgary Herald* which all contain job adverts, especially for dishwashers, waiting and bar staff. Free newspapers like the *Vancouver Courier* are also promising.

The Rocky Mountain resorts of Banff, Jasper, Lake Louise, Sunshine Mountain and Waterton are among the best places to try both summer and winter. Banff seems to absorb the largest number of foreign workers as catering and chamber staff, trail-cutters, etc. It is an expensive town in which to job-hunt but if you are prepared to walk you can find free campsites out of town and up the mountainsides. The huge Banff Springs Hotel alone employs 900 people, as do its sister hotels in the Fairmont group of luxury hotels (Chateau Lake Louise and Jasper Park Lodge). The Fairmont Group's website describes its recruitment needs (www.fairmont.com). Also try Lake Louise Inn, Inns of Banff Park, Banff International Hotel and Athabasca Hotel in Jasper. The standard wage at these hotels is $1-$1.50 an hour higher than the provincial minimum wage of $5.90. During the height of the season there may be very little time off. Employers are permitted to deduct $2.60 a day for staff accommodation plus $2 a meal.

One traveller to Western Canada reported:

> While on holiday in Banff, I met a lot of Australians and Britons staying at the youth hostel. All of them were just on holiday visas, and all of them had found work in the height of the tourist season. I was offered hotel work. There is a lot of work to be had in Canada and men in particular would have no trouble supporting themselves. Canadians are very warm towards foreigners and employers are generally prepared to risk hiring casuals 'black' if they can't get through the red tape. Wages are very good for this type of work.

Tourist industry jobs in the cities will be hard to find out of season as 18 year old Eric Lécuyer from Montréal found one autumn, proving yet again that word of mouth can be more productive than the official channels:

> Sadly I was not able to go to France, so I packed my hopes and dreams and left for Victoria. In the first week I toured all possible employment centres and always was told: 'it is going to be very hard to find any kind of job in the low season for tourism'. Not very motivating…in fact I gave up in the middle of the second week. Fortunately I met Manuel in the hostel's TV room, a Mexican guy that had just got hired by a window cleaning company. He told me to come with him to work on the next Monday and to my great surprise I was hired.

Ski Resorts

Ski resorts throughout Canada create a great number of seasonal employment vacancies which can't be filled by Canadian students since they're all studying. Unless you have an employment authorisation, your chances of picking up anything apart from very casual jobs like snow-shovelling and babysitting are minimal. As is the case throughout the world, affordable accommodation is in very short supply in the main ski resorts. Most of the accommodation in ski towns is full by October, well in advance of the start of the season. Two reasonably priced places to stay in Whistler are Shoestring Lodge and UBC Lodge.

The main ski resorts in western Canada are Banff/Lake Louise and Whistler/Black-comb. For Banff, consider Sunshine Village Resort which employs 300 staff, many of whom are provided with basic accommodation. Their website www.sunshinevillage.com has lots of useful information for prospective staff including dates of hiring clinics held at Banff International Hostel in late October. You can contact the Human Resources department for details at PO Box 1510, Banff, Alberta T1L 1J5 (403-762-6546; sunshineHR@skibanff.com).

Moving west to the Pacific, the contact address for the Whistler/Blackcomb Resort is 4545 Blackcomb Way, Whistler, B.C. V0N 1B4 (604-938-7366). Intrawest is the company that runs the ski operations at Whistler (as well as many other North American ski resorts). The website www.whistlerblackcomb.com/employment also gives dates of the annual recruiting fair and allows you to apply online; alternatively you can ring the jobline on 604-938-7367. A large number of workers leave after the Christmas rush so it is possible to get a job once the season begins even if you haven't lined anything up at the main hiring time of October/November.

A few jobs are available with UK ski tour operators though most are looking for staff who are at least 20, like the Specialist Holidays Group (overseasrecruitment@s-h-g.co.uk; www.shgjobs.co.uk) which recruits for Crystal Holidays, Thomson Ski & Lakes and Simply Travel among others; Skitopia/TJM (40 Lemon St, Truro, Cornwall TR1 2NS; 01872 272767; www.skitopia.com); Inghams Travel (10-18 Putney Hill, London SW15 6AX; www.inghams.co.uk) and Venture Abroad (Rayburn House, Parcel Terrace, Derby DE1 1LY; www.ventureabroad.co.uk) which hires reps to guide youth groups in Canada.

James Gillespie spent the winter and summer of his gap year working in Whistler. After taking the beautiful train ride from Vancouver, it soon became clear that getting a place to stay would be a major problem. But soon he had a job as a ticket validator which came with a free ski pass and subsidised accommodation: *'It was an excellent job and, although sometimes mundane, it was often livened up by violent and abusive skiers trying to get on the lift for free. Going there was the best thing I've ever done and I hope to be living there permanently eventually. I came home with a diary full of experiences, a face full of smiles, a bag full of dirty washing and pockets full of... well nothing actually. I was in debt, but it was worth it.'*

Jennie Cox from Derbyshire was unsure about what she wanted to do at the end of her degree at Durham University. After deciding to take a year out, she applied to Gap Challenge in October, attended a two-day selection course in December, completed a skills training course the following July and left for Canada in September.

On her return Jennie Cox described her seven months away:
I always wanted to go to Canada and had heard much about the country from friends and family. It's renowned for its friendly people; and Banff, in particular, looked beautiful. I was especially keen to ski and snowboard which influenced my decision. My placement involved housekeeping at Banff Park Lodge and general room cleaning, making beds etc. Overall I had an amazing time in Canada, and I certainly couldn't have asked for a more beautiful placement than the one I had in Banff. To wake up to vast snow-capped mountains each morning was such a luxury, that we had to be careful not to take it for granted. At times, of course, the work could be hard and exhausting, but you had to remind yourself why you were there: young friendly people to meet, lots of places to visit and days up on the slopes snowboarding, topped off by a pint of Canadian lager at night – who could ask for more? I've come back feeling relaxed, happy and refreshed and full of some great memories. Now I just have to find a job.

Applications for work in Ontario resorts like Blue Mountain near Collingwood (RR3, Collingwood, Ontario L9Y 3Z2; fax 705-444-1751; www.bluemountain.ca/employment.htm) are normally considered in November, whereas the deadline is somewhat earlier for work in western resorts since the season starts earlier. Blue Mountain employs up to 700 staff for the season which is running on full steam from Christmas to the March break. If considering ski resorts in Québec like Mount Tremblant, a knowledge of French is necessary.

Other popular holiday areas (summer more than winter) are the Muskoka District of Ontario centred on the town of Huntsville and the shores of the Great Lakes, particularly Lake Huron. Since most of the holiday job recruitment in Ontario is done through Canadian universities, and the resorts are so widely scattered that asking door to door is impracticable, it is advisable to concentrate your efforts in the west.

University Towns

Working out of a university setting, even if you're not a student, can provide a useful framework for making contacts and getting by. You might start by checking the university websites of universities like McGill in Montreal or Dalhousie in Halifax. Living in a university town and becoming involved in the life of a university often leads to a range of casual work opportunities. Almost all Canadian students hold part-time jobs to help fund their education and you may inherit this type of job when they leave university or temporarily while they go away for the vacations. Chances are good too that you will be able to find a cheap student house to live in especially if you arrive in the second semester when some students fall by the wayside.

Ann Sommerville stayed in Canada for four years altogether, mostly in the industrial city of Hamilton (near Niagara Falls) where McMaster University is located. She pieced together a living from a large variety of casual jobs, including part-time waitressing and washing up, bar work in the campus bar, babysitting and occasional house cleaning (which was easy to get through private advertising), essay typing (especially in December and March as terms draw to an end), and assisting at academic conferences, e.g. working a slide projector, manning a bookstall. Tele-marketing employs armies of people especially any who speak both French and English. A glance at the *Journal de Montréal* under the heading 'Emplois Divers' (Odd Jobs) will usually turn up between five and twenty telemarketing ads of possible interest to French speakers (www.vitevitevite.com).

Clinical research is often carried out in university towns by university medical departments and teaching hospitals. The website www.centerwatch.com gives easy-to-use links to major research centres in Canada such as the Clinical Research Centre at the McGill University Health Centre (514-934-1934; muhc.crc@mcgill.ca), the Queen Elizabeth II Health Sciences Centre in Halifax (902-473-8448) and Hill Top Research in Winnipeg (204-453-1835).

Universities can be found in the following Ontario towns: Toronto (two), Hamilton, St. Catharines, Waterloo (two), London, Windsor, Kingston, Peterborough, Ottawa (two), Sudbury and Thunder Bay as well as in the capitals and the biggest cities in all the other provinces.

Tree-Planting

The archetype of the working Canadian is the lumberjack. Nowadays there are fewer jobs for tree-choppers than tree-planters. In areas which have been logged or burnt, forestry officials are encouraging massive reforestation and every March planting contractors begin to recruit crews for the season which begins in April. The payment is piece work usually about 10-12 cents per tree though higher when the terrain is steep or uncleared. Rates are best in British Columbia and worst in Ontario. Novices can usually earn $80-$100 a day after a few weeks' practice. In some cases 'rookies' are earning more than $100 though you usually have to have done a few seasons before you're earning $150-$200 a day. A deduction is made for camp expenses, normally about $20 a day. You will need a waterproof tent and work clothes including boots and waterproofs. Many firms do not lend out the equipment, so the cost of shovels and bags (which will run to between $200 and $600) are deducted from your wages. The internet is a goldmine of insiders' information with extensive listings of companies and planters' comments on them; see www.canadiantreeplanting.com.

Prince George is an important centre for tree-planting. While travelling in Mexico on annual leave from her job in Germany, Brigitte Albrech met up with a van full of French Canadians who were heading for Prince George to plant trees, and decided to follow them rather than return to her job. She provided the names of a couple of companies: Bugbusters (www.bugbusters.ca) and Folklore Contracting; others are on the government's list of contractors (www.for.gov.bc.ca/hfp/planting/contract.htm).

Dates are uncertain due to weather. There is a spring and a summer season with two to four weeks in between. Some B.C. contractors start as early as late March and finish in August, though others don't begin until early May. Around Fort Frances and Thunder Bay in Ontario, the season is shorter, late April until the first week of July. An average season consists of 50 days of work.

Although Brigitte Albrech agrees that the work is hard and the hours long, she greatly enjoyed the team spirit and solved a few problems she didn't know she had. Chris Harrington paints a fairly negative picture (while concluding that he had a great time):

> Tree-planting itself consists of a ten-hour day starting about 6am, though overtime is available to masochists. This is awful work, make no mistake. The job is monotonous and weather conditions can be appalling (snow in June!). Coupled with the bugs, this can lead you to question your sanity. One of the worst aspects is 'down time' which occurs regularly between contracts, where you will find yourself hanging around expensive motels with no idea when and if you will be working again. How much you earn depends on how well you can motivate yourself. Not easy when you hate the job, it's been raining for a week, you are half way up a near vertical mountain and you've got bags full of trees which you can't find a suitable planting spot for.

Kevin Vincent and his brother both got jobs in the Slocan Valley in B.C. and disagree that tree-planting is one of the most miserable jobs in the world, which may have something to do with the fact that, in his first season, Kev's brother saved thousands of dollars in just two months:

> Tree planting is a job which can become a traveller's dream. It is a hard job, but not as hard as people say, no harder than construction work or heavy farm work. The food is great (sometimes outrageous) and camp life is very sociable with people playing music, etc. Whole families with babysitters come along. The money is good, there's no doubt about that. If camping out in Canada's forests and living a real healthy lifestyle for three or four months appeals, plus earning top wages, this is for you.

FRUIT PICKING

British Columbia

The fruit-growing industry of Western Canada takes place in decidedly more congenial surroundings. The beautiful Okanagan Valley of British Columbia is tucked away between two mountain ranges in the interior of British Columbia and supports 26,000 acres of orchards. The Valley stretches north from the American border at Osoyoos for over 200km to Armstrong. Cherries, peaches, plums, pears, apricots, grapes and apples are all grown in the Valley, with a concentration of soft fruits in the south and hard fruits (apples, pears) in the north. All of these must be picked by hand. The harvesting dates vary slightly from area to area, possibly as much as a fortnight or so earlier in Osoyoos than in Armstrong. A useful website is www.island.net/awpb/emop/harvest2.html entitled Harvest Information and Schedule for Okanagan and Kootenay Regions.

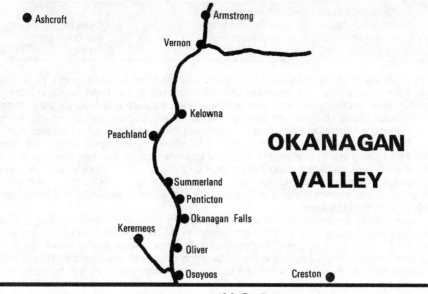

Anyone interested in summer seasonal employment should register with the Agricultural Labour Pool which runs a centralised province-wide placement service from its office in Abbotsford near Vancouver: Agricultural Labour Pool, No. 106, 2669 Langdon St, Abbotsford, B.C. V2T 3L3 (604-855-7281; info@agri-labourpool.com; www.agri-labourpool.com/jobseekers/alerts). Another valuable source of information in the Okanagan Valley is the Casual Labour Co-ordinator working at the Ki-Low-Na Friendship Society (442 Leon Ave, Kelowna, B.C. V1Y 6J3; 250-763-4905; marvbaker@shawcable.com). Lists of orchardists seeking workers are displayed in this office as requests come in; contact details of local farmers are not given out until there is a vacancy. The Society is a non-profit organisation working with and for First Nations people but their advice is available to anyone.

The harvests in Kelowna, a town approximately in the centre of the Valley take place at the times given in the chart below.

FRUIT HARVESTS IN BRITISH COLUMBIA		
Species of Fruit	**Approximate starting date**	**Approximate duration**
cherries	June 25	through July
apricots	mid-July	approx. 3 weeks
Vee peaches	August 5	2 or 3 weeks
Elberta peaches	August 28	2 or 3 weeks
Red haven peaches	July 20	6 weeks
Prune plums	mid-August	till mid-September
Bartlet pears	August 12	Sep/early Oct
Anjou pears	late September	October
Macintosh apples	early September	3-4 weeks
Spartan apples	late September	3-4 weeks
Newton apples	late October/November	3-4 weeks
Winesap apples	late October	3-4 weeks
Golden delicious apples	September	3-4 weeks

Red delicious apples	September	3-4 weeks
Rome beauty apples	September	3-4 weeks
Fuji apples	September	3 weeks
grapes	September 8	6 weeks

The Agricultural Labour Pool has offices in Penticton, Oliver and other towns. Of course you have to have legal status to make use of this service. As has been mentioned, immigration raids are frequent and merciless in this area, because it attracts so many illegal workers. Of course students with Employment Authorizations may want to consider trying for a job in the Okanagan, so here is more detailed information about the harvests.

Picking jobs are assigned by the Labour Pool office on a first come first served basis (all things being equal) and so it is important to arrive early in the day. Sometimes 100 hopeful job-seekers have gathered at the door by 7am. When the office is less busy, job-seekers are required to register, giving their name, social insurance number and contact address. Some attempt is made to screen applicants to avoid sending out a picker who has caused trouble elsewhere.

Iain Kemble recommends avoiding the employment office and instead hanging around the local fruit packing shed which all the farmers in the area visit at least once a day and asking for work as they arrive. Professional migrant pickers (many of whom are from Quebec) begin with the cherries in the south of the valley and move up the valley to pick only the peak cherries. Then they come south again to work the apricots in the same way and so on. The current going piece work rate for cherries is 20.5 cents per pound.

Almost all fruit-picking is paid piece work which can be lucrative, if gruelling in temperatures of 35°C. In order to make a lot of money you can't be afraid of heights, though most picking of soft fruit can be done from an 8ft ladder. The rate at present is about $16.50-$17.50 for half a bin. Inexperienced pickers usually start by earning not much more than $50 a day whereas the pros touch $200. Most people's wages are paid directly into a bank account, which is a further difficulty for casual workers without proper papers.

Apples are the Okanagan's most famous export product. There is continuous picking of one variety or another from mid-August to the end of October. Apple-picking can be slow and poorly paid. A basket is worn at the front of the body and this becomes very heavy as it fills up. Experience is not so important for the apple harvest, though if you confess to having none you may be given a job picking up windfalls for the provincial minimum wage of $8. Especially towards the end of the harvest when all the students have returned to university (approximately mid-September) and the weather is getting colder, the farmers begin to take almost anyone. Although most pickers do not live locally, not many farmers provide accommodation.

Raspberry, blueberry and cranberry picking and pruning take place nearer Vancouver in Richmond, Chilliwack, Abbotsford, Aldergrove and Langley between June and August, though this work is notoriously badly paid. Every year, tales of mass exploitation of farm labourers emerge, though this is changing in a market where there are acute labour shortages and growers complain that they have to push up statutory piece work rates to attract workers. Recently British Columbia has joined the government's Seasonal Agricultural Worker's Program which allows them to bring in mainly Mexican workers for the harvest. They must pay them a minimum of $8 an hour which is usually more than the piece work rates being paid to locals.

The official piece work rates in 2004/5 were 32.4 cents per pound of strawberries, 36.2 for blueberries and 14.9 for brussels sprouts, and skilled pickers can pick 400-500 pounds of berries a day. Most growers do not provide accommodation and campsite charges are considerable relative to wages. There are pickers' huts but these are mainly occupied by Asian immigrants. A further problem is the controversy over pesticides that may harm skin. A trawl of the internet will result in directories of fruit farms (e.g. http://bcstrawberries.com/FarmList.php). To take just two examples, Driediger Farms in Langley (604-888-1685) employs an average of 150 pickers in the season to harvest blueberries, strawberries and raspberries, while Greywal Farm in Abbotsford (604-504-3836) employs 325 pickers between July and November (and advertises on www.pickingjobs.com).

Ontario

The micro-climate in the fertile Niagara region bordering Lake Ontario is excellent for growing peaches, pears, plums, grapes (mostly for wine) and cherries. But it has already been pointed out that Niagara is an employment black spot, and it will be difficult to get a decent job, even though there is no shortage of fruit needing to be picked. To meet farmers, it is a good idea to go to the Saturday farmers' market (around the corner from the employment office on Main Street in Niagara Falls). Paul Donut had a compelling reason to stay in the area because he wanted to stay with a girl he knew:

> Even here in Niagara I managed to find work. I called around all the local farms listed in the phone book and got a job picking cherries. The pay was dismal as the harvest was poor (most of the time was wasted throwing out the bad ones and being paid only for the baskets we filled with good cherries). However the farm was beautiful, my workmates, all Caribbean, were great fun. The peach harvest was somewhat better and after a couple of months I had enough money to look around for better paying work.

Paul says he could have found a better-paid job if he had had transport from town to the farm, but since he didn't he had to accept work with the only farmer who would pick him up.

Elsewhere in the province there is a major tomato harvest in south-western Ontario, centred around Chatham and Leamington (pronounced Leemington), which starts in mid-August and lasts for six to eight weeks. Other fruit and vegetable harvests take place around the province, especially in the counties bordering Lake Erie. End-of-season bonuses are commonly paid. Below is a chart of harvests.

FRUIT AND VEGETABLE HARVESTS IN ONTARIO

Crop	Part of Ontario	Dates of Harvest
Asparagus	Chatham, Aylmer, Tillsonburg, Delhi, Simcoe, Alliston	early May to mid-June
Strawberries	Chatham, Simcoe, St. Catharines, Hamilton, Cobourg, Trenton	early June to mid-July
Cucumbers	Windsor, Leamington, Chatham, Aylmer	mid-June to mid-Aug
Cherries (sweet)	Chatham, Niagara Falls, St. Catharines, Hamilton	early July
Cherries (tart)	Chatham, Simcoe, St. Catharines, Hamilton	late July
Raspberries	St. Catharines, Hamilton, Cobourg	mid-July to mid-Aug
Plums	St. Catharines, Hamilton	Aug/Sept
Peaches	Windsor, Leamington, Chatham, Simcoe, St. Catharines, Hamilton	mid-Aug to end Sept
Tomatoes	Windsor, Leamington, Chatham, Simcoe, Picton	mid-Aug to end Sept
Pears	Leamington, St. Catharines, Hamilton	early Sept to mid-Oct
Apples	Leamington, Simcoe, Hamilton, Owen Sound, Cobourg, Trenton, Picton	early Sept to end Oct
Grapes	Niagara Falls, St. Catharines, Hamilton	mid-Sept to end Oct

Another seasonal agricultural job which needs to be done on Southern Ontario farms is detassling seed corn. During three or four weeks in July, people are needed for this work in the Chatham area. Busloads of students are brought in from cities 60 miles away, so if you were on the spot you would have a chance although local unemployment is high in this county.

The Maritimes

High unemployment in some Maritime areas has driven many locals west in search of employment. However if you are travelling in the eastern provinces in August/September, you might try to find paid work picking or 'raking' blueberries in the Nova Scotia towns of Parrsboro, Minudie, Amherst or Pugwash and elsewhere. Earlier in the summer (i.e. mid-June to mid-July), strawberry picking is available. In the autumn you can also look for work picking apples. Head for the Bay of Fundy coast of Nova Scotia around Annapolis Royal, Bridgetown and Middleton. If you're lucky, fruit picking wages will be paid cash-in-hand.

Another seasonal job which you can try for is fish processing as described by Stephen Boss, himself a Nova Scotian:

I am financing my round-the-world travels by working in a fish plant during the her-ring season (mid to late August until the end of September). This job consists of cutting open herring for the roe which is inspected and collected by Japanese techni-cians to be made into caviare. Cutters make good money. I was successful working for two fisheries in the town of Meteghan.

Stephen worked for I. Deveau Fisheries (902-645-3036). The website www.fishroute.org lists the names and emails of fisheries in the Maritime provinces (and worldwide).

OTHER FARM WORK

If you are interested in working your way from farm to farm and want to meet Canadi-ans, you might consider volunteering for WWOOF-Canada (World Wide Opportunities on Organic Farms). You can find the WWOOF Canada application form on the website www.wwoof.ca; membership costs C$35 (cash) plus $5 postage which should be sent to John Vanden Heuvel, 4429 Carlson Road, Nelson, B.C. V1L 6X3; wwoofcan@shaw.ca. You will then be sent a booklet that lists more than 500 farms across Canada including descrip-tions of the farms. All volunteers must have valid tourist visas.

Anyone with a background in agriculture might profit by placing an advert in small town newspapers as an enterprising Australian Mark Newton did. While waiting for his job to start at the Biting Fly Institute in Winnipeg, Mark put an advert in the Stonewall Argus, a small town north of Winnipeg and fixed up two weeks of work with a pig farmer.

The other harvest in Ontario which has also been traditionally assisted by migrant workers is the tobacco harvest in Southern Ontario. But times have been tough for tobacco farmers for some years now, mainly due to federal anti-smoking policies, and in 2004 became tougher when the big tobacco companies decided to source their tobacco elsewhere to keep prices down. Some growers in and around the towns of Tillsonburg, Aylmer, Delhi (pronounced 'Dell-high') and Strathroy were recently predicting the death of their industry, so it is probably not worth looking for work in August in this area near London Ontario any more.

Ontario is not the only place where tobacco is grown in Canada. There are about 80 tobacco farms in the small island province of Prince Edward Island in eastern Canada. While hitching around the region in May, Iain Kemble learned that there had been urgent messages on the radio asking for 800 tobacco planters. He pretended to the lady in the Montague Employment Centre that he had a work permit and was promptly assigned to one of many local farmers of Belgian extraction. He worked in the massive greenhouses from 7am to 8pm bending over a conveyor belt picking out plants at the appropriate stage of maturity. For this back-breaking work, he was paid considerably more than the minimum wage. Good meals and bunkhouse accommodation were provided for about $6 a day. The season lasted about a month until late June.

CHILDCARE

Live-in nannies and mothers' helps are in great demand in Canadian cities. However domestic employment in Canada is governed by a number of carefully formulated and strictly enforced regulations. A detailed leaflet about the 'Live-in Caregiver Program' may be obtained from the Canadian High Commission (www.cic.gc.ca/english/pub/caregiver/index.html). Qualifying nannies must either have six months of full-time training in a related field (teaching, nursing, childcare) or 12 months experience in full-time paid employment as a nanny or mother's help within the previous three years, at least half of which must have been continuously for the same employer. The other main requirements are that the nanny must have completed secondary school, speak English or French, sign a contract with her employers for at least one year and live in with the employing family.

If you are eligible and have found an employer (possibly through an agency), you can apply for an Employment Authorization for Canada valid for one year and renewable once. There is a handling fee of C$150 (which must be submitted as a bank draft in Canadian funds). The procedure for getting an Authorization usually takes three to four months and will include a very strict medical examination by an appointed private doctor who will charge about £130. The Authorization will be valid for one employer, though it can be changed within Canada as long as your subsequent job is as a live-in child-carer. At the end of two years as a care-giver, it is possible to apply for 'landed residency' i.e. permanent residence.

Working as a nanny or mother's help in Canada has more status attached to it than au pairing in Europe, and the conditions of work reflect this. The federal and provincial governments set out guidelines for hours, time off, holidays, minimum salary and deductions. For example nannies can expect to earn no less than the provincial minimum wage (given above) and in many cases above this rate. From a monthly salary of (roughly) $1,500, you might lose a fifth in taxes and up to the permitted maximum for room and board which in Ontario is $85.25 per week. That means that net wages are $900-$1,000 per month based on a 44-hour week.

A search of the internet will take you to some Canadian agencies though some are more experienced in bringing in nannies from countries like the Philippines, Hong Kong and Slovakia rather than the UK. In all cases, nannies must satisfy the government's Live-in Caregiver requirements. Here is a small selection of agencies:

ABC Nannies Agency, 11420 95A Ave, Delta, B.C. V4C 3V5 (604-581-1018; www.abcnannies.ca). Placements across Canada with offices in Calgary and Toronto as well as Vancouver.

Canadian Work Opportunities/Au Pair Canada, North York Square, 45 Sheppard Ave East, Suite 900, Toronto M2N 5W9 (416-590-7429; www.aupair.ca). Also place camp counsellors as well as nannies and au pairs.

Care Solutions Inc., 1055 Taylor Way, West Vancouver, B.C. V7T 2K2 (1-877-925-8474; www.absolutecarenanny.com).

International Nannies & Homecare Ltd. 515-119 West Pender St, Vancouver, B.C. V6B 1S5 (604-609-9925; www.internationalnannies.com). Other offices in Ontario and other provinces. Registered nannies mostly from Asia.

Nannies 4 You, 6701 Chisholm Ave, Unit 109, Halifax, N.S. B3L 2R7 (902-454-2544; www.alliedcaregivers.com). Job-seeking nannies must pay a non-refundable application fee of US$25.

Nanny Finders Directory Agency, 204-8055 Anderson Road, Richmond, B.C. V6Y 1S2 (604-272-1622; www.nannyfindersbc.com).

New Solutions Canada, 139 Grandview St. S, Oshawa, Ontario L1H 7C6 (905-725-9925; www.newsolutionscanada.com). Fee-charging immigration firm which assists prospective caregivers.

T&CS Canada, 62 Cassandra Boulevard, Unit 6, Toronto, Ont. M3A 1S6 (416-383-1856; www.tcscanadainc.com).

OptiMum Children & Nannies Inc., Vancouver, British Columbia (604-671-4965; info@opti-mum.com/ www.opti-mum.com). Nannies looking for work can add their details to a searchable internet database free of charge.

Scotia Personnel, Ltd., 6045 Cherry St, Halifax, N.S. B3H 2K4 (902-422-1455; www. scotia-personnel-ltd.com).

Selective Personnel International, 12 Irwin Avenue, Suite 300, Toronto, Ontario M4Y 1K9 (416-962-5133; www.selectivepersonnel.ca). Placement agency that recruits and markets caregivers, nannies, nurses and housekeepers from all over the world.

City newspapers are full of ads for nannies and babysitters, especially in August before the school term begins. When one reader replied to nannying adverts in the *Toronto Star,* she found that most were unwilling to employ her without papers. But by persevering she found a nannying and housekeeping job that allowed her to save a considerable amount.

VOLUNTEERING

Some interesting practical community projects are organised by Frontiers Foundation (419 Coxwell Ave, Toronto M4L 3B9; 416-690-3930; www.frontiersfoundation.ca) in low-income communities in Canada, including native communities in isolated northern areas. Some of the Operation Beaver projects consist of helping aboriginal people to build low-cost well-heated houses or community centres. Others take place on wilderness camps for Native children. More recently volunteers have been working in schools in the three northern territories (Yukon, Northwest Territory and Nunavut) tutoring in maths, science, English, music and drama. The accepted volunteer must commit to stay for at least five months from September or January and then only needs to obtain a medical certificate of fitness, fund a return flight to Toronto and get the appropriate volunteer visa. The Frontiers Foundation will pay all food, accommodation, travel and insurance expenses within Canada plus a modest allowance of $50 a week.

> **According to Sarah King, there was time left over to participate in some quintessentially Canadian backwoods activities:**
> *One of the great benefits about being a guest worker was that our activities became a focal point for the community. We played volleyball, helped break in wild horses, watched bears, made wild berry pies and rose-hip jelly, went camping, hunting, fishing and swimming, baked porcupine packed in clay, ate a delicacy of sweet and sour beaver tail, and all took up jogging around a local basketball park.*

Another contributor stumbled (or rather strode) across a different way to experience the Canadian bush. Obbe Verwer from Amsterdam spent part of the summer hiking in British Columbia:

> *After enjoying my visits to a couple of farms listed by WWOOF, I went on by myself to Vancouver Island. I set off to hike through the rainforest along the Clayoquot Valley Witness Trail. When I came to the trailhead, I met the trail boss who was working with a group of volunteers to build boardwalks at both ends of the trails. This was to enable more people to walk part of the trail which is important because this valley has to be saved from clearcut logging. I decided to join them. Actually you are supposed to go through the organising committee to become a volunteer worker but I just pitched my tent and joined on the spot.*
> *All the wood to build the boardwalk had to be carried into the trail, steps, stringers, nails and tools. We worked till 4pm, but it was not strict at all. Sometimes it was pretty hard, but it was fun. The forest impressed me more and more. The big trees, the berries, the mushrooms and the silence in the mist. It was just amazing. It was*

very satisfying to be helping to save this forest.

The Western Canada Wilderness Committee can be visited at 341 Water St in Vancouver (604-683-8220; volunteer@wildernesscommittee.org) though its postal address is 227 Abbott St, Vancouver V6B 2K7. Volunteers should bear in mind that while working in rainforests one is bound to get wet. The WCWC also needs people to work in roadside kiosks, selling T-shirts, etc. for fund-raising. These volunteers should expect a certain amount of hostility from local loggers.

Few international workcamps take place in Canada. One of the few organisations active in the field is in Québec, and the camps they arrange are bilingual French-English and for young people aged 16-25. The co-ordinating organisation that runs this International Exchange Program is Chantiers Jeunesse, 4545 avenue Pierre-de-Coubertin, CP 1000, Succursale M, Montréal, Québec H1V 3R2 (514-252-3015/1-800-361-2055; www.cj.qc.ca).

Latin America

Once the favourite stomping ground of adventurous North American travellers, South America has been gaining popularity among Britons and Europeans faster than almost any other regional destination. Many gap year students as well as older travellers are setting their sights on a trip to the Amazon or the Andes possibly in between a stint of teaching or volunteering.

Most Latin American nations do not need unskilled workers from abroad to perform the menial tasks associated with agriculture and industry. For every such job, there are several dozen natives willing to work for a pittance, and gringos (white westerners) will not be considered for such work. However, people who are bilingual in Spanish may find opportunities in the cities, especially bilingual secretaries. Because Britain has few colonial ties with Central and South America, there is a general cultural and economic orientation towards Uncle Sam which means that Americans tend to occupy many jobs rather than Britons. Apart from voluntary opportunities, the main sphere of employment in which foreign travellers have any prospect of gaining acceptance is the teaching of the English language.

TEACHING

Spanning 75 degrees of latitude, the mammoth continent of South America together with the Caribbean islands and the eight countries of Central America, offer a surprising range of teaching opportunities. All but Brazil have a majority of Spanish speakers and, as in Spain itself, there is a great demand for English teaching, from dusty towns on the Yucatan Peninsula of Mexico to Punta Arenas at the southern extremity of the continent, south of the Falkland Islands.

The countries of most interest to the travelling teacher are Mexico, Bolivia, Colombia,

Ecuador, Peru, Venezuela, Chile, Argentina and Brazil. Despite high levels of economic and often political uncertainty, demand for English language tuition continues to increase in the various kinds of institution engaged in promoting English, from elite cultural centres supported by the British and American governments to technical centres, from prestigious bilingual secondary schools to agencies which supply private tutors to businessmen. Experience is not always essential to land a teaching job on-the-spot. John Buckley, owner of a printing business in Blackpool, is just one traveller who was surprised at how welcome he was made to feel by a language school (in Brazil) when he had no TEFL training or experience:

> When I was in Brazil for Christmas and New Year, I thought I would go to the local English school to see what went on, armed with a bunch of roses for the teacher (luckily female) and a little knowledge of Portuguese. Before I knew it, I was teaching English, words, pronunciation, slang and English life in general. This carried on for a few days with the class getting bigger and bigger. I felt like an alien landed from Mars, but what a buzz. I have found my vocation in life and am now looking for a good TEFL training course.

After 20 years of corresponding with a pen friend in Brazil Lee Stewart finally made the journey from Northamptonshire to southern Brazil to meet her
I had no intention of working, as everyone had told me that it would not be possible to find work without speaking Portuguese. My friend works as a part-time teacher in Curitiba so I had an advantage. I approached CCLA, a very popular school in the city, and after only a five-minute chat I was offered part-time work for one or two evenings a week. The lessons comprised listening to adults having conversations in English while I waited for them to make mistakes and correct them. Teaching like this at least pays your youth hostel bills and gives you enough to eat, but you can't expect more than a few hours.

If you are going to take a more professional approach, make sure you bring your CV and qualifications with you, though not all schools will ask to see them. Obviously, you'll need a local contact number, so get yourself a mobile phone and then distribute your CV as widely as possible. When you drop your CV in, the school may ask you to take a written English test on the spot which is sometimes quite elaborate with a composition section. You may then be interviewed straightaway or the school may get in touch weeks later. If you pass the test, you may get invited to a group interview in which you will be asked to perform various tasks in small teams or pairs. If you are successful at this stage, you may then be asked to do a one- or two-week training course (usually unpaid). Only once this has been completed will you be offered work. Some of the smaller organisations will offer some hours if you pass their test and give a satisfactory demonstration lesson so try to bring some teaching materials with you.

You can also arrange jobs before arrival. Sheona Mckay managed to set up her own project as a volunteer teacher in Peru between March and June 2004 through a personal contact:

> Especially for people wanting to teach English, I think it is easy enough to find out the names of some schools in an area you are interested in working in. Then you can e-mail the school directly and hopefully come to an agreement with them. On the other hand maybe for first-time travellers the security of back-up from a placement organisation is necessary and worth the money. I wasn't expecting the school I taught in to be so well off and perhaps another time would try to find a poorer school where I would feel as though I had made a bigger difference to the children's education and lives.

More detailed information about teaching in Latin America can be found in the 2005 edition of my book *Teaching English Abroad* (£12.95 plus £1.50 postage from Vacation Work

Publications, or in libraries; $19.95 in the US).

The Job Hunt

In a land where baseball is a passion and US television enormously popular, American (and also Canadian) job-seekers have a distinct advantage. The whole continent is culturally and economically oriented towards the States and there is often a preference for the American accent and for American teaching materials and course books. On the other hand, many Britons have found themselves highly valued from Colombian universities to language agencies in Santiago. Business English is gaining ground throughout the region and anyone with a business background will have an edge over the competition.

The *Education & Training Group* of the British Council, 10 Spring Gardens, London SW1A 2BN; 020-7389 4596; assistants@britishcouncil.org) arranges for language assistants to work in a number of Latin American countries for an academic year. Applicants must be aged 20-30 with at least A Level Portuguese or Spanish. The level of placements and the nature of the duties are more suited to graduates than undergraduates. Application forms are available from October; the deadline is 1 December of the academic year preceding placement.

Some US-based organisations arrange for volunteers to teach in South and Central America. For example *Alliances Abroad* (1221 South Mopac Expressway, Suite 250, Austin, Texas 78746; 512-457-8062; www.allianceabroad.com) have voluntary teaching programmes in Brazil and Argentina while *World Endeavors* (2518 29th Avenue South, Minneapolis, MN 55406; 612-729-3400; www.worldendeavors.com) send paying volunteers to Costa Rica and Ecuador. For its 6 or 12-month Brazil programme, Alliances Abroad charges about $1,750-$2,000 though teachers are paid a monthly salary of $450. Unfortunately the Amity Volunteer Teachers Abroad programme (www.amity.org) has been put on hold for the present.

If you are looking for casual teaching work after arrival, check adverts in the English language press such as Mexico City's *The News*, the *Buenos Aires Herald* or the Caracas *Daily Journal*. English language bookshops are another possible source of teaching leads, for example the English Book Centre in Guayaquil (Ecuador), Books and Bits in Santiago and El Ateneo in Buenos Aires. Ask in expatriate bars and restaurants, check out any building claiming to be an 'English School' however dubious-looking, and in larger cities try deciphering the telephone directory for schools or agencies which might be able to use your services.

In Lima, Quito or Cusco visit the South American Explorers clubhouses (www.saexplorers.org; addresses in *Travel* chapter) which keep a list of language institutes and are staffed by expats who will be happy to share information with members. They also have a very valuable database called EVR (Explorer's Volunteer Resources) which members can access or non-members can consult (at least at the Cusco office at Choquechaca 188) if they donate $5 to a local charity. Many of the organisations listed will take on English teachers without a TEFL certification. SAE membership costs US$50 per year and residents outside the USA pay an additional US$10 for postage. Membership in the USA is via SAE at 126 Indian Creek Road, Ithaca, NY 14850 (607-277-0488/fax 607-277-6122).

The crucial factor in becoming accepted as an English teacher at a locally-run language school may not be your qualifications or your accent as much as your appearance. You must look as professionally turned out as teachers are expected to look.

Travellers working their way around the world are more likely to find a few hours of teaching here and there earning $3-$6 an hour, and have to patch together hours from various sources in order to make a living. If you have a good education, are carrying all your references and diplomas and are prepared to stay for an academic year, it may be possible to fix up a relatively lucrative contract.

Even when you land a paying job, be prepared for possible problems extracting your wages. Till Bruckner didn't manage to guard against the problem and offers this advice based on hard experience:

It's easy to find teaching work in these countries (Bolivia, Peru, Ecuador) but hard to get your pay if you're working for a cowboy outfit. Insist on weekly payment and make clear to the boss straight from the first day that it's against your culture to work if you're owed money. Make clear that you'll happily walk out the second you don't get paid. In Bolivia, I was stuck in a catch-22 where I had to go on working because if I stopped I'd definitely not get a penny of the money owed me (and boy was I broke). But if I continued, I might never get paid. The episode ended when the boss of the language school crammed a cool $60,000 into his briefcase and ran off to Argentina. I had a great time anyway.

Red Tape

Of course requirements vary from country to country but it is standard for work visas to be available only to teachers on long-term contracts after a vast array of documents has been gathered including notarised copies of teaching qualifications, police clearance, etc. This means that a high percentage of teachers work on tourist visas throughout Latin America. These must be kept up-to-date by applying for an extension from the immigration department or by crossing into and back from a neighbouring country. Occasionally extensions are available from the appropriate office, for example the 90-day visa given on entering Chile can in some cases be extended for a fee of $100. Shane Donavon, world traveller and editor of the admirable e-magazine *Jobs Abroad Bulletin* reported that in order to spend some months in Cusco Peru, he had to renew his visa stamp twice by crossing the border into Bolivia. Even though he had lost his Peruvian immigration card and the Bolivian officials sent him back, a well placed $5 bill fixed the problem with minimal inconvenience.

Mexico

The enormous demand for English teaching in Mexico increased dramatically in the wake of the North American Free Trade Agreement with the US and Canada. Companies of all descriptions provide language classes for their employees during all the waking hours of the week but especially in the early morning and at weekends. Roberta Wedge even managed to persuade a 'sleek head honcho in the state ferry service' that he needed private tuition during the siesta and that busy executives and other interested employees of a local company needed English lessons at the same time of day.

Demand is not confined to the big cities but exists in the remotest towns, at least one of which must remain nameless in order to preserve Roberta Wedge's dreams:

After doing a 'taster' ESL course in Vancouver, I set out for Nicaragua with a bus ticket to San Diego and $500 – no guide book, no travelling companion, no Spanish. On the way I fell in love with a town in Mexico (not for worlds would I reveal its name – I want to keep it in a pristine timewarp so I can hope to return) and decided to stay. I found a job by looking up all the language schools in the phonebook and walking around the city to find them. The problem was that many small businesses were not on the phone. So I kept my eye out for English school signs. I had semi-memorised a little speech in Spanish, 'I am a Canadian teacher of English. I love your town very much and want to work here. This is my CV...' Within two days I had a job at a one-man school.

Leaving England for the first time, Linda Harrison travelled on a one-way ticket straight from the picturesque Yorkshire town of Kirkbymoorside to the picturesque state of Michoacàn, and suffered severe culture shock. She and a Spanish-speaking friend had pre-arranged jobs at the Culturlingua Language Center (Morelos 636 Sur, C.P. 59680, Zamora, Michoacàn; tel/fax 351-512 3384; www.culturlingua.com) which has the advantage of offering its half dozen native speaker teachers accommodation. However it does not offer any pre-service training as Linda found out: *'The director told me that I might as well start teaching the day after I arrived. I stumbled into my first class with no experience, qualifications or books. Twelve expectant faces watched while I nervously talked about England. Twelve faces went blank when I mentioned soap operas.'*

The city of Monterrey held no appeal for Paul Donut when he was given the chance to teach there: *'A woman on the bus from Monterrey to Mazatlan gave me her phone number and said if I would teach her English, I could stay with her family in Monterrey and she would get me at least two paying students too. But even the prospect of a free bed and meals plus private students couldn't entice me back to a smog-ridden industrial city when I was heading for the Mexican Pacific Coast.'*

Mexico City is a thousand times more polluted, yet offers the best prospects for language teachers, some of which are advertised in the English language newspaper the *Mexico City News.* Rupert Baker answered an advert and was invited to attend a disconcertingly informal interview at a restaurant (to which he still wore his tie). He ended up working for six months.

Michael Tunison contacted half a dozen major teaching organisations from the Yellow Pages and was interviewed by Berlitz and Harmon Hall. The starting wage at the large chains will be the peso equivalent of US$400 though opportunities exist to make $700 in institutes specialising in executive language training.

The red tape situation in Mexico is bound to cause headaches. Visitors are not allowed to work or engage in any remunerative activity during a temporary visit. Established schools are not normally willing to contract people with only a tourist visa, unlike private institutes who often employ teachers on tourist visas and expect them to renew it every 90 days by crossing the border. Among the required documents for a work permit are a CV in Spanish, notarised TEFL and university certificates which have been certified by a Mexican consulate and, if you are already in Mexico, a valid tourist visa. Check the website www.mexicanconsulate.org.uk 'Visitors on a Profitable Trip'.

A volunteer placement organisation in the UK specialises in Mexico, placing people in teaching jobs as well as environmental and social projects. The £3,250 cost of a three-month placement with Outreach International (Bartlett's Farm, Hayes Rd, Compton Dundon, Somerset TA11 6PF; tel/fax 01458 274957; www.outreachinternational.co.uk) includes airfares, insurance and Spanish language course. Sarah Elengorn from Middlesex wanted to learn Spanish and so was attracted to a six-month project with Outreach International, working with street children in Puerto Vallarta, Mexico. She was the only female and the only non-Mexican on her placement at a shelter for street boys, so her Spanish (albeit street Spanish) improved very quickly. Sarah did some work on the streets but mainly worked at the shelter, organising, teaching (including safe sex) and playing with the boys. Six months after completing her project she returned to Mexico and now works part-time for Outreach International and part-time for the NGO that supports the street children.

Bolivia

Even the poorest of Latin American nations offers possibilities to EFL teachers, provided you are prepared to accept a low wage. In contrast to the standard hourly wage of $10-$20 in Europeanised cities like Rio de Janeira and Santiago, the wages paid by language schools in La Paz start at 16 bolivianos ($2). Because of the low salaries, many schools find it hard to attract teachers to Bolivia. However many travellers prefer the country to others in South America for cultural reasons, for its colourful social mix.

If you have a good standard of education, are carrying all your references and diplomas plus a CV translated into Spanish and are prepared to stay for an academic year, it is possible to fix up a teaching contract after arrival. Terms begin in early February and late September, so try to arrive a few weeks in advance of these dates. Look up the addresses of language schools in the *Yellow Pages,* deliver your application dossiers by hand to the directors and tell everyone what you are trying to do.

After graduating with a BA in Philosophy from Essex University, Jonathan Alderman chose Bolivia as the destination in which to become a volunteer teacher through Teaching & Projects Abroad.

He was so taken with Bolivia's second city ('it just *has* to be Cochabamba because of the perfect spring-like climate') that he obtained a TEFL Certificate in Spain and then returned to Bolivia to teach from January to October 2004:

I first went to Cochabamba as a volunteer to give conversation classes in the city's public university, San Simon. Everything was organised for me by Teaching & Projects Abroad before I arrived, including accommodation and Spanish lessons. Such a gentle introduction was great for someone new to the city and to teaching. In the university it is easy to settle in and make friends very quickly.

That only lasted for a few months, but I was sufficiently taken with Cochabamba to want to go back. Before arriving, I had already fixed myself up with a job teaching at the Pan American English Center in Cochabamba, which was a genuinely enjoyable place to work because of the relaxed atmosphere. The couple who run it are very warm and friendly and often have the teachers stay in their own home. However, the pay is pretty low, even by Bolivian standards (about $2 an hour) and I was rarely paid on time. I quickly became fed up with this and decided to leave after less than three months, despite enjoying the teaching. I wasn't breaking any contract, as there was none.

After I had explored South America for a while, I came back to Cochabamba and took a job in another institute, El Britanico Boliviano de Cultura (BBC) which paid $3.50 an hour (and paid on time). I taught mostly adults in the evenings, rather than kids and was lucky to get some daytime one-to-one classes through the school.

Contact details for the two schools at which Jonathan Alderman worked are Pan American English Center, Calle Beni No. 563, La Recoleta, Cochabamba (paec@supernet.com.bo) and BBC, Calle Espana No. 171, Cochabamba (043-422 0936; bbcbol@entelnet.com. bo).

The biggest language school in the country is the Centro Boliviano Americano (www. cba.com.bo) which has four locations in La Paz and schools in other cities like Sucre and Santa Cruz. Diana Maisel turned down a job offer here in favour of a more attractive one from the more relaxed Pan American English Center, Avenida 16 de Julio 1490, Edificio Avenida, 7° piso, Casilla 5244, La Paz (tel/fax 02-340796).

Brazil

The appetite for English has always been massive in Brazil though the country does well at producing its own highly qualified English language teachers. But there is always room for native speakers, as reported by Jon Cotterill (now resident in the country and working as a football commentator), even if long stay teachers inevitably come up against visa problems:

I first visited Brazil in 1995 but have been living here in São Paulo since September 2001. I am a qualified and experienced teacher (and a native speaker) and, as such, there are many opportunities for someone like me here. However, on a tourist visa, the maximum you'll be able to stay is six months. After three months, you will either have to leave the country or get an extension for your visa from the Federal Police. If you're coming to Brazil hoping to get a work visa, my advice is forget it. On your arrival, you may find that some organisations offer to apply for a work visa for you. The offer may be genuine (it happened to me a few times) but then the school discovers what's involved and the offer goes no further. If you want to stay here any longer than six months, your only viable option is to get married to a Brazilian, which is what I did.

In addition to recommending the Sunday edition of the newspaper *Folha de São Paulo*,

Jon has compiled a list of websites of potential employers in São Paulo: www.challenges. com.br; www.sevenidiomas.com.br; www.stgiles.com.br; www.welsys.com.br; and www. wizard.com.br/sub_sitewizard/escolas.htm.

Rates of pay for qualified and experienced teachers vary from R$12 ($4.50) an hour for classroom teaching to R$25 working for language agencies that will send you to companies like IBM. The majority of teaching takes place from Monday to Saturday from 7-9.30am and 6-9.30pm though you may be able to pick up a few hours in the daytime.

Chile

Unlike the economy of most other South American nations, Chile's economy is flourishing with a low rate of unemployment. The market for English language teaching is very healthy, with about 30 major language schools in the capital Santiago alone. Short-term casual teaching is not well paid: non-contractual work starts at less than 4,000 pesos per hour but rises to 6,000 pesos. To find private clients, it may help to advertise. The best results are obtained by putting a small ad in *El Mercurio,* the leading quality daily. Other newspapers such as *La Epoca* and *La Tercera* have classified ads sections which will cost slightly less than *El Mercurio.* The free ads paper is called *El Rastro.* A useful option is to put up a small ad in a supermarket like Almac or Jumbo.

If you are offered a job before arrival, there are two ways to obtain the appropriate visa permit. Either your employer submits the application at the Ministry of Foreign Affairs in Chile (Direccion de Asuntos Consulares y de Imigracion, Bandera 46, Santiago) or you apply at the Chilean Consulate in your country of origin. You will need a signed and notarised work contract and a full medical report. If granted, the visa will be valid for one or two years. After that you may be eligible for a *visacion de residencia* which allows an unlimited stay.

If you arrive to look for work, you will need to apply for a Temporary Residents Visa (cost varies according to nationality), for which you will need a written, notarised contract. Applicants will be given a card allowing them to work legally while they are waiting for their documents to be processed. This usually takes around 2-3 months. If you are able to commit yourself for a year, your employer may be willing to help. Most teachers who stay for shorter periods do not bother trying to change their visa status knowing that the immigration authorities are much less likely to raid language institutes than they are hotels and restaurants where migrant Peruvians work.

The following schools are among the best known language schools in Santiago. Typically these schools offer a newcomer a few hours and will offer them a full timetable only after a probationary three months.

Berlitz, Av Pedro de Valdivia 2005, Providencia, Santiago (02-204 4018). Berlitz has a substantial establishment in Santiago but prefers to interview only candidates who already have a work permit. Branch also in Concepcion (berlitz-biobio@entelchile. net).

British English Centre, Av. Providencia 1308, p.2. Oficina D, Providencia, Santiago (02-235 3039). Prefer teachers who are fluent in Spanish.

Burford English Centre, Avda. Pedro de Valdivia 511, Providencia, Santiago (02-223 9357/274 4603; www.burford.cl). A small 'agency-type' institute which favours British English.

EF English First, Hernando de Aguirre 215, Providencia, Santiago (02-374 2180). Up to 30 teachers.

ELADI Instituto Professional, José M. Infante 927, Providencia, Santiago (02-251 0365).

Fischer English Institute, Cirujano Guzman 49, Providencia, Santiago (02-235 9812/235 6667). Teaches both on and off-site. Offers plenty of structure in planning lessons.

Impact English, Rosa O'Higgins 259, Las Condes, Santiago (02-211 1925). Reputed to offer high rates of pay.

Sam Marsalli, Av. Los Leones 1095, Providencia, Santiago (02-231 0652). Hires only North Americans on one-year contracts.

Tronwell S.A., Av. Apoquindo 4499, 3er Piso, Las Condes, Santiago (02-246 1040; www. tronwell.com).

Wall Street Institute, Av. Apoquindo 3502, Las Condes, Santiago (02-362 9700; wsichile@netline.cl).

Although Diana Maisel had a disappointing response when she sent her CV from England to various schools, she had much better results when she arrived in Santiago, helped no doubt by her Cambridge ELT Certificate. She started gradually with a few hours from several of the above companies and after two months was teaching up to 35 hours a week and saving a lot of money. Meanwhile a friend from the US with no TEFL background failed to persuade any language institute to hire her and so turned to waitressing instead.

Ecuador

Compared to its neighbours, Peru and Colombia, Ecuador represents an oasis of political stability with its currency not only pegged to the dollar but it actually is the US dollar. The demand for English thrives more than ever, particularly American English in the capital Quito and in the picturesque city and cultural centre of Cuenca in the southern Sierra. The majority of teaching is of university students and the business community whose classes are normally scheduled early in the morning (starting at 7am) to avoid the equatorial heat of the day and again in the late afternoon and evening. Many schools are owned and run by expatriates since there are few legal restrictions on foreigners running businesses.

Teaching wages have climbed back so that most teachers earn at least $3-$4 an hour and a handful earn $7. Quito is not as large and daunting a city as some other South American capitals and it should be easy to meet longer term expats who can help with advice on teaching. Damaris Carlisle had no trouble finding work when she arrived in Quito because she had the Cambridge TEFL Certificate. She ended up working at the South American Explorers Club (as it then was) in Quito. Here is a brief list of language schools in Ecuador:

Centro de Estudios Interamericanos (CEDEI), Casilla 597, Cuenca (07-283 9003; www.cedei.org).

EF English First, Catalina Aidaz 363 y Portugal, Quito (02-22 71 140).

Key Language Services, Alpallana 581 y Whymper, Quito (Casilla 17-07-9770); fax 02-222 0956; kls@hoy.net.

If you want to get away from commercial language schools in the cities, several worthwhile projects in Ecuador place volunteer teachers. The Genesis Volunteer Program in the coastal town of Bahía de Caráquez invites foreign travellers to pay $300 for a four-week stay teaching in one of four local schools to subsidise their homestay costs. Contact Vladir Villagran for details (PO Box 13-02-8, Bahía; 05-269 2400; www.bahiacity.com/volunteer). Another scheme whereby paying volunteers of all ages teach English, art, computing, etc. at rural schools is run by Voluntarios de Occidente (voccidente@hotmail.com; www.geocities.com/vdovolun).

Technically you shouldn't work on a tourist visa but there is little control. Britons are entitled to a stay of six months on a tourist visa whereas Americans can stay 90 days though both of these can sometimes be extended. A tourist visa cannot be changed into another kind of visa without leaving the country. Many teachers work on a student or cultural visa valid for one year.

Peru

The threat of terrorist activities has subsided and Peru is once again a mainstream destination. Lima has many language institutes, especially in the port area of Miraflores, many of which hire and pay a salary to native speakers. The other main cities offer good opportunities too like Arequipa, Trujillo, Nazca and Piura. Check the display adverts in the 'Seccion Empleos' of the Sunday edition of the main daily *El Comercio*. Among the most prestigious are the Instituto Cultural Peruano Norteamericano (ICPNA), the Instituto Cultural Peruano Britanico and the Instituto de Idiomas de la Universidad Catolica but many other less well known schools offer pay at the lower end of the spectrum, i.e. US$6 rather than US$20 an hour. Setting up as a freelance tutor in the capital is potentially lucrative.

James Gratton arrived in Lima looking forward to what had sounded like a dream job. He had contacted the institutes included on the list sent by the Peruvian Embassy in London and was contacted enthusiastically by one (on the strength of a certificate earned from a one-week intensive TEFL training course in London and nine months of living and teaching in Venezuela the year before.) Despite the job not living up to expectations (many of his employer's promises were not honoured), he concluded that the experience could be used as a stepping stone to better opportunities. When he put a cheap advertisement (written in English) in *El Comercio* he immediately signed up two private clients.

The town of Cusco is a favourite among travellers, many of whom settle down for an extended stay. Among the academies to try are ICPNA on Tullumayo St, Excel on Q'era St and Amauta on Procuradores St near the La Tertulia Café. According to Mónica Boza, a Peruvian traveller who lived in Cusco for five years, wages will be non-existent even if you do find work. She made many friends who had decided to stay in Cusco teaching English, and the best pay they got was an exchange of Spanish lessons. She goes on to say that good places to stay are the districts of San Blas (Saphi St, Ataud St, Carmen Bajo St) and Tahuantinsuyo, a 20-minute walk from the main square, where rooms can be rented for $100 a month, provided the landlords don't treat you like a wealthy gringo and try to cheat you. For tips on living and working, pick up the new English language *Cusco Weekly*.

Venezuela

A general strike and continuing opposition to the government of President Chavez have left the economy reeling and now is not the best time to be conducting a job hunt in Venezuela. Proximity to the US and the volume of business which is done with *El Norte* mean a preference for American accents and teaching materials.

Nick Branch from St. Albans investigated most of the schools and agencies in Venezuela several years ago and worked outside Caracas where the pay was substantially less than in the capital: *'Merida is very beautiful and a considerably more pleasant place to be than Caracas. The atmosphere and organisation of the institute where I worked were very good. But alas. As with all the English teaching institutes in Merida, the pay is very low. Merida is three times cheaper to live in than Caracas, but the salaries are 5-6 times lower.'*

Check adverts in Caracas' main English language organ, the *Daily Journal*. Most give only a phone number, but a few addresses are included. Surprisingly, opportunities for English teachers also exist on the popular resort island of Margarita.

Most people work on a tourist visa which is valid for two months but extendable to six. James Gratton describes the process of getting a work permit as a nightmare: *'On no account attempt to get one on your own, since this involves dealing with the DEX, a truly horrific organisation housed in what resembles a prison and with appalling disorganisation. Once they lost 3,000 passports which, it turned out, had been sold on the black market.'*

Central America

If you keep your ears open as you travel through Central America, you may come across opportunities to teach English, especially if you are prepared to do so as a volunteer. Salaries on offer may be pitiful but if you find a congenial spot on the 'gringo trail' (for example the lovely old colonial town of Antigua in Guatemala), you may decide to prolong your stay by helping the people you will inevitably meet who want to learn English.

As the wealthiest country in Central America, Costa Rica is sometimes referred to as the Switzerland of the region and there are plenty of private language academies in the capital San José. The school year runs from March 1st to December 1st. Temporary six-month renewable working visas are sometimes issued to teachers working for established employers like the Instituto Britanico (Apartado 8184, San José 1000; 506-225 0256; www.institutobritanico.co.cr). After deciding that she needed a complete change from Hounslow and an office job, Jane Roberts signed up for a CELTA course at International House in London and had to decide where she wanted to job-hunt:

I wanted to work in a hot Latin country. IH had said don't expect to get a job straight-away in your dream destination, but I have proved this wrong. I got the address of

Instituto Britanico (from your book!), emailed them my CV and a covering letter, within two weeks was offered a job and a couple of weeks later I was here in Costa Rica. The working conditions are fine with a very well equipped library, cassettes, all necessary equipment for the classroom, and free email and internet access (when it works). My students are very motivated, lovely to work with, keen to learn, really want to speak a lot. I have the greatest admiration for them as they often come after a hard day at work to a 3-hour lesson and put a lot into it. I have to ensure that it is as interesting as possible for them. At first I didn't have much spare time as I was a new teacher and worked hard to prepare my lessons. However I have made time to visit various places in Costa Rica, mountains, volcanoes, the beach when I had a long weekend. My advice is to smile, relax, be nice to people. I have not found any problems with Latin Machismo, no hassles with men. They love my accent but have not been pushy or offensive. Costa Rican people are so friendly and helpful. It's a very chilled country.

Jessica Crisp from Hertfordshire taught at a primary school in Cristo Rey, Belize through Gap Challenge:

I had wanted to go to a developing country where I could be useful to the community and preferably work with children. I did Spanish A-Level and was keen to use it while I was away. I stayed with a young family in an adobe (mud) and tin house which the father, Tacio, had constructed himself. We did have electricity for lights and a telephone and even a television but we had no running water. The bathroom was a large bucket of cold water in a small stone outhouse. My class consisted of fifteen enthusiastic 8-10 year olds with lots of energy which was great for games and acting. Each weekend my friend and I travelled to a different part of Belize to explore the beautiful landscapes and find out more about the country.

VOLUNTEERING

Short-term voluntary work projects are scattered over this vast continent, though the two easiest countries in which to find organised projects are Ecuador and Costa Rica. Many of the opportunities that become widely known are concerned with conservation (treated separately below) and charge a substantial fee. But an approach to almost any environmental, health or childcare non-governmental organisation (NGO becomes ONE in Spanish) might be greeted warmly, especially if the enquiry is made in Spanish. The better funded of these projects might even be able to offer accommodation and expenses.

The internet has made it much easier to unearth opportunities for volunteering, whether from one of the mainstream databases like *WorkingAbroad.com* (see the introductory *Volunteering* chapter) or from indigenous organisations. A specialist advisory service based in Brighton will tailor-make a list of voluntary projects in Latin America to which clients can apply directly; see *www.volunteerlatinamerica.com* (prices from £22). The excellent online guide to Ecuador *www.EcuadorExplorer.com* has listings and links to teaching and voluntary projects as well as what to do. Another good source of opportunities is on *www.volunteeringecuador.org*. In some cases a centralised placement service makes choosing a project much easier, though you will have to pay for the service as in the case of *Volunteer Bolivia* (www.volunteerbolivia.org) located in Cochabamba. They encourage their clients to sign up for a month of Spanish tuition while staying with a local family before becoming a volunteer; a combined language course, homestay and volunteer placement programme costs $1,150 for one month.

ProWorld Service Corps (264 East 10th St, No.5, New York, NY 10009; 877-733-7378; www.proworldsc.org) offers a range of internships lasting one to six months with aid agencies in Peru and Belize. The fee of $1,950/£1,150 includes Spanish tuition followed by placement with an NGO and lodgings for the first four weeks. In fact combining a Spanish language course, homestay and voluntary placement over two to six months is a route favoured by many.

Spanish language course providers and cultural exchange organisations can often arrange interesting volunteer programmes. Among the largest are the following:

Amerispan Unlimited, PO Box 58129, Philadelphia, PA 19102 (800-879-6640; info@amerispan.com). Specialist Spanish-language travel organisation with great expertise in arranging language courses, voluntary placements and internships throughout South and Central America.

Amigos de las Americas, 5618 Star Lane, Houston, TX 77057 (800-231-7796; www. amigoslink.org). Summer training programme for 700+ high school and college student volunteers (minimum age 16) mostly in community health projects in Central America (Mexico, Costa Rica, the Dominican Republic, Honduras, Nicaragua, Panama) and Paraguay. Participation fee is $3,650 including travel from the US. All volunteers must have studied Spanish at school or university and undergone training.

Adelante LLC, 601 Taper Dr., Seal Beach, CA 90740 (562-799-9133; www.adelanteabroad. com). Internships, volunteer placements, teaching abroad and semester/summer study opportunities from 1-12 months in Costa Rica (San José), Mexico (Oaxaca) and Chile (Vina del Mar/Valparaiso). Prices range from $1,600 for 1 month in Chile and Mexico to include language classes, various housing options and work assignment placement.

Cactus Worldwide Ltd. No 4, Clarence House, 30-31 North St, Brighton BN1 1EB (0845 130 4775; www.cactusenglish.com). Spanish language courses followed by voluntary placements. Short and long-term placements in fields of healthcare, education, social work and conservation in Peru, Guatemala, Mexico, Bolivia and Ecuador. Examples include working at a hatchery for Leatherback turtles on Guatemala's Pacific Coast, helping in an orphanage for girls in Cusco, Peru and teaching English in a school in Oaxaca, Mexico.

Caledonia Languages Abroad, The Clockhouse, Bonnington Mill, 72 Newhaven Road, Edinburgh EH6 5QG (0131-621 7721; www.caledonialanguages.co.uk). Educational consultancy which books individuals of any nationality onto voluntary work projects as well as language courses in Brazil, Costa Rica, Mexico, Argentina, Bolivia, Ecuador and Peru.

EIL, 287 Worcester Road, Malvern, Worcs. WR14 1AB (0800 018 4015; www.eiluk.org). Provides community service opportunities in Mexico, Costa Rica, Argentina, Chile and Ecuador of varying duration and with differing requirements. Sample price for Argentina teaching programme is £1,166 for 3 months.

Individual language schools often have links with local projects and can arrange for students of Spanish to attach themselves to projects that interest them. Typically Carisa Fey started her big trip round South America with a short language course in Quito which led to some voluntary work afterwards teaching knitting to street kids. For example the Equinoccial Spanish School in Quito (Reina Victoria 1325 y Lizardo Garcia; tel/fax 02-2564 488; www.ecuadorspanish.com) arranges volunteer positions throughout Ecuador (for ESS language school clients) in a variety of fields from ecological studies to community work. Similarly APF Languages in Quito (www.apf-languages.com) combine a programme of Spanish tuition at $5 an hour with homestays ($14 per day) and ecological or humanitarian volunteering. For candidates with advanced Spanish and a keen interest in the Amazon, APF can fix up minimum six-month jungle-guiding jobs. Mundo Verde Spanish School, Nueva Alta, 432-A Cusco, Peru; (+51-84 221287; www.mundoverdespanish. com) has links with a development project in the rainforest and with many other voluntary projects to which students can be assigned for no fee.

Development organisations that are active in more than one country in the region and with offices outside Latin America include:

AFS Intercultural Programmes, Leeming House, Vicar Lane, Leeds LS2 7JF (0113-242 6136; info-unitedkingdom@afs.org; www.afsuk.org). Community service programme lasting 6 months in range of Latin American countries for volunteers aged 18-35. Accommodation is arranged with host families. The cost for participating is £3,300 which covers return airfares, orientation, language training, medical insurance and local support network.

Alliances Abroad Group, 1221 South Mopac Expressway, Suite 250, Austin, Texas 78746 (512-457-8062; www.allianceabroad.com). Sends mainly Americans to Ecuador, Brazil, Argentina, Peru and Costa Rica (8 weeks to a year) to live with local families, learn Spanish or do some voluntary work as an English teacher, to work or intern with various industries, etc. Fees are normally about $1,200-$1,600 for three months plus homestay fees (e.g. $12 a day in Peru).

American Friends Service Committee, 1501 Cherry St, Philadelphia, Pennsylvania 19102-1479, USA (215-241-7295/fax 215-241-7026; mexicosummer@afsc.org). Quaker organisation that recruits Spanish-speaking volunteers aged 18-26 to participate in long-established scheme with Mexican partner organisation SEDEPAC. Summer scheme lasts seven weeks; volunteers mostly work on building or teaching projects (programme fee $1,250 plus travel expenses). Application deadline mid-March.

Amizade Volunteer Vacations, PO Box 110107, Pittsburgh, PA 15232 (888-973-4443; www.amizade.org). Projects lasting 2-4 weeks in Bolivia, 1-12 months in Jamaica and 2 weeks in Brazil. Varying fees.

Casa Alianza, c/o Jim Harnett, SJO 1039, PO Box 025216, Miami, FL 33102-5216 (volunteer@casa-alianza.org; www.casa-alianza.org). Volunteers work with street children in Mexico City, Guatemala City, Tegucigalpa and Managua for 6-12 months. Accommodation varies according to country e.g. $70 a month in Nicaragua but up to $200 in Honduras.

Foundation for Sustainable Development, 870 Market St, Suite 32, San Francisco, California 94102 (tel/fax 415-283-4873; www.fsdinternational.org). Summer and longer term internships in all areas of development in Bolivia, Peru, Ecuador, Argentina and Nicaragua (as well as Tanzania, Uganda, Kenya and India). Sample fees are $2,000 for 8 weeks (June/July) in Nicaragua and $2,650 for 9 weeks in Peru.

ICADS, Apartado 300-2050 San Pedro Montes de Oca, San José, Costa Rica (506-225 0508; info@icads.org; www.icadscr.com). The well regarded programmes of the Institute for Central American Development Studies combine study of the Spanish language and development issues with structured internships in Costa Rica and Nicaragua lasting a semester ($8,500) or a summer ($3,800).

ICYE: Inter-Cultural Youth Exchange, Latin American House, Kingsgate Place, London NW6 4TA (tel/fax 020-7681 0983; www.icye.co.uk). Volunteers aged 18-30 spend a year abroad with a host family and undertake voluntary work placements, for example in drug rehabilitation, protection of street children and ecological projects. Placements available in Bolivia, Brazil, Costa Rica, Honduras, Colombia and Mexico.

Latin Link STEP Programme, 175 Tower Bridge Road, London SE1 2AB (020-7939 9014; step.uk@latinlink.org; www.stepteams.org). Self-funded team-based building projects in Argentina, Brazil, Cuba, Ecuador, Mexico and Peru, for committed Christians only. Spring programme runs March to July (£2,450); summer programme for 7 weeks from July (fee £1,850).

Peace Brigades International, The Grayston Centre, 28 Charles Square, London N1 6HT (020-7324 4628; www.peacebrigades.org). Supplies volunteers to accompany individuals in Mexico, Colombia and Guatemala who are in danger of persecution for their politics or religion.

Youth Challenge International, 20 Maud St, Suite 305, Toronto, Ontario M5V 2M5, Canada (416-504-3370; www.yci.org). Teams of volunteers carry out community development projects lasting from 5 weeks to 3 months in Costa Rica and Guyana.

As you travel throughout the region you are bound to come across various charitable and voluntary organisations running orphanages, environmental projects and so on, some of which may be able to make temporary use of a willing volunteer. The Quaker-run service centre in Mexico City, *Casa de los Amigos,* has information on volunteering opportunities throughout Mexico and Central America for Spanish speakers able to commit for at least three months.The initial fee is $50 plus $25 per month to cover admin expenses. The Casa is at Ignacio Mariscal 132, 06030 Mexico, D.F., Mexico (055-5705-

0521; amigos@casadelosamigos.org) and provides simple accommodation for 70 pesos ($6) per night to people involved in volunteer projects.

Many worthwhile social projects rely on volunteers. One of the most famous and long-established is *Casa Guatemala*, an orphanage and attached backpackers' hostel which relies on travellers to carry out maintenance, cooking, building, organic gardening, teaching the children English, etc. They can use as many as 100 volunteers a year preferably for a minimum of three months. The orphanage office in Guatemala City is at 14th Calle 10-63, Zona 1, 01001 Guatemala (Apdo. Postal 5-75-A; 502-232-5517; casaguatemal@guate. net; www.casa-guatemala.org), while the orphanage itself is about five hours north of Guatemala City, a short boat ride from the town of Fronteras on the road to the Petén region. The director is Angelina de Galdamez who warns that volunteers should expect a certain amount of hardship. Volunteers must pay a non-refundable fee of $180 however long they intend to stay.

Almost any Spanish language school in Guatemala can help arrange a volunteer position. To find links to many of these language schools, visit www.xelapages.com/schools. htm. Casa Xelaju, Apartado Postal 302, Quetzaltenango, Guatemala (502-761-5954; www. casaxelaju.com) runs Spanish courses and refers clients to internships and voluntary work in Guatamala. The city of Quetzaltenango offers many opportunities to do volunteer work in the community. In exchange for a fee of $25 the language school Casa Xelaju (Postal 302, Quetzaltenango, Guatemala; 502-761-5954; www.casaxelaju.com) will search for a suitable position.

Also in Guatemala the American charity *The God's Child Project* (721 Memorial Highway, PO Box 1573, Bismarck, ND 58502-1573; www.godschild.org) provides an education for slum children in Antigua and uses short- and long-term volunteers; volunteers staying for two years receive free homestay accommodation; otherwise the cost is about $50 a day.

Another children's charity is TASK Brasil (Trust for Abandoned Street Kids) whose UK address is PO Box 4901, London SE16 3PP (020-7737 5545; www.taskbrasil.org.uk) or in the US ring 215-732-5985. They are looking for volunteers over 21 to work on the streets of Rio. Placements cost £1,200-£2,500. If you want to work with children in Belize, the YWCA accepts volunteers to help teach and organise sports and arts activities in the school that they run in the capital (Education Department, YWCA, 119 St. Thomas & Freetown Road, PO Box 158, Belize City; 022-44971). While researching the *Rough Guide to Belize*, Peter Eltringham visited the Y and saw that the volunteers were doing a wonderful job adding to the basic teaching of sports, music, art and work skills. Another guidebook writer, Lan Shuder, author of *Fodor's Belize & Guatemala 2005*, lists a number of volunteer opportunities in Belize at www.belizefirst.com/indexvolunteer.html. The Belize Botanic Gardens regularly accept volunteers who pay $500 a month to cover their expenses (501-824-3101; www.belizebotanic.org/volunteer.html).

Conservation

An increasing number of organisations, both indigenous and foreign-sponsored, is involved in environmental projects throughout the continent. For opportunities in Ecuador investigate the Ecotrackers Network (www.ecotrackers.com) which charges $50 to register plus $2 a day while you're on a project, in addition to the daily average charge of $8 paid to the project organisers to cover board and lodging.

Many pre-arranged placement fees are equivalent to the price of a holiday. For example the Volunteer Galapagos programme (on which volunteers teach English, environmental sciences) costs about $50 a day for the first month, half as much thereafter. Nurses and biologists are also needed. Details are available in the UK from House of Ecuador, 94 Roman Way, London N7 8UN (0845 124 9338; www.voluteergalapagos.org). A cheaper way of spending time in those famous islands is to become an International Volunteer with the Darwin Foundation (External Relations Unit, Charles Darwin Research Station, Casilla Postal 17-01-3891, Quito, Ecuador; 011-593-552-6146/147; volunteer@darwinfoundation. org). Volunteers without relevant scientific skills have to pay their way with a contribution of $11 a day for food and dormitory accommodation and must stay for a minimum of six months.

The highest concentration of projects is probably in Costa Rica where the National Parks & Communities Authority runs a voluntary programme *Asociacion de Voluntarios para el Servicio en las Areas Protegidas* (ASVO). To be eligible you must be willing to work for at least one or two months, be able to speak Spanish and provide a copy of your passport and a photo. The work may consist of trail maintenance and construction, greeting and informing visitors, research or generally assisting rangers. There is also a possibility of joining a sea turtle conservation project. Details are available from the Volunteer Co-ordinator (alopez@asvocr.com), International Volunteer Program, Servicio de Parques Nacionales, Apdo. 11384-1000, San José 10104-1000 (506-233-4989; www.asvocr.com). Food and accommodation cost about $14 a day. The AVSO website is currently only in Spanish though there is a link to www.tropicjoes.com about short volunteer vacations planting trees.

A cultural exchange organisation in Argentina, *Grupo de Intercambio Cultural Argentino*, invites paying volunteers from abroad (normally with a working knowledge of Spanish) to work in Argentina's national parks as well as to take up internships in various fields or teach English. National park volunteers will be assigned to work within the Los Glaciares and Nahuel Huapi National Parks (both in Patagonia) and Iguaçu Falls National Park in northwest Argentina. Assignments last at least eight weeks and range from helping park rangers, to conducting guided visits, generally for four or five hours a day. Accommodation is provided for a fee of US$485 or US$515 a month. GICArg can also arrange short cooking courses at the Escuela Superior de Cocina de Alicia Berger in Buenos Aires followed by a short work experience placement in a four or five star restaurant. Details are available from the Cultural Exchange Group of Argentina, Lavalle 397, 1st Floor, Suite 1, Buenos Aires, C1047AAG, Argentina (tel/fax +54-11-4902 5153; info@gicarg.org/ www.gicarg.org)

BUNAC now has volunteering programmes in Costa Rica and Peru under the auspices of partner student organisations which provide back-up during the two to six month placement. Students (including gap year students) and recent graduates can participate if they have intermediate level Spanish. The Costa Rica programme fee for 2005 is £425 for three months, £525 for six months plus volunteers will need funds to cover their living expenses. The Peru programme costs £695 for two months and £895 for three. These costs do not include flights or insurance.

Other UK agencies like i-to-i run volunteer programmes in Costa Rica as well as in many other countries.

Trawling the internet for other eco-projects in Central and South America will turn up lots of lively possibilities. For example in a remote corner of Surinam you can monitor nesting sea turtles with *STINASU,* the Foundation for Nature Conservation in Surinam (c&f@stinasu.sr; www.stinasu.sr/volunteers_turtles.htm). They accept volunteers from February to September and expect a minimum contribution of $100.

The *Eco-Escuela de Español* in the Petén region of Guatemala arranges for language students to assist local conservation projects through Tikal Connection (Calle 15 de Septiembre, Ciudad Flores, Petén 17001; 502-7926-4981, fax 502-7926-4981; info@tikalcnx.com; www.tikalcnx.com).

A project in Brazil charges volunteers $310-$350 a month to donate their time to carry out rainforest conservation: *Iracambi,* C.P. No. 1, Rosário da Limeira, 36878-000 Minas Gerais, Brazil (055-32 3721 1436; www.iracambi.com). Volunteers at the remote *Picaflor Research Centre* in Peru (Casilla 105, Puerto Maldonado, Madre de Dios; picaflor_rc@yahoo.com; www.picaflor.org) can stay for $150 for ten days, provided they spend three hours a day clearing trails, painting boats, etc.

For animal lovers the *Inti Wara Yassi* wildlife reserve accepts volunteers to help care for injured animals (english@intiwarayassi.org). Many volunteer possibilities are available in national parks etc. through the *EcoVolunteer Program Brazil* (www.br.ecovoluntarios.org).

Organic farming has a healthy sprinkling of proponents in Latin America. In 2004 the newest national organisation was set up in Mexico; membership in WWOOF Mexico costs

$20 (wwoofmexico@yahoo.com; www.argos.net.mx/wwoof). Elsewhere on the continent you will have to turn to the International list of host farms (see introductory chapter Agriculture) as used by Rob Abblett, an inveterate organic farm volunteer. At present there are a handful of properties accepting volunteers in Belize, Brazil, Chile, Ecuador, Nicaragua, Panama and Peru.

The idea of visiting a few of these organic farms appealed to Rob Abblett:
The WWOOF list from Australia is without doubt the only book I would not leave England without. It includes some new addresses of potential volunteer work in countries which had previously been black holes for paid or unpaid work notably like Chile and Peru (among others). I stayed on a WWOOF farm in Paraguay for two weeks, living and working with a Swiss German family on a large isolated plot of land, learning about their many trials and tribulations as they struggled (in vain) to adapt from Swiss efficiency to third world conditions. Afterwards I became the first WWOOFer a German woman host in Uruguay had ever had. She worked as a teacher in Montevideo and had integrated well into the country. She provided great food and wine for working on her large garden, picking strawberries, weeding and painting. But I didn't stay long: I'd been robbed in Paraguay, got scared in Buenos Aires and decided that eight years of working around the world has been fantastic and worthwhile but now I need to do something different.

The *Nicaragua Solidarity Campaign* (129 Seven Sisters Road, London N7 7QG; 020-7272 9619; www.nicaraguasc.org.uk) organises two to four week work and study tours to assist fair trade co-operatives and environmental organisations in Nicaragua. The cost is £1,200 which includes airfares to and from Managua and all other expenses. Americans interested in this kind of programme in Nicaragua should contact *El Porvenir*, 48 Clifford Terrace, San Francisco, CA 94117 (415-566-3976; www.elporvenir.org) whose two-week work delegations cost $950 plus airfares.

OTHER OPPORTUNITIES

Apart from teaching, the only paid work available in Latin America tends to be for bilingual professionals. Engineers, business managers, highly specialised technicians have all found work in the private sector especially in international companies that operate in the mining, oil, hotel, banking and telecommunications sectors. Interesting voluntary opportunities are also available as Sara Ellis-Owen discovered when she decided she needed to get out of London, and the law firm that employed her was sympathetic to her desire to take a break. Not only did they give her three months of unpaid leave but they contributed financially to her placement by the Edinburgh-based charity Challenges Worldwide (www.challengesworldwide.com) with a legal NGO that advocated for the rights of all children in Belize. She was delighted to have plenty of free time to explore Belize which is an 'unspoilt, happy, relaxed place' and she loved every minute of it.

Work experience placements in Brazil are arranged by *CCUSA* (Camp Counsellors USA, 1st Floor North, Devon House, 171/177 Great Portland St, London W1W 5PQ; 020-7637 0779; www.ccusaweusa.co.uk). They offer a choice of office work, sports jobs, hotel/tourism placements or working with children mainly in Sao Paulo but also in Florianópolis and Vitória (both islands) plus Rio de Janeiro. The programme fee is £580 and earnings average R$150 (US$55) per month.

ELEP (Experiential Learning Ecuadorian Programs), Selva Alegre, 1031 y la Isla, Ecuador (593-9-940 0851/702 3926; info@elep.org, www.elep.org) arranges unpaid internships and volunteer placements in many fields in Ecuador such as media, tourism, computing, marine biology, event management, engineering, finance, medicine and law. Locations include the Highlands, coastal regions and Galapagos Islands. Participants must do a four-week course in intermediate/advanced Spanish (at a cost of about $1,500) before being assigned to a nine-week internship.

Unpaid work placements are available in Buenos Aires and Cordoba in Argentina via CDS International Inc. (871 United Nations Plaza, 15th Floor, New York, NY 10017-1814; 212-497-3502; www.cdsintl.org). Eligible candidates pay $500-$600 for a 12-week company placement or $1000-$1200 for a four week Spanish course followed by an eight-week internship in business, finance, hotel management, tourism, computer science, or engineering.

Bilingual secretaries who can produce letters in proper English are in demand from commerce and law firms. Americans should find out if there is a local American Chamber of Commerce (as there is in Caracas) and Britons may do likewise. For example the British-Chilean Chamber of Commerce will supply the names of British companies in Chile. The *US-Mexico Chamber of Commerce* (1300 Pennsylvania Ave NW, Suite 270, Washington, DC 20004-3021; www.usmcoc.org/usa/bvecino.html) sponsors a summer internship programme whereby bilingual American and Mexico students from certain universities are placed in companies in each others' countries.

Translators, particularly of scientific, medical and technical papers tend to be well paid by universities and large industrial concerns. Both types of vacancy are advertised in English language newspapers, which may themselves need proofreaders and editors or know of companies that do. In many large cities there is a sizeable English-speaking expatriate community, predominantly involved in international commerce. The bars and restaurants that they frequent are good job-hunting grounds: not only might you hear about opportunities for temporary work in business, but you could obtain work serving in the establishment itself.

Tourism

Only highly able candidates who have extensive Latin American travel experience and a knowledge of Spanish are hired as overland expedition guides with UK operators like the Australian-owned *Tucan Travel* (www.tucantravel.com) and *Journey Latin America* (12-13 Heathfield Terrace, Chiswick, London W4 4JE; www.journeylatinamerica.co.uk). In most cases, the company pays for food and accommodation plus a daily rate of $20-$25 but some companies do not cover all living expenses and tour leaders depend on being given free food and accommodation for bringing a group of clients to that particular restaurant or hotel. If you get to know an area well, you may be able to act as a freelance guide though, not surprisingly, this will probably incur the locals' resentment, as Mónica Boza found when she lived in Cusco Peru:

> If you have a good knowledge of the trails and want to become an outdoor guide, contact the tour agencies on arrival. But Peruvian guides are very jealous of foreign ones. I have known cases where they called the Migration Service and deportation followed. The adventure tour agencies are mainly along Plateros St or on the Main Square.

Foreign guides are occasionally hired by expatriate or even local tour operators. For example the *Tambopata Jungle Lodge* (PO Box 454, Cusco, Peru; tel/fax 084-245695; www.tambopatalodge.com) takes on guides for a minimum of six months who must have formal training in the natural sciences and (preferably) speak Spanish, all of which should be indicated on a CV. Information about the resident naturalist programme and research opportunities in the same area can be sought in the UK from TreeS, the Tambopata Reserve Society, c/o John Forrest, PO Box 33153, London NW3 4DR). Guides for the naturalist programme must be graduate biologists, environmental scientists or geographers over the age of 20. They receive free room and board throughout their stay.

Andrew James was lucky enough to spend the summer here some years ago:

> We lived in a jungle camp consisting of wooden lodges a four-hour boat trip up the Tambopata River from Puerto Maldonado. I was one of three English guides who took visitors of all nationalities in groups of about five on dawn walks to explore the rainforest and see the amazing plant life and the occasional animal. I was there for three months and was paid $150 a month for working 20 days a month with the other ten days free to do research or live it up in Puerto Maldonado (a town straight out of

the Wild West).

Paco Peña, himself a Peruvian, emerged at the beginning of the year from Manu National Park, in the remote south-east of Peru where he had been working as a park ranger. According to him, students of geography, biology and science from other countries can sometimes work as volunteer park rangers in the National Natural Protected Areas of Peru. You have to take in your own food and cover your travel expenses but accommodation will be provided at the Ranger's post; further information from INRENA (www.inrena. gob.pe in Spanish only).

Horse lovers should investigate riding holiday operators who may need people to exercise and look after the horses, for example Ride Andes (La Floresta, Pichincha, Ecuador; 99 738 221; www.rideandes.com) and a large ranch in the Corrientes region of Argentina (www.horse-riding-argentina.com) were both advertising in 2004/5 for general assistants. No salary is paid but room and board are free.

Local opportunities may crop up in one of the many places where tourism is booming. Many expat-style bars and clubs employ foreigners. For example Venezuela's Margarita Island in the Caribbean has dozens of places catering to package holidaymakers; try 4th of May Avenue and Santiago Marino Avenue, particularly between June and September and again December to March. In Caracas most foreign establishments are on the wealthy east side of the city in the Palos Grandes/Altamira area. Angie Copley was lucky enough to fix up a nannying job through a UK agency and was flown out to Caracas all expenses paid for a year. While admitting that Caracas is a stressful place to live (crime, traffic, pollution), she greatly enjoyed the tropical surroundings and the knowledge that the Caribbean coast was just an hour away and the Andes and Amazon a short flight.

Mónica Boza thinks that Cusco is a promising place with clubs like Mama Africa, Ukukus (which has the best bartenders in town), Eco, Up Town and Keros all near the main square. Few corners of the world have escaped the fashion for Irish pubs; in Cusco, try Paddy Flaherty and Rosie O'Gradys on Santa Catalina St. Similarly in the cities of Ecuador check at internet cafés such as Jamba, the Café Sutra or Pizza Net in Quito's 'Gringotown'.

The Chilean tourist industry also employs the odd gringo. Christine Hauser worked as a waitress in Santiago, though she found that the lack of a work visa was more of a problem than for English teachers since the authorities were wont to raid restaurants looking for illegal workers from other South American countries like Peru. She also landed a summer job at the beach resort of La Serena 500km north of the capital.

Mexico is another country in which travellers have been approached to work not as waiters or bar staff, but as hosts, entertainers and touts. Carisa Fey's stint as a singer at an upmarket restaurant in Puerto Vallarta is described in the *Tourism* chapter earlier in this book. While travelling in Mexico, Paul Donut was not expecting to work:

> *I stopped at Creél, a very small town in the Sierra Madre Mountains of north-west Mexico. It is about halfway through the Copper Canyon and looks like a town from a wild west movie. I was very surprised to find about a dozen travellers trying to entice people to stay at a group of small hotels known collectively as Margueritta's. In return for ambushing incoming trains, Margueritta (the owner) gave the travellers a free place to sleep and three excellent meals a day. I had a bit of luck here as I went to stay at a smaller place up the street. While we were on a tour the next day with the Irish manager, I was offered a job as tour guide, guest recruiter, wood cutter and general helper at the pension. I stayed for about a month, in a clean room with free meals and received a commission of $2 for everyone I brought back from the train. I would definitely recommend staying in Creél and going to the hotels for work. You won't make a fortune, but you should be able to stay here for free in return for some light duties.*

For information about living and working in Cancun, check out www.cancunassist.com/finding_a_job.cfm.

Anyone who can fix engines, especially on camper vans, should find no trouble earning a living in any touristy area of Mexico. Information on where and when to look for yachts that may be needing crew to sail from California to Mexico can be found in the chapter *Working a Passage*. You might be able to find day work on boats in harbours before the yachts set sail or perhaps an opportunity to boat-sit as Anne Wakeford did in Puerto Vallarta. She recommends asking boat owners to radio your request for work to their fellow yachtsmen in the morning. She also noticed that there might be work further south helping boats to navigate the locks of the Panama Canal.

Unexpectedly, you can make a tidy profit from collecting bottles and collecting the refunds. Just over half the millions of soft-drinks sold in Mexico are sold in returnable bottles. According to Bridgid Seymour-East who travelled along the Pacific coast of Mexico, you get back 3-5 pesos for every 660ml bottle of beer costing 10-15 pesos.

At the other end of the continent, reports from the Falkland Islands indicate that they are experiencing a mini-boom. Many of the tiny population have been drawn away from the countryside and into Stanley where a range of bars, shops and restaurants have opened. The island government is worried about rural depopulation and abandoned farms, so hard working people with agricultural experience might well be able to find work on the land. Sea Lion Lodge (Sea Lion Island, Falkland Islands; 500-32004; sealion_lodge@horizon. co.fk) was advertising in 2005 for hotel and nature reserve staff with the possibility of having your airfare paid.

The Caribbean

The Caribbean is far too expensive to explore unless you do more than sip rum punch by the beach. A host of Britons, Australians, South Africans, etc. are exchanging their labour, mostly on yachts, in order to see this exotic part of the world.

JOBS AFLOAT

Perhaps the easiest jobs to find are those working on the countless sailboats, charter yachts and cruise ships which ply the Caribbean each winter and spring. From November until May the Caribbean becomes a hive of marine activity. Christmas, since it marks the start of the main tourist season, is a particularly good time to look for work. The main requirement for being hired is an outgoing personality and perseverance in the search more than qualifications or experience. Hours are long and wages are minimal on a charter boat, but most do it for the fun. Board and lodging are always free and in certain jobs tips can be high. It would not be unusual to work for a wage of $50 a month and then earn $700 in tips.

Cruise Ships

For general information about cruise ship work see *Working a Passage*. Contracts are normally for six to nine months and the hours of work are long, often 14 hours a day, seven days a week living aboard the passenger ship with all onboard facilities provided by the ship owner. Most cruise ships active in the Caribbean contract their staff from Florida-based personnel agencies (known as concessionaires), some of which liaise with UK and European agencies. Workers aboard passenger ships require a C-1/D seafarer's visa issued by the United States Embassy which is only given through an employer or agency presenting a confirmed letter of appointment.

A long established cruise company which recruits its own staff is Windjammer Barefoot Cruises (Box 190120, Miami Beach, FL 33119-0120; 305-672-6453/ www.windjammer. com). One of the largest cruise lines in the world is Royal Caribbean Cruise Lines (RCCL,

1050 Caribbean Way, Miami, FL 33132-2096; 305-539-6000; http://royalcaribbean.hire. com/index.html).

Charter Yachts

The charter season in the Caribbean is November to May when an experienced deckhand can earn US$400 a week cash-in-hand plus tips. But there will be many weeks when the boat will not be chartered and the wage will fall to a third that amount while you may have to hang around a boring marina. It is important to stress that a deckhand job is not compatible with a great vacation. It's a tough job with long working hours during which you must never stop smiling. When the guests are snorkelling on the reef, the deckhand will be helping the skipper repair the toilet. While the guests are hiking up a volcano, the deckhand is polishing the winches.

The lack of a work permit can be a definite hindrance in the search for work with a charter company. Immigration authorities are consistently tough throughout the Caribbean. When you leave any boat as a crew you sign off the crew list in immigration where they want to see a ticket not only out of the country but one that connects with a flight to your home country. They also want to see an address where you intend to stay and may ask to see sufficient funds.

Yacht charter companies are unwilling to publicise vacancies, both because they have enough speculative enquiries on the spot and also they are forbidden by their respective island governments from hiring anyone without the proper working papers. However once you are on the spot, it is easier to hear of possibilities, and there are brokers and agents who match up crew with boats. The Danish traveller and sailor Kenneth Dichmann provided the following crew placement agency addresses (some of which may be out of date). They may be able to help people on-the-spot, particularly in late October, who complete an application form and pay the registration fee (usually $10-$20):

Hinckley Yacht Services, PO Box 2242, St. John's, Antigua (268-460-2711/fax 268-460-3740; antyact@candw.ag). $20 registration fee. Att: Jane Midson.

Cassandra's Yacht Services, Nelsons Dockyard, Antigua (809-462-9406/fax 809-462-9450).

Select Crew (Antigua Sails), Rena Night, Nelsons Dockyard, Antigua (809-460-1527/fax 809-460-1489). Must present yourself in person.

CCR St. Martin, Captain Oliver's Marina, St Martin (590-873049). Acts for Sun Yacht Charters between Antigua and St. Martin.

Captain & Crew, Yacht Haven, St. Thomas. Need CV, photo and $20 fee for one year's membership.

If you don't get anywhere with the agencies, it will be a case of implementing all the tactics outlined in the *Working a Passage* chapter to commend yourself to skippers, by asking at docks, putting up notices, following up leads learned in bars and so on. One way of breaking into the world of Caribbean yachties is to help with the drudgery of maintaining boats when at anchor. Try to find out when and where boat shows are being held as people are always in a rush to get their boats looking first class. Kenneth was offered a berth in Antigua by a German boat owner in exchange for a little polishing and barnacle scraping for three months but turned it down when the skipper was not willing to pay for food. Instead Kenneth spent a month at the end of the season (May) in Puerto Rico maintaining a boat in exchange for free food and accommodation.

JOBS ON LAND

People occasionally find work in nightclubs and hotels on the islands. The Cayman Islands are meant to be one of the best places to look for this sort of work, with over 1,500 Americans alone working there. Construction work may also be available on Grand Cayman; ask around at bars. Suzie Keywood from Surrey found work as a bartender at a lounge bar in Grand Cayman. Without a 'Gainful Occupation Licence' or work permit (difficult to obtain with hundreds of locals after the same jobs) you should not take for granted that you will be treated fairly. Plenty of horror stories circulate concerning maltreatment by employers, such as failure to pay wages and to honour agreements to provide a homeward flight. Keep your beach-scepticism handy, and don't hesitate to cut your losses and run, if you sense you're on to a bad deal.

The Dominican Republic has built up a flourishing package tour industry and jobs can be found by people with hospitality experience or a knowledge of several languages. There are 14 hotels in the resort of Playa Dorada and two more in Costa Dorado where you can ask for work which will pay only $50-$100 a month. Beware of promises of earning a fortune since these jobs will involve selling on commission.

There are some opportunities for voluntary service including in the Dominican Republic. For instance the Canadian charity the *Smiles Foundation* (www.smilesfoundation.org) accepts volunteers over 21 to join their projects in health care, education and social development. The *Bermuda Biological Station for Research Inc.* (Ferry Reach, St. George's GE01, Bermuda; 441-297-1880 ext 241; www.bbsr.edu) accepts students throughout the year to help scientists carry out their research in exchange for room and board. Applicants should make personal contact with the faculty member(s) for whom they wish to work and applications should be sent direct to those faculty members. The section 'Graduate/Undergraduate Opportunities' on the website provides a list of faculty members who are looking for volunteer interns. Volunteer interns are selected on the basis of their academic and technical backgrounds. Summer is the peak period (applications must be in by February); otherwise apply at least four months in advance. Note that immigration restrictions mean that the Station cannot hire foreigners to carry out work other than research.

Greenforce (11-15 Betterton Street, Covent Garden, London WC2H 9BP; 020-7470 8888; www.greenforce.org) recruits fee-paying volunteers to help with a biodiversity marine project in the Bahamas. Projects involve studying endangered species and habitats. No previous experience is necessary as training is provided. The cost is £2,700 plus flight.

With the beleaguered economy of Cuba, few opportunities will present themselves, though the *Cuba Solidarity Campaign* (c/o Red Rose Club, 129 Seven Sisters Road, London N7 7QG; 020-7263 6452) still runs its work/study 'brigade' twice a year in which volunteers undertake agricultural and construction work for three weeks either in July or December/January. No specific skills or qualifications are required but applicants must be able to demonstrate a commitment to solidarity work. The cost of the brigade is approximately £800 which covers the full cost of flights, visas, transfers, accommodation and food. For further information contact the Brigade Co-ordinator (tours@cuba-solidarity.org.uk).

A list of programmes and organisations in Haiti of interest to potential volunteers is available on the website www.vfp.org/directory/haiti.htm. The Hôpital Albert Schweitzer in Haiti (c/o 1360 Whitfield Avenue, Sarasota, FL 34243; 941-752-1525; hertha@hashaiti.org; www.hashaiti.org) uses voluntary work teams to help at this Haitian hospital run by the Grant Foundation.

Caribbean Volunteer Expeditions (CVE) is a non-profit organisation that recruits volunteers to work on historic preservation projects throughout the Caribbean (PO Box 388, Corning, NY 14830; 607-962-7846; www.cvexp.org) though its clientele is mostly retired.

St. Eustatius National Parks Foundation in the Netherlands Antilles has a volunteer programme to maintain park trails and a botanical garden, plus participate in a marine turtle monitoring programme.; contact the STENAPA Foundation, Gallows Bay, St. Eustatius (+599-318-2884; www.statiapark.org/stenapa/stenapa_volunteerprogram.html).

Volunteers collaborate with marine biologists at the Bimini Biological Field Station in the Bahamas studying the behaviour of lemon sharks and other captive animals for at least a month. For further information contact sgruber@rsmas.miami.edu (www.miami.edu/sharklab).

Visions Service Adventures (PO Box 220, Newport, PA 17074-0220; 800-813-9283; www.visionsserviceadventures.com) has summer volunteering programmes in the Dominican Republic, Guadeloupe and the British Virgin Islands, which cost about $4000 for one month.

Africa

At the beginning of 2005, Tony Blair wants Africa to be moved up the world agenda. But for travellers it has always been high on the list of desirable destinations. It is difficult to generalise about countries as different from each other as Morocco, Uganda and South Africa; however, the level of casual employment opportunities throughout the continent does not warrant a country-by-country treatment here. The red tape can be truly daunting in emergent Africa, and discouraging both in industrialised Southern Africa and Mediterranean Africa.

While travelling throughout Africa, be prepared for contradictions and aggravations. One traveller recommends carrying an official-looking list of addresses (whether invented or not), particularly of voluntary organisations, to show to suspicious immigration authorities. If you are given a job, you may be able to get a work permit though this is not always necessary.

You must also be prepared to cope with some decidedly uncomfortable conditions, whether you are staying in a cockroach-infested (yet still overpriced) hotel in Cairo while scraping together some money from English teaching; or enjoying the ten-hour truck ride into the Okavango Swamps of Botswana to look for work in the tourist bars and restaurants. As one contributor commented about this journey, 'it's an ordeal guaranteed to make you question whether working your way around some parts of the world is worth it after all.'

All travellers will have to come to their own conclusions about personal safety. Every so often a tragedy occurs in which a gap year traveller is mauled by lions or a safari jeep overturns in a ravine. Statistically, the level of violent crime in the urban areas of South Africa poses a more realistic threat at the moment, though victims tend to be the well-heeled types who stay in smart hotels. From having been at one time one of the favourite destinations for travellers, Zimbabwe has now been dropped by almost all of the volunteer-sending agencies and most people have no wish to spend time in what has become a despotic regime.

A tragedy of more far-reaching proportions is the spread of HIV/AIDS on the African continent. In 2004 an estimated 25.4 million people were living with HIV/AIDS in Sub-Saharan Africa and 2.3 million died. In much of Africa the teaching of safe sex has become far more important than the teaching of English. Many agencies are working tirelessly to spread the message and volunteers may well find themselves involved in raising awareness of the dangers of spreading the virus.

The concept of a true working holiday is well developed in Africa. Eco-tourism – where non-mass tourists pay for a holiday that may enhance not harm the local culture or environment – can take the form of participating in conservation projects or learning bush lore.

TEACHING

What makes much of Africa different from Latin America and Asia vis-à-vis English teaching is that English is the medium of instruction in state schools in many ex-colonies of Britain including Ghana, Nigeria, Kenya, Zambia, Zimbabwe and Malawi. As in the Indian subcontinent, the majority of English teachers in these countries are locals. Still there is some demand for native speakers in secondary schools, especially in Ghana, Kenya and Tanzania.

Vast stretches of Africa are not a promising destination for the so-called teacher-traveller. The majority of foreigners teaching in Africa are on one or two year volunteer contracts fixed up in their home country while a number of others are placed by recognised gap year organisations in the UK. Missionary societies have played a very dominant role in Africa's modern history, and some religious organisations continue active in the field of education and teacher recruitment, though even here the major organisations like Christians Abroad and the evangelical Africa Inland Mission (Halifax Place, Nottingham NG1 1QN; www.aim-eur.org) are being asked to supply fewer English teachers than previously.

Furthermore, conditions can be very tough and many teachers in rural Africa often find themselves struggling to cope at all. Whether it is the hassle experienced by women teachers in Muslim North Africa or the loneliness of life in a rural West African village, problems proliferate. Anyone who has fixed up a contract should try to gather as much up-to-date information as possible before departure, preferably by talking to people who have just been there. Otherwise local customs can come as a shock. A certain amount of deprivation is almost inevitable; for example teachers, especially volunteers, can seldom afford to shop in the pricey expatriate stores and so will have to be content with the local diet, typically a staple cereal such as millet usually made into a kind of stodgy porridge, plus some cooked greens, tinned fish or meat and fruit.

The agency Gap Challenge sent Sarah Johnson from Cardiff to Zanzibar one September to teach English and geography at a rural secondary school:

The expectations which Zanzibari children have from school are worlds away from those of British school children. They expect to spend most of their lessons copying from the blackboard, so will at first be completely nonplussed if asked to think things through by themselves or to use their imagination. I found that the ongoing dilemma for me of teaching in Zanzibar was whether to teach at a low level which the majority of the class would be able to understand, or teach the syllabus to the top one or two students so that they would be able to attempt exam questions, but leaving the rest of the class behind. Teaching was a very interesting and eye-opening experience. I believe that both the Zanzibari teachers and I benefitted from a cultural exchange of ideas and ways of life.

The US State Department (SA 44, Room 304, 301 4th Street, SW, Washington DC 20547; 202-619-5869; http://exchanges.state.gov/education/engteaching) runs English Language

Programs at its Bi-National Centers in a number of African countries, though this operation has been shrinking over the past few years. Normally they hire people who are already resident in the country. If teachers (British as well as American) are prepared to travel to an African capital for an interview, they have a chance of being assigned a few hours of teaching.

Obviously the British Council in the UK (Educational Enterprises, 10 Spring Gardens, London SW1A 2BN; 020-7389 4931/ www.britishcouncil.org) places a large number of qualified EFL teachers worldwide, and the Peace Corps in the US (Room 803E, 1111 20th St NW, Washington, DC 20526; 1-800-424-8580; www.peacecorps.gov) recruits hundreds of volunteer teachers every year. Also the major gap placement agencies, viz. Gap Activity Projects, Gap Challenge (with placements in Tanzania and South Africa), Project Trust (Namibia, Lesotho, Uganda, Malawi, Botswana, South Africa, Niger, Mozambique, Mauritania, Egypt and Morocco) and SPW/Students Partnership Worldwide (Tanzania, Uganda, Zambia and former South African homelands) are active on the African continent (see chapter *Volunteering: Gap Year Placements*). General voluntary agencies like Skillshare International, VSO and the Irish agency Concern Worldwide (52-55 Lower Camden St, Dublin 2; www.concern.ie) are also involved in the education field.

Cosmos Education is a relatively new charity which recruits professionals and university students in scientific fields to travel around Zambia, Kenya and Tanzania for short periods, visiting schools and youth institutions to extend science education in the developing world. See http://cosmoseducation.org for details.

Placement Organisations

The following organisations recruit teachers of English as a foreign language and/or student volunteers for schools in Africa. These postings are normally regarded as 'voluntary' since local wages are paid usually along with free housing. In some cases a substantial placement fee must be paid.

Africa & Asia Venture, 10 Market Place, Devizes, Wilts. SN10 1HT (01380 729009; www. aventure.co.uk). Places British school leavers as assistant teachers in primary and secondary schools in Kenya, Uganda, Tanzania, Malawi and Botswana, normally for 4/5 months. Programme includes in-country orientation course, insurance, allowance paid during work attachment and organised safari at end of teaching period. The 2005 participation fee is approximately £2,500 plus air fares.

Africatrust Bridge, PO Box 551, Portsmouth, Hants. PO5 1ZN (tel/fax 01873 812453; www. africatrust.gi). 3 or 6 month placements of graduate volunteers in Ghana, Cameroon or Morocco departing January or September, including teaching and working with needy children in schools and orphanages. Interviews held in London in July. Knowledge of French required (except for Ghana).

Daneford Trust, 45-47 Blythe St, London E20 0LL (tel/fax 020-7729 1928; dfdtrust@aol. com). Youth education charity sends students and school leavers from inner city London to Namibia, Botswana, Zimbabwe and South Africa for a minimum of three months. Volunteers must raise at least £2,000 towards costs.

Mondochallenge, Galliford Building, Gayton Rd, Milton Malsor, Northampton NN7 3AB (01604 858225; www.mondochallenge.org). Sends volunteers (average age 27) to help with teaching and business development programmes in Tanzania, Kenya, The Gambia and Senegal. Normal stay is 2-4 months and start dates are flexible. Fee of £900 for 3 months. Board and lodging in local family homes costs an extra £15 (approximately) per week.

Sudan Volunteer Programme, 34 Estelle Road, London NW3 2JY (tel/fax 020-7485 8619; www.geocities.com/svp-uk). Needs volunteers to teach conversational English to university students and adults in Sudan for 4+ months from September or January. Undergraduates and graduates with experience of travelling abroad (preferably in the Middle East) are accepted; TEFL certificate and knowledge of Arabic are not required. Volunteers pay for their airfare (about £585) plus UK travel expenses for selection and briefing. Local host institutions cover living expenses in Sudan; most are in the Khartoum area.

Tanzed, 80 Edleston Road, Crewe, Cheshire CW2 7HD (01270 509994; www.tanzed.org). Charity that sends voluntary teachers to work for a year in government primary schools in rural Tanzania (Morogoro region). £2,000 inclusive of flights.

Teaching & Projects Abroad, Aldsworth Parade, Goring, Sussex BN12 4TX (01903 708300; fax 01903 501026; info@teaching-abroad.co.uk; www.teaching-abroad. co.uk). Volunteer teachers work in Ghana, Togo and South Africa. Volunteers are provided with board and accommodation, placement and working arrangements and insurance. No TEFL background required but good spoken English and university entrance qualification. Three-month self-funded packages cost £1,600 plus airfares.

Trade Aid, Burgate Court, Burgate, Fordingbridge, Hants. SP6 1LX (01425 657774; info@tradeaiduk.org; www.tradeaiduk.org). Tanzanian address: The Old Boma, Mikindani, PO Box 993, Mtwara (oldboma@mikindani.com). Education charity in southern Tanzania that accepts both gap-year and mature volunteers who can offer a relevant skill e.g. as a teacher or cook. Length of stay is 6 months for gap year students, 12 months for older volunteers. All-in cost is £1,500-£2,500.

Tukae, 22 Hilgrove Road, Newquay, Cornwall TR7 2QZ (01637 874147; www.tukae. org). English teacher volunteer programme in Tanzania. £2,500 for a 3-4 month placement.

Village Education Project (Kilimanjaro), c/o Mint Cottage, Prospect Road, Sevenoaks, Kent TN13 3UA (01732 459799; www.kiliproject.org). Gap year programme which sends about 8 UK students each year to help teach EFL and other subjects in village primary schools in Tanzania for an academic year (8-9 months). Fee is £2,500.

Egypt

Respectable and dubious language teaching centres flourish side by side in the streets of Cairo and to a lesser extent Alexandria. Teaching jobs are not hard to come by, especially if you have a Cambridge or Trinity Certificate (and if you are thinking of doing the CELTA course, Cairo is one of the cheapest places to do it). Many parents enrol their children to do intensive language courses in the summer, so this is a good time to look for an opening (assuming you can tolerate the heat).

While the Australian Kate Ferguson was in Egypt, she was handed a leaflet advertising jobs with the International Languages Institute (ILLI) on Talaat Harb Street in central Cairo: *'I went there to make some initial enquiries and it was not the dodgy exploitative business that I expected. Instead it was quite professional in its appearance. I also got the impression that the Institute was nearly always looking for teachers. The pay was 10 Egyptian pounds an hour. Training, accommodation, medical care and a one-year work permit were all promised free of charge.'*

The British Council in Agouza (192 Corniche el-Nil, Aguza, near the Circus; 02-300 1666) is one place to check for work. The Director of TEFL may give you a form to fill in and then you may be asked to stand in for a practice lesson observed by the usual teacher. (You will be given a lesson beforehand to prepare.) If they think you are suitable they'll take you on which is more likely during the summer. During exam time there is also a need for paid invigilators. Also in Cairo try ILI, 4 Mahmoud Azmy St, Sahafeyeen, Mohandeseen (02-346 3087) or in Alexandria English Language Training Program, 3 Pharana St, Azarita (03-487 9655).

Dan Boothby has spent time in Cairo and found it almost alarmingly easy to find work:

I taught one-to-one lessons to several people and got about 5 hours a week work and charged £10 an hour. Frankly this was much more than I was worth but if you charge less than the market rate then it is felt that you are an amateur. I taught an isolated and lonely 5 year old, son of the Georgian Consul, where I was more a babysitter than a tutor. I felt so guilty about charging E£50 an hour that I spent an hour trying to get him to learn something. I didn't feel so guilty charging E£55 to tutor the Georgian Ambassador since he probably passed the bill onto his government. I got a lot of students through friends that I made who were teaching at the international schools. The kids at these schools are often in need of extra tuition towards exam times when their parents realise that they've been mucking about all year and are close to failing. The problem is that the kids tend to be very uninterested and so it is difficult to make them concentrate. But I enjoyed one-to-ones. One could build up a large group of students and earn a decent wage but equally teach less hours and have more time – one of the reasons for getting out of England.

One way of advertising your availability to teach might be to place an advert in the expatriate monthly *Egypt Today* (www.egypttoday.com) or the fortnightly *Maadi Messenger* published by volunteers and distributed through expat haunts like English-speaking churches. The American University, centrally located at the eastern end of Tahrir Square, is a good place to find work contacts. The University Press publishes a useful book for long-stay visitors *Cairo: The Practical Guide* by Claire Francy (2003, $15.95). Also try the notice boards at the Community Services Association (CSA No. 4, Road 21, Maadi, Cairo; csaegypt@intouch.com) where a range of adult education courses for expats is offered.

If you are looking for good causes to which you can volunteer your time, ask at All Saints Cathedral in Zamalek. Zamalek along with Heliopolis and Mardi are the best areas to look for private clients, as Ian McArthur found:

In Cairo I sought to work as a private English tutor. I made a small poster, written in English and Arabic, with the help of my hotel owner. I drew the framework of a Union Jack at the top, got 100 photocopies and then meticulously coloured in the flags. The investment cost me £3. I put the posters up around Cairo, concentrating on affluent residential and business districts. I ended up teaching several Egyptian businessmen, who were difficult to teach since they hated being told what to do.

Ghana

As one of the most stable countries in Africa, Ghana supports several organised schemes for volunteer teachers, since it has a long tradition of welcoming foreign students to participate in its educational and commercial life. Quite a number of exchange organisations, gap year programmes and charities operate to Ghana, many in co-operation with the Student & Youth Travel Organization in Accra (www.sytoghana.com). Individuals can apply directly to SYTO at least ten weeks before their intended arrival. The fee is $400 for both the Volunteering and Internship programmes.

The grass-roots Save the Earth Network (STEN) mentioned later in this chapter offers voluntary positions as English and maths teachers in primary and junior secondary schools in Ghana. Assin Endwa Trust UK (184 Maldon Road, Great Baddow, Chelmsford, Essex CM2 7DG; tel/fax 01245 475920; www.endwa.org.uk) has just started offering summer working holidays in the Central region of Ghana at a small village called Assin Endwa. Volunteers spend on average three weeks working with the schools in the village as teachers/assistants primarily working on conversational English, but also helping with building projects in the village, assisting the women's co-operative with farm work and (if qualified) helping with sports activities. The direct cost for all accommodation and travel within Ghana is £165; plus volunteers are expected to raise at least £250 through sponsorship to donate to the project. Flights from the UK cost around £450 (2004) plus food will cost around £30 per week.

Kenya

Kenya has had a chronic shortage of secondary school teachers for some time, mostly in Western Province. Although legislation has made it harder for unqualified teachers to find jobs, it may still be possible to fix up a teaching job by asking in the villages, preferably before terms begin in September, January and April. Be prepared to produce your

CV, diplomas and official-looking references. Basic accommodation and a monthly salary (local rates) may be provided, though not all schools can afford to pay it, especially non-government self-help *Harambee* schools. According to the Kenyan High Commission in London (45 Portland Place, W1B 1AS; www.kenyahighcommission.com), all non-Kenyan citizens who wish to work must be in possession of an Entry/Work permit issued by the Principal Immigration Officer, Department of Immigration, PO Box 30191, Nairobi, before they can take up paid or unpaid work.

The *American Universities Preparation Institute* (PO Box 14842, Nairobi; 02-374 1764; aupi@nbi.ispkenya.com) accepts a number of foreign teachers with university degrees on a 6 or 12-month volunteer programme where accommodation is provided.

A UK agency *VAE Teachers Kenya* sends school-leavers and university graduates on six-month teaching placements from January to poor rural schools in and around Gilgil in the central highlands of Kenya. The cost of about £3,000 is all-inclusive. Details are available from Simon Harris, Bell Lane Cottage, Pudleston, Nr. Leominster, Herefordshire HR6 0RE (01568 750329; www.vaekenya.co.uk) who spends half the year in Gilgil.

From the US, people can participate in volunteer vacations, short-term teaching assignments in rural Kenya through Global Citizens Network/Harambee, 130 N Howell St, St Paul, MN 55104 (651-644-0960; www.globalcitizens.org/kenya.html) or Global Routes (1 Short St, Northampton, MA 01060; www.globalroutes.org). Global Routes offer 12-week voluntary internships to students who teach English and other subjects in village schools in Kenya. There are no specific requirements apart from an ability to afford the programme fee of $4,250 for the summer and nearly $5,000 for the spring and autumn (excluding airfares). Ben Clark from the US participated in this programme between high school and college:

> Previous to my arrival at the Essabba Secondary School in the western provinces, there was no English teacher for the Form 1 students. My school was relatively well off and had most of the appropriate tools needed for learning (text books, notebooks, classrooms, etc.). I was surprised at the ease with which I was inserted into the school as teacher. They simply asked my co-intern and me what subjects we were best at, so I chose to teach English and math. It was a challenge for someone with no experience to manage a class of 37, particularly considering the students' different skill levels. Some of the kids were my age, and it was hard at first to earn the respect and trust of my class. Another problem I encountered was that of corporal punishment. In Kenya, caning is something that a lot of the schools practise as punishment for the students' bad behaviour. If students came in late, failed to do assignments or misbehaved, they were either sent to the Deputy Headmaster or sent out to do manual labour in the field. I chose not to apply these punishments and as a result many of my students did not do the homework that I assigned. The class was also too big for me to go around the room every day and check if each student had done their work. My host family is what I miss most about my time in Kenya.

Morocco

English is gaining ground despite Morocco being a Francophone country. Outside the state system there is a continuing demand for native speaker teachers especially in Casablanca and Rabat. Semesters begin in September and January and wages are higher than elsewhere in Africa, typically £5-£7 an hour. A number of commercial language schools employ native English speakers including the network of ten American Language Centers (www.aca.org.ma). The biggest branch in Rabat employs more than 50 teachers (half of them part-time), who must have an arts degree: ALC, 4 Zankat Tanja, Rabat 10000 (037-767103; dir@alcrabat.org) while the Casablanca branch at 1 Place de la Fraternité (022-277765; alc.casa@casanet.net.ma) employs mainly (but not exclusively) North American graduates with some TEFL certification and experience. Another possible employer is EF English First, 20 rue du Marché, Résidence Benomar, Maarif, Casablanca (022-254400) who pay 8,000 dirhams per month net (about £500).

TOURISM

Once again travellers' hostels are one of the few providers of casual work in the developing nations of the African continent. It is something that many independent trans-Africa travellers do for the odd week, from Dahab on the Red Sea to the backpackers' haunts of Johannesburg, and is a very nice way to have a break without having to pay for it. While cycling through Africa, Mary Hall stopped at a backpackers' hostel in Malawi where she was even offered a permanent job, but the road called.

Tourism is well established both on the Mediterranean coast of Africa and in the countries of East and Southern Africa where game parks are the major attraction. (Opportunities in South Africa are discussed separately below.) It is possible to find work in hotels and bars in resort areas; try the so-called trendy establishments rather than humble locally-staffed ones. A couple of years ago Jane Harris reported from Dahab on the Egyptian coast of the Red Sea that she had seen notices for a waitress at the Tota Dance Bar and for an English speaker to work in a travel agency helping to write leaflets in English. Wages were not high but living expenses here are very cheap.

French speakers have an advantage in North Africa, something that tempted Michel Falardeau from Quebec to investigate possibilities in Tunisia:

> I am currently in the major resort of Jerba and asked in the tourist office whether many English-speaking tourists come to Jerba. I was told that most English-speaking tourists go to Monastir, Sousse and Hammamet while Germans, Italians and French people favour Jerba. Since most Tunisians speak French I believe it would be useless for French speakers to compete with the locals for a job here. As far as timing is concerned, the best time to get a job in Tunisia would be late February or early March.

Purveyors of overpriced carpets in Morocco have been known to try to enlist the help of travellers whom they loosely employ to lure high-spending tourists into the shops. You approach a stranger and pretend to want advice on which carpet to buy yourself, and hope that the tourist will follow suit; most 'plants' find that they can't stomach this charade for long.

Anyone with a diver's certificate might be able to find work at Red Sea resorts like Sharm el Sheikh and Hurghada. If you aren't sufficiently qualified but want to gain the appropriate certificates, the Red Sea might be a good place to train. Emperor Scuba Schools (www.emperordivers.com) have five schools on the Red Sea at Hurghada, Sharm El Sheikh, Nuweiba, Dahab and Port Sudan. Once qualified as an instructor, they might hire you or help you make contact with diving schools worldwide. At local dive centres, you can sometimes get free lessons in exchange for filling air tanks for a sub-aqua club. It is possible to be taken on by an Egyptian operator (especially in the high season November to January); however the norm is to be paid no wage and just earn a percentage of the take. Stephen Psallidas confirmed this after spending a month in Egypt over Christmas:

> A few people were working in the scuba-diving schools in Dahab including an English guy who had been there three months and had worked his way up from complete novice to Dive Master. In the later stages, he was trained for free as long as he took some novices out diving. Several traveller types were working in the many cafés in Dahab.

Long-term possibilities may be available with the overland companies mentioned in the section *Overland Tours* in the chapter *Working a Passage*. For courier work, applicants are required to have first-hand knowledge of travel in Africa or must be willing to train for three months with no guarantee of work. Requirements vary but normally expedition leaders must be at least 23 and be diesel mechanics with a truck or bus licence. Some African specialists are listed here; others can be found on internet sites like www.go-overland.com.

Absolute Africa, 41 Swanscombe Road, Chiswick, London W4 2HL (020-8742 0226; www. absoluteafrica.com).

Acacia Expeditions, Lower Ground Floor, 23A Craven Terrace, London W2 3QH (020-7706 4700; www.acacia-africa.com).

Bukima Africa, PO Box 43963, London NW2 5WD (08707572230; www.bukima.com).

Economic Expeditions, 22 Craven Terrace, London W2 3QH (207 262 0177; www. economicexpeditions.com). Africa specialist.

Oasis Overland, The Marsh, Henstridge, Somerset TA8 0TF (01963 363400; www. oasisoverland.co.uk).

Phoenix Expeditions, College Farm, Far St, Wymeswold, Leicestershire LE12 6TZ (01509 881818; www.phoenixexpeditions.co.uk).

Truck Africa, www.truckafrica.com.

Anyone with skills as a mechanic might be able to find work with an overland company, especially if based along one of the major routes. Suitably connected people might be able to run their own safaris, something Jennifer McKibben observed in Kenya: *'Some entre-preneurial travellers used to make money by hiring a jeep and taking holidaymakers on mini expeditions. This would either be to places inaccessible by public transport or would undercut the travel agencies on standard trips. They found customers by placing notices in the youth hostel and cheap hotels.'*

In her whole year of volunteer nursing in Uganda, Mary Hall met only one foreigner who had found work on the spot and without a work permit. This woman was asked to manage a tourist lodge in the middle of nowhere and jumped at the chance since it was such a beautiful nowhere. More recently a luxury safari lodge has been advertising in Europe for catering staff: Uganda Safari Company, PO Box 23825, Kampala (fax +256 41 344653; tusc@africaonline.co.ug).

OPPORTUNITIES IN SOUTH AFRICA

Frightening levels of urban crime have prompted an enormous brain drain in South Africa. Hundreds of thousands of South Africans have emigrated over the past few years and more than two thirds of skilled and educated South Africans say that they are considering emigration, mainly to escape the crime but also the AIDS epidemic and an unemployment rate that has touched 40% (including people no longer looking for work). However affirmative action policies mean that it is very difficult for foreigners to land jobs (legally) which could be done by locals. Competition is intense from the formerly disenfranchised black population of South Africa. The openings that do exist are primarily for people with skills and experience, e.g. computer specialists, engineers, electricians and so on.

Check adverts in the Monday edition of the main dailies, the *Cape Times* in Cape Town, and the *Star* and *Citizen* in Johannesburg. The *South African Sunday Times* also carries employment ads and is distributed in the UK. Temporary employment agencies such as Kelly with 35 branches (www.kelly.co.za) might be willing to register likely candidates whom they are persuaded plan to settle in South Africa. Prospects are generally rosier outside the popular destination of Cape Town.

Red Tape

The government is (understandably) not keen to hand out work permits to Europeans and other nationalities when so many South African nationals are unemployed. Tony Forrester found the situation very discouraging: 'With affirmative action, it's a nightmare being a white male and looking for a job'. It is worth quoting the Director-General of the Department of Home Affairs, Billy Masetlhe, writing in the *Pretoria Times* several years ago:

Work permits are only granted in instances where South African citizens or perma-nent residents are not available for appointment or cannot be trained for the posi-

tion. Employment opportunities are, as a result of the prevailing economic climate in SA, extremely limited and there is at present no special drive or project to attract foreign workers to SA. Even as far as the so-called scarce employment categories are concerned, the position has worsened to the extent where professionally and technically qualified persons are being laid off and are finding it extremely difficult to secure alternative employment.

In recent years, the country has been flooded with Zimbabweans fleeing their own collapsed economy, willing to work for tiny wages.

Skilled and qualified people can apply to South African embassies for a Work Seeker's Permit (BI-159) provided they have a confirmed offer of a full-time job which the permit will allow them to assess face-to-face; the fee is $65. After a job is officially accepted, the foreigner can obtain a work permit from the nearest office of the Department of Home Affairs, which has a toll-free information number 0800 601190. Good information is available online at www.southafrica.info/public_services/foreigners. Detailed information on the scheme is available from the Consular Section (15 Whitehall, London SW1A 2DD; 020-7925 8910; www.southafricahouse.com).

Most people who do casual work have only a three-month tourist visa, which must be renewed before it expires. A 90-day extension can be obtained from the Department of Home Affairs in Johannesburg or Cape Town for a fee. If you try to do this more than once, the authorities will become suspicious.

One solution to the problem is to consider BUNAC's Work South Africa programme run in partnership with the South African Student Travel Services (11 Bree St, Cape Town 8000; 021 418 3794; www.sasts.org.za). The 12-month work permit is available to full-time university students under 30 of any nationality or those who have graduated in the past six months. The programme fee is £350 plus flights, special work permit (currently £33) and insurance. Participants are allowed to take any job they can find. BUNAC warns that finding a job can be tough, though easier in the high season between October and March.

Work Experience International (WEI, PO Box 3288, Somerset West, South Africa 7129; www.wei.co.za) arranges volunteer work placements for anyone aged 18-35 in boutique hotels, safari lodges and game reserves in South Africa. Inclusive fee for 3 month placement is £680.

Willing Workers in South Africa (WWISA) is a community service volunteer organisation based in The Crags, near Plettenberg Bay. Whatever their age and skills, volunteers work on projects alongside local villagers according to their interests, options and available dates, in the areas for example of schooling and education, youth development, business development, health care and environmental research. Programmes are geared to the social and economic enhancement of the local rural community of Kurland Village. Prices should be checked on the website www.wwisa.co.za, though as a rough guide participants pay £550 per month, £585 from 2006.

Another volunteer placement company is AVIVA (Africa Volunteering & Ventures Abroad, PO Box 60573 Flamingo Square, Table View, Cape Town 7439; 021-557 5996; www.aviva-sa.com). Their range of placement includes working with street children (fee of £1176/$2116 for 12 weeks) and working in a wildlife sanctuary (£873/$1613 for 4 weeks). Several other conservation opportunities in South Africa are provided at the end of this chapter under the heading 'Conservation and Wildlife'.

Tourism

Cape Town is the tourist capital of South Africa including for backpackers, though jobs are harder to find here than elsewhere. The Backpack Hostel & Africa Travel Centre at 74 New Church St (021-423 4530; www.backpackers.co.za) has been recommended for its notice board but many others will be able to advise, such as Oak Lodge (www.oaklodge. co.za). Roger Blake expected to stay in South Africa for three months but ended up spending seven:

There are more than 100 hostels in South Africa, many of which 'employ' backpackers on a casual basis. Within two weeks of arrival I was at a hostel in George on a work-for-keep basis. Through contacts made here I also sold T-shirts at the beach for a small profit and I did a few days at a pizza place for tips only. Then I was offered a job at a hostel in Oudtshoorn (Backpackers Oasis). They gave me free accommodation and 150 rand a week to run the bar and help prepare the ostrich braai (BBQ) that they have every evening. Also I did breakfasts for fellow travellers which was like being self-employed as I bought all the ingredients and kept all the profit. It was a small but worthwhile fortune after six weeks here.

Everyone who has looked for a tourist job in Cape Town recommends Seapoint, a beach suburb lined with cafés, ice cream kiosks, snack bars and other places which have high staff turnovers, though wages are low. (Ice cream is also sold from cycle carts; find out whom to contact for work by asking the sellers.) Also try using the door-to-door approach in the flashy Victoria & Albert Waterfront development, Camps Bay and the beaches along the Garden Route. People who can speak more than one language will be especially in demand. Long Street in Cape Town is lined with bars and restaurants where jobs crop up.

The summer season starts around the 10th of December and so the best time to look for restaurant/bar work is the last week of November. It took Mr. Rapp 27 minutes to find a full-time waiting job. He was promoted to head waiter after the Christmas rush, having never waited a table in his life before. Bear in mind that these high-profile tourist meccas have been the target of immigration raids. J.M. Rapp noticed that during the busy Christmas season, places on the Waterfront were not hiring people without a permit, though smart places downtown were, e.g. on posh Loop Street. Casual workers might prefer more discreet places. Suburban fast food restaurants such as Spur, Mike's Kitchen and St. Elmo's are often hiring, though the first two are liable to pay only commission. Suburbs to concentrate on are Observatory, Rondebosch, Wynberg and Plumstead.

Although Johannesburg is often maligned as a big, bad, city, it is the earning capital of South Africa with better job possibilities than many other places. Unfortunately some of the inner city areas where backpackers used to congregate and find jobs (Yeoville, Brixton) have succumbed to the crime and grime for which the city is known. Now the areas to head for restaurant and pub work are Sandton and Rosebank. Many travellers now prefer the northern suburbs to which hostels like the Ritz now in Dunkeld West (1A North Road, ritz@iafrica.com) and Rockey's have moved. Rockey's of Fourways (22 Campbell Road, Craigavon A.H., Sandton; 011-465 4219; www.backinafrica.com) is in an area where within a 5km radius there are more than 60 restaurants & bars, five huge night clubs, the new Montecasino complex and other backpackers' lodges. Travellers can often get jobs waiting tables, working on the bar, etc. as the owners of Rockey's of Fourways confirmed in 2005:

There are several work opportunities for travellers both at our lodge and in the neighbourhood. We are constantly building and improving so we can often offer jobs to electricians, carpenters, plasterers, gardeners and other artisans, either for free accommodation and/or a nominal wage. Also, from time to time we have positions open for bar, office & night staff. Payment is free board & lodging, a weekly wage and a percentage of commissions/profits.

Resorts along the east coast between Cape Town and Port Elizabeth and even as far as the Ciskei provide employment opportunities, as does the Natal coast especially Durban and Margate. Particularly recommended on the east coast are George, Knysna, Jeffreys Bay, Plettenburg Bay and of course Port Elizabeth. As in the cities, December/January is the high season.

Tekweni Backpackers & Ecotours in the Morningside area of Durban (168 Ninth St; 031-303 1433; tekwenihostel@global.co.za) sometimes employs foreigners for free rent and a small wage (which soon gets swallowed up in the happy hour at Bonkers on Florida Road, the local pub). If you stay any length of time in one place, you may be asked to act as relief manager or bartender as regularly occurs at Sani-Lodge in the Drakkensberg near Himeville (033-7020330) or Sani Top Chalet. The Backpack Hostel mentioned above has a Safari Lodge on the edge of Kruger National Park.

Gambling is a popular tourist pastime in South Africa, and there is reputed to be a continuous demand for croupiers. Casinos pay well, partly to compensate for the instability of the employment. Sun International is the main casino operator but does not pay cash-in-hand as some do.

Work may be available in the boatyards of Cape Town and other places, especially doing the dogsbody jobs of sanding and painting. Activity peaks before the Cape-to-Rio yacht race in the winter.

Selling

Judging from the number of stories of successful selling, South Africa sounds an excellent destination for budding entrepreneurs. It is possible to make a profit by selling anything from hotdogs and chocolates outside discos to lottery tickets bought in bulk at a discount and sold near post offices or liquor stores. Heideline Brisley (a native South African) offers some tips to travellers willing to consider sales work. She has found opportunities to sell clothes, crafts, jewelry, etc. at a number of coastal resorts between Cape Town and Port Elizabeth and beyond.

Tiring of his job as waiter at a Greek restaurant in Cape Town, Steve Psallidas answered an ad (posted up in hostels) for sales people. He was accepted to sell dodgy paintings door-to-door which he (like so many others who have done this job in various countries) described as a nightmare with low earnings. He also came across money-making opportunities in the markets of Cape Town: *'I've met several travellers selling arts and crafts items or doing hair-wraps in Greenmarket Square and St. George's Mall. In the latter you don't even need a licence; just turn up before 8am and pay a few rand for a patch of ground. In the Greenmarket Square market you have to work for a stall-holder.'*

Farm Work

The provinces of the Northern Transvaal, the Orange Free State and the Cape are rich agricultural areas where extra help may be needed at harvest time. The rural economy of South Africa is dominated by Afrikaaners, though most of them speak at least a little English. Generally speaking the slog work of fruit and vegetable picking will be done by local black labourers, but anyone with a background in agriculture might find an opening, especially if they have contacts.

The towns of Stellenbosch and Paarl to the east and north of Cape Town respectively are the centres of South Africa's wine industry. Around Stellenbosch picking begins in late January/early February and lasts for four or five weeks. Further inland (e.g. around Worcester) it starts a few weeks later, and continues well into March. If you find a farmer willing to put you up and give you work, the problem of work permits is unlikely to arise. A mango farming family was advertising on the internet for an energetic pair of gap year travellers to help during their busy season (November to February) 'ideal for someone looking for adventure and a crash course in sub-tropical farming'.

Rob Abblett worked briefly at an eco-community near Durban called Absolute Elsewhere (PO Box 807, Richmond 3780, Kwazulu-Natal; 031-209 6006). The residents were happy to accept working visitors from around the word and Rob helped them clear ground for fire breaks before moving on. Rob is a veteran traveller among intentional communities and earlier, in Malawi, had exchanged his labour for bed and board at the Tikondwe Freedom Gardens near Lilongwe (Box 70, Lumbadzi, Malawi), an organic fruit and vegetable farm which warmly accepted his help with the ground nut harvest. He was only the sixth foreigner ever to work here and the local villagers were filled with amusement and amazement to see a white man carrying sacks of peanuts on his head.

BUSINESS AND INDUSTRY

If you are interested in joining a business in Africa (especially if you have a technical or managerial skill) start by surfing the internet. For example the site www.africaguide.com/work.htm carries links to recruitment companies and some actual job vacancies. You can also of course contact the Commercial Section of the embassy of the country which interests you for information about job prospects. If you are on the spot, the expatriate community may be willing to offer advice or even more practical assistance. Information technology jobs are available in Morocco to people who know French as well as about computers.

Other work opportunities in Africa include translating business documents from and into French, German or English, depending on the particular country's position and trade. You could put an ad in the paper or visit firms. When Jayne Nash travelled in East Africa, she noticed many temporary employment agencies in big cities like Nairobi and reckons that accountants and secretaries might have a chance of finding work.

The Black Market

In most countries the black market in currency is not really worthwhile and likely to make you the target of rip-off merchants. You may also encounter a black market in consumer goods such as T-shirts, sneakers and jeans, though it is probably not worth stocking up on these things because people in-the-know (like overland couriers) have this trade sewn up. Keep your ears open for more local opportunities. For example bottled water is three times more expensive in Zanzibar than in Dar es Salaam so it might be possible to make a small profit. Apparently pens that click on and off (not just plain old biros) are all the go in Kenya, and watches are in demand too.

A scam which is common in Cairo and Alexandria is for hostel owners to approach travellers and ask them to go out to the airport to buy duty-free booze, especially the ever-popular Johnny Walker Black Label. Foreigners are allowed to buy up to four litres of spirits at duty-free prices at the airport within 24 hours of arrival and a further three litres within 48 hours from the airport or for slightly more money at the tourist Egypt Free Store in Mohandiseen. All purchases are stamped in your passport to keep you within the legal limits. In return for handing over your whisky allowance you are normally given a couple of free nights' stay. Be very careful being whisked into a duty-free shop by a stranger, since the paperwork is done in Arabic. Several people have reported that once they arrive at the airport, the hotel owner goes mad and buys hundreds of dollars worth of electrical equipment on the traveller's passport which can cause problems when they leave the country and are asked to pay the duty on it.

Film Extras

Egypt is the capital of the Arab world's film industry, and many of the films require Western extras, often to play drunken, drug-taking, promiscuous degenerates. Be prepared to wear some idiotic, ill-fitting costumes. This pays around £10 per day, which should cover a few nights' hostel accommodation. As usual the Cairo film agents looking for extras hang out in backpackers' haunts such as the hostels in Tawfikia Market. Make enquiries in budget hostels in or near Talaat Harb Square. Ex-soldier and Glaswegian Robin Gray was approached on his first night at a hostel. He was taken to the airport for a fruitless four-hour wait for the main actor to show up, but he was paid for his trouble.

Katherine Berlanny and a friend were approached and asked if they wanted to be extras in a television soap opera. During their one day of employment, they had to play guests at a dinner party which involved some chandelier-swinging on the part of the stars. They could have had more work but had to catch a train to Aswan.

According to Ian McArthur, Western models are also required for TV commercials in Cairo:

Models are normally recruited through the agencies listed in the Yellow Pages (which fortunately has an English language version). A portfolio is an advantage though not essential and a smart outfit is useful if only to create a good impression. I was offered this work at the Hotel Oxford (well-known for its long-term residents) but was told to come back the following day three times in a row, and lost patience. The pay is supposed to be high (£20-£25 a day) and can involve several consecutive days shooting, although it tends to be sporadic.

VOLUNTEERING

Africa is still very reliant on aid agencies and voluntary assistance. The majority of volunteers in Africa are trained teachers, medical staff, agricultural and technical specialists who have committed themselves to work with mainstream aid organisations like VSO (317 Putney Bridge Road, London SW15 2PN; 020-8780 7500; www.vso.org.uk) and Skillshare International (126 New Walk, Leicester LE1 7JA; 0116-254 1862; www.skillshare.org) for at least two years. Vacancies in Africa with various charities and aid agencies are posted on the internet, for example on www.volunteerafrica.org whose originator, Simon Headington, runs an NGO in Tanzania. The Health Action Promotion Association (HAPA) works with village projects in the Singida Region of Tanzania. Volunteers may join the project for four, seven or ten weeks for fees (respectively) of £950, £1,330 and £1,710, a large proportion of which is given as a donation to the host programme.

Conservation and environmental issues are a top priority in many African countries and many organisations, large and small, are involved in protecting the magnificent wildlife and landscapes of Africa. A very good starting point for locating interesting organisations is the website www.africanconservation.org which has a searchable database of organisations and vacancies in the field.

It may be possible to offer your services on a voluntary basis to any hospital, school or mission you come across in your travels, though success is not guaranteed. Travellers who have found themselves in the vicinity of a famine crisis have often expressed shock when their offer of help has been turned down. Passers-by cannot easily be incorporated into ongoing aid projects, but it is always worth asking the local OXFAM, Save the Children Fund or Peace Corps representative.

If you have a useful skill and the addresses of some suitable projects, you are well on the way to fixing something up. Mary Hall had both, so wrote to a mission clinic in Uganda offering her services as a nurse:

There wasn't a doctor so the work was very stressful for me. After a couple of weeks I was helping to run the clinic, see and examine patients, prescribe drugs and set up a teaching programme for the unqualified Ugandan nurses. There's an incredible need for any form of medical worker in Africa but especially in Uganda where HIV and AIDS are an increasing problem.

We had no running water, intermittent electricity and a lack of such niceties as cheese and chocolate. Obviously adaptability has to be one of the main qualities. Initially I worked on my visitor's visa which wasn't a problem, but when it became apparent that I would be staying for longer, the clinic applied for a work permit for me. Quite an expensive venture (£100) and I think very difficult without a local sponsor. The local bishop wrote a beautiful letter on my behalf, so I got one. A white person is considered to be the be-all and end-all of everyone's problems, and I found it difficult to live with this image. I'd like to say that the novelty of having a white foreigner around wore off but it never did. Stare, stare and stare again, never a moment to yourself. Still it was a fantastic experience. I've learnt an awful lot, and don't think I could ever do nursing in Britain again. My whole idea of Africa and aid in particular has been turned on its head. Idealism at an end.

This professed disillusionment with aid work has not prevented Mary from pursuing a career in development in Africa and the Middle East. It is worth quoting her more recent job-hunting experiences to illustrate the way that once you work for one aid project, it is easier to move to others:

> *While living in the wilds of Worcestershire I decided that life in England was not for me and got a job in Somaliland, largely as a result of my cycling experience in Africa. Unfortunately the security in Erigavo wasn't so good and we were evacuated after I'd been there for less than two months. It seems that after you have Somalia on your CV the job market opens dramatically so I had a lot of offers including in Rwanda. I'd met the director of International Co-operation for Development in Djibouti when working for Health Unlimited and been very impressed with them. He took a shine to me as I fixed the computer (well, I turned it off and turned it on again and it was fixed – Mrs. Engineer) and when ICD had a job in Hargeisa in Somaliland and another one in Yemen he got them to send me the application forms. It's a bit strange as I'd seen both advertised in the Guardian but hadn't bothered to apply.*

Specialist programmes exist to encourage this exchange. For example volunteer sports coaches, phys ed teachers, recreation leaders and sports organisers are placed by an organisation called SCORE (Sports Coaches' OutReach, PO Box 4989, Cape Town 8000; info@score.org.za; www.score.org.za). The work includes coaching, establishing sports clubs and organising tournaments and festivals in rural or urban settings. Suitable candidates over 20 must be interested in hands-on development work and willing to live with a host family. The work period is six months or a year starting in January or July. Participants pay a fee of €2,500 for six months (which includes living expenses and travel throughout) and €3,500 for 12 months; coaches also receive a nominal monthly stipend. Foreign volunteers can obtain application details from the Volunteer Exchange Manager, PO Box 1167, 1000 BD Amsterdam, Netherlands (score.europe@planet.nl).

Some UK agencies are becoming involved in the field of sports promotion. For example GSA (Gap Sports Abroad) Ltd, Willowbank House, 84 Station Road, Marlow, Bucks, SL7 1NX (0870 837 9797; www.gapsports.com) provides volunteers to a range of outreach programmes and coaching camps in football, rugby, cricket, tennis, basketball, hockey, athletics and boxing in Ghana and South Africa, as well as to some non-sports projects involving teaching, health care, art & design, journalism, psychology, conservation and physiotherapy. Stays lasting between five weeks and 12 months cost between £1,000 and £5,000. TackleAfrica, Estate Office. Pitt Hall Farm, Ramsdell, Basingstoke, Hampshire RG26 5RJ (01256 851144; www.tackleafrica.org) organises football tours around sub-Saharan Africa which fee-paying volunteers may join. Matches and tournaments are organised in collaboration with local NGOs and charities, which then mount HIV/AIDS awareness events on the back of the sporting event.

In 2004 Paul Edmunds signed up with Travellers Worldwide (7 Mulberry Close, Ferring, W Sussex BN12 5HY; 01903 502595; www.travellersworldwide.com) to join a cricket-coaching project on the outskirts of Accra in Ghana. He enjoyed the experience enormously and felt that it was extremely beneficial to the children to experience the structured framework of a sport. As well as bringing them pleasure, it also taught them discipline.

Sending Organisations

AFS Intercultural Programmes, Vicar Lane, Leeds LS2 7JF; 0113-242 6136; www.afsuk. org. Community service programme lasting six months in Ghana and South Africa. Work in residential centres with disabled children or those in need of remedial teaching. Volunteers contribute £3,300.

Azafady, Studio 7, 1A Beethoven St, London W10 4LG, U.K.; 020-8960 6629; www. madagascar.co.uk. 10-week Pioneer Madagascar programme allows volunteers to work on a grassroots level trying to combat deforestation and extreme poverty in Madagascar. Fundraising target is £2,000 excluding flights.

Blue Ventures, 52 Avenue Road, London N6 5DR (enquiries@blueventures.org/ www.

blueventures.org). Volunteers are needed for at least six weeks to carry out marine research, coral reef conservation and day-to-day management of field camps in South Western Madagascar. Fee for 6 weeks is £1,780 for non-divers; £1,580 for PADI divers. Blue Ventures has also co-ordinated marine projects in Tanzania, South Africa and the Comoros Islands.

BUNAC, 16 Bowling Green Lane, London EC1R 0QH (020-7251 3472; africa@bunac.org. uk). 3-6 month Volunteer Ghana programme for students and recent graduates and 8-week Volunteer South Africa programme.

EIL, 287 Worcester Road, Malvern, Worcs. WR14 1AB (0800 018 4015; www.eiluk.org) offers teaching and intern programmes in Nigeria. On top of the placement fee for 3-12 months (£363-£475), living expenses are £19 a week for an urban placement or £11 for a rural one.

Frontier, 50-52 Rivington St, London EC2A 3QP (020-7613 2422; www.frontierconservation. org). Tropical research training, field experience and conservation volunteering in Madagascar's forests and Tanzania's savannah or reefs. Volunteers carry out biological surveys and socio-economic research for 4, 8, 10 or 20 weeks; participation fees are respectively £2,100-£2,500 for ten weeks, £3,600-£3.950 for 20 weeks.

Global Vision International (GVI), Amwell Farm House, Nomansland, Wheathampstead, St. Albans, Herts. AL4 8EJ (0870 608 8898; www.gvi.co.uk). Wildlife expeditions in South Africa and voluntary projects in Namibia, Rwanda, Madagascar and Egypt. Sample prices for South Africa £1,275 for 4-week field guide course, £2,450 for 10-week wildlife research expedition and £2,995 for year-long internship.

Greenforce, 11-15 Betterton Street, Covent Garden, London WC2H 9BP (020-7470 8888; www.greenforce.org). Recruits volunteer researchers to join biodiversity conservation aid projects in Zambia for 10-week stints. Fieldwork assistants study endangered species and habitats. No previous experience needed as training is provided; £2,500 plus flight.

Inter-Cultural Youth Exchange (IYCE), Latin American House, Kingsgate Place, London NW6 4TA (tel/fax 020-7681 0983; info@icye.co.uk). Makes short volunteer placements as English teachers in Morocco and 12-month placements of volunteers aged 18-30 in Ghana, Kenya, Mozambique, Uganda and Nigeria working with children, in environmental work, etc. Fee is £3,300.

Madventurer, Hawthorn House, Forth Banks, Newcastle-upon-Tyne NE1 3SG (0845 121 1996; www.madventurer.com). Charity that arranges summer and 3-month expeditions to Ghana, Tanzania, Togo, Kenya and Uganda that combine development work and adventurous overland travel. The fee for a 5-week project is £1,480 plus flights.

Reefdoctor.org Ltd, 14 Charlwood Terrace, Putney, London SW15 1NZ (07866 250740; www.reefdoctor.org). New hands-on conservation programme for enthusiastic volunteers to become research assistants for 2-3 months in Madagascar. Based in Ifaty fishing village, volunteers help to survey the coral reef in the Bay of Ranobe. Non-divers can teach in the local school. Fee (2005) is £1100 a month.

African Legacy, 46A Ophir Road, Bournemouth, Dorset BH8 8LT (01202 554735; explore@africanlegacy.info). Fieldwork adventure holidays in Nigeria with research links to the School of Conservation Sciences, Bournemouth University. Explores and maps remote unsurveyed ruins of ancient civilisations, their culture and environment with Nigerian colleagues. Cost about £990 per month depending on airfares and funding levels. Visits tailored in length, itinerary and content to suit those coming.

Clare Ansell enjoyed her time in Tanzania with Frontier so much that she joined the London office after her expedition:

I joined Frontier as a self-funded volunteer and then stayed on for an extra three months as unpaid staff managing a field camp in the Coastal Forests and later returned to work for a time as UK Co-ordinator in the London office. I've learned a fantastic amount about the practicalities of the conservation world and personally collected a new species of toad! Scientific training isn't necessary. Interest and determination are what matter.

Greenforce's ongoing conservation project in Zambia is to assist the Zambia Wildlife Authority to carry out a large-scale wildlife survey, counting mammals and birds, and trapping small mammals, reptiles, amphibians and insects. When science teacher Nigel Hollington set off to join a Greenforce project in 2004, he knew that he would be expected to handle rodents, and decided to confront his phobia head on so packed an extra-strong pair of gardening gloves for the purpose and did not shirk when the moment came.

Even if you are not phobic about rodents, it is always sensible to do as much research about a project and an organisation to which you intend to commit considerable time and money. We are grateful to Amelia Cook who alerted us to serious problems encountered with a Scandinavian-based organisation Humana-Tvind which aggressively recruits volunteers under different names. The internet site at www.tvindalert.com warns people that the extensive training promised by the organisation never materialises and that, amongst other dubious practices, volunteers may be placed in dangerous situations in Africa and elsewhere and subjected to psychological pressure. Invariably the organisation requires volunteers to pay large upfront fees for training and placement. Humana has been declared a cult *(une secte)* by the French Parliament and the British Charity Commission has removed its charity status. This organisation operates under many names worldwide including One World Volunteer Institute and Humana People to People (both in Scandinavia) and the Institute for International Co-operation & Development or IICD (USA).

From the US, try any of these placement agencies:

Cross-Cultural Solutions, 2 Clinton Place, New Rochelle, NY 10801 (800-380-4777; www. crossculturalsolutions.org). Volunteer vacations in villages in Ghana and Tanzania to teach English, provide skills training or enhance recreation programmes in village schools. The programme fees cover expenses but not airfares: from $2,175 for 2 weeks to $4,655 for 12 weeks.

Operation Crossroads Africa, Inc, PO Box 5570, New York, NY 10027 (212-289-1949; http://operationcrossroadsafrica.org). Runs 7-week summer projects in rural Africa staffed by self-financing volunteers from the U.S. and Canada. Inclusive cost is $3,500. The deadline for applications is 1st February.

United Children's Fund, PO Box 20341, Boulder, CO 80308-3341 (1-800-615-5229; www. unchildren.org). East Africa aid organisation which places volunteers in Ugandan clinics, schools, farms, etc. for short periods or 6 months. Fees from $820 for 1 week to $6,750 for 6 months, excluding airfares.

Visions in Action, 2710 Ontario Rd., NW, Washington, DC 20009 (202-625-7402; www. visionsinaction.org). 6 and 12 month volunteer positions in Uganda, Zimbabwe, Burkina Faso, South Africa, and Tanzania plus short-term opportunities in Tanzania. Volunteers must have a degree or relevant work experience to fill positions in human rights, journalism, micro-enterprise, social work, health, environment and research. Participation fees from $3,400 for summer in Tanzania to $6,700 for 12 months in South Africa.

YMCA International, 5 West 63rd St, 2nd Floor, New York, NY 10023 (212-727-8800 ext 4303; www.ymcaglobal.org). Places volunteers for 2-12 months in Ghana and Gambia to work in education, youth work and computing. The programme fee is $500.

Workcamps

The kind of short-term voluntary work available to unqualified people is generally confined to workcamps that operate in many African countries. Most of the projects have to do with rural and community development. Normally you have to finance your own travel and pay a not insignificant registration fee to cover food and lodging for the three to six week duration of the camp. Camps are sometimes arranged in winter as well as summer. The work consists of building, installing water supplies, conservation or assisting in homes for disabled or underprivileged children and adults. The national headquarters are often good sources of local information, though not by post.

If you want to arrange a place on an African workcamp before leaving home, you may have to prove to an international organisation that you have enough relevant experience. The listing from VFP (see *Volunteering* chapter) for example contains information on workcamps in seven African countries from Botswana to Togo. The workcamp movement is particularly well developed in North Africa especially Morocco which has a number of regional organisations creating green spaces, building communal facilities, etc. Provided you can function in French, contact *Jeunesse des Chantiers Marocains* (+212 70-762757; internationalcamps@yahoo.com; http://perso.menara.ma/youthcamps) which arranges three-week summer workcamps in Morocco.

The *Kenyan Voluntary Development Association* (PO Box 48902-00100, Nairobi; +254-2-225379; kvdakenya@yahoo.com) publishes its list of short and longer-term camps each January. Short-term projects lasting up to three months are normally manual (digging foundations, constructing classrooms, making access roads) and cost $350 to join. Longer-term projects lasting three to six months ($450) or 12 months ($900) involve education, social work and health care, e.g. helping at a health centre in the Northern Rift Valley. An alternative Kenyan organisation to check out is Volunteers for Africa, PO Box 2044, 00100 Nairobi GPO (www.vfa.8m.net).

Uganda Volunteers for Peace (UVP, CPO Box 3312, Kampala, Uganda; +256 77-402201; uvpeace@yahoo.co.uk) oversees projects to help disadvantaged children, youth and women. Free lodgings are provided for volunteer. International membership costs $100 plus camp participation costs $200.

VOLU is the acronym for the *Voluntary Workcamps Association of Ghana* (PO Box GP 1540, Accra; 021-663486; www.volu.org). The summer and winter workcamps it organises last three to four weeks conducting AIDS awareness campaigns, building schools and community centres, planting trees in deforested areas, etc. Volunteers pay $200 to join one camp, $300 for two or more.

To find out about a large range of workcamps in Africa, it is a good idea to obtain the international list of projects from an international sending organisation in your country (or from its website). Sometimes even they find it hard to extract an answer from their counterparts in developing nations, so be prepared for receiving details at the last minute. If European organisations have to operate on a shoestring, African ones survive on a broken sandal strap, though in recent years many have gained internet access which makes communication infinitely cheaper and easier.

On-the-Ground Opportunities

If you decide to join a project once you are in an African capital like Maputo, Accra, Addis Ababa or Kampala, it should not be hard to track down the co-ordinating office. Start by asking at the British Embassy or British Council (especially if teaching interests you), at the YMCA or in prominent churches.

Roger Blake did exactly that when he travelled to Ethiopia and then Uganda, two countries which do not generally offer many voluntary opportunities:
I had contemplated a 'voluntary' placement fixed up through an agency at home but I find the modern concept of paying to volunteer your services a crazy idea. So I decided that I would go it alone. I have been in Ethiopia for almost two months now and have had a great time. On my return to Addis Ababa, I decided to ask at the British Council for any English teaching possibilities. Not expecting anything to come of if, they were welcoming of my two (basic) TEFL certificates and gave me the number of a highly qualified tutor. After some conversation into my background she recommended me to a charity who invited me to spend a week supporting their qualified local teacher in the classroom with physically disabled children. I did not get paid but they did make it worth my while by giving me three excellent meals a day and I got to stay in a wonderful house in an idyllic countryside location with magnificent gardens. My 'employment' was unofficial, thus the short stay. I have ascertained that there are casual opportunities to teach here in Addis but you must search hard to find them.

Continuing his trans-African journey, Roger next enquired about working possibilities in Kampala where he had already encountered the huge expatriate community and their attendant recreations – cinema, pubs, gyms, supermarkets:

> On the notice board of the Red Chilli Hideaway, a backpackers' hostel and campsite where I've been staying, Kabira School had an advert for a youth worker at their youth centre. Nothing ventured, nothing gained, so I applied and got the job (for a trial period). I've been working evenings and weekends with expat teenagers, in the same environment as a youth club at home. They would have been willing to arrange a work permit for me and pay me a very reasonable salary of 460 Ugandan shillings ($250) a month – enough to live on as I'm staying in my tent at the hostel. I was tempted but I decided to move on with the African trip, mainly because I didn't want to lose my non-refundable onward air ticket to Australia.

Another Ugandan possibility is Kasana Secondary School in Luwero (Buganda 72; 077-649000) which advertises on the website www.idealist.org for volunteers to teach English, science or computing, for a minimum of two months in marginalised rural areas.

Grassroots Organisations

Till Bruckner is another veteran world traveller who shares Roger Blake's fondness for fixing up teaching and voluntary placements independently rather than with the help of an intermediary:

> My advice to anyone who wants to volunteer in Africa (or anywhere else) is to go first and volunteer second. That way you can travel until you've found a place you genuinely like and where you think you might be able to make a difference. You can also check out the work and accommodation for yourself before you settle down. If you're willing to work for free, you don't need a nanny to tell you where to go. Just go.

However for those who find this prospect daunting (and unless you are a mature and seasoned traveller you probably will), you might like to pursue the middle way which is to make contact with small local organisations in Africa which actively look for volunteers abroad, though be prepared for problems in communication. The following are listed in alphabetical order by country:

AJVPE – Association des Jeunes Volontaire pour le Protection de l'Environnement, B.P. 4568, Lomé, Togo (901 2506; enquiries@ajvpe-togo.org; www.ajvpe-togo.org). Summer workcamps last 21 days carrying out projects like tree planting and building a municipal garden in the small town of Agbodrafo.

CYTOFWEA, Charity Youth Travel & Working Experiences Abroad, PO Box CO55, Tema, Ghana (cytofwea2001@yahoo.com). Self-funding international volunteers placed in range of development projects in Ghana, e.g. schools, wildlife rehabilitation centres and eco-tourist projects, for varying periods.

Future in our Hands (FIOH) Kenya, PO Box 4037, Kisumu, Kenya (03-40522; fiohk@hotmail.com). Volunteers needed for 5 weeks to 6 months. Branches also in Cameroon, Sierra Leone, Liberia and South Africa. UK link office is FIOH, 48 Churchward Avenue, Swindon, Wilts. SN2 1NH (www.fiohnetwork.org). The movement supports small charities in Africa with funding and volunteers.

RUSO (Rural Upgrade Support Organisation), c/o University of Ghana, PMB L21, Legon, Accra, Ghana (513149; www.interconnection.org/ruso). International volunteers join tree planting, AIDS awareness education, fish farming and other projects especially in the Kome area of Ghana. The cost to volunteers is a $300 registration fee plus $25 per week for stays of 1-3 months or $15 a week if staying 3-6 months.

Save the Earth Network (STEN), PO Box CT 3635, Cantonments-Accra, Ghana; +233-27-7743139; ebensten@yahoo.com). Promotes environmental preservation, sustainable development, international cultural exchange, solidarity and friendship through voluntary work placements and host family home stays in Ghana. Placements in teaching, orphanages, conservation, etc. last for between one week and four months; private accommodation and meals are provided free. The contribution to expenses ranges from $595 for 1-4 weeks to $1,995 for 4 months.

Sénévolu, Dakar (550 4885; fax 855 7172; www.senevolu.mypage.org). Involves foreign young people in local community projects and schools while living with a local family and spending weekends in cultural workshops in drumming, batik, etc. Minimum stay 3 weeks; fee €625/$750.

Women International Coalition Organisation (WICO), P O Box 1075, Limbe, Cameroon (+237 9580292; wicoafrica@yahoo.com; www.wicohome.org). Placements for all kinds of voluntary service including hospitality, conservation, community service and fundraising throughout Africa, especially Cameroon. Placement fee $350.

WWOOF Uganda, PO Box 2001, Kampala, Uganda (+256-346856; bob_kasule@yahoo. com). Membership fee of £10/$15 (bank drafts only).

Now that the political situation in Sierra Leone is heading towards stability, voluntary organisations are desperate for voluntary and (especially) monetary help. One such is PASACOFAAS (Pa Santigie Conteh Farmers' Community Development Association, 5a City Road, Wellington, PMB 686, Freetown) which needs manual and administrative help for its projects in the Bombali District.

Throughout Africa there are a great many volunteer workers with the mainstream aid agencies like VSO and the Peace Corps in hospitals, schools and agricultural projects who are sometimes willing to put up travellers. Probably the more remote and cut-off the volunteers are, the more welcoming they will be, but be careful not to abuse or presume on this kind of hospitality. Always offer to pay, or go armed with treats.

Foreign embassies might also be in a position to offer useful advice. According to an article in the bi-monthly magazine *Transitions Abroad* for example the American Embassy in Lusaka, Zambia has a Community Liaison Office who holds information about local charities and aid projects which may need volunteers.

Contacts are a great help here. Your path will be made smoother if you can procure an introduction from a church or family friend. Catherine Young spent a summer trying to set up a playgroup in a Nigerian village where a friend's father was setting up a medical clinic. But people have succeeded without contacts. One traveller we heard of went to Cape Town Central Library and looked through the 'green directory' which lists hundreds of environmental agencies. He then fixed up some voluntary work on a cheetah reserve near Johannesburg, where he was given free board and lodging but no wages. There is a myriad of plant and wildlife studies being carried out throughout Africa and you might be fortunate enough to become attached to one of these.

Conservation and Wildlife

A number of wildlife reserves in Southern Africa have introduced programmes for paying volunteers, especially gap year students, to get close to the animals by monitoring them and protecting their environment. The costs, which are usually substantial, are used to support the conservation of the reserve, many of which are privately owned. For example TrackAfrica (www.trackafrica.com) accepts volunteer 'wildlife custodians' to spend one to three months at their 1000 square kilometre reserve in the North West Cape province.

Some overseas agencies and workcamp organisations involved with conservation in Africa have already been mentioned. African Conservation Experience PO Box 28, Ottery St Mary, Devon, EX11 1ZN (0870 241 5816; www.ConservationAfrica.net) arranges conservation work placements lasting 4-12 weeks on game reserves in Southern Africa including South Africa, Botswana, Namibia and Zimbabwe. Tasks may include darting rhino for relocation or elephant for fitting tracking collars, game capture, tagging, assisting with veterinary work, game counts, etc. Alien plant control and the re-introduction of indigenous plants is often involved. The average cost for 12 weeks is £4,000 including flights, transfers, accommodation and all meals.

A new company called Bio-Experience aims to help South African nature reserves and wildlife rehabilitation centres by arranging for fee-paying international and local volunteers to spend a working holiday assisting them. International volunteers assist with various projects otherwise unaffordable to reserve owners due to a lack of funding. Volunteers can get involved in wildlife feeding and cage cleaning at wildlife centres and invader plant control and game counts at nature reserves. The inclusive participation fee differs but an example of two weeks monitoring baboons costs R3,000 and four weeks rehabilitating marine birds mainly penguins is R6,200. Further details are available from Natanya Dreyer (011-964 1900; natanya@cybertrade.co.za; www.bioexperience.org).

Wild at Heart in Kwazulu Natal (www.wah.co.za) offers hands-on opportunities to work with species such as lions, cheetah and elephants at wildlife rehabilitation centres in South Africa, Botswana and Namibia. About a thousand volunteers, many without specific skills, are placed in 15 projects every year. Further information is available from Wild at Heart, Old Main St, Suite 7A, Cowell Park, Hillcrest, 3610 Kwazulu/Natal (031-765 2947). UK bookings can be made through the Work & Travel Company, 45 High St, Tunbridge Wells, Kent TN1 1XL (01892 516164; info@worktravelcompany.co.uk). A sample fee would be £1,389 for four weeks on a project.

A survey carried out in 2003 asked people to rank the 50 things they wanted to do before they died. Well over half of these dream trips involved contact with wildlife, particularly African big game. Chris Giles and his wife Christine worked at Kwando Safari Camp in Botswana last year, arranged through The Leap Overseas Ltd (Windy Hollow, Sheepdrove, Lambourn, Berks. RG17 7XA; 0870 240 4187; www.theleap.co.uk), where they did menial work in the kitchen and grounds but had thrilling brushes with the wildlife:

> Our jobs were not strenuous or difficult but extremely important because it made us feel part of the team running the safari camp. Christine has been in the kitchen and I have been a waiter, scullery (washing up) and helped mend a walkway when an elephant wandered through during the middle of the night! As I have absolutely no practical skills, this was quite an achievement, although I'm not sure the maintenance manager, who showed great patience, was impressed with how long it took me.
>
> The scenery and wildlife in this remote part of northern Botswana are stunning so things that are normally mundane and routine suddenly become exciting. I was quite happy clearing plates, washing glasses, making fruit salad, serving drinks and chatting to guests from all around the world.

In Kenya, the Tsavo Conservation Trust (PO Box 48019, Nairobi, Kenya; 02-331191; www.originsafaris.info/community-volunteer.htm) runs a community volunteer programme which can make use of competent, but not necessarily qualified, volunteers in a variety of conservation and community projects in rural Kenya. The minimum stay is one month at a cost of $920. The Trust runs the Taita Discovery Centre in the wilds of Kenya where a number of gap year students are placed on organised schemes.

The Wakuluzu Trust in Kenya needs volunteers over the age of 22 who can stay for 6-12 months to work to save the Angolan Colobus monkey and preserve its coastal habitat. The cost of participating is modest: $300 per month plus about $20 a week for food. (Details are available from the Born Free Foundation, 3 Grove House, Foundry Lane, Horsham, W. Sussex RH13 5PL; www.bornfree.org.uk).

The US charity IDA Africa (In Defense of Animals), 700 SW 126th Ave., Beaverton, OR 97005 (503-643-8302; www.ida-africa.org/volunteer.html) sends volunteers who are able to communicate in French (rather than monkey language) to a chimpanzee sanctuary in Yaounde, Cameroon, for a minimum of six months.

Very few opportunities present themselves in the vast nation of Congo, but it is possible to join a project to release orphaned chimps into the wild. H.E.L.P. Congo (BP 335, Pointe Noire, Republic of Congo; help.congo@cg.celtelplus.com) accepts volunteers with no previous experience who are asked to contribute €310 per month for their keep and transport for a minimum of three months.

Israel

Israel is not a happy country. The conflict between the Israelis and Palestinians often seems beyond resolution. Predictably, as the Peace Process has unravelled, Israel has lost much of its appeal for travellers, and the number of young people choosing to head for what was a generation ago a favourite travellers' destination is drastically down. At present few if any opportunities exist in the Palestinian-governed Territories and many projects such as archaeological digs have been curtailed or cancelled because of the current situation in Israel. But behind all the shocking violence and retaliation in the headlines, thousands of individuals and groups do not consider the situation hopeless and are working patiently towards peace and reconciliation. Spending time in Israel will enable people from outside the region to gain more insight into one of the world's most bedevilling trouble spots. Personal security is bound to be a consideration but the statistics should be reassuring, that tourists and volunteers are rarely if ever the targets of violence. If entering the country under the auspices of for example a kibbutz placement organisation, you should seek up-to-the-minute advice about where it is considered safe to go.

The prospects for finding work are also much gloomier than they used to be, mainly because the government has made the visa situation much more difficult. A couple of years ago the Immigration Authority mounted a controversial ad campaign against employing foreign workers without permits. These ads implied that foreign workers harmed the Israeli economy, society, morality and even security. (It was later taken to the High Court of Justice for inciting racial hatred so the campaign has since been toned down.)

But the attitude of the authorities has changed utterly. To take just one example, the owner of a long-established au pair agency in Rishon-le-Zion south of Tel Aviv reported in November 2004 that she had been forced to close her agency (Hilma's Intermediary) due to the ferocity of the clampdown on all foreigners working in the country. Her account is strongly worded and very depressing for the working traveller:

Due to government regulations and severe actions against foreigners working here, there is NO WAY for any agency or individual to work in Israel as an au pair, mother's helper, etc. Basically it comes down to the fact that no one should even try to work on a tourist visa, because many people are just sent back at the airport. If they do receive a tourist visa, they may be able to stay for only two weeks or at most three months. No family wants a mother's helper for that short a period. Besides this, there is now a special police force that goes after anyone working that does not have a working permit and many people are being stopped in the streets or sometimes picked up from their homes (when a neighbour gives information!). Israel is at the moment a no-go country for those who want to work as nannies, au pairs, housekeepers or in a moshav. It is sad to see a foreigner getting into trouble and many Israelis are against this situation. But for the time being at least, I advise no one to come.

Not everyone takes such a negative view. The co-owner of a Tel Aviv hostel wrote in 2005 to say that, although it is not as easy as it once was, casual work in dishwashing, cleaning, construction is available. But he agrees that 'the problem is the immigration police because people who hire illegal workers risk big fines.'

Fortunately it is still possible to enter Israel as a volunteer. Most people associate working in Israel with staying on a kibbutz or a moshav. Although there are other working opportunities, these are the most popular ways of having a prolonged visit in Israel, and one of which many thousands of international travellers have taken advantage over the years. Although not everyone enjoys the work they end up doing in Israel (especially if they are there in winter and have been expecting hot sun), most agree that it is an excellent country in which to meet working travellers and (politics permitting) a good place to travel.

The Regulations

For anyone wishing to volunteer on a kibbutz or archaeological dig, it is obligatory to obtain a B4 Volunteer Visa (at a cost of NIS75/$17) within 15 days of joining a volunteer scheme. If you arrange a job after arrival in Israel or through official channels (e.g. the volunteer offices in Tel Aviv), it is fairly straightforward obtaining the visa, but may be difficult if you fix up something informally. If you stay more than three months, you must renew the B4 which will cost more than the first time. Currently only one renewal is permitted, giving a maximum stay in Israel of six months. But the regulations are always changing and, if you want to stay on and your employers are keen, they may be able to find a way to get a further extension. Note that when you leave the country, the B4 is cancelled even if it has time to run. If you plan to travel to Egypt or Jordan, you should plan to do it just before your volunteer visa expires.

It is virtually impossible to obtain a work permit for the kind of casual work travellers tend to do in Israel and increasingly risky working on a tourist visa. Those on tourist visas must leave the country before their visa expires and hope to renew it on re-entry. Some people cross into Egypt and get a new visa on returning. (If you are counting on receiving some wages owed to fund the trip, be warned that wages are often slow to come and you might find yourself trapped with a visa due to expire and no money to make the trip.) Others move onto a kibbutz or moshav and let the volunteer leader get the visa. Be careful not to let your visa expire, especially in Eilat. Contrary to what some people believe, a deportation order does not arrive with a free flight ticket.

On arrival, you may be asked to show enough funds to support yourself, which is when a pre-arranged letter of invitation from a kibbutz or moshav organisation can be very handy and you can obtain the B4 on entry. All visitors must be prepared for an unpleasant time both entering and leaving the country, with sometimes vicious interrogations, especially if you have been wandering around the country for a long period.

KIBBUTZIM and MOSHAVIM

Everyone has some idea of what a kibbutz is: it is a communal society in which the means of production are owned and shared by the community as a whole. For two generations, this idea has appealed to young people from around the world who have flocked to the 200+ kibbutzim of Israel to volunteer their services and participate in this utopian community based on equality. But the movement is in serious decline. Less than one-fifth of the number of foreign volunteers who came in the 1970s arrive in Israel now, 10,000 instead of 50,000.

Twenty-first century pressures mean that some of the founding principles have been abandoned and the economy of kibbutzim has increasingly become based on tourism and light industry rather than agriculture. Some argue that even if the ownership of the land is transferred from the state to the kibbutzim themselves, the spirit of communalism can be retained. Yet the consensus among volunteers is that they would be less inclined to donate their labour to a privatised profit-making community. Having said all that, thousands of young people from all over the world have continued to join kibbutzim for a couple of months and have enjoyed the experience. The majority of kibbutzim still accept volunteers and some recruit online e.g. Kibbutz Ketura (www.ketura.org.il). The unofficial site www. kibbutzvolunteer.com has links to about 25 kibbutzim with their own websites.

If the kibbutz is broadly based on a socialist model, the moshav is on a capitalist one, with members owning their own machinery and houses, though the produce is marketed co-operatively. Moshavim are flourishing; in fact nearly 40% of the rural population live on one (compared to 35% 40 years ago). The kind of experience the volunteer has on a moshav is very different and usually more demanding. Although the term 'volunteer' is used of moshavim, a wage is paid (normally the shekel equivalent of about $450 a month) and a frugal person can save up to half that amount to fund further travels (normally in Egypt) especially if he or she is prepared to work overtime (paid at about $3.50 an hour) and if you stay long enough to earn an end-of-season bonus. Paul Bridgland's travelling fund went from enough for a box of matches to $1,000 during the three months he worked on Moshav Pharan.

Arranging a Job in Advance

Two possibilities exist for fixing up a place on a kibbutz or moshav: application may be made through an organisation in your own country or you may wait until you get to Israel. The demand for volunteers fluctuates according to many factors including national politics, the point in the agricultural calendar when you arrive, competition from new Jewish settlers and so on. If you wait until you arrive in Israel, especially in the summer months, there may be a delay before you can be placed, though in the present circumstances, demand for volunteers is likely to outstrip supply.

There is no doubt that making contact with an organisation in advance will give you a certain peace of mind, especially if you do not have much money. Advance registration is recommended for any traveller who lacks confidence or whose circumstances are unusual such as the determined 56-year old Maureen Dambach-Sinclair who wrote such stroppy letters from her home in South Africa to the Volunteer Center in Tel Aviv about their discrimination on the grounds of age that they eventually gave her a chance. She ended up having a marvellous stay on a kibbutz and was invited back the next year by the volunteer leader.

In Britain the main kibbutz placement organisation is Kibbutz Representatives at 16 Accommodation Road, London NW11 8EP (020-8458 9235/fax 020-8455 7930; enquiries@kibbutz.org.uk). To register you must be between the ages of 18 and 40 (in some cases up to 50), be able to stay for a minimum of eight weeks and maximum of six months, attend an informal interview in London, and provide a signed medical declaration of fitness. Processing normally takes two to three weeks. The kibbutz package costs around £410 and includes flights and kibbutz insurance. You can either arrange to travel independently and present yourself at the kibbutz office in Tel Aviv, or you can book flights through KR, as an individual or as part of a group. Group participants are met at the airport.

American applicants should contact the Kibbutz Aliya Desk (633 3rd Ave, 21st Floor, New York, NY 10017; 1-800-247-7852; fax 212-318-6134; kpc@jazo.org.il; www.kibbutz-programcenter.org) which acts as a clearinghouse for American volunteers. The registration fee is $150 plus $80 insurance. Canadian Jewish people aged 18-26 might qualify for the Israel for Free programme operated by Canada Israel Experience (4600 Bathurst St, Suite 315, Toronto, Ont M2R 3V3; www.israelforfree.com).

The Kibbutz Adventure Centre in Sydney has been sending Australians to Israel for many years (mcohn@kibbutz.com.au; www.kibbutz.com.au). Unusually, they run a separate scheme for older volunteers aged 35-70. Depending on fitness and the amount of work contributed, older volunteers are asked to subsidise their stay, typically $20-$25 a day with four hours of light work. The head office in Israel is at 2 Gilboa St, Kochav Yair 44864; 09-749 2015).

South Africans may book through the Overseas Visitors Club (230 Long St, Cape Town 8001; 021-423 4477; www.ovc.co.za).

Arranging a Job on the Spot

Inevitably it is cheaper to arrange a placement independently than via an agency. First-time travellers typically turn to an agency but for subsequent visits to Israel arrange things themselves as Allan Kirkpatrick did:

While working as a packaging and bottling engineer in Glasgow, I contacted Kibbutz Representatives in London who arranged everything. I spent a very nice two months at Kibbutz Ein-Gedi next to the Dead Sea. Back home to Scotland to give up my flat and arrange everything for my world tour, starting back again in Israel. I didn't arrange my travel and job through Kibbutz Representatives this time. I got a really really cheap one-way flight to Tel Aviv and went to the kibbutz office to choose my next kibbutz. I wanted a kibbutz totally different from Ein-Gedi with its deserts, Dead Sea and dusty environment, and luckily got a place in Ein-Gev on the Sea of Galilee. I did many jobs at Ein-Gev such as gardener, dishwasher, laundry worker and holiday camp worker at a nearby village run by the kibbutz. It was so good that I stayed for four months and met a nice Japanese girl with whom I went travelling afterwards.

A number of offices in Tel Aviv are able to place volunteers who simply show up, particularly between October and May, provided they can pay the necessary registration and insurance fees. There may be a slight wait in the summer especially for those who request a particular kind of kibbutz.

The official volunteer placement office represents kibbutzim from both the main kibbutz movements Takam and Artzi: the Kibbutz Program Center, Volunteer Department, 18 Frishman St, Corner of 90 Ben Yehuda St, Tel Aviv 61030 (03-527 8874/ fax 03-523 9966; kpc@volunteer.co.il/ www.kibbutz.org.il/eng/welcome.htm). The office is situated in apartment 6 on the third floor, and the opening hours are Sunday to Thursday 8am-2pm. Bear in mind that if you arrive during religious holidays such as the week of Passover in the spring, working hours may be reduced or offices closed. The buses needed to reach the office are: number 222 from the airport, 10 from the railway station and 4 from the Central Bus Station.

To apply through the Kibbutz Program Center, you must take your passport, medical certificate, insurance policy (which must show that your insurer has an Israeli representative), an airline ticket out of Israel, two passport photos and registration fee of $60. This one-off fee covers you for a year, including if you move to another kibbutz (something the private agencies will charge for). They will also want to see proof of funds ($250), though if there is a shortage of volunteers they are unlikely to be strict about this. Comprehensive insurance cover is compulsory, so if your policy is not sufficient, you can buy a suitable policy at the KPC for $80 which provides cover for up to 12 months. A returnable deposit is payable to guarantee that you stay for the minimum period of eight weeks. Note that while the KPC discourages volunteers from applying directly to the kibbutz of their choice, many of the kibbutzim prefer direct contact. Many kibbutzim will want to see a recent HIV test or will arrange for or advise volunteers to have one done.

There are several private placement offices and agents which you will soon hear about in any of the Tel Aviv hostels. Try to get detailed instructions before setting off to find a certain address, since these offices tend to be hard to locate. Meira's Volunteers for Moshav/ Kibbutz is a long-established agency at 73 Ben Yehuda St, Ground Floor, Tel Aviv 63435 (03-523 7369/524 3811; fax 03-524 1604/ meiras@netvision.net.il); the entrance to the building is behind the restaurant through the orange terrace and the office is open Sunday to Thursday 9.30am-3.30pm. J. Hains described this office some time ago as 'extremely efficient and friendly' though no recent confirmation was forthcoming. Meira's is accessible by bus 222 from the airport; ask to be put off at the corner of Hayarkon and Mapu Streets. The charge for insurance here is NIS 250 (New Israeli shekels) plus a NIS200 handling fee, refundable after two months at the moshavim. Agencies can usually make placements on both kibbutzim and moshavim.

When in the past there has been a glut of volunteers, some Britons have reported that they are slower to be placed than other nationalities because of their reputation for hard-drinking yobbishness. Moshav farmers have always been less concerned than the agencies about the nationality of their workers. It is not too difficult to arrange independently to change from one kibbutz or moshav to another. Make sure you get a letter of recommendation from your last kibbutz to prove that you did not leave under a cloud.

If you are clued up when you visit the agencies, it is possible to request a certain kind of kibbutz or moshav (big or small, politically left or centre, well established or new) and in a certain location, though much depends on the individual volunteer leader and conditions change frequently. The vast majority are located in the fertile lands of central and northern Israel. It is best to be prepared for the climate; for example the north can be cold and rainy in winter, whereas the Jordan Rift Valley can be one of the hottest and driest places in the world.

Life on a Kibbutz

In return for their labour, volunteers receive free room and board and a small amount of pocket money (unchanged for some years at $90 a month). Most volunteers enjoy their stay, and find that some kibbutzim make considerable efforts to welcome volunteers. For example the majority of kibbutzim try to provide occasional organised sightseeing tours for volunteers, sometimes every month. Yet kibbutzim are not the holiday camps that some people expect them to be. The average working week is 48 hours though hours may be reduced in the hot summer or extended at busy times. You are entitled to a day off for every six hours of overtime you put in. Many kibbutzim give an extra two or three days off per month to allow their volunteers to travel (since travel is difficult on the sabbath when there is no public transport).

Jimmy Hill describes the variety of jobs he did in just two months at a small kibbutz south of Jericho: 'dining hall duties, baby house, chopping date trees, a lot of gardening, working in a vineyard, electrician, turkey chaser and guest house cleaner'. New volunteers are often assigned the undesirable jobs though most volunteer organisers are willing to transfer a dissatisfied volunteer to a different job. Catherine Revell claims that if you are assertive and show willingness to work hard, you can find yourself doing more interesting work; among the jobs she did on three different kibbutzim were kitchen manager, shepherdess and a sculptor's assistant. Increasingly, work is in factories or of an industrial nature, though it is impossible to generalise and interesting options crop up. For example Allan Kirkpatrick from Glasgow spent an enjoyable six weeks at Kibbutz Kfar Blum cleaning a theatre where a classical music festival was taking place. (What made his stay more interesting but less relaxing was that the town of Kiriyat Shemona, 3km away was being bombed by the Lebanese Army at the time, and he spent three days in the bomb shelter.) Another example of how varied a volunteer's work can be found at Kibbutz Yizreel south of Nazareth which has introduced an English-teaching programme for its growing number of Korean volunteers.

Agricultural jobs are still available at some kibbutzim. One unexpected hazard in the fields is the wildlife. The only job John Mallon was reluctant to do was to carry bunches of bananas since they housed rats and spiders. And although in most respects Deborah Hunter's kibbutz was no Garden of Eden, she recalls several shrieks and hasty descents of the ladder when volunteers encountered snakes in the fruit trees.

Facilities can differ radically from one kibbutz to the next as Kevin Boyd discovered when he moved from a kibbutz 2km from the Gaza Strip fence to another recommended by a woman he had met: 'My first kibbutz was very poor. Our rooms consisted of two pre-fab concrete huts with very thin plastic walls which meant that there was very little privacy in the rooms.' Although his second kibbutz had a swimming pool, barbecues, volunteers' pub, etc., these were all closed for the winter, and Kevin was made to feel that by arriving in the autumn, he had come just as the party was over. He was told that the best time to join a kibbutz is March, so that you can be well established by the time the hordes arrive in May/June.

Meeting people is the central theme of kibbutz volunteer life and everyone agrees that the social life on kibbutzim is seldom dull. It can be difficult to get to know the kibbutzniks (permanent residents) though if you happen to be around for a Jewish festival, you should be able to join in some of the celebrations. The kibbutz trip was definitely the highlight for Paul Bridgland: *'The kibbutz took us all on a three-day holiday to the south, gave us decent food, free beer and meals out. They were generous. We went sightseeing, snorkelling and hired out boats, one of which ended up being rammed through the side of another at high speed on account of the free beers.'*

Most of the necessities of life are provided by the kibbutz including stationery, tea, coffee, basic toiletries and cigarettes, though perks differ and have been generally shrinking as pocket money rises. The non-profit kibbutz shops and bars sell most items cheaply. On both kibbutzim and moshavim, it is a good idea to take along a few personal objects such as posters or a cassette recorder to humanise your life. Other valuable assets are an alarm clock since the working day gets underway as early as 4am to cheat the noonday sun and plenty of mosquito repellent. If you want to get rid of anything when you leave, you may be able to make a profit by selling it.

Julee Wyld from Canada is in a long line of volunteers who have ended up raving about kibbutz life:

I had an incredible experience on the kibbutz, one of the best things I ever did. I adapted well, loved my job (working in the zoo), got along very well with my volunteer leader, made friends from all over the world (many from Europe whom I will visit next month) and even made many kibbutznik friends. I also learned quite a lot of Hebrew, which is exciting to me. The volunteers on my kibbutz (approximately 30) were like family to me. We spent a lot of time together, looked out for each other, took care of each other and these people will be friends for life, something that is very special to me.

Many volunteers find that the communal lifestyle brings a feeling of relaxation and inner harmony, though after a few months some begin to tire of the menial nature of the work, the boss's attitude and to feel that all that can be gained from the experience has been gained.

Life on a Moshav

Life is very different on a moshav. As Alison Cooper says, 'getting up at 5am every day, working approximately 75 hours a week for a pittance, and doing your own cooking and washing is bloody hard work.' And there is no wild social life to compensate. On a moshav, you must be prepared for what Vaughan Temby calls the 'usual sweat and tears' kind of hard work. Usually there are few places to spend your money so they are a good place to save.

Moshavim differ as much from each other as kibbutzim do, so while some describe them as 'horrible places, soulless and depressing,' others find themselves working for charming and generous farmers. Sarah Protheroe's job sounds almost Biblical: trimming myrtle for the Jewish harvest festival of Sukkoth, which she thought was infinitely preferable to some of the jobs kibbutz volunteers she met had to do, such as working with battery chickens or in a factory. She also enjoyed the social life on her moshav which included a barbecue each Wednesday and a disco on Fridays, which compensated for the cramped accommodation (nine girls squeezed into a two-bedroom house). Paul Kington found himself working with cows in the Golan region in December, where it was cold and windy and he was the only volunteer. But he wasn't complaining since the work was easy, he had his own heated flat, a generous boss and lots of time to explore the best scenery he had very seen. The high season for most moshavim is November to April, so spring is when you are most likely to receive a bonus of up to two months' wages.

A few moshav volunteers live with the *moshavnikit* (moshav farmer) but most are housed in spartanly furnished volunteers' houses where they are responsible for buying and cooking their own food. Volunteers often have access only to the moshav shop where prices may be inflated and choice minimal. While staying on a moshav in the Negev, Lowenna Bartlett felt as though she were living in a goldfish bowl, and resented the way the Thai workers loitered and spied on her. After a rape took place on her moshav, she became especially wary.

TOURISM

The current situation in Israel and the Middle East generally has crippled the tourist industry, so the work described here may not be very plentiful until more peaceful times return. The best places for finding work in tourism are Eilat, Tel Aviv, Herzliya (a wealthy resort north of Tel Aviv) and, to a lesser extent, Haifa and Jerusalem. There is a plethora of cheap hostels around Israel, almost all of which employ two or three travellers to spend a few hours a day cleaning or manning the desk in exchange for a free bed and some meals. If you prove yourself a hard worker, you may be moved to a better job or even paid some pocket money. Heather McCulloch worked for a hostel in Tiberias, the main resort on the Sea of Galilee (where at that time it was easy to find restaurant, beach or hotel work). Julee Wyld did not find her summer job at a water park on the Sea of Galilee nearly as congenial as she had found her kibbutz:

> My one month there was definitely a learning experience. We worked 12-14 hours a day, seven days a week, some days receiving only one 30-minute break. We spent our days picking up garbage, cleaning toilets and watching the pools and slides. It was the worst job I've ever done, very hard work for less than £1 an hour. Crazy. The accommodation and food were included but it was very basic lodgings and the same food three times a day. I really saw Israeli culture and, although I met many nice people, many were rude, arrogant, inconsiderate and disrespectful. But I would like to end on a positive note because I did get the chance to meet many other foreign workers.

The Youth Hostel Association of Israel (1 Shezer St, PO Box 6001, Jerusalem 91060; 02-655 8400; www.youth-hostels.org.il) can provide a list of their 32 member hostels around the country which may be in a position to offer free accommodation, meals and pocket money in exchange for six hours of work a day.

Casual jobs in cafés, restaurants, bars and hotels can often be unearthed. As in Greece, these jobs are much easier to get if you're female. The pay is usually low and sometimes non-existent, but you will get free food and drink, and tips. There is no accepted minimum and, as throughout Israel, the price of a day's work has to be negotiated. The places that do pay wages on a monthly basis tend to make pay-day about the tenth of the month, so that is a good time to look for a job because lots of people move on after collecting their wages. Most working travellers also recommend collecting your wages (and paying your own hostel bills) on a daily basis to prevent aggravation later. Also be aware that many travellers have had their money stolen from hostels including one group who lost money entrusted to the hostel 'safe'.

Eilat

Eilat is the main holiday resort on the Gulf of Aqaba, with several large seafront hotels, numerous smaller establishments and a few under construction. Virtually all aspects of Israeli culture have been killed off, but it is still an established haven for the working traveller despite a general tightening of immigration rules. J. M. Rapp from the US reported that most of the big beach hotels were refusing to hire people without permits, though exceptions were made for clean-cut travellers (mostly couples).

Inevitably, women find it easier than men to pick up work in tourist-related places. Make the rounds of the hotel personnel managers as early in the season as possible. The Tourist Center near the Youth Hostel has lots of bars, restaurants and sandwich bars worth trying. Laura O'Connor describes the range of jobs she did in two months in Eilat: *'I had a variety of jobs: sold tickets for a boat cruise and handed out fliers for a restaurant (both for two days), waitressed in a fish restaurant for a week (had to leave as the chef would let me stay in the staff apartment only for sex), worked in Luna Park amusement park and cleaned in my hostel (Fawlty Towers).'*

The foreign tourist season lasts from late October to March. (When Israelis take their holidays, in high summer when the temperature is in the 40s every day, most workers will be expected to speak Hebrew.) There is such a ready supply of workers desperate for any excuse to stay on that some employers try to get away with murder, as Laura O'Connor describes: *'When in November it begins to get cold in the rest of Israel, there is a mass migration to Eilat which is a mega tourist trap. We are our own worst enemy since there are so many travellers looking for jobs that employers can be right bastards.'*

An additional problem for women is the level of hassle they must endure from male tourists from various countries who are attracted to Eilat on account of its thriving escort business.

Several travellers have warned also of the 'Eilat Trap' in which penniless travellers are sometimes caught, unable to extract owed wages from their employer and unable to leave before their visa expires. Like all international resorts, Eilat is expensive, and some backpackers end up sleeping on the beach, where every precaution must be taken to safeguard belongings and also to guard against the plague of mosquitoes. But there are showers, toilets and lockers next to the Underground pub in Eilat's New Tourist Centre.

Eilat is also an important yachting and diving centre. Vacancies are sometimes posted on the gates to the Marina or on the Marina noticeboard, but work as crew or kitchen staff, cleaners or au pairs is usually found by asking boat to boat. Sarah Jane Smith had the best time of her life in Eilat after she landed a job as a deckhand and hostess on a private charter yacht for scuba divers:

I was taken on cruises lasting between a week and a month to the Red Sea, Gulf of Suez, etc. to some of the best diving spots in the world. I was taught how to scuba dive and also did lots of snorkelling. I saw some of the most amazing sights of my life – the sun rising over Saudi Arabia as the moon sank into Egypt, coral reefs, sharks, dolphins, and so on. The social life on the marina was better than the kibbutz with hundreds of other travellers working on boats or in Eilat. Every night was a party and I hardly know how I survived it. The only bad thing is the low wages (if you get paid at all) and the hard work. But the harder you work and longer you stay, the better the wages and perks become.

This rosy view of marina work is echoed by Jane Harris who wrote from Dahab in Egypt to describe her experiences on the *Orionia*, the fourth boat at which she asked for work:

> *The marina is not the place to look for work if you want to save money. You get paid NIS30 per day plus free food and accommodation. But it's great work, cruising on the Red Sea. Our boat takes tourists on four or six hour trips with a stop for swimming, a barbecue and meal on board. To get these jobs we just walked down to the Marina and asked around, and started work the following day. A word of warning: always ask the crew what the skipper is like and how hard the work is. Our skipper was great but lots of them were absolute bastards to work for.*

Tel Aviv

Work is also plentiful at times in Tel Aviv as well. Hundreds of travellers spend some time working in this modern city doing everything from bouncing in clubs to au pairing. Work can be found in bars, restaurants and beach cafés, especially for women. It is a common practice for cafés not to pay any wages and to expect their staff to exist on tips, which are enough to live on providing the restaurant is sufficiently popular. Try to have a private conversation with the staff before taking a tips-only job.

The hostels along Hayarkon were once valuable sources of job information or jobs themselves though the employment situation is much tighter now and in fact many of the hostels have closed such as the Gordon Hostel and No. 1 Hostel which used to maintain Work Lists. At last report this system was still being used at Momo's Hostel at 28 Ben Yehuda St (03-528 7471; www.angelfire.com/il/momos) to which veteran traveller Jane Harris and her boyfriend Pete moved: *'Momo's had loads of work coming in, using a work list system. Pete got work loading and unloading containers, dishwashing and cleaning. I worked for Momo in the hostel. I'd recommend this hostel for work.'*

Another hostel worth trying is the Mugraby Hostel at 30 Allenby St (03-510 2443; www.mugraby-hostel.com) which is reputed to have among the cheapest dorm beds in Tel Aviv (NIS35/$8) as well as some doubles and an internet café. The Kibbutz Program Center recommends several hostels on its website including The Hayarkon 48 Hostel at 48 Hayarkon St (03-516 8989; info@hayarkon48.com) and Dizengoff Square Hostel at 13 Ben Ami St, Dizengoff Square (03-522 5184; www.dizengoffhostel.com).

Other places to visit which in the past have been recommended as places to pick up tips on work in Tel Aviv include the Buzz Stop Café at 86 Herbert Samuel St across from the beach, where many working travellers gather for cheap food and conversation. Cafés along the seafront might also be hiring. Tips are high here. This is also a good area for buskers and traders as is Nachalat Binyamin on Tuesday and Friday afternoons.

Jerusalem

Jerusalem has also been reported to be a possible centre for hotel and bar work, and girls have been offered jobs while wandering round the bazaars. Work is much easier to find in the Jewish rather than the Arab areas, though hostels in the Old City may employ people on a free-bed basis. Buskers and street sellers should head to Ben Yehuda St, the crowded pedestrian precinct in the New City.

Some good sources of information on jobs in Jerusalem are the New Swedish Hostel at 29 David St near Jaffa Gate (02-626 4124), the Petra Hostel also near Jaffa Gate with a fantastic view of the city, the Tabasco Hotel & Tea Room at 8 Aqabat at-Takiyah (02-628 1101) centrally located in the markets near the Damascus Gate and the Palm Christian Hostel (02-627 3189) on Ha-Nevi'im Street in Arab East Jerusalem which charges NIS25 a night. Also check out the notice board in the Goldsmith Building which houses the overseas students union just outside the campus. Jewish travellers might like to follow Amy Ignatow's example and stay at either the male or female Heritage House Youth Hostels (www.heritage.org.il) in the Old City. You pay no rent provided you can tolerate a constant barrage of orthodox Judaism and the midnight curfew.

The English language *Jerusalem Post* (Jerusalem Post Building, Romena, Jerusa-

lem 91000; www.jpost.com) carries a few job adverts from managerial positions to English-speaking secretaries, au pairs, etc. Friday is the best day. The classified ads can be
searched online.

Like buskers, sellers of handicrafts report good profits in Jerusalem. Amy Ignatow from
the US sold smooth stones she had collected from her moshav and decorated with a permanent marker for £3 each. She set herself up in the main square of the Jewish Quarter
under a sign that read 'Please Send me to Art School – Buy a Rock'. One man offered her
a job painting a sign for his restaurant, so she was pleased with her success.

Home-made jewelry is also popular. David Stokes had mastered macramé (a surprisingly easy skill) and earned his way by selling on the streets of Jerusalem, while Leda
Meredith sold woven string bracelets on Ben Yehuda St for a few shekels each. Also try
the evening market around the base of the main bank where it is possible to rent a stand
for a modest sum. Some shopkeepers hire English speaking assistants to help them sell
their wares to tourists.

One traveller's suggestion for getting an insight into Jewish culture while enjoying
a free meal is to visit the Western Wall on Friday evenings where mass worship takes
place. Apparently zealous Americans host shabbat dinners and passers-by are sometimes
invited into Jewish homes for a meal.

OTHER PAID WORK

Although the demand for live-in childcare is still strong, the visa issue referred to at the
beginning of this chapter has made things next to impossible. None of the agencies confirmed for this edition that they were able to make placements and Israel has no member
agency in the International Au Pair Association. Occasionally ads appear in papers like
the *Jerusalem Post*.

It is a good idea to meet several families if possible and choose the one with whom you
feel most comfortable. Hours are long (up to ten a day) but wages are relatively high, averaging $650-$800 a month. You should be prepared to learn how to keep a kosher kitchen.

Cleaning in private houses throughout Israel can be a lucrative proposition, though
it takes time to build up a clientele. Steve Hendry recommends placing advertisements
in shop windows or local papers. After persevering at this, Steve was earning above the
average wage in Israel. Religious Jews want to set their house in order for Passover in
April and so this is a particularly busy and profitable time for a house cleaner.

Not all field work is done on kibbutzim or moshavim. For example farms can be tracked
down (with difficulty) inland from Eilat that are dependent on a steady stream of transients
for their labour force and which pay good wages. Melon planting begins in early November
and lasts till mid-December, while the fruit is picked in the months of March, April and May.
At the busiest times, travellers are bussed in from Eilat to pick and pack melons, tomatoes
and zucchini.

Sometimes fruit harvesters can earn a premium rate at the height of a harvest, even
on a kibbutz. For example El-Rom Orchards in the Golan Heights is a kibbutz that wrote in
2005 to say that it needs people to undertake all aspects of orchard work year round:

> We also look for extra people during our peak harvesting season (May-Oct) when
> we begin with harvesting our pears and cherries, then onto our main crop which is
> apples. We also offer bonus incentives to people during this period. We have good
> clean accommodation with shared kitchen facilities, a TV satellite and computer
> room for the exclusive use of our volunteers, a communal dining room and a pub on
> the kibbutz.

Further information is available by phone on 04-683 8036; fax 04-683 8023 or email
mata@el-rom.org.il.

The British Council maintains a presence in Israel and has Teaching Centres in Tel
Aviv and Jerusalem which recruit qualified EFL teachers mainly from the local English-

speaking population. Like most other international organisations, they have withdrawn from the Palestinian Territories and their educational activities in Nablus, Ramallah, Gaza and East Jerusalem have been suspended.

Anyone with secretarial skills may be able to temp though work normally takes quite a while to come along. Manpower in Tel Aviv (110 Igal Alon St) are reputed to be helpful though their website is only in Hebrew.

Potential volunteers for paid clinical trials should make enquiries at the Clinical Pharmacology Unit, Simbec Israel Clinical Research Center, Tel Aviv Sourasky Medical Center (03-697 4845) or Harrison Clinical Research, 10 Plaut St, Rehovot Scientific Park, Rehovot, Tel Aviv (08-931 6330; info@harrison-cro.co.il). Male visitors may wish to investigate the possibility of donating to a sperm bank; Israeli hospitals are rumoured to pay up to £30. Most conservative rabbis prefer that non-Jewish donor sperm be used.

At one time many foreign movies and American television programmes were made in Israel, especially around Tel Aviv, Jaffa and Eilat. Check noticeboards at Tel Aviv hostels for ads for film or TV extras. Some years ago Katherine Berlanny followed up an advert and became a 'crowd artist' in an Agatha Christie movie. Xuela Edwards describes what she found in Eilat where a dodgy US cop show was being filmed:

There were lots of opportunities for work as an extra which pays 50 shekels a day plus a free breakfast. To find this work, you had to turn up at Eva's office, beneath the Neptune Hotel at 4pm and join the crowd. The selection process was pretty humiliating, but endured by everyone in town on the off-chance. New faces may well get work on the first attempt but you can't rely on getting work because they are reluctant to use the same people too often.

VOLUNTARY OPPORTUNITIES

The Jewish/Arab village of Neve Shalom/Wahat al-Salaam between Tel Aviv and Jerusalem accepts five or six volunteers to work in the guesthouse, school or gardens attached to the community's School for Peace for six or twelve months. In addition to board and lodging, volunteers receive $50 a month pocket money. Details are available from the Volunteer Co-ordinator, 99761 Doar Na Shimshon (02-991 2222; www.nswas.com).

The Friends of Israel Educational Trust (PO Box 7545, London NW2 2QZ; fax 020-7794 0291; www.foi-asg.org) have long run a gap year programme called the Bridge Programme for 12 British school leavers who are sent to Israeli cities to help on gardening, English teaching and other projects for six months from January. After being chosen at interview (in July), participants' expenses are covered apart from spending money (£600 is recommended).

Connect Youth International at the British Council (10 Spring Gardens, London SW1A 2BN; 020-7389 4030; connectyouth.enquiries@britishcouncil.org) has a programme of sending volunteers aged 18-25 from the UK to teach English to teenagers at summer language clubs in northern Israel. Volunteers work for five hours in the morning for between two and six weeks in July/August. Due to 'instability in the Middle East and other current circumstances', this programme is not available at present.

Palestinian Projects

The political situation has made it impossible for projects to continue in Palestinian territories. Unipal (Universities' Trust for Educational Exchange with Palestinians) runs a summer programme of teaching English to teenagers in refugee camps. Because the organisation cannot guarantee the safety of its volunteers in the West Bank or Gaza, it is concentrating its efforts on Lebanon (see chapter on the Middle East). Check the current situation with Unipal (BCM Unipal, London WC1N 3XX) whose website gives up-to-date news of its activities in the region (www.unipal.org.uk).

Friends of Birzeit University has assisted the Palestinian Birzeit University near Ramallah in the occupied West Bank to recruit international volunteers for summer work camps since the 1970s. In previous years volunteers, working alongside Palestinian students, built the area's first park and planted trees in the refugee camps. Further details and an application form are available from Friends of Birzeit University, 1 Gough Square, London EC4A 3DE (020-7373 1340; admin@fobzu.org; www.fobzu.org).

Jewish Projects

Kishor Village (M.P. Maale Hagalil 252149) is a former kibbutz now a sheltered centre for people with mental disabilities. The village accepts foreign volunteers (mainly Danes and Germans) to help in the plastics factory, kennels, goat farm and kitchens alongside village members and staff.

The Jewish Agency for Israel (www.jafi.org.il) is a repository of information for the Jewish community including a gap year scheme to Israel for Jewish sixth-formers (www.aj6.org) which is also offered by the Federation of Zionist Youth (www.fzy.org.uk). The latter's one-year 'course' involves a stint in the army and volunteering at a military base. For a range of voluntary opportunities in a Jewish context, the Israel Program Center in Philadelphia stores information about many projects. Contact the Community Center of Greater Philadelphia, 401 S. Broad St, Philadelphia, PA 19147, USA (215-545-1451).

The non-religious Shekel Association for the Disabled in Jerusalem provides assistance to disabled people in the community. Volunteers are needed to work at rehabilitation centres and in sheltered housing. Details are available from Shekel, 4 Yad Harutzim St, PO Box 53105, Jerusalem 93531; 02-672 0157).

The Weizmann Institute of Science (PO Box 26, Rehovat 76100; 08-957 1667; www.weizmann.ac.il) accepts research students with a minimum of one year of university study to assist with interdisciplinary scientific projects for 10-16 weeks in the summer, earning a small stipend.

A two-year Teach and Study Program (TASP) in Tel Aviv, enables students to combine 17 hours a week of interning in schools with study for an MA in TESOL at Tel Aviv University, as well as Hebrew language classes. Details are available in Israel from TASP (PO Box 2320, Kadima 60920, Israel; 011-972-9-899 5644; www.tasp.org.il) and in the USA from the Jewish Federation (Attn: Galia Avidar, 6505 Wilshire Boulevard, Suite 900, Los Angeles, CA 90048; 323-761-3183; GAvidar@JewishLA.org). The fees are from $8,250.

The Christian Information Centre in Jerusalem (PO Box 14308, 91142 Jerusalem; 02-627 2692; cicinfo@cicts.org) keeps a list of schools and institutes, mainly for people with disabilities, that take on volunteers; from their website www.cicts.org follow the links to Social Service. Try for example the Sisters of Charity in Ain Karem; contact Sister Susan Sheehan, PO Box 9209, Jerusalem 91190 (02-641 3280).

Archaeology

Volunteers are needed to do the mundane work of digging and sifting. In the majority of cases, volunteers must pay a daily fee of $35-$40 to cover food and accommodation (often on a nearby kibbutz) plus a registration fee (typically $50-$75). Most camps take place during university holidays between May and September when temperatures soar. Volunteers must be in good physical condition and able to work long hours in hot weather. Valid health insurance is required.

Information on volunteering at archaeological digs in Israel is most easily accessed via the Israeli Ministry of Foreign Affairs every January (www.mfa.gov.il/MFA/History/Early+History+-+Archaeology). After choosing an excavation of interest, you make contact directly with the person in charge of the research, some of them in the Department of Classical Studies at Tel Aviv University and others at universities elsewhere in Israel or abroad. Prices are posted on the website and are mostly $240-$280 per week. A longstanding project is at the ancient port site of Yavneh Yam (www.tau.ac.il/yavneyam).

Long-term excavations are taking place in Tiberias, in a region rich in antiquities, most recently to expose the Roman basilica and other buildings in use between the 2nd and 10th centuries CE. If interested in joining the excavations in March or November, contact the Volunteer Co-ordinator (shaitiberiasdig@netscape.net) or the dig director Prof. Yizhar

Hirschfeld (solari@alami.net); the all-in cost for four days is a steep $250 if you share a room, though students may be eligible for a discount.

Jennifer McKibben, who worked on a kibbutz, in an Eilat hotel and on a dig in the Negev desert, waxed most enthusiastic about the latter experience:
Actually the work was often enjoyable but not usually before the sun had risen (it gets incredibly cold at nights in the desert). It did seem madness at times when a Land Rover would take a team of us out to an unremarkable spot in the desert marked only by a wooden peg, and we would be told to start digging. I think the romance of excavations quickly fades once the blisters begin to appear and that long term camps are suitable only for the initiated or fanatic.

However despite the difficulties I really enjoyed the camp. Group relations were good – there were people of all nationalities – and there was normally a camp fire going with a couple of musicians. It was wonderful just to spend time in such a beautiful desert, to go off wandering over footprintless dunes, over great red hills to look and see no sign of civilisation. More practically, it was a cheap way to eat well for a couple of weeks, see another area and extend one's all-too-short stay in Israel.

Asia

For a continent as vast as Asia, this chapter may seem disproportionately short. That is simply because there are not many kinds of work open to the traveller in developing countries, as has already been noted in the chapters on Africa and Latin America. Third World economies struggle to support their own populations and can rarely accommodate novelty-seeking foreigners. Certainly the kinds of job which travellers get in the developed world (seasonal farm work, tourist resorts, as nannies, etc.) are not available in most of Asia.

The main exception is provided by those countries with a Western style economy, principally Japan, the Hong Kong Special Administrative Region and Singapore and increasingly China, Taiwan and Korea. While Japan was reeling at the beginning of the century with much higher unemployment than it had seen, the economy has made a strong recovery and in December 2004, unemployment was at a six-year low of 4.5%. One of the most surprising economic miracles has been taking place in India, where for the first time Europeans are being recruited to work in the 'offshore services industry' i.e. call centres.

Having made your fortune in an industrialised country, whether as a graphic designer in Singapore, an English teacher in Japan, a chambermaid in Switzerland or a mango picker in Australia, you should be able to finance many months of leisurely travel in the inexpensive countries of Asia. In most of Asia it is better to concentrate on travelling for its own sake rather than for the sake of working. The climate is another factor. Although Robert Abblett had carefully planned his trip to India and had the addresses of organic farms where he intended to work, he had not counted on the debilitating heat and decided to enjoy a holiday instead.

However, described below are a number of ways to boost your budget between enjoying the temples of Thailand and beaches of Turkey. Note that a working holiday visa scheme exists for Japan, plus young Australians and New Zealanders are eligible for a WH visa for certain countries of Asia (mentioned later in this chapter).

TEACHING

Although the English language is not a universal passport to employment, it can certainly be put to good use in many Asian countries especially China, Japan, Taiwan, Korea, Thailand, Vietnam and Turkey. Thousands of people of all ages are eager for tuition in English and native English speakers with a university degree or just a degree of enthusiasm have been cashing in for a generation. Serious teachers from the UK should always seek the advice of the British Council.

Outside the major cities, paid teaching jobs are rare. If you do end up working for a small locally run school, do not expect to find many teaching materials. You are likely to spend your evenings cutting up magazines and writing stories for the next day's lessons. Off the beaten track, it may be possible to arrange with locals, especially the local teacher, to stay with a family in exchange for conversation lessons.

> **Stuart Tappin travelled around South-East Asia doing this:**
> *In Asia I managed to spend a lot of time living with people in return for teaching English. The more remote the towns are from tourist routes the better, for example Bali is no good. I spent a week in Palembang (Sumatra) living with an English teacher and his family. You teach and they give you their (very good) hospitality. I did the same in Thailand. During the three months that I lived in Kanchanaburi (not far west of Bangkok) my only daily expense was a few baht for a newspaper.*

In addition to the information that follows on finding work with language schools in specific countries, it is also worth considering setting up as a private English teacher. Working as a self-employed freelance tutor is more lucrative but hard to set up until you have been settled in one place for a while and have decent premises from which to work. Steven Hendry, a long-time travelling Scot who has taught in Japan and Thailand, describes the steps to take: *'Be in town for at least a few months and get access to a telephone. Make up a little advertisement (half in English, half the local language) and plaster it all over town as quickly as possible, in universities, colleges, coffee shops, etc.'*

Extensive detailed information on teaching English in the countries of Asia is contained in the 2005 edition of *Teaching English Abroad* by Susan Griffith (Vacation-Work Publications, £12.95). For a list of useful TEFL websites see the introductory chapter on Teaching in this book.

Americans can investigate voluntary programmes such as Volunteers in Asia (VIA, Stanford University, PO Box 20266, Stanford, CA 94309, USA; 650-723-3228; www. viaprograms.org) which sends volunteer teachers to Indonesia, Vietnam and China on short (six week) and longer term (1-2 year) assignments; and Princeton-in-Asia (233 Frist Campus Center, Room 241, Princeton, NJ 08544; pia@princeton.edu) with placements in China, Hong Kong, Indonesia, Japan, Korea, Laos, Singapore, Vietnam, etc. The VIA fee starts at $1,500 for a summer placement and also for a two-year commitment.

TEACHING IN JAPAN

Teaching English in Japan is one of the classic jobs for working travellers. The demand for language tuition is very strong, and has been reviving again after a bad patch during the Far East economic crisis when several large language school chains went to the wall. Since then schools have generally become more selective, and competition for decent jobs can be fierce. The basic monthly salary of 250,000 yen for full-time EFL teachers may not have risen in more than a decade, but it is worth nearly £1,400/$2,000, considerably more than can be earned in most other countries. Wages are of course meaningless without balancing them against the local cost of living which is notoriously high. It is estimated that it takes between one and two months to land a teaching job which is a very long time to be supporting yourself in hyper-expensive Japan.

The key to success is a university degree; without one you will have an uphill struggle. A few years ago American Julie Fast described the drastic changes which she had witnessed:

> When I arrived in Tokyo, there were so many high paying jobs, prospective teachers (experienced or non-experienced) could pick and choose their work. This is no longer the case in Tokyo. I feel I should underline that sentence and write it in capital letters. Things are simply not as they were. When I first started managing a children's English school, I had a hard time finding a good teacher. Now teachers call me looking for work.

Normally newcomers find it a real struggle to acquire enough teaching hours to make substantial savings possible. To avoid an on-the-ground job-hunt you can try to fix up a job before leaving home with the government's JET programme or with one of the major chains of schools like Nova (described later in this section). Thousands of English schools in Tokyo, Osaka and many other Japanese cities are eager to hire *gaijins* (foreigners) to teach. A great many of these are willing to hire native speakers of English with no teaching qualification, though all expect teachers to have a university degree and preferably some teaching experience. Apart from a few schools (including the most prestigious ones) who advertise and conduct interviews abroad, most schools recruit their teachers within Japan. Because of the way that Japanese society works, using intricate networks of contacts, cold-calling is seldom successful.

The most common means of recruitment is by word-of-mouth among expat teachers and by advertising in newspapers, especially the English language *Japan Times* on Mondays and the magazine *Metropolis* (formerly *Tokyo Classifieds*) which comes out on Fridays and can be picked up free in record stores and restaurants (or read online at www.metropolis.co.jp). O-Hayo-Sensei (which means 'Good Morning Teacher') has pages of teaching positions across Japan at www.ohayosensei.com. Many of these are open only to candidates who are already in Japan. To find private students try www.findateacher.net which, according to one traveller, really works.

Joseph Tame was also pleased with www.gaijinpot.com:
The site is in English but has a few bits of Japanese here and there so it is an unfortunate necessity that you need the Japanese plugin. The first time that you go to their website you are invited to build an online CV. You can then browse their job listings, and simply click on 'Apply' so that your CV can be sent to the company who are looking to recruit. Through this website I have had seven invitations to interviews in four weeks, although unfortunately due to my visa status all have been unsuccessful. Every week I receive an email from gaijinpot.com with the new jobs listed. I really do recommend this service as they advertise widely in the press ensuring that they always have a decent selection of jobs.

The Japan Association for Working Holiday Makers (JAWHM) can be a great help to people with the working holiday visa stamped in their passport (see below). Also the Kimi Information Center, also described below, publishes its own newsletter *Kimi Job Opportunities*.

In order to shine over the competition, a number of practical steps should be taken when presenting yourself to a potential employer. These should be taken even more seriously than when trying for teaching work elsewhere in the world, if only because travelling to an interview in Tokyo is a major undertaking, often taking several hours and costing more than £10; so it would be a shame to blow your chances because of a simple oversight.

Dress as impeccably and conservatively as possible, and carry a respectable briefcase. Inside you should have any education certificates you have earned, preferably the originals since schools are catching on that forgery is a widespread practice. (If you apply for a working visa, you must have the original.) Also have a typed résumé which does not err on the side of modesty. Steven Hendry suggests converting 'travelling for two years' to 'studying Asian cultures and languages' and describing a period of unemployment as 'a chance to do some voluntary teaching with racial minorities'. Increasingly prospective employers ask interviewees to teach a demonstration lesson so it is well to arrive prepared for this. Always speak slowly and clearly.

One of the most often recommended places to start the job hunt in Tokyo is the Kimi Information Center (Oscar Building, 8th Floor, 2-42-3 Ikebukuro, Toshima-ku, Tokyo 171-0014; 03-3986 1604/fax 03-3986 3037; www.kimiwillbe.com) which offers a fax and telephone answering service as well as advising on cheap accommodation and jobs. Private rooms can be rented at nearby Kimi Ryokan – *ryokan* means Japanese-style guest house – for 4,500 yen single, 6,500 yen double. The address is 36-8 2-chome, Ikebukuro, Toshima-ku (03-3971-3766). Another office recommended for accommodation referrals is Fontana (03-3382 0151; www.fontana-apt.co.jp).

Other Tokyo gaijin houses offer dormitory accommodation for about half that price. Try to pick up a list of gaijin houses from the tourist office and look for ones that charge a monthly rather than a nightly rent since these are the ones that attract long-term residents. Because it is so difficult to rent flats, some teachers continue living in gaijin houses after they find work. Try to find a gaijin house favoured by teachers. Among those in Tokyo mentioned as being cheap is Mickey House (2-15-1 Nakadai Itabashi-ku; Tokyo; 03-3936 8889). Monthly rents typically start at 60,000 yen in a ryokan, 65,000/70,000 yen in an apartment. Note that a pub called Mickey House near Takadanobaba Station (4F Yashiro Bldg. 2-14-4, Takadanobaba, Shinjuku-ku; 03-3209 9686) holds regular social evenings when English speakers meet up with Japanese people which could be a good way to meet potential students.

Red Tape

Britons, Canadians, Australians and New Zealanders are eligible to apply for a working holiday visa for Japan. British citizens must be aged 18-25 (or up to 30 in restricted circumstances). The working holiday visa allows 400 single young Britons to accept paid work in Japan for up to 12 months. Applicants must show that they have sufficient financial backing, i.e. savings of £2,500. Note that applications are accepted from April and once the allocation of 400 has been filled, no more visas will be granted until April of the following year. Further details are available by ringing 020-7465 6565 or on the embassy website at www.uk.emb-japan.go.jp. Participants are entitled to make use of the services of the non-profit Japan Association for Working-Holiday Makers mentioned above; a large proportion of the jobs notified to the JAWHM offices in Tokyo, Osaka and Kyushu are as English teachers (www.jawhm.or.jp). Note that membership in the Association is free of charge but you must register in person and show your working holiday visa stamp.

For those ineligible for a working holiday visa, the key to obtaining a work visa for Japan is to have a Japanese sponsor. This can be a private citizen but most teachers are sponsored by their employers. Not many schools are willing to sponsor their teachers since they can safely rely on a stream of native speakers with the working holiday visa. If your work visa is to be processed before arrival, you must have a definite job appointment in Japan. Your employers must apply to the Ministry of Justice in Tokyo for a Certificate of Eligibility that they can then forward to you.

Many Britons without the WHV and Americans enter with a temporary visitor's stamp (valid for three months), find a job and sponsor and then apply for a work visa. Documents that will help you to find a sponsor are the original or notarised copy of your BA or other degree and résumé. The temporary visitor's stamp can be extended for another 90 days (for example at Kushiro immigration office) for a fee. In the past, many people worked on this temporary stamp which they kept extending. Now it is unlikely that someone who has stayed in Japan for six months and then leaves the country will be granted landing permission before a reasonable amount of time has elapsed. Those found to be overstaying as tourists can be deported. Furthermore, employers who are caught employing illegal aliens as well as the foreign workers themselves are subject to huge fines, and both parties risk imprisonment.

You are permitted to work up to 20 hours a week on a cultural or student visa. Cultural visas are granted to foreigners interested in studying some aspect of traditional Japanese culture on a full-time basis. In this case you must find a teacher of for example *shodo* (calligraphy), *taiko* (drumming), *karate, aikido, ikebana* (flower arranging) or *ochakai* (tea ceremony) willing to sponsor you and this is very difficult.

Placement from Abroad

If you want to arrange a teaching job in advance, the best bet is the government's JET (Japan Exchange & Teaching) Programme. Anyone with a BA who is under 39 and from the US, UK, Ireland, Canada, Australia or New Zealand (plus a number of other countries) is eligible to apply. In Britain contact the JET Desk, Embassy of Japan, 101-104 Piccadilly, London W1J 7JT (020-7465 6668/6670; www.jet-uk.org) to apply for one of the 400+ positions each year. Applications in Britain are due by the last Friday of November for one-year placements beginning late July. The annual salary is 3,600,000 yen (equivalent to about £18,250/$34,300).

Non-British applicants should contact the Japanese Embassy in their country of origin for information and application forms. US applicants can obtain details from any of the 16 Consulates of Japan in the US or from the Embassy in Washington (2520 Massachusetts Avenue NW, DC 20008; 202-238-6772/3; www.us.emb-japan.go.jp).

A number of the largest language training organisations recruit graduates abroad as well as in Japan. Some chains have been described as factory English schools, where teachers are handed a course book and told not to deviate from the formula. Demand for native speaker teachers is so great that they depend on a steady supply of fresh graduates who want the chance to spend a year in Japan. Often new recruits do not have much say in where they are sent and in their first year may be sent to the least desirable locations. The main employers include:

AEON Inter-Cultural USA, 1960 E Grand Avenue 550, El Segundo, CA 90245 (310-414-1515/fax 310-414-1616; www.aeonet.com). Recruits throughout the US and places 500 native English-speaking teachers in their 270 branch schools in Japan.

ECC Foreign Language Institute, Kanto District Head Office: 5th Floor, San Yamate Building, 7-11-10 Nishi-Shinjuku, Shinjuku-ku, Tokyo 160-0023 (03-5330 1585; www.ecc.co.jp though the website for job applicants is www.japanbound.com). 500 teachers for 150 schools throughout Japan.

GEOS Corporation, Simpson Tower 2424, 401 Bay Street, Toronto, Ontario M5H 2Y4, Canada (416-777-0109; geos@istar.ca; www.geoscareer.com). UK address: GEOS Language Ltd., St. Martin's House, St. Martin's Le Grand, London EC1A 4EN (020-7397 8405; london@geos.demon.co.uk). One of Japan's largest English language institutions employing 2,000 teachers for 500 schools, all of whom are hired outside Japan. Recruitment campaigns held in UK, Australia, New Zealand and North America.

Interac Co Ltd. Fujibo Building 2F, 2-10-28 Fujimi, Chiyoda-ku, Tokyo 102-0071 (03-3234 7857; www.interac.co.jp/recruit). 500 Assistant Language Teachers in a number of branches.

Nova Group, Carrington House, 126/130 Regent Street, London W1R 5FE (020-7734 2727; www.teachinjapan.com). Employ more than 5,000 in 520 Nova schools throughout Japan. Recruitment in North America via Interact Nova Group, 535 Boylston St, Suite 204, Boston, MA 02116 (617-437-7977); and 1881 Yonge St, Suite 700, Toronto, Ontario M4S 3C4, Canada (416-481-6000).

TEACHING IN TAIWAN

The hiring policy is virtually universal in Taiwan: all they are looking for is a BA and a pulse. The country remains a magnet for English teachers of all backgrounds. Hundreds of private language institutes or *buhsibans* continue to teach young children, cram high school students for university entrance examinations and generally service the seemingly insatiable demand for English conversation and English tuition.

Many well-established language schools are prepared to sponsor foreign teachers for a resident visa, provided the teacher is willing to work for at least a year. Only teachers with a university degree are eligible. Many people arrive on spec to look for work. It is usually easy to find a *buhsiban* willing to hire you but not so easy to find a good one. If possible, try to sit in on one or two classes before signing a contract. (If a school is unwilling to permit this, it doesn't bode well.) The majority of schools pays NT$500-$600 (roughly £8.50-£10) per hour.

The site www.taiwan-teachers.com belongs to a teacher placement agency based in Kaohsiung but which can conduct interviews in Canada and Boston. After arrival check the Positions Vacant column of the English language *China Post* and the *China News* though work tends to result from personal referrals more than from advertising. Word-of-mouth is even more important in Taiwan than elsewhere because there is no association of recognised language schools and no English language Yellow Pages. Linda Yee Recruiting (1000-5, 4F-3, Jungshan Road, Taoyuan City; 03-854 4558; yeelinda@yahoo.com) places between 50 and 100 degree-holders of all nationalities in full-time jobs.

One of the best notice boards is located in the student lounge on the sixth floor of the Mandarin Training Center of National Taiwan Normal University at 129 Hoping East Road. You might also make useful expat contacts in Taipei at the Community Services Centre, 25 Lane 290 Chung Shan North Rd, Sec. 6, Tien Mu (02-2836 8134) or at the Gateway Community Centre, 7Fl, 248 Chung Shan North Rd, Sec. 6, Tien Mu (02-2833 7444).

The following language schools hire on a large scale:

Hess Educational Organization, 235 Chung Shan Road, Chung Ho City, Sec. 2, No. 419, Chung Ho City, Taipei County (02-3234 6188; www.hess.com.tw). Specialise in teaching children including kindergarten age. 375 Native Speaking Teachers (NSTs) in more than 125 branches. Very structured teaching programme and curriculum. Quarterly intake of teachers in September, December, March and June.

International Avenue Consulting Company, 16F-1 No 499 Chung Ming South Road, Taichung City (04-2375 9800; www.iacc.com.tw). Recruitment agency with links to Canada which hires up to 150 teachers.

Kid Castle Language Schools, Min Chuan Road No. 98, 8F, Hsin Tien City 231, Taipei (02-2218 6996; http://personnel.kidcastle.com). 160 franchise branches throughout Taiwan.

Kojen ELS, 12 Kuling St, Taipei (02-2321 9005; www.kojenenglish.com). Employs 200-300 teachers at 19 schools, mostly in Taipei but also Kaohsiung and Taichung. Minimum starting salary for 25 hours per week is NT$52,000 per month (approx. US$1,600).

Todd's English School, Jung Shan Road No. 19, Tainan County, Yung Kang City 710 (06-232 3612; www.toddsenglishschool.com).

Visas

If you are entering Taiwan without a pre-arranged contract you should obtain a 60-day Visitor Visa before arrival which can be single entry or multiple entry (the latter costs twice as much). Otherwise you will be given permission to stay for just the two weeks (non-extendable) that tourists are granted. Once you sign a one-year contract with an employer, the school will apply to the local education authority for a working permit. When that is processed you can apply for a multiple-entry Resident Visa at the Ministry of Foreign Affairs (for a fee of NT$3,000) and then within 15 days to the foreign police for an Alien Resident Certificate (A.R.C.). Some schools will make a contribution towards the visa fees and help with obtaining official translations. Without an A.R.C. it will be impossible to exchange any excess earnings into dollars. Detailed information about visas should be requested from the Taiwan overseas office in your country of origin; the Taipei Representative Office in the UK is at 50 Grosvenor Gardens, London SW1W 0EB (020-7396 9152) or check the English section of the website of the Bureau of Consular Affairs in Taipei (www.boca.gov.tw).

Australians should note that since November 2004, they have been eligible to apply for a 12-month working holiday visa to Taiwan.

Having discovered the joys of world travel at age 30, Debra Fuccio from the US took the plunge and fixed up a teaching job with Todd's English School in Tainan via the internet. She found that good money could be earned and the cost of living really low, which had the disadvantage that many of the foreigners there were focussed on money to the exclusion of everything else. Her low overheads (in 2004) included $200 a month for a small apartment all to herself and a used scooter bought for $250. Meanwhile she was earning $17 an hour despite having no teaching certificate or experience. She stayed for most of an academic year but left a little early having tired of teaching only young children. She concludes that 'the whole country is simply gone mad with learning English'.

TEACHING IN KOREA

Although South Korea does not immediately come to mind as a likely destination for British TEFLers, it has been long known in North America as a country which can absorb an enormous number of native speaker teachers, including fresh graduates with no TEFL training or experience. Many English teachers have been getting the jitters about the aggressive stance taken by the unpredictable regime in North Korea (the border is only about 30 miles north of Seoul) but the demand for English is greater than ever. Wages in the Korean currency (the *won*) have increased though, with the sharp decline in the exchange rate, they are worth less than they were a few years ago. Young Australians and New Zealanders are eligible for a working holiday visa for Korea.

Hundreds of language institutes *(hogwons)* can be found in Seoul the capital, Pusan (Korea's second city, five hours south of Seoul, sometimes transliterated Busan) and in smaller cities. The majority of these are run as businesses, so that making a profit seems to be what motivates many bosses rather than educating people. Certificates and even degrees are in many cases superfluous, though a university degree will be needed in order to obtain the right visa. Native-speaker status may be sufficient to persuade the owner of an institute to hire an English-speaker, though having some letters after your name makes the job hunt easier.

The English Program in Korea (EPIK) is a scheme run by the Ministry of Education, and administered through Korean embassies in the US, Canada, Britain and Australia, to place about 190 native speakers in schools and education offices throughout the country each year. The annual salary offered is 1.7, 1.9 or 2.2 million won per month (depending on qualifications) plus accommodation, round trip airfare, visa sponsorship and medical insurance. Work starting dates are staggered over the summer with application deadlines falling between April and June. Current information should be obtained from the Education Director, Korean Embassy, 60 Buckingham Gate, London SW1E 6AJ (020-7227 5547; fax 020-7227 5503) or from the website http://epik.knue.ac.kr or contact the office in Korea (43-233 4516/7). Americans should contact any of the dozen Korean Consulates in the US. Other nationalities can contact the EPIK office in Korea (Center for In-Service Education, Korea National University of Education, Chongwon, Chungbuk 363-791. Note that EPIK does not attract the praise that the JET Programme does though it has been improving; for example the contract now lasts 52 rather than 50 weeks which means that teachers are entitled to severance pay of one extra month's salary. Check Dave Sperling's ESL Café website for details (www.eslcafe.com) and check its rating on EFL-Law (www.efl-law.com/epik_pages.html).

In North America and Korea a range of brokers and agents acts on behalf of institutes or groups of institutes to recruit teachers. Typically, advertisements placed by such intermediaries request only native-speaker fluency and a BA/BSc. Some charge a fee though these should be avoided. Identifying the good ones who are interested in more than collecting their commission from schools is tricky. A relatively new agent has been seeking teachers in the UK: contact Gary Morgan at Got The Bug (gotthebug@hotmail.

com) if interested in a one-year contract in Seoul, Suwon or Inchon. Also check out www. peoplerecruit.com based in Pusan and www.englishwork.com in Seoul.

Here is a list of Korea-based recruiters active at the time of writing:

HBS Company, 335-2 Sinsa-Dong, Unpyung-Ku, Seoul 122-082 (2-305-7971; www. hbscompany.com). Represents more than 500 institutes in Korea with a new intake of teachers every month.

Into Korea, 607 Union Center Bldg. 837-11 Yeoksam dong, Kangnam gu, Seoul (2-565-3058; www.intokorea.com).

Recruiting Busan Inc. (RBI), Busan (51-819-5656; jobs@rbi.co.kr). Client schools in Seoul, Daegu, Changwon as well as Busan.

Dozens of agents in North America recruit EFL teachers, particularly in Canada. To name just one of the longest-standing: Russell Recruiting based in Vancouver, Canada (www.asiangateway.net) recruits only for schools whose practices they can vouch for, mostly with big companies like YBM, Wonderland and Pagoda.

YBM/ELS International employs 400-600 native English teachers for English Conversation Centers and other kinds of institute throughout Korea. The central contact address is 55-1 Chongno 2ga, Chongno Gu, 3rd Floor, Seoul 110 122 (2-2264 7472; www.ybmhr. com).

> **William Naquin stresses the importance of arranging the details of a written contract before starting work:**
> *I found my present position in Korea in the classified section of the Seattle Sunday paper. A couple of Korean-Americans in Los Angeles calling themselves 'Better Resource' flew to Seattle two days after receiving my faxed CV. I cannot suggest strongly enough that teachers considering a position negotiated through a foreign broker get everything in writing. My contract was written in exceedingly poor English, and what it failed to stipulate in terms of housing conditions, medical insurance, etc. was only guaranteed orally. It was a mistake on my part to take the broker at his word. Living arrangements here are substandard, with three of us sharing a two-bedroom flat.*

William's ability to save $12,000 in one year helped him to tolerate the inconvenience.

One-year contracts arranged in advance are often lucrative. They can also be gruelling for those suffering acute culture shock and possibly also contending with an exploitative situation. Discontentment seems to be chronic among English teachers in Korea. So many American teachers have run amok of faulty contracts, that the US Embassy in Seoul issues a handbook offering guidance called 'Teaching English in Korea' which tackles the many pitfalls that have been brought to its attention over the years (which can be requested from the American Citizen Services Branch, 82 Sejong Road, Chongro-ku, Seoul, or seen on the internet at http://usembassy.state.gov/seoul/wwwh3550.html). Its wording has been toned down somewhat over the years, but it points out that disputes are very common and that an understanding of what constitutes a contract often differs depending on your culture. 'Many have observed that in the Korean context, a contract appears to simply be a rough working agreement, subject to change depending on the circumstances... Many employers will view a contract violation by a foreign worker as serious, and will renege on verbal promises if they feel they can.'

Despite contract language promising good salaries, furnished apartments and other amenities, many teachers find they actually receive much less than they were promised; some do not even receive benefits required by Korean law, such as health insurance and severance pay. Teachers' complaints range from simple contract violations, through non-payment of salary for months at a time, to dramatic incidents of severe sexual harassment, intimidation, threats of arrest/deportation and physical assault. The Embassy warns teachers to keep their passports in their possession after the visa processing has taken place.

If you wait until you get to Korea, it is usually easy to fix up a job without resorting to an agent. Every day adverts for teachers appear in the English language newspapers like the *Korean Herald* and *Korea Times.* A personal approach to language schools in Seoul or Pusan will usually be rewarded with some early morning and evening work within a week or two. Often new arrivals stay in one of the popular yogwons (hostels) and visit internet cafés to link up with the grapevine and learn about the English teaching scene. The Chongro area of Seoul contains a high concentration of both hostels and language schools and is a suitable area for a door-to-door job search.

Among the biggest language institutes are:

Berlitz Korea, Sungwood Academy Building, 2F, 1316-17 Seocho-Dong, Seocho-Gu, Seoul 137-074 (02-3481 5324; gerald.drabick@berlitzkorea.co.kr). About 40 native speakers employed.

Ding Ding Dang English School, 1275-3 Bummel-dong Soosung-gu, Taegu 706-100 (53-782 5200). 30-36 classes per week for minimum of one year. Branches in other cities.

English Friends, 733, Bang Hak 3 Dong. Do Bong Ku, Seoul 132-855 (2-3493 6567; tefaenglish@yahoo.co.kr). 30 franchise schools in northern Korea.

TEACHING IN CHINA

Recruitment of teachers for the People's Republic of China is absolutely booming in the private as well as the public sector. (For information about teaching opportunities in the Hong Kong Special Administrative Region, see the section below.) The internet is a prolific source of possibilities and expanding all the time. Any web search or a trawl of the major ELT job sites is bound to turn up plenty of contacts. Try for example Elite ESL (Qixing Yingyechu 1# Xinxiang, Guangxi, Guilin, Youzhengju 541004; www.elite-esl-teaching-in-china.com) part of the Buckland Group. It recruits nearly 100 teachers for 40-50 locations around China and gives detailed information on its website. Alternatively, the China TEFL Network at www.chinatefl.com/teach.asp has links to jobs mainly in state colleges and universities. Also check www.teach-in-china.cn based in Shenyang City but with vacancies throughout the country. Yakup International Trade Co. Ltd (www.yakup-international.com) recruits native speaker ESL teachers for positions at Chinese universities, colleges, high schools, junior schools and kindergartens. Package includes a furnished apartment with free internet access, monthly salary of RMB2,500-5,000, round trip air ticket, paid holiday, holiday allowance, medical allowance and Z-visa, in exchange for 12 hours teaching a week.

With the explosion in opportunities, the job hunt is far more straightforward than it was a few years ago when most teacher applications were for state-run institutes of higher education and had to go through the Chinese Education Association for International Exchange (CEAIE; www.ceaie.edu.cn) or one of its 37 provincial offices. Nowadays there are many private recruiters, foundations or China-linked companies, on and off the internet, eager to sign up native speakers (with or without relevant experience) for an academic year. Many English teaching posts in the Chinese provinces remain unfilled, though aid agencies like VSO and Christians Abroad do their utmost to fill vacancies. The requirements for these two-year posts are not stringent and, in return, teachers get free airfares, a local salary and other perks.

Some of the tried and tested old schemes are still in place and still work. The British Council places language assistants (who must be university graduates) to work with classes of 50 in secondary schools across China from September to June. Preliminary training is provided on an induction course in Shanghai which is paid for by the British Council. Participants receive free accommodation, a flight back to the UK and an expert's salary which will be a matter of negotiation between you and the hiring institution. The normal range is 2,500-3,500 Renminbi yuan (£160-£225) per month. Details of the application procedure and the registration fee (currently £48) can be obtained from the Assistants Department at the British Council (10 Spring Gardens, London SW1A 2BN; 020-7389 4595; fax 020-7389 4426; www.britishcouncil.org/languageassistants-china.htm).

If you apply widely you can expect to have to choose among job offers as William Hawkes did:

> During my last year at university, I obtained a list of Chinese universities and colleges looking to recruit foreign teachers, then faxed my CV and a letter to the ten which suited me most. I received several offers from around China (including a phone call at 3am) and eventually accepted an offer from Qingdao Chemical Institute on the east coast of China. The offer was quite standard: accommodation, unspectacular money... but a friend of mine had taught at this same institute and thoroughly recommended it, so I went and taught English from September to July.

IST Plus Ltd (Rosedale House, Rosedale Road, Richmond, Surrey TW9 2SZ; 020-8939 9057; info@istplus.com; www.istplus.com) runs Teach in China for graduates from the UK while CIEE in the USA places Americans in the same programme. Placements are in secondary and tertiary institutions mainly in the developed eastern provinces of Jiangsu, Zheijiang, Shandong and Hubei. Contracts last five months from February or ten months from August. The programme fee starts at £995 with the possibility of reimbursement for travel costs at the end of a 10-month contract. BUNAC also has a China programme operated in conjunction with Language Link (see introductory chapter on Teaching English) for candidates who obtain the TEFL Certificate; the cost including the four-week Certificate course is £1,700.

Some US-based placement programmes to consider are:

Amity Foundation, 71 Han Kou Road, Nanjing, Jiangsu 210008 (25-8332-4607; www. amityfoundation.org). Christian organisation that sends 60-80 people to teach English in China.

Colorado China Council, 4556 Apple Way, Boulder, CO 80301 (303-443-1108; www. asiacouncil.org). 20-35 teachers per year placed at institutes throughout China, including Mongolia. Council fees start at $3,250 (including TEFL training, Chinese course and domestic travel in China), $1,350 fee (administration only) for February start.

IEF Education Foundation, 18605 E Gale Avenue, Suite 203, City of Industry, CA 91748 (626-965-1995; www.ief-usa.org). Recruits mainly Americans with a BA to spend at least six months teaching English to junior high and high-school aged students in many Chinese cities.

WorldTeach, Centre for International Development, 79 John F Kennedy St, Cambridge, MA 02138 (617-495-5527; www.worldteach.org). Non-profit organisation sends volunteers to teach adults for six months in Yantai and runs Shanghai Summer Teaching Program. Volunteers teach small classes of high school students at a language camp in Shanghai. Volunteers pay about $4,000 for airfares, orientation, health insurance, living expenses and field support.

With an invitation letter or fax from an official Chinese employer (such as Elite ESL mentioned above), you will be able to obtain an F (business) visa. This permits you to work in China for up to six months. Otherwise you will simply get a tourist visa (L visa) from the Embassy of the PRC in your country. The cost of a multi-entry tourist visa (L visa) for Britons is £60 for six months, £90 for 12; all visas must now be applied for in person or through a travel or visa agent but not by post. It is possible to enter China on an L visa and then the Foreign Affairs Office at your institute or equivalent at a private company offering employment will arrange for an Alien Residence Permit (Z visa). Make sure this happens before your L or F visa expires; otherwise you will be liable to a fine and will have to leave the country to change status.

TEACHING IN THAILAND

Any university graduate can pre-arrange a teaching job in Thailand through IST Plus Ltd (address above) or CIEE in the US. Several hundred native English speakers with university degrees are sent to schools and tertiary institutions in Thailand (mainly in the Bangkok area). Five or ten-month renewable contracts start in May or October. The minimum salary is 10,000 baht (£140) per month plus free on-campus accommodation. The programme fee starts at £1,000.

Bangkok and other Thai cities are a good bet for the casual teacher. The most noticeable recent change in the market has been in the teaching of children so if you are prepared to enter the fray, you will almost certainly be able to find an opening, especially for weekend teaching. Finding a list of language schools to approach on spec should present few difficulties. The best place to start is around Siam Square where numerous schools and the British Council are located or the Yellow Pages which lists dozens of language school addresses.

One of the best all-round sources of information about teaching in Thailand with an emphasis on Bangkok and on inside information about the main hiring companies is the website www.ajarn.com with stories and tips as well as many job vacancies (www.ajarn.com/Jobs/jobs_offered.htm). The site is run and constantly updated by a teacher who has been in Thailand for many years. The English language *Bangkok Post* is as full as ever of advertisements for native speaker teachers (www.bangkokpostjobs.com). At the time of writing, an ad was appearing for the Teacher Recruitment Center on 02-970 8142.

The noisy Khao San Road is lined with expat pubs and budget accommodation, many with notice boards offering teaching work and populated with other foreigners (known as *farangs*) well acquainted with the possibilities. They will also be able to warn you of the dubious schools which are known to exploit their teachers.

If the Siam Square schools are not short of teachers, which may be the case in the slack season, you will have to try schools further afield. Travelling around this city of six million is so time-consuming and unpleasant that it is important to plot your interview strategy on a city map before making appointments. It may not be necessary to do much research to discover the schools with vacancies. Many of the so-called back street language schools (more likely to be on a main street, above a shop or restaurant) look to the cheap hotels of Banglamphu, the favourite haunt of Western travellers in the northwest of Bangkok. There is such a high turnover of staff at many schools that there are bound to be vacancies somewhere for a new arrival who takes the trouble to present a professional image and can show a convincing CV. As usual, it may be necessary to start with part-time and occasional work with several employers, aiming to build up 20-30 hours in the same area to minimise travelling in the appalling traffic.

Among schools to try after arrival in Bangkok are:

American University Language Centre, 179 Rajadamri Road, Bangkok 10330 (02-252 8170-3; www.auathailand.org). 200 teachers (must have a degree) for 4 branches in Bangkok and 11 upcountry, mainly at universities. Face-to-face interview required.

British American, 02-454 8973/81; www.british-american.ac.th. 100 teachers for 4 schools in Ransit, Bang Kapi, Ramintra and Bang Khae.

Chulalongkorn Go International with English, 19th floor, Wittyakit Building, Siam Square, Soi 9, Bangkok (fax 02-218 9935; recruitingyl@cec.chula.ac.th). Teachers of young learners earn 700 baht an hour for weekend work.

ECC (Thailand), 430/17-24 Chula Soi 64, Siam Square, Bangkok 10330 (02-253 3312; jobs@ecc.ac.th; www.eccthai.com). 500 teachers at 40 branches in Greater Bangkok, 20 elsewhere in Thailand. Prefer TEFL-certified teachers.

EF English First, Siam Square, Bangkok (02-658 4060). This branch and several others in Thailand are frequently hiring.

Siam Computer & Language Institute, 471/19 Ratchawithi Road, Rajthewee, Bangkok 10400 (02-247 2345 ext 370-373; www.siamcom.co.th). Teachers for 35 schools in greater Bangkok and 38 elsewhere in Thailand.

Tourist destinations like Chiang Mai are very attractive to job-hunting teachers and opportunities crop up in branches of the big companies and in smaller schools. A good source of leads is Eagle Guest House (16 Chiang Moi Gao Road, Soi 3) which is run by Annette Kunigagon who knows everything about language schools (and everything else). Annette's general advice for the job hunt is to dress conservatively and cultivate a reserved manner: 'too many gesticulations and guffawing are not considered polite'. She has developed a volunteer programme called 'Helping Hands Social Projects' in which volunteers teach at a centre for disabled people, school for the blind, etc. (www.eagle-house.com).

Outside Bangkok and tourist magnets like Chiang Mai and Phuket, there is far less competition from *farangs* for work, particularly in lesser known cities like Nakhon Sawan, Khon Kaen, Udon Thani and Ubon Ratchathani. For a job in a university you will probably have to show a degree or teaching certificate, neither of which will be scrutinised very carefully. The best places are Hat Yai (the booming industrial city in the south) and Song-khla. Hotels are always worth asking, since many hotel workers are very keen to improve their English. If you find a place which suits and you decide to stay for a while, ask the family who runs your guest house about the local teaching opportunities.

Sometimes the happiest and most memorable experiences take place away from the cities and the tourist resorts.

Brian Savage returned to England after a second long stint of teaching in Thailand and describes one of the highlights for him:
My most rewarding experience was teaching English conversation in a rural high school in Loei province in northeast Thailand. These children had rarely seen and had certainly never spoken to a farang before. My work during that week and a subsequent second visit was really appreciated by the pupils. The first visit came about after I was introduced to a teacher at the Chiang Mai school where I was teaching. If travellers get away from Bangkok and the resorts, they too can have experiences such as this, especially in the friendly towns of the north and north-east. A little voluntary teaching can really boost the confidence of students who are usually too poor to pay to study with native speakers.

In a country where teaching jobs are so easy to come by, there has to be a catch. In Thailand, the wages for *farang* teachers are uniformly low. The basic hourly rate has risen only slightly over the past six years to B200-B250 an hour though some decent schools and company work can pay considerably more. The norm is for schools to keep their staff on as part-time freelancers while giving them full-time hours; this is primarily to avoid taxes. Jobs that pay better often involve a lot of travelling, which in Bangkok is so time-consuming that it is necessary to work fewer hours. Most teachers conclude that it is just as lucrative and much less stressful to work at a single institute for the basic wage.

Alternatively, it is possible to work for no money at all. An interesting programme has been introduced by the Youth Hostels Association of Thailand called 'Giving English for Community Service'. Foreign volunteers with some basic English teaching experience spend three to five months teaching English to classes of low-paid workers in the hospitality industry. In exchange for teaching up to four hours a day, they receive all living expenses including travel between the provinces in which they work. Details are available from the Thai Youth Hostels Association, International Community Service Programme, 25/14 Phitsanulok Road, Si Sao Thewet, Dusit, Bangkok 10300 (2-628 7413-5; bangkok@tyha.org; www.tyha.org).

Officially you need a work permit for Thailand, though the majority of teachers continue to do a visa run to renew their tourist visas by crossing neighbouring border (e.g. to Penang in Malaysia) every three months. There is a fine of B200 for every day you overstay your tourist visa. With a letter from your school, you can apply for a non-immigrant visa, which is better for teaching than a tourist visa. It too must be renewed by leaving the country every 90 days for a fee of B500.

TEACHING IN SOUTHEAST ASIA

Indonesia

Most language schools in Indonesia (and Singapore as well) recruit only trained EFL teachers who are willing to stay for at least a year, though there are also many locally-run schools and colleges in Indonesia that are looking for a native speaker but can pay only a bare minimum. The currency which was so drastically devalued a few years back has been gaining strength and schools are again trying to attract professional ELT teachers from abroad. The site www.jakartaguru.com calls itself a one-stop shop for anyone interested in teaching in Indonesia.

Despite inflation and the devaluation of the rupiah, salaries paid by the 'native speaker' schools provide for a comfortable lifestyle including travel within Indonesia during the vacations and the possibility of saving. Most schools pay from 8,000,000 rupiah per month, after Indonesian tax of 10% has been subtracted. Since the cost of living is low, especially outside the cities, many teachers are able to enjoy a very comfortable lifestyle and travel in their free time. If you plan to complete a one or two-year contract, enquire about reimbursement for airfares and a possible tax rebate.

In 2003/4 Bruce Clarke worked for EF. Although he had no previous classroom experience, he was asked to become acting Director of Studies after only two months, although he would have preferred to carry on working 24 hours a week in the classroom. The starting monthly salary at EF was the equivalent of US$900:

> My school also agreed to reimburse me at the end of my contract for both the price of my plane ticket ($900) and my work visa ($60). Basic living is relatively cheap. I spend about half my salary on western luxuries like beer, CDs, movies, etc. I bank the rest so at the end of my year I expect to head home with a few thousand dollars saved. Most of the teachers I meet are in their early 20s, and are generally still at the 'let's party every night' stage of their lives. They complain about constantly being broke because they tend to nightclub two or three nights a week and waste a lot of money.

EF has been expanding quickly in Indonesia and has about 40 schools of which about a dozen are in greater Jakarta (Indonesian Head Office, Wisma Tamara Lt. 4, Suite 402, Jl. Jend. Sudirman Kav. 24, Jakarta 12920; 21-520 6477).

The most stable employment is in the oil company cities but opportunities exist in small towns too. At local schools unused to employing native speaker teachers, teaching materials may be in short supply. One of the problems faced by those who undertake casual work of this kind is that there is usually little chance of obtaining a work permit. It is also difficult for freelance teachers to become legal unless they have a contact who knows people in power.

Travellers have stumbled across friendly little schools up rickety staircases throughout the islands of Indonesia, as the German round-the-world traveller Gerhard Flaig describes:

> In Yogyakarta you can find language schools listed in the telephone book or you just walk through streets to look for them. Most of them are interested in having new teachers. I got an offering to teach German and also English since my English was better than some of the language school managers. All of them didn't bother about work permits. The wages aren't very high, but it is fairly easy to cover the costs of board and lodging since the cost of living is very low.

Indochina

The demand for English has exploded in Vietnam. Volunteers and teachers are needed in the private and public sectors, especially in academic institutes. Demand is strongest in the south where most of the wealth remains. A number of joint venture and independent language schools have been opened in Cambodia and Laos as well as in Vietnam. Whereas the opportunities a few years ago were mainly voluntary and in refugee camps, there is now a booming commercial market supplying English language training. Many joint ventures require varying degrees of professionalism in their native speaker teachers. In the provinces, there is very little competition to meet the demand for English.

Murray Turner described the huge demand for English teachers he encountered in Cambodia a few years back: *'In Cambodia they are so desperate for English teachers that I met more Dutch, Germans and Scandinavians teaching English than Brits or Yanks. Cambodia is one of the most beautiful South East Asian countries I visited and the people are among the friendliest.'*

Wages for casual teachers are about $6 an hour in a country where you can live comfortably on $8-$10 a day. Qualified EFL teachers can earn double that working for an established school like the Australian Centre for Education (PO Box 860, Phnom Penh, Cambodia; fax 023-724204) which employs about 30 teachers with TEFL Certificates. On entry, tourists are given one-month visas which are non-extendable and in some cases stamped 'Employment Prohibited.'

Matthew Williams visited Laos on one of his frequent visa trips from neighbouring Thailand and reported that the hourly rate was higher than in Bangkok which goes a long way in a tax-free country where long-stay residents can rent shared houses for $100 per month.

HONG KONG

With the birth of the Hong Kong Special Administrative Region (HKSAR) of the People's Republic of China on June 30th, 1997, Britons lost their preferential status. Like all nationalities (except New Zealanders and Australians who can obtain a one-year working holiday visa), Britons must now obtain a work visa prior to arrival if they wish to take up legal employment in Hong Kong. Without a pre-arranged job and a supportive employer, it will be very difficult to work in the former colony. Gone are the days when skilled Britons could find well-paid work in companies with relative ease.

However, it seems that the hundreds of expat bars and restaurants have not been able to attract suitable staff from the local Chinese population and there are reports that once again backpackers are finding work as bartenders and waiting staff, particularly at the Western-style bars in Lan Kwai Fong on Hong Kong Island.

Regulations

British citizens do not need a visa to visit Hong Kong for up to six months. But if they want to take up employment or join a business, they will have to obtain an appropriate visa for which they will have to persuade the Immigration Department that they possess special skills, experience or knowledge of value to and not readily available in Hong Kong or that they can make a substantial contribution to the economy of Hong Kong.

Applications for an employment visa may be submitted through the applicant's nearest Chinese diplomatic and consular mission or directly to the Immigration Department, Receipts & Despatch Unit, 2/F Immigration Tower, 7 Gloucester Road, Wanchai, Hong Kong (2824 6111; enquiry@immd.gcn.gov.hk; www.info.gov.hk/immd). The applicant is required to nominate a local sponsor, usually the prospective employer, to vouch for the application. The sponsor will be required to complete and sign a sponsorship form in support of the application. Each case will be considered on its merits. Visitors are not normally allowed to change their status after arrival except in unusual circumstances.

Teaching

The change in the visa situation has of course made it much harder to pick up easy-come easy-go English teaching work. Few employers are willing to risk the huge fines or threat of jail sentences if caught employing people illegally.

To meet the demand, the Hong Kong government employs hundreds of English speakers to teach in the Chinese-medium state education system as part of the NET scheme (Native English Teacher). Foreign teachers known as 'Netters' are assigned singly to government schools (primary and secondary) across Hong Kong and working conditions can be tough especially in a Band 5 school with low-achieving pupils. On the other hand salaries and benefits are generous. See current details on the website of the Education and Manpower Bureau (www.emb.gov.hk); at present the starting monthly salary for a TEFL teacher is about HK$16,165 (US$2,000/£1,100). Private agencies that also place native English teachers with a degree and/or specialised qualifications in HK schools include Mentor.net (www.mentor.net) and Talent Educational Services Co (www.talentedu.com. hk).

The Chatteris Educational Foundation (18/F Honest Motors Building, 9-11 Leighton Road, Causeway Bay; 2520 5736; www.chatteris.org.hk) offers teaching opportunities in Hong Kong at two levels. GELTAs (Graduate English Language Teaching Assistants) are recent graduates interested in teaching English in a Hong Kong school on nine-month contracts which pay a monthly salary of HK$14,000 (£950). ELTAs (English Language Teaching Assistants) are school leavers or current undergraduates who want to take a gap year to gain international teaching experience. ELTAs are given free accommodation and a monthly allowance (currently HK$3,800) to cover food and pocket money.

Other Work

Anyone who is prepared to try to find a Hong Kong employer willing to sponsor them for a work permit should check the two English daily newspapers, the *Standard* and the *South China Morning Post*, especially the bumper Saturday edition of the latter. Although the majority of adverts require fluent Cantonese, a few may not.

Secretarial and personnel agencies will be interested in you only if they are convinced you intend to stay for at least two years. Non-Cantonese speakers without visas will have difficulty in securing posts. Pay for secretaries varies from HK$8,000 a month at worst to HK$30,000 at best. A good English secretary with shorthand will earn HK$20,000. Hourly rates for temps are HK$55 for typists and HK$80-$90 for shorthand secretaries. Agencies to try are Sara Beattie Appointments for office personnel (Hennessy Centre, 8/F, East Wing, 500 Hennessy Road, Causeway Bay; 2507 9333; sba@sarabeattie.com) and Owens Personnel Consultants Ltd (1201 Double Building, 22 Stanley St, Central; 2845 6220; www. owens.com.hk) whose website lists actual vacancies especially in IT, finance, etc.

Film Extras

The Hong Kong film industry continues to crank out Chinese language movies at a remarkable rate. While the stars are invariably Chinese, *gweilos* (pale-skinned foreigners or ghosts) are sometimes taken on as extras, often to portray villains, fall guys or amazed onlookers.

Carolyn Edwards heard about a chance to be in the movies while staying (some time ago) at the sleazy Chung King Mansions, though from her description it was never going to go to the Cannes Film Festival:

After I'd been there about a week, I was asked if I'd like to be in a movie – wow. The scene took place in a restaurant on Hong Kong Island. Work started at midnight and we worked till 9am. Make-up and costumes came out and I was done up to look like a high class prostitute. For nine hours we had to walk around smiling, drinking imitation Champagne and saying 'cheers'. It seemed to be very amateurish and was quite tiring. We were starving but never fed as promised. When we weren't needed for a *scene we slept on the settees. Towards the end, our hair was looking messy and the make-up was all over the place but they still kept shooting. Eventually we were allowed to go and were paid HK$400.*

Obviously Carolyn acquitted herself well in her role since she was offered subsequent chances, one of which included a kissing scene and another participating in an aerobics class, but she decided one movie was enough. As usual take a book or pile of post cards for the inevitable long hiatuses between call-ups and possibly a packed lunch.

Casual Opportunities

The entrance to the Star Ferry and the corridors of the Mass Transit Railway stations are favourite locations for buskers. Official hassle should be minimal as long as you don't block thoroughfares. Kim Falkingham recommends being able to sing some songs in Chinese. She looks back fondly on one listener who dropped the equivalent of £80 in her cap, but also remembers long days when nobody contributed anything.

Each spring the Sevens rugby tournament draws huge crowds and many temporary bar staff are needed for the long weekend. You get a commission for every jug of beer you sell and can drink as much as you like. Call the headquarters of the major breweries (Fosters, San Miguel, etc.) before the event. People are also hired to sell commemorative shirts and souvenirs on the streets.

For casual opportunities to earn £30 for an hour and a half's work dressed as a clown to entertain at children's parties, check out Mike Abbott Leisure (www.abbottleisure.com). In the old days he regularly hired itinerants as costume characters to entertain at parties, deliver singing telegrams, etc. The Disney Corporation may provide more regular work for people who like to dress up in costumes since they are planning to open a Disneyland in Hong Kong at the end of 2005 that will create 35,000 new jobs (and probably take business away from Hong Kong's delightful theme park Ocean World).

ENTERTAINMENT

Many of the opportunities for film extras, buskers and models described above pertain to other countries in Asia as well as Hong Kong. Here are some scattered suggestions.

Hollywood does not have the world monopoly on film-making. There is an enormous film industry in the Hindi, Chinese and Japanese speaking worlds and it is just possible your services will be required, especially if you're blonde. Foreign travellers hanging around the Salvation Army Red Shield Hostel on Mereweather Road in Mumbai, the Broadlands Guest House in Madras, the main travellers' hotels in Goa, the Banglamphu area of Bangkok, Bencoolen St in Singapore or the Malate Pension in Manila may be invited by a film agent to become an extra. Danny Jacobson and his girlfriend Marion might have had a chance to be in a Thai movie a couple of years ago but never quite managed it:

Early on in my time in Bangkok, I met an Australian guy who told me about possible work as an extra in Thai films. He gave me a cell number; I called, and a guy said come to such and such a café – 'plenty of work'. About half an hour late a beer belly carried by a fast-talking Iranian guy leaped into the café on a cell-phone. I've since forgotten his name so I'll call him Mr. Agent. After a few calls on the cell-phone he sat down at our table and explained there was a war film going to be shot up near Chiang Mai and they needed Westerners as extras. Food and accommodation plus 500 Baht per day was the take. Not a lot of money, about $11US. But in Thailand that was enough to live very well on as a tourist for a day. We waited around while he made sporadic and seemingly non-pointless calls on his phone. He was the picture of what I assumed a casting agent would be like. Quick, up and down 'assessment' glances greeted all who approached him. He talked big, like everything was a done deal but then would become distant and confused. Later he filed us out onto the *street saying he was going to take us to an audition. He started talking on his phone again like he was returning a call, 'Yeah, when is the shoot to start? How many people do you need? Yeah, yeah, uh-huh...' and the Dutch guy with us whispered to me that Mr. Agent had been talking into a switched-off cell-phone. Eventually he spoke up that his cell-phone had just died and he had no idea where we needed to go. So we hopped out of the taxi.*

It is likely that agents like this one do occasionally find work for extras but can't predict when or where until the very last minute. They keep their young hopefuls hanging around so that if the summons does come, they will be ready to supply the right kind of extras and collect their commission. Without the services of an agent, you will simply have to find yourself in the right place at the right time, which can happen to anyone. Even the author of this book, while travelling in the Swat Valley of Northern Pakistan, had to disappoint a Pakistani film director also staying at the Heaven Breeze Hotel who wanted her to mount a horse and impersonate a colonel's daughter.

Bombay (now Mumbai) is probably the most promising destination for aspiring 'crowd artists' since every year 700 films are made in 'Bollywood'. Fast-talking agents with mobile phones lurk around the Salvation Army Hostel (022-284 1824) signing up prospective extras; this cheap hostel can be found on the corner of Mereweather Road and Best Street near the exclusive Taj Mahal Hotel. If signed up, you must take a rickshaw to the state-run Film City or wherever else in the vast city of Mumbai shooting is taking place. First-time extras are typically paid 500 rupees (£6) plus expenses. Expect to be kept hanging around much longer than originally told, often into the wee small hours.

Although not very common, busking can net some worthwhile profits. With a borrowed guitar, David Hughes busked in the subways of Taipei which earned him £10 an hour tax-free. But there was a catch: *'Things were fine until strange red graffiti appeared overnight near the spot where I stood. A man who 'represented' some people (gangsters? market traders?) told me to stop, or something might 'happen' to me. By this time we had just enough teaching to keep us afloat so I gladly yielded to his request.'*

Mimes, guitarists, dancers and musicians should go to Ginza in Tokyo or any Japanese city, especially in the evening. Once a few people gather, the Japanese herd instinct guarantees that the street will become all but impassable. Local taste favours old Beatles and Simon & Garfunkel songs.

Hostessing

A reasonably reliable way for a western woman to make money in Japanese cities is to work as a hostess. Catherine Quinn, a freelance journalist, enjoyed her stint as a hostess in Tokyo last year and has kindly provided this description of how it works. According to Catherine, hostesses and hostess bars are widely misinterpreted in the west. Most accounts suffer in the translation, and are rendered at worst as a method to lure unsuspecting girls into prostitution, and at best as a dubious activity to be approached with great caution. This was highlighted in press coverage of Lucie Blackman, the English hostess who was murdered in Tokyo in 2000. Her tragic death was mistakenly reported in the western media as a direct consequence of hostessing.

Hostess bars rely on a drinking culture completely alien to the west, where overworked salary-men pay for the company and attention of lively women. The preference is for European women, and prejudices can make it more difficult for 'non-Aryan' looking women. Generally, two types of hostess bar can be found. More traditional style bars open from about 8pm until midnight, pay around 2500 yen (around £13) an hour, and serve a small number of Japanese speaking clientele. These bars are more often the choice of women with full time English teaching jobs in the day, and often offer good chances to learn Japanese by talking with customers.

The second type of hostess bar is more in the style of a western nightclub. These bars attract groups of Japanese businessmen on high incomes, in search of a night on the town – although they also attract a steady flow of single regulars. Many clubs run shorter hours

(10pm-2am for example) if customers are scarce, and popularity is on the decline. Most clubs run a *dohan* (dinner date) reward system, which hostesses have to meet to earn serious money. Pressure to go on regular *dohan* has increased with economic necessity, with the strictest clubs operating fines for girls who don't make enough. Depending on the club, bonuses can be earned by drinking many drinks (these are charged to the customer) and persuading the customer to buy champagne. Many techniques abound for diluting the inordinate flow of alcohol, including the famous 'Lady's Special' (bar code for water), or the well-positioned pot plant in which to tip your drink.

Working hostesses are expected to wear nightclub style clothing which is glamorous rather than revealing, and to be well groomed. Appearance issues vary from club to club, with the top-end establishments often demanding a dizzying level of personal maintenance. Generally, work involves conversing with men who arrive at the bar, and acting as a drinking companion. Some clubs also like girls to sing karaoke with customers. For many hostesses, the major advantages of the job are the social company it provides and the unlimited drinks, a particular perk in a city where alcohol is so expensive. Although there is no guarantee that customers won't be tedious, to some extent your interest in the clientele will determine your enjoyment of the profession. Hours of speaking slowly can become tiring but, for some women, hostessing is an unrivalled method of earning money whilst experiencing another culture. Note that this kind of employment is forbidden under the terms of the working holiday visa scheme, as is bar work.

In Tokyo hostess clubs are scattered throughout Roppongi and Ginza, and can be difficult to distinguish from normal bars, nightclubs and strip-joints. Traditional hostess bars are virtually impossible to track-down without a knowledge of written Japanese. The best places to look for jobs are in the various English magazines scattered throughout youth hostels, such as *Tokyo Scene* and *Tokyo Classified*, both of which will advertise at least a few clubs looking for hostesses. Alternatively, you can find out the names of clubs by word of mouth, put your best dress on, and ask at the door. In Roppongi, Greengrass, Club Vincent, Casanova's and One Eyed Jack can all be fairly easily tracked down on the main strip (Minata-ku). It is even possible to apply online for a job at the latter via www.worldagency.tv.

Catherine Quinn, who prides herself on her ability to find employment at record speed in any country, gained three interviews for hostess work within two days of arriving in Japan and was working by the third evening. She soon realised that the hostess scene has changed greatly over the past two years, in particular the pay has dropped substantially in the wake of the severe economic downturn in Japan. It is not even necessarily better paid than teaching English. Apparently the increasing number of Russian women working as hostesses has helped to bring down earnings and demand. Still, Catherine found hostessing to be a viable source of income and 'one of the most refreshingly easy jobs' she has held abroad.

Lucie Blackman was a hostess who went for a weekend away with a customer who, it turned out, had drugged and raped several girls on previous occasions. When he drugged Lucie, she tragically suffocated. Catherine feels personally that hostessing is safe: *'Whilst I would stand by anyone's right to go away for a weekend with a customer, it's fair to say that this is not a regular activity amongst hostesses. I would say that there are no dangers peculiar to hostessing which do not also relate to common sense travelling behaviour for women and men.'*

Hostess bars also exist in Bangkok, Singapore and Hong Kong where it must be said that hostessing can shade into prostitution.

Modelling

Caucasian faces are sought after in the advertising industries of Singapore, Thailand, Japan, China, etc. Interested people should get some photos taken back home rather than risk being ripped off by agencies which charge you to put together a portfolio and then don't hire you. When you arrive, register with one of the numerous modelling agencies. The daily rate is high (usually around £80), and earnings good if you average more than one or two assignments per week. Jaime Burnell couldn't believe how easy it was:

When I was in Thailand, I was approached by an American scouting for white/blonde girls to have their photos taken for adverts. White faces sell in Thailand so even me who is not model material usually got paid for one day's work at a rate of 5,000 baht. It was all done very professionally and the photos are kept in a photo library for future use. As long as you don't mind it being used two years later in a soap commercial then go for it. That money let me travel for over two months with some left over. Scouts hang around Khao San Central Bar on the road of the same name.

Try to track down modelling agencies such as CalCarrie's in Siam Square, Red Modelling and the Pikanake Group which Vaughan Temby used a few years ago to find work as a magazine model and a film extra.

Similar opportunities exist in Japan. Again, you don't have to be particularly stunning, though obvious tattoos will probably disqualify you since these have connotations of gangster status. There are big agencies in Tokyo and Osaka; otherwise occasional jobs are passed on by word of mouth. The routine is you give them a call, go for an interview, they take your measurements, take a few photos and get you to sign a contract. Then they call you when they have work. To make good money you need to sign up with as many agencies as possible. No knowledge of Japanese is needed as you'll always be playing the foreigner.

TOURISM & BUSINESS

Brett Muir taught scuba in Phuket. Richard Davies funded his stay in expensive Singapore by recruiting travellers for the hostel he was staying at. Working as a croupier in Japan is said to be potentially lucrative because of the tips. Thailand affords the best chances as Vaughan Temby discovered:

We spent a great Christmas on the islands and although we weren't looking for work, we did come across some opportunities. On Koh Samui several bars along Chaweng beach needed staff during the peak season. The huge Reggae's Bar Complex, a little further inland hires some foreign staff. On Koh Pha'Ngan a friend of mine worked as a DJ and another as a waitress/kitchen helper in the excellent German-style bakery.

Later on Vaughan tried the hotels in Bangkok but was told that they had plenty of local labour and besides he would need a work permit. The Azure Corporation in Bangkok (www.azurecorporation.com) sometimes has hospitality vacancies.

Throughout Asia, especially in China, there are many ex-pat run restaurants and hotels. Often these are the most popular places to stay since they are tuned into providing what westerners want. Tim Leffel thinks that it is almost scary how easily they can dominate the market. He goes on to say that anyone who can obtain a long-term visa through local loopholes or by marrying a local, might try to capitalise on this situation.

Japanese ski resorts provide openings for people with a 'basic understanding of the Japanese language'. Rebecca Barber from Australia spent three months in the ski resort of Imajo, which was fixed up through an Australian agency. Young foreigners were employed to operate the ski lifts, as waitresses, golf caddies and, as in Rebecca's case, in fast food restaurants. Food and accommodation were provided in addition to a good salary. Rebecca's skiing and Japanese improved enormously and she went home with a good profit – she made A$6,500 in three months and spent little because most things were provided, including transport within Japan.

Another suggestion sent by Rebecca Barber based on a trip to Nepal is to volunteer to assist with one of the multitude of rafting trips which many companies run:
When I went on a rafting trip (which are fantastic but expensive by Nepali stan-

> dards – minimum $200 for ten days), I met a guy who had just done two free trips as 'safety kayaker'. No qualifications were needed apart from being confident of your ability to paddle the river. When in Kathmandu, simply walk into every agency you see and offer to work. You would be unlikely to get full-time or long-term work but as a way of getting a few free trips, living at no expense and getting some great paddling experience, not to mention the chance of future employment, it's ideal.

As has been well publicised, many major European companies have outsourced their call centres en masse to India, creating many training jobs for British and European citizens. One company that specialises in recruitment in this field is Launch Offshore (www.launchoffshore.com) with an office in Harley Street in London. It places graduates and anyone with six months call centre experience on ten-month assignments throughout India. The package includes return airfares, accommodation and a local salary.

VOLUNTEERING

Many people who have travelled in Asia or who have been moved by the Tsunami disaster are dissatisfied with the role of tourist and would like to find a way of making a contribution. In very many cases this is laudable but naïve. It may be worth quoting Dominique Lapierre, author of *The City of Joy*, the bestseller and later a film which movingly describes life in a Calcutta slum. Although he is talking specifically about India, a similar situation exists in all poor countries:

> Many of you have offered to go to Calcutta to help. This is most generous but I am afraid not very realistic. Firstly because Indian authorities only give a three-month tourist visa to foreign visitors. This is much too short a period for anyone to achieve anything really useful. Secondly because only very specialised help could really be useful. Unless you are a doctor or an experienced paramedic in the fields of leprosy, tropical diseases, malnutrition, bone tuberculosis, polio, rehabilitation of physically handicapped, I think your generous will to help could be more of a burden for the locals in charge than anything else. Moreover, you have to realise that living and working conditions on our various projects are extremely hard for unaccustomed foreigners.

As the director of a project working with forest tribal people in the Bangalore region of India wrote: 'As our work is in a remote area with no creature comforts, it is not easy for foreign visitors to stay there and work, and therefore I suggest that you not mention us in your book as it unnecessarily creates false hopes in the minds of your readers.'

It must be stressed that Westerners almost invariably have to make a financial contribution to cover food and accommodation as well as their travel and insurance. Some voluntary and travel organisations particularly in the US, can provide a more cosseted introduction to the business of volunteering in Asia.

The main difficulty with participating in local voluntary projects (of which there are many) is in fixing anything up ahead of time. And even if you do, the project staff may not know how to utilise the energy of an inexperienced volunteer. Some programmes will seem to western eyes almost completely unstructured, so volunteers should be able to create tasks for themselves. If you have not travelled widely in the Third World you may not be prepared for the scruffiness and level of disorganisation to be found in some places. If this is potentially alarming, try to find an organisation with an office abroad which can provide briefing materials beforehand.

India & Bangladesh

Several organisations in the UK send volunteers to teach English or undertake other voluntary work in India. For example *Teaching and Projects Abroad* (Aldsworth Parade, Goring, Sussex BN12 4TX; 01903 708300; www.teaching-abroad.co.uk) arranges short-term teaching and other workplace assignments in Kerala and Tamil Nadu, South India for a fee of about £1,300 excluding flights; *Travellers Worldwide* (7 Mulberry Close, Ferring, West Sussex BN12 5HY; 01903 700478; www.travellersworldwide.com) sends volunteers to teach conversational English (and/or other subjects like music, maths and sport) in India and Sri Lanka for £1,345 excluding flights; *i-to-i* (Woodside House, 261 Low Lane, Horsforth, Leeds LS18 5NY (0870 333 2332; www.i-to-i.com) sends teaching assistants who have done a TEFL course to Bangalore, Calcutta and Jaipur in India and to Sri Lanka. The fee for a four-week placement is £995 plus an extra £50 for each additional week (excluding airfares).

At an opposite extreme from a cushy attachment to an English-medium private school is working for Mother Teresa's *Missionaries of Charity* in Calcutta. It is possible to become a part-time volunteer at Mother Teresa's children's home in Calcutta (Shishu Bhavan, 78 A.J.C. Bose Road), in the Home for Dying Destitutes at Kalighat and other houses run by the Missionaries of Charity in Calcutta and other Indian cities, but no accommodation can be offered. The work may consist of caring for and feeding orphaned children, the sick and dying, mentally or physically disabled adults and children or the elderly. To register, visit the Mother House at 54A A.J.C. Bose Road, Calcutta 700 016. Further information is also available from their London office at 177 Bravington Road, London W9 3AR (020-8960 2644; www.tisv.be/mt/en/vol.htm).

Dustie Hickey found her brief time as a volunteer in India so affecting that she returned for an extended stay:

> When I was in Calcutta I decided to take a jar of horlicks to the hospital. The nuns were grateful and asked me to come back the following day to play with the children. So I went, taking with me as much paper, crayons and sweets as I could buy from the shop. I spent the morning drawing with them and it was a moving experience. In the afternoon I helped feed the babies. The nuns had their hands full. They invited me to go down to Mother Teresa's home which I did and where I met her.

As mentioned above, the visa problem can prove a difficult one for people who want to commit themselves to stay longer-term in India. If you do want to attach yourself to a voluntary organisation for more than three months, you should aim to enter India on a student or employment visa (see Indian Embassy website www.hcilondon.org). It is not possible to renew a tourist visa beyond six months or convert a tourist visa to a long stay visa within India.

The *Calcutta Rescue Fund* (85 Collins St, Calcutta 700016; info@calcuttarescue.com) works with destitute people in Calcutta, running street clinics, schools and training projects in and around Calcutta. For these they recruit volunteer health professionals. Occasionally other self-funding volunteers are recruited. Help is most needed during the monsoon. It is possible to slot in after arrival as David Hughes wrote from Calcutta:

> While in England we answered an ad for nurses but there is an ongoing need for volunteers in the street clinic where the only skill needed is the ability to communicate in English and read doctors' handwriting (and that's quite a skill). Anyone prepared to give assistance can meet both new and long-stay volunteers at the Khalsa Restaurant (opposite the Salvation Army Red Shield Guest House) between 7.30am and 8am weekday mornings. It's quite hard work (mostly due to the heat) but it can be good fun. You see another side of India.

A UK-based organisation Indian Volunteers for Community Service (12 Eastleigh Avenue, South Harrow, Middlesex HA2 0UF; www.ivcs.org.uk) sends willing volunteers on its DRIVE programme (Discover Rural India for a Valuable Experience). Volunteers over 18 start with three weeks at Amarpurkashi Polytechnic in Uttar Pradesh learning about development and then join a hands-on project in the region between September and March. The placement fee which includes orientation and training is only £175 while living expenses will be

£3 a day. The India Development Group (IDG, 68 Downlands Road, Purley, Surrey CR8 4JF; 020-8668 3161; www.idguk.org) runs a similar six-month programme in Lucknow for 5-10 volunteers over 21 concentrating on appropriate technology to support village life. Yet another organisation with a UK base is Development in Action, c/o Voluntary Services University College London, 25 Gordon St, London WC1H 0AY (07813 395957; www.developmentinaction.org) which can arrange attachments to various Indian NGOs for volunteers to spend the summer or five months from September in Delhi, Mumbai, Bangalore, Indore or Pondicherry. Fees are £550 for July/August and £1,000 for the 5-month placement.

An organisation that places graduates on a voluntary basis in Christian educational institutes in South India is *Jaffe Punnoose Foundation* (Kunnuparambil Buildings, Kurichy, Kottayam 686549, India; fax 0481-430470; jaffeint@sify.com). Volunteers teach for a minimum of four weeks in English medium high schools, hotel management colleges, teacher training centres, vocational institutes and language schools in Kerala State and also at summer schools in various locations in India. As with all projects in India, no wage is paid but you are billeted with a family. Volunteers must have a relevant degree or diploma in the subject (e.g. beauty therapy, gardening, photography).

A community service organisation in India which sends self-funding volunteers to projects is the *Joint Assistance Centre (JAC)*, C-7/150 Lawrence Road, Keshav Puram, Delhi 110035 (ajeets@vsnl.com). It recruits through a partner in California (510-237-8331; www.jacusa.org) and the participation cost is $300 for the one-month workcamp or $600 for a longer term placement plus a registration fee of $50. Andy Green's conclusions about volunteering in India after a stint with JAC are telling: *'I did two weeks' worth of workcamps and I feel that I was of no help to Indian society whatsoever. Due to differences in climate, food and culture, it is difficult to be productive. I could have paid an Indian a few pounds to do what I did in two weeks. It was however an experience I'll never forget.'*

Dakshinayan (c/o Siddharth Sanyal, F-1169 Ground Floor, Chittarangan Park, New Delhi 110019; tel/fax 011-262 76645; www.linkindia.com/dax) works with tribal peoples in the hills of Rajamhal and nearby plains. Volunteers join grassroots development projects every month and contribute $300 per month.

Geoffroy Groleau is an economist and consultant from Montreal who found his way to Dakshinayan via the internet:
The application process is simple and can be conducted fully over the internet. The registration fee which must be provided before setting out for the project is the primary source of revenues for Dakshinayan. So there I was in early March 2002, stepping onto a train from New Delhi heading to Jharkhand. The project provides an opportunity to acquire a better understanding of the myths and realities surrounding poverty in the developing world, and specifically about the realities of rural India. The tribal people of these villages do not need or want fancy houses or televisions, but simply an education for their children and basic healthcare in order to improve the life they have been leading in relative isolation for centuries. It was interesting for me to see that they lead a quiet and simple life based on the rhythm of harvests and seasons, in marked contrast to most westerners. The primary role for volunteers is to teach English for a few hours every day to the kids attending the three Dakshinayan-run schools. I should also mention the numerous unforgettable football games with enthusiastic kids at the end of another sunny afternoon. One should be aware that Dakshinayan is an Indian NGO fully run by local people, which in my view is another positive aspect. But it also means that volunteers will have to adapt to Indian ways.

Many travellers to India stay at monasteries, temples or ashrams, which are communities for meditation, yoga, etc. There may be no official charge or at least a very small one, but it may be assumed that you are a genuine seeker after enlightenment. The residential non-formal school *Samanway Ashram* (Bodh-Gaya 824 231, Bihar; 0631-400223) has links with various educational and sanitation projects in the state to which it sends volunteers. *Bombay Sarvodaya Friendship Centre* (701, Sainath Estate, Off Eastern Express Highway, Opposite Rao Saheb Balaram Thakur Vidyalaya, Mulund East, Mumbai 400081; 22-2563 1025/ 2563 1022; danielm@vsnl.com) is another Gandhian organisation that suggests that foreigners seeking placement in rural areas (preferably long-term) should try to learn some Hindi, be willing to work in difficult and novel situations and have a strong interest in environmental and peace issues and social change.

One of the most famous utopian communities is Auroville near Pondicherry in Tamil Nadu. Volunteers participate in a variety of activities to reclaim land and produce food, and are charged anything from $5 to $20+ a day for board and lodging according to their contribution. Information about volunteering is available from *Auroville,* Bharat Nivas, Tamil Nadu 605 101 (0413-622121; www.auroville.org). There is a relatively new *Volunteering, Internships & Studies (AVIS) programme for those who want to undertake an* educational programme in Auroville.

WWOOF (see Agriculture) lists 22 contacts in India. It no longer seems to be affiliated as it once was with a botanical sanctuary in south India which accepts volunteers who are interested in rainforest conservation to help in the garden, kitchen or office and to do maintenance or landscaping. A minimum donation of £7/$10 a day is requested to cover food and accommodation costs and to support the sanctuary's work. Details are available from Gurukula Botanical Sanctuary, Alattil PO, North Wynad, Kerala 670644 (04935 260426; gbsanctuary@vsnl.net).

The Devoted Organisation for Reforming Environment or DORE (196-b Khari Bazar, Ranikhet, 263645 Distt. Almora, Uttar Pradesh; 05966-20458) recruits up to 25 volunteers to help in a range of projects (including developing eco-tourism) for between one and six months, usually over the summer. The Viswadarsanam Centre for Humanity and Nature in Kerala hosts long and short term volunteers interested in experiencing an alternative lifestyle and helping with admin, gardening, teaching, etc.; details from Viswadarsanam, Nariyapuram PO, Pathanamthitta District, Kerala 689513 (0468 2350543/2353731; viswadarsanam@rediffmail.com). Volunteers contribute £170 for one month, £430 for three months.

A community organisation in the Himalayan foothills with the charming acronym ROSE (Rural Organization on Social Elevation, Social Awareness Centre, PO Kanda, Bageshwar, Uttar Pradesh 263631) can assist volunteers wishing to work with poor villagers, teaching children, carrying out environmental work and organic farming in this village in the Himalayan foothills. Volunteers pay £4 per day for board and lodging. Originally from London, Heather Joiner wrote to say how much she was enjoying her time with ROSE: *'I am a volunteer who is currently here working in the tiny school. I am also here at ROSE in order to improve my basic Hindi. In the morning we join the primary school children learning basic reading, writing and counting.'*

Youth Challenge (29-G Block, Sri Ganganagar, Rajasthan, India 335001; 0154-2471928/ 094140 52296; thedaxter@yahoo.com) is a social development organisation that places foreign volunteers in Udaipur, Jaipur and the Himalayas for 3-8+ weeks.

Few opportunities exist in the restricted Himalayan state of Sikkim. One exception is to participate in a programme run by the *Muyal Liang Trust* at the Denjong Padme Cheoling Academy in Pemayangtse at the beginning of a trekking route. Information about placements as volunteers to teach English or other subjects for up to two months is available in the UK from Jules Stewart, 53 Blenheim Crescent, London W11 2EG (tel/fax 020-7229 4774; JJulesstewart@aol.com). There is the possibility of teaching for longer periods in neighbouring Darjeeling.

Also in the Himalayas, the Ladakh Farm Project needs participants to work on a Ladakhi farm and live with a family for one month to help with farm and household work and take part in family life, as well as participating in educational workshops. Details are available from ISEC USA (International Society for Ecology and Culture), PO Box 9475, Berkeley, CA 94709; 510-548 4915; fax 510-548 4916; isecca@igc.org; the fee is $350.

A Swiss-based organisation, ROKPA International (www.rokpa.org), supports a number of primary schools, middle schools, colleges and universities in Tibet where priority is given to the very poor and orphans. ROKPA requires a small team of dedicated volunteers and places are strictly limited. Teachers must have completed a certificated TEFL course, preferably have had some experience of living in a third world country and be over 25. They also require a minimum commitment of six months to the project, usually starting in March. Further details on this programme are available from Cactus Worldwide Ltd (4 Clarence House, 30-31 North St., Brighton BN1 1EB, UK; 0845 130-4775; fax: 01273 775868; info@cactuslanguage.com; www.cactuslanguage.com).

The *Bangladesh Workcamps Association* (289/2 Work Camp Road, North Shahjahanpur, 1217 Dhaka, Bangladesh; fax 02-956 5506; www.mybwca.org) will try to place you on seven or ten day community development camps between October and February. The participation fee is at least $20 a day. They publish detailed camp information in English. Applications must be submitted at least by mid-September for autumn camps and by the end of November for January camps, enclosing a non-refundable $25 application fee. BWCA can also accommodate foreign volunteers on a medium-term basis (one to three months).

Sri Lanka

Short-term and long-term volunteers and interns can be accommodated at *Lanka Jatika Sarvodaya Shramadana Sangamaya* (98 Rawatawatte Road, Moratuwa, Sri Lanka; 11-264 7159/ 265 5255; ssmplan@sri.lanka.net; www.sarvodaya.org) to engage in social, economic and technical development activities in villages; and planning, monitoring and evaluation work at the head office in Colombo.

Samasevaya Sri Lanka (Anuradhapura Road, Talawa N.C.P., Sri Lanka; 025-227 6266; samasev@sltnet.lk) invites volunteers to their rural locations. Volunteers can be used rather loosely for their educational and development programmes, though it is more akin to a cultural exchange. If the volunteer wants to stay past the initial month of their tourist visa, it is sometimes possible to arrange a renewal. The organisation provides simple accommodation in their office complex in Talawa or with local families. They expect a contribution of $90 a month for meals.

As mentioned above *i-to-i* based in Leeds send teachers to Sri Lanka to teach in state schools and orphanages. To join, you must have a TEFL qualification (i-to-i run 20 hour courses for people with no previous training as well as online courses) and the ability to cover the training and placement fee, insurance and travel costs. Simon Rowland joined the scheme between school in Cambridge and university in York:

I am based in a private non-profit making English institute in a town called Binginya. The school, which opened 10 months ago, is run by a local school teacher of English. Additional classes were set up on my arrival for teachers and business people as well as children. The teaching is mostly enjoyable; classes are conducted purely in English except when they occasionally communicate in Sinhala, to my disgust and telling off. They are all willing to learn and, I like to think, have mostly improved quite a lot in the three months I've been here. The house I'm living in next to the school is wonderful, as are the meals which are brought to us from another house. The local people are all so friendly and falling over themselves to help me. I'd recommend rural Sri Lanka to anyone and think I've had a unique experience.

Despite reservations about the level of organisational back-up provided in relation to the high cost (for example Simon had no idea where he would be until he arrived in Sri Lanka), he had to conclude that without the UK agency i-to-i, he would never have been able to have the experience.

A new charity Volunteers for English in Sri Lanka or VESL (www.vesl.org) provides rural Sri Lankan schools with exposure to enthusiastic and creative native English speakers. VESL sent ten volunteers in the summer of 2004 and has plans to expand the programme in five rural communities in the North, East and Central Provinces, enabling projects to run within Sinhala, Tamil and Muslim communities. The cost inclusive of airfares is

£750 for a four-week experience. The charity is looking at ways of involving volunteers in the rebuilding of communities devastated by the Tsunami.

Internships for people 18-25 are arranged by a company in Colombo called Volunteer International Projects (148/1B Kynsey Road, Colombo 7; 74-720658; www.volunteerinternational.com). They offer a structured programme in the hospitality industry, business, conservation, teaching and so on. Participants pay £1,420 for three months and £2,395 for six months (plus travel). Some internship placements are available in the Maldive Islands for people fluent in French.

Nepal

Nepal is in turmoil at present with Maoist rebels perpetrating frequent acts of violence including the planting of bombs in Kathmandu. It is now estimated that they have between 10,000 and 15,000 fighters and their leaders have been refusing to rejoin peace talks. In December 2004 Maoist rebels staged a week-long blockade of the capital and a series of fierce clashes was reported from the western part of Nepal in early 2005. Close attention should be paid to the situation (e.g. on the Foreign Office website www.fco.gov.uk/travel) before deciding to spend time in Nepal as a tourist or a volunteer. It may be that some of the voluntary organisations listed below will have suspended their activities if the situation worsens. So far the rebels have not harmed foreigners though they do sometimes ask tourists (especially trekkers to Everest base camp) for a 'donation' of say $20.

If you avoid the areas of insurgency, Nepal is a promising destination for short-term volunteers and casual English teachers. Richard Davies came away from Kathmandu with the impression that anyone could get a job teaching in Nepal. He had made the acquaintance of an Englishman who had simply walked into the first school and got a job teaching children and adults. He was finding the work very rewarding, but not financially, since he earned less than £10 a month.

People who find voluntary openings in Nepal will be faced with a visa problem. Tourist visas (which can be purchased on arrival for $25 cash) are valid for 30 days whereupon they have to be renewed to a maximum of 120 days. A four-month visa is much less readily available but can be applied for at the Immigration Office in Thamel, Kathmandu. Normally these will not be granted unless the request is supported by an official organisation like the gap placement agencies which are very active in the country. People who overstay their visas have in the past been fined $4,000 or even put in prison.

Rachel Sedley spent six months between school and university as a volunteer teacher at the Siddartha School in Kathmandu (arranged through the UK organisation Gap Challenge) and greatly enjoyed the children and the local community, but concludes that 'it seems to me unnecessary to come to Nepal through an organisation, since everyone here is so keen to help.' Rachel's main complaint about her situation was that she was teaching in a private school for privileged children when she had been led to believe that she would be contributing her time and labour to more needy children. While there, she met several people from various schools and orphanages who would love to have English volunteers.

A range of organisations makes it possible for people to teach in a voluntary capacity. No indigenous organisations can afford to bestow largesse on foreigners joining their projects, so westerners who come to teach in a school or a village must be willing to fund themselves. Of course living expenses are very low by western standards, though the fees charged by mediating or gap year organisations like i-to-i and Africa & Asia Venture as well as by Nepali agencies (some listed below) can increase the cost significantly. If you want to avoid an agency fee you can make direct contact with schools on arrival. Note that the newly formed WWOOF Nepal organisation (GPO 9594, Kathmandu; 01-4363418; fdregmi@wlink.com.np) charges a one-off fee of $50 for trying to match a willing volunteer with a suitable volunteer placement. Of course it also distributes a list of about 100 organic farms in Nepal to members for the joining fee of $20.

Relevant organisations include:

Cultural Destination Nepal, PO Box 11535, Dhapasi, Kathmandu (01-437 7623; www. volunteernepal.org.np). Volunteer service work programme. Application fee €50 plus €650 fee includes 2-week pre-service orientation and homestay throughout. Placements last 2-4 months starting February, April, June, August and October.

Global Action Nepal, PO Box 2717, Ganeshchowk, Budhanilkantha, Kathmandu, Nepal; 01-370977; www.gannepal.org.). GAN is a charity working in the field of education in Nepal, providing dynamic volunteers to support village teachers in their work and also to improve school environments by building toilets, wells, etc. 2004/5 volunteers will be placed in the Kathmandu Valley only for security reasons.

Gorkha District & Educational Development Scheme, c/o Joy Leighton, Chairwoman – Fax 01277 841224; www.nepal.co.uk. Charity is always looking for volunteers to teach English to Nepalese school kids for a minimum of three weeks among other projects.

Insight Nepal, PO Box 489, Pokhara, Kaski, Nepal (insight@fewanet.com.np; www. insightnepal.org.np). 6-week and 3-month placements for all post A-level and high-school graduate native speakers of English. Participation fee of $840 for 3 months and $480 for 6 weeks. Full programme includes pre-orientation, placement in a primary or secondary school in Nepal to teach mainly English or in community development projects, a one-week village or trekking excursion and 3 days in Chitwan National Park.

International Mountain Explorers Connection, PO Box 3665, Boulder, CO 80307, USA (888-420-8822; www.mountainexplorers.org) Normally sends fee-paying volunteer teachers to Sherpa village schools where they live with local families from September to December and February to April. They cancelled their 2004/5 programme due to Maoist activity, but hope to resume in the near future.

Kathmandu Environmental Education Project (KEEP), PO Box 9178, Tridevi Marg, Thamel (01-4412944; fax 01-4413018; www.keepnepal.org). KEEP sends volunteers to different trekking villages in Nepal to teach the English language to lodge owners, trekking guides and porters and also as teachers in government schools, for a minimum of 2 months. Volunteers stay with mountain families. Volunteers must be totally self-funding. Membership fee £12/$20 and the placement fee is £18/$30.

New International Friendship Club, Post Box 11276, Maharajgunj, Kathmandu, (01-427406; fcn@ccsl.com.np). 40 English-speaking university graduates placed in schools or colleges. Volunteer teachers should contribute $150 per month for their keep (unless they become a project expert). Basic Nepalese standard accommodation is provided and Nepali (rice-based) meals.

RCDP Nepal, Kathmandu Municipality, PO Box 8957, Ward 14, Kathmandu (1-278305/ fax 1-276530; www.rcdpnepal.com). Paying volunteers and interns work on various programmes lasting 2 weeks to 5 months, including teaching English. Volunteers stay with families in villages. Also have volunteer programme in India, mostly in Delhi.

VSP/Nepal (Volunteer and Support Program Nepal), PO Box 11969, Kathmandu (fax 1-416144; vwop2000@hotmail.com). Willing volunteers looking for a cultural experience can be placed in variety of voluntary posts including teaching English in schools, in both urban and remote areas of Nepal. No special qualifications are needed. Volunteers stay with a local family and contribute $50 a month towards their expenses. Registration fee of $20 plus placement fee of $400 must be paid.

Eighteen year old Giles Freeman from Australia spent three months in Nepal through Insight Nepal: *'I would advise that applicants do have some teaching practice before coming. Classes easily reach 60 or 80 in many schools, making it necessary for the patient teacher to know what they are doing. With no teaching experience, this has proved a little hard, but it's a great challenge. All in all it has been extremely rewarding.'*

Southeast Asia

The mainstream London-based conservation expedition organisers all run projects in Asia. These expeditions are normally open to anyone reasonably fit who can raise the cost of joining (typically £2,500-£3,000):

Coral Cay Conservation Ltd, 13th Floor, 125 High St, Colliers Wood, London SW19 2JG (020-8545 7717; www.coralcay.org) recruit paying volunteers, expedition leaders, scuba instructors, etc. for its marine conservation projects in the Philippines, Malaysia and Fiji. Marine expeditions cost from £715 for two weeks to £2,900 for 12 weeks.

Frontier Conservation Expeditions, 50-52 Rivington St, London EC2A 3QP (020-7613 2422; www.frontierconservation.org). Places volunteers on 4, 8, 10 or 20-week phases on projects in Cambodia (among others) for a fee of between £1,500 and £3,950. Ian Wingate enjoyed his time in Southeast Asia so much that he joined the team in the London office after his expedition:

> *I joined Frontier as a self-funded volunteer and journeyed to the tropical forests of central Vietnam where I conducted biodiversity and socio-economic surveys. Frontier offered me the chance to gain practical conservation experience and the possibility of interesting employment afterwards. I learned a great deal about conservation in Asia and I also found out a lot about myself, my limits, strengths and weaknesses. Scientific experience or qualifications are not necessary. Higher value is placed on interest and determination.*

Greenforce, 11-15 Betterton St, Covent Garden, London WC2H 9BP (020-7470 8888; www.greenforce.org). Volunteer researchers are sent to join biodiversity conservation aid projects in Asia, i.e. Nepal and the marine environments of Fiji and Malaysian Borneo. Projects involve studying endangered species and habitats. The cost is from £2,300 for 10 weeks in Nepal plus flights.

Starfish Ventures, 199 Bishopsgate, London EC2M 3TY (020-7814 6641; www. starfishventures.co.uk). New company that places volunteers of all nationalities in development projects in Thailand including teaching, community development, construction and conservation. Fees are from £1,095 for 4 weeks to £1,495 for 12 weeks which include homestay accommodation, in-country supervision and (if appropriate) preparatory TEFL training weekend.

Trekforce Expeditions, 34 Buckingham Palace Road, London SW1W 0RE (020-7828 2275; www.trekforce.org.uk). Organise and run conservation projects in the rainforests of Sabah and Sarawak. The expeditions last between two and five months and are a combination of jungle training, adventurous trekking in the rainforest, conservation work and teaching. Each expedition's project varies and in the past has included work at an orangutan rehabilitation centre and construction of turtle hatching pens in one of the national parks. Fees from £2,590 for eight weeks to £3,450 for 17 weeks.

Working volunteers are welcomed by Bob Tillotson who has settled in Thailand with his Thai partner Soo Lee. After many years on the road (apparently he used the 1985 edition of this book in Taiwan), he has established a sustainable farm in northeast Thailand.

Rob Abblett's 12 day stay here was his introduction to third world living and he left feeling exhilarated:
My home was a three-sided bamboo hut with mosquito net. When I asked where the toilet was Bob gave me a spade. He likes to give WWOOFers a project which they can accomplish before leaving. Mine was to landscape around one of the sunken ponds on the property, planting, watering and making winding paths. I'm fascinated with alternative technology and I really admired Bob's simple style of living. While I was there he put together a bicycle-powered water pump which would draw water from a well to water his vegetables. 'There must be an easier way' was all I could think whilst the stiff pedals sucked the energy out of my body leaving me drenched in sweat, 'an electric pump, Archimedes screw, another WWOOFer!'

Bob has written in the past to say that readers who are sympathetic to the aims of his enterprise will be welcomed for a minimum of four weeks though he can accommodate only four volunteers at a time. Interested people (non-smokers) should write to him for an invitation before showing up, enclosing an IRC: Soo and Loong Bob, 268 Thamafaiwan, A. Kaeng Khro, Chaiyaphum 36150, Thailand. Also in the village is another organic farming community run on Buddhist principles: Rainbow House (Barn Sairoong) also accepts volunteers to help with farm work, teach English to the children and learn about Thai culture (PO Box 7, Chaiyaphum 36000).

Most of the activities of NGOs providing educational and other assistance to displaced persons in Thailand are located at the Thai/Burmese border. In the Burma Volunteer Program (Thailand), volunteers teach English to groups of Burmese refugees for at least 14 weeks near Mae Sot near the western Thai-Burma border; maesotel@loxinfo.co.th/ www.burmavolunteer.com. If in Bangkok, contact the Catholic Office for Emergency Relief & Refugees (COERR), 122-122/1 Soi Naksuwan, Nonsi Road, Chong Nonsi, Yannawa, Bangkok 10120 (fax 2-681 5306; coerr@mozart.inet.co.th) which provides services for refugees and poor Thai villagers. One of its projects is to provide English language teachers for a refugee camp called 'Safe Area for Burmese Students' in Maneeloy Village, Pak Tho District, Ratchaburi Province, Thailand.

Near Phuket at the other end of Thailand, conservationists are working to protect marine turtles, mangrove forest and coral reef on the island of Phra Thong. Though projects in this area were badly hit by the Tsunami, Naucrates plans to start work again soon. Prospective volunteers and student conservationists can obtain more details from the Italian organisation Naucrates, Via Corbetta 11, 22063 Cantù, Italy (+39 3334 306643; fax +39 031-716315; www.naucrates.org).

Mid- and long-term volunteering opportunities are available in the fields of teaching, eco-tourism, etc. through Greenway Cultural Exchange & International Living, PO Box 21, Had Yai Airport, Had Yai, Songkhla, Thailand 90115; 7447 3506; mltv@greenwaythailand. org; www.greenway.bizland.com. The cost is 20,000 baht ($500) for the first three months, with a maximum stay of one year.

Far East

The workcamp organisation in Japan has a reassuring name and acronym: Never-ending International Workcamps Exchange. It is probably not worth writing directly to Nice unless you are already in Japan (2-4-2-701 Shinjuku, Shinjuku-ku, Tokyo 160-0022; www.jah. ne.jp/nice-do) but via one of their corresponding agents such as Concordia or UNA Exchange.

An unusual opportunity is available at a farm in Hokkaido, the most northerly island of the Japanese archipelago, known as Shin-Shizen-Juku (Tsurui, Akan-gun, Hokkaido 085-12; 0154-64 2821), a place well known to the travelling fraternity. The owner Hiroshi Mine often welcomes short or long-term international travellers who work in various capacities, especially conducting conversational English lessons in the community or gardening, in exchange for their board and lodging. Joseph Tame was enthusiastic about the place:

Shin Shizen Juku provided a fantastic introduction to Japan. I was there with six other volunteers, all in our twenties. Japanese lessons were given, and the English teaching for local schools, colleges, evening classes, individuals, etc. was very laid back. Even an idiot could do it as it was almost entirely conversation. As it was getting pretty cold in early November, the gardening was quite limited but I can imagine that in the summer there would be loads to do on the huge plot of land. The building we lived in was a large 20-room dilapidated tin shack, but with numerous heaters and a wood burning stove it was quite cosy. The nightlife was great as a local family owned and ran (with the help of a volunteer) a restaurant which would frequently throw parties for us. Then we'd head for our local Onsen or hot springs to soak beside a vast lake of Siberian swans.

Japan and Korea have nascent WWOOF organisations, both of them web-based. It costs $40 to join WWOOF Japan (Honcho 2-jo, 3-chome 6-7, Higashi-ku, Sapporo 065-0042 Japan; www.wwoofjapan.com) whose list of member farms numbers about 50 and $50 for the Korean list from WWOOF Korea (No. 1008, Seoul B/D, 45 Jongno-1Ga, Jongno-Gu, Seoul 110-121; wwoof@wwoofkorea.com).

> **Just as his year's working holiday visa was about to expire, Joseph Tame went to a family-run pension called Milky Way in southwestern Hokkaido, as listed by WWOOF.**
>
> *WWOOF Japan have just relaunched themselves with a new detailed list and other services. Members can log in and then download details of the 33 hosts (one of which is a community organisation made up of 80 organic farms). I would thoroughly recommend Country Inn Milky House. The pay is average for Hokkaido (800 yen per hour) which meant that most months I was able to save about £700 for future travels. In addition to working an average of 7 or 8 hours a day, I spent three hours studying this funny language and my Japanese really improved. The various tasks I was given by the pension owner included putting up fences around tennis courts, acting as secretary for foreign guests, chain-sawing, erecting a big canopy on the veranda, shovelling snow, avoiding the phone when it rings, accidentally driving over big stones with the ride-on mower, cutting telephone lines with a bush cutter, operating the mini-digger, painting walls and planting flowers. For a few weeks I taught groups of visiting schoolchildren how to perform a traditional English Country Dance. It's been a great experience.*

The Korean International Volunteer Association organises voluntary placements throughout Korea. Projects include teaching English at an orphanage for at least a month and working in sheltered communities. Details are available from KIVA, 11th Floor Sekwang B/D, 202 Sejong-ro, Chongro-gu, Seoul 110-050 (02-723 6225; info@kiva.or.kr). More and more workcamps organisations in exotic places are coming to light, most recently the Mongolian Workcamps Exchange (mce-mn@magicnet.mn). An NGO in Ulaanbaatar that places volunteers is the New Choice Mongolian Volunteer Organization, Ikh toiruu, Building-15, Room-405, Ulaanbaatar, Mongolia (PO Box 159, Ulaanbaatar 210646; 991 18767).

Middle East

At the beginning of 2005 international job seekers may be a little more willing to consider the Middle East as a possible destination than they would have been two years ago as the Iraq war was pending. But with bitter anti-Western feelings running high in the wake of the US election in 2004 and ongoing tension between Israelis and Palestinians, the taste for travel and employment in the Middle East has been soured and many prospective travellers have been put off by fear for their personal security. Perhaps travellers and expats can play a small part in diminishing the distrust and tension between the two cultures, bringing people together, allowing individuals on both sides to gain some understanding of the complexity of the world's problems.

The areas of employment to consider are English teaching, nannying/nursing or a position in the petro-chemical or construction industries if you happen to have senior managerial experience. Oil wealth has meant that many of the countries of the Middle East like Saudi Arabia, Bahrain, Oman and the Gulf states have been able to afford to attract professional expatriate workers with superior qualifications and extensive experience. In fact most of these countries have been trying to reduce the number of foreign workers, which is bad news for all the semi-skilled and unskilled workers from the Indian Subcontinent, Philippines, Africa and so on. In recent years expatriate workers have accounted for 61% of the work force in Oman, 83% in Kuwait and 91% in the UAE.

Countries in the Middle East vary greatly in degree of Islamic restrictiveness. Bahrain and Oman, for example, are favoured by British expatriates for their relatively relaxed atmosphere and the United Arab Emirates are also politically stable and can provide a pleasant way of life. Accepting a TEFL contract in an oil state usually means first-class accommodation in a luxury apartment complex, cheap shopping, etc. Despite a strong EFL market throughout the region, there is seldom room for visiting job-seekers, since a tight hold is kept on tourist visas. It is usually essential these days to have an MA in TESOL or Applied Linguistics (or at least be enrolled in a distance learning ELT Master's degree) with at least three years of experience, preferably at university level. ELS Language Centers Middle East comprise 11 Centres in the region which employ a number of full-time teachers and many part-time teachers to teach American English; the regional office is at Khalidiya Street, Behind the Sheraton Residence, PO Box 3079, Abu Dhabi, United Arab Emirates; 02-666 9225; www.elsmea.com).

Saudi Arabia is a very different destination and the kingdom has been troubled in recent years by some high profile attacks on foreign residents. Women working in Saudi Arabia sometimes begin to feel that they are treated like prisoners. Liberalisation is coming very slowly to the region and it will be a long time before women are allowed to drive cars, let alone function as normal members of Saudi society. If trying to fix up employment directly with a company in the Middle East, try to be sure that you have a watertight contract.

Lebanon is struggling valiantly to recover from its long and painful war, and is looking to a prosperous future in which English will overtake French in popularity, so it may be worth investigating possibilities there. Similar opportunities exist in neighbouring Syria where there's an enthusiastic demand for private tuition in English. The American Language Center (PO Box 20, Damascus; 011-333 7936/fax 011-331 9327) runs American English courses for adults, and anyone with a TEFL background has a chance of getting some part-time hours with them. Occasionally they run their own training programme for EFL teachers and they may also know of individuals who want private tutoring in English. Dan Boothby lived in Syria for a year and found that the best place in Damascus to look for rooms and job advice was Bab Tourma, the Christian quarter of the old city.

Many people consider Yemen to be the most beautiful and interesting of all Middle Eastern states, though the risk of kidnapping discourages many. While Mary Hall was in Yemen working for an aid agency, she became familiar with the teaching scene:

There are more and more places teaching English here, the two main ones being YALI (Yemen American Language Institute) and the British Council, both of whom recruit mostly qualified teachers. The others hire any old bod who turns up, not many of whom are qualified TEFL teachers. Unfortunately they don't pay very well. If there is a Yemeni boss, the wages are even less and often not regularly forthcoming. I had a lodger who was teaching at one place for a pittance as the boss took money out of her wages to pay for her lodgings, even after she moved in with me. I think she was getting a couple of dollars an hour. This is something you sort of get used to. It can be very cheap living here, with rent about $50 a month or less if you're not fussy. The six-hour journey to Aden costs just $5. You can get a three month visa if you pay and are HIV-negative.

There is quite a thriving expat community so there are opportunities to pick up work there. Contact details for YALI are PO Box 22347, Sana'a (01-448039; www.yali.org.ye). A school that university graduates could try for teaching is the Modern American Language Institute (MALI, PO Box 11727, Sana'a, Yemen; 01-446103; www.arabicinyemen.com). Unlike most institutes in the Middle East MALI says it is willing to consider enthusiastic and adaptable graduates even if they lack an EFL qualification.

Because of the crisis in the Palestinian territories on the West Bank and Gaza, the educational charity for Palestinians UNIPAL (Universities Trust for Educational Exchange with Palestinians) has been directing its efforts at the refugee camps in southern Lebanon. Volunteers teach children aged 12-15 in the refugee camps in and around Sidon between mid-July and mid-August. Volunteers must be native English speakers, based in the UK and at least 20 years old. The approximate cost is £400 including airfares. Applications must be submitted to Unipal (BCM Unipal, London WC1N 3XX; www.unipal.org.uk) by the end of February in time for interviews at the end of March and two training days in the spring and summer.

TURKEY

Teaching English

Turkey's ambitions to join the European Union were given an enormous boost at the beginning of 2005 when several EU leaders came out in support of their case. Negotiations are due to begin at the end of 2005 but it is unlikely that Turkey would be ready for membership before another ten years, primarily because of its human rights record and the thorny problem of a divided Cyprus. But at least its economy has shown signs of recovery and on January 1st 2005, the Turkish lira lost six zeros against the dollar. A loaf of bread has gone from costing 350,000 lire to .35 new lire (or 35 kurus). The government was able to do this because for the first time in many years, the rate of inflation dropped to single figures (i.e. 9%).

For a number of years now, the Turkish middle classes have gravitated to all things Western including the English language. Teachers routinely earn $35 for a private lesson though obviously there is plenty of competition for privates. The boom in English is not confined to private language schools *(dershane)* but there are dozens of private secondary schools *(lises)* and a few universities where English is the medium of instruction. This has meant that Turkey has been an attractive destination for fledgling teachers of any nationality who could be fairly sure of finding employment and well-rewarded at that, often with free accommodation and free air fares (London-Istanbul) on completion of a contract.

But it seems that the market is over-provided with language schools, and fierce competition among the schools in the big cities has seen teachers' benefits pared away and hours raised to 30 a week, as Alan Hargreaves reported in 2004:

> Schools in Istanbul are cutting back on pay, free accommodation and holidays and increasing hours worked. The English Centre which was once the best school in Istanbul now can't pay teachers on time. It used to occupy four storeys, now just two and classes are tiny. Another main school, Dilko, no longer provides free accommodation or a sterling component to the teacher's pay packet. Interlang has been taken over by English Time calling its long term future into doubt.

Most of the mainstream schools will want to see a university degree and a TEFL Certificate of some kind, preferably the Cambridge (CELTA) or Trinity (TESOL) Certificate. This may apply to the established chains, but there are still many dodgy operators and swashbuckling and unscrupulous employers. One British teacher sets out what you should look for when choosing an employer:

> I worked at four different schools in Istanbul. You'll want a school that's professional (with good resources, support and teacher development), offers a good package (salary, accommodation, holiday entitlement) and has a timetable to suit you. Many schools like to boast about how professional they are and ignore their own faults. For example some provide a fake degree to a teacher with no degree, employ teachers without a degree, recruit travellers from youth hostels, fail to pay teachers, gossip about former teachers, and so on.

Although Istanbul is not the capital, it is the commercial, financial and cultural centre of Turkey, so this is where most of the EFL teaching goes on. On the negative side, there may be more competition from other travelling teachers here and also in Izmir than in Ankara or less obvious cities like Mersin and Bursa.

Among the main language teaching organisations in Turkey are International House with several big operations in Istanbul and the Turco-British Association in Ankara (www. tba.org.tr) and its American counterpart, the Turkish-American Association (www.taa-ankara.org.tr). Dilko, Kent English and English Time (addresses below) are all well established In Istanbul. Wall Street Institute has opened five branches in Istanbul and one in Ankara for which it has been recruiting staff (wsiinfo@pen.com.tr).

Most of the language chains have come in for criticism over the years, with words like 'cowboy,' 'unprofessional' and 'untrustworthy' being bandied about by disappointed teachers. For a rather dyspeptic lowdown on some of the schools, see the website www. geocities.com/antikenglish/schools.html which catalogues the problems including teachers sacked to save money, wages slashed for Turkish staff, contracts simply not honoured, certificates held by schools to prevent staff from leaving prematurely and teachers made to pay for their work permits. The accounts are undated so possibly too outdated to be of much use.

Without a degree and a TEFL certificate it will not be possible for English teachers to get a work permit and virtually impossible to get a residence permit. Most teachers work on a tourist visa which means that they must renew it every three months, either at the immigration office (by showing that they have the means to support themselves; for example having a Turkish friend undertake to support them) or more usually by leaving the country and obtaining a fresh tourist visa, which costs £10 in sterling at the point of entry. The cheapest border crossing is with Bulgaria which can be visited in one day from Istanbul.

For short-term opportunities, the Education Department of the youth travel and exchange organisation *Genctur* (Istiklal Cad. Zambak Sok. 15/5, Taksim 80080, Istanbul (212-249 2515; www.genctur.com) organises summer camps for children where English, German and French are taught by native speakers who work for seven hours a day in exchange for free board and lodging. Pocket money of $100-$350 is also given according to experience and skills. Applicants must have some experience of working with children.

Among the main indigenous language teaching organisations in Turkey are:

Active Languages, Ataturk Bulvari No 127, Kat:6-7, Bakanliklar, 06640 Ankara (312-418 7973; info@active-languages.com; www.active-languages.com). Small chain of private language schools conducts teacher interviews in Ankara or London.

Best English, Bayindir Sokak No. 53, 06640 Kizilay, Ankara (312-417 6063; www. bestenglish.com.tr).

Dilko English, Cumhuriyet Meydani Hatboyu Caddesi No. 16, 34720 Bakirköy, Istanbul (212-570 1270; dilkobakirkoy@dilko.com.tr). Branches also in Kadiköy and Besiktas, employing up to 60 teachers altogether.

English Centre, Rumeli Caddesi 92, Zeki Bey Apt. 4, 80220 Osmanbey, Istanbul (212-247 0983; www.englishcentre.com). 40 native speaker teachers. Online application form.

English Time, Istiklal Cad. No. 251, Kat: 6, Beyoglu, Istanbul (212-292 4778; molly@englishtime.com; www.englishtime.com). Other branches in Taksim (212-293 97 23) and Bakirkoy (212-542 61 60). Most teachers are paid €8-€12 an hour which allows teachers to live comfortably.

Istanbul Language Centre, Yakut Sok. no. 10, Bakirköy, Istanbul (212-571 82 84; ilm@ilm. com.tr). 40 teachers for 4 branches in greater Istanbul.

Kent English (Ankara), Selanik Cad. No. 7, Kat 3-4, Hamiyet Ishani, 06430 Kizilay/Ankara (312-433 6010; www.kentenglish.com.tr). Also in Istanbul: Kirtasiceyi Sokak No. 1, 34714 Kadiköy; www.kentenglish.com. Monthly wage $850.

Childcare

Demand is strong for English-speaking au pairs and also among wealthy Turkish families for professional nannies who have studied childcare and child development. The following agencies make placements in Turkey:

Anglo Nannies London, 2 St. Marks Place, Wimbledon SW19 7ND (020-8944 6677; www. anglonannies.com). Specialises in placing professional English-speaking nannies and teachers in Turkey. Support provided by Istanbul office.

Anglo Pair Agency, 40 Wavertree Road, Streatham Hnill, London SW2 3SP (020-8674 3605; anglo.pair@btineternet.com). Nannies and au pairs placed in Turkey and supported by agency's Istanbul office. Pocket money $90-$120 a week.

ICEP (International Cultural Exchange Programs), 2 Innes Lodge, Inglemere Road, London SE23 2BD (020-8699 0366; london@icep.org.tr). London office of Turkish organisation with offices in Ankara (Yuksel Cad. 9/10, Kizilay, Ankara; 312-418 4460) and Istanbul; www.icep.org.tr/english/aupairturkey.asp). Au pair in Turkey programme for 3-12 months. Minimum pocket money €200 a month. Internships and teaching positions also arranged.

English-speaking nannies are all the rage among the wealthy of Istanbul and to a lesser extent Ankara. The high salaries quoted sound very attractive, though the life of a nanny can be frustrating because of cultural differences. Some nannies have had to get used to having their freedom and independence curtailed, and also the extent to which Turkish children tend to be spoilt and babied. But despite this, many have thoroughly enjoyed their stint in Turkey, including C. Martin who was placed by Anglo Nannies and who commented about some of the cultural differences:

> Children are often idolised in Turkish families and are the centre of attention at family get-togethers. Usually you feel accepted straightaway even if people do not ask you a lot of questions about England. It's best to go with the flow. In Turkish (and all Muslim) culture, kitchen hygiene, child bathing and washing generally are very important. It is important to be flexible and open-minded. But the people are friendly, and working as a nanny in Turkey has been a good experience for me.

One persistent problem is that it may be considered unacceptable for young women to go out alone in the evenings. But Turkish families are normally very generous and allow their live-in child carers to share in family life on equal terms, even in their free time and on holidays.

Tourism

The main Aegean resorts of Marmaris, Kusadasi and Bodrum absorb a large number of foreign travellers as workers. Other places firmly on the travellers' trail like Antalya on the south coast and Goreme in Cappadocia are also promising; Heather McCulloch received three separate job offers in Goreme for the season after her visit, two in hostels and one in a copper shop. Antalya hostels regularly pay travellers $200 a month on top of a bed and one or two meals to man the desk or do other hostel chores. The best time to look is March or early April. Danny Jacobson met lots of foreign workers when he travelled in Turkey:

> I would say Turkey is a hot spot. I met loads of travellers working in the south and even in Selcuk. In Fethiye, Oludenez, definitely in Olympos, it was like an Aussie/ Kiwi resort complex. There are so many of them working and travelling down there, the Turkish people have started talking English with an Australian accent. I heard the authorities are pretty lenient on giving out permits and that the ones who work casual just leave and come back when the tourist visa runs out. There was one shaved-head tattoo-artist dude working the bar at Oludenez Camping who'd been working casual for years.

As in Athens, Istanbul hostels enlist the help of touts to fill their beds, of whom Roger Blake was one. After a trouble-free seven months in crime-ridden South Africa, he fell victim to a common scam within 48 hours of arriving in Istanbul, leaving him with a travel fund of almost zero:

> I found myself a job 'touting' for a new hostel. For this I got my accommodation and not much else (US$1 per person per night and 5% of trips and tours booked by them). I have been here for a month and have earned about $80. This is not much

considering the early start and long hours. In the mornings I'm at the tram stop; afternoons I go out to the airport and evenings are spent at the bus or train station. Whilst trying to entice potential customers, I was once picked up by the police who gave me a ride in their car. 'Work. Visa. Problem' they chanted. I insisted I had a visa. They drove me to my hostel and let me out, no questions asked.

'Help Wanted' signs can sometimes be seen in the windows of bars, travel agencies, etc. As elsewhere proprietors aim to use native English speakers to attract more customers to buy their souvenirs or stay at their hotels. In the majority of cases, this sort of work finds you once you make known your willingness to undertake such jobs. Roger Blake was given a few opportunities to be a 'lure' for those ever-determined carpet salesmen but declined, despite the earning potential in commissions.

Major Turkish yachting resorts are excellent places to look for work, not just related to boats but in hotels, bars, shops and excursions. (See section on Cyprus for information about Turkish Cyprus.) A good time to check harbourside notice boards and to ask captains if they need anyone to clean or repair their boats is in the lead-up to the summer season and the Marmaris Boat Show in May. Laura O'Connor describes what she found in Marmaris:

There's a large British community living there, retired and fed-up Brits who have sold their houses, bought a boat and are whooping it up. There's plenty of work opportunities in the Marina, especially for painting and varnishing in April. Also girls can do hostessing on the boats. I was cleaning boats with a friend for enough money to cover my accommodation and evenings in the pub. Just walk around the Marina and ask.

Paying and accepting commissions is the traditional way of doing business and not regarded as ripping off the punter because these commissions are built into the basic price of everything. Therefore it is possible for talented salesmen/women (preferably multilingual) to make good money in Turkey.

Doing a complete season on a yacht can also be lucrative according to Juniper Wilkinson from Canada who was pleased with the C$7,300 she made in just two months, but who warns that tensions on board can become intolerable:

My experience of working on a yacht was one that I am still having nightmares about two months later. My boyfriend and I were very fortunate to get in the same boat while travelling through Turkey. It was a very well known vessel in the yachting world and we were told we were lucky. However the crew of ten – mostly English – were brutal (drugs, depression, etc.) Our hours were long enough (7am-11pm) but having to put up with the behaviour of some of the other staff was degrading. I got off the boat feeling one inch tall

…and a lot richer. Despite her problems, Juniper says she would do it again but only after checking out the other crew beforehand. She wonders whether a smaller boat might be more conducive to peace of mind, though probably less money. If you can handle long hours, rich demanding guests and the politics of living and working with the same people for the whole four-month season, this is an excellent way to save a lot of money and see the Turkish coast.

Some UK tour operators hire people for Turkey. Sunsail Ltd (The Port House, Port Solent, Portsmouth, Hants. PO6 4TH; 01705 222308; hr@sunsail.com) has many openings for skippers, hostesses, mechanics/bosuns, dinghy sailors, cooks, bar staff and nannies to work in the watersports centres at Yedi Buku near Bodrum, Perili near Datca and a club at Marmaris. Applications for the summer season should be submitted by March. Similarly Mark Warner (08700 330750) employs seasonal staff for their sailing and watersports holidays and beach club hotels in Turkey. Occasionally resort jobs are advertised on the internet; try www.summerjobs.com where jobs as animators, DJs, instructors, etc. at resorts like the Aegean Holiday Village in Bodrum or the Hillside Beach Club or Lykia World in Fethiye may be posted.

Ian McArthur decided it would be an advantage while travelling in Turkey to be musical:

> There is a great demand for musicians, particularly guitarists, in places where the 'Marlboro, Levis and Coca Cola generation' predominates. I have travelled around with my friend Vanessa and she has found work playing in bars in Istanbul, Marmaris, Olu Deniz and Patara (near Kas). Marmaris was the goldmine – £30 a night. The problem was that we both hated Marmaris – too many bloody tourists! In Patara she got a job in a bar called the Lazy Frog and played for a place to stay, food and of course beer.

Voluntary Opportunities

The youth travel bureau Genctur mentioned above (workcamps@genctur.com) runs 30 international workcamps for manual and social projects as well as acting as a youth and student travel bureau and co-ordinating summer camps. GSM (Bayinder Sokak 45/9, Kizilay Ankara 06650; www.gsm-youth.org) is another workcamp organiser in Ankara with links to projects in Anatolia and throughout Turkey. Recruitment of volunteers for the fortnight long camps takes place through all the major workcamp organisations in the UK and worldwide. Full board and accommodation are provided in return for six hours of work six days per week. Most camps take place in small villages or towns where the traditional way of life persists. An optional three-day orientation takes place in Istanbul before the camps begin for a fee of €60.

On most camps you will have to work reasonably hard in the hot sun (and wear long sleeves and jeans in deference to Muslim customs). Mary Jelliffe recounts her experiences in Turkey:

> I applied to UNA (Wales) quite late (in May/June) and heard from Turkey just one week before my camp commenced in August. My workcamp, which consisted of digging an irrigation canal from the nearby hills to the village, took place in Central Anatolia. I was told that our camp was the most easterly, since the majority are in Western Turkey. Conditions in this remote village were fairly primitive. We lived in a half-built school-room sleeping on the floor and sharing the daily duties of collecting water and sweeping out the scorpions from under the sleeping bags. The Turkish volunteers were a great asset to the camp: through them we could have far more contact with the villagers and learn more about Turkish culture in general. In fact I later stayed in Istanbul and Izmir with two of the women volunteers I'd met on the camp.

An impressive new WWOOF exchange called Tatuta has started up in Turkey under the auspices of the (inauspicously-named) Bugday Association at Luleci Hendek Caddesi No 120/2, Kuledibi-Beyoglu, Istanbul (212-252 5255; www.bugday.org/tatuta). TaTuTa is a Turkish acronym for Agro Tourism and Voluntary Exchange. At present there are just 25 member farms but this is sure to increase.

IN EXTREMIS

The best protection against getting into serious difficulties is to have a good insurance policy (see *Introduction*). This is an expense that should not be shrugged off, given the findings of a recent study that revealed that almost a third of Britons who go backpacking or travelling independently are likely to face a serious problem at some point. One of the benefits of the International Student Identity Card and International Youth (under 26) Travel Card is access to a toll-free emergency helpline on which medical, legal or financial advice can be sought in a crisis. The ISIC and IYTC cards cost £7 and do not in any way replace the need for insurance. Details from any branch of STA Travel. Americans can obtain the International Student Exchange (ISE) card for $25 (www.isecard.com).

If you do end up in dire financial straits and for some reason do not have or cannot use a credit card, you should contact someone at home who is in a position to send money.

Transferring Money

Assuming your account at home remains in credit and you have access to a compatible ATM, it shouldn't be necessary to have money wired to you urgently. If you run out of money abroad, whether through mismanagement, loss or theft and cannot use a hole-in-the-wall money machine for some reason, you can contact your bank back home by telephone, fax or online, and ask them to wire money to you. This will be easier if you have set up a telephone or internet bank account before leaving home since they will then have the correct security checks in place to authorise a transfer without having to receive something from you in writing with your signature. You can request that the necessary sum be transferred from your bank to a named bank in the town you are in – something you have to arrange with your own bank, so you know where to pick the money up. Money can also be transferred by postal money orders or girocheques to bank accounts abroad. This is most useful when you want to transfer money home to your own bank account; you will need the bank sort code, a cheque card and cheque book. Expect to pay at least £20 each time.

If a private individual has kindly agreed to bale you out, they can transfer money in several ways. Western Union offers an international money transfer service whereby cash deposited at one branch (by, say, your mum) can be withdrawn by you from any other branch or agency, which your benefactor need not specify. Western Union agents – there are 90,000 of them in 200 countries – come in all shapes and sizes, e.g. travel agencies, stationers, chemists. Unfortunately it is not well represented outside the developed world. The person sending money to you simply turns up at a Western Union counter (it is not possibly by phone or online), pays in the desired sum plus the fee, which is £14 for up to £100 transferred, £21 for £100-200, £37 for £500 and so on. For an extra £7 your benefactor can do this over the phone with a credit card. In the UK, ring 0800-833833 and in the US 1-800-325-6000 for further details, a list of outlets and a complete rate schedule. The website www.westernunion.com allows you to search for the nearest outlet.

Thomas Cook, American Express and the UK Post Office offer a similar service called Moneygram. Cash deposited at one of their foreign exchange counters is available within ten minutes at the named destination or can be collected up to 45 days later at one of 60,000 co-operating agents in 160 countries. The fee is £12 for sending £100, £18 for up to £200, £24 for up to £300, £46 for between £750 and £1,000 and so on. Ring 0800 018 0104 for details or check the Post Office website (www.postoffice.co.uk).

Barclaycard holders are entitled to make use of their 24-hour International Rescue service (01733 294812) which will advise on a myriad of disasters including theft of money, tickets and cards, legal problems and medical emergencies. Customers of Barclays can use its Priority International Payment (PIP) to send cash to banks worldwide. The fee is £35 and the sender needs to quote the recipient's passport number. The Cooperative

Bank's electronic service is called Tipanet and costs a flat rate of £8 for any amount sent to its partner banks in Spain, Italy, Belgium, France, Germany or the US. Transfers take up to a week so it is useful only for non-emergencies.

US citizens can ring Overseas Citizens Services (202-647-5225), part of the State Department, which can wire cash from someone at home to any US embassy for a fee of $30; personal cheques are not accepted.

Despite the popularity of online banking, you may still find it necessary to open a local account for example if your employer pays by cheque. One way of simplifying this procedure is to set the wheels in motion before you leave home. Before setting off, you open an account at a large bank in your destination city, which may have a branch in London. Most won't allow you to open a chequing account so instant overdrafts are not a possibility. But knowing you have a few hundred pounds waiting for you in Sydney, San Francisco or Singapore is a great morale booster.

Embassies & Consulates

With luck you will never have to visit your consulate while travelling. But it is still a good idea to have the contact details handy especially if you are travelling in an unstable country where an incident might incline you to register with the consular officials. This can now be done quickly and easily via the FCO website (www.fco.gov.uk). The majority of people who do end up in consular waiting rooms are there because they have had their passports stolen. Note that it is much easier to arrange replacement documents if you have a record of the passport number and date and place of issue; even better is a photocopy of the relevant pages.

In an emergency, your consulate can help you get in touch with friends and relations if necessary, normally by arranging a reverse charge call. Consulates have the authority to cash a personal cheque to the value of £100 supported by a valid banker's card. But do not pin too much faith in your consulate. When Jane Roberts turned to the British Consulate in Toronto after having all her money stolen, they just preached at her about how she should have thought about all this before she left home.

If you are really desperate and can find no one at home or among your fellow travellers willing to lend you some money, you may ask your consulate to repatriate you by putting you on the first train or airplane heading for your home destination. If they do this your passport will be invalidated until the money is repaid. In fact permission is very rarely granted these days because of the thousands of unpaid debts incurred by indigent travellers; for example these days there are less than 100 repatriations to the UK a year. A British consular official advised us that in the 18 months she worked in India, only two repatriations were approved, despite the queues of desperate people.

The Foreign & Commonwealth Office of the UK government provides updated travel information and cautions for every country in the world and additional risk assessment of current trouble spots and advice on how to find consular help and legal advice. You can contact the Travel Advice Unit by phone on 0870 606 0290 or check their excellent website www.fco.gov.uk/travel.

General advice on minimising the risks of independent travel is contained in the book *World Wise_ Your Passport to Safer Travel* published by Thomas Cook in association with the Suzy Lamplugh Trust and the Foreign Office (www.suzylamplugh.org/worldwise; £6.99 plus £2 postage). Arguably its advice is over-cautious, advising travellers never to ride a motorbike or accept an invitation to a private house. Travellers will have to decide for themselves when to follow this advice and when to ignore it.

In the US, the State Department publishes its warnings and advisories on its website www.travel.state.gov highlighting any potential dangers to American travellers such as coups or terrorist activity. This same information is available in recorded messages on 202-647-5225. American citizens may request the Consular Information Sheets for any country by writing to the Office of Overseas Citizens Services at the Department of State (Room 4811, Washington, DC 20520-4811).

Legal Problems

Everyone has heard hair-raising stories about conditions in foreign prisons, so think very carefully before engaging in illegal activities. Currently 2,350 Britons are held in foreign prisons, half on drugs charges. If you do have trouble with the law in foreign countries, remain calm and polite, and demand an immediate visit from your Consul. He or she can at least recommend a local lawyer and interpreter if necessary. Britons should contact the charity Prisoners Abroad (89-93 Fonthill Road, Finsbury Park, London N4 3JH; 020-7561 6820; www.prisonersabroad.org.uk). Any travellers who would like to visit prisoners should contact these organisations for details, since many prisoners go years without a visit.

Dire Straits

Try not to be too downcast if destitution strikes. Elma Grey had been looking forward to leaving Greece and rejoining her old kibbutz, but she was unexpectedly turned away from the ferry because of her dire shortage of funds. She describes the 'worst down' of her travels:

> Back to the Athens hotel where I'd spent the previous evening, feeling utter despair. But I found that other people's problems have an incredible way of bringing out the best in total strangers. Everyone I came into contact with was full of sympathy, advice and practical suggestions regarding possible sources of work. And quite apart from this, the feeling of much needed moral support was probably what got me through the whole thing without my degenerating into a miserable heap. Although I'd never want to feel so stranded and desperate again, in a way it was all worth it just to experience the unique feeling of just how good fellow travellers can be in a crisis.

Several travellers have insisted that when you get down to your last few dollars/pesos/marks, it is much wiser to spend them in a pub buying drinks for the locals who might then offer useful assistance than it is to spend the money on accommodation or food. David Irvine found himself in Tasmania with just $10 in his pocket. He walked into a pub and bet two men $20 each that he could drink a yard of ale, a feat he was fairly confident that he could accomplish.

Less than 24 hours after Ilka Cave from South Africa arrived in Tel Aviv, all her luggage, money and documents were stolen. One of the girls in the hostel suggested that she contact an au pair agency and soon she was living with a nice family and earning a salary. Michel Falardeau wanted to live rent-free in Sydney, so he offered his assistance to a number of charities, one of which gave him a place to live. Mark Horobin was down to his bottom dollar in San Diego and queued up outside the Rescue Mission. Several days later he had signed on as a kitchen helper and stayed for some time free of charge.

It is to be hoped that you will avoid the kind of disaster that will require the services of a lawyer, doctor or consul abroad. If you find yourself merely running short of funds, you might be interested in some of the following tidbits of information, intended for entertainment as much as for practical advice.

HELP. Look out for churches that conduct services in English: the priest or vicar should be able to give you useful advice and often practical help. But be cautious about accepting help from fringe religious groups.

NIGHT SHELTERS. Most large towns and some railway stations in Western Europe and North America have a night shelter run by the Catholic organisation Caritas, the Salvation Army or similar which provides basic but free food and accommodation. They want to help genuine vagrants, not freeloading tourists, so you must appear genuinely impoverished or a potential convert. You can find out where to find these hostels by asking around – any policeman on the night beat should be able to help you. Be warned that many of these organisations are run by religious movements, and you may be expected to show your gratitude by joining in worship.

MONASTERIES & NUNNERIES. Monastic communities often extend hospitality to indigent wayfarers. Sometimes it is freely given but try to be sensitive as to whether or not a small donation is expected.

JAIL. Travellers have on occasion found a free bed for the night by asking at police stations if there are any spare cells. According to US law, all people (including non-citizens) have the right to demand protective custody. You are most likely to be successful (and escape unharmed) in peaceful country towns: the police may have other uses for their cells on a Saturday night in Glasgow or Miami.

SLEEPING OUT. It is illegal to sleep out on private property without the landowner's permission (except in Sweden); most farmers will grant their permission if you ask politely and look trustworthy. In cities try public parks and also railway or coach stations, though some are cleared by security after the last train or bus or you may be asked for an onward ticket. Many people try to camp discreetly near a proper campsite so that they can make use of the toilet and shower block. Ian Moody tried to avoid sleeping out on private property in Spain and one night chose a seemingly ideal shelter, a concrete covered ditch. At about 5am he was rudely awakened by a torrent of water which swept away his gear and nearly drowned him. Many people sleep on beaches; beware of early morning visits from the local constabulary and also large vacuum machines. Jonathan Galpin finds a mosquito net invaluable, not only as protection against biting insects but (when doubled over) from falling dew.

SQUATTING. Half-finished buildings usually provide enough shelter for a comfortable, uninterrupted kip. Robin Gray recommends garden huts in large garden centres which are often left open and provide a good night's shelter. Your luggage can be safely stowed in a locker at the station during the day.

FREE MEALS. Hare Krishna have free or heavily subsidised vegetarian restaurants (often called Govinda's) and take-away temples in many major cities from Sweden to South Africa. You may have to endure some minor attempts to convert you but their food is excellent. Sometimes charities such as the Red Cross and Caritas give out free food, as David Bamford discovered when he was stranded in Villefranche unable to find a grape-picking job, along with scores of North Africans.

Restaurants may be willing to give you a free meal if you promise to recommend them to a guide book or to correct the spelling on their menu (depriving future travellers of the delights of 'miscellaneous pork bowel,' 'grilled chicken with swing' and 'vegetable craps'). It may also be possible to do an hour's work in exchange for a meal by going to the back door, possibly at fast food outlets. Some will even give a hand-out if you are brazen enough to request one. If you know where to go, some supermarkets sell off very cheaply their unsold ready-made meals.

BUFFET RESTAURANTS. In some countries like Sweden, the USA and Australia, reasonable restaurants offer all-you-can-eat buffets. Diners have been known to share their second and third helpings with friends who have merely bought a soft drink.

FREE WINE. You may come across free tastings at the roadside in wine producing areas from California to France (where these tastings are called *dégustations*). There will sometimes be something to eat – perhaps bread and cheese, or a local speciality.

FACTORY TOURS. Ask tourist offices if there are any food or drink factories nearby that offer free guided tours; these tours normally end with the gift of free samples of whatever is being produced. For example, distilleries in Scotland hand out miniature bottles of whisky, and Kelloggs in North America provide a selection of miniature packets of cereal. Breweries are famous for their hospitality – try Carlsberg in Copenhagen (Castlemaine XXXX in Brisbane, Guinness in Dublin and Heineken in Amsterdam all charge admission.)

FREE SAMPLES. Look out for demonstrations promoting new foods or gadgets in supermarkets and department stores. This was another of Safra Wightman's survival tips in Israel:

> *In supermarkets it's acceptable to taste the pick'n'mix ranges from dried fruit and nuts to chocolate, sweets, olives, pretzels, etc. On several occasions my boyfriend and I stood for ten minutes 'tasting' then bought two apples on our way out. Everybody including Israelis does the same.*

HAPPY HOURS. To attract customers at off-peak times, bars and pubs sometimes offer free snacks as well as cut-price drinks.

FAIRS AND FESTIVALS. Watch for giveaways at annual fairs and festivals. To take just one example in Italy, there are often free snacks at *sagra* (fairs).

SCAVENGING FOOD. If you are not too fussy about what you eat you can look for stale or sub-standard food that has been discarded by shops, market stalls or even restaurants. This is especially worth doing around supermarkets in America, where a large quantity of perfectly acceptable food is thrown out after it reaches its sell-by date. Fancy resort hotels are also prone to throw out good food on a regular basis. Julian Peachey and many others camping at Eilat dined like kings out of the Club Med skips. While no one he knew suffered any ill effects, the residents of a local 4-star hotel all came down with salmonella.

RAIDING FRIDGES. When Roger Blake was broke in Brisbane, he became semi-reliant on the communal fridge at the backpackers hostel. Most hostels have a communal shelf for well meaning travellers to leave behind unwanted and perishable items. Apparently it is possible to live off unwanted food, especially in city hostels where there is a major departure airport.

WASHING UP. In hostels, everyone is expected to wash and dry his or her own dishes. If you make it known that you are willing to take over this chore in exchange for a small contribution, you may find lots of willing takers. Never underestimate the laziness of travellers. One night Roger Blake made $8 in 'tips' by doing this. He then asked the hostel owners whether he could set up as a 'dishy' for tips only. But they didn't welcome the idea as it went against their philosophy of getting everyone to muck in together.

SELF SERVICE RESTAURANTS. The publisher of this book had an odd experience in a huge New York self-service restaurant. Having eaten his Waldorf salad he went to the water fountain for a drink. On returning to his table to conclude his repast he found a tramp-like character, who had obviously assumed the customer had left for good, busily wolfing down the much anticipated apple pie: the unwanted guest promptly fled. On leaving the self-service emporium the victim spotted the culprit peering through the plate glass window with several pals, in search of customers who left their tables leaving uneaten remains still on the table.

CASINOS. Large casinos often put on a lavish spread in the staff canteen. Assuming the staff is large and changeable enough, it may be possible to infiltrate it on an occasional basis for a good binge. Paul Edwards has happy memories of the seven cuisines served to staff at the Crown Casino in Melbourne (see Australia chapter). Casinos from Istanbul to Las Vegas are also known to hand round free snacks to punters who may not be required to spend much money.

FREELOADING. It might be possible to follow in the footsteps of the penniless young Dutch traveller who set up a website www.letmestayforaday.com. At one point he confirmed that he had received 2,784 offers of hospitality as he toured the world. Ramon Stoppelenburg was on the road for more than two years without spending any money on accommodation. In 2004 he published a book of his freeloading travels, alas only in Dutch.

BEGGING. Straightforward begging is normally humiliating, boring, unprofitable and illegal. The best way of achieving results is to make yourself so unbearable that people will pay you to go away – for example, two people impersonating a lunatic and his keeper around the cafés of Paris, would be soon bribed to go away by pleasure-seeking Parisians and tourists.

IMPERSONATING PROPERTY BUYERS: Timeshare companies sometimes offer attractive sweeteners to potential investors simply to tour a property and sit through a sales spiel. While in Bali Jennifer and Eric decided to go for it:

> We've earned several free week stays in 5-star hotels by pretending we were going to buy a timeshare. On crowded streets in tourist resorts, locals are employed to find western tourist couples and offer them a free taxi ride to the complex. One guy that picked us up told us what the qualifications are so we could get our prizes and he a $100 fee. One of the couple has to be over 30 and fully employed; you must have been living together more than three years and your holiday on Bali no longer than four weeks. We pretended we were staying at a more expensive hotel than we actually were. You fill in your ID and agree to listen for 90 minutes to their blah blah (careful, very tricky talk). And you get your prize, whether you buy their timeshare or not. I felt a little nervous though, in my disguise covering tattoos and dreadlocks, but we managed. We got the holiday, parasailing tickets and ugly white T-shirts. A week later we did it again for another company and have collected holidays in India and Aussie. Too bad you have to pay a $50 administration fee but you're still getting a week's stay worth $800.

BEACHCOMBING. Beaches are a good place to look for lost property. After a storm in Greece, Sarah Clifford went beachcombing and found a gold necklace worth £150. A metal detector can be a valuable ally.

CLAIMING DEPOSITS. In Denmark, Sweden, Mexico, France, Spain, Italy, Australia, the US and many other countries you can earn some small change by taking wine, beer and coke bottles or aluminium cans for recycling back to shops for a refund of the deposit. It is best to look for bottles or cans after a beach party, a special event such as a festival or in the dustbins outside holiday villas early in the mornings.

PUBLIC TELEPHONES. In Austria, Spain and many other countries you have to insert money in a telephone before you dial a number, you then have to press a button to get a refund if you are not connected. It is always worth pressing this button when you pass a call box in case someone has forgotten to do this – the banks of telephones in railways stations are particularly recommended.

BOOKS OF TICKETS. You can buy a *carnet* of ten Metro tickets in Paris at two-thirds the price of buying the tickets singly, then sell the individual tickets to travellers, splitting the difference in cost. You may even get the full face value from busy commuters who don't want to queue for tickets at rush hour. Another trick is to buy group tickets for cable car rides in Switzerland at a substantial discount on the price of buying the tickets individually. For example the journey up Mount Titlis in Engelberg, Switzerland costs twice as much for a single traveller as for a group member ticket. You can then sell these tickets separately to individual travellers at less than the full rate. This has a better chance of success than selling single Metro tickets, since people will want to travel only once.

POSTCARDS. Tourists on beaches and in bars are often happy to pay over the odds for properly pre-stamped postcards and a pen with which to write them.

TRICKS AND SKILLS. If you know that you can drink a yard of ale, juggle four plates or smoke 27 cigars simultaneously, you might find people willing to have a sporting bet with you. For more ideas on this subject see the section on Gambling in *Enterprise*. We have heard of a traveller who erected a sign on the pavements 'Jokes – 25 Cents Each'.

RADIO QUIZZES. British Forces Broadcasting Services (BFBS) hold plenty of competitions and are generous with prizes. Jane Harris entered the daily quiz in Hong Kong and won a HK$400 food and drink voucher for a bar in Wanchai. She recommends tuning in to BFBS elsewhere in the world like Cyprus or wherever British forces are stationed.

MEDICAL RESEARCH. Private companies providing clinical trials to the pharmaceutical industry often pay volunteers handsomely to test new drugs and techiques. The website www.gpgp.net ('Guinea Pigs Get Paid') has a free directory listing hundreds of such places worldwide that pay healthy volunteers to take part in drug trials. Note that they are no longer able to maintain their list of UK centres and have delegated that job to Biotrax. To access the Biotrax database you have to pay a one-off membership costing £20/$39 (www.biotrax.co.uk). Also check www.clinicaltrials.gov and www.centerwatch.com or enquire at research hospitals and drug companies like Glaxo Smith Kline. You might also enquire at university psychology departments, where there may be a need for participants for perception tests, etc. No work permits necessary; only proof of human life.

SELLING BLOOD. Many countries pay blood and plasma donors handsomely, especially the USA and Middle East. Even if you donate your money free of charge, you are always given a free drink and a snack.

SPERM DONATION. In many countries, fertility clinics pay (typically £20) for sperm samples. Men should be aware that they will only be invited to donate after screening and analysis of potential fertility (which might be traumatic). Ian Smith did this in Denmark and was told if his sperm proved amenable to freezing (which it wasn't) he could have donated up to three times a week to a maximum of 30 times. In the UK one donor is allowed to 'father' no more than ten children. With new moves to do away with the anonymity of donors (so that any children born subsequently can trace their genetic fathers), men should focus on the psychological impact more than the immediate financial gain.

EGG DONATION. Egg donation is a much more serious business and is against the law in the UK. Private fertility clinics in the US have been offering upwards of $5,000 for donated eggs which involves hormone treatment and surgery. According to a recent article in the *Sunday Times* Jewish donors can automatically expect $10,000-$15,000 and Oxbridge students are also in great demand. A simple web search reveals sites with names like eggdonor.com.

SELLING BELONGINGS. By the end of your trip many of your belongings may have become expendable. You can try selling them to fellow travellers in hostels, to secondhand shops, or even to passing shoppers if you set yourself up on the edge of a market. Be ruthless about what you do and do not need: you have taken your photos, so you don't need your camera, and you can transfer your belongings from your expensive backpack to a cheaper bag. Be prepared to spend some time haggling.

THE LAST RESORT. Sell this book – but memorise the contents first! Better still, take a couple of spare copies as recommended by Kevin Boyd:

I have met so many other travellers who would have sold their mother into slavery for my copy of your book! You should recommend that people take as many copies as they can.

Peter McGuire sold this book's sister publication *Teaching English Abroad* for 5,000 won (then $6) in Korea to someone who was immediately offered double that amount by someone else. He in turn made copies of the relevant chapters and doubled his money.

Some Useful Phrases

English: Do you need a helper/temporary assistant?
French: Avez-vous besoin d'un aide/assistant intérimaire?
German: Brauchen Sie eine Hilfe/einen Assistenten für eine begenzte Zeit?
Dutch: Kunt U een helper/tijdelijke assistent gebruiken?
Spanish: ¿ Necesita usted un ayudante/asistente interino?
Italian: Ha bisogno d'un aiutante/d'un assistente provvisorio?
Greek: Khryázeste kanénan ypálliyo/prosorynó voythó?

GB: Do you know if there is any work in the neighbourhood?
F: Savez-vous s'il y a du travail dans les environs?
D: Wissen Sie, ob es in der Nachbarschaft irgendwelche Arbeit gibt?
NL: Weet u of werk is in de buurt?
S: ¿Sabe usted si hay trabajo por aquí?
I: Lo sa si c'e lavoro nel vicinato?
GR: Xérete an yaprkhy dhoulyá styn peryokhý?

GB: Where is the employment office?
F: Où se trouve le bureau de placement?
D: Wo ist das Arbeitsamt?
NL: Waar is het kantoor voor arbeidsvoorziening?
S: ¿Donde esta la Oficina de Empleos?
I: Dove sta l'agenzia di collocamento?
GR: Poú ýno to grafýo (evréseos) ergasýas?

GB: What is the wage? Will it be taxed?
F: Quel est le salaire? Sera-t-il imposable?
D: Wie hoch ist der Lohn? Ist er steuerpflichtig?
NL: Hoe hoog is het loon? Is het belastbaar?
S: ¿Cuanto es el salario? Esta sujeto al pago de impuestos?
I: Che e la paga? Sara tassata?
GR: Poso ýne to ymeromýsthyo? Tha forologhiyhý?

GB: Where can I stay? Will there be a charge for accommodation/food?
F: Où pourrais-je me loger? L'hébergement/les repas seront-ils payants?
D: Wo kann ich wohnen? Muss für Unterkunft und Verpflegung selb gezahlt werden?
NL: Waar kan ik onderdak vinden? Moet ik betalen voor huisvesting en maaltijden?
S: ¿Donde puedo alojar? Hay que pagar por el alojamiento/la comida?
I: Dove posso stare? Avra una spesa per l'alloggio/il cibo?
GR: Pou boró na mýno? Tha khreothó ya ty dhyamoný/to fagytó

GB: Are there any cooking/washing facilities?
F: Est-ce qu'il y a des aménagements pour faire la cuisine/la lessive?
D: Gibt es Koch/Waschgelegenheiten?
NL: Is er kook/wasgelegenheid?
S: ¿Se puede cocinar/lavar la ropa?
I: Ci stanno dei mezzi per cucinare/lavorare?
GR: Ypárkhoun efkolýes ya magýrema/plýsymo?

GB: When will the harvest/job begin? How long will it last?
F: Quand commencera la moisson/le travail? Combien de temps dure-t'il?
D: Wann beginnt die Ernte/Arbeit? Wie lange wird sie dauren?
NL: Wanneer begint de oogst/job? Hoe lang zal het werk duren?
S: ¿Cuando comenzara la cosecha/el trabajo? Cuanto durara?
I: Quando incomincia la messe/il lavoro? Per quanto tempo durera?
GR: Poté tharkhýsy o theryzmos/y dhoulyá? Póso tha dhyarkésy?

GB: What will be the hours of work?
F: Quelles seront les heures de travail?
D: Wie lange ist die Arbeitszeit?
NL: Wat zijn de werkuren?
S: ¿Cual sera el horario de trabajo
I: Che saranno le ore del lavoro?
GR: Pyéz tha ý ne y órez ergasýas?

GB: Thank you for your help.
F: Merci de votre aide.
D: Danke für Ihre Hilfe.
NL: Dank U voor Uw hulp.
S: Gracias por su ayuda.
GR: Sas efkharystó ya tyn vóythýa sas.

Appendix 1

Travellers' Itineraries

Roger Blake's Two-Year Working Holiday

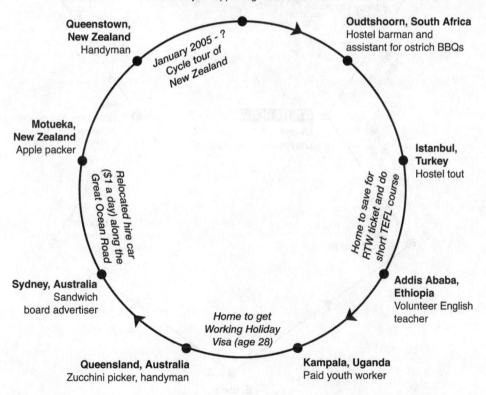

START HERE
Harrogate, UK
Leaves job supporting disabled adults

Queenstown, New Zealand
Handyman

January 2005 - ? Cycle tour of New Zealand

Oudtshoorn, South Africa
Hostel barman and assistant for ostrich BBQs

Motueka, New Zealand
Apple packer

Relocated hire car ($1 a day) along the Great Ocean Road

Istanbul, Turkey
Hostel tout

Home to save for RTW ticket and do short TEFL course

Sydney, Australia
Sandwich board advertiser

Home to get Working Holiday Visa (age 28)

Addis Ababa, Ethiopia
Volunteer English teacher

Queensland, Australia
Zucchini picker, handyman

Kampala, Uganda
Paid youth worker

Carisa Fey's Travels

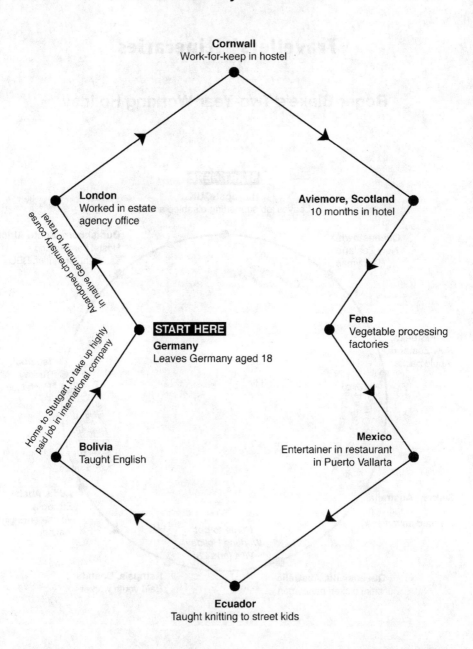

Cornwall
Work-for-keep in hostel

London
Worked in estate
agency office

Aviemore, Scotland
10 months in hotel

Abandoned chemistry course
in native Germany to travel

START HERE
Germany
Leaves Germany aged 18

Fens
Vegetable processing
factories

Home to Stuttgart to take up highly
paid job in international company

Bolivia
Taught English

Mexico
Entertainer in restaurant
in Puerto Vallarta

Ecuador
Taught knitting to street kids